Understanding Children and Adolescents

FOURTH EDITION

Judith A. Schickedanz

Boston University

David I. Schickedanz

Greater Lawrence Mental Health Center

Peggy D. Forsyth

Millersville University

G. Alfred Forsyth

Millersville University

Allyn and Bacon

Boston   London   Toronto   Sydney   Tokyo   Singapore

We dedicate this book, with love, to our children
Adam, Chris, Scott, and Holly, who make understanding children
and adolescents both interesting and delightfully fun.

Editor: Jeff Lasser
Editor-in-Chief: Karen Hanson
Editorial Assistant: Susan Hutchinson
Developmental Editor: Jodi Devine
Senior Marketing Manager: Caroline Croley
Composition and Prepress Buyer: Linda Cox
Manufacturing Buyer: Megan Cochran
Cover Administrator: Linda Knowles
Editorial-Production Administrator: Deborah Brown
Editorial-Production Services: Susan McNally
Typographic Services: Omegatype Typography, Inc.
Text Designer: Schneck-DePippo Graphics
Photo Researcher: Julie Tesser
Illustrator: Schneck-DePippo Graphics

Previous editions were published under the title *Understanding Children*, copyright © 1993,
1990 by Mayfield Publishing Company.

Library of Congress Cataloging-in-Publication Data

Understanding children and adolescents / Judith A. Schickedanz . . . [et al.].—4th ed.
    p. cm.
  Rev. ed. of: Understanding children and adolescents. 3rd ed. Boston: Allyn and Bacon, c1998.
  Includes bibliographical references and indexes.
  ISBN 0-205-31418-X
    1. Child development.   2. Child psychology.   3. Adolescence.   I. Schickedanz, Judith A.,
1944-
  HQ767.9.U53   2000
  305.231–dc21

                                            00-032275
                                            CIP

Printed in the United States of America
10 9 8 7 6 5 4 3   QW   05 04 03 02 01 00

Chapter Opening Photo Credits

Page 2: © Robert Harbison; 44: © VDG/SYNOPSIS/Photo Researchers; 86: © Rosann Olson/Tony Stone Images; 116: © Peter Vandermark/Stock Boston; 152: © Alan Carey/The Image Works; 190: © David Wells/The Image Works; 228: © David Young Wolff/Tony Stone Images; 264: © Elizabeth Crews; 294: © Penny Gentieu/Tony Stone Images; 332: © David Young Wolff/Tony Stone Images; 370: © Index Stock; 404: © Bob Daemmrich/Stock Boston; 436: © Will Faller; 480: © Penny Tweedie/Tony Stone Images; 508: © Robert Daemmrich/Tony Stone Images; 546: © Li-Hua Lan/The Image Works; 576: © Bob Daemmrich Photos, Inc.; 604: © Will Hart; 626: Robert Harbison

Brief Contents

Contents

Feature Boxes

An Introduction to

Understanding Children and Adolescents

We first undertook the task of authoring a development textbook because we experienced difficulty finding a book to use in our child and adolescent development classes. Some development books were not organized to suit our course. Others did not include the complete range of topics we thought important, or their presentation of material made children seem fragmented and remote. In still others, the writing was not as clear or as interesting as we wanted it to be. To make these books work for our students, we modified their organization or coverage to achieve the necessary coherence, compensated for the fragmented impressions the books conveyed, and provided additional illustrations and examples to achieve adequate coverage and make the material come alive. At last we resolved to write a book, one that would solve the problems we had encountered over the years. The success of the first three editions suggested that the book addressed not only our needs, but the needs of many other teachers. We think this fourth edition continues to do the same.

Aims

A primary aim in this edition, as in previous editions, has been to present a balance of theory, research findings, and applications, and to integrate all of these aspects of development by presenting a picture of the whole child situated in realistic, everyday contexts. *Understanding Children and Adolescents* is written primarily for students who will be living and working with children and adolescents, as teachers, parents, child-care providers, nurses, counselors, administrators of programs, and practitioners in a variety of other settings. Students who intend to pursue these types of work need comprehensive, accurate, and up-to-date information about children's development. They also need to understand the uses and implications of this information. Thus, the emphasis throughout this book is not only on current knowledge and theory, but on the working applications of this knowledge and theory.

Understanding Children and Adolescents invites students to engage deeply with the text. As a result, students read in such a way that they think, learn, and remember. Each chapter and many major topics are introduced with a vignette in which the essence of the information or issue about to be presented is captured in true-to-life situations involving children or adolescents and adults. Think-about-it paragraphs also occur throughout chapters. These pose questions intended to spark students' thinking.

Perhaps the most important goal in writing *Understanding Children and Adolescents* has been to convey our feelings about children. First, children are not miniature adults but individuals who have different ways of thinking and learning about the world. Second, children need considerable attention and care. These ideas are emphasized in the introduction to the book, entitled **Prologue: Why Study Children?** We encourage students to read this introduction to gain a preliminary orientation to the book.

Organization and Content

We think that students should be able to see children as whole human beings. This wholeness can be conveyed by presenting information about all aspects of development for each period of childhood. Therefore, *Understanding Children and Adolescents* is organized chronologically, introducing students to children as they grow, learn, and change, from earliest infancy to the threshold of adulthood. The book begins with the foundations for the study of child development (Part One)—theories of child development, and the biology of genetics, prenatal development, and birth. The remaining parts of the book cover four chronological epochs of childhood. Part Two addresses the development of the child between birth and age 3—infancy and toddlerhood. Parts Three, Four, and Five cover the development of the preschool child (age 3 to 6), the school-age child (age 6 to 12), and the adolescent (age 13 to 19), respectively.

Within this chronological framework, material on the different domains of development is presented topically. Parts Two through Five contain four chapters each, covering physical development, cognitive development, the development of language and communication, and social and emotional development.

Understanding Children and Adolescents provides comprehensive, in-depth coverage of a range of topics and issues in child development, always with an emphasis on the application of knowledge. Many topics discussed in previous editions continue to receive thorough coverage in the fourth edition. Included are such topics as the effects on the developing fetus of prenatal exposure to alcohol, cocaine, and other teratogens; advances in prenatal assessment tools and treatments for infertility; theories of infant and maternal attachment; information about the effects of temperament on socialization; differences found across cultures in children's motor development; knowledge about infant language, visual perception, and cognition; information about the development of cognitive abilities in preschool children, and the development of metacognitive abilities in school-age children; socialization processes and the learning of prosocial behavior; psychological effects of early and late maturing on adolescent girls and boys; concerns about alcohol and other drug use by adolescents; questions about bias in intelligence testing; and many, many more.

Special Features

Because the special features that distinguished the first three editions of *Understanding Children and Adolescents* from other textbooks have proven very successful, we have retained these in this edition, while also introducing some improvements. Primary among the useful and unique features in the first three editions were the vignettes included in each chapter and the **Knowledge in Action** boxes and the **Research Close-Ups.** We have retained the vignettes in this edition. We have added think-about-it paragraphs to spark students' thinking. You and your students will find five types of **Knowledge in Action** boxes: Education, Special Education, Health/Safety, Policy, and Parenting. **Knowledge in Action** boxes include topics such as:

> *The Human Genome Project*
> *Cross-Cultural Differences in Infant Crying and Carrying*
> *Detecting Hearing Problems in Infants*
> *The WIC Program*
> *Making Playgrounds Safe*
> *Children's Strategies for Retelling Stories*
> *Signs, Symptoms, and Long-Term Consequences of Child Abuse and Neglect*
> *Young Children's Drawings*
> *Explaining Cross-Cultural Differences in Mathematics Achievement*
> *Eating Disorders in Adolescence: Anorexia and Bulimia*

This edition also retains the **Research Close-Up** boxes. These make it possible for instructors to select for assignment only research topics that are of interest to them and their students. **Research Close-Ups** include such topics as:

Childbirth Practices around the World
Prenatal Assessment Techniques
Effects of Motor Development on Other Areas of Development
Infants' Knowledge about the World: Reactions to Impossible Events
Storybook Reading and Children's Vocabulary Development
Children and Violence
The Games Children Have Played: A Look around the World
Socialization of Gender Roles in Different Cultures
The Consequences of Teenage Pregnancy

Other Changes in This Edition

Of course, the entire book has been carefully reviewed, revised and updated. We have incorporated the latest research on important topics, new information on emerging issues, and material reflecting current thinking in the field. We also have strengthened in this edition information about child development across cultures. Cross-cultural information is included in discussions of topics such as physical, language, and social development in infants; the play of school-age children; the socialization of gender roles in preschool and school-age children; and academic achievement in school-age children. This information is not only integrated into discussions of many topics covered in the text, it is highlighted in several **Knowledge in Action** and **Research Close-Up** boxes.

Finally, this fourth edition of *Understanding Children and Adolescents* continues a trend toward more reliance on the systems approach found in the second and third editions. The systems approach is explained in Chapter 1, Theories of Child Development and Methods of Studying Children, and is used as a framework for discussing numerous topics throughout the book.

Learning Aids

Because the learning aids incorporated in the first three editions of *Understanding Children and Adolescents* have proven useful in helping students understand, organize, and remember material, we have retained them in the fourth edition. These learning aids include:

- A vignette to open each chapter and many main sections within each chapter. The vignette shows how a principle or issue to be discussed in the chapter translates into children's words, behavior, or beliefs; or how the principle or issue affects the adults in the child's world.

- Think-about-it paragraphs following the vignettes elsewhere throughout a chapter. Questions are posed to the student in the think-about-it paragraphs.

- A chapter outline on the chapter's opening page. This outline, coupled with the brief introduction of topics following the vignettes, gives the student a clear picture of what the chapter contains.

- Key terms appearing in bold type throughout each chapter. The terms are also listed in a glossary, with page numbers, at the end of the chapter, which provides for review.

- A detailed list of the chapter's key points in a summary at the end of each chapter.

- Annotated suggestions for further reading at the end of every chapter. These extend the boundaries of the material for the student. New titles have been added to these listings for the fourth edition.

▪ Numerous tables, charts, drawings, and photographs to provide graphic illustrations of the principles of child development. The captions inform and teach rather than simply label and identify.

Ancillary Package

A complete package of supplemental support material is available for *Understanding Children and Adolescents* to enhance both teaching and learning and to facilitate the application of knowledge to practical situations.

Supplements for Instructors

The **Instructor's Manual,** written by two of the co-authors, Peggy Forsyth and Al Forsyth of Millersville University, includes chapter summaries, learning objectives, and supplemental instructor's activities which include course activities using the Study Guide, student projects and activities, and topics for small-group discussions. Also included are questions for thought, debate, and discussion; demonstration topics for the instructor to present in the classroom, and suggestions for additional lecture topics. The Instructor's Manual also lists audiovisual resources that can be used in conjunction with the text, and free or inexpensive materials that can be obtained via the Internet or toll-free numbers.

The **Test Bank,** written by author Judy Schickedanz of Boston University and Molly Collins, a graduate student at Boston University, supplies over 2000 multiple-choice questions, as well as a selection of short-answer and essay questions. New to this edition of the Test Bank are practical problem-solving questions in which the student is given problem scenarios and is asked to evaluate them by applying the information from the text. The multiple-choice questions vary in difficulty and have been labeled easy, medium, or challenging. Key point rubrics are provided for the essay questions.

Computerized Testing: Allyn and Bacon Test Manager is an integrated suite of testing and assessment tools for Windows and Macintosh. You can use Test Manager to create professional-looking exams in just minutes by selecting from the existing database of questions, editing questions, or writing your own. Course management features include a class roster, gradebook, and item analysis. Test Manager also has everything you need to create and administer online tests.

The Allyn and Bacon Interactive Video for Child Development, 2001 Edition contains video clips which illustrate topics in each chapter and are tied to the text by a narrator who introduces the clips for each chapter and also provides a conclusion after the clips have been viewed. Critical Thinking Questions appear on the screen following related clips. A Video User's Guide accompanies each video and provides additional resources for instructors, such as page references to the text and additional lecture ideas. Contact your local Allyn and Bacon sales representative for information on other available videos, including the **Revised Films for the Humanities and Sciences Child Development Videotape.**

A set of 100 **overhead transparency acetates** was created specially for this text.

Supplements for Students

The SQ4R Guide to *Understanding Children and Adolescents:* Each chapter of this study guide is clearly organized in the SQ4R method of study, a proven strategy for improving academic performance. Students are provided with a **Survey** of the chapter, which is followed by the **Question** section, which uses the same learning objectives as outlined in the Instructor's Manual; the questions ask students to describe, explain, define, and apply concepts. Students **Read** the chapter and answer questions. Next comes the **Reflect** and Self-Reference section, which provides four to six exercises to help students use examples from their own lives to better understand and remember the information in the text. Students **Recite** by writing about four to six projects, all of which are more fully explained in the Instructor's Manual; at least two of the projects for each chapter have a worksheet for ease of completing the project. The **Review** section provides a review of the learning objectives and a practice multiple-choice and essay quiz.

Practice Tests: This manual of self-tests with answers provided helps students prepare for quizzes and exams. Available in value packs with the text.

Web Site: The Companion Website with Online Practice Tests, which can be accessed at www.abacon.com/schickedanz, offers a wide range of resources to both the instructors and students. Students will find learning objectives, practice tests, and links to stable URLs with brief descriptions of what will be found at each site, who the author is, and how it is relevant to the chapter material.

Also available in value packs with the text is an **Internet Guide for Child Development, 2000 Edition,** which identifies the most current URLs related to the study of child development. This easy-to-read guide helps point students in the right direction when looking at the tremendous array of information on the Internet as it relates to child development.

Acknowledgments

Many people have contributed to the development of the fourth edition of *Understanding Children and Adolescents*. Foremost among these are the co-authors from the third edition, David Schickedanz, Peggy Forsyth, and Alfred Forsyth. The book's authors consist of two husband-wife teams. This special circumstance allows close collaboration among the authors, a bonus for all concerned.

We are very grateful to the child development experts who provided detailed critiques of various chapters and offered useful suggestions in their review of the manuscript:

Third Edition User Survey Respondents

Pierrette Allison, *Napa Valley College*; Melita Baumann, *Glendale College*; Tena Carr, *San Joaquin Delta College*; Mellisa A. Clawson, *Syracuse University*; Donna S. Dent, *Virginia Western Community College*; Maribeth Downing, *Harding University*; Fred Foster-Clark, *Millersville University*; Barb Gregersen, *Hawkeye Community College*; Patricia A. Haught, *West Virginia University*; Judith Horowitz, *Medaille College*; Gretchen U. Kingsbury, *San Joaquin Delta College*; Paulete Kitchel, *College of the Sequoias*; Barbara K. Kraybill, *San Joaquin Delta College*; Linda Manzano-Larsen, *Glendale Community College*; Karen Olson, *St. Louis Community College–Meramec*; Barbara Paulding, *Indian Hills Community College*; Joanna Payne-Jones, *Chaffey College*; John Pfister, *Dartmouth College*; Eileen J. Reamy, *West Virginia University*; Sandra Waite-Stupiansky, *Edinboro University of Pennsylvania*; Barry H. Westfall, *Bradley University*; Virginia V. Wood, *University of Texas–Brownsville*.

Reviewers of Understanding Children and Adolescents, Fourth Edition

Diane Ashe, *Valencia Community College*; Diane Balin, *Aurora University*; Teresa Brito-Asenap, *Albuquerque TVI*; Rhonda D. Brown, *Texas Tech University*; Elda Buchanan, *Bradley University*; David Coddington, *Midwestern State University*; Ramie Cooney, *Creighton University*; Fred Danner, *University of Kentucky*; Linda

Flickinger, *St. Clair County Community College;* Diamantina Freeberg, *University of Texas at Brownsville;* Thomas Gerry, *Columbia-Greene Community College;* Marguerite Kermis, *Canisius College;* Richard Larcom, *Bloomsburg University of Pennsylvania;* Anne Law, *Rider University;* Sima Lesser, *Miami Dade Community College;* Robert McClure, *University of Texas at Tyler;* Lea McGee, *University of Alabama;* Jacquelyn Morales, *Methodist College;* Victoria Noriega, *University of Miami;* Jan Ochman, *Inver Hills Community College;* John Pfister, *Dartmouth College;* Vicki Ritts, *St. Louis Community College–Meramec;* Karen Gegner Rohr, *King College;* Debra Smart, *Tennessee State University;* Dolores Stegelin, *North Georgia College & State University;* Brock Travis, *Napa Valley College;* Laura Wagner, *University of Massachusetts–Amherst;* Gary Wilcox, *Anoka-Ramsey Community College;* Debra Zeifman, *Vassar College;* Christine Ziegler, *Kennesaw State University.*

The entire project has been greatly enriched by their suggestions, although any flaws or errors in the book are the responsibility of the authors.

Thanks are also due the staff of Allyn and Bacon. Carolyn Merrill, the executive editor, ensured a smooth transition to our new series editor, Jeff Lasser, who, along with Jodi Devine, the developmental editor, were thoughtful and considerate of our ideas, and helped us make them work. Their energy and enthusiasm inspired us, every step of the way. Deborah Brown and Susan McNally carefully shepherded the book through production, keeping us on schedule while also paying close attention to important details, such as the quality of the photographs and illustrations. We think the result is a very useful and beautiful book.

We also would like to thank the many students who have taken our child development classes over the years. We found that images of our students consistently came to mind when we were writing the textbook and preparing the ancillaries. It is for them that we undertook the writing of the first edition of the book. They continue to motivate us, and to provide essential feedback.

Finally, we would like to thank our children for their patience and understanding. Preparing a textbook involves considerable work, often produced under a tight schedule. Good humor and support from family members are absolutely essential to getting the job done. Peggy and Al Forsyth extend their thanks to Chris, Scott, and Holly. Judy and David Schickedanz extend their thanks to Adam.

PROLOGUE

Why Study Children?

As you read about children in the pages that follow, you may think of a child you know—a niece or nephew, a young cousin, even your own child if you are already a parent. Or, calling on your memories and the stories told to you by your parents, you may think of yourself when you were a child. You might know this child—even the child you once were—quite well or not so well. You might have daily contact with children or never see them at all.

No matter what your experience with children, you have one thing in common with all other adults: You will never again directly experience the "magic time" of childhood. Once we become adults, we can no longer see the world through children's eyes. We trade that vision for a more rational understanding of how things work, an understanding that allows us to function competently in the world.

When we were children, we were guided and cared for by our families and teachers. Now the responsibility for guiding the next generation of children to healthy adulthood passes to us. And even though we were once children ourselves, we do not understand many of the things children say and do. They charm and bewilder us. Their minds do not work the same way ours do. Even when we think we have explained things to them, we often discover that they have their own beliefs:

> . . . that after people die, they can "get alive" again
> . . . that when you tire of having baby brothers around, you can return them to
> the hospital where they were "boughted"
> . . . that blankets and stuffed bears can have their own thoughts and feelings
> . . . that dreams are "made by the night" when the lights go out
> . . . that children can be the secret but true reason for their parents' divorce

When we hear ideas such as these, we realize how profoundly different children's experience of the world can be from ours. We also realize that to provide conditions suitable for their growth, we must increase our understanding of them. Knowledge and understanding of children are what this book is designed to provide.

Our Approach to the Study of Children

Of course, children are not like cars on an assembly line, to be analyzed and put together piece by piece. They are whole people, living in the world, bringing themselves completely to their experiences. But this very complexity makes it difficult, at first, for the student to understand children. This is why we begin the study of child development by considering its different aspects separately. In this book, the study of children is divided into various domains—physical, cognitive, language and communication, social-emotional. Although it is convenient to treat the various aspects of development this way, we must not lose sight of the fact that children function as whole people.

We approach the study of children chronologically by organizing our material in "age-stages," from infancy to adolescence. Because we can see changes that set children apart at any point in time from their earlier and later selves, we discuss how children at one age-stage differ from children at another age-stage. But development is

also continuous in many ways, the accumulation of experiences that makes a child what she is today and what she will become tomorrow. Any single behavior or characteristic must, therefore, be considered as both a result of previous developments and a predictor of subsequent developments.

We also look at the many factors that interact to make children what they are, not the least of which are the unique characteristics that each one brings into the world. But a child's uniqueness is shaped by the many contexts in which the child lives—family, school, community, country, world. Each context leaves its mark and must be taken into account. Today we are more aware than ever of the complex reciprocal interactions between the child and her environment. The threads of a child's life are woven from all these elements into a fabric not easily—or even appropriately—taken apart for closer analysis.

This complexity in human development means that there are limits to our knowledge. Although we have theories, research studies, and a vast amount of information about child development, some questions have not been answered definitely in ways that help us know how to act. There are many questions that cannot even be studied experimentally. For example, children who watch a great deal of television tend to be poor readers. Does heavy television viewing *cause* low reading achievement? We cannot be sure. To find out, we would need to enlist large numbers of children and ask them to watch many hours of television every day for a fairly long period of time—perhaps five hours a day for a year. Very few parents would allow their children to participate in such a study, and a researcher proposing such an experiment, while believing that it would be harmful, would be acting unethically. Left with naturally occurring groups of children in real situations, we do not know whether low reading achievement is caused by the television viewing or whether some third factor causes both the low achievement and the heavy TV use. We also do not know if turning off the television would improve reading achievement or have no effect. Our knowledge is incomplete.

Making Connections: The Practical Aspects of Understanding Children

Even when research has provided clear-cut information about issues in child development, there is sometimes a gap between research and the everyday world of parents and teachers. Some of our daily interactions with children raise questions that either have not been investigated or have not been answered in ways that are useful to the practitioner. The connection between scientific information and the everyday situation sometimes seems to be missing.

Understanding Children and Adolescents helps to make these connections. From the huge body of information about children and adolescents—most of it important and relevant in one way or another—we have selected material that we judged to be particularly useful to the person who cares for and teaches children. We have then explicitly discussed the implications of this knowledge—the way it relates to what we do with children. Vignettes involving individual children—both actual children and composites of children we have known—illustrate and bring to life the principles of development discussed in each chapter. Our focus throughout is on the application of the research and theory we discuss.

Why We Cannot Account for Everything: The Role of Values

When we study children, we begin by watching them. We notice how they look, what they do and say, how they respond to what we do and say. We wonder what makes them the way they are. We find ourselves worrying, too, about whether they are the way they *should* be. When we ask these questions, we are no longer talking about research alone—we are talking about values too.

Whether they are explicitly stated or subtly implied, values are an ever-present element in the study of child development. All research reported, all topics covered, all actions recommended are based on values—ideas and beliefs about what constitutes the good parent or teacher, the good society, the best child. Sometimes we do not agree with the values implied in research studies. When this occurs, we find ourselves making decisions about children that do not seem to follow from findings about child development. Our choices reflect our own histories and ideals, as well as the information and theories we have learned. When we live and work with children, we take these factors into account too.

About Understanding Children and Adolescents

We begin our study of child and adolescent development with foundations—theories of child development and research methods. Then we consider genetics, prenatal development, and birth. Next, we discuss the neonate, before moving on to a discussion of the infant and toddler. Beginning with the infant and toddler part of the book, we address four areas of development, devoting a complete chapter to each one. These include physical development, cognitive development, development of language and communication, and social development. The same format is followed for the preschool child (3 to 6 years), the school-age child (6 to 12 years), and the adolescent (13 to 19 years). Summary charts showing some of the highlights of development are provided at the end of each age-stage period.

Despite limitations to our knowledge, the study of child development provides information of enormous importance to everyone who lives or works with children. It gives us a framework, a road map, with which to understand, guide, and support children on their journey through childhood—a journey on which it is our duty, privilege and pleasure to assist them.

We wish you well in your study of this important topic, and in your use of *Understanding Children and Adolescents*. We are confident that this book will help you understand children and adolescents. We suspect that it may increase your interest in them as well. We also hope that it will fill your life and work with children with more wonder and less worry than there might have been had we never met across the following pages of this book.

1

Theories of Child Development and Methods of Studying Children

"I DON'T *LIKE* tuna fish sandwiches!" Nicole announces.

"Stop that, Nicole," her mother whispers in her ear. "It isn't polite."

"But I only like peanut butter sandwiches!" Nicole protests. "Not these!"

"Nicole, you won't be able to visit Anabelle again if you don't stop acting this way, and I'm going to remove some stars from your reward chart at home if you keep this up."

"Why don't you like tuna fish?" Anabelle asks.

"Because it's yucky!" says Nicole. "It's yucky, yucky, yucky!"

"It is not," counters Anabelle. "It's good. I like it."

"That's great, Anabelle," says Nicole's mom. "It's important to learn to eat a lot of different things."

"I didn't need to *learn* to like it," offered Anabelle. "I *always* liked it."

"Here," announced Anabelle's mother, as she joined the others at the table. "Someone might like peanut butter and jelly sandwiches, or a sandwich with just cucumber slices in it."

"Miriam, Nicole needs to learn to eat a variety of things. You don't need to cater to her."

"Actually, I thought I might like cucumbers on my tuna fish sandwich."

After lunch, while the girls played, their mothers talk. "Her refusal to eat a variety of foods just drives me nuts," Claire confides to Miriam. "She'd eat peanut butter and jelly sandwiches, and nothing else, for breakfast, lunch, and dinner, if I'd let her. I've tried everything—favorite desserts if she will eat new foods, extra stickers on her star chart, and showing her how good new foods are by eating them myself. Nothing works."

"I don't know what to tell you," says Miriam. "My children just seemed to try things over time and learned to like them. Anthony and I also like almost anything. Perhaps it's genetic! Just relax about it. I always worry that conflicts around food will cause children to have serious eating disorders later in life."

"You know what? Let's suggest to Martha that one of the speakers at our preschool parent meetings this year be an expert on how to get children to eat without being so picky."

"Oh, that would be a great idea."

A few months later, a speaker did talk to the parents at the preschool Nicole and Anabelle attended. Afterwards, Claire said to Miriam, "Oh, boy! Wish I had known all of this earlier. I've been doing all the wrong things!"

"Oh, well, it's never too late to start doing things differently," said Miriam. "Some of us are just lucky. I had no idea that breast-feeding a baby had any-thing to do with a child's later acceptance of foods. I guess my children didn't inherit those food tastes—they experienced them early in life in my breast milk."

"I don't know why people don't tell you these things before you become a parent," said Claire. "I don't think I would have breast-fed Nicole, even if I had known, but I sure would have taken a different approach in handling her food aversions had I known that they are a normal reaction to new foods."

think about it   Why did Miriam and Claire have such different ideas about why Nicole did not want to try new foods? Why did these parents have trouble agreeing on how to get Nicole to eat differently? The way these two parents selected information about how to react to Nicole was undoubtedly guided by their theoretical orientations—the way they thought about the causes of children's behavior. In other words, each parent had one or more theories of behavioral development and tried to explain Nicole's behavior in terms of her own theory.

Sometimes people say, "That's just theoretical." They usually mean that a statement is unproven, unrelated to situations in which we typically find ourselves, or just someone's guesswork. It is true, of course, that theories often fail to hold up when tested, but even if we do not consider *our*selves scientists, we come up with explanations for why things happen. A **theory** is simply a set of systematically organized assumptions about why something happens or works the way it does.

Theories of child development are sets of assumptions about why children act the way they do, as well as why and how children change over time. Theories of child development are useful, first, because they prevent us from being overwhelmed by a collection of unrelated facts or observations. Second, theories help us formulate explanations for data about children, as we saw in Nicole's case. Finally, theories help us generate new ideas and questions that can lead to further discoveries—they influence us when we design studies to learn more about children.

In this chapter, we first discuss seven child development theories: (1) maturational, (2) psychoanalytic, (3) learning, (4) cognitive-developmental (Piaget), (5) sociocultural (Vygotsky), (6) information-processing, and (7) developmental systems (Bronfenbrenner). We place these theories in context and indicate how they have influenced the field of child development. Ethological theory (from animal behavior as determined by evolution) is discussed extensively in relation to relevant topics in chapters 7 and 11. An example of an ethological theory is that children's picky eating is a survival mechanism common to the human species.

Maturational Theory

Miriam initially described children's eating behavior as hereditary, meaning that children inherit preferences for the same foods their parents like. "My children just seem to try things over time and learned to like them," Anabelle's mother said, as if the inherited food preferences emerged when children matured enough according to their genetic timetable. Miriam's explanation is consistent with a genetic/maturational theory of child development.

G. Stanley Hall established the first formal laboratory of experimental psychology in the United States, but he was also interested in introspective approaches to psychology, including the work of Sigmund Freud. (*Source:* © Bettmann/Corbis)

Origins of Maturational Theory

Maturational theory, born in the late 19th century, was based on Charles Darwin's work on evolution (1859) and on his cousin Francis Galton's work on intelligence. Galton (1869) believed that people who are genetically similar have comparable abilities. He concluded that intellectual abilities are inherited and fixed at birth because he observed that people in the same family often were similar in terms of intelligence. But of course, members of the same family may be similar intellectually because their home environments are similar, not simply because they share the same genes.

According to maturational theory, the individual may be influenced by heredity either at birth, when certain genetically fixed characteristics are present, or later on, when genetically determined traits appear according to an inherited timetable. One example of a characteristic that is (usually) determined in large part by this developmental timetable is the age at which puberty begins. Another is final adult height.

Maturation is the process of biological change and development according to which new behaviors steadily emerge one after another. Maturational theory suggests that, within a broad range of normal conditions, the appearance of a particular behavior depends on genetically determined timetables, not on experience or environment.

Maturational Theory in the 20th Century

The most prominent advocate of maturational theory in the late 19th and early 20th centuries was the psychologist G. Stanley Hall (1844–1924). Hall was the first

POLICY

Genetic-Maturational Theory and the Uses of Intelligence Tests

So, because you're all related, although for the most part you'll produce offspring like yourselves, it sometimes happens that a silver child will be born from a golden parent, a golden child from a silver parent, and similarly all the others from each other. Hence the god commands the rulers . . . if a child of theirs should be born with an admixture of bronze or iron, by no manner of means are they to take pity on it, but shall assign the proper value to its nature and thrust it out among the craftsmen or the farmers; and, again, if from these men one should naturally grow who has an admixture of gold and silver, they will honor such ones and lead them up, some to the guardian group, others to the auxiliary, believing that there is an oracle that the city will be destroyed when an iron or bronze man is its guardian. (*The Republic of Plato,* in Bloom, 1968, p. 94)

Since ancient times, many people have thought that intelligence is inherited. Although Plato allowed that there might be occasional genetic "aberrations"—offspring who were either more or less intelligent than their parents or others in their social group—to him intelligence was something a person either did or did not have a lot of from the start. Early in this century, when intelligence tests and the psychometric (measurement of intelligence) movement were born, it was widely accepted that intelligence was inherited. This view was stated again in a controversial book called *The Bell Curve* (Herrnstein & Murray, 1994).

The Genetic-Maturational View of Intelligence: The Early 20th Century

A genetic-maturational view of development attributes intelligence directly to inheritance. Among the many psychologists who held this view of intelligence were Galton (1869), Terman (1916), and Spearman (1927). They assumed that intelligence was largely inherited and that it consisted of some unitary or single factor—what Spearman called "g" (for general reasoning)—that was applied to all thinking, no matter what kind. Thus, if a person demonstrated good memory, he or she was assumed also to be good at verbal definitions, mathematical reasoning, and spatial relationships.

Implications of a Genetic View of Intelligence

Imagine some of the actions that have followed from the belief that intelligence is completely inherited. In the 1920s, beliefs about the source of IQ differences, and information obtained from intelligence tests administered to army recruits, led to recommendations by The Immigration Restriction League that immigration into the United States be limited to people of Nordic and Anglo-Saxon descent. (It did not matter that immigrants' scores improved with years spent in the country.) Calvin Coolidge even said that "biological laws show . . . Nordics deteriorate when mixed with other races" (Steen, 1996, p. 43). The Johnson Immigration Restriction Act of 1924 put limits on immigration from Eastern and Southern Europe.

In the early 20th century, movements to improve the human race by eliminating those thought to be genetically inferior **(eugenics movements)** were fairly common in some countries. For example, by the 1930s, Adolph Hitler recommended killing German children who had physical defects or mental retardation. In 1930, the Committee for the Scientific Treatment of Severe Genetically Determined

president of the American Psychological Association and founded the first scientific psychological journal, *The Journal of Genetic Psychology.* He thought human behavior emerged in stages that unfolded in a predetermined way.

One of Hall's most famous students was Arnold Gesell, a physician who observed children throughout the 1920s and 1930s and described the ages at which different behaviors emerged. Gesell was one of the first to use motion pictures extensively in behavioral analyses (Cairns, 1998). He believed that skills, such as walking and talking, developed in accordance with the individual child's inner timetable and that learning could occur only *after* the individual was biologically ready.

Readiness, also called **neurological ripening,** was one of Gesell's major ideas. Until the nervous system was mature enough to accomodate a particular skill or behavior, Gesell thought, the child was not ready for it. In the 1930s, for example, it was suggested that children not be exposed to any type of reading instruction until they had reached a mental age of 6.5 years, as measured by intelligence tests (Mor-

Illness was formed, and by 1940, 5,000 children a year were being killed (Steen, 1996, p. 38).

In 1904, the state of Indiana passed a sterilization law that pertained to those institutionalized in state facilities who were insane, repeat criminals, or retarded. By 1931, 30 states had similar laws (Steen, 1996, p. 40). States also had laws against interracial marriages because it was assumed that children born to mixed-race couples would be genetically inferior (Steen, 1996, p. 40).

During the middle decades of this century, schoolchildren in the United States, and in many other countries too, were routinely administered intelligence tests. A low-achieving student scoring high on an intelligence test, for example, was called an "underachiever" and encouraged to do better. But a low-achieving student scoring low on an intelligence test was thought to be doing as well as could be expected. Still other children were classified as "overachievers." These children's achievement was higher than their IQ scores indicated should be possible!

During the 1960s and 1970s, children were placed in special education classes based on intelligence test scores and little or no additional information. Recommendations have also been made to abandon programs such as Head Start, because of claims that people live in poverty primarily because of low intelligence, determined by heredity, not lack of opportunity (Herrnstein & Murray, 1994).

Other Views of Intelligence

Today, most psychologists do not adhere to a strict genetic view of intelligence, nor do they think of intelligence as a unitary or single factor. Instead, they think intelligence is the product of complex interactions between an individual's heredity and experience, and they think that intelligence can be reflected in a number of different domains. For example, one theory of multiple intelligences describes seven different kinds (Gardner, 1991, 1995). (See chapter 13 of this text for a full discussion.)

Evidence supporting the importance of the environment in the development of intelligence comes from a variety of studies. Studies in which social factors such as poverty, maternal education level, and differences in children's learning experiences have been controlled show that IQ differences between racial groups virtually disappear (Brooks-Gunn et al., 1996). Number of years of schooling is strongly associated with IQ scores—increasing years and higher IQ are positively correlated—and the direction of effect seems to be from schooling to IQ scores, not the other way around (Ceci, 1991). Intervention programs, such as the one conducted by Campbell and Ramey (1994) for infants at risk for low IQ, show increases in IQ as a result of participation in this kind of experience.

Group differences in intelligence can be explained by something other than genetics. Given that racial and ethnic group membership has been highly correlated in the United States with educational and economic opportunity (and lack thereof), it is not surprising that group IQ differences favor those who have been privileged members of society. But this does not mean that group differences in intelligence are due primarily to differences in genetics. Differences among groups who experience different environments are likely to be due to differences in experience rather than to differences in heredity (Weiss & Mann, 1981).

The assumption that experience, rather than genetics alone, significantly affects the development of intelligence has implications for public policy. Here are just a few:

- Maintaining efforts to reduce poverty
- Improving educational opportunities for all children
- Making plans for children's educational placements based on the results of a variety of assessment instruments, rather than a single intelligence test

phett & Washburne, 1931). The 6.5 years landmark was thought to be determined by the biological maturation of the nervous system. No one seriously considered what we believe to be true today—that both readiness for reading and intelligence as measured by intelligence tests might be influenced by other, nonbiological factors, such as a child's experience with language.

Another student of Hall's was Stanford University professor Lewis Terman. Terman wrote an English translation of the intelligence test constructed by the Frenchmen Binet and Simon (1905). The test, known as the Stanford-Binet Intelligence Test (Terman, 1916), reported a person's intelligence as an "intelligence quotient" or IQ. Terman believed that intelligence was basically a genetically fixed characteristic. Although Terman thought children learned more the older they became, he thought their ability to learn—their IQ—was stabie. Today, this assumption is very much open to question. (See Knowledge in Action: Policy—Genetic-Maturational Theory and the Uses of Intelligence Tests.)

Arnold Gesell devoted his career to studying the orderly emergence of behavior patterns in infants and children. For example, he documented the locomotor progression of rolling over, sitting up, crawling, pulling up, walking with support, standing alone, and walking alone. He founded the Gesell Institute of Child Development at Yale University and popularized the idea that children can't learn or develop new behaviors until they reach the appropriate level of physical and neurological readiness. He did not think that experience contributed to readiness, but rather that it was determined solely by the genes the child inherited. (*Source:* Gesell Institute of Human Development)

Several observers have remarked that child psychology in the first half of the 20th century consisted merely of gathering data to establish age-related standards or patterns of behavior that apply to large groups—**norms**—without the guidance of a theory. However, to a maturational theorist, establishing norms is part of a developmental theory, one in which maturation determines when behaviors will occur. Gathering data about the emergence of physical or intellectual abilities, for example, was viewed as gathering data about the typical maturation of the nervous system, the undisputed explanation of the times for the development of intellectual and physical abilities.

Today few psychologists believe that abilities are fixed by genes for life without any influence from the environment. But some psychologists, parents, teachers, and pediatricians have ideas that lean in this direction. We still hear statements every day about child development that reveal strong beliefs in the power of maturation. Representative statements are listed in Table 1.1.

TABLE 1.1

Common statements based on a maturational view of child development

- "He will not accept children for kindergarten until they are at least 5 years old."
- "Children are not ready for reading until at least first grade."
- "Do not worry if your 2-year-old is not toilet-trained yet. When he is ready, he will practically train himself."
- "Oh, she will grow out of it. Just leave her alone."
- "They are born that way."

Psychoanalytic Theory

Miriam revealed a second theory about Anabelle's emphatic refusal of tuna fish when she said, "I think it's probably not a good idea to make too much of this sort of thing. I always worry that conflicts about food will cause children to have serious eating disorders later in life." Concern about potentially traumatic social and emotional scars of "pushing" was first expressed in psychoanalytic theory, which originated with Sigmund Freud. Later, Erik Erikson developed another theory, which, although based on traditional psychoanalytic ideas, differed in important ways from Freud's theory.

Sigmund Freud

In the early 20th century, while maturational theorists were absorbed in documenting intellectual and physical development, Austrian physician Sigmund Freud (1856–1939) was studying personality and emotional development. Like the maturationists, Freud recognized the importance of biology, but he also stressed the interaction of biology with the environment. Freud was interested in neurology and in psychological causes of loss of physical functioning. He learned that patients' nervous symptoms improved when the patients were encouraged to talk about them, and he developed a treatment based on this technique. This was the beginning of psychoanalysis, a therapy Freud referred to as "the talking cure."

Freud's Notion of Instinct   Freud focused on the biological components of the personality, which he called instincts. Other theorists use the term **instinct** to refer to an innate behavior in animals, but Freud gave this term a different meaning. Freud defined instinct as a mental representation of a body state or need, such as hunger or sexual arousal (Freud, 1925). The key to Freud's entire theory hinges on an understanding of his idea of instinct.

Freud thought that all actions are motivated by the desire to maximize instinctual, or need, gratification while minimizing punishment, guilt, and anxiety. Freud thought that these motivations drive behavior (Maddi, 1976). Because these needs are basically biological or physical, Freud's theory is a biological theory first of all. But because personality development depends on how the environment meets these biologically based needs, environment is important too.

The Parts of the Personality   Freud proposed that the psyche or personality has three parts, the id, the ego, and the superego. The **id** is the unconscious source of instincts. It operates according to the pleasure principle and demands immediate gratification of its instincts. It constantly propels the individual to relieve tension or excitation in the body—to satisfy needs. The life of the young child is dominated by the id and characterized by the tendency to gratify selfish instincts.

Sigmund Freud and his daughter Anna pioneered psychoanalysis. Anna, his youngest daughter, was the only one of Freud's six children to follow in his footsteps. She became a noted child psychotherapist and writer in London.   (*Source:* © UPI/Corbis-Bettmann)

The **ego**—the reality-oriented part of the personality—tries to direct the id to find satisfaction in appropriate ways, ways that will not be punished. Thus, the ego operates to transform or delay gratification of the id's instincts until their expression can be achieved in ways that do not elicit negative consequences from others. The rules for nonpunished behavior are taught to children by their parents. They become part of the moral component of personality, making up the part called the **superego.** The superego itself begins to provide anxiety and guilt to mildly punish the child's instinctual consideration of forbidden behavior and thus directs the ego, as the ego directs the id, in finding gratifications that will not be punished. At times, the superego blocks gratification altogether. When the superego effectively blocks direct instinctual gratification, the ego allows partial gratification by means of **ego defense mechanisms** (Table 1.2).

Stages of Development in Freudian Theory The instincts responsible for the child's conflicts with the punishing world change "location" as the child moves

TABLE 1.2

Freudian defense mechanisms

Defense	*Definition*	*Example*
Repression	Blocking out an unacceptable thought or feeling	A child feels he would like to get rid of his father so he can have his mother all to himself, but he keeps the thought from reaching his conscious mind.
Projection	Attributing an unacceptable thought or feeling to someone else; externalizing an internal experience	A child who dislikes a teacher feels that the teacher dislikes her.
Reaction formation	Doing the opposite of what one feels like doing to avoid experiencing an unacceptable impulse or feeling	A child who feels unsure of himself bullies other children and bosses them around.
Displacement	Transferring feelings from one event or person to a less threatening one	A child who is angry at her parents scolds her doll.
Acting out	Expressing an unconscious impulse directly rather than experiencing the emotion that accompanies it	A child sees his best friend playing with someone else and knocks down their block construction to avoid feeling jealous.
Intellectualization	Transforming thoughts about emotional conflicts into inaccurate, quasi-intellectual terms	A teenager rationalizes deep hostility toward her brother with a variety of extensive complaints.
Sublimation	Redirecting energy associated with an unacceptable feeling into a socially acceptable activity	A teenager feeling strong sexual urges focuses intensely on practicing the piano.

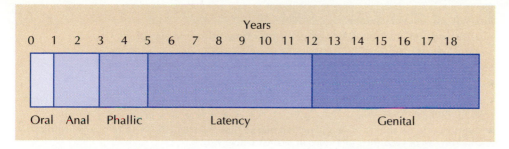

Years

0 1 2 3 4 5 6 7 8 9 10 11 12 13 14 15 16 17 18

Oral Anal Phallic Latency Genital

FIGURE 1.1

Stages of development in Freudian theory. Early psychoanalysts believed that if instinctual energy became blocked in any one stage, characteristics of that stage would become embedded in the individual's personality. For example, someone who was fixated at the anal stage, when toilet training is an important issue, might be stingy, compulsive, punctual, and unable to let go of possessions or relationships.

from one stage of development to the next. Freud identified these stages as oral, anal, phallic, latency, and genital (see Figure 1.1). Each is associated with the particular zone of the body that Freud thought was the source of troublesome instinctual energy during that period of life. In other words, Freud thought that the instinct likely to get the child into trouble changed as the child matured physically.

In the oral stage (birth to about 1 year of age), the mouth is the location of the most satisfying (or frustrating) experiences. In the anal stage (end of the first year to the end of the third), the anal region is the center of instinctual activity. Specifically, during this period, the child's developing sphincter control encourages the parents to attempt toilet training. The child, however, has an urge for immediate gratification of the instincts associated with defecation, so there is a conflict between child and parents. In the phallic stage, which lasts until about age 5, the genitals are the new source of prohibited instinctual activity. During the latency stage (age 5 or 6 until adolescence) no new instincts or activities emerge to create problems. Then, in adolescence, the genital stage begins, and mature love of others and socialized adult behavior become possible. Desires may still conflict with social rules, but the ego and superego keep the id in check.

If instincts are not overgratified or undergratified by the parents, the child progresses normally from one stage to the next, acquiring the defense mechanisms associated with each stage for keeping the id under control. These defense mechanisms largely determine the behavior we see. If the instincts are at any point overgratified or undergratified, however, the individual can become fixated at that stage. Being **fixated** means that some instinctual energy remains blocked in a previous zone rather than moving on to the next. As an adult, the individual continues to exhibit needs, defenses, and behavior more typical of individuals at an earlier stage. The early stages—oral and anal—were considered by Freud to be especially important for personality development. For example, an adult's overeating may be due to fixation at the oral stage.

The Meaning of Freudian Theory for Child-Rearing Practices Although Freud's theory asserted that fixation could result from either over- or undergratification, it was much more likely in the formal and rigid society in which Freud lived that instincts would be undergratified rather than overgratified. As a result

---

TABLE 1.3

Common statements based on a psychoanalytic view of child development

- "It's better to feed a baby on demand than on a rigid schedule."
- "Children who suck their thumbs were not allowed to suck the bottle or breast long enough when they were babies."
- "Nursery schools should have a punching bag so that children who tend to quarrel with other children can release their emotions in a constructive way."
- "Do not interfere with children's dramatic play; it is important for children to work out their emotional conflicts."
- "A child who is often angry must be displacing anger at his frustrating parents, which he carries around with him."
- "The goal of psychotherapy is to make the unconsious conscious."

Erik Erikson proposed that development proceeds through a series of stages, each with a crisis to be overcome, before identity is finally achieved. Many people in early childhood care and education programs find Erikson's theory particularly relevant to their work because it describes the kinds of tasks and expectations children will encounter at various ages and the balance of feelings and competencies children can achieve by engaging in them. *(Source:* © UPI/ Corbis-Bettmann)

application of his theory has usually involved a loosening of rules so as to gratify the child's instinct or wish to a greater extent.

Although there has been very little research that clearly supports Freud's ideas, Freudian theory exercised a strong influence upon 20th-century thought. His notion that childhood experiences influence a person later in life continues to influence developmental research and the thinking of teachers and parents (see Table 1.3).

Erik Erikson

Active in the 1940s through the 1960s, Erik Erikson did not agree with Freud that instincts, especially sex, were the driving force behind actions. Erikson focused more on how society affects the ego (an **ego psychoanalytic** emphasis). Erikson recognized that healthy adaptation to reality differs greatly from one society to another, something that would not occur if parental reactions to human biology were the primary factor determining personality. He also saw that society's demands on a person change as the person grows and that these demands can influence the course of development. Erikson's **psychosocial theory** of development reflects his emphasis on the individual's adaptation to differing social demands. In contrast, Freud's theory is **psychosexual**.

Erikson's theory involves eight stages (or "ages," to use Erikson's term) of development, each characterized by a major crisis or turning point, a time of both increased vulnerability and increased potential for psychological growth. The stages extend over the entire life span. From birth to about 18 months, the psychosocial conflict or crisis is between trust and mistrust. Depending on how the parent responds to the baby's needs, such as hunger, the baby will decide that he or she is either "all right" or "not all right." The appropriate resolution of Stage 1 is the development of trust, but not complete trust, because that would lead to behavior that is not truly adaptive. This kind of appropriate resolution applies to each stage.

In Stage 2, which lasts from about 18 months to about 3½ years of age, the conflict is between autonomy, on the one hand,

According to Erikson, a toddler who is allowed to explore, experiment, and try doing things for herself, without being reprimanded for mistakes, will develop autonomy without too much shame or guilt. Similarly, older children who succeed with effort in mastering school tasks will become industrious. Adults can help children meet society's challenge at each stage of development by understanding the tasks children face at different ages and responding appropriately. *(Source:* (LEFT) © Elizabeth Crews, (RIGHT) © Robert Daemmrich/Tony Stone Images)

and shame and doubt on the other. If the child is allowed to move around, make decisions, touch objects, and explore, the child develops a sense of being a separate person who can make choices and exert some control over the world. Table 1.4 summarizes the conflict or crisis to be resolved in Erikson's other stages.

TABLE 1.4

Erikson's eight stages of development

Psychological Conflict or Crisis	Pivotal Events	Age	What a Person Learns When Development Proceeds Successfully
Trust vs. mistrust	Caregiver response to physical needs of infant, especially in feeding	Birth to 18 months	I am all right.
Autonomy vs. shame or doubt	Toilet training, locomotion, exploration, and touching of objects in environment	18 months to 3½ years	I can make choices.
Initiative vs. guilt	Curiosity resulting from increased language, motor, and cognitive skills	3½ to 6 years	I can do and I can make.
Industry vs. inferiority	School tasks such as learning to read	6 to 12 years	I can join with others in doing and making.
Identity vs. confusion or diffusion	Learning one's vocational and professional orientation	Adolescence	I can be to others what I am to myself.
Intimacy vs. isolation	Love relationship	Young adult	I can risk offering myself to another.
Generativity vs. stagnation	Parenting, nurturing others, civic responsibility	Mature adult	I am concerned for others.
Integrity vs. despair	Reflection on one's life	Older adult	I can accept my life.

Source: Adapted from material in *Identity, Youth and Crisis,* by E. H. Erikson, 1968, New York: W. W. Norton.

Learning Theory

When Claire told Miriam, "I've tried everything—favorite desserts if she will eat new foods, extra stickers on her star chart, and showing her how good new foods are by eating them myself," she was describing a learning theory approach to eating novel foods. Providing rewards and modeling appropriate behavior are concrete actions parents can apply in the child's environment in order to change behavior.

In contrast to the psychoanalytic theorist's focus on inner personality developments over time, learning theorists focus on observable, external behavior and how specific environments affect it. Psychoanalytic theory proposes that biologically based events set personality development in motion. Learning theory, on the other hand, generally ignores biological aspects of development and proposes that developmental changes occur as a result of experiences. **Learning** is defined as a relatively permanent change in behavior that results from experience.

Origins of Learning Theory

Learning theory originated in studies with animals. Variations of learning theory have been known over the years as S-R theory, behavior theory, behavioral theory, and behaviorism. But no matter the specific name, learning theory refers to a focus on how a new behavior can be acquired. (In Nicole's case, the new learned behavior would be eating tuna fish.) The term *S-R theory* refers to the connection between a stimulus (S), generally in the environment, and a response (R), such as eating, on the part of the organism. The term *behaviorism* reflects the belief that psychological theories should be based only on observable behavior and should avoid references to inner states, such as thoughts, feelings, desires, and so on.

Classical Conditioning   The roots of learning theory can be found in the work of the Russian physiologist Ivan Pavlov (1849–1936). Pavlov showed that under certain circumstances an animal can learn a physiological response to a new stimulus in the environment. These circumstances involve the pairing of the new stimulus with another stimulus that naturally produces a particular response. After repeated pairings, the new stimulus produces the same response as the original stimulus. The response to the new stimulus is "conditional" on the previous pairing of the two stimuli. This type of learning is known as **classical conditioning.** Pavlov called the stimulus that produces the response naturally the **unconditioned stimulus** (often abbreviated UCS) and the new stimulus that is paired with it (often presented slightly before it) the **conditioned stimulus** (CS).

Pavlov's most famous illustration of classical conditioning involved teaching a dog to salivate at the sound of a bell. He rang the bell (the conditioned stimulus) immediately before he gave the dog some food (the unconditioned stimulus), which naturally caused the dog to salivate (the **unconditioned response,** or UCR). After several pairings of the neutral stimulus (bell) and the unconditioned stimulus (food), the sound of the bell alone caused the dog to salivate somewhat (the **conditioned response,** or CR).

We often see apparent examples of classical conditioning in child development. For example, classical conditioning is thought to be the basis of many irrational fears that develop in childhood. The classic example of this was John Watson and Rosalie Raynor's conditioning of "Little Albert" to fear a white rat that initially evoked no fear. By repeated pairings of the white rat (conditioned stimulus) with a loud gong (unconditioned stimulus) that naturally produced a startle response (unconditioned response), the presentation of the white rat alone eventually elicited a startle response (conditioned response).

Instrumental Conditioning   Pavlov studied how behavior was influenced by stimuli that occurred before the behavior. An American psychologist, Edward Thorndike (1874–1949), was interested in how behavior was affected by events that occurred after the behavior. He showed that he could increase or decrease the frequency of a behavior if he followed it consistently with a reward or a punishment. This type of conditioning, known as **instrumental conditioning,** provided the basis for behavior modification programs. **Behavior modification** requires that the reward follow only when the behavior, or a close approximation of it, actually occurs. When Claire proposed giving Nicole dessert or stars that could be exchanged for a toy, she was assuming that the frequency of eating new foods would be increased by rewards contingent on the desired eating behavior. If Claire gave Nicole dessert and stars even when she refused to eat new foods, she would not teach Nicole to eat tuna fish. For learning to occur, getting the reward must be contingent upon performing the appropriate behavior.

The Science of Behavior   Another American psychologist, John B. Watson (1878–1958), was sharply critical of the introspective methods that Freud and other psychologists used to study human behavior. First, he thought that people's reports of their own reactions to various stimuli were bound to be inaccurate. Second, these procedures could not be used with children or animals, the very subjects in which Watson was most interested. Above all, Watson wanted psychology to be a science of behavior. In **behaviorism,** only data obtained from the observation of behavior, those things that people actually do or say, are considered valid. Because of his revolutionary influence, Watson became known as the "father of behaviorism."

B. F. Skinner

The most influential behaviorist was B. F. Skinner (1904–1990). Skinner completely rejected concepts such as drives or needs that are inside the organism and therefore unobservable. Instead, his behaviorism, frequently referred to as radical behaviorism, attempted to explain behavior with no references to unobservable events.

Skinner replaced the concept of reward, which suggests drive reduction, with the concept of **reinforcement.** Reinforcement is defined as the process of increasing the probability of a response by presenting an observable event contingent on the response. A reinforcer is the observable event. It increases the frequency of a response when it follows that response (and no other). (Similarly, Skinner defined **punishment** as the process decreasing the probability of a response by presenting an observable aversive event contingent upon the response.) Skinner defined **operant conditioning** as either increasing the frequency of a behavior by following it with a reinforcing event or decreasing the frequency of a behavior by following it with a punishing event.

Behaviorists such as Skinner spoke of increasing the frequency of a given response with a reinforcer that was observed. Instrumental learning theorists such as Thorndike, on the other hand, spoke of increasing the frequency of a target response by following it with a "reward," defined as an event that reduces a "drive."

Some reinforcers are defined as positive because, following a child's response, they add something to, rather than take something away from, the environment. If a child

Russian scientist Ivan Pavlov demonstrated that animals could acquire new reflexes through a process of conditioning. His ideas and experiments formed the basis of the theory that behavior is the result of learning. In 1904, Pavlov won the Nobel Prize in physiology for his groundbreaking work. (*Source:* © Corbis-Bettmann)

B. F. Skinner, shown here as a young man at work in his lab at Harvard in 1933, built on the ideas of John B. Watson to develop a broad theory of animal and human behavior. Skinner believed that people's actions—even very complex actions such as learning to speak a language—could be explained in terms of learning principles, such as reinforcement. (*Source:* © UPI/Corbis-Bettmann)

is given a cookie only if she asks for it by saying "please," the cookie is said to be a positive reinforcer if using "please" in such requests increases in frequency. The cookie is a **positive reinforcer** because it increases the probability of a behavior—saying "please." The reinforcer is positive because it adds something to the environment.

Discovering what observable events tend to serve as positive reinforcers with a given species in a given situation allowed behaviorists such as Skinner to describe the general effects of various schedules or frequencies of reinforcement without referring to the organism's drives. Such study led, for example, to the general rule that continuously reinforced behavior is more easily learned than behavior that is only occasionally or intermittently reinforced. But after learning has occurred, behaviors that have been continuously rather than intermittently reinforced are less likely to continue when reinforcement actually stops. This is why some behaviorists have suggested to parents that they continuously reinforce appropriate behavior, such as saying "please," when they first teach it, then reinforce it only intermittently in various settings with various people. This schedule makes the behavior more likely to continue when no one is any longer actively reinforcing it. Among other things, Skinnerians have extensively described how behaviors change according to different schedules of reinforcement.

Other reinforcers are **negative**—they consist of removing something from the environment, following a response. Consider the case of a child and parent in a shopping mall. The child begins to whine. To stop the whining, the parent may buy the child a toy. If the whining stops when the parent gives the child the toy, something aversive has been removed from the parent's environment. If the parent then buys toys more frequently to stop whining, we say that the parent's toy-buying behavior has been negatively reinforced by the child. Both positive and negative reinforcers increase the likelihood that certain responses will occur again, the former by adding something, the latter by removing something.

Skinner and his followers became well known for teaching a new behavior by taking an existing, familiar behavior and reinforcing it to bring it closer and closer to the desired behavior. The process of reinforcing successive approximations until the desired behavior appears is known as **shaping.** For example, if researchers want a pigeon to walk with its head held very high, they give it grain first when it raises its head slightly higher than average, next when it holds its head considerably above average, and finally when it is stretched very high. Eventually, the pigeon can be taught to carry its head high almost all of the time.

In Nicole's situation, Claire might at first reinforce Nicole's behavior when Nicole eats very small amounts of tuna fish. Claire would then reinforce only successively larger portions until the desired behavior is reached. In other words, the mother would reinforce eating small amounts of new food in the early stages of the behavior modification program, even though Nicole's initial behavior only approximates the desired final result. Then the mother would further shape behavior, encouraging Nicole to eat larger amounts of tuna fish (closer and closer approximations of the desired behavior) before providing a positive reinforcer. Examples of common statements based on learning theory are given in Table 1.5.

Social Learning Theory

Subsequent to Skinner's work, some theorists concerned with human learning, notably Julian Rotter and Albert Bandura, were willing to talk about cognition (thinking, a behavior not directly observable). They elaborated descriptions of cognitive

TABLE 1.5

Common statements based on learning views of child development

- "You may watch television after you finish your homework."

- "In our math program, children learn just one small step at a time. Success is guaranteed, and children want to keep working with the materials."

- "When you finish your reading and math assignments, you may paint, play with blocks, or choose a learning game."

- "Ignore children when they are behaving badly; praise them when they are behaving well."

- "You will spoil the baby if you pick him up when he cries."

- "Children who answer correctly will receive a gold star on their papers."

- "It is important that children have good models of behavior."

processes involved in learning or changing the frequency of behaviors (Bandura, 1973, 1977; Rotter et al., 1961). Their ideas are fundamental to contemporary **social learning theory** (Cairus, 1998).

Bandura initially emphasized that many behaviors are learned quickly through observation and imitation of others rather than gradually through the shaping process that Skinner described. It is unlikely, for example, that many of us could learn to drive a car through shaping, which depends so heavily on trial and error. We might not live through the first lesson! Instead, we learn through cognitive processes related to modeling (imitating the general form of behaviors observed in others) and verbal instruction. A psychologist who warns, "If children see you hitting, they learn to hit," is using social learning theory to explain and predict behavior.

As social learning theory has progressed, it has placed more emphasis on the cognitive processes involved in learning. Walter Mischel (1976) suggested that an individual's behavior in a particular situation is determined not by the situation alone but by a complex of cognitive qualities that the individual brings to the situation. This includes abilities, values, expectations, interpretations, and plans. Mischel noted an observation first made long ago by Plato: The same stimulus or situation—for example, in modern times, a classroom test—elicits different responses from different individuals, depending on the abilities and interpretations they apply to it. Whereas the radical behaviorist would assert that the stimulus controls the response in a strict way, the social learning theorist allows room for individual variation due to different interpretations of the stimulus.

Bandura extended his theory into the realm of cognitive theory, even labeling it "social cognitive theory" (1986, 1994). Rather than describing individuals as determined strictly by the learning histories their environments have dealt them, Bandura described individuals who in large measure determine their own destiny by choosing their future environment, including the goals they wish to pursue. They reflect on and regulate their own thoughts, feelings, and actions to achieve those goals. The degree to which individuals are effective in thinking, motivating themselves, and feeling positively about their goal-directed actions is determined in large part by their own **self-efficacy belief**—that is, the belief that they can actively control events rather than endure passively whatever the environment provides (Bandura, 1995). Social learning theory accepts a number of the principles of behavioral psychology, such as the effects of reinforcement and other aspects of the environment on behavior, but it supplements these principles with ideas about cognition, which enables human beings to actively change their environment.

Cognitive-Developmental Theory: Jean Piaget

When confronted with picky eating like Nicole's, a cognitive-developmental theorist is likely to ask if she understands what is expected of her and why. The cognitive-developmental theorist may well probe the child's knowledge of the health advantages of eating a variety of foods and ask Nicole if she is interested in changing her behavior as a result of what she knows. If Nicole does not have these understandings, the cognitive-developmental theorist may take the position that rewarding her behavior would be of little use. However, if Nicole did understand the usefulness of eating a variety of foods, then her mother could remind her at appropriate times in order to encourage her to try a range of foods.

Interest in how cognition affects behavior grew rapidly in the late 1950s. Researchers from a number of traditions noted that exploration and learning often occurred best in situations unrelated to the satisfaction of commonly recognized reinforcers or primary rewards (those having to do with the satisfaction of physiological needs). For example, one researcher found that monkeys would learn a task when it was followed by an opportunity to look at something outside their cages (Butler, 1953). Similar behavior had been noted earlier in rats. They would cross an electrified grid to get to a maze filled with new objects (Nissen, 1930). Some theorists suggested that there might be a drive to play, explore, effectively manipulate, and become competent in mastering the environment (White, 1959). But other theorists looked for a different explanation. Cognition seemed to be a fruitful area to investigate in search of an explanation for the organisms' exploration in these situations.

At about the same time, information-processing theorists (Miller et al., 1960; Newell et al., 1958) began using a computer analogy to describe cognitive phenomena, such as selective attention, information gathering, and problem solving. We discuss information-processing theory later in this chapter as well as in later chapters on cognitive development.

Since the 1930s, however, Swiss philosopher and biologist-turned-psychologist Jean Piaget (1896–1980) had been studying the development of cognition. He was particularly interested in what knowledge is and how people acquire it. He approached the question of adult knowledge by investigating children's knowledge. He asked two basic questions: (1) Why do children and adults think differently in similar situations? and (2) What causes human knowledge to change with time?

Piaget's Explanation of Knowledge Acquisition

Piaget thought knowledge was constructed or created gradually, as maturing individuals interact with the environment. He considered children to be active in their own development. This view contrasted with other major theories. According to traditional maturational theory, the child is at the mercy of the genes that determine the rate of maturation. Only

Social learning theorists have pointed out that human beings learn many behaviors through verbal instruction, observation, and imitation. This young boy is imitating behavior that he has observed his father perform. (*Source:* © Will Faller)

when neural ripening has occurred can the child acquire knowledge quite easily from the environment.

Learning theorists consider knowledge to be external—acquired through experience and reinforcement. Piaget, on the other hand, did not consider knowledge to be independent of the child, to be lurking "out there" in the external world. He believed instead in **constructivism**, the creation of knowledge through interactions between the developing child's current understanding and the environment.

Processes by Which Knowledge Is Acquired   Piaget explained that knowledge is created by the child through two processes, assimilation and accommodation. **Assimilation** is the process of taking in information about the environment and incorporating it into an existing knowledge structure, which Piaget called a **scheme** or **schema**. A 2-year-old who is familiar with dogs, for example, can be said to have a dog scheme, which may

Jean Piaget, a Swiss psychologist, often observed children as they played games. He also developed tasks with which he could explore specific aspects of children's thinking. (*Source:* © Bill Anderson/ Monkmeyer)

cover medium-sized, four-legged animals often found in people's houses. Then, the first time the child sees a cat, she may call it a dog, assimilating it to her "dog" scheme. Gradually, as she sees more cats and notices how they differ from dogs, she develops two different schemes, one for cats and another for dogs. Piaget called the process by which children change their knowledge structures **accommodation.**

Because our schemes or cognitive structures are always inadequate to handle all our experiences (Piaget, 1963), assimilation tends to distort information from the environment to make it fit available schemes. Eventually, these distortions are corrected as we change the schemes to accommodate the new information. The 2-year-old changes her dog scheme to exclude animals that meow and climb trees, and she develops a cat scheme that includes these characteristics. Eventually, her schemes will accurately reflect all the noticeable characteristics of each type of animal. In this way, our schemes come to conform more closely to the world around us.

Piaget used the term *equilibration* to refer to the process by which assimilation and accommodation constantly balance each other. Experiences that promote cognitive development are those in which the child is in conflict or disequilibrium—current knowledge structures do not quite match the child's experience. This cognitive conflict leads the child to invent new structures or schemas, and equilibrium between experience (input) and knowledge (internal structure) is thus restored.

Piaget's Stages of Development   In Piaget's theory, assimilation and accommodation lead not only to more knowledge, but also to major reorganizations of knowledge—to different ways of thinking. Piaget considered the points at which major reorganizations in thinking take place to be the beginnings of different stages. Table 1.6 summarizes the four major stages Piaget proposed. (Each stage is discussed in detail in later chapters.)

TABLE 1.6
Piaget's stages of cognitive development

Stage	Description of Stage
Sensorimotor (birth–2 years)	Knowledge is acquired and structured through sensory perception and motor activity. Schemes involve actions rather than symbols.
Preoperational (2–6 years)	Knowledge is acquired and structured through symbols, such as words, but schemes are intuitive rather than logical.
Concrete operational (7–12 years)	Knowledge is acquired and structured symbolically and logically, but schemes are limited to concrete and present objects and events.
Formal operational (12 years and older)	Knowledge is acquired and structured symbolically and logically, and hypothetical/deductive ("if-then") thinking can be used to generate all the possibilities for a particular situation.

Piaget and Motivation for Knowledge Acquisition   Piaget's theories were enormously influential in many areas of child development. One implication of his ideas is that completely familiar events may be uninteresting to the child because they require no change in schemes. Completely unfamiliar events, on the other hand, may be incomprehensible because the child has no scheme into which to assimilate them. Piaget's theory predicts that children will prefer moderately novel events because these are the ones most likely to prompt accommodation (Hunt, 1965).

Piaget's ideas provide a theoretical basis for the notion of intrinsic motivation, or motivation that comes from information processing itself, rather than from external rewards (Hunt, 1965). In other words, a child might initiate actions without being motivated by hunger, thirst, sex, or pain and without being rewarded or punished for the actions. According to Piaget's theory, children will act simply to understand. When children express interest in something, Piaget's theory suggests that they are indicating both that they understand it in some sense and that they are trying to understand it in a better way.

Cognitive-developmental theory is evident in many child-rearing and educational practices and beliefs. Examples of its common applications are listed in Table 1.7.

TABLE 1.7
Common statements based on a cognitive-developmental view of child development

- ■ "Children learn best when they are interested in what they are doing."
- ■ "Children are active learners."
- ■ "When children answer questions incorrectly, ask them why they answered as they did before deciding how to help them arrive at a more accurate answer."
- ■ "Children seek stimulation."
- ■ "Do not put all of the new toys out in the classroom at once; add new ones gradually to renew interest."

Sociocultural Theory: Lev Vygotsky

Piaget tended to focus on the child's own construction of knowledge. He overlooked the social context in which knowledge is constructed (Valsiner, 1998), even in the acquisition of the most important cognitive structures. Other theorists have not shared Piaget's view that knowledge is acquired autonomously through interactions with the physical environment. For example, Lev Vygotsky, a contemporary of Piaget, had read the early writings of Gesell and Piaget, but felt that they minimized the importance of social interaction in cognitive development.

Vygotsky's Views of Knowledge Acquisition

Vygotsky received a degree in law from the University of Moscow in 1917, at the beginning of the Communist Revolution. He received his doctorate in the psychology of art in 1925. Vygotsky began writing in his native Russia just after the socialist revolution and led a young group of Marxists in the task of creating a psychology that would contribute to the development of a new socialist society. Despite this, his writings were suppressed because they were considered to be insufficiently Marxist. Specifically, Vygotsky had used intelligence tests in some of his research, a practice that was condemned by the Communist Party. Because of this political situation, and because Vygotsky died in 1934 at the age of 37, his influence worldwide was delayed. Only relatively recently has his work become widely known.

Like works by other Russians of his time, Vygotsky's first writings were marked by Marxist zeal, bent on pointing out how knowledge and even thought itself are socially mediated and constructed for each child throughout history. According to Vygotsky and Marxist philosophy, knowledge is acquired in a **dialectic** process—it is the product of interaction between two opposing tendencies existing within a problem-solving situation. The dialectic by which the knowledge in a culture is acquired is the interaction between the child and a more advanced member of the culture who usually uses language or a commonly understood sign to impart it. This dialogue is eventually internalized by the child as thought.

For Vygotsky, all knowledge, from the most important to the most mundane, is socially constructed. For example, suppose an adult reads a particular story to a child or describes how to do some aspect of homework. The child internalizes the essential features of these dialogues. Gradually, the child is able to work independently on these previously tutored activities.

An example of such internalization is the infant's nonverbal pointing to objects, which occurs near the end of the child's first year of life (Wertsch, 1985). Pointing begins with the baby's unsuccessful attempt to grasp an object, which a mother comprehends as an indication of the child's interest. The parent responds with her own attention to it, names it, gives it to the child, and so on. In other words, the mother, an individual more mature than the child, introduces meaning into the child's initial gesture. Subsequently, the child also sees the gesture as a sign (Leont'ev, 1981).

Internalization is the means by which culture (a social group's values and skills) is transferred from one generation to the next. The particular knowledge and even the ways of thinking transmitted from adult to child are thought to vary a great deal from culture to culture. Because knowledge is socially constructed by the child and others within the culture, Vygotsky's theory is usually described as **sociocultural**.

Vygotsky's theory is also cultural-historical. In addition to being a sociocultural theory of **ontogenetic development** (development of an *individual* child), his general theory encompasses a view of human evolution, plus a short human cultural history. Like Marx, Vygotsky indicated that tool use and labor in our history demarcated the beginning of human culture. But Vygotsky went on to say that the acquisition of language was the most important event in the development of the culture, just as it is in

Vygotsky agreed with Piaget that knowledge is constructed by children. However, he considered social interaction to be far more important to the process of knowledge acquisition than did Piaget. Because of this emphasis on the social construction of knowledge, Vygotky's theory of cognitive development is described as sociocultural.

the development of individual children. The breadth of Vygotsky's thinking allowed him to speculate not only about the relationship between linguistic signs and the development of thinking, but also about the nature of human consciousness itself.

Vygotsky believed that human consciousness did not exist prior to the development of the ability to use some sign (or mental "tool"), such as language, to form concepts, to generalize, or to describe events (Ratner, 1991). Without concept formation and linguistic description of events, Vygotsky thought mature human consciousness impossible. For Vygotsky, human consciousness was more than experience. The first development of human consciousness in the course of evolution and its subsequent manifestation in any given individual require the use of language, or at least some meaningful sign, which can be used to describe and operate on that experience. Human consciousness consists of thought about experience. In his typical literary style, Vygotsky (1926, p. 33) stated that a human's consciousness of his or her experiences means only that those experiences have been "changed into an object [a stimulus] for other experiences." In this way, he continued, "consciousness is the experience of experience in precisely the same way as experience is simply the experience of objects."

The cultural-historical aspect of Vygotsky's theory states that these important linguistic structures, thoughts, and ways of thinking are not developed independently by each child, but are instead the product of a long line of individual children's interactions with more advanced members of their culture. Any seemingly original thought or way of thinking is socially constructed both by the culture and by each successive child. For Vygotsky, this was true for voluntary attention, for concept formation, and for all other psychological (for Vygotsky, cultural-psychological) phenomena. "First [some psychological function] appears between people as an *inter*psychological category . . . then within the child as an *intra*psychological category" (Vygotsky, cited in Wertsch, 1981, p. 163).

We can say that Piaget's child constructs knowledge about the world. Vygotsky's child, on the other hand, internalizes knowledge that is socially and culturally constructed. As Vygotsky put it, "The path from object to child and from child to object passes through another person" (cited in Dean, 1994, p. 40).

The Zone of Proximal Development

Vygotsky is perhaps best known for his concept of a zone of proximal development, which is related to the social construction of knowledge. The **zone of proximal development** is the gap between the child's independent performance and the child's assisted performance (performance with adult help). Vygotsky stated that knowledge is socially constructed in a child's zone of proximal development only when the child receives assistance from a more skilled peer or adult.

Vygotsky suggested that classrooms not be grouped simply by achievement on the basis of the independent performances of the students, but that children's zones of proximal development also be considered. Children with narrow zones (slower learners), according to Vygotsky, should be in a different class from those with wide zones (fast learners) (van der Veer & Valsiner, 1991). Vygotsky said explicitly that instructional activities should be pitched to the top of each child's zone of proximal development. (See chapter 13 for an extensive discussion of Vygotsky's ideas and their application in educational settings.)

In reading Vygotsky, one realizes that the specific culture of the person who provides the path between object and child is extremely important for the child's understanding of the surrounding world. Vygotsky's emphasis on the cultural specificity of intellectual abilities suggests that research regarding the influence of diverse cultures on development is sorely needed today, just as it was during his time. (See Research Close-Up: Cross-Cultural Research in Child Development.)

RESEARCH

Cultural-historical theories of development, such as Vygotsky's, as well as the developmental systems or bioecological theories of Bronfenbrenner (Bronfenbrenner, 1977; Bronfenbrenner & Morris, 1998), Lerner (1986), and others, emphasize that the context in which the child and his or her caregivers exist affects child development. Researchers have tested these theories by gathering data on the development of children whose cultures vary in significant ways.

Among the best-known researchers who have investigated child development cross-culturally are John and Beatrice Whiting. They have published their data in several works, including *Children of Six Cultures: A Psycho-cultural Analysis* (Whiting & Whiting, 1975). In this book, the authors discuss observations of children from India, the Philippines, Mexico, Kenya, and the United States.

Among the many researchers who have collaborated with the Whitings over the years is Carolyn Pope Edwards. She worked with Beatrice Whiting on research and its publication in *Children of Different Worlds* (Whiting & Edwards, 1988). This book shows quite clearly the influence of different cultures on various aspects of child and adult/parent behavior. One of the most interesting differences in adult/parent behavior they describe concerns mothering. The authors describe this difference as a training-oriented versus a control-oriented approach to mother-child interactions.

related agricultural tasks and in household chores. Mothers whose workloads were heavy also trained children in behaviors to keep them safe and healthy. Because children growing up in these circumstances are kept fairly busy, they do not spend a great deal of time initiating their own independent activities to which mothers might respond, after the fact, with criticism of their behavior. Instead, the mother's interactions are dominated by instruction about tasks, both before children engage in them and while they are engaged.

A mother who is control-oriented, on the other hand, does not involve her young children in tasks nearly as much as do training-oriented mothers. Children are allowed instead to initiate their own activities to a greater degree. But during child-initiated episodes of behavior, control-oriented mothers often intervene to criticize or to alter behavior they think is inappropriate.

As might be expected, control-oriented mothers tend to be found more often in cultures where women's workloads are relatively light. Because they are not burdened heavily with work, their children's labor is not needed. Thus, children are more often left to initiate their own activities and perhaps to get into trouble, given the open-endedness of their activity. But the mother often gets involved after the fact, using controlling interventions, to get the child's behavior on a course she thinks is constructive and appropriate.

The Cultural Context of Training-Oriented versus Control-Oriented Mothering

A mother who is training-oriented tends to involve children rather constantly in tasks that reduce the workload of adults—especially the mother. For example, children might be asked to fetch water, gather kindling for cooking fires, tend the fire, feed farm animals, or watch over young children. Interestingly, mothers were more training-oriented in cultures in which their own workloads were very heavy. For example, they were responsible for tending food crops and for performing most household chores. Tending food crops usually includes planting, weeding, and harvesting. Household chores might include processing food (e.g., grinding grain to make flour), preparing food, cleaning the house and the immediate outdoor areas, and tending to children. Women also often needed to carry water quite a distance from its source, at a well or a stream.

When the mother's workload was heavy, children were included at a young age in economic- or subsistence-

Cultural Influences on Child-Development Theories

The larger cultural context no doubt influences the general view of child development that is held in a culture and the expectations that people have for children. In fact, Whiting and Edwards (1988) found that views about children, and expectations for them, were also associated with the workloads of women in a culture. They also found that religious and cultural practices and beliefs influenced adults' child-development theories. For example, mothers they studied in India held the most extreme view about which characteristics of children are determined at birth. Their view that practically everything is predetermined is consistent with the caste system that has shaped much of India. Mothers in the United States, on the other hand, were at the other extreme, believing that experience affects children's development. This is perhaps not surprising in a country where one finds strong beliefs about individual freedom and equality.

Information-Processing Theory

Information-processing theorists seldom claim to have as comprehensive a theory of cognitive development as Piaget or Vygotsky did (Lutz & Sternberg, 1999). Instead they examine how people of different ages process information or manipulate symbols. They tend to view the mind as a computer that has a memory into which information is fed. In this process, information from the environment is initially decoded (broken down), and parts of that information are encoded in memory where they are combined with previous information, stored, and eventually retrieved to solve a problem.

Development is thought of as acquiring new and more effective information-processing strategies. As age increases, the learner constructs new strategies, applies old strategies to new problems, and executes strategies (including "chunking" information into frequently used routines) more quickly as a result of practice. Some theorists also hypothesize that increasing age brings an ability to hold more information in working memory, which enhances problem solving. Information-processing theorists hold that development occurs continuously, rather than in stages. (Information-processing theory is discussed further in chapters 5, 9, and 13, all of which are concerned with cognitive development.)

This is how an information-processing theorist might explain why Nicole, a preschooler, has difficulty helping Claire count the number of chairs needed at the table for lunch with Anabelle and Miriam. If Nicole is told to check that four chairs are set at a table which in fact has only three, she is likely to count the first, second, and third successfully, yet continue around the table a second time, calling the first chair "Four." An information-processing theorist may point out that Nicole does not yet have enough working memory to both count chairs and notice where her starting point was. Later, Nicole's counting will become automatic enough to be "chunked" as a working memory that also will help her note which chair she counted first. In the meantime, Claire can help Nicole by pulling the first chair away from the table as a reminder of which chair Nicole counted first.

The Developmental Systems Approach

Each theory described so far differs from the others in significant ways, including scope. Scope refers to the range of issues and areas addressed by the theories—what they do and do not try to explain. An exhaustive comparison of the theories is not possible here, but two aspects of such a comparison are relevant because they relate to a new and broader approach to theorizing about children's development.

The Scope of Differing Theories

First, theories can differ in the scope or domain of behavior they try to explain and predict. Maturational theory focuses mainly on physical and intellectual development. Psychoanalytic theory focuses on emotional and personality development. Learning theory focuses primarily on social and intellectual development. Cognitive-developmental theory deals primarily with the child's developing intellectual understanding of the world.

A second difference between the theories is in the scope or extent to which they take into account the interacting systems that affect behavior. **Systems** are groups of elements that have similar rules for relating to each other. Each system has a boundary separating things "inside" from things "outside." The rules and relationships inside the system differ from the rules for relating to elements outside the system. Furthermore, systems tend to exist in hierarchies; that is, each system has smaller subsystems within it and is at the same time an element of larger systems beyond itself. For example, a body cell (such as a muscle cell) is a system within an organ (such as the heart). The heart is a system within a group of body structures (the cardiovascular system). The body structures are themselves a system within a particular human being. One important early model of living systems is shown in Figure 1.2 (Miller, 1971).

How can we understand and describe the systems and system interactions addressed by the major theories of child development? To answer this question, we identify four very general systems or levels of influence: (1) genetic/cellular, (2) neurological, (3) child/behavior, and (4) environment (see Figure 1.3).

Maturational theory proposes that behavior is primarily a result of neurological maturation. Individual differences result from genetic effects on neurological development. Behavioral learning theory spends little time describing anything other than

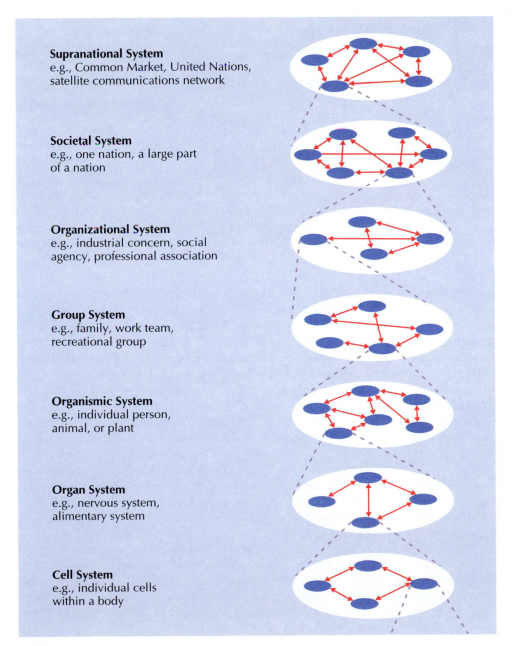

Supranational System
e.g., Common Market, United Nations, satellite communications network

Societal System
e.g., one nation, a large part of a nation

Organizational System
e.g., industrial concern, social agency, professional association

Group System
e.g., family, work team, recreational group

Organismic System
e.g., individual person, animal, or plant

Organ System
e.g., nervous system, alimentary system

Cell System
e.g., individual cells within a body

FIGURE 1.2

One model of levels of living systems. The systems approach suggests that human development occurs as a function of ongoing, mutual interactions among many systems. (*Source:* Adapted from *Clinical Psychology: Expanding Horizons 2/E* by Sundberg/Tyler/Taplin, © 1973. Reprinted by permission of Prentice-Hall, Inc., Upper Saddle River, NJ.)

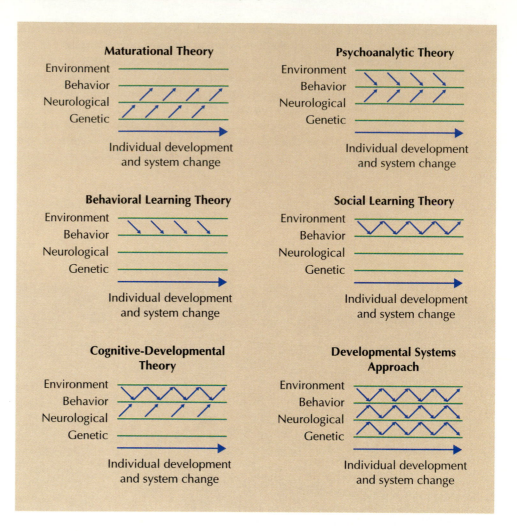

FIGURE   1.3

A simplified scheme show-
ing how major theories
address a
possible hierarchy of
four systems. Systems
above the level of the
immediate environment
and below the immediate
genetic level have not
been included.   (*Source:*
Adapted from *Individual
Development and Evolution:
The Genesis of Novel Behavior,* [Figure 14.3, p. 186], by
G. Gottlieb, copyright © 1992,
by Oxford University Press.
Reprinted by permission.

environmental influences on behavior, although social learning theory has begun to
address the effect of the individual on the environment.

Classical psychoanalytic theory proposes that the environment provides responses that may undergratify or overgratify the needs that appear as neurological
maturation proceeds. Cognitive-developmental theory suggests in a general way that
intellectual behavior is determined by the feedback the individual gets from small
changes he or she produces in the environment. Thus, Piaget claims there is an interaction between two systems, the individual's behavior and his or her environment.
Cognitive-developmental theory also acknowledges that neurological development
must have an effect on behavior, although it does not describe the precise nature of
neurological influences.

Because all of these theories have limitations in what they address or explain,
theorists in recent years have turned to a developmental systems approach as a framework for a more complete developmental theory. The major premise of this approach
is that a complete theory should take into account the reciprocal or mutual interaction that occurs constantly among all levels of the hierarchy of living systems (Gottlieb et al., 1998; Lewis, 2000). A single system influences both the systems within it
and the system of which it is a part. In other words, influences (or effects) go both to
the level above them ("bottom-up" influences) and to the level below them ("top-
down" influences). Those levels in turn act on the original system and on the levels
above or below them. An extremely simplified illustration of the developmental systems approach is shown in the last panel of Figure 1.3.

Because the systems approach captures much of the complexity of human relationships and development, it has been used by a number of child development theorists who have identified systems they think are particularly relevant. Other names for the systems approach include "developmental contextual" (Lerner, 1986), "transactional" (Dewey & Bentley, 1949), and "interactive" (Magnuson, 1988). Among developmental psychologists, the best-known systems theory has been Urie Bronfenbrenner's ecological or bioecological theory (Bronfenbrenner, 1977, 1993; Bronfenbrenner & Morris, 1998).

Bronfenbrenner's Bioecological Theory

Bronfenbrenner described the five systems shown in Figure 1.4. A **microsystem** is a pattern of activities, roles, and interpersonal relations that a child experiences in a face-to-face setting (Bronfenbrenner, 1979, 1993). For most children, the earliest influential

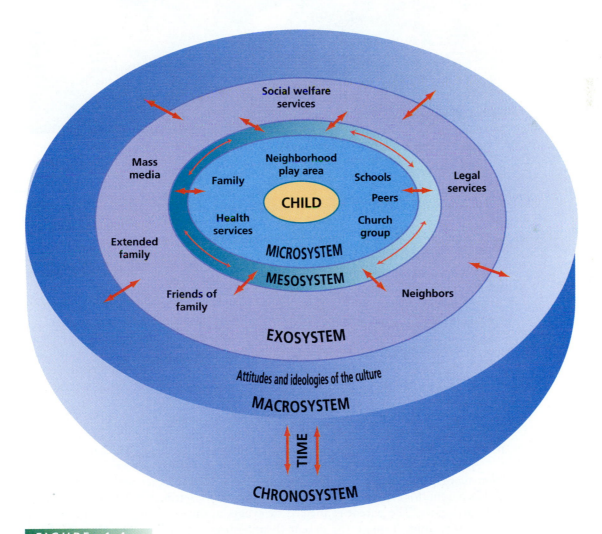

FIGURE 1.4

Bronfenbrenner's bioecological systems: *Microsystem* refers to relations between the child and the immediate environment; *mesosystem* refers to the network of interrelationships of settings in the child's immediate environment; *exosystem* refers to social settings that affect the child but do not directly impinge upon him or her; *macrosystem* refers to the attitudes, mores, beliefs, and ideologies of the culture; and *chronosystem* refers to time.   (*Source:* Adapted from *Child Development in the Social Context,* [Figure 12.1 from page 648], by C. B. Kopp and J. B. Krakow, © 1982 by Addison-Wesley Publishing Company, Inc. Reprinted by permission of Addison Wesley Longman Publishing Company, Inc.)

Urie Bronfenbrenner proposed a bioecological theory. Included in the theory is the notion that children elicit responses from the environment and, thus, influence their own development.   (*Source:* Chris Hildreth/Cornell University Photography)

microsystem is the family, followed by the child-care center or school. In Bronfenbrenner's bioecological model, the child is assumed to participate over a period of time in a number of such microsystems. Bronfenbrenner's theory has been used to classify, by system, the factors that enhance or interfere with a child's development (Garbarino, 1982). For example, parents who are not responsive to their child's signals, and those who respond with hostility, are examples of negative influences in the child's microsystem.

A **mesosystem** is made up of the interrelations among two or more settings in which the child participates (Bronfenbrenner, 1979). The child's most influential mesosystem is usually the one between home and school. In order to function effectively, there should be frequent positive interactions between parents and personnel in the home/school mesosystem. An absence of connections between microsystems, as well as the presence of conflicts in their values, presents risk to the child in any mesosystem, no matter whether the relationship is between family and school, family and child care, or child care and the neighborhood peer group (Garbarino, 1982).

An **exosystem** is a setting in which the child does not actively participate. But an element or person from the child's microsystem does interact with the setting. A child's parent, for example, might interact with a work setting in which the child does not participate. The parent is affected by events in the exosystem, which indirectly affects the child, through the parent (Bronfenbrenner, 1979). (See Figure 1.4.) A workplace that is stressful to the parent to the point of reducing the parent's responsiveness at home increases risk to the child's development. Exosystems also include not only parents' workplaces, but such things as a teacher's family.

The subculture and culture of which the child is a part is the **macrosystem.** Traditions of racism, sexism, violence, totalitarianism, or cut-throat competitiveness, communicated throughout the culture or subculture, will have obvious effects, particularly for vulnerable children—children already at risk due to difficulties they encounter at the microsystem and mesosystem levels.

Finally, Bronfenbrenner (Bronfenbrenner & Morris, 1998) saw development as taking place through processes of reciprocal interaction between the child and the child's environment, which become progressively more complex over long periods of *time*. The **chronosystem** (time) is the fifth system Bronfenbrenner proposed. But the chronosystem consists not only of patterns of stability and change over time at the microsystem level. It consists of changes at the mesosystem, exosystem and macrosystem levels as well. That is, examples of important events in the chronosystem include not only events occurring in the child's microsystem (e.g., change in one father's responsiveness to his daughter's signals), but events occurring in the macrosystem and other systems also (e.g., change in the degree to which a culture supports job advancement for women).

Bronfenbrenner brought the emphasis on bidirectional effects to center stage in developmental psychology. That is, like most developmental psychologists before him, he proposed examining the effects of the activities of others, such as parents and teachers, in a given microsystem, on the child. But he also defined as **developmentally instigative characteristics** those qualities of a particular child that affect others so as to set in motion repeated reciprocal interpersonal interactions that influence the course of that child's development (Bronfenbrenner, 1989, 1993). These characteristics include physical attractiveness, temperament, and activity level, which are thought to be determined largely by biology, as well as by the environment. He proposed that children influence their own subsequent environment, as well as their own subsequent biology. As a result, we see in developmental systems theory the complexity of the issue of how much of behavior is determined by heredity and how much by environment—the "nature-nurture" issue. We shall see in subsequent chapters that nature and nurture are very much intertwined.

The Major Research Methods

Sixth-grade teachers Ann and Kelly were concerned about the aggressive behavior of many children in their classes. In light of media reports that individuals who commit violent crimes often have a history of rejection and aggression during the elementary school years, Ann and Kelly begin discussing what they should do. Ann's behaviorist orientation leads her to suggest a behavior modification program of reinforcing prosocial behavior and punishing aggressive behavior. Kelly argues from her sociocultural (Vygotsky) perspective that they should set up a peer mediator program that couples children with poor conflict resolution skills with children who are good in conflict resolution.

Realizing that different theoretical orientations lead to very different action programs, Ann and Kelly decide to examine research studies that might help them select a course of action at their school. "Each journal article seems to use a different method," exclaims Ann. "I guess different research methods are used at different stages of research to answer different questions," concludes Kelly. "It seems you have to know about the research methods to understand the articles."

think about it

What kind of research methods are Ann and Kelly likely to find in reading journals? What kind of information can be obtained from each study? How will they know whether the information from the studies can be generalized to the children in their school?

This child's parents or teacher might keep an inventory of her book selections. Results from the study of this one case would provide detailed knowledge about this child, but results could not be generalized to other children. (*Source:* © Will Faller)

Ann and Kelly are searching the literature because they believe there are lawful relationships between the development of aggressive behavior and variables such as parenting style, school involvement, teaching strategies, and after-school programs. Understanding children and adolescents requires comprehending empirical research about development as well as the theories presented above. In this section we will examine the major research methods used in studying children. Each research method provides different kinds of information, and each is appropriate under different circumstances. To complement this portion of the chapter, a guide to understanding research on child and adolescent development is presented in Appendix A, page 659.

Case Studies

In a **case study,** the researcher focuses on only one of something—a child, a teacher, a school. The traditional case study, in which one child is studied in her or his natural environment, is the oldest method of child study. It was the method frequently used by Piaget and Freud, for example. A limitation of the case study is that its results cannot be generalized to other situations or children. The information it provides is about one case and one case only.

But the case study does have some notable advantages. The most important one is probably that it allows us to study something in great detail. When we study one child, we can collect much more detailed data, given the same amount of time, money, and human resources, than when we study 100 children.

One researcher used the case study method to study the development of literacy in her son between his second and third birthdays (Granucci, 1986). She taped nightly bedtime storytelling sessions. She kept track of the books he owned and the books he chose to have read to him. She kept a log, noting the toys he had and the ones he played with. She wrote down the questions he asked about print and kept all his scribblings. She did this day in, day out, for one year. By his third birthday, she had filled many file boxes with detailed descriptions of her son's behavior. With this information, she was able to put together a complete picture of one 2-year-old's literacy development during a one-year span of time. This researcher obviously could not have studied a large number of children in such great detail. Ann and Kelly would get lots of ideas from a case study of an aggressive sixth grader if the study recorded in detail what he watched on TV, what discipline his parents used, and how he spent his unstructured time.

The rich detail of the case study shows how complex and multifaceted human behavior is. Case studies often provide ideas about the developmental sequence of many abilities and behaviors. Finally, the ideas generated by case studies often generate hypotheses that can be examined with other research methods. But a case study never tells whether the information gained about this one case is characteristic of others.

Descriptive Studies

Descriptive studies are appropriate when a researcher wants to gather information about children without determining precisely whether there is a cause-effect relationship between variables. There are four kinds of observational techniques commonly used in descriptive studies—specimen records, behavior checklists, event sampling, and time sampling. We will briefly examine each one.

Specimen Records   When observers try to record everything a child does in a short period of time, the result is called a **specimen record**. This technique was extremely difficult before audio and video technology gave researchers the tools with which to observe a moment in a child's life, over and over again. The specimen record is used mainly to get a detailed picture of some aspect of a child's everyday behavior. Because any and all behaviors can be noted, it is considered an open observation method.

Behavior Checklists   Sometimes observers start out with a list of carefully defined behaviors that they are going to watch for and count. In order to carry out systematic observations accurately, a simple coding system is created to record the occurrence of specific behaviors of interest (Cozby, 1997). The **behavior checklist** is a closed method of observation, unlike the specimen record (Wright, 1960). It also does not provide the rich detail that specimen records give. On the other hand, the behavior checklist makes it easier to observe children accurately, and the resulting data are more precise and reliable. Behavior checklists are used for keeping track of specific behaviors, such as aggression, friendliness, or attention seeking. Ann and Kelly might use a behavior checklist in their own classrooms to record the frequency of name calling or intruding into another child's personal space.

Event Sampling   An observer notes the occurrence of a well-defined behavior using the descriptive technique called **event sampling**. Narrowing the range of behaviors to be observed helps to ensure that recording is very precise and accurate. One researcher used this method to study children's quarrels (Dawe, 1934). He observed children during free play in a nursery school. When quarrels occurred, he moved closer to note the details. Because Dawe carefully defined what he meant by a quarrel, comparisons of his data to data collected by researchers at other nursery schools could be conducted meaningfully. Ann and Kelly could use this method to obtain the details surrounding a disagreement between two sixth graders.

Time Sampling   Regular observations are made on a specific schedule in the **time sampling** technique. Observations may be made over a fairly long period of time to ensure that a child's behavior is seen across many different situations. Individual children may also be observed for specific lengths of time within one observation period. A researcher may observe one child for five minutes, then another for five minutes, and so on. In this way, the researcher observes each child in a variety of settings, rather than one child on the playground and another during snack time, which would make it difficult to compare their behavior.

One researcher used time sampling to see what kinds of play children engaged in (Parten, 1932). She defined four categories of play: (1) solitary play—children played alone; (2) parallel play—children played alongside other children; (3) associative play—children played with other children but without subordinating their own interests to the group; and (4) cooperative play—children played as a group. She set up a schedule allowing for one-minute observations of each child, every day for several days. She varied the schedule systematically so that each child was observed at a different time

When children are observed in a natural setting, the findings can be used as the basis for a descriptive study. A researcher observing these children might use event sampling to note every incident of a particular behavior on a checklist—for example, sharing, helping, quarreling, or other behaviors of interest.   *(Source: © Elizabeth Crews)*

Does watching violent shows on TV make children more aggressive, or do aggressive children watch more violent shows on TV? Or, does a third variable, such as parents' tolerance for both aggressive behavior and violent TV shows, cause children to be more aggressive? Correlational research can reveal an association between watching violent TV shows and aggression in children, but only experimental studies can determine if there is a causal link between two variables. (*Source:* © McLaughllin/ The Image Works)

during the free-play period on different days. Results from a careful data-collection strategy like this are likely to be very reliable. Such a method might help Ann and Kelly discover the overall frequency of specific aggressive events throughout the day.

Descriptive studies give a broad, rich picture of how children act. Because there is usually no intervention by the researcher, and often no direct contact at all, ethical issues—concerns about the effect of the study on the child—are kept to a minimum. On the other hand, descriptive studies do not readily lead to conclusions about the causes of children's behavior.

Correlational Studies

A **correlational study** is a study of the relationship betwen variables that are not manipulated by the researcher. Correlational studies measure two or more variables. If changes in one variable are associated with changes in the other variable, the two variables are said to be correlated. If both variables change in the same direction, either increasing or decreasing in value, they are said to be **positively correlated.** If both variables change, but in opposite directions—one increases as the other decreases—they are said to be **negatively correlated.** If one variable does not change systematically with changes in the other variable, the two variables are uncorrelated.

A correlational study can tell whether changes in one variable are related to changes in another, but a simple correlational study cannot report *why* the changes are related. For example, suppose a researcher wanted to explore the relationship between the amount that children were read to throughout the preschool years and the reading ability of those same children in the fourth grade. It is likely that a positive correlation would be found between these two variables. Although it would be tempting to conclude that more time spent reading with preschoolers causes them to have higher reading abilities in elementary school, such a conclusion would be inappropriate because of the correlational research method. Perhaps other confounding variables, such as parent vocabulary, amount of parent-child interaction, or number of educationally oriented family trips, also correlated with amount read to, and they accounted for reading ability differences.

A similar question about causality might exist in studies of aggression. If aggressive behavior is measured in groups of children who watch different amounts of cartoon violence on TV, and children who watch more are found to exhibit more aggression in play with peers, we cannot conclude that viewing violent cartoons causes the aggressive behavior. Perhaps children who are aggressive like to watch televised violence more than children who are not aggressive. Then aggressiveness would be the cause of watching more violent cartoons. Violent cartoons would not cause aggressiveness.

Correlational (also called classificatory) research methods are also used to examine naturally occurring variables which are not both numerical. For example, interested in accounting for differences in the social competence of sixth graders, a researcher might compare groups whose parents are classified as permissive, authoritarian, authoritative, or rejecting-neglecting. (Authoritative parents apply both parental authority and an explanation of their standards in specific situations.) Such a study may find that children raised with an authoritative parenting style have the highest social competence. That is, a relationship may be found between authoritative parenting and social competence. Again, it would be tempting to conclude that authoritative parenting caused the children to be more socially competent. But as in other studies using a correlational research method, it could be that other variables, such as socioeconomic level, number of social events attended, or parental education, might be confounded with parenting style.

Experimental Studies

To determine whether there is a causal relationship between two variables, researchers conduct an **experiment**. Experimental studies have two distinctive characteristics. The first is the use of two types of variables: dependent and independent variables. A **dependent variable** is the behavior the researcher observes or measures in the experiment. It is the behavior the researcher wants to predict or explain, and over which the researcher hopes to exert some control. An **independent variable** is the aspect of the environment manipulated by the researcher to observe its effect upon the dependent variable.

The second distinctive characteristic of an experimental study is the choice of subjects for the experiments. The groups receiving the different forms or amounts of the independent variable must be comparable *before* the study starts. The way to ensure that the groups are comparable is to assign large numbers of individuals randomly to different groups. A group that does not receive an experimental treatment is called a **control group.** Random assignment of children to a control and an experimental group controls for (or equates) all variables, other than the independent variable, that could explain any difference between the control and experimental groups on the dependent variable.

Many experimental studies are conducted in a laboratory setting. For example, in a study of the effects of viewing violent TV cartoons on children's behavior, groups of children might be brought into a special room to view videos. One group might be shown a violent cartoon, a second might be shown a prosocial video, and a third might be shown a neutral video. The type of video viewed is manipulated—it is the independent variable. The children's aggressive behavior in a free-play setting, after watching the various videos, is the dependent variable. If children who saw violent cartoons are observed to play more aggressively than children who watched some other kind of video, we can assume a causal link between watching filmed aggression and aggressive behavior exhibited by the child.

Sometimes experimental studies are conducted after a correlational study has been used to identify potential independent variables. Many developmental research programs use correlational and experimental studies in sequence. Where ethically appropriate, experimental follow-up studies are carried out to determine whether a relationship found in a correlational study is a cause-effect relationship.

Cross-Sectional and Longitudinal Research Designs

Regardless of the research *method* chosen for a study—case study, descriptive, correlational, or experimental—researchers interested in developmental changes throughout childhood and adolescence may choose to employ that method in one of two basic *designs*. The **cross-sectional design** uses groups of children of different ages—perhaps groups of 2-year-olds, 6-year-olds, and 10-year-olds. The **longitudinal design**, on the other hand, starts with a group of children of a specific age—perhaps 2-year-olds—and then follows them across the age span of interest—perhaps until

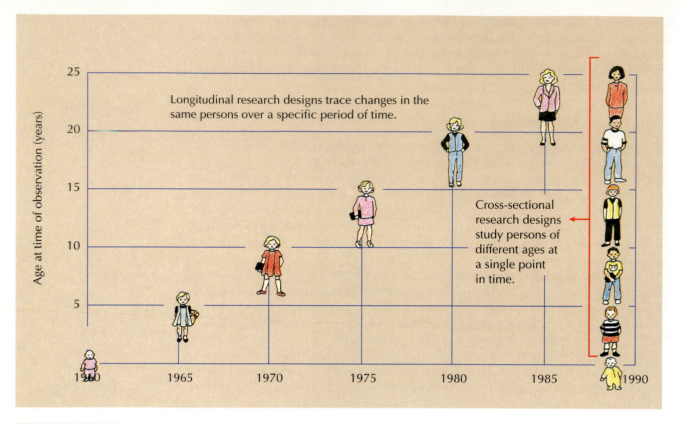

Age at time of observation (years)

Longitudinal research designs trace changes in the same persons over a specific period of time.

Cross-sectional research designs study persons of different ages at a single point in time.

1960   1965   1970   1975   1980   1985   1990

FIGURE 1.5

Longitudinal and cross-sectional research designs. In experiments with longitudinal designs, the same subjects are followed over a number of years, allowing researchers to focus carefully on the process of development. In experiments with cross-sectional designs, subjects of different ages are studied at the same time, allowing researchers to work more efficiently and reducing the likelihood of certain kinds of research errors.

they are 10 years old (Figure 1.5). Each design has its advantages and its disadvantages, and we consider both next.

Advantages of the Cross-Sectional Design

The cross-sectional design allows studies to be completed more quickly than does the longitudinal design, because researchers need not wait for the children to reach the upper age of interest. In a cross-sectional design, researchers simply study children of different ages at the same time. The cross-sectional design also lessens the possibility of biased sampling. In **biased sampling,** the children in the study are not representative of the population to which the researcher hopes to generalize the study's results. Parents who allow their children to participate in longitudinal studies may be different from parents who refuse to allow many observations of their children over a long period of time.

On the other hand, parents from a wide range of educational, social, and economic levels may agree to have their children participate in a one-time cross-sectional study. The smaller proportion of parents who consent to have their children participate in a longitudinal study may have more education or more time to spare. If they do, results from the longitudinal study may not be generalizable to as broad a population as would be results from cross-sectional studies.

Longitudinal study samples also can become nonrepresentative if some children withdraw over the course of the study. Families may move, or their circumstances may change in some other way that prevents them from continuing. If children withdraw during the course of the study, it makes the group under study different from what it was in the beginning. Therefore, if the group of children in the study shows a difference in behavior between, say, age 6 and age 8, we cannot know if this is an age difference—a difference due to *development*—or a difference due to the different composition of the groups of children who were included in the study at ages 6 and 8. We do not encounter this kind of problem with the cross-sectional design.

Advantages of the Longitudinal Design

The advantage of the longitudinal design over the cross-sectional design can be illustrated in studies of the preadolescent growth spurt. By following the growth of each of several individuals over time, a researcher would observe that very rapid physical growth begins for some children at age 11, but not for other children until age 14. Researchers using a cross-sectional design may focus on the mean rates of growth of 10-, 11-, 12-, 13-, 14-, and 15-year-old children and think, mistakenly, that there is a *gradual* increase in height across these years, rather than an abrupt increase in each individual. The longitudinal design charts the pattern of *change* that is undergone by each individual over time. The cross-sectional design reports only differences between groups of children at different ages, since no individual is observed more than once.

Another advantage of the longitudinal design is that it examines but one **cohort** of children—a group of children who are born in the same year and, as a result, have other statistical characteristics in common. That is, not only do members of a cohort have age in common, but also they have life experiences in common that are likely to be unique to the times in which they live. For example, a (hypothetical) cross-sectional study of a cohort of children born in 1990 and examined on computer skills at 15 years of age may show 15-year-olds to be as computer-literate as 25-year-olds born in 1980. One might conclude from this cross-sectional study that individuals do not improve in computer skills between 15 and 25 years of age. Yet a (hypothetical) longitudinal study following the 1980 cohort between ages 15 and 25 would show a difference in computer skills between 15 and 25 years of age, consistent with the increase in computer availability experienced by the 1980 cohort between 1995 and 2005. Powerful cohort effects may easily be ignored in a cross-sectional study of individuals of different ages if the results are simply attributed to age and not the unique experience of a given cohort. Studying a single cohort in a longitudinal design allows the researcher to attribute differences correctly to age and not to the differing experiences of each different cohort.

Selecting a Suitable Research Method

No single research method or design is clearly superior to the others under all circumstances. When doing research in child development, how do people decide which method is best for their purposes? The answer depends largely on two factors: (1) the research question and (2) the ethical considerations associated with the study.

TABLE 1.8

Examples of descriptive, correlational, and causal statements

Which of the following statements do you think are descriptive? correlational? causal?

1. On the average, babies weigh about 7 pounds at birth.
2. The incidence of Down syndrome in children increases as maternal age increases.
3. Older children tend to have more diseases than infants do.
4. When the drug thalidomide is given to pregnant women early in pregnancy, it prevents the formation of arms and legs in the fetus.
5. Girls mature physically faster than boys.
6. Boy toddlers own more vehicle toys than do girl toddlers.
7. Prematurity is a risk factor for problems in attachment.
8. Aggressive behavior can be reduced if children watch prosocial TV programs rather than violent ones.

Descriptive: 1

Correlational: 2, 3, 5, 6, 7

Causal: 4, 8

The Research Question

What kind of questions are to be answered about children? Do we want to know what children are like or what they do? This information could be obtained from a descriptive study. Do we want to know what behaviors are likely to be associated with each other? A correlational study could provide this information. If we want to know what causes differences in a specific behavior, we must conduct an experimental study.

These different methods allow us to make different kinds of statements about children—descriptive, correlational, or causal—after we have collected and analyzed data in a research study. We must always be careful to make only the kind of statement allowed by our research method. (Examples of each kind of statement are given in Table 1.8). The questions to be addressed in reading any research report are presented in Appendix A, page 659.

Ethical Considerations

Some questions cannot be investigated in the manner that would yield the most conclusive results because doing so might harm the research participants. We could not study the effect of protein in infants' diets on their growth by depriving a group of infants of protein, for example. Instead, we could compare the growth of infants in naturally occurring groups that have more or less protein in their diets. Our results in this case would be correlational. If we did find a relationship between growth and protein, we could not be sure it was a causal relationship. That is, we would not know whether differences in growth were due to differences in protein or to some other differences in the naturally occurring groups. These would be limits imposed on research by ethical considerations.

The ethics of research, especially research involving children, has been a concern over the years. The American Psychological Association, U.S. governmental agencies, and the Society for Research in Child Development have developed a code of ethics for research with children. The code includes the following guidelines:

1. Investigators may not use any research operations that may harm a child physically or psychologically. Before carrying out any study, a human subjects committee must review the proposed research for possible risks.
2. Investigators must obtain **informed consent** from the parent or legal guardian of the child before the child can be a participant in a study. This means that the study must be explained completely and accurately to the parent or guardian in language he or she can understand and that the parent must give consent for the child to be in the study. When older children and adolescents are involved, informed consent is sometimes obtained from the children, as well as from their parents.
3. Investigators cannot obtain consent by promising that the research will benefit the child.
4. Investigators may not force an unwilling child to participate in a study. The child has rights that supersede the investigator's.
5. Investigators should keep confidential all information obtained about the child.
6. When the experimental treatment is believed to benefit children, the control group should be offered the same or similar beneficial treatment. This applies even if it means providing treatment after data collection has been completed and if doing so substantially increases the cost of the study.

These guidelines are most likely to be violated by proposed research that involves some kind of treatment, interaction, intervention, or manipulation of variables—the kind of action typical in experimental studies. Correlational and descriptive studies, which tend to involve the observation of children in natural settings, are less likely to run into ethical problems or be met with resistance from parents. Regardless of the research question being asked or the kinds of results desired, ethical considerations must have top priority when choosing a research method.

Tying Things Together

It is perhaps obvious at this point in the discussion why it is so difficult to conduct flawless studies with children. No matter how brilliantly conceived the hypothesis, or how carefully executed the research, every study has limitations imposed by financial constraints or the reality of dealing with human participants. These difficulties help to explain why our knowledge of children is still limited, despite the vast number of studies that have been done on various aspects of child development.

Research is also constrained by theories, because data and theories interact in complex and subtle ways. Theories help organize and make sense of the world, but how we perceive the world is influenced by theories. Theories of child development provide a framework for interpreting the infinite variety of child behavior, and they give meaning to our observations. At the same time, theories can limit the ways we observe and attend to children's behavior. We can use theories of child development to expand rather than reduce our understanding by recognizing that each theory provides important insights yet has certain limitations in helping us study the growth and behavior of children.

In the final analysis our knowledge of children is based on research, but people who live and work with children will find the research useless unless they are able to understand and evaluate the studies. Teachers, parents, and caregivers must know how the results of different studies can be interpreted. They must be willing to think in critical ways when they encounter research findings in child development. Just as researchers must be careful in designing their studies, practitioners must be careful when they interpret and apply research conclusions to the children in their care.

KEY POINTS

- Child development theories include maturational, psychoanalytic, learning, cognitive-developmental, sociocultural, and information-processing theories. In addition, a developmental systems approach attempts to provide a framework for a more complete explanation of developmental processes than that provided by any of the other theories.

Maturational Theory

- Maturational theorists believe that particular behaviors emerge at predetermined times, depending on the individual's inherited biological timetable, and that the timing is unaffected by environment or experience.

- Based on the work of Charles Darwin and Francis Galton, maturational theory dates from the 19th century and was expounded in the United States in the early 20th century by G. Stanley Hall.

- Working in the 1920s and 1930s, maturational theorist Arnold Gesell described the regular emergence of different behaviors in children and explained them in terms of readiness, or neurological ripening, regardless of experience.

- Lewis Terman was responsible for the Stanford-Binet Intelligence Test, which was designed to measure a person's intelligence quotient, or IQ. Maturationists believe that IQ is determined at conception.

- Maturational theorists gather data to establish norms. Their research focuses mainly on physical and intellectual development.

Psychoanalytic Theory

- Developed by Sigmund Freud in the late 19th and early 20th centuries, psychoanalytic theory is based on understanding the gratification of instincts and is concerned mainly with personality development.

- Freud focused on the biological aspect of the personality, which he called instincts. He believed the body was driven by desires, particularly sexual desires, that were represented by mental images. The way people behaved was a result of their attempts to gratify these desires.

- Behavior is a function of the interactions of the id, seeking gratification; the superego, setting limits; and the ego, directing the id to find satisfaction in acceptable ways. The ego keeps the id in check by means of defense mechanisms, such as repression and sublimation.

- The instincts that drive the child change from one period of development to the next. Freud identified five stages of development—oral, anal, phallic, latency, and genital. Children progress smoothly from one stage to another, provided they do not become fixated—stuck—in one state by over- or undergratification.

- Erik Erikson's psychosocial theory focused not on instinct as the driving force behind actions, but on the interaction of the ego and society.

Learning Theory

- Behaviorists study how the environment affects behavior by focusing on observable behavior.

- Russian physiologist Ivan Pavlov demonstrated that animals can learn a new physical response to an environmental stimulus through a process known as classical conditioning. His most famous experiment involved conditioning a dog to salivate at the sound of a bell.

- American psychologist Edward Thorndike showed that he could increase or decrease the number of times a response occurred if he followed it with a reward or a punishment. This type of learning, known as instrumental conditioning, provides the basis for behavior modification programs.

- John B. Watson is known as the "father of behaviorism" because he argued that objective observation should replace self-report as the method of studying the effects of stimuli.

- The best-known modern exponent of behaviorism, B. F. Skinner, redefined rewards as reinforcers and instrumental conditioning as operant conditioning. Skinner demonstrated that new behaviors could be taught by reinforcing closer and closer approximations of a desired behavior until the behavior itself appears, a process known as shaping.

- Social learning theorists are willing to discuss conscious mental processes and inner experiences. They have pointed out that people learn things through observation and imitation, as well as through reinforcement and shaping. They see individuals as actively choosing and changing their environment, setting their own goals, and reflecting on and regulating their own behavior. Individuals are most likely to do this if they have a strong belief in their own self-efficacy.

Cognitive-Developmental Theory: Jean Piaget

- The idea that behavior and learning could be explained by something other than the satisfaction of drives or the reinforcement of responses to stimuli led theorists to begin investigating cognitive factors. The work of Jean Piaget tied in with these interests.

- Piaget discovered that children have different levels of understanding at different ages and that they do not think the same way as adults think. He also found that responses to the environment depend not simply on the situation, but also on the individual's understanding of the situation.

- According to Piaget, knowledge is constructed gradually through interactions with the environment. The child incorporates new knowledge into an existing knowledge structure, or scheme. This process is known as assimilation. Because schemes are inadequate to handle all new information, the child gradually adjusts schemes to make better sense of new information. This process is known as accommodation. Equilibration is the process by which assimilation and accommodation are kept in balance.

- Piaget proposed four stages of cognitive development, each characterized by a different, unique way of thinking—sensorimotor, preoperational, concrete operational, and formal operational.

- Piaget's findings suggest that children learn best when confronted with moderately novel events and that the desire to understand is a powerful motivating force behind children's behavior.

The Sociocultural Theory: Lev Vygotsky

- Like many present-day psychologists, Vygotsky disagreed with Piaget's emphasis on the child's autonomous cognitive development. Vygotsky emphasized instead the social mediation of knowledge that the child internalizes as a result of dialectic interaction with more mature members of his or her culture.

- Vygotsky emphasized the social construction of knowledge not only within the present generation, but also historically. He equated human cultural history with tool and language use. He thought concepts were constructed "between people" historically before they were constructed "within the child."

- Vygotsky thought children constructed knowledge in a "zone of proximal development," which is the gap between the child's ability to perform independently and when assisted by an adult or a more skilled peer. He saw the teacher's knowledge of each child's zone of proximal development as having major implications for the child's education.

Information-Processing Theory

- Information-processing theorists examine how children of different ages process information. Development occurs as the learner discovers which information-processing strategies are effective and which are not. Development occurs continuously rather than in stages.

- As age increases, the learner constructs new strategies, applies old strategies to new problems, and executes strategies more quickly as a result of practice and "chunking" information into frequently used routines. Increasing age also brings an ability to hold more in working memory.

The Developmental Systems Approach

- Systems theory has attempted to provide a framework for a more comprehensive approach to theorizing about human development. A system is defined as a group of elements with similar rules for relating to each other. These differ from the rules and relationships found in other systems.

- Systems are nested within one another. For example, each individual is a system, which is one element within a family system. The family system is an element of a neighborhood, and so on.

- Urie Bronfenbrenner found it useful to group important systems as follows: the microsystem (notably the home or the school), the mesosystem (the interaction of the elements making up two microsystems, such as school and home), the exosystem (systems that include elements of the child's microsystem, but not the child), the macrosystem (subcultures and cultures), and the chronosystem (time).

The Major Research Methods

■ Major methods of child study are the case study, the descriptive study, the correlational study, and the experimental study.

■ In the case study the researcher studies only one person or situation, but in great detail. Because any one person or situation is unique, the results of the case study cannot be generalized.

■ Descriptive studies provide information about how people act. Descriptive studies include specimen records, behavior checklists, event samples, and time samples. Descriptive studies give a broad, rich picture of children's behavior without establishing causation.

■ Correlational studies measure two variables of interest. If the variables consistently change in the same direction, they're said to be positively correlated; if they change in opposite directions, they're said to be negatively correlated. Data for correlational studies can come from descriptive studies, questionnaires, or interviews. Simple correlational studies do not firmly establish cause-effect relationships.

■ In experimental studies, the researcher manipulates an independent variable by applying more of the treatment to one group than to another, the control group. Experimental studies allow researchers to make statements about causes of changes in the dependent variable.

Cross-Sectional and Longitudinal Research Designs

■ The two basic research designs are cross-sectional and longitudinal. In the cross-sectional design, researchers study groups of children of different ages at the same point in time. In the longitudinal design, researchers follow the same group of children over a period of time.

■ Cross-sectional studies can be completed more quickly than longitudinal studies. They are also less likely to be affected by biased sampling, which occurs when groups that were originally comparable change over time.

■ Longitudinal studies allow researchers to observe changes in individual children over a fairly long period of time. They also eliminate the possibility that cohort effects will be confounded with age effects— that is, that differences between groups will be attributed to developmental changes when they're really the result of different life experiences.

Selecting a Suitable Research Method

■ Researchers decide on a research method by considering two factors—the research question and the ethical considerations.

■ Experimental studies are suitable if researchers want to discover causes of behavioral differences. Correlational studies are suitable if they want to know what behaviors are associated with other behaviors. Descriptive studies are appropriate for learning what children do.

■ Ethical considerations have highest priority when a research method is being chosen. Experimental studies are much more likely to raise ethical problems than correlational or descriptive studies, because experiments usually involve some intervention in the child's life.

Tying Things Together

■ Every study has limitations. It is important that practitioners be aware of these limitations when they interpret and apply research conclusions to the children in their care.

GLOSSARY

accommodation: in Piaget's theory, a modification in a knowledge structure or scheme that results from taking in new information (p. 19)

assimilation: in Piaget's theory, the taking in of new information about the environment and incorporating it into an existing knowledge structure (p. 19)

behavior checklist: a list of defined behaviors that a researcher focuses on in a study (p. 31)

behaviorism: the science of behavior based on observable behavior (p. 15)

behavior modification: bringing about a change in behavior by using rewards and punishments that are contingent on the child's behavior (p. 15)

biased sampling: procedures that result in a nonrepresentative sample for a study (p. 34)

case study: a study in which the researcher studies something in just one individual, just one classroom, or one family (p. 30)

chronosystem: the time over which reciprocal interactions take place durng the life span, including sociohistorical conditions (p. 29)

classical conditioning: a type of learning in which a new and neutral stimulus is repeatedly paired with another unconditioned or meaningful stimulus to eventually produce a conditioned or learned response to the previously neutral stimulus (p. 14)

cohort: a group of research subjects born at about the same time, e.g., the same year (p. 35)

conditioned response: a reaction to the conditioned stimulus in the classical conditioning paradigm, which is similar to the unconditional response (p. 14)

conditioned stimulus: in classical conditioning, an initially neutral stimulus that comes to produce a conditioned response after being paired repeatedly with the unconditioned stimulus (p. 14)

constructivism: the belief held by Piaget and other cognitive-developmental theorists that knowledge is not "out there," but is created by the individual through interactions with the environment (p. 19)

control group: a group in an experiment that does not receive the experimental treatment (p. 33)

correlational study: a study of the relationship between variables that are not manipulated by the researcher (p. 32)

cross-sectional design: a design in which children of different ages are included in a study (p. 33)

dependent variable: the behavior a researcher is trying to explain in an experiment (p. 33)

developmentally instigative characteristics: qualities of a particular child that affect others so as to set in motion repeated interpersonal interactions (p. 29)

dialectic: dialogue in which two opposing tendencies interact in a problem-solving situation, according to sociocultural theory (p. 21)

ego: in Freud's theory, the conscious, reality-oriented part of the personality; the experiencing self; the part of the self that organizes personality (p. 10)

ego defense mechanism: ways of guarding the ego against overwhelming negative feelings that are housed only in the unconscious portion of the ego (p. 10)

ego-psychoanalytic emphasis: psychoanalytic study focused on ego, a conscious part of the personality (p. 12)

eugenics movements: movements described by proponents as planning the betterment of the human race by eliminating those thought to be genetically inferior (p. 6)

event sampling: a descriptive technique in which the researcher notes the details of each occurence of one well-defined behavior (p. 31)

exosystem: in Bronfenbrenner's bioecological theory, the systems level in which the child does not participate directly but that affects him or her through interactions with others who interact with that exosystem (p. 28)

experiment: a study in which participants are randomly assigned to groups which receive differing treatments by the researcher (p. 33)

fixated: a condition in which instinctual energy remains blocked in a previous zone rather than moving on to the next one (p. 11)

id: in Freud's theory, the unconscious source of instinct (p. 9)

independent variable: a characteristic that is manipulated in an experiment and might influence the dependent variable (p. 33)

informed consent: permission given by informed parents, and sometimes by children themselves, for participation in a research study (p. 37)

instinct: a mental representation of a body state or need, such as hunger or sexual arousal (p. 9)

instrumental conditioning: a means of changing behavior by following the behavior with a reward or a punishment (p. 15)

learning: the relatively permanent change in behavior that results from experience (p. 14)

longitudinal design: a research design in which children of a specific age are followed across ages of interest (p. 33)

macrosystem: in Bronfenbrenner's bioecological theory, the systems level that is the subculture and culture of which the child is a part (p. 28)

maturation: the process of biological change programmed genetically and thought to cause some new behaviors to emerge (p. 5)

mesosystem: in Bronfenbrenner's bioecological theory, the systems level in which two microsystems interact (p. 28)

microsystem: in Bronfenbrenner's bioecological theory, the systems level in which the child has experiences (p. 27)

negatively correlated: a relationship between two variables in which the level of one variable decreases as the level of the other variable increases (p. 32)

negative reinforcer: a reinforcer (an event contingent upon a given response and increasing its probability) that consists of removing something aversive from the environment (p. 16)

norms: age-related standards or patterns of behavior (p. 8)

ontogenetic development: the development of an individual child in contrast to the historical development of human culture (p. 21)

operant conditioning: increasing the frequency of a behavior by following it with reinforcement or decreasing the frequency of a behavior by punishment (p. 15)

positively correlated: a relationship between two variables in which the level of one variable increases as the level of the other variable increases (p. 32)

positive reinforcer: a reinforcer (an event contingent upon a given response and increasing its probability) that consists of adding something to the environment (p. 16)

psychosexual theory: Freud's theory, which attributes development to adaptation to biological changes he called instincts (p. 12)

psychosocial theory: Erik Erikson's theory, which attributes human development to changes in society's demands on the individual rather than biologically based instincts (p. 12)

punishment: decreasing the probability of a response by presenting an observable event contingent on that response (p. 15)

readiness or **neurological ripening:** peak receptiveness to experiences due to maturation of the nervous system (p. 6)

reinforcement: the process of increasing the probability of a response by presenting stimuli contingent on that behavior (p. 15)

scheme or **schema:** a generalized knowledge structure in Piagetian theory (p. 19)

self-efficacy belief: belief by a person that he or she actively controls the events that affect him or her (p. 17)

shaping: the process of reinforcing successive approximations of a desired behavior (p. 16)

social learning theory: a learning theory in which observation, imitation, reinforcement, and cognitive processes play a major role (p. 17)

sociocultural: a term used to describe Vygotsky's theory, which posits that knowledge is socially constructed by the child and others within the culture (p. 21)

specimen record: a descriptive study in which the researcher attempts to record all of a child's behavior (p. 31)

superego: in Freud's theory, the part of the personality that contains society's rules and other ideals and that causes anxiety and guilt for misdeeds (p. 10)

systems: groups of elements with similar rules for relating to each other (p. 24)

theory: a set of systematically organized assumptions about why something happens or works the way it does (p. 5)

time sampling: a procedure of making observations on a regular schedule (p. 31)

unconditioned response: a natural reaction in response to an unconditioned stimulus (p. 14)

unconditioned stimulus: a stimulus that naturally elicits a response (p. 14)

zone of proximal development: a major construct in Vygotsky's theory that refers to the gap between what a child can do independently and what the child can do when assisted by a more expert other (p. 22)

SUGGESTIONS FOR FURTHER READING

Bentzen, W. R. (1997). *Seeing young children: A guide to observing and recording behavior* (3rd ed.). New York: Delmar. This book is an excellent introduction to techniques useful for doing descriptive studies of children.

Bornstein, M. H., & Lamb, M. E. (Eds.). (1999). *Developmental psychology: An advanced textbook* (4th ed.). Hillsdale, NJ: Erlbaum. This comprehensive textbook contains excellent chapters on history, theory, culture, and research design in developmental psychology.

Bronfenbrenner, U., & Morris, P. A. (1998). The ecology of developmental processes. In W. Damon & R. Lerner (Eds.), *Handbook of child psychology: Vol.1. Theoretical models of human development* (pp. 993–1028). New York: Wiley. This chapter presents Bronfenbrenner's evolving bioecological model as it focuses on the need to study important forms of repeated bidirectional interactions between child and environment (proximal processes), including child characteristics that influence those proximal processes. The remaining 18 chapters of the *Handbook* include the views of a number of contemporary developmental systems theorists.

Daniels, H. (Ed.) (1995). *An introduction to Vygotsky.* New York: Routledge. This book combines reprints of journal and text articles, with the editor's comments, providing an excellent overview of Vygotsky's work.

Forsyth, G. A., & Bohling, P. H. (1999). *Interpreting statistics and behavioral research* (2nd ed.). Acton, MA: Copley Publishing. This easy-to-understand, humorously written book helps students learn how to interpret behavioral science research and related statistics. Most examples are from child and adolescent research.

Group for the Advancement of Psychiatry. (1999). *In the long run . . . Longitudinal studies of psychopathology in children.* Washington, DC: American Psychiatric Press. This book gives good examples of longitudinal studies of ten groups of children, such as those in Head Start, those with neonatal disabilities (including prematurity), and those with chronic medical illness, mentally ill parents, and each of several psychiatric diagnoses.

Plomin, R. (1994). *Genetics and experience: The interplay between nature and nurture.* Thousand Oaks, CA: Sage. This scholarly discussion of research and theory on the nature-nurture debate reviews considerable research, including twin and adoption studies. The author's theory is that inheritance mediates interactions with the environment, what he calls "the nature of nurture." This is an interesting book for the serious student.

Stake, R. E. (1995). *The art of case study research*. Thousand Oaks, CA: Sage. This book is a readable introduction to doing case study research, written by one of the leaders in the field.

Steen, R. G. (1996). *DNA & destiny: Nature and nurture in human behavior*. New York: Plenum. This very readable book about the influence on behavior of inheritance and the environment includes material about the history of genetically based racist views, as well as current research from a variety of fields (medicine, education, criminology). It presents a very balanced discussion about the development of intelligence and issues relating to social responsibility on this matter.

Whiting, B. B., & Edwards, C. E. (1988). *Children of different worlds*. Cambridge, MA: Harvard University Press. This book describes children's behavior and parent practices in different cultures around the world. It provides interesting insight on how cultural differences affect development.

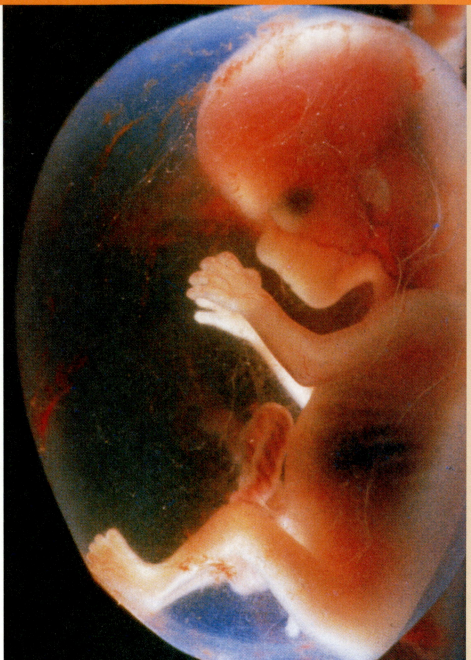

2

Genetics, Prenatal Development, and Birth

CLARA HAD JUST returned from a session with her son's learning-center teacher, where she had learned that Seth's short attention span, poor memory, and high activity level were causing problems for his teacher. Seth was 11 years old now and he seemed to be getting more impulsive every day.

Clara reached for Seth's baby-book and leafed through the pages, noting that the drooping eyelids, short eye openings, and underdeveloped face were quite evident even in his first photos. Clara remembered that, during infancy, Seth had feeding and sleeping problems and was irritable a lot of the time. She looked at the photo of Seth in a cast when he was 2 years old. His poor motor coordination and his active and distractible nature had led to a bad fall and a broken leg.

"I didn't think," she whispered to herself as she closed the book, "that it could happen with just two or three beers or some wine each day." The tears came faster now as these thoughts combined with those about Seth's probable reaction to the new plans for him in the learning center.

Is Clara's story unusual today? Are many women having this same experience? Suppose Seth had been born in 1965. Would he have been classified as exhibiting fetal alcohol syndrome? Might genetics have contributed to Seth's problems? As we shall see in this chapter, extensive research has been done on the prenatal effects of alcohol and other drugs and on the fetus's vulnerability at various stages of prenatal life. There have also been many changes in parents' experiences of pregnancy and birthing, in prenatal testing, and in genetic trends.

Consider these practices and trends:

- Couples thinking of starting a family can consult a genetic counselor to find out if they are likely to transmit a hereditary disease or abnormality to their child.
- Couples can choose when and whether to have a child by using any of a number of birth control methods, which places the size of their family under more control.
- Infertile couples can try a variety of conception methods, including artificial insemination, in vitro fertilization, sperm injection, and gamete transfer.

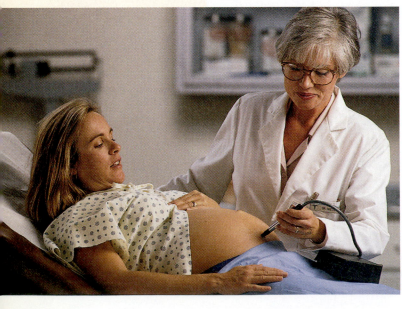

Ultrasound allows a physician to view the developing fetus. Gestational age can be assessed using ultrasound, and certain physical problems, such as cleft palate, can be detected. (*Source:* © Bruce Ayers/Tony Stone Images)

- Women can determine whether they are pregnant within 20–30 days of conception by using a urine test.
- Pregnant women can find out the sex of their baby and whether certain physical problems or genetic abnormalities are present through the use of ultrasound, amniocentesis, chorionic villus sampling (biopsy), and nuchal translucency scans.
- Pregnant women are advised to eat well; get adequate exercise and rest; avoid hot tubs; abstain from alcohol, cigarettes, and other drugs; avoid secondhand smoke; and reduce the amount of stress in their lives.
- Women who attend prepared childbirth classes can participate actively in the birth process with reduced use of pain-relieving drugs.
- Fathers can be present at births, even when cesarean sections are performed.

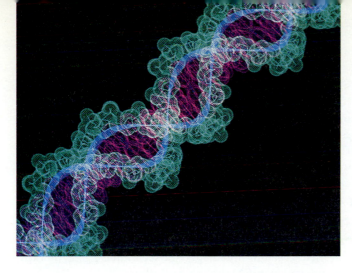

In this chapter, we discuss genetics, prenatal development, and birth. Each of these areas influences the child that a baby eventually will become. These three aspects of development have undergone profound changes in recent years, as a result of research discoveries, new technologies, and changing attitudes and social policies. Now more than ever we have an opportunity—and a responsibility—to see that all children are in the best environment right from the start.

Genetics: Biological Inheritance

Incredible variation exists within our human species. People differ in body size and build; skin color; eye, nose, and head shape; hair texture and color; and many other visible traits. Within the organism, beyond our observing eye, are variations such as blood type, hormone levels, mental abilities, personality traits, and predispositions to contract diseases or to suffer from some psychopathology.

What accounts for this wide array of differences? What makes every human being a unique individual, unlike any other person who has ever lived or will ever live on the planet? One part of the answer to these questions is genetic inheritance. Genetic inheritance does not *determine* everything a person is and becomes, but it does *influence* what a person is and becomes. We referred to the **nature–nurture controversy** in chapter 1, and we will refer to it in subsequent chapters, as well, when we discuss the effects of genetic inheritance on various aspects of development. To appreciate the controversy, and to understand an important part of development, one must know the basics of genetics.

Genes and Chromosomes

Genetics is the study of the transmission of biological traits from one generation to the next. Sex, eye color, left- or right-handedness, and thousands of other characteristics are encoded in **genes**. Every gene is a sequence of nucleic acids (DNA), which encodes the information needed to produce a protein, the basic building block of the cell. Genes themselves are contained on chromosomes. Chromosomes are long enough to be visible in a dyed cell under a powerful microscope. These extremely long strands of DNA are coiled up in the nucleus of each cell of our body (see Figure 2.1).

Chromosomes occur in pairs, of which every normal human body cell contains 23. The genes on one chromosome have counterparts on the other chromosome in the pair. Pairs of genes on the two matching chromosomes interact to determine which characteristics a person will inherit (see Figure 2.2). Some genes are **recessive**—the information they carry will not be translated into a particular biological trait unless they are paired with another recessive gene. Blue eye color is an example of a recessive trait.

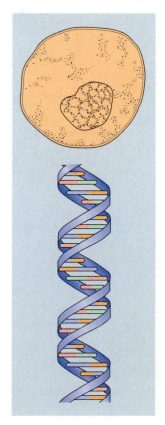

47

Thus, to have blue eyes, a person must inherit a recessive gene for this eye color from each parent.

Other genes are **dominant**—they override their gene partner so that their characteristic is always expressed. Brown eye color is dominant. A person with brown eyes may have inherited the recessive gene for blue eyes from one parent, but the dominant gene inherited from the other parent overrode that recessive gene.

Cell Division and Conception

Each of us has over 100,000 genes. The 15-year Human Genome Project was begun in 1988 to map the genes and their relation to diseases and behaviors. This genetic technology has three applications: screening and diagnostic techniques, gene therapy, and the possibility of genetic enhancement (Mehlman & Botkin, 1998).

In every one of our cells each of us has a unique set of genes that makes us distinct individuals. This unique set is produced at the moment of conception when an egg contributed by the mother and a sperm contributed by the father combine. Eggs and sperm are known as **germ cells** because they are involved in reproduction.

Germ cells differ from body cells—**somatic cells**—in the way they divide. For example, when we grow new skin cells or hair cells, a parent cell (or original cell) divides to produce two new cells, each containing the same 23 pairs of chromosomes as the parent. Each new cell, with its 46 chromosomes, is identical to the parent cell. This type of cell division, in which the original cell is duplicated exactly, is called **mitosis** (see Figure 2.3).

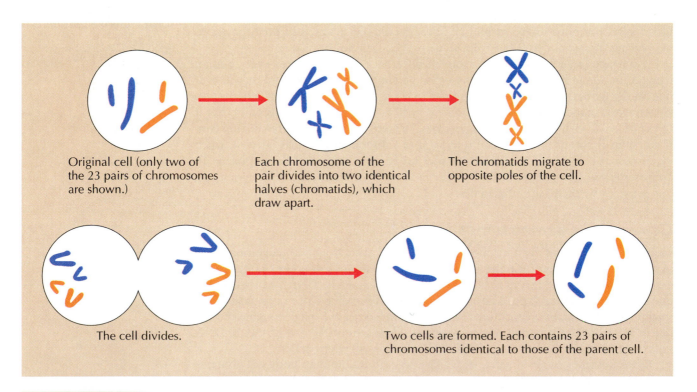

Original cell (only two of the 23 pairs of chromosomes are shown.)

Each chromosome of the pair divides into two identical halves (chromatids), which draw apart.

The chromatids migrate to opposite poles of the cell.

The cell divides.

Two cells are formed. Each contains 23 pairs of chromosomes identical to those of the parent cell.

FIGURE 2.3

Body cells replicating by mitosis. This is the process by which bone, muscle, skin, and other cells of the body grow and repair themselves.

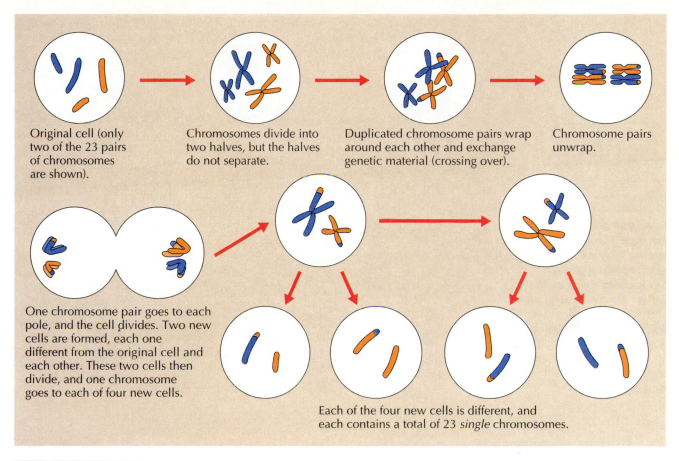

Original cell (only two of the 23 pairs of chromosomes are shown).

Chromosomes divide into two halves, but the halves do not separate.

Duplicated chromosome pairs wrap around each other and exchange genetic material (crossing over).

Chromosome pairs unwrap.

One chromosome pair goes to each pole, and the cell divides. Two new cells are formed, each one different from the original cell and each other. These two cells then divide, and one chromosome goes to each of four new cells.

Each of the four new cells is different, and each contains a total of 23 *single* chromosomes.

FIGURE 2.4

Germ cells replicating by meiosis. The resulting cells contain 23 single chromosomes rather than 23 pairs of chromosomes, and they are genetically different from the original cell. Thus eggs and sperm combine to create a genetically new human being.

Germ cells are designed to combine with other germ cells to produce an altogether new cell. If each germ cell brought 46 chromosomes to conception, the resulting organism would have 92 chromosomes! But because germ cells are prepared for conception by a different kind of cell division—meiosis—this does not happen. In **meiosis,** the number of chromosomes in the cell is reduced by half (see Figure 2.4).

Meiosis provides the biological mechanism for the mixing and combining of characteristics that make each individual unique. During the crossing-over step shown in Figure 2.4, chromosome pairs in the parent cell wrap around each other and exchange genetic material. When they unwrap and the cell divides, the new cells contain genes that make them different from the parent cell and from each other. This accounts for some of the differences we see between parents and children and among siblings. Crossing over makes the possibilities for unique combinations virtually limitless (Silver, 1998). A scientific investigation of gene disorders and inherited diseases is described in Knowledge in Action: Health—The Human Genome Project.

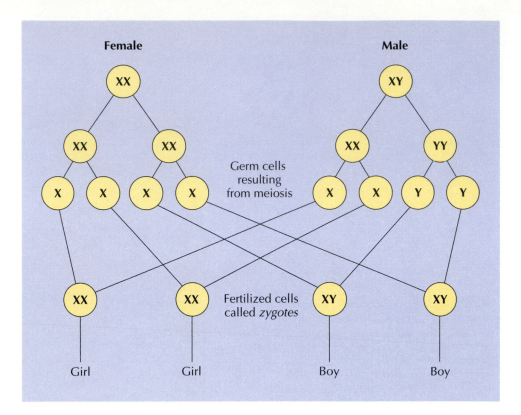

FIGURE 2.5

Sex chromosomes. Germ cells (eggs and sperm) have just one sex chromosome each. Sex is determined by the father if a sperm with an X chromosome fertilizes the egg,; the child will be a girl. If a sperm with a Y chromosome fertilizes the egg, the child will be a boy.

In figure: Female, Male, Germ cells resulting from meiosis, Fertilized cells called *zygotes*, Girl, Girl, Boy, Boy

Determination of Sex

One of the 23 pairs of chromosomes determines whether a fetus will be female or male. Females have a matching set of sex chromosomes, called XX (from the way they look under an electron microscope). Males have one X chromosome and one Y chromosome. After meiosis, eggs always contain an X chromosome; sperm may con-

HEALTH/SAFETY

The Human Genome Project

The National Institutes of Health/Department of Energy Human Genome Project is the largest scientific project funded by the federal government since the Apollo Moon Project. The project has a $3 billion dollar budget and involves scientists from several countries. All are searching for new information to be used to diagnose and treat gene disorders and other inherited diseases (DOE, 1999a & 1999b; Hagerman, 1996; Mehlman & Botkin, 1998). The scientists hope to map the entire set of genes and molecule sequences that make up human genetic information. This task includes indexing genetic chemical instructions, and mapping and se-

quencing all of the estimated 3 billion base pairs that make up the human genome. Researchers have already located the genes associated with many hereditary disorders, such as cystic fibrosis, muscular dystrophy, fragile X syndrome, hemophilia, and Huntington's disease. These problems and others, such as coronary artery disease, diabetes, cognitive ability deficiencies, antisocial personality disorders, and some forms of cancer, may be prevented or treated. Thus, this project should be quite beneficial to humankind.

The Human Genome Project has established a program to deal with the ethical, legal, and social implications of the research. Patient anonymity, prenatal diagnosis, and the possibility of a eugenics movement must be considered with the advent of new genetic information. Suppose, for example, that nations wanted to set up a sperm

tain an X or a Y chromosome. If the sperm contributes an X chromosome to the new organism at conception, the baby will be a girl. If it contributes a Y chromosome, the baby will be a boy (Figure 2.5). The sex of the child, then, is always determined by the father.

About 120 males are conceived for every 100 females. By birth, the ratio has dropped to 105 males for every 100 females. The reason for this is that the sex chromosomes carry many genes other than the ones that determine sex. If one of these genes is defective on an X chromosome in a female, a corresponding healthy gene on the other X chromosome can often compensate for it. A female would have to inherit two defective chromosomes to express the defect and suffer adverse effects from it.

If a male has a defective gene on the X chromosome, on the other hand, there may not be a corresponding healthy gene on the Y chromosome. Thus, the male would be more likely to express an abnormality encoded on the X chromosome. As a result, a higher mortality rate exists for males, and more of them have to be conceived if a roughly equal number of males and females are to be born. This is also why more boys than girls are affected by the fragile X syndrome. Girls must inherit two X chromosomes with the problem gene to be affected; boys, on the other hand, are afflicted with the disease if the one X chromosome they inherit carries the gene for the disease. Children affected by this syndrome are mentally retarded, autistic, and they exhibit attention deficit hyperactivity disorder–type behaviors (Hagerman, 1996).

Characteristics encoded by genes that are carried on the sex chromosomes are known as **sex-linked characteristics.** Many of these are encoded by recessive genes carried on the X chromosome. They can be expressed in males because males do not have a second X chromosome with a matching dominant gene to override the problem recessive gene that is inherited. Hemophilia and some forms of color blindness are examples of sex-linked traits that normally occur only in males.

Multiple Births

At conception only one egg and one sperm usually unite to produce one fertilized ovum, known as a **zygote.** But sometimes a woman's ovary releases two or more eggs during monthly ovulation. If both eggs are fertilized, two babies develop. These twins

bank that accepted samples only from Nobel laureates, or to sterilize chronic alcoholics, or selectively abort fetuses with genetic disorders (Garver & Garver, 1994). Although advances in understanding genetics may contribute to better physical and psychological well-being for children and adolescents, some scientists are concerned about potential uses of genetic technologies. For example, the cloning of the sheep Dolly is seen as a symbol of the power of genetics. Dyson (1999, p. 105) described such genetic manipulation as "a long-term threat to the autonomy of the human spirit." Gosden (1999) pointed out the need to differentiate two potential uses of genetic technologies: (1) for correcting inherited disease and disorders in order to avoid suffering and (2) for eliminating trivial individual differences. Rothman presents this per-

spective in the following way: "We're being asked to think about what kinds of children we want to bring into the world, what kinds of people we want on our planet. We're being asked to look at all the bits and pieces of ourselves and choose which ones to keep and which ones to discard in the generations to follow. There are no maps" (1998, p. 41).

The debate about using genetic technology to improve the human condition is made more complex by the interplay of genes and the environment. Indeed, the studies of genetic influences on behavior have been important in identifying environmental influences and the role that genetics plays in influencing children's and adolescents' sensitivity to different environments (Plomin et al., 1997a; Rutter, 1997).

will be no more alike than siblings born at different times, because each came from a different fertilized egg. They are called **fraternal twins** and may be two girls, two boys, or a boy and a girl.

Multiple births, sometimes caused by fertility drugs, make up about 10 percent of all births (Pasquariello, 1999; Smith, 1998). Women whose body chemistry prevents them from ovulating (releasing an egg) may take these drugs when they want to become pregnant. Fertility drugs trigger ovulation, and sometimes overstimulate the ovaries. Several ova can be released. If all ova are fertilized, the woman may find she is carrying twins, triplets, or even more fetuses. In fact, the world's first surviving septuplets were born by cesarean section in 1997 in Carlisle, Iowa (McCaughey et al., 1998).

Twins also result if the two cells resulting from the first division of the zygote separate and develop independently. Because mitosis involves the exact replication of the genetic material in the original cell, these babies will be **identical twins.** These twins are genetically alike in every way and are the same sex (see Figure 2.6). Identical triplets develop if the original zygote separates by mitosis twice in a row (producing four identical cells), and then one cell dies. If one embryo in a multiple pregnancy does not survive, it may be reabsorbed into the body (early in pregnancy) or will remain in the uterus until the remaining babies are born (Pasquariello, 1999).

Twins occur once in about every 89 births. Of twin births, about one third (one in every 250 births, worldwide) involve identical twins. Triplets occur about once in every 8,000 births. Quadruplets are rare, occurring only once in about 400,000 births

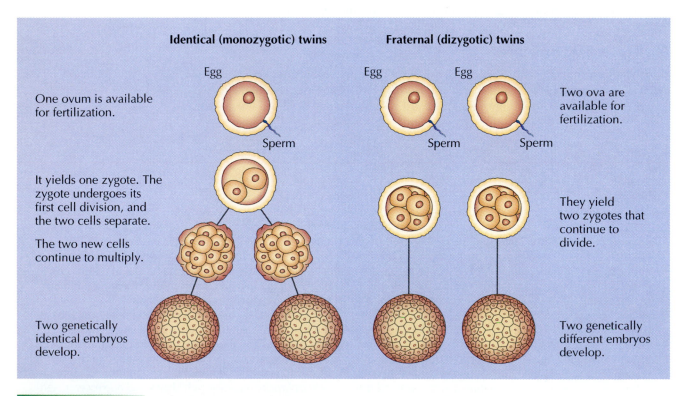

Identical (monozygotic) twins

One ovum is available for fertilization.

It yields one zygote. The zygote undergoes its first cell division, and the two cells separate.

The two new cells continue to multiply.

Two genetically identical embryos develop.

Fraternal (dizygotic) twins

Two ova are available for fertilization.

They yield two zygotes that continue to divide.

Two genetically different embryos develop.

FIGURE 2.6

Zygotes of twins. Identical twins are produced when a fertilized egg divides and forms two cells, each containing the same genetic material. Fraternal twins result when two different eggs are fertilized at the same time and develop side by side in the womb. Their genetic material is as different as that of any two siblings born at different times.

(Curtis, 1997). The incidence of multiple births varies among different population groups. For example, they are more frequent among Nigerians and quite rare among Chinese and Japanese (Stern, 1973). The chances of multiple births increase with age (chances peak between ages 35–39), the mother's family history of multiples, and having a heavier, taller physique (Smith, 1998).

Genetics and the Environment

Developmentalists have long debated whether specific abilities, personality traits, or psychopathologies are primarily due to genetics or the environment. It is now generally agreed that both must be considered in understanding any aspect of behavior (Gottlieb, 1998). Gottesman (1974) proposed a limit-setting model to replace the idea that behaviors are a function of genetics *versus* the environment. He introduced the concept of **range of reaction,** which means that a trait can vary as a function of the environment only to the extent of the limits set for that trait by genetics. Thus, genetics may establish the interval or range within which musical ability might fall, while environmental factors, such as the mother's alcohol consumption (negative) or music provided in early life experiences (positive), determine where within the genetically established range of reaction the child's musical ability will fall. This view suggests that genetic and environmental factors both contribute to specific levels of mental ability, personality traits, or psychopathology (Platt & Stanislow, 1988).

These identical twins resulted when the cells separated and developed independently, after the first cell division in the zygote. Fraternal twins develop when two different eggs are fertilized by different sperm. (*Source:* © D. E. Cox/Tony Stone Images)

Three types of developmental relations may lead to environmental support of the level of any behavior that is established by genetics (Scarr, 1992; Scarr & McCarthy, 1983). **Passive relations** of the environment support the genetic blueprint when the child's environment is controlled primarily by the biological parents who also share a similar genetic background. For example, a child who is genetically endowed with musical ability may have parents who provide a rich musical environment.

The **evocative relations** of the environment support the genetic blueprint when the child's behavior evokes responses from others that are consistent with and supportive of the genetically determined level. For example, a child who has a genetic push toward being happy, smiling, and gregarious elicits more smiles and friendly responses than a child who has a genetic push toward being shy and withdrawn. These return smiles from others support the child's initial bias to be gregarious.

Active relations involve the child in picking the niche or set of activities that best supports the child's genotypically determined area of greatest strength. For example, one individual with genetically strong mathematical aptitude and poor athletic or spatial-figural aptitudes may pursue mathematics activities, while a second individual with a greater athletic than academic genetic environment may pursue athletic activities more than academic ones.

Some developmentalists (Baumrind, 1993; Huston, McLoyd, & Coll, 1997; Jackson, 1993; Maccoby, 1992) think that environmental influences cause a child to be different from what might be predicted based on genetics. For example, negative effects might result from the mother's or father's smoking during pregnancy, from the mother's consumption of alcohol, or from poverty. Parents may also respond insufficiently to the infant during the first year of life. Positive influences result from the avoidance of harmful substances during pregnancy, from appropriate parenting, and from early experiences that provide stimulation.

The longitudinal research by Ramey and associates provided a dramatic example of positive environmental influence. Beginning with a population of pregnant women with below-average IQs (average IQ = 80), children were randomly assigned to the two groups; half of the offspring were cared for at a high-quality child-care center and were given dietary supplements and medical care. The control group children, who were reared only at home, received the same dietary supplements, medical care, and family social services. Food supplements were provided to both groups because other studies showed positive effects for dietary enrichment (Super et al., 1990). Positive effects of attending the stimulating child-care center were evident in mental ability differences found at both 3 years and 5 years of age, and by differences in both mental ability and academic achievement by the time the children were 12 years old (Campbell & Ramey, 1994).

In summary, genetic and environmental factors interact, and these effects may become evident at different stages of development. An interaction of genetic and environmental factors has been reported for language ability (Hohnen & Stevenson, 1999), antagonism and interpersonal unresponsiveness personality traits (Jang et al., 1996), emotional temperament (Goldsmith et al., 1997), aggressive and violent behavior (Cadoret et al., 1997; Gjone & Stevenson, 1997), depression (Thapar & McGuffin, 1997), and obesity (Maes et al., 1997).

One 20-year longitudinal adoption study demonstrated the importance of examining the genetic-environmental interaction at different stages of development. Plomin and colleagues (1997b) gave cognitive ability tests to children at ages 1, 2, 3, 4, 7, 12, and 16. The adopted children's cognitive abilities were more like those of their adoptive than their biological parents in early childhood, but in adolescence their abilities were more like those of their biological parents. The adolescent similarity to biological parents was equal to that of nonadopted controls. This pattern was especially pronounced for verbal ability, but also existed for spatial ability and recognition memory. Plomin and colleagues concluded that genes related to these cognitive abilities may not have their effect until adolescence.

Other studies have provided data on these abilities. Petrill and colleagues (1998) also found increasing genetic influence on general cognitive ability in a longitudinal study of twins at 14, 20, 24, and 36 months. In his examination of genes and the environment in life span development, Loehlin (1997) concluded that the relative effect of genetics increases across the life span and that this effect is especially apparent with cognitive ability measures.

Prenatal Development: Life in the Womb

"Hey, Reggie, feel this. Put your hand right here. Can you feel it?"

"I don't know. I don't think so. Do it again, Latoya."

"What do you mean, 'Do that again'? I'm not making the baby move, silly. It moves when it wants to. It has stopped, I think. Wait, let me concentrate and see if I can feel anything. No, no, I can't now. It has stopped. I'm sure the baby was moving. I know that's what I felt."

"Well, let me know when it happens again. I want to feel it."

"I will. I promise I will."

This couple is experiencing one of the dramatic events of prenatal development—the first movements of the fetus that can be felt by the mother. How far along is the fetus when the expectant mother can feel its kicks and movements? Are they dramatic enough for anyone but the mother to feel them? Actually, it is not until about 16 or 17 weeks of prenatal development have passed that the mother feels the first tickle of fetal movement. But this does not mean that life in the womb has been uneventful.

Figure 2.7 indicates how quickly prenatal development proceeds. Even though we sometimes think of birth as the beginning of a person's life, the basic biological blueprint is laid down at conception, when the ovum is fertilized by a sperm. Thus, the individual's unique genetic makeup is established at that moment. Then, the

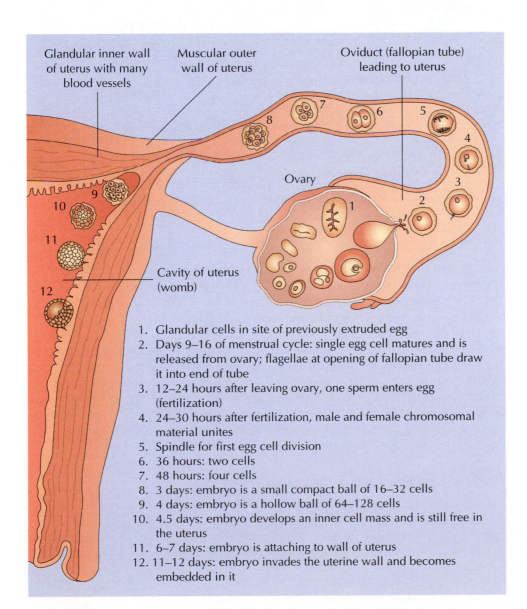

Glandular inner wall of uterus with many blood vessels

Muscular outer wall of uterus

Oviduct (fallopian tube) leading to uterus

Ovary

Cavity of uterus (womb)

1. Glandular cells in site of previously extruded egg
2. Days 9–16 of menstrual cycle: single egg cell matures and is released from ovary; flagellae at opening of fallopian tube draw it into end of tube
3. 12–24 hours after leaving ovary, one sperm enters egg (fertilization)
4. 24–30 hours after fertilization, male and female chromosomal material unites
5. Spindle for first egg cell division
6. 36 hours: two cells
7. 48 hours: four cells
8. 3 days: embryo is a small compact ball of 16–32 cells
9. 4 days: embryo is a hollow ball of 64–128 cells
10. 4.5 days: embryo develops an inner cell mass and is still free in the uterus
11. 6–7 days: embryo is attaching to wall of uterus
12. 11–12 days: embryo invades the uterine wall and becomes embedded in it

FIGURE 2.7

Ovulation, fertilization, and cell division in the oviduct and implantation of the embryo in the wall of the uterus.

There have always been couples who wanted to have children but couldn't. Ways of trying to bring about conception have ranged from herbal remedies to ritual practices to ingenious sexual positions. Today, the problem of **infertility**—the inability to conceive a baby—is approached more scientifically but with no less compelling interest. Infertility is a problem for 20 percent of all couples in the United States. Women have a higher risk of infertility after the age of 30. For example, 15 percent of women between 30 and 35 may not be able to bear a child.

Treatment for infertility enables about half of the couples who seek help to have a child. But in many other cases, there is nothing physicians can do.

Identifying the Cause of Infertility

A variety of conditions can cause infertility. In women these conditions include a failure to ovulate, endometriosis (a condition in which abnormal tissue in the fallopian tubes, vagina, or uterus prevents conception), endocrine imbalances, and scarred fallopian tubes. Some women have physical abnormalities, such as an oddly shaped uterus, that make it more difficult for them to carry a pregnancy to term.

Infertility can be due to a problem in men. For example, some men have too few sperm or sperm that have a problem with their ability to move. These problems sometimes can be traced to a case of mumps in adolescence or early adulthood, to untreated gonorrhea, or to an endocrine imbalance.

Sometimes, infertility is due to some problem in carrying a child to term, not in a failure to conceive. From 15 to 20 percent of all pregnancies end in miscarriage, which often occurs in the first days or weeks of pregnancy. Many women have miscarriages and later experience successful pregnancies. But, occasionally, one parent will have a chromosomal abnormality that causes repeated miscarriages. Hormone imbalances also may be linked to repeated miscarriages.

Miscarriage in the fifth or sixth month of pregnancy may be due to abnormalities in the cervix (a condition known as cervical incompetence) or uterus. Some studies have linked late miscarriages with certain infections; many women who have these infections are subsequently treated with antibiotics and can have successful pregnancies.

Treatment of Infertility

Some kinds of infertility can be treated; others cannot. Surgery can sometimes repair oviducts, clear up endometriosis, and correct problems in anatomy. Fertility drugs can help a woman ovulate, although they carry the risk of causing multiple births. Male infertility can be treated by collecting the father's sperm, concentrating it, and artificially inseminating the mother. Sometimes immature sperm are removed from the testes, allowed to mature in vitro, and are then injected into the egg (Gosden, 1999).

Other treatment techniques include in-vitro fertilization, the use of frozen embryos, and laser surgery, which can sometimes be used in men to reverse a vasectomy (a sterilization method in which the small ducts that carry semen from the testes are severed) or to repair oviducts in women. Two of the more controversial techniques used in cases of infertility are in-vitro fertilization and surrogate motherhood.

individual begins the nine-month period of growth and development that we refer to as **prenatal development.** During this period, development proceeds in a genetically determined pattern common to all human beings, but it is critically influenced by interactions within the context of the mother's body.

Over the past 30 years, there has been an explosion of knowledge about prenatal development. Now embryologists can tell us exactly when the heart, lungs, and other organs are formed, when the eyes open, and when the fetus can cry and suck its thumb in the womb. Researchers can tell us how the fetus is affected by environmental factors, such as alcohol, cigarettes, stress, radiation, drugs, and chemicals in the environment. Developmental psychologists understand a wide range of genetic and developmental problems, and genetic counselors provide information and advice to parents whose babies may have genetic disorders.

Periods of Prenatal Development

Every month an egg is prepared in one of the woman's ovaries and released sometime between the 9th and 16th day of her menstrual cycle. The egg is drawn into the open end of the **oviduct,** or **fallopian tube,** and moved down the tube to the uterus. If not fertilized, the egg is flushed out of the body at the end of the monthly cycle.

In vitro fertilization involves extracting eggs from the mother and mixing them with the father's sperm in the laboratory. (Babies born this way are commonly called "test tube babies.") One of the embryos is then implanted in the mother's uterus. Although this procedure is often successful, it is very tedious and expensive. First, not all embryos grow and thrive in the lab, and second, not all implantations become successful pregnancies. Any unused embryos that do thrive are often frozen and stored for the couple to use later. This practice has led to debates about moral and legal issues. A case in Australia involved the legal status of frozen embryos as heirs to the estate of their parents, who were killed in a plane crash before the embryos could be implanted. Debate has also focused on the moral implications of allowing research to be conducted on frozen embryos.

Another technique, implantation testing, mixes a couple's sperm and ova in the laboratory and then tests the zygotes for problem genes. Healthy zygotes are inserted into the woman's uterus for implantation and development (Lee, 1993).

Using **surrogate mothers** is a controversial approach to infertility. It involves a contract between a fertile woman, who agrees to carry a fetus, and an infertile woman whose husband provides the sperm. The surrogate mother is impregnated by the father's sperm through artificial insemination, agrees to carry the child for the couple, and names the couple as legal guardians of the child who will be born.

Some people see surrogate motherhood as an arrangement essentially to "sell" a baby, and they fear the psychological consequences for children who learn that their biological mothers "sold" them. They also point to the pos-sibility that a woman will change her mind after having the baby, and will refuse to fulfill the contract she has signed.

In 1986 Mary Beth Whitehead of New Jersey refused to give up a baby to the couple who had contracted with her for the child. She said that she hadn't realized how she would feel about giving up the baby, and she argued that she had the right to keep the baby because she was the biological mother. After a lengthy battle, the court awarded the baby to the couple and granted the surrogate limited visitation rights.

The Trauma of Infertility

Infertility is painful, and its treatment can be stressful. Ovulation is monitored, sperm samples are collected and analyzed, intercourse practices are studied, and surgery may be performed. A couple may feel vulnerable and out of control; their sex life may become an unpleasant routine.

Solutions that seem radical to outsiders, such as in vitro fertilization or surrogate motherhood, become acceptable options, if the couple can afford them. Many couples remain childless or turn to adoption. Older couples often have more difficulty adopting a baby than younger couples and may turn to less restrictive orphanages. Adoption regulations vary dramatically across agencies and from country to country (Jones, 1998). Other issues faced in treatment for infertility include lack of insurance reimbursement, lack of regulations to control clinic standards, misleading advertisements, high cost, and the large number of multiple births (Wiscot & Meldrum, 1998). Support groups for infertile couples can provide help in this difficult situation.

Through sexual intercourse (or artificial insemination or in-vitro fertilization), millions of sperm are available to fertilize an egg. But only one will penetrate the surface of the egg. If the egg is fertilized, prenatal development begins, lasting 38 weeks for the full-term infant. Prenatal development, also known as gestation, is usually divided into three periods. Each has a different focus of activity.

The Period of the Ovum: Conception to Week 2   The first period of prenatal development, called the **period of the ovum,** begins in one of the oviducts (see Figure 2.7). It is here that fertilization occurs, when a sperm penetrates the egg. The fertilized cell begins to undergo cell division as it continues moving toward the uterus. In about three days, the cluster of 20 to 30 cells enters the uterine cavity, where it organizes itself into a hollow ball. In one area of this single layer of cells is a group of larger cells, called the **embryoblast,** which will develop into structures such as the placenta and chorion, which nourish and support the developing embryo. About six or seven days after fertilization, the embryo attaches itself to the uterine wall. Within four to five days, it becomes embedded there.

Sometimes the developing embryo does not reach the uterus because it attaches itself to the wall of the oviduct. These are called **ectopic pregnancies** and are dangerous because the developing embryo causes the oviduct to burst. If the embryo is not removed surgically prior to this bursting, the mother can die from internal bleeding. Ectopic pregnancies are the leading cause of pregnancy-related death during the first trimester. Those who survive one ectopic pregnancy are at increased risk for another, and for future infertility (National Center for Health Statistics, 1995). An exam conducted by the end of the second week can reveal whether the embryo is growing properly in the uterine wall. The embryo is only about the size of the period at the end of this sentence, but it has already begun to form the remarkable system by which it will draw nourishment and oxygen from the mother for the next 36 weeks. The course of prenatal development is shown in Figure 2.8.

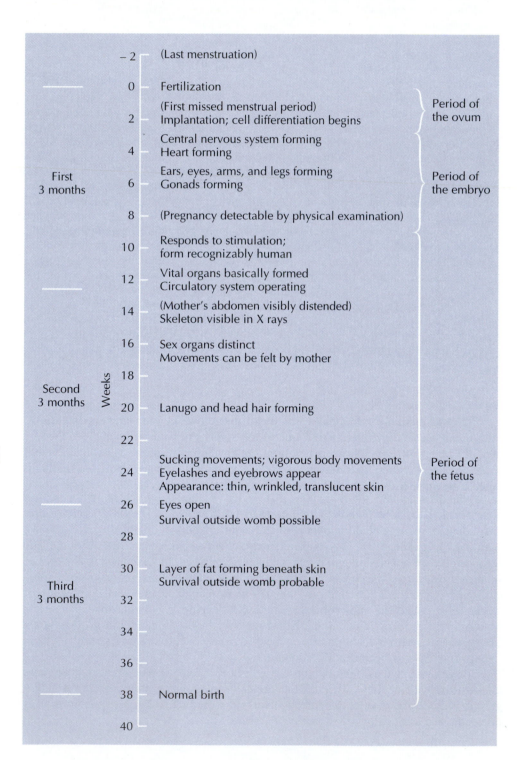

	Weeks		
	– 2	(Last menstruation)	
	0	Fertilization	
	2	(First missed menstrual period) Implantation; cell differentiation begins	Period of the ovum
First 3 months	4	Central nervous system forming Heart forming	
	6	Ears, eyes, arms, and legs forming Gonads forming	Period of the embryo
	8	(Pregnancy detectable by physical examination)	
	10	Responds to stimulation; form recognizably human	
	12	Vital organs basically formed Circulatory system operating	
	14	(Mother's abdomen visibly distended) Skeleton visible in X rays	
	16	Sex organs distinct Movements can be felt by mother	
Second 3 months	18		
	20	Lanugo and head hair forming	
	22		
	24	Sucking movements; vigorous body movements Eyelashes and eyebrows appear Appearance: thin, wrinkled, translucent skin	Period of the fetus
	26	Eyes open Survival outside womb possible	
	28		
Third 3 months	30	Layer of fat forming beneath skin Survival outside womb probable	
	32		
	34		
	36		
	38	Normal birth	
	40		

FIGURE 2.8

The three periods of prenatal development. The baby's anatomy is almost completely formed during the first three months of prenatal life, although the fetus is only a few inches long at the end of the first trimester. During the second trimester, the fetal heartbeat can be heard with a stethoscope, and the mother feels vigorous kicking and turning in her abdomen. The largest weight gain occurs during the last few months of prenatal development.

The Period of the Embryo: Week 2 to Week 9   The second period of prenatal development, called the **period of the embryo**, lasts from the second week to the end of the eighth prenatal week. The embryo differentiates rapidly during this time. All the major body structures, including the heart, the brain, the liver, the lungs, and the ovaries and testes, begin to form during this period. Some organs begin to function—the heart starts to beat, the liver begins to make blood cells, and the testes produce sex hormones. The eyes, nose, ears, tooth buds, and jaw are formed. Arms and legs appear; eyelids seal the eyes shut.

Because body structures are forming during this period, the structures are extremely vulnerable to damage from environmental influences. These include drugs, infections, and irradiation (X rays). Later in this chapter we discuss how many outside agents can damage the embryo. Despite the important developments that occur during this second period, the embryo at the end of the eighth week is only 1½ inches long and weighs less than ⅒ of an ounce.

The Period of the Fetus: Week 9 to Birth   The third and final period of prenatal development, called the **period of the fetus**, lasts from the ninth week until birth. During this period, structural development continues. Hands, fingers, feet, and toes are formed; bones develop; neural cells multiply and migrate; and hair and nails appear. All body systems begin to function; even the lungs make breathing movements, moving fluids in and out (see Figure 2.9). Beginning in the fifth month, the expectant mother can feel the baby's movements. Most of the fetus's increase in weight and length takes place during this third period, especially in the ninth month. By the end of the 38th week, the average baby weighs a little over 7 pounds and is about 20 inches long.

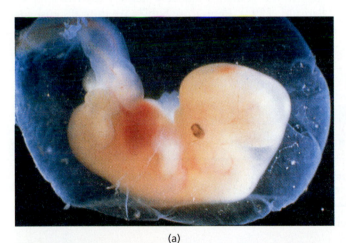

(a)

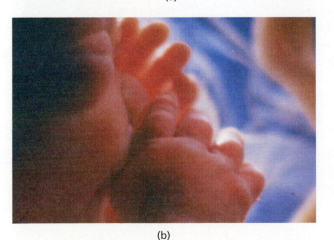

(b)

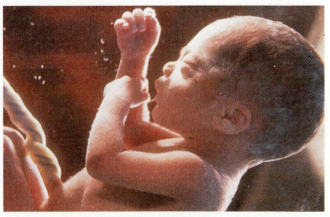

(c)

FIGURE 2.9

Physical changes. During the period of the ovum, all basic body structures are laid down (a). During the period of the fetus, structures such as arms and hands continue to grow (b). Late in the fetal period, the infant grows rapidly and accumulates a layer of fat under the skin (c).   (*Source:* (TOP) © Petit Format/Nestle/Science Source/ Photo Researchers, (BOTTOM LEFT) © Petit Format/Nestle/Science Source/Photo Researchers, (BOTTOM RIGHT) Petit Format/Nestle/ Science Source/Photo Researchers)

Various parts of the body grow at different rates during the prenatal period. At first, the head region grows very quickly compared to the trunk and legs. Later, the lower parts of the body begin to grow faster than they do at first. The head remains more fully developed than the other parts of the body throughout the entire prenatal period. This head-first pattern of development continues after birth. Thus, babies and young children appear "top heavy" compared to older children and adults, whose heads account for only about 10 percent of their total height.

Critical Periods of Prenatal Development

A **critical period** is a limited time when rapid development takes place in an organ, a body part, or a behavior. For example, a critical period for neural migration in the brain is between the 8th and 16th prenatal weeks. A developing system is especially sensitive to environmental influences when it is undergoing rapid development. **Teratogens** such as alcohol or radiation can cause severe damage to the developing brain during this time. A teratogen is a substance, organism, or physical agent capable of causing birth defects in a fetus. Fetal and maternal biochemistry, exposure level, teratogen interactions, and time of exposure all play a role in the effects of teratogens (Guttmacher, 1999). Table 2.1 presents information about the fetus's vulnerability to environmental hazards during various periods of prenatal life.

Prematurity

Gestation usually lasts 38 weeks. But some babies are born after a shorter gestation period. The **age of viability** refers to the youngest age at which a baby can survive outside the womb (Moore & Persaud, 1993). **Premature babies** are thin, because fat tissue does not begin to develop under the skin until the 30th to the 34th week. This absence of fat, plus their low body weight in general, makes premature babies more

---

TABLE 2.1

Critical periods in prenatal development

Structure	Period in Which Major Abnormalities May Develop	Period in Which Minor Abnormalities May Develop
Brain and central nervous system	Conception to week 16	Weeks 17 to 38
Heart	Weeks 2 to 6	Weeks 6 to 8
Arms	Weeks 3 to 5	Weeks 5 to 8
Legs	Weeks 4 to 6	Weeks 6 to 8
Eyes	weeks 4 to 8	Weeks 8 to 38
Teeth	Weeks 6 to 8	Weeks 8 to 38
Palate	Weeks 6 to 9	Weels 9 to 16
Ears	Weeks 4 to 9	Weeks 9 to 36
External genitals	Weeks 7 to 9	Weeks 9 to 38

Source: Adapted from *Before We Are Born,* by K. L. Moore and T. V. N. Persaud, 1993, Philadelphia: Saunders.

susceptible to cold temperatures and to dehydration than full-term babies are (Hunter et al., 1994).

Also critical to the survival of premature babies is development of their lungs. The terminal air sacs in the lungs, called alveoli, do not develop until about 32 weeks of gestation. Surfactant, a chemical essential for proper breathing, is not present in the lungs until about the 34th week. But despite formidable problems, premature babies are being saved at earlier and earlier dates.

Numerous differences exist between premature and full-term individuals throughout childhood and adolescence. For example, in the area of language, comparisons of children born before 32 weeks' gestation with full-term children showed that premature children had lower skills in expressive language, vocabulary, short-term memory, speech production, and comprehension (Briscoe et al., 1998; Luoma et al., 1998). A more extensive discussion of premature babies is presented in chapter 3.

Postmaturity

When labor does not occur until long after the baby is fully mature and able to survive on its own, the baby is considered **postmature**. When a baby remains in the uterus too long, the placenta may not provide enough oxygenated blood. This can result in brain damage or even death. The stillbirth rate for postmature babies is twice that of babies born on time. Labor may be started artificially for postmature babies, or a cesarean section may be performed. The cause of postmature delivery is generally unknown (Beers & Berko, 1999).

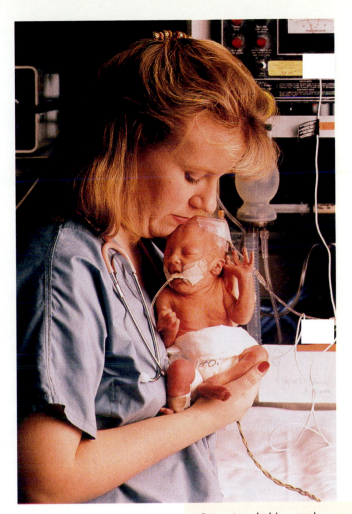

Premature babies need various kinds of support for several weeks, or even several months, after birth. This premature baby is being fed through a tube. (*Source:* © Terry Vine/Tony Stone Images)

Birth: Transition to Life in the Outer World

The journey down the birth canal out of the mother's body marks the end of life in physical union with the mother—a state in which food, oxygen, and hormones are obtained from her body—and the beginning of life as a separate individual. Birth is a complex process, one during which many remarkable changes occur that enable the baby to take up this new, physiologically independent existence.

The Physical Process of Birth

The birth process occurs in three stages (see Figure 2.10). Labor starts when hormonal changes in both the baby and the mother initiate strong, rhythmic uterine contractions. These contractions exert pressure on the cervix, the neck of the uterus, causing **dilation**—a gradual opening. The contractions also put pressure on the baby, which causes it to descend into the mother's pelvis (in first babies, this descent usually occurs well before labor even begins). This first stage is the longest part of the birth process.

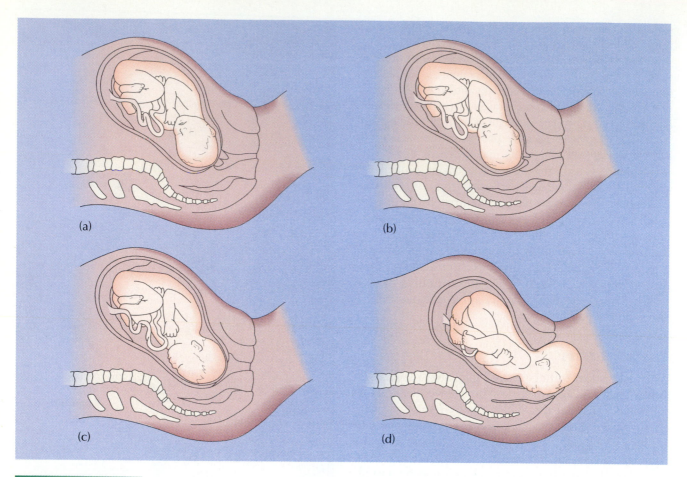

(a)

(b)

(c)

(d)

FIGURE 2.10

Stages of labor. Before labor begins, the full-term fetus rests comfortably in the uterus, typically in a head-down position (a). In the first stage of labor, uterine contractions pull the cervix open and push the baby downward (b). In the second stage of labor the baby is pushed further down (c) and out of the mother's body (d). The baby's head turns toward the mother's back during the birth process and is completely turned as it emerges, or crowns.

When the cervix is completely dilated, the second stage of birth, referred to as **expulsion**, begins. The baby moves slowly down through the bones of the pelvic ring, past the tight, muscular cervix, and into the vagina, which stretches open from the pressure. The baby's back bends, the head turns to fit through the narrowest parts of the passageway, and the soft bones of the baby's skull actually overlap as it is squeezed through the pelvis. The baby's head finally emerges from the vagina, followed quickly by the rest of the body. A new human appears in the world!

When the cervix is opening during the first stage, the woman having an unmedicated birth is encouraged to relax as much as possible, despite the contractions, to allow labor to proceed. When the baby is being expelled during the second stage, the woman can "bear down" with the contractions to help push the baby out. When the top of the baby's head appears at the vaginal opening, the baby is

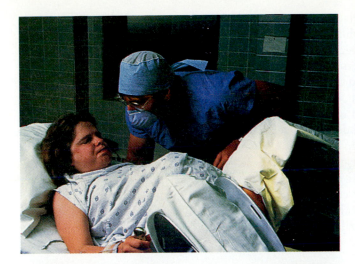

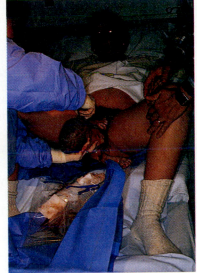

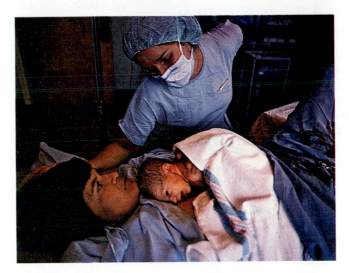

The birth process progresses in stages. In the second stage, which culminates in the actual birth of the baby, the mother bears down to help push the baby out. Once the baby's head emerges, the shoulders and body slip out easily. Immediately after birth, most babies spend some time in contact with their mother's body. (*Sources:* (TOP) © SIU/Photo Researchers, (BOTTOM LEFT) © Scott Camazine, Sue Trainor/Photo Researchers, (BOTTOM RIGHT) © John Eastcott/YVA Momatiuk/The Image Works)

said to be **crowning.** Because the head is the largest part of the baby's body and wider than the shoulders, the body slips out after the head emerges. The third stage of birth, which usually begins within 10 to 20 minutes of the baby's birth, is known as **afterbirth.** During this stage, the placenta is delivered. The whole birth process takes an average of about 12 hours for a first baby and about 7 hours for subsequent babies.

As the infant is squeezed through the pelvis, cervix, and vagina, the fluid in the lungs is forced out by pressure on the baby's chest. When this pressure is released as the baby emerges from the vagina, the chest expands and the lungs fill with air for the first time. This process ensures that the baby starts breathing immediately after birth. A cesarean baby (surgical delivery) may retain some amniotic fluid in the lungs because it did not pass through the birth canal (Goldberg, Brinkley, & Kukar, 1998).

Not all babies are born vaginally. A variety of conditions can result in birth by **cesarean section,** the delivery of the baby through an incision in the mother's abdominal wall. Situations that may lead to a cesarean delivery include atypical positions of the baby or placenta, a pelvis that is too small for the baby's head to pass through, lack of cervical dilation, fetal distress, and certain medical conditions of the mother such as diabetes, high blood pressure, heart disease, and toxemia. In the past, a cesarean was also performed if a woman had previously had a cesarean birth. Because it is now understood that the pressure of labor and vaginal delivery is not likely to rupture the old incision, many women now deliver subsequent children vaginally even after an earlier child was delivered by a cesarean section. In the United States, the percentage of women delivering vaginally after cesarean increased from 15 percent to 33 percent between 1980 and 1998 (Smith, 1998).

Cesarean births are usually safe and healthy for both mother and child. Despite the success of the cesarean procedure, there is still some controversy about its use. Critics argue that many cesareans are performed unnecessarily and for convenience rather than the mother's or the baby's health. The length of stay in the hospital for the mother and baby after cesarean section is usually 3 to 4 days (Goldberg et al., 1998).

The Evolution of Childbirth Practices

Until about a hundred years ago, birth was treated as a normal event in a woman's life, usually experienced at home with the help of a midwife and other attendants. But mortality for both infants and mothers was high. As progress was made in medical knowledge and techniques, physicians attempted to lower the number of deaths of infants and mothers by increasing medical intervention in the birth process. The use of drugs, forceps, and surgical techniques removed birth from the realm of natural events and placed it in the hands of medical specialists.

By the 1940s, birth was treated as a medical emergency requiring lengthy hospitalization. Hospital personnel pursued efficient, safe births, without much thought to the emotional consequences. For example, women were routinely separated from their husbands during labor and birth, given no information about what was happening to them, and sedated during delivery. Immediately after birth, the mother was sent to her room; the baby was whisked away to the nursery. The father had no direct contact with his baby during the hospital stay—he could look at the baby only through the nursery window. The baby was brought to the mother at scheduled feeding times and then returned to the nursery, where the hospital staff cared for all the newborns together. Any older children in the family were not allowed in the mother's hospital room. After two weeks in the hospital, the mother was sent home with a baby whom she was still getting to know.

Prepared Childbirth   Almost all the hospital childbirth practices just detailed have been modified in the past 30 years. The typical childbirth experience differs considerably from what it was several decades ago. Women are no longer routinely sedated during childbirth. The current belief is that the less medication used, the better. Usually, general anesthesia is not administered even for cesarean births. Instead of relying on drugs, many women learn techniques in childbirth preparation classes that help them deal with the discomfort and rigors of labor and delivery.

One method of prepared childbirth was developed by Dr. Dick-Read, who believed that the pain experienced during birth was the result of a woman's learned fears and anxieties that interfered, through tension, with the natural process of birth. To dispel these fears, childbirth educators teach parents the details of the birth process, as well as physical and respiratory relaxation techniques. The **Dick-Read method** strongly discourages the use of pain-relieving drugs.

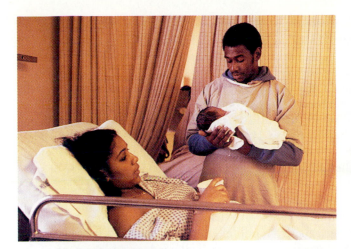
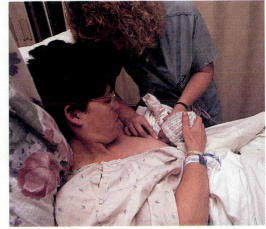

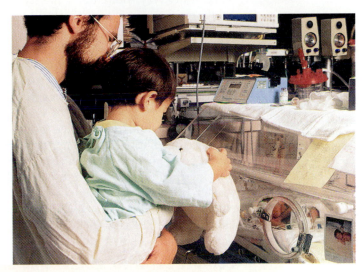

Today's hospitals typically include fathers and siblings in the birth of a new baby. Hospital staff also help mothers learn to breast-feed their infants.   (*Source:* (TOP LEFT) © H. Gans/The Image Works, (TOP RIGHT) © David Wells/The Image Works, (BOTTOM LEFT) Jake Rajs/Tony Stone Images, (BOTTOM RIGHT) © Jonathon Selig/Tony Stone Images)

Another approach to prepared childbirth was developed by Lamaze. Unlike Dick-Read, Lamaze acknowledged that childbirth involves some inherent pain and tension. The **Lamaze method** uses conditioned-response training to teach positive responses to labor contractions rather than tension responses (Goldberg et al., 1998). Like the Dick-Read method, it also teaches parents about the birth process, on the assumption that ignorance breeds fear and knowledge dispels it. The Lamaze method advocates minimal use of pain-relieving drugs to help ensure that both mother and baby are alert during the birth, and to reduce risk to the baby. But limited drug use is not discouraged, because the mother's comfort is an important part of prepared childbirth.

Robert Bradley developed another method of childbirth preparation, known as the **Bradley method,** which stresses relaxation. Women learn techniques, such as massage, relaxation exercises, and breathing control and are encouraged to practice all of the techniques they learn in childbirth classes. Medication during pregnancy, birth, and breast-feeding is discouraged. In one survey, 94% of women attended by Dr. Bradley were unmedicated (McCutcheon, 1996). Fathers are actively involved as coaches and attend weekly classes with the mother starting in the sixth month of pregnancy (AAHCC, 1999).

Most hospitals and clinics instruct parents in a combination of relaxation techniques. Childbirth classes are now almost a routine part of the prenatal experience. When present, the father typically acts as a coach, supporting the mother emotionally and helping her with her breathing. He might also be ready with various comforts, such as wet washcloths or ice chips. He remains with the mother throughout labor and delivery, even when a cesarean section is performed. A labor nurse or midwife also attends the labor.

The **Leboyer delivery method** was developed by a French doctor, Frederick Leboyer, to reduce the trauma of labor and delivery. His recommendations include indirect, dim lighting, gentle handling of the baby, minimum noise, a warmer delivery room, delay in severing the umbilical cord, and placement of the newborn in a warm water bath. Some physicians disagree with the Leboyer techniques on the grounds that the bath may chill the newborn, and that delivery shock into the environment stimulates the breathing process. This method should not be confused with the fad for delivering babies under water, which is not recommended and is potentially dangerous. Babies may take water into their lungs and drown because there is no way to tell when the placenta has been separated (Hotchner, 1997).

Other methods for childbirth include alternate relaxation techniques such as massage, meditation, mental imagery, and hypnosis. Walking during labor and using varied body positions for delivery are preferred by some women. Supported squatting, kneeling on all fours, or even standing upright are birthing positions that some women prefer. Birthing chairs or beds are sometimes used along with less intrusive environments, which may include lower lighting and homelike settings (Bean 1990; Hotchner, 1997; Pasquariello, 1999).

Contact between Mother and Baby   Babies are no longer rushed off to the nursery right after they are born. They spend time with the mother and sometimes the father immediately following birth. They are taken to the nursery to be weighed and examined, and then they are often returned to the mother. **Rooming-in** is the practice of leaving the baby with the mother for as much time as she desires.

Fathers are also encouraged to hold and care for the newborn in the hospital. Many hospitals offer classes on infant care and fathering to new parents during the mother's hospital stay. Fathers can usually visit at any time. Siblings can visit too, but usually only during regular visiting hours. Some hospitals allow the newborn to remain in the room when brothers or sisters are visiting. This practice gives the older children a chance to meet the new member of the family and also a chance to see and talk to Mom.

Even if they do not have rooming-in, mothers today have more contact with their babies during the days after birth than mothers used to, simply because they do not stay in the hospital for nearly as long. Some states have mandated length-of-stay regulations, and many insurance companies encourage no longer than a 24-hour hospitalization. Federal law requires insurance companies to pay for no less than a 48-hour stay (96 hours for cesarean delivery). Some birthing centers may discharge the mother and baby as early as 4–6 hours after delivery and then provide daily phone consultations (Goldberg et al., 1998). Both mother and baby must be medically stable, of course, before leaving the hospital or center. Unfortunately, a large proportion of families living in poverty have no health insurance and receive inadequate care.

Home Births and Other Alternatives   Some parents decide not to have their babies in hospitals at all, but to have them at home or in alternative birth centers, attended by a midwife or a physician. Here, the surroundings are comfortable, the atmosphere is casual, and the company is familiar. Friends, family members, and children can be present at the birth if the parents wish. **Doulas** are professionals who provide informational, emotional, and physical support to the mother and family throughout the childbirth experience. A doula may help with questions, homekeeping, or errands during pregnancy; may assist during labor; and may give help and services after delivery, such as aiding the mother in breast-feeding techniques. (Dona, 1999; Smith, 1998).

Physicians, midwives, doulas, and other personnel who participate in alternative births usually have some medical backup planned in case of emergency. For example, birth centers may have a car available at all times for immediate transport to the nearest hospital. They also carefully screen out high-risk cases to ensure that mothers and babies who are likely to have problems go through labor and delivery where they will have the medical resources they may need.

Benefits of Various Childbirth Practices

There is debate about the advantages of various childbirth practices. No one questions the benefits of reducing medication during birth. The involvement of fathers in labor and delivery is also considered to have psychological and emotional benefits for both parents. There is also a financial advantage to shorter hospital stays. But there are some misgivings over the increase of home births, which tend to be less safe than hospital births. The importance given to early contact between mothers and babies has also been questioned. During the 1970s and 1980s, an emphasis was placed on uninterrupted contact as a requirement for attachment and "bonding" (an early emotional tie between mother and child). Some people claimed that if bonding did not occur immediately after birth, the baby might never form a proper attachment.

More recent research has contradicted these beliefs. Premature babies and babies with physical problems at birth are usually placed in neonatal care units, and women who have had general anesthesia are unable to interact with their babies immediately after birth. But attachment still forms between these mothers and babies, and early separation seems to have no permanent detrimental effects (Goldberg, 1983). (We discuss attachment and bonding in chapter 7.)

The positive side of current childbirth practices is that parents now have choices. Mothers who choose rooming-in can have their babies with them virtually every minute of their hospital stay. But it is acceptable for mothers not to choose rooming-in. Mothers who have older children or have no spouse to share responsibilities at home may feel that they need to use the hospital stay to rest and regain their strength. Still others may want to have their babies with them for short periods of time until they become confident that they can care for them. In most hospitals today, parents can decide for themselves what kind of childbirth experience they want to have.

Of course, childbirth practices vary considerably from culture to culture around the world. To learn more about these cross-cultural variations, see the Research Close-Up: Childbirth Practices around the World.

RESEARCH

Childbirth Practices around the World

Most mothers and fathers view childbirth as a very special event, and it is treated with great interest in many parts of the world (Callister, 1995). But the specific way in which the event is treated varies a great deal from one culture to another. For example, cultures vary in terms of the degree to which the mother is isolated at the time of birth, the access to the birth allowed the baby's father, the extent to which birth is considered a natural, nonmedical event, and the many practical ways in which the mother is aided as she goes through labor and delivery.

Cultural Variations in the Isolation of Childbirth

In some tribal cultures, birth takes place in the midst of everyday life. For example, the Jarara (South America) mother may give birth in a shelter or passageway, in full view of the entire tribe. There are no special facilities for giving birth, nor are women isolated in their own homes during this time. Moreover, special birth attendants, such as midwives, are not used (Mead & Newton, 1967). The !Kung (Kalahari Desert of Africa) also provide no special physical place or facilities for births. Women in this tribal society may simply go out alone to the bush, give birth, cut the cord, and begin care of the newborn with no assistance (Komner & Shostak, 1987).

The Gusii, a tribe living in southeastern Kenya, also have no special facilities to which mothers go to deliver their babies. Instead, they give birth in their homes while squatting on the floor and supporting themselves by clinging to ropes hanging from the ceiling beams. Gusii mothers may give birth alone, or they may be attended by another woman or child (Keefer et al., 1991).

The practices common in these tribal cultures differ markedly from those found in larger cities in Western industrialized countries. In these contexts, birth takes place in a hospital or at home, and it is considered important to have trained medical personnel, such as a doctor or a midwife, present. The Netherlands, although an industrialized country, is unique in having a high proportion of home deliveries (56 percent), though many are assisted by midwives (43 percent). Most Dutch women neither expect nor receive any type of medication (Jordan, 1993; Van den Boom, 1991).

In contrast, pain relief, sedation, and labor stimulation methods are common in Sweden where less than 1 percent occur outside of hospitals. Many hospital births are managed by well-trained midwives (Jordan, 1993). Relaxation training and information for pregnant women are readily available, free of charge (Munck et al., 1991).

The Father's Participation in Childbirth across Cultures

It is common today in the United States for fathers to be present at the birth and to assist the mother throughout labor.

In traditional Javanese (Indonesia) culture, husband and wife also share the responsibility for the birth. The woman sits on a mat (on the floor or wide bench), with her husband behind her. She leans against his legs to push while the midwife massages her abdomen and legs. Relatives and older children may be present to observe, but the father and midwife are the only participants in the birth (Piessens, 1991).

Yucatecan (Mexico) fathers also help with the birth of their children. Privacy for the event is obtained by hanging a blanket from the rafters of the family's one-room house. Occasionally, the entire house is off-limits to all but the husband, midwife, and helpers. The helpers are usually mothers and daughters or other kin of the woman (Jordan, 1993).

In other cultures, the father's presence at a birth is prohibited. For example, in some of the small, rural Zulu villages in southern Africa, where people live in mud-walled, thatched-roof huts, women give birth in their living hut, often with the grandmother supervising the delivery. Usually, no one else may enter the hut for a 10-day period following the birth. Men especially may not enter, because the Zulu believe that only women may be involved in the birth process. The new mother and baby are cared for by the female relative who assists at the birth for the 10-day period following the birth (Niestroj, 1991).

Many other peoples in South Africa are similar to the Zulu in the belief that birth is strictly an event for women. From maternity clinics to large hospitals, nurses and midwives create a warm, homelike atmosphere, but family members are not permitted to be present during labor or the postpartum period (Niestroj, 1991).

In Nepal, men, as well as all children and women who have not yet had children, are prevented from attending or witnessing the birth of a baby. It is also believed that men should be kept far enough away that they cannot hear any cries of the woman (Escarce, 1989).

Cultural Variations in Practices to Aid Labor and Delivery

During labor, Yucatecan (Mexico) women lie crosswise in a hammock with legs drawn up and apart. "As the woman begins to feel some discomfort, a helper takes her place (or his place, if the husband is there) on a chair beside the hammock, at the woman's head. . . . With her arms under the woman's shoulders, the 'head helper' supports the woman's hammock-encased body on her lap. The hammock's flexible compactness permits her to pull the woman up at the height of a contraction, raising her to almost a sitting position. As the contraction fades away, she gently lets her down to rest. Meanwhile, the midwife and another helper are occupied with rubbing her abdomen, her back and her legs" (Jordan, 1993, p. 34).

In other cultures, such as in southeastern Kenya and in Nepal, women give birth in a squatting position (Escarce,

1989; Komner & Shostak, 1987). In still others, birth takes place while the woman sits (Piessens, 1991). In Western, industrialized cultures, women have traditionally given birth while lying on their backs on a bed. In more recent years, however, women have been given some freedom in hospital birthing rooms to position themselves as they wish during labor and delivery.

Special Customs Associated with Pregnancy, Labor, and Birth

In many cultures, special rituals and customs are commonly associated with pregnancy, labor, and birth. For example, at traditional Navajo births in the special hogan, ceremonies and celebrations take place, and the placenta is buried in the ashes of the hogan fire to combat evil spirits. Today, Navajo women are more likely than in the past to be in or near a hospital for labor and delivery, but a Navajo elder must also be present at the birth to deliver the special chants (Dempsey & Gesse, 1995).

In traditional Javanese (Indonesia) culture, the woman is to eat very peppery food during the seventh month of pregnancy and must avoid eating some foods, such as sugar cane and certain fruits, to guard against a difficult birth or a deformed baby (Piessens, 1991). In some South African groups, silence during labor is part of the tradition. Calling out or vocalizing in other ways during labor is believed to be harmful to the newborn child and thus to be avoided by the mother and all others in attendance (Niestroj, 1991).

In Nepal, a country tucked between India and China, Hindu traditions dictate many practices associated with the reproductive lives of women. During menstruation, women are considered polluted, and thus contact with them is taboo. For three days during the month, they must not prepare food or even enter the kitchen. During the later stages of pregnancy, a woman is also not to cook certain foods for elders, nor is she to handle their drinking water. For 10 days following birth, the woman is again untouchable by anyone except a woman who comes to massage her body with oil. Even these women must wash thoroughly and change their clothes when leaving the house (Escarce, 1989).

During labor and delivery, women in Nepal are to avoid facing north or south, because these are not thought to be good astrological directions. After birth, the baby may not be shown to its father for several days if it was born under an unlucky astrological sign (Escarce, 1989).

Changes in Birthing Practices

Birth practices change as cultures change. In the 1800s, childbirth in the United States was treated as a social event, with help provided by friends and neighbors. Often, the entire family was present for the birth, which occurred at home. In 1900, only about 5 percent of babies born in the United States were born in hospitals. By 1993, 99 percent were born in hospitals (Jordan, 1993; National Center for Health Statistics, 1988; Wertz & Wertz, 1977).

In recent decades, women in Westernized cultures have questioned the practices of hospitals, asking for more home birth facilities and more control over the birthing process, including who can be present. At the same time, in some traditional cultures, especially in developing countries, there has been some eagerness for information about Western birth practices and some interest in acquiring more technology to assist birth. It seems that different cultures are perhaps trying to put together the best of both worlds—naturalness and support for the mother, on the one hand, and increased assurance of her health and safety, on the other.

Problems in Early Development: When Things Go Wrong

You read at the beginning of this chapter how one mother was affected by a problem in the prenatal development of her baby. Not all prenatal problems are as devastating as fetal alcohol syndrome, but many create difficulties for an entire lifetime for the child, the child's family, and the community. Some of these problems result from genetic abnormalities, others from chromosomal errors, and still others from environmental factors. No matter what their origin, and no matter how they show up later in life, these problems can never be erased from the child's makeup.

Genetic Problems

As the name implies, genetic problems result from the inheritance of particular genes from the parents. Most common genetic problems are due to the inheritance of a pair of abnormal recessive genes. The probability of inheriting a disease carried by two **recessive genes** is diagrammed in Figure 2.11.

Four common recessive-gene disorders are **sickle-cell anemia, cystic fibrosis, phenylketonuria,** and **Tay-Sachs disease.** Some genetic disorders occur disproportionately among certain groups, because recessive genes develop within a particular gene pool and tend to remain in it. For example, sickle-cell anemia, a disease of the red blood cells, occurs mainly in people of black African ancestry. Tay-Sachs disease, a fatal disorder of the central nervous system, primarily afflicts people of Eastern European Jewish ancestry. The probability that a child will inherit any of these four genetic diseases when both parents are carriers (healthy, but recipients of one recessive gene for the disease) is 25 percent. Table 2.2 describes these diseases and gives the prognosis for children born with them.

Rh disease, a genetically related disorder, is not caused by inheriting abnormal recessive genes. The **Rh factor** is a protein found in the blood. If an Rh-positive father and an Rh-negative mother conceive an Rh-positive baby, the baby's blood will be incompatible with the mother's. If some of the baby's blood enters the mother's bloodstream during delivery, she will develop antibodies to it just as she would toward a virus. The first baby is not affected, because at the time the antibodies are not yet in the mother's bloodstream. But subsequent Rh-positive babies will suffer. The antibodies in the mother's blood, passing through the placenta, destroy the fetus's red blood cells, which carry oxygen throughout the fetus's body. Jaundice, anemia, and other problems, sometimes leading to mental retardation or death, can result (Hotchner, 1995).

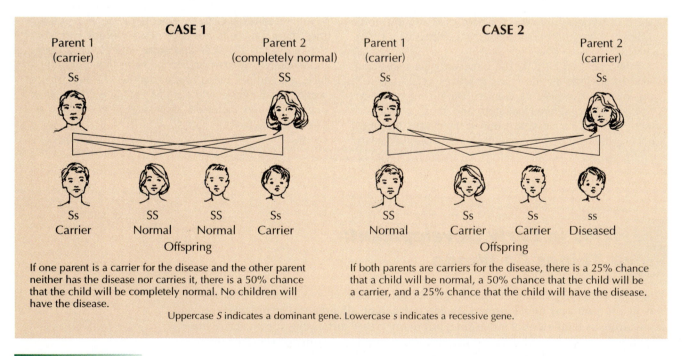

If one parent is a carrier for the disease and the other parent neither has the disease nor carries it, there is a 50% chance that the child will be completely normal. No children will have the disease.

If both parents are carriers for the disease, there is a 25% chance that a child will be normal, a 50% chance that the child will be a carrier, and a 25% chance that the child will have the disease.

Uppercase *S* indicates a dominant gene. Lowercase *s* indicates a recessive gene.

FIGURE 2.11

Inheritance of recessive gene diseases. The probability of inheriting a disease carried by recessive genes depends on whether one or both parents is a carrier.

TABLE 2.2

Diseases caused by the inheritance of two abnormal recessive genes

Disease	Incidence	Description and Consequences of the Disease	Prognosis for Children Who Are Afflicted	Population at Risk
Sickle-cell anemia	1 in 625 live births among African Americans	Abnormal hemoglobin in red blood cells sickels (changes shape) during periods of stress caused by such factors as low oxygen. Sickled cells stick together and impair blood flow to organs. Children may have swollen abdomens and a yellowish cast to their eyes.	Many children with this disease do not survive into adulthood.	The recessive gene is carried by a disproportionate number of African Americans.
Cystic fibrosis	1 in every 2,000 live births, 1,500–2,000 per year	Essential enzymes of the pancreas are deficient. Thick mucus develops in the lungs and intestinal tract. Sweat contains a higher than typical concentration of sodium and chloride. Absorption of food is impaired. Susceptibility to respiratory infections is greatly increased because salt and water are removed from lungs too fast.	Many victims die in early childhood, although antibiotic and enzyme therapies are increasingly successful in prolonging life into adolescence and early adulthood. Some cases remain relatively asymptomatic until early adulthood.	The disease is the most common of the serious recessive diseases afflicting Caucasians.
Phenylketonuria (PKU)	1 in 10,000 live Caucasian births	The enzyme needed to metabolize an amino acid (phenylalanine) into another (tryosine) is absent. Toxins accumulate in nerve tissue and destroy it. Mental retardation can result.	PKU can be detected early in infancy with a urine test. (All newborns are rountinely screened in most states.) Foods high in phenylalanine are resticted so that toxins are not formed.	This condition is most common among Caucasians. It rarely afflicts children of African American or Asian ancestry.
Tay-Sachs	1 in 3,600 live births for Eastern European Jews	Victims cannot metabolize fat properly. The brain and other nerve tissue deteriorate as a result. Children have motor weakness initially, followed by blindness, seizures, and death.	The condition results in death, which usually occurs by age 3 or 4.	The recessive gene causing this disease is carried primarily by Jews of Eastern European ancestry.

Source: Data from "The Challenging Epidemiology of Cystic Fibrosis," by S. C. FitzSimmons, 1993, *Journal of Pediatrics, 122,* pp. 1–9; *Human Molecular Genetics,* by T. Srachan and A. P. Read, 1996, New York: Wiley; *Access to The Genome: The Challenge to Equality,* by J. Mehlman and J. R. Botkin, 1998, Washington, DC: Georgetown University Press.

A serum called Rh immune globulin destroys Rh-positive cells as they enter the mother's body. Thus, this serum prevents the development of antibodies if it is administered to an Rh-negative mother within a few hours after she gives birth to an Rh-positive baby (Beeson, 1989). Before this vaccine was developed in the 1960s, about 40,000 babies were affected each year by complications due to Rh incompatibility. Today, the condition is almost nonexistent.

This child is enjoying his art activity. He has the most common chromosomally-related-problem, Down syndrome. (*Source:* © Ellen Senisi/The Image Works)

Chromosomal Problems

There are other problems when errors occur in the egg or sperm cell during meiosis. Sometimes complete chromosomes do not separate, and they go to different cells than intended. At other times, pieces of chromosomes break off, leaving extra genetic material in one cell and a shortage in another. Obviously, children with errors in their chromosomes will have serious problems.

The most common chromosomally related problem is **Down syndrome,** which occurs about once in every 600 births (Stratford, 1994). Down syndrome is caused by an error in the number 21 chromosome, usually the presence of three chromosomes at this location instead of the normal two (Kerkay et al., 1971; Lilienfield, 1969). Usually, two of those chromosomes come from a defective ovum with an extra chromosome and one comes from a normal sperm. Children with Down syndrome are mentally retarded and have a characteristic physical appearance.

The older the mother (after reaching 30 years of age), the greater the chance that she will have a Down syndrome baby. It is believed that this is caused by the sex cells weakening over time or by exposure by either parent to harmful agents in the environment. The extra chromosome is contributed by the father approximately 25 percent of the time (Hotchner, 1995).

Sex chromosome abnormalities create physical, cognitive, and psychopathological problems (Kumra et al., 1998; Milunsky, 1992). Some of these are caused by an extra sex chromosome (XYY, XXY, or XXX), others by a missing sex chromosome (XO). Males with XYY are usually tall and large-bodied, and they usually have a low verbal intelligence. Klinefelter's syndrome is a disorder that results when a male receives an extra X chromosome. Males with this chromosomal error are mentally retarded and develop some female characteristics at puberty (Johnson et al., 1970). Girls with the sex chromosome abnormality XXX (an extra X chromosome) have smaller head circumferences at birth and lower verbal IQs than normal children do. Girls with Turner's syndrome (XO) have all or part of one X chromosome missing. They have incomplete sexual development and low spatial intelligence, but average verbal intelligence.

In addition to the selected cognitive ability deficiencies, individuals with these four sex-chromosome disorders have a higher incidence of schizophrenia than occurs in the normal population (Kumra et al., 1998). In **fragile X syndrome,** children have an abnormal break in one or both of the X chromosomes. These children may have a spectrum of difficulties, including lower intelligence, autism, attention disorders, sensory motor disorders, and facial abnormalities. Thus, the presence of an extra sex-related chromosome or the absence of one appears to impair some mental abilities (Harris-Schmidt & Fast, 1998; Hotchner, 1995; Ratcliffe et al., 1994). Approximately 7 percent of autistic boys have the fragile X syndrome. Research from the Human Genome Project indicates that individuals with fragile X syndrome have mild mental retardation in childhood and a moderate range of mental retardation by adulthood (Harris-Schmidt & Fast, 1998).

Problems Due to Environmental Factors

Infectious Agents   Environmental factors that contribute to problems in early development include infectious agents, chemicals, and radiation. Infections known to be harmful to the fetus include the rubella virus, which can cause hearing loss, blindness, heart and nervous system defects, and even death soon after birth (Iconis, 1995). In 1964–65 an epidemic of rubella (German measles) swept through the United States, and nearly 50,000 children died in utero or were born with birth defects as a result.

Other harmful infectious agents are not viral. **Toxoplasmosis,** which is caused by a parasite, exhibits only coldlike symptoms or symptoms similar to mononucleosis in the mother. But the infection can be devastating to the infant, for whom it can cause abnormal brain and head growth and mental retardation (Whitley & Goldenberg, 1990). Expectant mothers may be infected with this organism through contact with animals or through eating raw or undercooked meats.

Noninfectious Environmental Hazards   Environmental agents (**teratogens**) can interfere with the normal development of the prenatal child. One teratogenic hazard is prescription drugs. In the 1950s and 1960s, hundreds of European mothers who had taken the tranquilizer thalidomide gave birth to babies without arms or legs (Lenz, 1966). Other drugs also can cause problems in development. Almost all prescription drugs now carry warnings to pregnant women, telling them to check with their doctors about the safety of the drugs during pregnancy.

Other noninfectious teratogens include chemicals, such as paint vapors, garden chemicals, and pesticides. Industrial compounds known as PCBs and heavy metals such as lead and mercury and radiation also can cause problems in the developing fetus. Pregnant women must also avoid vapors given off by glue, gasoline, contact cement, cleaning fluids, and oven cleaners (Hotchner, 1995; Stoppard, 1998). Exposure to radiation during pregnancy can slow physical growth of the fetus and also cause an undeveloped brain and other physical malformations and miscarriage. Even low levels of radiation may cause later childhood cancer (Smith, 1992). The specific effect of radiation depends upon the period of prenatal development during which radiation exposure occurs.

Exposure to Cocaine   Among the babies who have been exposed to harmful substances prenatally, there has been an alarming increase in the number exposed to cocaine. Compared to babies not affected by teratogens, cocaine-exposed babies have a lower average birth weight, a smaller average head circumference, and a greater likelihood of being born prematurely or stillborn. They are more likely to show either impaired or excessive motor activity, impaired information-processing ability, and less responsivity (Tronick et al., 1996). They also are extremely irritable and tend to be ultrasensitive to noise and touch. As a result they do not seem to be able to respond or relate to people the way normal babies do. They are more fussy and difficult at one year than are other babies, and they are very difficult to comfort or console (Beeghly et al., 1995; Richardson et al., 1995).

Children can be harmed by parental cocaine use not only in the womb, but before conception. Infants whose fathers used cocaine prior to the child's conception can have birth defects, because cocaine can affect the sperm (Yazigi et al., 1991).

Other serious problems also have been observed in cocaine-exposed children. However, so many other negative prenatal factors may be involved in this population of mothers that it is difficult to sort out the exact cause-effect relationship between prenatal cocaine exposure and later developmental difficulties. For example, cocaine users tend to be less well nourished than other mothers (Frank et al., 1988), and they may receive little or no prenatal care. Furthermore, babies born to cocaine-abusing mothers may be neglected or may live in impoverished or dangerous environments. Any of these factors, alone or in combination, can cause serious problems in the child's development.

Exposure to Alcohol   Although Clara, the woman we met at the beginning of the chapter, did not fully comprehend the importance of not drinking during pregnancy, the effects of alcohol on the developing fetus are well documented. Alcohol

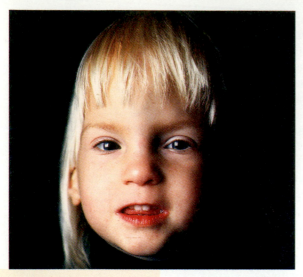

Children exposed prenatally to alcohol may suffer from fetal alcohol syndrome. Children with this syndrome have a unique set of features, including deformities of the face. (*Source:* © George Steinmetz)

can affect the reproductive capacity of the mother and father, can affect the developing fetus directly, or can have indirect effects by altering the metabolism and nutrition of the alcohol-consuming mother (Williams et al., 1994).

Studies indicate that alcohol can interfere with a prospective mother's ability to conceive and that alcohol can reduce the male's sperm count by acting as a direct toxin to sperm (Cicero, 1994; Grodstein et al., 1994; Pasquariello, 1999).

Alcohol's effects on prenatal development include attention and processing disorders, physical alterations, behavioral problems, and learning problems. Indeed, consumption of alcohol during pregnancy has been labeled as the leading cause of mental retardation in the Americas and Europe (Nevitt, 1998). Binge drinking has very severe effects and frequently occurs before the mother is aware of her pregnancy (Bookstein et al., 1996).

Children who have the unique set of physical features and problems associated with prenatal alcohol exposure are said to have **fetal alcohol syndrome** (FAS), whereas those with only a few of the problems are said to suffer from **fetal alcohol effects** (FAE). Noticeable characteristics of FAS include microcephaly (a small, underdeveloped brain), facial and limb defects, and a wide range of emotional and cognitive disorders. Characteristic facial features include widely spaced eyes, narrow eyelid openings, a flattened nose, and an underdeveloped upper lip. Table 2.3 presents a summary of prenatal alcohol effects on different stages of life.

TABLE 2.3

Effects of a woman's alcohol consumption during pregnancy

Effects on the Fetus	Effects on the Infant	Effects on the Child	Effects on the Adolescent	Effects on the Adult
Slowed prenatal growth	Slowed physical growth	Poor motor coordination	Mental retardation	Mental retardation
Facial malformations	Slowed brain growth	Visual-spatial deficits	Poor school performance	Learning disabilities
Body malformations	Sudden infant death syndrome	Head banging	Poor planning skills	Hyperactivity
Organ malformations	Infant leukemia	Rhythmical rocking	Communication difficulties	Restlessness
Central nervous system disorders	Brain wave abnormalities	Mental retardation	Difficulty in interactions	Attention problems
Kidney abnormalities	Seizures and tremors	Slow information processing	Attention problems	Poor social skills
Microcephaly (small brain)	Alcohol withdrawal symptoms	Learning disabilities	Adjustment problems	Poor interpersonal interactions
	Hearing problems	Poor short-term memory	Impulsive behavior	Poor planning skills
	Poor sucking response	Short attention span	Decreased social competence	Adjustment problems
	Feeding problems	Restlessness	Serious behavior problems	Difficulty keeping a job
	Sleep disturbances	Irritability		
	Irritability	Hyperactivity		
		Distractibility		

Sources: Becker et al., 1994; Bookstein et al., 1996; Matthews & Simpson, 1998; Moore et al., 1997; Nevitt, 1998; Olson et al., 1998; Pasquariello, 1999; Shu et al., 1996; Tishler et al., 1998.

Approximately 12,000 FAS babies are born in the United States each year, and the number with FAE is even higher (Nevitt, 1998). Alcohol is the most frequently used teratogen in the Western world (Streissguth et al., 1999). The severity of FAS and FAE problems vary, depending on the amount of alcohol consumed, the frequency of binge drinking, and the specific weeks during prenatal development when the fetus was exposed to alcohol. The timing factor is associated with the critical period hypothesis: The body system that is developing most quickly at the time of exposure is the one that will be most affected by a teratogen. For example, the prenatal period between 8 and 16 weeks is the period of rapid neural migration in the formation of the brain. Alcohol (or radiation) exposure during this period results in a microcephalic brain, distorted information-processing abilities, and mental retardation. Exposure to multiple teratogens at the same time may have **synergistic effects.** That is, the combined effect of two or more teratogens is greater than the additive effects of each. Because of this and the possibility that even very low levels of alcohol use may have some effects, the Surgeon General of the United States has advised that pregnant women completely abstain from drinking alcohol throughout pregnancy.

FAS was first identified only 30 years ago. There is now extensive information that should be made available to all individuals facing pregnancy and distributed during prenatal checkups (Russell, 1994). Prenatal clinic programs, community prevention efforts, and training programs for health providers and teachers hold promise for reducing alcohol consumption during pregnancy (Ma et al., 1998).

Exposure to Cigarette Smoke   Cigarette smoking has also been studied intensively as a teratogen because it has been associated with several adverse conditions in newborns. The risk of low birth weight increases with the number of cigarettes smoked by the mother during the third trimester (Lieberman et al., 1994). Birth weight also is affected by the number of cigarettes smoked by the father during the child's prenatal period, when the mothers themselves are nonsmokers (Martinez et al., 1994).

Prenatal exposure to cigarette smoke has been associated with other problems. The fetus's breathing and movement patterns become more rapid and agitated when the mother's nicotine level is high (Erickson et al., 1983). Studies suggest that prenatal exposure may predispose the child to later cigarette addiction during adolescence (Kandel et al., 1994), and to poorer auditory maturation during the school years (McCartney et al., 1994).

It seems obvious that neither parent should smoke during or after pregnancy. In addition to the problems already noted, the U.S. Environmental Protection Agency has found that fumes given off from lighted cigarettes have concentrations of cancer-causing chemicals as high as smoke actually inhaled by the smoker (Dreher, 1995). These chemicals create health risks for children whose parents smoke. Some researchers also report synergistic effects of tobacco and alcohol use. This combination can result in smaller infants and less cognitively capable children than the use of either drug individually (Day & Richardson, 1994).

Smoking tobacco increases the level of carbon monoxide in the mother's blood, and this, instead of oxygen, is carried across the placental barrier. The increase in carbon monoxide coupled with the decreased oxygen resulting from nicotine constricting the mother's capillaries affects brain development, which causes later deficits in learning and memory. Researchers have found that lung damage to the offspring can last into adulthood (Cunningham et al., 1994). Table 2.4 presents a list of other environmental factors associated with impairments during prenatal development.

Smoking during pregnancy is associated with a higher risk for low birth weight in the infant, and deficits in learning and memory later in childhood. (*Source:* © Michael Newman/Photo Edit)

TABLE 2.4

Environmental factors associated with impairments during prenatal development

Agent or Condition	Effects
Accutane (13 cis-retinoic acid, for treating acne)	Small or absent ears; small jaws; heart defects; mental retardation
Addictive drugs	Low birth weight; possible addiction of infant; hypersensitivity to stimuli; higher risk for stroke and respiratory distress
AIDs virus	Death, often within two years of birth
Alcohol	Mental retardation; growth retardation; miscarriage; microcephaly; structural abnormalities in the face; lower IQ; attention and learning disorders
Anticoagulant	Miscarriage
Aspirin	Miscarriage; newborn hemorrhage
Barbiturates	Congenital malformations
Caffeine	Low heart rate; less alert and active; malnourished
Chemotherapy	Miscarriage
Clozapine	Problems in bone marrow
Cortisone	Abnormalities or stillbirth
Cytomegalovirus (CMV)	Microcephaly (smaller than normal head); motor disabilities; hearing loss
DES (diethylstilbestrol)	Increased incidence of vaginal cancer; impaired reproduction
Diet pills	Heart defects; blood vessel malformation
Diuretics	Blood disorders; jaundice
Endocrine disorders	Cretinism; microcephaly
Environmental chemicals (e.g., benzene, formaldehyde, PCBs)	Chromosome damage; miscarriage; low birth weight
Inadequate diet	Reduction in brain growth; smaller than average birth weight; decrease in birth length; rickets
Irradiation	Physical deformities; mental retardation
Malnutrition	Low birth weight; abnormal reflexes; altered brain growth
Maternal age over 35	Increased incidence of Down syndrome
Maternal age under 18	Prematurity; stillbirth; increased incidence of Down syndrome
Quinine	Deafness
Smoking tobacco	Prematurity; low birth weight and length; decreased attentiveness
Streptomycin	Eighth cranial nerve damage (hearing loss)
Sulfa drugs	Jaundice
Syphilis	Mental retardation; physical deformities; in utero death and miscarriage
Tetracycline	Discoloration of teeth
Thyroid medication	Goiter
Valium	Cleft lip and palate

Sources: Berger & Goldstein, 1980; Bookstein et al., 1996; Herbst, 1972; Herbst et al., 1975; Hotchner, 1995, 1997; Jacobson & Jacobson, 1996; Joos et al., 1983; Kitzinger, 1997; Lenz, 1966; Meredith, 1975; MOD, 1999a; Naeye, 1983; Naeye et al., 1973; Plummer, 1952; Siegel et al., 1971; Snyder et al., 1945; Streissguth et al., 1995; Walters, 1975; Zeskine & Ramey, 1978.

Maternal Conditions Affecting Prenatal Development

Nutrition and Exercise   Good nutrition is especially important for the pregnant woman because the baby depends completely on its mother for nutrition during the prenatal period. The earlier in life infants are malnourished, the greater the adverse effects on development (Marin et al., 1995). A good prenatal diet includes regular, well-balanced meals, consisting of foods rich in iron, calcium, folic acid, protein, and vitamins A and D (Hotchner, 1997). One study demonstrated the negative effects of low protein in maternal diets. These effects included poor fetal growth rate, poor brain development, and faulty fatty acid metabolism (Marin et al., 1995). An insufficient amount of folic acid in the diet may cause spina bifida (incomplete vertebrae development, resulting in a spinal gap with an underdeveloped section of chord), anencephaly (brain did not develop), or other birth defects (Jacobson, 1995). Women should have 400 micrograms of folic acid daily before conception and during pregnancy. Natural sources include orange juice, beans, peanuts, and enriched grain products. Folic acid can reduce the risk of having a baby with neural tube defects (defects of the brain and spinal cord) (MOD, 1999b, 1999e). In 1999 the March of Dimes (MOD) launched a multiyear national education campaign to spread this important information because many women do not consume enough folic acid.

A variety of ingredients can affect prenatal development. The flavoring MSG (monosodium glutamate) can cause dehydration, and it is recommended that pregnant women avoid foods processed with it, as well as highly salted foods and foods containing sodium nitrate. Sodium nitrate can reduce the oxygen-carrying power of the blood. Because tea contains tannin, which interferes with iron absorption, pregnant women should avoid tea, especially with meals (Stoppard, 1998). Tea also containes caffeine, as do coffee, chocolate, and many soft drinks. Caffeine is not recommended for pregnant women because when it is ingested during pregnancy, it may increase the risk that babies will have a lower heart rate, less alertness, and lower birth weight than they should (Mann, 1997; MOD, 1999c).

In a survey of women's eating habits during pregnancy, researchers found that many women do not consume enough high-calcium foods or fruits and vegetables. They receive only two thirds of their need for folic acid and less than half of their requirements for iron (Somer, 1995). Enriching the diets of pregnant women, especially with calcium, iron, protein, and vitamins, can help prevent malnutrition and its negative results in infants (Sigman, 1995).

Regular, moderate exercise is recommended for pregnant women, and many childbirth education programs offer exercise classes. Exercise improves respiration, muscle tone, and circulation. Recommended exercises during pregnancy include walking, stationary biking, and swimming. Exercises for strengthening the pelvic floor muscles (Kegel exercises) and for reducing tension, as well as gentle abdominal exercises, are also appropriate. Pregnant women should avoid jogging, scuba diving, weight-bearing sports, skiing, diving, waterskiing, and mountain biking (Hotchner, 1997).

Exposure to Excessive Heat   There has been increasing concern over the use of hot tubs and spas that raise the body temperature. Ten to 15 minutes of exposure is sufficient to cause central nervous system damage to the fetus. Malformed babies are increasingly likely with even moderate heat exposure that lasts longer than 45 minutes. Pregnant women should avoid saunas, hot tubs, and excessively hot showers or baths (Pasquariello, 1999).

Parental Age   Increased maternal age is associated with an increased chance of giving birth to a baby with Down syndrome. Women may also have more difficulty becoming pregnant after age 30, although first births to women in their 30s increased in the past 25 years, and 11 percent of births are by women age 35 and older. The highest age at which a woman gave birth after conceiving naturally has been recorded as age 57 (Jones, 1998). Adolescence is another time for concern. Infants born to adolescents have a mortality rate double that of infants born to mothers in their 20s. Moreover, infants born to adolescent mothers are often premature. These problems can be caused by a lack of prenatal care, poor nutrition, health problems, stress, and low income. Interestingly, the father's age is also important, as there is greater likelihood of sperm problems as age increases.

Emotional Stress   Babies may be at risk for a variety of difficulties if their mothers experience emotional stress during pregnancy (Crnic & Acevedo, 1995; Pasquariello, 1999). Physiological changes occur in response to fears, anxieties, and other emotions. Because blood flow to the uterus is reduced as more blood is sent to other parts of the mother's body, the fetus receives less oxygen and fewer nutrients. Emotional stress also influences the secretion of hormones and adrenaline, which pass through the placenta and affect the fetus. The birth process itself may be influenced by stress, leading to irregular contractions and a more difficult labor (Lobel et al., 1992). All of these physiological effects restrict blood flow and deprive the fetus of oxygen.

Hormones   Sometimes hormonal abnormalities during pregnancy expose the fetus to atypical levels of hormones, which can cause problems. For example, an overproduction of androgens during pregnancy causes congenital adrenal hyperplasia (CAH). This condition causes female fetuses to develop enlarged sex organs and show more "masculine" behavior traits as children and adolescents (Berenbaum & Hines, 1992). Some research even suggests that there can be hormonal influences from an opposite-sex twin. Miller (1998) reported that opposite-sex twins are less sex-typical in their abilities and emotions than same-sex twins or single-borns. He interpreted the research as supporting hormone transfer and prenatal hormone effects.

Diabetes   Women with poorly controlled preexisting diabetes (diabetes before pregnancy) are more likely to have a baby with heart or neural tube defects, and they are at increased risk of miscarriage and stillbirth. Women with gestational diabetes (diabetes develops during pregnancy) are at somewhat less risk, especially if insulin treatment is not required. Both types of poorly controlled diabetic women are at increased risk of having an extremely large baby (10 or more pounds) or a baby with breathing difficulties, low blood sugar, or jaundice. Most pregnant women with controlled diabetes and good management of their pregnancy have a good chance of delivering a healthy baby (MOD, 1999d).

Problems in the Birth Process

Lack of Oxygen   One danger to the baby during birth and immediately afterward is oxygen deprivation, or **anoxia.** The baby may not get enough oxygen if the umbilical cord is compressed during delivery, if breathing does not start immediately after birth, or if breathing is impaired by respiratory distress in the first days or weeks of life, as it might in a premature birth.

Anoxia affects most severely the brain centers where motor functioning is controlled. Anoxia during or just before birth can cause cerebral palsy, a disorder of the motor system (Paneth, 1986). Children with cerebral palsy have problems controlling their muscles, which affects their speaking and other motor-related behavior.

Infections   Any infection of the mother's reproductive tract can be contracted by the baby during or before birth. The most serious infections are syphilis, gonorrhea, chlamydia, herpes simplex virus, and AIDS. Syphilis can infect and kill the fetus during the prenatal period. If the baby is born alive, it will have syphilis. Penicillin given to the mother during pregnancy will cure the disease in both mother and fetus.

Gonorrhea can infect the baby during delivery and cause blindness. It can be present in the mother without any symptoms, so the danger to the baby may not be apparent. Because of this uncertainty, all newborns are treated with silver nitrate drops in their eyes soon after birth. Silver nitrate destroys the gonorrheal bacteria.

Chlamydia is a sexually transmitted disease that, if untreated, can cause pelvic inflammatory disease, which has been linked to infertility and to potentially fatal tubal pregnancy. Prenatal exposure to chlamydia can cause problems such as neonatal conjunctivitis and pneumonia (CDC, 1999j).

Herpes simplex virus can be transmitted to the baby during delivery if the mother's infection is in the active phase. If this is the case, the baby is delivered by cesarean section to keep it from contracting the virus in the birth canal. Herpes can damage the baby's eyes and brain. No cure has yet been discovered for the infection. (In adults the virus causes open sores on the skin or mucous membranes, but no organ damage.)

Currently, the most serious infection affecting newborns is **acquired immune deficiency syndrome** (AIDS). This fatal disorder of the immune system is transmitted in blood and semen. The **human immunodeficiency virus** (HIV), which causes AIDS, can be passed to a fetus by an HIV-infected mother, because viruses from her body can cross the placenta into the developing baby. Some infants may contract the virus during delivery. Populations of infants at high risk for this fatal disease consist of those whose mothers are IV (intravenous) drug abusers or who have sexual partners who are infected with HIV. Intravenous drug abusers often acquire the disease by sharing dirty needles with someone who already has the virus.

If a pregnant woman is HIV infected, she has a 30 percent risk of transmitting HIV to her child during delivery. However, two doses of the drug nevirapine can drop the risk to a 13 percent chance. The drug stays in the body a long time and may also help prevent HIV transmission through breast milk (CNN, 1999).

Birth Defects   Birth defects are the leading cause of infant death and a major cause of disability in young people. They affect more than 150,000 babies each year. Fortunately, the rate of infant deaths due to birth defects has been cut in half since 1960 (MOD, 1999b). Advanced technologies, better management of maternal medical conditions, increased focus on good nutrition, avoidance of teratogens such as alcohol and cigarette smoke, immunizations against diseases such as rubella, and new fetal treatments are leading to fewer incidents of birth defects. Television, radio, computer, magazine, and billboard advertisements, as well as magazines such as *Mama* (March of Dimes annual magazine for parents-to-be), make important information available to prospective parents. The International Centre for Birth Defects located in Rome, Italy, represents more than 30 malformation-monitoring programs worldwide and helps identify and prevent birth defects (ICBD, 1999).

Prenatal Diagnosis and Genetic Counseling

Many couples know well before birth whether their baby has a genetic or chromosomal problem. Modern technology has given us the tools and knowledge to assess prenatal development quite accurately, but moral and ethical dilemmas have accompanied these advances.

Prenatal Assessment Techniques

Several techniques can be used to examine fetuses and detect prenatal problems. **Ultrasound** is a technique in which sound waves are bounced off the fetus and are shown on a TV monitor. Ultrasound can reveal the number of fetuses in the womb, the position of the fetus, and certain problems in anatomy, such as cleft palate.

Amniocentesis involves the extraction of some amniotic fluid from the uterus through a needle inserted into the mother's abdomen. The fluid surrounding the fetus contains fetal cells with the same genetic and chromosomal makeup as the fetus itself. By analyzing the fluid, technicians can detect a variety of abnormalities, including Down syndrome, Tay-Sachs disease, and sickle-cell anemia. These techniques, alpha fetoprotein screening, and chorionic villus sampling are discussed in detail in the Research Close-Up: Prenatal Assessment Techniques.

RESEARCH

CLOSE-UP   *Prenatal Assessment Techniques*

Physicians and parents have rushed to take advantage of prenatal assessment techniques as they have been developed. One of the first to be commonly used was ultrasound. In this technique, very high frequency sound waves, far beyond the hearing capacity of the human ear (thus the name *ultra* sound), are bounced off the fetus in the uterus. Sound waves are deflected or absorbed at different rates, depending on the density of the object they strike (e.g., bone, soft tissue, fluid). For example, they bounce off bone but are absorbed by soft tissue, water, or blood. These differences are converted into electrical signals, which are converted into a visual image.

In prenatal diagnosis using ultrasound, a technician passes a handheld transducer over the mother's abdomen. The transducer emits pulses of ultrasound. The deflected ultrasound waves are converted into an image of the fetus on a TV monitor. The image reveals the fetus's position in the womb, its size and gestational age, and whether anatomical problems are present. For example, the image will reveal an abnormally large head, an improperly formed spine, or a heart with certain defects. The newest ultrasound techniques also reveal problems such as a cleft lip or palate.

Ultrasound appears to be a very safe procedure. Data have failed to confirm any harmful effects on mothers or children. The benefits to patients who undergo diagnostic ultrasound outweigh the slight possibility of risk (Reece et al., 1990).

Whereas ultrasound gives a picture of the fetus, amniocentesis provides a genetic profile. In this procedure, a technician extracts a sample of amniotic fluid from the mother's uterus through a needle inserted into her abdomen. The fetal cells in the fluid are cultured in a lab for several weeks, and then their genetic, chromosomal, and biochemical makeup is analyzed.

Amniocentesis can reveal a variety of genetic and chromosomal abnormalities, including Down syndrome, Tay-Sachs disease, and sickle-cell anemia. Many hospitals routinely advise all mothers over age 35 to have an amniocentesis because of their higher probability of passing on a chromosomal disorder. The procedure can also be used to determine the fetus's maturity. For example, if a physician wants to deliver a baby as soon as possible because the mother's health is endangered by the pregnancy, amniocentesis can reveal whether the fetus's lungs are mature enough for the baby to survive outside the uterus (Kogon et al., 1986).

Amniocentesis is relatively safe. It's even safer if ultrasound is used to determine the position of the fetus so the needle is not stuck into the unborn infant or the placenta. The main drawback of amniocentesis is timing. It cannot be performed until the fetus is at least 14–16 weeks old because until then there isn't enough amniotic fluid to permit extraction. Then the cells have to be cultured for an additional 3–5 weeks before they can be analyzed. By the time the results are available, the woman is in her 20th or 21st week of pregnancy— her 5th month. If she chooses to terminate the pregnancy, a saline procedure abortion has to be performed.

Another prenatal assessment test is known as **chorionic villus sampling** (or chorionic biopsy). This alternative to amniocentesis also provides for genetic analysis (see Figure 2.12). Chorionic sampling can be performed as early as the 10th week of pregnancy, a full month earlier than amniocentesis (Pasquariello, 1999). Results are available within one to seven days.

To perform the biopsy, a tube is inserted into the uterus and a small amount of chorionic tissue is extracted. Tissue from the chorion, part of the fetal support system in the uterus, is genetically identical to the fetus itself, because both originated from the zygote. Any genetic or chromosomal abnormality in the chorionic cells indicates an abnormality in the fetus too.

Some hospitals offer a nuchal translucency scan, which measures the thickness of the back of the baby's neck. Because babies with Down syndrome tend to have extra fluid at the back of the neck, this measurement may indicate that further testing is needed (Pasquariello, 1999).

Blood tests also are used for prenatal assessment. The **alpha-fetoprotein (AFP) test** is a screening test performed at 16 weeks, using blood drawn from the mother. The test measures a protein produced in the fetus's liver. If the level is high, it may indicate the presence of a neural tube defect. When it is low, the baby may have Down syndrome. While this test is useful as a screening tool, high or low levels do not always indicate a problem. As with all screening tests, a positive result requires follow-up assessment. The waiting period for AFP results is from two to three weeks. Blood and chemical tests for use in prenatal diagnosis also hold good potential for identifying problems such as hemophilia and muscular dystrophy (Hotchner, 1995).

Ethical and Social Issues in Prenatal Assessment

When a fetus is assessed, one implication is that the pregnancy may be terminated if a defect is found. This is not always what happens, of course. Some parents use the information to prepare themselves to accept and care for a child with a disability. Many parents go into prenatal testing without having decided what they will do if the results indicate a problem. They are hoping, naturally, that there will not be any decision to make.

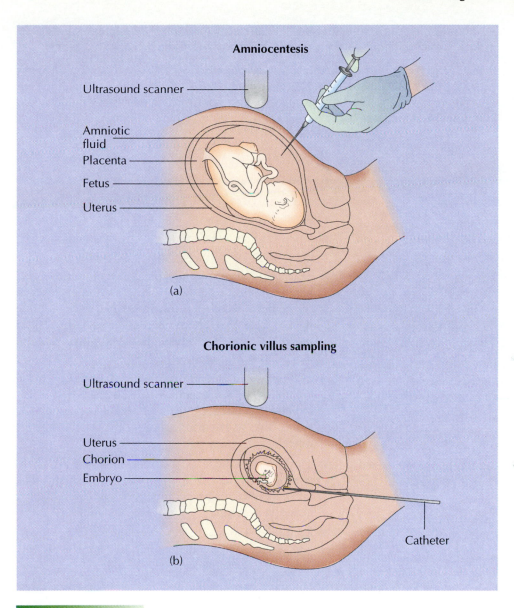

FIGURE 2.12

Amniocentesis and chorionic villus sampling. In the amniocentesis procedure, amniotic fluid is extracted and cultured. In chorionic villus sampling, a small amount of the chorionic tissue is taken and analyzed.

The difficult decisions associated with prenatal assessment have wide-ranging moral, social, and political implications for both the parents and the larger society. Consider just some of the questions that arise with this technology:

- Which genetic disorders are likely to cause problems severe enough to warrant termination of a pregnancy?
- Can a civilized society decide that individuals below a certain level of development are incapable of living a worthwhile life?
- If so, what level of development is sufficient to ensure a worthwhile life—worthwhile in what terms, and from whose point of view? Who decides?

- Should more research be devoted to treatment methods for people born with genetic disorders, or should such births be prevented altogether? Who decides?

- If research on treatment methods is to be pursued, which disorders should receive top priority? If a disorder that occurs more frequently in a particular ethnic or racial group is given higher priority than another disorder, what are the social and political consequences of this choice?

KEY POINTS

Genetics: Biological Inheritance

- Every person on earth is unique, in part because of genetic inheritance. But how much people are affected by their genetic makeup, as opposed to their experiences, is a matter of debate—a question referred to as the nature-nurture controversy.

- Biological traits are transmitted in genes (sequences of DNA), which are carried on chromosomes. Human body cells contain 23 pairs of chromosomes.

- A dominant gene always expresses its own characteristic; a recessive gene expresses its characteristic only when it is paired with another recessive gene.

- A child's genes come from two cells, one contributed by the father and the other contributed by the mother. Germ cells (ova and sperm) differ from body cells in the way they divide. Germ cell division, called meiosis, results in a new cell that contains only 23 single chromosomes, not 23 pairs.

- Individual genetic differences are the result of the crossing over that occurs during meiosis.

- The sex of a child is determined by the sex chromosomes. A female inherits an X chromosome from each parent; a male inherits an X from his mother and a Y from his father. Sex-linked characteristics are traits encoded by recessive genes on the X chromosome that can be expressed in males because there is no second X chromosome to override them.

- Fraternal twins occur when two different eggs are fertilized. Identical twins occur when a single fertilized egg divides after conception.

- Multiple births often occur when a woman has taken fertility drugs, because these can stimulate the ovaries to release more than one egg. Multiple births also are linked to maternal age, and they occur more frequently in some ethnic populations than in others.

Prenatal Development

- For couples who cannot conceive a child, many treatments are available, including surgery, fertility drugs, in vitro fertilization, and surrogate motherhood.

- Once a child is conceived, it develops over a 38-week period, which is divided into three stages.

- The period of the ovum, from conception to week 2, begins in one of the fallopian tubes and ends when the embryo becomes firmly implanted in the uterine wall. If the embryo becomes implanted in the wall of the fallopian tube, the result is an ectopic pregnancy, which must be ended surgically.

- The period of the embryo, from the second to the eighth week, is the time when all the major body structures begin forming. The organism is especially susceptible to environmental influences during this time.

- The period of the fetus, from the ninth week to birth, is a time of growth and further development. The body systems begin to function, and the external genitalia develop.

- Rapid development takes place during critical periods, a time when a developing system is especially sensitive to teratogens.

- Different parts of the body grow at different rates, but the head is more fully developed than the rest of the body throughout the entire prenatal period.

- Babies born as early as the 22nd week of gestation have survived, but most premature babies face difficult problems.

- The age of viability is the youngest age at which the baby can survive outside the womb.

Birth

- The birth process occurs in three stages. During the first and longest stage of labor, the cervix dilates and the baby moves down into the mother's pelvis. During the second stage, the baby moves down through the birth canal and out of the mother's body. The third and final stage is the expulsion of the placenta.

- A variety of conditions can necessitate birth by cesarean section, delivery of the baby through an incision in the abdominal wall.

- Prior to the early 1970s, birth was treated as a medical emergency. Women were heavily sedated and gave birth in hospital delivery rooms. Babies were taken to a nursery after delivery and brought to the mothers only at scheduled feeding times. The father and any siblings had little or no contact with the baby during the hospital stay.

- Problems in early development can result from genetic abnormalities, chromosomal errors, or environmental factors.

- Today many parents take childbirth education classes in which they learn special breathing and relaxation techniques to use during labor, reducing the need for pain-relieving drugs. Women are often assisted by their husbands or partners, and they may labor and deliver in special birthing rooms if their deliveries are uncomplicated.

- If the baby is full-term and healthy, the mother can usually keep the baby with her immediately after birth. Rooming-in is available in most hospitals, and fathers and siblings have contact with the new baby before it comes home.

- Mothers stay in the hospital for two or three days following a normal, uncomplicated delivery, and women who have had a cesarean section stay from three to four days.

- Some women who have normal, low-risk pregnancies choose to give birth at home or in alternative birth centers. They may be assisted by a midwife or physician.

- Some families are assisted by doulas, professionals who provide information and support throughout the childbirth experience.

- The main benefit of the new childbirth practices is the reduced use of medication. There are also psychological and emotional benefits to giving birth in a relaxed setting and having the father involved during the birth.

- Early contact between mother and baby is important, but studies have shown that mothers who couldn't have contact with their babies immediately after birth have no trouble establishing a strong attachment once they do have contact.

Problems in Early Development

- Prenatal problems can be genetic, chromosomal, or environmental.

- Many genetic problems result when the child inherits an abnormal recessive gene from both parents. The most common recessive gene diseases are sickle-cell anemia, cystic fibrosis, phenylketonuria, and Tay-Sachs disease.

- Chromosomal problems stem from errors that occur during meiosis. The most common chromosomal abnormality is Down syndrome, which is more common in mothers under age 20 and over age 35 than in mothers between 20 and 35.

- Environmental problems occur when a fetus is exposed to teratogens, including viruses, drugs, alcohol, environmental chemicals, and stress.

- The two major problems at birth are insufficient oxygen and infections.

- Maternal conditions such as nutrition, parental age, and stress may affect the prenatal child.

- Infections can be passed from the mother to the baby during or before birth. The most serious infections are syphilis, gonorrhea, chlamydia, herpes simplex virus, and AIDS.

Prenatal Diagnosis and Genetic Counseling

- Techniques for detecting prenatal problems include ultrasound, which gives a picture of the fetus, and amniocentesis and chorionic villus sampling, both of which provide a genetic profile.

- These techniques have created ethical and political questions, such as how to decide when a prenatal problem is severe enough to warrant termination of a pregnancy.

GLOSSARY

acquired immune deficiency syndrome: an extremely serious viral infection that attacks the immune system (p. 79)

active relations: a child's picking activities that best support his or her strengths or aptitudes (p. 53)

afterbirth: the third stage of the birth process during which the placenta is expelled (p. 63)

age of viability: age at which a fetus can survive outside the mother's womb (p. 60)

alpha-fetoprotein (AFP) test: a maternal blood test used to detect a number of central nervous system defects, such as spina bifida (p. 80)

amniocentesis: a prenatal test based on analysis of cells shed by the fetus into the amniotic fluid (p. 79)

anoxia: oxygen deprivation (p. 78)

Bradley method: a prepared childbirth method in which the mother learns to relax by learning how to breathe and to benefit from massage (p. 65)

cesarean section: delivery of the baby through an incision in the abdominal wall (p. 63)

chorionic villus sampling: a prenatal diagnostic procedure in which cells taken by biopsy from the chorion are cultured and analyzed (p. 80)

chromosomes: bands of DNA that contain the genes (p. 47)

critical period: a period of extremely rapid development in an organ, a body part, or a behavior (p. 60)

crowning: appearance of the baby's head at the vaginal opening during the second stage of birth (p. 63)

cystic fibrosis: a recessive genetic disease causing excessive mucus in the lungs and problems with the pancreas (p. 70)

Dick-Read method: a childbirth preparation method in which the woman is taught relaxation techniques (p. 64)

dilation: the widening of the cervix that occurs during the birth process (p. 61)

dominant gene: a gene that can be inherited singly to express a trait (p. 48)

doula: a professional who provides support to the mother throughout childbirth (p. 67)

Down syndrome: a chromosomal abnormality resulting in mental retardation (p. 72)

ectopic pregnancy: an embryo developing within the oviduct or some other structure outside the mother's uterus (p. 57)

embryoblast: a group of cells within an outer ring of cells in the early development of the embryo (p. 57)

evocative relations: environmental conditions that support the child's genetic blueprint because the child evokes responses from the environment (p. 53)

expulsion: the second stage of the birth process, during which the baby is born (p. 62)

fetal alcohol effects: impairment occurring prenatally due to the mother's alcohol consumption (p. 74)

fetal alcohol syndrome: a pattern of birth defects associated with a mother's drinking of alcohol during pregnancy (p. 74)

fragile X syndrome: a chromosomal abnormality involving a break in the X chromosome (p. 72)

fraternal twins: twins resulting from fertilization of two ova (p. 52)

genes: carriers of DNA for all inherited traits (p. 47)

genetics: the study of how biological traits are transmitted from one generation to the next (p. 47)

germ cells: the cells involved in reproduction—sperm and ova (p. 48)

human immunodeficiency virus: the virus that causes the AIDS infection (p. 79)

identical twins: twins resulting from fertilization of one ovum and the division of the zygote after the first cell division (p. 52)

infertility: difficulty in conceiving a child (p. 56)

in vitro fertilization: a procedure in which eggs are extracted from the mother, fertilized outside of the mother's body with the father's sperm, and inserted into the mother's uterus (p. 57)

Lamaze method: a prepared childbirth technique in which the mother is taught how to breathe and the father is taught to coach the mother (p. 65)

Leboyer delivery method: a method of birthing in which the child is delivered in dim light in a warm, quiet delivery room, and is placed in a warm bath (p. 66)

meiosis: cell division involved in reproduction (p. 49)

mitosis: typical cell division of body cells in which a cell is duplicated (p. 48)

nature-nurture controversy: the long-standing debate over whether behavior is determined by genes, by the environment, or by some combination of the two (p. 47)

oviduct or **fallopian tube:** the structure in which an ovum is fertilized and through which it travels from the ovary to the uterus (p. 56)

passive relations: environmental conditions that support the child's genetic blueprint due to consistency between the child's and the parents' biology (p. 53)

period of the embryo: the second period of prenatal development, lasting for 2 to 8 weeks, during which the major bodily structures are differentiated (p. 59)

period of the fetus: the third period of prenatal development, which lasts from the eighth week until birth (p. 59)

period of the ovum: the first 2 weeks of prenatal life, from conception to implantation (p. 57)

phenylketonuria (PKU): a recessive genetic disease affecting the metabolism of an amino acid (p. 70)

postmature baby: a baby who stays in the womb longer than the normal gestational period (p. 61)

premature baby: a baby born prior to full gestation (p. 60)

prenatal development: development in the womb, from conception to birth (p. 56)

range of reaction: the degree to which a trait can vary within the limits set by genetics (p. 53)

recessive gene: a gene that must be inherited in a pair to express traits (p. 70)

Rh factor: a protein in the blood that can cause difficulties for the baby if the mother's blood lacks the factor (p. 70)

rooming-in: a hospital housing arrangement in which the baby stays in the mother's room rather than in a nursery of newborns (p. 66)

sex-linked characteristics: characteristics encoded on genes carried on the sex chromosomes (X and Y) (p. 51)

sickle-cell anemia: a recessive genetic disease affecting the shape of the red blood cells (p. 70)

somatic cells: body cells—cells not involved in reproduction (p. 48)

surrogate mothers: a contracted arrangement with a woman to gestate a baby conceived from the surrogate's ovum and sperm from the infertile couple (p. 57)

synergistic effects: the combined effect of two or more teratogens, which is greater than the additive effects of each (p. 75)

Tay-Sachs disease: a recessive genetic disease affecting the nervous system (p. 70)

teratogen: any environmental agent that interferes with normal development during the prenatal period (p. 73)

toxoplasmosis: an infection that, when transmitted from infected animals or raw meat to pregnant women, can cause birth defects (p. 73)

ultrasound: high-frequency sound waves used to image the developing fetus for diagnostic purposes (p. 79)

zygote: the single cell resulting when a sperm fertilizes an ovum (p. 51)

SUGGESTIONS FOR FURTHER READING

Belsky, J., & Kelly, J. (1994). *The transition to parenthood*. New York: Dell Publishing. This book chronicles the story of three couples who become first-time parents, including what happens in their lives and marriages during and after the birth of their child.

Benson, M. (1995). *Pregnancy myths: What not to expect when you are expecting*. New York: Marlowe and Company. Countering many of the mistaken notions concerning pregnancy, this book explains the problems of myths such as "exercise can cause miscarriage" or "women are more likely to go into labor during a full moon." A very readable book.

Bing, E. (1994). *Six practical lessons for an easier childbirth*. New York: Bantam Books. This book clearly describes and teaches the Lamaze method of childbirth. It includes excellent photographs of exercises and also provides information about labor.

Gosden, R. (1999). *Designing babies: The brave new world of reproductive technology*. New York: Freeman. This book reviews and analyzes the history of reproductive technologies, discussing the social and ethical considerations. Interesting and easy to read.

Harris-Schmidt, G., & Fast, D. (1998). Fragile X syndrome: Genetics, characteristics, and educational implications. In F. Anthony & J. O. Schwenn (Eds.), *Advances in special education: Vol. 11. Issues, practices, and concerns in special education* (pp. 187–222). Greenwich, CT: Jai Press. This chapter describes the causes of, characteristics of, and interventions related to fragile X syndrome. It also discusses treatment and school programs for those who have the syndrome, as well as indications for future protein and gene therapy interventions.

Hotchner, T. (1997). *Pregnancy and childbirth*. New York: Avon Books. This book describes pregnancy and childbirth, with advice on proper prenatal care, including an excellent section on the importance of good nutrition.

McCaughey, K., McCaughey, B., & Lewis, D. (1998). *Seven from heaven: The miracle of the McCaughey Septuplets*. New York: Nelson. Written by the parents of the septuplets, this book describes the stages of pregnancy, birth, hardships, and joys of the McCaughey family. Includes excellent photographs.

Mehlman, M. J., & Botkin, J. R. (1998). *Access to the genome*. Washington, DC: Georgetown University Press. This well-written book clearly describes the practical applications of the Human Genome Project, discusses the impact of genetic technology, and describes the possible future problems of genetic engineering.

Pollock, L. (1987). *A lasting relationship: Parents and children over three centuries*. Hanover, NH: University Press of New England. The book uses diaries, memoirs, autobiographies, and letters to provide a portrait of children from the early 1600s to the mid-1800s. The first section covers views of pregnancy and childbirth. Fascinating reading.

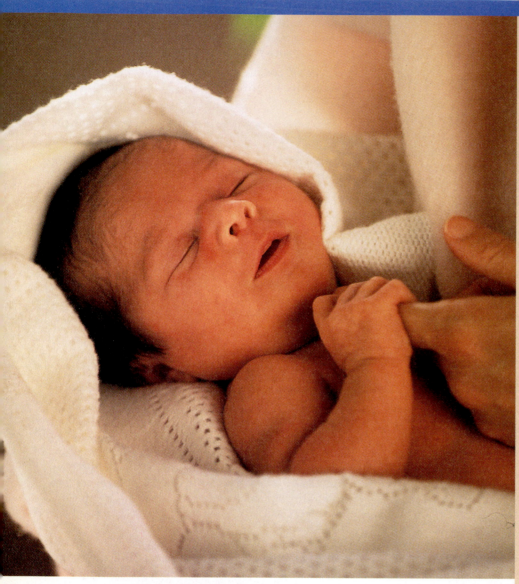

3

The Neonate

LEW HARDING'S WIFE had gone into labor the previous night. He had been deeply moved when the baby was born. Now, he was just beginning to relax as he and Susan gently rubbed the baby's back.

Lew soon realized that the baby in front of him did not look at all like the baby he had imagined so many times nor like the pictures of infants in books. His son Patrick's skin, bright red, chafed, and creased at the wrists and elbows, was covered with a white coating that looked like old soap. His black hair was matted against his head, and there was a coating of fine black hair all over his body. His eyes were swollen shut, his nose was flat, one of his ears was pasted forward on his cheek, and his head was pointy!

think about it

What causes newborns to look the way they look? Are some of their features helpful in the warm, wet life in the womb? Are others simply marks from the long, hard journey from the uterus to the outside world? How long does it take for a newborn to begin to look more like the baby that most of us imagine?

In this chapter we first describe neonates and discuss why they look the way they do. We then discuss the many changes they go through to adjust to life outside the womb. Later in the chapter, we consider the unique experiences of the premature baby. We also discuss how parents cope with an infant's crying and sleeping patterns. Finally, we discuss neonatal assessment—ways in which physicians can evaluate a newborn's physical and behavioral well-being.

Physical Characteristics

Patrick, like all newborns, looked somewhat different from older infants and remarkably different from older children and adults. Newborns also have some unique internal physiological characteristics that we cannot readily observe. In this section we discuss how neonates look and what goes on inside them as they adapt to their new world.

Appearance

There is an explanation for everything about the appearance of newborns. The white, greasy covering on their bodies, called **vernix caseosa**, is accumulated sebum, a secretion from glands surrounding the hair follicles in the skin. Vernix forms a protective barrier between the fetus's skin and the fluid in the mother's womb. It also provides lubrication during the birth process and helps to protect the skin from infection after a baby has been born.

A newborn often has a misshapen and pointed head because the head is squeezed as it passes through the mother's pelvis. Because the bones in the newborn's skull are not completely formed by the time a baby is born, they can move, even to the point of overlapping. This **molding** of a baby's head allows it to fit through the pelvis at birth, even if it is as much as an inch larger in its uncompressed state. Thus, molding permits a baby to have a larger, more mature brain at birth than would be possible if the bones in the skull were fused at this time.

The open spaces (**fontanelles**) in the newborn's skull are covered with a tight protective web of skin and tissue (see Figure 3.1). These "soft spots" on the head disappear as the bones of the skull grow together (fuse) and harden during the first two years of life.

The puffiness in a newborn's face and eyes is caused when fluids accumulate during the hours that the infant spends in the head-down birthing position. Additional puffiness is created by the silver nitrate drops that are put into each newborn's eyes immediately after birth. The drops are administered to protect the baby's eyes from gonorrhea, an infectious disease that can be contracted during delivery if the baby's mother is infected.

A newborn's appearance begins to change during the first few weeks. The head gradually assumes a normal rounded shape, the puffiness disappears from the eye-

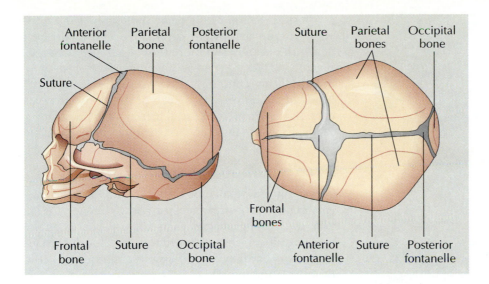

Newborn's skull, showing the fontanelles.

lids, and the fine body hair, known as **lanugo,** falls out. A baby will still be recognizable as a newborn for some time to come, however, because other unique physical characteristics endure for a while.

Body Proportions

When the nurse held Patrick before placing him on his mother's stomach, she made sure she supported his neck with her hand. Without this support, Patrick's head would have fallen backward, and he would have been unable to bring it up again. This is due not only to the weakness in Patrick's neck muscles (Prechtl, 1982), but to his very large and heavy head. The head grows faster than other parts of the body during the prenatal period. The head of a newborn is almost one fourth of its total body length. In an adult, the head is only one tenth of body length (Figure 3.2).

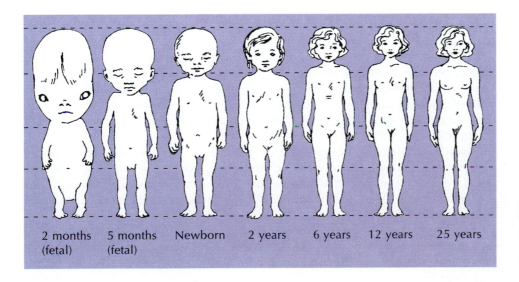

Body proportions from 2 months prenatally through early adulthood.

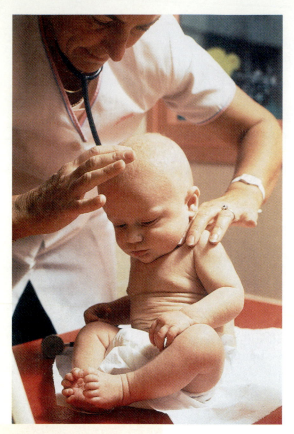

The newborn's head is almost one fourth of the baby's total body length. Given the size (and weight) of the newborn's head, and the weakness in the neck muscles, a young baby must be handled with great care. Jostling of a baby's head can damage the brain and even result in death. (*Source:* © Owen Franken/Tony Stone Images)

Just as the top of the newborn's body is more fully developed than the lower portion, the upper portion of the newborn's head is also more fully developed than the lower portion. Babies' jawbones are underdeveloped, they have practically no chin, and their necks are very short. Their heads sit almost directly on top of their very narrow shoulders. As they grow, their facial features and body proportions gradually evolve into those of the older baby and child.

Feeding and Digestion

Newborns are capable of eating food and absorbing nutrients immediately after they are born, although they can digest some things better than others. For example, they produce enough enzymes to digest and absorb both proteins and sugars but they cannot absorb saturated fats efficiently (Katz & Hamilton, 1974).

Beginning late in pregnancy, women's breasts produce **colostrum,** a thin, yellowish liquid, high in protein and low in fat. Its composition makes it perfectly suited both to newborns' nutritional needs and to their digestive capacities. A mother's milk is also an ideal food for newborns because it contains antibodies to specific diseases as well as some nonspecific protective factors (Hamosh, 1998; Xanthou, 1998). Ingestion of antibodies from their mothers makes breast-fed babies more resistant than formula-fed babies to gastrointestinal and respiratory infections and to other infections as well, especially during the first six months of life (Cunningham et al., 1991). Because premature babies are more vulnerable to disease than are full-term babies, some experts think that all premature babies should receive human milk (Goldman & Smith, 1973; Lucas et al., 1992).

In the first few days of life, a newborn might lose up to 10 percent of his birth weight. This weight loss occurs because babies use up stored glycogen, throw off fluids, and excrete feces. Bottle-fed babies start gaining weight sooner than breast-fed babies because the latter group must wait until mother's milk starts to flow. Premature babies gain weight more slowly than full-term babies because they can eat only a little at each feeding.

Most newborns eat every 2½ to 4 hours. Average-size infants under 5 months of age typically eat seven times in a 24-hour period (Michelsson et al., 1990). Smaller than average babies eat more frequently.

All newborns, of course, have a limited capacity for what they can eat at one feeding because their small stomachs will not hold very much. Newborns compensate for eating little at each feeding by eating more frequently. The less they eat at one time, the more frequently they eat. The less they eat at one feeding, the more they are likely to eat the next time, up to the limit imposed by the capacity of their stomachs (Birch & Fischer, 1995).

Newborns often fall asleep repeatedly while they eat. When they do nurse, they may gag frequently on mucus in their throats. But, luckily, not eating much the first few days does not harm a newborn because the baby has stores of glycogen. This is a starch the baby's body transforms easily into sugar when the baby needs energy. A full-term baby also has reserves of extra fat and fluids. As the baby's sleep begins to increase at night and decrease during the day (Parmalee & Stern, 1972), nighttime feedings begin to be separated by longer intervals than daytime feedings (Birch & Fisher, 1995). Almost all babies require nighttime feedings for several months.

Parents often wonder whether they should feed an infant in response to a signal such as crying ("on demand") or on some predetermined schedule. **Scheduled feeding** may help to organize the daily routines of the baby, prevent overfeeding when parents tend to pacify all cries with food, and aid the baby's adaptation to the sleeping and eating patterns of family members. But **demand feeding** may be especially beneficial at this young age because it places priority on responding to the baby's signals, which builds the baby's trust in caregivers and helps the baby adjust to life outside the womb.

Most parents today respond to the baby instead of following a rigid schedule and are more responsive to a newborn than to an infant of 5 or 6 months of age. They gradually establish some regularity in the baby's feeding schedule by taking into account the baby's immediate signals and preferences ("I'm beginning to cry because I'm hungry."); judging the baby's capacity for reasonable delay ("I'm hungry, but I can stop crying if you play with me or take me for a stroller ride."); and considering a better schedule as a goal to be reached as soon as circumstances allow ("I'm hoping these feedings can be spaced at about every 4½ hours before too much longer.").

Researchers probably would say that this approach, which considers both baby and adult, is reasonable. Among those who study nutrition, feeding, and eating behavior are some who are concerned that a problem might develop if early feeding is divorced from internal, bodily signals. This is a risk if feeding is guided completely by a rigid schedule (Birch & Fisher, 1995). Obesity as well as eating disorders, such as anorexia nervosa and bulimia (see chapter 16), may be related to early feeding practices in which the parent completely controls the feeding times, the food selection, and the amount of food consumed. In these situations, the infant (and later, the child, if high parental control continues) may not learn to associate eating with internal hunger and satiety cues, which should regulate when and how much a person eats.

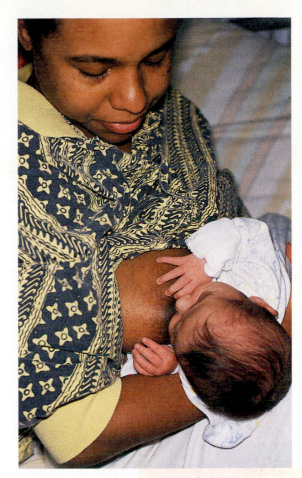

Breast milk's immunoglobulins help protect the infant from infectious diseases. Human milk also has less fat than does cow's milk and for this reason is better suited to the infant's digestive system. (*Source:* © Suzanne Arms/The Image Works)

Respiration and Circulation

When Patrick took his first breath, his lungs filled with air and he let out a healthy cry. Later, as he settled down into his first long sleep, his breathing became more irregular, rapid, and shallow, and it was punctuated by long, deep breaths. Sometimes, he stopped breathing altogether for a few seconds, a normal and apparently harmless occurrence known as **apnea.** He also coughed and sneezed frequently, in response to mucus in his nose and throat.

Before birth a baby's oxygen comes from his mother, through the placenta. The fetus's blood does not even pass through his own lungs. Immediately after birth, air fills the baby's lungs. From that point on, the baby obtains oxygen from the air (Wennberg et al., 1973). Because oxygen obtained directly from the air is richer, babies need fewer red blood cells after birth than they needed prenatally to carry the oxygen through their bodies. To adapt to this environmental change, the baby's body destroys excess red blood cells. In the process, the baby's body produces a by-product called **bilirubin.** If the liver cannot convert the bilirubin into an excretable form quickly, the baby's bilirubin level goes up, causing **hyperbilirubinemia.** This condition causes a yellowing of the skin (**jaundice**).

Within a few days, most newborns' livers break down the bilirubin, which makes the jaundice disappear. But some babies develop moderate jaundice and also have a

CLOSE-UP   *The Premature Baby*

Premature babies—those born before the 37th week of gestation—account for almost 7 percent of all births (Kliegman, 1996). In 1960, only 10 percent of the babies born weighing less than 1,000 grams (2 pounds) lived. By the early 1990s, the survival rate had climbed to about 50 percent (Hack et al., 1991). Since the early 1990s, survival rates have increased somewhat more because of a new treatment, known as **surfactant therapy** (see the following discussion).

One cause of prematurity is multiple births at a given delivery. About 1 percent of mothers have multiple offspring, and 99 percent of these are twins (Phipps, 1996). Multiple offspring have become more frequent as pregnancies resulting from infertility treatment have increased. These pregnancies often involve more than one fetus, and mothers who carry two or more fetuses often deliver prematurely. The mortality rate among multiple offspring is about six times that of singletons, mostly due to very low birth weight caused by the shorter than normal gestation (Phipps, 1996).

Physical Problems of Premature Babies

Premature babies, vulnerable both during birth and postnatally, are particularly susceptible to **hypothermia,** a dangerous drop in body temperature. To keep them warm, premature infants are placed in incubators where the temperature can be carefully controlled.

About 15 percent of premature babies also suffer from a serious breathing disorder known as **hyaline membrane disease.** Recall from chapter 2 that although lung development begins early in the prenatal period, the alveoli, or air sacs, at the very ends of the branches of the lungs, are not completely formed until a few weeks before birth (Hallman & Gluck, 1982). The alveoli produce surfactant, a substance that keeps the lungs from collapsing when a breath is expelled. Because premature babies lack surfactant (Kogon et al., 1986), their lungs tend to collapse when they breathe, which reduces the amount of oxygen they receive.

Hyaline membrane disease is potentially fatal. In recent years, the condition has been treated by delivering surfactant directly to premature infants' lungs either soon after birth or as a treatment when respiratory distress appears. Surfactant therapy has reduced respiratory distress in premature infants and has led to higher rates of survival (Bregman & Kimberlin, 1993; Halliday et al., 1998).

Because babies with respiratory distress syndrome (RDS) get less oxygen than they need from regular air, they are treated with concentrated oxygen. When this treatment was new in the 1940s and 1950s, doctors did not realize that high levels of oxygen damage the blood vessels in the eye and cause **retrolental fibroplasia blindness** (ROP—retinopathy of prematurity). Today, a baby's blood is monitored carefully to make sure oxygen levels do not rise too high. In addition, antioxidants, such as vitamins A and E, are administered. These improvements in oxygen therapy appear to help prevent blindness in premature infants (Keith & Doyle, 1995).

Long-Term Effects of Prematurity

Children born prematurely seem to catch up to their genetically intended size as they grow. In fact, early size disadvantages disappear by early school age (Ross et al., 1990). Premature infants also do not seem destined to have disrupted attachment relationships with their mothers, although premature infants do present parents with a more

rising bilirubin level. If the baby's blood-binding capacity for bilirubin is exceeded, bilirubin can pass into the brain and damage it. Placing the newborn under special lights—**phototherapy**—helps the baby's liver excrete bilirubin faster than it otherwise could (Cashore & Stern, 1982). Another therapy uses an enzyme that slows the body's breakdown of red blood cells, which gives the baby's body a better chance to clear bilirubin as it is produced (Kappas et al., 1988).

Several conditions or situations increase the risk of jaundice. One of these conditions is Rh incompatibility (see chapter 2). Rh incompatibility causes the destruction of red blood cells, thus adding to the number that are being destroyed soon after birth. The risk of jaundice also increases if the baby is bruised during the birthing process because the body breaks down the red blood cells in bruises. General anesthesia, administered during childbirth, can also increase the risk of jaundice because these drugs compete with the processing of bilirubin by the liver. As a result, less bilirubin can be disposed of in a given amount of time, causing bilirubin to increase and jaundice to worsen.

challenging social partner (Eckerman et al., 1994). (See chapter 7 for a detailed discussion of attachment in infancy.) Hospitals now allow contact between premature babies and their parents, and this reduces the risk of later attachment difficulties (Scafidi et al., 1990; Watt, 1990).

Premature babies as a group, however, are at higher risk than full-term babies for social and behavior problems at 7 and 8 years of age. In one study researchers considered such variables as participation in sports and other activities, number of friends, and school performance. Premature children had significantly lower social competence scores than did the normative groups. Premature boys, especially those born to low-income families, had significantly higher scores on conduct disorders. Lack of family stability was actually the best predictor of which babies born prematurely would have these later social difficulties (Ross et al., 1990).

Premature babies have also been followed to see if their later ability to learn is the same as other infants. No differences have been found in some studies on overall intelligence test performance (such as on the WISC-R) between extremely low-birth-weight babies and babies who were less premature (Papageorgiou et al., 1991). But other researchers have found a link between premature birth and the risk of a learning disability at school age, especially in the areas of memory and motor integration (Field et al., 1983; Papageorgiou et al., 1991). Still other studies have found an association between hyperactivity and very low birth weight (McCormick et al., 1990). It appears that the rate of learning difficulties in premature infants is about 25 percent higher than the rate in infants not born prematurely (Cohen & Parmelee, 1983; Leonard et al., 1990). But what predicts which infants in the premature group are more or less at risk?

In general, studies point to the postnatal environment as a strong determiner of learning outcome in children born prematurely. According to one researcher who reviewed several studies, "the single most potent factor influencing developmental outcome turns out to be the environment of the child, as expressed in the socioeconomic status and parental educational level" (Sameroff, 1981, p. 392). Another researcher drew similar conclusions: "social influences and family factors have a much more profound influence on a child's subsequent development than any of the biological factors that result in a child being born even extremely light-for-date" (Hawdon et al., 1990, p. 951). These conclusions have been drawn not only by researchers who have studied outcomes of extremely low-birth-weight infants. Especially with respect to long-term difficulties in learning, socioeconomic variables are better predictors than gestational age (Msall et al., 1991). But when specific medical complications are taken into account, biological risk increases in importance as a predictor of long-term outcomes. The greater the medical problems, the more likely a baby will have long-term learning difficulties (Taylor et al., 1998).

But why should there be such a strong association between socioeconomic circumstances and premature infant outcome? It seems that parenting is affected by the economic circumstances of the family. Harsh economic circumstances can create considerable stress in parents, which then reduces their ability to be attentive and responsive to a baby. Premature newborns are more difficult to care for in the first place than are full-term babies—they eat more often, their cries are more unpleasant, and they are less responsive to social interaction. When the baby is needy, and the economic circumstances of the family severe, there is an increased risk for poorer outcomes.

Temperature Regulation

Even though the temperature of the room in which Patrick was born was approximately 80 degrees, the nurse still covered him immediately with a warm blanket. Then his mother held him closely against her body, and his father rubbed his back. Patrick needed all this warmth because babies are not able to maintain a normal body temperature by themselves until they are about 8 or 9 weeks old.

No one knows exactly why newborns have trouble keeping warm. Some researchers think the temperature-regulating mechanism in the brain is immature or that it works differently than the adult mechanism. Others note that the ratio of the body's surface to its mass is so high that heat escapes rapidly from the surface. Still others point out that the baby's body has very little fat under the skin to provide insulation (Mestayan & Varga, 1960; Perlstein et al., 1974; Sinclaire, 1975). Premature babies have special difficulty keeping warm, which is why they are kept in incubators. (See Research Close-Up: The Premature Baby for more information about the problems that premature infants have.)

It is difficult to tell if a young baby is too hot or too cold, because they do not shiver or perspire (Klaus & Fanaroff, 1973). Instead, neonates must burn a specialized fat their bodies have stored during the last trimester of prenatal life (Hunter et al., 1994). This nonshivering **thermogenesis** (heat production) helps to keep them warm.

If a parent thinks a baby may be too cold, holding the baby is an excellent way to warm him up. Holding not only enhances temperature regulation (Phillips, 1974; Rovee-Collier & Lipsitt, 1982), but it also soothes an upset baby and helps the baby conserve energy needed to maintain growth. Holding also enhances social interaction and learning. Parents should also wrap babies quickly in a towel when removing them from bathwater, and dress them in hats and coats for even brief excursions out into the cold.

Sensory Abilities

Patrick's eyes were open when he was born, and he seemed to be looking around the room. When his mother held him in her hospital room, his eyes came to rest on his mother's face, or at least she thought they did. "Hi, there," she said. "What are you doing?

Susan wasn't sure how much Patrick could see, but she thought he was looking at her, especially at the top of her head. Once, she looked around to see if something on the hospital wall had caught his attention. But the spot was bare—hospital white wall, nothing more. "I guess you like to look at my dark brown hair," she said to him. "That's a funny thing to look at. Look at me, why don't you?" She held him out farther away from her body and more directly in front of her face. She thought at that moment that Patrick changed his gaze and was looking more at her eyes. But she could not be sure. Soon, his eyelids closed. "Sleepy again?" she asked. Just then he opened his eyes again and seemed to squint up at her. "Is this light too bright?" she asked, as she reached up to switch off the lamp above the bed. "We can turn this off if you don't like it." In the dimmer light, Patrick's eyes stayed open longer, and he seemed more comfortable as he looked up at Susan.

think about it

Was Susan right that Patrick could see her? Was she also right that he preferred to look at the top of her head, not at her eyes? In what condition are a newborn's other sensory capacities? Do newborn infants hear? Can they feel pain? Do they feel our touch and what their own fingertips embrace?

In this section, we discuss the newborn's sensory capacities. These include vision, hearing, taste and smell, and touch and pain. We will see that the infant enters the world equipped remarkably well to take it all in.

Vision

The human newborn can see at birth, although vision is somewhat limited at this early age due to immaturity in various aspects of the visual system. For example, the receptor cells in the retina (rods and cones), on which light reflected from objects lands, are themselves immature. There is also immaturity in the visual cortex—the part of the brain that receives electrical impulses from the retina. Over the course of the first few months of life, visual stimulation causes the visual cortex to organize and fine-tune itself in ways that are necessary for mature visual functioning (Johnson, 1999). The eye itself also grows over the course of childhood, and most of this growth takes place during the first year of life (Larsen, 1971). This growth causes the distance between the front of the eye, where light enters (cornea), and the back, where light lands (retina), to increase. The greater the distance between the front and the back of the eye, the larger is the image that is formed on the retina. The larger the image, all other things being equal, the sharper it will be. Sharpness makes keen detail detection possible (Kellman & Arterberry, 1998).

We will discuss first the basic visual sensory capacities of the newborn infant and then some initial visual preferences—what very young infants like most to look at. These initial preferences are driven by the visual sensory capacities themselves. Within a few months, though, visual preferences change. Once the visual capacities themselves are more mature, contrast in stimuli becomes less of a factor in determining what infants will look at. As infants begin to store information about the world, they begin to respond to visual experiences in terms of what they know and how novel or familiar various stimuli are in relation to their knowledge.

Basic Visual Sensory Capacities
The pupillary reflex, an automatic change occurring in the diameter of the pupil when light changes in brightness, functions well in the newborn (Aslin, 1987; Haith, 1980). Babies also blink, just as adults do. Susan may have been right that Patrick was bothered a little by the bright light and closed his eyes in response to it.

Other basic visual capacities, including binocular fixation, acuity, and accommodation, operate much less fully at this early age. By about 1 month of age, however, babies have **binocular fixation**—they are able to look at an object with both eyes simultaneously (Slater & Findlay, 1975). But babies do not yet actually see a fused visual image—one image instead of two—because their brains do not fuse images until about 4 or 5 months of age (Aslin & Smith, 1988; Fox et al., 1980).

It takes even longer for a baby's eye to provide sharp visual images. The resolving power of the eye determines the sharpness of images we see. **Visual acuity** is defined as the eye's capacity for spatial resolution. In other words, acuity refers to how well the elements of a pattern can be seen by someone at specific distances (Kellman & Arterberry, 1998). Acuity is measured in older children and adults with an eye chart containing lines of alphabet letters. The lines of letters vary in size. Adults and older children are asked to read the letters arranged in lines on the chart, starting with a line set in larger print and proceeding to lines set in increasingly smaller print. At some point, the letters appear so blurred to the viewer that their specific features can no longer be detected. Infant acuity is measured by presenting pairs of stimuli, one always a patch of gray, the other always striped (black lines on a white background). This procedure is based on our knowledge that infants prefer to look at patterned versus nonpatterned visual displays (i.e., at surfaces with marks on them rather than at plain surfaces). Thus, if infants can see stripes, researchers know that they will look at the striped stimulus and not at the patch of gray. At the point where the stripes appear blurred to the infant, the striped stimulus will not actually look like a pattern but rather very much like the patch of gray. When this occurs, the infant should look as much at the solid gray stimulus as at the striped one.

Researchers vary the striped stimulus by decreasing the width of the stripes while keeping the contrast (how dark the stripes are) the same. They start with wide stripes with a lot of white space between them and then present narrower and narrower stripes separated by less and less white space. They then can pinpoint the size of the pattern (stripes) that an infant can actually resolve. Using this procedure, researchers have determined that acuity in newborns is at best about 20/400 (i.e., an adult can see clearly at a distance of 400 feet what an infant can see clearly only at 20 feet)

(Kellman & Arterberry, 1988). Acuity improves to 20/100 by about 3 months of age, but it does not reach the 20/20 mark of adults until about 12 months of age (Banks & Salapatek, 1983; Fantz et al., 1962; Norcia & Tyler, 1985, 1990).

Infants' vision also differs from the vision of adults in terms of contrast sensitivity and temporal resolution. **Contrast sensitivity** refers to the amount of contrast needed for a pattern to be detected (Kellman & Arterberry, 1998). For example, the lines in a pattern can range from very bold to very faint. If lines are very faint against a background, no pattern can be seen. Newborns need far more contrast—boldness in the lines—than adults do in order to detect a pattern. By about 3 months of age, however, contrast sensitivity in the infant and the adult are similar.

Temporal resolution refers to the ability to detect that a light is actually flashing on and off rather than shining constantly. Even 1-month-olds can detect a flashing rather than a constant light almost as well as an adult. By 2 months of age, the infant's detection matches that of an adult (Kellman & Arterberry, 1998).

Another basic visual process, **visual accommodation,** refers to the change in the shape of the lens to bring objects at varying distances into focus. The lens in the eye of a newborn baby does not change as the distance of an object changes because the newborn's brain does not respond to out-of-focus, blurred images the way that the brain of an adult does. Thus, the newborn's view of objects or faces is always somewhat blurry, but not so blurry that contrast goes undetected. Newborns have been thought for some time to focus best on objects that are about 7 to 8 inches from their faces (Haynes et al., 1965). Some research, though, suggests that accommodation in the very young infant might be better than this (Hainline et al., 1992). By the time babies are about 2–3 months of age, they can accommodate almost as well as adults (Banks, 1980).

Newborns can also track a moving object. Movement is also one of the properties of visual stimuli that can grab a newborn's attention (Aslin & Shea, 1990; Kellman & Arterberry, 1998). If an object is held in front of a newborn until her eyes fix on it, and then moved, the baby gazes at and tracks it. In **tracking,** the baby's eyes, or head and eyes, move to keep the object in view (Brazelton, 1973; Salapatek, 1968). In neonates, the visual pursuit of objects is not entirely smooth. Jerky movements, known as **saccades,** are interspersed with smooth movements (Aslin, 1987).

Later, at about 8 or 10 weeks of age, a baby's eye movements become smoother. At this time, eye movements are affected by attention—the baby's interest in a stimulus. Eye movements related to the baby's attention apparently are controlled by areas of the visual cortex different from the areas that control the neonate's movements. The early, jerky eye movements of the neonate are reflexive (Richards & Holley, 1999). Once the smoother system of movement control begins to operate, the baby can target eye movements to focus on features of a stimulus that he or she wishes to inspect, and the baby can linger on one feature rather than another one (Berg & Richards, 1997).

Visual Preferences Newborns and very young infants show several preferences for visual displays. These preferences reflect the basic visual sensory capacities. We discuss two preferences here, one for pattern and contrast and one for the color red as opposed to the colors blue, green, or yellow. Visual perception—initial understandings about the world of objects and their organization in space—will be discussed in chapter 5.

PREFERENCES FOR PATTERN AND CONTRAST. R. L. Fantz (1963) was the first to demonstrate that babies can notice the difference between patterned and unpatterned visual displays. He showed babies six different stimuli, three patterned (a face, concentric circles, and a piece of newspaper) and

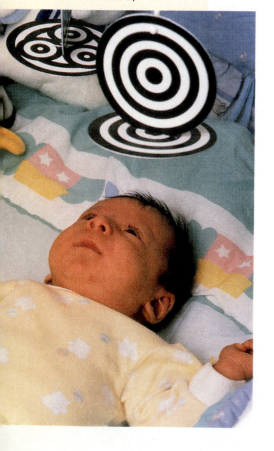

A baby's preference for pattern and contrast makes this mobile especially appealing. (*Source:* © Barbara Peacock/ FPG International)

three unpatterned (white, yellow, and red). The babies (ages 10 hours to 5 days old) looked at the patterned displays longer than the unpatterned ones. Of the patterned displays, they liked the face best (see Figure 3.3). Of the unpatterned displays, red was preferred over white and yellow.

Other studies have shown that babies prefer contrast. These studies featured displays with large differences in brightness between background and foreground. The brighter and bolder the lines placed on a white background, the more a young baby will like the display. Greater contrast is needed between figure and background for an infant to be able to detect a pattern. Estimates of the difference between adult and neonate vision, in terms of contrast sensitivity, suggest that the adult capacity is about 20 times greater (Wilson, 1993). Immaturity of the young baby's retina accounts for some of this limitation. Cones, the basic light receptors in the retina of the eye, are smaller in a young baby than they are in the adult, and farther apart. As a result, less light is absorbed by the baby's eye than by the adult's (Banks & Crowell, 1993; Kellman & Arterberry, 1998). Thus, more light must be reflected off the stimulus—the stimulus must be brighter—if it is to be seen by the baby. Young infants fix their gaze at the edges of figures, where black and white meet, because this is an area of high contrast (Salapatek & Kessen, 1966).

COLOR PREFERENCES. To study color preferences, researchers present pairs of stimuli, equal in brightness, and observe how long an infant looks at each one. Infants under about 8 weeks of age do not distinguish most colors from others (Clavadetscher et al., 1988; Peeples & Teller, 1975), although babies this young can discriminate red from white (Adams et al., 1994; Teller et al., 1978). In Fantz's (1963) study of visual preferences, newborns looked significantly longer at the plain red circle than at the white circle, but not much longer at the yellow circle compared to the white one. Thus, we can say that newborns show some sensitivity to red, although color detection, overall, is not very good at this very early age. The situation improves fairly rapidly, however. Between 8 and 12 weeks of age, infants begin to discriminate a number of colors (Kellman & Arterberry, 1998).

Hearing

Newborns can hear, but to be heard by a young infant, a sound must be louder than the level required for an adult to hear it (Kellman & Arterberry, 1998). Although sound sensitivity increases considerably over the course of the first 6 months of life, adult levels of sensitivity are not reached until well into childhood.

There is probably some adaptive value in having a lower sensitivity to sound early in life. Low sensitivity probably decreases distractions, for one thing, which can heighten attention to things close at hand (Kellman & Arterberry, 1998). Additionally, a lower sensitivity may allow babies to sleep without being disturbed as much as they would be if their hearing were as keen as an adult's.

When newborns do hear a sound, they turn toward it and look alert, as if searching for its source (Brazelton, 1969; Kellman & Arterberry, 1998). A good way to elicit this response is to hold a bell or rattle out to the side of a baby's head while she sits in an infant seat, for example, and ring or shake it several times in succession. It

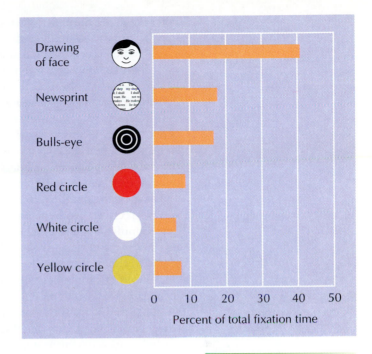

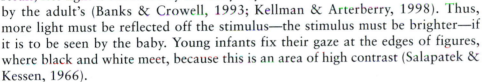

will take a newborn just a few seconds to begin to turn in the direction of the sound, but the response is quite clear.

Newborns can distinguish between sounds based on qualities such as frequency (i.e., high or low) and intensity (i.e., loud or soft) (Hirschman & Katkin, 1974). Researchers have been able to uncover these abilities by using a procedure called **habituation.** In this procedure, researchers first expose the baby to a sound that is within the range of stimuli to which a baby can respond. Then the researcher repeats this same sound several times until the baby's response to it decreases substantially. When the response lessens to a certain level, the researcher concludes that the baby has become habituated to this sound. At this point, the researcher introduces a different sound, one just a little bit louder or softer, or higher or lower, depending on the quality of sound the researcher is studying. If the baby becomes alert again—recovers from the habituation instead of generalizing the habituation to the new stimulus—the researcher concludes that the baby senses the difference between this new sound and the sound that was presented earlier during the habituation phase of the procedure.

Habituation can be explained by assuming that the baby is building a store of information—a mental model—about a stimulus and compares this model repeatedly to the stimulus itself (Bornstein & Arterberry, 1999; Cohen & Gelber, 1975). Researchers assume that when the model is refined enough to match the stimulus itself, the baby stops paying attention to the stimulus because there is no more information to be gained. If a baby becomes alert again when a new stimulus is introduced, we can assume that general fatigue or a change in state does not explain the initial response decrease. Instead, we can infer that the decrease in attention to the first stimulus was due to model building by the infant and also that the new stimulus does not, in the infant's mind, match the model. The infant's attention increases as the baby starts building a new or expanded model to accommodate the new stimulus. This activity requires more alertness than was needed to respond when the previous stimulus had become "old" (Berg & Berg, 1987).

It is clear that babies can hear quite well at birth. Can they hear sounds while in the womb? It seems that they can. Evidence comes from researchers who have found that newborns show a preference for a familiar voice, usually their mother's (DeCasper & Fifer, 1980; Simon & Butterworth, 1998). Although this could be a natural preference due to genetic similarities between mother and child, the preference could also be developed from exposure to the mother's voice during prenatal life. By using equipment that allows infants' sucking to control how much of various taped voices they hear, researchers demonstrated that French newborns could discriminate between their native language and another language, even when spoken by someone other than their mother (Mehler et al., 1988). English and Spanish newborns also prefer listening to their native language (Moon et al., 1993). There is no good reason to believe that babies would have a genetic-based preference for their native language. The preference must be due to familiarity acquired prenatally.

Taste and Smell

Newborns prefer a sweet fluid to fluids that are sour or bitter, and they prefer sugar water to plain water (Desor et al., 1975). Newborns demonstrate these preferences by sucking less when offered fluids with sour, bitter, and salty tastes, and sucking more when offered sweet tastes (Lipsitt & Behl, 1990). The preference for sweetness is inborn (Steiner, 1977). The newborn does not show a reaction to a salty solution in comparison to water, although, by 4 months of age, an infant prefers salty water to plain water (Beauchamp et al., 1994; Harris et al., 1990).

Newborns can distinguish other tastes as well. Infants as young as 1 month of age nurse longer and consume 20 percent more milk during the three hours following their mothers' ingestion of vanilla flavor (Mennella & Beauchamp, 1996). Researchers suggest that breast-fed infants may become familiar with flavors consumed by their mothers, which possibly affects future food and flavor preferences.

Infants have a natural preference for sucrose, and it has a calming effect on most infants' crying. Crying begins to subside within the first minute of sucrose solution ingestion, and it stops within 2 minutes. Additionally, infants do not resume crying for about 5 minutes after sucrose ingestion has stopped. During this time after ingestion, newborns are typically calm and alert, and they engage in hand-to-mouth activity. Even though plain water is somewhat effective in reducing crying in newborns, infants' eyes do not remain open as widely, nor do infants engage in as much hand-to-mouth activity. They also start to cry much more quickly after water ingestion has stopped (Blass & Ciaramitaro, 1994).

The sense of smell is also present at birth. Newborns turn away from certain smells, such as ammonia (Rieser et al., 1976), and they can distinguish different odors (Lipsitt et al., 1963). Neonates orient their heads to amniotic fluid, colostrum, and transitional milk rather than to control substances. Their sense of smell is so highly developed that they orient themselves longer toward the odor of their own amniotic fluid than to that of another fetus's (Marlier et al., 1998). The well-developed sense of smell found in newborns, and their ability to learn quickly to recognize certain smells, is also seen in their rapid identification of their own mothers' milk and bodies (Cernoch & Porter, 1985). There may be few innate preferences for odors. Rather, specific odor preferences may be learned (Bartoshuk, 1990). Researchers have been able to demonstrate the rapid development of various odor preferences in newborns by repeatedly exposing the infants to them (Balogh & Porter, 1986).

Touch and Pain

Newborns are highly sensitive to touch, especially in the head region. For example, when a newborn's cheek is stroked beside the mouth, about 93 percent of the time the newborn turns its head toward the side that was stroked (Kisilevsky et al., 1991). This reflexive responding is the rooting reflex. Newborns respond to the stroking of other body parts, too, although sensitivity to touch in other body regions is not as keen as it is on the newborn's face.

Touch is used by parents to calm a baby, such as when a parent rubs the baby's back while holding it forward against shoulder and chest. The benefits of touch are considered so important to development that premature babies are typically rubbed or massaged as part of a planned program of stimulation. Premature infants who are handled while in their incubators gain weight faster then those who are not (White & Labarba, 1976). In one study, infants stimulated by massage gained 47 percent more weight than nonstimulated premature infants, and they also performed better on an infant assessment scale (Field et al., 1986).

A sensation less pleasant to contemplate than the others we have discussed is pain. Newborns

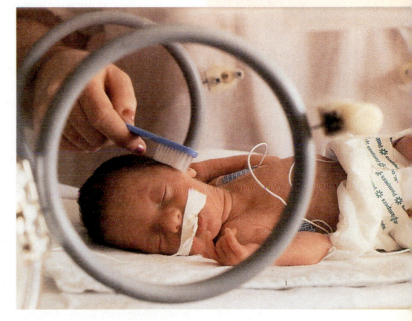

Stimulation by touching facilitates development in premature infants. The soft brush used here provides a different sensation on the baby's skin than does a massage with the fingertips. (*Source:* © Joseph Nettis/ Photo Researchers)

respond to stimulation known to cause pain in older children and adults by display-ing a typical facial expression and crying (Grunau et al., 1990). Newborn boys ex-perience pain during circumcision, which is why some doctors give the baby a shot of novocaine to anesthetize the penis before performing the procedure. All newborns experience pain from the pinprick in the heel for the PKU test that is administered routinely after birth.

Newborns cry less during and after the heel prick for blood collection if they drink a sucrose solution a few minutes before the prick. The sucrose taste may release calming and pain-reducing opioids (Blass & Shah, 1995). Infants' temperaments, be-havioral states, and wellness states also influence their responses to pain (Grunau et al., 1994; Stevens et al., 1994). As babies grow older and their nervous systems be-come more developed, their sensitivity to pain increases (Lipsitt & Levy, 1959).

Motor Capabilities

Newborns are quite helpless at birth. They cannot hold their heads up, nor can they stand upright, or reach out to take hold of something. These abilities develop over the first year of infancy. But newborns can make some voluntary movements, and they exhibit quite a number of reflexes.

Voluntary Movements

During the last few weeks in the womb, the fetus develops a considerable amount of muscle tone, or **tonus,** the continuous tension normal in muscles at rest (Dargassies, 1966). In the fetal position, a newborn's legs are crossed at the ankles and bent at the knees so that they touch the baby's abdomen. Arms are bent at the elbow and raised up. Fists are clenched.

A newborn baby can move voluntarily by turning the head from side to side, while sitting up or lying down with the back and head supported. He will also attach himself to a nipple that is just touching his mouth by pulling back slightly from it until the mouth is just out of contact. Then he moves toward it while opening his mouth, reestablishing contact, usually with the mouth around the nipple. This is done in one smooth motion (Koepke & Bigelow, 1997).

But even though a neonate can make these movements with the head and mouth, he has little control over the movement of arms, hands, and legs. A newborn's limb movements are like the gradual unwinding of a tightly wound spring. Arms and legs jerk and flail, and the newborn cannot quite get his hand and fingers to his mouth. As he gains control over his muscle activity, he becomes more successful at reaching his mouth with less excess motion. (Milestones of voluntary motor development dur-ing infancy are discussed in detail in chapter 4.)

Reflexive Behavior

Inborn motor responses, or **reflexes,** help newborns to survive. Some reflexes were probably useful at some time during human evolutionary history. Today, they are used as an index to the baby's neurological well-being. If these reflexes are present, the baby's nervous system is presumed to be intact and working properly; if they are ab-sent or are abnormal in some way, this indicates that something might be wrong.

One reflex found in the newborn is the **tonic neck reflex.** To test for this reflex, the doctor lays the baby on her back and turns the baby's head to one side. The baby stretches out her arm and leg on the side she is facing and flexes the arm and leg on the other side.

Another reflex, the **Moro,** is elicited by a loud sound or a sudden dropping back of a newborn's head. Apparently, the Moro is triggered when internal receptors sense movement in the neck muscles. The reflex involves a series of actions, which begins

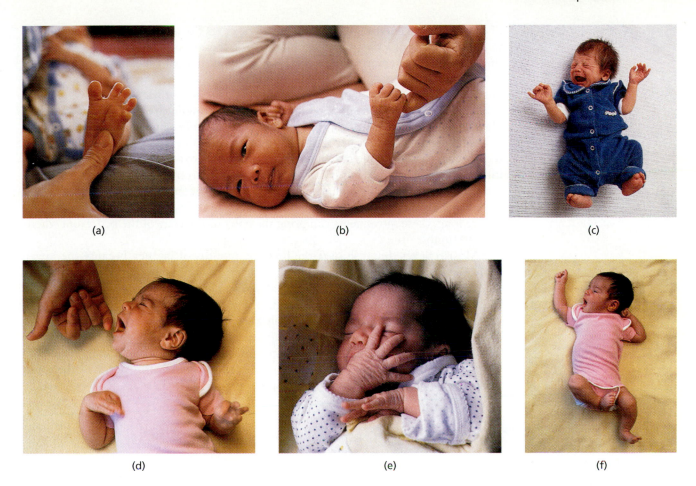

(a)   (b)   (c)

(d)   (e)   (f)

The infant has a variety of reflexes. The Babinski reflex (a) is elicited by stroking the outer edge of the sole of the infant's foot. The newborn infants palmar grasp (b), which can be elicited by placing something against the palm of the infant's hand. When the Moro reflex (c) is elicited, the infant throws out his arms. Loud noises, or a sudden drop back of the infant's head, will elicit the Moro response. The rooting reflex (d) is elicited by stroking an infant's cheek. The infant turns its head toward the stimulus and opens its mouth. The newborn's sucking reflex (e) is elicited by objects placed in the infant's mouth. In this case, the object is the baby's own thumb. The tonic neck reflex (f) involves flexion of two limbs, and the extension of the other two, in the characteristic "fencing" pattern seen here.   (*Sources:* (TOP LEFT) © Elizabeth Crews, (TOP MIDDLE) © Elizabeth Crews, (TOP RIGHT) © Elizabeth Crews/The Image Works, (BOTTOM LEFT) © Elizabeth Crews, (BOTTOM MIDDLE) © Elizabeth Crews., (BOTTOM RIGHT) © Elizabeth Crews)

when the baby throws out her arms. Then the baby fans out her fingers, extends her neck and lets out a cry, before bringing her arms back to "embrace" or clasp her chest (Dargassies, 1966).

Other reflexes are seen in the baby's feet and hands. One of these is elicited by stroking the outer edge of the soles of a newborn's foot, which makes the toes fan out in a display (the **Babinski reflex.**) Another, the **palmar grasping reflex,** is elicited by pressing and stroking the palms of the newborn's hands. This grasping reflex is so strong that the baby can be lifted up from a flat surface if she has been lying on her back. A toe grasp can be elicited by pressing on the bottom of a newborn's foot, just below the toes.

In addition to the reflexes just discussed, whose current roles in adaptation are unclear, newborns have several reflexes whose adaptive functions are very clear. The **rooting reflex** is one of these. This reflex is elicited by stroking a baby's cheek. The rooting reflex consists of the head turning toward the stimulation, and movements of the baby's lips and tongue. The rooting reflex gets the newborn in a good position to put the nipple of a breast into her mouth. The sensation of the nipple in her mouth then triggers the **sucking reflex,** a complex behavior involving a combination of pressure and suction. A **gag reflex** helps newborns clear mucus from their throats. Newborns also sneeze and cough reflexively, just like the rest of us.

Another reflex that supports survival is the **crawling reflex.** If a newborn is placed face down on a surface, and the nose and mouth become obstructed, she raises and turns her head, raises her shoulders, and extends and flexes her arms and legs in movements that resemble crawling. This series of reflexive actions helps prevent an infant from suffocating, but it can also get infants into trouble if they are left unattended in the middle of a bed. The baby's face may become obstructed when turned face down on the bed. The baby will then "crawl" reflexively each time to clear it. Before long, these movements can bring the baby to the edge of the bed, from where she can tumble off.

Most reflexes diminish over the first few months of infancy because the lower brain centers (midbrain, pons, medulla, and cerebellum) come under the control of the cerebral cortex, which inhibits reflex action. Because of changes brought on by brain maturity, it is difficult by 6 months of age to elicit the Moro reflex; by 8 or 9 months of age, it is impossible. The Babinski reflex is usually gone by 4 months. (See Table 3.1 for a description of the developmental course of reflexes.) If these reflexes persist longer than typical, it may indicate that the brain is not functioning normally. One of the early signs of cerebral palsy, for example, is the persistence of the tonic neck, the Moro, and the palmar reflexes (Barabas & Taft, 1986).

TABLE 3.1

Infant reflexes and their developmental course

Reflex	Description	Developmental Course
Blinking	When a light is shone into the baby's eyes, she closes them.	Permanent
Rooting	When the baby's cheek is touched or stroked, she turns toward the touch. The baby moves her lips and tongue to suck.	Gone by 4 months
Sucking	When a nipple or other object is placed in the baby's mouth, she sucks, with both pressure and suction.	Sucking becomes voluntary by 2 months
Gagging, coughing, sneezing	The baby clears air passages automatically when mucus or other material blocks them.	Permanent
Crawling	When the baby is placed face down, and her nose and mouth become obstructed, she raises and turns her head and shoulders and alternately extends and flexes her arms and legs.	Voluntary maneuvers take over by 3–4 months
Tonic neck	When the baby is laid on her back with the head turned to one side, she stretches out her arm and leg on the side she is facing and flexes the other arm and leg.	Gone by 4 months
Moro	When there is a loud noise or the baby's head is dropped back suddenly, she throws out her arms, fans her fingers, extends her neck, cries, and then brings the arms back to the chest and closes her fingers as if clasping something.	Weak by 5 months; gone by 8 months
Babinski	When the baby's foot is stroked from the heel to the toe, her toes fan out.	Gone by 12 months
Grasping	When the palms of the hands are stroked or pressed, the baby closes her fingers around the object in a strong grasp. When the feet are pressed just below the toe, the baby curls her toes down.	Begins to weaken by 3 months; gone by 12 months
Stepping	When the baby is held upright with one foot touching a surface, she makes stepping motions as if walking.	Gone by 3 months

Behavioral States

Typically, newborns are awake and alert when they are born. After about an hour, they fall into a long, deep sleep for a day or longer (Brazelton, 1961; Stratton, 1982; Wolff, 1965). After this sleep, their behavior becomes increasingly organized into recurring patterns of wakefulness and sleep called **behavioral states**. Behavioral states involve varying degrees of alertness and sleep. Researchers define the behavioral states in terms of specific variables. These usually include eye movements, position of eyelids (open or closed), regularity of breathing, brain wave patterns, and motor activity (Prechtl & O'Brien, 1982). One of the classification systems devised to assess babies' behavioral states is shown in Table 3.2. It labels the states with descriptive terms, such as regular sleep, irregular sleep, drowsiness, alert inactivity, waking activity, and crying (Wolff, 1966).

Regularities and Variations in Behavioral States

Behavioral states are organized and cyclical—they appear in a predictable order, not at random (Berg & Berg, 1987). For example, alert inactivity typically follows

TABLE 3.2

Behavioral states in the newborn

State	Motor Activity	Muscle Tone	Skin	Eyes	Face	Respiration	Vocalization
Regular sleep	No movement of limbs and trunk; startle reflexes present	Relaxed	Pink, but pale	Closed; no movement	Relaxed	Regular; 36 breaths per minute	
Irregular sleep	Movement of trunk and limbs between periods of rest	Moderate degree of tension	Flushed during activity	Closed, but movements present	Grimaces such as smiles and frowns	Irregular rhythm; 48 breaths per minute	
Drowsiness	More movement than during regular sleep but less than during irregular sleep	Moderate degree of tension		Eyes open and close; dull, glazed, and unfocused		Generally regular	Occasional high-pitched squeal
Alert inactivity	Inactive	Moderate degree of tension		Eyes open, bright, shining, attentive; move together in horizonal and vertical plane		Faster than during regular sleep	
Waking activity	Activity occurs in spurts	Higher degree of tension	Flushed during activity	Eyes open but not bright and shining		Irregular	Moans, grunts, whining but no sustained crying
Crying	Very active	Considerable tension	Flushed bright red	May be open or closed; tears in some babies	Grimaces	Fast and irregular	Crying

Source: From "The Causes, Controls and Organization of Behavior in the Newborn," by P. Wolff, 1996, *Psychological Issues, 5,* pp. 1–105.

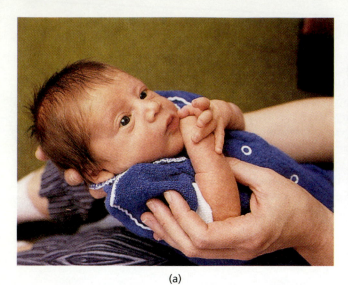

(a)

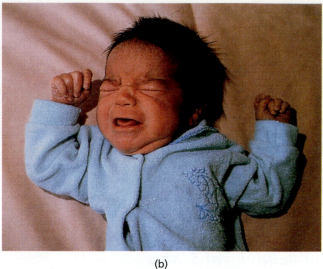

(b)

(a) Infants in the alert inactive state have bright, wide eyes that seem to be taking in sights of the nearby world. (b) Infants in a crying state have fast and irregular heartbeats, often close their eyes, and move their limbs. An infant's skin also flushes to a bright red if an infant cries for very long. (*Source:* (LEFT) © Elizabeth Crews, (RIGHT) © Elizabeth Crews)

waking activity, and drowsiness typically follows crying (Prechtl & O'Brien, 1982). But even though behavioral states are organized similarly in all infants, some babies cry more than others, some sleep more than others, and some are alert for longer periods than are others.

Specific events may explain some of these variations. For example, babies whose mothers were anesthetized during the birth tend to be less active and alert for the first few days after birth than are babies whose mothers were not (Brazelton, 1970; Desmond et al., 1963; Richards & Bernal, 1972). Babies born to mothers who were anesthetized also tend to be less **consolable** (more difficult to bring out of an upset, crying state) (Brackbill et al., 1974; van den Boom & Grovenhorst, 1995). Of course, we cannot know for sure if these differences in babies are due to the drugs themselves or to differences in mothers' behavior or even genetics. Mothers are not randomly assigned to different birthing procedures. More anxious or irritable mothers may elect more often than calmer mothers to have anesthetized births. Thus initial differences in mothers, rather than differences in drug use, could account for differences in their babies.

Child-rearing practices may also influence the baby's states. For example, **swaddling** (wrapping the baby tightly in a blanket) helps babies maintain control of their arms and legs and prevents startling (Brazelton, 1969; Friedman et al., 1981). Hospital nurses usually wrap babies tightly because they know it keeps them calmer.

Individual Differences in Behavioral States

Different babies have different **temperaments.** Temperament affects the intensity and length of time babies spend in the various behavioral states (Fox & Stifter, 1989). Some babies are more active and alert than others. Some babies cry more than others and are also more difficult to calm. These differences in temperament, in turn, can affect caregivers (Bell, 1971; Crockenberg, 1981). An irritable baby, or a baby who responds weakly to touching, might affect a parent negatively and thus affect the baby's own subsequent development negatively, just as a baby who is responsive and calm may have a positive effect both on the parent and on his own long-term development.

A positive, nurturing relationship, and parental ability to adapt to the baby as an interactional partner, probably keep the baby calmer and better able to take advantage of the sights and sounds available in the environment. Holding the baby up to the shoulder, for example, often stops crying and induces the alert inactive state, in which the baby is most likely to observe the surroundings (Hunziker & Barr, 1986). Thus, individual differences in babies' temperaments affect their behavioral states. These, in turn, can affect the kinds of relationships babies develop with caregivers and also the opportunities they have to learn during their earliest months. In chapter 7 we discuss in detail the importance of the mother-child relationship and the many factors that influence it.

Parental Coping with Infant Sleeping Patterns

"Oh, no. Not again. I just put you down."

Natasha climbed out of bed and made her way in the dark to her 2-week-old baby's cradle. It was 3:25 A.M. She had been awakened by Molina's crying earlier, at 1:30 A.M. Then, she nursed Molina for about 10 minutes, until she fell back asleep. "Maybe," Natasha thought to herself, "I should have jiggled her or something, to encourage her to eat more."

"I'll take her out to the rocking chair and try to calm her down again" Natasha told her husband. "You go back to sleep."

When Natasha tried to nurse Molina, she fought the breast and seemed to intensify her crying. So Natasha put her up to her shoulder and started to rock, gently patting her back as well. Soon Molina was calm again and seemed to be sleeping. "Should I risk putting her down?" Natasha wondered. "Or will she wake up again? Maybe I'll just try to doze off out here," she thought to herself. But she reconsidered this idea as thoughts of dropping the baby while she slept flashed through her mind.

Natasha walked slowly back into her bedroom, heading toward the cradle. But just as she put Molina down, she thought she heard and felt Molina's breathing quicken. She stood for a moment and then decided she would simply go to bed and take Molina with her. As Natasha leaned back on her pillow, Molina snuggled into the crook of her mother's neck.

But Natasha could not fall asleep. She wondered how she would ever be able to return to work in just six more weeks when her maternity leave ran out. She felt a knot in her throat and tears running down the side of her face, right toward Molina's forehead. "If this continues," she thought, "I'm never going to make it."

think about it   Is Natasha's experience unusual? Or do most newborns wake up several times during the night? And when might she reasonably expect the interruption of her sleep to end? Will she be able to return to work well-rested each day in just six more weeks, or are Molina's nighttime awakenings likely to continue for several more months?

One of the biggest adjustments new parents make is a reduction in their sleep. Some babies sleep through the night, or most of it, from their first week of life. But most do not. It takes several weeks for babies to get into some semblance of a schedule, and even then, it is not something a parent can count on.

Even though newborns typically sleep as much as 15 to 17 hours a day (Bamford et al., 1990; Berg & Berg, 1987), their sleep schedules do not necessarily overlap neatly with parents' schedules. In one study, researchers found that about 40 percent of babies under 9 months of age woke up at least twice between 11:00 P.M. and 6:00 A.M., the time period when most parents try to sleep. By 9 months of age, 30 percent of the infants continued to wake up during this time period (Michelsson et al., 1990).

Infant Sleep Routines Recommended in the United States

In the United States, pediatricians often tell parents to prepare a separate room for the baby and to place the baby in it from birth, or at least within the first 2 or 3 months, if the baby begins by sleeping in the parents' room (Spock & Rothenberg, 1992). They claim that several negative consequences will follow if parents hold infants while they fall asleep or take a young baby into their own bed during the night, or have the baby's crib in the parents' room. Some experts claim that babies might form a habit of depending on parent contact to fall asleep or that they may develop sleep problems or show a decrease in the development of autonomy and independence (Wolf et al., 1996). There is actually little evidence on which to base such advice.

Factors such as family size, house size (number of rooms), feeding method (i.e., breast or bottle), and parental values and beliefs about autonomy and interdependence seem to influence parental behavior concerning sleeping arrangements (Abbott, 1992; Wolf et al., 1996). For example, infants and toddlers in African American families often sleep with their parents (Medansky & Edelbrock, 1990), as do eastern Kentucky Appalachian infants and toddlers (Abbott, 1992). Thus, as Wolf and colleagues (1994) note, "sleep management practices even in the United States are heterogeneous, despite the uniformity of child-care recommendations" (p. 366).

Cross-Cultural Studies in Parental Management of Infant Sleep

Expectations for independent and isolated sleep in infants are not found in some parts of the world. One extensive review of parents' sleep expectations for infants included 119 societies (Barry & Paxson, 1971). In 64 percent of those societies, mothers and infants slept in the same bed. In all of the societies studied, except the United States, the expectation was that mothers would help babies fall asleep at bedtime. Only in the United States was there the expectation that infants would be put in their own room to fall asleep.

Other researchers have found similar variation across cultures. Rebecca New (1988) found cosleeping (children sleeping in the same bed with parents) to be very common among families in her study of a small Italian town. New noted that parents thought it "unkind to put an infant to sleep alone in a room" (p. 58). Japanese mothers and infants also cosleep. This practice seems to be based on their belief that the infant is at first independent and must be brought into interdependent relationships with other human beings (Caudill & Weinstein, 1962).

In another study of cosleeping among mothers and infants in Japan, Italy, and the United States (Wolf et al., 1996), differences were found both within the

U.S. sample and across the different countries. Three samples were included in the U.S. group: (1) white parent-baby dyads, (2) African American parent-baby dyads, and (3) white, breast-feeding parent-child dyads. Results showed that the U.S. white and African American groups were most likely to have a set bedtime. The Italian parents were least likely to establish a set bedtime for their infant—they seemed to lack a bedtime routine.

The researchers found that infants of Japanese mothers were much more likely than infants in any of the other groups to fall asleep in their mother's bed, in bodily contact with the mother. The Italian mothers were the most likely to have the baby's bed in their own room. (Japanese mothers were also likely to have the infant's bed in their room, but their infants usually fell asleep in the mother's bed.) The highest rates of cosleeping were found among Japanese and African American mothers, who were the only ones likely to cosleep all night. (In other groups in which cosleeping was found, it lasted only part of the night.) The white groups (breast-feeding or not) in the United States were less likely than the other groups to have the baby's bed in the parents' room, and these mothers and infants also coslept less than did mothers and infants in the other groups (Wolf et al., 1996).

In some cultures, infants cosleep with their mothers. In other cultures, infants are helped to fall asleep, sometimes by rocking them in a rocking chair, but they are put in their own cradle or crib once they have fallen asleep. (*Source:* © Tom McCarthy/ Photo Edit)

Explaining Cultural Differences in Infant Sleep Management   Researchers have suggested that children are put in their own beds in cultures where parents believe strongly in developing autonomy and independence. Where these beliefs are not so strongly held, cosleeping is thought to be more common. But this variable may not be the only one that affects parent-child cosleeping patterns. Data on household composition may provide clues about other factors. For example, consider that among the three U.S. samples, there were fewer fathers living in the African American households than in the two white U.S. samples. Consider, as well, that a grandmother was more likely to reside in Italian, Japanese, and African American households in the study than in white U.S. households.

In white U.S. households, where fathers were frequently present, perhaps mothers were required to a greater extent to balance their relationship with the baby and the relationship with the baby's father. In a household where a male partner does not reside or is absent for significant portions of the evening due to work (Japanese households), perhaps mothers focus more on the relationship with the baby. Similarly, perhaps a grandmother's presence in a household (Japanese, Italian, and African American) influences the balance between the adult partner relationship and the mother's relationship with the infant. For example, grandmothers might encourage mothers to focus more on the baby and less on a spouse or partner.

PARENTING

Soothing the Newborn

When a baby cries, parents try to figure out what is wrong. Parents of older babies often say they can tell why their baby is crying, and babies actually cry differently for different reasons. One study of infant crying distinguished three kinds: the basic, or hungry cry; the angry cry; and the pain cry (Wolff, 1966, 1969b). A baby who is startled or who is being overstimulated, for example, might give an angry cry. A baby with colic (gastrointestinal pain) would give the pain cry.

All the mothers in this study responded immediately to the pain cry and were worried or alarmed by it. All the mothers responded to angry cries, too, but they were not worried about this kind of cry. The basic or hungry cry usually got a quick response from first-time mothers, but experienced mothers sometimes waited a while before responding.

Caregivers often wonder how best to quiet a crying baby. The effectiveness of a method depends in part on why the baby is crying. Hunger cries can be stopped by feeding the baby, although holding the baby or putting a pacifier in the baby's mouth might stop the crying for a short time. (An angry cry may follow soon if some food doesn't supplement the pacifier!) A crying baby who is undressed and flailing his or her limbs can often be soothed by swaddling or by being held closely so the limbs stay in control. A pacifier can also soothe a baby and inhibit diffuse motor activity, which can leave a baby upset and awake (Wolff, 1966).

Many times babies who are dry, fed, and being held continue to cry. It is difficult to know why they are crying or how to stop it. Parents must often be ingenious. Although smooth and airy lullabies have long been used to regulate infant states and communicate positive emotional information (Rock et al., 1999), recordings of a beating heart or sounds of the womb may also soothe the baby. The sound of a rattle or the sight of a bright light will also inhibit the crying. But these maneuvers may work for only a short while when a baby is very young. Parents often rock a baby in a rocking chair, as Natasha did, or they walk around while holding the baby, push the baby in a stroller, or take the baby for a ride in a car.

A maneuver that is often effective in stopping crying is picking up the baby (Korner & Grobstein, 1966; Korner & Thoman, 1972). When babies are picked up, they also become alert and begin to look around. Because babies are most receptive to stimulation while they are in the alert inactive state, parents who pick up their crying babies give them a chance to observe and learn about their world. Thus, how the parent soothes a crying baby may affect not only the baby's emotional state, but also the baby's early learning. (See Research Close-Up: Cross-Cultural Differences in Infant Crying and Carrying for a discussion of why babies in different cultures may cry different amounts.)

The mother's career status and the length of a maternity leave may also affect mother-child cosleeping. If mothers are concerned about returning to work, it may decrease their tendency to allow infants to sleep with them.

Using a developmental systems theory of child development, researchers are likely to discover that the phenomenon of mother-infant cosleeping is embedded in a set of complex and interacting family and cultural situations and events. Until there is additional cross-cultural research on sleep management in infants, and until this research takes into account more variables and their interaction, we cannot fully explain cross-cultural, or intra-cultural, differences in parent-child cosleeping.

Learning

What can newborns learn? How do they learn it? Does newborn learning provide evidence for one or another of the major child development theories? Many behaviorists have tried to show that newborns can learn things through classical conditioning.

RESEARCH

In some countries, including the United States, babies cry more and more each day until they are about 6 weeks old (St. James-Roberts et al., 1994). After this peak, infant crying gradually decreases. Babies in the United States cry more in the afternoon and evening than during other parts of the day. In the United States, babies are expected to cry a certain amount, and adults consider the typical amount of crying normal.

In other countries, such as southern Mexico and urban Zambia (Africa), babies cry considerably less than they cry in the United States. Hewlett and colleagues (1998) found similar differences in crying in two adjacent African cultures, the Aka hunter-gatherers, who carry their infants extensively, and Ngandu farmers. Researchers have wondered if babies in some cultures cry less because they are carried extensively, and if U.S. babies cry so much because they are carried about relatively little.

To test this hypothesis, Hunziker and Barr (1986) recruited a number of mother-infant pairs and assigned them randomly to one of two groups: (1) a control group with no increased carrying and (2) a treatment group with increased carrying. The mothers in the treatment group were asked to carry their babies at least three hours a day, not just in response to crying. The extra carrying was spread throughout the day and was in addition to the time the mothers normally held the baby during feeding. Infant carriers were provided for the treatment group. The researchers collected baseline data from both groups in order to obtain initial rates of crying for all babies.

Control group babies (no additional carrying group) increased their crying until the characteristic 6-week peak. But babies in the supplemental carrying group did not increase their crying—they never exhibited a 6-week peak. Their crying began to decrease after the third week of life, which was the week the supplemental carrying began. Moreover, although babies in both groups cried the most during late afternoon and early evening, the carried babies cried significantly less than the control babies (54 percent less during the sixth week; 47 percent less during the eighth week).

Hunziker and Barr (1986) suggested that increased carrying "provided postural change, repetitiveness, constancy and/or rhythmicity, close proximity between mother and infant, and involvement of many sensory modalities" (p. 645). Increased carrying may also have given mothers more information about their babies. This may have increased mothers' skills in understanding what was wrong and helped them to soothe their babies when they cried. Finally, because holding induces the inactive alert state, babies may have been less fussy because they were interested in observing their surroundings.

The researchers concluded that the amount of infant crying considered normal in the United States is "only normal in the sense of being typical for infant caregiving practices in our society" (p. 646). They recommend that parents soothe their crying infants and prevent excessive crying by increasing the amount that they carry their babies. Aside from the obvious agitation and upset of the crying baby, crying is energy depleting, and excessive crying competes with growth for energy (Blass & Ciaramitaro, 1994). Crying is considered by ethologists (i.e., theorists with an evolutionary/biological view of behavior) to be a potent signal that prompts caregiving from adults. Even though crying has high energy costs, it is effective in eliciting energy-replenishing responses. From an ethological perspective, there is no benefit and many costs (energy expenditure, less alert attention to the environment, and so on) associated with sustained crying.

Blass and Ciaramitaro (1994) note that, in the wild, primate infants are carried almost constantly by their mothers. They cry only when dropped or if they are hurt very badly. In such cases, their mothers respond to them instantly. It is dangerous in the wild for infant crying to be sustained, for it alerts other animals to the primates' location. Researchers who hold an ethological theory of development wonder if what has become the acceptable standard for infant crying in the West (two hours a day) is in the best interest of an organism who evolved to cry only when a high threshold of distress had been crossed.

Parents can increase the carrying of their infants, and decrease their crying, by using an infant carrier. For very young infants, these carriers are designed as pouchlike sacks that the parent straps onto the front of his or her own body. An advantage of these devices is that the parent's hands are free even while carrying the baby. Thus, the baby experiences the security and warmth of the parent's body and can be carried more, but the parent can also tend to necessary tasks.

Carrying babies in soft carriers reduces crying and also increases the rate of secure attachment in low socioeconomic status mothers (Anisfeld et al., 1990). (See chapter 7 for an extensive discussion of attachment.) Unfortunately, babies with established patterns of colic (i.e., considerable crying, often concentrated during a specific time of day) do not seem to be helped by increased carrying (Barr et al., 1991).

Recall from chapter 1 that this technique involves the pairing of a new stimulus with another stimulus that automatically elicits a certain response. After repeated pairings, the new stimulus alone elicits the response.

Newborns are prime candidates for investigations of various aspects of the nature-nurture controversy—questions of whether preferences and reactions are innate or learned—because they have as yet experienced the environment only minimally. Because human behavior is the result of complex interactions between children and their biological and environmental systems, these studies provide us with important information about the state of all these systems before children are exposed directly to the environment beyond the uterus.

Studies of the relatively simple behavior of newborns help developmentalists understand how behavior is organized and how this organization changes with time and experience. For example, a preference for visual contrast is present at birth, but visual preferences several months later reflect not only the innate preference but also the experiences—the specific visual patterns—to which the baby has been exposed. The baby's behavior has been reorganized by experience. In this section we review some of what is known about learning in the newborn.

Researchers have paired the ringing of a bell or gentle forehead stroking with giving a baby sugar water or a nipple. If the baby could be classically conditioned, the bell or stroking alone would later elicit sucking after repeated pairings. Although classical conditioning is difficult with newborns because they do not stay awake and alert for very long periods, researchers have been able to elicit sucking with stimuli like bells and stroking (Blass et al., 1984; Rovee-Collier & Lipsitt, 1982).

Other researchers have tried to show that babies can learn through instrumental conditioning, the technique in which a response is followed with reinforcement. This kind of learning seems to be easier for newborns than is classical conditioning (Millar, 1974; Sameroff, 1972). In one study, newborns were given a nipple when they turned their heads as part of the rooting reflex. The babies turned their heads more often as a result (Papousek, 1967; Siqueland & Lipsitt, 1966).

Other studies have shown that babies change their sucking response, depending on whether or not a nipple provides food (Rovee-Collier & Lipsitt, 1982). If the nipple is attached to a bottle of milk or sugar water, babies squeeze the nipple with their tongues and cheeks *and* suck on it. If the nipple is attached to a pacifier, they just squeeze it. Experiments such as these show that babies can respond to the environment in intelligent ways and that they learn from experience. Further questions about infant learning have been raised and addressed by other studies, summarized in chapter 5.

Assessing the Newborn

Physicians and researchers have developed several instruments, or procedures, for examining newborns. These instruments help physicians evaluate the newborn's physical well-being. They also help physicians and researchers determine what conditions and behaviors in the neonate are associated with later problems in development.

Assessment Instruments

Three instruments are especially well known for their reliable assessment of three different aspects of infant functioning. The **Apgar scale** (named for the physician Virginia Apgar, who invented it) measures the new-born's physical well-being in the delivery room at 1 minute and 5 minutes after birth. The baby is scored from 0 to 2 for heart rate, respiratory effort, muscle tone, reflex irritability, and color (see Table 3.3). The five scores are summed to obtain a total score ranging from 0 to 10. A higher score indicates a better condition (Apgar, 1953).

Another instrument used to assess the baby's neurological condition is the **Neurological Examination of the Full-Term Newborn Infant.** It was developed in 1964 by Prechtl and Beintema (revised in 1977 by Prechtl). This test, often referred to as the Prechtl, is used to evaluate babies within 10 days of birth. It has two parts: (1) an observation period during which spontaneous movement and posture are noted, and (2) an examination period during

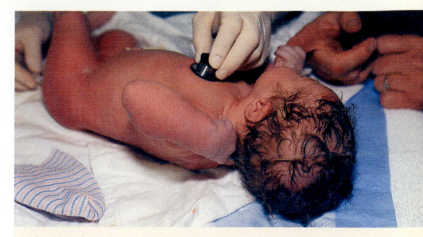

Physicians have a variety of ways to assess the well-being of newborns. This baby, like all born in hospitals in the United States, was assessed with the Apgar at birth. On subsequent days, other instruments, such as Prechtl's Neurological Examination, can be used.   (*Source:* © Myrleen Ferguson/Photo Edit)

TABLE 3.3

The Apgar scale

Sign	*Criterion**	*Score*
Heart rate (beats/minute)	100 or more	2
	Less than 100	1
	Not detectable	0
Respiratory effort	Lusty crying and breathing	2
	Any shallowness, irregularity	1
	Not breathing	0
Reflex irritability	Vigorous response to stimuation (e.g, sneezing or coughing to stimulation of nostrils), urination, defecation	2
	Weak response	1
	No response	0
Muscle tone	Resilient, limbs spontaneously flexed and resistant to applied force	2
	Limpness, lack of resistance	1
	Complete flaccidity	0
Skin color	Pink all over	2
	Partially pink	1
	Bluish or yellowish	0

*Observations made at 60 seconds after birth.

Source: From "Evaluation of the Newborn Infant—Second Report," by V. Apgar, D. A. Holaday, L. S. James, I. M. Weisbrot, and C. Berrien, 1958, *Journal of the American Medical Association, 168,* pp. 1985–1988. Reprinted with permission.

which reflexes and other motor behavior are checked. As mentioned earlier, the presence or absence of the various reflexes provides information on the baby's neurological functioning.

A third assessment instrument is the **Brazelton Neonatal Behavioral Assessment Scale** (Brazelton et al., 1984). This test is given when the infant is three days old and again several days later. It provides information about the baby's general neurological condition, capacity for self-organization, and reactions to a caregiver.

Specific items on the BNBAS assess the baby's behavioral state, major reflexes, and habituation to repeated visual, auditory, and tactile stimuli. It also assesses the baby's activity level, muscle tone, and orientation to the human face and voice. For example, one part of the test involves ringing a bell loudly overhead when the baby is awake and lying on a flat surface. The baby will usually be startled the first time the bell is rung. The examiner then rings the bell again. This time the baby is startled but typically not as much as the first time because the baby becomes habituated to the sound of the bell after a few rings. To score the baby's response, the tester notes how many presentations occurred before the baby stopped reacting. The longer it takes for the reaction to stop, the poorer the rating. A long time may indicate that the baby has difficulty in processing information and learning.

Brazelton stresses the importance of taking the baby's behavioral state into account when giving this test. Results obtained when a baby is drowsy or crying would not be comparable to results obtained when the baby is in an inactive alert state, which is the ideal state for testing. If a baby starts to cry, the tester must stop testing and hold the baby or provide some other comfort. If the baby becomes less irritable, the testing can continue; otherwise it has to stop, at least for the time being.

Adequacy of Assessment Instruments

Unfortunately, it is often difficult to know which early behaviors actually predict future problems. Neurological exams, such as the Prechtl, measure reflexes, noting simply whether or not they occur. Because instruments such as the Brazelton include items that assess newborns' ability to inhibit responses to a repeated stimulus, to escape a stimulus, to quiet or console themselves, and to orient themselves toward or seek out stimulation, they may predict later functioning better than the basic neurological exams do. This is because the behaviors the Brazelton measures are important to mother-child interactions, which continue to influence development for years. (See chapter 7 for further discussion of this topic.)

Other assessment instruments have similar problems. The Apgar measures the most general aspects of physical well-being and reveals only the most obvious difficulties. Timing is also a problem with the Apgar, which is administered at 1 and 5 minutes after birth. A baby's functioning two hours after birth may be radically different from functioning immediately after birth (Desmond et al., 1963). The later score may be a better predictor of future behavior.

Different instruments are appropriate for different purposes. The Apgar gives a quick assessment of physical condition immediately after birth. The Prechtl reveals clinically important neurological problems during the neonatal period. The Brazelton scale may be most useful for predicting long-term problems related to difficult parent-child interaction (Prechtl, 1982). As long as their appropriate uses and limitations are kept in mind, all of these assessment instruments can provide important information.

KEY POINTS

Physical Characteristics

■ A white, greasy coating called vernix caseosa protects the neonate's skin before, during, and after birth.

■ Two fontanelles allow the bones of the fetus's skull to squeeze together, or mold, as the baby passes through the mother's pelvis.

■ Newborns' eyes and faces are often swollen and puffy from the accumulation of fluids and from silver nitrate drops in the eyes. Their skin is bright red because they have so little subcutaneous fat.

■ The newborn's head is very large in proportion to his body, and the upper portion of his head is more developed than his chin, jaw, and neck.

■ Newborns are able to absorb nutrients. Mothers produce colostrum, an antibody-containing liquid perfectly suited to the newborn's needs. Breast milk, high in protein and low in fat, is the ideal food for infants.

■ The average neonate weighs 7½ pounds and measures 20 inches in length.

■ Newborns require frequent, small feedings, and most need night feedings for a few months or more.

■ Different feeding approaches, demand or scheduled, might affect the infant's later eating behavior.

■ The neonate's breathing is characterized by rapid, shallow breaths interrupted by periods of long, deep breathing and even brief periods of apnea.

■ The respiratory system takes time to adjust to breathing oxygen-rich air. A by-product called bilirubin often accumulates in the blood. The liver can have difficulty metabolizing and excreting the bilirubin, and the baby may develop hyperbilirubinemia, or jaundice, which sometimes requires treatment to protect against brain damage.

■ Newborns cannot maintain their own body temperatures until they are about 2 months old. Care must be taken to keep them warm.

■ Babies are considered premature if they are born before 37 weeks of gestation. About 7 percent of all babies are born prematurely, and more and more premature babies are surviving due to advances in medical technology.

■ Premature babies are prone to problems such as hypothermia, brain hemorrhages, and hyaline membrane disease, a serious lung disorder. Administration of oxygen has to be carefully monitored to prevent retrolental fibroplasia blindness.

■ The best predictor of outcome for premature babies is the social-emotional and educational environment provided by the baby's family, rather than physical condition at birth.

Sensory Abilities

■ Newborns can see right from birth, but images remain blurry. Focus is best on objects about 7 or 8 inches from their face. Newborns can track a moving object.

■ Babies have binocular fixation by about 1 month and see fused visual images by about 4 months. Their visual acuity is as good as an adult's by about 12 months, and their eyes can accommodate as well as an adult's by about 2 months.

■ Newborns have size constancy. They also like to look at patterns, especially the pattern of faces, as well as areas of contrast. These preferences are innate and support the development of parent-child attachment.

■ Babies can hear at birth and apparently even in the womb. They respond to new sounds and then gradually become accustomed to everyday noises, incorporating them into their repertoire. Researchers use habituation to conduct studies on their hearing and other senses.

■ Newborns prefer sweet tastes over sour, bitter, and salty tastes. Newborns stop crying almost immediately when fed sucrose solution, and they become calm and alert. They do not give those responses to plain water.

■ Newborns can distinguish odors at birth and soon learn to know the smell of their mother's milk.

■ Newborns feel physical pain; their sensitivity to pain increases as they mature.

Motor Capabilities

■ Babies are born with innate responses known as reflexes, which help them survive.

■ Newborns have a rooting reflex, which allows them to find the nipple, and a sucking reflex, which allows them to suckle and ingest food. The gag reflex prevents them from choking on mucus or extra milk.

■ A "crawling" reflex prevents newborns from suffocating if their mouths and noses become obstructed, as they lie prone on a bed, for example. It can also create enough movement to topple them off a bed if they are left unattended.

■ Other reflexes include the tonic neck, the Moro, the Babinski, and the grasping reflex. As the baby matures, reflexes gradually disappear; their presence or absence at different times is a good indicator of the infant's neurological functioning.

■ Newborns have little control over voluntary responses.

Behavioral States

■ When newborns awaken from their first long sleep after birth, their behavior is characterized by recurring periods of wakefulness and sleep known as behavioral states.

■ Typical behavioral states include regular sleep, irregular sleep, drowsiness, alert inactivity, waking activity, and crying. These states are cyclical, not random.

■ Infants' overall behavioral patterns, including how long they spend in each state, are probably influenced by heredity and by their parents' responses to them. Their patterns, in turn, affect the parent-child relationship. A baby who spends a lot of time crying is more difficult to care for and requires more creative parenting.

■ The initial parent-child interaction is affected by obstetrical drugs. Pain-relieving drugs given to mothers in labor quickly cross the placenta and enter the fetus. Newborns of medicated mothers tend to be less alert, less responsive, and less consolable than the newborns of nonmedicated mothers.

■ Newborns sleep for many hours a day, but not continuously through the night.

■ Pediatricians in the United States typically advise parents to establish a sleep routine in which babies go to sleep in their own beds in their own rooms. Other sleep management customs found in different cultures are probably due to several factors, such as parental values and beliefs and the composition of the household.

■ Babies cry differently, depending on whether they are hungry, angry, or in pain.

■ An effective way to stop infant crying is to pick up the baby, thus inducing the alert inactive state. Carrying the baby in an infant carrier also seems to reduce crying.

Learning

■ Newborns are capable of learning through both classical conditioning and instrumental conditioning.

Assessing the Newborn

■ Babies are assessed at birth to see if they require any medical or developmental intervention.

■ The Apgar scale is used to assess the baby's overall physical condition.

■ The Neurological Examination of the Full-Term Newborn Infant (known commonly as the Prechtl) is used to evaluate the baby's neurological condition.

■ The Brazelton Neonatal Behavioral Assessment Scale provides information about the baby's neurological condition and behavioral patterns.

■ Each neonatal assessment instrument has limitations, but each provides important information about newborns.

GLOSSARY

acuity: the resolving power of the eye that determines the sharpness of images (p. 95)

Apgar scale: an instrument to assess the newborn's overall physical condition (p. 110)

apnea: cessation of breathing, usually for short and harmless periods of time (p. 91)

Babinski reflex: the fanning out of the infant's toes when the outer edge of the sole of the foot is stroked (p. 101)

behavioral states: cyclical levels of being awake and asleep, found in young infants (p. 103)

bilirubin: a by-product of red blood cell destruction (p. 91)

binocular fixation: looking at the same object with both eyes simultaneously (p. 95)

Brazelton Neonatal Behavioral Assessment Scale: an assessment instrument that includes neurological and behavioral items (p. 112)

colostrum: the thin yellowish substance that appears in mother's milk, prior to milk production (p. 90)

consolable: able to be comforted (p. 104)

contrast sensitivity: the amount of contrast needed for a pattern to be visually discernible (p. 96)

crawling reflex: pattern of movements of the arms and legs that is elicited when the face is obstructed (p. 102)

demand feeding: feeding the baby in response to signals of hunger, such as crying (p. 91)

fontanelles: the open spaces in the young baby's undeveloped skull that make possible the molding of the head during birth (p. 88)

gag reflex: involuntary movement elicited by mucus or other material in the back of the throat (p. 102)

habituation: a lessening of response that occurs after repeated presentations of a stimulus; helps determine which stimuli an infant can discriminate (p. 98)

hyaline membrane disease: a breathing difficulty common in premature infants, whose lungs do not yet contain surfactant (p. 92)

hyperbilirubinemia: a condition in which the blood has a higher than normal level of bilirubin (p. 91)

hypothermia: a dangerous drop in body temperature, which is a danger for premature infants (p. 92)

jaundice: a yellowing of the skin caused by high levels of bilirubin in the bloodstream (p. 91)

lanugo: the fine body hair found on the newborn (p. 89)

molding: the squeezing together of the bones in the baby's skull during birth (p. 88)

Moro reflex: a reflex elicited by a loud sound or a sudden drop, involving the throwing out of the baby's arms and an extension of the fingers and neck (p. 100)

Neurological Examination of the Full-Term Infant: an assessment instrument used to determine the neurological well-being of newborns; also known as the Pretchl (p. 111)

palmar grasping reflex: the reflexive closing of the hand when the palm is pressed or stroked (p. 101)

phototherapy: light therapy used to treat hyperbilirubinemia in the newborn (p. 92)

reflexes: built-in responses to stimulation in certain areas of the body (p. 100)

retrolental fibroplasia blindness: a type of blindness caused in newborns from overexposure to concentrated oxygen (p. 92)

rooting reflex: head turning and movement of the lips and tongue in response to stroking of the cheek (p. 101)

saccades: jerky movements seen in the newborn's eyes as a moving object is tracked (p. 96)

scheduled feeding: feeding the baby on a predetermined and set schedule (p. 91)

sucking reflex: pressure and sucking movements elicited by placing something in the infant's mouth (p. 102)

surfactant therapy: a treatment to prevent hyaline membrane disease in premature infants (p. 92)

swaddling: tight wrapping of an infant with cloth to hold the limbs close to the baby's body (p. 104)

temperament: each infant's unique levels of activity, consolability, and sociability (p. 104)

temporal resolution: the abilitiy to detect that a light is flashing on and off, rather than shining constantly (p. 96)

thermogenesis: nonshivering heat production based on the burning of a special fat found in the neonate (p. 94)

tonic neck reflex: a reflex involving a specific pattern of extension and flexion of limbs (p. 100)

tonus: muscle tone (p. 100)

tracking: visual following of a moving object (p. 96)

vernix caseosa: a white, greasy covering found on the newborn's skin (p. 88)

visual accommodation: the change that occurs in the eye's lens to bring objects at varying distances into focus (p. 96)

SUGGESTIONS FOR FURTHER READING

Brazelton, T. B. (1969). *Infants and mothers*. New York: Dell. This book about the first year of life devotes four chapters to the neonatal period. Good discussion of individual differences among infants, with emphasis on adaptation to the baby.

Field, T. (1990). *Infancy*. Cambridge, MA: Harvard University Press. This short paperback book contains good information about the newborn period.

Harkness, S., & Super, C. M. (1996). *Parental cultural belief systems: Their origin, expression, and consequence*. New York: Guilford. This book presents studies of parental beliefs and behavior in a variety of cultures around the world. Parent-infant behavior, including behavior relevant to the newborn period, is described and discussed in some of the chapters.

Kellman, P. J., & Arterberry, M. E. (1998). *The cradle of knowledge: Development of perception in infancy*. Cambridge, MA: The MIT Press. This book is written for the serious student. The first four chapters provide very good information about the very young infant's visual perception abilities and their physiological foundations.

Kopp, C. (1994). *Baby steps*. New York: W. H. Freeman. The first section of this book discusses infant cognitive, physical, and socioemotional development from birth to 3 months of age.

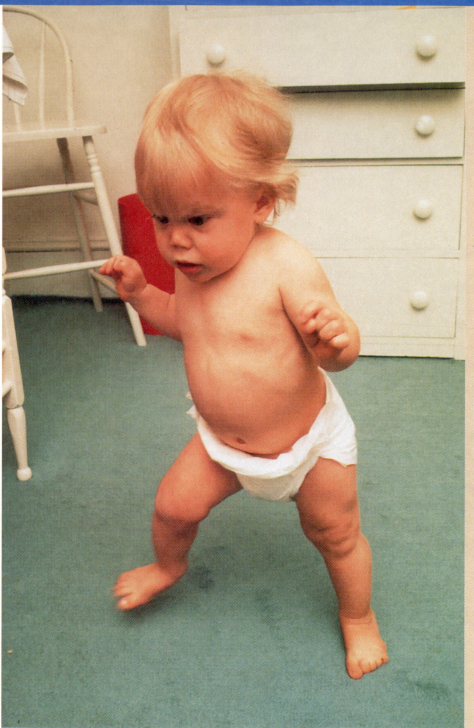

Physical Development in Infants and Toddlers

"DR. MARQUEZ WILL see Sabrina now, Mrs. Austen," the pediatric nurse called from the open door.

"Put the puzzle back on the table, Sarah. We need to see the doctor now." As Ursula Austen gathered her things, Sarah picked up her puzzle pieces from the floor and placed them on the puzzle frame. Then she leaned forward on her hands to raise herself from a sitting position. Once up on her feet, she squatted down, knees bent, and picked up the puzzle with both hands. She carried it to the toy table in the corner of the waiting room.

Ursula, meanwhile, had made her way to the door leading to the examination rooms. She held Sabrina carefully up against her shoulder, supporting the back of her head with her other hand. Sarah toddled quickly to her mother and reached up to take hold of the diaper bag strap hanging from Ursula's shoulder.

In the examination room, Ursula placed Sabrina on the table to undress her. Sarah stepped up on a small stool beside the table to get a better look. She put her finger in her sister's hand, and Sabrina's fingers closed tightly around it. She had to pull it out to allow her mother to pull Sabrina's sleeper over her hand.

As Sabrina began to cry, her hands were squeezed into tight fists and her arms waved in jerky arcs. Ursula talked softly to her, hoping to reduce her distress. Sarah stepped down from the stool to walk over to the large medical scale and began to climb on the sturdy wooden chair beside the scale. She reached across the seat, took hold of the far side with her hands, and then pulled herself up and across it. When her legs were pulled up far enough, she bent her knees under herself and sat up on them. Then, turning toward the back of the chair, she put her hands on its top, and stood up. She was reaching up to get hold of the wall-mounted blood pressure cuff when her mother caught sight of her.

"Sarah! Get down from there!" she called. "That's not a toy. And you might fall!"

think about it

Both of these girls are infants, but they are at opposite ends of the time span that marks the period called infancy. How old is each girl? What changes have taken place in Sarah since she was Sabrina's age that allow her to maneuver in her environment with such physical skill? What changes in a parent-child relationship might be prompted by an infant's mobility or the arrival of a new sibling?

In this chapter we discuss the dramatic changes that occur during infancy and toddlerhood, a time period that spans birth to 2½ years of age. In addition to growth and early physiological adaptations to life outside the womb, we focus on the motor skills that allow infants and toddlers to reach and grasp and to move around with ever-increasing agility and speed. We also discuss patterns of wakefulness and sleep in the newborn, appetite and nutrition in babies, and toilet training, the achievement that comes at the end of toddlerhood.

How Do They Grow?

Of the remarkable changes that take place in babies during their first years of life, physical changes are the most visible, and for that reason probably the most astonishing. A person who has not seen a baby in a few weeks or months often remarks,

Toddlers can climb stairs by crawling before they have learned to walk. When toddlers begin to walk, they climb even more. Parents must be very, very vigilant once an infant is on the move, and they should block entry to stairs by using gates. Toddlers can topple off stairs after they climb up on them. Falling from a height presents a grave danger to infants and toddlers. (*Source:* © Stephen Frisch/Stock Boston)

"Look how she's grown!" A person who has not seen a baby for a year or so since birth might even fail to recognize her.

Increases in Weight and Length

The most obvious difference between the two girls in the doctor's office is that 15-month-old Sarah weighs more and is taller than 6-week-old Sabrina. Babies usually double their birth weight in their first 4 months and triple it by their first birthday (Overby, 1996). The increase in terms of pounds is from an initial weight of about 7 pounds at birth to about 21 pounds by 12 months. Sarah, at 15 months of age, already weighs a little more than three times what 6-week-old Sabrina weighs.

From 12 months to 2 years, weight continues to increase, but at a slower rate. The average 2-year-old weighs 28 pounds (Overby, 1996), not a whopping 63, which would result if the growth rate remained at first-year levels. Between 2 and 3 years of age the growth rate slows down even more. The average 3-year-old weighs about 32 pounds. This is a relatively small increase from the weight of the 2-year-old, especially when compared with the difference between a newborn and a 1-year-old. The growth charts shown in Figure 4.1 illustrate these changes graphically. Notice that the lines are very steep in the first year and then flatten out somewhat after that.

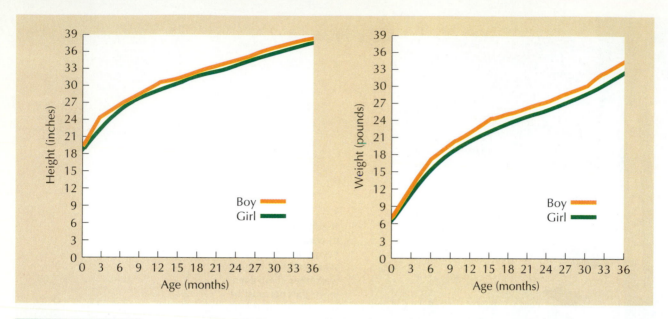

FIGURE 4.1

Height and weight for boys and girls from birth through 36 months of age. The graphs show heights and weights for children who are average (50th percentile). Between birth and 9 or 10 months, the slope of the line is quite steep, reflecting the rapid rate of growth during this time. After 1 year of age, the slope flattens out. If prenatal growth were shown, the slope of that line would be even steeper than the line showing the first 9 months after birth.

Variations in Growth   Although the trends we have described are typical, some infants and toddlers grow either more or less than the average amount. Among the causes for departures from the norm is the fact that birth weight is determined more by the mother's own size and the conditions of uterine life than by the child's genetic inheritance. Thus, if a fetus is cramped in the womb, or if the mother's nutrition is inadequate during pregnancy, a baby may not grow prenatally as much as its genetic potential would have allowed under other circumstances. However, if nutrition is adequate after birth, such a baby will grow much faster than average in the first months of life because the child's genetic inheritance is able to exert more control. This pattern of growth can occur in cases where the baby has a small mother and a large father (Tanner, 1970).

On the other hand, if a baby's inheritance pushes the child in the direction of being smaller than average, but the uterine environment is especially ideal, such a baby may be larger at birth than would have been predicted from the baby's genetic inheritance alone. After birth, this baby's growth is likely to be slower than average, as the baby's genes exert more control (Maggioni & Lifshitz, 1995).

Failure-to-thrive is a significantly slower than average rate of growth that is due to caregiving and feeding problems rather than to disease or an infant's adjustment after birth to inherited growth patterns (Valenzuela, 1997). Failure-to-thrive can occur if parents neglect their infants, failing to feed them frequently enough. Other parents feed their infants frequently enough, but nutrition is compromised because they dilute the formula in order to save money. Diluted formula retards the infant's growth. When evaluating a baby's growth, pediatricians take into account prenatal conditions, family history of stature, and other normal variations in growth, in order to distinguish between slow growth that is truly failure-to-thrive and slow growth that is normal for a specific baby (Maggioni & Lifshitz, 1995).

Effects of Growth Rate on Appetite

Very young infants seem to be hungry just about all of the time and need to be fed usually about every three or four hours. Toddlers, on the other hand, sometimes eat so little that their parents worry about their health. This difference between infant and toddler appetite parallels the normal decrease in the growth rate between 1 and 2 years of age. Toddlers are simply not as hungry as infants, because they are not growing at such a rapid pace.

Good nutrition is important throughout childhood. As the growth rate slows and appetite wanes in late infancy, parents must be especially careful about what their children eat. Early in infancy, babies drink only milk, either from their mothers or from infant formula. The baby does not select foods to eat. But by 2 years of age, a wider range of foods is offered to the child and the child begins to exert more control over what and how much is eaten. As a consequence, good nutrition begins to depend more and more on making sure that the child is offered a good selection of foods. (See the Feeding and Toilet Training during Infancy and Toddlerhood section.)

Tissue Growth

In addition to differing in size, toddlers' body proportions are radically different from those of younger infants. Toddlers are also stronger and have more stamina. These physical characteristics reflect neurological changes and patterns of tissue growth in the first year of life. Because of these changes, the older infant and toddler can move in ways that younger infants cannot.

Changes in Body Fat, Muscle, and Bone

Subcutaneous fat, the layer of fat just below the skin, begins to form in the fetus about 6 weeks before birth. Recall from chapter 3 that premature babies do not have the benefit of this layer. This is why they look unusually scrawny at birth. Subcutaneous fat continues to accumulate rapidly in the first 9 months of life, making the baby look rounded and filled out. After 9 months, it accumulates more slowly.

No new muscle cells are formed after birth, but changes do occur in muscle fibers during infancy. For example, the proportion of water, salts, and protein found in the fibers changes, with water decreasing and salts and proteins increasing. This change increases muscle strength.

Bones are changing too. At birth, babies have soft bones composed mostly of cartilage. During infancy, cartilage is gradually changed to bone as minerals are deposited through a process called **ossification**. As the bones in the baby's skull harden and fuse, the fontanelles gradually close. The large fontanelle at the top of the head usually closes completely by about 2 years (Wennberg et al., 1973).

Six-week-old Sabrina looked about like this. A baby this age has usually gained a pound or two since birth, and will double its birth weight by 4 months of age. Sustaining this growth rate requires frequent feeding, usually every 3 or 4 hours during the early months of the first year. (*Source:* © Myrleen Ferguson/Photo Edit)

knowledge *in action*

HEALTH/SAFETY

Teething and the Care of Teeth

"Ouch!" squealed Cathy one afternoon as her 7-month-old chewed on her finger. She ran her finger along Evan's slippery bottom gum. Right in the middle she felt the hard edges of his first two teeth.

"You're getting teeth!" she exclaimed.

Patterns of Teeth Eruption

Teething begins at about 7 or 8 months of age. By their first birthday, children have 4 teeth on the top gum and 2 on the bottom. By 1½ they usually add 6 more, and by age 3 they have their full set of 20 deciduous (i.e., baby) teeth.

First molars do not erupt until 10 months; second molars not until 20 months at the earliest. This is why babies have to be fed minced or chopped meat and cooked vegetables. Not until they have their full set of teeth, between 2½ and 3 years of age, can they chew meat reasonably well. (See Figure 4.2 to see the order in which all 20 baby teeth erupt.)

The Effect of Diet and Fluoridation

Over 8 percent of children between 18 and 23 months have caries. By 3 years, almost half of all children have them (Miller & Rosenstein, 1982). The development of caries is influenced by diet and by fluoride in the drinking water. Sugar in sticky form, such as in chewy candy, cake frosting, and chewing gum with sugar, is the most pernicious form, in contrast to nonsticky forms of sugar found in fruit juice, milk, ice cream, and so on (Herrmann & Roberts, 1987). Bathing the teeth in sugar, by sucking lollipops, for example, is particularly conducive to tooth decay. If babies fall

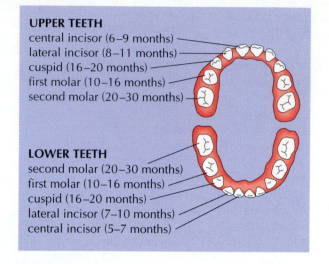

UPPER TEETH
central incisor (6–9 months)
lateral incisor (8–11 months)
cuspid (16–20 months)
first molar (10–16 months)
second molar (20–30 months)

LOWER TEETH
second molar (20–30 months)
first molar (10–16 months)
cuspid (16–20 months)
lateral incisor (7–10 months)
central incisor (5–7 months)

FIGURE 4.2

The 20 baby teeth and the dates when they appear.

asleep while sucking a bottle of milk or juice, they are likely to have "nursing bottle" caries, a particular pattern of cavities in those teeth most directly exposed to the flow of liquid from the bottle (Crall, 1986).

Water fluoridation reduces tooth decay by 50 to 70 percent (Shelton et al., 1982). Where water is not fluridated, fluoride drops or tablets can be used to obtain the same effect (Herrmann & Roberts, 1987).

Toothbrushing and Visits to the Dentist

Frequent brushing—at least twice a day—helps fight tooth decay. Parents should begin cleaning their babies' teeth as

Bone growth continues throughout childhood and adolescence (Stoner, 1978). It is essential that children's diets contain adequate minerals, especially calcium, to support bone growth. (For a discussion of the development of teeth, whose proper development also requires minerals such as calcium, see Knowledge in Action: Health/Safety—Teething and the Care of Teeth.)

Because some bones and bone parts ossify before others in a regular pattern, ossification provides an index of children's physical maturity. The extent of ossification can be determined by X rays (taken when children are examined for possible broken bones or other medical problems), because the denser ossified areas show up on the X-ray film. Using this technique, researchers have confirmed that girls' physical matura-

soon as they erupt, at first with a washcloth, then with a soft toothbrush. Toddlers can learn to brush their own teeth, although they do not have the coordination to do a very good job. A technique parents can use to ensure clean teeth without interfering with the child's budding confidence is saying, "You did a good job with that one, and that one, and that one," while checking (and quickly re-brushing) each tooth.

Dentists often recommend that parents bring children in for a visit at about the age of 3. The dentist looks at the teeth, perhaps touches each one with a dental tool, and records the teeth on a dental chart. With a particularly co-operative child, the dentist might be able to do some quick scraping of plaque. The dentist might also be able to give a fluoride treatment, which consists of having the child bite down on some toothpaste-like material that contains fluoride.

Effects of Thumb Sucking

Parents often worry that thumb or finger sucking will harm the alignment of a child's baby teeth. But if the habit stops by the age of 5 or 6, the teeth self-correct (Schneider & Peterson, 1982). Parents need not worry about thumb or finger sucking in the toddler or take any drastic action to stop it. Parents who provide an emotionally secure and intellectually stimulating environment for the toddler's play and development lay the foundation for the day when thumb and finger sucking will disappear.

In summary,

- Caregivers need to feed infants and toddlers minced or cooked foods to be sure the foods can be safely swallowed before the child has a full set of teeth.
- To help prevent dental caries, parents should avoid feeding babies "sticky" sugar. Babies should not fall asleep while sucking a bottle of milk or juice.

- Fluoride drops can be used to help prevent tooth decay if local water sources are not fluoridated.
- Parents should see that children's teeth are cleaned twice daily.

It is not too early for parents to begin cleaning baby's teeth as soon as they erupt, first with a wash cloth, then with a soft toothbrush. (*Source:* © Dennis O'Clair/ Tony Stone Images)

tion proceeds faster than boys'. At birth, girls' skeletal maturity is about four weeks in advance of boys'. By age 5 or 6, the gap has widened to about one year (Tanner, 1990).

Brain Development   Brain cells begin to develop early in the prenatal period. In fact, soon after conception the hollow ball of cells formed out of the zygote as a result of cell division begins to organize itself into three layers. From one of these, the **ectoderm,** the skin and the nervous system will be formed. Within the nervous system, the neural tube is formed first. This tuble differentiates into the brain and the spinal cord. The different structures of the brain itself can be seen as bumps and indentations by about 5 weeks after conception (Elman et al., 1998).

Growth of brain cells. These cells continue to increase in size and number during the first year of life and beyond, as can be seen in these drawings made from photomicrographs. Both nutrition and sensory stimulation must be adequate during this important time to ensure proper growth and development of the brain. (*Source: Postnatal development of the human cerebral cortex*, Vols. 1–8, by J. L. Conel, 1939–1967, Cambridge, MA: Harvard University Press. © 1939–1967 by the President and Fellows of Harvard College. Reprinted by permission of the publisher.*)

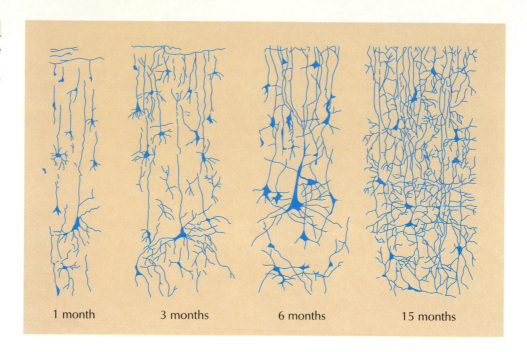

1 month   3 months   6 months   15 months

Neurons, or nerve cells, which make up about 10 percent of the brain, develop between the second and seventh month of prenatal life (Dobbing, 1984). Dendrites and axons, the fibrous extensions from these cells, continue to grow for about 9 months after the child is born. These fibers carry impulses to and from the cells (see Figure 4.3). The major development after birth is the organization of synapses (Johnson, 1999). **Synapses** are the narrow spaces between neurons; across them, signals pass that prompt neurons to fire.

The rest of the brain consists of **glial cells.** These begin to appear early in the prenatal period (Elman et al., 1998) and multiply rapidly through the second year, and then develop more slowly (Spreen et al., 1984). Glial cells supply nutrients to neurons or remove neural waste materials, and they help to repair nervous system damage. They also aid in the migration of neurons from their production site to where they belong in the brain (Elman et al., 1998). They produce myelin, a fatty substance that forms a sheath around nerve fibers, increases the speed with which impulses are transmitted, and aids interaction between separate parts of the brain (Casaer, 1993; Johnson, 1999). **Myelination** of some parts of the brain begins before birth, but most is completed postnatally. Myelination of some parts of the brain (associative areas of the cortex) is not complete until many years after birth (Elman et al., 1998).

At 15 months, Sarah is well into what is called "the brain growth spurt." This is the period of most rapid brain growth, which extends from the last three months of prenatal life through the first year and a half of postnatal life. During this time, more than half of the adult brain weight is achieved (Dobbing, 1984). By 5 years of age, the brain is almost at full adult weight (Tanner, 1978). See Table 4.1 for a breakdown of this weight gain.

Because it is still growing, the infant's immature brain contains fewer glial cells than the more mature brain, and there are larger spaces between brain parts than is true in the older child and adult.

Growth of the brain

Age	Percentage of Weight of Adult Brain
Birth	25
6 months	30
12 months	60
20 months	75
5 years	90

knowledge *in action*

Shaken Baby Syndrome

One form of physical abuse in infants is shaking. Because the infant is top-heavy, and the brain is not yet mature, even a small amount of shaking can harm an infant seriously or cause an infant to die. This type injury is known as **shaken baby syndrome (SBS)**. About 1.6 children per 1,000 suffer from the syndrome, which is the leading cause of death among children who are under 6 months of age (Conway, 1998).

Several physical symptoms indicate shaken baby syndrome. These include hemorrhages in the retinas, bleeding inside the skull, bulging fontanelle, and seizures. Behavioral indicators include staring episodes, irritability, and lethargy (Conway, 1998).

The outcome of SBS is often quite poor. The death rate varies from study to study, but is estimated to be about 25 percent (Conway & Bello, 1996). Children who survive often suffer long-term consequences of the shaking episode. They may have developmental delays, loss of both hearing and sight, and mental retardation (Conway, 1998).

Caregivers who have been identified as having shaken a baby report, when interviewed, that the infant's crying was what precipitated the shaking episode. Some of these caregivers may not have known that shaking can cause severe injury to a baby. Others simply lose self-control when dealing with an irritable baby and physically abuse the infant. Seventy percent of the adults who abuse an infant by shaking are men (Starling et al., 1995).

To reduce the incidence of this injury to infants, public health workers, pediatricians, and parents can take these measures:

- Inform parents about the dangers of shaking an infant.
- Use brochures, posters, and videos to help get the message out.
- Stress in their instructions to babysitters the need for very gentle handling of an infant's head.
- Be alert to signs of stress in the family, and encourage family members to seek help to solve their problems.

This immaturity, coupled with immaturity of the neck muscles, makes the young infant extremely vulnerable to head trauma, especially to shaking. (See Knowledge in Action: Health—Shaken Baby Syndrome.)

NUTRITION AND BRAIN GROWTH.   Good nutrition must be maintained throughout the period of rapid brain growth in order to ensure proper brain development (Dobbing, 1984). A good diet is also important because metabolic processes in the brain are controlled by enzymes, and enzyme production depends on the availability of specific nutrients. In their absence, brain function is impaired.

Studies have shown that learning is impaired in malnourished children (Grantham-McGregor et al., 1994; Sigman et al., 1989) and that negative consequences to learning become more obvious with the child's increasing age (Pollitt et al., 1993). This is probably because the demands on conceptual learning become greater as the child progresses through school. The longer the malnutrition continues in early childhood, the more severe the negative effect on later learning (Pollitt et al., 1993). (See Knowledge in Action: Policy—The WIC Program, for a discussion of a program designed to prevent nutritional problems in infants.)

STIMULATION EFFECTS ON BRAIN DEVELOPMENT.   Factors in the environment other than nutrition also affect brain development. A stimulating environment can produce growth in brain cells and increase brain functioning. Studies with rats have shown that environmental factors have a direct impact on the weight of the brain cortex, the chemistry of the brain, and problem-solving abilities (Greenough et al., 1987, 1993; Rosenzweig, 1984).

POLICY

The WIC Program (Special Supplemental Food Program for Women, Infants, and Children)

Children's health is a matter of such consequence to the larger society that many different government assistance programs have been established over the years to support good health and nutrition in children. In 1972, U.S. Public Law 94-105 was passed to create one of the most successful of these, the Special Supplemental Food Program for Women, Infants, and Children, commonly known as the WIC program. As the only nutrition program that provides both food and health service, the WIC program is unique (Egan, 1977). It serves pregnant women, nursing mothers, infants, and children under the age of 5 who meet low-income guidelines and who are judged to be at risk for health and nutrition problems. State health departments distribute funds to appropriate health agencies, which serve parents and young children.

Foods Available through the WIC Program

A specified amount of food is distributed to the participants each month. But only certain foods are made available. These include iron-fortified infant formulas; iron-fortified cereal; fruit or vegetable juices high in vitamin C; and foods, such as milk, cheese, dry beans, and eggs, that are high in protein, calcium, and iron. These foods were selected because iron-deficiency anemia, insufficient vitamin C, and low protein intake are common among low-income populations. These are also the nutrients necessary for healthy prenatal development, rapid growth during infancy and early childhood, and protection against disease (Select Committee on Hunger, 1988).

The WIC program also educates parents in the use of food supplements, the relationship between nutrition and health and disease, and the importance of good nutrition in children's growth and learning.

Benefits of the WIC Program

The WIC program has been associated with several health improvements (Egan, 1977, p. 237):

- Infants in the program gained weight and grew more quickly than similar infants not enrolled in the program.
- Fewer infants had anemia, and the mean blood hemoglobin concentration of infants in the program increased.
- Women gained more weight during pregnancy than similar women who were not in the program.
- Newborns weighed more at birth than similar newborns not in the program.
- Participants took greater advantage of health services than they had prior to enrolling in the program.

In summary, research has shown that enrollment in the WIC program improves the intake of essential nutrients in populations of women at risk for deficient diets (Farrior & Ruwe, 1987). Program enrollment also increases length of gestation and birth weight (Batten et al., 1990). Health professionals have also used their contact with WIC program mothers to increase immunization rates among low-income children (Goldberg, 1995).

Like all publicly funded programs, the WIC program is reviewed periodically and is subject to the political and social views of changing administrations. But because of its success, the program would probably be one of the last nutrition programs to be cut back or discontinued. It appears to be an effective way to prevent nutritional problems when they are most likely to lead to serious impairment of physical and mental growth.

Stimulation apparently has similar or even greater effects on human babies. Studies in which both nutritional status and intellectual stimulation have been altered in severely malnourished infants have found independent effects for both variables (Grantham-McGregor et al., 1994; Sigman et al., 1989). Even when the brain has been affected in some physical way by malnutrition, changes in both the nutritional environment and the care and stimulation the baby receives seem to compensate somewhat for disturbances (Colombo et al., 1992; Elman et al., 1998; Winick et al., 1975). As with other aspects of development, many factors, including both nutrition and social stimulation, interact to form the intellect (Dobbing, 1984, 1987; Galler, 1987; Johnston et al., 1987). Unfortunately, children who are malnourished are often the same ones who receive less than optimal stimulation. And, of course, babies who are hungry or unhealthy due to poor nutrition also are less active in exploring their environments. This reduces the stimulation they receive from their environment (Frank & Zeisel, 1988).

Changes In Body Proportions and Shape

The proportions of a toddler's body differ greatly from those of a very young infant. These changes occur because different parts of the baby's body grow more quickly than they did before, while parts that had earlier grown faster begin to slow down. The head grows the fastest of any body part, both prenatally and during infancy, but a toddler's head is not as top-heavy as the head of a young infant because the baby's trunk grows faster during infancy than it grew prenatally. The toddler's head is still larger in proportion to her body than is an older child's or an adult's, but it now constitutes a smaller proportion of overall height than it did in infancy. During the preschool and school years, the legs and trunk actually grow faster than the head, and this changes a child's appearance greatly.

The various body tissues grow at different rates, too, giving the child a different appearance at different ages. Toddlers have lost some of the "baby fat" they accumulated during the last few weeks of prenatal life and the first 9 months after birth, and their bodies also have more muscle and bone. Although they still look pudgy compared to a 3- or 4-year-old, 2½-year-olds look much leaner than do 1-year-olds. The chubbiness that remains in toddlers is especially noticeable around their middles. This is not simply fat, but a bulge made by the internal organs. Internal organs grow quite a lot during the first two years of life, while the trunk does not grow quite enough to allow room for them. Additionally, underdeveloped muscles of the abdomen offer little resistance. Thus, the organs push out, creating the tummy bulge that is so characteristic of the toddler. Children keep this silhouette until they are 3½ or 4 years of age. By then, their trunks have lengthened enough to provide more room for their organs, and their abdominal muscles have become strong enough to hold the organs in their place.

Toddlers' body proportions affect not only their appearance, but how they walk. Children start walking when they are 12 or 13 months of age, but they walk flat-footed with short, wide steps and a wobbly gait. Toddlers walk this way because top-heaviness, caused by their relatively large head, makes it difficult for them to keep their balance. They compensate, and thus maintain their balance, by placing their feet far apart to create a wide base of support. As the trunk and legs grow longer during the preschool years (and growth of the head slows further), the child's **center of gravity**—the point around which the weight is evenly distributed—moves lower in the body, and balance improves. Due to this gradual change in bodily proportions, the toddler's characteristic stance (swaybacked) and walk (wide and wobbly) evolve into the surer, more graceful movements of the preschooler.

A toddler's middle sticks out because his internal organs have grown large, and his trunk is short. As the trunk grows longer and muscle tone improves, children lose some of the roundness we see in this 19-month-old. (*Source:* © Bob Daemmrich/The Image Works)

Development of Motor Abilities

During infancy, great advances in motor abilities occur. Motor development proceeds in two directions: (1) from the center of the body out to the arms, hands, and fingers; and (2) from the top of the body downward. Development in the outward direction is known as **proximodistal** (literally, "near" to "far") development. This trend leads to ever-increasing skill in using the hands. Development in the downward direction is known as **cephalocaudal** (literally, "head" to "tail") development. This trend eventually leads to using the legs to stand and walk.

Fine Motor Development: Reaching and Grasping

Fine motor development refers to development in the use of the hands. A newborn infant can grasp an object if it is placed in her palm, because the grasping reflex causes the fingers to curl forward to close the hand. But voluntary reaching and grasping—and letting go—take quite a while to develop. The first milestone of fine motor development is reaching out and enclosing an object with the hands.

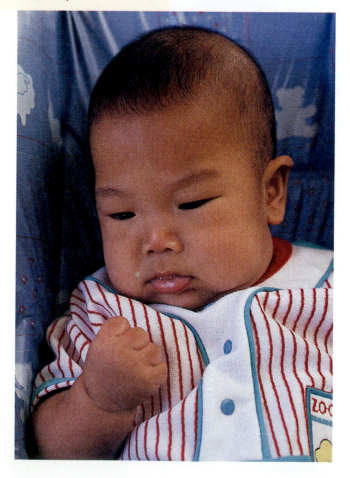

This baby has discovered his hand and is enjoying looking at it. Before long, he will be using his hands to reach out and grasp objects. (*Source:* © Elizabeth Crews)

Developmental Course of Reaching and Grasping

Although newborns show some tendency to direct arm movements toward objects, they are not skilled in executing reach and grasp motions (Hofsten, 1982; Hofsten & Ronnquist, 1989). Gradually, their abilities improve. By about 2½ months, they reach for objects by swiping at them, and by about 4½ months, they can reach for and grasp an object.

One of the long-held assumptions about reaching is that vision guides it. Of course, infants do reach for objects they can see, and they adjust the positioning of the fingers and the extent of reach, depending on the features and location of the object. But apparently, increasing skill in reaching is not primarily the result of better eye-hand coordination, as once was thought (McCarty & Ashmead, 1999). In one study (Clifton et al., 1993), no difference in infants' reaching was observed in light versus dark conditions. According to these researchers,

> by about 4 months . . . infants have a unified spatial coding system within which visual, auditory, and proprioceptive stimulation is integrated in a way that does not require vision as a mediating process. Although the most typical reaching situation provides congruent stimulation through all three modalities, infants are quite successful at reaching when stimulation is removed. . . . They can reach for objects heard but not seen, or seen but not heard, and they can do this whether or not their hands are visible during the reach. (p. 1106)

A major obstacle to smoothly executed reaching is lack of control of the arms when infants first begin to reach. Improvement in reaching depends on practice—on learning to control the energy expended by the muscles, so as not to overshoot or undershoot the object. Infants must also learn how to coordinate different parts of their arm, such as the shoulder and elbow regions. Finally, reaching and grasping improve as control of the trunk and other systems improves (Goldfield, 1995). For example, the achievement of stable sitting (without supports) frees the upper limbs from the encumbrance of maintaining balance, allowing coordinated action of the upper limbs and trunk in reaching (Rochat & Goubet, 1995).

The gradual development of arm control in making reaching movements has been studied extensively by Esther Thelen and her colleagues (1993). They have found that by about 5 months of age many babies are able to execute a reasonably accurate reach—one that gets them to the target object—and also to judge whether an object is within reaching distance. Some babies take into account not only the length of their arm, but the amount by which their reach can be extended if they lean forward!

To study infants' judgments about objects within and outside of their reach, one team of researchers (Yonas & Hartman, 1993) divided babies into two groups—leaners and non-leaners—and then positioned objects at various distances. Objects were positioned in one of three ways: (1) within arm's reach, regardless of whether the infant leaned forward; (2) within reach *only* if the infant leaned forward while reaching; and (3) outside of an infant's reach, even if the infant leaned forward.

Most 5-month-olds reached much more frequently for objects placed within their reach than for objects placed outside of it. Moreover, babies who tended to lean forward when reaching also reached much more frequently than did non-leaning babies if objects were in fact within reach.

Knowledge about the distance of a reach and of its extension through leaning forward is acquired by babies as they gain experience in reaching. (See the Research Close-Up: Effects of Motor Development on Other Areas of Development later in this chapter for more examples of how motor experience is likely to affect a baby's cognition.)

Development of a Baby's Grasp   Babies first grasp objects awkwardly by surrounding them with their fingers and pressing them into the palms of their hands. Later, they use their thumbs to help hold objects. By about 9 months of age, babies can grasp small objects by holding them between the thumb and index finger (or forefinger). This grasp is known as the **pincer grasp.** To execute a pincer grasp, babies must be able to separate the forefinger from the other three fingers (see Figure 4.4).

Separating the forefinger from the other fingers comes in handy not only for picking up objects with more precision, but for communication. Infants now are able to point to objects in the environment. This gesture is useful for language development because it enables the child to point to an object while verbalizing. Together, the gesture and vocalization can mean, "What is that?" or "Look at that." The pointing augments information provided by the infant's gaze and helps adults figure out what the infant is referring to (Carpenter et al., 1998). (See Chapter 6 for more information about development of language and communication.)

With the disappearance of the grasping reflex, at about 1 year the infant can also begin to release objects. Most 2-year-olds can build sturdy block towers and also do many other things with their hands.

FIGURE 4.4

The pincer grasp. Between 9 and 12 months the baby perfects her pincer grasp, which allows her to pick up small objects (and, most likely, put them in her mouth).

For example, they can snap pop-beads together, make marks on paper with a crayon, and work simple puzzles (two to four pieces). They can even string large beads into a necklace if the end of the string is stiff enough to pass completely through a bead. (If the end will not pass through the bead, the child must work it through with her fingers. This takes considerably more skill.)

With increased skill in using their hands, infants can manipulate objects in various ways. These manipulations provide the baby with a great deal of information about objects. (See Table 4.2 for a summary of the manual manipulations infants apply to objects.)

Factors Affecting the Development Reaching and Grasping   Disappearance of the palmar grasp and emergence of the pincer grasp may lead observers to think that motor development is solely a matter of maturation. Recall from chapter 1 that the proponents of the maturational theory of development took much of their evidence from the realm of physical development. But although motor development is influenced considerably by maturation, experience is also important (Konner, 1982; Thelen & Ulrich, 1991). Studies of blind babies have given us some information about the factors influencing motor development. Additional informa-

---

TABLE 4.2

Types of manual manipulation found in infants

Manipulation	Description
Rotation (second month)	Twists of the wrists cause a held object to take on different angles.
Translation (third month)	Objects are moved closer to or farther away from the infant.
Vibration (fourth month)	Objects are shaken or waved.
Bilateral hold (fifth month)	Both hands are employed to hold or explore different objects.
Two-handed hold (fifth month)	One object is held with both hands.
Hand-to-hand transfer (sixth month)	One object is passed from one hand to the other.
Coordinated action with one object (sixth month)	The object is held by one hand while the other hand performs some action on it (e.g., fingering, patting, pulling apart).
Coordinated action with two objects (eighth month)	Two objects, one held in each hand, are related to each other (e.g., one object is topped by the other).
Deformations (eighth month)	The hands are used to alter the shape or size of objects (e.g., by crushing or ripping).
Instrumental sequential actions (ninth month)	Two hands perform different acts, in sequence, to accomplish a goal (e.g., object is held up while something under it is removed by the other hand).

Source: From "The Role of Manual Manipulative Stages in the Infant's Acquisition of Perceived Control Over Objects" by R. Karniol, *Developmental Review, 9,* pp. 205–233, © 1989 by Academic Press, reproduced by permission of the publisher.

tion has come from studies in which the environments of sighted babies were modified to add more visual stimulation.

STUDIES OF REACHING AND GRASPING IN BLIND BABIES.   Blind babies attempt to reach and grasp early in life when they hear a sound. But because the sound does not tell the baby how far away the object is, the baby frequently fails to touch the object when reaching out. Without feedback that the object is "out there," the baby soon stops reaching (Bower, 1977). Psychologist Selma Fraiberg (1975) found that the ability to reach for an object on the basis of sound alone requires a higher level of conceptual development than reaching for an object on the basis of both sight and sound. This is because sound alone does not convey the sense that something is an object and can be grasped. Blind babies must be helped to acquire this concept. Fraiberg's studies have shown how this can be done:

> For a perilously long time in the first year of life the blind baby behaves as if the musical toy in his hand is one object and the sound of the musical toy "out there" is another object. . . . Toys that united tactile and sound qualities were sought out by us and the parents to encourage a sound-touch identity for objects. . . . Through the devices of a special play table and playpen we created "an interesting space" in which a search or sweep of the hand would guarantee an encounter and interesting discovery. . . . one day . . . the sound of the bell would motivate the hands. A grasping-ungrasping motion would appear. . . . There was not yet reach, but we knew the idea was emerging. A few days later, a few weeks later . . . without vision, a baby would discover that the sound that we call "a bell" and the bell which he could not experience in his hand were "out there" in space. (p. 48)

Because blind babies do not have the same physical equipment as sighted babies, they cannot work out the "unified spatial coding system" that Clifton and colleagues (1993) suggest underlies the sighted infant's reaching. Therefore, the environment must be adapted to the abilities of blind babies to ensure their development.

Fraiberg's studies are important not only because they provide a procedure for helping blind babies learn to reach and grasp, but because they shed some light on child development theory—on explanations for what causes development to occur. These studies have helped us to understand that motor skill development depends on stimulation and feedback that babies get from the environment as well as on maturation.

STUDIES OF REACHING AND GRASPING IN MODIFIED ENVIRONMENTS.   Further evidence for the role of experience in motor development comes from investigations of the effects of added visual stimulation, beginning when infants were just a few months old (White, 1971). The increased stimulation consisted of multicolored sheets on the infants' crib mattresses, additional time on their stomachs (a good position from which to view the world), and large stabiles (stationary mobiles) above their cribs. One group of infants received the stabile during their second, third, and fourth months. A second group received an attractive pacifier centered on a disk at both sides of the crib during their second month and the stabile during their third and fourth months. A control group did not receive any additional stimulation.

Babies in both experimental groups began reaching and grasping with the hand out of view when they were about 4½ months old, a month earlier than is typical. Babies in the control group reached and grasped at 5½ months of age, which is right in line with the norm. Again we see that the environment has an effect on development that might seem to be purely a matter of biology.

An important side effect of this study was that the babies who received the stabile in their second month cried more at first than did infants in any other group. The stabile may have been too stimulating—too novel or frightening—for them. If a baby expresses extreme surprise or fear, or if she frequently looks away from the stimulation, it is probably too novel. If she gazes continuously, the level of stimulation is probably just about right.

Locomotor Development: Up and About

A baby's first unassisted steps are usually celebrated as the major achievement of infancy. Walking is an important milestone of infancy, but it is preceded by an equally impressive—and orderly—series of developments. Before they can walk, babies must be able to stand. Before they can stand, they must know how to sit; to sit, they must be able to hold up their heads. The cephalocaudal trend in development means that the head, neck, trunk, and leg muscles come under control in a head-to-tail order. The cephalocaudal development of locomotor skills (skills used in moving from place to place) is shown in two classic illustrations done by researchers working in the 1930s. Figure 4.5 shows the development of creeping (Ames, 1937); Figure 4.6 shows the development of walking (Shirley, 1933).

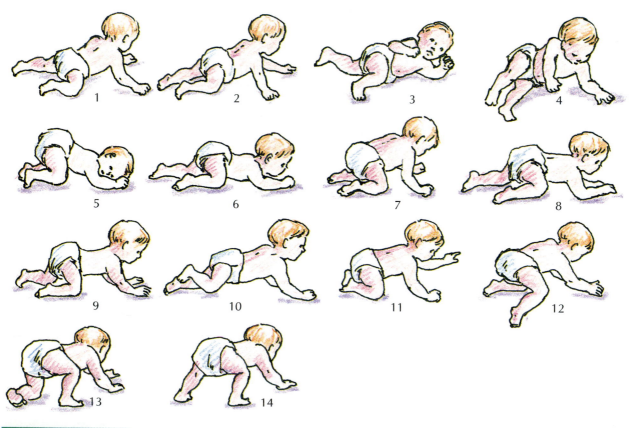

FIGURE 4.5

The development of creeping. One milestone of locomotor development is broken down here into 14 steps. The baby's persistence pays off first with crawling (step 9) and then with creeping on the hands and feet (step 14).

Birth
Fetal posture

1 month
Lift head
(2 weeks to 2 months)

2 months
Lift chest
(1½–3 months)

3 months
Reach and miss
(2–4 months)

4 months
Sit with support

5 months
Sit on lap,
grasp object

6 months
Sit in high
chair, grasp dangling object

6½ months
Sit alone
5–6½ months)

8 months
Stand with help

8 months
Stand holding furniture
(5–9 months)

8 months
Pull to stand
(6–9 months)

10 months
Creep on hands
and knees

11 months
Climb stairs

11 months
Walk when led

11 months
Stand alone
(10–13 months)

12 months
Walk alone
(11–13½ months)

FIGURE 4.6

Milestones of locomotor development. The cephalocaudal trend in development
can readily be seen in this chart. As the baby's brain and muscles mature, and as she
practices moving, her achievements center on progressively lower parts of the body,
leading eventually to walking.

This 4-month-old baby is able to hold his head up for long periods of time. He uses his arms to push his chest up off the floor. This allows him to raise his head for a good look around. It won't be long before he will be able to roll over from front to back. (*Source:* © Elizabeth Crews)

Today, babies seem to reach these milestones earlier, perhaps because nutrition is better and babies also have more opportunities to move around on the floor. For example, in the 1993 manual for the Bayley Scales of Infant Development, Second Edition, the norm for walking while led is 9½ months. The norm for walking without support, at least a few steps, is 11 months (Bayley, 1993).

The one milestone that today's babies reach later than their 1930s counterparts is that of rolling over. The delay in rolling over has occurred because parents have been advised to place their baby in the side or supine (face up) sleeping positions to reduce the probability of sudden infant death syndrome (SIDS). Infants placed in the side or supine position are less likely to roll over than infants who sleep primarily in the prone position (Jantz et al., 1997). (See Research Close-Up: Sudden Infant Death Syndrome later in this chapter.)

The order in which babies achieve the milestones is usually the same for all infants, although some babies exhibit a particular behavior in the sequence for a relatively short time or not at all. For example, some babies crawl for a long time, while others become upright fairly quickly. Some babies crawl for a while, dropping their bellies to the floor; others are up on hands and knees without a belly-crawling stage.

An interesting individual difference is seen in how different babies move themselves forward, using their arms and legs, when they crawl. Some babies coordinate their arms in making a movement and then move their legs. Other babies first move the limbs on one side of the body and then move the limbs on the other side. Still others use both arms and legs, coordinating the movement of the arm on one side of the body with the leg on the other. Most babies settle on using the last approach, apparently because it is the one that best helps them keep their balance (Freedland & Bertenthal, 1994).

A baby who has just started walking must give her full attention to remaining upright and taking a few steps. She often stops and presses her toes forward to keep from falling down. As she gains experience, she begins to move faster and with less effort. The difference between these two levels of skill can be seen in children's use of two different kinds of toys. A baby just starting to walk can use a push toy, but

This 13-month-old must place her feet wide apart and hold her arms out in order to maintain her balance. As her trunk and legs grow and the center of gravity moves lower in her body, she will become less top-heavy. Then she will narrow the base on which she walks and swing her arms at her sides.   (*Source:* © Robert E. Daemmrich/Tony Stone Images)

cannot manage a pull toy, which requires that one arm be extended behind the child. A more experienced walker who is at less risk of falling over backward can manage to use both push and pull toys.

Factors Affecting Locomotor Development   Changes in motor skills have traditionally been attributed almost solely to biological maturation—to maturation of the nervous system. But within the past few decades, this "neurological causality" explanation of motor development has been questioned by some theorists, most notably by Esther Thelen (Thelen & Ulrich, 1991). Thelen acknowledges, of course, that many dramatic changes occur in the nervous system during infancy. But she questions the "assignment of final causality to the central nervous system" (p. 37). As she and others have pointed out, and as we noted early in this chapter, changes in the brain are themselves "caused" in part by experience (Edelman, 1987; Greenough et al., 1987). Thelen asks, "What do infants do in their first 8–12 months to produce specific timing and patterns of brain anatomy?"

Thelen thinks that "the developmental milestone of learning to walk is not the result of a dedicated 'locomotor switch' turned on somewhere in the central nervous system." Instead, each milestone is the result of the coming together of several "relatively autonomous processes, each with its own developmental history" (Thelen & Ulrich, p. 40). Motivation, supportive body proportions, strength of the child's legs, and visual and vestibular (i.e., balance) feedback all influence a child's ability to walk. Studies of the development of walking in blind babies, and in babies who have been reared in orphanages, illustrate that maturation of motor ability interacts with such things as motivation and an understanding of the world.

For a baby beginning to walk, this push toy is a lot easier to use than a pull toy. (*Source:* © Will Faller)

Cross-cultural studies of motor development also shed light on the interaction of biology and experience.

STUDIES OF LOCOMOTOR DEVELOPMENT IN BLIND BABIES. The research of Fraiberg and others (Bigelow, 1992; Fraiberg, 1975, 1977) with blind babies provides information about how heredity and experience both affect motor development. Fraiberg explains that in "normal development . . . there is a smooth transition to bridging and creeping" (Fraiberg, 1975, p. 48). But this development does not proceed smoothly in blind babies:

> Most of our babies achieved stability [sit] in well within the range for sighted babies. Then, something that should appear on the developmental timetable did not appear. The baby did not creep! The sighted child will reach for the out-of-reach toy which propels him forward. . . . At every point where vision would normally intervene to promote a new phase in locomotor development we had to help the blind baby find an adaptive solution. The prone position, for example, is not an "interesting" position for the blind baby. . . . We build in "interest" in prone through speaking to the baby, through dangle toys or other devices.

> Practicing pulling to stand and cruising will be more "interesting" in the familiar space of a playpen with favorite toys offering sound-touch incentives.

Other studies of blind infants provide additional insight into the effect of experience on the attainment of motor milestones. In one study (Bigelow, 1992), three blind infants began to walk at different ages, one at 17 months, one at 32 months, and one at 36 months. In each case, walking followed, or occurred together with, a major cognitive transition in spatial/object knowledge. (See chapter 5 for a discussion of object permanence in infants.) Thus, age of walking was not determined solely by physical maturation. It depended on spatial/object knowledge too. Interestingly, this level of cognitive understanding occurs at about

12 months of age in sighted babies, the age at which sighted infants typically begin to walk.

STUDIES OF LOCOMOTOR DEVELOPMENT IN INSTITUTIONAL SETTINGS. Babies' motor skills are delayed when they are raised in nonstimulating environments. Wayne Dennis (1960), a well-known psychologist, studied orphan infants in three institutions in Iran. In Institution I, 600 children under the age of 3 lived in conditions that provided only one attendant for every eight children. Babies who could not yet sit up were left lying on their backs in their cribs. They were never propped up or given toys. They even were fed in their cribs with bottles propped on pillows.

When babies managed to pull themselves into a sitting position, they were placed on the floor when awake, but they were given no toys. Only 42 percent of the 1- and 2-year-olds could sit up; none could walk. When they turned 3, most of these children went to Institution II, where conditions were just as bad. Only 15 percent of the children between 3 and 4 years of age at Institution II could walk.

Institution III was opened as a model of improved child care. Babies in Institution I whose motor development was the most severely retarded had been transferred to Institution III very early in their infancy. In Institution III there was one attendant for every four babies, and babies were held while fed, placed on their stomachs or in a sitting position in their cribs, put in playpens when they were 4 months old, and given toys. At Institution III, 90 percent of the children could sit alone by 2 years of age (as compared with only 42 percent at Institution I), and 15 percent could walk (none of the infants in Institution I could walk at this age). By age 3, all children could walk alone (compared with 8 percent at Institution I). Dennis attributed the more normal development of children in Institution III to better child care. While awake, babies who are placed in the prone position can push themselves up and learn to sit up, roll over, and crawl. (See the Research Close-Up: Sudden Infant Death Syndrome for cautions about placing young infants in the prone position for sleeping.)

Studies have shown that retarded motor development in early infancy can be overcome if the baby is later placed in better conditions (Dennis, 1960; Kagan et al., 1978). Dennis's institutional study demonstrates powerfully how child-care practices affect motor development.

CROSS-CULTURAL STUDIES OF INFANT MOTOR DEVELOPMENT.   Motor milestones are reached at different ages in different cultures. For example, U.S. norms trail behind infants reared in the African countries of Kenya and Uganda. These infants achieve the milestones of sitting, standing, and walking about 1 month earlier than U.S. babies. What is interesting about the precocity of babies in some countries is that mothers in these cultures are more active than are U.S. mothers in stimulating an infant's motor development. For example, both the Baganda mothers of Uganda and the Kipsigis mothers of Kenya start early to teach their infants to sit. Mothers must at first hold the babies in the sitting position on their laps. Later, they prop them up in a tub or in special holes dug in the ground (Kilbride & Kilbride, 1975; Super, 1981).

Motor development in babies reared in South India also seems to be influenced positively by their mothers' handling. As Landers (1989) explains:

> The Indian bath is an elaborate, formal routine of daily massage which starts in the first few days of life and continues throughout the first year. It begins with the infant lying prone on the mother's outstretched legs. Each part of the infant's

body is stretched and prodded. Then, with tepid water and soap, the feet and legs are massaged, followed by the arms, back, abdomen, neck, and face. Exhausted from the intensity of this stimulation, the infant is swaddled and then enters into a prolonged sleep. (p. 186)

Motor precocity is also common among West Indian (Jamaican) infants, whose mothers perform specific handling routines during the first few months of infancy (Hopkins, 1991). These routines include massaging the baby, throwing the baby up in the air and catching her, holding the baby upside down by the heels, and holding the baby upright with feet on a solid surface (this encourages "stepping" motions). There are also exercises to stretch the neck (the head is held between the two hands and gently raised up). (See Figure 4.7.)

In contrast, Ache infants living in a nomadic tribe in the Paraguay rain forests receive little motor stimulation. They are carried almost everywhere and are allowed to explore only a few feet away from their mothers. These infants are delayed in several motor skills and begin walking almost a year later than children living in the United States (Kaplan & Dove, 1987).

Motor Development: Maturation and Experience

That motor development seems to depend in part on experience is a relatively new idea. Genetic-maturational theory has dominated views of physical and motor development throughout most of this century, in part because of several studies on the effects of experience that were conducted in the 1920s.

In one classic experiment on maturation and learning, maturational theorists Arnold Gesell and Henry Thompson (1929) compared the stair-climbing skill of children with and without stair-climbing experience. They used identical twins as subjects in order to hold constant genetic or biological contributions. They gave one twin six weeks of daily practice in climbing stairs, beginning at 46 weeks of age. By the fourth week of practice, this twin climbed stairs alone. After six weeks of practice, when 52 weeks old, he climbed them in just 26 seconds.

The other twin, who had never been allowed to climb stairs, was introduced to them at 53 weeks of age. On his first attempt, he climbed them in 46 seconds. Two weeks later, at 55 weeks, he climbed them in just 10 seconds. In other words, without any experience of stairs at all, he equaled or surpassed his brother's performance at a particular age.

The conclusion drawn was that maturation alone was responsible for motor development. But the researchers did not take into account the possibility that ability to climb stairs might be influenced not only by practice in climbing stairs but by practice in other motor skills as well. The twin who received no practice climbing stairs had just as much practice crawling, creeping, and walking as his brother did. Moreover, both twins had similar visual and cognitive stimulation from the environment, a condition that we now know affects motor development. Thus, even though the researchers demonstrated that learning a behavior does not require a specific experience, they did not prove that the behavior will occur without any experiences at all (Bower, 1974).

In our society most parents provide the environment and experiences that foster fairly rapid motor development. Without the ability to compare this rate of growth to that of infants whose growth follows another pattern (e.g., a faster rate of development in infants in other cultures), we conclude that normal motor development occurs spontaneously and inevitably, as a result of neurological maturation. But, as we have seen, children's development can be either slowed or accelerated by environmental conditions. Although maturation is an extremely important influence on

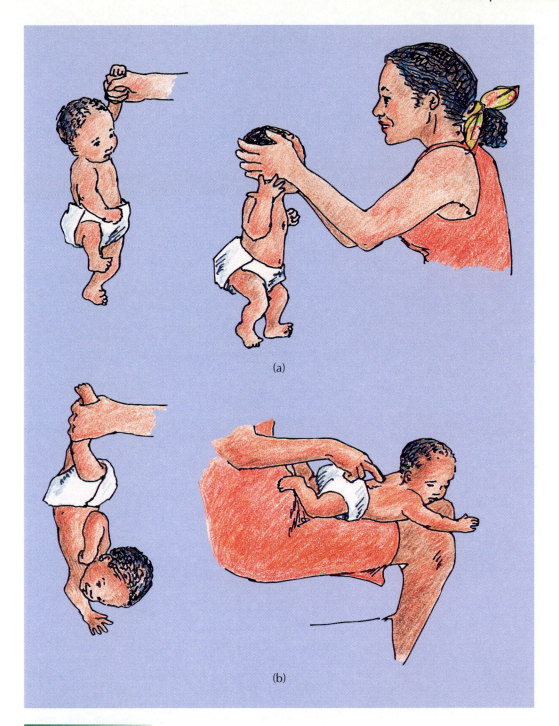

(a)

(b)

FIGURE 4.7

Babies growing up in the West Indies are exercised by their mothers according to specific routines. Their motor precocity may be due to this early experience. (*Source:* Adapted with permission from Ablex Publishing Corporation.)

motor development, experience also affects motor skill development. (For a discussion of a question that has not received as much attention as variations in the rate of motor development, see the Research Close-Up: Effects of Motor Development on Other Areas of Development.)

RESEARCH

CLOSE-UP

Effects of Motor Development on Other Areas of Development

Considerable research has been devoted to investigating the environmental and inborn factors that influence motor development. Research has also explored relationships between motor development and development in other areas.

Early Animal Studies

The first studies to indicate that motor development might have a profound effect on other systems were done on animals. Researchers found that kittens that were prevented from walking had impaired visual development (Held & Hein, 1963). Researchers also learned that locomotion was critical in some species for providing feedback necessary for normal social development (Schneirla, 1957; Schneirla et al., 1963).

But what about in humans? Of course, researchers cannot blindfold human babies, nor can they prevent them from walking in order to get answers to their questions. But other situations are available to researchers who wish to study these questions.

Studies of the Effects of Human Infant Mobility on Other Aspects of Development

Human studies have indicated that infants' avoidance of drop-offs, as demonstrated in the visual-cliff experiments (see chapter 5) (Gibson & Walk, 1960), is learned quickly after infants have some experience crawling (Campos et al., 1978). Apparently, infants' spatial knowledge increases after they begin moving around independently because they experience so many different spatial orientations (Acredolo, 1978; Adolf, 1997).

Other studies indicate that there can be a change in social relationships as infants become more mobile. For example, researchers have found that some parents increase both positive and negative statements to babies as they begin to walk (Biringen et al., 1995). As we saw in the doctor's office episode with Sarah, her mother scolded her mildly about climbing up on a chair and fiddling with the blood-pressure cuff. In contrast, not a word of reprimand was directed toward her not-yet-mobile, 6-week-old sister, Sabrina.

A study designed specifically to probe the effects of locomotion on other behavior involved the use of mechanical walkers (Gustafson, 1984). Babies who were not yet crawling independently were placed in a walker in a laboratory equipped with several wall posters, a popular "activity center" toy mounted on the back of a chair, and toys in a pan on a shelf. Babies were observed to see how much they traveled around the room; what they looked at and for how long; what objects they manipulated and how they manipulated them; and how much they vocalized, smiled, gestured, or fussed.

Babies traveled much more when in the walkers than when out of them. They entered more areas of the playroom and approached the activity center and the adults more often (their parents, as well as a research assistant, were present). They looked more at the people and at non-toy aspects of the room (e.g., wall posters) when in the walkers. They also smiled more and directed more vocalizations toward adults.

In this study, Gustafson (1984) showed that the ability to move around independently affects babies' social interactions, language development, and cognitive and perceptual development. Other researchers have wondered if there are similarly profound effects on development of infants' increasing ability to explore objects with their hands.

The Effects of Infant Object Manipulation on Perceptual and Cognitive Development

The ability to manipulate objects increases tremendously the information and knowledge gained by an infant, thus providing a potentially important support for cognitive development. Even before they develop the ability to reach and grasp, infants explore objects that adults place in their hands. (Their grasp reflex allows them to hold the objects.) Recent studies show that exploration of objects held by 2-month-old infants consists largely of oral contact. But by 3 or 4 months of age, infants begin to inspect visually the objects they hold before moving them to their mouths. In fact, they move objects back and forth between the visual field and the mouth. Also at about 4 months of age, infants finger objects—one hand holds or supports an object, while the fingers of the other hand explore it (Karniol, 1989; Rochat, 1989). This maneuver surely provides considerable information to the infant.

Infants also use a wide range of other actions to explore objects they hold. They dangle, squeeze, wave, bang, drop, scratch, and pull objects, and they pass them from one hand to the other. They also adapt their manipulations to the properties of the objects they are offered. For example, they switch textured objects more than nontextured objects from hand to hand. They also wave objects more if they make a sound. They tend to dangle objects more if they have something such as a tail to hold onto (Palmer, 1989).

Bushnell and Boudreau (1993) suggest that there is a relationship between object manipulation and the develop-

Parental criticism of their toddler's exercise of new locomotor skills should be supportive and informative so as to teach the child that, in the long run, he or she is capable of making appropriate autonomous choices. (*Source:* © James P. Blair/ Corbis)

ment of **haptic perception** (i.e., obtaining information from handling objects versus looking at them). Properties such as temperature, hardness, texture, weight, and the contours of shape are obtained by haptic perception. Bushnell and Boudreau have hypothesized that specific hand movements are required for infants to obtain certain kinds of information about objects. For example, placing and holding a hand on top of an object provides information about the object's temperature; moving the fingers back and forth over the surface of an object provides information about texture. Pressing the object provides information about its hardness, and so on. The developmental courses of specific hand movements and various aspects of haptic perception seem to be related, but additional research is needed before concluding that they are causally related. Bushnell and Boudreau think that certain aspects of perceptual and cognitive development might be delayed if motor development is delayed for some reason. "Motor development . . . may serve as a 'control parameter' within the larger system of the whole developing organism" (p. 1007).

This theory has profound implications for child development. It suggests, among other things, that decreases in energy level, which result from malnutrition, have both indirect and direct effects on cognitive development. In other words, poor nutrition delays motor development directly, which, in turn, depresses motor activity and exploration. Second, poor nutrition decreases energy levels, which also depresses exploration and mobility, even if certain motor skills have been acquired by the child. Lower levels of mobility and object manipulation then decrease the child's access to information about the world (Eppler, 1995; Pollitt et al., 1993). In addition, malnutrition directly affects cognitive development because brain growth is hindered and brain chemistry is altered. Recall as well that stimulation alters both the anatomy and chemistry of the brain (Greenough et al., 1987). These alterations no doubt affect the child's ability to take advantage of experiences by moving around in the environment and manipulating objects.

Ensuring Health in the Infant and Toddler

"Oh, my. She's burning up; she's pink all over. Phil, come here!"

"What? What's the matter, Elaine?"

"Get the thermometer out of the medicine cabinet. It's on the top shelf in that little plastic box."

Elaine started to undress Alex, who was still half asleep but beginning to cry. "It's okay. It's okay, honey," Elaine said, as she picked her up. "You're sick. I wondered why you were so fussy this afternoon."

"Here it is. How do we do this?"

"Under her arm," Elaine instructed, as she turned so Phil could reach Alex's right side. "Hold it there for a few minutes."

Fourteen-month-old Alex rested her head on her mother's shoulder. She was not at all her bright, bouncy self. There was not a trace of her typical alertness, or her smile.

"Okay, that's probably long enough. What does it say?"

Phil removed the thermometer from under Alex's arm and held it up to read it. "One hundred five and—"

"Oh, my gosh, and that's under the arm! Get Dr. Eisenberg on the phone. The number is on the wall. Ask if we should go to the emergency room or what. I'm going to give her a dose of Tylenol and then start sponging her down. Her temperature has never been this high."

Dr. Eisenberg instructed Phil to give the age-appropriate dose of infant Tylenol to Alex and to sponge her down for a few minutes. "Then take her in to the office. Dr. Katz is on duty. I'll call in to tell her you are on your way. It's probably nothing more than the virus that's going around, and she'll be better in a few hours. Kids can spike a high fever, but it doesn't necessarily mean there's something serious going on."

Elaine and Phil's experience is very familiar to most parents. Children get sick and run high fevers. Parents become alarmed. Elaine could hardly believe how scared she had felt the evening before as she watched Alex play the next day. "They sure bounce back," she laughed to herself. "I shouldn't have panicked."

Children are actually relatively healthy during their first 2 years of life. In fact, they have fewer illnesses at this time than at any other time during childhood. Good health during the first 6 months is due in part to the passive immunity a baby gains from the mother in utero. Breast-fed infants gain additional immunity because breast milk carries the mother's antibodies. Young infants' low illness rate is also due to their relatively low exposure to other children and to people in general. Compared to preschoolers and school-age children, infants usually are not out and around in the world very much.

Whenever exposure to groups of other children occurs, children suffer from an increase in respiratory infections. Such infections are most likely when children are first exposed to many other children and have not yet built up their own immunities (Hurwitz et al., 1991). Of course, sharing toys in preschools and in play groups makes contagion more likely.

When children under 2 years of age do get sick, the illness can be more serious than illnesses in older children, mainly because of the baby's small body. Infants have narrow air passages that can easily become blocked from respiratory infections, and they **dehydrate**—lose water rapidly—when they vomit or have diarrhea. These conditions require careful monitoring and prompt medical attention, especially in young infants.

Common Childhood Diseases

Childhood physical disorders are typically grouped into four categories: (1) respiratory (colds, bronchitis, tonsillitis, and so on); (2) communicable (mumps, German

RESEARCH

CLOSE-UP   *Sudden Infant Death Syndrome*

Probably nothing fills parents with more dread than the thought of something terrible happening to their baby. This fear becomes reality in **sudden infant death syndrome** (**SIDS**). In the 1980s, roughly 1.5 out of every 1,000 infants died of SIDS in the United States. The rate declined over the first half of the last decade to 0.84 of every 1,000 infants in 1995 (Weese-Mayer, 1998). Still, in the United States this disease is the major killer of infants between the ages of 1 and 12 months.

The Mystery of SIDS

SIDS usually strikes infants between 2 and 4 months of age, at night, while they are asleep. The mystery of the disease is that it suddenly strikes apparently healthy infants (Kelly & Shannon, 1982). Prolonged apnea—periods when breathing stops—are associated with increased risk for SIDS, although it is not clear what causes the apnea in these infants (Freed et al., 1994). SIDS has been a "diagnosis of exclusion"; it is given as the cause of a particular death when no other disorder can be found. One hypothesized cause is some abnormality in the central nervous system's regulation of breathing during sleep (Obonai et al., 1998). These abnormalities, according to some specialists, are accompanied by heart arrhythmias (Freed, 1999).

Some additional research suggests that the swallowing reflex, and its coordination with breathing, is controlled by different receptors in different sleep positions, and that a collection of fluid in the larynx sets in motion a series of reactions in the very young infant when fluid is not cleared properly (Jeffrey et al., 1999).

Even though researchers do not know the cause of SIDS, they know some factors that predict which infants are at higher risk than others for the disease. These risk factors have been determined by analyzing characteristics of previous SIDS victims (Freed, 1999; Grether & Schulman, 1989; Guntheroth et al., 1990). Infants in the following groups are at increased risk:

- Infants of mothers less than 20 years of age
- Infants whose mothers smoke cigarettes
- Infants whose mothers abuse narcotic drugs
- Premature infants
- Small-for-date infants (full term, but low birth weight)
- Infants who are twins or triplets
- Infants with a sibling who died of SIDS
- Male infants who also have some of the above risk factors

Apnea Monitoring

High-risk infants may be monitored for sleep apnea at the hospital or at home. Short periods of apnea are common in all infants, but prolonged periods are not. SIDS victims occasionally have experienced prolonged periods of apnea before the actual SIDS event (Ariagno & Glutzbach, 1996). The monitor is attached to the infant during periods of sleep. If the infant stops breathing, an alarm sounds to alert parents, who then resuscitate the infant. Monitoring has been associated with decreased risk of SIDS (Freed at al., 1994).

The Association between Infant Sleep Position and SIDS

In 1992, a task force established by the American Academy of Pediatrics recommended that infants not be placed prone (on their stomachs) to sleep. This recommendation was based on the findings of several studies (Engleberts & de-Jong, 1990; Freed et al., 1994). Specifically, a higher incidence of SIDS was found among infants placed in the prone position to sleep. Subsequent studies conducted in the United States have shown a 30 percent reduction in SIDS deaths since recommendations to place infants on their backs to sleep have been in effect (Maugh, 1996).

One study, which reports a concerted effort to educate parents about the hazard of prone placement, has reported even better results. In this small but impressive study (Skadberg et al., 1998), one county in Norway was examined before and after parent education regarding prone placement in January 1990. The SIDS rate dropped from 3.5/1000 in the period 1987–1989 to 1.6/1,000 in the period 1990–1992. It dropped further to 0.3/1,000 in the period 1993–1995. Of the 6 deaths reported in 1993–1995, 5 infants were found in the prone position. The authors noted that infants of an age of particular risk for SIDS frequently spontaneously turn from side to prone. They also noted that babies commonly slip under bedding during sleep, and this is thought to be another risk factor for SIDS, particularly because soft bedding favors rebreathing of exhaled gases (Kemp et al., 1998).

The data from Skadberg and colleagues (1998) suggest a 10-fold decrease in SIDS possibly associated with the intervention program to avoid prone sleeping. This level of decrease is relatively consistent with results presented by Ariagno and Glotzbach (1996), who describe the increase in relative risk of SIDS associated with using the prone sleeping position to be 3.5- to 9.3-fold. Both Skadberg's limited data and Ariagno and Glotzbach's risk analysis suggest the importance of avoiding the prone position unless it is recommended by a physician because of another medical condition.

measles, whooping cough, and so on); (3) gastrointestinal (those affecting the stomach and intestines to cause vomiting and diarrhea); and (4) accidents. (For a discussion of a disease that does not fit one of these categories, but is largely a mystery, see the Research Close-Up: Sudden Infant Death Syndrome.)

Immunization against Childhood Diseases

Children today are immunized against many communicable diseases. The DPT immunization protects against diphtheria (an upper respiratory illness), tetanus (an infection causing contraction of facial muscles), and pertussis (an upper respiratory illness, commonly known as whooping cough). Another immunization (MMR) contains vaccines that protect children against measles, mumps, and rubella. Children are also immunized against polio and *Haemophilus influenzae* type B, the organism primarily responsible for meningitis. A vaccine against chicken pox has also become available and is now being added to the routine series of immunizations children receive.

Immunizations are given during regular checkups at 2 months, 4 months, 6 months, and 1 year. "Booster" shots and a shot for influenza type B are given at 18 months and again when the child is 5 years old. An additional booster against rubella is now given to children when they are in the seventh or eighth grade, unless their serum level of antibodies against measles demonstrates immunity. Children (and adults) should receive a tetanus booster about every 10 years.

CHILDHOOD IMMUNIZATION PROGRAMS   In 1962, the first federal assistance for childhood immunizations was provided by the Vaccine Assistance Act. Funds were targeted specifically to children in rural areas who were not receiving immunizations as part of school-based immunization programs (Goldberg, 1995). The funds were not continued under this act in 1968, but Congress appropriated other monies to help states control communicable diseases and provide immunizations. Then, in the late 1970s, concern increased because too many children were not being immunized (as many as 65 percent of low-income children were not receiving their full series). A federally funded program, the Childhood Immunization Initiative, was begun to increase the number of children under 5 years of age who were immunized. Within a few years, less than 10 percent of children lacked immunizations (Bumpers, 1984). Since then, many states have passed laws requiring that children be immunized before they are permitted to attend child care, preschool, or elementary school.

According to a survey conducted between 1996 and 1997, about 78 percent of children in the United States are immunized against polio, diphtheria, tetanus, measles, mumps, and rubella. Among poor urban children, however, the rate can be lower (Altemeier, 1998). Pediatricians are encouraged to be especially proactive in helping to ensure immunization among children who are at higher risk for low immunization rates. These are children whose mothers have a high school education or less and who move frequently (Miller et al., 1994). An incentive tied to distribution of foods in the WIC program has been effective in increasing rates of immunization among this population (Goldberg, 1995).

IMMUNIZATION SAFETY   Although we refer to them as common, childhood diseases can be serious and costly. When complications arise, they can cause permanent disabilities and death. Public health officials are anxious for as many children as possible to be immunized so that the spread of infectious diseases is controlled. Some parents resist having their children immunized. For example, in 1989–1991, the low rate of immunization among some preschoolers resulted in a dramatic increase in measles among preschoolers (Miller et al., 1994).

Although some parents do not have their children immunized because of religious beliefs, other parents have concerns about the safety of vaccines. This concern is based on the fact that a child can contract the disease itself from the vaccine. This outcome is extremely rare, but this concern has prompted a change from the use of live (attentuated) vaccine to the use of inactivated (dead) polio virus vaccine (Prevots & Strebel, 1997). Children's reactions to vaccines usually consist of fever, headache, nausea, and other flulike symptoms, which occur as the body begins to develop antibodies toward the diseases against which the immunizations protect. As troublesome as these risks can be, immunizations are quite safe, especially when viewed in terms of actual probability of contracting the disease from the vaccine.

REDUCING OTHER DISEASES   Many diseases, such as the common cold, are caused by viruses and cannot yet be prevented by immunizations. Various gastrointestinal diseases also sometimes afflict children. These can also be caused by a virus, but other organisms cause them too. Control of most serious gastrointestinal diseases depends on good personal hygiene, especially hand-washing, and on proper handling of food (e.g., keeping perishables properly refrigerated and cooking ground meats and chicken thoroughly).

Control of diseases in child-care settings is discussed in Knowledge in Action: Health—Keeping Children Healthy in Child-Care and Preschool Programs, in chapter 8.

Feeding and Toilet Training during Infancy and Toddlerhood

In addition to the typical diseases we have already discussed, toddlers face two other health-related situations: feeding and toilet training. How these aspects of child care are handled can have long-range consequences for a child's well-being.

Feeding the Toddler   As noted earlier, appetite begins to wane by 2 years of age because children are growing more slowly than they grew in early infancy. What children eat becomes especially important because they eat relatively little. Not surprisingly, children eat less food after they have eaten a food that is "energy dense" (i.e., contains a high concentration of calories in the form of fat) than after the same amount of less energy-dense food (Birch & Fisher, 1995). This means that a child who snacks on fat-rich cookies or crackers before a meal can be expected to eat less at mealtime than a child who snacks on apple or orange slices. Thus, parents and other caregivers would be wise to offer nutritious snacks so that the child's nutritional health can be maintained. This is especially true for the 24 percent of 2-year-olds reported to have problems with feeding ("pickiness" about eating) (Howard, 1996).

In addition to rejection of food due to decreased appetite, toddlers often reject new foods simply because they are new. This situation does not arise during infancy, especially at first, because young babies drink only milk. Later in

With parental encouragement, children will usually continue to try new foods until they develop a taste for them. (*Source:* © David Young Wolff/Tony Stone Images)

infancy, parents begin to offer a wider variety of foods. Later still, after children have a full set of teeth, they typically eat at the family dinner table, where little consideration may be given to their food preferences. It is during this time that a child can develop a solid reputation as a picky eater.

When toddlers resist eating new foods, parents sometimes bribe them ("You may have a cookie if you eat all of these carrots"). Sometimes they force them to eat ("Open up. You are going to eat all of these carrots even if I have to feed them to you myself!") Sometimes they cajole them ("Open wide—the train is going into the tunnel!"). But rewards do not prod children into forming good eating habits, nor is punishment effective.

Children who are rewarded with desserts or other things for eating their food later show low preference for exactly the foods they were made to eat to obtain the rewards. When forced to eat foods they say they do not like, children often end up liking *less* the very foods parents want them to like the most (Birch & Fisher, 1995). How, then, can children be helped to develop good eating habits?

Luckily, children do expand the range of foods they prefer if they are exposed repeatedly to new foods over a period of time. The most frequent and effective setting for this exposure is the family dinner table, where parents themselves eat a variety of foods and offer a small taste of new things to children. Typically, children initially show aversion to almost any new food, unless it is sweet (this is the one preference that seems to be innate). This reaction to new foods probably was important long ago when humans located food in the wild, because many plants that humans might have nibbled on to quell a pang of hunger could have been toxic. A natural inclination to eat little of something new until a taste for it had been developed helped to ensure that humans did not consume large amounts of some unknown—and toxic—substance (Birch & Fisher, 1995).

Because of the natural aversion to new foods that is part of our evolutionary history, parents should expect children to reject new foods when they first taste them. But parents can continue to make the new foods available and can encourage children to take just a little taste (even a sniff and a lick can count!). One contributor to a pediatric textbook (Howard, 1996, p. 103) states that "it takes more than 10 to 15 tasting exposures to increase the likelihood that a child will eat a previously rejected food." Parents should, of course, eat the foods themselves. Children will usually continue to try new foods; in time, they will develop a taste for them, gradually broadening the range of foods they prefer (Birch & Fisher, 1995).

One interesting finding from studies of the development of children's food preferences is that children who are breast-fed develop a taste for new foods faster than children who are bottle-fed (Sullivan & Birch, 1994). Apparently, a mother's milk changes in flavor, depending on variations in her diet. Thus, a breast-fed infant experiences a much wider range of tastes during early infancy than does a formula-fed infant (Mennella & Beauchamp, 1991). Because this experience with a variety of tastes early in life apparently familiarizes the child with a range of new tastes, a breast-fed baby is later more accepting of new foods.

Toilet Training   In young infants, the **sphincter muscle** of the rectum or bladder relaxes reflexively, permitting the contents to escape. As infants mature physically, neurologically, and socially, they learn to inhibit these reflexive actions. This control requires an awareness of the sensations associated with a full rectum or bladder, which depends both on maturation of the cerebral cortex and socialization to pay attention to these sensations. The cephalocaudal order of development applies to sensory, as well as to motor, areas of the brain. Sensory development of the leg area in the brain is not fully achieved until age 2 or even a little later (Tanner, 1990).

Humane and systematic toilet training requires patience on the part of both child and parent. (*Source:* © Laura Dwight/ Photo Edit)

Sometime before the age of 2, most toddlers begin to be aware of the feeling of a full bladder. But the bladder still releases urine reflexively in children of this age. A child this young usually cannot retain urine nor anticipate the need to use the toilet. By about age 3, and sometimes earlier for girls, children become able to retain urine for a short period of time after sensing a full bladder. Children can now begin to anticipate the need to use the toilet, and parents or caregivers can help them get there in time. This is when most parents start to teach their children how to use the toilet.

Children usually do not achieve nighttime dryness until 6–12 months after daytime bladder control has been achieved. Many 4- and 5-year-olds still wet the bed during the night, though most do so fairly infrequently (Verhulst et al., 1985). The frequent inability to control bladder function during the night after age 4 is known as **enuresis**. From 15 to 20 percent of 5-year-olds and 5 percent of 10-year-olds still wet the bed, with boys having more difficulty than girls. Some children's sleep patterns prevent them from waking up to go to the bathroom at night. Other children may have a genetic predisposition toward immaturity in bladder control (Doleys & Dolce, 1982).

Some children—one or two out of every one hundred 4-year-olds—have trouble gaining bowel control, a difficulty known as **encopresis**. This problem, again more common in boys than in girls, can have serious consequences and requires medical attention to help the child achieve appropriate control (Bishop & Nowicki, 1999; Parker, 1999).

knowledge *in action*

HEALTH/SAFETY

Preventing Accidents

As infants and toddlers gain mobility, they are at increased risk for sustaining injuries from accidents. Keeping an infant or toddler safe requires making adaptations in the environment and keeping a close eye on the child. Many steps can be taken to make the environment safe for young children.

■ Never leave a baby unattended on a bed, on a table, or in a crib with the side down. Even newborns can move reflexively and plunge over the edge.

■ Place gates at the tops and bottoms of stairs and in doorways to areas that are off-limits to children.

■ Place barriers around heating stoves, floor grates, and radiators. Babies might be able to roll close enough to touch a hot surface but then not be able to move away.

■ Don't use tablecloths. Babies might pull themselves up on tablecloths and can pull dishes and hot food down on themselves.

■ Store medicine in locked cabinets or well out of a child's reach. Buy medications in the smallest available quantity. Keep purses, which may contain medications and other toxic substances, out of children's reach.

■ Strap infants and toddlers into government-tested car seats when driving them in cars. Never hold a child in your lap while a car is moving. In the event of an accident, holding on to a 10-pound infant in a car going 30 miles per hour requires the same strength needed to lift a 300-pound weight. If you are not wearing a seat belt and are holding an infant, your body will continue to move forward at the speed the car was moving before impact. The infant would be crushed between your body and the interior of the car (Robertson, 1985).

■ Keep small objects out of reach of children under 3, and do not feed them raw carrots, nuts, popcorn, or hard candy. These items are difficult to chew, and large, hard pieces can get caught in the airway.

■ Inspect toys carefully for small parts that could come loose and be put in the mouth. Many toys are labeled to indicate small parts unsuitable for children under the age of 3. Also, do not give balloons to young children. Balloons break when children bite them, and the explosion can force a piece of the balloon into the child's throat.

■ Inspect hand-me-down furniture to make sure it is free of lead-based paint and other hazards, such as spaces where a young child's head could become stuck.

■ Do not put babies to bed wearing jackets with drawstring hoods. The strings could strangle them. Also, cut or tie up high cords hanging from window blinds. Move a child's crib away from windows where cords or curtains might be within reach.

■ Do not use talcum powder. It contains a substance that damages the lungs.

■ Keep cleaning solvents, laundry detergents, furniture polishes, and all other toxic substances in locked cabinets or in places inaccessible to infants and toddlers.

■ Never leave buckets of water, such as one used to mop floors or wash a car, where a baby can reach it. Infants lean over head first, can get stuck, and can drown. Never leave a baby or young child unattended in a bathtub or sink.

■ Keep the number of the poison control center near your telephone. In the event that an infant in your care ingests a substance you think might be harmful, call the poison center immediately for expert information about steps to take.

■ Keep a bottle of ipecac syrup on hand. Use it to induce vomiting in the event of accidental poisoning, but do not use it if the child has ingested a caustic substance. These products will burn the esophagus more if they pass through it again. In these cases, it is better to dilute and neutralize the substance by giving the child something to drink. (A poison control center can provide specific information.)

■ Use covers on electrical outlets. Move floor lamps to out-of-the-way places where infants will not attempt to use them as support for pulling themselves up to stand.

KEY POINTS

How Do They Grow?

■ Babies triple their birth weight by their first birthday and then grow more slowly in their second and third years. Length also increases rapidly at first and then proceeds at a slower rate.

■ Variations in growth among different babies can result from either genetic or nutritional factors. Babies whose growth was limited in the prenatal period will catch up to their genetic potential after they are born, given adequate nutrition. Infants who genetically were intended to be smaller can have a slower rate of growth after birth if uterine conditions had been especially supportive of prenatal growth.

- Failure-to-thrive is slow growth due to lack of proper caregiving, not slow growth due to disease conditions or a normal slowing due to a child's genetic inheritance.

- As the growth rate slows down, toddlers' appetites diminish. They begin to eat less.

- Body tissue grows and changes in a particular pattern. Subcutaneous fat accumulates rapidly in the first 9 months, giving babies their rounded look; muscle fibers lose water and gain in salt and protein, making them stronger; and soft, cartilaginous bones begin to ossify, providing the support structure needed for walking. The fontanelles on the top of the head are fully closed by the time children are about 2 years old.

- Teething begins at about 7 months, and most babies have their full set of 20 deciduous teeth by the time they are 3 years old. A lifetime of healthy teeth can begin in toddlerhood with proper brushing, a good diet, fluoride treatments, and regular trips to the dentist.

- The brain is about one quarter of its adult weight at birth. The "brain growth spurt," during which more than half of the adult brain weight is achieved, takes place between the last 3 months of prenatal life and the first year and a half of postnatal life. The brain reaches 90 percent of its full adult weight by the time the child is 5 years old.

- Adequate nutrition, both prenatally and postnatally, is crucial to proper brain growth and functioning, as is environmental stimulation during infancy.

- Different parts of the brain mature at different times. This pattern of maturing influences motor development.

- The proportion of fat to muscle and bone decreases in the second and third years of life, making toddlers look leaner than younger infants. But because of rapid growth and undeveloped abdominal muscles, toddlers keep their protruding tummies and swayback silhouettes until they are about 4 years old.

- Toddlers are still top-heavy, although not as much as infants. Their body proportions cause them to set their feet wide apart when walking and to walk with quick, short steps. They have a characteristic "toddle."

Development of Motor Abilities

- Motor development proceeds in two directions: (1) from the center of the body out to the fingers, known as proximodistal development; and (2) from the top of the body downward, known as cephalocaudal development.

- Proximodistal development results in reaching and grasping with the hands and fingers. At first, babies swipe at objects; later they reach and grasp. Once babies acquire the pincer grasp (at about 9 months), they can pick up tiny objects. After they lose the palmar reflex, at about 1 year, they can voluntarily let objects go, which allows them to develop skill in building a tower of blocks, for example.

- Although the emergence of reaching and grasping is influenced considerably by maturation, experience plays a part as well. Research has shown that babies develop these skills earlier if there are stimulating objects in the environment that they want to grasp. Research also indicates that blind babies reach motor milestones later than sighted infants, due to a lack of information about objects and their location in the world.

- When babies have mastered standing up and controlling their leg muscles, they can learn to walk. They reach all developmental milestones somewhat earlier than babies did years ago, except for the ability to roll over.

- Like fine motor development, locomotor development is influenced by both biological maturation and environmental factors. Stimulation and opportunities to move around are necessary for normal motor development. Delayed motor development in early infancy can be overcome if the environment is improved or adapted to special needs, such as blindness.

- Research has shown that the development of motor skills affects other areas of babies' development and experience, including their social interactions, language development, and cognitive and perceptual development.

Ensuring Health in the Infant and Toddler

- Infants and toddlers are relatively healthy, but they can suffer from a variety of illnesses.

- Immunizations can protect infants and toddlers from many communicable diseases. Immunizations are very safe, especially when risks of the diseases they protect against are considered.

- Toddlers have little appetite because their growth rate has slowed considerably. They also often reject new foods.

- Offering a nutritious selection of foods to toddlers is important. Fat-rich foods satisfy appetite quickly, without providing adequate nutrition.

- Neither rewarding children for eating certain foods nor forcing them to eat are effective ways to help them develop good eating habits. Offering a wide variety of foods to children, and encouraging them to take a little taste, works in the long run to develop preferences for a wide range of foods.

■ Breast-fed children accept new foods better than do formula-fed children, apparently because breast milk varies in flavor, depending on the mother's diet.

■ Toddlers can become toilet trained only after a certain level of neurological development has been reached. Toddlers must gain control of the sphincter muscles of the bladder and bowel to achieve toilet training.

■ Bowel control is usually achieved before bladder control. Girls are typically toilet trained earlier than boys, at about age 2½. Boys usually aren't ready until about age 3. Night control is not achieved until after daytime control, even a year or more later in some children.

■ When the child is ready, toilet training will take several months, with many accidents and relapses. For some children it takes longer. Some have considerable difficulty with staying dry during the night or with establishing bowel control.

GLOSSARY

center of gravity: the point around which body weight is evenly distributed (p. 127)

cephalocaudal trend: motor development that proceeds from the head to the tail or feet (p. 128)

dehydrate: to lose water from the body through vomiting, diarrhea, or perspiration caused by extreme heat or high fever (p. 142)

ectoderm: layer of cells formed in the zygote from which the skin and nervous system will be formed (p. 123)

encopresis: difficulty in establishing appropriate bowel control (p. 147)

enuresis: frequent failure to control the bladder during the night after the age of 4 especially during the night (p. 147)

failure-to-thrive: a slower-than-normal rate of growth due to feeding or problems with caregiving (p. 120)

fine motor development: development of motor skill in the hands (p. 128)

glial cells: cells in the brain that produce a fatty subtance called myelin (p. 124)

haptic perception: getting information by handling objects (p. 141)

myelination: the process by which nerve cells become encased in a fatty sheath of myelin (p. 124)

neurons: nerve cells (p. 124)

ossification: the process of mineral deposition in cartilage that changes it to bone (p. 121)

pincer grasp: a grasp involving the index finger and the thumb (p. 129)

proximodistal trend: motor development that proceeds from the center of the body outward to the hands (p. 128)

shaken baby syndrome (SBS): harmful effects suffered by a baby who is shaken, including bleeding, seizures, and even death (p. 125)

sphincter muscle: a circular muscle found at the end of the rectum and at the opening of the bladder that opens reflexively until the child learns to control it (p. 146)

sudden infant death syndrome (SIDS): The sudden death which occurs while an infant is sleeping (p. 143)

synapse: the narrow space between neurons across which signals pass, prompting neurons to fire (p. 124)

SUGGESTIONS FOR FURTHER READING

Cratty, B. J. (1986). *Perceptual and motor development in infants and children* (3rd ed.). Englewood Cliffs, NJ: Prentice-Hall. This book contains detailed information about early brain growth, how brain development affects movement capability, the reflexes found in infants, and the factors that affect movement development.

Goldfield, E. C. (1995). *Emergent forms: Origins and early development of human action and perception.* New York: Oxford University Press. This book describes a contemporary ecological, dynamic systems, and developmental theory of human action systems, and applies the theory to locomotion and manual activity.

Johnson, R. V. (1994). *The Mayo Clinic complete book of pregnancy and baby's first year.* New York: Morrow. This book provides much good information about physical development during the first year, as well as information about nutrition, immunizations, and so on.

Kalverboer, A. F., Hopkins, B., & Geuze, R. (Eds.) (1993). *Motor development in early and later childhood: Longitudinal approaches.* New York: Cambridge University Press. An interdisciplinary statement of the fundamental principles for the development of motor skills, including risk factors for adaptive motor development. Disciplines represented in the 21 chapters include pediatrics, neurology, ethology, and psychology.

Tanner, J. M. (1990). *Fetus into man: Physical growth from conception to maturity* (2nd ed.). Cambridge, MA: Harvard University Press. Here is another thorough discussion of physical growth at all stages of life.

Perceptual and Cognitive Development in Infants and Toddlers

EIGHT-MONTH-OLD ERIC AND his mother, Gillian, had just arrived at a friend's house. As Gillian settled into a chair in her friend's living room, she placed her purse upright on the floor and dropped her large set of keys into it. They fell down and were not visible from the open top of the purse. Next, she placed Eric on the floor. He liked to sit up by himself and also to turn onto his tummy and push himself up on his hands and knees. Before long, Eric grabbed the purse and removed the set of keys. He began chewing on them and then held them in one hand as he put his hands and knees to the floor.

"That's a bit dangerous, Eric," said his mother as she removed the keys from his hand and put them back in the purse. "Those keys are kind of sharp at the end, and you're going to poke your hand with them, before you know it. You won't like that!"

Soon, Eric had set himself upright again near the purse, and he began reaching to get the keys.

"You are persistent, aren't you?" said his mother, as she took the keys out of his hands once again. This time, rather than put them back in the purse, she put them under a pillow on the seat of her chair. Eric tracked the keys' path as they moved from his hand to under the pillow, but then he looked away and began rubbing his hand against the textured fabric on the side of the chair. Then he got on his tummy again and pushed himself up on his hands and knees. From this vantage point, he spotted the fringed edges of a rug. He dropped down to his tummy to feel it with both hands. He seemed to have lost interest in the keys.

think about it

Why did Eric stop pursuing the keys once they were under the pillow? It wasn't the keys' new physical location that stopped him. He had been pulling himself up to stand for a couple of weeks and thus could have managed to get into position to reach beneath the pillow. Why didn't he? Had he simply gotten the message from his mother that he wasn't to play with the keys? Or might he have been completely puzzled about where they were? If Eric was puzzled when his mother hid the keys under the pillow, why wasn't he puzzled when he couldn't see them inside his mother's purse? Might it be more difficult for a baby to understand the spatial relationship *under* than to understand the relationship *inside*?

The discussion of infant cognition in this chapter will shed some light on the different problems presented by keys placed in these two positions. But before we discuss problem solving and other examples of infant cognition, we will discuss how young infants perceive the world of objects. Recall that in chapter 3 we discussed the basic sensory capacities of the newborn infant—sight, sound, smell, taste, and touch. We also discussed the neonate's preferences for viewing pattern and contrast. In this chapter, we start with a discussion of infant **visual perception**—the descriptions of the world that the infant's brain presents or allows. Then we discuss how infants process or manipulate perceptual information and the knowledge they construct as a result of mental activity. **Cognition,** which involves thinking or reasoning of one kind or another, enables the infant to adapt to the world and to solve problems. As we shall see, the infant is very busy making sense of the world.

Infant Visual Perception

We know that babies can see at birth and that they prefer to look at high-contrast patterns rather than at plain displays. We also know that vision improves rapidly over the course of the first few months of life. But does the infant see a world of separate objects arranged coherently in space, as adults do, or does the world appear at first to be a mass of undifferentiated and constantly changing images? Do infants perceive the size of an object as remaining the same, no matter whether the object is close or far away? Do they know that a bicycle parked behind a telephone pole on the street is one bicycle, rather than two separate wheels with one attached to a set of handlebars?

In this section, we describe what is known about the infant's ability to discern objects and maintain their size and shape constancy, once they have been detected. We also review what scientists have been able to learn about infants' perception of faces.

Object Perception

Suppose that there is a desk in the room. On top of it sits a computer, a stapler, a tape dispenser, a telephone, and a lamp. Would an infant see these individual items as we see them? Or would the objects we see as separate from the desk appear to an infant to be part of the desk itself?

Because different objects are made out of different materials and because they also differ very often in color and texture, each reflects light somewhat differently. These variations in reflected light mark object boundaries or edges, and this information allows adults to perceive objects as separate units in the world, even when the objects touch each other (Kellman & Arterberry, 1998).

Infants younger than 9 months of age cannot detect object boundaries by using only surface information, although they can use two other kinds of information. If they see one object move while another remains stationary, they judge that these are two different objects. Motion catches the attention of even a newborn infant, as we learned in chapter 3. Infants are also helped to make this judgment if they can see objects arranged in front of or behind each other, so that depth cues are present (Spelke et al., 1993; von Hofsten & Spelke, 1985). Depth cues are salient to infants by the time they are a few months old. (See Research Close-Up: Depth Perception.)

Adults also understand that what they might see as separate images are actually two parts of just one thing. A partially occluded object, such as the bicycle parked behind a telephone pole, is a good example of this situation. An adult would conclude that one object, rather than two, is present, even though the continuity of the two parts cannot actually be observed. This understanding is called **object unity.** What information is used to detect object unity?

Adults, of course, have seen a bicycle in its entirety. Knowledge obtained from direct experience helps adults judge that two such discontinuous images are actually the two ends of one continuous object. But what do adults do when they have no direct knowledge of an object and its specific parts? Can they use perceptual clues to judge whether two images are two different objects or simply two different parts of the same one? Apparently they can.

First, if boundaries of the parts have similar spatial orientations, adults are likely to think they belong to one object rather than two. The height of the two wheels of

---

RESEARCH

CLOSE-UP   *Depth Perception*

Because we perceive depth, we know how far away things are, and we understand that one plane can drop to another. Without depth perception, we might tumble down stairs, fail to judge how much time we have to pass a car on the highway, or miss catching a baseball that is hurtling toward us. Are we born with the ability to make judgments of depth, or do we develop this ability?

Appreciation of Depth

In the classic study of this question, babies who were 6 to 14 months old were placed on a special surface that appeared "shallow" on one side and "deep" on the other (Gibson & Walk, 1960). (See Figure 5.1.) Because the deep side was covered with Plexiglas, it was possible for babies to crawl across to the side of the apparent cliff without falling over an edge. Babies were first placed on the shallow side of the cliff apparatus. Their mothers were instructed to stand on the far edge of the deep side and to encourage them to crawl across it to reach them. But babies would not crawl across the deep side, even though they could feel with their hands the supporting glass on top of the drop-off. It was obvious that they perceived the drop and were afraid of it.

Gibson concluded on the basis of this experiment that depth perception and fear of cliffs are innate. But the babies she studied were already 6 months old. Perhaps babies developed depth perception during the first 6 months of life. Other researchers used younger infants (all infants in the Gibson and Walk study were already crawling) in additional experiments. They placed them onto either the deep or the shallow side of the visual cliff and measured their heart rates. A difference in the heart rates of infants placed on the shallow versus the deep side would suggest that infants perceive the difference in the depth of the two sides. The researchers found a difference in heart rates in infants who were only 2 months old (Campos et al., 1970).

Although depth perception might be innate, given that 2-month-olds apparently have it, many scientists still think it is not. Scientists have found that infants younger than 3–4 months of age have difficulty using some depth clues, though not all of them. They think that infants might use optical and stereoscopic clues. Optical clues arise as objects at different distances create images of different sizes on the retina. As an object approaches, its image gets bigger and bigger. Infants who are about 4 months of age seem to perceive this change in an object's distance or depth as it moves closer. For example, a baby will try to dodge an oncoming object (or a visual image that appears to the baby to be a solid object) by moving her head as the object approaches (Yonas, 1981). She will also blink, as if antici-

the bicycle, for example, would be quite similar. This observation would lead an adult to think they were the two ends of one object. Second, if surface qualities (color, texture, material) are the same for the two parts, adults are likely to think they are looking at one object rather than at two. Because the materials (metal, spokes, rubber tire) do not change from one end of the bicycle to the other, adults are likely to conclude that there is just one object sitting behind the telephone pole. Although some objects have very different surface qualities at their two ends (e.g., a floor lamp with a lampshade at one end and a wooden or metal base at the other), many have similar surface qualities from top to bottom or end to end. These similarities provide vital clues for adults. Finally, if one end of the bicycle moves and the other end follows instantaneously, adults are likely to conclude that the appearance of two things is actually one.

As it turns out, infants younger than 1 or 2 months of age cannot use any of these clues. They basically perceive any visible parts of occluded objects as different objects entirely. It is somewhat surprising that young infants cannot take advantage of motion clues to make object unity judgments because we know that even newborns are sensitive to motion. (Recall that moving objects attract a newborn's attention.) Apparently, though able to detect motion, infants younger than 2 months of age do not notice the direction in which two objects are moving or that their movements are simultaneous (Johnson & Anslin, 1995). Infants who are older than

---

pating a collision with the oncoming object. Blink reactions reliably indicate depth perception earlier than do head-dodging reactions. Based on eye-blink data, it appears that infants might perceive depth based on optical cues as early as about 1 month of age (Kellman & Banks, 1998).

Stereoscopic cues for depth depend on the convergence of the two eyes on the same target. Objects that are placed at different distances, but in the same visual display, will cause disparity calculations—differences in images based on their different locations. It appears that such cues about the relative positions of objects from foreground to background are available to infants by about 2 to 3 months of age (Held et al., 1980).

Researchers now think that depth perception depends on a variety of clues, including binocular fixation, fused visual images, and stereoscopic information (Yonas & Owsley, 1987) and that the infant makes considerable progress in using a number of depth cues between 2 and 4 months of age. As for the visual cliff, 2-month-olds perceive depth, as noted earlier, but they do not fear it. Fear of cliffs is not present until the infant starts to crawl. Thus, by 9 months of age most infants are reluctant to cross over the cliff—they seem afraid to go over it. The infant becomes fearful of the cliff very quickly after the onset of crawling, perhaps because

the infant's experience quickly demonstrates the value of having support under the feet and hands (Campos et al., 1978).

Perception of Depth in Pictures

Photographs present an interesting situation. Even though all of their images are on the same surface (there is no actual depth to a picture), we perceive the picture as having depth. The overlapping of the objects pictured and variations in their shading guide us in judging that the pictured scene has depth. We also use our knowledge of various objects to judge their sizes in pictures. Do infants perceive photographs similarly?

Infants can use overlapping and familiar size cues by about 7 months of age (Granrud et al., 1985; Granrud & Yonas, 1984), and they can use information from surface features of objects (shading, in this case) by about 9 months of age. Apparently, infants do not need to learn about the nature of pictures from experience with pictures, but rather "see through them" to the objects they depict, using the same clues that they use to judge depth in the three-dimensional world (Gibson, 1979).

Deep side   Shallow side   Glass over pattern surface

Floor pattern seen through glass

FIGURE 5.1

Gibson's visual cliff.

2 months of age, and especially infants within the 3- to 5-month range, can utilize motion clues quite well to detect object unity, although their object unity judgments are better when the object parts are close rather than far apart (Kellman & Spelke, 1983; Van de Walle & Spelke, 1996). Additionally, up until about 6 months of age, infants can use motion information only if the two parts move together in a back-and-forth motion. When two parts spin around behind a screen and thus appear alternately above and below and on each side of it, infants under 6 months of age do not perceive the parts as belonging to the same object (Eizenman & Bertenthal, 1998).

By 7 months of age infants are able to use information about the spatial orientation of the two parts of a partially occluded object (e.g., similarity in height of the two bicycle wheels), and by about 9 months, they can use surface quality information (i.e., variations in light caused by texture, color, and material differences) (Spelke et al., 1993). Scientists do not know if use of these clues depends solely on maturation of some part of the visual cortex or on experience (Kellman & Banks, 1998).

Despite their limitations during the first few months of life, it appears that by about 2 months of age, infants can begin to perceive the world as encompassing many different objects and that they begin to understand that objects remain unified despite appearances that suggest the presence of two objects rather than just one. Infants can use motion clues before they can use surface and spatial information. Infants' object-perception and object-unity detection abilities improve greatly after 6 months of age because at this time they can begin to use multiple sources of information.

Object Constancies

think about it

As the infant begins to perceive that the world contains objects, what constancies or stabilities does the infant assign to them? For example, does the infant think that objects change in size as they move farther away because the image the object casts on the retina gets smaller? Or do they perceive that objects stay the same size, regardless of the variation of the image created by the light reaching the eye? And what happens when an object is turned about in various orientations? Do the different views make the infant think the object actually changes shape? Or does the infant perceive the overall shape of an object as stable, despite seeing variations in its appearance from moment to moment?

As it turns out, **size constancy**—the perception that the size of the object stays the same whether it is moved closer to or farther away—appears to be present from birth. Researchers have drawn this conclusion on the basis of two kinds of information. First of all, newborns perceive that same-sized objects placed at different distances are constant in actual size (although the retinal images of the objects change in size as their actual distance from the baby changes). Second, newborns perceive objects of varying sizes the same as like-sized objects placed at different distances as changing in size.

Shape constancy—perceiving the overall shape of an object as staying the same, regardless of changing views of it—is not present in the newborn. Shape constancy appears fairly early in the first year, however, sometime between 3 and 4 months of age (Kellman & Short, 1987).

Face Perception

The infant's perception of the human face has intrigued both parents and scientists for a long time. Researchers have learned quite a lot over the last few decades about what infants know about the human face, and when they know it. (See the Research Close-Up: The Infant's Perception of the Human Face.)

CLOSE-UP   *The Infant's Perception of the Human Face*

Researchers have tried to answer several questions about infants' perception of the human face. Many studies have focused on finding out *when* a baby recognizes faces and especially when a baby recognizes her own mother's face. And because the face is the source of a great deal of information about emotion, researchers have also wondered when infants can detect various facial expressions and when they begin to understand their meanings. We review some of this research here.

Development of the Concept of a Face

In the Fantz (1963) demonstration of visual preferences in the newborn (chapter 3, p. 97), infants looked at the face longer than at any other stimulus. Apparently infants were attracted to the face simply because it provided a pattern with a fair amount of contrast, not because they recognized it as a face (Easterbrook, 1999). Scientists have concluded this because babies under 2 months of age look as long at facial features that have been scrambled in a drawing of a face as they look at facial features that have been arranged to match how faces look naturally (Haaf, 1974; Haaf & Bell, 1967; Maurer, 1985). (See Figure 5.2.)

Not until about 3 months of age do infants consistently show a preference for naturally arranged, rather than scrambled, facial features. At this age, it is accurate to say that infants have a concept of a face because they know that specific features are located in a specific relationship to each other. It is not surprising that infants show no preference for a natural versus a scrambled arrangement of facial features until about 3 months of age because until about 2 months of age, they do not scan the internal features of figures, including a face. Instead, they scan the edges. (See Figure 5.3.) One-month-olds gaze mostly at the upper hairline or at the lower part of the chin. They look very little at the eyes and even less at the nose and mouth. Two-month-olds, in contrast, fixate on the eyes (Haith et al., 1977).

Interestingly, when babies do begin to scan the internal features of the face, they concentrate first in the region of the eyes, perhaps because of the contrast they provide. For a while, infants behave as if they expect a face to have only eyes—they do not look any longer at a schematic drawing of a face with eyes, mouth, and nose than they look at a face with only eyes. At about 4 months of age, infants expect all of the features to be there, where they belong (Haaf, 1977; Maurer, 1985). By about 5–6 months of age, babies also begin to recognize specific faces, and they show greater recognition of these familiar faces than of their toys (de Haan & Nelson, 1999).

This development seems rather late when compared to mothers' impressions that their newborns recognize them. Of course, many clues other than facial features could be used by an infant to recognize a specific person. As we discussed in chapter 3, an infant can recognize his mother's breast milk by odor, within a matter of days. But could mothers be right in thinking that their babies recognize their faces too? Researchers have tried to find out.

How Newborns Recognize Their Mothers

In one study (Field et al., 1984), the researchers had each infant's mother and a female stranger sit in an apparatus that revealed only their faces. The infant sat in an infant seat from

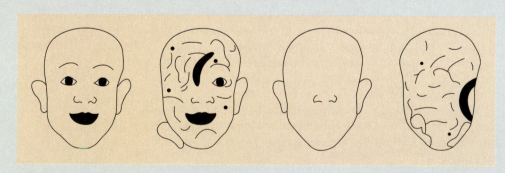

FIGURE 5.2

Faces with and without scrambled features. Babies under 2 months of age will look as long at a face with scrambled features as at a face with features placed properly. Apparently they like to look at faces simply because they contain areas of contrast, not because the infants perceive a face as a face.   (*Source:* "A Facial Dimension in Visual Discrimination by Human Infants" by R. A. Haaf and R. Q. Bell in *Child Development, 38* 1967. Copyright © The Society for Research in Child Development, Inc. Adapted with permission.)

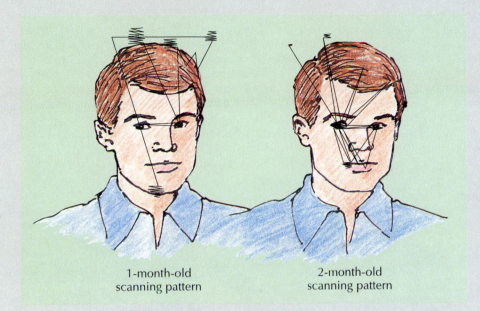

1-month-old
scanning pattern

2-month-old
scanning pattern

FIGURE 5.3

Scanning patterns.   (*Source:* "Infant Perception: Methods of Study" by P. Salapatek in *Infant Perception: From Sensation to Cognition,* L. B. Cohen and P. Salapatek, eds. Adapted by permission of Academic Press.)

which he or she could see both of the women's faces. In this situation, infants were not being held by their mothers, and thus would not have odor cues by which to recognize them. The mothers also remained silent in one condition so that the infant's reaction to the mother's face alone could be determined. Infants just 2 days old distinguished their mother's face from the face of a female stranger.

Other researchers (Walton et al., 1992) thought that changes in expressions, not the discrimination of specific facial features, were what attracted the infant more to the mother's face rather than to the stranger's. To eliminate this possibility, these researchers recorded one image each of the mother's and the stranger's faces on videotape and then used a computer to control changes in each one. Infants in this study could look at the videotape they liked best by sucking to turn on the video of the mother and by stopping their sucking to turn on the video of the stranger. Newborns still showed a preference for the mother's face.

This study might have clinched this issue if its results could have been reconciled with information about infant scanning. Why would infants scan the internal features of their mothers' faces if they do not ordinarily scan the internal features of other faces and patterns? What might infants use to discriminate the mother's face from the face of a stranger if not its internal features?

Some researchers hypothesized that infants might recognize features of the hairline and the outline of the head (Pascalis et al., 1995). They asked mothers and strangers to wear head scarves covering the hairline and the outer edge of the head. Infants did not prefer their mothers' faces under these conditions. Thus, it is not his mother's face but the outer contour of her head that a newborn recognizes.

Recognition of Facial Expressions

Knowledge of facial features helps an infant to distinguish one human face from other faces. Infants also learn how facial features change when people express different emotions. When do infants begin to distinguish faces that express happiness, surprise, fear, and anger? Is it early in infancy or later on?

We should not expect the discrimination of facial features to appear very early in infancy. First, facial features appear somewhat blurred to young infants because they have poor visual acuity. Second, infants' tendencies to fixate on and scan the hairline and chin limits their knowledge of internal feature changes. Not surprisingly, infants do not begin to discriminate different facial expressions until about 4 months of age (C. A. Nelson, 1987). This is about two months after scanning behavior has shifted fixations on the edges or borders of figures to their internal features. Acuity also has improved greatly by this time.

In one study (Kuchuk et al., 1986), 3-month-olds showed a strong preference for smiling faces rather than neutral expressions. Seven-month-olds who had been habituated to different models with a happy face became realerted when presented with a new model who showed a fearful expression (C. A. Nelson, 1987). Other researchers have also found that 7-month-olds can distinguish happy from fearful

(continued)

expressions (Nelson & Dolgin, 1985), and happy expressions from expressions of surprise (Caron et al., 1982).

Of course, the ability to distinguish differences among various facial expressions tells us only that infants can distinguish the different looks of faces on which these expressions are displayed. Infants seem to begin to understand the meaning of parents' expressions sometime late in the first year. Evidence comes from visual cliff studies in which parents were instructed to show different expressions when coaxing their 12-month-old infants to cross the deep side. They had more success when they smiled or looked interested than when they appeared angry or fearful (Sorce et al., 1985). Other evidence of infants' understanding of the meaning of facial expressions comes from studies of social referencing, a process in which an infant looks at the parent's face to read expressions in situations that pose some threat or expose the infant to extreme novelty. Social referencing starts at 9 months of age. (See the discussion of social referencing in chapter 7.)

This 10-month-old is no doubt beginning to learn the meaning of her mother's facial expressions. (*Source:* © David Young Wolff/Tony Stone Images)

Infant Cognitive Development

The difference between perception and cognition is often debated (Haith & Benson, 1998) because it is not always easy to tell the difference. Perception yields descriptions of the world. These are obtained by the structure imposed on sensations coming to the infant's eyes and ears by the sense organs themselves and by the parts of the brain that receive impulses from sensory organs. Cognition, on the other hand, involves the addition of specific meanings to perceptions.

Drawing the line between perception and cognition tends to be based on the methodology used to obtain information from infants. When an infant's looking behavior is used to obtain clues as to the categories an infant forms, the physical knowledge an infant possesses, or the reasoning an infant seems to employ, some researchers hesitate to consider the observed phenomena to be cognitive rather than perceptual. Functional behavior—that is, a child's actions on objects—is thought by these researchers and theorists to be a better indicator of what a child knows and understands about the world (Haith & Benson, 1998).

This section gathers, in a rather large net, several areas of research on perception and cognition in infancy. We start with a review of research on infants' ability to form categories based on their interactions with pictures and model objects. We then consider how infants approach problem solving, with a review of Piaget's sensorimotor view of early development and his work on object permanence and what the infant knows about how the world works. We include a review of some researchers' views on an infant's knowledge about objects in the physical world and their abilities to reason about physical events.

Perceptually Based Categorization in Infants

When infants **categorize** visual stimuli, they recognize similarity across nonidentical instances. For example, all cats are more similar to each other than they are to dogs, even though cats often differ greatly from each other. When infants categorize cats, they notice the similarities among cats despite their differences.

We begin our discussion of infants' ability to form categories with an explanation of the two methodologies researchers use when they study categorization based on perceptual features of animals or human-made artifacts (e.g., furniture or vehicles). Then we describe the details of a few illustrative studies before summarizing what scientists have learned from them.

Methods for Studying Categorization of Visual Stimuli

The method used in visual categorization studies is a variation of the habituation procedure. In simple discrimination studies, researchers present one stimulus repeatedly until the infant becomes habituated to it. This is the **habituation phase** of the procedure. Then a different stimulus is shown. This is the **test phase** of the procedure. If the infant becomes realerted by the new stimulus, researchers know that the infant can detect the difference between the first stimulus and the second.

In visual categorization studies, researchers use a series of stimuli rather than just one stimulus during the habituation phase. For example, if the researcher wishes to find out if infants can form a category for cats, the researcher might use 10 or 12 color photographs of different cats for the habituation phase (Eimas & Quinn, 1994). This phase gives infants an opportunity to become familiar with the physical features of cats and to see if they can learn the constellation of features (e.g., long tail, whiskers at the mouth, four furry feet, small pointed ears, and so on) that sets cats apart from some other kind of animal, such as dogs or horses. When infants have decreased their looking at the photographs shown in the habituation phase to the level the researchers have set, the **test phase** of the experiment begins.

In the test phase, the infant is shown two stimuli: (1) a new example from the habituation phase series (e.g., a picture of a cat)—one not included in the habituation phase series—and (2) a stimulus from a different category (e.g., a dog). If the infant generalizes habituation to the new example (fails to become realerted to the new example of a cat), but does not generalize it to the stimulus that is a member of a new category (the dog), then we can conclude that the infant has developed category knowledge for cats. Of course, we must be certain that infants do not see all of the cats as exactly the same cat, but rather as different examples of cats, and that they have no initial preference for one category. If they prefer dogs to begin with, and we use a picture of a dog in the test phase, infants might look at the dog simply because they like very much to look at dogs, not because they recognize it as something new—as something that does not fit the cat category.

The Model Examination Method for Studying Categorization Ability

Several other methods have been used to study infants' ability to form categories. The examination method involves the presentation of small models of one kind of thing (e.g., cats, dogs, or sea animals) for infants to examine briefly (Mandler & McDonough, 1998; Oakes et al., 1997). Babies are usually seated in a chair with a tray. One object from the set is put out on the tray, and the infant is allowed to examine it for about 30 seconds. Then this item is removed, the next item from the set is put out, and so on, until the child has seen all of the items that make up the familiarization set. (Usually four to six items are used.) Then the process is repeated, perhaps five or six more times.

After this familiarization phase, there is a test phase. Just as with the visual habituation procedure, two novel items are presented during the test phase in model examination studies. One novel item is a new example from the familiarization phase category; the other is a member of a different category. The test stimuli are placed on the infant's tray one at a time and are left there for 20 or 30 seconds each. Observers record how long the baby examines each of the items. If the baby examines the novel item from the different category longer than the novel item from the old category (i.e., the familiarization phase category), the researcher concludes that the infant formed a category of the familiarization phase items and recognized that the item from the new category did not belong in it.

What Objects Can Infants Categorize?   Babies as young as three- to four-months of age can form perceptual categories for a great number of things, including faces (Cohen & Strauss, 1979), birds (Roberts, 1988), and dogs and cats (Quinn et al., 1993). Infants in the study by Quinn and colleagues were shown the habituation stimuli series of cats or dogs (actual color photographs) repeatedly until they showed habituation at a specific level. Then the infants were shown a novel exemplar of the habituation/familiarization category (i.e., a photograph of a dog or a cat not included in the habituation series), as well as a photograph of a bird (the stimulus from a new category). The infants became realerted to the bird photograph, but not to the new example of a dog or a cat. And when the researchers tested infants to see if they simply preferred birds to cats or dogs, they found no such preference. The failure to be realerted to the photograph of the dog or cat, and the realerting to the bird stimulus, must have been caused by the infants' recognition of the bird as being something different from a cat or dog.

In one examination-method study (Oakes et al., 1997), 10- and 13-month-old infants were familiarized with either a set of land animal models (rhinoceros, cow, tiger, sheep, bear, and so on) or a set of sea animal models (walrus, seal, dolphin, whale, and so on). In the test phase, infants were presented with a novel sea animal and a novel land animal, or with a novel land animal and a novel sea animal (if they had been in the land animal familiarization group), and also with a truck. The 13-month-olds were able to form categories for either animal set, and they demonstrated this by examining longer the novel, out-of-category test item. Ten-month-olds had a little more difficulty but were able to form categories for both sets of animals when some were eliminated from each set. (This made the animals within each category more similar to each other and the entire set more distinctive from the other kind of animal.)

In a second examination-method study (Mandler & McDonough, 1998), 7-, 9-, and 11-month-old infants made categorical judgments about animals versus vehicles, animals versus furniture, and furniture versus vehicles. The set of animals included a horse, a cat, a bird, a dog, and a whale. The furniture included a dresser, a pedestal table, a bed, a rocking chair, and a couch. In this study (Mandler & McDonough, 1998), and also in a study conducted by Behl-Chadha (1996), the categories were global—they were **superordinate categories** (animals versus vehicles or animals versus furniture). In most studies of infant categorization, animals or furniture for the familiarization phase have contained all dogs or all cats, or all chairs or all tables. Then, in the test phase, comparison is made between a new item from the familiarization series category and a new item from a different **basic-level category** (dogs versus cats, or tables versus chairs).

What We Know about Infants' Categorization Abilities

Infants are able to form categories based on perceptual features of visual stimuli they are shown or of objects they are allowed to inspect and examine. Apparently they can detect correlated features among a kind of animal or vehicle or furniture. For example, ducks have feathers, wings, two webbed feet, and beaked mouths. Dogs have fur, a tail, four feet, a mouth that does not have a beak, and ears with external flaps. None of these features of ducks overlap with the unique features of dogs. Similarly, vehicles do not have heads; they have wheels and a cavity or seat of some kind. By noticing the correlated features of one kind of thing, infants can distinguish it from other kinds of things (Younger, 1990; Younger & Cohen, 1983, 1986).

Of course, it is very doubtful that infants of only 3 or 4 months of age are exposed to enough exemplars from either basic- or superordinate-level categories to form many categories. But by late in the first year, when parents begin, for example, to look at books with children or take them on outings to the zoo, it appears that children are quite well equipped to learn from these experiences and to connect with words some of the typical features by which adults organize the world. Babies still have much to learn about categorizing. They cannot yet organize by subtler distinctions, such as hidden internal features of animals, or understand the fact that physical features can sometimes be misleading (an earthworm may slither like a snake, but it is a far different type of animal). Children will also need to learn to categorize items based on similarity of function based on what we use them for, rather than by their physical features. Toys or cooking utensils may have few visual similarities yet form useful categories.

Objects and animals also can be members of many different categories. A category of things that are long and thin could include an eel, an earthworm, a snake, and also a piece of rope and a yardstick. Infants have a long way to go in learning the many characteristics by which people group things, as well as different subgroups within categories and the reasons behind these distinctions (a cocker spaniel is a dog because . . . ; a dog is a mammal because . . . ; a mammal is an animal because . . .). It is nevertheless remarkable that young infants can form categories at all and that children who are just a year or so old can form them about so many things, apparently at both basic and more global levels.

Children who are somewhat older than infants have been included not only in habituation and examination-method studies, but in situations where they can display what they know by touching objects. These studies are reviewed in Research Close-Up: Which Objects Do Toddlers Group in Categories?

RESEARCH

CLOSE-UP *Which Objects Do Toddlers Group in Categories?*

How do infants and toddlers respond to a collection of objects containing two different groups of identical or related items? Do they manipulate the objects at random, picking up one and then another, without regard to each object's category? Or do they touch or manipulate all identical objects in a sequence? Several studies have been conducted to answer these questions.

Object Sorting by Infants under 18 Months of Age

In one study (Ricciuti, 1965), one collection of objects consisted of four cube-shaped yellow beads and four gray balls of clay; another collection consisted of four yellow ellipses and four yellow parallelograms. As these examples illustrate, some of the four collections of objects contained objects differing on just one dimension; others differed on several dimensions.

Starkey (1981) used eight different collections of objects because he wanted to vary more systematically the number of dimensions on which the two groups of objects differed. Two sets consisted of objects differing in only one way (shape or size) (e.g., four large red Masonite ovals and four small red Masonite ovals). Other sets consisted of objects differing in two or three ways (form and color, or color, shape, and texture, etc., such as four metal bottle caps with black-and-white stripes paired with four yellow plastic cubes).

In both studies, infants were given only one collection at a time. Objects were placed in recessed compartments on a tray, in random order. Infants could play freely with the objects, for 2½ to 3 minutes. Their sorting ability was inferred from two behaviors: (1) a tendency to touch or manipulate sequentially objects from a single group and (2) a tendency

to separate the identical objects into piles or other physical groupings.

At 9 months of age, almost all of the infants touched or manipulated sequentially at least three items from one of the two groups contained in the collection, while not touching items in the other group in the same manner. By 12 months of age, many infants not only touched all three or four objects of one kind, but then touched at least three objects of the other kind. Object grouping showed a similar pattern, although somewhat fewer infants actually picked up and grouped objects than manipulated or touched them sequentially.

In a study of 18-month-olds (Mandler et al., 1987), the researchers used objects whose group membership was not based on perceptual features, but on a common context of use. For example, groups of objects consisted of "kitchen things" or "bathroom things." Fourteen- to 20-month-old infants touched objects within these groups sequentially, not randomly, which suggested that the babies knew which items were similar with respect to function.

Object Sorting by Toddlers 18–30 Months of Age

In some sorting/categorizing studies conducted with children 18–30 months of age, researchers have presented collections containing two groups of objects that, though not identical, were still all of a kind—all animals or all vehicles, or all dogs or all birds (Mandler et al., 1991). The degree of similarity between the two groups of objects has been varied across the collections. In some collections, the overall grouping was based on global characteristics—superordinate categories (e.g., animals, vehicles, furniture). For example, infants were given four objects from the animal category (cow, turtle,

Sensorimotor Intelligence: Piaget's Studies of Infants and Toddlers

Jean Piaget took a very different approach to the study of infants' cognitive abilities. He tried to sketch the developmental course of various abilities, such as the ability to act on the environment to produce certain effects and the ability to represent an object when it cannot be seen. He was rather demanding with respect to the criteria used to credit the infant with knowing something, and his research methods apparently create barriers that prevent the younger infant from showing us all that he or she knows. Piaget also did not work with a variety of tasks. He used tasks in which infants manipulate things with their hands or move other parts of their bodies to create some effect in the world, and no other kind.

Piaget, like all researchers, also worked from the perspective of a specific theory. In Piaget's theory, knowledge is thought to be constructed from the infant's own

seal, chicken) and four objects from the vehicle category (ambulance, train engine, off-road vehicle, bus). In other collections, infants were given two groups of objects from different basic-level categories (four dogs—poodle, German shepherd, terrier, and bloodhound paired with four birds—sparrow, bluejay, seagull, and cardinal). Some of the basic-level collections contained groups that were low in contrast (e.g., dogs and horses, or cars and trucks), whereas others contained groups that were higher in contrast (dogs and birds or cars and airplanes).

Eighteen-month-olds distinguished animals versus vehicles; 22–24-month-olds distinguished animals versus plants and furniture versus kitchen utensils. Eighteen-month-olds responded differentially only to high-contrast basic-level groups (dogs versus birds, or cars versus airplanes). Twenty-four-month-olds responded differentially to basic-level categories of only moderate contrast (cars versus motorcycles or dogs versus rabbits), not to basic-level categories with low contrast (dogs versus horses or cars versus trucks). Even at 30 months of age, children responded only slightly to these different groups.

In another study of this kind (Rakison & Butterworth, 1998), 14- and 18-month-olds responded differently to animals and vehicles, but not to furniture and animals, presumably because both animals and furniture items such as chairs and tables have legs. Twenty-two-month-olds, on the other hand, distinguished animals from furniture, animals from vehicles, and vehicles from furniture.

Summary of Infants' and Toddlers' Object-Sorting Behavior

At around 9 months of age infants begin to sort two groups of objects differing from each other on rather obvious perceptual features. The more the features of the two sets of objects differ, the more young infants are likely to respond. By about 14 months of age, infants begin to group objects that are used together or that occur together in a context (e.g., the bathroom or the kitchen), regardless of whether the objects look alike. By 18 months of age, toddlers begin to group objects that are "of the same global kind," though not identical (e.g., animals with other animals, not with vehicles), although they still confuse animals and furniture because both have legs. At the same age, they begin to respond differentially to objects from categories that are more closely related to each other if their difference is fairly high in contrast (dogs versus birds or cars versus airplanes) rather than low (dogs versus horses or cars versus trucks).

Infants' sorting or categorizing abilities, based on manipulation of objects, lag behind their sorting/categorization of visual stimuli. Infants can manipulate objects in any way they wish when presented with object-sorting tasks. As a result, they might get distracted or simply want to explore each object for its own sake. Moreover, object-sorting tasks do not direct the infant's attention to features of a certain kind, as visual perception studies do. Recall that in visual category studies, infants see many exemplars of one kind of item during the habituation/familiarization phase, before they are shown a noncategory item during the test phase. Thus, infants are basically instructed first on the category and then have an opportunity to indicate whether new stimuli are category members. In object manipulation studies, on the other hand, infants are given two kinds of things without any "instruction" on category features or group membership. Infants simply must notice for themselves that the two groups of things differ in some way.

actions on the world. Piaget did not think that infants come into the world with innate ideas, as some researchers have suggested. Piaget thought the "givens" at the beginning are mental processes (i.e., assimilation, accommodation, and equilibration) that infants used to construct ideas. Piaget also did not think that the infant is able to learn by simply looking and paying attention to what happens to objects. He thought knowledge originated in the infant's own actions on objects. Other researchers have used remarkably different methods to probe some of the domains of knowledge that interested Piaget (e.g., categorization). We will consider some of this research after we discuss Piaget's research methods and his conclusions about infants' cognitive abilities.

As we mentioned briefly in chapter 1, Piaget built a theory of how children think and acquire knowledge. The data he used to construct his theory were collected through careful observations of infants in natural contexts. Based on these observations, Piaget called the first two years of life the **sensorimotor period.** He chose this

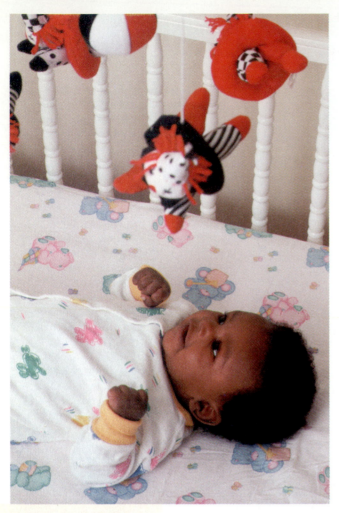

When infants notice that the items on the mobile over their crib move, they typically try to reinstate the movement by flapping their arms down by kicking their feet against the mattress. When some action works, the infant repeats it in an action-effect, action-effect cycle. This is a secondary circular reaction, because the spectacle or effect takes place in the environment as the result of one action. (*Source:* © Laura Dwight/Corbis)

name because he thought that thinking during this period consists of simple coordinations between what babies sense and how they react physically. Through sensing and acting, babies build intelligence. Piaget proposed that within the sensorimotor period, which extends from birth to about 2 years of age, babies develop increasingly complex forms of sensorimotor thinking through six levels, or substages.

Dimensions of Infant Cognition Studied by Piaget

Piaget described several dimensions of infant intelligence. For each dimension, he described six substages. Piaget called one "means for achieving desired environmental events;" he called a second "object construction" or "object permanence." We describe infant behavior on these two dimensions in detail in order to explain Piaget's work and to reveal its flavor. We then discuss some of the questions that other researchers have raised about Piaget's research methods and conclusions.

MEANS FOR ACHIEVING DESIRED ENVIRONMENTAL EVENTS.

This dimension of cognitive activity involves figuring out ways to make things happen. Another name for it might be problem solving. Babies become progressively more skilled at influencing their environments as they acquire behavior typical of Piaget's six sensorimotor substages (all ages are approximate).

Stage 1: Reflexes (Birth to about 1 Month). At this age, babies' behavior is dominated by the reflexes. The sucking reflex, for example, is elicited by placing a nipple or a finger into the baby's mouth. But babies learn quickly that not all objects they suck provide food. They soon stop sucking a pacifier and thrust it out of the mouth with the tongue, if they are hungry. Piaget saw this simple action as evidence of the infant's ability to "think" because it is based on the infant's prior experience with things inserted into the mouth. To Piaget, intelligence involved the ability to change behavior in response to feedback and circumstances.

Stage 2: Primary Circular Reactions (1 to 4 Months). Soon, the infant's behavior involves deliberate actions, not only reflex action. Piaget described the first deliberate actions as "circular" because they involve the repetition of an action-event-action sequence. A **circular reaction** sequence is primary if it involves only the baby's own body, not an object in the environment.

A circular reaction starts when an interesting result follows from something a baby does accidentally. To achieve the result again, the baby repeats the original action, which leads to the interesting result, which makes the baby repeat the action, and so on. A **primary circular reaction** occurs when a baby touches his tongue to his lips (accidentally), notices the sensation, touches them again, notices the sensation again, and so on. Cooing, an early vocal behavior, is another example. The baby makes a sound, hears or feels it, makes it again, and so on.

Stage 3: Secondary Circular Reactions (4 to 8 Months).   Circular reactions are "secondary" if they involve objects in the environment, not just the baby's body. A common **secondary circular reaction** occurs when the baby's normal spontaneous movement in the crib makes a mobile shake. The baby notices the mobile's movement. When it stops, he tries to make it move again. He discovers that banging his legs or feet on the mattress makes the mobile move. He bangs his feet, watches, bangs his feet, watches. The reaction is circular—it involves an action-event-action sequence. It also involves an event or response of an object in the environment beyond the baby's own body.

Stage 4: Coordination of Secondary Circular Reactions (8 to 12 Months).   In this stage Piaget found the first acts of true intelligence, because a child who exhibits behavior characteristic of Stage 4 performs actions intentionally—has a goal in mind. In contrast, in the earlier primary and secondary circular reactions, the first action and its result occur accidentally. For example, the mobile moves by accident the first time. The baby's goal is to reinstate the event, *after* he notices the accidental event.

By 8 to 12 months of age, the baby begins to conceive a goal in his mind without first having seen the event occur. Having a goal or idea before any result accidentally presents itself is new. He pursues the conceived goal with familiar means—actions he can already perform. For example, Piaget placed a piece of paper on the hood of his son Laurent's bassinet. Laurent wanted the paper—that was his goal. He had previously experienced pulling on a string attached to the hood. With his new goal in mind, he used the string (the familiar means) to get the paper (Piaget, 1952, p. 214).

In this case, the paper did not come down accidentally the first time. Instead, Laurent saw the paper and had the goal of making it come down. After several unsuccessful attempts to reach the paper, Laurent *thought* of a way to achieve his goal. He coordinated two familiar actions—pulling the string and picking up the paper. His thinking consisted of "schemes" to get hold of the paper.

Because the object of Laurent's efforts was located in the environment, and because the two behaviors used were already in the child's repertoire, Piaget considered it to be a secondary circular reaction. Because Laurent also combined or coordinated two actions to achieve his goal, Piaget used the name **coordination of secondary circular reactions** to designate Stage 4 behavior.

We often see this kind of means-end action in babies between 7 and 12 months of age. For example, a baby crawls to an object (first action) and then grasps it (second action) when it is within reach. Or a baby lets go of one object (first action) in order to pick up another (second action), or knocks away an object that is blocking a toy in order to get to the toy. In each case, the baby has a goal and then thinks of two sequential actions to achieve it.

Stage 4 behavior also includes infants' use of their mothers or other people as tools (means) to obtain objects or to make objects work. In one study (Mosier & Rogoff, 1994), mothers were instructed to demonstrate toys, but to do it out of their infants' reach. The researchers wondered if infants would use the mother to obtain the toy. They did.

Babies used several means—leaning forward, reaching out with the hand, and vocalizing—to get the mother to hand over the toy. These researchers found a large increase in instrumental use of the mother between 6 and 9 months and an additional, smaller increase from 9 to 13 months. These times coincide with the behaviors typical of Stage 4.

Stage 5: Tertiary Circular Reactions (12 to 18 Months).   In this stage, babies are interested in experimenting with different ways to achieve results. In the course of these experiments, they often invent or discover new ways to act on the world. Stage 5 behavior involves the object-dropping experiments most parents recognize (Piaget, 1952). Babies younger than 18 months of age deliberately drop spoons from high-chair trays, but they simply pick up the spoon, let it fall, and listen for the crash. They repeat this sequence for as long as someone is willing to pick up the spoon. Behavior that is characteristic of Stage 5, however, involves more than simply dropping the spoon. Babies experiment with and study the effects of different amounts of force on the spoon's trajectory.

Stage 6: Invention of New Means through Mental Combinations (18 to 24 Months). Stage 6 marks the end of the sensorimotor period and the beginning of the period in which the child uses mental representation to solve problems. The child invents—thinks of—ways to accomplish goals. The invention does not come about as the result of physical experimentation—trial and error—but through "insight." What is new at Stage 6 is the creation of the means to achieve a goal through thinking rather than by acting. The idea of a goal is not new. That was the achievement of Stage 4 thinking, but at that stage children used familiar means to achieve a goal. In Stage 6, the means are novel, and they come to the child through insight.

Consider Laurent in the following example provided by Piaget:

> Laurent is seated before a table and I place a bread crust in front of him, out of reach. Also, to the right . . . I place a stick about 25 cm long. At first Laurent tries to grasp the bread without paying attention to the instrument, and then he gives up. I then put the stick between him and the bread; it does not touch the objective but nevertheless carries with it an undeniable visual suggestion. Laurent again looks at the bread, without moving, looks very briefly at the stick, then suddenly grasps it and directs it toward the bread. But he grasped it toward the middle and not at one of its ends so that it is too short to attain the objective. Laurent then puts it down and resumes stretching out his hand toward the bread. Then, without spending much time on this movement, he takes up the stick again, this time at one of its ends (chance or intention?) and draws the bread to him. He begins by simply touching it, as though contact of the stick with the objective were sufficient to set the latter in motion. But after one or two seconds at the most he pushes the crust with real intention. He displaces it gently to the right, then draws it to him without difficulty. Two successive attempts yield the same result. (1954, p. 335)

When Laurent picked up the stick the second time, he quickly adjusted the position of his hand. He seemed to know by thinking that this position would be more effective than the way he had held the stick previously. Also, having seen that simply making contact with the bread had no effect, he immediately moved the stick more effectively.

We see in Stage 6 the budding ability to judge and anticipate actions that will have a desired result. With this ability, children can take much more control of their world. For example, when playing with a shape box (a toy with holes of different shapes and pieces that fit in each one), older toddlers can inspect the individual pieces and decide where they go. Of course, children still benefit from taking action. The difference now is that their problem solving does not depend entirely on trial and error. Instead, they can benefit by observing the results of many fewer actions because they can think ahead of action. Thus they anticipate the results of various actions, were they to take them.

OBJECT PERMANENCE. Piaget was also interested in infants' thinking about the permanence of objects. **Object permanence** refers to the knowledge that objects

Because of their repetitive nature, games provide a good context for language development. This caregiver and infant are enjoying a game of peek-a-boo. (*Source:* (LEFT) © Will Faller, (RIGHT) © Will Faller)

exist even when we cannot see them. Piaget said that the 1-year-old had object permanence, but that the 6-month-old did not. Piaget provided detailed descriptions of how object permanence develops across the six substages of the sensorimotor period.

Stage 1.   Newborns track a moving object continuously with their eyes over a short arc in an attempt to keep it in view. If it goes out of sight, they do not keep searching for it. Piaget assumed that infants this young have no conception that objects are permanent.

Stage 2.   Babies between 1 and 4 months of age continue to stare at the place where an object disappears as it leaves their field of vision. For example, if a red ball is slowly moved back and forth in front of a 3-month-old's face, the baby moves her head and eyes to follow it. But if the ball is made to disappear behind the baby, her eyes linger for only a moment at the spot where she last saw the ball before its disappearance, and then she looks away. The lingering glance suggests that the baby thinks the ball still exists, but presumably the awareness is fairly short-lived.

Stage 3.   Babies 4 to 8 months old search for a partially hidden object. If we partially cover a baby bottle with a cloth so that the bottom of the bottle still shows, the baby will search for the bottle. But the Stage 3 baby will not search for a completely hidden object. Piaget interpreted this behavior to mean that objects have not yet become permanent for the baby. (See Figure 5.4.)

Stage 4.   Sometime between 8 and 12 months of age, babies begin to search for completely hidden objects when the objects are placed under a screen. But it is fairly easy to confuse babies and cause them to stop their searching. For example, if a toy is first hidden under one screen and then is moved in full view of the attentive baby to a position under a second screen, the baby will look for it under the first screen (A) and then stop searching (**perseveration error**). Even though the baby saw the

Finding hidden objects. Between 8 and 12 months of age, babies learn to search for and find a completely hidden object.

object moved to the position under the second screen, (B), he searches only under the first one.

Stage 5.   Between 12 and 18 months the baby goes directly to the last screen where she saw the toy disappear. But other situations confuse the Stage 5 child. If the screens themselves are moved around, and the hidden toy with them, the baby looks under the screen that ends up in the position where the toy was originally left (switching error). Not finding it there, an infant simply gives up the search. The child in this stage is also confused if the tester hides the toy in his hand or in a box before placing it under the screen. The child sees only the hand or the box pass under the screen; he does not see the toy placed there. If the first screen he lifts does not reveal the toy, he gives up.

Concealing the object in the hand or a box before placing it under a screen is known as **hidden or invisible displacement.** The infant sees the object go into the hand or the box but does not see the displacement that follows. The infant must imagine the path of the object when presented with the empty box or hand, after it has passed under all of the screens.

Stage 6.   By 18 to 24 months of age, the baby is not fooled by switched screens or hidden displacement. If she fails to lift the correct screen the first time, she flips up the others until she finds the toy, as if to say, "It's got to be here somewhere!" Apparently her new ability to imagine actions allows her to understand the unseen path of the toy. (A summary of sensorimotor development is provided in Table 5.1.)

Other Views on Object Permanence   No one disputes Piaget's observations of how infants and toddlers behave when presented with the standard Piagetian task. And no one disagrees with Piaget in thinking that an understanding of the permanence of objects is of central importance. However, other researchers offer different interpretations of infant behavior on these tasks and what this behavior means.

TABLE 5.1

Summary of two dimensions of sensorimotor development

Stage	Development of Means to Achieve Desired Environmental Events	Object Permanence
1. Reflexes Birth–1 month	Elaboration of reflexes	Follows object with eyes over short arcs
2. Primary circular reactions 1–4 months	Use of means to produce interesting effects involving own body	Glance lingers where an object disappears
3. Secondary circular reactions 4–8 months	Use of means to produce interesting effects involving objects in environment	Uncovers partially hidden object
4. Coordination of secondary circular reactions 8–12 months	Novel coordinations of familiar schemes	Uncovers hidden object but shows perseveration error
5. Tertiary circular reactions 12–18 months	Progressive modification of familiar schemes to produce novel schemes as means to an end; groping	Uncovers hidden object but shows switching error
6. Invention of new means through mental combinations 18–24 months	Insight without groping	Uncovers object hidden through invisible displacement

Neo-Piagetians, for example, believe that changes in infant thinking involve the acquisition of specific knowledge that allows them to solve certain kinds of problems in certain situations.

Changing the design of the object concept task using different materials and procedures—causes children to behave differently. If infants' behavior changes as the result of these kinds of maneuvers, then neo-Piagetians think it is not accurate to say that object permanence develops in the stagelike way that Piaget described.

When one researcher tried hiding the toy *behind* a screen rather than *under* it (Brown, cited in Bower, 1974). Stage 3 babies (aged 4 to 8 months) searched for an out-of-sight toy. Babies did not search for an object that was placed under a screen, as Piaget had placed it. Bower concluded that infants fail to search for hidden objects in the standard Piagetian task not because they think that unseen objects no longer exist, but because they think two objects cannot be in the same place at the same time. They think that the screen occupies the space that the object previously occupied, because they do not yet understand the concept "under." But apparently babies this age do understand the concept "behind." Thus, when the toy is placed *behind* the screen, they search for it even though it is completely out of sight. The difference in the infant's behavior in these two situations suggests that a baby's progress in tackling object permanence tasks depends on the acquisition of specific knowledge or information, and that perhaps young babies do think that objects exist even when they cannot see them.

Other researchers have questioned Piaget's tasks entirely, claiming that their manual nature introduces barriers that mask the infant's intellectual competence. In order to remove a screen (cloth) from atop a hidden object and then reach for it, the infant must plan and execute two motor actions. This takes time, if nothing else, and even a short delay, these researchers claim, could cause a baby to forget where he saw

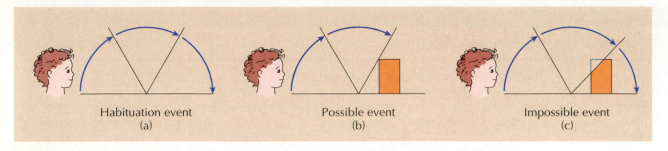

Habituation event
(a)

Possible event
(b)

Impossible event
(c)

FIGURE 5.5

Baillargeon's moving screen experiment. Renee Baillargeon uses visual behavior—looking time—in her experiments. Piaget, in contrast, required infants to manipulate objects.

the object disappear. Some researchers have reduced the motor difficulties by hiding the object in the dark (Goubet & Clifton, 1998). In this approach, only one action (reaching), rather than two coordinated actions (removing a barrier, followed by reaching), is required. To get around motor barriers and delays completely, some researchers have probed the infant's object permanence by using tasks that require a baby only to look at events (Baillargeon, 1985, 1987, 1993).

An ingenious example of this approach involved a task in which 4- to 8-month-old infants were seated so that they could view a tabletop on which a screen could be raised and lowered in an arc of 180 degrees. The researchers first habituated the infants to the movement of the screen by moving it back and forth, time after time. (See Figure 5.5a.) Then the infant watched as a box was placed on the tabletop opposite them, in a position that should have kept the screen from going all the way down to the tabletop on that side. (See Figure 5.5b.) Finally, the screen was made to move again. It was raised from the side of the tabletop near the infant and then lowered to the other side of the table, following the usual arc (see Figure 5.5c). With the box now there, the screen should not have been able to go down all the way to the tabletop. But because a trap door in the tabletop allowed the box to be removed in trials presented to some infants, the screen went down to the tabletop—an **impossible event condition**—just as it had in the familiarization trials. Thus, some infants saw what would be an impossible event, assuming, of course, that they thought the box was still there (had the idea of object permanence).

The researchers reasoned that infants who had object permanence would be surprised by the impossible event and would look longer at it as they tried to figure out what in the world was going on. If, on the other hand, they lacked object permanence, they would think that the box had simply disappeared when they couldn't see it. Lacking the concept of object permanence, they would not be surprised when the screen was lowered all the way, and they would not look very long at the screen, given their lack of surprise. Five-month-olds in this experiment (and babies as young as 3.5 months of age in other experiments of the same general kind) were surprised when the screen continued to move beyond where the box should have blocked its path.

Researchers who have conducted these studies claim that babies just entering Stage 3 (4 to 8 months of age) have object permanence, even though Piaget thought it did not begin to develop until Stage 4 (8 to 12 months of age). The **impossible–possible events methodology** has generated considerable research on infants' physical knowledge and reasoning. (See the Research Close-Up: Infants' Physical Knowledge and Their Capacity to Reason about It, for a brief review.)

CLOSE-UP

Infants' Knowledge about the World: Reactions to Impossible Events

The looking behavior methodology in which impossible and possible events are presented to infants was first developed by Baillargeon (1985, 1987, 1993). Since her first studies, the methodology has been used by many researchers to probe what infants know about how physical objects actually behave in the world, and whether infants try to think about why things happen.

In this methodology, infants are shown two events in an experimental condition, a possible one and an impossible one (made possible in the research demonstration by some behind-the-scenes maneuvering out of the infant's view). If infants look longer at the impossible event than at a contrasting possible event, researchers conclude that an expectation the infants hold for how things are supposed to work has been violated. Scientists then infer from infants' prolonged looking, prompted by their surprise and attempts to figure out what is going on (i.e., reasoning), that they have knowledge about the movement of physical objects in the world.

A variety of experiments have probed several aspects of infants' physical knowledge, such as whether they know objects need support if they are to stay suspended in midair and whether they know that an object is likely to move immediately if another object collides with it. We will discuss some specific studies in which infants' physical knowledge has been explored.

Infants' Knowledge about Object Support

In one experiment (Baillargeon, 1994), 6½-month-olds saw an index finger of a gloved hand push boxes along a platform (see Figure 5.6). In the impossible event condition, one box was not pushed beyond the edge of a platform, while a second box was. This second box should have fallen off (this constituted the impossible event). It did not fall because it was held in place by a device at the back of the box, where infants could not see it. A second group of infants (the control group) saw two boxes being pushed the same distance along their platforms, but a gloved hand grasped each box. In this case, the box that was moved off the supporting edge of its platform would not be expected to fall because the hand was still holding onto it. The researchers found that infants did look a lot longer at the impossible event than at the possible event.

A rather surprising result was obtained with infants who were only 3½ months old. These infants

EXPERIMENTAL CONDITION
Test Events

Possible Event

Impossible Event

CONTROL CONDITION
Test Events

Full-Overlap Event

Partial-Overlap Event

FIGURE 5.6

Baillargeon's tests for 6½-month-old infants. (*Source:* From "Physical Reasoning in Young Infants: Seeking Explanations for Impossible Events," by R. Baillargeon, 1994, *British Journal of Developmental Psychology, 12,* pp. 9–33.)

did *not* look longer at the box that remained suspended in midair beyond the edge of its supporting platform than at the box remaining supported on the platform. However, they did look a lot longer at *both* of these events than at the control events in which a hand grasped both boxes. For some reason, both of the test events looked impossible to these young infants. The researchers wondered whether these young infants thought the index finger was attached to the box that remained suspended over the edge of the platform. But if the infants reasoned in this way, they probably were puzzled about the orientation trials they had seen at the start of the research. In these, the finger came in contact with the boxes before beginning to push them along the platform. (See Figure 5.7.) The fingers were not attached to the boxes.

EXPERIMENTAL CONDITION

Orientation Event

CONTROL CONDITION

Orientation Event

FIGURE 5.7

Baillargeon's tests for 3½-month-old infants. (*Source:* From "Physical Reasoning in Young Infants: Seeking Explanations for Impossible Events." by R. Baillargeon, 1994, *British Journal of Developmental Psychology, 12,* pp. 9–33.)

(continued)

CLOSE-UP

Infants' Knowledge about the World: Reactions to Impossible Events (continued)

In other words, the infants had originally seen an event that would lead them to believe that a finger was not attached to a box. But assuming that the finger was attached to the box was the only way they could explain why the unsupported box did not fall. Because of the discrepancy between the unattached finger in the orientation trials and the presumably attached finger in the experimental trials, the infants might have inspected both events in the experimental condition in an attempt to figure out more about the relationship between the fingers and the boxes.

To find out if this was what the infants had been thinking, the researchers did another experiment. This time, after the two boxes had been moved to their final resting places, one at the end of its platform, the other off its platform's edge, the index finger was bent back to join the other fingers of the hand (Figure 5.8). This time, the infants looked much longer at the box that was off the platform's edge than at the box that was still on the platform because now they apparently had no explanation for why it remained suspended.

The researchers conducting these experiments suggested that the impossible–possible event methodology can be used to reveal not only what the young infant knows about how physical objects should behave, but also whether young infants can reason. In the object support experiment, infants seemed to account for the fact that an object remained suspended in midair when it should have fallen. The infants apparently reasoned that the finger was stuck to the box. With this possibility removed in the second experiment, they could no longer explain the atypical event and apparently remained surprised or puzzled because of it.

Though Baillargeon's experiments are impressive, other researchers, using different research tasks, have not found evidence of knowledge about object support in infants under 9 months of age. For example, when Sitskoorn and Smitsman (1995) used open containers of different sizes and then tested infants' expectations about whether boxes of different sizes would either fit in or be supported (and prevented from going in) by a container's edges, they found that 9-month-olds, but not 4- or 6-month-olds, anticipated the effect of a support. Young infants also do not know exactly where and how much support specific objects may need. For example, 9-month-olds did not judge correctly the support needed by asymmetrical objects to keep them from falling (Baillargeon & Hanko-Summers, 1990). Other researchers (Keil, 1979) have also documented infants' failure to judge adequacy of support (i.e., whether there is enough support

FINGER-BENT CONDITION
Orientation Event

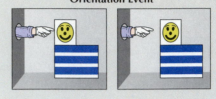

Test Events

Possible Event

Impossible Event

FIGURE 5.8

Baillargeon's test with bent index finger. (*Source:* From "Physical Reasoning in Young Infants: Seeking Explanations for Impossible Events" by R. Baillargeon, 1994, *British Journal of Developmental Psychology, 12,* pp. 9–33.)

or whether a support is placed where it will prevent an object from falling). Much of this particular understanding would seem to rest on an infant's own exploration of objects, which, of course, does not start in earnest until after 6 months of age when infants develop more dexterous use of their hands and can sit up well enough to free their hands for this use.

Physical Causality: Movement of One Object When Contacted by Another

The methodology used to probe physical causality in terms of object contact employs two objects, one of which is stationary at first, the other moving. Upon contact, the initially stationary object moves, and the initially moving object stops. The onset of movement by the originally stationary object is understood by adults to have been caused by the force involved when the moving object contacted it. Researchers have wondered if infants have this understanding.

If researchers prevent the originally stationary object from moving immediately, infants' expectations for contact causality (if they have any) would be violated. Researchers can also manipulate the moving object to stop after contact, sit still for a while, and then move back in the direction from which it came. Of course, sometimes when the stationary object is large and heavy, collision with a smaller object will not move it, and the smaller object will be deflected backward. But this happens immediately. The object does not stop for a period of time and then start to move backward! Researchers also can make an approaching object stop before it actually touches the second object, and then make the second object begin to move, without the two objects ever coming into contact. This, too, should violate infants' expectations of how objects actually behave, if they have such expectations.

In experiments of this kind, researchers (Cohen & Oakes, 1993; Leslie, 1984; Leslie & Keeble, 1987; Oakes, 1994; Oakes & Cohen, 1990; Spelke et al., 1994; Spelke & Van de Walle, 1993) have observed that infants as young as 6 months of age expect that movement of one object in response to another requires physical contact and that movement in such situations will be immediate rather than delayed. But some researchers have found that, even at 10 months of age, infants do not always conclude that contact between objects will cause movement. Their judgments vary somewhat, depending on the objects involved (Cohen & Oakes, 1993). These researchers suggest that infants observe specific relations between specific objects and the actions resulting from their movement, and then gradually sort out the particulars of causality. Infants may realize from early on (6 months of age) that things "happen for a reason" (Haith & Benson, 1998). Although under most circumstances, contact and immediacy of movement seem reason enough, to infer that one event caused the other, infants apparently pay attention to the particulars of objects and begin to learn that contact between a moving object and a stationary object (one capable of movement) does not always cause the contacted object to move (picture a light foam ball rolling into a heavy bowling ball). Knowledge about objects themselves is required for a rich understanding of causality, but it seems that infants have some global expectations about physical causality fairly early in the first year of life.

What Else Do Infants Know about Object Movement?

Other experiments have probed various aspects of physical knowledge, including whether infants know that objects cannot pass through solid surfaces or other solid objects (Caron et al., 1988; MacLean & Schuler, 1989; Spelke, 1991; Spelke et al., 1992) and whether infants understand rigid versus compressible, and that a rigid object cannot fit into a container that is smaller in width than the object itself (Aguiar & Baillargeon, 1998). Researchers have also probed infants' understanding of the continuity in the path of a moving object (Spelke et al., 1994).

Taken together, this research suggests that especially by the last quarter of their first year, infants know far more than theorists once thought, and much of this early knowledge is acquired in the absence of the infant's active motor involvement. Still, infants certainly learn a lot from acting on their environments, and some things cannot be learned in any other way. Their knowledge is enriched deeply once they start to handle and act on objects in various ways. It certainly has been eye-opening for most of us to learn how much babies pick up about how things work from simply watching closely as the world goes by. We know, though, from our experience with preschoolers and school-age children, as well as with infants, that infant knowledge provides just a beginning, that deep and full understandings depend on a child's complete and sustained engagement with objects and people in the world.

There is considerable debate among child development researchers and theorists about whether Piaget's view of the child is correct (Haith & Benson, 1998; Munakata et al., 1997). Is the infant highly precocious, as some researchers and theorists now claim, or are these claims too strong? Some researchers and theorists (Haith & Benson, 1998) have suggested that the behavior of longer looking might be a reaction to two perceptual events—trace image of the box still in the child's mind and the screen going past where the box should have stopped it. These critics contend that as long as a perceptual trace image of the box remains, one cannot assume that the infant has gained the idea of object permanence—the idea that objects exist *when they cannot be seen*. The trace image still allows the object *to be seen*—in the infant's mind.

It is necessary to distinguish between such a perceptual trace, which will disappear in a short time, and an actual *representation* of the box. Perceptual traces do not endure; representations endure longer and can continue for a long or a short time, depending on their strength. Critics of the "precocious infant" view caution that "it is an error to assume that cognition necessarily begins when perceptual input ends. Perceptual processes can outlast perceptual input" (Haith & Benson, 1998, p. 242).

Some researchers (Munakata et al., 1997) have suggested that the different results obtained with different tasks used to probe object permanence are due to both task variables and representational variables. In other words, they suggest that infants' representations of objects do in fact develop over the first year of infancy, becoming more and more robust. Success on some tasks, such as those requiring means-end reaching (lift the screen and reach for the object), depends on stronger representations than do other tasks, such as those requiring only looking. Or, they suggest, representations may be involved in both the reaching and grasping and the looking situations, but perhaps different representational systems (i.e., brain pathways) are involved, and perhaps one develops later than the other (Goodale & Milner, 1992; Munakata et al., 1997). By comparing infants' behavior on various kinds of tasks, researchers can gradually begin to understand all of the underlying mechanisms that constitutes a baby's "knowing." A great deal more research will be needed to sort this out. In the meantime, we can expect to see an increase in the variety of tasks used to probe infant cognition, as well as in the explanations provided to account for infants' uneven performances.

The Enduring Value of Piaget's Work   Although Piaget's behavioral timetables and interpretations have been questioned, virtually everyone agrees that his work has been enormously important and influential. Piaget focused attention on the cognitive abilities of the very young child. According to one developmental psychologist (Beilin, 1994, p. 284), "Piaget, more than anyone before him, changed our conception and understanding of the cognitive resources of children." He may have underestimated the young infant's cognitive skill, and he may have been mistaken in some of his conclusions about infants' capacities. He was responsible, nevertheless, for focusing attention on infant cognition in a way that was virtually unknown before him, and he may turn out to have been right about more things than it now appears to many. Only time will tell.

Cognitive Development Revealed by Play with Objects

Mark and Samantha are playing with toys on the living room rug. Ten-month-old Mark clutches a red plastic ring from a set of stacking rings. Nearby, his sister Samantha, age 2½, holds her baby doll and feeds it with a toy bottle.

Mark looks at his red ring, passes it from one hand to the other, chews on it briefly, and taps it on the floor. Samantha looks up at Mark, then glances down at her doll. She sets the doll on the floor and reaches over to take the ring out of Mark's hand. In exchange, she offers him the orange ring from the stack. He drops the red ring as he reaches for the orange one. Samantha picks up her doll again and says, "Bracelet, baby," as she pushes the red ring onto the doll's wrist. Then she lifts her baby and turns her face so that she can see the wrist of her own left hand: "See my bracelet? See? Pretty?"

think about it

What did the ring mean to Mark? If we could have peered into his mind, what might we have found him to be thinking? What does this thing look like? How does it feel? How would it taste? What sound will it make if I tap it on the floor? What might Samantha have been thinking? How was she able to fashion the simple red ring into a bracelet? If we peered into her mind, might we have seen her contemplating questions such as "What can I make of you?" or "What do I wish you to be?"

Children's play with objects provides another window through which we can observe their thinking and knowledge development (Lloyd & Goodwin, 1995). We will discuss first two kinds of play that emerge before 2 years of age—exploratory play and pretend play. In exploratory play, as Mark's actions demonstrate, children do not relate objects to each other in socially determined ways, nor do they use them for social purposes. The second kind of play—symbolic or pretend play—is symbolic and social: Objects are used to stand for things.

The Infant's Exploratory Play with Objects

Observers see that babies wave objects, bang them, and poke, squeeze, chew on, and rub them. In many of the studies of infants' object exploration, researchers have provided specific items, such as a pot with a lid, cups and saucers, and spoons. They have been interested in learning when infants relate various objects in social or functional ways (i.e., in ways typical of how the objects are used in the real world) rather than simply manipulating each object for its own sake. (Fein & Apfel, 1979; Fenson et al., 1976)

Infants under 12 months of age rarely engage in functional play with toys. Instead, they explore each item separately and apply behaviors (e.g., banging, waving, shaking, mouthing) to each one. After about 12 months of age, babies begin to relate objects in functional ways; for example, they put the lid on the pot, or they put a cup on a saucer (Fenson et al., 1976; Tamis-LeMonda et al., 1995). Even at 12 months, though, infants rarely use the objects symbolically. In other words, they rarely tip the cup and bring it to their lips, as if taking a drink of an imaginary substance; and they rarely move the spoon around in the cup or the pan, as if stirring some kind of food or drink. Infants are able to engage in this sort of symbolic or pretend behavior by about 1 year of age, but they do not do so very often. They focus on manipulating objects rather than using them in pretend activities. Some researchers (Vondra & Belsky, 1989) have suggested that the question on the mind of most children between 1 and 2 years of age is "What can I do with this?" We would add that toddlers are also interested in what effect an object will have on something else. Toddlers are intrigued, for example, by marking tools—crayons and markers—and by the designs they can create on a surface. (See Research Close-Up: Toddlers' Scribbles: A Look at a Special Kind of Object Play.)

This older infant is likely to bang these metal cooking utensils against each other more than he would bang soft toys together, because metal objects banged together create sound while soft objects do not. (*Source:* © Mike Neveux/Corbis)

RESEARCH

CLOSE-UP   *Toddlers' Scribbles: A Special Kind of Object Play*

Twenty-four-month-old Adam sits in his high chair. His mom gives him a blue felt-tip marker and a white piece of paper. Adam eagerly begins by making a patch of circular marks on the upper left portion of the paper. He pauses for a moment to inspect what he has done, and then he creates another patch to the right of the first one. A second pause for inspection is followed by the creation of a third circular pattern, placed practically on top of the first patch. Then, he draws horizontal lines. The first line begins in the right-hand circular patch, a second begins above that patch, and a third is placed at the very top of the upper left portion of the paper. Several more horizontal lines are added lower on the paper.

Next, a different sort of experiment—vertical lines. Adam adds two on the left side of the paper. Then he draws one line straight through the middle of the first circular patch and another line diagonally down from the patch. Finally, he adds a series of "combination" lines. One starts as a vertical line, drawn from the top, but then turns and makes its way horizontally to the right before looping around to make a tiny, irregular circle. It continues horizontally, then around, to create a larger circle. Before it stops, it continues upward, then bends to the right horizontally. Adam then adds several more lines that combine the separate vertical, horizontal, diagonal, and circular lines that he used when he first began to draw. At last, apparently finished, he sits back and looks at his creation. (See Figure 5.9.)

Many observers of children (Golomb, 1992; Kellogg, 1967; Smith, 1983) have noted the keen interest that toddlers take in the marks they can make with writing or drawing tools. In his book *Artful Scribbles* (1980), Howard Gardner describes in detail the drawings of his son, Jerry, beginning at 18 months of age. Once, at the beginning of this period, Jerry produced more than two dozen drawings in just ten minutes, each one somewhat different from the others. Many showed experimentation with the same movements as well. On his second birthday, Jerry produced what his father referred to as "one super picture—a many-colored, full-page effort which contained within it instances of every one of the schemes he had hitherto practiced" (pp. 33–34).

FIGURE 5.9

Adam's experiments with a felt-tip marker. These markings give us clues about his intellectual development.

Rhoda Kellogg, the well-known authority on children's art, collected well over 1 million samples of paintings and drawings made by children from all around the world. She found that all children begin to make marks by 2 years of

In the first studies of children's exploratory play with objects, researchers assumed that the baby's prerelational and presymbolic explorations of objects were random and "indiscriminate." They thought that babies applied a set of behaviors—banging, mouthing, waving, poking—to all objects, in a rather stereotypic way. Subsequent research has shown that young infants actually adapt their exploration of objects to object properties, and that they use information gained from one episode of object exploration in their subsequent explorations of objects. The beginnings of

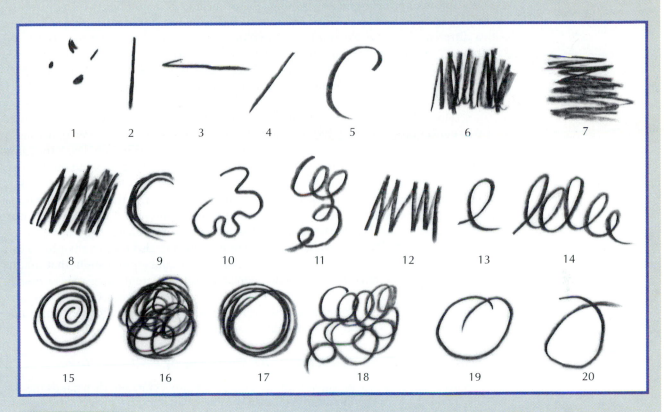

The 20 kinds of scribbles created by 2- and 3-year-olds.

age and that children's first scribbles consist of about 20 basic types. (See Figure 5.10).

Children repeat their lines, and they cross one line over another. They move back and forth, and up and down. They find that jabbing at the paper has one result and that pulling the tool across the paper has another. Moving the tool around and around, without lifting it, produces still another result. Through this process, toddlers learn what kind of mark will be left by a movement of a certain kind and duration. Later, they will use these scribble forms to represent many things, such as smoke swirling from a chimney, curls on top of someone's head, teeth in the mouth of a jack-o'-lantern, or blades of grass swaying in the wind. For now, though, the whole process is just one grand experiment, a delightful form of play with a very special kind of object.

adaptation to objects with different properties may begin as early as 4 months of age (Rochat, 1989). For example, infants wave objects more and mouth them less if the objects make a sound. They also mouth objects more if a table surface is covered with foam than if it is left bare; and they bang and scoot objects more if the table's hard surface is exposed. Presumably, a foam covering on a table limits the sound that can be created by banging an object and also makes it difficult to scoot objects along the table's surface. The infant adapts to these conditions in the environment and explores objects in different ways under the two sets of conditions (Palmer, 1989). Adaptation to the characteristics of the toy has been noted in a variety of research studies involving infants under 12 months of age (Baldwin et al., 1993; Kimmerle et al., 1995).

Infants appear to be able to infer the properties of new objects using information obtained from previous exploration of similar but nonidentical objects. Thus, a different, but new, toy horn is not explored in the way that a first toy horn is explored. The new horn's bulb is squeezed rather immediately to produce the expected sound. The infant infers the sound-making property of the new horn from experience with the previous horn and applies to it the actions that he or she learned (Baldwin et al., 1993).

This inferential behavior is similar to the behavior that infants exhibit on visual perception tasks that involve correlated features (two or more features that usually occur together on specific types of objects). This means that infants learn to distinguish some objects from others, not on the basis of one feature alone, but on the basis of features that typically occur together. For example, a giraffe has a long neck, a small head with knobby horns, and a short tail (compared with the features of a horse or a cow, for example). Birds have wings and a beaked mouth. A horn-type toy usually has a soft, bulblike part, plus a bell-shaped protrusion. These two features occur together in hornlike toys, and a specific action applied to this type of toy produces a sound. Laboratory studies on the categorization of visual stimuli show that infants begin to use correlated features to distinguish among different categories of objects by about 9 or 10 months of age (Younger, 1990). (See Research Close-Up: Which Objects Do Toddlers Group in Categories? earlier in this chapter for more information about infants' ability to form object categories.)

Using Objects Symbolically: The Dawning of Pretend Play

> An adult picks up an empty teapot, "pours" tea into a cup, and then hands the child the cup. One might expect a child to be bewildered by such bizarre behavior. . . . In the course of such a tea party, the adult may also produce strange remarks. For example, if the child inadvertently knocks the cup over, the adult might exclaim, "Uh oh, you've spilled your tea. You'd better wipe it up"— even though there is no tea, no spillage, and nothing to wipe up. . . . Children's willingness to go along with such overtures—to sip from the empty cup or to wipe up a perfectly dry table—suggests that they . . . realize that it is pretend tea that has been poured or spilled and that the adult is inviting them to drink or wipe up an imaginary liquid rather than the real thing. (Harris & Kavanaugh, 1993, p. 1)

The ability to engage in pretend play or **pretense** marks a revolution in the infant's way of thinking. Piaget (1962) emphasized that pretending involves the use of symbols—the use of one thing to stand for or represent something else. A child uses a toy cup to stand for an actual cup or a long block to represent an airplane. Unlike symbols used in language, the symbols used in pretend play share some physical similarity with the objects they are used to represent.

The first pretend play in which the child engages is simple. The child pretends with objects—suspends reality—but the child does not pretend to *be* someone else, nor does the child collaborate with partners who themselves have taken on pretend roles. Mark, for example, had no idea what his sister, Samantha, was up to.

The first social play is seen sometime between 15 and 21 months (McCune, 1995) and involves such simple acts as extending an empty spoon to the lips of the child's mother. Or the child might place an empty cup up to the mouth of a doll and tip it. **Sociodramatic play,** which involves taking on roles and coordinating actions with others, is well beyond the grasp of the infant and toddler. (See chapter 9, Cognitive Development in the Preschool Child.)

This young 3-year-old is engaging in pretend play with his doll. The script he is playing was no doubt inspired by observations of his mother and father as they cared for his baby sister. (*Source:* © Goodwin/ Monkmeyer)

Assessing Infants and Toddlers and Providing for Their Play

"I'm worried," Veronica confided to her best friend, Margerita. "Willie doesn't seem to play like Jeremy. Look at him. He's banging the pot on the floor, chewing on the lid, and spinning it in front of his eyes. When Jeremy played with that pot just a few minutes ago, I saw him put the lid on the pot where it belongs."

"Well, Jeremy is two months older than Willie," Margerita said, reassuringly. "I think Jeremy used to do that too when he was younger."

"I don't know. He just looks different to me. I wonder if I could get him evaluated by somebody?"

"He's pretty young. I don't know if there's any way they can test a 14-month-old to see if his thinking is okay. Ask Dr. Frankl. Maybe he would know."

think about it

As we have seen, infants and toddlers learn an incredible amount about their world. Are there ways to assess what they know and what they can do when a child's parents or pediatrician suspects that perceptual and cognitive development might not be proceeding as it should? And how can parents and child-care workers support perceptual and cognitive development in infants? Do children this young need playthings? If so, what kind?

In this section, we discuss assessment procedures that are used with infants and toddlers, as well as some difficulties in predicting later cognitive functioning from infant tests. We also discuss some of the alternatives to traditional infant tests that seem to result in more accurate predictions of later intellectual functioning. In addition to the discussion of infant and toddler assessment, we also discuss materials that can be provided for infant and toddler play, either at home or in the child-care center.

Infant and Toddler Assessment

Several instruments have been available for quite a long time for use in assessing the development of infants and toddlers. If Willie's mother is able to find someone to evaluate him, the person might use the best-known instrument, the *Bayley Scales of Infant Development*. These scales were devised by Dr. Nancy Bayley at the University of California at Berkeley, in the 1930s. The instrument is used to assess children from birth to about 3½ years of age. The 1993 edition of the scales provides assessment in three areas: (1) mental development, (2) motor development, and (3) the child's response to the testing experience itself (behavioral rating scale). The mental scale tests sensory abilities, such as the child's response to sound and light (habituation), ability to solve problems, communication attempts, and classification of objects. The motor scale assesses basic locomotor milestones, such as pulling up, sitting, crawling, and walking; and fine motor skills, such as reaching and grasping and building towers with blocks. For the behavioral rating, the examiner makes notes of the child's interest in the testing materials, the child's wariness of the situation and attention to the tasks, and the child's cooperation with the tester.

The Bayley Scales, as well as other tests of infant intelligence, are poor predictors of a child's later performance on IQ tests. Perhaps intelligence is simply not stable from infancy to later childhood, or perhaps the infant tests themselves do not tap the kinds of skills that later intelligence tests measure. For example, infant scales of development rely very heavily on motor and sensory items, which cannot be expected to be very good predictors of later language skills, reasoning, and problem solving (Bornstein & Sigman, 1986).

Research indicates that it is possible to predict later IQ better by using measures that have not typically been included on infant tests. Measures that are better predictors of later IQ include such things as habituation rate (faster rates predict higher later IQ) (Bornstein & Sigman, 1986); reaction to novelty (McCall & Carriger, 1993); and length of fixation to visual stimuli (shorter fixations predict greater competence later) (Colombo, 1995). Mastery behavior—the way an infant approaches a problem-solving situation—may also predict later IQ test performance. Babies who manipulate objects more, and who are more engaged in and persistent on tasks, tend to be the ones who are judged later in childhood to be more competent (Messer et al., 1986).

The revised edition of the Bayley Scale (1993) contains habituation items in the mental scale and aspects of mastery behavior in the behavior rating scale. Future studies of the predictive power of the Bayley Scale might show a stronger relationship between infant scores and later IQ scores than was found with the 1969 edition of the test. But even though measures with better predictive validity have been identified, this does not mean that infant measures of intelligence will predict later performance levels with a high degree of certainty. Even during the school-age years, when IQ remains relatively stable, IQ scores can change considerably under some conditions. (See the discussion of IQ tests in chapter 14.)

The extensive work that is currently being conducted in neuroscience should help inform assessment in the years ahead. Neuroscientists are trying to link infant and toddler behaviors to specific neural pathways and specific parts of the brain. It appears that some domains of development are quite plastic—very "activity-dependent" (Johnson, 1999). Other domains are more tightly fixed. More knowledge in this area will help us take the best measures to support development and to design interventions when development strays from typical paths (Johnson, 2000). According to one neuroscientist, "studying the postnatal emergence of cortical specialization for different cognitive functions offers the possibility of new perspectives . . . for social development, education, and atypical developmental pathways" (Johnson, 1999, p. 224).

Play and Play Materials for Infants and Toddlers

Most toys for babies are designed to provide sensory stimulation. Crib mobiles became popular after research on babies' visual perception was publicized. Rattles are another popular toy for very young babies, given their action-response-action nature. A 6-month-old will grasp a rattle placed in her hand, look at it, put it in her mouth, feel it with her free hand, and shake it. She will like the sound it makes or, perhaps even more, the mystery of what makes the sound.

When babies start to crawl, they enjoy pushing a colorful ball in front of them. They like the changing colors or patterns and the moderately predictable path the ball takes in its movement. Another good push toy for crawlers is a nonbreakable mirror attached between two wheels. As the mirror moves, it reflects a variety of stimulating displays to catch the baby's attention.

With their improving fine motor coordination and cognitive abilities, toddlers start to enjoy simple puzzles, boxes with shapes to sort and fit, stacking toys (such as the graduated rings that fit over a post), small blocks, and crayons and paper (under supervision, of course). Dolls and stuffed animals give children something soft to hug and objects with which to pretend play when this ability emerges during the second year of life. Old hats, purses, shoes (to prevent tripping, avoid those with raised heels), and clothes suggest roles to older toddlers. Play dishes, pots and pans, vehicles, and small figures of people and animals will also be used by toddlers. Babies also like common household objects, such as pots and pans and plastic bowls. They seem to get enormous pleasure at times out of simply poking their hands and fingers around in empty boxes and cardboard tubes.

Play and Play Materials: A Cross-Cultural Perspective

Research on play in various cultures has often raised questions such as, "Where, how, and with whom do children have opportunities to learn . . . and in which ways do these settings provide unique opportunities for learning and development?" (Bloch & Adler, 1994, p. 162). These questions have been explored by a number of researchers, including Bloch and Adler, who studied the Lebou, a group in a small village in Senegal, Africa; and Farver and Wimbarti (1995), who studied Indonesian children in Yogjakarta, a working-class, urban village in Indonesia.

Toys for young infants provide sensory stimulation—interesting sights and sounds. But an older toddler, like the child shown here, enjoys toys that allow him to act on them. A set of blocks and some toy people, added to this child's dump truck and ready-made buildings, would provide for hours of creative play. (*Source:* © Elsa Peterson/Stock Boston)

The economy in the African village studied in Senegal is based mostly on agriculture. The social organization is patrilocal, with cluster households consisting of the eldest male of a family, his wife (or wives), and their male children and families. Thus, children in the village have many adults and children with whom to interact and play. There is a sharp division of labor among the adults, based on gender. Thus, girls' play is dominated by cooking, house cleaning, shopping, and child-care content and themes; boys' play is dominated by hunting and vehicle themes (Bloch & Adler, 1993). Beginning at a relatively young age, both boys and girls are assigned as helpers in doing actual work. Even as early as 2 years of age, Senegalese children perform simple errands. For example, they carry an item to someone, or transporting an item from outside to inside the house. Later, at age 4, children might be assigned to help wash cooking pots or feed the farm animals.

Much of children's play (especially that of girls) is "play-work"—play that is directly related to tasks the children are later asked to perform. For example, at 2 years of age, girls are given a small tin can of water to carry on their heads; a little later, a larger container is used (Bloch & Adler, 1993. Similarly, when very young, a little girl is given some grain to pound but is allowed to experiment under the watchful eye of the mother, who gives a little instruction. Later, pounding grain becomes real work and not play.

Compared with U.S. midwestern city children, Senegalese children spend somewhat less time in play, presumably because they are engaged more often in real work. In both cultures, girls engage in responsible work to a greater extent than do boys. The amount of work young children are assigned depends on the workload of their mothers in the culture. When the workload is heavy, young children are assigned work at a younger age than when the mothers' workload is light (Whiting & Edwards, 1988). In some cultures, as we have seen, this child work begins at a very young age—during toddlerhood.

In Indonesian culture, older siblings have considerable responsibility for taking care of younger children, and the culture values harmonious sibling relationships. Children engage in pretend play more frequently with other children than with mothers. Older siblings often play with younger siblings, and researchers have judged them to be quite skilled in "scaffolding" the younger child's engagement in pretend play. They make suggestions for the younger child's participation in play. They comment to the younger child about actions they are performing, they demonstrate what to do with materials, and they hand materials to the younger child, with specific instructions for what to do. They also sometimes join in the younger child's initiation of new play ideas. (Farver and Wimberti, 1995)

In their study of play among Indonesian children, Farver and Wimbarti (1995) were especially interested in who played with young children. Children who live in extended family households often are cared for by older siblings. In these contexts, children's pretend play is more frequent and more complex in the company of older siblings than in the company of their mothers (Farver, 1993; Gaskins, 1994).

These cross-cultural examples remind us that specific toys, of which there are a multitude on the shelves of many toy stores, are not essential for infant and toddler development. Materials at hand, along with the typical sights, sounds, tastes, smells, and tactile sensations, provide appropriate stimulation. Perhaps the best toy of all is another human being. Our eyes open and close, we make noise, and we can hide and reappear again. We can clap our hands, smack our lips, cluck our tongues, tickle a tummy, and say "ah-boo" at just the right time. Adults keep such social games interesting by varying the pace of the clapping, tickling, or booing. No jack-in-the-box can take the place of all that.

Babies even like to chew our fingers, run their fingers through our hair, feel the buttons on a blouse or shirt, touch a flowing scarf, and explore our eyeglasses. They stick their hands in our pockets when they find them, and they latch onto our pant legs or skirts to keep from falling down as they begin to toddle about. When they do fall, they learn that some surfaces are soft, such as a carpet or a bed of grass. Babies learn that other surfaces, such as concrete or packed earth, are not so forgiving. Water streaming down their face at bath time, whether its source is a crock used to carry water from a well or a cup filled from a modern home's faucet, no doubt feels the same to children the world over. Shadows are created everywhere by objects that obstruct the sun; it's a trivial matter what images are actually cast. As long as adults care about children, are attentive to them, and bring to their eyes and hands, and therefore to their minds, the objects of importance to their particular time and place on this planet, children's play with objects will surely support their development.

KEY POINTS

Infant Visual Perception

- Very young infants have size and shape constancy.

- Infants can parse the world into separate objects by using motion and depth cues.

- Scientists think that depth perception is not innate but develops over the first few months.

- In a classic study, depth perception was measured in infants by using an apparatus called the "visual cliff."

- Newborns fixate, over and over, on one restricted area of a visual display. At 1 month, babies look at the edges of a figure, but at 2 months they look at its internal features.

- Babies' preferences for faces change. When given a choice between normal and scrambled faces, newborns and 1-month-olds show no preference. They have no concept of a face, because they do not scan internal features. They look at the outer edges of faces simply because they are patterns with contrast. Babies 3 months old prefer facial features arranged normally. They have a concept of a face.

- Newborns show a preference for their mother's face versus the face of a stranger, based on knowledge of the mother's hairline and the shape of the outer contour of her head.

- Babies begin to discriminate among several facial expressions by 4–7 months of age.

- Babies' understanding of the meaning of various facial expressions does not develop until late in the first year.

Infant Cognitive Development

- On the basis of habituation studies, researchers have concluded that babies are able to form concepts about objects beginning at about 3 to 4 months of age.

- Older infants indicate by sequential touching which objects they think go together.

- Piaget suggested that infants build intelligence and learn about the world during their first two years by sensing and acting.

- According to Piaget, infants develop through six substages of development during the sensorimotor period: Stage 1: reflexes (birth to 1 month); Stage 2: primary circular reactions (1 to 4 months); Stage 3: secondary circular reactions (4 to 8 months); Stage 4: coordination of secondary circular reactions (8 to 12 months); Stage 5: tertiary circular reactions (12 to 18 months); and Stage 6: invention of new means through mental combinations (18 to 24 months).

- Piaget described several dimensions of infant intelligence, including means for achieving desired environmental events, imitation, and object permanence.

- The dimension of intelligence referred to as "means for achieving desired environmental events" involves solving problems or learning to make things happen.

- A circular reaction is an action-event-action-event sequence that is repeated.

- Piaget thought the first intentional acts occur in Stage 4. Babies also start to use adults as "tools" in Stage 4.

- Babies develop new means rapidly in Stage 5, as they explore the effects of various actions.

- Object permanence refers to knowing that an object still exists even when it cannot be seen. Babies begin to demonstrate object permanence during Stage 4.

- Researchers sometimes use the technique of hidden or invisible displacement to test object permanence. This technique fools the Stage 5 child, but not the Stage 6 child.

- Some researchers think babies have object permanence well before Piaget said they did. They think infants can't locate objects manually because their spatial and temporal concepts are not yet well developed or because their means-end planning is poor. A technique used to measure object permanence in young infants uses demonstrations of possible and impossible events.

- Even young babies seem to try to figure out impossible events.

- During the first year of life, babies seem to develop considerable knowledge about how objects behave in the world.

- Babies explore and manipulate objects at first, without relating them functionally and without engaging in pretend play.

- Studies of infants' exploration have shown that infants adapt the actions they use with objects, depending on the characteristics of the objects and their previous experience with objects.

- Symbolic or pretend play begins at about 12 months of age, but infants engage in it infrequently at this young age.

- One kind of object play enjoyed by toddlers is scribbling with a writing/drawing tool.

- Children's object and pretend play is affected by their culture. In cultures in many parts of the world, children's play partners are more often children than adults and their toys are objects used in daily life.

Assessing Infants and Toddlers and Providing for Their Play

- The *Bayley Scales of Infant Development* is one instrument that is commonly used to assess developmental progress in three areas in children from birth to 3½ years.

- Tests of infant development have not been good predictors of later IQ scores. Researchers have found in recent years that such things as habituation rate, response to novelty, visual fixation time, and mastery behavior predict later competence better than the motor and sensory items that have dominated traditional infant tests.

- Research in neuroscience probably will further inform our assessments and interventions.

- Many infant toys provide stimulation. Crib mobiles and rattles are common toys for very young infants. Toys for infants and toddlers include balls, mirrors, simple puzzles, shape boxes, and dolls.

GLOSSARY

basic-level category: a category of quite similar items, such as dogs or cats (p. 165)

categorize: putting together items that are similar though nonidentical (p. 163)

circular reaction: an action-response-action sequence that is repeated (p. 168)

cognition: how infants process or manipulate perceptual information and gradually construct systems of knowledge (p. 154)

coordination of secondary circular reactions: actions in which the infant combines two behaviors already in his or her repertoire in order to achieve a goal (p. 169)

habituation phase: the first part of the habituation procedure used in research during which the infant is shown one stimulus, or a series of stimuli, until he loses interest in looking at it (p. 163)

hidden or invisible displacement: concealment of an object in a box or the hand before placing it under a screen in the object permanence task (p. 172)

impossible–possible events research methodology: a methodology in which naturally impossible events are made to occur in order to gauge infants' physical knowledge about what usually happens (p. 174)

neo-Piagetians: researchers and theorists who agree with some of Piaget's observations of children's behavior while disagreeing with his interpretations, especially his lack of emphasis on task features and the role of specific knowledge (p. 173)

object permanence: knowing that objects exist even though out of our sight (p. 170)

object unity: the perceptual understanding that allows us to know that a continuous object is there when we can see only discontinuous object parts (p. 156)

perseveration error: a mistake infants make in object permanence tasks when they return to the screen where the object was last found, not where it was last seen to disappear (p. 171)

pretense: pretend play (p. 182)

primary circular reaction: an action-response-action sequence involving only the infant's own body (p. 168)

secondary circular reaction: an action-response-action sequence involving objects in the environment, not just the baby's body (p. 169)

sensorimotor period: the period of cognitive development in which thinking consists of simple coordinations between sensations and actions (p. 167)

shape constancy: the perceptual realization that an object's shape remains the same despite the different views of it we see from different perspectives (p. 159)

size constancy: the perceptual realization that objects stay the same size when their distance from us varies (p. 159)

sociodramatic play: pretend play involving the taking on of roles and collaboration among players (p. 182)

superordinate category: a category of objects (animals, vehicles, etc.) grouped together because they share global characteristics (p. 165)

test phase: the second part of the habituation procedure during which an infant is shown a new stimulus or stimuli that differ from the stimulus or stimuli shown in the habituation phase (p. 163)

visual perception: the descriptions of the world that the infant's brain presents or allows (p. 154)

SUGGESTIONS FOR FURTHER READING

Flavell, J. H., Miller, P. H., & Miller, S. A. (1993). *Cognitive development.* Englewood Cliffs, NJ: Prentice Hall. The section on infant cognition gives an excellent discussion of sensorimotor schemes, cognitive motivation, Piaget's six stages, and other concepts. It also includes infant perception.

Goswami, U. (1998). *Cognition in children.* Philadelphia, PA: Taylor & Francis Group. This book covers basic cognitive processes in infant cognition, conceptual development, and the development of causal reasoning. Piaget's theory is also presented. This book provides a good, clear overview of cognitive development in children, with considerable coverage devoted to infancy.

Kellerman, P. J., & Arterberry, M. E. (1998). *The cradle of knowledge.* Cambridge, MA: The MIT Press. This book focuses on perceptual processes and their development in the infant. It is an excellent resource for the serious student who wants to know more about this topic. Chapters cover physiological and sensory foundations of perceptual development, space perception, pattern perception, auditory perception, and several other topics.

Roopnarine, J. L., Johnson, J. E., & Hooper, F. H. (Eds.). (1994). *Children's play in diverse cultures.* Albany: State University of New York Press. This book contains 10 chapters, each devoted to children's play in a different cultural setting. It covers preschool as well as the toddler period and provides interesting information about variations in conceptions of play in different cultures.

Sawyers, J. K., & Rogers, C. S. (1988). *Helping young children develop through play.* Washington, DC: National Association for the Education of Young Children. This very practical book was written to help caregivers provide for children's play.

Wadsworth, B. J. (1996). *Piaget's theory of cognitive and affective development* (5th ed.). White Plains, NY: Longman. This book provides a very readable overview of Piaget's stages of intellectual development. One chapter covers the sensorimotor period.

6

The Development of Language and Communication in Infants and Toddlers

JUST A MINUTE, Travis; just a minute. I'm coming.

"I bet you're hungry. Just give me a minute to get this frozen yogurt into the freezer. Ohhhhh, and there's a knock at the door. Kimberly said she was coming down here today.

"Come in, Kimberly."

Kimberly, Rhonda's 8-year-old niece, lives in the upstairs apartment with her grandparents, Rhonda's mother and father.

Rhonda carries Travis to the sofa and sits down to nurse him.

When Rhonda puts Travis up to her shoulder to pat up the bubbles from his stomach, Kimberly moves on the sofa to a position somewhat behind Rhonda, where she can talk to Travis.

After listening to her for a minute, Rhonda asks, "Do I sound squeaky and high-pitched like that when I talk to him?"

"Yes. I'm talking just like you," said Kimberly.

"Everybody talks to babies like this."

think about it

Was Kimberly correct in saying that everybody talks to babies in a high-pitched, singsong voice? The attention of young babies seems to be captured quickly by the human voice, especially if it is pitched in a high register. Is a high-pitched voice actually more appealing to infants, or do people just think it is?

In this chapter, we discuss the development of language and communication from birth to about 2½ years of age. We also discuss language development theories—the explanations researchers have proposed for how human babies are able to produce and understand language within just a few short years.

Communication and Language Development during the Infant's First Year

From the moment they are born, infants respond to the human voice and also begin to use their own voices. Because vocalizations during the first year of life are wordless, this early phase of language behavior and development has been called the **prelinguistic period.**

Most of us have little idea of what has gone on behind the scenes in preparation for the first word that our ears finally hear when a baby is about 12 months old. Such remarkably rapid accomplishment can make us think that the script for language is so completely written in each child's brain that language simply blossoms without aid of a baby's active participation or ours.

Babies are actually hard at work long before they utter a first word, using their remarkable language and cognitive powers to make sense of language and other information provided by the physical and social worlds. Babies acquire a tremendous amount of knowledge about both language and the world by listening, watching, and actually participating in social events that transpire around them. A baby's opportunities for social interaction, as well as a baby's vocal play when alone, provide speech and language practice of various kinds. Thus, in one way or another, virtually thousands of preliminary acts prepare a baby for the big event that all of us recognize.

We start our discussion of communication and language development during the first year by going behind the scenes to learn about young infants' capacities to react to the speech they hear and to acquire knowledge about many of its organizational characteristics. Then we turn our attention to a discussion of the development of the vocalizations that infants produce.

Speech Perception: What Infants Make of the Speech They Hear

Phonology refers to all of the sound features of language and the rules for how they work together. The individual sounds that make up words are called **segmental features.** The overall sound of language, the features that determine the rhythm and flow of our speech, are called **suprasegmental features.**

During the first year of life, infants show an amazing ability to detect and respond to both segmental and suprasegmental features. An infant's responses to the speech she hears reveal **speech perception** abilities. We start our discussion of the infant's speech perception with the infant's ability to detect variations in suprasegmental features of language; then we discuss the infant's ability to distinguish segmental features.

The Infant's Perception of Suprasegmental Features   Do infants listen attentively to speech that is uttered at a typical adult pitch, or do they prefer to listen to speech that is higher in pitch? Can infants detect pauses in sentences and stress placed on syllables? These are some of the questions we explore next.

SENSITIVITY TO CHILD-DIRECTED SPEECH.   In most cultures, adults adjust their speech when talking to young infants. This special way of talking is sometimes called **motherese**. Language researchers typically use a broader term, **child-directed speech (CDS)**, when referring to this unique way of talking to babies because mothers are not the only ones who engage in this behavior. Almost everyone speaks differently when speaking to a baby than when greeting an adult neighbor or the clerk in a retail establishment.

Adults make numerous alterations in their speech when they produce CDS (Ferguson, 1964; Snow & Ferguson, 1977). Only some of these adjustments involve suprasegmental features. Other adjustments alter different aspects of the language. For example, adults use simple rather than complex terms. They rarely say to a baby, "You'd better get ready because I'm going to tickle your *abdomen*." Instead they say, "Get ready—get ready—I'm going to tickle your *tummy*." They also are inclined to say, "*Grandma* is going to tickle your tummy," which makes the sentence simpler by deleting the personal pronoun. Adults also repeat words and phrases. For example, Grandma might say, "Tickle, tickle," as she actually tickles the baby's tummy, and then she might say, "And Grandma's going to tickle your feet. Tickle, tickle. And your nose. Tickle. Tickle." Like most CDS, this example of speech concerns the here and now, not the past or the future.

CDS also alters several suprasegmental features found in adult-directed speech. For example, when speaking to young infants, adults lengthen vowels. This exaggerates phrase and clause boundaries in sentences. Adults also say hard-to-hear consonants more carefully than usual (Bernstein-Ratner, 1984, 1986). This makes these sounds stand out more. When speaking to a young infant, adults also speak in a higher-pitched voice than they use normally, and they also increase the range of **pitch** and make more sudden pitch changes. Adults also lengthen pauses and exaggerate stress on syllables in words (Fernald & Kuhl, 1987; Fernald & Simon, 1984; Fernald et al., 1989; Papousek et al., 1991).

These alterations in the suprasegmental features of language give CDS a special sound quality that is very effective in getting and maintaining a young baby's attention (Cooper & Aslin, 1990; Fernald & Kuhl, 1987; Pegg et al., 1992; Werker & McLeod, 1989; Werker et al., 1994). Babies also smile and vocalize more in response to CDS than to typical adult speech (Masataka, 1992). Apparently pitch, which is actually about 30 percent higher in child-directed speech than in adult-directed speech, is the characteristic that makes CDS appeal so much to babies (Clarkson, 1992; Fernald & Kuhl, 1987; Papousek, 1992). Of course, cues other than language, including raised eyebrows and broader-than-usual smiles, also help to capture the baby's attention (de Boysson-Bardies, 1999).

How Pervasive Is Child-Directed Speech?   Child-directed speech has been found in many different language communities, including those that speak Arabic, Spanish,

Japanese, Mandarin Chinese, French, and Italian (Ferguson, 1964, 1978; Fernald et al., 1989; Fernald & Morikawa, 1993; Greiser & Kuhl, 1988). Deaf parents who use American Sign Language (ASL) with their deaf infants and toddlers also use child-directed language. They sign more slowly, shorten sentences, repeat words and phrases frequently, and use proper names instead of personal pronouns (Erting et al., 1990; Masataka, 1992). When not signing, deaf parents alter facial expressions when they communicate with deaf infants. For example, a furrowed brow typically indicates that a question is being asked. But when signing to young deaf infants, deaf parents rarely display this facial expression, apparently because it also accompanies the emotion of anger. In order to make clear to the infant that the parent is not angry, the parent simplifies the language signed to the child under 2 years of age by removing grammatical markings when they overlap negative expressions of affect (Reilly & Bellugi, 1996).

Even though a unique register for communicating to infants has been found just about everywhere researchers have looked (Snow, 1995), the cluster of features that distinguishes CDS from adult-directed speech in one culture or language community is not always the same cluster that distinguishes it in another. For example, pitch contrasts are greatly exaggerated in many cultures but are not exaggerated at all in others (Ingram, 1995). In Qu-iche Mayan culture, high pitch is not found in CDS because it is used to show deference to people of very high status (Ratner & Pye, 1984). Another example of a cultural variation in CDS is the prohibition on baby talk (i.e., talk composed of nonsense syllables) found in the Kaluli culture of New Guinea. In Kaluli culture, anything resembling bird talk (nonsense talk) is to be avoided because it evokes a mythic connection between birds and dead children's souls (Schieffelin, 1986).

Does Child-Directed Speech Aid Language Learning?   Ever since Noam Chomsky claimed in 1965 that children must have a built-in language acquisition device because the language input they hear is too ill-formed, complex, and sloppy to support learning, language researchers have been trying to determine whether this is true. Child-directed speech is actually quite well formed (i.e., it is grammatical) and is appreciably simplified, compared to typical adult talk (Newport et al., 1977; Snow, 1972). But the question of whether CDS serves an instructional function, or merely supports parental communication with an infant who might otherwise fail to attend, has not yet been answered.

Because specific relationships between aspects of CDS and children's language development have not been found consistently in all studies (Murray et al., 1990; Plunkett, 1993; Furrow et al., 1979; Gleitman et al., 1984), some language researchers believe that "there is little correlation between child-directed speech of the mother and the linguistic development of the child" (de Boysson-Bardies, 1999, p. 90). But other researchers say that the question about how CDS might aid language learning cannot yet be answered. According to Catherine Snow (1995), "We have not even begun to analyze whether variations within the culturally prescribed forms of CDS in every society relate to differences in speech or ease of language development by children in that society" (Snow, 1995, p. 186). We can expect to see a great deal more research conducted before the question of whether CDS helps infants learn language is fully answered.

PREFERENCES FOR FAMILIAR VOICES AND THEIR NATIVE LANGUAGE.   The auditory system begins to function in the human fetus during the last trimester of pregnancy (Pasman et al., 1991). Because the fetus can hear best the voice of its own mother (Lecanuet & Granier-Deferre, 1993), the unborn baby becomes familiar with the suprasegmental features her voice. The fetus also becomes familiar with the native language, and can even become familiar with a specific story or poem. (If you read aloud two stories, such as *Dr. Seuss's ABC* and Sendak's *Where the Wild Things*

Are, you will see how the suprasegmental features of your speech form a distinctive pattern with each one.) This prenatal experience then seems to account for the newborn's language preferences (Jusczyk, 1997).

Newborns prefer to listen to their native language rather than to other languages (Mehler et al., 1988; Moon et al., 1993) and to their mother's voice rather than to other female voices (DeCasper & Fifer, 1980; Spence & DeCasper, 1986). They also prefer to listen to a story that was read to them during the last 6 weeks of prenatal life rather than to a story not read to them during the prenatal period (DeCasper & Spence, 1986). And when a mothers reads a specific poem to her unborn child from the 33rd to the 37th week of pregnancy, the unborn child prefers to listen to it rather than to a different poem. Researchers discovered this last preference when they asked mothers to read a poem to their unborn babies and then made a tape of the familiar poem and a different poem, in alternating and repeating sequences. When the researchers played the taped sequences to the fetuses at 37 weeks of gestation, the fetuses' hearts decelerated when they heard the familiar poem and then resumed their normal rhythm when the unfamiliar poem played on the tape (DeCasper & Spence, 1986).

In studies of this kind (Mehler et al., 1988), the taped language played for the fetus is sometimes filtered later to remove segmental features (i.e., the features we need to distinguish particular words) and then played again. The infants still recognized and preferred the familiar language when the segmental features were removed. Thus, suprasegmental features of language—intonation, rhythm, and stress—seem to be used by newborns to distinguish their own language from an unfamiliar language as well as a specific passage of prose or poetry drawn from their native language.

There is a bit of evidence, however, indicating that some segmental information also gets through to the fetus. Researchers have found that 36- to 40-week-old fetuses can distinguish between the bisyllables *babi* and *biba* (Lecanuet & Granier-Deferre, 1993; Lecanuet et al., 1993, cited in de Boysson-Bardies, 1999, p. 24). (The researchers measured fetal reactions to the bisyllables by tracking changes in fetal heart rate.) But despite this demonstration of the fetus's capacity to detect some segmental information, newborns probably use this information very little. Even adults who listen to tapes made of mothers' voices as they sound in utero can detect only 30 percent of the phonemes. In contrast, adults make almost no errors when they use suprasegmental features (Querleu, et al., 1981, cited in de Boysson-Bardies, 1999, p. 23).

PERCEPTION OF PAUSES AND STRESS.   Suprasegmental features include the insertion of pauses to mark off clauses and phrases, and the placement of stress on syllables in multisyllabic words. To test infants' sensitivity to pauses in natural speech, researchers (Hirsh-Pacek et al., 1987; Jusczyk et al., 1992) have made tapes with identical language content, but with pauses placed correctly in one tape and incorrectly in the other (e.g., "Peter tried and tried to whistle // but he couldn't" and "Peter tried and tried to whistle but he // couldn't"; Keats, *Whistle for Willie*, p. 4). The infant can turn on one speaker or the other by looking toward a speaker. Researchers can learn which tape is preferred by recording which one is turned on more frequently and stays on longer.

By 5 or 6 months of age, babies prefer to listen to stories in which pauses are inserted correctly at clause boundaries, rather than incorrectly within a clause (Hirsh-Pacek et al., 1987). By 9 months of age, infants indicate a preference for language in which natural rather than unnatural phrase boundaries are marked with pauses (e.g., "He saw a boy // playing with his dog," rather than "He saw a boy playing with // his dog"; Keats, *Whistle for Willie*, p. 3) (Jusczyk et al., 1992). Pauses marking off clauses may be appreciated earlier by infants than pauses marking off phrases because clause boundaries are emphasized more in CDS (Fisher & Tokura, 1996).

Infants exposed to English should develop a preference for words in which the first syllable is stressed because the first syllable of about 75 percent of multisyllabic English words is stressed (e.g., *in*lay, *ta*ble, *so*fa), and these words are used more frequently in speech than words in which the second syllable is stressed (Cutler & Butterfield, 1992; Cutler & Carter, 1987). By 9 months of age, infants show a preference for the typical English pattern of word stress (Jusczyk et al., 1993; Mattys et al., 1999; Morgan and Saffran, 1995.)

Researchers think that infants are able to divide the stream of speech into manageable segments based on their detection of pauses and stress. The typical strong/weak syllable pattern found in English words seems to be especially important in helping infants find the boundaries separating one word in a sentence from the next one (Mattys et al., 1999). Anyone who has visited a foreign country without knowledge of the language knows that the words seem to run together. This is how speech must first sound to the infant. Infants' remarkable perceptual powers, however, apparently help them locate words in the sentences they hear.

Infants' Perception of Segmental Features

Infants' Perception of Segmental Features   Difference between the bisyllables *babi* and *biba* can be detected by fetuses who have reached a gestational age of 36 to 40 weeks (Lecanuet & Grainer-Deferre, 1993). But even though segmental features of speech can be perceived somewhat by the older fetus, the amniotic fluid and other barriers in the womb filter out much of the segmental speech information before it reaches the fetus. After birth, when physical barriers no longer stand in the way, infants have good access to segmental information.

We start our discussion of the infant's capacity to detect and use segmental information with a consideration of the speech contrasts an infant can hear. Then we discuss the development of the infant's specific preferences for segmental features found in the native language. Finally, we comment on how the infant uses this information, in combination with knowledge about suprasegmental features, to perform the important task of isolating words in the speech stream.

PERCEPTION OF ISOLATED SPEECH CONTRASTS.   Think for a moment about the words *bin* and *pin*. Even though these words are very much alike, we perceive them as two different words. Our perception of their difference is based on our ability to discriminate between two categories of speech sounds, two **phonemes**, /b/ and /p/. If you say these sounds to yourself, you will note that the sounds differ only slightly (say the sounds themselves as they are uttered in pronouncing the words—do not name the letters used to write them). One of them (/b/) is voiced; the other (/p/) is not. We say that /b/ and /p/ differ in terms of the voiced/voiceless speech contrast. (**Voicing** involves vibration of the vocal cords. Hold your fingers on your throat while saying /t/, then /d/, and /b/, then /p/.)

Now say *truck* and *top* and *pit*. Try to feel the position of your tongue when pronouncing the /t/ in each of these different word contexts. Notice that the position of your tongue differs slightly in each case. This causes the sound of the /t/'s you produce to differ a little. Yet despite these small variations in /t/'s, we recognize all of these sounds as belonging to the same phoneme category. That is, we don't misperceive any of these /t/'s for the similar, but voiced, phoneme /d/.

Apparently, infants are born with the capacity to categorize this sort of variation in sound. Researchers discovered that infants have this innate capacity by systematically presenting variations within a phoneme category until the variation reaches the boundary of what constitutes a new category for adults. Using the phoneme pairs /t/, /d/, and /p/, /b/, a machine makes sounds that vary over a continuum from voiceless to voiced because this is the dimension on which these phoneme categories differ. Because even newborns like to receive somewhat novel stimulation, they will suck harder to turn on a new stimulus when they tire of listening to an old stimulus. If the infant perceives the next speech sound presented by the researchers as essentially the same as the speech sound last heard (i.e., as belonging to the same category), then the infant's sucking will not increase. But if the infant perceives that the next speech sound belongs to a different speech category, sucking increases. By using this method, researchers can determine when infants perceive one speech sound to be different from another (Siqueland & DeLucia, 1969). The increment of change between each and every speech sound presented on the continuum (e.g., from voiced to voiceless) is exactly the same. Interestingly, infants do not perceive sounds within a category to differ. But at exactly the points where adults would say, "Hey, that's now a /b/, not a /p/" and "That's now a /d/, not a /t/," young infants indicate the same answers by changing their sucking. Thus, speech perception in infants is **categorical,** just as it is in adults.

One-month-olds can differentiate between the speech categories of /b/ and /p/, /d/ and /t/, and /b/ and /g/ (Eimas et al., 1971; Eimas, 1974; Moffit, 1971; Trehub & Rabinovitch, 1972). The first two pairs (/b/, /p/ and /t/, /d/) differ on the voiced/voiceless contrast. In /b/ and /p/, /b/ is voiced, whereas /p/ is not. In the second pair, /d/ is voiced, whereas /t/ is not. Everything else about the two speech sound pairs is exactly the same. The sounds in the third pair (/b/ and /g/) are the same with respect to voicing, but differ in terms of where in the mouth they are formed (place of articulation): /b/ is articulated at the lips; /g/ is articulated in the back of the throat. Infants can also distinguish pairs of vowels, whether they are presented in combination with consonants (/pa/, /pi/) or alone (/a/, /i/) (Trehub, 1973). In fact, researchers have demonstrated that very young infants can perceive any potential phonemic contrast found in any language in the world (Jusczyk, 1985). Thus, infants come into the world prepared to learn whatever language is spoken in their own community.

NATIVE LANGUAGE EFFECTS ON INFANTS' SPEECH PERCEPTION.   Because each language has speech contrast boundaries that differ from the set used in other languages, infants who are exposed to just one language (which is typical of most infants) are exposed to some sound contrasts, but not others. What happens to infants' initial speech discrimination ability under these conditions? Do they retain the ability to hear all of the speech contrasts used in languages around the world, or do they lose the ability to hear contrasts that are not used in their native language?

Infants actually begin to lose the ability to detect contrasts not utilized in their native language (Burnham et al., 1991; Eilers et al., 1979). These native language effects become evident sometime between 6 and 9 months of age (Kuhl et al., 1992; Polka & Werker, 1994; Werker & Lalonde, 1988; Werker & Tees, 1984). Because these speech perception abilities lessen with age, it becomes increasingly difficult with age for someone to learn to speak a new language without an accent.

PERCEPTION OF SOUND SEQUENCES WITHIN WORDS.   Languages differ not only in terms of speech sound contrasts, but in terms of the sound sequences that are used to form syllables. For example, an English dictionary does not contain the letter combination *cylz*, because this combination is not used in English. Moreover, some permissible sequences are found very frequently in words; others appear only rarely. Knowledge about the sound sequences used in a language to create syllables is called **phonotactic knowledge.** Using this information, infants might recognize words used in their native language long before they know the meanings of any specific words or can say a word. If infants recognize sound sequences used to form syllables in their native language, they should prefer listening to words composed of these familiar sound sequences to listening to unfamiliar or rarely used sound sequences.

The first studies to probe infants' phonotactic knowledge found that 2-month-olds can detect variations in the ordering of sound sequences that make two syllables.

One group of 2-month-olds was presented first with the syllables /ba/ and /dae/. A second group first heard the syllables /bae/ and /da/. After the infants were habituated to this order of the two syllables, the order was reversed. Infants in both groups became realerted to the reordered syllables (Bertoncini & Mehler, 1981; Miller & Eimas, 1979).

Studies have also confirmed that infants learn to identify words in their native language by using phonotactic information (Friederici & Wessels, 1993). For example, in a study of both Dutch and American preverbal infants (Jusczyk et al., 1993, 1994), 9-month-olds preferred words composed of native language sound sequences over words found in the other language.

Speech Comprehension

Understanding of the meanings conveyed through speech is called **speech comprehension.** We commonly think of speech comprehension in terms of an infant's understanding of specific words. For example, if we ask, "Where's the doggy?" when looking at a picture book with a baby, we would judge that the baby comprehends this word if he points at the picture of the doggy rather than at the picture of the bird. But getting meaning from speech actually begins long before infants can perform at this level.

Comprehension of Meanings Expressed through Pitch Contours   To study infants' understanding of the affective meaning of utterances, researchers have presented approvals or prohibitions. Infant-directed speech containing approvals has a gradual change in pitch. In contrast, prohibitions contain very abrupt pitch changes (Trehub et al., 1993). The speech is filtered (i.e., passed through a machine) so that only suprasegmental features can be heard. Thus, researchers can determine whether the language's "melody" alone can convey specific meanings.

In one study, 5-month-olds who had been exposed only to English were presented with approvals and prohibitions in five different languages: German, Italian, nonsense English, natural English, and Japanese (Fernald, 1993). Changes in the infants' facial expressions were noted as they listened to approvals and prohibitions in each language. Infants showed more positive affect when they heard approvals and more negative affect when they heard prohibitions, although infants' reactions to the Japanese utterances did not follow this pattern. Because Japanese speakers use less contrast in their infant-directed approvals and prohibitions than do speakers of other languages, infants accustomed to hearing only English (with its greater contrasts) failed to respond to the reduced contrasts found in Japanese. Japanese babies learn to respond to the narrower contrasts because these are the contrasts to which they are exposed.

In a second study, 4-month-olds were more attentive to approval than to disapproval utterances (Papousek et al., 1990). Together these studies indicate that quite young infants attend to suprasegmental features that convey different affective meanings and that characteristic changes in pitch might help the child learn various social meanings (Papousek, 1992). For example, infants are likely to know that "Stop!" and "No!" are similar in meaning, even though they do not know the specific meaning of either word.

Comprehension of Words   Near the end of their first year, infants begin to comprehend specific words. In **word comprehension,** infants match specific familiar sound sequences to specific meanings (Jusczyk et al., 1994).

Picture books provide a wonderful opportunity for an older infant or a toddler to name objects. Joint visual attention is easy to establish in the context of a book. (Source: © Kathi Lamm/Tony Stone Images)

Estimates of words comprehended by young infants are usually obtained from parental reports, not from laboratory studies. Parental reports typically overestimate actual comprehension of words because parents observe words used in a specific context and do not test whether the infant also understands the word in different contexts. Based on parental reports, the number of words comprehended by young infants who are learning English is about 36 words at 8 months of age, 58 words at 10 months of age, 126 words at 13 months of age, and 210 words at 16 months (Bates et al., 1995; Fenson et al., 1994). There are, of course, rather large individual differences: At 10 months of age, reports obtained in the study by Bates and colleagues (1995) contained estimates ranging from 8 to 183 words.

American parents' estimates of their young children's word comprehension tend to be relatively high compared to estimates provided by parents in other countries (de Boysson-Bardies, 1999). For example, in a study of 228 Swedish infants (Eriksson & Berglund, 1999), parents reported that, on average, 8-month-olds understood only 4.5 words, 10-month-olds understood 18.5, and 12-month-olds comprehended 44. By 14 months of age, the number of words comprehended had reached 107.5. By 16 months, infants on average comprehended 169 words. The range at 10 months of age was from 0 words to 84 words.

The first indications of a baby's comprehension of a word are seen by parents in specific contexts. It is difficult to determine whether the child truly understands the meaning of the word well enough to generalize it to unfamiliar circumstances. Researchers have sometimes gotten around this problem by assessing word comprehension in a laboratory (Golinkoff et al., 1987). While mothers hold their infants on their laps, a woman's voice, heard over a speaker, commands the infant to "Find the _____." Then images of two objects, only one of which has been named by the woman's taped voice, are shown (one each on two different screens). The woman's taped voice then says, "Which is the _____?" If the infant looks toward the image of the object named, rather than toward the screen showing the image of the unnamed object, researchers judge that the infant understands the word's meaning. In the study by Golinkoff and colleagues (1987), only rarely did 9- or 10-month-olds look at one image (the correct one) more than the other. Only half of the infants who were between 12 and 14 months of age looked at the correct screen. Not until 15 to 17 months of age did 80 percent of the infants look at the correct screen.

Of course, infants are in the process of acquiring knowledge of the phonotactic patterns of words well before this age. As we saw earlier, infants reveal phonotactic knowledge—knowledge of specific sound sequences in syllables—by 9 months (Jusczyk et al., 1994). Linking these patterns to specific meanings seems to begin somewhere between 8 and 10 or 11 months of age (Halle & de Boysson-Bardies, 1994; Huttenlocher, 1994), or perhaps earlier for sounds in the names of highly familiar animated subjects, such as parents (Tincoff & Jusczyk, 1999). Infants gradually link more and more sound sequences to meanings but confuse the meanings of words that have very similar phonetic form (e.g., *dish* and *fish*), until about 20 months of age (Stager, 1995). Clearly, familiar contexts help infants respond to words they hear often in these contexts. The laboratory situation, in contrast, provides quite a stringent test of an infant's word understanding.

Vocal Production: What Babies Say

"Dat?" asks Morgan, as she points up to the sky.

"That's an airplane," her father tells her. "It's making a loud noise, isn't it?"

"Pane? Pane?" Morgan says, as she continues to follow the airplane with her eyes.

"Yes, that's an airplane. It's a very noisy airplane."

"Voom, voom," Morgan answers back.

think about it

How old is Morgan? How long ago might she have said her first word? We know from this conversation that Morgan can say three words—"dat" (*that*), "pane" (*plane*), and "voom" (*vroom*). How many others might she be able to say?

Infants do not actually produce their first word until near the end of the first year of life. Of course, throughout the first year, infants vocalize in many ways. They cry, coo, and babble. Infants also use a variety of gestures to communicate. They shake their heads, reach, raise their arms (to be picked up), and point. In this section, we discuss these early preverbal vocalizations and gestures.

Crying and Cooing: The First Vocalizations   Infants' first vocalizations are uttered at birth when they cry. Noncrying vocalizations appear soon after birth, but the infant has little voluntary control over their features. Very young infants can "emit only reactional sounds that signal their well-being or discomfort" (de Boysson-Bardies, 1999, p. 37). Starting at about 2 months of age, infants can vocalize more, but only while lying down (de Boysson-Bardies, 1999). Because infants do not at first use their lips or tongues to control production of different sounds, they emit only open, vowel-like *ooohs* and *ahhhs* and raspy, consonant-like sounds resembling /g/ and /k/ (de Boysson-Bardies, 1999; Cruttenden, 1970; Oller & Eilers, 1988). At about 4 or 5 months of age, infants begin to use their lips to produce sounds (e.g., /w/, /p/, /m/). Other vocalizations, such as squealing and vocalizing while vibrating the lips (i.e., making "raspberries"), also appear at around 4 or 5 months of age. All of these early single sounds are known as coos.

By 4 or 5 months of age, infants begin to play with the sounds they can make by engaging in vocal games. By varying the pitch, duration, and loudness of their **cooing,** they can emit sharp cries, grunts, and howls. They can also click their tongues and open and close their mouths (de Boysson-Bardies, 1999). At around 6 months of age, they practice at starting and stopping their vocalizations (de Boysson-Bardies, 1999), and they can imitate intonation patterns provided by a model (Masataka, 1992). By using the variations they have learned to produce, they can communicate how they feel, what they notice, and what they want.

Babbling: Syllable Repetition   Between 6 and 10 months of age, infants no longer utter isolated sounds. They begin to combine consonant- and vowel-like sounds to form syllables. Infants repeat these syllables to create long chains (e.g., "ma-ma-ma-ma-ma," "da-da-da-da-da-da," "ba-ba-ba-ba-ba"). This language behavior, called **reduplicated babbling,** reflects the sequences found in the child's native language for forming syllables (Oller & Eilers, 1988; Oller & Lynch, 1992). Thus, an infant's babbles can sometimes sound like words, especially near the end of the babbling phase when the long chains of repeated syllables give way to only one or two repetitions (e.g., "ba-ba" or "da-da"). Although these **protowords,** which appear just before most infants say their first real words (Kamhi, 1986), sound like actual words, they are not actual words because the infant does not associate these sound sequences with any specific meanings.

IS BABBLING INFLUENCED BY THE LANGUAGE ENVIRONMENT?   Because different languages utilize somewhat different sound contrasts, sound sequences, and suprasegmental features, infants growing up in different language environments might babble somewhat differently. If they do, it would indicate that babbling is influenced by the infant's language environment. If they don't, it would mean that babbling is controlled by maturational processes and is not influenced by language input. The dominant opinion from the 1940s to the 1980s was that babbling was unrelated to language input. The famous linguist Roman Jakobson put forth this belief in his book *Child Language, Aphasia, and Phonological Universals* (1941). As it turns out, Jakobson was wrong. Babbling is related to the language a baby hears and also to the first words a baby produces.

Researchers have discovered that the sound quality of infant babbling is indeed related to the features of the infant's native language. French, American, Japanese, and Swedish babies babble differently, and these differences reflect differences in the place and manner of articulation of consonants in their languages (de Boysson-Bardies et al., 1992). De Boysson-Bardies (1993) also found that infants growing up in Nigeria, learning to speak Yoruba, produce more vowel-consonant-vowel babbles than consonant-vowel babbles (62 versus 38 percent). In Yoruba, most words begin with a vowel, not a consonant. Infants learning French, Swedish, and English, on the other hand, produce babbles beginning with consonants up to 75 percent of the time because most words in these languages begin with consonants. Other studies have shown that suprasegmental features characteristic of the native language are also evident in infants' babbling (de Boysson-Bardies et al., 1984; Levitt & Wang, 1991).

Researchers have also studied the relationship between language environment and babbling by comparing hearing and deaf infants. If babbling is a spontaneous, internally driven behavior, we would expect both the onset and the sound quality of babbling in hearing and severely hearing-impaired infants to be the same. But if babbling is influenced by language exposure, we would expect to find that deaf infants babble later than hearing infants, or perhaps not at all.

Hearing infants produce their first syllable repetitions (i.e., babbles) sometime between 6 and 10 months of age. Deaf infants, on the other hand, almost never produce reduplicated babbles in speech within this time frame. Instead, their babbling is delayed for many months (Oller & Eilers, 1988). Much later, when deaf babies can take advantage of visual observation, they begin to produce syllables beginning with labial consonants (those produced by the lips and mouth, such as /m/, and /p/), (de Boysson-Bardies, 1999). Deaf babies who have been exposed to sign language from birth begin to babble in sign at about 8 months of age. Researchers who have studied signed babbles think that they resemble the counterparts produced by babies who speak (Petitto & Marentette, 1991). Like the speech babbles produced by hearing infants, signed babbles use sublexical units found in signed words, but they are not used systematically to refer to particular meanings (de Boysson-Bardies, 1999). Deaf infants' signed babbles are clearly distinguishable from typical manual gestures (e.g., pointing, reaching, showing, and so on) used by both hearing and deaf children to aid communication in its early stages. (See Knowledge in Action: Education—Detecting Hearing Loss in Infants.)

Researchers have also found differences between the babbling of infants raised in extreme poverty and infants raised in more advantaged economic circumstances. These groups of infants differ in *how much* they babble after they start, not in when they start to babble (Oller et al., 1995). Infants reared in extreme poverty hear less talk because their mothers talk less to them (Hart & Risley, 1992, 1995; Rosser & Randolph, 1989). As a consequence of this low level of stimulation, they babble less than infants reared under other circumstances. The fact that the onset of babbling is not delayed in infants reared in extreme poverty suggests that infants have a strong biological disposition to babble.

Researchers have wondered whether babbling a little bit is just as advantageous as babbling a lot. If the sound combinations practiced in babbling influence the words

EDUCATION

Detecting Hearing Loss in Infants

Hearing loss can have a profound effect on an infant's language development. If a hearing loss is found, two steps can be taken: (1) residual hearing can be augmented with a hearing aid and (2) an alternate form of communication can be taught to the infant.

Diagnostic Tools

If there is a family history of deafness, or if prenatal conditions suggest that there might be a hearing problem, newborns can be screened for a possible hearing loss. The **Crib-O-Gram** and the **Brain Stem Evoked Response** test a baby's brain waves to see if sounds elicit typical brain activity (Downs, 1978; Murray, 1988; Stein et al., 1983). Babies are also observed visually to see whether they respond to sounds. Because only infants who are at risk are screened, some infants with profound hearing loss are not diagnosed at this early age.

Deaf and hearing babies both produce about the same kinds of early vocalizations. Both groups of infants cry, and they also coo, screech, and make "raspberries" with their lips. Parents and pediatricians sometimes think that if infants make these sounds, they hear them. But before the stage of reduplicated babbling, vocalizations are prompted by internal factors, such as physical exploration of the vocal tract, as well as by social factors. Because deaf infants make these physical explorations, they produce many of

the same sounds that hearing infants produce even though there is a difference in phrasing (Lynch, 1996). But at about 6 or 7 months of age, hearing and deaf children's vocalizations begin to differ. Reduplicated babbling (syllable repetition) is severely delayed in deaf infants. The absence of this kind of babbling by 10 months of age can alert parents and pediatricians to the possibility of a severe hearing loss if they have not noticed earlier that an infant is unable to hear.

An Alternate Mode of Communication

Infants find it easy to learn sign language, once they have been immersed in it. Obviously babies will have an advantage if a profound hearing loss is diagnosed soon after birth, rather than later, and they are exposed to sign language from the very beginning. But a later introduction also produces good results (Dale, 1976; Petitto & Marentette, 1991).

Babies babble in sign before they sign their first words. Deaf babies also use one-word signs to convey the whole range of meanings used by hearing infants. (See p. 000 for a discussion of holophrases.) Deaf children also express the same relations in the two-sign strings as hearing children express in their 2–3 word "sentences" (Schlesinger & Meadow, 1972). Deaf children learn sign language at about the same rate that hearing children learn oral language, and the processes are similar.

Because deaf babies are so capable of learning language (although in a different mode), it is very important to detect hearing losses early so that they are provided with appropriate language input in manual form.

---

an infant produces, then we might expect word production to be delayed and vocabulary development slowed in infants who babble little. We discuss this topic next.

BABBLING AND WORD PRODUCTION. There are strong correlations between the production of sound during the babbling stage and development of language during the single-word stage. The first words children are likely to say, as well as how they pronounce them, can be predicted quite well from the sounds infants produce in their babbling (Bloom, 1998; de Boysson-Bardies 1999; Oller et al., 1976; Viham et al., 1985). This research indicates a relationship between the sound sequences an infant has practiced when babbling and the sound sequences found in the infant's first words. It also indicates a relationship between amount of babbling and the rate at which new words are added, at first, to the baby's vocabulary.

Preverbal Communication: Intentional Vocalizations and Gestures

Newborn communication is limited to crying, stiffening, and turning the face away. Within a few weeks, infants add gazing to their signaling repertoire. Looking at a person signals the person to continue to interact; looking away signals the person to

Children point in order to draw an adult's attention to objects of interest. Adults can most easily establish joint reference with a baby by looking at objects to which the infant is attending.   (Source: © D. Greco/The Image Works)

stop. By 3 months of age, infants can also smile or look sober to communicate their willingness to interact or their unwillingness to do so.

The infant's expressions of emotion also serve to regulate the behavior of others, and infant reactions also begin to vary in response to the facial expressions displayed by others. By 3 or 4 months of age, infants respond differently to a smiling face accompanied by words of encouragement than to a sad face (Termine & Izard, 1988). Between 10 and 12 months of age, infants comprehend affective expressions and use these to regulate their behavior. For example, their approach to or withdrawal from novel objects and people is influenced by the expressions they read on a familiar caregiver's face (Klinnert et al., 1983).

Of course, messages etched on the face are typically accompanied by vocal expressions (Fernald, 1993; Haviland & Lelwica, 1987; Walker-Andrews, 1986). Infants may rely more heavily on information expressed vocally than on information expressed visually to determine the meaning of emotional expressions (Caron et al., 1988). By 4 or 5 months of age, specific changes in intonation (i.e., changes in pitch), used routinely by parents, have acquired specific meanings for an infant. Infants understand whether what is said is a prohibition or an approval, whether it signals discouragement or encouragement, or when it is meant to soothe (Fernald, 1993; Papousek, 1992). Infants understand meanings from these suprasegmental features before they understand the meanings of specific words. By 9 or 10 months of age, infants begin to vary their own intonation when they vocalize, and in this they can communicate different meanings. Soon after the first birthday, infants also begin to use specific gestures to signal to others and to communicate various intentions (See pp. 204–205).

Intentional Vocalizations

Over the course of the first year of life, as crying itself becomes differentiated, infants can communicate different intentions with their cries. In detailed case studies, Demos (1986) described how crying is used by infants to express different emotions and to communicate intentions. By 3 months of age, for example, one infant varied her crying between a lower-intensity distress cry and a more intense protest cry, which she combined with looks at the mother, who was preparing food. Demos interpreted the distress cry as an expression of annoyance aimed at the mother, a message to her to "hurry up!" At 5½ months, the child could control the intensity of her cries and varied them from weak to intense. On one occasion, at 6 months of age, when the infant was alone, she cried moderately, probably because she was hungry. When her mother reentered the room, she emitted a sharper, more intense "protest" cry and then resumed her distress cry until her mother fed her (Demos, 1986).

Thus, as infants learn to change the loudness, duration, and onset of their crying, cries of distress begin to differ from cries of protest or cries intended merely to signal to a caregiver. Cries used to signal to a caregiver apparently are used specifically to communicate intentions or emotions (Demos, 1986).

By late in the first year, infants have gained a measure of control over the sounds they can produce through engagement in a great deal of vocal play (de Boysson-Bardies, 1999). They use this vocal control to vary the intonation accompanying their babbles and thus are able to communicate various intentions to others (Konopezynski, 1995). Infants are able to produce calling types of vocalizations, which they use, for example, when their mothers are not in sight (D'Odorico, 1984). They also have vocalizations that communicate demands, requests, and protests (Bruner, 1977; Masataka, 1992). They also can use a flat or falling pitch at the end of sentences to comment.

Gestural Communication
By about 1 year of age, infants also begin to use a variety of gestures. **Deictic gestures** communicate to another person the infant's intent. **Representational gestures**, on the other hand, stand for or symbolize an object, request, event, or attribute. A sniffing gesture, for example, can mean "flower." Shrugging the shoulders, while extending the arms and hands with palms turned up, can mean "I don't know." Deictic gestures—reaching, pointing, showing, and giving—are accompanied by gaze, which is directed back and forth between the person to whom the infant is communicating and the object or event about which the infant is communicating. The deictic gestures will be discussed here.

FEATURES OF DEICTIC GESTURES AND THEIR APPARENT MEANINGS.
Pointing consists of an extension of the arm while the index finger is extended. Pointing serves a declarative (commenting) or interrogative (questioning) function, and it is used often when objects or events are at a distance, clearly out of reach. An exception occurs in the context of looking at a picture book, in which "objects" can be referred to or called to someone's attention, but cannot, of course, be taken in hand. In pointing, an infant communicates "Look at that" or "What is that?" (Bates et al., 1975; Franco & Butterworth, 1996).

In **reaching,** the arm is also extended, but the fingers and thumb are held away from the palm, which is turned down. The infant uses reaching to give commands, which mean something akin to "Give that to me" (Franco & Butterworth, 1996). Sometimes reaching is used along with pointing when objects are close at hand—almost within reach.

In the **giving** gesture, the arm and hand are extended toward another person while an object is in hand. The object is released momentarily to the person, for the purpose of calling the person's attention to it (Capirci et al., 1996). **Showing** involves essentially the same movement as giving and seems to be motivated by the same intention (i.e., calling the other person's attention to the object). But in showing, the object is moved only into the other person's line of vision; it is not released.

Of all the deictic gestures, pointing has received the most attention because infants point more than they reach, give, or show, and because pointing is perhaps the most important of these gestures. It is significant because it helps people establish **joint attention**—the focusing of gaze by two people on the same object or event. **Gaze** alone helps to direct another person to an object that has grabbed our attention, but it is not as obvious or effective a gesture as pointing.

THE DEVELOPMENTAL COURSE OF POINTING.   Some infants begin to point at about 10 months of age (Bates et al., 1979; Fenson et al., 1994). In the context of picture-book reading, pointing has been observed just a bit earlier, at about 9 months of age (Murphy, 1978). Although present in some infants prior to the first birthday, most infants do not point very much until sometime between 12 and 14 months of age (Carpenter et al., 1998; Leung & Rheingold, 1981; Murphy & Messer, 1977). Once it is established, the frequency of pointing increases for several months (Gelman et al., 1998). Gazing, which accompanies pointing, also increases with age. In one study (Franco & Butterworth, 1996), a little less than half of infants' pointing at 1 year of age was accompanied by visual checking with the adult whose attention the infant was trying to direct. By 16 months of age, visual checking accompanied 65 percent of the infant's pointing gestures.

With increasing age, the timing of visual checking also moves from *after* the pointing (at 1 year) to *during* the pointing (at 14 months), and then, finally, to *before* the pointing (at 16 months) (Butterworth & Franco, 1993). By 16 months, the infant apparently has begun to realize that it is wise to check before pointing, in order to assess whether the other person is likely to see the pointing gesture. Infants also vocalize while pointing about 75 percent of the time, and this also alerts the other person to the pointing (Franco & Butterworth, 1996). Infants probably also learn to visually check the other person's gaze and to alter their vocalization, if necessary, to get more attention.

When objects are pointed out to them, do infants understand the gesture? Between 6 and 9 months of age, they are much less inclined to fixate on the target than to look at the mother's finger (Butterworth & Grover, 1990). Sometime between 9 and 11 months of age, infants attend more reliably to objects indicated by another person's pointing (Bates et al., 1979; Carpenter et al., 1998). Infants succeed most often in fixating on the actual target when the target is nearby and is located between the adult and the child (Lempers, 1979). Otherwise, infants under 1 year of age tend to look at the adult's finger, not at the object pointed out, especially if the adult is pointing across or forward, in front of the infant. Not until about 14 or 15 months of age do infants follow a point to the intended object regardless of whether the point is away from, in front of, or across from them (Morissette et al., 1995; Murphy & Messer, 1977).

Language Development during the Infant's Second Year

"And there's the doggy. And a cat. 'Meow, meow.' And a chicken, a chicken. And a duck, a duck."

"Duh," Reggie repeats. "Duh, duh."

"Yes, that's a duck, just like your bathtub duck."

"Duh," Reggie says again, as he points to the picture in the book.

"There's a lamb." 'Baaaa, baaaa.'

"And there's a horse, a horse.

"Shall we do that again?

"Oh, and a doggy. 'Woof-woof.' "

"Ooof-oooof," Reggie repeats.

think about it

How old is Reggie? Why did he repeat some animal names his mother provided, but not all of them? Are all children somewhat selective at first, as Reggie was, or do they repeat most of the names of items pictured in their books after adults name them? Should we even count Reggie's utterances as words? After all, he did not pronounce "duck" or "woof" accurately. How can we know if a child has said a real word or if he has not?

Babies usually speak actual words near their first birthday. They add other words slowly for several more months, before they begin to combine them to form multi-word utterances. In this section, we discuss the single-word stage of language development. We also discuss other language milestones that most children achieve during the second year of life.

RESEARCH

CLOSE-UP *Children's First Words*

In one study (Fenson et al., 1994) the words that appeared among the first 50 for at least half of the children were grouped into about 15 categories. (See Table 6.1.) The largest category of words was games and routines. Animal names and names for food and drink tied for second place, with six items each. Next were names for people. Three categories ranked next—sound effects, names for toys, and animal sounds. Words that were names for clothing, body parts, or vehicles were next. Categories with the fewest items—two each—were small household items and prepositions.

Nelson (1973) found that names for food and drink (e.g., *juice, milk, cookie, water*) and animals (e.g., *dog, cat, duck, horse*) topped the list (90 and 67 items, respectively) of the first 50 words. Names for clothing items (e.g., *shoes, hat, socks*) and names for toys and play equipment (e.g., *ball, blocks, doll, teddy bear*) ranked next. Vehicle names (e.g., *car, boat, truck*) and names for furniture and household items (e.g., *clock, light, blanket*) followed closely. Names for personal items (e.g., *key, book, watch*) ranked next, with names for eating and drinking utensils (e.g., *bottle, cup, spoon*) not far behind. The categories "outdoor objects" and "places" contained the fewest items (15 and 6, respectively).

Lois Bloom (1973, 1993) found many of these same words among the first uttered by the children she studied. The five words used by all 14 children were baby, ball, down, juice, and more. Thirteen of the 14 children all produced the words *mommy, no, oh,* and *up.* Many said *bye, hi,* and *yum,* and half produced the words *moo, woof, uh-oh, whee, cookie, truck, boom, daddy,* and *eye.*

Why Might a Word Be Learned First?

Many first words are those encountered frequently in a baby's environment. When playing peek-a-boo, for example, an adult hides and reappears several times in succession and says "peek-a-boo" each time. Babies hear other words, such as *eye, nose,* and *ear,* when parents label body parts.

Mere existence of an item in the child's environment, no matter how pervasive, does not explain everything about why children learn some words but not others. Children wear diapers, shirts, pants, and pajamas, but names for these items do not appear in children's early vocabularies, nor do the names of many household items. Children tend to learn first the names for only some of these items (e.g., *clocks* and *lights*). Why?

Nelson (1973) suggested that children are likely to name first the things that move, make a sound, and can be manipulated. Balls roll; cars and trucks move and make noise. Keys rattle and clang; clocks chime or "tick-tock" (not true of digital clocks, of course).

Candidates for first words must also be easy to pronounce. First words tend to be short, and they contain sound sequences that are used frequently in the language. Bloom (1993, 1998) suggested that the most frequently occurring sound sequences in the language probably became frequent because they are the easiest to learn. These sound sequences are the ones babies tend to babble, and they are also the ones contained in babies' first words.

The Single-Word Stage of Language Development

Thirteen-month-old Reggie has recently begun to talk. His first words, like those of most children, include names for highly familiar animals ("duh") and sounds he has learned to associate with animals ("baa-baa" and "oof-oof"). (See Research Close-Up: Children's First Words.) If Reggie's language development proceeds like most other children's, he will add other words slowly for several more months, before he begins to combine words into 2- and 3-word utterances. In this section, we discuss the single-word period of language development. We consider how the child's vocabulary increases during this period, as well as how children communicate during this time, using the relatively few words they have at their disposal.

First, real words have a symbolic quality, which means that what an infant says must be understood by the infant to stand for something. Researchers assume that infants are using words symbolically when they apply the same word to several different instances of an object or action. If a word such as "ba" is used only in relation to a very specific ball that is found in only one context (e.g., perhaps one used in a routine play context with a parent), the child is simply using a vocalization as a

---

TABLE 6.1   Children's first words by category

Games and Routines (7 items)	Animal Sounds (4 items)	Sound Effects (4 items)	Food and Drink (6 items)
bye	woof	uh-oh	banana
hi	moo	ouch	juice
no	baa-baa	yum-yum	cookie
night night	grrr	owie	cracker
bath			apple
peek-a-boo	**Body Parts (3 items)**	**Clothing (3 items)**	cheese
thank you	eye	shoe	
	nose	sock	**Toys (4 items)**
People (5 items)	ear	hat	ball
daddy			book
mommy	**Animal Names (6 items)**	**Small Household Items (2 items)**	balloon
baby	dog		boat
grandma	kitty	bottle	
grandpa	bird	keys	**Vehicles (3 items)**
	duck		car
	cat		boat
	fish		truck
			Preposition/Location (2 items)
			up
			down

Source: Adapted from "Variabilty in Early Communicative Development," by L. Fenson, P. S. Dale, J. S. Reznick, E. Bates, D. J. Thal, and S. J. Petnick, 1994, *Monographs of the Society for Research in Child Development,* Serial No. 242, *59*(5).

Naming routines aid vocabularly growth in infants. This mother is naming parts of the face for her infant. The infant is repeating each name and also touching each body part. (*Source:* © Elizabeth Crews)

procedure to get the parent to play a game. But if the infant uses "ba" when she sees other round objects, or when she looks at circles or pictures of balls in a book, then we might safely assume it is used as a symbol or name for a type of thing.

Second, a child's vocalization counts as a word if the sound sequence resembles somewhat the adult pronunciation of the word. Here, though, we find some cross-cultural variation in the extent to which adults are willing to accept a sound sequence as a word when it departs from the adult rendition of it. Researchers and parents alike in the United States tend to be quite liberal, accepting the sound sequence as a word even when it departs dramatically from the adult standard, as long as the child uses it consistently to indicate a specific meaning (Carter, 1975; Ferguson & Farwell, 1975; Winitz & Irwin, 1958). American mothers' tendencies are quite liberal in what they count as evidence of a child's "knowing how to talk" (de Boysson-Bardies, 1999, p. 179). De Boysson-Bardies wonders if this tendency to count almost any pronunciation as a word might be responsible for cases in which inaccurate pronunciations persist for quite a long time in some children (pp. 157–158). In contrast to American mothers, French mothers tend to count a sound sequence as a word only when it matches fairly closely the adult pronunciation (de Boysson-Bardies, 1999).

General Patterns of Vocabulary Growth

Because of differences in the standard used to judge sound sequences, vocabulary size estimates differ somewhat from culture to culture. Such variations would not occur were vocabulary assessed directly by researchers who applied a single standard. But because researchers need to collect data from large numbers of children, they cannot assess each child directly. Instead, they ask parents to indicate on standard inventories of words when their child produces a particular word (Eriksson & Berglund, 1999; Fenson et al., 1994). This heavy reliance on parental report increases the possibility that somewhat different cultural norms will emerge.

Vocabulary Size

In one study of vocabulary size at various ages (Bates et al., 1994), most children between 8 and 11 months of age almost never produced a word, although a few children produced 1 or 2 words. At 12 months of age, the median number of words produced by infants was 6, although the range was enormous (0 to 52 words). By 16 months of age, the median number of words produced was 40. The range, which was 0 to 347, was even greater than at 12 months. At 20 months, the median number of words was 170, and the range was 3 to 544 words. At 2 years of age, the median number of words had reached 311; at 2½ years of age, it had reached 574. The range at age 2½ was from 208 to 675 words. Researchers who conducted a second large study in the United States at about the same time (Fenson et al., 1994) obtained similar results. Both studies relied on parental report to obtain their estimates of vocabulary size at different ages.

In a study conducted in Sweden (Eriksson & Berglund, 1999), most 8-month-olds rarely produced any words, but a few produced 1 to 3 words. At 10 months, the median number of words was about 2 words, with a range from 0 words to 7. At 12 months, the median number of words produced was 4; the range was from 0 to 20.

At 14 months, the median number was 8, with a range of 40 words to 0. At 16 months, the final age covered by the study, the median number of words was 18, and the range was from 120 words to 0. These estimates of productive vocabulary (based on parental use of a standard checklist) are significantly lower than those found in U.S. studies. The contrast illustrates a difficulty inherent in parental reports about children's vocabularies. There is considerable variation in parental reports (Feldman et al., 2000).

A striking similarity across all studies of early vocabulary acquisition, however, is that all reveal enormous individual variation. Some is due to individual differences found among children—to what has been called "learning styles." Other variations are due to differences found in the social environments of different infants.

The second striking finding in all studies is that vocabulary increases slowly at first. After the first word is produced, only 3 or 4 more are added in the next 1 or 2 months. In the following 2 or 3 months, another 20 words might be learned. After about 50 words have been acquired, however, new words are added much more rapidly. In the 4 months following the 50-word milestone, an infant typically adds 120 new words. In the next 4 months, an infant is likely to add 140 (Boysson-Bardies, 1999). Fenson (Fenson et al., 1994) has estimated that, between 16 and 23 months of age, infants add 0.81 words per day. Between 23 and 30 months, the rate is 1.64 words per day. (We will see in chapter 10 that vocabulary acquisition continues to increase at an accelerating rate throughout the preschool and school-age years.)

Different Approaches to Word Learning   Children who tend to be oriented toward objects, inclined to learn objects' names, and focused more on phonetic elements and syllables in the speech stream than on larger segments are said to have a **referential style** of word learning (Bates et al., 1994; de Boysson-Bardies, 1999; Nelson, 1973.) Not surprisingly, names for people, animals, places, and things—nouns—make up most of their first 50 words. Other children are described as having an **expressive style.** These children focus more on the suprasegmental features of speech, rather than objects in the environment. Their early words tend less often to stand in isolation from one another. Instead, they are found in **formulaic chunks**—whole phrases they have heard repeatedly. These might include "Just a minute," "It's okay," and "See you later." Because these children focus on chunks of speech, they have a wider variety of words in their early vocabularies than do children with a referential style. Their vocabularies include verbs, adjectives, pronouns, and some nouns, rather than predominantly nouns, although it cannot be said that they have analyzed the formulaic chunks into specific words or word categories.

The tendency for children to adopt one or the other of these two basic approaches to word learning has been documented in a number of different language communities around the world, although the proportion of children who adopt each approach varies somewhat, depending on the characteristics of the native language. Some languages, such as French, lend themselves more to global rather than to fine-tuned segmentation, and more children in this language community adopt an expressive, more holistic, style of early word learning than is typical of English-speaking children (de Boysson-Bardies, 1999). Parents also differ in terms of their tendency to provide word-level segmenting information in their child-directed speech. Some parents provide more information than others do about segmenting the speech stream into words; they do so by producing more single words (e.g., "Lamb"). They also repeat a noun in more than one sentence frame (e.g., "Oh, see the lamb. It's a pretty lamb. Nice lamb.") and use different labels in the same sentence frame (e.g., "See the lamb? See the kitten?"). Children of these parents tend to adopt a referential style of early word learning. Children of parents who tend to talk more in whole phrases or sentences, without inserting repetitions of this kind, tend to adopt an expressive style (Pine et al., 1997).

The exact proportion of nouns in relation to verbs in the early vocabularies of children who adopt a referential style also seems to be influenced somewhat by characteristics of the native language. Korean and Japanese children have fewer nouns and more verbs in their first 50 words than do English-speaking, referential-approach children, according to some studies. These languages permit verbs and adjectives alone to refer to an object when the object is in view. As a result, nouns are used less frequently in these languages than in English. Verbs are also found often in the final position in Korean sentences (Au, et al., 1994; Gopnik & Choi, 1990). Words are more likely to be noticed in this position than when embedded in the middle of a sentence (Fernald et al., 1998; Goldfield, 1993). Korean parents also provide more labels for actions than for objects, whereas American parents tend to provide more labels for objects than for actions (Gopnick & Choi, 1990). Parents who speak Mandarin Chinese also have been found to provide more labels for actions than for objects, compared to American parents (Tardif, 1996, 1999).

Parents goals for their children may also differ. Mothers in the United States, particularly those with higher levels of education (Bates et al., 1994; Hampson & Nelson, 1993), stress the teaching of object names. In fact, a large proportion of American parent-child exchanges consists of name-learning routines: "What is that?" "Can you say 'duck'?" In other cultures, learning the names of a vast array of things at an early age is not considered as important as learning to attend to the feelings of others, to observe rules of politeness, and to appreciate the poetic or musical quality of one's language (de Boysson-Bardies, 1999). These different goals probably influence the amount of time parents spend with their children in some contexts versus others, and different contexts appear to elicit different kinds of language behavior from parents. In a study comparing parents who speak English and those who speak Mandarin Chinese, researchers found that both used more nouns than verbs in a picture-book context than in a mechanical-toy context, where they used more verbs than nouns (Tardif et al., 1999). Thus, the relative amount of time that different infants and their parents spend in various contexts would influence the proportion of nouns to verbs found in infants' early vocabularies.

Children with a referential style typically show a spurt in vocabulary growth after they have accumulated about 50 words or after they start to combine words. The vocabulary spurt in toddlers correlates closely with object-sorting behavior. Children who have begun to sort objects into groups are the same ones who show a marked increase in naming things (Gopnik & Meltzoff, 1992). Children might also suddenly realize that there are parts to an event (objects, actions, people). With this insight, many things may appear suddenly to need a name (Nelson & Lucariello, 1985).

Children who exhibit the expressive style add words more incrementally. They do not show a spurt in vocabulary growth until after they have accumulated about 100 words. A quicker versus a slower start, or a preponderance of one kind of word versus another, seems to have no long-term consequences. Apparently, different children simply start in different places, tackling one thing first rather than another (Bates et al., 1994; de Boysson-Bardies, 1999).

Of course, parents and others worry when a child who has reached the age of 2 years, for example, has not begun to talk. This does not necessarily indicate that a child will have problems later on. Only when a combination of certain factors exists does a delay in talking suggest a significant problem. (See Knowledge in Action: Special Education—Indicators of Significant Language Delay in Infants.)

The Meanings Children Give to Their First Words   When children first learn new words, they typically use them either more narrowly or more broadly than adults use the same words (Anglin, 1983; Bloom, 1998; Clark, 1975). When a child

SPECIAL EDUCATION

knowledge in action

Indicators of Significant Language Delay in Infants

Some children say their first word at 8 months; others wait until their first birthday or later. To illustrate how great are the differences among children, consider that, at 16 months, children in the top 10 percent produced about 180 words, whereas children in the bottom 10 percent produce fewer than 10 (Fenson et al., 1994). But both parents and researchers routinely encounter children who are slow to speak and then turn out to be perfectly all right in every respect. Is there any way to predict when a delay indicates a child will have problems in later development and when it does not?

Different approaches to solving this diagnostic puzzle have been proposed. Some researchers have collected extensive data from which they have developed language norms—the number of words the average or typical child understands and produces at various ages, or the typical age at which children produce multiword sentences (Fenson et al., 1994). Most norm-based screening tools suggest that the production of fewer than 50 words by age 2, or a failure by age 2 to produce multiword sentences, is reason for concern (Rescorla, 1989). But only a few studies have been done on children with these delays at age 2 to see how many and which ones of them actually have language difficulties later on.

In one recent longitudinal study (Pearson & Basinger, 1995), three groups of children were followed up: (1) both full-term and premature babies from low and middle socioeconomic, monolingual families; (2) bilingual babies, learning English and Spanish; and (3) premature infants who were living in extreme poverty, some of whom were exposed to drugs prenatally.

Babies who were premature and who lived in bilingual families under middle socioeconomic circumstances developed vocabularies in line with typical norms. But premature birth coupled with low, and especially very low, socioeconomic conditions was related to slow rates of word acquisition. The group of premature infants living in extreme poverty also showed the biggest delay in the onset of multiword utterances.

In this longitudinal study, lacking 50 words by age 2, or failing to combine words by age 2, was not related to a significant language delay at age 4 or 5. But if a child did not have a vocabulary of at least 50 words and failed to combine words by age 2, there were problems at age 4 or 5. Thus, although relatively uncommon, some children combine words by age 2, even though their productive vocabularies have not yet reached the 50-word mark.

When keeping an eye out for indicators of a significant language delay, some things to watch for are these:

- an absence of a 50-word vocabulary *and* failure to combine words by age 2
  By itself, a small vocabulary does not predict later language problems as well as these *combined* factors do (Pearson & Basinger, 1995).
- difficulty in learning verbs (Oetting et al., 1995)
- absence of use of the intentional communicative gesture of pointing
  An absence of pointing can indicate a delay in developing intersubjectivity (i.e., awareness of others' minds), which appears to be necessary to prompt word acquisition (Bloom, 1998; Locke, 1996). An extreme example of a lack of intersubjectivity occurs in children with autism. Children with autism do not seem to comprehend that pointing has a declarative function, nor do they use pointing (Baron-Cohen, 1989). Not surprisingly, they also engage in very low levels of joint attention with caregivers.
- low levels of word comprehension between 12 and 18 months (de Boysson-Bardies, 1999)
  Low levels of production can be caused by production problems—problems in organizing and producing sound sequences. Low levels of comprehension, on the other hand, can indicate a general lack of understanding about the symbolic function of words and about the use of language to communicate. These latter difficulties disrupt language learning more seriously than many other snags in language production.

restricts the use of a word more narrowly than is customary, we say that the child has **underextended** the word. When a child uses a word more broadly than is customary, we say that the child has **overextended** the word. Underextension has occurred, for example, when a child who has learned to call sneakers and saddle oxfords "shoes" does not apply the same term to sandals. An example of overextension has occurred if a child calls a horse "dog."

Sometimes, what appear to be underextensions are actually instances in which words are not being used symbolically. These instances should not be counted as words at all because the child does not use the word to represent or stand for something. Because children learn to repeat some words in the course of participating in routines, they often repeat the sound form of these words when in this context. But these vocalizations are not actual words in the representational sense—are not symbols that stand for something—because they are restricted to the specific routines in which they have been learned (Bloom, 1998).

True underextensions can occur if children "cut" categories a bit differently than the adults do in a particular language community (Bloom, 1998). Children often apply or generalize new words to new circumstances when they perceive similarities between a newly encountered object and a familiar object to which they have attached a specific label (Gelman et al., 1998; Golinkoff et al., 1995; Landau et al., 1988; Soja et al., 1991). Though adults may consider certain objects to be similar enough in kind to have the same label, this connection may not be obvious to a young child. For example, if a child learns the label "shoe" during the wintertime in a cold climate, the label might first be used to name a closed and laced shoe, such as a sneaker. The following summer, it would not be surprising if the child does not immediately use the same word to name a sandal; a sandal looks remarkably different from a closed and laced-up shoe, and it is worn without a sock. The two items are similar in function, to be sure, but functional similarity does not always mean that the same label applies to the items. The difference between a jacket and a long-sleeved shirt or blouse does not lie in overall shape or in the part of the body each one covers. Their thickness and their position on the body in relation to each other make them distinct; they cannot both be called jackets. Naming objects can get rather complicated for children! Calling a sandal a "shoe" in the child's presence helps the child override an initial reluctance to generalize "shoe" spontaneously to sandal. If nothing else, hearing a term applied in an unexpected way might cause children to compare items more closely and draw conclusions about the similarities among objects (Gentner & Rattermann, 1992).

Children may overextend new words because the categories they form for things in the world are global rather than detailed (Barrett, 1995; Mervis, 1987). For example, children probably call horses "dogs" because both animals have four legs and thick body hair. At the same time, children may not call birds "dogs" because these two animals differ from each other in terms of legs, mouth structure, and body covering. As children increase their skill in detecting finer distinctions among things, overextensions diminish (Mandler et al., 1991).

Overextensions may also begin to diminish as children gain a larger vocabulary and no longer need to "borrow" a known label to fill in some lexical gap. Even as they are overextending *dog*, for example, children might actually know that a horse does not look exactly like a dog. But lacking a unique word for the new animal (the horse), they call it "dog" anyway. It may, after all, be the best word among the few they have for use in this situation (Clark, 1990; Gelman et al., 1998; Naigles & Gelman, 1995). Once they have *horse* and *dog* in their vocabularies, however, their tendency to use *dog* too liberally declines. Similarly, a child who has the words *worm* and *lizard* in his or her vocabulary is much less likely to overextend *snake*.

The reduction in overextensions might result not only from increases in vocabulary, per se, but from information children are given together with a new word. For example, when a child calls a lizard "snake," an adult is apt to say, "Well, actually, that's a lizard. Snakes don't have legs, even though they have a tongue that sticks out like a lizard's, and they also have scaly skin like a lizard's."

Communicating with Single Words   Children use single words not only to label objects, actions, and people, but also to express complex meanings. For example, Morgan, whom we met earlier, used the single word "Dat?" to mean "What is that?" Single words interpreted by adults as expressing a complex thought are called **holophrases** (Anisfeld et al., 1998; Halliday, 1975). For example, a child who says, "milk," when sitting in his high chair, might mean "Is this milk?" or "This is milk," or "I want more milk." The child's intonation helps adults understand which meaning is intended (Galligan, 1987).

Communication at this early stage requires adults to engage in a fair amount of interpretation. Observant adults pay attention to how infants say words they already know and also consider the situation in order to understand what meanings an infant is trying to convey. Adults do not always get it right. At some point, children may realize that communication would become easier if they adopted the conventions shared by the other speakers around them. Such an awareness may spur a child to try to combine words (Anisfeld et al., 1998). In turn, this might cause a child to learn a lot of new words quickly, in order to express more clearly the intentions they had earlier expressed using just one word at a time (Anisfeld et al., 1998). This new focus on grammar—how words go together—might, in turn, increase the child's word learning because the grammatical context of a word provides information about its meaning (Gleitman & Gillette, 1995). The rapid increase in vocabulary, which occurs after a fairly incremental start, has been found in some studies to coincide with the first 2- and 3-word utterances (Anisfeld et al., 1998; Caselli et al., 1999; Halliday, 1975).

Multiword Utterances: Infants Combine Words

Sometime between 18 and 24 months of age, infants begin to combine words to create multiword utterances. At first, children often just put together two of the words they have in their vocabulary. For example, they might say, "more cookie" or "no eat." The meanings are obvious. Some of children's early multiword utterances are also pat phrases they have picked up. These might include "See you, bye-bye" or "all gone" (Bloom, 1998). Production of such multiword utterances does not indicate appreciation for the meaning implied in word order. Utterances such as "I go," "Daddy go," or "I cry" are better indicators of budding appreciation for grammatical relations (Bloom, 1998). Acquisition of verbs is essential for early use of grammatical structures (Bloom, 1998; Tomasello, 1992). Children who are slow to move into using sentences often have trouble learning verbs (Oetting et al., 1995).

Although the number of words in the first utterances is quite limited, toddlers can communicate quite a few meanings and relations between objects or people. For example, they can indicate where something is, to whom it belongs, what someone is doing, and what they do or do not want to do (Bloom et al., 1975; Schlesinger, 1974). These and other meanings that toddlers are able to express in the two-word stage are listed in Table 6.2.

Two- or three-word utterances, such as "Doll cry," "Mommy go," and "No eat," are called **telegraphic** because they resemble sentences adults write when composing telegrams. The words omitted both in telegrams and children's telegraphic utterances are grammatical morphemes. A **morpheme** is the smallest meaningful unit in a language. For example, *dogs* has two morphemes, one for the root word (*dog*), and one (-*s*) to indicate that more than one dog is being referred to.

Grammatical morphemes can be word parts or whole words. Suffixes (green*ish*, good*ness*, and *insightful*) are grammatical morphemes that are word parts. Grammatical morphemes that are whole words include articles (e.g., *the, a, an*), verbs (e.g., *is, are, to be*), and pronouns (e.g., *this* and *that*). If "Daddy car" means "That is Daddy's car," the child's utterance lacks the grammatical morpheme used to mark possession (*'s*), the pronoun *that*, and the verb *is*.

TABLE 6.2	
Meaning expressed by toddlers in the two-word stage	
Category of Meaning	**Example**
Identification	That plane See man
Location	Kitty here Bottle [on] chair
Recurrence	More juice Tickle again
Nonexistence	Nomore cookie Milk allgone
Negation	No bed
Possession	Sarah book
Agent, action, object	Mommy throw Throw ball
Attribution	Big clown Go truck
Question	Where bottle? What that?

Source: Adapted from *A First Language,* by R. Brown, 1973, pp. 168–180. Cambridge: Harvard University Press.

This baby and his father are having fun, and the baby is learning about language. (*Source:* © Elizabeth Crews)

Practicing the Sounds of Sentences: Variegated Babbling

Between 14 and 16 months of age, some children produce nonsense words and string them together. As in the case of their earlier syllable repetition babbling, this **variegated babbling** contains sound sequences that are permissible in the language, even though actual words are rarely formed (Jusczyk, 1997; Kent & Bauer, 1985). But unlike their earlier babbling (repetition of the *same* consonant-vowel syllable), variegated babbling consists of a great variety of syllables tucked into sentencelike intonation patterns. Infants sound very much as if they are actually talking when they engage in variegated babbling because they vary the pitch contour of utterances, insert pauses to mark clauselike clusters of "words," and stress the first syllables of their made-up words, if they are learning English.

A very detailed example of a young child's variegated babbling is provided by de Boysson-Bardies (1999, pp. 158–162). Simon joined in "conversations" with adults, using his variegated babbling, commenting appropriately, it seemed, although no one knew what he was saying because there was so little "correspondence between his productions and words or sentences in adult language." Simon was somewhat unusual in his tendency to talk most of the time in this variegated babbling style, rather than in real sentences. Many children slip into this mode of speaking when engaged in soliloquy, but not when engaged in dialogue with others. For example, when alone, some young children can be heard having pretend conversations and to be pretend-reading their picture books. Because written language differs from conversational language in several ways, the suprasegmental features used when reading aloud to children differ from those used to converse with them (Jusczyk et al., 1992). Thus, when looking at their books, children often verbalize in ways that make them sound as though they are reading (Schickedanz, 1986).

Learning How to Join in Conversation with Others

The baby is lying quietly in his baby seat. His face is serious. When his mother comes into the room, she begins to talk with him.

"Hello" [she says] in a high-pitched but gentle voice . . . he follows her with his head and hand and eyes as she approaches him. . . . His mouth opens wide and his whole body orients toward her. He subsides, mouths his tongue twice, his smile dies and he looks down briefly, while she continues to talk in an increasingly eliciting voice. During this, his voice and face are still but all parts of his body point toward her. . . . He looks up again, smiles widely, narrows his eyes, brings one hand up to his mouth, grunting, vocalizing, and begins to cycle his arms and legs out toward her. She begins to grin more widely, to talk more loudly and with higher-pitched accents, accentuating his vocalizations with hers. . . . The grunting vocalizations and smiles, as well as the cycling activity of his arms and legs, come and go in two-second bursts. . . . Meanwhile, with her voice and her face . . . she both subsides with and accentuates his behavior with her own. He looks down again, gets sober . . . makes a pouting face. She looks down . . . then comes back to look into his face as he returns to look up at her. . . . He bursts out with a broad smile and a staccato-like vocalization . . . she . . . smiles broadly, her voice getting brighter too. (Brazelton et al., 1975, pp. 141–142)

think about it

What is this mother trying to teach her infant? What assumptions does she make about a very young baby? Does she assume, for example that he is social from the very beginning? Do all mothers in the world think about young babies in the same way?

So far we have concentrated on infants' knowledge of speech sounds and on the words and word relations they comprehend and produce. But children might learn more than this about language. Among other things, they learn to cooperate in various ways when talking with someone. For example, speakers might be expected to take turns when talking with others, to stick to the topic of conversation, to add something during their turn, and to signal topic changes.

All of these behaviors are concerned with how language is used in social contexts—in other words, with **pragmatics.** The particulars of this social learning vary across cultures. For example, more overlapping is allowed among speakers in some cultures than in others, and the length of pauses used to signal the transition from one speaker's turn to another's also can differ quite dramatically. But all children are socialized with respect to language use, no matter where they live.

In this section, we discuss early face-to-face interaction between mothers and babies. Such social interaction is found in many parts of the world, but certainly not in all. We point out several notable exceptions where they are especially relevant.

Some infants receive specific tutoring in turn-taking when their parents talk to them and then leave slots for them to respond. (*Source:* © Andy Cox/Tony Stone Images)

Turn-Taking

By using signals, speakers avoid overlapping each other's utterances and interrupting one another. Infants might begin to learn these rules of conversation during early social interactions with their parents or other caregivers. In this section, we discuss the young infant's ability to detect contingent versus noncontingent responding. Then we discuss whether early parent-child interactions fit a turn-taking format and whether mothers tutor their infants in its use. Finally, we discuss how turn-taking is signaled by conversational partners and when children begin to use these signals themselves.

The Effect of Contingent Responding on Infants' Vocal Behavior
Recall from chapter 3 that even very young infants can detect a contingency between their behavior and some event. (A **contingent event** is one that follows consistently, and fairly

quickly, an infant's behavior.) For example, if music is played only in response to pauses of a certain length occurring between bursts of infant sucking, infants soon begin to insert pauses of this length between their sucking bursts in order to turn on the music (DeCasper & Carstens, 1981). In conversational contexts, infants learn that their pauses are filled by a partner's utterances and that a partner invites the infant to respond by pausing.

Under contingent conditions (adults vocalize, smile, and touch the infant in response to the infant's behavior), 3-month-olds pause after vocalizing, are quiet and attentive to the adult during the pause, smile after the adult makes a response, increase their activity level, and then vocalize again. This behavior pattern is repeated in cycles, as parent and child interact (Bloom, 1977; Bloom & Esposito, 1975). Infants' acquisition of turn-taking, which requires that they learn to pause and to notice pauses, seems to depend on contingent responding from adults. Interestingly, contingent responding affects only the organization and distribution of infant responses, not quantity.

The Infant's First Year: Parental Tutoring of Turn-Taking   Learning to join someone in conversation takes time and tutoring. During the first weeks of infancy, some parents work hard to get their infant to notice and attend to them and to get their infants to respond with smiles and vocalizations.

VOCAL CO-ACTING.   During the first few weeks of infancy, parents do not always follow a turn-taking format. Their responding is wavelike instead, rising and falling as the infant's attention and activity levels change. The mother described in the opening episode often continues talking quietly as a backdrop to the cycling of the baby's smiles and glances away from and back to her. Although the mother's talking changes in intensity, depending on the baby's response, it does not always go off when the baby vocalizes, moves, or smiles. The mother responds, but in a way that is most likely to keep the baby pulled into interaction. The mother rarely ever lets go completely, perhaps because the young infant's attention is fragile. Thus, turns in these very early interactions often overlap rather than alternate (Ginsburg & Kilbourne, 1988; Stern et al., 1975; Trevarthen, 1977). By about 12 weeks, turn-taking changes from this predominantly **co-acting** or chorusing pattern to a pattern in which there is a mixture of co-acting and alternating responses (Ginsburg & Kilbourne, 1988). By the end of the first year, the alternating conversational pattern dominates (Broerse & Elias, 1994).

SPECIFIC TUTORING OF TURN-TAKING.   The first lessons in conversational turn-taking seem to be provided in face-to-face interactions between mother and child when no object intervenes. Once the baby's gaze locks onto his mother's, the mother increases her vocalization, smiles, opens her eyes more broadly, and raises her eyebrows. While the mother vocalizes, the infant's body tends to remain relatively calm, and facial expressions become heightened and more positive (Kaye & Fogel, 1980). When the mother stops speaking, the infant often puts forth a flurry of movement, as if responding to the mother's pause (Condon, 1979).

If infants have been engaged in face-to-face interactions since the neonatal period, the pattern of response to a mother's gaze and initial vocalization can be reasonably complex by 2 months of age. The infant begins with a smile and increased bodily movement, which includes movements of the mouth. Then the infant vocalizes in some way. When the infant's burst of activity and vocalization have subsided, the mother vocalizes back. The infant responds, and so forth. Alternations of infant and mother responses can continue for several rounds (Trevarthen, 1977). Mothers tutor turn-taking by responding vocally after a baby has vocalized and by making their own vocalizations short to create many pauses during which the infant can insert a response.

Because very young infants do not always respond to their mothers' greetings and other vocalizations, mothers often coax them into responding (Snow, 1977). Mothers of the 3-month-old girls whom Snow studied vocalized to all of their baby's burps, yawns, sneezes, coughs, vocalizations, smiles, or laughs. If the mother received no vocal response—or no sneeze or burp or yawn—she typically took the infant's turn, paused, and then took another turn herself (Snow, 1977).

By 7 months of age, infants respond more frequently to the pauses mothers provide, and they also fill their turn more often with vocalizations than with other noises. But even at 7 months, infants often fail to take their turns (Snow, 1977).

CROSS-CULTURAL STUDIES OF EARLY MOTHER-INFANT INTERACTION.

There is considerable variation across the world with respect to early mother-child interaction. For example, the Efe people who live in the Ituri forest in northeastern Zaire do not engage in face-to-face interactions with their newborns. Efe newborns are fed often and comforted quickly when they cry. But adults in this culture do not have as a goal drawing newborns or very young infants into face-to-face social interaction. The Efe believe that young babies should sleep because it helps them gain weight, become strong, and later open their eyes (Winn et al., 1989, p. 94). Not until about 4 months of age, when Efe infants are considered to be social beings, do Efe mothers and other members of the Efe camp begin to interact socially with infants.

Similarly, Hmong (Laotian and Cambodian) mothers living in the United States tend to nuzzle their babies, rather than kiss or stroke them as Caucasian mothers tend to do. These differences affect the amount of eye contact between mother and baby (Caucasian mothers establish more eye contact). Hmong mothers also do not try to elicit social interaction as Caucasian mothers do. Even though they vocalize and smile to greet their babies, they then become quiet, waiting patiently and attentively for the baby to vocalize or change expressions. Then they imitate the baby's behavior. Caucasian mothers, on the other hand, typically respond with a behavior that differs from the baby's rather than with an imitation of the baby's behavior, although they sometimes do respond by imitating (Muret-Wagstaff & Moore, 1989).

Of course, even mothers such as the ones described by Brazelton in the vignette do not spend a great deal of time each day interacting with their newborn babies. Because newborns sleep up to 17 or 18 hours a day, no matter where in the world they live, even Western mothers probably spend relatively little time engaged in face-to-face interaction with their infants during the first month or two of life.

Contingency learning of the kind required in conversational turn-taking can be learned in other contexts. For example, mothers in villages in southern India are similar to the Efe people of northeastern Zaire in that they do not engage in face-to-face interactions with newborns. Like babies living in the Efe village, babies raised in Kannada-speaking villages in the south of India are fed on demand and are constantly "held, cuddled, and talked to" (Landers,

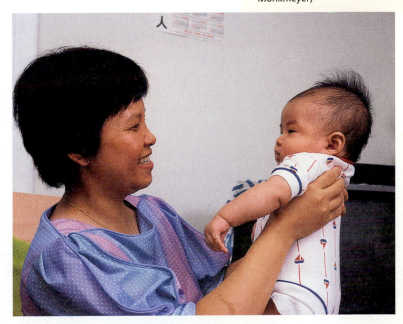

In some cultures, parents do not spend much time face-to-face with their young infants. In other cultures, parents typically spend quite a lot of time gazing into their infant's eyes while talking to them.   (*Source:* © Shackman/Monkmeyer)

1989, p. 173, 185). Thus, the mother's care of young infants in these instances is highly contingent on the baby's signals—more contingent, in fact, than is common among many mothers living in Western cultures who tend more often to feed on schedule rather than strictly on demand. Mothers in some cultures do not vocalize directly to the very young infant while face to face, even though their infants hear human speech almost constantly and surely learn about contingent responding from their mothers' highly responsive caregiving (Landers, 1989).

The Second Year: More Reliable Responding and Mastery of Turn-Taking   By 12 months of age, infants who have experienced face-to-face interaction usually respond to their mothers' utterances and also initiate many verbal interactions. By 18 months, infants begin to use gaze to help regulate conversations. For example, they look at their mothers as they finish their own verbalizations (this is referred to as a "terminal look"). In one study, 18-month-olds used a terminal look two and one-half times more frequently than did 12-month-olds (Rutter & Durkin, 1987). Twenty-four-month-olds used a terminal look four times more frequently than the 12-month-olds. Eighteen-month-olds also began to continue looking at their mothers as their mothers began their turn (Rutter & Durkin, 1987; Schaffer et al., 1977). This sent the message "I'm listening to you."

Between 18 and 24 months of age, babies coordinate gaze with their own vocalization in just about the same way as do adults in their culture. They look away from the listener as they begin their turn. Then, during the turn, the speaker looks intermittently at the listener, apparently to check the listener's attention. The listener typically looks attentively at the speaker throughout the speaker's turn. This lets the speaker know that the listener is attending. Then, when the speaker finishes a turn, he or she looks at the listener. The speaker's terminal look signals yielding of the floor (Rutter & Durkin, 1987).

By 18 months of age, the child is so reliable in responding to and initiating verbal interactions that mothers no longer tutor this behavior. Instead, they begin to tutor accurate content. For example, if a child calls coffee "tea," the mother is likely to tell the child, "No, that's not tea. That's coffee." (Snow, 1977).

Learning to Initiate Verbal Interaction

When people wish to tell someone something or to strike up a conversation, they must attract the potential partner's attention. A person can approach and look at the person, or call the person by name. One of the surest ways to get a conversation going is to ask a question, because questions require a response.

Tutoring on these conversational strategies sometimes begins very early in the context of parent-child interaction. Recall that mothers in Western countries gaze at their babies almost constantly when interacting with them face-to-face. When the baby's gaze meets the mother's, she typically greets the baby: "Well, hello. How are you today?" At 6 weeks of age, infants respond very infrequently to greetings. But by 13 weeks of age, infants often respond to the mother's greeting with a return greeting. By 26 weeks of age (7 months), infants are just as likely to offer a greeting spontaneously when they first gaze at their mother during face-to-face play as they are to respond to a greeting offered by the mother (Kaye & Fogel, 1980). Quite early in life, then, babies can learn to vocalize to greet someone whose gaze meets theirs. And even though they cannot carry on a real conversation, they can start a social interaction.

Book-reading routines also provide parents with opportunites to demonstrate how to get a conversational partner's attention. Mothers attract the baby's attention with verbalizations such as "Look!" and follow it by a question such as "What is that?" (Ninio & Bruner, 1978) Mothers answer their own questions at first because the baby is not yet able to talk. But as soon as the baby can talk, the mother pauses and allows the baby to respond.

By the time they are toddlers, many children already have a long history of verbal interaction in which they have seen and practiced different attention-getting strategies. Given some mothers' strategies, it is no wonder that many toddlers attempt to open conversations by using such tactics as standing close and looking at the person whose attention they seek to attract, by commenting on what the listener is doing, and by saying, "Hey!" "Look!" or "Guess what?"

Theories of Language Development

Like theories for other aspects of children's behavior, theories of language development vary in their emphasis on whether language acquisition depends on innate structures that are specific to language or on learning that utilizes more general cognitive abilities. They also vary in their treatment of internal and external factors—on what the child brings to the situation and what the environment (the child's experiences) contributes. Four theories have been used to explain language development. *Learning theories* claim that language development occurs primarily as a result of contact with the environment. *Nativist theories* claim that language acquisition is determined primarily by structures within the child, by biological "givens." *Cognitive theories* claim that language is but one aspect of cognition and that understanding of relations among objects in the world provides the foundation for grammatical relationships. *Social theories* stress the interactional context in which language is used and the fact that communication itself rests on understandings about the contents of other people's minds. In our discussion of language theories, we treat learning and nativist theories separately because they provide the extreme contrasts on the continuum. We then discuss cognitive and social theories together. We now take a closer look at these four major theories of language development and at the evidence supporting or contradicting each one.

Learning Theory

Following the lead of B. F. Skinner, learning theorists believe that children learn to speak by imitating what they hear. These imitations are then shaped by explicit feedback, such as reinforcement, punishment, or lack of response. Above all, learning theory assumes that the language children encounter in the environment is the primary support for their language learning. That is, a learning theorist assumes that language learning results largely from input (experience), not from what the child brings to the input (innate ability to acquire language).

The environment obviously influences some aspects of language learning. The language we learn as our mother tongue, for example, is the one that is spoken to us. But language learning theories must explain a great deal more than such trivial variations. It must explain how children learn grammatical rules, even though they are exposed only to sentences. Children are not directly taught what seems essential about sentences—how to form them according to a set of rules—nor do parents explicitly disapprove of children's grammatical errors. For example, when a child says, "Mommy purse," a parent usually does not say, "No. It's Mommy's purse. Say 'Mommy's purse,' not 'Mommy purse.'" Instead, the parent typically says, "No, that's not Mommy's purse; that's Aunt Susan's." In other words, parents look past the grammar itself and focus on the content of the utterance (Brown et al., 1969). Parents sometimes do recast or reformulate ill-formed utterances, and some theorists think that these responses could provide indirect feedback to a child about grammar, even though the feedback is not in the form of specific corrections (Bohannon & Stanowicz, 1988; Moerk, 1991). (See the discussion about research on indirect feedback—what is called negative evidence—in chapter 10, p. 343.)

Still, traditional learning theory simply does not account well for some basic aspects of language learning. In fact, it has been virtually impossible for anyone to explain grammatical development without positing a number of biological constraints. The ability to produce utterances never heard, based on rules of grammar, does not necessarily indicate that specific structures of the brain are dedicated—are "hard wired"—to handle specific language functions, and only these. It does indicate, however, that there are aspects of language that traditional learning theory cannot explain. Some form of nativist theory seems to be required.

Nativist Theory

Nativist theory contrasts sharply with traditional learning theory. It is located at the opposite end of the nature-nurture continuum. According to **nativists,** language development depends on what is in the child—on what the child brings to language encountered in the environment—not on what is in the environment. Noam Chomsky proposed this language acquisition theory when he sharply criticized learning theory (Chomsky, 1959, 1965).

Chomsky and other nativists noted that imitation does not explain children's creative utterances and that parents do not explicitly approve or disapprove children's grammar. Nativists argued as well that parents do not simplify or carefully sequence language for their children, and their utterances are often not grammatical. These characteristics of parents' language behavior make it highly unlikely, according to a nativist, that children learn grammar from parental input. Chomsky argued that children's basic knowledge of grammar must come from an innate **language acquisition device (LAD),** a structure in the brain dedicated specifically to language learning (McNeill, 1966).

Support for the nativist view comes from information about the universal and orderly progression of language development (Slobin, 1982). No matter what the specific language, many language forms emerge in the same order in virtually all children. And despite wide variations in the environment, all children acquire a grammar for their mother tongue unless they have a severe cognitive deficit. But several aspects of nativist theory do not quite hold up. Whether the claim is that parents provide complicated, messy grammatical input, or that grammatical learning occurs spontaneously and extremely quickly, or that grammatical learning is unrelated to prior learning, there is some evidence to dispute it (de Boysson-Bardies, 1993, 1999; Oller et al., 1976; Snow, 1977; Vihman et al., 1985).

First of all, speech directed to infants by parents and other adults is not very sloppy or messy. In many cases, it consists of short, well-formed (i.e., grammatical) utterances, cast in a high pitch (Furrow & Nelson, 1986). If this simplified register serves a teaching function (Kemler-Nelson et al., 1989), the infant's experience of conversational give-and-take with adults may be important in language development (Ginsburg & Kilbourne,

1988; Snow, 1995). The suprasegmental features of child-directed speech might help infants find words as well as the general outlines of major grammatical units (i.e., phrases and clauses). The simplified and repetitive nature of child-directed speech might aid infants in acquiring specific sound sequences. In turn, learning grammar might be aided considerably by this phonological knowledge (Jusczyk, 1997; Jusczyk et al., 1992).

A second major claim of biologically based theories of language acquisition is that word production and knowledge of grammar appear suddenly and spontaneously and are virtually unrelated to language-related phenomena that precede them. If there is no continuity between earlier and later behavior, then a specific language acquisition device must "kick in" quickly at some predetermined maturational moment. But some research suggests that language development might be more continuous than nativists have claimed. For example, as we have seen, phonological development that occurs through babbling is related to later word production (de Boysson-Bardies, 1999; Jusczyk, 1997). Additionally, phonotactic knowledge (knowledge of sound sequences) predicts when an infant will begin to comprehend words. The size and composition of a child's vocabulary are related not only to the amount of speech the infant hears, but also to when multiword utterances appear, and thus to the onset of grammatical development (Anisfeld et al., 1998; Caselli et al., 1999; Fenson et al., 1994; Huttenlocher, 1995). Some researchers think that phonotactic, suprasegmental, and lexical (i.e., vocabulary) knowledge might help children acquire grammatical knowledge.

Language acquisition might be better described as **innately guided learning** (Gould & Marler, 1987; Jusczyk, 1993) than as "hard wired." In other words, learning directed by biological constraints need not take the form of specific language structures in the brain (Elman et al., 1996). Recent connectionist models of language learning consider language to be "innately constrained" but not "pre-wired," as Chomsky first envisioned (Elman et al., 1996, p. 348). By "innate," a connectionist theorist does not mean that "there is a single genetic locus or set of genes which have the specific function of inducing the behavior in question, and only that behavior" (Elman et al., 1996. p. 357). Instead, connectionist theorists think that nature can "maximize the likelihood of good solutions to difficult problems" (Elman et al., 1996, p. 357), while, at the same time, depending quite heavily on input.

"All students of language acquisition would acknowledge," according to Jusczyk (1997, p. 27), that the "cognitive and perceptual resources of the learner affect the course of language acquisition." The disagreements occur over whether specific structures in the brain are dedicated to grammatical learning. In Jusczyk's view, what is "given" is not necessarily specific to language: "Nonlinguistic cognitive and perceptual resources play a leading role" not a "supporting role" (Jusczyk, 1997, p. 27). If this turns out to be true, then a specific structure in the brain is not dedicated to grammatical learning, as Chomsky originally claimed. "More general cognitive and perceptual capacities will suffice." (Jusczyk, 1997, p. 27).

Cognitive and Social Theories

As these names imply, cognitive and social theories do not assume that language learning is accounted for by specific, biologically dedicated language structures. Instead, more general cognitive abilities account for language learning. Initial theories about possible cognitive foundations for language proposed that the cognitive schemes constructed during the sensorimotor period provide information about relations of objects and events in the world, and this knowledge provides a foundation for grammatical learning (Bates, 1976; Bruner, 1975). Early cognitive theories also claimed that language was but one instance of the development in the child of a general capacity to engage in symbolic activity (Piaget, 1924, 1954).

CLOSE-UP   *Joint Attention and Word Learning*

Joint attention is the focus on an object or event shared by an infant and an adult. Researchers have been interested in learning when and how infants track the gazes of their caregivers and the consequences on language learning of the sheer amount of time infants spend in joint attention. Researchers have also wondered whether variations in caregiver styles of establishing joint attention—following the infant's current gaze (at an object or event) or redirecting the infant's gaze to something else—have any effect.

Development of Infants' Gaze-Following Abilities

In an early study of infants' ability to follow the gaze of someone else, an adult established eye contact with an infant and then turned away to look at some part of the room (Scaife & Bruner, 1975). One hundred percent of the 11- to 14-month-olds followed the adult's line of regard—looked out into the room when the adult looked—but only 30 percent of infants who were 2 to 4 months of age did so. Only infants older than 8 months of age looked back to the adult, from time to time, to check the adult's gaze. This checking behavior probably indicates true gaze following, whereas mere turning in the direction of the adult's gaze does not.

Other studies have focused on infants' gaze in contexts where adults have looked at specific object targets. (Adults in the Scaife and Bruner study looked only at small marks on the walls.) The number of targets, their distance from the infant, and their specific location affect the success infants have in following an adult's gaze. In several studies (Butterworth & Grover, 1988; Butterworth & Jarret, 1991), infants as young as 6 months of age redirected their gaze to look *in the direction of* the mother's gaze, but they looked at the first object that caught their attention. Not until 12 months of age could they reliably pinpoint the correct target with their gaze. Not until 18 months of age did they turn around to gaze at an object when their mother gazed behind them.

In another study (Morissette et al.,1995), infants younger than 12 months of age often continued to look at the mother rather than redirect their gaze in the direction of hers. At 12 months of age, infants both looked in the direc-

tion of the mother's gaze and focused on a target, but often not the target at which the mother was looking. Not until between 12 and 15 months of age did they fixate reliably on the correct target. When targets were positioned quite far from infants, or at unusual angles, only 18-month-olds succeeded in following the mother's gaze to a specific target.

With regard to pointing, 9 months is the earliest age at which infants can be aware of what to look at when someone points to something. Comprehension of pointing improves steadily after that, as does development of checking the gaze of the adult. By 16 months, infants are sophisticated enough to know that they should check the other person's gaze before they themselves point at something.

Joint Attention and Word Learning

A high positive correlation has been found between word learning and time spent in joint attention (Nagell, 1995; Saxon, 1997; Smith et al., 1998; Tomasello & Todd, 1983). Engagement in picture-book reading and infant games, such as peek-a-boo and pat-a-cake, provides excellent opportunities for establishing joint reference with infants. Many parents in the United States begin to engage their infants in looking at picture books during the first year of life, and naming routines are also commonly employed in this context (Bridges, 1986). Not surprisingly, words used in infant games and highly ritualized routines are often among the first words that infants speak. Early story reading, which provides an ideal situation for establishing joint attention, is also positively correlated with greater word comprehension (DeBaryshe, 1993).

A caregiver's style of establishing joint attention also affects language development. First of all, babies talk more in situations in which parents actively respond to infant vocalizations. Responsive parents observe the infant closely, react contingently to infant vocalizations, and establish joint attention by **following in** rather than by **redirecting** an infant's attention (Tomasello & Farrar, 1986; Wendland-Carro et al., 1999). Infants seem to learn more words when adults use a following rather than a redirecting approach to establishing joint attention (Bakeman & Adamson, 1984; Carpenter et al., 1998; Dunham et al., 1993; Harris et al., 1986; Tomasello & Todd, 1983), at least for ages under about 20 months.

Once cognitive theories had pushed the language learning discussion into the domain of knowledge construction, language theories were broadened to encompass the child's interactions with others in a social context. But before long, social theories, with their main emphasis on the contributions of social interaction to the child's language learning, began to stand apart from cognitive theories, which restricted their attention primarily to the child's capacity for creating knowledge (Bloom, 1998).

Parents who issue many directives to their infants might delay the development of the insight that language has a referential function, whereas parents who are less directive might convey this idea better to their infants. Differences in developing this insight could, in turn, affect word-learning rates (Nelson, 1981).

Another possibility is that the infant's fragile attention-following abilities simply cannot make necessary adjustments when redirected (Tomasello, 1988). As infants get older, however, they are better able to shift attention in response to requests to do so (Akhtar & Tomasello, 1996; Baldwin, 1993). By 19 or 20 months, infants have gained more skill in responding, and by 24 months they are faster still in directing their gaze to fixate on an object (Fernald et al., 1998). Not surprisingly, then, at these later ages a mother's tendency either to follow in or redirect an infant's attention and the infant's word acquisition are not as strongly correlated as they are at earlier ages (Carpenter et al., 1998). By this time, infants are not only better able to follow redirection, but also they also have more word-learning supports at their disposal. For example, because their understanding of grammar is increasing quite rapidly, a word's position in a sentence can help them understand its meaning.

Even for infants younger than 19 or 20 months, directing instead of following in does not have negative effects *after* following in had been used to establish joint attention. In other words, if a parent joins an infant in looking at a book on which the infant has been focusing and then directs the infant's attention to various objects pictured in the book, there is a positive, not a negative, effect on word learning (Akhtar et al., 1991). Only when the parent redirects a young infant's attention away from an object currently of interest, to another object, does directing have a negative effect on language acquisition (Pine, 1992).

Mothers at Risk for Unresponsive Interactions and Low Levels of Talk

Adolescent mothers, as a group, talk less to their infants than do adult mothers (Culp et al., 1988, 1991, 1996; Garcia Coll et al., 1987; Osofsky & Osofsky, 1970). This tendency reduces word learning because **speech density** alone—the sheer number of words an infant hears—is highly correlated with rate of vocabulary growth (Akhtar et al., 1991; Huttenlocher et al., 1991). Adolescent mothers, as a group, also engage in less responsive (i.e., contingent) vocal interaction with their infants (Barrett & Roach, 1995; McAnarney et al., 1986). By 1 year of age, infants of adolescent mothers vocalize a lot less than infants of adult mothers, thus giving their mothers many fewer opportunities to respond. Low levels of vocal engagement with their infants during the early months of infancy apparently result in less vocalizing by these infants at 1 year of age (Culp et al., 1996).

Mothers who suffer from depression tend to talk less to their children than do nondepressed mothers (Breznitz & Sherman, 1987; Kaplan et al., 1999; Lundy et al., 1996), and mothers who live in poverty talk relatively little to their children compared to mothers who live in more affluent circumstances (Hart & Risley, 1992, 1995). Mothers living in poverty are also less responsive to their infants when they interact verbally and socially. That is, they offer fewer contingent responses overall.

Because speech density and vocabulary acquisition are positively correlated, it is important to increase responsive caregiving in at-risk mothers. Early intervention in the immediate postpartum period can raise the level of parent-child interaction in adolescent mothers and in mothers living in poverty. "Vocal exchanges between infant and mother may encourage the mother to respond to the infant as an interactive partner whom she imagines may understand her. . . . The infant's responsiveness . . . may lead to a general increase in mutual stimulation" (Wendland-Carro et al., 1999). Mothers who suffer from depression need other kinds of intervention, such as counseling and drug therapy.

The relationships between responsive interaction and levels of infant vocalizing, and between speech density and vocabulary development, also underline the importance of establishing stringent criteria for adult-child ratios in infant child care. Quality child care for infants is defined in part by adult-child ratios of 1:3 or 1:4—no more than 6 or 8 infants with 2 caregivers (Bredekamp, 1987). When there are fewer adults per child, adults are forced only to supervise groups of children and to provide minimal (usually not responsive) physical care.

The attention that social theories of language learning have given to social interaction, including the general development of intersubjectivity, has resulted in many studies on joint attention and its effects on language development, especially on word acquisition. (See Research Close-Up: Joint Attention and Word Learning.) Social theories have also created interest in variations in adult levels of social interaction with babies, the effects of these variations on specific aspects of language development, and ways to alter both the amount and quality of interaction.

Summary of Language Acquisition Theories

According to Hirsh-Pacek and Golinkoff (1996, p. 2), "the major debates in language acquisition theory today concern not *whether* there are some sensitivities to syntactic information (grammar) but which sensitivities children are endowed with and how they might be translated into the organizing principles that get syntactic learning off the ground."

Bloom (1998, p. 314) even suggests that a theory to account for language development needs to "reach beyond language. . . . The disparate threads of explanation in language acquisition can begin to come together only when theory and research embrace the wholeness of the child in the larger context of the child's overall development." Such a comprehensive theory would require considerations of the "child's intentionality and the necessary convergence of developments in affect, cognition, and social connectedness to other persons." Intersubjectivity—some appreciation for others' states of mind—develops in the first year through affective expressions between the child and caregivers. . . . As a consequence of cognitive development during the first year, infants have "more elaborate intentional states that require expression and need to be articulated if they are to be shared. . . . Thus, if language is to keep up with developments in cognition and social connectedness . . . children need to acquire words and the procedures for sentences for expression and interpretation" (Bloom, 1998, p. 314).

KEY POINTS

Communication and Language Development during the Infant's First Year

■ Infants respond to the human voice from birth, and they use their voices to signal to others.

■ Infants do not speak in words during the prelinquistic period, but they make significant strides in their language learning.

■ A language's phonology includes segmental and suprasegmental features.

■ Infants discriminate among speech sound contrasts categorically, just as adults do.

■ Over the first year of life, infants lose the ability to distinguish contrasts that are not in the native language, and they increase their skill in making distinctions that were weak at birth, if these are in their native language.

■ Infants begin to prefer the sound sequence patterns of their native language by the end of their first year. They also prefer frequently heard sound sequences to those heard less frequently. Infants may learn sound sequences best when language is structured to contain many repetitions of the same words.

■ Infants prefer human speech to other sounds, their mother's voice to the voice of other females, and child-directed speech to adult-directed speech.

■ The high-pitch characteristic of infant-directed speech is not universal, but some kind of adjustment in language directed toward infants is found in virtually every language community that has been studied.

■ Infants have learned the typical placement of clause pauses in sentences by 7 or 8 months of age.

■ By 8 or 9 months of age, infants recognize the typical pattern of stress applied to English words.

■ Infants can comprehend some meanings that are expressed in language on the basis of suprasegmental features alone, before they can understand the words themselves.

■ Babies and toddlers comprehend words before they speak any.

■ Parental reports of infant word comprehension vary considerably.

■ Babies' vocalizations during the first year are called prelinguistic because they do not contain words. Crying and cooing are two early forms of prelinguistic behavior.

■ Reduplicated babbling, a type of vocalization consisting of consonant–vowel strings, emerges at about 6 months. By about 10 or 12 months, babies shorten their babbles to one or two syllables.

■ Reduplicated babbling reflects characteristics of the baby's native language.

■ Deaf infants babble later than hearing infants; infants reared in poverty begin to babble at the same time as infants raised in more favorable economic circumstances, but they babble less.

- Sounds practiced in babble predict the first words that babies will speak and how words are pronounced.

Language Development during the Infant's Second Year

- Crying changes over the course of the first few months, and infants communicate different intentions through their different cries.

- Infants communicate before they use words by varying their intonation while babbling. These intentional vocalizations can communicate different intentions.

- Pointing, reaching, giving, and showing are deictic gestures used by infants to communicate before they can speak in words.

- Pointing appears between 12 and 14 months of age. The timing of the gazing that accompanies pointing changes between 12 and 16 months from after the pointing to before it.

- Infants comprehend the pointing of others sometime between 9 and 11 months of age, but they are not reliable in fixating on targets until sometime between 14 and 15 months of age.

- Most babies say their first word at about 12 months.

- Joint attention aids word learning in infants.

- Directing styles of establishing joint attention are not as effective as following styles for infants under 19 or 20 months of age. After 20 months of age, directing versus following styles do not appear to affect word learning differently.

- Speech density affects vocabulary acquisition.

- Young children often underextend or overextend the meanings of words. Infants' understanding and use of words change as they progress to new cognitive levels.

- Vocabulary size varies greatly among infants.

- Vocabulary increases slowly at first, after the first word is spoken.

- After several months, words are added more rapidly.

- Some infants exhibit a referential style of word learning and have many nouns among the first words they learn. Other infants exhibit an expressive style. They have a wider range of word types in their early vocabularies.

- The proportion of nouns to verbs in early vocabularies varies around the world, depending on characterstics of the native language and mothers' tendencies to label objects or actions.

- Children use single words to communicate complex meanings.

- Between 18 and 24 months, English-speaking children begin to combine words into primitive, telegraphic sentences.

- In telegraphic sentences, grammatical morphemes are omitted.

- Between about 14 and 18 months, children practice the intonation patterns of sentences by engaging in reduplicated babbling. Babies who have been read to use both conversational babble and book babble.

- Significant language delay seems to be indicated by small vocabulary combined with delay in combining words, but not by a small vocabulary alone.

- Difficulty in learning verbs can indicate a problem in learning language.

Learning How to Join in Conversations with Others

- Infants figure out contingencies—that a behavior consistently follows their behavior.

- The amount of infant vocal behavior is the same in the contexts of either contingent or noncontingent social behavior from adults, but only contingent social responding seems to teach turn-taking.

- Infants seem to learn conversational turn-taking in the context of early parent-child interaction.

- Mothers at first count almost anything as an infant's conversational "turn."

- Early vocal interchanges between parents and babies take the form of co-action more than turn-taking.

- Before 1 year of age, a turn-taking pattern of vocal interaction begins to dominate parent-infant interactions.

- Infants begin to respond—to take their turn—more and more as the months of the first year pass by. By 12 months of age, they are quite reliable in making a response when it is their turn.

- Face-to-face interaction between mothers and young infants is not common in all cultures, but all cultures have ways to teach young babies about contingencies. In many cultures, babies learn about contingent responding from responsive caregiving.

- Infants have learned to coordinate gaze and vocalization to regulate turn-taking by about 18 or 24 months of age.

- Infants learn from their parents' gazes and greetings how to initiate conversations. They also probably learn how to initiate conversation from such things as picture-book-reading routines.

Theories of Language Development

- Learning theorists believe that babies acquire language through the learning mechanisms of imitation, reinforcement, extinction, and punishment.

- Nativists believe that human beings are born with specific language learning abilities.

- One challenge to the strict nativist view comes from cognitive theorists who claim that sensorimotor learning provides a basis for language learning.

- Social theories of language stress the importance of social interactions to language development. They also stress the central role of intersubjectivity in communication.

- Small caregiver-to-child ratios in child care centers is especially important during infancy when language is being learned.

- Adolescent mothers, depressed mothers, and mothers who live in poverty talk less to their babies than do other mothers.

- Interventions can sometimes increase mother-infant interaction and language development.

- Picture-book reading and infant games can increase verbal interaction between mothers and babies.

- A complete explanation for language acquisition requires complex systems theories.

GLOSSARY

Brain Stem Evoked Response: brain wave reactions to sound, used to assess hearing during the neonatal period (p. 202)

categorical speech perception: sensitivity to categories of speech sound rather than to absolute differences between one sound and another (p. 197)

child-directed speech (CDS): speech that has elevated pitch and other characteristics that appeal to infants (p. 193)

co-acting: vocal overlap during interactions (p. 216)

contingent event: an event that is responsive to—that follows—another person's behavior (p. 215)

cooing: early vocalization consisting of single sounds (p. 200)

Crib-O-Gram: a special instrument used to assess hearing during the neonatal period (p. 202)

deictic gestures: gestures, such as pointing and reaching, that are used to signal to others and to communicate intent (p. 204)

expressive style: an approach to word learning in which children repeat formulaic utterances and include more than nouns in their initial vocabulary (p. 209)

following style: an approach to establishing joint attention in which the adult directs his or her gaze to an object of current interest to the baby (p. 222)

formulaic chunks: multiword segments of language the child has heard often and repeats in entirety, without analyzing them (e.g., "eat your lunch"; "stop that") (p. 209)

gaze: the direction of looking (p. 204)

giving: a deictic gesture consisting of an extended arm and hand, with the object in hand available for release to another person (p. 204)

grammatical morphemes: articles and pronouns and word parts that mark verb tense, possessive, and plural (p. 213)

holophrases: single words used by children and interpreted by adults as expressing a complex thought (p. 212)

innately guided learning: learning influenced considerably by biological constraints, but not dependent on function-specific structures in the brain (p. 221)

joint attention: a shared focus between adult and child on an object or event (pp. 204 and 222)

language acquisition device (LAD): a metaphor for the nativist view that the brain is structured to enable the child to learn grammar (p. 220)

morpheme: the smallest unit of speech that has meaning in a language (p. 213)

motherese: an informal term for child-directed speech (p. 193)

nativist: one who thinks language development is due primarily to characteristics of the child, not to the child's experience (p. 220)

overextended words: words used to encompass broader meanings than they do when used by adults (p. 211)

phonology: the sound system of a language (p. 192)

phoneme: a category of speech sound, including, for example, all of the variations of /b/ or /p/ (p. 196)

phonotactic knowledge: knowledge of the sequences of sounds used in a language to create syllables (p. 197)

pitch: the quality of highness or lowness of the voice (p. 193)

pointing: a deictic gesture consisting of an extended arm and index finger, typically used to communicate "that is _____" or "what is that?" (p. 204)

pragmatics: the aspect of language having to do with language use in social contexts (p. 215)

prelinguistic period: the period typically encompassing the first year of life when infants vocalize but do not say actual words (p. 192)

protowords: consonant-vowel syllables that are repeated only 2 or 3 times (p. 200)

reaching: a deictic gesture consisting of an extended arm with fingers and thumb held away from the palm, used to communicate "I want that" or "give me that" (p. 204)

redirecting style: an approach to establishing joint attention in which the adult redirects an infant's current focus of attention to a different object (p. 222)

reduplicated babbling: consonant-vowel combinations (syllables) that are repeated over and over (p. 200)

referential style: an approach to word learning in which many nouns are learned first, as if the child views language learning as a naming game (p. 209)

representational gestures: gestures that stand for or symbolize an object, event, or attribute (p. 204)

segmental features: the sounds and sound combinations that make up the words in a language (p. 192)

showing: a deictic gesture consisting of an extended arm and hand, with object in hand, available only for viewing at by another person (p. 204)

speech comprehension: understanding the meanings conveyed by speech (p. 198)

speech density: the sheer number of words a child hears spoken by others (p. 223)

speech perception: the ability to detect individual speech sound categories and various aspects of sound organization, as well as the rhythm and flow of language, designated by intonation, pauses, and stress (p. 193)

suprasegmental features: the sound features that include stress, intonation, and pauses (p. 192)

telegraphic speech: speech consisting of only content words, not function words, such as grammatical morphemes (p. 213)

underextended words: words used to express narrower meanings than they do when adults use them (p. 211)

variegated babbling: vocalizations consisting of nonsense words that nonetheless honor rules for syllable formation and use intonation patterns resembling sentences (p. 214)

voicing: speech sounds, such as /d/ and /b/, that involve the vibration of the vocal cords (p. 196)

word comprehension: the matching of specific sound sequences with specific meanings (p. 198)

SUGGESTIONS FOR FURTHER READING

Bloom, L. (1993). *The transition from infancy to language.* Cambridge: Cambridge University Press. This book includes an overview of language-related events during the first year of life and data from a study of children during the single-word stage—from 9 months to 2 years. It emphasizes the effects of cognition and affect on language development during this period.

de Boysson-Bardies, B. (1999). *How language comes to children.* Cambridge, MA: The MIT Press. This introduction to language in the child from birth to age 2 covers all aspects in a very engaging style. Cross-cultural examples abound. Research is integrated throughout.

Gleason, J. B. (1993). *The development of language.* New York: Macmillan. This book provides a good overview of many facets of language.

Hirsh-Pacek, K., & Golinkoff, R. M. (1996). *The origins of grammar: Evidence from early language comprehension.* Cambridge, MA: The MIT Press. This thorough discussion of language theories and the commonalities and differences among them is a helpful resource for students interested in language theory.

Jusczyk, P. (1997). *The discovery of spoken language.* Cambridge, MA: The MIT Press. This book covers speech perception and early vocal production from birth to the end of the first year of life. Detailed research is reported in a readable style. A picture of the infant as an active constructor of knowledge about language is presented. Jusczyk provides an alternative view to that held by theorists who assume that innate structures specifically dedicated to language are responsible for language development.

Pinker, S. (1994). *The language instinct.* New York: HarperCollins. This is a readable and even entertaining book about the nature of language and language acquisition. It tackles in a sophisticated though accessible way many of the basic questions about language and the mind that have occupied linguists and cognitive psychologists. The author provides a wonderfully informative and thoroughly fascinating discussion of language.

7

Social and Emotional Development in Infants and Toddlers

IT'S THE FIRST day of play group! Excitement fills the brightly colored room as parents and 2-year-olds explore activities. Wooden puzzles dot the tabletops in one corner, and two boys head for them eagerly. Dumping the pieces out on the table makes a loud "ker-plop!" Then comes the hard part—putting the puzzles back together. After a few tries, Juan turns to his mom, who is sitting nearby watching him, and says, "Where this goes?"

"Try it here," she suggests, pointing to an empty spot. He smiles as the piece slips in.

Daniel also tries to reassemble his puzzle. He forces a piece into a spot, but it resists. He throws it down and tries another, then a third. His mom picks up the first piece, hands it to him, and says, "This will work. Just turn it around."

Daniel shouts, "No!" and pushes her hand out of the way.

In a few minutes, Juan has his puzzle back together. He says, "All done! I do again!" Daniel, meanwhile, has abandoned his puzzle for the block corner, leaving the empty frame on the table and the pieces on the floor. His mother calls to him, "Daniel, come here! I'm not going to pick up this mess for you!" But Daniel keeps playing with the blocks, while his frustrated mother sits.

By the end of the morning, Juan, tired and happy, leaves hand-in-hand with his mother. But Daniel leaves in an angry frenzy. He darts out of the room ahead of her, ignoring her calls to wait and to say good-bye to the teacher. She chases after him, shouting, "Daniel, stop! Get back here right now, young man!"

When all the children are gone, the teacher turns back to the disordered room. She wonders if Daniel was having a bad day or if there's a bigger problem. Closing the door behind her as she leaves for the day, she thinks, "If he still seems to be this difficult after the first week, I'll talk to her to see how he behaves with other adults and how long he has been this way. He and his mother may need some help learning more positive ways of interacting. I think there may be a lot of work ahead for Daniel and his mother, and for me too."

think about it

Why did Juan and Daniel behave as they did? Have they always been as different as they seemed to be today? Were they different from birth, one calm and social, the other irritable and determined to conquer the world on his own terms? Do they behave like this no matter where they are or with whom they interact, or are they different when with adults other than their mothers? What if they had been interested in the same puzzle? Would they have been considerate of each other, perhaps working it together or waiting for turns? Or would one of them have been more likely to grab it from the other?

The teacher did not know why Daniel was behaving as he was, but she wondered if one possibility involved his relationship with his mother. Perhaps he had also been a difficult baby. Because of this, perhaps Daniel and his mother failed to "click." Perhaps instead of building a consistent give-and-take relationship, they often become locked in a struggle that eroded their good will and made them angry. We would say they had a problem in their attachment relationship.

Attachment is the relationship a baby and his primary caregiver develop with each other. This chapter explores various aspects of attachment, including how it forms, what each partner brings to the relationship, and what associations have been found between attachment and other aspects of the child's development. The chapter also addresses infants' and toddlers' interactions with each other and their growing ability to play together.

We also consider the development of empathy in young children—their ability to respond to others' distress. Finally, we discuss sex-stereotyped behavior, particularly how parents might teach their children to act "like boys" or "like girls." Taken together, these topics provide a comprehensive picture of the emotional and social underpinnings that shape children's personalities and influence how they interact with others as they grow.

Attachment

There are many theories about how and why an emotional tie develops between a child and parent or other important caregivers. We discuss these next. We also focus on details of the two sides of an attachment relationship, the infant's and the adult's. Finally, we discuss the relationship between attachment and other aspects of the child's behavior.

Theories for Explaining and Understanding Infant Attachment

Three major theories of attachment have been offered over the years. Two of these, the learning theory and psychoanalytic explanations, have in common drive reduction in the feeding situation. The ethological explanation differs from these—it assumes that attachment is based on signals that ensure the survival of the species. We discuss these theories and the evidence for and against each one.

The Learning and Psychoanalytic Explanations
Early learning theorists proposed that babies develop a strong emotional tie—attachment—to adults who satisfy their basic needs, especially hunger. According to their theory of **drive reduction,** inner needs (hunger, for example) create tension, which in turn generates activity to reduce the tension. The baby seeks to reduce the tension by satisfying the need (by eating). The adult who gratifies the baby's needs becomes a **secondary reinforcer.** A secondary reinforcer acquires reinforcing properties as a result of its association with a primary reinforcer. In the case of hunger, the primary reinforcer is food. According to this theory, then, babies are thought to become attached to their mothers because babies associate their mothers with being fed.

Psychoanalytic theory takes a similar position. Feeding was thought to be the primary source of pleasurable (oral) feelings in infancy. But unlike learning theory, psychoanalytic theory also assumes that each child has a limited amount of mental energy for attachments, an idea based on the observation that a baby becomes attached to only one person, usually the mother. Later, the child comes to identify with the parent of the same sex, but in the case of boys only after having worked through conflicts associated with this first emotional tie with the mother.

Also unlike learning theory, psychoanalytic theory assumes the first relationship with the mother to be extremely important for personality development and for later love relationships. The first attachment is thought to become an enduring part of the psyche. According to Freud, the mother and father continue to be present in the individual's mind as objects of love, admiration, and fear, long after the child grows up or the parent dies.

The Ethological Explanation
Ethology is the study of animal behavior, particularly the aspects of behavior relating to ecology and evolution. The ethological explanation for attachment focuses on the ways young keep in touch with their mothers (Waters & Deane, 1982). The ethological explanation for attachment, first proposed by John Bowlby in 1969, claims that infants are **preprogrammed**—genetically "wired"—to form attachment to the adult who best ensures their survival.

The ethological explanation accounts both for the way babies stay near their mothers and the way they separate to explore (Ainsworth, 1990). Babies must be able to explore if they are to learn about their environment and become independent. But they also need to be safe, or they may not survive. As the human species evolved, the babies and mothers who survived were those who learned best how to send and read signals about feeding, danger, and so on. They then passed on their genes to succeeding generations.

Ethological theory predicts that babies will become attached most strongly to adults who respond the best to their signals. Rather than claim that human babies have an innate attachment to their biological mothers or that they **imprint** (follow or become attached to the first moving object they see during an early critical period) on their mothers, it suggests that babies are born with certain capabilities for building relationships with adults and that adults are able to respond to the subtle signals babies send.

Human babies keep in touch with their parents by sending signals—crying, gazing, smiling—and parents respond by reacting to the signals—holding, feeding, smiling back. Babies prefer adults who read their signals accurately, interpret what they need, and respond with appropriate care and stimulation. Although signals often revolve around feeding, attachments need not be based on the feeding situation. Babies can develop strong attachments to adults who are not the ones who feed them or provide them with other basic physical care.

Bowlby claimed that the essence of attachment is strong affection between the adult and the baby. According to Bowlby, the goal of the baby's attachment behavior is to maintain the availability of the adult attachment figure (Ainsworth, 1990).

Over time, the child's experiences with her caregiver lead her to form expectations about future social interactions. These expectations form the basis of her **internal working models** of a caregiver and herself. If primary caregivers are generally responsive to her signals, she will build a model of them (and of others, based on them) as responsive and trustworthy. She will build a complementary model or schema of herself as competent and worthy of her caregivers' responsiveness (Bowlby, 1980).

The outcome of early social interactions may sound quite similar to the results that would be expected according to Erik Erikson's psychosocial theory of development, which we reviewed in chapter 1 (p. 12). In Erikson's theory, early caregiving resolves the first psychological conflict of trust versus mistrust. According to Erikson, responsive caregiving leads to the development of trust in the infant and to the feeling that says, "I am all right." Unlike ethological theorists, however, Erikson focused on feeding and other physical needs of the infant in considering the contexts in which parental responsiveness mattered. Ethological theorists consider more contexts than these, including, for example, the caregiver's ability to provide appropriately responsive social stimulation.

Evidence for the Theories The drive reduction explanation for attachment that lies at the heart of both the psychoanalytic and the learning theories was struck down when Harry Harlow, a psychologist at the University of Wisconsin, conducted studies with baby monkeys to determine why they became attached to a caregiver (Harlow, 1958). He used two types of surrogate (substitute) mothers, one made from a tube covered with terry cloth and the other made of wire mesh (see Figure 7.1). In one condition of the experiment, the baby monkeys were fed from a bottle placed on the wire mesh surrogate; the cloth mother provided only cloth "contact comfort." If the monkeys showed a preference for the surrogate who

FIGURE 7.1

Baby monkey with cloth "mother." Harlow's studies of infant monkeys provided evidence against the drive reduction theory of attachment. When frightened, monkeys preferred wire mothers covered in cloth to bare wire mothers, even though monkeys had not received any nourishment from the cloth surrogate mothers. (*Source:* © Martin Rogers/ Tony Stone Images)

fed them, it would support the drive reduction explanation for attachment because it would indicate that they developed an emotional tie to a caregiver who fed them. A preference for the cloth mother would not support this explanation.

The baby monkeys spent more time on the cloth mother, and when a frightening wind-up toy was placed in their cage, they ran to the cloth mother. This experiment undermined both the secondary reinforcement and psychoanalytic explanations for attachment because both are based on the satisfaction associated with eating. Further evidence against the secondary reinforcement and psychoanalytic hypothesis came when it was learned that 30 percent of the infants in a study were attached to an adult other than the one who took care of them most of the time. Additionally, 22 percent of the infants were attached to someone who had *never* performed for them any basic caregiving activity, such as feeding or diapering (Schaffer & Emerson, 1964).

Currently, the best explanation we have for infant attachment is the ethological one. Babies come into the world equipped to build relationships with people who will respond to them. They send signals to adults, and they build the strongest relationships with adults who respond most sensitively to these signals.

Several questions come to mind at this point in our discussion. First, how do we know when an infant has become attached to an adult? What does the baby do that indicates attachment? Second, what signals do babies send to adults, and what are the sensitive responses? Finally, what makes some adults respond sensitively and others insensitively? A discussion of these questions follows.

Infant Attachment Behavior

Infants reveal their sense of danger or need and the expectations they have for the adults' responses to their signals in several ways. These attachment behaviors, and how they are measured, are discussed next.

The Strange Situation   Mary Ainsworth was the first person to study differences among infants' attachment behavior (Bretherton, 1992). In the 1960s, she and her colleagues developed a standard method to study and describe attachment behavior in babies between 1 and 2 years of age (Magai & McFadden, 1995). The laboratory situation they developed to assess attachment is called the Strange Situation. The Strange Situation involves seven episodes and three participants—the mother, the baby, and an adult stranger.

The experimental procedure begins when the mother and baby are introduced to the laboratory playroom, where there are some toys. (See Table 7.1.) Then the mother and baby are left alone in the room, but the mother does not play with the baby.

TABLE 7.1

Strange Situation episodes and their sequence

Episode	Situation
Episode 1:	Parent and child are alone in the playroom. (3 minutes)
Episode 2:	Stranger enters (stranger, parent, and child are in the playroom). (3 minutes)
Episode 3:	Stranger and child are alone (parent leaves the room—first separation). (3 minutes or less)
Episode 4:	Parent returns and stranger leaves (first reunion). (3 minutes)
Episode 5:	Parent exits and leaves child alone (second separation). (3 minutes or less)
Episode 6:	Stranger enters (child and stranger are alone—second separation from parent continues with stranger present). (3 minutes or less)
Episode 7:	Parent returns; stranger leaves (final reunion episode). (3 minutes)

Next, a stranger enters, talks with the mother a bit, and then focuses her attention on the baby. The mother leaves; the adult stranger and the baby are now alone in the playroom. The first reunion follows very soon, with the mother's return. The mother talks to and comforts the baby if the baby has become distressed. (If the baby is very distressed at any point, the experiment is terminated.) Then the mother leaves again. During this second separation, the baby is left completely alone for a few moments. Then the stranger, not the mother, enters the room first after this separation. Then the mother returns, and the stranger leaves.

Several features of infant attachment become apparent in the Strange Situation: (1) the extent to which the baby uses the mother as a secure base for exploration, (2) how much the baby prefers the mother to the stranger, and (3) how likely the baby is to consider the mother a haven of safety when frightened (Connell & Goldsmith, 1982).

Researchers have identified and described three major patterns of response. These patterns, which indicate the quality of babies' attachment to their mothers, have been labeled secure attachment, insecure/avoidant attachment, and insecure/ambivalent attachment. (See Table 7.2.)

In **secure attachment,** the baby separates from the mother to explore the toys in the playroom when mother and baby are introduced to the laboratory situation. But the baby touches base with the mother periodically. When the mother leaves, the baby is moderately distressed and either cries or plays in a more subdued way. When she returns, the baby greets her warmly and accepts comfort if upset. Sixty-five to 70 percent of low-risk, middle-class, North American infants who are assessed in the Strange Situation are classified as securely attached (Rosen & Burke, 1999; van IJzendoorn & Kroonenberg, 1988).

TABLE 7.2

Patterns of attachment observed in 12- to 18-month-olds in the Strange Situation

	Exploratory Behavior before Separation	*Behavior during Separation*	*Reunion Behavior*	*Behavior with Stranger*
Secure	Separates to explore toys; shares play with mother; friendly toward stranger when mother is present; touches "home base" periodically.	May cry; play is subdued for a while; usually recovers and is able to play.	If distressed during separation, contact ends distress; if not distressed, greets mother warmly; initiates interaction.	Somewhat friendly; may play with stranger after initial distress reaction.
Insecure/Ambivalent (resistant)	Has difficulty separating to explore toys even when mother is present; wary of novel situations and people; stays close to mother and away from stranger.	Very distressed; hysterical crying does not quickly diminish.	Seeks comfort and rejects it; continues to cry or fuss; may be passive—no greeting made.	Wary of stranger; rejects stranger's offer to play.
Insecure/Avoidant	Readily separates to explore toys; does not share play with parent; shows little preference for parent over stranger.	Does not show distress; continues to play; interacts with the stranger.	Ignores mother— turns or moves away; avoidance is more extreme at the second reunion.	No avoidance of stranger.

Source: Compiled from "Attachment and Exploratory Behavior of One-Year-Olds in a Strange Situation," by M. D. S. Ainsworth and B. A. Wittig, 1969, in *Determinants of Infant Behavior* (Vol. 4), edited by B. M. Foss. London: Methuen.

In **insecure/avoidant attachment,** the baby readily separates from the mother to often explore toys and does not show a preference for the mother over the stranger. When the mother leaves, the baby often shows no concern. When she returns, the baby ignores or avoids her. If an avoidant baby cries, no comfort is sought. About 20 percent of low-risk infants are classified as insecure/avoidant based on their behavior in the Strange Situation (Fox et al., 1991; Rosen & Burke, 1999).

In **insecure/ambivalent** (also called insecure/resistant) attachment, the baby stays close to the mother and does not explore the toys. When the mother leaves, the baby reacts with great distress; when she returns, the baby seeks her, but then resists or rejects her offers of comfort at the same time (that is, the reaction is ambivalent). Between 12 and 14 percent of low-risk infants are classified as insecure resistant/ambivalent (Fox et al., 1991; Rosen & Burke, 1999).

A fourth pattern, called **disorganized/disoriented attachment,** has also been proposed (Main & Hess, 1990; Main & Solomon, 1990). It includes elements of both ambivalence and avoidance. The disorganized/disoriented pattern and two other patterns of insecure attachment are described in Table 7.3.

TABLE 7.3

Criteria for atypical attachment categories

Disorganized (Type D)	Avoidant/Ambivalent (Type A/C)	Unstable-Avoidant (Type U-A)
Strong or frequent manifestation of one or more of the following: 1. Sequential display of contradictory behavior patterns 2. Simultaneous display of contradictory behavior patterns 3. Undirected, misdirected, incomplete, and interrupted movements and expressions 4. Stereotypies, asymmetrical movements, mistimed movements, anomalous postures 5. Freezing, stilling, and slowed movements and expressions 6. Direct indices of apprehension regarding the parent 7. Direct indices of disorganization or disorientation	1. Moderate to high avoidance combined with moderate to high resistance during reunions 2. Moderate to high proximity seeking and contact maintenance, as is typical of securely attached infants	1. Marked avoidance in the first reunion (5–7 on Ainsworth's interactive rating scales), followed by at least a 4-point drop in avoidance in the second reunion (1–3 on the rating scales)

Source: From "Atypical Attachment in Infancy and Early Childhood among Children at Developmental Risk," by J. I. Vondra and D. Barnett, 1999, *Monographs of the Society for Research in Child Development,* Serial No. 258, *64* (3), p. 16. © 1999 by the Society for Research in Child Development. Reprinted with permission

Babies' behavior in the Strange Situation is influenced not only by the quality of their attachment, but also by aspects of their daily experiences. For this reason, conclusions reached about a baby's attachment relationship based on behavior in the Strange Situation must be viewed with caution. (See Research Close-Up: The Strange Situation in Cross-Cultural Perspective.)

THE RELATIONSHIP BETWEEN INFANT ATTACHMENT AND THE PARENT'S BEHAVIOR.   The parent's overall pattern of behavior toward the baby influences strongly the kind of attachment the baby will develop. Each attachment pattern seems to reflect different histories of parental response. When parents respond sensitively to the baby's signals, the baby tends to become securely attached. When parents respond inappropriately, or not at all, the baby tends to form an insecure attachment of some kind. Appropriately responsive caregivers (1) pay attention to the baby's signals, (2) interpret the signals accurately, (3) give appropriate feedback, and (4) respond contingently, that is, promptly enough for the baby to feel that his signals caused the response (Ainsworth et al., 1978).

RESEARCH

CLOSE-UP   *The Strange Situation in Cross-Cultural Perspective*

The Strange Situation has been used to study attachment patterns of infants in different countries. Researchers have wondered whether Ainsworth's attachment categories show **construct validity** in other cultures. High construct validity of Ainsworth's attachment categories means that attachment patterns found in the Strange Situation are related systematically to important variations in parent-child behavior wherever attachment is studied.

Data from Cross-Cultural Attachment Studies

In these studies, the majority of babies have been classified as securely attached; a minority are classified as insecure. The cross-cultural findings, however, sometimes show a different distribution of babies in the two insecure categories—ambivalent and avoidant—for different countries. Specifically, in some cultures, more of the insecure babies are classified as insecure/avoidant, while in other cultures, more insecure babies are ambivalent or resistant. In Germany, more avoidant than ambivalent babies have been found, overall, whereas in Japan, more insecure babies are ambivalent than avoidant.

Table 7.4 lists the percentage of babies in several different countries who show the various types of attachment patterns. (Pattern A is insecure/avoidant, Pattern B is secure, and Pattern C is insecure/ambivalent) (Magai & McFadden, 1995). The percentages were found using studies reviewed by van IJzendoorn and Kroonenberg (1988) In some cases, such as Sweden, Great Britain, and China, data from only 1

TABLE 7.4   Attachment patterns across different cultures

Country	Insecure Avoidant Pattern A (%)	Secure Pattern B (%)	Insecure Ambivalent Pattern C (%)
Germany	35	57	8
Great Britain	22	75	3
Netherlands	26	67	6
Sweden	22	74	4
Israel	7	64	29
Japan	5	68	27
China	25	50	25
USA	21	65	14

Source: Adapted from *The Role of Emotions in Social and Personality Development* (p. 51), by C. Magai and S. H. McFadden, 1995, New York: Plenum Press. Reprinted with permission.

study were used. In the case of the United States, the percentages were based on 18 studies.

Very low rates of insecure/avoidant babies have been found in Israel and Japan, and relatively high rates of avoidant babies have been found in Germany. The figures are averages across several studies—2 each, in the case of Is-

Responsive parents also cooperate with the baby's ongoing activity rather than intrude or interfere. Mothers of securely attached babies "are more responsive to their infant's cries, hold their babies more tenderly and carefully, pace the interaction contingently during face-to-face interaction, and exhibit greater sensitivity in initiating and terminating feeding" (Crockenberg, 1981, p. 857; de Wolff & IJzendoorn, 1997; Isabella & Belsky, 1991). Across cultures, caregiving is highly responsive even where face-to-face interaction is uncommon. Babies in these cultures are often in bodily contact with the mother, day and night. Feeding is on demand, and babies' cries are responded to immediately. Thus, the baby learns that her initiations are followed by responses of the caregiver (Landers, 1989; Winn et al., 1989).

Parents of insecurely attached babies may ignore the baby's signals, or they may respond, but not in an effective or appropriate way. For example, a mother may take the opportunity to read the newspaper every time she feeds the baby, holding him loosely and not noticing his gaze or sucking. A father may consistently ignore the baby's cries in the middle of the night to get some extra sleep. A parent might bounce a baby vigorously when the baby prefers to be cuddled or end a feeding when the

rael and Japan; 3 in the case of Germany. Interestingly, there is wide variation among the German studies. In one study done in the northern region (Bielefeld), a high proportion of avoidant infants was found. But in a second study done in Regensburg, in southern Germany, the distribution of insecure/avoidant and insecure/ambivalent attachment is very much like the distribution found in U.S. samples.

The Significance of Cross-National Variations in Attachment Patterns

Studies have revealed variations both within and between cultures that seem to reflect ecological conditions of different geographic regions within a country and among different social classes (Thompson, 1998).

As has been noted by Miyake and colleagues (1985, p. 281), "the investigator must be very careful not to confuse the contextual determinants of strange situation performance with 'quality of attachment.'" One must be aware that specific experiences can influence the meaning of the Strange Situation for various infants. Attachment theory suggests that infants' reactions to the strange situation will vary across cultures (Waters & Cummings, 2000).

Because Japanese babies are rarely left in the care of a babysitter (Miyake et al., 1985; Vogel, 1968), the Strange Situation is likely to induce a great deal of distress. This distress then is an index not only of the mother-child attachment relationship, but of the infant's general lack of experience in being left alone with a stranger. In the case of some German babies, an emphasis on independence training may lead to

a higher level of avoidant behavior in the Strange Situation. Greater avoidance in these babies may not indicate a higher incidence of problems in the attachment relationship, but a higher rate of experience in being separated from and reunited with parents.

With few exceptions, mothers who are most sensitive and responsive to their babies tend to be the ones whose babies are classified as secure, no matter where they live in the world. Thus, it would seem that insecure categories, whatever their distribution, tend on average to indicate less optimal mother-child relationships than the secure classification, although their specific interpretation must be made within a cultural context.

Variations in attachment across cultures may suggest the existence of (1) cultural expectations that actually interfere with attachment, as well as (2) cultural expectations that are irrelevant to the attachment relationship, but nonetheless affect a baby's behavior in the Strange Situation. Within a country, the varied experiences of different groups of babies may alter the behavior of a baby in the Strange Situation without actually altering the attachment relationship. Receiving child care outside the home during infancy may be one instance of this kind of variation. The exact reasons for the increase in avoidance behavior among U.S. babies who spend time in child care as compared with U.S. babies reared only in the home are not known. (See the Research Close-Up: How Does Child Care Affect Parent-Child Attachment on p. 248 of this chapter.)

baby only wants to rest. Or the parents might continue to stimulate the baby when the baby has had enough and wishes to stop.

Serious problems in attachment can occur when a parent's behavior is disturbed. For example, some mothers have "restricted affect," which means that they express fewer emotions, especially positive, joyful ones, than other mothers (Ainsworth et al., 1978; Main, 1981). Some mothers dislike physical contact with their babies or treat them in an angry or threatening way (Bretherton et al., 1986). Some mothers even mock their babies' behavior, speak sarcastically to them, handle them roughly, and "stare them down." Babies treated in these ways are likely to have severe problems in their emotional and social development. (We describe parental histories that can lead to such behavior in a subsequent section of this chapter.)

Sensitivity in parenting may have two dimensions: (1) responding versus not responding and (2) responding appropriately versus responding inappropriately (Lamb, 1982). Babies whose parents do not respond contingently or consistently seem to show the ambivalent (or resistant) pattern of insecure attachment (Isabella & Belsky, 1991). The response they receive may be appropriate when it comes, but they cannot be sure when it is going to be given or if it will come at all. Because they cannot be sure the parent will give the desired comfort, they seek it intensely but then resist it, as if both testing for consistency and anticipating disappointment.

The second dimension of sensitivity in parenting—responding appropriately versus responding inappropriately, in combination with contingent responding—also affects the development of the infant's trust in others. Babies whose parents respond to them inappropriately may learn to expect that people will not react to them in desired ways. Babies whose parents are intrusive or rejecting, for example, may stop sending signals and may even try to avoid the parent, perhaps as protection against getting an inappropriate response (Cassidy, 1994; Isabella & Belsky, 1991). Ainsworth explained insecure avoidant behavior as a defense against anxiety. Ainsworth said that anxiety continues to be present but is repressed (Ainsworth, 1990), a response the baby finds more desirable than calling upon a parent who responds inappropriately.

Observations of mothers of insecurely attached babies are consistent with these predictions. Mothers of insecure ambivalent babies have shown few mutual and reciprocal interchanges. They have also been less involved, more inconsistent, and more limiting of their baby's exploration than expected (Cassidy & Berlin, 1994; Magai & McFadden, 1995). And mothers of insecure avoidant babies have been more intrusive, less inclined to establish body contact, and less responsive than might be expected.

We do not yet fully understand all of the links between specific maternal behavior and each insecure pattern of attachment. But we do know that the quality of parenting in the early months is an important predictor of the child's long-term development and future happiness; therefore, we need to be alert to situations in which a parent and child seem headed for trouble.

In order to identify situations and the circumstances that contribute to troublesome attachment, we will first examine behavior exhibited by the baby. We will look at how babies generally signal their needs to their caregivers. Then we will look at individual differences in temperament shown by babies and discuss how these differences may affect their signaling.

The Infant's Early Signals

While talking and looking at me the mother turned her head and gazed at the infant's face. He was gazing at the ceiling, but out of the corner of his eye he saw her head turn toward him and turned to gaze back at her. This had happened before, but now he broke rhythm and stopped sucking. He let go of the nipple and the suction around it broke as he eased into the faintest suggestion of a smile. The mother abruptly stopped talking and, as she watched his face begin to transform, her eyes opened a little wider and her eyebrows raised a bit. His eyes locked on to hers, and together they held motionless for an instant. The infant did not return to sucking and his mother held frozen her slight expression of anticipation. This silent and almost motionless instant continued to hang until the mother suddenly shattered it by saying "Hey!" and simultaneously opening her eyes wider, raising her eyebrows further, and throwing her head up and toward the infant. Almost simultaneously, the baby's eyes widened. His head tilted up and, as his smile broadened, the nipple fell out of his mouth. Now she said, "Well, hello! . . . Heeelloooo!" so that her pitch rose and the "hellos" became longer and more stressed on each successive repetition. With each phrase the baby expressed more pleasure, and his body resonated almost like a balloon being pumped up, filling a little more with each breath. The mother then paused and her face relaxed. They watched each other expectantly for a moment. The shared excitement between them ebbed, but before it faded completely, the baby suddenly took an initiative and intervened to rescue it. His head lurched forward, his hands jerked up, and a fuller smile blossomed. His mother was jolted into motion. She moved forward, mouth open and eyes alight, and said "Oooooh . . . ya wanna play do ya . . . yeah? . . . I didn't know if you were still hungry . . . no . . . noooooo . . . no I didn't . . . " And off they went. (Stern, 1977, p. 3)

think about it

How can a young baby communicate with an adult? Did the mother read the baby's signals and adjust what she did to the level desired by the baby? What did the baby do when the mother reduced stimulation below the level the baby wanted? How did the mother interpret the broadening of the baby's smile?

This example illustrates how babies can be partners in even the earliest social interactions, attempting to regulate their partner's action and responses by deploying their repertoire of signals. Parents must be able to read and respond to the signals. What happens to the relationship when parents are insensitive to the baby?

The baby in the example was not a newborn. Newborns have fewer signals at their disposal, but even they are equipped to signal. Some of the newborn's signals are subtle; others are not. Perhaps the least subtle and most powerful signal is crying. Adults usually move quickly to quiet a crying baby. Parents usually can tell whether the crying indicates hunger, anger, or pain. Their judgments are based on how suddenly the crying starts, how loud and high-pitched it is, and how long it lasts (Wolff, 1969a). Parents also consider the context of the crying. For example, they know when the baby was last fed. Taking this and other information into consideration, the parent decides what might be causing the crying and begins to do something about it.

Most parents respond to crying by picking up and holding or rocking the baby. This not only soothes the baby (Hunziker & Barr, 1986; Korner & Thoman, 1972) but also induces the alert inactive state. The baby opens her eyes and searches, often fixating on her parent's eyes if the parent is looking at her.

The tendency of parents to gaze into a newborn's eyes is common in some cultures but not at all in others (Landers, 1989; Winn et. al, 1989). For example, the Efe, who live in the Ituri forest in Zaire, believe that the newborn's job is to sleep. A newborn is not perceived to be social during this early stage of life. Newborns are fed on demand and cared for with great tenderness and responsiveness, because upsets and lack of sleep are thought to hinder their growth. But mothers do not gaze into their babies' eyes to try to elicit social interaction. This kind of response comes later, at around 4 months of age, after the intense sleeping period has passed and the baby is thought to have become a social being (Winn et al., 1989).

But babies are capable of gazing, even during the very first weeks of life, and their capacity to use gazing to help regulate interaction increases rapidly (see Figure 7.2). Steady, intent attention to another's face suggests that the baby wishes to engage in social interaction. The parent will probably gaze back at the baby and smile or speak; a baby who is 2 or 3 months old may smile or coo in return. Parents in some cultures like this eye contact, perhaps because it makes them feel that the baby is enjoying their company. Many parents will gaze back at the baby as long as the baby gazes at them (Robson, 1967).

Babies signal their wish to reduce stimulation or end the interaction by looking away. Sensitive parents who have been interacting with their baby reduce stimulation when the baby looks away. But some parents miss the signal or do not respond to it in a way that lets the baby regulate the interaction.

Besides crying and gazing, babies have other ways to make adults pay attention to them and to regulate their responding. When they are eating, for example, babies suck in rhythmical bursts and then pause. Mothers often jiggle babies during the pauses. This biologically based sucking pattern, with its alternating bursts and pauses, may keep the mother actively involved in the feeding. The turn-taking nature

FIGURE 7.2

The endogenous smile and the social smile. (LEFT) The first smile seen in an infant is not elicited by social stimuli. (RIGHT) It is fairly easy to coax a smile from an infant of 3–4 months of age; the infant will respond to talking or smiling. (*Source:* (LEFT) © Elizabeth Crews, (RIGHT) © Michael/Photo Edit)

RESEARCH

The Developmental Course of Smiling

Newborns often smile in their sleep, but these spontaneous smiles, known as **endogenous smiles,** are triggered by changes in their internal sleep states (Emde & Gaensbauer, 1981). Between 6 and 8 weeks of age, there appears a **social smile**—a smile given in response to something outside the baby (see Figure 7.2, right frame). The baby smiles more and more frequently over the next few months (Anisfeld, 1982; Konner, 1982; Wolff, 1969). Babies smile more fully in social contexts than in nonsocial ones (Messinger et al., 1999).

At first, the social smile is indiscriminate: The baby smiles at familiar and unfamiliar adults alike, as long as they make some friendly gesture—gaze, smile, or talk. Then from 2 to 4 months of age, babies begin to react more positively to familiar figures than to unfamiliar ones (Mizukami et al., 1990). The baby begins to search the faces of unfamiliar people and to become a bit sober (Emde et al., 1976; Kurzweil, 1988). By 6 to 8 months of age, the baby's reaction to unfamiliar people may be so intense that he cries if a stranger approaches (Konner, 1982; Lamb, 1982). The baby's smile is now very selective, reserved only for familiar people. Unfamiliar people are likely to make the baby cry. When a baby reacts this way to a stranger (usually between 6 and 18 months of age), he is showing **stranger anxiety.**

What makes a baby start to smile? Does the baby learn to smile by seeing smiles, or is the impulse to smile innate?

The answer comes from a study of smiling in premature babies. Researchers hypothesized that smiling is an innate capability, programmed to emerge at a certain point in the baby's development. They calculated this point in weeks from conception. They suggested that babies born 8 weeks prematurely would smile not at 6 weeks postnatally, when full-term babies smile, but at 12 to 14 weeks, when their developmental age would match that of 6-week-olds. This is exactly what they found (Anisfeld, 1982). Other research shows that social smiling begins at about the same time that certain portions of the brain develop. (See Konner, 1982, for an excellent discussion of this topic.)

It appears that one of the baby's most powerful social signals is not especially social in origin. But parents read the smile as a friendly social gesture. Commenting on the parent's point of view, one researcher writes, "fantasies are not to be disparaged. Fantasies are, in fact, part of the evolved apparatus with which parents are provided (the evolution in this case being cultural, not only genetic), so that they treat the infant as a person from the start. . . . Parents capitalize on certain aspects of the newborn organism that, so far as we can tell, evolved for that very purpose, so as to involve the infant in social frames" (Kaye, 1982b, p. 196). In other words, smiling is another behavior that may have evolved to help ensure the survival of the baby and the species.

of the feeding interaction may help mothers learn to observe their babies closely and adjust their responses to the babies' behavior (Kaye, 1982a).

As the newborn matures, another powerful signal—the social smile—emerges. It begins to appear by about 2 months of age. (See the Research Close-Up: The Developmental Course of Smiling.) When the smile starts to fade and the baby becomes sober, something may be amiss. Smiling and becoming sober, and gazing and gaze aversion, are the signals with which the baby can participate in regulating her interactions with her parents and other adults in the early months. These signals may not seem like much in comparison with the virtually infinite variety of signals older children and adults use to communicate. But they are powerful enough to elicit and regulate responses from responsive caregivers.

Attachment Reaction: Stranger Anxiety and Separation Distress

Babies between 6 and 12 months add a whole new set of actions to their repertoire as they begin to creep, crawl, and finally, walk. Now they need not wait for their parents to come to them or just watch them as they move away. They can follow them. At the same time, babies start to discriminate sharply between familiar and unfamiliar adults (see Research Close-Up: The Developmental Course of Smiling). When approached by someone unfamiliar, they grow sober and may even cry. Babies can also gain information now about new people and situations by engaging

knowledge *in action*

"How Do You Feel about Her, Mom?"

As 12-month-old Anthony plays with brightly colored plastic rings, the doorbell rings. His mother answers the door. When their new neighbor enters the room, she begins to chat with Anthony. "Well, hello there," she says, as she kneels down on the floor. "What are you doing?"

Anthony stops playing and begins to clutch the yellow ring in his hand. He looks toward his mother, who has sat down on the sofa. She smiles at Anthony and says, "Say hi to Mary Beth, Anthony. Say, 'Hiiii, Mary Beth.' "

Anthony stares at Mary Beth. Then he casts a glance back toward Mom, who smiles as she talks now with Mary Beth about Anthony. Anthony looks back toward Mary Beth, led there by the direction of his mother's gaze. Anthony slowly raises the hand that holds the ring, and then extends it toward Mary Beth. "Oh, what a pretty yellow ring!" Mary Beth exclaims. "Does it go on this post?" Mary Beth reaches for the post as she asks and tilts it toward the ring held out by Anthony. Anthony looks up at Mary Beth, then back at his mom. As he slips the ring over the end of the post, his face breaks into a smile.

What Is Social Referencing?

Anthony's strategy of using information about how another person feels about a third event—in this case, Mary Beth—is called **social referencing** (Clyman et al., 1986; Flavell & Miller, 1998). Social referencing involves scanning the face of a familiar and trusted person to pick up information about a new situation. From that person's emotional reaction to the situation, the child can form his response. Babies 9 months of age and older often use this strategy. They are also likely to look to the parent before touching unfamiliar toys (Walden & Baxter, 1989; Walden & Ogden, 1988).

Studies of Social Referencing

In one study mothers were asked to pose different expressions as their babies were presented with a new toy (Klinnert, 1981). When mothers looked happy or joyful, their babies were more likely to accept the toy. Babies react similarly to fathers' signals (Hirshberg & Svejda, 1990). Babies' reactions to strangers have also been linked to their mothers' facial expressions (Feinman & Lewis, 1983).

Mothers' facial expressions also influence babies' willingness to cross over the "visual cliff." (Recall from chapter 5 that this is a laboratory apparatus, designed for the study of infant depth perception.) When babies get close to the part of the surface where the cliff appears, they look up at their mothers for clues about this novel situation. In studies of social referencing, researchers asked different mothers to show emotions, such as interest, anger, or fear, as their babies approached the cliff. When mothers looked pleased or interested, babies were much more likely to cross the cliff than when mothers looked angry or afraid.

Babies' Ability to Read Facial Expressions

Babies who engage in social referencing recognize and can respond to facial expressions. Babies start discriminating among facial expressions by the time they are 4 or 5 months old, but they probably do not attach meanings to different expressions at that age (Appel & Campos, 1977). Somewhat later, between 6 and 9 months of age, they begin to respond differently to different expressions, which indicates they understand some of the meanings attached to the expressions. A baby might cry, for example, on seeing an angry face, or smile on seeing a joyful one. At this point, they start to be able to communicate with someone else, via emotional expressions, about an uncertain third event (Campos et al., 1983).

in social referencing. (See Knowledge in Action: Parenting—"How Do You Feel about Her, Mom?")

Sometime between 8 and 10 months of age, babies start to express on their faces the emotions of joy, surprise, and anger (Hiatt et al., 1979; Stenberg et al., 1983). Now they can combine facial expressions, sounds, and movement to produce the full-blown attachment reactions that parents and babysitters know so well. When they see their parents after a separation, they greet them with joy and stretch out their arms or crawl to them. When separated from their parents, or when concerned that a separation may be coming, they show **separation anxiety**—they sob, cry, cling, or try to follow. The older infant and the toddler show attachment by walking or running to keep in contact with the parent. With the acquisition of language, the child adds words of protest: "Mommy! Daddy! Stay here! I go!" These kinds of scenes are practically the hallmark of the toddler years, when separation distress is at its height.

Temperament in Infancy

Unique tendencies differentiate one baby from another. **Temperament** is made up of those characteristics which show consistency across situations and stability over time. Even neonates differ reliably on emotionality (sensitivity and intensity of reaction), activity level, and sociability (Bates, 1994; Woroby, 1993). Temperament is largely what most of us consider emotional responsiveness. (Magai & McFadden, 1995). It might be thought of as an infant's style of responding to environmental stimuli.

It is generally agreed that these initial individual differences in temperament have a constitutional, or biological, basis and that this is determined in large part by genetics. Precisely how much heredity contributes to temperament is controversial. Some researchers believe that genetic influences on behavior are extensive in the general population, whereas other researchers point out that biology and environment are so intertwined even in infancy that it is difficult to separate their effects. Possibly some aspects of initial temperament are more amenable to environmental influences than others are (Magai & McFadden, 1995), but temperament is thought to be influenced by genetic inheritance, with contributions from maturation and experience.

In a classic study of the stability of temperament and the influence of experience over time, Jerome Kagan studied shyness—inhibited responses to unfamiliar events. He found that an infant who cries, stiffens her muscles, and arches her back in response to an unfamiliar stimulus at 4 months is likely to be shy in her second year (Kagan, 1971; Kagan & Snidman, 1991). Average differences in shyness between the infants who showed motor activity and distress and those who remained relaxed and did not fret were apparent in a social situation in their fifth year (Kagan, 1997; Kagan et al., 1998).

Kagan (1998) has pointed out that shyness may be influenced by two biochemical factors: (1) the concentration of at least one neurotransmitter (a chemical that carries impulses from one nerve cell to the next) in parts of the brain that control crying and motor activity and (2) the density of neurotransmitter receptors on those nerve cells. These factors, which are at least partially determined by genetics, would explain individual differences in both negative temperament beginning at birth and in exploratory behavior in the second year (Kagan & Snidman, 1991).

Of course, individual history also influences shyness or lack of it: A child who is rejected by her parents may become anxious and introverted regardless of her genetic makeup (Kagan & Snidman, 1991), and a child who was initially shy may become less so, with supportive parenting.

Dimensions of Temperament   Researchers have long discussed how many specific traits make up the important aspects of temperament (Kagan, 1998; Rothbart & Bates, 1998; Strelau & Anleitner, 1991). Alexander Thomas and Stella Chess (1977), who conducted one of the longest longitudinal studies in history, identified newborns as "easy," "difficult," or "slow to warm up," based on nine characteristics: rhythms of biological function (e.g., hunger, sleep), approach or withdrawal from new stimuli, adaptability, distractibility, activity level, quality of mood, persistence or attention span, intensity of reaction, and sensory threshold of responsiveness.

Chess and Thomas (1984) also pointed out that the infant's temperament affects the parent's response and choice of socialization techniques. They proposed that the "goodness of fit" between the child's temperament and the parent's responses is a major factor in successful child rearing, a position echoed by developmental systems theorists and supported by considerable research (Seifer et al., 1996; Vondra & Barnett, 1999). The parent's ability to adapt to a baby with a specific temperament mediates the effects of temperament on the child's development, including the forming of attachment. For example, parents with a baby who is not especially outgoing may misinterpret the baby's low level of initiating and responding in interactions to mean that the infant is understimulated. The parent then provides too much stimulation for the baby, causing the baby to avoid the parent (Smith & Pederson, 1988) and thus demonstrating an avoidant pattern of attachment. A level of stimulation to accommodate the more sensitive baby can result in a different attachment relationship. Similarly, a child who is very emotionally reactive and irritable may at times cause a parent to lose confidence, respond inconsistently, and provide less stimulation than the baby might prefer. This inconsistent pattern of parental responsiveness is related to insecure/ambivalent attachment (Vondra et al., 1995).

In this "goodness of fit" or contextual or systems model of parent-child interaction, temperament influences the parent-child relationship, but it does not directly determine the type of attachment relationship that is formed. Although specific initial temperaments tend to be associated with specific patterns of attachment, a parent's behavior—how the parent adapts to the specific temperament of the baby—appears to be the most powerful influence on the kind of attachment a child will develop (Vondra & Barnett, 1999).

Temperament and Self-Regulation One description of temperament includes individual differences not only in emotional and motor behavior, but also in self-regulation (Rothbart & Bates, 1998). A distinction is made between **attentional reactivity,** the relatively passive arousability of emotion, motor activity, and attention when confronted with stimulation, and **self-regulation,** the process by which the child actively tries to control that reaction. In self-regulation, an infant directs her attention to modify her emotional and motor response to stimulation. Kochanska et al. (1997) describe this active self-regulation component of temperament as inhibitory or effortful **control of arousal** (Kochanska et al., 1997). Rothbart (1989) suggests that inhibitory or effortful control first becomes apparent at the end of the first year, when the infant actively suppresses the urge to approach a person or a thing, even at the cost of pleasure. Inhibitory or effortful control first appears at a time when parents expect children to begin to regulate their conduct somewhat. It is thought to be related to several factors, including the maturation of certain neurological systems and increased understanding of the meaning of verbal prompts (i.e., prohibitions).

Measures of inhibitory or effortful control include a 2-year-old's waiting for an experimenter to ring a bell before getting an M&M from under a glass cup, not peaking while a gift is being wrapped, and whispering the names of cartoon characters presented, all as instructed by an adult (Kochanska et al., 1996). Tests measuring such inhibitory or effortful control of arousal are highly correlated during the toddler, preschool, and early school years. This component of temperament is also correlated with measures of conscience at early school age, such as complying with the mother's request to clean up items others have spilled, completing a mundane task even when the child thinks he is alone, and not cheating in a game (Kochanska et al., 1997).

Clearly, temperament can be influenced by the child's interactions with caregivers, despite the biological underpinnings of temperament itself. Self-regulation is shaped in part by caregivers who sensitively respond to a baby's signals, as we shall see (Fox, 1994).

Even though babies come into the world with different temperaments, we can say that they generally are well equipped to interact with adults and to regulate those interactions. The baby's signals—gazing, smiling, crying, and becoming sober—motivate the parent to respond, and then the give and take of the interaction keeps them both going, if all proceeds smoothly. But what ensures that a parent will respond appropriately? And what happens when things do not go well? These questions are discussed next.

Theories of Individual Differences in Attachment: The Parent's Side

Newborns turn life upside down. They sometimes cry many hours a day, challenging the patience and ingenuity of even the most resourceful adult. Old family patterns break down and new ones emerge as the baby takes her place in the household. Parents are helped through the difficult parts of parenting by their own feelings of attachment to their baby. When parents lack feelings of attachment, it is more likely that the parent will respond to the stresses of parenting with child abuse or neglect (Crittenden & Ainsworth, 1989; Lieberman & Pawl, 1990).

Like infant attachment, parental attachment has been of great interest. What causes parental attachment to form? Three explanations for its development have been proposed: the biological explanation, the parental history explanation, and the developmental systems explanation. Each is discussed here.

The Biological Explanation

One biological explanation, also known as the critical period explanation, claims that maternal attachment is based on hormones. The theory is that hormones released at the end of pregnancy or soon after birth "prime" the mother to bond with her baby. **Bonding** is the dramatic and immediate emotional tie that mothers often feel toward their newborn babies, according to the proponents of this explanation (Klaus & Kennel, 1976). Bonding is supposedly triggered in the hormonally primed mother by contact with her baby within a **critical period** immediately after birth, when the hormones are at their highest level. If the mother bonds with the baby during this early period, her love will continue to grow, and she will be able to provide the responsive care that ensures the baby's attachment to her.

This biological theory of maternal attachment originated in research on sheep, goats, and rats. Mothering was disrupted when the young were separated from their mothers immediately after birth, even for only one to two hours (Collias, 1956; Hersher et al., 1958). Mothering was not disrupted, or the disruption was less serious, when some contact was allowed before mothers and young animals were separated. The identification of a critical period for maternal attachment emerged from these studies.

Researchers have also found a higher level of maternal behavior in pregnant rats than in nonpregnant rats, and, when blood plasma from pregnant rats was injected into nonpregnant rats, these rats also exhibited maternal behavior (Rosenblatt, 1969). This research established a hormonal basis for maternal behavior in rats.

Researchers soon investigated whether the findings from animal studies could be applied to humans. One research group wanted to know if there was a causal relationship between severe disruption in maternal attachment—the kind that results in child abuse—and separation at birth. This question arose because physicians who cared for premature newborns in the neonatal intensive care unit of a large city hospital noticed that an unusually high number of the premature infants later returned to the emergency room as victims of child abuse. They wondered if the mothers of these babies had been unable to bond with them because they were separated during a critical period for bonding.

In pioneering studies to test the critical period theory in humans, these physicians (Klaus et al., 1972; Klaus & Kennell, 1976) manipulated the amount of contact between mothers and their newborns in hospitals. Some mothers were kept on traditional schedules, which involved contact mainly at regular feeding times; others were given contact immediately after birth and for increased periods of time in the days that followed (Carlsson et al., 1978; Hales et al., 1977; Leifer et al., 1972; Rode et al., 1981).

In general, results of these studies did not provide strong evidence for a critical period during which bonding must take place. Researchers and theorists have concluded that hormones are probably more important in determining behavior in lower animals than in humans. Maternal behavior in humans seems to depend not on one critical event but on many different factors occurring over time. Early contact between mother and baby is probably beneficial, but it does not seem to be absolutely essential to the formation of attachment (Goldberg, 1982; Svejda et al., 1982).

The Parental History Explanation Other theorists and researchers think that maternal attachment is closely related to the mother's previous life experiences. A mother's ability to form a close, nurturing tie with a baby is seen as a function of her personality and of how she was cared for when she was a child. This explanation comes from observations and studies of disrupted attachment, such as in cases of neglect and abuse, rather than from observations of healthy mother-child relationships. Mothers who have a poor-quality attachment with their children are seen as lacking in parental skills, knowledge about children, or the ability to act responsibly because of their own immaturity. Sometimes these mothers have psychological problems or personality disorders. Or perhaps these mothers have acquired internal working models that represent others as untrustworthy and themselves as ineffective.

In support of the parental history position, it can be said that abusive parents as a group are more likely to have been poorly parented than nonabusive parents (Green et al., 1974; Oliver & Taylor, 1971). Furthermore, the children of abusive parents tend to show more insecure/avoidant attachment than do nonmaltreated infants (Magai & McFadden, 1995). (See also Knowledge in Action: Health/Safety—Signs, Symptoms and Long-Term Consequences of Child Abuse and Neglect, in Chapter 8.)

Additionally, mothers who suffer from major depression, psychosis, or drug abuse may well have difficulty being effective parents (Field et al., 1989; Field., 1994; Musick et al., 1981). One study found a higher proportion of insecure/avoidant and resistant babies among children of depressed mothers than among children of mothers who were well. This was especially true if a depressed mother was separated from her husband (Radke-Yarrow et al., 1985). In another study, the specific effects of a mother's depression were influenced by her level of stress. Infants of depressed and stressed mothers were likely to develop an insecure/ambivalent attachment, whereas infants of depressed but unstressed mothers were likely to develop an insecure/avoidant attachment relationship (Rosenblum et al., 1997).

The mother's capacity to form a good attachment relationship with her child is also influenced by the father's alcohol use. When the father's drinking is heavy, the mother's relationship with the child is less optimal (Eiden & Leonard, 1996). Generally, it has also been confirmed that past childhood relationships, at least the reconstructed memories of those relationships, influence how individuals parent their own children (Ricks, 1985; Simons et al., 1991).

Parental histories do not, however, completely explain attachment behavior. The majority of abused children apparently do not become abusive parents (Kaufman & Zigler, 1989). Moreover, although some abusive and depressed mothers and fathers develop poor attachments to their babies, others do not appear to suffer from such obvious problems. Parental history and personality characteristics may provide part of the explanation for attachment, but not the whole story (Parke & Lewis, 1981).

The Developmental Systems Explanation

As in other areas of child development, researchers working in the area of attachment are increasingly formulating systems (contextual/ecological) explanations for events. They have proposed a model—the developmental systems explanation—suggesting that parental attachment is a function of several interacting factors: (1) characteristics of the parent (personality traits and psychological well-being); (2) characteristics of the baby (health, degree of development at birth, and temperament); (3) characteristics of the family (number of children, role of the father in child care, and economic resources); and (4) social supports beyond the immediate family (extended family, friends, and medical resources) (Belsky, 1984; Cooley & Unger, 1991; Feldman, et al., 1997; Rauh et al., 1990; Seifer et al., 1996).

Babies differ in terms of initial temperament. Interactions with parents and others during infancy and childhood can alter the extent to which an initially shy or outgoing child stays that way. It appears that this toddler's outgoing disposition is being encouraged by involving her in social play. (*Source:* © Bob Daemmrich/Stock Boston)

These factors are thought to interact in two directions to determine the kind of attachment the mother forms and the extent of her ability to nurture attachment in the baby. For example, correlational evidence indicates that a baby can affect his mother's responsiveness and that the mother's responsiveness in turn can affect the quality of the baby's attachment. One study found that babies classified as highly irritable in the first two weeks of life were less sociable with their mothers at 1 year of age and tended more often to be anxiously attached, whereas nonirritable babies were more sociable and tended more often to be securely attached (Van den Boom, 1989).

When babies have a negative or difficult temperament, however, parents can overcome this difficulty. In a study of irritable babies, some mothers were visited by a worker 6 to 9 months after birth. The worker encouraged the mother to pay attention to the baby's signals, interpret them, choose an appropriate response, and then act on it. The worker also encouraged the mother to imitate the baby, repeat vocalizations, be silent when the baby looked away, and soothe the baby when he cried. Mothers who received this intervention became more responsive, and their babies became more sociable and exploratory and less irritable, when compared with control babies who initially were just as irritable. At 1 year of age, 68 percent of the program babies were securely attached, but only 28 percent of the control babies were.

These results are consistent with the positions of attachment theorists and others (e.g., Wendland-Carro et al., 1999) who believe that parents can take the lead in social interchanges during the baby's first few months. Irritability in a baby can be considered a developmentally instigative characteristic (a behavior of the baby that brings behavior back on itself from the environment) (Bronfenbrenner, 1993). Characteristics of the baby are partially responsible for a poor "goodness of fit" in the attachment situation (Chess & Thomas, 1984), although many parents override the baby's characteristics with their own ability to adapt flexibly. Thus, they achieve a "goodness of fit" even with a difficult baby. (See pp. 243 for a discussion of temperament.)

To see how a number of factors interact to determine the kind of attachment that develops between a parent and infant, it is helpful to consider the case of the premature baby. Premature babies overall are more difficult to parent than are full-term babies. They signal their needs less clearly, avert their gaze more often, and smile less (Brown & Bateman, 1978; Crnic et al., 1983). Adults find their cries more unpleasant and their faces less attractive or cute (Frodi & Lamb, 1978). The premature baby cannot respond as much in a relationship as the full-term baby. But if the premature baby is born to parents with adequate parenting skills, healthy personalities, a stable relationship, a supportive extended family, a network of friends, and a secure economic situation, the baby's initial deficiencies probably will not stand in the way of the development of a secure attachment (Belsky & Vondra, 1989).

Similarly, if an extremely robust and "easy" baby is born into a situation that is not ideal or to a parent who is barely able to keep an interaction going, the baby might be able to contribute enough to make the relationship work. But a problem can occur when a difficult baby is born into difficult circumstances (Crockenberg, 1981; Vaughn et al., 1979). Any baby with a difficult temperament may be at risk for developing attachment problems because such a baby needs parenting under ideal circumstances, which not all caregivers can provide. When a relationship is found between early temperament and later poor attachment, it is likely that a difficult baby provided too great a challenge for a parent whose per-

RESEARCH

CLOSE-UP   *How Does Child Care Affect Parent-Child Attachment?*

Researchers interested in how child care affects attachment have posed the question, "Is there a difference in attachment relationships between babies reared full-time at home and babies reared both at home and in full-time child care?" Even though numerous studies have been conducted to explore this question, debates about it continue.

Studies of Child Care and Attachment

One of the first studies to document a difference between these two groups of babies used Ainsworth's Strange Situation to assess attachment behavior (Blehar, 1974). In this study, more of the children in the child-care group than in the home-reared-only group were judged to be insecurely attached to their mothers.

Many studies followed soon after this first one (Brookhart & Hock, 1976; Doyle, 1975; Kagan et al., 1978). Overall, they showed no significant deleterious effects from the childcare experience (Clarke-Stewart & Fein, 1983; Rutter, 1981). Then, in the early 1980s, two studies again found a difference in attachment between child-care and home-reared infants (Schwartz, 1983; Vaughn et al., 1980). Child-care infants showed a greater tendency to avoid their mothers upon reunion after separation. Several subsequent studies also found a slight increase in avoidance during reunion in infants placed in child care more than 20 hours per week during their first year (Belsky, 1988). Although more infants who were enrolled in child care exhibited avoidance, the amount of avoidance observed was not usually enough to change the infants' overall attachment classifications. In other words, most child-care infants had secure attachment patterns overall, although their behavior at reunion showed more avoidance than did the behavior of home-reared-only infants (Thompson, 1988). Moreover, secure attachments were more likely when the infant was an "easy" baby, when the father was the caregiver in the absence of the mother, and when the mother showed high levels of responsiveness and empathy to her children (Belsky & Rovine, 1988).

The NICHD Study of Early Child Care

In order to address discrepancies in previous studies of child care and attachment, a large longitudinal study was

sonality or current life circumstances limited the response to the infant (Sroufe et al., 1983).

The developmental systems explanation for attachment focuses on the complex interweaving of many factors, both those that create stress and those that provide support. The balancing of these elements seems to "buffer" parenting because if one part of the system is weak, another part can compensate for it. However, if something does go wrong in the system and only one part can be intact, it will be best if the intact part is the parent (van IJzendoorn et al., 1992). The most vulnerable situation occurs when the only strong part of the system is the baby (Belsky, 1984).

The developmental systems model is currently the favored explanation for attachment. In its complexity, it reflects what we see in real families, where nothing happens in a vacuum. It also makes sense from an ethological point of view. If we think of parental attachment in terms of its role in preserving the species, we realize that nothing as important as parent-child attachment would be left to only one or two determining factors. (See the Research Close-Up: How Does Child-Care Affect Parent-Child Attachment? for more discussion about factors that may affect attachment.)

Implications of Early Attachment

If a baby's attachment at 1 year is judged to be insecure on the basis of behavior in the Strange Situation, what kind of child might she be at 2 years? What will she be like later in life? Many studies have shown that the quality of early attachment is

begun by the National Institutes of Child Health and Development, an agency of the U.S. government. The Study of Early Child Care began in the 1990s (NICHD Early Child Care Research Network, 1997), and, to date, more than 1,000 infants and their mothers have participated. Types of care included care by mother (i.e., children not in regular child care), care by father, care by other relative, care by in-home nonrelative, child-care home, and child-care center.

Mothers were interviewed and observed in the home when their infants were from 1 to 15 months of age. Babies were observed in child care at 6 and 15 months and in the Strange Situation at 15 months. There were no overall effects of child-care experience on attachment security or on avoidance, regardless of the child-care quality, amount, age of entry, stability, or type of care. There were, as expected, significant positive effects on attachment of maternal sensitivity and responsiveness. Additionally, when low maternal sensitivity and responsiveness were combined with (1) poor quality child care or (2) more than one care arrangement, attachment was influenced negatively, as would be expected.

What Should Parents Do?

Nonparental child care per se does not appear by itself to be associated with infant-mother attachment difficulties. Other factors (e.g., low maternal sensitivity, parental anxieties about employment or separation, and so on) may, together with nonparental child care, affect the attachment relationship. Thus, a comprehensive understanding of the effects of infant child care on the parental attachment relationship awaits further research. Such research will need to take a number of variables into account and follow children longitudinally to test the validity of Strange Situation attachment assessment for infants who are not reared primarily by their mothers at home (Lamb, 1998).

Making an effort to find a child-care arrangement in which the caregiver or caregivers are warm and responsive should help ensure that the baby will not suffer harmful consequences, and that parents, too, will feel comfortable with the situation. Nonparental child care for infants apparently does not harm the mother-child attachment relationship if the care is responsive and appropriate, if the mother is responsive and empathic to the baby, and if the caregiver can deal well with a child's temperament.

correlated with the child's later social and cognitive development (Lamb et al., 1999; Magai & McFadden, 1995).

Table 7.5 gives a sampling of some of the relatively early studies that have reported on the later behavior of children whose attachment was evaluated in infancy. Later studies have been consistent with these.

As Table 7.5 shows, children who were securely attached as infants tend to grow into toddlers and preschoolers who are more affectively positive and curious

TABLE 7.5

Later behavior of children whose attachment was assessed in infancy

Behavior of Children Securely Attached as Infants	Behavior of Children Insecurely Attached as Infants	Current Age at Follow-Up	Study
When separated from mothers, cried less and played more than insecurely attached peers.	Cried more, played less.	1½	Jacobson & Willie, 1984
More likely to engage in play sessions with stranger; IQ, language, and social relations intercorrelated and related to stimulating and positive maternal behavior.	Less likely to play with stranger.	2	Clarke-Stewart et al., 1979
Engaged in more pretend and imaginative play; accepted mothers' suggestions in problem solving; showed more enthusiasm and persistence in problem solving.	Engaged in less symbolic play; ignored mothers' problem-solving suggestions.	2	Matas et al., 1978
Approached problems with enthusiasm; were more persistent; used mothers to help them.	More likely to throw tantrums, act aggressively, ignore mothers' suggestions.	2	Sroufe, 1982
More likely to engage in purposeful behavior, be more involved in activities, and get along well with others.	More likely to be aggressive with peers, to be on the fringes of activities, and to use materials in destructive rather than purposeful ways.	3½	Sroufe, 1982
More flexible in handling feelings and impulses; more independent in helping selves and managing social relations; more compliant; more empathetic.	More likely to create problem behaviors and exhibit aberrant behavior.	3	Sroufe, 1981
Appropriately independent: sought contact with teacher when ill or hurt or when they needed help, but otherwise functioned autonomously.	Showed emotional dependence that interfered with autonomous functioning; needed teacher's constant attention and support.	3	Sroufe et al., 1983
	Toddlers in child-care setting who were abused as infants showed anxious attachment; they were more aggressive, more inhibited in approach to adults, and more resistant to friendly overtures than peers who were not abused.	2–3	George & Main, 1981
Lower risk of becoming bullies or the victims of bullies at school during the preschool years.	High risk for becoming a bully or a victim of a bully at school during the preschool years.	4–5	Troy & Sroufe, 1987
Lower risk for developing attention deficit disorder with hyperactivity in kindergarten.	Increased risk for developing attention deficit disorder with hyperactivity in kindergarten.	5	Jacobvitz & Sroufe, 1987

during free play and who show an attentive, persistent, and apparently confident approach to solving problems. They show greater social competence with peers and more compliance with adults, suggesting trustfulness. Thus, overall, they are more competent and well adjusted than those classified in either of the insecurely attached groups (Lamb et al., 1999; Magai & McFadden, 1995; Thompson, 1998).

Few studies have used samples large enough to differentiate the later correlates of insecure/avoidant from insecure/ambivalent attachment classified in infancy because ambivalent babies tend to make up only some 7 to 15 percent of the subjects (Cassidy & Berlin, 1994). As a result, later correlates of insecure avoidance in comparison with insecure ambivalence in infancy are rarely described, though the few reports available are consistent with what would be expected from early attachment classification. For example, preschoolers who had been classified as insecure/ambivalent during their first year showed more dependency on teachers, whereas those classified as insecure/avoidant tended not to seek help from teachers (Magai & McFadden, 1995; Sroufe, 1983).

Strength of the Relationship between Infant Attachment and Later Behavior

Attachment theorists suggest that if a child develops an internal working model that depicts others as untrustworthy and herself as ineffective, this model will consistently undermine later opportunities to learn that others are trustworthy and that she can be effective. As a result, theorists have proposed that attachment classification in infancy will tend to remain the same as the child gets older. Some have suggested that early attachment history is correlated with later social and intellectual behavior because parents who were inconsistent in their responsiveness to an infant will also be inconsistent later in setting limits and socializing the child (Ainsworth, 1990). Both suggestions imply that a positive attachment classification in infancy should be strongly correlated with later desirable behavior, just as it is strongly correlated with desirable behavior in infancy.

The link between infant attachment behavior and later desirable behavior in childhood is, however, surprisingly modest. And the older the child becomes, the weaker these associations become. Even though positive infant attachment would seem to indicate later positive behavior, this connection is often not strong (Belsky, 1997). As time passes, a smaller and smaller proportion of children who were securely attached in infancy manifest the expected positive behaviors, and some children who had insecure attachments during infancy begin to show positive behavior. This changing picture makes sense if one adopts the developmental systems model. The availability of caregivers often varies over time because life circumstances of families (ecological conditions) change and because the child comes in contact with numerous other adults (Thompson, 1998). As Rosen and Burke (1999, p. 442) have pointed out, "By 4–5 years of age, the organized patterning of attachment behaviors that has been achieved during infancy is renegotiated and modified with changes in autonomy, cognitive and linguistic abilities, . . . and with multiple experiences in relationships with siblings, peers, and other adults."

Because infant attachment is not a good long-term predictor of behavior, researchers have studied attachment behavior at later ages and looked at its correlates at those ages. In other words, the attachment relationship with the parent is assessed at various times during childhood and correlated with the child's behavior with peers, with other adults, and so on. Attachment behavior is measured at these later ages by observing behaviors similar to those used to classify infant attachment behaviors, but with age-appropriate adaptations of the Strange Situation. These studies tend to show correlates consistent with their age-related attachment classification. For example, studies of adults have been successful in identifying attachment styles analogous to insecure/avoidant, secure, insecure/ambivalent, and disorganized/disoriented and relating them to expected differences in social behavior, quality of contemporary relationships, and parenting attachment styles with their own children (Cassidy & Berlin, 1994; Magai & McFadden, 1995; Pederson et al., 1998; Slade et al., 1999; West & Sheldon-Keller, 1994).

Overall, children who were insecurely attached as infants have a harder time getting along in the world unless their family circumstances change for the better. Like Daniel, whom we met at the beginning of the chapter, they are more likely than others to become difficult children, avoidant, distrustful, and/or aggressive with people. They evoke reactions from others that maintain negative relationships and that prevent them from developing more positive social behavior and possibly more trust in others. Unfortunately, these same strained relationships may lead to such children being rejected by their peers. According to one researcher, "Not all anxiously attached children later show acting-out behavior problems, but a young child manifesting such problems in an extreme form is likely to have a history of avoidant or resistant attachment relationships" (Sroufe, 1981, p. 15).

Emergence of Prosocial Behavior

One of the characteristics we sometimes observe in securely attached children is **empathy,** the ability to understand how another person is feeling. Babies at first are purely without empathy. They are unable to realize that others have their own points of view and their own emotions. When children start to show empathy, we know that certain social understandings are beginning to dawn on them. Late in the second year of life and early in the third, children begin to demonstrate considerable prosocial behavior, especially when another person shows distress. In this section we discuss research about this aspect of infant and toddler development.

Early Empathic Behavior

"Ouch!! Oooh. Oh, dear. My ankle."

Jocelyn had stumbled on the raised section of sidewalk as she walked hand-in-hand with her 18-month-old, Annette. She grimaced in pain and sat down on a patch of grass in a neighbor's yard.

"Let's sit here for a minute, Annette. Mommy hurt her foot."

Jocelyn removed her shoes and began rubbing her ankle. "Ooohhhh," she said. "That hurts."

"Mommy hurt?" Annette asked, snuggling into her mother's side.

Jocelyn could feel the tap of little fingers on her back under her shoulder blade, as Annette patted her. The thumb of Annette's other hand was in her mouth, a sure sign that she was upset.

"Yes. Mommy is hurt, Annette. Mommy twisted her ankle. But it will get better. We'll just sit here for a minute until it feels a little better. Mommy will be okay."

"Mommy okay?" Annette repeated.

"Yes, Mommy will be okay."

Empathy refers not only to understanding the negative feelings of another but the positive feelings as well. The older children pictured here have noticed the toddler's interest in something inside the fence and appear to be sharing that interest with some enthusiasm. (*Source:* © Michael Siluk/The Image Works)

think about it

We see empathy when a child hugs or pats a friend who is crying or shows sympathy when a parent is hurt or upset. This kind of behavior involves at least four things: (1) the ability to perceive the distress, (2) some idea of what might be causing the distress, (3) what might be done to help, and (4) the willingness and emotional wherewithal to go to someone's aid. But when do children start to notice that someone is sad or hurt? And what do they do once they notice? What kinds of differences in empathic responding exist among children?

One study reported that 12-month-olds responded to another's distress about half the time, although their response consisted of crying, frowning, or looking toward their mothers (Radke-Yarrow et al., 1983). They could not take any action, but they

Parents who are responsive to a young child's distress seem to have children who are themselves responsive to the distress of others. (*Source:* © Robert Harbison)

clearly noticed the distress and were aroused by it. By the time they were 18 months old, children in the study began trying to do something for the distressed person, such as touching or patting. By 2 years of age, children sometimes offered an object, said something supportive, or went to get help. If their first efforts did not work, they tried something else. By 2½ years, children communicated verbally about emotions and provided comfort with words: "Baby crying. Kiss. Make it better," "I love Mommy. I want to hold Mommy," and "No cry, Mom. It will be all right" (Bretherton et al., 1986, p. 536).

In another study (Zahn-Waxler et al., 1992), the responses of babies of age 13 to 24 months to the distress of others were observed both in the home and in the research laboratory. In some instances, the distress of the mother or the experimenter was not linked with the babies' actions. In other instances, the distress of others was made to appear as if it was caused by the infant. The researchers coded infants' prosocial behavior (asking if the person is okay, providing physical comfort in the form of kisses or hugs, and removing the stimulus that is making a person sad); hypothesis testing (asking what happened and visually searching the environment and connecting some object with the distressed person's injured body part); and showing empathy (saying "I'm sorry" and speaking in a sympathetic tone).

The researchers found that infants "express concern, attempt to comprehend or experience the situations, and engage in behaviors directed toward alleviating distress in others" (Zahn-Waxler et al., 1992, p. 130). When infants thought they had caused the distress, they were less likely to engage in empathic responses or to test various hypotheses about what to do. They were also more likely to respond aggressively. They also showed more self-distress when they had caused the distress than when they had not.

Although children are capable of empathic responses before the age of 2, they do not always respond, especially in some situations. Children of ages 2 through 4 at child-care centers have shown surprisingly low rates of response to other children's distress. This may be because teachers usually take care of the crying child. When the children themselves do respond, most of their actions are prosocial. They approach, comment, mediate, or console (see Table 7.6).

TABLE 7.6

Responses of children to peer crying at one child-care center

Category	Definition
Stare	Child stands near crying child and watches but takes no action and remains silent.
Approach	Child walks over to child and observes silently.
Comment	Child talks about the episode with another child or tells teacher a child is crying.
Mediate	Child tries to remove the source of pain or conflict or takes the crier to the teacher.
Console	Child offers physical or verbal comfort by patting or hugging the crier, offering an object, or apologizing when the child has caused the distress.
Ignore	Child appears unaware of or ignores crying, even when near the crying child.

Source: Compiled from J. S. Phinney, N. D. Feshback, and J. Farver: "Preschool Children's Response to Peer Crying," *Early Childhood Research Quarterly, 1* (3), p. 211, 1986, with permission from Elsevier Science.

Accounting for Variations in Empathic Responding

Infants and toddlers differ greatly in their responses to others' distress. Some children respond prosocially; others leave the scene where a child is crying or even attack the crying child (Radke-Yarrow et al., 1983; Zahn-Waxler et al., 1992). These different responses may reflect how much the child's own needs had been met at the moment, the reaction the child has received to prosocial gestures in the past, the general level of nurturing provided to the child by the adult with whom the child routinely interacts, and the child's temperament (Young et al., 1999). In a study of 2-year-olds, children's empathic responding was related to the mother's sensitivity and her tendency to reason with the child (Zahn-Waxler, 1979).

As Zahn-Waxler's data on the link between empathy in young children and maternal sensitivity suggest, the most important factor in children's development of empathy may be their attachment history. If a parent has been responsive to a child's distress, the child will tend to be more responsive to the distress of someone else (Roberts & Strayer, 1987). If the parent has been relatively non-nurturing, the child will tend to be unresponsive to the distress of others (Crockenberg, 1985).

All in all, we can say that prosocial response to others' distress *begins* in the late toddler period. The seeds of empathic understanding are present in children well before they are 2 years old. Such understanding continues to develop throughout childhood and beyond.

Baby to Baby: Peer Interaction among Infants and Toddlers

Rebecca, a bouncy 16-month-old, arrives in the pediatrician's office in her mother's arms. Her mother sits down in a chair in the crowded waiting room, holding Rebecca on her lap. She reaches into her purse and retrieves a small stuffed rabbit, which she places in front of Rebecca. But Rebecca does not grab it. She is looking at a baby sitting across the room on her mother's lap. Rebecca's mother taps her softly on the head with the stuffed rabbit to get her attention. Rebecca turns around, sees the rabbit, and takes hold of it. But she immediately turns around again to look at the baby. Then she waves her rabbit-filled fist as she squeals a greeting to her peer. The other baby looks serious for a moment, but then her face breaks into a smile. She slaps her hands against her lap and gives out a friendly squeal in answer to Rebecca's greeting.

think about it Is it common for babies to notice and interact with other babies? How early do they show interest in each other? Are they skilled in their interactions? We look more closely now at this aspect of social and emotional development.

Signals, Responses, and Interaction

Babies begin watching other babies and sending them social signals when they are about 10 months of age. They smile, laugh, or vocalize to them. Or they cry or fuss while watching another baby.

Many times the interactions among infants and toddlers involve a toy. Toddlers often offer a toy to another child, reach for the toy the other child is playing with, or attempt to play with a toy while the other child is playing with it (Bronson, 1981). Occasionally, a toddler strikes another baby (Eckerman et al., 1975).

Social interaction requires both a signal and a response, but infants and toddlers are not very adept at responding. Their most frequent response to a social gesture from another infant or toddler is to ignore it (Bronson, 1981). They also sometimes look at the other child or passively grasp an offered toy. Sometimes they hit, poke, or pull hair. All in all, responses that seem to reciprocate the social intention of the other child are fairly rare in the first or second year of life. When a child of this age responds to a social gesture, it is most often with a single response. Sometimes a second "contact burst" occurs between the same two children, involving a different toy or theme. Parallel play, in which two children play with similar toys near each other, is very rare at this age, as are "contact chains" in which children engage in a series of back-and-forth actions and reactions that are true social interactions (Bronson, 1981).

What we see, then, is that children up to about 2 years of age lack the ability to sustain social interaction with peers. Interactions are more frequent when children are brought together more than once and have a chance to become acquainted (Mueller & Brenner, 1977; Rubenstein & Howes, 1976). They also sometimes get caught up in **social games**—activities that involve taking turns, repetition, and imitation, accompanied by much smiling and laughing (Fein & Rivkin, 1986). Consider this example, in which two 22-month-old boys discover the fascination of spinning a wheel on an overturned doll carriage:

> David approaches the overturned doll carriage. After exploring the spokes of the wheel, he discovers that the wheel can be made to spin. Sam wanders over, watching David's motion on the wheel and the resulting spin. David looks up at Sam, grinning. The wheel is no longer spinning, and Sam timidly puts his hand on it, giving it a push. He laughs, looks at David, who is smiling broadly. As the wheel slows down, David gives it a push, and when it slows again, looks at Sam who again makes it spin. The children continue to take turns, but soon they begin to overlap. After five turns, Sam moves the wheel continuously, studying its motion. David fingers the spokes, then wanders off to another toy. (Fein, 1984, p. 97)

What were the characteristics of this interaction that made it possible for the children to sustain several rounds of play? First, the actions were repetitive and those that parents often practice with their children, such as taking turns. (Recall from chapter 6 how hard parents work during the first year of life to establish turn-taking behavior in their babies.) Then, after the children established a **shared meaning**—an understanding about the content of the game (Brenner & Mueller, 1982)—they coordinated and maintained the action. If pretend play had been involved, these children probably could not have managed it. Children between 2 and 3 years of age start to engage in pretend play (see chapter 5), but play is fairly solitary until about age 3.

Peer Interaction and Attachment History

We know that children's attachment history has a powerful effect on their social and emotional development. But specifically how does it affect their relationships with other children? By the time children are in elementary school, some of them are popular and preferred as playmates and others are disliked and rejected. (Popularity in school-age children is discussed in chapter 15.) Popular children are often the ones who have positive, friendly personalities and who do not engage in much aggressive, hostile, or harassing behavior (Coie et al., 1990). Children's social behaviors with peers are related to a child's attachment history.

Toddlers who were securely attached as infants seem to be more positive toward other children than toddlers with histories of insecure attachment (Pastor, 1981). They are friendlier and more cooperative, more outgoing, and more flexible in struggles over toys. On the other hand, when avoidant and resistant toddlers try to initiate social interactions, they more often get negative results than do secure children (Fagot, 1997). In other words, the positive initiatives of the insecurely attached children are less effective than those of their securely attached peers.

Toddlers with secure attachment histories also behave differently with respect to symbolic play. They pretend play for longer periods of time, and they spend more time planning and creating make-believe scenes (Slade, 1987). Their greater ability to plan may be related to a greater capacity to delay action and control impulses. Older children who are popular also are good at sizing up ongoing play situations and accurately timing their requests to be included.

Attachment history is also associated with a child's tendency to be a bully or a victim. A study of 4- and 5-year-olds found that victimizers, or bullies, had insecure/avoidant attachment histories at 12 and 18 months (Troy & Sroufe, 1987). Furthermore, most victims—children who are consistently passive in the face of aggression—had insecure/ambivalent attachment histories. In fact, in all of the cases in which a child with an insecure/avoidant attachment history was paired with a child with an insecure/ambivalent attachment history, one victimized the other. Children with secure attachment histories did not exploit or bully others, and they also did not respond passively when others tried to bully them.

Sex-Role Stereotyping in Infancy

Today, Benjamin is 4 weeks old. His mother puts him in his cradle for a nap and then sits down to write some thank-you notes for baby gifts. As she mentions each gift in the notes, it dawns on her that Benjamin received very different baby presents than his older sister received three years ago. Back then, there were not any soft hammers or squeezable choo-choo trains, nor was there a sturdy metal dump truck to put away for later. She could not recall a single item of clothing that had been blue. Everything was pink, white, or pale yellow. "Well," she thought, "the birth announcement did say, 'IT'S A BOY!' "

think about it

The first thing most parents ask about their baby is whether it is a boy or a girl (Itons-Peterson & Reddel, 1984). This information is proclaimed on the birth announcement along with weight, length, and other vital statistics. There is little question but that everyone is interested in the baby's gender. But does this information affect in any way how people act toward the baby? Do people treat boy babies differently from girl babies? And, if they do, what are the consequences of this different treatment?

We have all seen 2- or 3-year-olds acting "like boys" or "like girls." At a nursery school, for example, we might see more boys than girls playing with trucks and cars, building with blocks, or chasing each other outdoors. We might see more girls than boys caring for dolls, having tea parties, or playing house. Caldera and colleagues (1989) report gender differences in toys selected for play during the toddler years.

Where do children learn to act this way? Many of these apparently sex-appropriate behaviors are probably not "built into" the biological makeup of boys and girls, but are instead acquired during childhood. The question is whether children learn these different behaviors because their parents—consciously or unconsciously—treat them differently right from the day they are born.

How Adults See Boy and Girl Babies

Adults do seem to have different perceptions and expectations of boy and girl babies. In some studies with actor babies (babies who were not the children of the adults being observed), adults were told the baby was a boy when it was a girl, or vice versa, and then their reactions to the baby were observed. When a 6-month-old boy was presented as a girl to some women and as a boy to others, they played differently with him, depending on how he had been labeled (Will et al., 1976). The women who thought he was a girl offered him a doll rather than a train or a fish. The women who thought he was a boy offered the train. In another study, adults encouraged "boys" to walk, crawl, or engage in physical activity more than they encouraged "girls" to do so (Smith & Lloyd, 1978). Stern and Karraker (1989) report that different personality characteristics and physical traits ascribed to the infant are influenced by the sex label given to the infant.

Parents perceive their own babies differently, too, based on whether they are boys or girls. In one study, parents rated their newborns on a questionnaire, and they made a clear distinction between the sexes. Although the babies did not differ in their newborn measurements or their Apgar scores, girls were judged to be weaker, prettier, softer, and more delicate, and boys were judged to be firmer, more alert, stronger, hardier, and better coordinated. Fathers' ratings showed even more differences for the sexes than mothers' ratings did (Rubin et al., 1974).

Even though adults do perceive and treat babies differently based on their sex, these experimental situations may not be good ones for inferring a great deal about parents' everyday behavior with their babies. When actor babies are involved, the brief interaction with a strange child might be expected to evoke a stereotypical reaction (Frisch, 1977). And when parents are new and inexperienced, they may be forced to rely on sex-role stereotypes when answering questions about their newborns (Rubin et al., 1974). It is probably more important to know whether parents treat their own children in stereotypical ways over longer periods of time.

How Parents Treat Their Own Boy and Girl Babies

Some studies have revealed no differences in how parents treat their boy and girl babies; other studies have turned up a few differences. For example, researchers have observed that fathers play in more active, physical ways with their sons than with their daughters (Parke & Suomi, 1980; Power & Parke, 1982). Boys and girls also have different toys, most of them presumably bought by their parents (Fein et al.,

1975). And mothers have been observed to respond differently to their sons' and daughters' emotions. When their infant girls showed pain, mothers matched their expressions with furrowed brows. But they almost totally ignored their infant boys' expressions of pain. When their boys showed anger, on the other hand, mothers responded with expressions of concern and sympathy. Girls' anger, on the other hand, was met with a return of anger (Haviland, 1982). Similarly, mothers have been found to be more likely to respond to their infant daughter's crying than are mothers of infant boys (Ruddy & Adams, 1995). Although we can only speculate at this point about the effects of these reactions, it seems reasonable to conclude from such studies that some mothers in the United States may teach boys to hide their pain and show their anger and teach girls to show their pain and hide their anger—the stereotypes of "masculine" and "feminine" emotional expression.

The mixed results of these studies do not give us clear answers to our questions about the origin of the sex-typed behavior we see in children and adults. We can note that studies turning up no differences in how parents treat their boy and girl babies are the ones in which researchers were observing basic, daily caregiving and social interaction. The studies that found differences focused on activities such as playing and shopping for toys or clothes. It may be that the job of taking care of a baby is so demanding that it overrides all other considerations. Most parents are so busy that they treat their babies just as babies, not as girl babies or boy babies.

However, the few occasions when they do treat them differently may be important, such as when they respond to their child's emotions. This subtle kind of teaching and learning may contribute to the differences that do exist in sex-typed behavior. Future research in many areas of child development, psychology, and biology, in many parts of the world, will probably shed more light on how boys and girls come to adopt the behaviors that fit the sex roles accepted in their society.

KEY POINTS

Attachment

- Attachment is the emotional relationship between an infant and a caregiver. It is a crucial factor in the social and emotional development of the growing child.

- Early theories of attachment assumed that infants develop a preference for the adult who feeds them. The psychoanalytic and early behavioral theories were based on notions of drive reduction and secondary reinforcement, respectively.

- Ethological explanations of attachment focus on behaviors that would have enhanced chances of survival as the species evolved. They suggest that adults who are skilled in identifying and responding appropriately to babies' signals are the ones most likely to foster healthy attachments and trust of others.

- Harlow's study of surrogate mothers among monkeys discredited the secondary reinforcement explanation of attachment. Ethologists have used this study as support for their view.

- Infant attachment is assessed in a standard laboratory procedure known as the Strange Situation, which highlights the way infants use their mothers for both safety and exploration.

- Three basic patterns of attachment—one normal and two deviant—emerged from experiments involving the Strange Situation: secure, insecure/ambivalent, and insecure/avoidant. Securely attached infants use their mothers as a home base from which to explore and as a source of comfort when they are distressed. Infants exhibiting the insecure/avoidant pattern rarely interact with their mothers during play and show no distress when separated. Infants exhibiting the insecure/ambivalent pattern show extreme distress when separated from their mothers but don't accept comfort from them when they return.

- It has been suggested that the insecure/ambivalent pattern of attachment may result when parents fail to respond contingently to a baby's signals. The insecure/avoidant pattern may be more likely when parents routinely respond inappropriately/intrusively to a baby's signals.

- Crying, gazing, and averting the gaze are among the earliest social signals at the infant's disposal. Smiling emerges by 2 months of age, apparently as a result of maturational factors followed by social factors.

- Children usually exhibit "stranger anxiety"—wariness of unfamiliar adults—between 6 and 18 months of age.

- Social referencing—scanning the face of a familiar and trusted person to pick up information about a new situation—begins at about 9 months. Infants can discriminate among facial expressions by the time they are 4 or 5 months old, but they do not know their meaning until they are between 6 and 9 months old.

- Temperament comprises individual differences in behavior that are based on one's constitution and are relatively consistent over time. Temperament may have an indirect effect on attachment by contributing to the degree of responsiveness shown by the caregiver.

- The hormonal theory suggests that maternal attachment is a result of bonding with the baby in the first hours after birth. This theory has not been supported by research.

- A mother's history has an effect on her parenting behavior, but it is not the sole determining factor in the kind of attachment she forms with her baby.

- The currently accepted developmental systems theory suggests that many factors interact to influence attachment. Characteristics of the parent seem to have a stronger influence on parenting behavior than do characteristics of the baby or those of the environment. Temperament—the child's inborn characteristics—can influence the attachment relationship, but it is not necessarily a crucial factor.

- Children with insecure attachment histories are at a higher risk of becoming emotionally dependent, aggressive, noncompliant, easily frustrated in the face of challenging tasks, inattentive, and overactive.

- The experience of nonparental child care appears to have no overall effect on attachment in general. However, when maternal responsiveness is low, poor-quality child care makes the development of an insecure attachment relationship even more likely.

The Emergence of Prosocial Behavior

- Signs of empathy—the understanding of another person's feelings—reflect the child's social and emotional development.

- At 12 months, babies tend to respond to the distress of others by showing distress themselves. By 18 months, they begin to focus on the distressed person and try to provide comfort. By 2 years, children share, help, and look concerned often enough to indicate that the seeds of empathy are present.

- When parents have been nurturing and responsive in calming their child's distress, the child is better at responding to others' distress.

Baby to Baby: Peer Interaction among Infants and Toddlers

- Children between 12 and 24 months of age have a repertoire of social signals that they can use with peers, but true social interaction is rare in this age group.

- Children under 3 years of age enjoy social games, which involve actions familiar to them from their games and play with adults.

- Pretend play is usually solitary prior to the age of 3.

- Social "style" seems to be related to attachment history. Toddlers with secure attachment histories are more positive toward peers than are toddlers with insecure attachment histories. They engage in more planning during pretend play, sustain their play episodes for longer periods of time, and tend to be neither bullies nor victims in later social interactions.

Sex-Role Stereotyping in Infancy

- Sex-role development is the learning that results in children's acting "like boys" or "like girls."

- Adults perceive babies differently, depending on whether they are labeled boys or girls.

- When basic caregiving is examined, only a few gender-related differences in how parents treat their babies have come to light.

- An important area in which boys and girls do seem to be treated differently is emotional expression.

GLOSSARY

attachment: the emotional relationship that babies develop with their caregivers (p. 230)

attentional reactivity: the passive arousability of emotion, motor activity and attention when confronted with stimulation (p. 244)

bonding: the immediate reaction of affection that mothers sometimes feel upon seeing their newborn (p. 245)

construct validity: the degree to which the measure is related to other measures that are also thought to be associated with the behavior of interest (p. 236)

critical period: a specific period of time in which a certain behavior or behavioral system is developing rapidly and is most likely to be influenced (p. 245)

disorganized/disoriented attachment: an attachment pattern that is a combination of behaviors found in the other classifications (p. 235)

drive reduction: the elimination of tension caused by inner needs, such as hunger, brought about by satisfying them (p. 231)

empathy: the ability to understand the feelings of another person (p. 252)

endogenous smile: a spontaneous smile, thought to be triggered by changes in internal sleep states (p. 241)

ethology: the study of animal behavior, particularly in regard to the evolution of behavior (p. 231)

imprint: to follow the first moving object seen, which is characteristic of the young of some animal species (p. 232)

insecure/ambivalent attachment: a pattern of infant behaviors exhibited in relation to a primary caregiver, including becoming upset in a new playroom, extreme distress in the mother's absence, and inability to accept comforting (p. 235)

insecure/avoidant attachment: a pattern of infant behaviors in relation to a primary caregiver, including lack of wariness toward a stranger, absence of upset in the primary caregiver's absence, and no attempt to get close to the primary caregiver when that person returns (p. 235)

internal working models: a system of expectations or schemes derived from early interactions with caregivers (p. 232)

preprogrammed: built into the brain through genes (p. 231)

secondary reinforcer: something or someone whose reinforcement value is obtained through association with a primary reinforcer, such as food for hunger (p. 231)

secure attachment: a pattern of behavior exhibited in babies in relation to primary caregivers that involves touching base during play, acceptance of comfort after separation, and preference for a primary caregiver over a stranger (p. 234)

self-regulation: process by which the child actively modifies her attentional reactivity (p. 244)

separation anxiety: behavior, including becoming sober, crying, clinging, and following, exhibited by infants when their primary caregiver leaves them (p. 242)

shared meaning: an understanding between two people about what social game they are playing (p. 256)

social games: activities shared by two people that involve turn-taking, repetition, and shared meaning (p. 256)

social referencing: the infant's checking of the facial expressions of the primary caregiver in novel or threatening situations (p. 242)

social smile: a smile that is clearly elicited by social stimuli (p. 241)

stranger anxiety: distress shown by infants when they see or are left in the company of a strange person or anticipate that they will be left (p. 241)

temperament: individual differences in behavior that are based on a person's own constitution and are relatively consistent over time (p. 243)

SUGGESTIONS FOR FURTHER READING

Bates, J. E., & Wachs, T. D. (Eds.). (1994). *Temperament: Individual differences at the interface of biology and behavior.* Washington, DC: American Psychological Association. An excellent discussion of the issues surrounding the concept of temperament.

Bowlby, J. (1988). *A secure base: Parent-child attachment and healthy human development.* New York: Basic Books. In the nine lectures in this book, Bowlby describes the implications of his attachment theory for clinical psychology and personality development.

Eisenberg, N. (Vol. Ed.), & Damon W. (Series Ed.). *Handbook of child psychology: (Vol. 3). Social, emotional, and personality development.* New York: Wiley. This volume contains (among others) excellent chapters by Rothbart and Bates (on temperament), Kagan (on biology and the child), Thompson (on early sociopersonality development), and Eisenberg and Fabes (on prosocial development).

Fox, N. A. (Ed.). (1994). The development of emotion regulation: Biological and behavioral considerations. *Monographs of the Society for Research in Child Development, 59* (2–3, Serial No. 240). This monograph defines emotion regulation, describes its physiological correlates, and suggests how (e.g., attachment) relationships with caregivers contribute to it.

Magai, C., & McFadden, S. H. (1995). *The role of emotions in social and personality development.* New York: Plenum. This wonderful book gives an excellent overview of both attachment and empathy in describing the role of emotions in development from a functionalist or evolutionary point of view.

Thompson, R. A. (1999). The individual child: Temperament, emotion, self, and personality. In M. H. Bornstein & M. E. Lamb (Eds.), *Developmental psychology: An advanced textbook* (4th ed., pp. 377–409). Mahwah, NJ: Erlbaum. Thompson's chapter addresses the topics of temperament, emotion, and self as they relate to infancy. He also describes changes in these in the context of later development.

MILESTONES *in Infant and Toddler Development*

AGE	PHYSICAL	COGNITIVE	LANGUAGE	SOCIAL-EMOTIONAL
0–6 mos.	Holds head up when on stomach Rolls over from front to back Reaches for objects Exhibits many reflexes	Demonstrates primary circular reaction stage of sensorimotor intelligence Scans within a face Shows preference for contrast in visual displays Prefers looking at normal face	Cries and coos Recognizes human voice Prefers "baby talk" Can discriminate /d/ from /t/	Signals needs with crying and gazing Becomes attached to caregiver Smiles in sleep Smiles at people but indiscriminately
6–12 mos.	Demonstrates fewer reflexes Gets first tooth Sits up Develops pincer grasp Creeps, crawls Stands holding on	Demonstrates secondary circular reaction Demonstrates coordination of secondary circular reactions Imitates new behavior if scheme is familiar Searches for completely hidden object Looks longer at scrambled face	Repeats consonant-vowel syllables Varies intonation Says protowords Says first word	Smiles selectively Begins to use social referencing Shows stranger anxiety Responds to distress of other by showing distress, crying
12–18 mos.	Walks Climbs stairs	Demonstrates tertiary circular reactions Includes others as recipients of play behaviors	Uses holophrases Uses expressive jargon	Experiences peak of separation distress
18–24 mos.	Begins to run	Demonstrates invention of new means through mental combinations Finds hidden objects through invisible displacement Shows deferred imitation Activates toy or doll in pretend play	Uses telegraphic speech Understands multiword utterances	Demonstrates less separation distress Begins to show empathic responses to another's distress
24–36 mos.	Jumps Begins to ride a tricycle	Shows ability to substitute objects in pretend play Shows greater ability to substitute objects in pretend play Shows ability to integrate themes in play	Uses verbal strategies to start a conversation Uses less telegraphic speech	Begins to respond verbally to another's distress Includes others in pretend play

8

Physical Development in Preschool Children

"PUSH US, PUSH us," sang out a trio of girls on swings.

"I can't push all of you," called Monique as she walked toward them across the nursery school yard. "Someone's going to have to pump."

"Oh, I know how to pump," said one. She backed up against the swing and then plopped onto it just as it began to swing forward. She thrust her short legs awkwardly out in front.

Monique watched as the others struggled to coordinate their movements with the swings. "You're getting it," she called to them.

As they practiced, Monique kept an eye on other activities in the yard. Two children were climbing a jungle gym, and a third was hanging upside down by her knees from the top bar, about four feet above the sandy ground. Nearby, a child was standing on top of a seesaw, trying to find a spot in the middle where it would balance.

Over at the sandbox, four children were digging canals and filling them with water from a hose. In some places, the canals were so wide that children had to use boards as bridges. They ran back and forth across the boards or jumped over the canals as they scurried from one place to another, pushing sand banks higher in an effort to keep the water from overflowing.

think about it

Preschoolers usually keep quite busy, both indoors and outdoors. The preschool years, from 3 to 6 years of age, are the play years. When children play outside, we can see clearly some of their physical skills. What can preschoolers do with the large muscles of their bodies that would be impossible for children only a year younger? Run? Hop? Jump? Pump a swing? And what can they do with their hands? Cut with scissors? Guide a paintbrush? Fashion something out of clay?

In this chapter, we examine the physical growth of preschoolers, their physical appearance, and their range of movement. We also discuss some of the diseases that are common among preschoolers and some of the precautions that parents and other caregivers can take to keep them healthy and safe.

The boy in the striped shirt seems to have mastered the art of pumping a swing. With coaching and encouragement, the others will soon learn. These swings have safe, soft seats, not dangerous hard rubber or wooden seats. This play area would be safer still if it were surrounded by railroad ties or short bushes to mark off a boundary beyond which children should not pass while other children are swinging. (*Source:* © Robert Harbison)

Appearance and Growth

If a toddler and a preschooler were to stand side by side, the differences in their physical appearance would be striking. The preschooler's legs and trunk are also longer than the toddler's, and they will continue to grow faster than his head for the next several years. This differential growth of body parts changes a child's body proportions dramatically over the course of the preschool years. The preschooler is longer and leaner than the toddler, and his head is not as large in proportion to the rest of his body as is the toddler's (see Figure 3.2).

Although their appearance changes quite a lot, preschoolers do not actually grow very much, compared to how much babies grow. In fact, the rate of growth is slower during the preschool years than it has been at any time during the child's short life.

Of course, preschoolers do gain weight and grow taller. The average preschooler gains from 3 to 5 pounds per year (compared with 14 pounds gained between birth and the first birthday)—a total of 9 or 10 pounds over the 3-year preschool period. The average child in the United States weighs 31 pounds at the beginning of the preschool period (age 3), 35 pounds at age 4, 38 pounds at age 5, and 43 pounds at age 6 (see Figure 8.1).

Increases in height are moderate too. The child grows about 2½ inches per year from the age of 3 until the age of 10 (Lowrey, 1978). At age 3, the average child is 37 inches tall. At age 4, the average child is about 42 inches tall. By age 6, a child may be 45–46 inches tall (Allen & Marotz, 1999). Compared with the gain of 10 inches between birth and 1 year, 4½ inches between 1 and 2 years, and 3½ inches between 2 and 3 years, the preschooler's growth rate is quite modest.

Recall from our discussion of physical development in the toddler (chapter 4) that slower growth reduces a child's appetite. Preschool children usually eat relatively little; sometimes, they eat very, very little. Sometimes they eat heartily for a period of 1 or 2 months, and then they show little interest in food for a while. This is normal. Fluctuations in appetite, though exasperating for parents, usually correspond to bursts of faster and slower growth.

Preschoolers need high levels of calcium and other minerals to support bone growth; they also need iron, vitamin C, and protein to maintain health and sustain growth. To make sure that children are adequately nourished, even though they eat relatively little, parents can curtail non-nutritious between-meal snacks and offer children wholesome foods. If children have a choice of only nourishing foods, their appetites can be the guide to how much they need to eat. When parents provide non-nutritious foods as choices, children's small appetites are satisfied, but the foods do not provide the nourishment they need. Because the preschooler is still not very skilled in the use of eating utensils, including finger foods at meals is a good idea (Marotz et al., 1993)

The most effective way to increase the number of foods that preschoolers like is to expose them to a food as other people eat it. For example, when children who initially

The short trunk and legs of this toddler contrast with the long legs and trunk of her school-age brother. The "stretching out" process begins in earnest during the later preschool years. By 5½ years of age, this child's body will look leaner.
(*Source:* © Mary Ellen Lepionka)

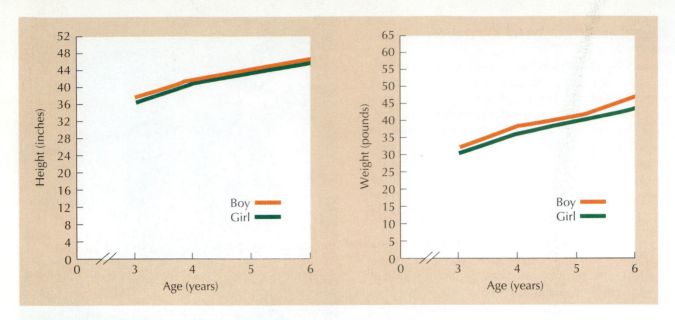

FIGURE 8.1

Height and weight for children 3 to 6 years of age. The graphs reflect height and weight for children who are average (50th percentile). Growth is slower during the preschool years than it was during toddlerhood.

prefer one vegetable to another eat with children who have the opposite preference, they change their preferences within days to match those of other children. They maintain the preference for the new food even weeks later (Olson, 1986). Eating with adults who like a food that they dislike also increases children's interest in the food, although the effect is not as great as when they see another child eat a food. The more frequently the child is exposed to new foods and to people who eat them, the better are the chances that the child will taste the new food and learn to like it (Olvera-Ezzell et al., 1990).

Motor Development

How do preschoolers use their stronger, more coordinated bodies? How can adults help them develop their motor skills in appropriate ways? We look more closely now at the development of preschoolers' motor skills, both gross and fine, and will consider the implications of these developments for parents and teachers.

Gross Motor Development: Locomotor Skills

The **center of gravity**—the point in the body around which the weight is evenly distributed—is very high in the newborn, near the bottom of the breastbone. As children's trunks and legs grow and the head takes up less of the total body length, their center of gravity moves lower on their bodies. By the time children are 5 or 6 years of age, it is below the navel (Lowrey, 1978). As long as the center of gravity is higher, the child's top-heaviness makes it difficult for the child to maintain balance. The toddler's top-heaviness causes her to fall over if she walks with her feet close together or if she stops or turns suddenly while running. These problems fade during the preschool years when the center of gravity moves lower.

Walking and Running   Children learn to walk when they are toddlers. Between the ages of 2 and 3, they start running. (They appear to run before age 2, but at first when running, neither foot ever actually leaves the ground at the same time.) By age 3, children run, but they cannot change direction while continuing to run. Instead, they must stop running (but not too quickly or they will fall forward), turn in the new direction, and then start running again. By age 4½ or 5, preschoolers can dash first in one direction and then in another, while continuing to run the whole time. They can also come to an abrupt stop and remain upright (Cratty, 1986).

Children's increased ability to move during the preschool years results from a narrowing of the base on which children walk. Toddlers must walk with feet spaced widely apart, to create a wide base that offsets a large head. The more steady (i.e., less top-heavy) preschooler need not make this accommodation. Balance has improved so much by about 3½ years of age that children can even place one foot in front of the other and walk on a line drawn on the floor. Walking in this way is difficult because it narrows the base of support. By age 4, they can walk a curved line, which is harder than walking a straight line because children must place one foot in front of the other while turning at the same time. Turning requires that feet be placed a bit at an angle, which alters the base of support and presents a challenge to balance. It is even more difficult to walk on a balance beam (a board raised off the ground). To accomplish this, children must place one foot in front of the other while making adjustments in distributing their weight to each side. Younger preschoolers have a hard time walking a balance beam—they usually step off to the ground several times to regain balance as they make their way from one end of the beam to the other (Cratty, 1986). In all of these cases, children hold out or withdraw their arms, shifting as they step first with one foot and then with the other, which helps them to maintain their balance.

Jumping   The children digging canals in the sandbox were fairly accomplished jumpers. Before they are 2 years old, children step down from low heights with one foot while keeping the other in contact with the higher surface. By age 2, they jump with both feet suspended off the ground for just a moment. By age 3, children can jump higher from a low step or platform, but they throw their arms back behind them and lean backward rather than forward. This "winging" movement creates an awkward jump that tends to leave the child off balance for the landing.

By about midway through the preschool years—around age 4½—children have learned how to move their arms forward and up at takeoff for a two-footed jump, leaning forward as they go into the air. When leaping over obstacles, children start by leading with one foot. Later, they can jump over things with both feet together. By age 5, most children can perform a whole repertoire of jumps. The movements involved in jumping with both feet are illustrated in Figure 8.2.

FIGURE 8.2

Execution of a skillful broad jump.

This 4-year-old is pretty steady on his feet, but needs to hold onto the railing of this suspended, swaying walkway. If he wanted to walk it without holding on, he would no doubt widen his base of support by moving his feet farther apart. (*Source:* © Susan McGee/Unicorn Stock Photos

Climbing   Children begin to climb stairs about as soon as they can walk, but they usually go up stairs by climbing a step with one foot and then bringing the other foot up to the same step, before moving to the next step. This is **marked-time climbing.** By the beginning of the preschool period, children no longer need to use marked-time climbing; they can walk up stairs by alternating their feet. Because balance is a greater problem when walking down stairs than when walking up, children use marked-time climbing as they descend stairs until they are about 4 years old.

Children also use marked-time climbing to get up ladders, climbers, and jungle gyms before they climb by alternating their feet; and they can get up before they can get down. At the beginning of the school year, preschool teachers must watch for children who have climbed up bars by themselves but cannot figure out how to get down. Gradually, preschoolers come to feel comfortable on climbing structures. The girl at the beginning of this chapter who was hanging upside down from a climber was an older preschooler, perhaps a 5-year-old.

Coordinating More Difficult Movements

Hopping, skipping, and galloping require better balance and coordination than do the basic skills of walking and running. Hopping, for example, requires very good balance, because, like walking up or down stairs, it narrows the base of support to one foot when the other leaves the ground entirely for a moment. By age 3½, children can hop a few steps on one foot; by age 5, they can hop 8 to 10 steps. **Rhythmic hopping** (hopping while alternating feet) requires balance and coordination beyond the ability of most 5-year-olds.

Galloping involves an uneven rhythmic movement with a leading foot. Skipping requires alternation of the feet and coordination of a step forward and a hop. Galloping and skipping are hard because they require coordination and shifts in balance. Most 4-year-olds can gallop, although few can skip. Skipping appears at about 6 years of age (Cratty, 1986).

Preschoolers also learn to move while they sit or stand atop various kinds of equipment, such as tricycles and scooters. Most 3-year-olds can learn to ride a tricycle; most 6-year-olds can ride a bicycle. Older preschoolers can maneuver a scooter quite well. Older preschoolers can even begin to learn to roller-skate, ice-skate, and ski. The development that occurs in large motor skills during the toddler and preschool years is summarized in Table 8.1 on p. 271.

Supporting Motor Development   Preschoolers' physical abilities and motor skills emerge in a regular pattern. Their bodies grow, they develop more muscle tissue, and the motor areas of their brains continue to mature. Skill development is supported by stimulation from the environment and opportunities for practice, as well as by physical changes and maturation.

Parents sometimes wonder whether they should enroll their children in movement or gymnastics programs. In pre-gymnastics programs, children walk on balance

TABLE 8.1

Gross motor skills

Age	Walking	Running	Jumping	Pedaling	Climbing	Throwing
8 months–1 year	Walks in a wide stance like a waddle				Climbs onto furniture and up stairs as an outgrowth of creeping	
1–2 years	Walks in a toddle and uses arms for balance (does not swing arms)	Moves rapidly in a hurried walk in contact with surface	Uses bouncing; steps off bottom step of stairs with one foot		Tries climbing up anything climbable	Throws items such as food in a jerky sidearm movement
2–3 years	Walks up stairs, two feet on a step	Runs stiffly; has difficulty turning corners and stopping quickly	Jumps off bottom step with both feet	Sits on riding toy and pushes with feet	Tries climbing to top of equipment, although cannot climb down	Throws ball by facing target and using both forearms to push; uses little or no footwork or body rotation
3–4 years	Walks with arms swinging; walks up stairs, alternating feet; walks down stairs, two feet on step; walks straight line	Runs more smoothly; has more control over starting and stopping	Springs up off floor with both feet in some cases; jumps over object, leading with one foot	Pedals and steers tricycle	Climbs up and down ladders, jungle gyms, slides, and trees	Throws overhand with one arm; uses body rotation; does not lose balance
4–5 years	Walks up and down stairs, alternating feet; walks circular line; skips with one foot; gallops; walks balance beam	Displays strong, speedy running; turns corners, starts and stops easily	Jumps up, down, and forward	Rides trike rapidly and smoothly	Climbs up and down ladders, jungle gyms, slides, and trees	Uses more mature overhand motions and control but throws from elbow
5–6 years	Walks as an adult; skips with alternating feet	Shows mature running; seldom falls; displays increased speed and control	Jumps long, high, and far; jumps rope	Rides small bicycle	Displays mature climbing in adult manner	Steps forward on throwing arm side as throws

Source: From *Observing Development of the Young Child,* fourth edition, by Beaty, J. J. (1998). Reprinted by permission of Prentice-Hall, Inc., Upper Saddle River, NJ.

beams, crawl through tunnels, tumble on mats, roll on balls, climb ladders, and interact with other children. For older children, real gymnastics classes are available. Most children develop their motor skills by using whatever they find at hand—at home, on their local playground, or in the play yard of their nursery school or child-care center. As long as there is space to run, a few things on which to climb, and a soft place to fall, children attain a fair degree of motor skill by the time they leave their preschool years. If parents and children enjoy something like pre-gymnastics, these experiences are suitable too. (For a discussion of what to look for in a safe playground, see Knowledge in Action: Policy—Making Playgrounds Safe.)

POLICY

Making Playgrounds Safe

Skinned knees, scraped elbows, bruises, and bumps are the battle scars all children wear at one time or another as they develop their physical skills. Parents and teachers usually find that a few words of sympathy, some antiseptic spray, and perhaps an ice cube wrapped in a washcloth are enough to ensure a speedy recovery. These occasions of being hurt and healed are actually an important part of the child's early experience.

More serious injuries at play often are the result of unsafe playgrounds. Approximately 150,000 children per year are seen in hospital emergency rooms for injuries sustained on playgrounds. Most injuries are caused by swings and swing sets. Climbing equipment comes in second, followed by slides and seesaws. Other injuries are caused by protruding bolts and sharp edges on play equipment and by play equipment that entraps a body part. The most serious injuries (and the most deaths) are caused by falls from a height (Greensher & Mofenson, 1985).

Safety standards have been issued jointly by the American Public Health Association and the American Academy of Pediatrics (1992). Both sets of standards recommend that surfaces under play equipment be given special attention. Concrete, asphalt, brick, and packed earth are hazardous and unacceptable. Minimally acceptable are gravel, wood chips, 2-inch-thick gym mats, and 1⅛-inch-thick rubber mats. The only fully acceptable safe surface is sand to a depth of 8 to 10 inches. The height from which a child can fall before the critical limit for receiving a concussion is expressed as 50 G (G stands for gravity) (Reichelderfer et al., 1979). As shown in Figure 8.3, a child would need to fall from over 11 feet to receive a concussion if the surface below were sand, but from less than a foot if the surface were concrete or asphalt.

Playground standards also suggest that safety zones should surround play equipment, such as swings, to prevent children from running into the path of moving swings. Low bushes, railroad ties partially sunk in the sand, or some other barrier should mark the zones. Climbing structures built over a certain height should have protective railings or be completely enclosed to prevent falls. Young children are thrilled to be 4 or 5 feet off the ground—heights of 10 or 12 feet are unnecessary.

Adults should inspect equipment for exposed bolts, rough or rusty surfaces, or deteriorated parts. Broken glass, crushed soda cans, and other trash in sand or wood chips also are hazardous. Adults should remove these items. Although, children should never go barefoot where these dangers are possible, even if adults check the areas daily. Small pieces of broken glass may be missed and can cut children. Splinters from all types of wood chips are unpleasant; those from redwood chips quickly become inflamed.

The relationship between playground hazards and children's injuries was demonstrated in a study of children enrolled in child-care centers in Atlanta. In child-care centers with 5 or fewer hazards, about 43 percent of the centers reported a playground injury. In centers with 6 to 11 environmental hazards, the percentage of centers reporting an injury rose to about 52 percent. In centers with more than 12 hazards, about 60 percent reported injuries (Sachs et al., 1990).

Even when playgrounds are safe, young children need supervision and guidance in using them. A safety zone around a swing will do little good if children are not instructed to stay out of it. Children need to be taught not to climb over railings, roughhouse at the top of the slide, or ride tricycles outside of set paths. When the equipment itself is safe, adults can concentrate on helping the children learn to play safely.

Playgrounds can be made safer by raising public awareness of the dangers. A demonstration project in New York

Gross Motor Development: Upper Body and Arm Skills

"Okay, Alecia. I'm going to throw the ball again. Get ready." Rick stands about 5 feet away from his daughter and gently tosses a soft ball to her.

Four-year-old Alecia stands with her arms extended straight out in front of her body. As Rick throws the ball, Alecia continues to look at her dad's face rather than at the ball. As the ball approaches, she turns her head to the side and squeezes her eyes shut.

"Ohhh, you missed! Throw it back."

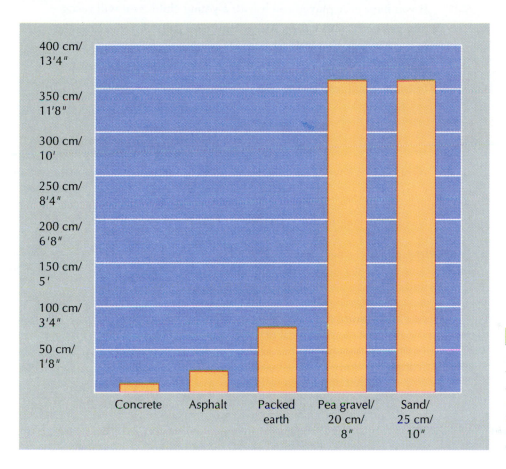

FIGURE 8.3

Distance a child could fall before receiving a concussion on various playground surfaces. (*Source:* Adapted from Kompan Inc. 1985–1986 Catalogue, p. 75.)

State illustrates what is possible (Fisher et al., 1980). People inspected the playgrounds in one community, gave seminars and provided literature about playground safety to community personnel, and dispensed information to the public through the local newspapers. The community covered hard surfaces under play equipment with softer materials and reduced other hazards by 42 percent. Local hospitals subsequently reported that playground-related injuries had dropped by 22 percent. By training personnel and providing information to the public, safety can be improved in local playgrounds.

Alecia runs to get the ball. She extends her arm up above her head and throws the ball onto the ground in front of her. It rolls to her dad. Rick picks it up and gets ready to throw again.

"Okay, are you ready?" he asks.

Alecia smiles and nods.

"Put your arms out in front of you," Rick instructs. "Now, this time, keep your eye on the ball." He tosses the ball. Alecia watches Rick's face again as the ball approaches, and again turns her head away and shuts her eyes as it bounces softly against her chest.

"Oooohhhhh, almost!" Rick shouts. "Let's try it again!"

think about it

If you have ever played catch with a young child, you will recognize this scene. Why does Alecia have such difficulty catching the ball? How much practice do you think it will take for her to master this skill? Or is it even possible for a 4-year-old to learn to catch a ball, even with extensive practice?

As long as the child is having fun and the adult encourages her, a game of catch can be a positive experience for a preschooler. Some ball skills are so difficult to master that older children and adolescents are still learning and practicing them. Preschoolers have their hands full in trying to learn the rudiments of throwing and catching a ball.

Throwing a Ball   Between 1 and 2 years of age, children start to throw or toss objects in the air from a sitting position. Older toddlers stand and toss a ball with both hands without shifting their weight as they throw the ball. If they were to shift their weight, they probably would not remain upright due to their high center of gravity.

Once a child around Alecia's age starts using a one-handed throwing strategy, we can observe a four-stage pattern of development (Williams, 1983). At first, she holds her body stiffly and throws the ball with a simple, fast arm extension (at age 3). She does not rotate her body or "get behind the ball." In the next stage, she twists her shoulder a bit to follow her arm as it moves forward, but she does not shift her body weight or change her footing.

In the third stage, she takes a step forward with the leg on the throwing-arm side as she extends her arm and releases the ball. She rotates her shoulder slightly but does not turn her body very much. Finally, she starts to rotate her body, first back as she pulls her arm back, then forward as she throws. As she rotates her body, her arm moves through a fairly wide arc, increasing the ball's velocity (age 6–8). Illustrations of this developmental sequence are shown in Figure 8.4.

These developments take from three to five years. Although throwing skills continue to develop during the school-age years and adolescence, the first basics can be mastered during the preschool period if the skill is practiced.

Catching a Ball   Catching begins when babies sit and capture a ball that rolls between their legs. Then children try to catch a ball when they are standing upright. Preschoolers find it easier to catch a large ball tossed straight at them than a smaller ball thrown up like a fly ball (Randt, 1985). Even so, they extend their arms stiffly to try to trap the ball with their arms, hands, and body. They do not reach out to grasp the ball with their hands. Like Alecia, they are also unable to follow the ball very well with their eyes, and they often turn their face away in a protective gesture as it approaches.

Somewhat later, they start to watch the ball as it approaches and use just their hands, rather than their arms and their chest, to grasp it. Later still, usually at about age 5, they place their feet wide

This two-and-one-half-year-old is not twisting her body to get ready to throw this ball, nor is she likely to step forward as she throws the ball. Her arm is likely to move straight down as she lets go of the ball. Otherwise, she might fall over as she throws the ball, even though she's holding her left arm out to help maintain her balance.   (*Source:* © Gale Zucker/Stock Boston)

Stage 1

Stage 2

Stage 3

Stage 4

FIGURE   8.4

Stages in learning to throw a ball. Throwing a ball isn't as easy as it looks. Skill develops over a number of years and progresses through the stages shown here.

apart on the ground in anticipation of needing to move to one side or the other to catch the ball. When they actually close their hands around the ball, they pull their arms back against their bodies to cushion the force of the ball (Cratty, 1986). Older children and adolescents are able to execute maneuvers such as jumping and extending one gloved hand to catch a fly ball. Most preschoolers cannot make these movements.

Reaction Time   In addition to mastering the physical movements needed to catch a ball, children must respond quickly when a ball is thrown. **Reaction time** consists of

Scissors are a challenge for preschoolers. Developmental delays make it even more difficult to use scissors. The teacher is holding the paper to make it possible for this child to concentrate fully on opening and closing the scissors. (*Source:* © Will Faller)

the time it takes the child to assimilate the stimuli (such as the appearance of an oncoming ball), make judgments about the throw, and then decide which movements to make in order to catch the ball or hit with a bat. It also takes time for the child's mental plan to reach the muscles (Cratty, 1986).

Even a ball thrown slowly from a short distance requires a judgment the instant it is in the air, or there will not be time enough to make the adjustments necessary to catch it (Whiting, 1969). As we saw, reaction time in a 4-year-old such as Alecia is very slow. It improves quite a lot between ages 3 and 5, but the reaction time of a preschooler still lags well behind the reaction time of older children and adults. The throwing, catching, and batting skills seen in many older children can be attributed to their faster reaction time.

The upper body and arm skills of throwing and catching develop gradually as the child grows. The center of gravity continues to move lower in the body, muscle tissue increases, and fat decreases. The nervous system matures, which results in better coordination and improved reaction time. All the child needs from the environment is a ball, a willing and patient companion, and plenty of opportunities for practice.

Fine Motor Development

A group of preschoolers is sitting at a table in their classroom. Some are drawing with markers; others are using hole punchers. Still others are cutting with scissors. A girl who is 3 years and 3 months old attempts to cut a piece of construction paper. Irina positions her thumb in one of the holes of the scissors handle and then sticks her index finger in the other hole. She positions the paper between the scissor blades and moves her hand, in an attempt to close them. But the scissors are positioned sideways, not straight up and down, and they do not close firmly on the paper. It is folded a bit, but remains whole.

Irina removes the paper and repositions her grip by putting her thumb in the bottom hole of the scissors and placing two fingers, her index finger and the next one, in the other hole. The scissors are positioned straight down toward the table as she attempts to insert the paper. It doesn't work. She turns the scissors to give them a more horizontal slant and ends up pointing them toward herself. With this rotation of the scissors, Irina's thumb ends up being in the hole that is on top. She inserts the paper once again with her other hand and attempts to cut. She manages once again to close the scissors, catches the paper, but does not cut it.

Irina's mouth opens, and she sticks her tongue out. She licks the corner of her mouth. She retracts her tongue, takes a deep breath, and exhales through her mouth. This is hard work.

She repositions the scissors, this time putting one side of the scissor handle in each of her hands. Now, with neither hand free, she attempts to deal with the paper while it rests on the table by moving the scissors so that the paper is between the blades. But as soon as she tries to close them, the paper slips out.

A teacher reaches over to take the paper: "Here, I'll hold that for you, Irina." The teacher positions the paper between the scissor blades. Irina closes them, using two hands. This time, she makes a cut in the paper. She stops for a moment to inspect it, then opens the scissors, and makes another snip. Next she places the scissors on the table. Then she takes the piece of construction paper from the teacher's hand and pulls it apart at the line she had cut with the scissors.

"I cutted it!" she announces, as she smiles broadly at the teacher. "I cutted it!"

Put a pair of scissors in your own hand, and think about the movements you make when cutting a piece of paper. Which fingers do you put in the holes of the scissor handles? How much tension do you feel in the muscles of your hand as you hold the scissors? When you cut, do you close the scissor blades completely (way up to their tip), or do you cut using the portion of the blades nearest the handle? In cutting a piece of paper in half, how many times do you open and close the scissor blades? Do you use the supporting hand to turn and reposition the paper as you cut farther into it? If you try cutting out a circle instead of simply cutting straight across a piece of paper, what changes do you notice in the movements of your supporting hand?

During infancy, the child learns how to grasp, let go, wave, and point. But infants and toddlers lack flexibility in moving their fingers. Even young preschoolers hold a tool stiffly with their fingers; they do not move by moving their fingers. Instead, they use the muscles in their upper arm, or they move their wrist. The major change in prehension (grasping) during the preschool years involves increasing skill in moving the fingers (Carlson & Cunningham, 1990).

When the movement of an object is controlled by the upper arm or the wrist muscles, the movement is large, because the distance between the pivot (point of movement) and the object that is being moved (e.g., paintbrush) is relatively long. But when an object is moved with the fingers, rather than by the muscles in the upper arm, the distance between the pivot and the object being moved by the hand is shorter. Therefore, the movement can be much more precise. As a result of their increasing finger skills, preschoolers become fairly adept at putting pegs in pegboards, cutting, stringing beads, and manipulating markers and pencils. It takes some practice, as we saw in the scissors episode, but children make steady progress.

The increasing use of finger movement enables preschoolers to become more independent in dressing themselves. They can button large and easily accessible buttons, zip up and snap their pants (if the snaps are not too stiff), and pull on and take off their socks and shoes. Connecting the two ends of a zipper on a jacket or coat presents quite a challenge to the young preschooler, but many 5-year-olds master even this difficult task. Because tying shoes and the straps of winter hats are beyond the abilities of most preschoolers, they still need help.

If parents choose clothes wisely, preschoolers can begin to dress themselves. If interested in nurturing a child's physical independence, parents can avoid buying clothing that has tiny buttons, difficult snaps, openings in the back, and strings to tie. (For a discussion of how parents and teachers can help children with disabilities achieve independence, see Knowledge in Action: Special Education—Adapting the Environment to the Child with Disabilities.)

Young preschoolers often use a stiff finger grip to hold a crayon or a marker. This child's arm is resting on the tabletop, and the movement of the crayon is coming from wrist and finger action. It probably won't be long before she will be able to adjust the crayon to a more mature finger grip and move it entirely with the fingers. She has already learned how to use her other hand to hold the paper steady. (*Source:* © Will Faller)

SPECIAL EDUCATION

Adapting the Environment to the Child with Disabilities

Parents and teachers often must restrain themselves from rushing to help young children who are struggling with buttons and zippers, forks and spoons, combs and toothbrushes. It is even harder for adults to watch the struggles of children with physical disabilities. Children work hard to master the daily tasks of taking care of themselves, and children with disabilities, including those with impaired motor control or limited use of their arms or legs, are no exception. How can adults help these children attain the fullest possible measure of independence and self-sufficiency?

First, parents can make sure that their child's clothing is adapted to specific needs. It should fit properly, allow easy movement, be strong enough to withstand abrasion from braces or other mechanical aids, and have openings and fasteners the child can reach. A physically challenged preschooler may be able to dress herself as efficiently as her able-bodied age-mates if her shirt is fastened in the front with Velcro instead of buttons. She may be able to zip a zipper if a large ring, such as the kind used to hold papers together, is inserted through the tab at the end. She may be able to get her coat on by herself if she sits down with the coat in her lap and flips it over her head. (A child with delayed physical development may be top-heavy and will fall over if she tries to flip her jacket while standing.)

Some simple adjustments in equipment and tools can also help the preschooler with disabilities do the same things the other nursery school children do. For example, a child who has poor wrist rotation (a common problem among children with Down syndrome) may be able to pour her juice from a pitcher if the lid is attached so the spout is 90 degrees from the handle rather than opposite it. A child with poor balance or muscle tone may be able to use a toilet more confidently if there is a low stool in front of it where she can rest her feet. Children who have difficulty grasping objects can be given eating utensils and toothbrushes with extended or thickened handles (Schleifer, 1987).

Children with disabilities often have poorer coordination and slower reaction time than other children. They can benefit from practicing T-ball—batting a ball from a stationary holder rather than a ball that is moving. Movable playground equipment can be taken apart and the pieces placed flat on the ground. Children who otherwise could not use parts of play structures can practice walking across them when they are on the ground.

Teachers often have one or more mildly disabled children in their regular classrooms. Teachers can help them be part of the group by meeting their needs in many ways. Many items of special equipment and clothing are now made for children with disabilities, and many parents and teachers take advantage of it. A good source for information about these materials is the journal *The Exceptional Parent* (209 Harvard Street, Suite 303, Brookline, MA, 02146–5005).

Ensuring the Preschooler's Health and Safety

The preschooler is usually busy and on the move. This can present some challenges for caregivers, but also great joy. The adult must now think of play materials and how to aid the child while also nurturing independence. Adults must think of ways to occupy children with challenging and safe activities, help them develop healthy eating and sleeping patterns, keep them as free as possible of infectious diseases, and nurse them back to health when they get sick. We discuss these topics in this section. We also discuss the signs and consequences of child abuse. People who work with or treat children are bound by law to be alert to signs of child abuse and neglect and to report suspected cases to appropriate child protection agencies.

Health and the Preschool Child

The preschool years are typically healthy years for most children, although children do get sick with various infectious diseases. Children also are sometimes exposed to

This tricycle has been adapted to the needs of a child with motor difficulties by adding lap and shoulder belts, a box-style seat, and straps to hold the feet on the pedals. Such adaptations make it possible not only for a child to ride a tricycle, but also to enter into play with peers. (*Source*: © Will Faller)

harmful substances in the environment. Parents also worry about the health risks of various sleeping and eating behaviors. In this section, we discuss (1) communicable health problems (head lice, middle-ear infections, chicken pox, meningitis, and others) and their control in child-care and preschool programs, (2) lead poisoning, and (3) sleeping and eating patterns.

Communicable Health Problems   Illness in preschoolers is fairly frequent but usually not very serious. Compared to other periods of childhood, the preschool years have the highest incidence of illness, perhaps because this is the age when many children first interact frequently with other children in group settings. As more and more children enter child care at younger ages, the incidence figures are beginning to change such that frequency of illness in toddlers and preschoolers is about the same for children in child care (Nafstad et al., 1999).

HEAD LICE.   Tiny, wingless insects called **head lice** are the source of one communicable health problem in preschoolers. The female lays eggs (nits) on the shaft of the hair near the scalp. When the eggs hatch, the lice that emerge burrow quickly into the scalp to get a meal of blood from their host. The toxin they produce as they feed causes the intense itching that accompanies lice infestation. Special shampoos must be used to kill the lice and the nits. Nits must be removed from the hair with a fine-tooth comb provided with the shampoo.

Hats, clothing, bedding, and all other items that have come in contact with the lice must be washed in very hot water to kill them, or items can be sealed in a plastic bag for two weeks. Because lice need blood to survive, they die inside the plastic bag because they cannot attach themselves to a host to feed. Insecticidal sprays are available for items such as furniture and car upholstery, which cannot be washed or sealed.

Because lice do not have wings, they are passed from one child to another by direct contact, not by flying from one child to another. Pillows, combs and brushes, and dress-up hats are all potential sources of infection in child-care centers and preschool classrooms. Teachers should suspect head lice if they see children scratching their heads frequently. Many schools and teachers simply conduct regular "head checks" to guard against infestations.

MIDDLE-EAR INFECTIONS.   Known as **otitis media,** infections of the middle ear are another common problem among preschool children. They are, in fact, the illness most frequently diagnosed in young children (Chartrand & Pong, 1998). Middle-ear infections are often caused by bacteria and are usually treated with antibiotics. Because some strains of bacteria have become resistant to antibiotic therapy, treatment in the future may include vaccines. These are currently being developed (Chartrand & Pong, 1998).

Young children's facial anatomy makes them susceptible to ear infections. The problem is that the **eustachian tubes,** the tubes connecting the middle ear to the throat, are in a nearly horizontal position during infancy, toddlerhood, and most of the preschool years. Fluid accumulates in the middle ear when the child has a cold because the position of the eustachian tubes hinders good drainage through the tubes into the throat. Trapped fluid provides a medium for bacterial growth, which can lead to recurring ear infections. As the lower face grows more during the last year of the preschool period and the first few years of the school-age period, the eustachian tubes become more vertical, which allows fluid to drain more easily. Consequently, school-age children have many fewer ear infections than preschoolers.

If a child has chronic ear infections despite careful treatment with antibiotics, surgeons will sometimes insert tiny tubes into the eardrum to allow fluid to escape through the ear canal. Treatment is necessary in severe cases because ear infections can impair hearing. Good hearing is especially important in early childhood when language is developing. Many studies have found a relationship between a history of middle-ear infections and language delay (Teele et al., 1984), although a language delay is not inevitable (Roberts et al., 1986). Many other factors affect language development, including the amount of verbal stimulation that is available to the child.

CHICKEN POX INFECTION.   Chicken pox is a common viral disease among preschool children. It has a characteristic rash, which starts out as clusters of tiny blisters that soon change into whitish fluid-filled pimples. In four to five days, the blisters break or dry out, then crust over. The worst symptom for children with chicken pox is usually intense itching.

The chicken pox virus is very contagious, and once it breaks out in a child-care center or a preschool classroom, many children often contract it. Luckily, it is rarely serious, though it can be if a child's immune system is already impaired by some other disease, such as leukemia (Law et al., 1999). Though rare, complications of chicken pox do occur, even in otherwise healthy children. Complications can include bacterial infection of the skin lesions and brain or kidney inflammation. In the United States, chicken pox causes about 100 deaths each year (Arvin, 1997). Because of its danger in these few cases, and because an infected child cannot attend a child-care center or preschool program for 7 to 10 days (the time it takes the lesions to scab over), a chicken pox vaccine (**varicella vaccine**) has been developed and is now available to all children (Arvin, 1997).

In addition to these risks, especially among vulnerable children, the economic costs of chicken pox outbreaks are greater than one might expect. In one study, the costs were estimated to be $122.4 million per year in the United States and $109.2 million per year in Canada (Law et al., 1999). Most of this cost consists of lost productivity by parents who miss work because of the extended period of time (7–10 days) that children cannot attend child care.

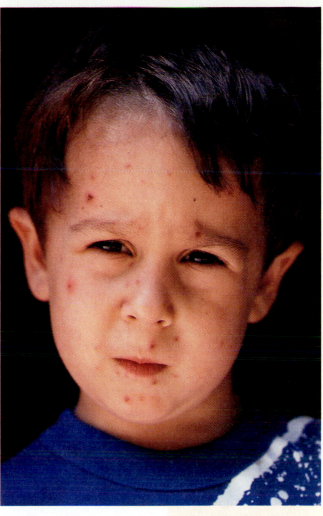

This child's chickenpox lesions appear to be scabbed over. He probably can start attending preschool again, because he can no longer infect others. (*Source:* © Carey/ The Image Works)

MENINGITIS.   Children can contract meningitis, an inflammation of the membranes covering the brain and spinal cord. It is caused most frequently in young children by the bacterium *Haemophilus influenzae* type B. Like the common cold, this organism is spread through respiratory secretions. Meningitis is prevented effectively with an immunization (Hib), which many children now receive routinely at 2, 4, and 15 months of age (Humiston & Atkinson, 1998). In one study of immunized children who were enrolled in child-care centers in New York State (excluding New York City), Hib infections declined from 216 cases in 1987 to 42 cases in 1991 (Schulte et al., 1994). Many states require children enrolling in group programs, including Head Start, to be immunized with the Hib vaccine (Bisgard & Wenger, 1997). From 1989 to 1995, there was a 99 percent decline in Hib infections. In other words, this vaccine has nearly eradicated Hib infections in children in the United States (Bisgard & Wenger, 1997).

HEPATITIS.   There are two main types of **hepatitis**, which is a viral infection of the liver. Hepatitis A is transmitted orally and through the feces, by food, by contact with contaminated diaper surfaces, and by contaminated toys. There has been a relatively high incidence of hepatitis A in child-care centers (Hurwitz et al., 1994). Since the late 1980s, more aggressive measures have been taken to increase surveillance for this disease and to curtail spread of the disease by taking such steps as administering immune globulins. In some studies, this has resulted in a marked reduction of the disease, although the percentage of infections attributed to child-care transmission (child to child, as well as child to adult) has not changed very much (Hurwitz, et al., 1994).

knowledge *in action*

Keeping Children Healthy in Child-Care and Preschool Programs

Attending a child-care center or a preschool program does carry some risk of illness. Almost every study conducted has found a higher incidence of respiratory infections and otitis media in children who attend child care compared to children reared solely at home (Nafstad et al., 1999; Turner, 1998). It is not the case that children in child care get sick, and home-reared children do not. Rather, children in child care are at increased risk for infection. This increased risk was calculated in one Norwegian study to be 14 percent for episodes of the common cold and 26 percent for episodes of otitis media (Nafstad et al., 1999). Child-care personnel can take steps to reduce this risk. We discuss here what can be done to reduce illness in child-care facilities and how to cope when it does happen.

Features of Child-Care Centers and Rates of Illness

Some types of child-care centers have higher rates of infectious diseases than others. One type is the center that serves non-toilet-trained children under 2 years of age. At this age, children mouth everything, come in close contact with each other, and eat with their hands. Staff must also change diapers for children this age, and poor hand washing and treatment of diaper-changing surfaces can spread disease (Laborde et al., 1994).

All other things being equal, large child-care centers may have higher rates of disease than smaller centers simply because children come in contact with larger numbers of children. But in some studies (Collet et al., 1994), children in very small centers have been found to contract more infections, not fewer, than children in larger centers. One critical factor related to size may be the separation of children into different age groups. In fairly small, age-organized centers, children contract fewer infections than children in larger centers simply because there are fewer children in the center to come into contact with each other. But in very small centers, where children are not divided into age groups, children contract more infections than do children in larger centers that are organized by age groups.

The specific design of the facility also probably matters. For example, a building designed as a child-care center could have such things as diapering facilities and sinks located optimally to help prevent spread of disease. Smaller centers are more likely to operate in buildings not designed specifically as child-care facilities. When larger versus smaller centers differ in terms of this factor, smaller centers may have higher rates of infection than larger centers (Collet et al., 1994).

Centers that allow drop-ins, such as children who cannot attend their regular center because they are sick, have higher rates of infection as well.

Hepatitis B is transmitted through contact with blood and is quite rare in young children. Both adults and children can be immunized against the disease. Recent evidence shows that the vaccination for hepatitis B given in infancy can reduce the lifetime risk of contracting hepatitis B by almost 70 percent. If immunization is delayed until preadolescence, the risk is lowered by about 45 percent (Margolis et al., 1995). Newborns are given the first of three doses. The other two are given at 1 and 2 months of age (Humiston & Atkinson, 1998).

GASTROINTESTINAL INFECTIONS.   Gastrointestinal infections involve vomiting and/or diarrhea. These infections, usually caused by a virus, are spread orally and through the feces. But the most serious gastrointestinal diseases are caused by bacteria when food is not cooked or stored properly, or when food handlers do not wash their hands after using the toilet.

For information about steps that child-care-center staff can take to control contagious diseases, see Knowledge in Action: Health/Safety—Keeping Children Healthy in Child-Care and Preschool Programs.

Procedures Child-Care Staff Can Follow to Control Disease

Health experts have recommended the following procedures for controlling the spread of disease in child-care centers:

- Hand washing is the most effective way to limit the spread of disease in child-care centers because hands are the most common means of spreading infections (Laborde et al., 1994; Turner, 1998). Child-care staff should wash their hands frequently, using soap and running water. Workers should wash their hands when they arrive at the center; before eating, preparing, or serving food; after using the toilet and blowing their noses; and after diapering a child, wiping noses, or being outside. Children also should wash their hands after using the toilet, before meals, and after playing outside. Hands should not be washed in a sink where food is prepared.
- Child-care workers should change diapers carefully, as soon as they are soiled. The changing table should be covered with a disposable surface and used only for changing diapers. The table top should be cleaned and disinfected after each use. Diapers should be properly disposed of in plastic bags and put in a plastic-lined trash can with a lid. The diaper-changing table should be near a sink (which is not used for food preparation) so that caregivers can wash their hands immediately after changing a diaper.
- Child-care staff should wash and disinfect toys and equipment daily. They should disinfect high-chair trays after each use.
- Tables used by older toddlers for eating snacks and meals should be washed with soap and water, sprayed with a disinfectant solution, and dried with throw-away toweling before each use.
- Child-care centers should establish and maintain a sick-child policy. Staff should screen children as they arrive for the day. Parents also need information about symptoms that indicate a child should stay home. Children who become ill at the center should be isolated until a parent can take them home.
- Child-care centers should require that all children be vaccinated against *Haemophilus influenzae* B, the virus that causes meningitis.
- Center employees should show proof of negative tuberculosis skin tests before they can care for children.
- Child-care centers should make sure they employ enough people. When workers are extremely busy, they may have so many responsibilities that they neglect to wash hands, clean the diapering area, and so on. Centers should also avoid overcrowding among the children because this increases contact and the spread of germs.
- Child-care staff should be educated about how diseases are transmitted and how they can be controlled. (The National Centers for Disease Control in Atlanta provides excellent training materials.)
- Centers should have a pediatrician or nurse as a health consultant to provide training and advice and to be on call for emergencies.

Lead Poisoning   Even in low concentrations, lead can impair mental functioning and cause overactivity. At high levels, it can make children very sick and even cause death. Children under 6 years of age are the most vulnerable to the harmful effects of lead poisoning because their brains are growing rapidly.

Children ingest lead in several ways. Water can be contaminated by lead pipes or lead soldering on pipes. Some factory workers carry lead dust on their clothing to their homes, where it can mix with regular household dust. Children ingest the lead when they mouth toys and household objects. By far the most common source of lead is lead-based paint, which was used in houses before World War II. When lead-based paint crumbles, young children can pick up chips and eat them, or the paint chips can be crushed underfoot where the pieces combine with household dust to be inhaled or ingested. When older homes are renovated, the lead-containing airborne dust can be hazardous (Landrigan, 1981). The deleading of older houses can create problems of airborne lead particles, unless safety procedures are followed (Williams, 1989). Lead paint in old buildings is now often contained by painting over it with a special protective paint, rather than removing it.

Despite measures to protect young children from lead paint in buildings, lead poisoning is still a serious and common problem, especially among young children who live in older dilapidated buildings in urban areas. It is estimated that 3 to 4 million children age 5 and under have levels of lead in their blood that are toxic (Bellinger et al., 1991).

Sleeping and Eating Habits

The day has started in the preschool room at the child-care center. Children are playing with puzzles, painting pictures, and pretending that they are going on a trip to the supermarket. The door opens. Lilly walks in, bagel in hand. Her mother follows closely behind. The teacher approaches. "Hi. We wondered where you were today, Lilly. Glad you got here."

"It was one of those mornings," her mother explained. "She didn't want to go to bed last night, and she was up in the middle of the night. The last time was 4 o'clock this morning. She was sleeping so soundly at 7:30 that I hated to wake her. Any suggestions?"

"We can talk later. Give me a call this afternoon around 1:30, if you can. The children will be napping then, and I'll have time to talk."

"Okay. I don't need to be at the hospital until about 7 tonight. I'm working the late shift."

think about it

Are sleeping problems common among preschoolers? Or do most preschoolers take delight in going to bed and then sleep through the night? If they awaken during the night, do they go right back to sleep? Or do they call parents and hop into their bed? What should parents do to ensure sufficient sleep for their preschooler?

In this section, we discuss sleeping and eating patterns among preschoolers because these issues are often a source of concern to parents and other caregivers. Adults worry that children will not get enough rest, or that the parents themselves will not, if they are awakened during the night. They also worry about both the small amount of food preschoolers sometimes eat and their dislike for certain foods, particularly those that adults consider especially nutritious.

SLEEP PATTERNS.   Sleep is one of the most common topics that parents of preschoolers discuss with pediatricians (Mindell et al., 1994). Parents and other caregivers often worry about the amount of sleep a child gets, when a child should stop taking naps, how to get children to go to bed and to sleep, and what to do when a child wakes up crying in the middle of the night.

Researchers have found that 40 to 50 percent of preschool children engage in bedtime routines, such as listening to stories, using the toilet, and getting a drink of

It often takes a pre-schooler 30 minutes or more to fall asleep. Hearing a story can help. (*Source:* © Jennie Woodcock/Corbis

water, and that these routines take more than 30 minutes. Most of the children take a comfort object—a stuffed animal or a doll—to bed with them. Almost all children take at least 30 minutes to fall asleep. Some children have night lights. The percentage of children who need night lights increases between the ages of 2 and 4 and then begins to decline at age 5. Many children call to their parents for an additional kiss or drink of water after being put to bed, and almost all go through periods when they cry or call out during the night (Beltramini & Hertzig, 1983). Sleep disturbances are often associated with an upset in the child's life, such as a change in routines, an illness or accident, or a family move (Kataria et al., 1987).

Sleep-related behaviors concern adults, even though they are quite common among preschoolers. Preschoolers resist going to bed, call for a drink or a kiss after they are in bed, take a long time to fall asleep, and wake up and cry in the middle of the night—at least occasionally.

Bedtime and naptime routines make falling asleep easier for children. A specific set of events leading up to bedtime—using the toilet, brushing the teeth, having a story read, getting a comfort object, and kissing and hugging—can help manage and prevent problem behavior, both at home and at the child-care center. Dimming the lights and putting on some quiet music can also help. But sometimes, the reality of family life makes it difficult for a preschool child to establish a regular sleep routine. For example, Lilly's difficulties could be related to her family's circumstances in her life.

Lilly's mother is a nurse who sometimes works from 7 in the morning to about 3 in the afternoon, sometimes from 3 in the afternoon to 11 at night, and sometimes from 11 at night to about 7 in the morning. At other times, she does not work at all for three or four days in succession. Lilly also spends some nights with her father at his apartment, where she has a different bedtime routine. A babysitter sometimes picks Lilly up from the child-care center when her mother is working the late afternoon or evening rotation. Even though she tries to follow her mother's routine, Lilly often falls asleep on the living room sofa. On most of these occasions, the babysitter has told Lilly's mother, "She wouldn't get in her bed because she wanted to be up when you got home from work." Lilly's mother wishes the babysitter would be a little firmer in insisting that Lilly sleep in her bed, but she is dependable, mature, attentive, and loving, and Lilly adores her. For these reasons, Lilly's mother does not insist that the babysitter follow the routine exactly, although she plans to discuss this further with her.

EATING HABITS.   Problems with eating can affect a preschooler's short- and long-term well-being and can also cause anxiety among adults. Like toddlers, preschoolers have periods of relatively slow growth when their appetites are small. A sensible approach when children are not eating much is to limit non-nutritious snacks and then let the child's appetite be the guide. Adults can also influence children's food preferences in several ways. Contrary to popular beliefs and practices, forcing or bribing children to eat something they dislike is not an effective way to change their eating habits. Children's ratings of disliked foods drop even lower when they are bribed with desired food to eat foods they dislike. The rating of the food already desired, on the other hand, rises. Forcing or bribing children to eat vegetables to get some dessert apparently teaches them only to like vegetables less and dessert more (Olvera-Ezzell et al., 1990).

Safety and the Preschool Child

The hazard we focus on here is child abuse. (Other hazards threaten preschoolers' safety, but the precautions described earlier in the book, in Knowledge and Action: Health/Safety continue to apply during the preschool years. See p. 148.) Stories and descriptions of child abuse have existed throughout history. But not until 1962, when Dr. C. Henry Kempe described the "battered child syndrome," did this problem receive widespread official attention in the United States and Europe (Kempe et al., 1962).

Causes of Child Abuse and Neglect   Efforts to understand the complex causes of child abuse continue (Korbin et al., 1998). Many factors are involved, and one of the most comprehensive attempts to describe them is the systems or ecological approach of Jay Belsky (1980). Belsky drew on Bronfenbrenner's ecological approach to the study of child development (1977, 1979) to organize the risk factors contributing to abuse. As shown in Table 8.2, Belsky considered risk factors at four levels: ontogenetic (characteristics of the caregiver), microsystem (characteristics of the immediate setting), exosystem (characteristics of the community), and macrosystem (characteristics of the society or culture). Table 8.2 shows factors that increase the likelihood of child abuse and neglect or buffer a child against such treatment.

The Success of Mandated Reporting Laws   The first laws required only physicians to report cases of suspected abuse to state authorities. The laws were later widened to include more **mandated reporters,** which now include teachers, dentists, social workers, law enforcement personnel, psychologists, nurses, and child-care workers. In addition, the laws were broadened to include not only physical abuse, but other kinds of abuse and neglect. (For a list of types of abuse and their definitions see Table 8.3.)

Experts estimate that mandated reporting laws and increases in federal appropriations for protective services have resulted in a decrease of deaths from child abuse and neglect in the United States from between 3,000 and 5,000 a year to about 1,100

TABLE 8.2

Determinants of abuse: compensatory and risk factors

Ontogenetic Level	Microsystem Level	Exosystem Level	Macrosystem Level
Compensatory Factors			
High IQ	Healthy children	Good social supports	Culture that promotes a sense of shared responsibility in caring for the community's children
Awareness of past abuse	Supportive spouse	Few stressful events	
History of a positive relationship with one parent	Economic security/savings in the bank	Strong, supportive religious affiliation	
Special talents		Positive school experiences and peer relations as a child	Culture opposed to violence
Physical attractiveness		Therapeutic interventions	Economic prosperity
Good interpersonal skills			
Risk Factors			
History of abuse	Marital discord	Unemployment	Cultural acceptance of corporal punishment
Low self-esteem	Children with behavior problems	Isolation	View of children as possessions
Low IQ	Premature or unhealthy children	Poor social supports	
Poor interpersonal skills		Poor peer relations as a child	Economic depression
	Single parent		
	Poverty		

Source: From "The Intergenerational Transmission of Child Abuse," by J. Kaufman and E. Zigler, 1989. In I. D. Cucchetti and V. Carlson (Eds.), *Child Maltreatment: Theory and Research on the Causes and Consequences of Child Abuse and Neglect* (pp. 129–152). New York: Cambridge University Press. Reprinted with the permission of Cambridge University Press.

a year (Besharov & Laumann, 1996). Still, child abuse and neglect are the sixth most common cause of death in children between birth and 14 years of age (Besharov & Laumann, 1996).

The number of reported abuse cases rose dramatically after the laws were passed. In California the number increased from 4,000 in 1968 to 40,000 in 1972. In Michigan, reports increased from 741 to 30,000 during the same time frame. In the United States as a whole, cases reported in 1993 (3 million) were 20 times the number reported in 1963 (150,000) (Besharov & Laumann, 1996). (See Table 8.4.) But in many cases, authorities find no evidence of abuse or neglect when they investigate the case. Currently, 60 to 65 percent of reports filed are not substantiated (Besharov & Laumann, 1996). Some of these cases actually involve child abuse or neglect, but investigators are unable to confirm it. In other unsubstantiated cases, there is, in fact, no abuse or neglect.

The high number of **unsubstantiated reports** is due in part to the fact that the professionals mandated to report abuse are encouraged to report abuse when they *suspect* it, not when they are very sure that it has occurred. According to some experts, one of the most pressing problems relating to child abuse is overreporting. All reports received by child protection agencies must be investigated. This takes considerable time and resources. As a consequence of overreporting, actual cases of serious abuse

---

TABLE 8.3

Reportable child abuse and neglect

Physical abuse: physical assaults (such as striking, kicking, biting, throwing, burning, or poisoning) that caused, or could have caused, serious physical injury to the child

Sexual abuse: vaginal, anal, or oral intercourse; vaginal or anal penetrations; and other forms of inappropriate touching or exhibitionism for sexual gratification

Sexual exploitation: use of a child in prostitution, pornography, or other sexually exploitative activities

Physical deprivation: failure to provide basic necessities (such as food, clothing, hygiene, and shelter) that caused, or over time would cause, serious physical injury, sickness, or disability

Medical neglect: failure to provide the medical, dental, or psychiatric care needed to prevent or treat serious physical or psychological injuries or illnesses

Physical endangerment: reckless behavior toward a child (such as leaving a young child alone or placing a child in a hazardous environment) that caused or could have caused serious physical injury

Abandonment: leaving a child alone or in the care of another under circumstances that suggest an intentional abdication of parental responsibility

Emotional abuse: physical or emotional assaults (such as torture and close confinement) that caused or could have caused serious psychological injury

Emotional neglect (or"developmental deprivation"): failure to provide the emotional nurturing and physical and cognitive stimulation needed to prevent serious developmental deficits

Failure to treat a child's psychological problems: indifference to a child's severe emotional or behavioral problems or parental rejections of appropriate offers of help

Improper ethical guidance: grossly inappropriate parental conduct or lifestyles that poses a specific threat to a child's ethical development or behavior

Educational neglect: chronic failure to send a child to school

Source: From *Recognizing Child Abuse* (p. 30), by D. J. Besharov, 1990, New York: The Free Press.

---

sometimes fail to get the attention they need. Besharov and Laumann (1996) describe the situation:

> Some reports are left uninvestigated for a week and even two weeks after they are received. Investigations often miss key facts, as workers rush to clear cases, and dangerous home situations receive inadequate supervision, as workers must ignore pending cases as they investigate the new reports that arrive daily on their desks. Decision making also suffers. With so many cases of unsubstantiated or unproven risk to children, caseworkers are desensitized to the obvious warning signals of immediate and serious danger. . . . These nationwide conditions help explain why from 25 to 50 percent of child abuse deaths involve children previously known to the authorities. . . . Tens of thousands of other children suffer serious injuries short of death while under child protective agency supervision. (p. 43)

Proposed Solutions to the Problem of Overreporting   A group of child protection agency professionals met in 1987 to develop ideas for solving the problem of overreporting. They recommended that better materials be developed to help people who are required to report abuse become more skillful in recognizing actual child abuse and neglect. They also recommend that reports be screened by child protection agency personnel to determine which failed to meet certain criteria. The goal is to improve reporting so that resources can be expended on more cases that are likely to be substantiated. Some cases of child abuse will, of course, be missed when more stringent criteria are used to determine which reports are to be investigated. But, currently, serious cases of child abuse are not investigated promptly or thoroughly because the volume of cases is overwhelming (Besharov & Laumann, 1996).

Child Abuse in Cultural and Family Context

It can be difficult to evaluate the meaning of parental and child behavior in a society with diverse ideas about what actions are appropriate in rearing and disciplining children. In general, unreasonable punishment involves blows to a body part that is vulnerable. A slap to the head or the face, for example, is always considered unreasonable for infants, and may be considered unreasonable for older children, as well, if too much force is applied. Throwing children, punching them with the fists, and pulling their hair is always unreasonable. But spanking a child on the buttocks with the palm of a hand is not considered unreasonable under state laws, even though it may offend people who think that children should not be subjected to physical punishment of any kind (Besharov, 1990).

Reporters sometimes confuse conditions of poverty with child neglect and thus overreport parents who are poor. For example, eating unbalanced meals, not eating breakfast, and eating non-nutritious foods is undesirable, but it does not legally constitute parental neglect. Nor does dressing the child in ill-fitting or torn clothing, or failing to dress a child in a pair of boots constitute neglect. Living in a home that is generally unkempt by some people's standards does not constitute neglect (but severe unhygienic and unsafe conditions in the home do). *Delay* in seeking medical attention for childhood illnesses, such as colds or ear infections, while undesirable, does not constitute neglect. However, ignoring conditions that should have medical treatment does constitute neglect (Besharov, 1990). In many of these cases, families need help. School nurses can provide clothing and food items, and parents can be informed about low-cost or free school breakfast or lunch programs. Social service agencies can advocate for repairs to apartments. But needing help and being neglectful are two quite different things. Reporters must be careful to differentiate between these two situations if they are to be of help to families.

Child-rearing and child discipline practices differ greatly across cultures. In some cases, child protection agencies will need to intervene with a family whose disciplinary practices, though accepted in their culture, are harmful to children. These cases need to be treated with sensitivity. For example, parents need to be informed that the practice is not acceptable, and why. In such cases, supervision by child protective agency personnel during a period of acculturation of the parents is usually more appropriate than removing children to foster care. (For specific information about signs of various forms of child abuse and neglect, see Knowledge in Action: Health/Safety—Signs, Symptoms, and Long-Term Consequences of Child Abuse and Neglect.)

TABLE 8.4

Reports of child abuse and neglect (1976–1993) in the United States

Year	Number of Children Reported
1963	150,000
1976	669,000
1979	989,000
1981	1,225,000
1985	1,928,000
1987	2,178,000
1993	3,000,000

Sources: Adapted from *Recognizing Child Abuse* (p. 10), by D. J. Besharov, 1990, New York: The Free Press; and "Child Abuse Reporting," by D. J. Besharov and L. A. Laumann, 1996, *Society, 33* (4), pp. 40–46.

Signs, Symptoms, and Long-Term Consequences of Child Abuse and Neglect

Those who work with and care for children are mandated by state laws to report suspected cases of child abuse and neglect. Professionals are sometimes uncertain about the signs of abuse and neglect. Because of this uncertainty, they may fail to report a situation in which a child is indeed in harm's way, or overreport situations in which abuse or neglect have not actually occurred. Familiarity with signs of abuse, and knowledge about the level of specificity of various signs, can help with the correct identification of child abuse and neglect. Better reporting allows child protection agencies allocate resources to serve children who are in much need of help.

Child abuse and neglect take many forms. Twelve types are considered serious and worthy of making a report. These are listed and described briefly in Table 8.3 (p. 289).

Specific Indicators of Child Abuse and Neglect

Indicators for four kinds of abuse/neglect are reviewed here: (1) physical abuse, (2) sexual abuse, (3) physical neglect, and (4) emotional maltreatment.

Indicators of Physical Abuse

Young children sustain many injuries in the normal course of their daily activities. They fall, bump into things, scratch or scrape themselves, and so on. However, some injuries are "suspicious"—not what one would ordinarily expect to find. Children's accidental injuries, such as scrapes, scratches, and bruises, usually occur on the fronts of their arms or legs and on their foreheads (from falling and bumping their heads) not on the backs of their arms and legs, in the middle of their back, around their eyes, or in their genital area. When injuries are located in these areas, they are most likely due to physical abuse. Child abuse should also be suspected when marks occur on several different areas of the body at the same time, or when there are multiple marks in one region (Besharov, 1990).

Suspicious injuries also include those in which a mark seen on the body matches the shape of an object. For example, a slap leaves finger marks (see Figure 8.5). A hot iron leaves the imprint of the iron on the child's skin. Beatings with cords or belts leave welts that match the cord or belt (see Figure 8.5). Cigarette burns leave characteristic marks, often in different stages of healing (see Figure 8.5). Burns from liquids, such as water, tend to leave splash marks, if accidental. Liquid burns are typically more serious when caused by abuse because the child's hands or feet are held in the hot water. These burns have glovelike boundaries between burned and unburned regions (Besharov, 1990).

Indicators of Sexual Abuse

Sexual abuse is recognized through both physical and behavioral signs. The physical indicators include torn, infected, or bloody vaginas; swollen, inflamed, or infected penises; infected, swollen, or torn anal areas; and venereal diseases (Besharov, 1990, p. 92) The mouth is also a common site of sexual abuse (Ad Hoc Workgroup on Child Abuse and Neglect, 1999). Behavioral indicators include knowledge of sexual behavior that is beyond what would typically be known by a preschool child and seductive behavior that is not appropriate for the age of the child; fear of going home; very dramatic changes in behavior or achievement in school; and wariness of people (Besharov, 1990, p. 97).

Signs of Physical Neglect

Signs of physical neglect include severe developmental lags, such as failure-to-thrive; evidence of hunger, or begging for or stealing food; extreme and chronic fatigue and listlessness; untreated infections or injuries; severe and untreated dental problems; dirty and unbathed bodies that smell of urine or feces; inadequate clothing for severe winter weather; being left alone at home without care; parental addiction to alcohol or drugs; and home conditions in which feces are on walls or floors, garbage is strewn about, no electricity or water are available, and toileting and washing facilities are inoperable (Besharov, 1990, pp. 102–103).

Signs of Emotional Maltreatment

Signs of emotional maltreatment include excessively compliant or aggressive behavior; phobias, compulsive behavior, and hysteria; failure to engage in play; head banging or body rocking; failure-to-thrive and other lags in growth; behavior that is too adultlike or too infantile; extreme changes in school achievement or behavior; lack of desire by parents to know where the child is and what the child is doing; and parental behavior that provides an environment that is extremely inappropriate for a child (Besharov, 1990, pp. 117, 120).

Long-Term Consequences of Child Abuse

The signs of abuse represent the immediate effects of the abuse or neglect on the child. Long-term consequences include subsequent mistrust of self and others, poor self-regard, lack of social skills, a sense of helplessness, and problems with identifying and talking about feelings, especially anger, guilt, and depression (Leehan & Wilson, 1985; Porter et al., 1982). Physical abuse also often leads to aggression toward others (Briere & Runtz, 1990).

The precise effects of abuse depend on the age when the abuse occurred, relationship of the child to the offender, the severity and duration of the abuse, and on the buffering effects of the family and other systems, including any treatment the child receives (Cohen & Mannarino, 1998; Harter et al., 1988; Trickett & McBridge-Chang, 1995).

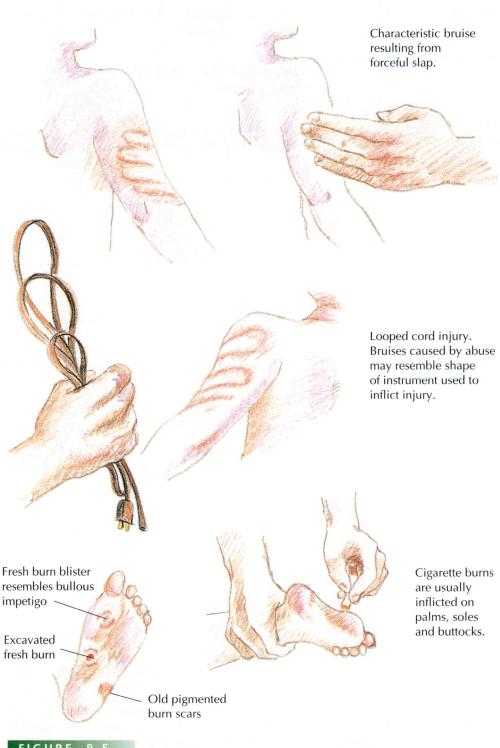

Characteristic bruise resulting from forceful slap.

Looped cord injury. Bruises caused by abuse may resemble shape of instrument used to inflict injury.

Fresh burn blister resembles bullous impetigo

Excavated fresh burn

Old pigmented burn scars

Cigarette burns are usually inflicted on palms, soles and buttocks.

FIGURE 8.5

Signs of physical child abuse.   (*Source:* Based on *Recognizing Child Abuse* (pp. 77, 80), by D. J. Besharov, 1990, New York: The Free Press.)

KEY POINTS

Appearance and Growth

■ Preschoolers are taller and thinner than toddlers, and their heads are more in proportion to their bodies.

■ Preschoolers continue to grow, but at a slowed-down rate. They gain about 3 pounds and grow about 2½ inches a year.

■ Preschoolers often have small appetites. They should be given a nutritious diet and not be pressured to eat. Seeing other children eat a new food helps increase a reluctant child's interest in it.

Motor Development

■ The preschooler's center of gravity has moved down to the abdomen, reducing top-heaviness and increasing balance needed for many locomotor activities.

■ Preschool children become increasingly adept at running, jumping, and climbing. Movements requiring more coordination, such as galloping, hopping, and skipping, take longer to master. Children's improving balance makes skill acquisition possible.

■ Motor skills emerge as more muscle tissue develops and as the brain matures. Motor skills are nurtured by a stimulating environment and opportunities to practice. Adults should make sure that playgrounds are safe and free from hazards. Injuries increase when environmental hazards are present on playgrounds.

■ Preschoolers begin to master the basics of throwing and catching a ball. By the age of 6, they are able to get their body behind the ball to throw it, can maneuver to catch it and respond more quickly. Children's reaction time also improves during the preschool years but major improvements occur later.

■ Children gain more control of their fingers during the preschool years and use this ability in many fine motor activities, such as drawing, cutting, and stringing beads.

■ Preschoolers also gain the ability to dress themselves. Parents can support independence by providing manageable clothes as well as any necessary help and supervision. To accommodate children who have disabilities, parents and caregivers may have to make certain adaptions in the environment to help them become independent.

Ensuring the Preschooler's Health and Safety

■ Preschoolers typically have more illnesses than infants and toddlers, although earlier exposure to child care is changing this pattern. Illnesses in child-care settings can be reduced by following certain precautions.

■ The Hib vaccine and the vaccine for hepatitis B can reduce the incidence of disease in children in child care.

■ Head lice are a minor health annoyance in preschool age children.

■ Chicken pox is a common disease among preschool children. The disease is not serious, but it causes parents to miss considerable work because lesions take 7–10 days to heal. Chicken pox is likely to decrease in incidence now that a vaccine is available to protect children against it.

■ Meningitis is a serious disease that affects the lining of the brain and spinal cord.

■ Lead in the environment presents a safety hazard to many preschool children.

■ Sleep problems are extremely common among preschool children.

■ Many of the same precautions used to keep infants and toddlers safe can also be taken to ensure the safety of the preschool child.

■ Preschoolers, as well as both younger and older children, can suffer from child abuse and neglect. Professionals are mandated to report suspected cases of child abuse and neglect to child protection authorities.

■ Since they were passed in the early 1960s, child abuse reporting laws have saved the lives of many children.

■ Overreporting of suspected child abuse is overwhelming the child protection system's ability to respond. Better information for people required to report abuse, and screening of initial reports by child protection agency personnel, could help solve the problem of overreporting.

GLOSSARY

center of gravity: the point around which the weight of an object is distributed (p. 268)

eustachian tubes: the hollow tubes that connect the inner ear to the throat and allow for drainage (p. 280)

head lice: wingless insects that infect hair follicles and cause intense itching (p. 279)

hepatitis: a viral infection of the liver (p. 281)

mandated reporters: professionals, such as physicians, teachers, and social workers, who must report suspected instances of child abuse and neglect (p. 286)

marked-time climbing: climbing accomplished by bringing one foot up or down to a step or rung on which the other foot rests, rather than placing the second foot on the following step or rung (p. 270)

meningitis: inflammation of the membranes covering the brain and spinal cord, which is often caused by the *Haemophilus influenzae* type B bacterium (p. 281)

otitis media: infection of the middle ear (p. 280)

reaction time: the time it takes to assimilate a stimulus, decide what to do, and then transmit the message to muscle for action (p. 275)

rhythmic hopping: hopping on one foot and then the other in an alternating pattern (p. 270)

unsubstantiated reports: reports of child abuse or neglect that are not supported by evidence when caseworkers investigate the report (p. 287)

varicella vaccine: the vaccine used to immunize children against the chicken pox virus (p. 281)

SUGGESTIONS FOR FURTHER READING

Besharov, D. J. (1990). *Recognizing child abuse: A guide for the concerned*. New York: The Free Press. This comprehensive book about child abuse and neglect provides detailed lists of signs of different forms of abuse and neglect. It discusses mandated reporting laws, how to keep records, and how to make a report. An excellent resource.

Capaldi, E. D., & Powley, T. L. (1993). *Taste, experience, and feeding*. Washington, DC: American Psychological Association. The book contains chapters on taste perception, taste preferences, food aversions, the social context of food habits, and obesity. Though fairly dense in some spots, the book is largely accessible and very informative.

Cratty, B. J. (1986). *Perceptual and motor development in infants and children* (3rd ed.). Englewood Cliffs, NJ: Prentice-Hall. This highly readable classic provides a thorough discussion of physical growth and motor development. Chapters on hands, visual perception, and the effects of exercise provide interesting information.

Kalichman, S. C. (1993). *Mandated reporting of suspected child abuse*. Washington, DC: American Psychological Association. This book includes a discussion of the legal and ethical aspects of reporting child abuse. It reviews definitions in various state laws and provides some cases, with commentary.

9

Cognitive Development in Preschool Children

"A FIVE AND a two," Margaret says, as she looks at the dots on the upturned faces of two dice. Then, she counts to find the sum of the dots and moves her token on the game board: "One, two, three, four, five, six, seven."

Next, Margaret's dad rolls a four and a three. "Seven," he says.

"Hey!" Margaret protests. "You have to count the dots."

Her dad complies. "Four," he says, as he gestures once with his hand toward the die with the four pattern on its face. "Five, six, seven," he continues, pointing to each of the dots on the other die. "See? Four plus three is seven."

"But you have to count that one, too," Margaret insists, pointing to the die with four dots.

"I do?" asks her dad. "Why?"

"To see how many it is," she explains.

"Don't we already know that it's four?" her dad asks.

"No, we don't," Margaret says.

think about it

In some ways, Margaret's cognitive abilities seem quite sophisticated. She recognizes the number value of various arrangements of dots on die faces; and she can count at least to seven. But even though she announces that she has rolled "a five and a two," Margaret counts the group of dots whose numerical value she already seems to know. If Margaret knows beforehand that there are five dots on one of the dice and two on the other, why not take five as a given and count up from there? Why count both groups of dots? And why insist that her dad do the same?

Margaret appears quite illogical, and most 4-year-olds behave just as Margaret behaves. Piaget called preschoolers' thinking **preoperational** to indicate that it is inflexible, illogical, fragmented, and tied to specific contexts. In this chapter, we begin our discussion of preschoolers' cognitive behavior by considering their difficulties with seemingly simple tasks that probe their understanding of number, classification, and physical perspective-taking. We also discuss preschoolers' understanding of pretend play and living and nonliving things. Finally, we examine preschoolers' understanding of thinking itself. From these discussions, we will obtain an overall picture of the child's cognitive development between ages 3 and 6.

Cognitive Development in Preschool Children

Because many of our general beliefs about the preschool child's thinking have come from the work of Piaget, we begin with a discussion of Piaget's classic contributions. Then we will discuss differing perspectives on young children's cognitive abilities in each of his areas of inquiry, painting a somewhat different picture of the preschool child's cognitive activity than the one offered by Piaget.

Piaget's Research on Conservation

Among the best-known of Piaget's studies are his investigations of **conservation**. These probe the understanding that the mere rearrangement of items in a set, or the mere redistribution of the material in a mass, leaves the quantity of the set, or the amount of material in the mass, unchanged. Adults, of course, know that it does not matter whether a set of ten blocks, originally arranged in a row, is rearranged into a circle, a tower, a longer line, or a shorter one. There will still be ten blocks, unless blocks are added or removed. And no matter into what shape we mold a piece of clay, we know that unless clay is added or taken away, the *amount* of clay will remain the same.

Piaget wondered how rearrangements of items and redistributions of a continuous material would affect children's judgments about the number of items or amount of material. Would children understand that mere rearrangements of items do *not* alter quantity? Or would they think otherwise? With his conservation experiments, Piaget probed this understanding.

Piaget investigated the conservation of number, continuous quantity or mass, length, area, weight, and volume. He found that even the first-occurring conservation—that of number—is not attained by most children on the standard Piagetian task until they are between 6 and 7 years of age. But what does it mean, in Piagetian terms, to say that a preschooler is unable to conserve? How is a conservation task presented to children? What is the typical performance of a 3-year-old, for example, or a 4-year-old?

In the classic number conservation task, the experimenter arranges 8 to 10 objects in a row and asks the child to make a second row containing just as many objects as the first one. The child is not instructed to use a specific procedure. The child decides how to make the row. Young children who establish a row that is equal in number to the experimenter's row achieve this by matching each item they put out to one item in the experimenter's row. This procedure for establishing equal sets is called **matching one-to-one**. But most 3-year-olds, and even some very young 4-year-olds, do not use this strategy. Instead, they focus only on the lengths of the two rows, making sure that the ends of their new row are exactly opposite the ends of the experimenter's model row. As a consequence of their focus on the rows' lengths, they may have more items or fewer items in their row, compared with the experimenter's row (see Figure 9.1a).

Without two equal sets, the experimenter cannot continue the task because subsequent questions probe the child's understanding of whether physical manipulations disturb the original number equivalence of the two sets. Only when the child has created a second row equal to the first row can the experimenter proceed with the task. If a child has created a row equal in number to the experimenter's row, the experimenter continues by asking the child if he or she is sure that the two rows have the same number of items. If the child confirms that this is the case, the experimenter then says, "Okay. I'm going to do something to one row. Watch!" The experimenter then rearranges the items in one of the rows. This rearrangement disturbs the direct, physical, one-to-one correspondence between the individual items of the two sets (see Figure 9.1b). After rearranging the items, the experimenter asks the child if the two rows still have the same number of objects, or if one has more or fewer than the other.

If a child says that the rows now contain *different* numbers of objects, the child clearly does not conserve number—does not understand that the equality of two sets is left undisturbed by mere rearrangement of the items in one of the sets. Children who focus on the *density* of the rows—how close together the items in each set are—say that the shorter row contains more objects. Children who focus on the *length* of the rows say the longer row has more objects. The child does not take length *and* density into account, in either case. Piaget referred to this tendency of the child to focus on one attribute, in isolation of the others—the length of the rows *or* the density of items in the rows—as **centering**.

Piaget found that most children between ages 4½ and 6 deny the equality of the two rows when the direct, physical, one-to-one correspondence between the items in the two

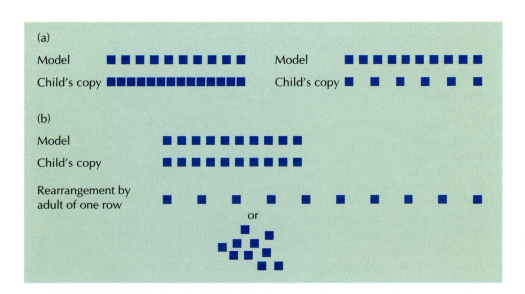

FIGURE 9.1

Piaget's conservation of number task.

sets is destroyed. The tendency to base judgments about number on how the situation *looks,* rather than on the logical consequences of the manipulation that has occurred, led Piaget to claim that the young child's thinking is **perceptually based** rather than logical.

By the age of 6 or 7, children typically begin to say that the two rearranged rows still contain the same number of items. If asked why they think the rows remain equal in terms of the number of their items, even though they appear to be unequal, children this age usually give one of three logical explanations: (1) No item was taken away or added to either group of items (the **identity argument**); (2) the longer row has big gaps, while the shorter row has smaller ones (the **compensation argument,** which results when children stop centering); or (3) the items could be put back the way they were (the **reversibility argument**).

According to Piaget, any one of these three responses indicates that a child conserves number and engages in **operational thinking.** The stage of thinking characterized by such **mental operations** is called the **concrete operational stage.** Children who explain their judgments in the conservation task by using at least one of the ways listed above are engaging in operational thinking. The term *concrete* is used in the label because children are thinking about actions performed on objects they observe. Not until later, in the **formal operational period,** can children think about possible actions to be taken on objects without actually seeing the actions. The ability to perform mental operations or mental actions on objects not previously seen allows the formal operational child to formulate hypotheses systematically. This thinking allows the child to imagine actions—to think of possible actions—rather than think only about actions he can observe. For example, when designing a scientific experiment, it is necessary to alter just one variable at a time while holding other things constant. The thinking involved in planning such an experiment requires formal operational thinking (see chapter 17, p. 000, for a good illustration).

Post-Piagetian Research on Children's Understanding of Number

Some researchers have altered Piaget's standard task to see if different ways of presenting it affect children's performance. Others have provided training before children are administered the task, to see if this has any effect. Still other researchers have abandoned the Piagetian tasks entirely and have devised other tasks to probe children's understanding of number. These different approaches to studying children's understanding of number have been taken by researchers who questioned both Piaget's number conservation task and his theory about the development of the concept of number.

Alterations of Piaget's Task and the Training Relating to It In one study that altered the standard Piagetian number conservation task, children were asked about the equality of the rows only once, after the transformation, not before and after. This change trimmed more than a year off of the age at which children demonstrated conservation of number (Rose & Blank, 1974).

In another study, McGarrigle and Donaldson (1975) made a stuffed animal (Naughty Teddy) jump out of his box and "mess up" one row of items (rather than have the experimenter alter one of the rows in the standard manner). After Naughty Teddy had altered one row, the experimenter put him back in his box and said to the child, "Now, where were we? Oh, yes, I remember, I was going to ask you, 'Are there just as many items in this row as here, or does this one have more or less than this one?'" In the Naughty Teddy condition of the study, 50 out of 80 children between 4 and 6 years of age conserved number. Only 13 out of 80 children conserved number on the standard task. Apparently, telling children to "watch carefully what I do" in the standard task (watch the experimenter rearrange a row of items) leads children to believe that the experimenter is doing something that is significant in relation to the questions the child is asked. When the methodology is changed to avoid creating a false expectation in children, they are much less likely to judge that the quantity of the items in the two sets has changed.

In another study, Gelman (1969) trained children to make judgments about the equality of two sets by having them focus on both length cues and number cues, and on comparing the two. Training significantly improved children's performance on the number conservation task. Apparently, the standard Piagetian number task leads children to believe somewhat that they should focus on length or physical alignment when they actually should focus on a different attribute (number of items). Other researchers have provided training in counting the items and on using counting to compare the equality of two sets whose items are not physically aligned. About two-thirds of the 5-year-olds in one study of this kind conserved number; none of the 5-year-olds in a no-training control group (the standard Piagetian task) conserved number (Gold, 1978).

A different study involving training encouraged children to reason about specific actions. The goal was to draw children's attention to the relevant details in the conservation task. One group of 5-year-old non-conservers (Siegler, 1995) received feedback indicating only whether the response was correct or incorrect. A second group of children received feedback indicating whether the response was correct or incorrect, accompanied by a request that the child explain his or her reasoning. A third group received feedback about the correctness or incorrectness of their response, with a request that the child explain the *experimenter's* reasoning (i.e., how the experimenter was thinking when judging the child's response). The children who were asked to explain the experimenter's reasoning improved the most in their own reasoning about the conservation of number task. In general, children who understand explanations they are given generalize strategies better than children who do not understand them (Crowley & Sielger, 1999). Asking a child to explain the adult's reasoning might be an effective way to increase understanding.

Tasks Used to Probe Children's Number Understanding

In a study involving plates of items, even 3- and 4- years-olds demonstrated knowledge of the difference between transformations of item sets that are number-relevant (items added or taken away) and number-irrelevant (items rearranged, but none added or subtracted) (Gelman & Gallistel, 1978). These results contradict Piaget's claims that children this young have no understanding that some transformations simply rearrange the items in a set, without altering their number.

In other studies, researchers have devised tasks to probe directly children's ability to reason about number. For example, in one study children were asked to infer one-to-one correspondence between the items in two sets from information about the number of items the sets contained (Becker, 1989). In one task, children were told, "There are X cups and X spoons." Then they were asked, "Will every cup have a spoon?" If the experimenter said 8 cups and 8 spoons, then the answer should be yes. But if the experimenter said 6 cups and 8 spoons, the correct answer would be no. In a second related task, children were told the number of items in one set (e.g., 9 spoons) and were asked to match these items with items in a second set (e.g., cups). Children were asked to name the items as they matched them one-to-one to prevent them from counting the items. After children had matched the items in the two sets, the experimenter asked, "Are there 9 cups?" If given only 6 cups, children would not have had a cup to match to each spoon. The child should say, "No, there are not 9 cups."

Becker's goal in this research was to determine whether children could infer number information from matching one-to-one information, and matching one-to-one from number information. Children who were between ages 4 and 4½ drew accurate inferences on both kinds of tasks, and most children between ages 4½ and 5 could justify their answers.

Preschoolers usually learn to count small sets of objects. They make many errors along the way. (*Source:* © Laura Dwight/ Corbis)

What We Have Learned from Post-Piagetian Research Much of the post-Piagetian research suggests that specific knowledge and skills affect children's performance on a conservation task. Several researchers have pointed out that "what has been taken as evidence of structural deficits [deficits in mental operations or reasoning] has turned out to stem instead from knowledge deficits" (Deloache et al., 1998, p. 802). In other words, these researchers and theorists do not expect to see general, overarching cognitive changes as children mature, which will then affect how the child reasons across many domains. Instead, they expect children's reasoning to improve in a specific domain as children gain knowledge about each one. If knowledge in a specific domain is impoverished, reasoning in that domain should be limited as well (Deloache et al., 1998).

A more domain-specific theory about the development of children's reasoning has led some researchers who are interested in children's learning about number to focus more squarely on specific skills, such as counting, and on children's gradual construction of detailed knowledge about number relationships (e.g., how 6 is related to 4 or how 3 is related to 5) (Case, 1998). These researchers think that counting at first consists of isolated motor and verbal routines, without any conceptual understanding (Case, 1998). As children acquire experience in thinking about the relationship of one number to other numbers, they gradually construct an ordered view of number—a mental number line. For example, if a child has selected 3 pieces of candy in a candy store and has been told by his parent that he may have 5 pieces, the child often takes another piece and counts how many he now has, and then takes another piece and counts again.

Through engagement in many experiences of this kind, a child gradually gets each number in its proper place in a number line from 1 to 10. Then children can begin to think of one number as being both one more than a certain other number, and one less than a different one (e.g., 5 is one more than 4 and one less than 6—it is in between these two numbers on the child's mental number line) (Case, 1998). This understanding provides the basis for an operational understanding of number—for knowing that adding items or taking away items is what changes the number of items in a collection, and that mere rearrangement of items does not alter their number.

Other studies have revealed that development in logic, in general, or in any other general cognitive ability, does not distinguish experts in a domain from novices. For example, expert chess players have very detailed knowledge of chess and a keen memory for the position of chess pieces on a chessboard. But chess experts are no better than novice chess players in remembering the positions of chess pieces on a chessboard when they are placed there randomly, out of context of an actual game (De-Groot, 1966). What distinguishes novices from the expert, in chess or medicine or anything else, seems to be the degree to which the expert has detailed and specific knowledge. The expert does have a firmer grasp of principles, but these seem to be derived from knowledge of the specifics. General logic does not appear first, as Piaget proposed, with the acquisition of details following behind. It seems that development proceeds the other way around (Chi et al., 1989; Chi & Rees, 1983).

Post-Piagetian views have opened the door for studies on how children acquire detailed knowledge about number and number relationships, and on how specific experiences, language, and cultural contexts affect this acquisition. An overview of the development of counting and of knowledge about base-ten organization and place-value notation can be found in the Research Close-Up: Learning to Count and Learning to Think about Large Numbers.

Piaget's Research on Classification

Piaget also studied children's ability to separate objects into groups or classes according to certain attributes. If asked to **classify** a large red felt circle, a large blue felt circle, a large blue felt square, a little red felt square, a little blue felt square, a little red felt circle, a paper clip, an elastic band, and an eraser, an adult might first separate the shapes from the objects. Then the adult might work within the class of shapes to create finer categories—red shapes and blue shapes, for example—which could then be further divided into circles and squares or big shapes and little shapes. These groupings can be represented schematically as shown in Figure 9.2. This kind of grouping is known as **hierarchical classification** because subclasses are created within larger, superordinate classes.

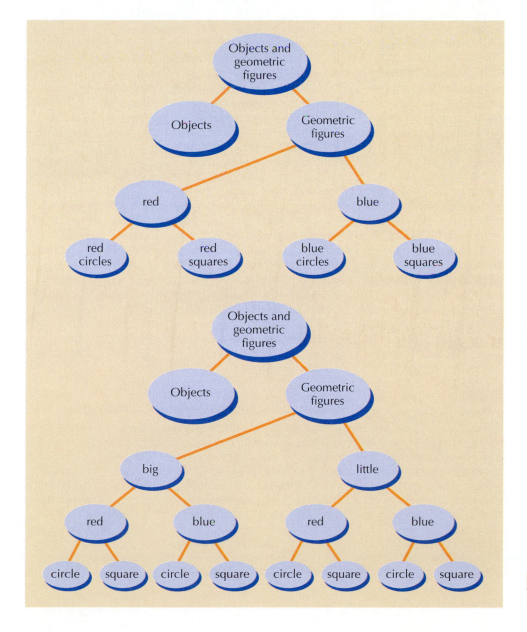

FIGURE 9.2

Hierarchical classification.

RESEARCH

CLOSE-UP

Learning to Count and Learning about the Composition of Larger Numbers

The understandings and skills required for true counting are acquired during the preschool years. Once children can count beyond 10, they are positioned to learn about how numbers are grouped by tens. On their way to these achievements, children make some characteristic errors. Moreover, some specific features of a child's experience in learning to count seem to affect the acquisition of other understandings about number.

Three Kinds of Counting Errors

Children make errors in reciting the numeral sequence (**sequencing errors**), in keeping track of which items have been counted and which ones are yet to be counted (**partitioning errors**), and in coordinating numerals recited to items tagged (**coordination errors**). In an attempt to count a collection of objects, a young child might make one of these errors, or two of them, or all three.

Errors of omission are the most common of the sequencing errors. Many 3-year-olds, for example, recite the first five number words (Saxe et al., 1987) and then jump ahead: "One, two, three, four, five, eight, nine, ten" (Gelman & Meck, 1983). Children gradually fill in the number words that fall in the gap between these two chunks of the 1–10 numeral sequence. A second sequencing error involves the **reordering** of numerals. When children make this error, they alter the standard numeral sequence (e.g.,"one, two, three, six, five, eight, ten"). A third type of sequence error involves the **reuse** of number words ("one, two, three, two, three").

There are two kinds of partitioning errors, **skipping** and **double-counting.** When a child makes a skipping error, the child places a "yet to be counted item" on the "already counted items" side of a mental **partition**—an invisible line separating items already counted from those yet to be counted—when the item should remain on the other side. When a child double-counts an item, the partition has mistakenly been kept in place, causing the child to count again an item that has already been counted. It is usually hard for a child to keep track of a large set of small items that cannot be moved; a small group of large items is easier to manage. Items organized in a straight line or in some other orderly arrangement are also easier to count than randomly arranged items.

Even when a child recites numerals correctly and knows how to count each object once and only once, she may fail to match the recitation of numerals and the tagging of objects.**Tagging** involves pointing or nodding at, or casting the eye toward, an object as a numeral is recited, in order to associate one and only one numeral to each item as one counts an entire set.

Usually, children recite numerals faster than they tag objects, probably because numerals have become a memorized chain of associations—each one prompts recall of the next one in the sequence. If the child slows her recitation of numerals, she might forget which one comes next. When numerals are recited quickly enough to prompt their recall, the child may not move her finger from one object to the next at the same speed. Coordination errors result.

Learning to Count beyond Ten

Many older 4-year-olds have learned to count to 10 and are learning to recite the conventional number words up to about 15 (Saxe et al., 1987). But they tend to make errors when they get to the teen numbers: "twelve, fifteen, sixteen, thirteen, twenty." Because some of the teen numbers do not match their 1-to-10 counterparts (we say "thirteen" rather than "threeteen," for example), English-speaking children must memorize many of the number words between 10 and 20. Because it is difficult to memorize so many unique names, it takes children quite a long time to master the teen number names (Baroody, 1987).

Learning to count beyond 10 is considerably easier for children who speak some Asian languages (e.g., Japanese, Chinese, Korean) because names for numbers between 10 and 20 are composed of "ten" and the appropriate item from the basic counting sequence. Instead of the name "eleven," the name is literally "ten-one." For "twelve," it is "ten-two," and so on. The decade names are also compounds of basic counting words. For example, "twenty" is "two-ten," and "thirty" is "three-ten" (Miura et. al., 1993). When counting in the 20s, one would say, "Two-ten-one, two-ten-two, two-ten-three," and so on.

Given the special difficulties the English counting names present, parents and teachers can expect English-speaking 4-year-olds to make omission and reordering errors when they attempt to count through the teen numbers. They also can expect many 5-year-olds to falter at the beginning of each new decade as they attempt to count to 100. It takes considerable practice for children to learn the numeral sequence.

A Conceptual Understanding of Counting

At first, counting consists of verbal and motor routines. For example, a child may be able to count 15 or 20 objects without making any kind of error. But if asked which is more, 8 or 6, the child may be stumped. When asked, "What would you need to do to have 6 items, given that you have only 4 right now," a typical 4-year-old cannot answer. Despite the fact that the child has the skill to count much larger sets accurately, which would seem to inform the child that 8 is *more* than 6, and 6 is 2 more than 4, the child draws a blank. The child needs experiences other than mere counting in order to develop an understanding of the relationship between one number and other numbers. Counting itself, especially when the child is first learning, does not seem to require that a child reflect about the relationship of one number to another. Situations that ask a child to relate one number to another (e.g., getting the correct number of pieces of candy in the candy store) seem to be required to prompt the kind of reflection that is the source of this conceptual knowledge about number.

For example, suppose that a child is told that he may buy 6 pieces of candy at the candy store, and he takes 3 to start. His father then asks, "How many do you have so far?" The child glances at the candy in his hand and says, "Three." His father reminds him that the total number of pieces he may have is 6. "How many more should you take?" his father asks. The child says, "I don't know." His father then takes out 3 more pieces of candy and puts them in the palm of his own hand. "Okay, '3 (pointing to the pieces in the child's hand as he says this), 4, 5, 6' (pointing at one piece at a time as he recites these 3 numerals). *Three* more pieces makes 6 altogether."

A child will not grasp the exact distance separating 3 and 6 from just one episode. He may grasp that 6 is more than one space away from 3, but he is unlikely to remember exactly how many. Slowly, a child builds a mental model of the numbers from 1–10 and can picture each in its position in relation to the other numbers. Plus 1 and minus 1 relationships are easiest to calculate, once numbers are in position on a conceptual number line. Plus 2 and minus 2 relationships take longer to construct, and distances of 3 more and 3 less (i.e., knowing which number occupies a position this far from a target number) take even longer to master.

The Development of Understandings about the Base-Ten Organization of Number

After children have learned to count past 10, adults have the opportunity to help them begin to think about numbers in terms of groups of tens and ones. This understanding rests on several related understandings. As children gain experience in counting up to 40 or 50, they begin to realize that the basic number words one through nine repeat as soon as a new decade starts. At this point, children can begin to think about larger numbers as composed of tens and ones. For example, 12 consists of one group of ten and two ones; 15 consists of one group of ten and five ones. Twenty consists of two groups of tens.

Young English-speaking children (as well as children who speak many other languages) have considerable difficulty understanding that a larger number can be thought of in terms of groups of tens and ones. Children who speak an Asian language have much less trouble, probably because the number names Asian children use reveal explicitly each number's composition. By the time Asian children are 6 years old, they have little difficulty making models of multi-digit numbers in terms of groups of tens and ones. If given **tens blocks** and **units,** and told to make the number 45, Asian children tend to use 4 tens blocks and 5 units. U.S. children, on the other hand, tend to make a model of the number by counting out 45 units (Miura et al., 1993, 1994), unless they are prompted to think in terms of grouping by tens (Saxton & Towse, 1998). Even when prompted, 6-year-old English-speaking children lag behind Japanese children of the same age in performing this task.

Not surprisingly, failure to think about numbers in terms of their tens and ones composition affects children's understanding of place value. **Place-value notation** indicates whether a specific numeral represents its face value or some multiple of that (10, or 100, or 1,000 times the face value). Even third-graders in the United States have great difficulty identifying correctly the value of numerals in different positions (e.g., in ones place, tens place, or hundreds place) (Kamii, 1989; Kouba et al., 1988). Asian children understand place value notation much earlier than this, apparently because Asian number names provide tutoring on base-ten ideas (i.e., number words explicitly indicate a number's composition in terms of tens and ones) (Fuson & Kwon, 1992a).

Implications of the Research

No matter what teachers or parents do, the young preschool child cannot understand large numbers in terms of groups of ones and ones, or that a number's value changes depending on its position or place. But both research and Vygotsky's sociocultural theory suggest that the timetable for these understandings is related to the nature of previous counting experience, including whether counting words used in the language make explicit the concept of grouping by tens. Teachers of English-speaking children might use counting language that resembles that of Asian languages (e.g., "ten-one, ten-two, ten-three") and explain to children that this is a different way to say "eleven, twelve, thirteen." Teachers can also provide math manipulatives that do not restrict counting to 10 or fewer items. Moreover, manipulatives that allow counting to higher numbers should organize items in groups of tens. For example, pegboards (10 × 10 grids) and Unifix cubes provided with a hundreds board (10 × 10 grid) can be useful to 4-, 5,- and 6-year-olds as they explore the concept of number. Some researchers have suggested that the limitations imposed by the difficult number names in the English language can be rather easily overcome by thinking carefully about the instruction of young children (Saxton & Towse, 1998).

A classification system is constructed and imposed on objects. We must think in terms of attributes such as red and blue (color), or big and little (size), or circles and squares (shape). Any object might be a member of a number of different classes, depending on the classification scheme. An object can also be a member of a subclass and a member of one or more superordinate classes, all at the same time. To understand this, children must understand **class-inclusion,** the nesting of subordinate groups of objects (red squares and blue squares) within superordinate, or larger, classes (all of the squares) of which they are parts.

Children under 4 years of age make selections based on an attribute, but they switch attributes across a series of selections (Inhelder & Piaget, 1969). For example, a child might first select and set aside a *red* square, then a *red* circle, and then a blue *circle.* A common attribute (red) is shared by items 1 and 2, but a different attribute (circle) is shared by items 2 and 3. The child might pick up a blue *triangle* next, having focused this time on the color of the last item (blue *circle*), rather than its shape. The groupings of objects made by children who switch attributes across selections are **collections,** not true **classes.**

Children between 5 and 7 years of age put all the red shapes or all the squares together, without losing track of the attribute across selections (Freund et al., 1990). They even organize subclasses within classes, such as when they make groups of red squares, blue squares, and yellow squares, after first having grouped together all of the squares. But children at this age still have trouble thinking about class-inclusion—about the fact that both red squares and blue squares are members of the larger class, squares.

The difficulty that children have with class-inclusion becomes particularly noticeable when they are asked questions like these about a group of red trucks and green trucks: "Would we have any trucks left if we lost all of the red trucks?" "Of which are there more, green trucks or trucks?" (See Figure 9.3.) Prior to 7 or 8 years of age, children tend to say that the subclass is larger (green trucks) than the superordinate class, because items are observable in the subclass position. To solve these verbal problems, children must keep the larger superordinate class in mind and make distinctions between the parts (the two subclasses, red trucks and green trucks) and the whole (the superordinate class, all of the trucks) (Ginsburg & Opper, 1988).

Post-Piagetian Research on Classification

Like his conclusions about conservation, Piaget's conclusions about young children's ability to classify have also been challenged. Recall from our discussions in chapter 5 that even infants are capable of categorizing visual stimuli, such as pictures of dogs and birds. Of course, dogs and birds differ in many more features than do red squares and blue squares. Thus, infant categorization studies are not quite like the difficult

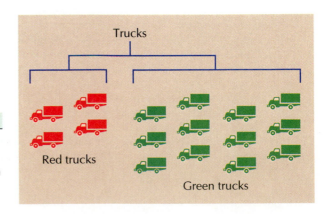

FIGURE 9.3

Arrangement of trucks. When asked, "Are there more trucks or more green trucks?" preschoolers answer, "Green trucks."

single-attribute classification tasks Piaget presented to preschoolers. Nor are the object-sorting studies (e.g., vehicles versus furniture) done with toddlers as difficult (Mandler et al., 1991).

Even when object-sorting studies conducted with older toddlers have used abstract features as the basis for defining category membership, objects have differed from one another in more than one attribute (Ricciuti, 1965; Starkey, 1981). For example, objects belonging together might be both red and large or both yellow and small. When objects that belong together have more than one feature in common, and these features are not found in objects belonging to another group, categories are much easier to establish. (Review the Research Close-Up: Which Objects Do Toddler's Group in Categories?, in chapter 5, pp. 166–167.)

Experiences That Influence the Development of Classification Abilities

How does the rudimentary ability to classify familiar objects, shown in studies by children 3 years and younger, develop into the 7-year-old's ability to answer class-inclusion questions? For one thing, experience in sorting objects with respect to abstract attributes, taken one at a time, influences children's subsequent classification behavior. For example, if children are asked to sort blocks and toys by color, shape, or size, and then to sort them again using a different attribute, many 3-, 4-, and 5-year-olds stick with one attribute at a time. They do not switch categories in the process of making groups, which is typical of children who have not received training in the concept of attributes (Nash & Gelman, cited in Gelman & Gallistel, 1978, p. 18).

Children's ability to think about relationships among the classes in a hierarchical classification scheme seems to be influenced by training. In some class-inclusion training studies, children have been asked questions such as "How many red squares are there?" "How many squares are there?" and "Are the red ones squares?" (Siegel et al., 1977, cited in Gelman & Baillargeon, 1983, p. 178).

In yet other studies, after children have answered that a group constituting a part is larger than the whole, they have been asked to count the items in the subordinate and superordinate classes. They also have been asked to explain the inconsistencies between the result of their counting and their previous answers (Judd & Mervis, 1979). Under these task conditions, children younger than 7 or 8 years of age have correctly answered class-inclusion questions.

Another process of learning has been proposed by Johnson and colleagues (1997). They suggest that the child initially learns the correct labels of objects in basic and subordinate categories. As children learn to divide the basic-level category (e.g., trucks, dogs, boats, and so on) into subordinate categories, they are likely to focus attention on class-inclusion relationships. "Learning that fire trucks differ from other trucks because the former have a particular cluster of properties (siren, ladder, and hoses) highlights the fact that properties indicative of a subordinate concept are not necessarily shared by all members of the basic-level concept" (p. 760). Once children have identified the relationships between categories, they can generalize this knowledge to categorize new items.

Once a child has learned about basic superordinate and subordinate categories in relation to at least one kind of familiar object, the child can then think by analogy to solve the Piagetian class-inclusion question (e.g., the child learns the characteristics of parent and child and considers these to be subordinate categories for the superordinate category of family members) (Halford, 1993). Halford (1993) suggested that when a child is asked, "Are there more apples or more fruit?" the child may draw an analogy to a familiar mental model of class-inclusion, such as the family, with its subcategories of parent and child. According to Halford (1993), young children are likely to understand that all of a subcategory (e.g., apples) is included in a superordinate category (e.g., fruit), just as all of the Smith children are included among the members of the Smith family.

This child seems to be organizing objects she has taken from a tub into groups that are the same color. Sorting objects in terms of attributes, such as color, shape, or size, aids children's ability to classify objects on these attributes. (*Source:* © Will Faller)

What We Have Learned from Post-Piagetian Studies of Classification

All of these studies suggest, once again, that specific and detailed knowledge influences the child's ability to engage in certain kinds of logical thinking. For example, it can be expected that the more that a child knows about trucks and has been exposed to different kinds of trucks (or cars, or dogs, or dinosaurs, or anything), the better that child will perform in classification tasks involving trucks. It appears that the young child gradually acquires relevant knowledge and works by analogy from known and differentiated categories to establish new ones, thus gaining proficiency in solving class-inclusion problems.

Piaget's Studies of Children's Understanding of Physical Point of View or Perspective

To study children's understanding of the fact that another's physical point of view can differ from their own, Piaget designed a display of three mountains (Piaget & Inhelder, 1967). Each of the three mountains differed from the others in height, color (green, brown, gray), and the artifact placed at its peak (e.g., a house, a red cross, or snow). (See Figure 9.4.) Extending up and down the side of one mountain, and visible from only one position, was a zigzagging path. A small stream was on the side of another mountain. When facing the tallest mountain, a person cannot see the smallest mountain. When facing the shortest mountain, a person can see all three moun-

FIGURE 9.4

The Piagetian mountain experiment. In this experiment, the child looks at all sides of the display before taking a seat on one side. Questions are then posed about what the child can see and what a doll who is seated on the opposite side can see.

tains, with the largest mountain forming a backdrop for the other two. Thus, depending on which mountain is faced, different artifacts can be seen, and the composition of the scene of the three mountains appears different.

During administration of the task, the child is first asked to walk around the display and to look at it from every vantage point. Next, the child is seated on one side of the mountain display table, and a doll is placed opposite the child. The child is asked to indicate what the doll sees in each of the three positions the doll eventually occupies (the doll is moved to each position that the child does not occupy, as the experiment proceeds) and also what the child sees from her stable position. To answer, the child (1) selects a photo from a collection showing various visual perspectives on the mountains or (2) uses a cardboard display to re-create a scene. Through these methods, the child answers questions of the doll's view and the child's own view.

The 4-year-olds created or selected displays at random, sometimes selecting the doll's view, sometimes their own, and sometimes a view not seen by either of them. By age 5, children can sort out the views somewhat, but they seem unable to dissociate themselves from their own view to indicate what the doll sees. By age 6 or 7, children seem to realize that the doll cannot see what they can see, but they often select the wrong photo or compose the wrong scene. Not until the age of 9 or 10 are children reliable in selecting the doll's actual view.

Piaget concluded that preschoolers are unable to take another's visual perspective. They are wholly **egocentric**—mistaken in thinking that another person sees the view that they see, when in fact the person cannot. Piaget also thought that children failed at visual perspective-taking because they understand spatial relations only topologically. This means that they notice if objects touch each other, overlap, or are close, but do not conceive and project lines on which to order objects (Newcombe & Huttenlocher, 1992). (See Knowledge in Action: Education—Young Children's Drawings to see how a topological conception of space is expressed in children's artwork.)

EDUCATION

Young Children's Drawings

Preschool children's first drawings and paintings consist of splotches or lines of color. When children start to make representational pictures, at around the age of 4, their pictures differ quite a lot from the drawings and paintings of older children. Preschool children seem to conceptualize and organize space differently. For example, young children seem to think more about proximity or distance between items, what parts enclose other parts, and whether a part itself is opened or closed. They do not consider whether one object is smaller than another in real life or how to scale the objects with respect to each other when pictured.

In their first representational drawings and paintings, young children may draw a person whose arms and legs are attached to the head (see Figure 9.5a.), or they may draw a head with eyes, nose, and mouth not placed where they belong. Body parts that are actually connected may not be connected in the child's drawing, as when a cat's tail is not attached to the cat. (See Figure 9.5b.)

Somewhat later, **topological relationships**—relationships about what things are close together and what things touch or overlap—are well understood. Eyes, nose, and mouth are placed in correct relationship to one another. However, proportions and relative distances are still not understood. Thus, in children's drawings people are as big as the houses. (See Figure 9.5c.) Children also lack an understanding of perspective (viewpoints in projective space). For example, a child might draw the outside of a house, but then include, within the frame of the house, what one would see only if inside the house. In other words, conflicting physical views are all included in the same picture. (See Figure 9.5d.)

Before the age of 4½ or 5, children's paintings and drawings lack a baseline around which objects in the picture are organized. Thus, people and houses float in the air. (See Figure 9.5e.) When a baseline is added, it usually appears first at the bottom of children's pictures, and most items in the picture are placed right on it. (See Figure 9.5f.) Later, the child indicates an understanding of a plane from foreground to background. By the age of 7 or 8, objects in children's drawings are scaled to each other, with objects in the distance being drawn smaller than those in the foreground. Drawings also have a consistent view. For example, only one eye is drawn on a dog's head if the dog is pictured from the side.

(a) Boy with blue hat

(b) Cat without attached tail

FIGURE 9.5

Children's understanding of spatial relations revealed in their paintings and drawings. Very young children often fail to connect things that are actually connected, such as a cat's tail and its body. They also may draw arms protruding from a person's head or attach legs to the head, completely leaving out a neck and trunk. Eventually, children connect parts accurately, maintain size relations, and learn how to place objects in perspective, which requires that they project a line from foreground to background on which to order objects.

Some researchers have documented cultural differences in young children's drawing skill. One study (Huntsinger et al., 1995) included three groups of preschool and kindergarten children: Euro-American children, second-generation Chinese American children, and Taiwanese children. Children were administered the Goodenough Draw-A-Person Test (Harris, 1963). Their drawings were scored for both maturity (i.e., for their detail and accuracy) and creativity. Chinese American and Taiwanese children outperformed Euro-American children on both maturity and creativity ratings. Parent interview data revealed that Euro-American parents set aside only about 6 minutes a day for drawing and writing activities, compared with 54 minutes per day set aside by Chinese American parents and 28 minutes a day set aside by Taiwanese parents. Chinese American and Taiwanese parents were also less reluctant than Euro-American parents to provide explicit instruction in both drawing and name writing.

The study did not rule out the possibility of ethnic differences in the maturation of fine motor skills. If fine motor skills develop more rapidly in children of Chinese descent than in children of European descent, then Chinese parents might be encouraged by this rapid development to provide more opportunities for their children to draw and write. They also might be less reluctant to provide specific instruction because they think their children are capable of following it, given their good fine motor skills. Of course, these differences could be cultural—children could learn to draw differently due to different parental beliefs.

(c) Large person standing beside house of same height and the sun in sky with face

(d) School bus, showing inside and outside, mixed perspectives

(e) Houses floating in air—no baseline

(f) Ferry boat sitting on baseline of waves of water

Post-Piagetian Research on Visual Perspective-Taking in Young Children

What alterations in the standard Piagetian task might help children perform better? Would more landmarks on the mountains make each view more distinctive? Would some practice in identifying a view of someone else, coupled with corrective feedback, improve performance? What if children were allowed to rotate the actual model to show someone's view rather than being asked to identify it in a photo? Would this alteration affect a young child's performance?

Modifications in Piaget's three-mountains task have revealed that preschoolers are somewhat more competent than Piaget concluded. Performance improves, for example, when children are asked to rotate an actual model of the mountains rather than pick a photo of the scene out of a collection (Fishbein et al., 1972; Huttenlocher & Presson, 1973). Performance also improves when modifications are made in the visual display itself. For example, simpler and more distinctive displays, as well as familiar and engaging objects and characters, result in better performance. Performance also improves when training is provided prior to presentation of the main task.

In one study (Borke, 1975), children were first shown a fire engine. Next, Grover, the *Sesame Street* puppet, drove his car around the fire engine and stopped and got out occasionally to look at it. The child, who remained seated in one position near the stationary fire engine, was asked to orient a second fire engine (mounted on a turntable) to show the view that Grover saw each time he got out of his car. If the child did not select the correct view, he was able to look at the fire engine from Grover's vantage point. If the child still indicated the incorrect view, the experimenter turned the fire engine on the turntable and said, "This is the way that Grover sees the fire engine from where he is parked" (Borke, 1975, p. 241).

After giving the child practice in taking Grover's perspective, the experimenter showed the child three other displays, one of a small lake and a sailboat, another of a horse and a cow, and a third of three mountains. The mountains in this study were set with many objects, including objects familiar to the young children in the study (e.g., people, trees, a barn and animals, a woman feeding some chickens). Children were again seated in one position as Grover moved around each display and stopped three times. Children were asked to rotate an identical display to indicate the view that Grover saw each time he stopped.

Three- and 4-year-olds were more accurate in reporting Grover's perspective on the first two displays than on the third display (the mountains), but they still performed much better than children perform on Piaget and Inhelder's mountain experiment. Borke concluded that display features and response mode both have an effect on children's performance on visual perspective-taking tasks. There were more features on Borke's mountains than on those used by Piaget and Inhelder, and children rotated an exact replica of a display to select Grover's view, rather than compose the view out of pieces or select a photo representing the view.

The results of a visual display study by Newcombe and Huttenlocher (1992) also differed from Piaget's. Children were asked to view items in a display and then to answer questions about both their specific locations (closest, farthest, left side, right side) and the specific view one would see from various positions around the display. Children selected photos to respond to the second question. Three-, 4- and 5-year-olds responded more accurately to questions about the locations of specific items in relation to others' positions; they responded less accurately to questions requiring them to select photos showing various views. The researchers' results were consistent with Piaget's in that children's performance on perspective-taking tasks involving the selection of a total view continued to develop through about 10 years of age. But the researchers found that much younger children exhibited knowledge of the specific items in a display that the other person could see.

Together, these studies suggest that the young child has some difficulty, but not as much as Piaget thought (Newcombe & Huttenlocher, 1992). Given more information, familiar objects, and training, preschoolers display some skill in physical perspective-taking.

Piaget's Studies of Animism and Artificialism in Childhood

Piaget referred to the young child's tendency to attribute thoughts, feelings, and intentions to inanimate objects as **animistic thinking.** Because their animistic thinking about objects grows especially strong when an object appears to move on its own (Piaget, 1969, 1972), cars and trains seem as alive to young children as animals do. Plants, on the other hand, seem to children to be unlike animals, cars, trains, and clouds because they do not move through space. Thus, when asked to place together the things that are alive, young children often separate plants (not alive in their judgment) from animals and cars and trains (alive in their judgment).

Piaget probed children's attributions of **consciousness** (the capacity to have thoughts and feelings, including intentions and motives) by asking children whether things such as water, stones, animals, or clouds can feel a pinprick, heat from fire, or the force of impact when they are dropped. Young children attributed consciousness to all inanimate objects, although what they thought a specific object could feel differed, depending on its characteristics. For example, a stone could not feel a pinprick, according to one child, "because it is hard." But it could feel fire, "because it would get burnt" (Piaget, 1960, p. 176).

Post-Piagetian Research on Childhood Animism

Piaget thought young children are confused about which things are and are not alive because they cannot distinguish between self-initiated movement and movement caused by some external force. But perhaps preschoolers misunderstand how to apply the word *alive,* or perhaps the unfamiliarity of the remote objects about which Piaget questioned them make the children appear more confused than they actually are. The work of other researchers suggests this is the case.

In one study (Bullock, 1985), the researcher showed 3-, 4- and 5-year-olds videotapes of several objects, some animate (a rabbit and a girl) and some inanimate (a wind-up worm and a pile of colored blocks). The movement of some objects (toward a bowl

Because plants do not move spontaneously the way animals do, children might think they are not alive. Involvement in the care of plants can help children attend to other attributes that distinguish animate from inanimate things. (*Source:* © Andy Sacks/Tony Stone Images)

of crackers) was made to appear spontaneous, whereas the movement of other objects was made to appear as if it were physically caused. In the spontaneous movement condition, inanimate objects were moved by hidden wires and other devices. In the physically caused condition, the objects were pushed or pulled by a visible stick or rope.

After viewing the films of object movement, children were interviewed. The experimenter began by saying, "We need to tell our friend some things about the X. Let's see . . . " Following this introductory statement, each child was asked eight questions, including these: "Does X have a brain?" "If there was a fire, could X run away?" "Can X grow bigger?" "If we put X on a shelf, will it stay there?" After children responded to the eight questions, they were shown 15 photos (4 objects used in the experiment, plus 11 more). When shown each photo, children were asked, "Is this alive?" (Bullock, 1985, p. 219).

Four-year-olds answered correctly about 94 percent of the time when asked whether an object was alive; 5-year-olds responded accurately about 98 percent of the time (Bullock, 1985, p. 222). The researcher suggested that the 3-year-olds' errors were not due to a general tendency to consider *all* inanimate objects animate, but to "a general uncertainty about the precise properties of many objects, regardless of object type" (Bullock, 1985, p. 224).

Other researchers have reached similar conclusions. For more information, see Research Close-Up: What Do Preschoolers Know about Biology?

Piagetian and Post-Piagetian Studies of Childhood Realism

Piaget was also interested in what children know about thoughts. Do children distinguish between thoughts and things thought about, or do they confuse thoughts with things in the material world? Piaget called such confusions **realism.** To find out if children have such confusions, Piaget asked them about dreams and whether something named one thing could just as well be named something else, if everyone agreed to call it that.

To probe children's understanding of dreams, Piaget (1969) asked them several questions:

1. "Do you know what a dream is?"
2. "Where do dreams come from?"
3. "Where do dreams happen?" "Where is the dream when you are dreaming?"
4. "Could someone else see your dream?"
5. "What do you dream with?"
6. "Why do you dream?" "What sends them?"

Children under 7 years of age often said that "the night makes the dream," that a dream happens "in my room," and that dreams come "from the sky." Children an-

RESEARCH

| CLOSE-UP | *What Do Preschoolers Know about Biology?*

In addition to evidence contradicting Piaget's theory of animism, evidence has also been accumulating to show that Piaget's hypothetical structures of reversibility, identity, centering, and egocentricity are less important than once was thought. As more and more research has shown that Piagetian theory fails to show that such structures account for behavior across domains, researchers have started to examine what children actually know about relatively specific domains of knowledge. Researchers have studied children's naive knowledge of physics, biology, and psychology to find out what they know about the behavior of objects, plants and animals, and human thought.

Researchers have discovered that preschoolers know considerably more about physical, biological, and psychological realms than Piaget suggested. We described in part children's knowledge of the physical realm (e.g., object permanence) in chapter 5. We turn now to preschoolers' knowledge of biology.

In addition to probing children's understanding of the relationship between the nature of an object (animate or inanimate) and self-generated movement, researchers have examined children's knowledge of a number of biological phenomena. For example, Backscheider and colleagues (1993) asked children whether various animate and inanimate objects can repair themselves spontaneously if they break or are scratched. The potential for spontaneous and systematic growth or repair is a characteristic of living things but not of inanimate objects. In other words, someone must glue together a doll's broken arm or sand and repaint a scratch on an automobile. But a rosebush can grow another rose, and a dog whose hair has been trimmed can grow more hair.

When asked to categorize animate objects as distinct from inanimate objects that were human-made artifacts, based on their capacity for spontaneous growth or repair, 4-year-olds indicated an understanding that both plants and animals belong together in an "alive" or animate category, whereas artifacts do not. Three-year-olds indicated less understanding than 4-year-olds did. This study suggests that children use information from several dimensions to judge whether an object is animate or inanimate. Accuracy in judgment about whether an object is "alive" or "not alive" may depend on integration and coordination of these dimensions (Backscheider et al., 1993). By asking one overarching question, Piaget failed to uncover the budding knowledge that preschoolers actually possess.

By preschool age, children understand that animals become larger and more complex with age, not smaller or less

complex. Four- and 5-year-olds usually understand something of the biological importance of the dimensions of movement, illness, growth, and inheritance (Johnson & Solomon, 1997; Wellman & Gelman, 1998). Some children as young as 3 and 4 years of age realize that the movements of animals are truly self-generated, whereas the movements of human-made objects are not (Gelman & Gottfried, 1996). These aspects of biological forms involve the entire visible organism rather than specific inner parts (e.g., the stomach) or obscure processes (e.g., digestion). And, by 4 or 5 years of age, children generally understand the distinction between living things (including plants) and nonliving things (Wellman & Gelman, 1998). Young children who do not understand this distinction may not yet be integrating completely the biological dimensions of knowledge they have (e.g., knowledge about movement, illness, growth, inheritance).

Wellman and Gelman (1998) suggested that children show an early understanding of biological processes, at least when considering qualities of animals that (1) involve the whole organism, (2) are related to important everyday behaviors, and (3) are topics frequently discussed with others. Aspects of biology that do not share these three characteristics are less likely to be well understood. For example, 4- and 5-year-olds tend to believe that any familiar cause of illness will inevitably produce the illness in every case. That is, preschoolers consider outcomes of typical causes of illness to be definite rather than based on probability (Kalish, 1998). Eating cookies contaminated with germs or playing with a child who is sick is believed by preschoolers to lead inevitably to illness (of this they are very sure), whereas adults know that the rate of actual illness will be considerably lower than the number of people who ate the cookies or played.

Because the probabilistic nature of typical causes of illness is seldom a topic of discussion at this young age, it is poorly understood. In fact, germs or contagion as a cause of illness is discussed with preschoolers in order to guide their everyday behavior. Parents and teachers tell children to wash their hands before they eat, so they will be free of germs. They admonish children not to eat items that have fallen to the floor or the ground "because they are dirty, have germs, and will make you sick." As a result, preschoolers show an early (though incomplete) understanding of the relationship between such familiar causes of illness and illness itself, and they believe more strongly than adults do that an effect will likely result from a cause in a very high number of instances.

swering in these ways indicate that they believe both the source of the dream and its physical location are outside of the head. Somewhat older children, those between 8 and 10, said that dreams come from them, but they still answered that dreams take place outside of them—in their room, under their bed, or in their closet. Finally, by about 11 years of age, children's answers reflected the mature understanding that dreams are formed in one's mind and also take place there (Piaget, 1969).

Piaget greatly overstated young children's tendency toward realism when he suggested that they consistently confuse things and things thought about. Actually, 2- and 3-year-olds have comparatively little difficulty in making this distinction (Wellman, 1990). They understand the difference between things and thinking about things. Moreover, by 3 to 5 years of age, children know that thinking takes place *inside* someone (Flavell et al., 1995). Interviewing children about their dreams is apparently not a very good way to find out whether or not they can distinguish between thoughts and material things. Perhaps it is especially difficult to talk about dreams, or perhaps children speak metaphorically when they discuss dreams. Moreover, questions such as "Where does your dream take place?" are misleading. Children could interpret the question to mean "In the dream that you had, where in the physical world did you picture yourself having the fight with the monsters?"

Summary: How Much Do Preschoolers Actually Understand?

Despite the validity of criticism of the Piagetian tasks, Piaget did put his finger on a significant difference between the thinking of young preschoolers and the thinking of children who are 5 to 7 years of age. Piaget referred to the preschool child's thinking as preoperational, that is, as not coordinating two aspects of a relationship (such as length and density of rows of pennies) or not reversing an action to link two different positions of the same objects (such as close together and far apart). Whether preschoolers' problems with thinking are due to the absence of such operations or to gaps in specific knowledge and strategies is still being debated. At issue is Piaget's *theory* of development—his *explanations* of what accounts for change.

Piaget thought changes in children's performance on his tasks depended on changes in mental operations. He also assumed that these changes very heavily depended on maturation. Other research reviewed here suggests that some changes Piaget noted probably resulted from task features—children actually had certain competencies all along but could not display them in Piaget's tasks. Where actual changes in children's thinking do take place, other theorists are more inclined than Piaget to think that they result more from the integration of ever-increasing information than from maturation. They think that changes in the young child's thinking depend more on experience than on maturation, on help in reflecting on experience, as Vygotsky suggested.

Those who think maturation does play a major role in changes in children's performance on Piaget's tasks also believe that maturation increases information-processing capacity. They do not think it directly makes available the specific mental operations of the sort proposed by Piaget. Information-processing capacity refers to memory and **executive functioning capacity**. Executive functioning capacity helps the child keep the overall task in mind and direct her attention to relevant aspects (Case, 1998). As knowledge and skill become more automatic (overlearned), information-processing demands are reduced. When full attention must be directed to fewer things, the child can focus on the coordination and integration of knowledge; this helps the child perform tasks better.

Pretend Play

The ability to engage in pretend play, or **pretense**, marks a revolution in the infant's development. As we noted in chapter 5, pretend play is seen first at around 12 to 14 months of age, although the child does not at that age yet pretend to *be* someone else. Rather, the child pretends to sleep or eat when not actually engaged in these real acts and signals that she is pretending by laughing or smiling. The first truly social pretend play is seen between 15 and 21 months of age, when a child includes others (e.g., a doll or an adult) in her play and begins to incorporate into her play repertoire some behaviors not typically performed in her own daily life (e.g., stirring in a pan on the stove). But **sociodramatic play**—play marked by role enactment and collaboration with others—emerges later, during the preschool period.

In answering these questions we will describe in this section how pretend play changes and develops from about 12 months onward, in terms of a framework based on Piaget's research and theory. In the following section, we discuss the social context of play and its development, emphasizing Vygotsky's contributions to our understanding.

Piagetian Conceptions of Pretend Play

Piaget's ideas about preoperational thinking contributed a framework for describing developments in children's pretend play. Specifically, changes over time in the child's egocentrism and realistic thought have been applied to pretend play. Pretend play develops away from egocentrism to allowing others to share or take over center stage (decentration), and it moves from the use of realistic objects to allowing object substitutions (decontextualization). In this section, we discuss trends in these two dimensions of play, and also in a third dimension—the complexity of the action scenarios the child creates when playing.

Decentration

The **decentration** dimension of play is concerned with the place or role the child occupies in the pretend play scenario and with the source of the content of the child's play. At first, the child himself takes center stage as the only actor in the pretend play (Tamis-

LeMonda et al., 1995). For example, a 12-month-old might pretend to feed himself or to be asleep. When toddlers do this, they may smile or giggle, as if to say, "This is funny. I'm not really eating (or sleeping). I'm only pretending" (Bretherton, 1984). The child's very early pretend play is egocentric, not only because it involves just one actor—the child—but because the content of the play is drawn from the child's own daily activities. The child includes in his early play only actions he himself has performed, not actions he has seen others perform (Fein, 1981; Fenson, 1984; McCune-Nicolich, 1981).

Children first begin to share the play stage by making others the recipients of their own playful actions. This behavior is seen somewhere between 13 and 15 months of age, when a child feeds a doll or puts a doll to sleep in a bed (Fein, 1981; Fenson & Ramsey, 1980; Tamis-LeMonda et al., 1995). When children first make dolls or other play figures the recipients of their play behavior, they do not make the figures "come alive"—appear to act on their own. For example, the child does not make the doll talk, nor does the child attempt to make the doll simulate walking or waving by arranging its arms or legs (Bretherton, 1984).

By about 20 months of age, children do animate their dolls, first by making them talk (Fenson & Ramsey, 1980). Later, they also make them move (Fenson, 1984). A child might also begin to put a spoon in his doll's hand and make it look as if the doll is feeding itself. The child no longer simply does things *to* the doll; he makes the doll do things to itself. In this way, the child removes himself somewhat from center stage—he is beginning to decenter and become less egocentric in conducting pretend play.

At the same time that children begin to animate recipients of their play actions, they begin to perform actions they have seen others perform in real life but have never actually performed themselves (Bretherton, 1984). For example, they pretend to cook food in pots on a play stove, place calls on their play telephones, and sweep the floor with a toy sweeper.

At around 30 months of age, children begin to pretend to be someone else. Pretending to be someone else requires that the child adopt behaviors and intentions that differ from the child's own (Dunn, 1998). The child plays Mommy or Daddy or plays the big sister or brother. Children adopt the tone of voice of the person they are pretending to be, they dress up to get "in role," and they behave in ways that are characteristic of the actual people they know who occupy the roles they adopt.

As the child adopts roles to play, she often creates two roles, perhaps one for herself and a doll, a role for each of two dolls, or one for herself and another child or adult player. To do this, she must stand back a bit and consider one role in relation to another because the roles must complement each other. For example, if playing Mommy, there usually must be children. If playing doctor, there must be patients. If playing store, there must be customers. Creating complementary roles for play, and playing within a framework of roles, requires some **intersubjectivity**—sharing understanding with other players of the roles and how they fit together (Goncu, 1998).

The ability to play a role and to begin to coordinate it with another player is usually seen in rudimentary form by 30 months of age (Bretherton, 1984; Miller & Garvey, 1984). Skill in role playing and in coordinating one's play with others continues to develop over the course of several years (Goncu, 1998).

Decontextualization   The decontextualization dimension in pretend play is concerned with object substitution. In pretend play, children often use one thing to stand for or represent another. Very young pretenders, age 12 to 18 months, need real objects, or realistic replicas of them, to support their pretend play (Fein, 1975; Fenson, 1984). They do not typically pretend, for example, that a cube or a leaf is a cup. They need a toy cup if they wish to pretend that they are drinking something from a cup. Between 18 and 24 months of age most children begin to substitute one object for another object, rather than rely on replicas (Fein, 1975; Tamis-LeMonda et al., 1995; Ungerer et al., 1981).

Children's ability to take objects out of their original context and pretend they are something else is quite limited at first but gradually increases as they get older. At first, the child may be able to use a Popsicle stick as a pretend spoon when feeding a realistic doll, but she may not be able to pretend two things—that a block is a doll and that a Popsicle stick is a spoon. When too many **object transformations**—changes from reality—are required, the youngest pretenders cannot play. Children under age 3 can use a few substitutions all at the same time, but only if many other items in the play situation are realistic (Fein, 1975).

The child's ability to use one object to stand for another also depends at first on how much an available object resembles the object needed in the pretend play. Children under 26 months of age will substitute one object for another only if the object they select looks somewhat like the needed object. For example, a seashell might be accepted as a cup because a seashell's cavity makes it resemble a cup somewhat (Fenson, 1984). But a 2-year-old will not use a solid wooden cube to stand for a cup, nor will a 2-year-old typically use a piece of construction paper to stand for a hat.

By 26 to 34 months of age, children can substitute objects more easily. A 3-year-old will even select objects to represent other objects when there is little or no resemblance between the two (Ungerer et al., 1981). The child is able to decontextualize the object's actual use and features in order to use it in the new pretend context—as if it were a different object.

By 4 years of age, an interesting twist of events occurs with respect to the child's selection of substitute objects. If an object has a specific and well-known use, a child is not likely to use this object to stand for any other. At the same time, the child is more flexible than ever in her tendency to use ambiguous objects to stand for just about anything. This explains why a 4-year-old might resist using a plastic golf club as a fishing pole but be willing to use a rolled-up newspaper as a fishing pole (this object has no clearly defined or contradictory use in the child's life).

Completely imaginary objects and substances are created by 3 years of age and this behavior continues to develop during the preschool years. At first, the imaginary objects or substances must be supported by other objects (Fenson, 1984). A cup can support the idea of pretend hot cocoa or tea. Somewhat later, children invent imaginary substances and objects when there is no support for them from other objects in the situation (Fenson, 1984). A child might look across the room and say, "You sit over there, doggy," when there is nothing to sit on, and when the doggy itself is a complete fabrication. Or a child might knock in the air, pretending to knock on an imaginary door to the house-play area in a preschool classroom. In these cases the imaginary objects are created literally "out of thin air." Imaginary playmates are good examples of such creations, and parents of creative 4- and 5-year-olds may find themselves setting an extra place at the dinner table or even buckling an imaginary playmate into a seat of the family's car.

Integration of Play   Integration of play refers to the child's ability to combine actions in increasingly complex sequences. Children use different kinds of action combinations in their play as they get older (Fenson, 1984; McCune-Nicolich, 1981). Children who are 15 to 24 months of age are likely to use mostly **single-scheme combinations.** In these action sequences one action (scheme) is repeated and applied to several things: The child pretends to feed a doll and then pretends to feed his mother. By 24 months of age, children begin more and more to combine several different actions (schemes) in a sequence and direct all of these toward the same recipient (Tamis-LeMonda et al., 1995). These action sequences are called **multischeme combinations** (Fenson & Ramsey, 1980; McCune-Nicolich & Fenson, 1984). We see a multischeme combination when a child holds a doll, feeds it, gives it a bath, and then puts it to bed.

Research Based on Vygotsky's View on the Origins of Pretend Play

Conceptions of the origins of pretend play have been influenced greatly by Piagetian theory. Recall from our earlier discussion that Piaget tended to think that the process of cognitive development occurs primarily as the result of the child's maturation and his or her autonomous interactions with the environment. With respect to pretend play, two researchers (Haight & Miller, 1992) have noted that "Piaget's [1962] otherwise meticulous observations omit information about the social context of early pretending, with the implication that pretend play develops regardless of whether anyone pretends with the child" (pp. 331–332). Vygotsky, on the other hand, proposed that a social partner or tutor is needed for the development of social pretend play.

Some researchers have attempted to determine whether the Piagetian assumption of spontaneous development is accurate or whether the development of pretend play depends on tutoring in a social context. Researchers interested in the possible social origins of pretend play have also studied play cross-culturally. If children's play varies across cultures—across variations in social context—then we would have reason to believe that play does not emerge spontaneously as a result solely of advances in a child's cognitive development, but is socially constructed through experiences in playing with others.

Playing Alone versus Playing with an Adult Partner

In Piagetian-inspired studies of children's pretend play, adults have been instructed to stay very much on the sidelines (O'Connell & Bretherton, 1984). But Vygotsky's theory has prompted many researchers to compare children's solitary play to their play with others. Recall from chapter 1 that Vygotsky contrasted the child's level of independent action with the child's level when assisted by more expert others (the child's zone of proximal development). Consistent with Vygotsky's theory, many researchers have found that children's play is more complex when they play with an adult partner than when they play alone.

In a study involving 20- and 28-month-olds (O'Connell & Bretherton,1984), mothers were instructed in the collaborative session to "play with the child and show him or her how to use the toys." Mothers made suggestions for what the child could do, and they demonstrated actions. Rather than follow all of a mother's suggestions, children chose only some things from the mother's suggestions: "Mothers provide their children with far more suggestions than the children ever implement in their play. . . . Children pick over this flow . . . for things that will get them a little bit farther along than they already are" (O'Connell & Bretherton, 1984, p. 360). The same kinds of selective response to the mother's suggestions have been found in other studies (Haight & Miller, 1992).

Play episodes also tend to be longer when the mother is available as a play partner than when she is not, and they also are less exploratory and more symbolic (Bornstein et al., 1994, cited in Bornstein & Tamis-LeMonda, 1995; Haight & Miller, 1992; Nicolich, 1977; Slade, 1987). Some researchers have also found that toddlers engage more often in pretend play when their mothers are available to play with them than when they are not (Fiese, 1990).

The Effects of Non-Intrusive versus Intrusive Interactions

think about it But are the adult's presence and participation enough? What happens if an adult dominates the play? Does a child's more mature play behavior depend on *how* the adult interacts with the child?

Adult presence and participation appear to have positive results only when the adult's actions are reciprocal (marked by sensitive give-and-take) (Fein & Fryer, 1995; Haight & Miller, 1992). If the mother or other adult becomes too directive, the child's play becomes less symbolic. One researcher summed it up like this: "It is not just the more sophisticated player's skill in directing play that influences the toddler's play, but the willingness to allow the toddler self-direction within the context of turn-taking and reciprocity" (Fiese, 1990, p. 1654).

For example, suppose that a child is playing with kitchen props in a playroom. Further suppose that he is making stirring motions with a spoon in a pot on the toy stove when a parent approaches and says, "Oh, if you're going to cook dinner for us, you'll need to set the table. What dishes will we need? Plates or bowls? What are you cooking?"

When the child ignores the parent's queries, the parent says, "Okay, if you won't tell me, I will just guess. I'm guessing that you are cooking soup. I'm putting bowls out. Am I right?" The child continues to stir in the pot for a few more seconds and then abandons the toys and heads for the puzzles.

This episode might have evolved differently had the adult approached the child at the toy stove, sniffed the air, and said, "Mmmmm, something smells good." In response to this, the child might have offered, "I'm making pudding."

"Mmmmmm, no wonder it smells so good. I can't quite tell what flavor it is. Vanilla? Chocolate? Butterscotch?"

"Chocolate," the child might have said, excitedly.

"Chocolate!" the adult might have said. "My very favorite kind of pudding."

"Want some?" the child might have queried.

"Sure," the adult might have said.

Before the adult could get a bowl, the child might have said, "Here" as he pulled the spoon out of the pot and held it close to the adult's lips.

The adult might have pretended to lick the spoon and then said, "Mmmmm, that is delicious, absolutely delicious. Can't wait to have a great big bowl of this."

In the first scenario, the adult was intrusive. Although interested in the child's play and a source of suggestions for play ideas, the adult directed the child's play too much. In the second scenario, the adult was more responsive and sensitive to the child and his ideas. To be supportive of a child's play, the adult "takes responsibility for guiding pretend actions," but is "sensitive to the child's moment-by-moment contributions to the interaction" (Haight & Miller, 1992, p. 344).

Consequences of Adult Participation in Children's Play

In most studies, the observations of the child's solitary play and collaborative play with an adult caregiver have been made virtually within the same day or within a few days. This leaves unanswered an interesting question about whether the effects of adult collaboration on children's play can be detected in the longer term. For example, if a child played collaboratively at a higher symbolic level when playing with his mother than when playing alone at age 20 months, would the child's own independent play be at a higher level at 26 or 28 months than it would be if the child had only played alone?

Only a handful of studies have addressed this question, and their results are inconclusive (Belsky et al., 1980; Bornstein et al., 1994, cited in Bornstein & Tamis-LeMonda, 1995; Tamis-LeMonda & Bornstein, 1994). Additional research is needed on children's play with a variety of play partners before researchers will be able to answer questions about the effects of more expert players on the development of play in young children.

Play in Cross-Cultural Perspective

think about it

Do children play the same, no matter where in the world they grow up? Or can we find differences both in the content of children's play and in how children treat each other as they play? Is there any relationship between the values and beliefs in the larger culture and how children conduct themselves while playing? Studies have been designed to discover whether culture influences the nature and expression of pretend play.

Play among children in a village in Senegal and among children in Indonesia was described in chapter 5 (p. 186). Another example is provided here. It is drawn from a study conducted by Farver and Shin (1997) of Korean American and Anglo-American preschoolers. The parents of the Korean American children had immigrated to the United States about 10 years prior to the study. The parents of the Anglo-American preschoolers were not recent immigrants.

Farver and Shin (1997) observed Korean American and Anglo-American preschooler dyads (pairs of children) during an "experimental" play condition. The researchers provided a toy castle with small human figures, animals, and furniture. The frequency of social pretend play, the communication strategies used by the children, and social play complexity themes were observed in over 20 dyads from each cultural group.

The researchers found no cultural differences in the frequency of the children's engagement in social pretend play. But researchers did find significant differences in the children's communication strategies and in the play themes observed in the experimental play condition. Anglo-American preschoolers more often described their own actions, rejected their partner's suggestions, and gave directives. In contrast, Korean American children tended more often to describe their partner's actions, make statements that added new elements to their partner's play, state agreement, ask for approval of their ideas, and make polite requests.

The researchers concluded that each group of children used communication strategies that are consistent with some of their culture's norms for social behavior. The Korean American culture is characterized by group interdependence and a desire to keep social conflict to a minimum. The Korean American children's communication reflected these cultural values. On the other hand, Anglo-American culture is characterized by independence, individual initiative, and self-expression, and the Anglo-American children's communication reflected these cultural values.

The play themes also differed across the two cultural groups. The Korean American preschoolers tended to focus on everyday activity and family roles, whereas the Anglo-American preschoolers tended to enact themes of danger in the environment, as well as fantastic themes. Several culture-related explanations were proposed by the researchers to account for these differences. These included two hypotheses: (1) that Anglo-American preschoolers are more experienced and skilled than are Korean American preschoolers in complex social pretend play and (2) that Anglo-

American preschoolers may have more exposure to su-
perhero cartoons and similar fantastic television programs than Korean American preschoolers have.

The researchers pointed out that their data were
drawn from a short (20-minute) videotape of just one
play session in a particular context and that the children in both groups were drawn from middle-class
families. They also pointed out that there is variation
within any cultural group, and their data indicate
group tendencies, not behavior found in all of the individual children. The results of this study, however,
are consistent with other cross-cultural studies in
showing that variations in play are correlated with the
child's culture. These results provide evidence for those
who believe that play does not simply emerge spontaneously, with maturation, but is socially constructed,
as is consistent with Vygotsky's sociocultural views of
development.

Young Children's Understanding of Thinking

Three-year-old Adam and his 9-year-old brother Barry
were playing in their bedroom when their 8-year-old
sister Samantha came in and took Barry's large, new
box of crayons to her room. "Mom!" yelled Barry,
"Sam just stole my crayons!"

Mrs. Leonard came into the boys' bedroom and said,
"If you weren't using the crayons, Sam can use
them." "But, Mom," Barry protested, "she always
takes the paper off to color with them sideways!"
"Barry, don't be so selfish," his mother said. "You can
still color with them even though the paper is taken
off." Having heard that the crayons were safely in her possession, Samantha
walked past the boys' room to the girls' bathroom downstairs.

Barry was unhappy. "Sam always gets her way 'cause she's a girl," Barry said to
Adam. "Let's play a trick on her!" "Come on," he said to Adam, and the two boys
went into Sam's room. "Shhh!" said Barry, "don't tell." He then proceeded to pick
up the few crayons spread about, plus the crayons still in the box, and dump them
in the top drawer of Samantha's desk. Then he went to the boys' bathroom near
his room, got a bar of soap, brought it back to Sam's room and put it in the crayon
box. "Now when Sam comes back, I'll ask you what's in the crayon box. You say
'crayons.' Then when she opens the box, boy will she be surprised!"

When Sam returned to the room she asked the boys what they were doing
there. "We wanted to watch you color," said Barry. "Adam," he continued, "do
you know what's in the box there?" "Soap!" Adam said excitedly, much to
Barry's dismay.

Preschoolers are often frightened by things that look real but aren't, because they can't make appearance-reality distinctions very well. This child is so frightened by the big dinosaur model that she wants to get completely away from the exhibit area. (*Source:* © Elizabeth Crews)

think about it

Was Adam trying to give away Barry's secret, perhaps knowing that once before Barry had tried to blame him for Barry's dirty tricks? Or could it be that 3-year-old Adam had trouble representing a falsehood as true? Do young children understand that their beliefs and those of others are representations of the real world and that, as representations, those beliefs can be false? How can children be helped to understand that others can have beliefs that differ from their own?

In answering these questions we note that the study of children's thinking about thinking has a history extending back at least as far as Piaget and Vygotsky. In one of his first books, *The Child's Conception of the World* (1969), Piaget concluded that young children do not think that thoughts differ from reality. Instead, as we saw in our previous discussion of children's thinking about dreams, Piaget claimed that the young child thought dreams actually occurred in a person's room rather than in a person's head. Although Piaget's claims about young children's misunderstandings about thoughts were greatly overstated, his work focused attention on children's cognition and sparked an area of very extensive research.

Vygotsky emphasized that children must think about thinking in order to develop mature human consciousness. According to Vygotsky, young children experience things, but they do not have mature consciousness until they *think about thinking*. Some awareness of the mind's activity appears to usher in the self-consciousness Vygotsky described as being essential to mature consciousness (Astington, 1993).

What Do Preschoolers Know about Psychological Causes of Behavior?

Adults reason about psychological causes (in contrast to physical or biological causes) using a belief-desire reasoning system. That is, adults think that a person's beliefs and desires cause his or her actions. These actions in turn are intended to produce desired emotional effects. An adult might use this reasoning to explain a person's behavior: "He was *hungry* [desire] and *thought* [belief] that there was food in the refrigerator, so he went to the fridge. He was *happy* [emotion] to find a sandwich." In other words, the adult predicts that a person acts in a certain way because he or she *believes* that the act will satisfy particular *desires*. Researchers have been particularly interested in whether preschoolers, like the adult, reason about psychological causation using belief-desire reasoning, in contrast to the way they reason about causes of events in the physical or biological realms.

According to some researchers (e.g., Gopnik & Meltzoff, 1997), though very young children (e.g., 3-year-olds) explain simple actions in terms of desires and emotions, they have little understanding of beliefs. Considerable research in this area, known as research on the child's **theory of mind**, has focused on whether 3-year-olds understand that people can have **false beliefs** (e.g., "he thought that there was food in the refrigerator, but there was not").

In introducing the term theory of mind, researchers (Premack & Woodruff, 1978) stated that "an individual has a theory of mind if he imputes mental states to himself and others" (p. 515). In other words, they defined an elementary theory of mind as a theory about mental states. Philosophers subsequently suggested that an accurate test of the presence of a theory of mind requires that one set aside one's own accurate representation of the world and represent to oneself an actor's false representation, and then act accordingly. This suggestion prompted a number of studies on children's understanding of false beliefs.

The scenario presented in the first of these (Wimmer & Perner, 1983) is outlined in Figure 9.6. Most 3-year-olds suggest that Maxi will look in the kitchen box Y (box on the right in the figure) where *they* last saw the chocolate disappear. They do not believe that Maxi will have a false belief about where the chocolate is, even though he left before his mother put the chocolate in kitchen box Y (on the right). Three-year-olds do not have a theory of Maxi's mind, whereas the average 4-year-old does.

Gopnick and Astington's (1988) study with Smarties and pencils was done subsequently. It was formulated to show that 3-year-olds do not even recognize their *own* previous false belief. In this study, children were shown a Smarties candy box (familiar to the British and Canadian children who participated in the study) and were asked what they thought was in it. Of course, they said, "Candy." But when children opened

FIGURE 9.6

Sequence of events with Maxi and the chocolate bar.

the box, they found pencils, not candy. Later, they were asked what they had *first* thought was in the box, *before* they opened it. Amazingly, 3-year-olds usually said that they thought at first that the box contained *pencils*. In other words, they seemed to hold a false belief about their *own* previous thought. Four-year-olds, on the other hand, distinguished between their previous and their subsequent beliefs of what was in the box, and 5-year-olds did even better than the 4-year-olds (Gopnick & Astington, 1988).

Children were also asked what they thought *another* child would think was in the box. This question probed children's understanding of the false beliefs of *others*. Because another child had not yet seen what was actually in the candy box, he or she should have a false belief about what the box actually contained.

The 4- and 5-year-olds reported accurately that the naive child would have a false belief about the box's contents. But the 3-year-olds said that the other child would guess that the box contained pencils! In other words, the 3-year-olds seemed to have no understanding that a person could have a false belief (Gopnik & Astington, 1988). Of course, we should not be surprised to learn that 3-year-olds fail to realize that another child will hold a false belief about the contents of the candy box. After all, they did not realize that even *they* had held a false belief before seeing what was actually inside the box.

When these procedures have been repeated with other materials, the results have been the same. Apparently, the 3-year-old does not realize that other people can be unaware of some fact that he himself knows about a situation. Similar studies have found clear differences on false belief tasks between 3- and 4-year-olds in several different cultures, including non-Western ones, such as those of Japan and Cameroon (Avis & Harris, 1991; Naito et al., 1994). Only when the 3-year-old is given very straightforward and specific questions or procedures to help him does he respond correctly (Chandler & Hala, 1994; Lewis, 1994).

Explaining the Three-Year-Old's Inability to Understand False Beliefs

Why are 3-year-olds unable to predict false beliefs of others or even to remember their own? Some researchers suggest that it is because 3-year-olds do not have a representational theory of mind. In other words, 3-year-olds have difficulty representing that someone may have any of several differing beliefs about a specific issue. Because they consider a thought to be a *direct* internal statement of the way the world actually is (Astington, 1993), they think only one thought about the matter is possible, namely, the way the real world is. They do not understand that their thoughts are merely representations produced by the mind (Perner, 1991). Without this understanding, they do not realize that thoughts can conflict with the world—can be false—or that thoughts can change (Astington, 1995; Flavell et al., 1995).

In order to consider another's belief about the world to be false, the child must understand that thoughts are representations of reality (Moore & Frye, 1991; Perner, 1988). The child must have a **representational theory of mind.** The child who has this kind of theory about the mind can represent people's different and incompatible beliefs about the same thing and understands that some of the beliefs that people hold are false (Wellman & Gelman, 1998).

Other researchers (e.g., Lewis, 1994) believe the 3-year-old's poor performance is due simply to an exaggeration of an information-processing problem shown at times by older children as well. That is, they reject the theory that a child must acquire a representational theory of mind (the "theory theory"), suggesting that the child has a representational theory of mind all along but has difficulty demonstrating this knowledge. Perhaps, they suggest, 3-year-olds' memories are too fragile to allow them to remember the details of what occurred on false-belief tasks. If this is the case, they would have difficulty recalling their previous thought and may be inclined to guess incorrectly (Lutz & Sternberg, 1999).

Regardless of the explanation, children age 3 and younger tend to have difficulty in understanding at least some of the beliefs of others. This limitation in understanding psychological causes can lead to errors in their predictions of others' behavior.

Helping Children Develop the Understanding That Thinking Is Representational

Some people have suggested that exposure to narratives (stories with a plot) in the preschool years may be a useful device for helping children come to understand theory-of-mind concepts, including false belief. Listening to stories read from books would seem to create an ideal context for children to reflect about the thoughts and feelings of others. In fact, when one group of researchers (Cassidy et al., 1998) examined the books read by parents to their 3- through 6-year-olds, they found that 78 percent of the books contained references to internal states and 34 percent contained false beliefs. A look at some specific children's stories reveals how they might help children understand the representational nature of thinking.

In the book *Blueberries for Sal* (by Robert McCloskey), a little bear and a little girl are out in the wild with their mothers, gathering blueberries. At one point in the story, Little Sal and Little Bear have a false belief. Each thinks that she is following the right mother when she is actually following the wrong mother. Additionally, the two mothers think it is their own child's footsteps they hear behind them, even though this is not true. The child listening to the story can see that both Little Bear and Little Sal and their mothers have false beliefs—thoughts that do not match reality.

Corduroy, a story by Don Freeman about a teddy bear who lives in a toy department and wants very much to be taken home by a child, also provides insight into thinking. In this story, a little girl named Lisa asks her mother to buy the teddy bear, but her mother says no, in part because Corduroy is missing a button on his overalls. As Lisa and her mother walk away, Corduroy says to himself, "I didn't know that I was missing a button." He decides to try to search for it that night. During the journey in search of his button, he mistakes the escalator in the store for a mountain, the furniture department for a palace, and a button on a mattress for the one missing from his overalls. Not only does the book include a character with false beliefs, but also it is ideal for discussions of how both the little girl and Corduroy feel, and what they think about each other.

Such stories would seem to provide children with rich opportunities to talk with adults about what people think, about the fact that people often have false beliefs, and about the fact that one person's beliefs often differ from and conflict with those of another. Books provide opportunities for children to observe characters who think and change their minds. Some research suggests that experience with storybooks does help children develop the idea that thinking is representational.

Sabbagh and Callanan (1998) found picture-book reading to be particularly productive in eliciting talk about mental states. They also found that parents gave responses concerning mental states when children said, "I don't know" (e.g., "I don't know what happens next"); when children contradicted their parents; or when children corrected themselves. Parental responses apparently provided a zone of proximal development in which representational thought could develop. In particular, the 4-year-olds of parents who took the opportunity to discuss multiple perspectives of thought when the 4-year-olds contradicted the parents' thinking or when the 4-year-olds contradicted their own previous thinking were more likely to show representational thinking (to frequently contrast two different mental states) than other 4-year-olds whose parents did not do this.

Other predictors of a child's showing understanding of representational thinking or false belief at an early age include high verbal ability and positive teacher ratings of the child's ability to get along with others (Watson et al., 1999). A rich fantasy life (Taylor & Carlson, 1997) and having older siblings to talk to in play also predict early understanding of the representational theory of mind (Ruffman et al., 1998).

Whatever the specific causes of the change, we see a remarkable transformation in thinking between the ages of 3 and 5. This transformation includes the apparent discovery of the representational mind (Astington, 1993). Without the ability to realize that thoughts are subjective and changeable, human beings would be unable to think the way they do—to reflect about thinking, to correct their misperceptions and misunderstandings, to allow their ideas to change and evolve, and to accept that other people may have different ideas than they do about the same thing. We see only a faint glimmer of such understanding in 3-year-olds. But in the 5-year-old, who understands that both her thoughts and the thoughts of others can be wrong, we see the dawn of the mature thinking that is to come.

Other Limitations in Young Children's Understanding of Thinking

In addition to their difficulty with false beliefs, 3-year-olds lack other important knowledge about thinking (Flavell et al., 1995). For example, very young children are not aware of the source of their knowledge. When they know something, they cannot say whether they actually saw it with their own eyes, whether someone told them about it, or whether someone gave them clues and they drew an inference (Gopnik & Graf, 1988; Woolley & Bruell, 1996). Instead, they focus on the object represented by the thought and seem to be unaware of the thought's source.

Three- to 5-year-olds even have difficulty recognizing when a person is engaged in thinking. Although preschoolers can state that thinking is not the same as talking, seeing, or knowing (Flavell et al., 1995), they do not recognize thinking as private mental activity. Instead, they tend to associate thinking only with someone's observable problem solving. For example, they do not think that someone who has been sitting quietly in a chair for a while is thinking, but they think that a person who abruptly stops an on going activity to consider how to answer a question is thinking. If children understand thinking to be only an occasional, isolated mental event, they must not experience thinking in the Vygotskian sense—as a stream of consciousness. But how do children begin to understand thinking as being a stream of consciousness?

Some experts appeal to Vygotsky's theory to explain this development. At first, children are told or asked to think about their thoughts in conversations with adults. For example, after reading a story to a young child, a parent might ask, "Were you surprised when the little red hen ate all of the bread herself? Did you think she was going to share it with the animals?" Or a parent might ask a child what he or she thought or felt in a recent situation: "Well, did you like your music movement class? Did you think it was fun?" "What did you think about that seal who bounced that ball on the end of his nose?" This kind of experience is followed by children's own self-reflection and by school instruction. School instruction, particularly in reading and writing, encourages children to reflect on their own thinking in addition to thinking about story characters in the ways we described earlier.

KEY POINTS

Cognitive Development in Preschool Children

■ Piaget investigated children's understanding of the fact that the quantity of a group of items does not change when the items are rearranged. This understanding is called conservation.

■ Piaget found that children between ages 4½ and 6 cannot judge the equivalence of two sets based on number considerations. But by 6 or 6½ years of age, children begin to realize that rearranging the objects in a group does not affect how many objects there are—they conserve number.

■ Piaget referred to preschoolers' thinking as preoperational, meaning that they do not use mental operations to make sense of their experiences. Limitations in their operational thinking, such as their tendency to center, and their inability to reverse transformations mentally, make preschoolers' thinking illogical.

■ Some researchers have modified Piaget's conservation experiments to see just what those tasks actually tested. Their results indicate that many children can conserve number during the preschool years and that they can easily be confused, distracted, or misled by the experimenter.

■ Studies show that training in making length-number distinctions also affects how well preschoolers do on number conservation tasks. Having children explain their own or the experimenter's reasoning also helps children perform better on the number conservation task.

■ Studies show that preschoolers know the difference between manipulations of sets that change the number of items and manipulations that don't. Studies also show that preschoolers can use one-to-one correspondence information to infer information about number, and vice versa.

■ Preschoolers learn to count and, in the process, often make three kinds of counting errors: sequencing, partitioning, and coordinating.

■ Children learn the standard counting sequence, 1–10, in chunks and only gradually master the entire sequence. At first, counting consists of a verbal and a motor routine. Gradually, children develop a conceptual understanding of number in which each number's position on a mental number line, and its relationship to other numbers, is understood.

■ English-speaking children, unlike children who learn Asian languages, must learn unique number names for the teens and the decades. Learning so many number names makes number-word learning more difficult for English-speaking children and for other children whose language does not use compound names for larger numbers. This, in turn, is related to later difficulties in learning base-ten organization and place-value notation.

■ Materials that make grouping of items by ten explicit to children should help them develop a base-ten organization of number.

■ Piaget's classification task involves thinking of an attribute and selecting items with respect to it. Piaget found that preschool children have difficulty sticking with one attribute across all of their selections when making a group of objects. They change attributes as they continue to select items. Thus, the groupings they make are collections of objects rather than true classes.

■ Class-inclusion involves relating superordinate and subordinate classes. It is a matter of understanding part-whole relationships. Children under 7 or 8 years of age have difficulty responding correctly to the verbal probes included in Piaget's classification task.

■ Research shows that preschoolers can make distinct groups of objects when the objects differ from each other on more than one attribute. Experience in sorting by single attributes helps children perform better in Piagetian classification tasks.

■ Piaget used a display of three mountains to study children's ability to judge the visual perspective of others. He found that preschool children are extremely limited in their ability to differentiate their physical view from the physical view of someone else. Piaget explained children's poor performance on his mountain display task in terms of their egocentrism and topological conception of space.

■ Preschoolers are not as egocentric as Piaget thought with respect to physical perspective-taking. If given more detailed and familiar displays, and a variety of ways to indicate what they think another person sees, preschoolers show that they understand the perspective of another person. Preschoolers are better at indicating the location of a specific item in relation to themselves or another person than they are at selecting a photo of a view seen by another person.

■ Preschool children often attribute thoughts and feelings to inanimate objects. This tendency is referred to as childhood animism.

■ Piaget studied whether children made distinctions between animate and inanimate objects, in the way that adults do, by asking them to answer questions about whether such things as water and stones can feel certain things.

■ Preschoolers actually seem to have quite a lot of information about the distinctions between animate and inanimate objects. Researchers have found that certain task features help children reveal what they know.

■ Researchers who ask children about specific dimensions of animate and inanimate things find that preschoolers know more than Piaget thought; they have acquired some types of information, but lack others. Because Piaget asked children to judge, overall, whether something was "alive" or "not alive" and provided only certain types of models in his tasks, he underestimated what preschoolers know. Preschoolers must integrate several dimensions of knowledge to answer the question "Is it alive?" Inability to answer this global question does not mean that a preschooler understands nothing about the characteristics that differentiate animate and inanimate things.

■ Piaget thought that children confused thoughts with the things thought about—children considered thoughts to be concrete objects. The tendency to endow thoughts with material substance was called realism by Piaget. Preschoolers are able to think better than Piaget thought they did, though they have limitations that older children and adults do not have.

■ Other researchers and theorists think that the development of children's thinking may not be linked as closely to maturation as Piaget thought. Those who consider maturation to be quite important think so because maturation increases information-processing capacity. They do not think it leads directly to the specific (logical) mental operations proposed by Piaget.

■ Many researchers think that preschoolers' thinking is impeded mostly by their incomplete and fragile knowledge. As they gain specific knowledge relevant to a specific domain, their reasoning improves, according to these researchers.

Pretend Play

■ Changes in children's pretend play occur along three dimensions: decentration, decontextualization, and integration.

■ Decentration refers to the child's gradual removal of herself from center stage in her play.

■ As children's pretend play becomes less egocentric (they decenter more), the child gradually uses actions from his own daily activities less and less. Decentration is seen first when the child makes someone else the recipient of actions. A later indication of greater decentration is seen when children play a role.

■ Decontextualization refers to the child's increasing ability to take an object out of context and let it stand for something else.

■ Children at first must have replicas of actual objects to use in their play because they cannot handle many object transformations. When they first move beyond the need for replicas, they will choose an object with features similar to the object it represents. Gradually, children become able to use an object to stand for another even when there is no resemblance between the two objects.

■ Around 4 years of age, children begin to resist using a very familiar object for anything but its usual purpose, although ambiguous objects are used very flexibly to stand for just about anything.

■ Integration refers to the child's ability to combine actions in increasingly complex sequences.

■ Multischeme combinations involve more than one theme and are seen in the play of older toddlers and preschool children.

■ Infants and toddlers engage more frequently in dramatic play when adults play with them. When adults play with children, children reject many ideas the adults suggest but pick up on others. Adults who respond to children's cues contribute to children's play. Adults who are intrusive decrease rather than increase the amount of pretend play the child engages in.

■ The content of children's play is affected by their culture. The communication strategies children use in their play are also influenced by the values taught in the child's culture.

Young Children's Understanding of Thinking

■ Young preschool children have a limited understanding of the psychological causes of people's behavior. They seem to think that people are prompted to act by their desires and emotions, but they do not understand that humans also act in response to their beliefs.

■ Because 3-year-olds are unaware of their own current and previously held false beliefs, as well as the false beliefs of others, theorists say that they do not have a representational theory of mind. When a person has a representational theory of mind, the person understands that thoughts are representations of reality, that they can be false, and that they can change.

■ Four- and 5-year-olds have indicated in studies such as the one involving a Smarties candy box that they do have a representational understanding of mind.

- Adults can aid the development of children's thinking by helping them learn basic information and procedures and also by helping them to reflect about what they know.

- Listening to and discussing storybooks probably helps children learn about some of the characteristics of thinking.

- In addition to having difficulty understanding false beliefs, 3-year-olds do not know where they obtained the knowledge they have. They do not know whether someone told them something or whether they obtained it directly from their own observations.

- Young preschoolers even have trouble understanding that thinking can occur without being accompanied by overt problem solving.

- Asking children what they think and what they like probably helps them reflect on their own thinking and to begin to understand the representational nature of thought.

GLOSSARY

animistic thinking: thinking in which inanimate objects are considered to be alive (p. 311)

centering: the tendency of preoperational thinkers to focus on only one attribute of a physical relationship at a time (p. 297)

classes: groups of objects all of which possess the same defining attribute (p. 304)

classify: to place objects into different groups based on a specific attribute (p. 301)

class-inclusion: the nesting of subgroups within superordinate groups (p. 304)

collections: a grouping of objects based on changes in a defining attribute (p. 304)

compensation argument: an argument stating that the greater density of items in one row makes up for the greater length of items in another in order to explain why the two rows are still equal with respect to the number of items they contain (p. 298)

concrete operational stage: according to Piaget, the period between about 6 and 11 years of age when thinking is logical but is based on observations of actions the child has seen performed on objects (p. 298)

consciousness: the ability to have thoughts and feelings (p. 311)

conservation: understanding that rearranging items or a mass does not alter the number of the items or the quantity of the mass (p. 296)

coordination error: a counting error in which the number word sequence is not coordinated with pointing at the objects (p. 302)

decentration: the decline in egocentrism seen in a child's play as others become the recipient of the child's actions and the child enacts behaviors not performed by the child in real life (p. 315)

decontextualization: a trend in pretend play related to the child's willingness to use one object to stand for or represent another (p. 316)

double-counting: a partitioning error in which an item is counted more than once (p. 302)

egocentric: being mistaken in one's thinking that other people see the world and think about it in the same way as we do (p. 307)

errors of omission: a kind of sequencing error in which numerals in the standard counting sequence are left out ("1, 2, 3, 6, 7, 9, 10") (p. 302)

executive functioning capacity: the child's ability to deploy attention effectively and to coordinate other aspects of thinking (p. 314)

false beliefs: mistaken representations of what actually is true in the world (p. 322)

formal operations: logical and systematic thinking of the kind needed to formulate hypotheses about causation and to design an experiment to isolate a cause (p. 298)

hierarchical classification: a classification scheme in which subgroups are nested within superordinate groups (p. 301)

identity argument: an argument stating that because no objects have been added or subtracted from two sets that were equal at the start, the sets must still be equal (p. 298)

integration of play: the child's ability to combine actions in increasingly complex ways when engaging in pretend play (p. 317)

intersubjectivity: shared understanding between two or more people (p. 317)

matching one-to-one: a procedure, involving the physical matching of items in one set with the items in a second set, used in order to establish or check the equality of two sets (p. 297)

mental operations: logical thinking processes, using arguments such as reversibility, compensation, and identity (p. 298)

multischeme combinations: play behavior in which more than one behavior is applied to the same person or object (p. 317)

object transformations: the mental activity of imagining that one object is another in pretend play (e.g., popsicle stick for a spoon) (p. 317)

operational thinking: thinking that is controlled by logic—mental operations—rather than by perception—how things appear to be (p. 298)

partition: an invisible line separating items already counted from those yet to be counted (p. 302)

partitioning error: losing track of which objects have been counted and which still need to be counted (p. 302)

perceptually based thinking: thinking that is swayed more by how things appear than by logical consideration of a situation (p. 298)

place-value notation: a representational system in which the value of a number is determined by its place as well as by its face value (p. 303)

preoperational thinking: inflexible, illogical, fragmented, and perceptually based thinking found typically in children under 6 or 6½ years of age (p. 296)

pretense: pretending or acting "as if" (p. 314)

realism: confusing thoughts with their concrete referents, or considering thoughts themselves to be material—made of something (p. 312)

reordering counting error: a kind of sequencing error in which the numbers are recited in something other than the conventional counting sequence (p. 302)

representational theory of mind: knowing that thoughts are representations of reality and therefore can be false (can misrepresent reality) and can change (p. 324)

reversibility argument: a mental operation in which the result of an action on objects can be replayed so as to represent the objects' original arrangement (p. 298)

reuse: a kind of sequencing error in which a number is used more than once to tag two or more different objects (p. 302)

sequencing errors: errors in the use of the conventional sequence of numbers in counting (p. 302)

single-scheme combinations: play behavior in which one behavior is applied to more than one person or object (p. 317)

skipping error: a kind of partitioning error in which an item is not counted at all because it has been placed mistakenly in the already-counted group (p. 302)

sociodramatic play: pretend play involving the taking on of roles and collaboration with other players (p. 315)

tagging: pointing at items in a set, or using other means to associate one and only one numeral to each item, as one counts a set of items (p. 302)

tens blocks: instructional materials designed to be the equivalent of 10 units blocks (p. 303)

theory of mind: imputing mental states to oneself and to others (p. 322

topological relationships: spatial relations involving proximity, enclosure, and overlapping (p. 308)

units: instructional materials designed for use with tens blocks and hundreds blocks and equivalent to ⅒ of a tens block and ¹⁄₁₀₀ of a hundreds block (p. 303)

SUGGESTIONS FOR FURTHER READING

Astington, J. W. (1993). *The child's discovery of the mind.* Cambridge, MA: Harvard University Press. This readable little book presents an interesting introduction to information about the young child's developing theory of mind. In addition to her own theory of the development of the representational mind, Astington introduces other theorists, including those who believe that the child is born with a (representational) theory of mind but does not use it.

Donaldson, M. (1978). *Children's minds.* New York: Norton. This researcher/author thinks the Piagetian tasks underestimate preschoolers' reasoning ability. This readable book presents some of the research that has been conducted to support this conclusion.

Flavell, J. H., Green, F. L., & Flavell, E. R. (1995). Young children's knowledge about thinking. *Monographs of the Society for Research in Child Development, 69* (1, Serial No. 243). This series of 14 studies describes what young children do and do not know about thinking, including the important implications of their lack of understanding of the stream-of-consciousness, cause-and-effect relation of thoughts to other thoughts. For the student who is serious about this topic.

Ginsburg, H. P., & Opper, S. (1988). *Piaget's theory of intellectual development* (3rd ed.). Englewood Cliffs, NJ: Prentice-Hall. This readable book discusses Piaget's theory and stages of development. The book covers constructs such as conservation and seriation.

Gopnik, A., & Meltzoff, A. N. (1997). *Words, thoughts, and theories.* Cambridge, MA: The MIT Press. This little book describes and defends the theory that young children, like scientists, learn about the world, including the minds of others, by forming and revising theories. The authors also describe competing theories of the origins of knowledge and compare them to their "theory theory."

Lewis, C., & Mitchell, P. (Eds.). (1994). *Childrens' early understanding of mind: Origins and development.*

Hillsdale, NJ: Erlbaum. This extensive book looks in detail at the precursors of a representational theory of mind, elucidates the "representational theory theory," and describes other theories (e.g., limited information-processing capacity) to account for the young child's difficulty on false-belief tasks.

Wellman, H. M., & Gelman, S. A. (1998). Knowledge acquisition in foundational domains. In W. Damon (Series Ed.), D. Kuhn, & R. S. Siegler (Vol. Eds.), *Handbook of child psychology: Vol. 2. Cognition, perception, and language* (5th ed., pp. 523–573). NY: Wiley. The authors make the case that the young child organizes foundational knowledge into specific domains, which include the physical, the biological, and the psychological. By foundational knowledge, they mean knowledge important to everyday interactions, which constrains other conceptual understandings. They describe what children know about each of these specific domains at an early age and present general theories about how children learn about each domain.

10

The Development of Language and Communication in Preschool Children

"**WHAT DID YOU** do today?" Kate's dad asked.

"Oh, nothing," she replied.

"You must have done something," her dad continued. "You were at school all morning, and I see that you have a painting there."

"I painted this picture the last day, and I put it on the rack to dry. Today, I clayed."

"Oh, you played with clay today. What did you do after you played with clay?"

"Mmmmmmmmmm. Well, Jessica taught me how to staple papers together for a book."

"You and Jessica used a stapler?"

"Yes! You press it very very hard on the top. Then you pull the papers out, and they stay sticked together because a staple holds them."

"I hope you didn't stick your finger."

"No, we didn't."

"That's good. What did you do after that?" her fathered continued.

"Mmmmmm . . . I can't remember." With that and one last suck on the straw in her juice box, Kate ran off to play.

think about it

Kate has no trouble carrying on a conversation with her father, but she talks differently than an older child or an adult. What is it about her speech that makes it stand out? Are her sentences ill-formed and incomplete? Or are some of her words a bit peculiar? Do the words she coins have anything in common? Think about it. In this chapter, we look at the characteristics of preschoolers' oral language and at the origin of the distinctive mistakes they make. We also discuss children's first understandings about written language, another milestone of the preschool years.

Oral Language Development

Language continues to develop at an extremely rapid pace during the preschool years. Children are able to say more as the preschool years pass by, and they also understand more of what others say to them. In this section, we discuss major developments in language production and comprehension.

Language Production: What Preschoolers Can Say

think about it

What advances do children make in the language they use during the preschool years? What are some of the conditions that help children move forward in acquiring language?

General Vocabulary Development   Children learn an amazing number of words between 18 months and 6 years of age. It has been estimated that preschoolers—children between 3 and 6 years of age—learn as many as 6 to 9 words a day. At this rate, children can learn as many as 3,000 words per year (Carey, 1978; Templin, 1957). By 6 years of age, when most children enter first grade, their vocabularies are estimated to be 10,000 (Anglin, 1993) to 14,000 words (Carey, 1978), depending on how researchers have done their studies.

Prior to 2 years of age, children learn most of their words through direct teaching—parents and others point to specific objects and label them while in the child's presence. As we discussed in chapter 6, infants and toddlers learn words by associating a word they hear with some concrete referent they can see. Adults explicitly label objects, actions, and events, often repeating them many times. Joint attention is highly correlated with word learning at these young ages. After 2 years of age, children learn most new words by inferring their meanings from context (Werner & Kaplan, 1952). To do this, they use their budding understanding of the world and of language.

Verbs present an especially challenging situation. Some verbs, such as *walk, run, eat,* and *cry,* describe specific actions. These kinds of verbs are not confusing. But the meaning of other verbs depends on the perspective of persons in the situation. For example, although *buy* and *sell* and *give* and *take* describe actions, the meaning of each word in a pair depends on the role each occupies in the event. Children figure out the meanings of these verbs by paying attention to the other words used with them in sentences (Fisher et al., 1994; Naigles & Hoff-Ginsberg, 1995). For example, we say, "I will give this *to* you" and "I will take that *from* you." We also say, "I will buy that coat *from* you" and "I will sell that coat *to* you." (Fisher et al., 1994; Fisher, 1996) The unique preposition used in each case provides a clue about the different meanings of each of the verbs in the verb pair.

After about 2 years of age, children pick up the meanings of most new words from hearing them in the context of natural conversation or storybook reading. (*Source:* © Ken Fisher/Tony Stone Images)

Children as young as age 3 also learn new words because they notice that they occupy the same positions in a sentence as a word or two they already know. For example, in one study (Landau & Stecker, 1990), children heard two sentences, "This is a *corp*" and "This is *acorp* my box." In the first case, the novel word was interpreted as a noun—as a name for an object—because this is the position nouns occupy in sentences of this kind. But the pronunciation, which is exactly the same in the two sentences regardless of whether *a* is attached to *corp* or not, was interpreted as a preposition when it was heard in the second sentence because prepositions, rather than nouns, occupy this position in a sentence.

Under the age of 2, caregivers speak such sentences slowly and emphasize the particular noun and preposition to be learned. They choose specific words and repeat them while pointing to objects in the environment or to the position of one thing in relation to another ("This is a *turtle*. A *turtle*. He's sitting *on* the rock, isn't he?"). Later, children use the few exemplars they already know to learn new words that can fill the same slots (Bloom, 1998). Based on their previous experience in learning words that occupy a specific slot in sentences ("This is a *turtle*." "This is *on* my turtle."), children assume that new words occupying the same slots are the same kinds of words—nouns or prepositions—as those they already know. This knowledge helps them narrow down the range of possible meanings for the new words they hear. For example, if a child recognizes that a new word is the same kind of word as two familiar words, turtle and ball, she is likely to guess that the new word is also the name of something. This process of learning words has been called **syntactic bootstrapping** (Gleitman, 1990) because children use their knowledge of sentence structure to help them guess what kind of word a new one might be.

Because young children learn new words so quickly, often from only one exposure, the process has been called **fast mapping** (Carey, 1978). Fast mapping was illustrated in a study that exposed children to a new word—*koob*. The word was used to name an object used in a game the children were invited to play (Dollaghan, 1985). This object was the only new one used in the game, and its name was the only new word introduced. Thus, the conditions for fast mapping were ideal. The novel object was called by its name only once. Acquisition was tested in recognition, comprehension, and production tasks. Comprehension scores were higher than production scores for 3- and 4-year-olds (83 percent versus 0 percent and 91 percent versus 45 percent, respectively). Comprehension and production scores were exactly the same for 5-year-olds (71 percent).

Four- and 5-year-olds are much more likely than 3-year-olds to say (produce) a novel word after one or just a few exposures. Because 3-year-olds *understand* new

RESEARCH

CLOSE-UP   *Storybook Reading and Vocabulary Development*

Storybook reading provides a good word-learning context. Specific features of storybooks, and certain ways of reading them, affect children's word learning in this context.

Rate of Word Acquisition from Simply Hearing a Story Read

By simply hearing a previously unknown word as it appears in the text as a story is read, children often learn its meaning. In one study of 4- and 5-year-old Canadian children, the researchers wrote a text for a wordless picture book, using ten target words. The story was read just once. Four-year-olds learned on average about 3½ words from this brief exposure. Five-year-olds learned on average a little more than four words (Senechal & Cornell, 1993).

In a second study (Senechal et al., 1995), two books were read to 4-year-olds. Thirteen target words were introduced in each story, and each book was read twice. Based on testing before they participated in the study, children were classified as either high or low on word knowledge. The children with low word knowledge learned about two words from hearing the stories read twice. The children with high word knowledge learned a little over three words.

In a third study (Robbins & Ehri, 1994), kindergarten children heard one storybook read twice on two different days, within the same week. The 11 target words were not discussed as the book was read, although the stories themselves were discussed briefly, using the prompts, "What did you like about the story?" and "Tell something that happened in the story." Children's vocabularies were assessed with the Peabody Picture Vocabulary Test before they heard the story.

When the researchers compared children's performance on 11 new words that were *not* included in the story with the 11 words that were included in the story, children performed significantly above chance only with the words they heard. Children who had better vocabularies at the start learned more words from listening to the story than children who had poorer vocabularies. This result is consistent with the study by Senechal and colleagues (1995).

Book Characteristics That Affect Children's Word Learning

In the Robbins and Ehri (1994) study, words occurring four times in the storybook were learned at a higher rate than words heard just twice. Others have also found that words repeated more in a storybook are learned better than are words occurring only once (Elley, 1989).

If word meanings are captured in the illustrations, words also tend to be learned better. The extent to which the context in which the word is introduced defines or explains the word also affects the likelihood that it will be learned (Elley, 1989).

Storybook Reading Conditions That Affect Vocabulary Acquisition

Variations in reading can include defining or not defining new words as they are encountered, and engaging or not engaging children actively in the story reading by discussing the story or by asking children to label or point to pictures. These practices make a difference in word learning.

Defining Words as the Story Is Read

To define new words for children, the reader can provide a synonym immediately after reading them in the story ("*A ferocious lion* is a lion who is very, very fierce or mean"), or a reader can indicate a word's meaning by using intonation. For example, in the *The Very Hungry Caterpillar,* the egg on the leaf goes "Pop!" when the caterpillar hatches. The reader can say "pop" in a way that emphasizes the explosive quality captured by this word. A reader can also explain a word's meaning by pointing to the picture that shows the object or action to which a word refers.

Elley (1989) used all three devices to define words and compared children in this explanation condition with children to whom a teacher simply read the story without explaining new words. The explanation condition was considerably more effective than the no-explanation condition. Pemberton and Watkins (1987) and Dickinson and Smith (1994) also found higher levels of vocabulary learning in chil-

words reasonably well, even after only an exposure or two, the stumbling block for them seems to be in figuring out how to say the new word. Apparently, they need more repetitions of new words than do 4- and 5-year-olds to learn how to pronounce them. Fast mapping does not, of course, yield complete information about the meaning of words; finer points are picked up over a longer period of time. But fast mapping works well enough that it is possible for preschoolers to understand and use the new words after one or two (4-year-olds) or a few (3-year-olds) exposures. Because storybook reading provides an excellent context for hearing new words several times and also for discussing them, it provides a good context for learning new words and for refining their meanings. (See Research Close-Up: Storybook Reading and Vocabulary Development.)

dren whose preschool teachers defined words as they were encountered in the story.

Ways to Engage Children in Story Reading

Some studies have investigated whether active engagement of children in story reading increases word learning. In one study of 2- and 3-year-olds (Arnold et al., 1994), parents were taught to ask questions to encourage their child to talk and also to expand upon what children said. Children in the experimental group showed significantly greater gains in receptive vocabulary than children in a control group whose parents did not receive training.

In other studies (Senechal, 1997; Senechal & Cornell, 1993), researchers provided different story-reading conditions, including one in which children were asked *what* and *where* questions. Active engagement was effective in enhancing receptive vocabulary.

Dickinson and Smith (1994) also found that the development of preschoolers' story comprehension and vocabulary depended on the way in which teachers read stories to them. Children whose teachers used a **performance style** showed good gains in vocabulary and comprehension. These teachers read the story through first without discussion; then they discussed and sometimes reconstructed the story after the first reading, as they went back through the book. During the first reading of the story, teachers using a performance style also commented about word meanings, using the word-explanation strategies developed by Elley (1989).

Parental styles of engaging preschoolers in story reading also have an effect. Two styles of story reading—**describer** (mothers described and pointed to pictures) and **comprehender** (mothers stressed story meaning and asked questions requiring the drawing of inferences)—have been identified in mothers of 3- to 5-year-olds (Haden et al., 1996). Mothers who used a comprehender style when reading storybooks had children with larger vocabularies and better story comprehension several years later, compared with children of mothers who used a describer style.

In a subsequent study of 4-year-olds (Reese & Cox, 1999), children's word knowledge level was assessed prior to the experiment. The describer style was correlated with better vocabulary growth in children whose initial word knowledge was low, whereas the performance style was associated with better vocabulary growth in children who started out with higher levels of word knowledge.

Because word knowledge is related to a child's ability to use sentence structure to infer word meanings, children who are not yet very good at doing this would have lower vocabulary knowledge and would not be able to utilize sentence structure to learn more words from the story itself. Younger children, and children who are not as skilled in understanding language, need more explicit object and action labeling if they are to learn new words. Once children's language skills have improved, they would seem to benefit more from the performance style in which the teaching of words is less explicit than in the descriptive style, and in which the discussion is wider ranging.

Summary of Research on Story Reading and Vocabulary Acquisition

Storybook reading can aid children's word learning. Though small in some studies, the effects are very consistent across many studies. Children's learning of new words from books can be greatly enhanced if the reader defines words briefly when they are encountered, rereads books, engages children in conversations about the stories after reading them, and adjusts strategies to match the word-learning skills of the children. It is important for researchers to continue to study effective ways to help young children acquire vocabulary because size of vocabulary greatly affects reading comprehension. Word recognition skills (e.g., alphabet recognition, phoneme segmentation, and letter-sound associations) are the best predictors of success in beginning to read—in learning how—but after an initial stage of learning to read, vocabulary is the best predictor of reading achievement (Bast & Reitsma, 1998).

Young children learn many new words from hearing them in the context of stories adults read to them. Discussing a story, during or after reading it, enhances overall language development, as well as vocabulary acquisition.   (*Source:* © Ken Fisher/Tony Stone Images)

Advances in children's social cognition—in their awareness that others have thoughts and that these can be influenced in various ways—also motivate children to learn more and more language. Playing with toys in the company of others, eating meals (Beals & Tabors, 1995), and sharing picture books are contexts for learning words, but they are more than that. They are occasions for learning about people and about what is required to interact with them (Bloom, 1998). The motivation to talk and to acquire vocabulary is probably driven in large part by a desire to maintain contact and to share our thoughts and feelings with others (Locke, 1996).

Children's Increasing Sensitivity to Phonology   Children actually produce most of the sounds of their language by the time they are 3 years old. But children this age often make some articulation errors (de Boysson-Bardies, 1999). Children are fairly adept at producing enough of the sounds in new words they hear to repeat them after only one or two exposures. This is especially true for 4- and 5-year-olds.

Language-Based Sound Play.   Children reveal their budding phonological skills when they play with language. They deliberately vary phonology, often while participating in gamelike social exchanges with peers. They play with suprasegmental features (stress, pauses, etc.), with the forms that words take, with rhyming syllables, and with phoneme substitutions.

Catherine Garvey (1990) gives several examples of language-based sound play in her book *Play*. In the following example, two 5-year-olds play with the word *mother* and with words that rhyme.

Child One	*Child Two*
"And when Melanie and . . . you will be here you have to be grand mother grand mother. Right?"	
	"I'll have to be grand momma, grand momma, grand momma."
"Grand mother grand mother grand mother."	
	"Grand momma, grand momma, grand momma."
(Later in the sequence of interactions . . .) "Momma."	
	"Momma I . . . my mommy momma. Mother humpf."
"Hey."	
	"Mother mear (laugh) mother smear."
(laugh)	
	"I said mother smear, mother near, mother tear, mother dear." (laugh)
"Peer."	
	"Fear."
"Pooper."	
	"What?"
"Pooper. Now that's a . . . that's a good name."	
	(Garvey, 1990, pp. 68–69)

These children played with forms of a word (*momma, mommy, mother*), and with rhyme (*fear, tear, smear, peer*).

Preschoolers often take great delight in language play. In one episode of language play, a mixed group of 4- and 5-year-olds was having a snack immediately following music time in their preschool. During music time they had sung *Willoughby-Wallaby-Woo*. In this song, people's names are rhymed by altering their first sound. For example, the song says, "Willoughby-Wallaby-Woo, an elephant sat on Sue; Willoughby-Wallaby-Bydney, an elephant sat on Sydney," and so on. The children began by changing their own names into other names for the song (e.g., Sydney to Bydney, Sasha to Zasha, Billy to Silly, and so on). This continued for several minutes, amid much laughter. When the children had exhausted their ideas for varying each others' names, they began to change the names of objects in the room—table/zable, cup/mup, pitcher/litcher, floor/sploor. They continued until they had practically worn themselves out.

THE DEVELOPMENT OF PHONEME-LEVEL AWARENESS.   Awareness of the individual sounds making up words begins to emerge during the preschool years if the written form of the language makes use of an alphabet. This awareness is a kind of **phonological awareness**—an explicit focus on the sounds of language instead of on its meaning. The language play set off by the song *Willoughby-Wallaby-Woo* required that the first phoneme of a name be deleted and another put in its place. This kind of phonological activity is called **phoneme substitution.**

An easier level of phonological awareness involves breaking words at their syllable boundaries, such as when children clap once for each syllable in words as they and a teacher recite them (e.g., ba-by, um-brel-la, chry-san-the-mum). Recognizing words that rhyme (**rhyme detection**), and creating rhyming words to match a target word (**rhyme generation**) (*boat*—goat, coat, moat, vote), requires more skill than does breaking words apart at syllable boundaries. Creating words that begin with the same sound (*ball*—big, banana, balloon, bag) requires even more skill. It is harder still to delete a phoneme, such as when children are asked, "What would be left if you took the /b/ out of *bat*?" (Yopp, 1988, p. 164).

A very high level of phonological awareness is seen in the ability to segment an entire word into its constituent phonemes (**phonemic segmentation**), as children do when they sound out words to try to spell them. In order to segment a word into its constituent phonemes, children must start at the beginning of a word and work systematically to the word's end, isolating each phoneme, in turn, as they go. At first, children are not able to isolate all of the phonemes. Adults must help a child sound out words before the child can begin to engage in the process by herself. The help must be provided for several months.

Phoneme segmentation and manipulation tasks are much better predictors of beginning reading than are syllable segmentation or rhyme detection tasks (Bryant et al., 1989; Muter et al., 1997). Experience with rhyming is vitally important, however, because it probably primes the child's awareness of individual sounds within words and thus paves the way for children to develop higher-level phoneme segmentation and manipulation skills (Bryant et al., 1989). Involvement in rhyming does not by itself lead automatically to the ability to segment all of the phonemes within a word or to manipulate them in a phoneme deletion task. Additional experiences, such as being helped to sound out words in order to spell them, are required to develop the higher levels of phonological awareness.

When a child's native tongue is not written with an alphabetic writing system—with a system that codes spoken language at the individual sound (i.e., phoneme) level—an explicit awareness of phonemes does not develop (Bentin et al., 1991; Read et al., 1986). But when the written form of a language codes the sound at the phoneme level, children must become aware of sound at this fine-grained level if they are to learn to read and write. Word games and listening to adults sound out words that children have asked them to spell help children develop phonemic awareness.

Phonological tasks focusing on the phoneme level are difficult for children under 5½ or 6 years of age, although some children develop phonemic awareness this early or even earlier. In one study, 3-year-olds sounded out words (segmented them into phonemes) and used alphabet letters to spell them (Read, 1975, 1986). Because it is very unusual for such young children to have phonemic awareness, we can surmise that the population of children included in Read's study probably had had early experience with nursery rhymes as well as experience in hearing adults sound out words to spell them. We know that phonemic awareness does not develop naturally or spontaneously (Adams et al., 1998). It must be specifically tutored, first, by engaging children in language experiences that involve rhyme and alliteration, and then by engaging them in spelling words and playing word games.

Development of phonemic awareness also seems to be aided by general vocabulary development. As a child's vocabulary gets larger over the course of the preschool years, she may begin to compare words that are closely related in their sound sequences. **Phonemes** are the smallest unit of sound that make a difference to meaning. For example, *bat, rat, sat,* and *cat* are perceived to be different words—to have different meanings—because they differ by one phoneme. As children acquire many words that overlap a great deal in sound, they must store words in memory with more segmental (i.e., sound) information. Otherwise, they will confuse words when they try to retrieve them, and they may misunderstand words they hear. Words that are in one of the child's dense phonological neighborhoods—words that are close in sound to many other words the child knows—are usually segmented more fully than words that are members of a child's sparse phonological neighborhoods—words that are not similar in the sounds they contain (Metsala, 1999; Metsala & Walley, 1998). (See pp. 358–360 for discussions about phonemic awareness in relation to learning to read and to write.) Variations in children's phonological development are due to some combination of individual differences in phonological sensitivity and differences in the activities children are provided.

Acquisition of Grammatical Morphemes

When Kate, whom we met at the beginning of this chapter, was a toddler, she said "Mommy sock" if she meant "This is Mommy's sock." At age 4, she speaks in sentences that contain the grammatical morphemes she omitted when she was younger. These begin to appear early in the preschool period. Children's use of grammatical morphemes continues to improve for several months thereafter (Peters & Menn, 1993).

Recall from Chapter 6 that a morpheme is the smallest unit of meaning in a language. **Unbound morphemes** are whole words (e.g., dog, elephant); **bound morphemes** consist of only a few sounds and must be attached to a larger morpheme. When attached to a larger morpheme, bound morphemes change the meaning of the original morpheme (e.g., the s indicates plural in the noun *dogs,* the -ed indicates past tense in the verb *walked,* and so on). During the preschool years, children learn to use articles, prepositions, and auxiliary verbs (unbound morphemes); they also learn to use bound morphemes to change nouns from singular to plural form, mark possessive, and change the tenses of verbs. (See the list in Research Close-Up: The Grammatical Morphemes Young Children Acquire.)

The appearance of grammatical morphemes in children's sentences is a major advance in language development. But even with this advance, preschoolers' speech

---

RESEARCH | **CLOSE-UP**   *The Grammatical Morphemes Young Children Acquire*

Children's oral language emerges in a definite, predictable way. A child who now says, "Daddy go," will soon be saying, "Daddy going," and later, "Daddy is going." With each new utterance, the child has learned a new morpheme and made a linguistic leap. The following list includes 14 morphemes that young children learn to use, in the order in which they learn to use them (Brown, 1973).

Name of Morpheme	Example	Name of Morpheme	Example
Progressive (-*ing*)	Daddy going.	Articles (*the, a*)	The pail has a hole.
Locative (*in*)	Bat in room.	Regular past (-*ed*)	Daddy walked home.
Locative (*on*)	Hat on head.	Regular third person (-*s*)	He runs.
Regular plural (-*s*)	Boys there.	Irregular third person	He does that.
Irregular past	Ran home.	Uncontractible copula	She is running.
Possessive (-*'s*)	Adam's shoe.	Contractible copula	She's afraid.
Uncontractible copula*	Susan is here.	Contractible auxiliary	She's running.

*That is, the child does not form contractions with the copula ("is")

T A B L E 1 0 . 1		
The words children invent		
Situation	*Invention*	*Model*
Child was referring to cheese that had to be weighed.	"You have to scale it first."	"You have to drill it first."
Child was hitting a ball with a stick.	"I'm sticking it and that makes it go really fast."	"I'm batting it to make it go really fast."
Child was using tongs to remove spaghetti from a pan.	"I'm going to pliers this out."	"I'm going to hammer this out."
Mother was sweeping child's room.	"Don't broom my mess."	"Don't mop the floor."
Child was putting crackers in soup.	"I'm going to cracker my soup."	"I'm going to dye my hair."
Child was putting beads in play dough.	"I think I'll bead it."	"I think I'll salt it."
Child wanted chocolate syrup in milk.	"Will you chocolate my milk?"	"Will you salt my eggs?"
Child was taking stocking from a fireplace (Bowerman, 1985).	"I will unhang it."	"I will untie it."

remains somewhat imperfect. Their speech is distinctive because it contains words never heard in the language of adults and older children (see Table 10.1).

ACQUIRING MORPHOLOGICAL RULES.

think about it

How do preschoolers go about creating new words? Do they do it randomly, out of thin air? Or do they have an organized approach?

Preschoolers actually are quite organized and systematic in coining new words, basing them on **morphological rules** that govern word formation. They refer to teeth as "tooths," to feet as "foots," and to mice as "mouses." They might say that something is the "funnest" thing they have ever done. Or they might say that they "runned" around outside or "teached" someone to do something.

Preschoolers learn the morphological rules that are applied to words in general, applying them incorrectly to words whose past tense or plural versions are formed differently, when they cannot recall the irregular forms. Irregular verbs, for example, have completely different present- and past-tense forms. In these cases, the ending *ed* is not attached to the root word (e.g., *run/ran, teach/taught, go/went*) to form the past tense of the verb. If a preschooler does not know or cannot remember at the moment the past tense of run, she draws upon her general knowledge of morphological rules. Because she has heard "walk" and "walked," "play" and "played," and "jump" and "jumped," she says "runned." Use of bound morphemes (i.e., -s and -ed) to form the plurals and past tenses of irregular nouns and verbs is called **overregularization.**

Interestingly, children first imitate the irregular forms they have heard (Fenson et al., 1994). But as children are exposed to more language, they begin to develop rules and then start to use these strategically, as cognitive theories would predict. When children cannot recall an irregular form, or if they have never heard the irregular form of a specific verb, they employ the "default decision"—the general rule rules. "Do what I usually do in these situations, given that I cannot recall that I should do something else instead in this particular case." A default decision results in an overregularization of the rules when a child applies them to an irregular noun or verb (Marcus et al., 1992).

THE INCIDENCE OF OVERREGULARIZATION.   Most children overregularize inflections for nouns and verbs only about 10 percent of the time (Fenson et al., 1994; Marcus et al., 1992). Even children who overregularize a lot compared to other children do so only about 25 percent of the time (Marcus et al., 1992). Thus children actually tend to "suppress overregularization, contrary to common belief" (Marcus et al., 1992, p. 35). We may tend to think that preschoolers overregularize more than they actually do, perhaps because unique words grab our attention. When children use standard forms, on the other hand, they blend in.

The Effect of Feedback on the Development of Children's Grammar
Kate's father did not correct her grammar directly when she said that she had "clayed" at school. Instead he used the correct form himself as he conversed with her. It is probably beneficial that he did not correct Kate's grammar directly because such effort is rarely effective, as the following examples illustrate:

Episode 1:

A child said, "My teacher holded the baby rabbits and we patted them."

I asked, "Did you say your teacher held the baby rabbits?"

She answered, "Yes."

I then asked, "What did you say she did?"

She answered, again, "She holded the baby rabbits and we patted them."

"Did you say she held them tightly?" I asked.

"No," she answered. "She holded them loosely."

(Gleason, 1967, cited in Cazden, 1972, pp. 4–5)

Episode 2:

Child: "Nobody don't like me."

McNeill: "No, say 'Nobody likes me.' "

Child: "Nobody don't like me." (eight repetitions of this dialogue)

McNeill: "No. Now listen carefully; say 'Nobody likes me.' "

Child: "Oh! Nobody don't likes me!"

(McNeill, 1966, p. 69)

Parents generally do not directly correct their young children's poor grammar (Brown & Hanlon, 1970). Soon after researchers made this discovery, researchers found that even though parents do not provide direct disapproval, they behave in ways that children might perceive as corrective. These researchers called implicit parental responses that might be perceived as corrective **negative evidence.**

Negative-evidence responses differ somewhat from responses to sentences that are error free (Bohannon & Stanowicz, 1988; Nelson, K. E., 1987, 1988). Rather than simply take a turn in a conversation after a child utters a poorly formed sentence, a parent may **recast** (reorganize) or expand it (add to it). If a child says, "There the doggy," the parent might recast it by saying, "There is the doggy." Or the parent might recast and expand the utterance by saying, "Oh, yes. There's the doggy over there by the tree." But if the child's utterance is well formed, the parent is more likely to move on with his or her turn ("Oh, yes. I see him").

But negative evidence may not be perceived as such by a child. For one thing, recasting and **expansions** are not distinctive. That is, they do not involve a unique kind of sentence or other language structures used only to provide negative evidence. Negative feedback is negative only by the nature of its place in the order of a conversation—*after* a child's ill-formed utterance. Some people doubt that children even notice negative evidence, or that they are able to compare their utterance with the improved one provided by the parent (Morgan et al., 1995).

Corrective feedback follows only about one-third of children's errors (Bohannon & Stanowicz, 1988). Some researchers have wondered whether negative feedback follows ill-formed utterances regularly enough to be of value to children. Other researchers say that this is not a problem because no matter what the area of learning, corrective feedback never follows children's errors 100 percent of the time (Bohannon et al., 1990).

The value of negative evidence has also been questioned because parents sometimes recast children's well-formed utterances, and sometimes even recast their own. How, then, could children interpret recasts that follow their ill-formed utterances as corrective if recasts also occur after well-formed sentences? These facts create problems for the hypothesis that negative evidence provides feedback for children about their grammatical errors (Bohannon, 1996; Morgan, J.L., 1996; Morgan et al., 1995).

But negative evidence provided by parents is associated with higher levels of language development (e.g., Farrar, 1990, 1992; Moerk, 1991; Robeson, 1995). How are we to explain the positive correlations between recastings and expansions and language development? Some researchers think that negative evidence is especially useful to the child because it provides an immediate contrast between the child's error and the correct form of the word. **Positive input**—correct instances of a word form used by parents in their own speech—also provides information about language to children. But positive input may not be noticed as much as contrasting utterances. Negative evidence—information about language *that follows a child's error*—provides language information contingently. Apparently, information provided contingently affects a child's language development more than the very same information provided in positive-input (i.e., noncontingent) situations (Saxton et al., 1998). Although parents do not follow children's errors with negative input every time they make an error, every occasion on which they do may provide a situation in which children are likely to notice a contrast between two different language forms (Saxton, 1997).

Creating Questions and Negative Sentences

When asking a question in English, the order of subject and verb are reversed from that used in declarative sentences. For example, we say, "Where <u>is she</u> going?" rather than "Where <u>she is</u> going?" Similarly, in creating negative sentences, children must figure out where to place *no* or *not* (e.g., "I won't go to the movies." "I do not like him.").

Children's first negative sentences often have the word *no* at the beginning: "No break." "No eat." "No go." In these instances, *no* is placed at the beginning of an utterance that lacks a subject. Even though children use subjects in declarative sentences (e.g., "I break it"), the additional challenge of dealing with negation could cause them to delete the subject. According to information-processing theory, children include only the parts of the sentence that are vital to communicating their message (Bloom, 1998). Later, as familiarity with this form of sentence increases, the information-processing load lessens, and children can add a subject to the utterance. Another hypothesis—the one favored by linguists rather than information-processing theorists—is that young children do not use subjects because they do not yet know that English grammar requires them. Not all languages do, and young English-learning children might think they also do not need subjects (Bloom, 1998).

No matter the reason, negative sentences soon change from the earliest kind that begin with "no" to another form that is illustrated by statements such as, "I no want go" or "I no like bed" or "I no eat." Eventually, at 3 to 4 years of age, children add and rearrange words within negative sentences. At this point, a child says, "I don't want to eat."

Children use negative sentences for three different purposes: (1) to express refusal ("No go bed"); (2) to indicate that something is all gone or doesn't exist ("No daddy"); or (3) to disagree with someone ("No cracker"). In the last case, a child may actually be trying to say "No, that's not a cookie—it's a cracker," in response to someone who has just said, "That's a cookie" (Bloom, 1970, 1998). Children use negative sentences to refuse and express nonexistence before they use negative sentences to disagree or deny. This order has been found not only in children who are learning English, but in children who are learning Japanese (Clancy, 1985; McNeill & McNeill, 1968).

When children first ask *wh-* questions, they say, "Where you go?" or "What it?" Somewhat later, children insert the auxiliary verb, but they put it in the wrong place, leaving it where they observe it in declarative sentences. Thus, children say, "What it is?" or "Where you are going?" Finally, children place the auxiliary verb properly: "Where are you going?" "What is it doing?"

Children formulate questions using *what, where,* and *who* before they ask questions involving *when* or *why.* This order is probably related to children's understanding of the world. *What, who,* and *where* are used in queries about objects, people, and their locations. Questions about *when* and *why* deal with time and causality that are more remote and harder for children to comprehend.

Discourse Development: Sticking to the Topic in a Conversation

The teacher is conducting a group meeting with 4-year-olds. On a tray she has various red objects: a toy car, a scarf, a pencil, a felt-tip marker, a paper bag, and a glove. She asks, "How are all of these objects alike?"

"You keep them in your room," one child offers.

"Well, yes, but not everyone has all of these items in his room. There's something else about them that makes them all alike. Something about how they look."

"They are red," another child offers.

"That's right! I had that in mind when I selected them. I wonder if you can think of other red things."

One child says an apple; another says cherry candy. A third child says a fire engine. Then Jill chimes in: "I got one for my birthday. It has a real siren, too, and you can wear the siren hat. But it doesn't work if the batteries are dead. My car has batteries but it doesn't have a siren."

"Wait a minute, Jill" the teacher says. "We're not talking about sirens right now, but about things that are red. Let's put our thinking caps on. Who has some more ideas?"

think about it

What happened in this situation? Why did Jill get off track? How did her teacher help her to get back on track? Should she have allowed her to change the topic of the conversation? Or should she have pulled it back to the original topic?

Preschoolers probably are capable of maintaining the topic of conversation more often than they actually do it. Perhaps their own interests push them in the direction of getting off the topic. Or perhaps parents are interested mostly in encouraging their children to talk and simply tolerate their tendency to stray from the topic. Teachers may tolerate it less than parents because they are trying to involve a whole group of children in a conversation, which is difficult if each child goes off on a tangent.

We discussed in chapter 6 how children can learn turn-taking during the first two years of life. By age 2, children do not overlap or interrupt the other speaker. But moving a conversation along still rests very much on the shoulders of the adult. Even though 3-year-olds contribute to a conversation, about half of their turns consist of comments that are not contingent—are unrelated to what has been said by their conversational partners (Bloom et al., 1976). Some of these noncontingent comments are deliberate topic changes—children know they are changing the topic—but others occur simply because children like Jill cannot maintain a topic very easily.

Children's first contingent comments are repetitions of a part of an adult comment, in question form (Bloom et al., 1975). For example, if a parent says, "I'm going to eat my cake," the child might say, "Eat your cake?" More sophisticated strategies for coordinating comments with the comments of a conversational partner appear over the course of the preschool years. But coordinating comments with the content of a conversation is not seen as frequently in young preschoolers as it is in older children and adults. Exactly how and why children get better at this is not completely clear. Experience in group discussions in preschool settings would seem to have an effect, though research on this question has not been conducted.

Tutoring on coherence and completeness when relating personal narratives also may help children learn to comment on topics that come up in discussions with others. For example, if a child tells about the accident that resulted in the bandage that appears on his knee, a teacher might ask, "Well, where did this happen, on the rocks at your house or at the park?" Research on parents' elicitations of personal narratives (i.e., stories about one's own past experiences) from their young children indicates that they ask for more information and help structure the retellings in chronological order (Burger & Miller, 1999; Hudson, 1993; Minami, 1996; Peterson & McCabe, 1992). Even though parents may not consistently demand that children be coherent in conversations, they often take steps consistent with their own cultural and language conventions to help their preschool children improve on completeness and coherence when relating personal episodes. This experience may help preschoolers learn to stick to a topic.

Preschoolers' somewhat limited cognitive ability, compared with that of older children and adults, probably constrains their capacity to maintain a topic of conversation skillfully. Background knowledge, including knowing what things are related, is required if one is to stay on a topic. Children must also be able to integrate information in rather sophisticated ways. Whatever the many skills involved, children gradually improve their skill in sticking to the topic of conversation as they proceed through the preschool and early school-age years (Hickman et al., 1996; Hobbs, 1990; Reichman, 1990).

Language Comprehension: What Preschoolers Can Understand

Children's understanding of words and sentences they hear improves dramatically during the preschool years. By about 18 months of age, the average toddler comprehends between 200 and 300 words (Fenson et al., 1994). By the end of the preschool period (age 6), children comprehend about 14,000 words.

Understanding Words

But during the preschool years, and even beyond, there are some words whose meanings are difficult for children to understand. What are these words? Why do they cause problems?

LOCATIVE EXPRESSIONS.   Words such as *in, on, under,* and *beside* provide information about the location of things. Young preschoolers are just beginning to learn the meaning of **locative expressions** as they are used in such phrases as "in the box," "on the sofa," and "beside the chair." Children interpret verbal instructions containing locatives differently, depending on which objects they see when the instructions are given. When children see any kind of container, they are inclined to place something in it, even when the instructions are to put the object *on* or *under* something. Preschoolers also interpret an instruction to mean *on* when the object they see has a supporting surface, even if they are told to place something *under* or *in* it (Clark, 1978).

Clark's study showed that children do not understand the meaning of any of these words until they are about 2½ years old. Before this time, they interpret these words in terms of what objects are available in the situation. When children begin to understand the actual meanings of these words, they learn *in* first, then *on* and *under.* Not until 4½ or 5 years of age do they begin to master *beside, between, in front of,* and *in back of* or *behind,* which they learn in this order (Johnston & Slobin, 1979).

Children may find it especially difficult to learn prepositions because there are no cues in the sentence to help them determine their specific meaning. For example, in the sentences, "Put the toy in the box," "Put the toy on the shelf," and "Put the toy under the table," each preposition occupies exactly the same slot in an identical sentence frame. The sentence context itself does not help a child figure out the meaning of one term in contrast to another. Children must observe the relationships in the environment to learn the specific meaning of each one. Because preschoolers often misinterpret linguistically based location information (e.g., they put an object *on* something when the direction was to put it *beside* something), their teachers often provide additional information by giving children a physical prompt about the relationship they are trying to specify.

UNDERSTANDING OPPOSITES SUCH AS MORE AND LESS.   Until about 3½ years of age, children do not understand that the word *more* refers to the greater of two amounts, although they have a better understanding of *more* with countable objects, such as pennies or blocks, than with substances whose individual parts are not counted (clay or sand) (Gathercole, 1985). By the age of 4½, children use *more* accurately with both countable items and mass quantities. That is, they indicate correctly which of two groups has more items, and which of two masses of clay is larger. By age 5, children use *more* when they mean greater in number—more items—and *bigger* when they mean greater in mass.

It takes children even longer to understand the word *less.* When asked which of two quantities is less, children sometimes point to the quantity that actually is more.

Perhaps they know only that both *less* and *more* refer to quantity. Thus, they use the terms interchangeably. Only later—at about age 4½—do they distinguish the two terms, using *more* to indicate the greater of two quantities and *less* to indicate the smaller. Preschoolers also confuse other words that indicate opposites (*hot/cold* and *bigger/smaller*), in the same way that they confuse *more* and *less*.

CONFUSIONS BETWEEN WORDS USED TO NAME OBJECTS WITH SIMILAR FEATURES OR FUNCTIONS.   Children (and adults) also find it difficult to sort out exactly which of two terms refers to very similar objects. The words *cup* and *glass* provide good examples. Three-year-olds use *glass* and *cup* almost interchangeably, regardless of whether the container is tall or short; has a handle or lacks one; is made of glass, ceramic, or plastic; or contains a cold or a hot drink (Nelson & Nelson, 1978). Five-year-olds pay attention to both physical features and contents in using these two words, but they are not as precise in their specifications of these matters as 10-year-olds.

Many words that exhibit fine distinctions in meaning must be learned through observation of several features as well as occasions of use. Words such as *pen* and *marker* are sometimes used interchangeably by preschoolers, or both are called by the name of the writing tool children use most frequently (often *markers,* these days). Because both tools are used for the same function, preschoolers do not seem to notice that the inks differ in each.

Understanding Sentences: Word Order   When we hear, "Kim hit the ball," we know that *Kim* is the subject and *ball* is the object of her action. Such sentences employ the *active* voice. We can convey the same meaning in a different way, by saying, "The ball was hit by Kim." When do children begin to understand the meaning of sentences of the second kind, those employing the *passive* voice?

The response of 2-year-old English-speaking children to passive verb constructions is correct only 50 percent of the time—they are guessing (Bever, 1970; de Villiers & de Villiers, 1973). Not until about 5 years of age do children finally understand the passive voice. But even at this age, the specific verbs used in the sentence influence children's comprehension. Mastery of verbs used in the active voice is secure with action verbs by about age 5. But when passive verb constructions are involved, mastery is not achieved until a few years later (Maratsos et al., 1979).

Sometimes, children younger than 5 years of age appear to understand some passive sentences, but in these cases only the passive interpretation makes sense. For example, children correctly interpret the sentence, "The baby was fed by her mother," because mothers feed babies; babies do not feed their mothers (Strohner & Nelson, 1974).

Although English-speaking children master the passive form fairly late, children learning other languages master it quite early. In some languages, whether a word is serving as subject or object is marked by grammatical morphemes rather than word order. Recall from our earlier discussion that grammatical morphemes are acquired early in the preschool period. It is not surprising, then, that young preschoolers can understand passive sentences when their language marks whether a noun is a subject or a direct object by using grammatical morphemes rather than position (Demuth, 1990).

Decontextualization and Comprehension

A group of preschool children, mostly 4-year-olds, is cutting grapes in half in preparation for squeezing to make grape juice. As the children and a student teacher cut the grapes open, they occasionally find seeds.

"Seeds make plants grow; that's what they are for, right?" the student teacher asks the children.

Sasha turns to the teacher and says, "Well, not *these* grapes. Seeds make new grape trees grow, and then you have to water them and make sure they have sun. These seeds didn't make these grapes grow, right?"

"Yes, that's right, Sasha," the student teacher confirms. "We get seeds from the old plant, and then we can grow new ones. In the case of grapes, we plant seeds and get new grape vines. And then we water the vines and maybe put fertilizer on them—that's sort of a plant food."

"Well," Sasha continues, "you don't even need to have seeds sometimes, because you can have a bulb. Or, sometimes, you just cut a plant and put it in water and it grows roots. Then you have a new plant that way, not even with a seed. I know because we did that once when you weren't here."

think about it

What accounted for Sasha's rather remarkable ability to think about the ambiguity in the student teacher's first statement that "Seeds make plants grow"? What made it possible for him to think about the two possible meanings (one correct and the other incorrect) of the student teacher's statement? Was he able to do this because of his previous experience in starting new plants and in nurturing the growth of sprouted seeds?

Background knowledge, like the knowledge of plants demonstrated by Sasha, helps children comprehend language in oral or written form. Children also gradually begin to use linguistic structure to understand what is being said. Snow (1991, p. 7) suggests that participating in discussions, telling someone about past experiences, and creating dramatic play scenarios may be especially beneficial for developing **decontextualized** language skills—skill in understanding language that describes something other than the "here and now." Sasha was discussing a situation about seeds that was not before him as he helped prepare grapes. This episode fits Snow's idea of a context that is not about the "here and now."

In the beginning, language comprehension is necessarily **context bound**—it is understood in terms of the extralinguistic context, not in terms of linguistic structures alone (Bates, 1979). (Think of our earlier discussion about how English-speaking children interpret passive sentences.) Language comprehension also depends at first on face-to-face contexts. If a child does not comprehend what someone says, the adult can say it again, say it in a different way, explain further, point to objects, demonstrate, and so on.

But over time children must become less dependent on immediate context and clarification from others in comprehending language, especially if they are to understand the language in books. Adults can help children to develop decontextualized language skills by engaging them in recounting immediate past experiences. Parents often begin to talk with their children about the immediate past when they are about 2 years old, even though parents must at first provide a lot of details to prompt a child's memory (Fivush et al., 1987; Miller & Sperry, 1988). The recountings produced are called personal or **autobiographical narratives** because they take the basic form of a story—settings are recalled, the people who were present are described, and events are related in chronological order.

Children's skill in recounting past experiences improves considerably over the course of the year between ages 2 and 3, and it continues to develop over the entire preschool period if children are provided with the relevant experiences (Peterson et al.,

Mealtime is a good time to talk with children about recent past experiences. This provides opportunities for them to use language to talk about something other than the immediate here and now.   (*Source:* © E. Crews/The Image Works)

1999). Both decontextualized language skills and knowledge of the basic structure found in many stories are related to later school achievement, especially to story comprehension (Dickinson, 1991; Reese, 1995; Snow & Dickinson, 1990).

Written Language Development

A teacher is reading Maurice Sendak's *Where the Wild Things Are* to 4-year-old Matt and Amy. When he gets to the pages with pictures but no print, and begins to comment about the Wild Things' claws, Matt says, "You can't read these—turn the pages to where the words start again."

"No!" Amy objects. "He has to read all of the pages."

"He can't read those pages," protests Matt. "They don't have any words on them!"

"Yes, he can!" Amy insists.

think about it

Amy thought there was no difference between pages with text and pictures and pages with pictures only. Or perhaps she had not even noticed the print. To her, a page with pictures but no print can be "read." Matt, on the other hand, thought that the text tells the story and is read, whereas the pictures illustrate or confirm the text. Is Amy's view of the situation typical of young preschoolers? Or is Matt's view of the world of reading more typical of children during the preschool years? How did Matt develop his more accurate view of the reading process? What experiences will help Amy progress to Matt's level of understanding?

Actually, preschoolers often think that adults read the pictures, not the print (Ferreiro & Teberosky, 1982). As children gain experience with books, they gradually come to understand that there is print on the pages and that the reader gets the meaning of the book from looking at the print.

Many people have thought that preschoolers are incapable of understanding very much about written language. But they actually understand quite a lot. After researchers made this discovery, the term **emergent literacy** replaced the term **reading readiness**. The latter term implied that children needed to learn many things *before* they could begin to read or write. The former term suggests that even very young children engage in "real" reading and writing activities (Teale & Sulzby, 1986).

In this section, we discuss emergent literacy in preschoolers. We also discuss the knowledge children must have if they are to make the transition from emergent to conventional reading.

Emergent Reading of Familiar Storybooks (Retellings)

As Jonathan, age 4, reads Eric Carle's *The Very Hungry Caterpillar* out loud to himself, he misses only a few of the words printed on the page. He mixes up the days of the week, saying "Tuesday" where the book says "Wednesday"; and he says "one *piece*" of watermelon, instead of "one *slice*." Jonathan even sounds as if he is reading a story. But how can Jonathan read this book if he cannot decode words?

Jonathan has heard this story many times, and the book is quite memorable because its text is highly **predictable**. Children's books are made memorable when they contain rhyme or many repetitions of sentence frames. For example, in this book, the following sentence repeats many times:

"On (＿＿＿＿＿＿), he ate (＿＿＿＿＿＿) (＿＿＿＿＿＿),
  day of the week   number of   name of fruit
but he was still hungry."

The illustrations on each page of predictable books also match everything that is mentioned in the text. When predictable books contain rhyming words these help to jog a child's memory about particular words that come next in sentences.

Given an unfamiliar book, Jonathan would not be able to read it. But he can retell this very familiar book. (A closer look at emergent or "pretend" reading, which gradually changes in form over the preschool years, is provided in Knowledge in Action: Education—Children's Strategies for Retelling Stories.)

Children's Strategies for Retelling Stories

At first, preschoolers retell familiar stories by looking at the pictures. The pictures prompt the child's recall of the story's text. Only gradually do preschoolers begin to pay attention to the print itself.

Pretend-Reading Strategies

Sulzby (1985) described the strategies children use to pretend-read storybooks before they actually pay attention to the print:

1. *Attending to pictures but not telling a story*
   The child "reads" by labeling and looking at the pictures in the book, but the child's speech is only about the picture in view. The child does not weave the pictures into any kind of a story.

2. *Attending to pictures and forming an oral story*
   The child looks at the pictures and weaves a story across pages but the wording and intonation resemble storytelling, not story reading.

3. *Attending to pictures and forming a written story*
   The child still "reads" by looking at the pictures but the child's wording and intonation sound consistently like reading. The child uses his or her own words to retell the written story, or repeats the actual story word for word, if it has been heard a number of times and especially if it has rhyming words and sentences that repeat.

Finally, the child begins to attend to the print, perhaps at first passing a finger under the print, as he or she has seen adult readers do. But the child does not try to map the retelling of the story to specific words.

Sometimes children do try to find specific words they already know how to read by sight. Several substages of following the print usually precede the final step of reading familiar books, which is called fingerpoint-reading. Once children are that far along, they can usually begin to read print in unfamiliar books, such as those designed for early or beginning readers. (See chapter 14, pp. 497–501.)

Accounting for the Shift in Attention from Pictures to Print

Educators have been particularly interested in what causes children to shift from picture-governed to print-governed strategies only because then are they actually reading, or learning to read, in a conventional sense.

In one study (Ehri & Sweet, 1991), an experimenter read a rhyming text many times to children, pointing to the words and also engaging the children in reading along in chorus. Children were also tested for alphabet recognition and to see if they could segment orally presented words into their phonemes.

After training and testing, children were asked to read the rhyming text themselves. The researchers were particularly interested in whether the children would simply repeat memorized text, without pointing to the print, or simply point globally to the print, without concern for finding specific words as they said them. Exact matching between words said and pointed-at words is called **fingerpoint-reading.** The researchers wondered how many of the children would reread the familiar text in this sophisticated way.

Over 70 percent of the children (who were between 4½ and 6 years of age) recited lines verbatim, and 44 percent pointed globally at the text. Twenty-three percent of the children fingerpoint-read the text.

This study illustrated how repeated readings of predictable storybooks help children pretend-read picture books verbatim, using pictures as prompts. It also clarified why so many children who learn familiar storybooks "by heart" never actually learn to read by doing so, whereas other children move into actual reading by using their storybook experience. The key is in the other skills that children possess. Children who fingerpoint-read the rhyming text recognized letters of the alphabet and could segment speech into phonemes.

It makes sense that alphabet letter recognition and phoneme segmentation skill are positively correlated with fingerpoint-reading, because the process goes something like this:

- Children listen to a story many times, until they can read it verbatim, using picture clues.
- Children segment the first phoneme of key words as they say them—"/D-/own in the /j-/ungle where the /r-/iver /r-/uns /b-/lue."
- Children use their letter name knowledge to map an alphabet letter to the phoneme they have isolated (Thompson et al., 1999; Treiman et al., 1998).
- Children use their knowledge of how alphabet letters look to locate the letter.
- Children find the word that begins with this letter and point to it as they say it, thus voice-point matching their oral recitation of each word with its printed version in the text.

What Preschool Teachers Can Do to Promote Fingerpoint Reading

- Parents and preschool teachers should read to children daily. Reading provides an opportunity for children to hear book language, to relate events in their own lives to events in the story, and to learn the story line.

Fingerpoint-reading a familiar storybook indicates that a child can segment words into phonemes, can associate various phonemes with an appropriate letter of the alphabet, and can recognize letters of the alphabet. (*Source:* © Will Faller)

Preschoolers enjoy hearing the same story read repeatedly, and they need opportunities to hear the same story.

- Predictable books should be among those adults read to children. **Predictable books** are easy to memorize because they contain repeating sentences, rhyming words, and relatively little print per page. Their illustrations also closely match the text.
- Parents and teachers should engage preschool children in language play by inviting them to think of words that rhyme with or start with the same sound as a target word (e.g., "What words can you think of that start with the same sound as *turtle*?" "What words can you think of that sound like—rhyme with—*cat*?"). This experience helps children become sensitive to similar sounds across words and may provide the foundation for phonemic segmentation and manipulation skill development.
- When parents and teachers sound words out when children ask for spellings, they illustrate to children that words are composed of individual sounds, and they demonstrate how words can be segmented into their individual phonemes.
- Parents and teachers can help children learn to discriminate among the alphabet letters and learn letter names. (See pp. 354-356 for a discussion about ways to accomplish this.)

Distinguishing Writing from Nonwriting

Recognizing writing and distinguishing it both from pictures and from other kinds of marks is one of the earliest literacy learnings. In a study (Lavine, 1977) designed to find out how English-speaking preschoolers recognize writing, children ranging from 3 to 6½ years of age were shown various combinations of letters, numbers, pictures, and doodles printed on cards. Children were asked to sort the cards into two piles, one for cards they thought had writing marks, and one for cards with marks they thought were not writing.

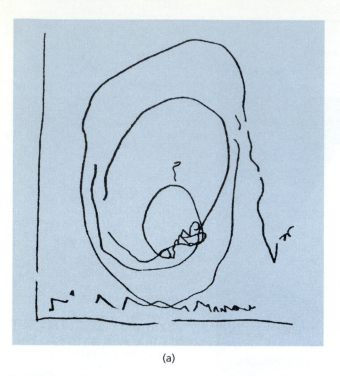

(a)   (b)

Drawings with scribble-writing. (a) A picture and the artist's signature (at bottom) produced by a 3-year-old (Harste, Burke, & Woodward 1981, 421). (b) Scribble-writing is tucked
under the lower right portion of this scribble drawing (Schickedanz, personal collection)

Even 3-year-olds who could not yet name letters or read words labeled as writing any display that had the general features of writing. Apparently, children first
identify writing in terms of the overall characteristic of linearity. This understanding
is reflected in children's early scribbles. A "picture" consists of many marks, running
in many directions all over the page. But the scribbles that serve as the child's signature or commentary about a picture are organized in lines, usually placed horizontally across the paper. (See Figure 10.1.)

Learning to Recognize Letters of the Alphabet

To appreciate the difficulty of this task, we need only examine a writing sample from
a language that uses an alphabet unfamiliar to us. Suddenly, the letters are indistin-
guishable—we do not know one from another. This task is not insurmountable, by
any means, but adults must understand why learning to distinguish among alphabet
letters is difficult for young children.

Distinctive Features Used in Alphabet Letters   Children learn to distinguish one letter from another by gradually differentiating various **distinctive features.**
Distinctive features are the characteristics of a set of similar things (such as our al-

phabet) that make that set different from other sets (such as the Greek alphabet). Specific features from the set are combined in different ways within the set to create individual units (in this case, the letters) that differ from each other, sometimes only minimally.

The distinctive features of the English alphabet include straight or curved lines; open or closed curves; and diagonal, horizontal, and vertical lines (Gibson, 1969). Some letters are closed (*D, O*), but others are open (*C, L*); some letters have curved lines (*C, S, O*), but others have straight lines (*L, E, T*); and some straight-line letters contain diagonal lines (*K, N, M*), but others do not (*L, E, T*).

When children are first exposed to letters of the alphabet, they often consider letters to be "the same" if they share many distinctive features. For example, if children are given two sets of letters with instructions to put letters together that are the same, they put *D* and *O* together because both letters are closed figures containing curved lines. They also tend to confuse *E* and *F* because both are made from straight horizontal and vertical lines. *M* and *N* might also be viewed as the same because both are made from straight diagonal and vertical lines. Children also tend to confuse *M* and *W* because these letters differ only in terms of **spatial orientation**—their position in space. The letters *b* and *d* are often reversed. Letter **reversals** are a type of spatial orientation error. Preschoolers can have considerable difficulty coming to appreciate this feature.

Why do children find the distinctive feature of orientation in space so hard to detect? It contradicts all their previous experience with three-dimensional objects. To understand the child's problem, imagine that you are going to a cupboard to get two identical coffee mugs. There are four mugs on the shelf (see Figure 10.2): (1) a tall brown plastic mug sitting upside down with its handle to the left; (2) a short brown ceramic mug sitting upright with its handle to the right; (3) a second tall brown plastic mug sitting upright with its handle to the right; and (4) a second short brown ceramic mug sitting upside down with its handle to the left. Chances are you would pair mugs 1 and 3 or mugs 2 and 4, completely ignoring whether the mugs were upside down or had their handles turned to the left or the right.

This example shows that orientation is not a distinctive feature for three-dimensional objects. The print context is just about the only one where children encounter objects whose identities change when their orientation in space changes. Nearly the only example in the three-dimensional world is a floor, a wall, and a ceiling. But these surfaces would be confusing only in an empty house. In a completed and furnished house, distinctive features are provided by furniture and rugs (floors); pictures, light switches, and various openings, such as windows and doors (walls); and light fixtures (ceilings). When children first begin to look at print, all their previous experience

1   2   3   4

Which two cups would you pick as "identical"?

FIGURE 10.2

The challenges of orientation. Which two cups would you consider "identical"?

involves objects. Although they see that some letters are reversed versions of others, they assume that this difference does not matter, just as it does not matter in the case of three-dimensional objects.

Learning to Attend to Letter Differences   To distinguish one letter from another, children must pay attention not to what letters have in common, but to what makes them different. Typically, we make the world more manageable by lumping similar things together and making sense of them as members of a group. As we saw in chapter 5, a lot of learning requires that we form categories of things that are similar. Even infants are very good at doing this.

When children first see alphabet letters, they note similarities and ignore differences, which leads them to group together letters that are different. They behave just as we might in considering all utensils with tines and a handle to be forks, regardless of whether they have three tines or five, or long ones or short ones. Children must actively compare letters in order to notice (1) that they differ from one another, and (2) exactly how they differ (Gibson, 1979; Schickedanz, 1998). Alphabet puzzles in which each letter must be fitted into a space cut in its shape lead preschoolers to make such comparisons. Teacher-made letter-matching games also can help. Teachers should place easily confusable letters together on the same board because this helps children notice differences between letters that they tend to confuse. (A background board has the letters printed on it. Matching letters are printed on small tiles that can be placed beside the letters on the matching board.)

Discovering How to Make Words with Alphabet Letters

Even after children know the names of many alphabet letters, they still must solve the puzzle of how letters are combined to make words. Even though children may know the names of letters, they often do not know how letters function in writing. Very young children observe that strings of letters are used to make words, but they do not understand that the sequence of a letter string is determined, in large part, by the sequence of sounds in the oral version of the word. English **orthography**—the spelling system—codes speech at the phoneme level much of the time. Of course, it does not always code phonetically. For example, the word *helped* is spelled with *d* at the end rather than *t*. Sometimes, a word's spelling is related to meaning rather than sounds. For example, *helped, played, hammered,* and *walked* are all past-tense forms of verbs. English orthographic rules require that we ignore the fact that these words sound different at the end (*helped* and *walked* end with /t/, whereas *played* and *hammered* end with /d/), so that similarities in their meanings (all indicate that actions have been done) can be directly observed.

There are other irregularities in English spelling as well, although the relationship between sounds and letters is consistent enough that children (and adults) can use letter-sound associations to produce a sound approximation of many words. The understanding that, much of the time, alphabet letters function to code individual phonemes is known as the **alphabetic principle.** With this basic insight, children can get started with reading and writing. The complications of spelling are gradually worked out as children learn to read, write, and spell. Among other things, children learn that pairs of letters are often used to code some phonemes. The sound coded by *t* and *h* in the word *the* and the sounds coded by both the pair *c* and *h* and the pair *c* and *k* in the word *chicken* are good examples. (See chapter 14 for more information about children's early spellings.)

Levels of Speech Coded by Characters

In Chinese, each character represents an idea or word. Children learning to write Chinese must memorize thousands of different characters (Taylor, 1981). In Japanese writing, characters represent syllables. Coding syllables rather than whole words or ideas certainly reduces the number of characters needed, because a single syllable can appear in many different words. But even fewer characters are needed in writing systems that use an alphabet. In English or Spanish or French, for example, just a few characters are used to represent a small set of phonemes. This small set of characters is then combined in many different ways to create all the words in the language (Taylor, 1981). Although quite efficient, an alphabet is very abstract, which makes learning to read and write rather difficult (Treiman, 1993).

Children's Assumptions about How Characters Code Language

Children reveal how they think alphabet letters work as they try to write. At first, children's writing indicates that they have no idea that English is coded at the phoneme level (more or less). Gradually, children begin to understand that sound-symbol relationships dictate letter selection and organization in written words. (For a discussion of this topic, see Knowledge in Action: Education—How Children Create Written Words.)

This 4-year-old is writing his name on the picture he has drawn. Trying to account for why these particular letters are used to spell his name is likely to help this child learn that graphemes—letters and letter pairs—represent sounds in words. (*Source:* © D. Young-Wolff/Photo Edit)

EDUCATION

How Children Create Written Words

Most 6- or 7-year-olds know that many English words are made by selecting and ordering alphabet letters to represent the sounds heard as words are spoken. Before children arrive at this insight, they entertain other ideas about how words are formed (Ferreiro & Teberosky, 1982; Levin & Korat, 1993; Lundberg & Torneus, 1978; Schickedanz, 1990).

Children's Word-Creation Strategies

Physical Relationship Strategy (Semantic Strategy)
At first young children relate the number and appearance of marks to some physical aspect or property of the object or person the word represents. For example, a 3-year-old might use three marks to write her own name, but five marks to write her father's name, explaining, "He's bigger." (Lundberg & Torneus, 1978)

Visual Design Strategy
A child who uses this strategy assumes that each word has its own "design." Children try to copy words, such as their own name and the names of friends or family members. Because children do not yet appreciate that a small set of letters is used to make all words, they often claim that any word beginning with the same letter as their name *is* their name.

Syllabic Strategy
Children who use a syllabic strategy notice a relationship between the oral and written versions of words, but they break spoken words apart into their major beats or syllables. Children use one mark to represent each syllable. Because the same letters reappear in different "words" written by children using this syllabic strategy, it is clear that children understand that a small set of letters can be used to form many, many words. They have yet to learn, however, how to think of spoken words in terms of individual sounds—phonemes—rather than in terms of syllables.

Visual Rule Strategy
Children group letters in ways that look like actual words. They are guided by several rules: (1) do not use too many or too few letters; (2) use a variety of letters (no more than two of the same letter in succession); and (3) rearrange the same letters to make different words. See Figure 10.3. Children who experiment with making words in this way often ask adults what words they have made. Typically, children's letter strings do not form actual words, although children sometimes get lucky.

Authority-Based Strategy
This strategy often follows on the heels of the visual rule strategy, probably because children discover that letter strings rarely form an actual word. Thus, children become somewhat discouraged about the prospects of creating actual words by using visual rules as a guide. It might be more productive to ask adults for spellings or to copy words from signs or food cartons, or from titles of their favorite storybooks.

(a) (b)

FIGURE 10.3

The two children who wrote these mock words honor visual rules when making words. They do not use too many or too few letters, they do not use the same letter more than twice in succession, and they reorder the same letters to make different words. But neither child's "words," when sounded out, resemble actual words, because letters are not selected to match the series of phonemes found in an actual word.

Early Phonemic Strategy

Children segment words into their individual phonemes and code these sounds, in sequence, with alphabet letters. Knowledge of letter names gives children information about letter-sound associations, because letter names contain a sound that the letter is used to represent (Treiman et al., 1996). If wishing to write *cake,* the child is very likely to write *kk* or *kak* because, in saying this word, the child hears the sounds that he or she hears when naming the letters *K* and *A*. Because these spellings are not conventional, they are called **invented spellings** (Figure 10.4).

Transitional Phonemic Strategy

Using visual information, children judge that their invented spellings do not look right. This dissatisfaction is often seen in older kindergarten and first-grade children who are beginning to read, and in preschoolers who learn to read early.

Integrated/Conventional Spelling Strategies

Children begin to combine knowledge of permissible letter sequences found in standard spellings with sound-based spelling strategies. They learn many common words by sight and also learn word endings, such as *-ed* and *-ing.*

Development of Children's Word-Creation Strategies

The shift away from thinking that words must in some way represent physically the objects they represent probably occurs after children encounter several instances in which someone reads to them a short printed word whose meaning is a large object or a long printed word whose meaning is a small object. These violations of expectations prompt children to question their initial hypothesis and replace it with a new one (Schickedanz, 1990; Treiman et al., 1996).

A child's shift from the syllabic strategy to the visual rule strategy might depend on seeing considerable print in the environment. Words coded syllabically are shorter on average than most words the child sees in the environment. Thus, these short words may not look right to the child. Children also see specific words spelled in full that contradict their own syllabic versions of them. For example, children see their own names written with many more letters than would be required simply to record a mark for each syllable or "beat." The shift from the visual rule to an authority-based strategy might depend on the availability of an adult, first, to respond to questions about letter strings, and second, to answer spelling questions. A child who receives feedback indicating that most of his letter strings are not words is likely in time to give up on this strategy.

Making the shift from an authority-based strategy to an independent, phonemic-based strategy may depend on how adults answer children's spelling questions. If they segment phonemes—sound out the words—that children ask them to spell, children would gain information about the sound-based nature of spelling. But if an adult simply dictates a list of letters or writes down words for children to copy when requested, they may not gain information that is necessary for them to create phonemic-based spellings.

Thus, shifts from one strategy to the next seem to "occur because of active comparisons that the child engages in" (Clay, 1983, p. 263). Adults are involved in getting children to make these comparisons. In sum, "development seems to depend on a series of adult-child transactions that take place within a print-rich environment" (Schickedanz, 1990, p. 12).

Source: Adapted from "The Place of Specific Skills in Preschool and Kindergarten" by J. Schickedanz, 1989. In D. S. Strickland and L. M. Morrow (Eds.), *Emerging Literacy* (p. 103). Newark, DE: International Reading Association.

Grappling with the Graphics: Learning to Produce Writing

Apart from learning what level of speech is represented by alphabet letters, children must learn how to form the alphabet letters and arrange print on a piece of paper. Young preschoolers usually cannot create conventional alphabet letters, but they do play with writing, and they learn to create approximations to alphabet letters if they have access to paper and marking tools. Remarkably, preschoolers' early writing captures many aspects of print conventions, though not all of them. Slowly the preschool child moves toward greater conventionality in his or her writing. In this section, we discuss some of the progress that preschoolers make.

From Scribble Marks to Alphabet Letters   Many children first represent a message with **scribble-writing**—chains of zigzags or loops placed horizontally

FIGURE 10.4

Examples of invented spellings.

across a page. Children's early writing also includes mock letters. **Mock letters** resemble actual alphabet letters and indeed would make good candidates for a 27th or 28th letter of our alphabet, should we ever need one. Examples of both scribble-writing and mock letters are shown in Figure 10.5.

Children often mix scribble-writing, mock letters, and conventional letters as they learn to write, using one, then another, then the first again (Clay, 1987; Schickedanz, 1990). Many children who can form the alphabet letters quite well turn to scribble-writing in certain situations, such as when creating a very long story. Temporarily reverting to an earlier, more comfortable strategy—in this case, scribble-writing—is common in childhood. We see the same thing when beginning walkers drop to their hands and knees to crawl when they want to get somewhere in a hurry. We also see it when first- and second-graders spell words. They use a variety of strategies, and the number at their disposal increases with age. That is, new strategies often overlap old ones for a time, rather than immediately replace a previous one, as is suggested in views that consider development to proceed in distinct stages that are qualitatively different from each other (Rittle-Johnson & Siegler, 1999). In a non-stage view of strat-

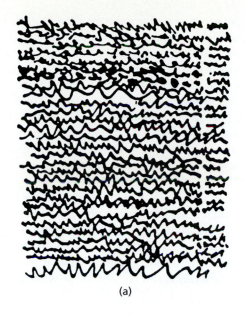
(a)

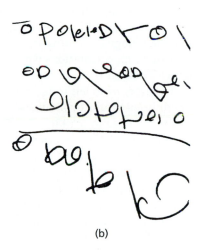
(b)

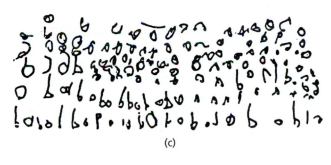
(c)

(d)

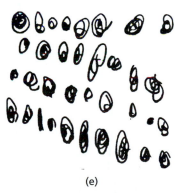
(e)

FIGURE 10.5

Examples of preconventional writing:
(a) continuous scribble-writing;
(b and c) mock letters;
(d) conventional letters with a few mock letters intermingled;
(e) individual scribble marks.

egy development, a number of strategies are available, and their number increases over time. The strategy chosen on a specific occasion depends on variables such as how much processing of new information is required in the situation. Gradually, as the child's skills improve and new tasks are better accomplished by a new strategy rather than an old one, old strategies may disappear and be completely replaced by new ones.

Learning Print Conventions: How Words Are Organized on a Page

Children must also learn how print is organized on a page. Does it go from right to left, from left to right, or both, sweeping back and forth on alternate lines like a computer printer? And how is the page filled vertically? From top to bottom or from bottom to top?

FIGURE 10.6

Examples of preconventional writing by a 5-year-old. His messages are
(a) "I love you, Mommy, I love you forever";
(b) "Dear Badgie, I miss you. Love, Adam";
(c) "Dear Bullfrogs, Hi. I think I can visit at Beaver Camp." In the last message he ran out of room, when he finished up on the other side of the paper with mirror writing. (Numbers in illustrations indicate the order in which lines were created.)

Although there is no universally right way to arrange print on a page, each language has a convention. Some languages, such as Hebrew, are written from right to left; others, such as Chinese, are written in columns, from top to bottom. Still others, such as English, use a left-to-right, top-to-bottom organization.

Preschool children's writing often appears quite disorganized because they violate their language's convention about how print is to be placed on a page. Preschoolers often mix orientations when writing, perhaps writing the first few letters of their name from left to right across the top of a page, and then turning the page to write more letters from left to right across what had been the bottom of the page. Because the finished product contains writing in several different orientations, the reader must rotate the page to read it.

Children who mix orientations this way often lack a spatial concept that Piaget (1967) called **projective space**. As we discussed in chapter 9, a person who conceptualizes space projectively knows that there are different points of view, and the person can adopt a view and stick with it. Children who mix points of view in the same writing sample often do not know that there are specific points of view or that their writing contains inconsistencies. Mixed orientations can be seen in the writing samples in Figures 10.6 and 10.7.

When preschoolers reverse the typical, left-to-right direction of writing and work from right to left, they often reverse the orientation of the alphabet letters as well, although not all letters in a line are reversed (Figure 10.6). Exactly why children tend to reverse letters when writing in the wrong direction has not been explained by researchers so far. A good example of the *mirror writing* children produce when they write in the wrong direction and reverse each and every letter is shown in Figure 10.7.

Even if children can adopt a point of view and stay with it consistently, they still must learn that specific conventions are correct in the English language. One 5-year-old who invited an adult to write a book with him asked if they could write from left to right so they would not be "confusing to each other." This child realized that internal consistency was a good idea. He thought the organization of writing on the page was something to be decided each time a person sits down to write, perhaps because many children in his kindergarten could also write in Hebrew, which is placed from right to left.

Another print convention marks where one word ends and the next begins. Dots, slashes, hyphens, and specific letters have all been used in various languages to indicate word endings. In English, words are separated by space. Preschoolers, kindergartners, and even young first-graders sometimes string their words together without leaving spaces between words (Figure 10.6). With help from adults who point out the conventions, children learn to separate words. Sometimes adults say, "This is hard to read. I don't know where one word stops and the next word begins. Show me. Try to leave a little space between them the next time, to make it easier. Okay?"

FIGURE 10.7

Mirror writing. This writing is common among preschoolers and shouldn't be taken as a sign that a child has a learning disability. Children who write this way simply haven't acquired a strong sense of where to begin or which way to go when they start to write.

Variations in Language and Literacy Learning during the Preschool Years

As we have seen, preschoolers can make great strides in learning about oral and written language. Children who have a variety of experiences as well as adults who interact and talk with them have a decided advantage over children whose experiences are less stimulating. Children who enter school with less well-developed oral language and few beginning literacy understandings have more difficulty learning to read and typically fall farther and farther behind their peers with each passing year (Juel, 1988; Walker et al., 1994). A person *can* be taught to read at any age. But because schools have an age-grade curriculum, a child who enters school having had few literacy experiences, and thus few literacy skills, has great difficulty ever catching up (Whitehurst & Lonigan, 1998). This is why parents, teachers, and policy makers have been particularly interested providing experiences that support literacy development during the preschool years.

These kindergarten children are using print props in their play store. Young children's interactions with print can be increased if print props are included in their play. These children might also make sales signs, indicating the prices of various items available in their store. (*Source:* © D. Young Wolff/Photo Edit)

Studies of Low-Income Preschoolers' Language and Literacy Knowledge

Many low-income children are far behind their more advantaged middle-class peers in language and literacy development when they enter kindergarten. In one study (Whitehurst, 1997), children from Head Start programs scored on various language and literacy measures at about the 17th percentile. There was a great deal of variability among the children—scores ranged from the 1st percentile to the 97th! The Head Start children made substantial gains during their kindergarten year, but their scores, on average, were still only at about the 27th percentile. In this study, the knowledge that separated the more competent children from children who were less competent was made up of two components: (1) vocabulary size and knowing that print in books represents words; and (2) basic phonemic sensitivity (i.e., judging whether two words sound the same or not the same).

In a second study (Robinson & Dixon, 1992), researchers compared middle-class children attending preschool with low-income children attending Head Start programs. Although there was a group storytime in all of the preschool classrooms, none of the classroom environments was particularly print rich, none planned any activities to engage children in using print, and none incorporated print props (e.g., menus, supermarket sale bills, food coupons, telephone message pads, empty food cartons, etc.) in dramatic play settings.

All groups of children were assessed in the fall and the spring of the year on letter names; invented spelling (i.e., sounding words out and coding them with alphabet letters); recognition of environmental print (e.g., a stop sign, popular fast-food restaurant logos, etc.); judgments of whether a string of letters on a card was "a word" or "not a word" (similar to Lavine's study); and literacy object functions ("What is this?" asked about a telephone book, a store receipt, etc.).

The middle-class children scored significantly higher than the Head Start children in the fall assessment on most measures, but not on invented spelling and identifying words in isolation (i.e., printed on cards). Both the low-income Head Start children and the middle-income children did well on environmental print tasks.

In the spring assessment, the middle-class children scored significantly higher than the Head Start children on the invented spelling task, which indicated that their phonemic awareness had developed during the year. Moreover, the gap between the low-income children and their middle-class peers had widened on other measures that had shown a difference in performance in the fall testing. In the fall testing, 25 percent of the scores in the top quartile had been earned by the low-income children. By spring, only 7 percent of the scores were earned by children in the low-income group. Thus, many low-income children had lost ground with respect to many of their middle-class peers, even before they entered kindergarten.

Even though preschool programs for low-income children distinguish low-income children who attend them from low-income children who do not, they often fail to boost low-income children's learning to the level of their more advantaged peers. One solution is to increase the activities related to language and literacy that are provided in programs such as Head Start.

Recall, for example, that Robinson and Dixon found fairly meager support for print-related learning in both middle-class and low-income preschool programs. This finding suggests that middle-class children obtained their increased knowledge from activities that took place at home or elsewhere, *outside* of the preschool classroom setting. The Head Start children, whose eligibility for the program was based on the low-income status of their family, apparently had fewer opportunities to obtain literacy knowledge and skills at home. Their parents would be less able than middle-income parents to buy books and educational games, and the stress of managing obstacles in everyday life reduces the time they can spend focusing on educational activities for their children. Preschool education programs can provide experiences that may not be plentiful in children's homes.

What Preschool Teachers Can Do
Preschool teachers can provide a number of activities to help facilitate language and literacy development in preschool children. Chief among these activities are: (1) talking to children as they play; (2) reading stories to and talking with children about them; (3) singing songs and reciting poems that include rhyming words and words that begin with the same sound; (4) exposing children to alphabet letters through puzzles and such things as play with magnetic letters; (5) providing paper and writing tools with which children can play; (6) incorporating literacy-related materials as props for children's dramatic play (food coupons, pads of paper beside the play telephone, etc.); and (7) playing language-related games, such as the one provided by the song *Willoughby-Wallaby-Woo*.

In all of these activities, adult interaction is the key to children's learning. As we have seen, children can pick up new words simply from hearing stories read, but they learn considerably more words if adults define words briefly, immediately after the words are encountered in the text. Children's comprehension of stories they hear also improves when the adult discusses the book with the children while going back through it again after an initial reading.

Other interactions can include responding to children's requests for various kinds of help when children draw and write using available paper and writing tools. When children ask teachers to show them how to write their names, teachers can name the letters they use and can relate the letters to the oral version of the child's name: "Let's see. Michael . . . /m/m/m/m/m . . . we need an *M* at the beginning." Then "Mi /i/i/i/ . . . we need an *I* next," and so on. Teachers also can describe their actions as they form the letters.

Children's names can be used to label their coat hooks and any personal spaces set aside for children's paintings and drawings. Helpers' charts (for snack, watering plants, feeding fish, etc.) can be made, and the children's names posted on them can be changed each day.

At snacktime or lunchtime, children can be engaged in conversation about how they made something or what they played with during the earlier part of the day. It also is appropriate, at times, to engage children in language games, such as "I'm thinking of . . . " Teachers can use clues that describe physical features of objects ("I'm thinking of something that we eat. It is a fruit and it is crunchy. Sometimes it is red and sometimes it is green or yellow. It grows on trees, but it is not an apple"). Teachers also can include as clues phonological features of the object's name ("Its name starts with /p/").

Teachers can use rich, descriptive language when they talk with children, and they can talk with children after reading to them. When supervising children as they play with blocks or water table items or various art materials, teachers can comment about what children are doing and ask children to tell them about their buildings or pictures. Teachers also have many opportunities to give children directions. Responding to directions requires attentive listening and experience in holding in mind one or more things at a time.

Parent Programs Can Help   Some preschool programs help parents learn to read stories effectively to their children and encourage them to increase the number of books available in their homes (Edwards, 1989; McCormick & Mason, 1989). Other programs help parents improve their own reading skills and learn how to share books with their children (Lonigan & Whitehurst, 1998; Paratore, 1991). These efforts help preschool children become more successful in reading and writing when they go to elementary school. In one meta-analysis, about 8 percent of the variance among children in language growth, emergent literacy skills, and actual reading achievement was attributed to parental book reading (Bus et al., 1995).

Many libraries also support parent-child story reading by providing story hours and by helping parents select books to check out and take home. *Sesame Street* and other television programs also include many literacy-related episodes, such as those in which a character writes a message or creates a sign or reads one. Parents can be encouraged to watch along with their children. This enhances the child's learning.

The Importance of Variety and Balance in Literacy Experiences in the Preschool and at Home

Both language and literacy learning involve many different skills. Sometimes preschool teachers and parents focus too narrowly on one aspect of language or literacy learning and neglect others, or one kind of educational material is used to the exclusion of others. For example, even though predictable books foster pretend-reading better than unpredictable books and also provide a high concentration of rhyming words (which enhances children's phonological development), they may not be as effective as nonpredictable books for exposing children to new words and complex sentence structures (Dickinson & Smith, 1994). Wise teachers use both types of books.

Similarly, balance must be kept in mind when thinking about helping young children acquire print-related knowledge. Children cannot learn to read until they have acquired some specific print-related knowledge, including knowledge of alphabet letters and letter-sound associations (Crain-Thoreson & Dale, 1992). But reading achievement after the first few primary grades depends on oral language skills. In other words, no child can learn to read without some technical knowledge about how the writing system works. After these basic technical skills are in place, however, reading level is influenced more by vocabulary size and other aspects of the child's oral language (Snow, 1991).

It is shortsighted to focus on specific print-related skills during the preschool years while ignoring broader experiences that develop oral vocabulary, background knowledge, and facility in understanding complex sentences, such as those found in good children's stories. At the same time, it is foolish to focus only on oral language learning during the preschool years when children's success in *learning* to read requires some technical skill and print-related knowledge (Meyer, et al., 1994). Variety and balance should be provided in literacy programs for young children (Snow et al., 1998).

KEY POINTS

Oral Language Development

■ Oral vocabulary increases at the rate of eight or nine words a day during the preschool years if word meanings are acquired through incidental learning from conversations with parents, listening to storybooks, and watching children's television programs. Preschoolers seem able to learn new words with only a few exposures.

■ Children seem to be aided by sentence structure in learning word meanings.

■ Words are learned best from storybooks when the adult reader defines the word in context and engages the child in discussions about the story after reading it.

■ Children become increasingly sensitive to phonological aspects of language during the preschool years. The highest level of phonological sensitivity involves the ability to isolate phonemes within words. High levels of phonological development are related to better progress in learning to read.

■ Preschoolers' speech is no longer telegraphic. Their sentences are longer and more complete than those of toddlers.

■ Children acquire grammatical morphemes early in the preschool period. Preschoolers overregularize morphological rules governing how words are changed to their plural or past-tense forms if they cannot retrieve an irregular word from memory. This is why children sometimes produce the ingenious usages for which they are famous.

■ Children learn grammar as they are exposed to language. Parents' recastings and expansions of children's utterances may not be perceived by children as corrective, but they do provide children with alternative ways of saying things.

■ Preschoolers gradually learn how to formulate questions and negative sentences.

■ Young preschoolers have difficulty sticking to a topic in a conversation. Older preschoolers are better at sticking to a topic, perhaps because they have been tutored in how to be coherent and thorough when they talk about past experiences.

■ The locative expressions *in, on,* and *under* emerge at about age 2½, but *beside, between, front,* and *back* are not understood until age 4½ or 5.

■ It takes children many years to acquire some word meanings.

■ An understanding of passive verb construction in sentences is not attained by English-speaking children until about age 5. Children learning other languages understand sentences in the passive voice earlier because the subject of a sentence is marked by grammatical morphemes rather than by word order alone.

■ Preschoolers often use context to figure out what is said to them. Listening to stories and talking with others about past events can help children become more skilled in understanding decontextualized language.

Written Language Development

■ The term *emergent literacy* has replaced the term *reading readiness* to describe all the literacy activities in which children engage before becoming conventional readers and writers.

- At first children refer to pictures when they pretend-read familiar stories; later they realize that reading involves looking at the print.

- Fingerpoint-reading of familiar storybooks occurs only if children have specific skills, including letter name knowledge, letter-sound association knowledge, and the ability to segment words into phonemes.

- Children as young as 3 years of age recognize general features of writing and can distinguish writing from nonwriting using the feature of linearity.

- To figure out how English print works, children must learn that letters of the alphabet code phonemes rather than whole words or syllables.

- Recognizing letters of the alphabet requires children to differentiate distinctive features. One of the hardest features for children to understand is orientation in space, a difficulty that accounts for the confusions about *M* and *W*.

- Scribble-writing, mock letters, mixed orientations, and lack of space between words are seen frequently in young children's writing.

- Group differences in the levels of language and literacy development between low-income and middle-income children seem to be related to variations in language and literacy experiences.

- Parents and preschool teachers can support literacy development with the many reading and writing activities offered both at home and in the classroom. It is important to include a wide variety of experiences, because both oral language and literacy involve a multitude of different skills and understandings.

GLOSSARY

alphabetic principle: the understanding that alphabet letters represent the sound of oral language at the phoneme level (p. 356)

autobiographical narratives: recollections of personal experiences told in a storylike format (p. 349)

bound morphemes: one letter or a group of letters attached to a longer morpheme to change its meaning (p. 341)

comprehender: a label given to adults who stress comprehension of the story as they read books and discuss them with young children (p. 337)

context-bound language: language about the "here and now" shared by speakers who are face to face (p. 349)

decontextualized language: language that cannot be understood in terms of the "here and now" situation or by seeking clarifications from someone with whom we are face to face; language related to a different context (p. 349)

describer: a label given to adults who focus explicitly on teaching new words to children as they read stories to them (p. 337)

distinctive features: characteristics of a set of things that can be combined in different ways to form distinct members of the set (p. 354)

emergent literacy: a description for the early period of literacy learning when children read and write using nonconventional strategies (p. 351)

expansion: a response to a child's utterance in which new information is added to what the child said (p. 344)

fast mapping: the name given to the process in which word meanings are learned through one or a few exposures (p. 335)

fingerpoint-reading: perfect matching of words said while reading their printed versions in the text (p. 352)

invented spellings: spellings derived by isolating phonemes in words children say and using alphabet letters to record what they hear, without regard to some of the conventions used in standard spellings (p. 359)

locative expressions: words indicating the spatial position of objects or persons (p. 347)

mock letters: graphic forms that are not alphabet letters, even though their parts are selected from the set of distinctive features used to make alphabet letters (p. 360)

morphological rules: rules governing word formation (p. 342)

negative evidence: the terms used to refer to recasts of children's ill-formed utterances (p. 343)

orthography: the rules for spelling words in a writing system (p. 356)

overregularization: the extension of morphological rules to form plurals and tenses using unbound morphemes for words that take irregular forms (p. 342)

performance style: a style of reading to children in which the story is read through without discussion and then discussed extensively afterward, often by going back through the book (p. 337)

phoneme: an individual speech-sound category (p. 340)

phoneme segmentation: the ability to isolate, one by one, the phonemes that make up a word (p. 340)

phoneme substitution: replacing a phoneme in a word with a new one (p. 339)

phonological awareness: ability to focus on the sounds of language, such as syllable segments or rhyming words, rather than on meaning (p. 339)

positive input: the correct language usage children hear their parents employ, though not as an immediate follow-up to the child's grammatical error (p. 344)

predictable books: books whose texts are easy to recall because they contain rhyming words, repeated sentence frames, and clear text-illustration correspondences (p. 353)

projective space: a framework for thinking about space that includes an understanding of different perspectives (p. 362)

reading readiness: a description of the early period of literacy learning used by those who think that children cannot read and write at all until prerequisite knowledge is in place (p. 351)

recast: responding to a child's utterance by reorganizing the child's original statement or using correctly a word the child misused (p. 343)

reversals: writing alphabet letters backwards (p. 355)

rhyme detection: the ability to match words heard to target words provided, when only some actually rhyme with the traget (p. 340)

rhyme generation: the ability to think of words that rhyme with a target word (p. 340)

scribble-writing: looped and curved marks arranged horizontally across a page (p. 359)

spatial orientation: the position of letters in space (p. 355)

syntactic bootstrapping: use of sentence structure knowledge to help determine the meanings of new words (p. 335)

unbound morphemes: morphemes which can stand alone, such as whole words (p. 341)

SUGGESTIONS FOR FURTHER READING

Clay, M. (1987). *Writing begins at home.* Portsmouth, NH: Heinemann. This short book is full of samples of preschoolers' writing. It's an excellent introduction for anyone unfamiliar with young children's writing.

Gleason, J. B. (Ed.). (1994). *The development of language.* New York: Macmillan. This comprehensive yet readable text covers all aspects of language development in children, from birth through the school years.

Schickedanz, J. (1998). *Much more than the ABCs: The early stages of reading and writing.* Washington, DC: National Association for the Education of Young Children. This short paperback provides an overview of research on emergent literacy and suggests ways that parents and teachers can support young children's curiosity about written language.

Slobin, D. I. (Ed.). (1997). *The cross-linguistic study of language acquisition* (Vols. 4 and 5). Mahwah, NJ: Erlbaum. These books provide many examples of variations across languages. Each chapter is devoted to a single topic, such as morphological differences, syntactic differences, or differences in phonology. Variations in children's language acquisition are discussed in terms of differences in the languages themselves and in socialization practices. This interesting book is for the serious student who is interested in language.

Snow, C. E., Burns, M. S., & Griffin, P. (Eds.). (1998). *Preventing reading difficulties in young children.* Washington, DC: National Academy Press. This book provides a comprehensive overview of the components of emergent literacy and of the conditions necessary to help young children learn to read and write. A very comprehensive picture of emergent literacy is provided, and recommendations for improving literacy experiences for young children are discussed.

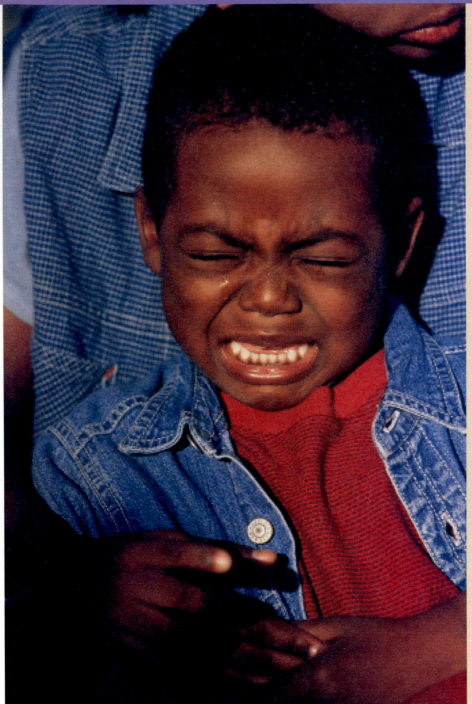

11

Social and Emotional Development in Preschool Children

CODY AND SEBASTIAN, age 2½, were playing together at Cody's house. They seemed to be enjoying each other's company as they scooted their toy cars across the floor (usually in opposite directions). Cody's mom, Carol, was making sandwiches and dishing up some Jell-O nearby in the kitchen.

Soon, Cody stopped playing and looked around. He spotted Sebastian by the stroller, exploring the contents of his mother's purse. "No! Mommy's purse. Mommy no touch! No play Mommy's purse."

Cody grabbed the purse by its long strap and dragged it to the kitchen. "Mommy," he announced, "Sebastian no play purse" (meaning, "I told Sebastian not to play with your purse").

Carol had left her purse in the stroller seat, and had left the stroller in the family room. She forgot to fold it up and put it away in the hall closet.

She dashed to retrieve the items that Sebastian had dumped out of her purse. She knew there was nothing dangerous to a child, but she dreaded the thought of finding lipstick smeared on the carpet and perhaps all over Sebastian's face.

Carol began picking up items and putting them back in her purse. She glanced over at Sebastian, who had moved away from the stroller and the other side of the room. She noticed his sober expression and that he was not playing with his car.

"Sebastian," she said. "It's okay. You probably didn't even know this was my purse. It looks like an old bag, doesn't it? And sitting in the stroller, you probably thought it had some toys in it. It's okay. Come on over and help me put things back. Then I'll put it away where it belongs, which is what I should have done when we came home."

Sebastian took Carol's outstretched hand, and they made their way slowly across the room. She held the purse open, turning it first in one direction and then in the other, to accept items as the boys picked them up. "There, everything is all picked up now. Thanks, boys."

"Cody, I'm glad you remembered not to play with Mommy's purse; and, Sebastian, I'm glad you stopped playing with it as soon as Cody told you to. Thanks, boys. You were good helpers today.

"Now, who is ready for some peanut butter and jelly sandwiches and cherry Jell-O?"

think about it

How would you characterize Cody's behavior? Would most children behave as Cody behaved? Or would most children participate in doing what they know they were not supposed to do, perhaps even using their friend's ignorance of a family's rule as a good excuse? What parental teaching methods might promote internalization of standards of behavior in a young child? What parental teaching methods might not "take?"

The process of teaching children what they should and should not do, both inside and outside their families, is called **socialization.** Socialization begins during the child's second year, soon after the first birthday, when children begin to walk. It increases between 2 and 3 years of age because children are able by this time to understand more of what is said to them and to exercise a little self-control (Gralinski & Kopp, 1993). Socialization continues throughout the preschool, school-age, and adolescent years, as children are helped to adapt and expand what they have learned previously. As children's social horizons broaden, they must learn how to do what they are asked to do; how to share and be fair; how to express themselves and solve problems; and how to trust, enjoy, and care for people.

In this chapter, we discuss the methods that parents and other adults use to teach appropriate social behavior to children. We also discuss what is known about how different methods of socialization and discipline affect children. But first we briefly review the foundation that the attachment relationship provides for the development of moral behavior.

An Overview of Socialization and Early Moral Development

Recall from chapter 7 that the child's secure attachment in infancy predicts positive social behavior during the preschool years. Attachment history in infancy and social behavior during the late toddler and preschool years are related, in part because babies develop rudimentary **script knowledge**—expectations for how events usually unfold in familiar contexts (Bauer, 1995). These are carried forward from infancy to the later toddler and preschool years. These scripts provide internal working models of relationships with primary attachment figures. When there is a secure attachment, the baby also has a positive regard for the content of these scripts, which include the adult's standards for the toddler's behavior. This positive regard for the adult's standards supports adoption of them as his or her own, a process called **internalization**. This early internalization of an adult's standards constitutes the beginning of the moral self because these are the child's first ideas about how she should act (Emde et al., 1991). Internalization of parental standards eases the socialization process during the second and third years of life because the child has already begun to think that she should behave as the adult thinks she should.

The correlation between a secure attachment history in infancy and positive social behavior during the preschool years is also due to the fact that the quality of interaction between a child and a primary caregiver tends to be consistent over time. Quality interactions in infancy are responsive. As the child matures, high-quality responsive interactions involve allowing the child appropriate autonomy (Ainsworth, 1990). A responsive parent of an infant reads signals indicating discomfort or the baby's desire to maintain or reduce social interaction. The same responsive parent in also likely to read the older infant's wish to explore, to communicate verbally, and to make some decisions. The first words, for example, require attentive observation by the parent and sincere attempts to understand what the infant is trying to say.

Of course, complete consistency in parenting across time periods is rare. New siblings can arrive, and older siblings' needs can change. Parents' relationships with each other can change, and parents' work situations and events in the world can also change. Parents differ individually, too, in terms of their responses to a young and demanding baby, as compared to an autonomous and adventurous toddler. Some parents respond better as a baby gets older and is less demanding in some ways, whereas other parents respond better to a young baby than to a more independent toddler who sometimes challenges their authority.

Cultural and social-class demands vary, too, and these interact in complex ways with early relationships. For example, late in the second year, beginning between 18 and 24 months, parents actively prompt children to recount personal events in **autobiographical narratives,** stories about the child herself (Hudson, 1990). This personal storytelling serves as a socializing experience (Miller et al., 1997). Researchers have found differences in the extent to which parents allow children to have thoughts about events that differ from their parents' thoughts (Wiley et al., 1998). In working-class families, children are sometimes allowed little autonomy of

RESEARCH

Emotional self-regulation apparently begins with mutual regulation in the attachment context. It then continues to develop throughout the toddler and preschool years as children gain practice in inhibiting actions in various contexts as they learn to respond to increasing parental expectations (Rothbart, 1989).

Attachment as a Context for Turn-Taking

Rules involving reciprocity, for example, develop from procedures for how to engage, maintain, and terminate social interaction (Emde et al., 1991). In this way, turn-taking that is part of the attachment relationship contributes to the mutual regulation of emotions in the attachment system.

These early emotional communications have important effects on the child, long before verbal communication is possible. For example, by 6 months of age, babies frown, become sober, and even cry when adults frown or look angry at them (Charlesworth & Kreutzer, 1973). By 9 months of age, infants begin to read the expressions on caregivers' faces to judge the safety of novel situations and people.

Social Referencing's Contribution to Self-Regulation

A number of researchers (e.g., Kochanska, 1994) have recently commented on the importance of social referencing (see p. 242 in chapter 7) in communicating that an event is socially significant. These events include prohibitions (Barrett & Campos, 1987). When given a prohibition, the toddler repeatedly looks toward and away from the caregiver, testing the authority and clarity of the prohibition (Emde et al., 1991).

Twenty-four-month-olds respond to familiar prohibitions when the parent is present and can be referenced (Emde et al., 1988). Older children can remember prohibitions and parental emotion about a particular stimulus even when the parent is absent. Cody, whom we met at the beginning of this chapter, regulated his own behavior in terms of emotions, even when his mother was not around.

Emde suggests that strategies of "negotiation" used during emotional communication, and the consequences of such strategies, are gradually internalized by the child. The child solicits procedural knowledge from the caregiver about what is permissible in various situations. Parents consistently set limits and children learn how to observe them. In the process, children acquire an early morality which is in large measure an "executive we" (Emde et al., 1991). Cody displayed this kind of behavior.

Emde suggests that through reciprocal interactions involving prohibitions the child acquires a sense of what "feels right." That is, children at first react to their violation of prohibitions with nonspecific distress, and later with more differentiated arousal responses, such as shame, guilt, avoidance, concern, and sadness (Kochanska, 1994). Toward the end of their second year, toddlers show distress when they perceive another's discomfort, and they attempt to provide comfort. This reaction is known as **empathy** (Radke-Yarrow et al., 1983; Zahn-Waxler et al., 1992). Many theorists believe that there is a strong maturational component to the initial appearance of empathy and that it has been an adaptive process in human evolution (Porges et al., 1994; Thompson, 1999). But it is also influenced considerably by experience (Hoffman, 1993).

---

thought. When conflicts occur about events themselves (i.e., what had happened) or about the meaning or interpretation of events, working-class parents tend to demand that the child adopt the parent's view. In middle-class families, on the other hand, parents more often indirectly prompt a child to speak more accurately or simply end the conversation by commenting that the child's version was funny or odd (Wiley et al., 1998). Middle-class mothers seem willing, according to researchers, "to sacrifice accuracy rather than infringe on the child's right to articulate his or her view of the past experience" (p. 843). Or perhaps middle-class mothers do "not treat children's past transgressions as a didactic resource" (Miller et al., 1997, p. 565). Instead, they deal with children's transgressions, in context, when they occur.

Thus, different conflicts arise for different parents during the toddler and preschool years, based somewhat on cultural groups and social class. Conflict about events and their interpretation must be navigated carefully if the child is to adopt the

Appropriate mutual regulation in the moral sphere involves a child's adequate perception of parental messages plus a sense of reciprocity and empathy guided by the caregiver. These lead to internalization of standards of behavior and of what "feels right" (Emde et al., 1991). Internalization allows **self-regulation**—behavior in relation to a standard one has adopted for oneself (Asendorpf & Nunner-Winkler, 1992; Kochanska, 1994).

Further Development of Self-Regulation

Self-regulation moderates emotional and other kinds of reactivity, including approach, avoidance, attention, orientation, and selection. **Simple reactivity** is the child's characteristic reaction to stimulus change, reflected in how the somatic, endocrine, and autonomic nervous systems characteristically work (Rothbart et al., 1994). Kagan's fearful child (see chapter 7) appears to be a manifestation of reactivity, at least at the earliest ages (Kochanska, 1995).

A second kind of reactivity involves inhibiting action. This kind of reactivity is not an emotion. It is, rather, the ability to inhibit inappropriate behavior voluntarily and to execute socialized alternatives (Kochanska, 1993). This kind of inhibition is known as **effortful** or **inhibitory control** (Kochanska et al., 1996, 1997). When a parent tells a child to stop doing something, the child must inhibit, or stop, an action. Gradually, the child inhibits actions that would violate prohibitions even before initiating them and when the socializing agent is absent. Of course, self-control is not a matter of all or nothing. Self-control is typically exercised in some situations, but not in others—and in some situations some of the time, but not all the time.

Some children seem to have more difficulty than others in exercising effortful control, perhaps because of temperament. Temperament, however, does not determine directly the outcome of self-control. "Temperament must operate through transactions with the socializing environment" (Bates et al., 1998). This means that parents must adjust their attempts at socialization based on the child's temperament. If a child complies readily with prohibitions, a parent can exercise control in a low-key way. This level of control then allows the child to develop appropriate autonomy of functioning (i.e., to learn to self-regulate in response to an internalized standard). If, on the other hand, a child resists complying with parental prohibitions, the child's self-control will improve in the long run if the parent increases the firmness of control over the toddler (Bates et al., 1998). In other words, according to one theorist, "'temperament' itself is modifiable by experiental factors, particularly by the child's transactions with meaningful caregivers, and it should be viewed as an open system that is influenced by experience, rather than a purely biological construct, despite its biological underpinnings" (Kochanska et al., 1997).

Wise caregivers require a reasonable set of age-appropriate expectations, and they enforce them, using the level of control a child seems to require. They "up the ante" as children establish control at one level and can handle more. Wise caregivers also seek cooperation and allow for autonomy, as much as they can, because children also strive for competence and mastery (Thompson, 1998). Offering alternative activities and engaging the child in them—that is, being proactive with respect to socialization—also is effective (Holden, 1983; Kuczynski & Kochanska, 1995).

parent's values and standards. Allowances for autonomy must be handled carefully as well. To avoid excessive conflict, the parent must convey expectations regarding the child's actual behavior, whether or not the parent grants a child some autonomy in self-expression. Skill in accomplishing these tasks is not necessarily similar to a parent's ability to be responsive to a young baby. Thus, discontinuities in some parent-child relationships are likely to occur as a child matures.

There are, in fact, four stages of attachment. The first is the *phase of undiscriminating social responsiveness* (1 to 2 months of age). The second is the *phase of discriminating sociability* (2 to 7 months of age). The third is the *attachment/ proximity-seeking phase* (from 7 to 24 months of age). The fourth and final stage, the *phase of goal-corrected partnership*, begins at about 25 months of age (Schaffer & Emerson, 1964). The goals of children and their caregivers will sometimes be at odds, which sets the stage for conflict. Moral behavior becomes refined in the dialectic that follows situations of conflict with others.

Socialization in the Family during Childhood

The child's conflict with others over the goals of actions, much of which takes place in the family, calls for the parent to discipline the child. Parents usually begin disciplining their children around the time the children begin to walk (at about 1 year of age). Everyday discipline apparently constitutes the beginning of moral development because the child's compliance with parental requests and demands between 2 and 3 years of age predicts later conscience very reliably (Kagan, 1987; Kochanska et al., 1995). **Conscience** refers to self-control in situations where a standard of conduct should be applied. When children have a conscience, they do what they know they should do, even if they know that nobody else will ever find out if they did not (Kochanska, 1991).

Patterns of Child Rearing During Childhood

A useful scheme for thinking about differences in patterns of parental discipline was developed by Baumrind (1967). The three patterns she identified are (1) authoritative, (2) authoritarian, and (3) permissive. Each pattern is unique in terms of its mixture of parental control and maturity demands, parental warmth and nurturance, and clarity of parental communication. The **authoritative parent** is nurturant and warm, exerts a high level of control, and makes high maturity demands. The **permissive parent** is nurturant and warm but makes few maturity demands and exerts little control. The **authoritarian parent** exerts high control, but is not very nurturant or warm. A fourth pattern of parenting based on Baumrind's dimensions is **neglectful/uninvolved** (Maccoby & Martin, 1983). Neglectful and uninvolved parents are disengaged, and their goal seems to be to reduce interactions with a child to the minimum.

Both authoritarian and authoritative parents exert high control, but they exert it differently. Authoritative parents give reasons for prohibitions and requests, and they describe the effects that children's behavior has on others. This approach to teaching appropriate social behavior to children is an **inductive approach**—children are given information about specific cases from which they can formulate general principles of behavior. Authoritative parents also permit children to express their views, and they often discuss these views with them, even though these parents expect children to comply with their requests. These discussions provide another opportunity for children to consider the details of situations and how their behavior might affect others.

Authoritarian parents, in contrast, give few reasons for their demands. Instead of explaining their demands in terms of the effect of the child's behavior on others, they appeal to an authority: "Do this because I said so." Authoritarian parents also do not allow children to express their views, which reduces children's opportunity to think about situations. These parents also frequently use force to maintain their position. Parents who use these discipline strategies are said to use a **power-assertive approach** to discipline. This approach contrasts sharply with the reasoning approach used by authoritative parents. Reasoning relies on the child's capacity to arrive at general principles from thinking about details of specific situations. Authoritative parents use enough power assertion to ensure that they have the child's attention, but they do not rely primarily on power-assertion to discipline their children.

Other researchers have found additional differences in parents' approaches to disciplining their children. For example, parents differ in terms of whether they are proactive or reactive in exerting control. Proactive parents keep children busy, anticipate problems, and teach children actively what to do, rather than tell them simply what not to do (Holden, 1983). They control more with demands for action ("do's") than with prohibitions ("don'ts"). Proactive parents are likely to become involved in activities with their children, especially when the children are very young, as a way to ensure compliance. For example, if a parent asks a toddler to play with a toy as an alternative to engaging in some inappropriate behavior, the child's compliance usually depends on the parent's willingness to play along, at least for a time (Kuczynski & Kochanska, 1995). Reactive parents, on the other hand, simply tell the child to stop the inappropriate behavior, but make no effort to engage the child in acceptable behavior.

Methods of Discipline and Their Effect on the Child

Baumrind (1967, 1991a) found striking differences in the behavior of children whose parents used different discipline methods. The least competent children, both socially and cognitively, were those whose parents were permissive or neglectful/uninvolved. They exhibited less self-control than the other children, and they were less self-reliant. Children of neglectful/uninvolved parents showed especially poor achievement and social skills. Children with authoritative parents were the most competent. They were very self-reliant and exhibited high levels of self-control. They also explored their environments actively and were the most assertive children, even though their parents asserted firm control—expected them to comply with their reasonable demands. Children of authoritarian parents typically took their schoolwork seriously and were more competent cognitively than children reared by permissive parents. But when compared with children of authoritative parents, they were more apprehensive about doing things and more hostile when experiencing stress. They were also less skilled in social situations with peers.

Reasoning about expectations—the approach used by authoritative parents—predicts high rates of compliance and internalization of adult standards. Parents who discipline primarily by asserting power, on the other hand—especially those who express anger and hostility and frequently use force—have children who apparently do not internalize very well what parents are trying to teach them. Without giving reasons for behaviors, there is no genuine teaching. As a consequence, these children comply less with adult standards than do children whose parents have given them reasons for their expectations and demands (Crockenberg & Litman, 1990; Holden & West, 1989; Londerville & Main, 1981; Power & Chapiewski, 1986).

Baumrind (1989, 1991a, 1991b) has followed samples of children through adolescence and has expanded the categories of parenting behavior to adapt to various age levels. The results of her studies of older children are similar to those found with preschoolers. (These are discussed in depth in chapter 15.)

Baumrind's conclusion that authoritative parenting produces better outcomes is not based simply on correlational evidence. Correlational evidence alone would be problematic because the child's behavior may elicit the parent's behavior rather than the other way around. But studies suggest that previous appropriate, authoritative maturity demands enhance compliance and result in fewer behavior problems, even after the influence of child temperament has been controlled (Koenig, 1995). And parenting that utilizes mostly power assertion during toddlerhood predicts behavior problems even better than power assertion during preschool. It seems, then, that power assertion is both a correlate and a predictor of children's low compliance.

Baumrind's findings fit Hoffman's (1993) theory that power assertion interferes with children's moral development because it preoccupies them with fear and anger rather than with the empathy and understanding that can be elicited when reasons are provided and the child is encouraged to think about these. A model of parental discipline that leads to good internalization of adult standards has been provided by Grusec and Goodnow (1994). (See Figure 11.1.)

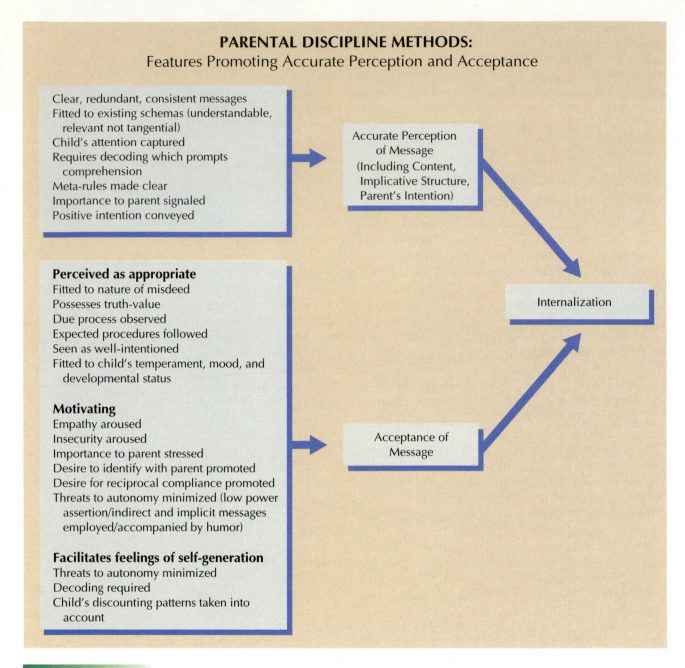

PARENTAL DISCIPLINE METHODS:
Features Promoting Accurate Perception and Acceptance

Clear, redundant, consistent messages
Fitted to existing schemas (understandable,
    relevant not tangential)
Child's attention captured
Requires decoding which prompts
    comprehension
Meta-rules made clear
Importance to parent signaled
Positive intention conveyed

Accurate Perception
of Message
(Including Content,
Implicative Structure,
Parent's Intention)

Perceived as appropriate
Fitted to nature of misdeed
Possesses truth-value
Due process observed
Expected procedures followed
Seen as well-intentioned
Fitted to child's temperament, mood, and
    developmental status

Motivating
Empathy aroused
Insecurity aroused
Importance to parent stressed
Desire to identify with parent promoted
Desire for reciprocal compliance promoted
Threats to autonomy minimized (low power
    assertion/indirect and implicit messages
    employed/accompanied by humor)

Facilitates feelings of self-generation
Threats to autonomy minimized
Decoding required
Child's discounting patterns taken into
    account

Internalization

Acceptance of
Message

FIGURE 11.1

Features of parental disciplinary actions promoting accurate perception and acceptance
(internalization) of parent's message.   (*Source:* From "Impact of Parental Discipline Methods
on the Child's Internalization of Values: A Reconceptualization of Current Points of View," by
J. E. Grusec and J. J. Goodnow, 1994, *Developmental Psychology, 30* (1), p. 15. Copyright © 1994 by
American Psychological Association. Reprinted with permission.)

One of the difficulties with Baumrind's conclusions about patterns in parenting
is that their correlations with later child behavior do not hold up completely across
different cultural and social-class settings (Thompson, 1998). For example, the authoritarian pattern results in fewer negative, and even some positive consequences,
for children when applied by parents of lower socioeconomic status. The dangers in

their neighborhoods may create dynamics that require different approaches to parenting, changing the outcomes of the authoritarian pattern (Furstenberg, 1993). The authoritarian pattern is also found frequently in Chinese culture, where it yields quite positive child outcomes (Chao, 1994). Baumrind's warmth dimension may not capture entirely the devotion found in the Chinese parent. When intense devotion to the child is combined with warmth, perhaps the reasoning and induction aspect of the authoritative approach is less important in helping the child internalize adult standards than when warmth exists without such intense devotion.

Baumrind's categories of parenting approaches are very useful, nevertheless, because they predict the worst child outcomes, which result from permissive and neglectful/uninvolved patterns. However, the specific outcomes of authoritarian and authoritative approaches seem to interact in complex ways with culture and other aspects of a child's socialization environment. We must say that the specific effects of these approaches vary, depending a child's cultural and social circumstances (Parke & Buriel, 1998).

Socialization Processes

So far we have provided a general outline of effective parenting. Here we will discuss some specific socialization processes that parents and teachers often hear about and use, and we will indicate how these relate to some of the parenting behaviors we have already discussed.

Socialization processes do not operate in a vacuum, of course. They are part of a child's history of relationships with adults. The attachment relationship with parents is especially critical, because it determines children's willingness to be attentive to adults and the feelings they have for them. These feelings affect a child's imitation of adult behavior, their tendency to listen when adults explain the reasons for an admonition, and how dissatisfied they feel when they fail to meet their parents' expectations, or their own. The attachment relationship also influences the extent to which parents are likely to teach appropriate social behavior to toddlers and preschoolers. Parents who have been consistent in responding to their baby's signals, and thus have supported the development of a secure attachment with their child, tend to be consistent and clear in setting and maintaining limits as the child gets older (Sroufe, 1983, 1988). Perhaps this continuity is found because their children are responsive to them, given their good attachment, which encourages the parent to continue socialization efforts. Some of the contextual factors that support a parent's responsive behavior during the child's infancy also support parents in being consistent during the rest of their child's childhood.

Social learning theorists (e.g., Bandura, 1977) agree with attachment theorists about the factors that influence children's social behavior, especially that the quality of their relationships with others is important. Both also agree that children's internal working models of themselves and others shape how they interpret subsequent social experiences (Youngblade & Belsky, 1990). Even though attachment theorists emphasize emotion and bonds of affection, whereas social learning theorists emphasize social skills, both agree that specific methods of disciplining children affect children's behavior.

Verbal Instruction

During a free-play period in school one day, Joanne and Amelia began chasing each other around a table. Their laughter got louder and louder. Their teacher approached them, took hold of their hands, and said, "Let's stop the running. You might hurt someone or fall down and hurt yourselves. Let us find something else to do. There is clay on the art table, or you could play in the block corner, or read a book in the library area. What will it be?"

"Let's build with blocks," said Joanne. "We can make cages for animals!"

"Okay," agreed Amelia.

"Good idea," said their teacher as they hurried off. "Tell me when the cages are ready. I'll be interested to see how you made them."

think about it

What strategy did this teacher use to change Joanne and Amelia's behavior? What additional strategy do you think she will use when Joanne and Amelia call her over to view the completed cages?

Beginning at about age 2, parents and children may experience frequent "clashes of will." Perhaps this mother is explaining why it is dangerous to go head-first down the slide. Parents who watch their children closely, enforce prohibitions, and give reasons for them, tend to have children who develop good self-control. (*Source:* © Joseph Nettis/Photo Researchers)

The teacher instructed these two girls verbally about why they should stop running, and what they could do instead. In many situations, verbal instruction is the quickest and most effective way to discourage inappropriate behavior and teach and encourage positive alternatives. The teacher's concrete suggestions helped the girls find something else to do.

Verbal communication can also help children to think of themselves in certain ways. A parent might say, "You're a good helper. I don't know what I'd do without your help. It would take me forever to fold all this laundry by myself." Or a teacher might say, "You're such good listeners. I don't think I've ever seen such good listeners as you are today."

Children often respond to these **positive attributions** or **dispositional praise** by thinking of themselves in the favorable terms mentioned and by trying to live up to this image (Grusec et al., 1978; Jensen & Moore, 1977; Miller et al., 1975). Comments like these must be made sincerely, though, when children are helping or listening well (gauged in terms of what is reasonable for their age, of course). Children usually know whether they are behaving well in terms of an appropriate standard. If they are praised when they know they are not behaving well, they will see no reason to improve, and perhaps, worse, will view the adult as insincere and unreliable.

Verbal instruction *alone* can be effective in getting children to behave in appropriate ways. But many studies indicate that verbal instruction is more effective when it is *combined* with other techniques, such as reinforcement and modeling.

Observational Learning

Children imitate the adults and older children they know—their parents, teachers, neighbors, brothers and sisters, and people who work in their community. Children learn a lot about how to behave through **observational learning**—by watching how others behave. The social process by which one person demonstrates behavior that another imitates is called **modeling.** When children watch another person act a certain way and receive reinforcement for it, they are likely to imitate the person's actions (Bandura, 1977). They are most likely to imitate persons whom they think are similar to themselves because they think it is possible to become like these models.

Children's motivation to imitate others has been explained in various ways. Freud believed that imitation occurred because children identified with the same-sex parent. During the phallic stage of psychosexual development, a boy competes with his father for the mother's attention. This creates what Freud called the Oedipal conflict. The little boy even contemplates killing his father, but because this is too frightening, he decides instead to become like his father—to adopt many of his behaviors, attitudes, and beliefs. Freud called this process **identification.**

Social learning theorists agree that children imitate their same-sex parent, but they think children imitate behavior because of incentives—reinforcement and punishment—and because the model has status or value. A parent who is nurturant and helps a child solve conflicts by serving as a source of good suggestions, for example, is likely to be held in high esteem by a child. A child who holds a parent in high regard is likely to copy the parent's behavior.

Reinforcement

One Saturday morning, 3-year-old Susan turned the knob of the TV and watched the screen light up. Then she turned it off, and then on again. She was intrigued by the dot of light that appeared and spread across the screen. In the next room, her dad heard what was going on and came in to investigate.

"Susan, where's your Play-Doh?" he asked. "Weren't you going to make some cookies this morning out at the picnic table?"

Susan ran to get her Play-Doh and pushed open the back door. Her dad went with her and helped arrange her place mat and cookie cutters. Then he settled into a nearby chair to read.

After a while he got up and approached the table. "Looks like Valentine cookies. May I have a bite?"

Susan offered a cookie, and her father took an imaginary bite.

"Mmmmmmm," he said. "These taste delicious."

Susan laughed in delight.

Her father returned to his chair to read, and Susan continued playing with the Play-Doh for the next half-hour, apparently having forgotten all about the TV knob.

A learning theorist would say that Susan's responses in this situation were reinforced. **Reinforcement** is providing a consequence to a response that increases the probability that the response will occur again in the same situation or a similar one. The interesting light appearing on the screen **positively reinforced** Susan's turning of the TV knob; her father's attention, and the interesting results obtained from manipulating the Play-Doh, positively reinforced her play with Play-Doh.

Susan's dad did not simply tell her to stop fiddling with the TV knob. He redirected her instead to an interesting alternative, one in which she was likely to stay engaged for some time. By doing this, he helped her avoid play that was inappropriate. The Play-Doh activity was also one for which her father could easily provide attention that served as a positive reinforcer, even though he wanted to do some reading. Effective discipline depends in large part on the adult's skill in organizing situations and redirecting behavior so that they give children positive feedback. This is an example of the proactive versus reactive parenting we noted earlier.

In **positive reinforcement,** something that is added to the environment after the person acts maintains the person's action. The interesting sight on the television screen added novelty to Susan's environment and led her to turn the TV knob on again. Her father's attention while she played positively reinforced her engagement with the Play-Doh.

A person's behavior might also be maintained by negative reinforcement. In **negative reinforcement,** an action results in the removal of something the child finds noxious—does not like. Let's suppose that Susan has a toy drum, in which she did not show any interest until her baby sister arrived. Suppose her sister cried a lot, and Susan often got her drum and plastic drumsticks and banged on her drum whenever her sister cried. She seemed to choose to make noise that would drown out the baby's crying. In this case, we can say that Susan's drum playing was negatively reinforced—that it increased in frequency after the arrival of her baby sister because the noise she could create with the drum removed her sister's crying (covered it up with Susan's own noise-making).

Extinction

Adults can reduce inappropriate behavior by arranging the environment so that the child receives no response at all for a behavior. In the case of a whining child who has already received an explanation for why another cookie will not be forthcoming, a parent simply stops explaining and goes about his business. When a behavior does not produce any interesting consequences, it often disappears. When behavior declines or disappears because it has received no response from the environment, we say it has been extinguished or that **extinction** has occurred. In the classroom, a teacher who ignores a child's obnoxious behavior is attempting to extinguish the behavior—hoping it will disappear if it gets no response. Teachers or parents need to be prepared for the undesirable behavior to escalate when they first ignore it. Children seem to think that if they scream more loudly, for example, they will make the adult respond. If the adult can hold out through this initial escalation, the child will realize that the adult has resolved to ignore the behavior, and extinction has a chance to work.

Adults do not use extinction as often as they use some other socialization processes. Some misbehavior simply cannot and should not be ignored because it hurts or endangers other people or the misbehaving child. Parents and teachers also know that children need practical ideas about what they should do instead of doing the things that are troublesome. Susan's dad apparently sensed that she needed a suggestion. He mentioned an engaging activity that took Susan outside, away from the TV, where she would not be tempted to turn the knob again. If Susan's dad had simply ignored her behavior, it is doubtful that she would have stopped. For one thing, the effect of the knob-turning was interesting and apparently reinforcing; second, Susan would probably not think about something else that might be interesting to do. Extinction is useful at some times, especially if the adult feels that the child knows alternative behavior and is engaging in troublesome behavior simply to get the adult's attention. But extinction is not effective or appropriate in many other situations.

Punishment

Susan's dad might have slapped her hand or sent her to her room to teach her not to play with the TV knob. If Susan's knob-turning behavior decreased after these actions, we would say that they were punishers for her behavior. **Punishment** involves providing a consequence that decreases the probability that a response will recur.

There are two kinds of punishment. One kind adds stimuli to the environment (a slap on the hand). The other kind removes stimuli from the environment. Sending Susan to her room, where she could not play with the TV or the other toys in the family room, would be an example of this kind of punishment.

Punishment of the second kind—removal of reinforcers—is referred to as **response cost** (Reese & Lipsitt, 1970). In other words, the child's response costs the child positive reinforcers. When children are sent to their rooms, or sent to sit by themselves someplace in the classroom, the procedure is called **time out from positive reinforcement,** or more commonly, **time out.** Because children's normal environments at home or school have so many interesting activities, including social interactions with people, taking them out of these environments for misbehavior usually serves as punishment.

Although punishment gets results, it has several drawbacks. First, it can backfire, producing exactly the behavior the parent wishes to eliminate. We have all witnessed scenes like this one:

Kevin approaches the TV set and clicks the remote. His father, Edward, looks up from his book and tells him, "No!" Kevin stops playing with the remote, and Edward returns to his book. Kevin again clicks the remote, but Edward doesn't notice right away. Finally, Edward notices and intervenes again, once more telling Kevin, "No!" He returns to his book, and Kevin begins to play with some toys. Kevin then approaches the TV, turning to look at his dad. Edward looks back at him. Kevin smiles broadly and grabs the remote. Edward intervenes, says, "No!" again, picks Kevin up, and puts him down on the other side of the room. Kevin runs to the TV, laughing in delight, and turns it on. Edward by now is very angry and spanks Kevin hard.

Edward's responses reinforced Kevin's behavior; that is, they *increased* his involvement with the TV; they did not serve to decrease it. Kevin was pleased that he could get his dad's attention. The "class clown" often behaves this way. The teacher's attention results in an increase in the child's misbehavior—it reinforces rather than punishes it. When this happens, the parent or teacher often escalates the punishment to a harsher level. Kevin's father finally spanked him for playing with the TV remote.

But did Kevin deserve the punishment? And will he learn not to play with the remote as a result of this consequence? Actually, there are many problems associated with physical punishment. These are discussed in Knowledge in Action: Education—Disadvantages of Using Physical Punishment.

EDUCATION

Disadvantages of Using Physical Punishment

Problems are associated with physical forms of punishment, especially if punishment is used as the primary means of socializing children. The most important of these problems are discussed here.

Punishment Interferes with Reasoning

The period of time following misbehavior is often a unique one for instruction, and learning during this period can be generalized to other situations. We can use this time to help the child understand how inappropriate behavior adversely affects others, and what else a child should or could do in a particular situation. One problem with physical punishment is that it upsets children, and we simply cannot explain or teach very much to a crying and angry child. The opportunity for learning is wasted. An explanation might reduce the inappropriate behavior just as effectively as physical punishment, especially if the child has never before received that instruction.

Punishment May Reduce Initiative and New Learning

A second problem with punishment—including time out—is that it may reduce exploration and initiative, especially if it comes without warning. A child in a new sit-uation must be given the chance to find out what behaviors are appropriate and inappropriate. Consider the following example:

Two preschoolers were each attempting to look in a small, round mirror that both were holding. They started tugging it back and forth.

"Let me have it," shouted Katie.

"I want it," Andy responded.

Katie's mother came over and took the mirror. She put it on the table and showed the children they could both see themselves in the mirror if they stood back a little. The two children played happily together for the next several minutes, as they both looked in the mirror.

Later, Andy relayed the incident to his mother, who asked him why he had not shared the mirror with his friend in the first place. "Well, I didn't know how to do that before Katie's mom 'splained it to me," he said.

If Katie and Andy had been punished with time out or a spanking for their quarreling, they may have learned that to avoid punishment it is wise to avoid new situations altogether, or to be quiet and sneaky when taking a desired object away from someone else. Children who are punished when they have not yet had a chance to learn how to behave in a variety of situations may develop only a limited repertoire of responses when they find themselves again in conflict situations over toys.

Other Factors Influencing Socialization

How children behave in a particular situation depends on more than the socialization strategies parents use. For one thing, children's level of cognitive development influences their responses to socialization strategies. As children's ability to understand and reason increases, they are better able to respond in appropriate ways. Of course, a higher level of cognition does not automatically result in better behavior. The values children are taught, and the socialization processes parents have used, influence whether children use their improving cognitive abilities for prosocial or antisocial purposes.

Genetic and biological factors also influence the child's behavior, which in turn influences adult behavior. For example, it is usually more difficult or complicated to teach children when Down syndrome affects their intelligence, or when a sensory impairment limits their ability to communicate. Some researchers (e.g., Lytton, 1990) believe that biological influences on behavior are very extensive even in the general population, although biology and environment are so intertwined that it is difficult to separate the effects of each (Dodge, 1990; Wahler, 1990).

When Katie's mom demonstrated how two children could use the mirror, she not only helped them solve their current problem, but also taught them the general idea that sometimes a way can be found to use a toy together. Obviously, children learn more when they do not avoid situations out of fear and when adults provide suggestions for alternative behavior.

The Punisher Can Become an Ineffective Socializing Agent

Punishment can also create hostility and resentment, making the adult an **aversive stimulus** for the child—a stimulus the child will seek to avoid. A punishing adult will become particularly aversive if the child thinks the punishment is harsh, unnecessary, or motivated by anger rather than concern for the child. If Katie and Andy had been spanked for quarreling, they may have felt hostility and resentment. After all, as Andy explained, they did not know how to share the mirror until Katie's mom gave them an idea. They played cooperatively with the mirror after being shown how, which indicated that they had not wanted to fight with each other. They were simply two young children without the means to solve a problem.

Punishment Can Lead to Child Abuse

Punishment can also lead to child abuse. Child abuse sometimes occurs in disciplinary situations that simply go too far (Gil, 1970). If the punishment is severe or is seen as coming from anger or hostility, so that the parent becomes an aversive stimulus, then any positive reinforcement the parent tries to initiate will have limited effect.

A vicious cycle can sometimes be set up. The parent begins to control less through rewards and positive involvement with the child, and more by using punishment. The level of punishment necessary to have an effect increases because an angry and resentful child resists the parent's authority. Because an angry and resentful child is often willing to absorb quite a lot of physical pain rather than submit to the adult, physical punishment often escalates. The adult feels compelled to increase the physical punishment—to hurt the child even more—to make sure it has an effect (Brehm, 1981). The result is likely to be abusive.

Punishment Models Aggression

Physical punishment is also undesirable because it models aggressive behavior. Correlations between parents' use of physical punishment and children's aggressive behavior have been documented repeatedly (Eron et al., 1971; Trickett & Kuczynski, 1986) and are especially likely when parents are low on warmth (Deater-Deckard & Dodge, 1997). Children of parents who use aggressive discipline techniques often grow up to use similar techniques with their children (Simons et al., 1991). Because the evidence is correlational, we do not know if more aggressive children cause parents to use more physical punishment, or if more physical punishment produces more aggressive children. But we do know that a lot of aggression can be learned by imitation. Therefore, the assumption that physical punishment produces more aggressive children is consistent with these findings.

Selecting Socialization Strategies

The most effective discipline strategy is telling children how their misbehavior affects others and why they need to change it. This is the reasoning approach used by authoritative parents. Reasoning leads to induction and internalization of standards.

But what if children ignore adults when they are trying to explain something to them? Should adults be content with having their admonitions ignored? Of course not. Recall Baumrind's finding that effective parents not only provide reasons, but exert firm control—they expect compliance with their requests.

If reasoning is not effective, adults can use a firm voice, withdrawal of privileges, or time out. Mild punishment is especially appropriate if the child has the ability to understand the situation and if the parent knows the child is capable of behaving better. Mild punishment is useful because parents must first get children to stop what they are doing and pay attention to what they are saying to them. Hoffman thinks that "too little power assertion or love withdrawal may result in children's ignoring the parent. On the other hand, too much can produce fear, anxiety, or resentment in children" (Hoffman, 1984, p. 304). These intense feelings can interfere with the development of empathy and understanding. Erikson also warned about the possibility of "oversocializing" children in ways that might interfere with their budding initiative. But what is too little or too much depends on the child because children with different temperaments respond differently to the same amount of punishment. Very sensitive children often respond to a quiet and firm voice. Children who are not very sensitive typically need a firmer voice and even physical restraint if their attention is to be secured (Bates et al., 1998). When parents do not exert higher levels of control when a child's temperament indicates a need for it, the child is more likely to exhibit behavior problems later on (Bates et al., 1998).

Aggression: How It Is Learned and Controlled

Is aggression an inborn trait, or do children learn to be aggressive? Biology no doubt plays some role in aggressiveness. Some children seem to be born with stronger emotions, more volatile personalities, or less ability to control their impulses, all of which might make them more difficult to socialize than children who are calmer and more inhibited in their responses to events in their lives (Bates et al., 1998; Lytton, 1990). But aggressive behavior is learned. That is, temperament does not affect later behavior directly. Instead, it influences parent-child interactions by affecting the parent's behavior. When parents adapt appropriately to a child's difficult temperament, the child's behavior is likely to have a more positive outcome than when a parent finds it difficult to make appropriate adaptations (Bates et al., 1998; Patterson, 1995; Snyder & Patterson, 1995). Aggression can be accounted for by the same principles we have been discussing—reinforcement, punishment, and observation of aggressive models. Early attachment history also sets the larger stage for how socialization processes affect a child. In this section, we discuss how children learn aggressive behavior and how adults can help prevent this learning.

Reinforcement, Punishment, and Aggression

Dolores is playing with her dolls in the living room, near her little sister, Rhonda. Rhonda is playing a toy xylophone with a small wooden mallet. Dolores stops playing for a moment to listen to the sounds her sister is making. Then she reaches over and grabs hold of the mallet. Rhonda, surprised, resists, gripping the mallet more firmly and scrunching up her face and squealing. But Dolores persists. She pushes Rhonda with her free hand and pulls harder on the mallet. Rhonda releases her grip on the toy, and Dolores starts playing with her sister's xylophone.

Reinforcement   Dolores's success in using force to take away her sister's toy is likely to reinforce her aggressive tactics. The extent to which children are reinforced or punished for aggression influences whether they learn to be aggressive or nonaggressive. In addition to material rewards, such as possession of a toy, aggression can yield **intrinsic reinforcement**—nonmaterial changes in the child's environment. For example, with just a little aggression, children can make other children cry and move away, make objects fly across the room and shatter, and make adults come running. Aggression can quickly produce a little excitement in what might otherwise be a boring environment (Roedell et al., 1977). The child becomes the center of attention, even though the attention received is negative.

Aggression sometimes increases when children are initially gathered into a group, apparently because their aggression is reinforced. In a classic study of preschool children's free play, 80 percent of children's aggressive actions were rewarded by victims' giving up objects or leaving the field (Patterson et al., 1967). Children who were not aggressive at the beginning of the year became more aggressive if they were frequent victims. Apparently, they imitated aggression to defend themselves, and also found that it worked when they wanted to get objects themselves. The only children who did not become more aggressive were those who failed in their first attempts at defensive aggression. This study and others underscore exactly how reinforcement increases behavior—if a behavior works to obtain desired goals, it will increase.

Positive reinforcement—getting a desired reward—is not the only kind of reinforcement for aggressive behavior. Negative reinforcement—removal of an aversive (undesired) stimulus—is a second kind. Studies of especially aggressive children indicate that parents who do not attend to their child's misbehavior, or fail to stop it immediately, teach their children that if they are sufficiently assertive and aggressive, they can put an end to their parents' demands for good behavior (Patterson & Reid, 1984; Youngblade & Belsky, 1990). In these cases, the child's aggression is rewarded, sometimes by positive reinforcement (they get and retain things they want) and sometimes by negative reinforcement (a parent's demands disappear).

If children's aggressive acts result in a gain in materials or territory, they are likely to repeat the aggressive behavior. Other children, not initially aggressive, are likely to begin to act that way, both to protect themselves and to gain objects and territory. If preschool teachers are not vigilant, aggression among a group of preschoolers is likely to increase over the first few weeks of school, and to remain high. (*Source:* © Elizabeth Crews)

Punishment   Punishment is the least effective strategy for reducing children's aggression. But if a child's aggressive behavior continues after parents and teachers have tried to reason with the child and have reinforced appropriate behavior, they may need to use mild punishment, such as time out. Time out, like any form of punishment, should not be used for first infractions, when the child might not have known that the behavior was wrong or what behavior would have been more appropriate. Redirecting the child's behavior (giving an idea for something else to do) and reasoning are more effective under these circumstances. If the inappropriate behavior continues, and the adult is satisfied that the child cannot be excused on the basis of naivete or ignorance, then time out might be appropriate.

Punishment must also be reasonable. If a teacher denies a misbehaving child the opportunity to participate in a special activity that had been planned for the class later in the day, the child may have no incentive to behave well for the rest of the day. The child might also become so resentful about losing the privilege that he has more difficulty controlling his behavior, and thus acts even more aggressively.

To prevent these problems, teachers can explain any contingencies that are associated with special activities or routine activities. Adults can also relate the loss of privileges or participation to the specific offense. For example, if a child is harassing a classmate, it makes sense to restrict the child's privileges by confining him to an isolated area of the classroom for a few minutes. But it makes little sense to tell him he cannot go on a scheduled trip to the park later in the day. On the other hand, if a child misbehaves at the park, despite efforts to suggest other ways of behaving and to reinforce these, then it may make sense to decide that there will be no trip to the park the next day.

It is most effective to use the minimum removal of privileges—the minimum response cost—that will end the misbehavior, but no more (Roedell et al., 1977). A longer period of time out may not be needed to stop the child's inappropriate behavior, and it may work against any positive effect of the punishment by increasing the child's anger and frustration to undesirable levels. With a child's pride intact, his emotions under control, and his feelings for the adult still positive instead of hostile, the child is more likely to think about the situation and thus learn from it. The child may even identify with the adult's positive standards (Lepper, 1973). When adults do not follow appropriate guidelines in using punishment, the effects may be wiped out (Hyman, 1995).

Also, punishment can backfire in reducing aggression in children, especially if it is the only or the primary strategy that a parent or other adult uses. First, physical punishment models aggression. Second, it can lead to anger, resentment, and frustration, which can increase noncompliance. Very aggressive children often have a history of severe punishment. Their aggression is perhaps due to the combined effects of modeling and resentment. Although they copy the aggressive behavior of adults, they are so angry and resentful that they do not adopt the standards that the punishing adult tries to impose. (See the earlier discussion of disadvantages associated with the use of punishment in Knowledge in Action: Education—The Disadvantages of Using Physical Punishment.)

Observational Learning of Aggression

There is no question that children learn aggression by observing it in others (Bandura & Walters, 1963; Reiss & Roth, 1993). Even when an aggressive model is not reinforced, children may learn the aggressive response and use it when they think it may lead to reinforcement. According to some researchers and theorists (Huesmann, 1988; Rule & Ferguson, 1986), children learn aggressive scripts as they watch aggressive models. **Scripts** are generalized memories for ways of behaving in specific circumstances. They specify sequences of actions for particular situations or events, and they indicate role slots and who may fill them (Nelson, 1993; Shank & Abelson, 1977).

Children develop scripts for all kinds of situations. For example, they learn bath time, bedtime, and mealtime scripts, as well as scripts for what to do at the playground or when visiting at a friend's house. They also learn scripts for what to do about disagreements. Once scripts are acquired for specific situations and events, they guide children's behavior. Thus, scripts can be thought of as formulas for "what to do" in various situations. When aggression is part of the behavior the child witnesses repeatedly in specific situations, aggression becomes part of the child's script for behavior in those situations. When opportunities present themselves, the child practices the scripts, and this develops the child's script knowledge further.

According to Coie and Dodge (1998, p. 797), "Living in a violent family or in a neighborhood in which the heroes are violent, interacting with antisocial peers who present repeated chances to act aggressively, and watching television violence all represent opportunities to learn aggressive scripts." In this section, we examine how aggressive behavior is learned in two of these contexts—the family and on television.

Aggressive Behavior in the Family

Many parents use physical punishment to discipline their children, which can provide children with impressive models of aggressive behavior. When physical punishment is harsh and coupled with low involvement with the child and low parental warmth, it is especially likely to be associated with aggressive behavior in the child (Deater-Deckard & Dodge, 1997; Dodge et al., 1994). Many parents also model verbal aggression, telling their children they are stupid or saying things such as "I'm going to kill you if you don't start listening to me."

Many children also witness violence between their parents, between a parent and another adult, and between siblings and their friends and acquaintances. Children also are sometimes physically abused by their parents.

Children who grow up in violent homes seem to develop a heightened sense of arousal to conflict. When they are in situations of conflict, they are less capable than other children to judge the intentions of others and routinely assume that others are hostile. They seem overly concerned with watching for possible threats to themselves, they see threats when none are there, and they are more inclined than other children to strike out at others when angry or in distress, rather than think of alternative ways of responding (Cummings & Zahn-Waxler, 1992; Dodge et al., 1995). Thus, physical abuse seems to alter a child's ability to process conflict cues, and this impairment helps to maintain the child's aggressive behavior over time (Dodge et al., 1995).

Television as a Source of Aggressive Models

The ever-present television set brings additional aggressive models into the home. Children watch a lot of TV. Even though some parents regulate the number of hours their children are allowed to watch TV (Huston et al., 1983), many others place no restrictions whatsoever on

These young children are engrossed as they watch television. If they are typical of other 3- and 4-year-olds, they will watch television between 2 and 4 hours each day. (*Source:* © Robert Daemmrich/ Tony Stone Images)

TV viewing (Lyle & Hoffman, 1972). When households have cable TV, the amount of viewing appears to be higher still (Kerkman et al., 1983).

HOW MUCH TELEVISION CHILDREN WATCH.   Children begin to watch TV systematically at about 2 or 2½ years of age (Huston et al., 1999). Some studies have indicated that children between 2 and 5 years of age watch anywhere from 13 to 27 hours per week, or 2 to 4 hours per day (Anderson et al., 1985; Huston et al., 1992). Other studies show even higher rates—as many as 35 hours a week for children between 2 and 3 years of age (Huston et al., 1999). Some studies show that TV viewing peaks during the kindergarten year and then declines during the school years (Calvert & Wright, 1982). In a 1994–95 study of young children's TV viewing behavior, 3- and 4-year-olds watched about 16 hours a week of adult programming. There was a decline to about 10 hours a week by age 5 or 6, and then an increase again between 6 and 7 years of age. Children also watch about 10 additional hours of television each week, including cartoons and educational children's shows, such as *Sesame Street*. This yields a total of about 26 hours per week of TV viewing for children between 2 and 4 years of age, and about 20 hours a week for children between 4 and 6 (Wright & Huston, 1995). In a later study (Huston et al., 1999), the number of hours of television viewing per week was somewhat higher for all ages. Two- to 3-year-olds watched almost 36 hours each week. Three- and 4-year-olds watched about 30 hours. Four- and 5-year-olds watched, on average, about 29 hours. Five- and 6-year-olds watched TV for about 22 hours each week; 6- and 7-year-olds watched about 20 hours each week.

By the time the average American child is 18 years old, she has spent more time watching television than in any other activity except sleep (Huston et al., 1992; Liebert, 1986). At age 70, she will have spent a total of 7 to 10 years watching TV (Strasburger, 1992). Traditionally, family, religion, and school have been the primary influences on a child's intellectual and moral development. Today, in terms of time spent, the biggest influence is likely to be the television set (American Medical Association, 1996).

STUDIES OF THE EFFECTS OF TV VIOLENCE ON CHILDREN.   Violence on television has been studied extensively. There are many violent episodes in children's cartoons and in the adult programs that children often watch. For the past two decades, children's Saturday morning TV has contained 20 to 25 violent acts per hour, while the average prime-time hour has shown 3 to 5 (American Academy of Pediatrics, Committee on Communications, 1995). The average child growing up in the United States will see more than 200,000 acts of violence on television, including 16,000 murders, by the time he or she turns 18 (American Medical Association, 1996; Huston et al., 1992).

Correlational studies show that children of all ages who see more violence on TV tend to behave more aggressively, and experimental studies indicate that viewing TV violence increases aggression in the viewer. These experimental studies indicate that the increased violence found among children who watch a lot of television is not simply a matter of more aggressive children watching greater amounts of television.

In one classic study of cause-effect relationships between child characteristics and television viewing (Friedrich & Stein, 1973), researchers divided nursery school children into three groups and showed them television programs of three different types: aggressive cartoons, such as *Batman* and *Superman;* prosocial programs, such as *Mr. Rogers' Neighborhood;* and neutral programs, such as nature films. Each group watched a 20-minute program of a particular type every day for four weeks. Researchers collected baseline data on children's interactions during free play before the study began and then observed the children's behavior every day during the study.

After four weeks, they found that among the children who were initially above average in aggression, those who saw the violent TV programs showed more aggression than those who watched the other programs. All the children who saw the violent films also showed less self-control in waiting for materials or adult attention, regardless of their initial level of aggression. And these same children had more difficulty obeying.

In other classic studies of the effects of filmed violence on children's behavior, children increased their aggressive behavior after watching only one violent TV show (Ellis & Sekyra, 1972). Children who watched a violent sequence from the TV series *The Untouchables* were more willing to do things they believed were hurting other children than children who watched an athletic competition (Liebert & Baron, 1972).

The results of numerous other studies, including statistical meta-analyses of a number of these taken together, indicate that TV violence increases aggression of the viewers (Gunter, 1994; Paik & Comstock, 1994; Reiss & Roth, 1993). Overall, the evidence is conclusive: Watching violence on TV is causally related to aggression (see Table 11.1). It has been estimated that TV violence explains about 10 percent of the variance in aggression in children (Wood et al., 1991). This means that other factors help explain the difference between those children who are aggressive and those children who are not. Nevertheless, 10 percent of the variance constitutes a sizable chunk.

TABLE 11.1

U.S. organizations that have concluded that violent entertainment causes violent behavior

- American Academy of Child and Adolescent Psychiatry
- American Academy of Pediatrics
- American Medical Association
- American Psychological Association
- Centers for Disease Control and Prevention
- National Institute of Mental Health
- Surgeon General's Office

Sources: From *Physician Guide to Media Violence,* by the American Medical Association, 1996, Chicago: AMA; and *Television and Behavior: Ten Years of Scientific Progress and Implications for the 1980s,* by the National Institute of Mental Health, 1982, Washington, DC: U.S. Government Printing Office.

LONG-TERM EFFECTS OF WATCHING TV VIOLENCE.   The effects of viewing TV violence appear to be deep and long lasting. For one thing, children become desensitized to violence and accept it more willingly. In one classic experimental study, researchers showed one group of third- and fourth-grade children a violent cowboy movie and another group a nonviolent film (Drabman & Thomas, 1974). They then asked the children to observe a group of younger children and to seek adult help if the children began to fight. Children in the group that had seen the violent cowboy movie were less likely to summon help when the children fought.

Another study reported correlations between high amounts of TV watching and desensitization to violence (Cline et al., 1972). Researchers tested groups of 5- and 12-year-old boys for their emotional reactivity, measured by pulse rate and other physiological signs of arousal, while they were watching a violent film. Boys of both ages who watched high amounts of TV had milder physical reactions to the violence than boys who did not watch much TV. Although correlational, this and similar evidence are consistent with the conclusion that frequent TV viewers grow accustomed, in both mind and body, to observing violence without much reaction.

Concern about the harmful effects on children of viewing TV violence has prompted a number of citizen efforts to influence TV programming. The most visible efforts have been carried out by an organization called Action for Children's Television. (For a discussion of various public policy efforts regarding children's television, see Knowledge in Action: Policy—Improving Children's Television.)

knowledge in action

Improving Children's Television

Children's television programming has been debated over the years. Public policy makers have tried to reduce TV violence, increase the number of children's shows, especially educational ones, and limit commercials on programs designed for children. Broadcasters and advertisers have often resisted many of these efforts.

Concerns about Violence

Television sets were common in U.S. homes for little more than a decade when concern arose about the violence depicted in programs. In 1969, the National Commission on the Causes and Prevention of Violence issued a report stating that televised violence affected children's aggressive behavior. The report rated television shows for violence and recommended that programs be rated on an annual basis. Over the years, the violence rating indicated that shows were becoming more violent.

During the 1960s and 1970s, most research on children's television focused on the effects of violence. Many people were concerned not only about violent episodes in cartoons, but about children watching violent shows intended for adults. Legislators were urged to control televised violence through regulation, but these efforts failed. Television stations asserted that programming decisions were matters of internal policy, and some lawmakers felt that regulation would violate the stations' First Amendment rights of freedom of speech.

Programming and Advertising Concerns: The Birth of Public Television

In 1960 the Federal Communications Commission (FCC) recognized children as a segment of the public needing special attention from TV broadcasters. Programming for children got a boost when the Corporation for Public Broadcasting was founded. A 1967 Carnegie Commission study called for the creation of a federally funded network of public and educational television stations that would air more and better children's programs. The Public Broadcasting System (PBS) is the network within this system that carries such acclaimed shows as *Mr. Rogers' Neighborhood, Sesame Street,* and *Reading Rainbow.*

Action for Children's Television: Efforts to Limit Advertising

In 1970 a grassroots group called Action for Children's Television (ACT) lobbied the FCC to require all stations to provide certain minimal programming for children every day. ACT also proposed that advertising be abolished during children's programs. As a result, the FCC issued its 1974 Children's Television Report and Policy Statement. This nonbinding ruling established guidelines for children's programming. Among other things, it instructed TV stations to use "separators" between children's shows and commercials (to help children perceive that a commercial is not part of the show) and to stop using characters from children's shows to push products (a practice known as "host selling").

Broadcasters ignored many of the guidelines. In 1976, ACT succeeded in getting the Federal Trade Commission (FTC) to consider children a special population with respect to advertising. The FTC proposed a ban on television advertising directed toward children under 8 years of age. But the proposal met with such strong resistance that the FTC abandoned its efforts to encourage regulation of TV commercials directed at children (Hymes, 1982).

Efforts to Improve Children's Shows: The Children's Television Education Act

Subsequent efforts to develop a policy for children's television have focused on improving its educational value. In 1984, Rep. Timothy Wirth of Colorado introduced the Children's Television Education Act of 1983 in the House of Representatives. This bill called for TV stations to provide a minimum of one hour of children's programming every weekday. The bill died in 1984.

Rep. Wirth and his cosponsor, Senator Frank Lautenberg, reintroduced the bill in 1985. Under the revised act, broadcasters' licenses would not be renewed if they failed to provide minimal children's programming every day. The bill also called for the FCC to investigate the effects of children's programs produced solely to promote toys or other products—the so-called "program-length commercials." This bill died in 1986.

Finally, in 1990, two laws were passed regarding children's television. One, the Children's Television Act of 1990, limited the number of commercials that can be aired during children's programs. During the week, the limit is 12 minutes per hour; on weekends, the limit is 10.5 minutes per hour. When stations apply for renewal of their broadcast licenses, they must also provide information about how they address children's educational and informational needs. Finally, the act created a National Endowment for Children's Educational Television (National Association for the Education of Young Children [NAEYC], 1991).

The second law, the Children's Television Violence Act, exempts broadcasters from antitrust laws, which had been invoked after the National Association of Broadcasters developed a self-regulating code in 1980 to limit violence on TV and encouraged all broadcasters to adopt it (NAEYC, 1991). This law was needed because any agreement among competing broadcasters is generally seen as an il-

No matter how good the programs on television, children can spend too many hours watching it. Active play is important during all the years of childhood. This parent and child are busy shoveling snow. Such activities can give children something else to do besides watch television.   (*Source:* © Nancy Richmond/The Image Works)

legal attempt to form a "trust" or association to control competition.

In 1996, the FCC approved more stringent rules for the Children's Television Act. They stipulate that broadcasters must provide a minimum of three hours each week of educational programming for children. Importantly, "educational programming" was defined more narrowly to ensure that television stations cannot substitute adult programming that was not meant to be educational for children (NAEYC, 1996).

What Can Adults Do?

Adults who are concerned about children's TV watching can take the following steps:

- Limit the amount of time children spend watching TV. Active play is preferable to TV watching for children of all ages. Experts recommend that adults limit preschoolers to no more than one hour a day and school-age children to no more than two hours a day.

- Do not allow children to watch shows that contain a lot of violence. Make adult shows off-limits. For preschoolers, these might include news broadcasts, as well as situation comedies, some game shows, all talk shows, and many documentaries. Preschoolers cannot comprehend most adult programming and often find it upsetting or frightening.

- Watch television with children and explain what is real and what is pretend or make-believe.

- Encourage children to watch educational programs and shows with a prosocial message.

- Support public policies that protect children by making improvements in children's television.

- Substitute high-quality videotapes (children's story tapes, information tapes about animals, and so on) for television programming.

Prosocial Behavior

Behavior that benefits others rather than, or in addition to, oneself is called **prosocial behavior.** It includes helping, sharing, comforting, and cooperating. Children may have an inborn inclination to be helpful, nurturing, and consoling, but most prosocial behavior, like most aggressive behavior, is learned. And many of the same socialization processes are at work. A child's level of cognitive development also plays an important part. In this section, we discuss how parents and teachers can support children in this aspect of their development.

Reinforcement, Punishment, and Prosocial Behavior

When adults notice and comment approvingly on children's prosocial efforts, children are motivated to act that way again. Smiles, approving looks, and simple comments, such as "It was thoughtful of you to give Johanna some of your markers so that she could draw too," can be as reinforcing to children as elaborate rewards. Adults often overlook children's positive behavior, perhaps because it seems like normal courtesy to them, at the same time that they are quick to criticize misbehavior. If they get in the habit of expressing their appreciation for children's thoughtfulness, helpfulness, and other prosocial attempts when they occur, adults will probably increase the likelihood that those behaviors will occur again.

Teachers can also build opportunities for helping into the structure of their classroom day. Children can help prepare and serve the snack for the class, with different children counting out cups and napkins, making juice, and distributing crackers. Children enjoy being given this kind of responsibility, and the teacher has a chance to teach and verbally reinforce working together.

Punishment is not an effective way to teach prosocial behavior, for all the same reasons that it is ineffective in discouraging aggression. There is usually a way to support sharing and cooperating without resorting to punishment. Consider the following example:

One day during the first week of nursery school, Emily was sitting at a table drawing with crayons. Karen sat down nearby and pulled a piece of paper toward herself. Then she reached over to get a crayon from the box Emily was using.

"No, they're mine!" Emily snapped, grabbing them away. "You can't have any!"

"But I want to draw," Karen protested.

The teacher approached. "Emily," she said, "could Karen use the red crayon while you're using the blue one? Then both of you could draw at the same time."

"Well, okay," Emily slowly replied. She pushed the crayons toward Karen. After a few moments, she looked over at Karen and said, "What are you going to draw?"

Now imagine that instead of suggesting a way to share the crayons, the teacher took the crayons away from Emily, saying, "Those crayons belong to the whole class. If you cannot share them, you cannot use them at all!" It is easy to see that Emily would learn very little about prosocial behavior from this "lesson."

Verbalization and Prosocial Behavior

If, after Emily shared the crayons, the teacher made positive comments to her about her behavior, she would teach the prosocial behavior even more effectively. "You really are a good sharer," she might say. "You know just how to make sure you and Karen both have fun. You use one color and she uses another, and then you trade." As we saw earlier, attributing positive characteristics to a child (positive character attribution) can make the child want to live up to the image in the future (Grusec, 1991).

Another technique parents and teachers use to increase prosocial behavior is **empathy training** (Grusec, 1991). Prosocial behavior can be expected to increase when children are made aware of the effects of their behavior on the feelings and welfare of others (Hoffman, 1982). The teacher might say, for example, "Emily shared the crayons with Karen, so Karen had a chance to draw too. Everyone in the classroom is happier when all children are able to play."

Parental talk about emotions, and the ways in which parents socialize their children's emotions, also seem to affect children's prosocial behavior. For example, when parents modulate their discussions of negative emotions, taking into account the child's developmental level, children seem better able later to react with sympathy in situations where someone else is distressed. When parents do not buffer young children from too much negative emotion, children seem to react with distress rather than with sympathy in the face of another's distress (Eisenberg & Fabes, 1998). Prosocial responding also seems to be enhanced when parents probe to find out why their children are feeling sad, and when they listen to their children when they are upset about something (Eisenberg et al., 1993).

Observational Learning of Prosocial Behavior

Verbal instruction, especially of the inductive type, helps children learn prosocial behavior. Seeing prosocial behavior modeled is even more effective, although some kinds of models and modeling situations are more effective than others. An elaborate study undertaken with preschoolers showed that adults who are warm and nurturant are the best models. It also showed that seeing helping modeled in real life is more effective than seeing it depicted in fictional situations, such as books, films, or puppet plays (Yarrow et al., 1973).

A classic study of kindergarten children showed that the level of nurturance of the adult model is a critical factor in how actively helpful a child is (Staub, 1971). It seems that if the adult is warm and accepting, the child attempts to help in a situation even if he does not know exactly what to do. If an adult is distant and unfriendly, the child is more hesitant, apparently because he is afraid his efforts will be criticized. Both of these studies are discussed in detail in the Research Close-Up: How Children Learn to Help Others.

Sharing is also influenced by modeling. One study found that children shared significantly more after they saw a film in which a boy shared his candy with someone who did not have any (Elliott & Vasta, 1970). Even more sharing occurred among children who saw the film and who then saw the boy rewarded with a toy and heard why he was being rewarded. In other words, the research showed that the highest level of prosocial behavior resulted from observational learning combined with reinforcement and verbalization.

Although studies show that helping and sharing are both influenced by modeling, sharing is not influenced by the nurturance of the model the way helping is. In fact, the more nurturant the relationship with the model, the less likely a child sometimes is to share. This phenomenon can be understood by noting that sharing requires some sacrifice on the part of the child. He must give up part of something he has, and he may not want to do this. If he does not do the socially accepted thing, the adult model may express disapproval of him. But if he has a warm, accepting relationship with the adult, he may not fear the adult's disapproval. Therefore, he does not share.

These boys are helping their mom with the dishes. Her tolerance for little mistakes, such as not thoroughly drying a plate or splashing a little water on the sink counter or floor, provides the nurturance that encourages children to pitch in and help. She has also made the situation safe by placing the chair back against the sink rather than behind the child. Additionally, the water heater in the house is set at a safe level to prevent the possibility of burns at the kitchen sink or in the bathtub. (*Source:* © Stephen Marks)

RESEARCH

To learn how we can teach children to help others, one group of researchers set up a study with pre-schoolers (Yarrow et al., 1973). They began by collecting baseline data on the children's helping behavior. Children were tested individually to see how they responded to pictures of animals, adults, and children in distress. The child was asked, "What's happening in this picture?" and "If you were there and saw that happening, what would you do?" Real-life incidents of distress also occurred during the pretesting session. For example, the tester knocked a vase of flowers to the floor, and a kitten tangled in yarn was brought into the room. The child's responses to the pictures and incidents were rated in terms of helping behaviors.

In the next phase of the experiment, an adult interacted with groups of 8 to 10 children in a playroom for half an hour a day for two weeks. Half the groups interacted with a nurturing adult who offered help, gave attention and praise, and was friendly and sympathetic. The other half interacted with an adult who was not nurturing, did not give attention, and criticized achievements.

Next, the adult who interacted with the children modeled prosocial behavior either symbolically only or symbolically and in real life. The symbolic situation involved a diorama (a small box depicting a situation). For example, a toy monkey was helped to reach some bananas. In a real-life situation a person might enter the room and bump her head; the adult model would comfort her and ask her if she would like to sit down.

In summary, the experiment involved four sets of conditions:

1. Nurturant adult behavior paired with symbolic modeling (the friendly adult showed the diorama).
2. Non-nurturant adult behavior paired with symbolic modeling (the unfriendly adult showed the diorama).
3. Nurturant adult behavior paired with symbolic and real-life modeling (the friendly adult showed the diorama and helped the person in the room).
4. Non-nurturant adult behavior paired with symbolic and real-life modeling (the unfriendly adult showed the diorama and helped the person in the room).

During post-testing—the period when changes in behavior are observed in a study—the children were allowed to play with the diorama and were also taken to a nearby house to visit a mother and baby. During the visit, several "accidents" occurred, such as toys falling out of the baby's crib. The children's helping behavior was recorded in both the symbolic situation with the diorama and the real-life situation with the baby's toys.

Only the children who interacted with the nurturant adult and who saw helping behavior modeled in both the diorama and the real-life incident increased their helping behavior in the real-life situation with the baby. This indicates that nurturant adults are more effective models than non-nurturant adults and that children must actually see adults helping others in real situations to become helpful themselves. When helping is modeled symbolically, children seem to learn only the principle of helping, not the idea that they can do it too.

A study with kindergarten children turned up similar results (Staub, 1971). First, individual children played games with the experimenter, who was nurturant with some children and non-nurturant with others—task-oriented and unfriendly. After they played for a while, the experimenter said he had to do one of two things: check on the child in the next room, or respond to a child's crying in the next room, which the child playing games could hear. This was the distress-modeling situation.

When the experimenter returned, he explained that the child had fallen but that he had helped her up and she was all right. Then he said he had to go do some work but that the child could continue playing. He also told the child that more crayons could be found in the next room.

After he left, the child heard a crash from the next room, followed by crying. This was the post-testing situation. Children who went to the next room to try to help the crying child saw the tape recorder and were told by the experimenter that he wanted to see how children felt when they heard another child cry. Children who did not offer direct help, including those who described the incident to the experimenter when he returned, were told that someone else had helped the crying child and that she was okay.

Children who saw the adult demonstrate helping by going to the assistance of the "crying child" were more helpful than children who thought the adult was just checking on another child. In addition, children with whom the adult had been nurturant were much more likely to offer active help rather than just tell the adult about the crying. Even children in the nurturant group who had not seen helping modeled were more likely to go to the crying child's aid than were children in the non-nurturant group.

Being nurtured gives children the confidence to try to do something in new situations, even if they do not know what to do. Fear of disapproval for doing the wrong thing inhibits children who have not been nurtured. This experiment also underscores the importance of practicing ourselves the behaviors we verbalize to children.

Helping, on the other hand, often involves empathy—the understanding of someone else's feelings. When we see or hear someone else's distress, we remember how we felt in similar situations and we feel distress too. Helping or comforting the other person relieves our own feelings of pain or sadness, and thus it is in our own interest to help. A child often does not know what to do to help someone in distress, and he may worry that he will do the wrong thing. But when he has a nurturant relationship with the adult model, he does not fear that the adult will ridicule or disapprove of his attempts. He will show the initiative Erikson sees as important to develop at this stage, initiative without fear of making a mistake as the result of goodwill efforts (Grusec & Skubinski, 1970; Staub, 1971, 1975).

If this explanation is correct, nurturance encourages children to act in their own best interest without fear of consequences. Young children often consider helping to be in their own best interest, but think sharing is not.

How should parents and teachers teach children to share? If they are nurturant, children learn to help others in distress, but they do not learn to share. The children in the studies never expected to see the experimenters again, and they could act just as they wished at the moment (Baumrind, 1972). Luckily, in their own lives, children have long-term relationships with adults who have definite expectations of them and whose approval they want. Parents and teachers show by their consistent encouragement of sharing that this is a behavior they expect children to learn.

Learning Self-Control

Eli, Sam, and Rebecca were trudging along the darkened street in their Halloween costumes, behind their dads. It was late and they were cold and tired. The giddy excitement of dressing up and going trick-or-treating was gone, but the pleasure of eating all that candy drove them on toward home.

"Can I eat a piece of my candy, Daddy?" piped up Rebecca.

"No, not now, Becca," Mike replied. "Wait till we get home."

"Just one piece?" she wailed.

He turned around and looked at her. "You know we talked about this before. Your mom and I want to look at all your candy before you eat any. And we want to make sure you do not eat too much tonight. You will get a stomachache." He turned back and continued his conversation with Sam and Eli's dad.

When they got to their door, Rebecca and Mike said good night to their neighbors. Looking down at his daughter in the porch light, Mike saw that she had chocolate smeared across her face.

"Hey," he said, squatting down in front of her. "I told you not to eat any candy until we got home."

Rebecca looked down at the ground. "Sorry, Daddy," she said. "I just ate one piece."

think about it

Was there something Rebecca's dad might have done differently to help her resist temptation? Can self-control become so strong that we can count on children or adults never to do what they shouldn't? Or are external supports also important to help people maintain self-control?

Developing self-control of all kinds is important. When we help young children learn self-control, we give them a stronger foundation for self-control later. How can the socialization processes we have been discussing be used to support self-control?

Verbal Instruction and Self-Control

Distractions and diversions help children control their impulses. Rebecca's dad could have helped her if he had suggested that she think about something else on the way home. "Don't think about the candy or it will be harder not to eat any," he might have said. "Why don't you see how many jack-o'-lanterns you can count? Or we could sing one of your Halloween songs."

In one study, children were told they would receive a large reward later if they could forgo a smaller reward immediately (Mischel & Ebbesen, 1970). Children did everything from covering their eyes to making up games with their hands and feet to avoid taking the smaller reward. In another study, children were helped to delay taking rewards like pretzel sticks and marshmallows by being told to think about them as little brown logs and white cotton balls or clouds (Mischel & Baker, 1975).

Other researchers gave children a repetitive task to work on to win attractive rewards (Patterson & Mischel, 1976). They created a temptation dilemma for the children by placing a "Mr. Clown Box" in the same room. The clown made noises and friendly comments and lit up to show toys within the box. Children who paid attention to the clown instead of doing the task would lose out on rewards later.

Researchers gave the children two different self-instructional plans to help them resist the temptation to watch the clown. One was the temptation inhibition plan, in which the child's attention was directed away from the clown. The other was a task facilitation plan, in which the child's attention was directed toward the task. The temptation inhibition plan was more effective in helping the child resist the temptation.

Various strategies, ranging from putting the temptation out of sight to helping the child think about something besides the temptation's desirable characteristics (for example, thinking about candy as rocks), can help children resist temptations. Younger children do not know that these strategies might work (Glucksberg et al., 1975; Patterson, 1982). An adult can help preschoolers by stressing the consequences their actions will have (Meichenbaum & Turk, 1976), by consistently modeling resistance, and by helping them think through strategies for dealing with temptations when adult support is needed.

Self-Control in the Long Term

Although many studies have looked at children's self-control as a function of such socialization techniques as modeling, reinforcement, and verbal instruction, other studies have focused on the relationship between self-control and attachment. Correlational studies of the kind described in chapter 7 have shown that children who were securely attached as infants are especially persistent in working on difficult or frustrating tasks, which is another aspect of self-control. In one such study (Arends, 1984, cited in Sroufe, 1990), 3-year-olds with secure attachment histories clearly remained on-task more than did anxiously attached preschoolers. They kept "expecting well" in the face of what was actually an impossible task (a "barrier box").

Although some children consistently show more self-control than others, self-control is also strongly influenced by situations. Adults often manage children's environments to reduce temptation. For example, parents keep cookies and candy out of sight until they want children to have some, and teachers closely monitor students during class exams. These are wise practices, because even adults are apt to yield when social controls and external sanctions are absent. We should "discard any simplistic notion that a person's internal moral standards persist unchanged through life without environmental support," writes one observer, "and accept the fact that internalized standards are vulnerable to external pressure and temptations" (Hoffman, 1984, p. 307). We should not give up on supporting internal controls but we should realize that *both* internal and external controls are important when children—or adults—face difficult situations. (See Knowledge in Action: Education—Guidelines for Helping Children Develop Self-Control in Preschool Settings.)

EDUCATION

Guidelines for Helping Children Develop Self-Control in Preschool Settings

Young children need to learn self-control, but it takes a long time and requires the help of adults. The preschool years are an important time for this learning, and there is much that preschool teachers can do to help children. Here are some guidelines.

■ Think carefully about your place in children's conflicts. Do not hesitate to let children know when you think a behavior is right or wrong, but incorporate the children's ideas in thinking of how they might right a wrong.

■ Emphasize how children's appropriate and inappropriate behavior affect others. At times, adults must express negative emotions when prohibitions and standards are violated. But it is never excusable or effective to belittle children, to be punitive, or to hold a grudge.

■ Young children will make a lot of mistakes. When an incident is over, it should be over. Criticizing the child's acts, rather than the child herself, also is important for letting children know that they can make a fresh start.

■ Use enough authority-assertion to get a child's attention in a situation where a prohibition or a standard has been violated. Deal with individual children in private as much as possible, adapting levels of authority-assertion to individual needs.

■ Provide interesting activities to engage children. Prevent unnecessary conflicts by providing adequate materials. The ability to share materials and wait for a turn does not develop well in children accustomed to deprivation.

■ Avoid the trap of thinking that you cannot begin implementing an interesting curriculum until children's social and emotional development is under control. Remember that providing interesting and challenging things for children to do is a very good way to distract them from doing what you do not wish them to do.

■ Use tactics that make compliance easier for young children. Keep rules to a few basic, necessary, and understandable ones. Organize the classroom to make cleaning up easy. Give children some choice, but also enforce expectations. Enable children to predict events and expectations by being consistent and following a daily routine. Children cannot learn self-regulation if they experience nothing regular or consistent.

■ Give reasons for your prohibitions, but do not wait for children's agreement as a condition for following through. Baumrind's (1967) effective, authoritative parent "does not base her decisions on group consensus or the individual child's desires," although this parent does "share with the child the reasoning behind her policy" (p. 168).

■ Interact with children as they play. Adult interaction increases children's learning, and redirection and suggestions in the midst of play can help children play with each other and resolve conflicts in constructive ways. Teacher interaction with children also is important for forming teacher-child affective bonds (Moss, 1992).

Source: Adapted from "Helping Children Develop Self-Control," by J. A. Schickedanz, 1994, *Childhood Education, 70* (5), pp. 274–279. Used with permission.

KEY POINTS

An Overview of Socialization and Early Moral Development

■ Attachment sets the stage for later moral development because it leads to internalization of the caregiver's values and behavior.

■ Face-to-face turn-taking during early phases of attachment provides the first opportunity for a child to learn "rules" of reciprocity.

■ It is during the fourth stage of attachment that moral behavior begins, because at this time the child's initiative may conflict with adult standards for behavior.

Socialization in the Family during Childhood

■ Parents begin to discipline children early in the second year of life, at about the time children begin to walk.

■ Moral development begins in everyday discipline contexts.

■ Baumrind developed a scheme for thinking about parenting behavior in terms of three styles—permissive, authoritative, and authoritarian.

■ Control, nurturance/warmth, and maturity demands vary among parents who use different discipline approaches. The most competent children tend to receive authoritative parenting. The least competent have permissive or uninvolved parents.

Socialization Processes

- Currently favored methods of socialization are based largely on learning and social learning theory.

- The main socialization processes are verbal instruction, reinforcement, punishment, extinction, and observational learning.

- The effect of the socialization processes is influenced by other factors, such as children's attachment relationships with their parents, their level of cognitive development, and temperament.

- In verbal instruction children are told what behaviors are desirable. Verbal instruction can also be used for attributing positive characteristics to children when they have been observed behaving in desirable ways.

- Verbal instruction combined with reinforcement and modeling is more effective than verbal instruction alone in motivating children to behave in a desired way.

- In observational learning, children observe how adults act and then imitate their actions. When an adult demonstrates a behavior, we say the adult is modeling that behavior. Children are more likely to imitate a model who is nurturant and helpful and whom the child perceives to be like himself.

- Reinforcement occurs when a response increases the likelihood that a child will respond the same way again in the same or in similar situations. Socialization is fostered when children receive positive reinforcement for their desirable behaviors.

- Punishment decreases the likelihood that a child will respond the same way again. Some punishments (such as a spanking) add stimuli to the environment; others remove stimuli from the environment (such as time out, a process also known as response cost).

- Reinforcement of behavior incompatible with misbehavior is generally considered the best learning method for socializing children.

- Extinction refers to the reduction of a behavior due to lack of response to it. This might be accomplished by arranging the environment so the child's undesirable behavior receives no response at all.

- Extinction is difficult to use, since it is not always possible to ignore a child's misbehavior.

- Physical punishment, used as a primary socialization strategy, has some problems. Physical punishment can reduce a child's initiative and drive; restrict him to a few limited responses in difficult social situations; and create hostility between him and the punishing adult.

- The most serious problem with physical punishment is that it can lead to child abuse.

- Physical punishment models aggressive behavior. Researchers have found a positive correlation between aggression in children and the use of physical punishment by the parent.

- The most effective way to discipline children is to use reasoning about how the child's behavior affects others and how the child can change it in positive ways.

- Children's behavior is influenced by their level of cognition, the values they have been taught, the socialization methods their parents have used, and genetic and biological factors, including temperament. No single factor explains how a child behaves.

Aggression: How It Is Learned and Controlled

- Children are reinforced for aggression when their aggressive behavior is effective in helping them achieve their goals. Aggression sometimes increases when children are brought together in a group for the first time.

- Inattentive parents of very aggressive children tend to reward aggressive behaviors by giving up parental demands.

- Severe physical punishment is associated with very high levels of aggression in children, probably due to the combined effects of modeling and hostility.

- A time-out can be an effective punishment, but it must be used appropriately and moderately to minimize the child's anger and frustration and to increase the chances that a child will think about the situation.

- Much aggressive behavior is learned through observation. Aggression observed in the family includes physical punishment, verbal abuse, violence between adults, and violence among siblings.

- Correlational studies reveal that all children, regardless of age, level of intelligence, or socioeconomic status, act more aggressively after they watch very violent TV programs than after they watch programs that have prosocial or neutral content. Experimental studies show that watching violent TV shows is causally related to children's aggression.

- Preschoolers do not have the cognitive ability to understand violence on TV or its consequences, nor can they distinguish between real and nonreal events depicted on TV.

- In the long run, children who watch a lot of violence on TV become desensitized to it—they accept aggressive behavior. They also obey adults less than children who have not been exposed to filmed violence.

Prosocial Behavior

■ One of the best ways to discourage aggression is to model prosocial behavior—behavior that benefits others besides oneself, such as helping, sharing, comforting, and cooperating.

■ Reinforcement promotes prosocial behavior by recognizing it and making the child want to attempt it again. Punishment of antisocial behavior is not effective as a primary means to teach prosocial behavior.

■ Verbal reinforcement of prosocial behavior helps children understand why their behavior is desirable.

■ Children also learn prosocial behavior by observation and imitation. Effective models are warm and nurturing and demonstrate prosocial behavior in real-life situations.

■ Nurturant models make children more likely to help others but less likely to share with others because, in each case, children feel comfortable acting in their own best interest. A young child seldom sees any long-term interest in sharing, so concentrates instead on the immediate reward of keeping materials to herself. To encourage sharing, adults can make clear that sharing is expected in many situations.

■ The best way to teach prosocial behavior is through a combination of modeling, reinforcement, and verbalization.

Learning Self-Control

■ Learning to exercise self-control is important, especially in adolescence and adulthood, when people face potentially dangerous temptations.

■ Adults can help children use diversions and distractions to control their impulses. They can guide the children's thoughts, redirect their actions, or remove the temptation from view.

■ Adults can help children by explaining the consequences of their behaviors and by working out strategies of resistance with them. The more internal control children have acquired from responsive parenting, the more likely they are to resist a temptation when external controls are absent.

■ Both attachment theory and social learning theory propose that early experience helps produce children who create experiences that maintain their internal working models and patterns of social behavior.

■ Preschool teachers and child-care workers can use specific strategies to help children develop self-control and prosocial behavior.

GLOSSARY

authoritarian parent: a parent who exhibits behaviors that include high levels of control coupled with low warmth (p. 376)

authoritative parent: a parent who exhibits behaviors that include warmth, a high level of control with respect to child compliance with parental expectations, and high maturity demands (p. 376)

autobiographical narratives: personal stories about past events that serve in some families and cultures as socialization opportunities (p. 373)

aversive stimulus: a stimulus to which a person responds with intense negative feelings (p. 385)

conscience: self-control exercised by a person in situations where the person's wrongdoing would go undetected (p. 376)

dispositional praise: positive comments about the child that indicate the kind of person the adult thinks the child is; similar to positive attribution (p. 380)

effortful control: control of actions by stopping them, once they are in progress, or before they are started (p. 375)

empathy: understanding how others feel or what they think (p. 374)

empathy training: making children aware of the effects of their behavior on others (p. 394)

extinction: the disappearance or reduction of a behavior when it receives no reaction at all from the environment (p. 382)

identification: in Freudian theory, this term refers to the adoption of behaviors, attitudes, and beliefs of the same-sex parent (p. 81)

inductive approach: an approach to discipline that involves reasoning with the child to explain how behavior affects others (p. 376)

inhibitory control: same as effortful control, in which actions violating standards are stopped in progress or not initiated at all (p. 375)

internalization: the acceptance by the child of standards of conduct caregivers teach them (p. 373)

intrinsic reinforcement: reinforcement that comes from the individual's own pleasure following the behavior, rather than from reinforcement provided by materials or by other people (p. 386)

modeling: displaying behavior that others copy (p. 381)

negative reinforcement: something that, when removed from the environment following a person's response, results in an increase in the person's response (p. 387)

neglectful/uninvolved parent: a parent who does whatever it takes to minimize interaction with the child (p. 376)

observational learning: learning by watching and imitating others (p. 381)

permissive parent: a parent who exhibits behaviors that include high warmth and nurturance, as well as low control and demands for maturity (p. 376)

positive attribution: a verbal socialization technique in which the adult describes the positive behaviors of a child, with the result that the child then begins to think of himself in these terms and to live up to them (p. 380)

positive reinforcement: something added to the environment following a person's action, which results in an increase in the action (p. 382)

power-assertive discipline approach: an approach to discipline in which the parent does not give reasons for demands, uses physical force often, and appeals to authority (p. 376)

prosocial behavior: behavior that benefits others, rather than or in addition to the self (p. 393)

punishment: providing a consequence for a behavior to decrease the likelihood that it will occur in the future (p. 383)

reinforcement: providing a consequence for a behavior to increase the likelihood that it will occur in the future (p. 382)

response cost: the level of reduction in reinforcement in a punishment situation in which reinforcement is removed from the situation (p. 383)

script or **script knowledge:** knowledge of action sequences and behaviors that are typical of people in various familiar contexts (pp. 373 and 388)

self-regulation: moderation exercised by a person who engages in effortful inhibition (p. 375)

simple reactivity: the child's characteristic reaction to stimulus change—novelty in the environment (p. 375)

socialization: teaching children what they should and should not do (p. 372)

time out: removal of a child from access to positive reinforcement (p. 383)

time out from positive reinforcement: descriptive name for the procedure known commonly as time out (p. 383)

SUGGESTIONS FOR FURTHER READING

Bates, J. E., & Wachs, T. D. (1994). *Temperament: Individual differences at the interface of biology and behavior.* Washington, DC: American Psychological Association. The 12 chapters of this book about the biological underpinnings of temperament are written by authors such as Robert Plomin (on genetics) and Mary Rothbart (on self-regulation).

Eisenberg, N., & Mussen, P. (1989). *The roots of prosocial behavior in children.* New York: Cambridge University Press. This little book summarizes research on the influences of parents, peers, culture, biology, personal characteristics, situational determinants, and the media on prosocial behavior in children.

Emery, R. (1989). Family violence. *American Psychologist, 44,* 321–328. This article places child abuse in the context of family violence in general, discussing the development of violence between family members and what to do about it.

Grusec, J. E., & Lytton, H. (1988). *Social development: History, theory, and research.* New York: Springer-Verlag. This paperback was written to be used as a text in courses on social development. It has good chapters on socialization and the family, and on the development of self-control and the problem of aggression.

McCord, J. (Ed.). (1995). *Coercion and punishment in long-term perspective.* New York: Cambridge University Press. This book contains individual chapters on various topics, all relating to the short- and long-term consequences of coercion and punishment on aggressive behavior. The book provides an interesting and informative treatment of the topic.

Wilson, J. Q. (1995). *On character: Essays by James Q. Wilson.* Washington, DC: American Enterprise Institute. Several essays in this readable volume are concerned with the family context in which character is formed in children. Interesting more for its breadth of coverage than for its depth of insight.

MILESTONES *in Preschool Development*

AGE	PHYSICAL	COGNITIVE	LANGUAGE	SOCIAL-EMOTIONAL
3 yrs.	Demonstrates true run, with both feet leaving ground Walks upstairs alternating feet Walks downstairs using marked-time climbing Can take most clothes off	Begins to demonstrate preoperational thinking Knows conventional counting words up to 5 Can solve nesting cup problem by reversing two cups or by insertion	Understands *in, on,* and *under* Speaks in more complete sentences Distinguishes graphics that are writing versus graphics that are pictures Begins to overregularize rules for creating verb tenses and plurals	May begin preschool Uses physical aggression more than verbal aggression Can remember a prohibition when the parent is absent
3 yrs. 6 mos.	Can hop a few steps on preferred foot Can button large buttons Can put easier clothes on	Can't easily distinguish false beliefs Can count five objects before making a partitioning error	Might use syllable hypothesis to create written words Rereads favorite storybooks using picture-governed strategies Often uses scribble-writing	Has difficulty generating alternatives in a conflict situation Will learn aggressive behavior rapidly if these means succeed
4 yrs.	Appears thinner due to longer trunk Can walk a curved line Walks downstairs alternating feet Can gallop Can cut straight line with scissors	Can make a row of objects equal to another row by matching one to one Cannot make true classes	Creates questions and negative sentences using correct word arrangement Might create " mock" letters	Watches, on average, 2 to 4 hours of TV per day
4 yrs. 6 mos.	May begin to hold writing tool in finger grip Leans forward more when jumping from a height Can button smaller buttons	Knows conventional counting words up to 15 Understands false beliefs	Often reverses letters when writing Understands *beside, between, front,* and *back*	Self-control often depends on removal of temptation
5 yrs.	Can stop and change direction quickly when running Can hop 8 to 10 steps on one foot	Selects own view in three-mountain task Creates classes of objects based on a single defining attribute	Understands passive sentences May begin to use invented spellings	Inhibitory or effortful control should be well-established for familiar prohibitions
5 yrs. 6 mos.	Can connect a zipper on a coat May be able to tie shoes	Can count 20 objects without making a partitioning error May display conservation of number	May begin to make print-governed reading attempts with favorite books	

Physical Development in School-Age Children

AS STEVE ATKINSON set up orange cones at the ends of the playing field, he heard the first-graders from his first physical education class of the day coming out of the school.

After he led them in some warm-up jumping jacks and torso twists, Steve asked, "We can play either color tag or freeze tag. Which do you want?"

"Color tag!" they all seemed to shout at once.

"Okay, color tag it is."

"Mr. Atkinson, Yolanda and I want to be the chasers today," piped up Sharon, an energetic 6-year-old.

"Let me check my list," Steve replied. "Everyone needs to have a turn . . . yes, that looks okay. Now, look at your clothes to see what colors you're wearing, and then we'll divide into two sides."

When the class was ready, Yolanda and Sharon stood whispering in the middle of the field for a moment and then called out "Red!" From the opposite ends of the field, children started running directly for the other side, and the two girls tagged as many as they could.

Sharon and Yolanda conferred again and this time called out "Yellow!" The field once more became a blur of children running, laughing, and trying to dodge the taggers. Sometimes a child would run wide, out to the edges of the field, but most headed straight for the other end of the field. Sharon and Yolanda had no trouble tagging all but two of the children in four rounds, and those two became the next taggers. By the end of the class, when Steve had them walk around the field to cool down, the children were pink-cheeked and tired, ready to return to their classroom.

Steve's next class was a group of third-graders, and he offered them a choice of capture the flag or elbow tag. They chose elbow tag, a more complicated game that they were just learning to play. Steve liked elbow tag because it required a combination of quick thinking and maneuvering. After the children had jogged once around the field to warm up, they linked arms at the elbow with a partner and spread out over the field. Steve asked Cindy to be the first chaser, and Miguel agreed to be the first one chased.

As they started running, Miguel was able to keep ahead, but when Cindy started to close in, Miguel ran over to a pair of classmates and linked elbows with one of them. The other child in the pair pulled her arm free and ran off, and Cindy now ran after her. But she was starting to get out of breath, and soon she too linked elbows with a classmate. The boy on the other end of that chain became the new chaser.

As the game continued, Steve watched the children running, dodging, and stopping short, then taking off in another direction after a different child. Sometimes he marveled that they were able to keep track of what was going on as well as they could. They too were ready for a rest by the end of the class.

Steve met his last morning class in the gym. The sixth-graders had started learning some basic basketball skills two years earlier, dribbling first with one hand, then with alternate hands, then dribbling around the body while remaining stationary, and finally dribbling while running. Later they practiced dribbling around obstacles, changing directions, and dribbling against an opponent. They practiced a series of throwing and shooting skills too.

Just this year they were starting to put together the understanding, coordination, and skills really required to play the game. After warm-ups, Steve had them practice dribbling and shooting lay-up shots, and then they played a short game. As he watched them play, Steve noted that many of their skills were built on earlier experience in games like color tag, played not so many years ago.

How do Steve's physical education classes compare with those with which you are familiar? Why didn't Steve have his first-graders play basketball? What were the skills required in each kind of physical activity that Steve offered to the different classes? It appeared that Steve had all classes warm up before beginning to play their games. Why did he spend time on this?

Physical education teachers and youth sports coaches must be aware of changes in fine and gross motor skills and the increasing complexity of physical tasks that can be undertaken as children develop during the school-age years—the years from approximately ages 5 to 12. They also must be skilled in dealing with individual differences so that all children can enjoy positive and healthy experiences despite large variations in size and physical skill. Children's continued participation in activities depends on their enjoyment of them when they are young. Parents, teachers, and coaches help determine whether children view sports with a competitive, play-to-win orientation or as opportunities to engage in enjoyable physical activities and improve their skills.

How Do They Grow?

The school years are a period of steady physical growth and rapid skill acquisition. The first-grader turns into the taller, more muscular child of the later elementary school years who is able to begin playing complex games such as basketball. This transformation is supported by a physical education program like Steve's, built around games and physical skill development. As children grow, their increasing strength and motor coordination can contribute to good health.

This chapter covers the typical growth of middle childhood as well as typical and atypical variations in these patterns, such as the preadolescent growth spurt and childhood obesity. This is followed by a discussion of motor development.

These school-age girls are learning and practicing basic skills that will contribute to good health and a sense of well-being. (*Source:* © Robert Harbison)

In groups of 12- and 13-year-olds, girls often tower above boys because they begin their pubertal growth spurt first. After age 14, however, when boys experience their growth spurt, they become taller, as a group, than girls. Of course, there is great variation in height among both boys and girls at all ages, as shown in this photo of a school-age musical group. *(Source:* © Michael Newman/Photo Edit)

Finally, this chapter discusses some of the ways to keep school-age children safe and healthy.

Increases in Height and Weight

The growth rate during the first part of the school years is even slower than the growth rate found among preschool children. The average 6-year-old weighs about 43 pounds and is about 44 inches tall—almost 4 feet. Six years later, at the age of 12, the average child weighs a little over 80 pounds and is about 5 feet tall. An average school-age child's height increases by 2 to 3 inches per year, while weight increases from 5 to 7 pounds per year.

By the time children are 6 years old, they have attained about two thirds of their adult height. By the end of the school-age years, they are much closer to adult height due to the preadolescent growth spurt. Girls begin their pubertal growth spurt around age 10 or 11. Because boys do not start their growth spurt until two to three years later, girls as a group are taller and heavier than boys for a few years. But when boys do begin their growth spurt, around age 13 or 14, the tide begins to turn—boys on average become taller and heavier than girls. Girls are usually as tall as they are going to become when by around age 16 their growth spurt comes to an end. For boys, height continues to increase until around age 17 or 18 (Tanner, 1990). There are large individual differences in these patterns. For example, two basketball players recruited in the 1999 NBA draft grew 9 inches during their college years. Because there is little difference in physique and weight between girls and boys during the school-age years, they should be able to participate together in most physical activities (Gallahue & Ozmun, 1998).

Weight gain during the school-age years is concentrated more in muscle than in fat. As a consequence, strength increases considerably. Because boys as a group have more muscle cells than girls as a group, they are stronger during the later school years, as well as during adolescence (Michael, 1990). The increase in muscle and the lengthening of the legs cause many to look slimmer than they did during the preschool years. However, there has been a three-decade trend, especially among girls, toward obesity during the school-age years (Bar-Or et al., 1998; Freedman et al., 1997; Halpern et al., 1999). This problem is discussed in the section on abnormal variations in growth patterns.

Changes in Body Proportions

Recall from chapter 4 that the brain achieves about 90 percent of its adult weight by age 5. Brain weight equals adult levels by age 6. In the school years, growth of the head is very, very slow, although many changes, including **lateralization** (dominance of one or the other of the brain's two hemispheres with respect to specific functions) and **myelination** (growth of a fatty sheath on the outer surface of nerve cells), will continue for several years (Cratty, 1986).

During the school years, the trunk and especially the legs grow more quickly. The face also undergoes some changes. Unlike the pattern in earlier years, when the upper part of the head grew more rapidly than the lower part, it is the lower face—the jaw—that grows during the school-age years. As the face elongates, the cheeks slim down. The eustachian tubes connecting the middle ear to the throat also begin to assume a more vertical position. Because fluids now can drain from the ear more easily, school-age children tend to have fewer ear infections than preschoolers do. The tiny plastic tubes that some preschoolers must have surgically inserted in their ears to promote drainage of fluids and thus reduce the incidence of ear infections are rarely needed by children who are 7 years or older.

The Eruption of Permanent Teeth

Losing the first baby tooth is a rite of passage into the school-age years. Even though a few children lose one or two teeth soon after their fifth birthday, when they are in kindergarten, losing the first tooth is more commonly a 6-year-old phenomenon. First- and second-grade classrooms are usually full of "toothless grins." The process of tooth loss continues over the entire course of middle childhood. By about age 11 or 12, all permanent teeth except for two sets of molars have erupted.

Care of the permanent teeth is especially important because they need to last for the child's entire life. It is expensive to treat heavily decayed teeth, and gum disease can cause damage to the bones that support the teeth. This is why good oral hygiene, including twice-daily brushing and flossing, is stressed throughout childhood. With the eruption of permanent teeth, dental caries becomes more common. By age 12, the average child has more than four decayed or filled teeth (Brown, 1994). Children exposed to lead are more likely to have cavities (Sternberg, 1999). For this reason and those discussed in chapter 8, efforts must be made to reduce exposure to lead. Fluoridation of water, oral fluoride supplements provided to infants and toddlers, and topical fluoride treatments administered as part of dental care during the preschool and early school-age years have helped considerably to improve the

Losing baby teeth and acquiring permanent ones are hallmarks of the school-age child. One of these third-graders is still missing a front tooth. All of these girls will experience tooth loss and gain until they are about 12 years old. After age 12, they will acquire two sets of molars. (*Source:* © Will Faller)

dental health of children. Unfortunately, dental health care benefits are not available to many children.

As discussed in chapter 4, if thumb and finger sucking do not stop by the time the permanent teeth have come in, **malocclusion** (improper alignment) may result. If a child does not give up this habit, parents may want to obtain counseling for the child. Even without thumb or finger sucking, some children will have overbites and other misalignments of their teeth. Braces may be needed by some older school-age children to correct the problems. Indeed, increasing numbers of late school-age children have orthodontic appliances to correct misalignments.

Normal Variations in Growth Patterns

It's the week for taking school pictures. Mr. Fontaine's seventh-graders are heading to the gym for their group picture. The photographer sizes up the children quickly and begins to tell them where to stand.

"Okay, stand over there, please," he says to the tallest child in the class, a girl with curly brown hair. "You're going to be right in the middle of the back row."

"You over there," he says to another girl. "Please stand to her right."

"Now, let's see . . . We still have a problem here . . . need a few more taller kids there in the back. Let's see, do we have any? . . . Yes, you over there in the yellow blouse. Could I get you to move to the back row? Better, that's better, but let's get a row of chairs in the front so I can get some of these kids to sit down. A fourth level will work better."

Finally, the scene is set, and the photographer starts snapping shots. "Smile, everyone," he calls out. "Just a few more. Look over here, please. Uh, put the hands down by your sides. We don't need any finger rabbit-ears on anyone's head. Now, are we ready? Hold it! Okay, I think that should do it."

think about it

Why were girls picked to form most of the back row in the photo? Will the arrangement of these same children in their class picture be different two or three years from now, when they are 14 and 15 years of age rather than 11 and 12 years? To what degree did anxiety about physical appearance and size contribute to the rabbit-ears behavior?

The Preadolescent Growth Spurt   The photographer probably noticed more than would casual observers the variations found among late school-age children. He used these variations to create a pleasing composition for the class picture. Throughout the whole course of childhood, children of the same age vary in height and weight simply due to genetic differences and to differences in health and diet. Poverty and poor nutrition contribute to large individual differences in height and weight (Peck & Lundberg, 1995). As a result of improved health conditions across the decades, males are now 2 inches taller and females 1½ inches taller than were school-age children 80 years ago (Steckel, 1997). Because older school-age children grow at different rates, typical differences in size are exaggerated during the **preadolescent growth spurt.**

Some children, usually girls, shoot up and begin to develop sexually by the age of 9 or 10. Other children retain their childish proportions longer. The age at which the growth spurt occurs among children can vary by several years. This is why the photographer picked mostly girls to form the back row for the photo. (The growth spurt and other aspects of puberty are discussed in more detail in chapter 16.)

Implications of the Growth Spurt   The rapid physical change of the later school-age years is both exciting and frightening to children. When one mother discovered that her sixth-grade daughter was concerned about a topic that began with the letter *D,* she hastened to assure her that she and her husband had never considered divorce. But the 11-year-old informed her in exasperation that the topic of interest was development.

The physical changes of puberty, such as the development of breasts, pubic hair, and genitalia, can affect how children are regarded by their peers (Lackovic-Grgin et al., 1994; Rodriguez-Tome et al., 1993). Children's concern is heightened by the wide variation in timing of the growth spurt and in the onset of puberty. Some girls show early stages of breast or pubic hair development by age 8, and 2 to 3 percent begin menstruating at age 10 or younger (Herman-Giddens et al., 1997). The average age of menarche (onset of menstruation) is 11.4 years for African Americans and 11.8 years for white Americans (Halpern et al., 1999). A national longitudinal study of youth health revealed that 84 percent of African Americans and 80 percent of white Americans reach menarche by age 14 (Bearman et al., 1997). If a child develops either sooner or later than her peers do, she may feel awkward and self-conscious. Studies have indicated that early-developing females are often embarrassed by breast growth, may be more anxious or depressed, and, when coupled with overweight, may be less popular than later-maturing girls (Ge et al., 1998; Halpern et al., 1999). Late-developing males experience more social anxiety about their physical development than do early-developing males.

Added to this self-consciousness about physical development is a strong desire to belong—to be like others. By about the fourth or fifth grade, school-age children also begin to have a heightened awareness of other people's opinions of them. All of these developments can interact to make older school-age children vulnerable to wide fluctuations in how they feel about themselves. Adults can ease children's feelings of discomfort by making sure they understand their physical development and emerging sexuality and by providing a supportive environment in which developmental changes are an accepted part of each child's life.

Abnormal Variations in Growth Patterns

Although wide variations in children's growth are normal, some children's growth falls outside of the normal range. Some children fail to grow or grow too slowly; others gain too much weight during childhood.

Retarded Growth   Retarded growth can be caused by social-environmental factors or by organic (physical) factors. Children whose growth is far below what is typical for their age are known as **failure-to-thrive** children. Failure-to-thrive children are small for their age, appear undernourished, and may be lethargic or listless. In infancy, this syndrome is most often caused by parental neglect and can continue throughout childhood. The syndrome is treated by working with the parents or by placing the child in a foster home where proper care can be provided.

A very serious form of malnutrition, known as **kwashiorkor,** is caused by severe dietary deficiencies in both protein and calories. Children with kwashiorkor suffer from edema (collection of water in the tissues) and have large, protruding abdomens and very skinny arms, hands, and legs. Many children in poorer regions of the world, where there are frequent famines or prolonged wars, suffer from this condition. Many starve to death.

Severe malnutrition not only harms the child's health and developing brain directly by limiting growth, but makes the child extremely weak and listless. Weakness and listlessness are secondary effects of malnutrition and the related problem of iron-deficiency anemia. They reduce children's activity level and their ability to sustain interest in the world. This reduces considerably the child's stimulation and thus restricts the child's opportunities for learning (Frank & Zeisel, 1988; Tanner, 1990). Supplemental nutrition can improve such children's growth and cognitive performance. However, the later in childhood the correction in nutrition is undertaken, the smaller the chance that the child will catch up in development (Peck & Lundberg, 1995; Steckel, 1997; Super et al., 1990).

As many international news stories reliably indicate, inadequate food is a major problem for children in many countries throughout the world. Even children in countries with considerable wealth can suffer from malnutrition if there is great disparity in life conditions between the rich and the poor. The Child Protection Report (1995) indicates that about 4 million low-income children in the United States are not getting enough to eat. They estimate that another 9 million—about 30 percent of low-income children in the United States—are hungry or are at risk for hunger. Government-sponsored food stamp programs for low-income families, and free or reduced-cost school breakfast and lunch programs, are designed to help prevent hunger, poor nutrition, and impaired growth. These programs also help prevent the secondary effects of hunger and malnutrition, which include low energy and lack of stamina.

Retarded growth during the school-age years can also be caused by a disturbance of the pituitary gland, which supplies growth hormone to the body. Children with low levels of growth hormone are short for their age and often overweight for their height. Because growth hormones are secreted during non-REM sleep and are stimulated by exercise, good sleeping conditions and a regular exercise program are important for growth (Gallahue & Ozmun, 1998).

The best indicator of a problem in growth hormone is an extreme deviation from the norm for the child's age. Pediatricians or school nurses plot a child's growth on standard growth charts. They can tell easily from these records if the child's growth is substantially below the norm. A child with a growth problem due to hormonal difficulties can be given a synthetic hormone, but physicians must monitor growth carefully to control the child's response to this drug (Cara & Johanson, 1990; Raiti et al., 1987).

Childhood Obesity   Obesity is defined as an excess of body fat relative to lean tissue (Hassink, 1999). Obesity can be measured by using skin-fold calipers to compare the amount of body fat to normal standards. A child's weight is less crucial than the ratio of fat to lean tissue (Gallahue & Ozmun, 1999). Effective diet and exercise programs reduce body fat mass while leaving body-fat-free mass unchanged (Figueroa-Colon et al., 1998). Obesity is the most common deviation from normal growth found among school-age children in the United States. Estimates of the number of obese school-age children vary from 20 to 40 percent of this population (Robinson & Killen, 1995). There has been a three-decade trend toward greater obesity among U.S. school-age children. While in the late 1960s, 17.5 percent of 6- to 12-year-olds were obese, that percentage rose to 29 percent by the late 1990s. This increase in childhood obesity has been greater for girls than for boys, and the proportion of African American girls who are obese is significantly greater than the proportion of white girls who are (Bar-Or et al., 1998; Freedman et al., 1997; Popkin & Udry, 1998). It is discouraging that the problem of obesity continues to increase during a period of increasing emphasis on health and fitness and decreasing total fat consumption.

Do children outgrow their childhood obesity? Unfortunately, they do not. Most overweight children become overweight adults (Gallahue & Ozmun, 1998; Popkin & Udry, 1998), probably because the eating and physical activity habits that children form during the school-age years stay with them into adolescence and adulthood. Overweight Children are more likely to be rejected, teased, or ridiculed than are normal-weight children. In one study, school-age children described silhouettes of obese children as ugly, lazy, and stupid (Stunkard & Sobol, 1995). Obese children also have a lower than average academic performance, poorer self-image, and persistent concerns with dieting. Increased body fat is also associated with a lower probability of dating when they reach the seventh and eighth grades (Gallahue & Ozmun, 1998; Halpern et al., 1999). Obese children usually run more slowly than other children and cannot move quickly in games because of their excess weight. They can become dissatisfied with their lack of skill and with other children's reactions and then withdraw even more from physical activity. Such withdrawal is more common when children experience sport programs that emphasize winning rather than individual development.

Childhood obesity is caused in part by low levels of physical activity in some children. These two overweight boys may get their weight under control by curtailing their snacking while watching television, and by running every day. (*Source:* © Will Hart)

What causes children to gain extra weight in the first place? Researchers have found that the problem is not simply that overweight children eat a great deal more than their normal-weight peers; the problem is that obese children exercise less than do normal-weight children (Bar-Or et al., 1998; Siedentop, 1999). Not surprisingly, perhaps, obese children also tend to watch more television than their normal-weight peers (Dietz, 1990; Nemours Foundation, 1999), and not get as much exercise as their peers (Smith, 1997). A TV habit not only takes up time that could be spent in physical activity, thus reducing the number of calories a child burns in a day, but it also increases snacking, particularly of calorie-dense junk food (Barcus & McLaughlin, 1978; Dietz, 1986). The majority of additional eating in which obese children engage is often done in front of the television set. Obese individuals also tend to be more susceptible to external food-related cues than are normal-weight individuals (Ballard et al., 1980). Simply seeing food or food advertisements leads such individuals to want food.

On average, obese children put on their excess weight during the school-age years at a rate of 5 pounds per year. This amounts to an excess of about 50 calories a day. A 20-minute bike ride would more than offset that many calories, as would one less snack of chips and a cola drink while watching TV. Twenty minutes of aerobic exercise three or more times per week raises metabolism, helping the body to burn more calories (Nemours Foundation, 1999).

Even though it is true that some of the variability in school-age children's weight can be accounted for by knowing the children's activity level and caloric intake, data from the Colorado Adoption Longitudinal Study suggest that two thirds of the variability in weight and height is determined genetically (Cardon, 1994).

knowledge *in action*

Overcoming Childhood Obesity

Obese children have some of the same health risks that are found in obese adults, including high blood pressure and elevated total cholesterol levels. Moreover, childhood obesity predicts adult obesity and adult cholesterol levels (Kelder et al., 1994). An additional risk of childhood obesity appears to be emotional disturbances. Data from one study indicated that adults who developed obesity in childhood showed more psychopathology than those who developed obesity later in life (Mills & Andrianopoulos, 1993). All of these facts underline the urgency of solving childhood weight problems as early as possible.

In contrast to the disappointing long-term results obtained with obese adults, it may be easier to teach children healthy eating and activity habits (Wilson & Terence, 1994). Epstein and his associates developed the **Child Weight Control Clinic** at the University of Pittsburgh School of Medicine (Epstein et al., 1985, 1994). The program has three components: healthy eating, exercise, and behavior modification. The healthy eating component uses a "traffic light" system to manage eating. "Go" foods can be eaten in unlimited amounts; "Caution" foods can be eaten in moderate amounts; and "Stop" foods should be avoided.

The exercise program works on a point system. Different activities are rated according to how many calories they burn. Children are given a point goal for the week, but they can choose the exercises they prefer to reach their goal. The behavior modification component has several parts: (1) information mastery, which includes knowledge about healthy eating; (2) self-monitoring, which involves keeping a log of foods eaten; and (3) contracting, which requires parents and children to earn back money paid at the beginning of the program by attending weekly training sessions.

Studies of this program indicated that parental restriction of sedentary activities, such as TV watching, and parental involvement in exercising with children have been the most effective components in reducing childhood obesity (Epstein et al., 1995).

Programs like this one obviously call for considerable commitment and investment of time by both the child and the family. Comparative studies have shown that programs involving the parents are more successful than those involving only the child. But when children are approaching adolescence, it is especially important that the child and parents attend separate training sessions, even though they are enrolled in the same overall program (Brownell et al., 1983). This separation gives the child independence and control and shifts responsibility for weight control to the child, who increasingly will be the one who must maintain it.

The bad news is that some people may indeed have a natural tendency toward obesity. The good news is that environmental factors play a large role in determining whether a person actually becomes obese. People can exert some control over their weight. That is, there is a wide range of reaction to one's genetic endowment. With rigorous weight-control measures, including physical activity, no individual is destined to become overweight. Good habits of physical activity developed during the school-age years may play an especially important role in lifelong fitness. (See Knowledge in Action: Health/Safety—Overcoming Childhood Obesity.)

Motor Development

In the vignette at the beginning of this chapter, we saw that children's physical abilities develop impressively over the course of the school-age years. Children can handle greater physical demands, thanks to bone and muscle growth, and they gain more control over their movements, due to brain development and practice. Steve probably understood that his first-graders were not only enjoying color tag, but also were developing running speed, balance, and "faking" skills when they were tagging and avoiding being tagged (Belka, 1998). The third-graders in Steve's gym class showed more precision of movement and coordination than the first-graders, and the sixth-graders showed even greater maneuverability. All of these growing abilities enable school-age children to learn games and sports involving gross motor skills. Changes in fine motor skills also enable them to engage in games, hobbies, and crafts. Programs have been designed to increase children's interest and involvement in activities that develop motor skills and physical fitness (Hodges & Henderson, 1999; McKenzie, 1999). A common finding is that when the enjoyment stops, the exercise program also stops. The children in Steve's physical education classes enjoyed the activities and also remained active throughout most of the class. Steve's approach contrasts with reports of time utilization in physical education classes—in many, only 8 to 16 percent of class time is devoted to vigorous activity.

Large Motor Skills

Large motor skills include running, jumping, twisting, bending, and turning the body. All of the maneuvers required to play baseball, basketball, tag, and soccer are gross motor movements. Quickness, balance, speed, and strength all continue to improve during the school-age years. The acquisition of these basic skills enables school-age children to play an increasing number of physical games.

Physical Activities and Sports

School-age children's favored activities range from soccer and swimming to tennis and baseball. Many **youth sports programs** are sponsored by schools, community agencies (e.g., boys' and girls' clubs, scouts, YMCA/YWCA), or recreation associations. Involvement in soccer, basketball, cheerleading, gymnastics, swimming, softball, baseball, track, tennis, hockey, and floor hockey can positively influence children's physical appearance, athletic competence, and general feelings of self-worth (Seidel & Repucci, 1993). The beginning of the WNBA in 1997 and the record-breaking spectator interest in the women's 1999 World Cup soccer teams provided motivation for girls to become involved in sports. The proportion of girls participating in sports has traditionally been lower than that of boys. In addition to exercise, sports participation provides opportunities for developing friendships, learning to follow rules, and learning to cooperate with team members and coaches. Sometimes, of course, pressure to win or to be the best player can have negative consequences. Parents or coaches who place too much emphasis on winning, who criticize or punish mistakes instead of teaching children strategies to overcome them, or who pressure children beyond their abilities provide a negative experience for children (Exline & Lobel, 1999).

Sleek (1996) summarized research that demonstrates the benefits of having individuals focus on competing with themselves, with improvement as the measure of success, rather than competing against others, with winning as the measure of success. In addition to maintaining involvement for a longer time, those who focus on improvement enjoy the activity more and are more likely to develop a positive self-concept. A reliable finding across many studies is that a cooperative, rather than competitive, orientation leads to better achievement on motor skill tasks and a higher level of positive interpersonal relationships among group members. This finding is especially strong for competitive tasks on which a single winner emerges. Studies also show that developing quality interpersonal relationships among those working on a motor skill task leads to higher performance (Stanne et al., 1999). Parents, physical education teachers, and youth sport coaches also help determine whether the school-age child develops a cooperative, improvement, or winning orientation to sport involvement. (See Knowledge in Action: Education—Coaching Young Athletes.)

Soccer is a favorite sport among school-age children. By participating in such games, children develop physical skills, build a healthy lifestyle, and have opportunities to make friends. (*Source:* © Elizabeth Crews)

EDUCATION

Coaching Young Athletes

Sports participation among young athletes can have a number of benefits. It can provide fun, exercise, cooperation, sportsmanship, friendships, and new social and physical skills (Saffici, 1998; Slade, 1999). But whether such benefits are realized depends in large part on the orientation of the coach.

If participation in sports is to provide adequate physical activity, coaches must include a sufficient amount of training and physical activity during practice. Unfortunately, practices do not always engage children in physical activity. In one Canadian study, researchers found that only 33 percent of each coaching session was devoted to actual physical activity, with the rest of the time being spent observing and organizing (Trudel & Cote, 1994). A minimum level of physical activity can be ensured for all children who participate in sports, not only by using practice time well, but by establishing equal-playing-time requirements (i.e., all players play the same amount of time) for games. These requirements benefit children and also support many coaches who have broader goals (Strear, 1995).

Children's willingness to participate in sports over a period of several years can depend on **coach effectiveness** in motivating children and in helping them build positive self-perceptions. Coaches who give information following good performance, and encouragement with information following poor performance, build player competence, enjoyment, higher levels of perceived success, and a preference for optimally challenging activities (McMahon, 1998; Saffici, 1998).

In one study, training in supportiveness and instructional effectiveness was provided to one group of coaches, while no training was given to a control group of coaches. The researchers then examined the effect of these coaches on elementary school boys who played baseball on these coaches' teams. Researchers who interviewed the boys at the end of the season found that those with trained coaches evaluated their coaches more positively, had more fun, and felt more team cohesiveness. Teams with treatment and control group coaches did not differ in terms of their won-lost records. The study also found that boys with low self-es-

teem who played for the trained coaches showed significant increases in general self-esteem, while the control group boys with low self-esteem did not (Smoll et al., 1993).

Children who believe that their coaches support their efforts show greater enjoyment in the sport. When coaches are trained in support techniques, such as positive rather than aversive control, and when they have a conception of success related to effort rather than to winning, children like the coaches more, rate them as better teachers, report having more fun with the sport, and like their teammates more than do children with nontrained coaches (Smith et al., 1995).

These studies indicate that coaches who provide instruction during practices and games, support their players, and involve everyone, rather than play mainly a first string, are the most effective in getting children to invest time and effort in practices and games. The children they coach also enjoy participating more, and they develop more commitment to the team and the sport. Table 12.1 presents a checklist for effective coaching.

TABLE 12.1   Coach's Checklist

- Be patient, caring, and understanding.
- Be encouraging and supportive, and use lots of praise.
- Have a sense of humor.
- Ensure equal involvement of all players.
- Be a role model of good sportsmanship.
- Pay attention to relationships with and between players.
- Stay calm when players or officials make mistakes.
- Be energetic and enthusiastic.
- Demonstrate what to do, rather than what not to do.
- Create a cooperative, rather than competitive, orientation.
- Teach one new skill at a time.
- Help parents keep all comments positive.
- Stress fun and improvement.

Sources: Burnett, 1999; Rudd & Stoll, 1998; Saffici, 1998.

Do school-age girls and boys differ in their ability to play various sports? For example, can girls pitch as well as boys in a baseball game? Although some girls may throw the ball with less body motion and force than some boys, it is a myth and an "insidious stereotype" that girls "throw like a girl" because of the way their bodies are constructed (Milano, 1995). The body parts—muscles and tendons—used in the throwing motion are the same in girls and boys. Because throwing is a learned skill (see stages of ball throwing in chapter 8), the difference between a good and poor throw is mechanical, not physiological. From an early age, boys practice throwing things more than girls do. Boys are also more likely than girls to learn from coaches and by imitating pro players and older children (Milano, 1995). If school-age girls are taught to throw, and if they have the same opportunities to learn from experience, their throwing abilities should be the same as those of boys. A much higher proportion of boys than girls participates in organized sports. Thus, the benefits of physical skill-development activities for girls must be a continued focus in sports, schools, and after-school programs (Bialeschki, 1999; Posner & Vandell, 1999).

The development of specific motor skills depends on both maturation and experience. Thus, children need practice opportunities to master particular sports.

Physical Fitness

Despite widespread knowledge about the **benefits of exercise,** including physical, cognitive, and psychological health effects, recent surveys indicate that school-age children exercise less and are less physically fit than children were 25 years ago. Unfortunately, the majority of American school-age children do not meet minimum fitness standards (Ernst et al., 1998). In response to the poor physical condition of children at the beginning of the 1990s, Healthy People 2000 established goals to be met by the year 2000 (Davis et al., 1994). These goals include engagement in daily vigorous physical activity for 20 minutes or more per occasion, greater participation in daily physical education, and more lifetime fitness activities. However, at the close of the century, these goals were far from being met (McKenzie, 1999). The school-age years represent a critical window of opportunity for the rapid development of motor skills. Involvement in appropriate physical activities during these years is important for later skill mastery, as well as for improving immediate physical and psychological well-being.

Increased participation in after-school programs may provide some hope for meeting these goals. In a longitudinal study comparing third-, fourth-, and fifth-graders in after-school programs with those in mother's care, informal sitter's care, or self-care found that children in after-school programs spent more time in physical activities, extracurricular activities, coached sports, and academically oriented activities. The single most common after-school activity for those not in the program was watching TV (Posner & Vandell, 1999). After-school programs are discussed more fully in chapter 15.

Regular physical activity improves health and quality of life by reducing the risk of heart disease, colon cancer, diabetes, and high blood pressure. It also builds healthy bones, muscles, and joints, and it increases HDL ("good") cholesterol levels. Regular exercise reduces feelings of anxiety and depression and promotes psychological well-being (Ernst et al., 1998; Strand et al., 1998). Studies also report that physical activity is associated with other positive behaviors. For example, children who are physically fit perform at a higher level academically and show more enthusiasm than do children who do not exercise regularly. In one study, students reported that exercise led to better mood states and a greater ability to concentrate on tasks (Moore, 1993). In another study of African American fourth- and fifth-graders, children who exercised and followed a proper diet were one-third less likely to have smoked tobacco or drunk alcohol than their peers who did not engage in these healthful activities (D'Elio et al., 1993). Rathbun (1995) has even proposed that physical activity promotes the development of synapses (nerve connections) critical to learning and thinking and that it increases the number of capillaries that deliver blood, oxygen, and nutrients to the brain.

Fine Motor Skills

Fine motor skills continue to improve during the school-age years, especially between 6 and 8 years of age. Many activities that were not possible a few years earlier are enjoyed by school-age children.

Rapid Skill Acquisition   School-age children enjoy everything from origami to jewelry making to model building. Many children also begin to learn to play musical instruments, many of which require considerable dexterity.

The manual dexterity needed in tying shoes is usually present in children who are between 5½ and 6½ years of age. (*Source:* © Will Faller)

The rapid development of fine motor skills during the early school-age years enables children to handle writing tools quite skillfully. (*Source:* © Will Faller)

The increased skill in using the hands and fingers opens up an amazing array of hobbies and other activities to the school-age child, and allows young school-age children to reach a new level of independence. By first grade, most children can dress themselves without any help at all, unless an item of clothing presents some unusual problem. Children also become independent at the dinner table, even learning how to cut their own meat and to eat skillfully with a spoon and fork or chopsticks.

Handwriting The ability to control and manipulate a pencil or pen usually improves rapidly during the early school-age years as children acquire a mature grip and increased ability to manipulate their fingers (Carlson & Cunningham, 1990). Younger children often use a full-palm or fist grip on a pencil. They move the pencil with the muscles of the upper arm rather than with the fingers, and they keep their hands and arms up off the tabletop. Because the distance from the pivot (source of movement) to the pencil is so great, their marks are very large. As the movements begin to originate in the wrist rather than the upper arm, children rest their arm on the tabletop and make smaller marks. Writing becomes smaller still when children begin to rest the side of their hand on the tabletop and move the pencil with their fingers. With this superior control, they can make finer marks and confine their writing to a smaller and smaller amount of space.

Handwriting is influenced by visual-motor, tactile-kinesthetic, and cognitive planning abilities (Tseng & Cermak, 1993; Tseng & Murray, 1994). Difficulty with handwriting is one of the most frequent reasons for referring elementary school children to occupational therapy. Several types of interventions have been developed by physical therapists to help children with handwriting problems (Tseng & Cermak, 1993).

One of the many drawbacks of including formal handwriting programs in the kindergarten classroom is that some children do not yet have the fine motor control required for this activity. Preschool and kindergarten children like to draw and write, but their enjoyment will be dampened if they are asked to confine their creations to a restricted area, such as the lines on ruled paper. To see the dramatic change in size and precision that takes place in children's handwriting between the ages of 2½ and 7½, look at the samples in Figure 12.1.

Play and Motor Development

Play activities provide opportunities for school-age children to develop both gross and fine motor skills. Involving children in enjoyable activities such as soccer, basketball, tennis, hide-and-seek, jump rope, bicycling, swimming, bowling, skiing, ice-skating, in-line skating, baseball, softball, and Frisbee throwing help develop gross motor skills. To support fine motor development,

FIGURE 12.1

Development of fine motor control. As this child's fine motor control improved, he was able to write his name smaller and smaller. His age at the time of writing the different samples (shown reduced here) was (a) 2 years, 9 months; (b) 3 years, 6 months; (c) 4 years, 4 months; (d) 5 years, 7 months; (e) 6 years, 2 months; (f) 7 years, 7 months. Not until he was well over 7 years old was his writing small enough to fit on regular lined paper.

parents, teachers, and adults who run youth programs might provide school-age children with marbles, jacks, yo-yos, model and jewelry craft kits, drawing and art materials (e.g., markers, paints, paper, scissors, transparent tape, and glue), doll-making materials, and construction materials, such as Legos, Tinkertoys, and Erector sets.

Cultural traditions play a part in the play materials made available to children. For example, kite flying, a traditional physical activity among Chinese children, is still engaged in today by children living in Taiwan (Pan, 1994). In a village in Senegal, Marianne Bloch (1989) found that children used leftover fish bones in their pretend play and that parents made dolls out of corncobs and fabric scraps. Children also used sand, sticks, rocks, and trees (to climb) as play materials. They even ran with and chased their family's sheep and chickens!

Too few children have safe access to activities such as climbing trees, hiking on trails, jumping over streams, and riding horses (Gallahue & Ozmun, 1998). As modern forms of entertainment, such as television and video games, creep farther and farther into all corners of the world, changes inevitably occur in children's play. One interesting example has been documented among Eskimo girls living in southwestern Alaska. In decades past, village girls between 6 and 12 years of age spent many hours on the riverbanks, engaged in an activity called "storyknifing." Each girl within a group started this game by working a spot of mud on the riverbank into a suitable palette. When the palettes of soft mud had been made ready, each girl in the group told a story, illustrating it as she went along by carving pictures into her mud palette (deMarrais et al., 1994). Today, this traditional form of play is virtually gone in many villages, as children spend increasing amounts of time viewing television and videos.

Researchers studying other cultures have noted the disappearance of other traditional forms of children's play. For example, in Japan, Takeuchi (1994) has noted

RESEARCH

CLOSE-UP   *The Games Children Have Played: A Look around the World*

The playing of games seems to be a universal pastime among children. Hopscotch, hide-and-seek, blindman's bluff, and jacks are found in diverse cultures separated by great distances. Researchers can only speculate about whether the widespread occurrence of some games is due to the natural inclination of children everywhere to invent them or to the dispersion of games as people migrated from one part of the world to another (Sierra & Kaminski, 1995).

Children's Traditional Games

Hand games are among the traditional games passed on from generation to generation. One popular hand game is rock, scissors, and paper, in which children hold their hand out as a fist (rock), two fingers extended (scissors), or all fingers together and extended (paper). According to the rules, scissors cut (beat) paper, paper covers (beats) rock, and rock crushes (beats) scissors. Two players each thrust one hand out at the same time to see who wins. Traditional games also include games using strings, tops, shells, and stones. Spinning top games involve attempts to hit and damage other players' tops, knock down objects, maintain spinning for a long time, and race tops by whipping them with a leather thong. In England during the Middle Ages, special tops were raced once a year, during Lent, after which they were put away "to sleep." Hence came the term "sleeping like a top" (Sierra & Kaminski, 1995).

Chasing games, played all over the world, are the most universal of all games (Sutton-Smith, 1972). They began in Rome, in the second century A.D., and include hide-and-seek,

fox and geese, and colors. In the Netherlands, over 300 versions of hide-and-seek, each known by a different name, have been identified (Sierra & Kaminski, 1995).

Hopscotch, another traditional game, is called *Marelles* in France, *Ekaria Dukaria* in India, and *Tempelhupfen* in Germany (Arnold, 1972). The name *hopscotch* contains the old English word *scotch,* meaning "scratch." Originally, hopscotch diagrams were scratched in dirt or sand. One ancient hopscotch diagram was actually found inscribed in the pavement of the Forum in Rome (Arnold, 1972). The markers children often place in the hopscotch diagrams may be flat stones, pebbles, bits of pottery, or even shoe-polish tins filled with sand (Sierra & Kaminski, 1995). Many versions of this game are still played today by children all around the world. One researcher found 19 versions when studying hopscotch play among children in San Francisco.

The game of jacks, which originated in ancient Greece, is still played today in many parts of the world. Children in Malaysia use flat seashells for jacks, Scottish children use whelk shells, and children living in India use beans or small wooden cubes. Tiny beanbags filled with rice are used as jacks by children in Japan and China (Sierra & Kaminski, 1995).

Children learn many things from engaging in traditional games. For example, creativity is encouraged in some games, such as storytelling, word games, and pantomime. Games also provide a framework for children to learn how to get along without considerable adult intervention. The rules or rituals of games provide a structure for children's interactions (Sierra & Kaminski, 1995). Good examples of such rules or

that group play, such as rope skipping, top spinning, hide-and-seek, and tag, have all but disappeared in urban areas. Space to support such play no longer exists, and the availability of video and computer games also encourages children to spend more time indoors. Watching television and playing computer games are sedentary activities that interfere with the variety of movement experiences needed to foster motor development (Gallahue & Ozmun, 1998).

The challenge for parents today is to find motor activities that are suitable for the surroundings in which they live. Indoor games such as tiddlywinks and pick-up sticks provide a measure of physical activity and challenge. Table tennis and other physical tabletop games can also be utilized. And, of course, many varieties of throwing materials are relatively safe for indoor use. These include soft balls that stick to a target with Velcro and safe dart games. Parents might even consider purchasing or renting exercise videos and joining with their children to exercise in front of the television set! For a discussion of games played by children since ancient times, many of which have modern versions, see the Research Close-Up—The Games Children Have Played: A Look around the World.

rituals are the ways in which a player or a team is chosen to go first—to make the first move. Selecting players to be leaders or to be "it" and deciding the order of play can be accomplished in many different ways, from tossing a pebble or coin to counting rhymes such as "one potato."

Ball Games

Many games involve moving a round object by tossing, kicking, rolling, or hitting it. These games have been handed down from generation to generation in virtually all parts of the world. London's British Museum displays one of the first balls used in a game—it is a shaped and polished stone more than 5,000 years old. Throughout the ages, balls have been made of many materials, including wood, marble, pottery, papyrus, plaited rushes, animal hides, inflated bladders from an ox or a pig, carved yucca root, woven rattan, and linen filled with hay, cut reeds, sawdust, beans, feathers, seeds, or shavings (Arnold, 1972; James & Thorpe, 1994; Sierra & Kaminski, 1995). Modern materials used to make balls include rubber and synthetics such as plastic and foam rubber.

Games using balls have been documented since the time of the ancient Egyptians. Hurling, originally played by the Romans, was the forerunner of football and rugby (Arnold, 1972). The earliest version of golf was played in ancient Rome, using a ball consisting of a leather case stuffed with feathers.

Polo, which originated in Persia (today's Iran), sometime before 500 B.C., is played while riding horseback. The rider uses a long-handled stick of some kind to knock a ball through goal posts. Polo became a popular sport among princes in China by the eighth century, and special horses were bred and maintained for use in the game (James & Thorpe, 1994). Croquet, a mallet-and-ball game played while on foot, was devised in England during the seventeenth century. A croquet course is set up by inserting wire hoops in the ground. Several people play the game; the winner completes the course first.

A game considered to be the forerunner of soccer—*t'su chu*—was played in China in the third century B.C. A version of this game, played by women, was called "Eight Immortals Crossing the Sea." The net used in playing games of *t'su chu* was made of silk. In order for a team to score, the ball had to pass through a small hole in the net (James & Thorpe, 1994).

Other ball games include bowling and tennis. The earliest games of bowling originated in Europe during the Middle Ages and were similar to the Italian game of bocce. In the original game of tennis, a ball was struck with the open palm of the hand. A gloved hand was later used; finally, strings were stretched across the glove, foreshadowing today's tennis racket. This game was played in France as early as the twelfth century, where it was a popular game in monasteries (James & Thorpe, 1994; Sierra & Kaminski, 1995).

Basketball, now played by children in many countries, was invented by James Naismith in 1891. As a physical education teacher at Springfield College (Massachusetts), Naismith was asked to create a team sport that could be played indoors. Using a soccer ball, two peach baskets, and simple rules for dribbling and shooting, the new sport became popular in short order.

Health and Safety

Parents and teachers have several concerns about school-age children. These include coping with children's diseases and promoting their health by supporting healthful eating and adequate physical activity. Concerns and responsibility also include keeping children safe, both from accidental injuries and from acts of violence. Poor housing, substandard child care, inadequate educational opportunities, and drug abuse are also topics now viewed as health concerns (Zigler & Hall, 2000).

Ensuring the Health of the School-Age Child

Middle childhood is a time of relatively robust energy and good health. Most children have been immunized against the childhood diseases—mumps, measles, whooping cough, chicken pox, diphtheria, and polio—that formerly punctuated children's lives. There are some common illnesses during the school-age years, and disorders such as attention deficit hyperactivity disorder can be a problem. But perhaps the biggest health-related task during the school-age years is helping children build healthy lifestyles that will prevent chronic diseases later in life.

Diseases in Middle Childhood   The main illnesses with which school-age children must contend are virus-based colds, virus-based influenza (a respiratory infection), and bacteria-based strep throat. Children who are basically healthy and whose illnesses are properly cared for with rest, fluids, and nutritious food usually do not have much trouble recovering from colds and flu. Physicians usually control strep throat with antibiotics to keep it from turning into a more serious respiratory infection or rheumatic fever. Some children develop tonsillitis—tonsils that become abscessed and susceptible to repeated infections—and may even need to undergo a tonsillectomy. For the most part, however, school-age children do not suffer from serious illness, although one very serious disease—AIDS—increased dramatically among children during the past half-century. See a discussion of this disease in Knowledge in Action: Health/Safety—Children and AIDS.

Asthma   Asthma is a chronic condition marked by difficulty in breathing, tightness in the chest, and wheezing (Wenar & Kerig, 2000). More than 100,000 children are hospitalized each year due to asthma, making it one of the leading causes of school absenteeism. In 1999, the first comprehensive plan (The Asthma and Environment Strategy) to fight childhood asthma set the goal to reduce asthma by protecting children from environmental triggers such as smoke, pesticides, and outdoor air pollution (Francis, 1999). Other factors such as cold temperature, exercise, rapid breathing and ingested substances (e.g. milk, chocolate or wheat), may trigger an asthma attack (Wenar & Kerig, 2000).

Attention Deficit Hyperactivity Disorder   Although activity rates differ greatly among children, sometimes a child seems to be constantly in motion, has a very short attention span, and is easily distracted. In group settings, these conditions may interfere with learning, affecting all the children in a classroom (Boyles & Contadino, 1998; Nahmias, 1995).

CHARACTERISTICS AND INCIDENCE OF ADHD.   A child who exhibits an inability to inhibit behavior, difficulty in focusing, and distractibility may be suffering from **attention deficit hyperactivity disorder (ADHD)**. These children may also exhibit excessive levels of physical activity and a short attention span. Unlike normal inattention, ADHD behaviors are more dramatic and may include developmentally inappropriate impulsivity, excessive inattention, and hyperactivity (Mulhern et al., 1994; Wachtel, 1998; Zigler & Hall, 2000). Some children with ADHD also exhibit

knowledge in action

Children and AIDS

Even very young children are victims of **acquired immune deficiency syndrome,** or AIDS. AIDS is caused by the human immunodeficiency virus (HIV), which destroys the immune system. Worldwide, over 6 million persons have died from AIDS. Over 33 million were infected with HIV by 1999. AIDS was first diagnosed in the United States in 1981, and since then, over 600,000 cases of AIDS have developed per year in this country. Approximately 8,000 of these cases in one year involved children less than 13 years of age (Centers for Disease Control and Prevention [CDC], 1997; Laurence, 1999). AIDS is one of the top 10 causes of death in children under age 5 (Jesse et al., 1995).

HIV is found in body fluids, specifically, in semen and blood. The virus is transmitted from one person to another through sexual contact or through contact with the blood of infected individuals. Children contract AIDS prenatally from their mothers in 90 percent of childhood cases. The virus can also be transmitted postnatally to infants by their mothers through breast milk (CDC, 1995). Blood transfusions and blood components used to treat coagulation disorders such as hemophilia have been the sources of HIV transmission in some children. Approximately 14 percent of infants born to HIV-infected women are infected by the virus. Prenatal treatment paired with cesarean delivery can reduce the transmission rate to 4 percent (CAAF, 1999).

Prenatal infection is expected to remain the major source of HIV infection in children because more women of childbearing age are becoming infected through intravenous drug use or contact with infected sexual partners. Infection from blood supplies has decreased dramatically as blood-screening tests have improved.

When a child who is infected with HIV enrolls in a child-care center, a preschool, or an elementary school classroom, parents often worry that noninfected children will contract the virus from the infected child. Teachers also sometimes worry that they might become infected. All available evidence indicates that AIDS is not contracted through casual, everyday contact. No known cases of AIDS have been transmitted in schools or child-care centers (CDC, 1995). Because of this fact, the Centers for Disease Control recommends that HIV-positive children not be barred from school. This recommendation has been endorsed by the U.S. Department of Education.

Because there is no requirement that HIV status be revealed to school authorities, children who are HIV-infected are not always known to teachers. Teachers who work with young children in child-care centers must, therefore, follow universal precautions, as a matter of course, when children have nosebleeds and cut themselves. Problem behavior, such as biting, should be taken seriously by teachers because an HIV-infected child with open mouth sores could transmit HIV to a child or an adult who is bitten.

When a child is known to be HIV-positive and has a tendency to bite, the child should not be placed in the regular child-care, preschool, or elementary classroom. If a child who is known to be HIV-infected has open sores that cannot be covered, the child should be kept at home or isolated from other children at school until the sores heal. Most state departments of public health have developed specific policies regarding school attendance by children with AIDS. School districts can obtain information from these departments, from state departments of education, or from child-care licensing agencies.

Although it can cause birth defects, AZT (an antiviral drug) has been found to reduce prenatally transmitted AIDS by 75 percent. HIV-infected children taking **zidovudine** or **dideoxyinosine** are more likely to remain symptom-free and to function at more normal developmental levels. But special precautions should be taken to reduce the transmission of childhood diseases to HIV-infected children because their depressed immune system can make normal childhood diseases, such as the flu or chicken pox, fatal. For example, these children should receive flu shots and the chicken pox vaccine, and special care should be taken to protect them from individuals who have viral or bacterial infections. Because it is not possible for child-care or school officials to know which children are at risk because of depressed immune system functioning, from HIV infection or other conditions (such as chemotherapy for cancer), schools and child-care centers should notify all parents of potentially contagious diseases occurring in the school.

---

aggression and may be at increased risk for developing conduct disorder, oppositional defiance disorder, depression, and anxiety (Boyles & Contadino, 1998; Dykman & Ackerman, 1993; Wachtel, 1998). Usually, the intelligence of ADHD children is normal or above normal. A major problem in ADHD is the inability to inhibit behavior. Children with ADHD have difficulty keeping themselves from prohibited or inappropriate behavior and stopping the behavior once it is started. They also have trouble with restraining reaction to a compelling stimulus (Barkley, 1997). Children with ADHD often have difficulty staying focused on a task. For example, such a child might be sent upstairs to get a towel and might be found 20 minutes later, looking at a magazine he found on the way to get the towel (Wachtel, 1998). Children with self-regulation and impulsively problems not only suffer educational underachievement, but also are at a greater risk for behaving in unsafe and societally unacceptable ways (Baumeister & Heatherton, 1996).

Metcalf and Mischel (1999) have proposed a "hot/cool system" for understanding self-regulation. The hot system provides the basis for emotional, impulsive, and reflexive responding. The cool system is cognitive, reflective, and strategic. The cool system develops during the school-age years, with the growth of self-awareness and ability to reflect on one's own actions. According to this theory, the child with ADHD appears to be dominated by the hot system. Such children are more likely to show higher levels of interpersonal verbal and physical aggression.

Estimates of the incidence of ADHD in the population of school-age children range from 5 to 10 percent. Boys are diagnosed with ADHD six times more than are girls. Girls may be diagnosed at a lower rate because they tend to be distracted by inner thoughts and sit quietly without disturbing anyone. Boys are more likely to be distracted by external stimuli and respond to them (Boyles & Contadino, 1998).

ADHD is diagnosed by assessing the presence of several critical behaviors. Information is gathered from those having extensive contact with the child or by observing the child's responses on specific tasks. Table 12.2 presents the behavioral characteristics of ADHD. If a significant number of these are present, the child may be diagnosed with ADHD, and possible behavioral and medical interventions should be explored.

Oppositional defiance disorder often accompanies ADHD. A comparison of children with ADHD only, oppositional defiance disorder only, and both ADHD and oppositional defiance disorder revealed that those having both disorders were rated poorest on academic performance, social functioning, attentiveness in class, and homework. Aggressiveness was higher for boys with these disorders than for girls (Carlson et al., 1997).

TABLE 12.2

Characteristics of ADHD

If a significant number of these behavioral characteristics are present, the child may be classified as having ADHD.

Inattention	Hyperactivity	Impulsivity
■ Has trouble maintaining sustained attention in play or to tasks	■ Fidgets with hands or feet; squirms in seat	■ Blurts out answers before questions are completed
■ Does not give attention to detail and makes careless mistakes	■ Leaves seat often when expected to remain seated	■ Begins tasks before they have been explained
■ Cannot selectively attend to tasks	■ Reports feelings of restlessness	■ Has difficulty waiting for a turn
■ Has difficulty listening when spoken to	■ Often prefers standing to sitting	■ Speaks out of turn; interrupts others
■ Fails to complete tasks	■ Runs or climbs excessively at inappropriate times	■ Often intrudes on others
■ Has difficulty organizing tasks and activities	■ Has difficulty playing or engaging in quiet activities	■ Often responds without thinking about the situation
■ Avoids dull, repetitious tasks or tasks requiring sustained mental effort	■ Often talks excessively	■ Often gives apologies and expressions of remorse
■ Tends to lose things, especially items necessary for tasks	■ Is often on the go, as if "driven by a motor"	■ Fails to learn from mistakes
■ Is distracted by external stimuli or own thoughts	■ High levels of inappropriate activity	
■ Is often forgetful		
■ Reports thoughts that flit about; has flights of imagination		

Sources: Boyles & Contadino, 1998; American Psychiatric Association, 1994; Wachtel, 1998; Zigler & Hall, 2000.

CAUSES OF ADHD.   ADHD does not have a single cause. Because ADHD runs in families, and both identical twins are more likely to have it than are both fraternal twins, ADHD is believed to have a hereditary basis (Hauser et al., 1993; Samuel et al., 1999). Research has substantiated that ADHD is a neurobiological disorder occurring because of difficulty in the regulation of neurotransmitters in the frontal lobe of the brain (Aman et al., 1998; Boyles & Contadino, 1998).

ADHD may also be caused by prenatal damage, such as exposure to teratogens or complications during pregnancy. Factors such as head trauma, family stress, exposure to lead, and encephalitis may also cause children to be inattentive and more active than is typical. Sugar and chemical food additives, once thought to trigger ADHD, have been shown to be unrelated (Boyles & Contadino, 1998; Ingersall & Goldstein, 1993; Wachtel, 1998).

INTERVENTIONS TO HELP CHILDREN WITH ADHD.   ADHD can cause a great deal of difficulty for children. For example, the behaviors of children with ADHD can lead to peer rejection. One study with 6- to 12-year-old boys showed that as early as the first day of interaction, boys with ADHD were overwhelmingly rejected by other boys (Erhardt & Hinshaw, 1994). Parents and siblings may also react negatively to ADHD. Teachers may expect children with this condition to behave in ways that pose great difficulties. A child with ADHD often truly cannot "be quiet and sit down right now." The disadvantages of physical punishment that were discussed in chapter 11 may be especially disadvantageous for ADHD children.

Many different kinds of behavioral interventions, such as social skill training, behavior modification, cognitive strategy training, stimulation, exercise and movement, and computer use, have been developed. In skill-training interventions, children are taught to become increasingly aware of appropriate social behaviors. A variety of techniques are available on computer to help maintain active involvement and attention. Computer techniques can also facilitate organization and overcome writing difficulties that are typical for children with ADHD (Boyles & Contadino, 1998; Wachtel, 1998).

Medication can decrease the symptoms of children with biochemically based ADHD. Medication includes stimulants (e.g., Ritalin, Dexedrine, and Pemoline) and antidepressants (e.g., Wellbutrin, Prozac, and Effexor). Individual children respond differently to the various drugs, but stimulants or combined stimulants and antidepressants appear to be most effective (Wachtel, 1998). Because of the difficulty in determining a neurochemical basis for a specific child's ADHD symptoms, the high rate of prescribing these drugs to treat ADHD is a controversial issue.

Children can learn about components of a healthy diet by helping to prepare foods. In fact, helping children learn to select healthy foods to prepare may be the most important part of the process. (*Source:* © Myrleen Ferguson/ Photo Edit)

Promoting Health through Good Eating Habits

Diets high in salt, fat, and cholesterol have been linked to heart disease and elevated cholesterol levels. Studies show that 80 percent of children consume more fats and cholesterol than the recommended 30 percent or less of total calories (Thompson & Dennison, 1994). Children must be educated and encouraged to avoid foods containing these ingredients (Wills, 1998).

Schools often teach the principles of good nutrition, and health education programs starting in the early grades significantly improve health knowledge (Schall, 1994; Gidding et al., 1995). Some schools are incorporating the **Heart Smart intervention program** into their curriculum. This program presents cardiovascular health information to children and provides information about the health effects of various eating behaviors and exercise (Ross, 2000). Another program, Gimmie 5, is a school nutrition education program designed to help children consume more fruits, juice and vegetables. Techniques include role playing, taste testing, preparation of meals and snacks, making recipes at home, watching videos, analyzing television commercials, and writing commercials concerning consumption of more fruits, juice, and vegetables. Produce managers of grocery stores make presentations and suggestions, and families are directly involved (Barahowski et al., 2000). Schools can also set a good example by offering school lunch menus that include low-fat foods, skim milk, and low-salt foods.

Parents can make fruits and vegetables available for snacks in place of fat-rich, nutrient-poor foods, such as chips, candy bars, and cookies. Finally, they can demonstrate healthful eating habits in their own lives. Simply switching from whole to skim milk and from regular to low-fat cheese for family meals can significantly lower everyone's intake of saturated fat, thus promoting good eating habits that can benefit children for a lifetime. However, because fat intake is not usually a problem before the school-age years, care should be taken not to lower the fat intake for children under the age of 2 nor for most preschool children (Wills, 1998).

Many school-age children respond to food-related environmental cues by heading for the refrigerator or snack shelf. In addition to the commercial influence from TV itself, some parents try to help their children cope with frightening segments of TV programs by telling them to get something to eat or drink (Spireck, 1993). When food is used as an emotional crutch, children may learn to eat when faced with an uncomfortable situation or other problems. The increasing popularity of dining out requires that parents help children make healthful choices. Compared with foods prepared at home, most restaurant foods are higher in fat and lower in fiber, calcium, and iron (Lin, 1999).

School-sponsored field days can encourage children to engage in physical activity, but too much emphasis on winners and losers can put a damper on children's interest in physical games. It might be better to recognize children for the number of events in which they participate rather than for how many they win. (*Source:* © Will Faller)

Promoting Health through Exercise   Many schools still provide very little in the way of physical education programs; some have reduced them due to budget cuts. Reading, for example, is often taught for an hour every day, but physical education may be taught only 45 minutes once a week. Studies of activities in elementary school physical education classes showed that 64 percent of the class time was spent in sedentary activity (e.g., waiting or watching others), while less than 10 percent was spent on moderate to vigorous physical activity (McKenzie, 1999). (See Knowledge in Action: Education—Physical Education Revisted.)

Approximately one-half of U.S. children do not vigorously exercise on a regular basis, and one-fourth do not vigorously exercise at all. Participation in physical activity decreases during the school-age years. In light of the many health risks associated

EDUCATION

Physical Education Revisited

knowledge *in action*

To meet current health goals, **physical education programs** should include more activities such as running and rope skipping, and fewer games such as dodge ball and red rover. Some physical activities used traditionally by teachers involve too little physical activity. In addition, they often lead to negative feelings about physical activity in some children, usually those who are chosen last by other children to be on teams (McHugh, 1995).

To assist physical education teachers in eliminating activities and games that do not support physical education goals, Neil Williams (1994) established the Physical Education Hall of Shame. To be inducted into the Hall of Shame, a game or an activity needs to possess at least one of the following criteria:

- low participation time factors
- high likelihood for injury or harm
- lack of emphasis on teaching motor skills
- lack of emphasis on teaching lifetime physical fitness skills
- focus on eliminating students from participation
- embarrassing a student in front of other class members
- absence of purported objectives

Some inductees include dodge ball, relay races, duck duck goose, musical chairs, red rover, and Simon says.

If the development of physical health and good exercise habits is the goal of field days held by schools and recreation departments, it would be wise for them to emphasize participation and improvement rather than which children can run the fastest or throw the farthest. For example, children could record their participation in activities and receive recognition based on the number of activities they complete (Jackson & Rokosz, 1995). Children could also be recognized for improvement in an event, from one time to another.

The National Association for Sport and Physical Education recommends 30 minutes of vigorous activity per day for school-age children (Friedlander, 1994). Therefore, the ideal physical education program should spend 50 percent or more of class time on activity, and physical education classes should meet on all five, rather than just two or three, days each week. This level of physical education is not attained in many schools. To encourage a healthier lifestyle among children, schools should do all that they can to devote more resources to basic physical education for elementary school-age children.

---

with physical inactivity, the following recommendations have been made for promoting health through exercise:

- Teach children about the health problems that are reduced through exercise.

- Increase the safe and attractive places available for exercise (e.g., swimming pools, gyms, tracks).

- Integrate appropriate exercise in sports activities.

- Encourage moderately vigorous, enjoyable exercise rather than optimal-performance exercise.

- Involve parents in exercise programs with children.

- Encourage involvement in several different types of exercise.

- Ensure that supervising adults have appropriate knowledge about safe exercise.

- Teach students about the relationship between exercise, appearance, and social acceptance.

(Halpern et al., 1999; Hodges & Henderson, 1999; Siedentop, 1999; Strand et al., 1998)

Physically challenged children also need opportunities to participate in physical activities. Basketball is one of the many physical activities that children in wheelchairs can play. (*Source:* © Lawrence Migdale/Tony Stone Images)

Exercise needs apply to **physically challenged** children as well as to typical children. Children with a physical disability cannot perform some typical physical behaviors, such as running, jumping, swinging a bat, or sometimes simply walking. Some children who can perform these behaviors have poorer coordination, slower reaction time, or poorer balance and muscle tone than other children.

Paralysis may be responsible for the physical difficulties experienced by some children. Other children have visual or hearing impairments or orthopedic difficulties (including joint problems such as those caused by rheumatoid arthritis, or bone problems). A whole array of problems, including brain damage, amputation, cerebral palsy, spina bifida, or neuromuscular diseases may be the cause of a specific child's problem.

Special equipment can be adapted to help these children move and stay physically active. For example, leg and back braces and wheelchairs have been available for a long time. Motorized equipment and other newer devices are becoming increasingly available. Examples include motorized wheelchairs, hand-propelled tricycles, orthopedic cycles, power mobility aids, and full-body floatation suits for water activities. Young children can use such equipment to participate in many activities that provide exercise important for good health. Older children who have multiple disabilities can use a motorized wheelchair for sports events, for pulling younger siblings in a wagon, for hauling branches, and even for riding on trails during camping trips (Carson, 1995).

A number of organizations and recreational facilities provide special activities for physically challenged children. These include Junior Wheelchair Sports Camps in San Clemente, California, the Pocono Mountain Summer Camp in Pennsylvania, and the Children's Specialized Hospital in New Jersey. Each of these places offers recreation, sports, and cultural and performing arts activities for children with physical disabilities. Numerous U.S. communities also sponsor Special Olympics events. Just as professional sports and the Olympics encourage sports participation among nonphysically challenged children, the **Paralympics** provides models for physically challenged children. In 1996, the Paralympics was the second-largest sports event in the world (the Atlanta Olympics was the largest). More than 3,500 physically challenged athletes from 120 countries competed in 17 medal sports (Allen, 1996).

Special equipment and facilities can change the lives of children with physical disabilities in significant ways. One child, who was using a wheelchair, said to her mother after her first two-week camp session, "You know what, Mom? For the first time in my whole life, I felt like a regular, normal kid. I did everything the other kids did, and my chair was no big deal" (Peck, 1994, p. 51).

Ensuring the Safety of the School-Age Child

Adults are often concerned about the physical safety of school-age children. There is good reason for their concern because accidents are the leading cause of death in this age group (Bryn & Gallagher, 1999). Although school-age children have more knowledge and skill than do toddlers or preschoolers, they also have certain other pressures with which to contend. For example, because school-age children care very much about being accepted by their peers, they may act without thinking carefully about the harm they may cause to themselves. When they were younger, they may have been more interested in "doing what Mom said." By school age, they may be led into danger by their great desire to be part of the group.

School-age children have more autonomy from adult supervision than do younger children. This new level of independence means that they have less access to adult judgment and planning than they did when they were younger and more dependent. Risk-taking behaviors increase during the school-age years because children have more opportunities to act in unmonitored, unfamiliar situations. Such activities require that children regulate their own behavior and resist the temptation to take unwise risks. Males are at greater risk for harm in such situations than females because males feel greater pressure to succeed at physical tasks and generally spend more time in unsupervised settings where poor judgment may result in physical injury (Byrnes et al., 1999).

Warm-up exercises are very important for school-age children whose bone growth pulls muscles tightly. If muscles are not warmed up, they are more likely to be pulled or torn. (*Source:* © Will Hart)

Pedestrian Accidents   One of the most common accidents among children is being hit by a car while on foot. The best way to protect children from these **pedestrian accidents** is a matter of some debate. Some adults think children should be taught safety rules and then allowed to negotiate streets by themselves. Others argue that even school-age children do not apply safety information carefully enough. These developmentalists say that 6- and 7-year-olds cannot understand or follow rules necessary for crossing safely at intersections and that even 9-year-olds sometimes forget to look both ways before crossing a street (Rivara et al., 1989).

Adults probably should begin to teach children safe pedestrian rules early in the school years but not allow them to cross streets alone until they are 9 or 10 years old. Even at this age, children should be shown the safest way home from school and taught to cross busy streets where a crossing guard is available.

Eye Injuries   Most eye injuries occur in children who are between the ages of 6 and 14 (Grin et al., 1987). Many more eye injuries occur among boys than among girls. The highest percentage of these injuries occurs during a sports activity, closely followed by incidents involving sticks or branches and BB guns. They also occur when a child is struck in the eye by a thrown object, such as a rock or a snowball, or when the child is jabbed in the eye with a pen or pencil. Baseball is the leading cause of sports-related eye injuries in the United States. It accounts for 40 percent of all eye injuries occurring in children between 11 and 15 years of age (Rome, 1995).

The importance of good eyesight to everyday living makes the prevention of eye injuries especially important. Most sports-related injuries can be prevented, according to the National Society to Prevent Blindness, if safety guidelines are followed. This organization recommends that children wear safety helmets with face protectors for baseball, hockey, and football, and eye guards for other sports. Eye injuries from air-powered guns (BB guns) could be reduced if children were not allowed to use them.

Bicycle Accidents and Head Injuries   Ninety percent of all fatal bicycle injuries involve collisions with a car. Approximately 75 percent of these fatalities are due to head injury (Rome, 1995). It has been estimated that between 70 and 90 percent of head injuries could be prevented by wearing helmets (Ginsburg & Silverberg,

This girl is wearing a helmet and wrist and knee guards. This safety gear decreases considerably her chances of being injured during in-line skating. (Source: © Tim Davis/Photo Researchers)

1994; Rome, 1995). The following recommendations have been made to reduce head injuries:

- Riders should always wear helmets no matter when or where they ride.

- Bicycle helmets should meet the standards of independent testing organizations, such as ANSI (American National Standards Institute), the Snell Memorial Foundation, or SEI (Safety Equipment Institute).

- States and communities should implement programs to promote helmet use (NSKC, 1997).

Safety precautions should be observed as well for any activity that puts a child "on wheels." In-line skating is one of the fastest-growing recreational sports in the United States and the world. Forty percent of skaters are between 6 and 11 years of age (Fried-Cassorla, 1995; Schieber & Branch-Dorsey, 1995). Helmets, wrist guards, and knee and elbow pads should be used during in-line skating. Wrist guards can reduce the odds of injury for roller bladers, roller skaters, and skateboarders by more than six times (Schieber & Branche-Dorsey, 1995).

Head injuries result from many recreational activities involving special equipment. The large number of injuries involving seesaws, swings, trampolines, wagons, and scooters has led to recommendations that multipurpose helmets be used in such activities (Baka et al., 1994).

Overuse Injuries During the school-age period, many children begin to participate in organized sports, such as Little League baseball, gymnastics, and tennis. Although school-age children have the cognitive and motor skills to play sports, their bones and muscles can easily be injured.

Immature bones are softer than the fully ossified bones of teenagers and adults, and they can be deformed from strain. Immature muscles can also be strained or torn, although it is more likely that school-age children will sustain bone injuries rather than muscle or ligament injuries. This is because soft tissues are usually stronger in school-age children than are bones, which are in the process of growing. A growth plate—the **epiphyseal growth plate**—is near the end of all of the long bones. These cartilaginous plates do not disappear until after the preadolescent growth spurt. Because these plates are the weakest parts of the skeletal-muscular system in children (Rome, 1995), it is here that children are most likely to sustain injury in the form of fractures. Weight training may damage the epiphyseal plate, especially if improper techniques are used (Gallahue & Ozman, 1998).

Injuries to a growth plate are especially serious because they can stop the bone from growing or deform the bone. Improper healing also can create roughness in a joint, which can lead to arthritis (Kunz & Finkel, 1987).

Prolonged use of one area of the body can lead to **overuse injuries,** such as sprains, tendinitis, and stress fractures (small breaks) in the bones (Rome, 1995). Distance running, gymnastics, and distance swimming have the potential to cause overuse injuries (Gallahue & Ozmun, 1998). If handled improperly, these injuries can lead to long-term disability. In one study, researchers found that gymnasts who trained for more than 18 hours per week in early puberty had an abnormal growth spurt resulting in shorter final height (Rome, 1995). For these reasons, restrictions are placed on the amount of time a child can pitch in a Little League game.

It also is important for children to do warm-up exercises before participating in physical activities. Children lose flexibility between 5 and 13 years of age because bones grow a little faster than muscles (Teitz, 1982). Without proper warm-up, injury is much more likely. Steve Atkinson, the physical education teacher whose classes were described at the beginning of this chapter, understood the importance of warming up. Most coaches ask that children arrive at least half an hour before a game is scheduled to start, in order to do warm-up exercises. If children arrive late, just as the game is starting, coaches should have them warm up individually before putting them in the game.

Reducing the Threat of Violence Against Children   Violence is a serious threat to the physical and emotional well-being of children. The homicide rate in the United States, for example, is the highest in the industrialized world. Troublesome behavior, such as school truancy and fighting, begins as early as first grade and predicts similar behavior in high school. In today's world, children shoot other children, are afraid to go outside after school because of the violence in their neighborhoods, and are sometimes abused by their parents or other adults. Schwartz and colleagues (1997) found that 10-year-olds who were physically aggressive bullies or were victims of bullies experienced a more punitive, hostile, and abusive family environment than those who neither bullied nor were bullied. (See Knowledge in Action: Health/Safety—Signs, Symptoms, and Long-Term Consequences of Child Abuse and Neglect in chapter 8.)

Some of the violence children experience also results from conflicts they have with each other. A survey designed to find out how students settle arguments found overwhelming acceptance for fighting and for not involving adult authority (Bracey, 1995). Children often resort to violence because they know of no other way to resolve conflict. Helping children to identify feelings, to empathize, to solve problems, and to anticipate potential consequences of their actions supports the development of nonaggressive behavior (Shure, 1994).

Cognitive factors are also involved in aggressive behavior. Thoughts that encourage aggression are strongly associated with aggressive behavior (Egan et al., 1998). Similarly, children who hold negative beliefs about unfamiliar peers are more likely to initiate aggression toward them. Such belief systems tend to be more prevalent among boys whose interaction with their mothers is very negative. Generally, the research on thought processes associated with aggression supports the theory that aggressive children enter social interactions with negative expectations about the other person's behavior (Mackinnon-Lewis et al., 1999). The media contribute to many thought patterns associated with aggression. News programs tend to focus on killings, terrorists, bombings, and injuries from fights and massacres, rather than on stories about programs that have reduced violence and aggression (Aronson, 1999; Garbarino, 1996). For example, the Columbine (Colorado) High School massacre story was on the news and special programs for several weeks. The first 10 minutes of most local TV news programs focus on violence. This focus can lead to a war zone mentality and negative thoughts about other groups. The dominance of the hot system (response based on emotion and impulse) over the cold system (reflection before response) (Metcalfe & Mischel, 1999) and lack of self-regulation are associated with negative affect and negative thoughts. Lack of self-regulation is central to most social problems, including violence (Baumeister, 1999). School-age children who are regularly the victims of aggression have cognitive thought processes different from those of other children. Nonvictimized children use the strategy of getting a friend or an adult to help resolve a problem, whereas victimized boys take a "fighting back" approach (Kochenderfer & Ladd, 1997). Having friends and being liked by one's peers are important factors in the prevention of victimization. Schools in which students do not tolerate bullying (e.g., defend victims, interrupt bullying bouts, and tell authorities) have lower rates of victimization (Pellegrini et al., 1999).

Despite the epidemic of youth violence and aggression, Garbarino (1999) stresses that we can do more than observe and record it. Based on his research with violent youth, Garbarino emphasizes the importance of being attentive to warning signs such as lack of connectedness, withdrawal, rage, hypervigilance, trouble with friends, cruelty to other children and animals, and a belief that violence is necessary for survival and thus the "right thing to do." Preventive actions that are most effective include instilling in children a sense of purpose, fostering a spiritual or religious connectedness, organizing life experiences that develop empathy and social interest, and teaching strategies for being resilient without violence in situations that might trigger aggression (Garbarino, 1999).

One program of many designed to help children overcome violence is called **Enough Is Enough,** Inc. This program educates children about guns, violence, peer mediation, and self-respect. In the Washington, D.C., public schools, free conflict resolution classes are also offered as part of the program. Schools that have completed this program now have almost no incidents of violence (Kline, 1995). Another program, "Kids without Violence," educates children, teachers, and parents about the causes of and solutions to violence (Arnow, 1995).

Sadly, in some parts of the world, children are exposed directly to physical violence as the result of war. One study analyzing Lebanese children's war experiences reported posttraumatic stress syndrome, depression, and maladaptive adjustment resulting from exposure to shelling or combat, violent acts, separation from parents, physical injuries from war, and involvement in hostilities themselves (Macksound & Aber, 1996). Exposure to violence via the media can also have negative effects on children. See the Research Close-Up: Children and Violence for more information.

RESEARCH

CLOSE-UP   *Children and Violence*

James Garbarino's (1996) studies of children who have been exposed to violence identified three kinds of threats that are suffered by them. First, exposure to violence, or a belief that violence is likely to be experienced, decreases children's future orientation. For example, those experiencing violence-related trauma expected to live about seven years less than those not so exposed. Indeed, 50 percent of African American children surveyed believed that being shot will keep them from reaching old age. One consequence of this expectation is that programs designed to address the dangers of drugs or unsafe sexual practices are less likely to be effective.

The second theme identified by the research is a decline in children's confidence that adults can be counted on to protect them from violence. That is, children who observe adults who are anxious about violence, or who experience it directly or know friends who have experienced it directly, conclude that parents are incapable of controlling the problem. This belief often leads to child and adolescent vigilanteism—to relying on peers and weapons for protection.

The third theme is that increased exposure to violence develops in children a sense that the probability of violence is very high. Associated with this belief is a desensitivity to violence. This desensitivity unleashes aggressive behavior toward others under the guise of self-defense.

These themes emerge even when children's fear of violence is much greater than the actual threat. Fears of violence can be fanned by exposure to media violence, as well as by direct experience with violence. Both kinds of exposure contribute to children's sense that they are living in a war zone (American Psychological Association, 1993). Although most studies of televised violence have focused on entertainment programming, news reports of violence are likely to contribute to the three themes reported by Garbarino. One study of televised news reported that more than half of news programming contained visual images dealing with violence and conflict. This violent content was more likely to be presented earlier rather than later in a news broadcast, thus implying that it is pervasive.

KEY POINTS

How Do They Grow?

■ Children grow more slowly during the school-age years than they did as preschoolers. By the age of 6, they have reached almost two thirds of their adult height.

■ Most weight gain is concentrated in the muscles, so children increase in strength. Boys have more muscle cells than girls do, which tends to make them stronger.

■ The growth of the head slows, and the trunk and the legs grow more rapidly. The face becomes longer and slimmer as the lower face and jaw come into balance with the upper part of the head.

■ Most children start to lose their first teeth at about age 6, and by age 11 or 12, they have all their permanent teeth except for two sets of molars.

■ All children grow at their own individual rates. Normal variations are particularly apparent toward the end of the school-age period when the preadolescent growth spurt occurs.

■ Some children do not grow properly. Children who grow much more slowly than average are called failure-to-thrive children. If their retarded growth is caused by environmental factors, it can be treated by providing counseling to the parents or placing the child in a foster home. If it is caused by physical factors, it can often be treated medically, by administering a growth hormone.

■ The most common abnormal growth pattern in school-age children is obesity. Studies have shown that obese children exercise less and watch more television than is typical of their normal-weight peers. A positive correlation exists between obesity in parents and obesity in children, suggesting that this condition has a genetic as well as environmental basis.

■ Obese children may have to take extraordinary steps to keep their weight under control. Programs for obese children often use behavior modification techniques that help them take responsibility for their eating habits.

Motor Development

■ School-age children rapidly acquire many gross and fine motor skills, and they use and practice these skills in their sports, games, and activities. As their fine motor skills mature, their handwriting becomes smaller and more precise.

■ Children should be encouraged to participate in physical activities and physical education programs. Physical activity promotes cognitive development, increases physical strength, helps develop motor coordination, improves self-esteem, and provides opportunities for peer interaction. Ideally, schools should devote some part of every day to physical education.

■ The role of play is important in the development of both large and fine motor skills.

Health and Safety

■ School-age children tend to be healthy and active. Adults can help them develop and maintain healthy lifestyles by teaching them about nutrition and encouraging them to participate in sports and other physical activities.

■ AIDS is a problem among children, who most often contract it prenatally. Currently, the Centers for Disease Control recommends that children with AIDS attend school unless they have a tendency to bite, have open sores, or are under 3 years of age.

■ ADHD involves an inability to inhibit behavior, difficulty in focusing, and distractibility. Boys are diagnosed with ADHD more often than girls. Stimulants and antidepressants as well as behavioral methods are used to reduce symptoms.

■ Accidents are the leading cause of death among school-age children. Adults can enforce a variety of measures to keep children safe.

■ Certain injuries are associated with excessive exercise during the school-age years because bones and muscles are still immature. When children overuse one part of their bodies, they can suffer stress fractures and sprains, which can lead to long-term disabilities. For this reason, knowledgeable adults should supervise children's sports programs.

■ Violence is a serious health problem, and children often resort to violence because they know of no other way to resolve conflicts. Conflict resolution programs are important interventions.

GLOSSARY

acquired immune deficiency syndrome (AIDS): a fatal disease in which the immune system is gradually destroyed by HIV (human immunodeficiency virus) (p. 423)

attention deficit hyperactivity disorder (ADHD): a disorder involving the inability to inhibit behavior, difficulty in focus, and distractibility (p. 422)

benefits of exercise: the positive physical, emotional, and cognitive outcomes that have been associated with exercise (p. 417)

Child Weight Control Clinic: a weight-control program developed at the University of Pittsburgh, which consists of healthful eating, exercise, and behavior modification (p. 414)

coach effectiveness: ability of a coach to motivate children to participate in physical activity and to help them build positive views about their physical abilities (p. 416)

dideoxyinosine: a drug used to treat pediatric AIDS patients (p. 423)

Enough Is Enough Program: a violence-prevention program that educates children about guns, violence, and peer mediation (p. 432)

epiphyseal growth plate: the growth plate that is found at the ends of long bones (p. 430)

failure-to-thrive: a slower-than-normal growth rate usually caused by problems in caregiving, including neglect (p. 411)

Heart Smart intervention program: a program that provides children with information about healthful diets and cardiovascular health, and also involves children in aerobic exercise (p. 426)

kwashiorkor: a severe form of malnutrition caused by deficiencies in both protein and calories (p. 411)

lateralization: development of dominance of one or the other of the brain's hemispheres with respect to a specific function (p. 408)

malocclusion: improper alignment of teeth that causes various kinds of atypical bites, which can be corrected with dental appliances (p. 410)

myelination: the process by which the outer surfaces of nerve cells become covered by a fatty sheath as a normal part of brain maturation (p. 409)

obesity: a condition involving an excess of body fat relative to lean tissue (p. 412)

overuse injuries: fractures, sprains, and so on, that result from too much use of one body part in sports activities (p. 430)

Paralympics: Olympic games for the physically challenged (p. 428)

pedestrian accidents: accidents involving a motor vehicle and a person on foot (p. 429)

physical education programs: organized programs of physical activity, ideally provided daily in schools (p. 427)

physically challenged children: children who are not able to perform typical physical behavior due to some physical disability (p. 428)

preadolescent growth spurt: a marked and sudden increase in growth, especially in height, that occurs late in the school-age period, as puberty approaches (p. 410)

youth sports programs: organized and supervised sports activities sponsored by schools, community agencies, and recreation associations (p. 415)

zidovudine: a drug used to treat pediatric AIDS patients (p. 423)

SUGGESTIONS FOR FURTHER READING

Bolig, E. E., Borkowski, J., & Brandenberger, J. (1999). Poverty and health across the lifespan. In T. L. Whitman & T. V. Merluzzi (Eds.), *Lifespan perspectives on health and illness* (pp. 88–103). Mahwah, NJ: Erlbaum. This study presents important poverty-based health problems of school-age children. The major risk factors for each critical health problem are presented, and preventive intervention programs are discussed.

Boyd-Franklin, N., Steiner, G. L., & Boland, M. G. (Eds.). (1995). *Children, families, and HIV/AIDS: Psychosocial and therapeutic issues.* New York: Guilford. This book addresses the cultural, psychosocial, and medical needs of HIV-infected infants, children, and adolescents. It contains several case studies.

Carroll, S. (1994). *The complete family guide to healthy living.* New York: Dorling Kindersley. This easy-to-read book contains sections on exercise and children, healthful snacks and drinks, immunization protection, and other good health information.

Metcalfe, J., & Mischel, W. (1999). A hot/cool-system analysis of delay of gratification: Dynamics of willpower. *Psychological Review, 106*(1), 3–19. This article presents a two-system framework related to self-regulation behaviors. The later-developing cool system is the basis for self-regulation and control.

Posner, J. K., & Vandell, D. L. (1999). After-school activities and the development of low-income urban children: A longitudinal study. *Developmental Psychology,*

35(3), 611–619. This article examines the differences in after-school activities for low-income children attending after-school programs, those in the care of a mother or an informal sitter, and those in latchkey situations. The implications for children's health are discussed.

Stanne, M. B., Johnson, D. W., & Johnson, R. T. (1999). Does competition enhance or inhibit motor performance: A meta-analysis. *Psychological Bulletin, 125*(1), 133–154. The impact of cooperative, competitive, and individualistic orientations on motor skills performance is examined across several different types of tasks.

Van Cleave, J. (1995). *The human body for every kid*. New York: Wiley. A collection of projects, activities, and ideas for exploring the human body. The projects are easy and fun for children to do.

Wachtel, A. (1998). *The attention deficit answer book*. New York: Penguin Putman. This book discusses the diagnosis and treatment of ADHD, and the types of drugs used in treatment. It also examines the experiences of the child with ADHD at home, at school, and with friends. The last chapter includes information about ADHD associations, government help, newsletters, and Internet Web sites.

Zigler, E. F., & Hall, N. W. (2000). *Child development and social policy*. NY: McGraw-Hill. This book emphasizes the connections between what is known about healthy child development and what is being done (or not done) to strengthen the nation's families.

13

Cognitive Development in School-Age Children

BILL ARRIVED JUST as Desserae began to tell her mom about the cooperative homework project that she and her friend Bill had been assigned. As Desserae and Bill began work on the project, Desserae's mother listened to them.

From what she could gather, the assignment by Mrs. Caskie required Bill and Desserae to roll two dice 100 times and record how often they obtained (1) two *5s*, (2) a *2* or a *3*, and (3) a *1* and a *6*. Before rolling the dice, they were supposed to predict how many times they would get each of these three outcomes and then explain to each other the basis for their predictions. Desserae's mother could hear them discussing this. Then the rolling began. The two children called out the numbers that turned up each time. Then, after the rolling and recording were finished, they discussed why they thought they had obtained their pattern of results.

On that same afternoon, Ellen, a fourth-grader in another school district, descended the stairs from her school bus and trudged up the walk to her home. She had been inside for no more than a minute when she began complaining that she didn't understand anything in math class today. Before long she was sobbing about the math test scheduled for the next day. Her mother comforted her, telling her that she, too, had experienced difficulty with math.

Her mother's sympathetic words helped, but Ellen continued to tell her mother of the anguish she was experiencing: "Mr. Huber talked about an additive law and a multiplicative law of probability, and I don't even know what he was saying. And nobody else does either. We don't know when we're supposed to use one law and when we're supposed to use the other. I can't even figure out what I'm supposed to multiply or add. Mom, I don't want to go to school tomorrow and take that test!"

"That doesn't sound like a good solution," her mother counseled. "I think you should go. Study your book tonight. Perhaps you can figure all of this out. If you can't, well, you can't be good in everything. Perhaps math just isn't your cup of tea. A lot of girls aren't very good in math. There are a lot of things you do very, very well. Remember the 96 you got on your reading test last week?"

think about it

Desserae and Bill's understanding and enjoyment of math may differ dramatically from Ellen's. What might be the source of these differences? Could Desserae and Bill have inherited more natural ability than Ellen? Might they have matured more quickly, with the result that their cognitive skills match more closely the demands of school? Or could the differences we see in these children's understanding of math, and in their emotional response to it, be due to variations in their experiences? Could the instructional programs in their schools be different, and might their teachers and parents have different expectations for children's math achievement?

Children make dramatic gains in cognitive skills during the school-age years. Their cognitive development is facilitated when they are asked to generate solutions to problems, explain and elaborate upon their solutions, collaborate with others, and employ metacognitive skills (e.g., Brown, 1997; Karpov & Haywood, 1998). Children's learning depends upon the context in which learning opportunities are provided, on the degree to which they are involved in tasks, and on the task's potential to motivate them (e.g., Voss & Wiley, 1995; Wentzel, 1999). It depends, as well, on the relation of to-be-learned concepts to children's life experiences (e.g., Hunt & Ellis, 1999; Symons & Johnson, 1997). Cognitive skill development depends upon children's general knowledge, their attitudes about learning information, the value they place on the material to be learned, and having the expectation that success is attainable (Reif & Allen, 1992). Ellen's mother may have communicated that learning math is not valued highly and that she does not expect Ellen to master this school subject.

In this chapter, we examine changes in cognitive abilities during the school-age years, some factors that influence these changes, and how motivation can affect school performance. We also discuss the concept of intelligence and review approaches to facilitating cognitive development in school-age children.

Piaget: The Acquisition of Operations

The thinking of school-age children is more logical than the thinking of preschool children. We saw in chapter 9 that preschoolers often understand and evaluate situations on the basis of appearance, not logic. By the beginning of the school-age years, with the emergence of what Piaget called **concrete operational thinking**, children begin more and more to use logic and mental operations to understand situations and to think about how things work.

A Gradual Transition

Many children begin their transition from preoperational to concrete operational thought prior to beginning first grade, as we discussed in chapter 9. The transition from preoperational to concrete operational thought is actually quite gradual for most children. That is, children display competence on an increasing number of tasks over the course of several years.

Figure 13.1 presents several of the conservation tasks used to assess children's use of preoperational versus concrete operational thought. Conservation is the knowledge that changes in the appearance of a substance do not change its amount. In other words, it involves knowing that changes in the arrangement of items or in the shape of a quantity of material do not affect the number of items or the amount of material. As shown, children do not apply concrete operational thinking simultaneously to all conservation tasks. Instead, they demonstrate it first on one or two tasks, then on one or two more, and so on, until all conservation tasks are approached at this level. For example, the behavior of 6-year-old Chris illustrates the unevenness with which school-age children apply concrete operational thinking to different tasks. When Chris was tested on the number conservation task, he explained quite logically why the two rows still had the same number of marbles, even though one row had been rearranged. But later, at home, he demonstrated vestiges of preoperational thinking in making judgments about area. Chris spread out a green cloth and began to set up his play farm. He set out his 10 cows, and then placed the farmhouse, two barns, and a garage on the green cloth so that they were touching, as are the items in the first area representation shown in Figure 13.1. His older brother, Scott, suggested that he spread out the buildings. He demonstrated what he meant by placing one of the four buildings in each of the four quadrants of the green cloth. Chris argued that Scott's arrangement of buildings was not as good as his own earlier arrangement because the cows now had less grass to eat. When Scott asked why, Chris said, "Well, see [pointing to the farm scene], there's not as much grass now as there was before."

Type of Conservation	Dimension	Change in Physical Appearance	Average Age at Which Invariance Is Grasped
Number	Number of elements in a collection 	Rearranging or dislocating elements 	5–7
Substance (mass) (continuous quantity)	Amount of a malleable substance (e.g., clay or liquid) 	Altering shape 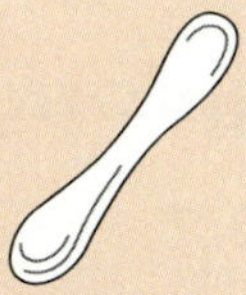	6–8
Length	Length of a line or object 	Altering shape or configuration 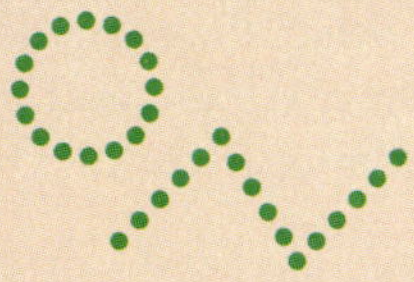	6–8
Area	Amount of surface covered by a set of plane figures 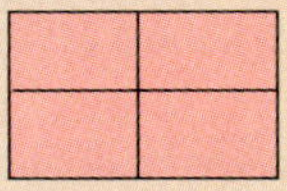	Rearranging the figures 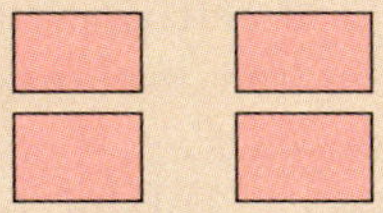	7–9
Weight	Weight of an object 	Altering its shape 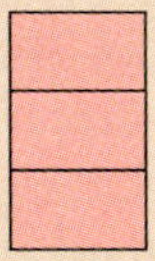	8–10
Volume	Volume of an object (in terms of water displacement) 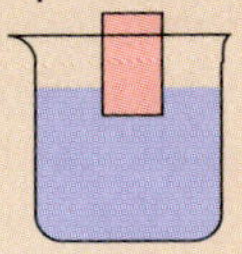	Altering its shape 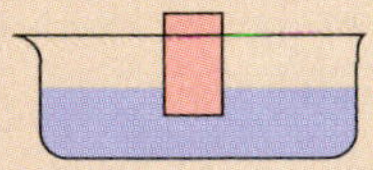	10–14

FIGURE 13.1

Types of conservation. Piaget found that different types of conservation were mastered at different ages, most of them during the school-age years. Conservation is one of the hallmarks of Piaget's concrete operational stage of cognitive development.

School-age children are able to play games, such as checkers and chess, because they can think about what the other person is thinking, and about the results of a move in terms of the moves it opens up for an opponent. Possibly the most brilliant chess match in the history of the game was played by Bobby Fischer at the age of 13. Preschool children, in contrast, are usually able to play only games of chance, such as Candyland™ and Go Fish.   (*Source:* © Laim Druskis/Photo Researchers)

Several years typically elapse between children's mastery of their first conservation task and mastery of a very difficult task such as volume conservation. Interestingly, most children master the various conservation tasks in the same order, even though the ages at which different children master each task vary quite a lot. This typical progression across tasks in the transition from preoperational to concrete operational thought is referred to as the **horizontal decalage.**

Piaget noted that the transition to concrete operational thought also occurs on classification and seriation tasks (arranging different objects by graduating them based on size). He also differentiated the concrete operational thinking of the school-age years from more sophisticated abstract thinking. Piaget called abstract thinking without concrete referents **formal operational thought.** He believed that the transition from concrete operational thought to formal operational thought begins for most children during early adolescence. Desserae and Bill's teacher understood that they were concrete operational thinkers who needed to solve problems using dice.

Limitations of Piaget's Theory

Many child development theorists and researchers believe that Piaget's theory does not address all of the important changes in intellectual performance that occur during the school-age years and that some aspects of Piaget's theory need more elaboration. Neo-Piagetians have attended more to task specificity, to the role of training versus maturation in advancing children's thinking, and to the effects of culture and education on the age at which children demonstrate various levels of cognitive performance (Case, 1993; Flavell et al., 1993; Gelman & Brenneman, 1994). Bidell and Fisher (1992) pointed out that although group averages support the transition from preoperational to concrete operational thought as Piaget described it, individuals reach specific cognitive stages at different ages and in different order. Children of different cultures also vary in their performance of cognitive tasks. For example, 90 percent of 8-year-old Inuit children (of northwest Canada) understand the concept of horizontality (the surface plane of water will always be horizontal, no matter the tilt of the vessel), but only 60 percent understand conservation of liquids, even by age 15. However, by age 10, 100 percent of Baoule children (Ivory Coast) understand conservation of liquids, but only 50 percent understand horizontality even by age 15

(Dasen, 1984). These skills may be related to the interest in and use for specific skills in daily activities.

To account for children performing at or beyond their stage of cognitive development inconsistently across contexts, Thelen and Smith (1997) and van Geert (1998) have proposed a dynamic systems model that takes into account children's interactions with different aspects of their environment. Children are challenged by trying to understand and interact with the environment and are at the same time supported by environmental systems, such as family, school, state interest in education, or global concerns for environmental issues. According to this model, expertise is gained by interacting with specific aspects of the environment; stages in development do not result simply from maturational processes. Piaget did acknowledge the need for such a modification to his theory and believed that development occurs as children strive to understand contradictions between what they already know and interactions with the environment that push them to add to or refine this knowledge.

Cognitive developmentalists have also been giving increased attention to children's problem-solving strategies, to their information-processing strategies, and to the effect of specific knowledge on patterns of cognitive development (Granott & Gardner, 1994; Hirschfeld & Gelman, 1994). Aspects of cognition now being examined include growth in the number of facts or amount of information a child knows and increased capacity and efficiency of memory and cognitive processing (e.g., older children can remember more numerical digits in a series than can younger children, and they can memorize a list of items more easily). More expert knowledge facilitates cognition by supplying ready-made solutions or strategies and by freeing mental capacity. "When concepts, technical terms, problem patterns, and other domain-specific data are highly familiar, they require less time and mental energy to process" (Flavell et al., 1993, p. 143).

Researchers have also been interested in the developmental course of **attentional focus,** the idea that an individual focuses attention on just one thought or thing at a time. Older school-age children show more understanding of the focused nature of attention and realize that they can physically see something, but not think about or pay attention to it (Flavell et al., 1995).

Piaget considered language as a means of understanding a child's thinking but has been criticized for neglecting the role of language in directing the school-age child's thought. In addition, his research placed a heavy emphasis on logical and scientific thinking without giving sufficient attention to the independent development of musical, spatial, bodily-kinesthetic, social, or quantitative aspects of intelligence (Lutz & Sternberg, 1999) or to motivational factors that affect performance on cognitive tasks (Kanfer & Heggestad, 1999). Approaches that address these limitations in Piaget's theory are presented in the remaining sections of this chapter.

Piaget contributed significantly to our understanding of cognition in school-age children, and his work prompted research by many others. But current research efforts to understand cognition in the school-age child go well beyond the basic areas that were probed by Piaget.

Approaches to Cognitive Processing

A second major perspective on cognitive development is taken by developmentalists who seek to explain how children of different ages process information. Three major approaches are taken within this perspective: (1) the development of metacognitive skills, (2) memory strategies, and (3) information-processing operations.

Metacognitive Skills

The child's ability to allocate mental effort and to select and execute strategies in solving problems increases during the school-age years (Kuhn, 1988; Sternberg, 1992). Being strategic when attacking familiar problems is perhaps what most distinguishes school-age children's thinking from that of preschoolers.

Metacognition refers to the ability to think about thinking, to play with thoughts, and to monitor and deploy mental effort strategically. Metacognition helps to regulate and control problem-solving processes and memory (Frederiksen, 1994). When a child plays chess or checkers and considers her moves in terms of her opponent's likely responses, not only is she thinking—she is thinking *about* thinking. When a child makes up a joke or laughs at one, she is playing with thoughts. When children decide to relate new material to their life experiences, to use mnemonics, or to reorganize information, they are deploying mental effort strategically. Bill and Desserae deployed mental effort strategically when they predicted outcomes for their dice tosses and when they explained their predictions to each other. According to the metacognitive skills approach, their experience in completing the dice throwing assignment results in the development of a schema for organizing the knowledge gained. This schema is then recalled and applied to solve future problems (Hunt, 1999). Metacognitive skills also include awareness of what other people may be thinking, the different strategies that could be used to solve a problem, and the monitoring and regulation of one's own thinking (Flavell, 1999; Flavell & Miller, 1998).

The development of metacognitive abilities enables children to allocate mental effort and to select strategies to solve problems. School-age children typically get better and better at studying because they can monitor what they do and do not know and, thus, can pinpoint trouble spots needing extra practice and review. (*Source:* © Elizabeth Crews)

Metacognitive skills are important in oral communication, oral comprehension, reading comprehension, writing, language acquisition, perception, attention, memory, mathematical reasoning, problem solving, logical reasoning, social cognition, and various forms of self-instruction and self-control (Flavell et al., 1993; Sternberg, 1995). Because the ability to understand jokes and riddles is a specific type of metacognition known as **metalinguistic awareness,** we discuss this behavior in chapter 14. Because the ability to think about what someone else is thinking helps determine how children relate socially to other children and adults, we consider this aspect of metacognition in chapter 15. We focus in this chapter on the metacognitive abilities that allow children to monitor their own thinking and to use thinking about thinking to aid their learning and problem solving.

Memory Strategies

"How can I remember this?" "What are the important ideas here?" "What points are irrelevant?" The ability to think in this way about information and the ability to direct mental effort strategically are both aspects of metacognitive functioning.

Children under 6 or 7 years of age cannot easily remember something as simple as pictures from a collection. When asked to study the pictures so that they will be able to name them from memory, kindergartners say they are ready, but then cannot recall many of the items (Baker-Ward et al., 1984). They are not as likely as older children to organize the items into categories, to make associations between the items, or to rehearse to see if they have in fact memorized the items (Siegler, 1991). Older children have better short-term memory than younger children do. The older children are, the faster they can pronounce words in rehearsing them, and the more words they can hold in short-term memory (Siegler, 1998). Older children also learn that practice in retrieval of information is more effective than more input time, such as rereading (Hunt & Ellis, 1999). Second-graders, on the other hand, tend to make use of some of these memory strategies, although their strategies are not as sophisticated as those of older children or adults (Schneider & Bjorklund, 1998).

Older children do better at memory tasks, because they have a larger knowledge base (they know more facts), and because they use a wider range of strategies and use them more effectively. For example, older children are better than younger children at rehearsing to remember and are more likely to use **elaboration,** strategies through which the information to be learned is linked to existing knowledge. Of the various elaboration strategies, **self-referencing** has been found to produce the strongest effect (Symons & Johnson, 1997). Self-referencing involves relating new information to one's own life experiences in one of the following four ways:

- Recognizing how a concept is illustrated in one's own life experience
- Describing how the concept could be used to improve one's life experience
- Recognizing how a concept is illustrated in everyday observable societal events
- Describing how a concept could be applied to address a societal problem

(Forsyth & Forsyth, 1999)

Moreover, when new terms must be organized in a particular order, older children are better than younger children in using the **method of loci,** a strategy in which the learner attaches each new term to locations along a familiar route. Older children are better at applying mnemonics, self-referencing, and chunking to encode to-be-learned information. Younger children are simply not as aware as older children of "rules of the game" that can be used in memory and problem solving (Brown & Kane, 1988).

However, young children can be taught some strategies such as rehearsal, which can improve their memory considerably. They also can be given mnemonics (memory devices), such as "Roy G Biv" for the colors of the rainbow and "My Very Educated Mother Just Served Us Nine Pizzas" for the names of the planets. They can use the keyword method or an imagery strategy to increase the number of items remembered (Levin, 1980). Teaching memory strategies to children makes a difference in their memory performance. Evidence for this comes from cross-cultural data. For example, in one study, German children exhibited more memory strategies than one typically finds in young U.S. children, apparently because teachers in German schools stress these more than do U.S. teachers (Carr et al., 1989). But it is not simply training in memory strategies that makes a difference. For example, to use the strategy of relating new information to previously learned material or to their own life experiences, children must first have a wide store of knowledge. It takes time and experience for children to build this storehouse.

Individual differences in using memory strategies have been found between males and females, across cultures, and across elementary school ages. For example, males tend to rely more heavily on self-referencing, whereas females use a broader range of elaboration and self-referencing strategies. As a result, females perform better than males on memory tasks involving neutral or female-oriented concepts, and males perform at the level of females only when male-oriented concepts are to be memorized (McGivern, et al. 1997). North American children tend to rely more on rehearsal strategies than do Guatemalan or Australian Aboriginal children, who rely on spatial location and arrangements of objects. Instruction in the use of memory strategies leads to better performance on memorizing unrelated materials but has not been shown to affect recall for well-structured stories (Cole, 1999). Younger children do not use memory strategies as much as older children do and are not as likely to transfer the use of a learned strategy to a second memory task (Lutz & Sternberg, 1999).

People sometimes have quite vivid memories of practicing addition or multiplication facts by using flash cards. But practice of this sort, in which children try literally to learn math by practicing facts over and over, is not highly effective if children do not understand the basis for the numerical operations. Children learn mathematics best when they can use various representations—concrete models—for tasks such as multiplication and division, and when they can explain the relationships among these representations (Kouba and Franklin, 1995). When children are introduced to multiplication, teachers can have them add together equal groups of concrete objects, perhaps six groups of three objects each, or five groups of two objects each. This concrete experience helps children develop a model for what multiplication actually entails. To introduce children to division, teachers might ask, "How could you divide these bags of marbles equally among your group of seven children?" After providing relevant concrete experiences, teachers can help children link these experiences to formal symbols and procedures needed to perform these computations on paper.

Although children benefit from practicing math facts and from performing computations, they must also understand thoroughly the basis for the procedures used in more abstract and formal contexts. Kouba and Franklin (1995) suggested that teachers give children rich concrete experiences and help children constantly build from their experiences. It is important for teachers to present examples, both typical and unusual, and to encourage children to make observations and formulate ideas (Banchoff, 2000). Children should also be challenged to invent and discuss their own solutions to problems (Caliandro, 2000). We saw earlier in this chapter how much trouble Ellen was having in mathematics. Apparently, her teacher approached the material formally, without first providing appropriate experiences to which Ellen could have related abstract laws and procedures.

Another school context often associated with remembering is one in which children are asked to read to acquire information. For example, children read science and social studies textbooks, and they also read stories. In these contexts, children are asked to define terms, to recall facts or events, and to explain how and why things happen. Remembering what one reads involves high-level skills. For one thing, the reader must first sort out what is important to learn—what he or she should try to remember.

To study effectively, children must weed out irrelevant information, notice redundancies to avoid noting the same thing twice, create categories, and use category markers, such as topic sentences and headings. These mental activities require metacognitive abilities that are not within the independent reach of children in the first several grades of elementary school. Even though fifth-graders (9- and 10-year-olds) are quite good at deleting irrelevant and redundant information, they are not yet very good at creating categories or using category markers provided by a text.

The **imagery** memory strategy involves visualizing an event or object and storing it in a visual code. This is especially helpful in remembering concepts or words that have a concrete referent. Imaging provides a second memory code, and two codes are better than one. The visual images aid memory because of their ease of storage and the amount of detail available in the image (Hunt & Ellis, 1999).

Information Processing

Many of the researchers who are exploring ways of fostering cognitive development take an **information-processing approach** which focuses on operations of the mind that manipulate information coming into it and information stored in it. Rather than focus on stages of cognitive development, information-processing researchers examine the mental activities involved in attending to, taking in, mentally manipulating, storing, and acting on information. They examine how children represent information, how they use it to achieve a goal, and how their information-processing operations limit their thinking ability (Lutz & Sternberg, 1999).

Developmentalists who take an information-processing approach to cognitive development are interested in knowing the specific life experiences that foster the abilities needed to succeed at cognitive tasks. Those who have used Piagetian tasks with children living in different cultures have noted large cross-cultural differences in the ages at which conservation tasks are mastered at a concrete-operational level. For example, in cultures where few children go to school or where sharing materials equally is uncommon, children may be delayed by as much as four or five years in producing concrete operational responses (Light & Perrett-Clermont, 1989; Rogoff, 1990). The absence of universality in cognitive development has led many information-processing developmentalists to explore specific environmental factors that may limit changes in information-processing abilities. Rather than focus on stages of cognitive development, as Piaget did, information-processing researchers examine the factors that influence changes in the ability to perform a specific task (Case, 1992).

Some information-processing developmentalists think of cognitive processes as the management of information through multiple stages of processing. They describe memory as consisting of stages of encoding, storage, and retrieval. **Encoding** addresses how information gets into memory. It involves selective attention to certain aspects of the information to be learned, in order to form a memory code. Many children today encode more information from electronic visual displays than from the same information encoded from printed text. (Walma, van der Molen, & van der Voort, 2000). **Storage** addresses the issue of how encoded information is maintained in memory. Information-processing researchers view encoded information as flowing through three different memory stores. First, information is held for a fraction of a second in the sensory store. Second, the information enters a short-term store that may last a couple of minutes (long enough to read and dial a telephone number). This short-term store is often called our **working memory**. Third, the information finds its way into a long-term store from which it can be recalled at some future date (Lutz & Sternberg, 1999; Massaro & Cowan, 1993). **Retrieval** is the process of recovering information from any of the three memory stores. (For more information about what researchers are exploring in this area, see the Research Close-Up: Information Processing.)

The information-processing approach is closely linked to the cognitive neurosciences in trying to locate brain structures and identify neurochemical processes that are involved in the development of cognitive activities. This involves looking at the brain activity changes that occur as participants in a study attempt to complete different cognitive tasks (Smith & Jonides, 1997). The information-processing approach assumes that anatomical locations exist for working memory and for long-term memory, which function differently. Such neuroimaging studies have demonstrated that working memory capacity and the ability to control attention involve the forebrain structures, whereas long-term memory operations involve the hippocampus and associated medial temporal lobes (Hunt, 1999). Such findings aid in our understanding of cognitive behavior differences among school-age children. For example, the lag in myelinization of the frontal lobe area for males compared to females may account for gender differences in attention. Relatedly, the neurosciences aspect of in-

CLOSE-UP   *Information Processing*

Information-processing researchers examine variables that affect children who are at different ages or who have had different experiences. Researchers have taken a **depth-of-processing approach** in studying the impact of differences on encoding. The classic study upon which this line of research has been built instructed one group of individuals to attend to perceptual features of written words (e.g., capital versus lowercase letters). A second group was instructed to attend to phonemic features of the same words (e.g., children were asked to think about what rhymes with each word). A third group was asked to attend to semantic features of the words—to think about their meanings. These three different instructions were assumed to produce increasing levels of depth-of-processing information during the encoding phase. As expected, recall of the words increased with greater depth of processing (Craik & Tulving, 1975).

Whether the child can process information by using deeper self-referencing depends on the experiences of the child. The greater the knowledge and experience children have, the more they are able to relate new information to their already existing knowledge. This was demonstrated in a study by researchers who presented a list of words to soccer-experienced and soccer-inexperienced elementary school children. The list contained words related to soccer and words related to other subjects. In a test of words remembered, children with soccer experience remembered more soccer-related words than did children without soccer experience, but both groups remembered the same number of words unrelated to soccer (Schneider & Bjorklund, 1992).

Some information-processing developmentalists interpret such research in terms of scripts. **Scripts** are reconstructed memories that combine many repeated experiences or events, such as playing soccer or making fudge (Fivush et al., 1992). As children repeatedly experience working at a task, their mental representations of the task become more detailed and better organized. These generalized mental representations or scripts indicate how information is cognitively organized (Shank & Abelson, 1977). The more experiences children have with a task, the more elaborate are their scripts (Fivush, 1984; Fivush et al., 1992). For example, a child with little guided experience in cooking may simply describe making candy by saying, "Fudge is mixed up and cooled and then you have candy." Another child who has helped many times with culinary tasks may say, "To make fudge, you mix sugar, chocolate, and butter. Then you boil it and add nuts. Then you mix it and spread it out. When it gets cold, you cut it." As children become very familiar with an event, they are even able to maintain the correct sequence of tasks if asked to recall the sequence in reversed order (Bauer & Thal, 1990).

This research suggests that scripts provide an important tool for understanding the world (Flavell et al., 1993). Research also indicates that repeated experiences provide a foundation for success in mathematics (Fuson, 1992; Resnick, 1989; Siegler, 1991). Indeed, the ever-increasing number of life experiences throughout the elementary school years contributes to a steady improvement in general information-processing speed and complexity (Kail, 1991). The script resulting from Bill's and Desserae's repeated experimentation with dice, for example, will no doubt make it easier for them to learn the formal laws of probability.

formation-processing research is leading to new understandings of brain functioning and biochemical modifications that can help people overcome deficits in specific information-processing and mental ability tasks.

Social Interaction and Cognitive Development

As indicated in chapter 1, the **sociocultural theory,** developed in the 1930s by the Russian psychologist Lev Vygotsky, has been receiving attention from developmental psychologists as they attempt to understand cognitive development during the school-age years. This increased interest in Vygotskian theory is due to increased communication with Russian researchers since the collapse of the Soviet Union, translation of Vygotsky's writings, and developmental research that has been generated by his theory. In this section, we review the details of Vygotsky's theory that we introduced in chapter 1, along with some of the ways that it has been applied, especially in educational settings.

Applying Vygotsky's Sociocultural Theory

Vygotsky (1934/1987) emphasized the importance of social interaction and language on the school-age child's cognitive development. Vygotsky emphasized that learning occurs in an interpersonal, social context. Children's **level of potential development** is what they can do with assistance; their **level of actual development** is what they can do on their own. He considered the difference between what children can do independently and what they can do with help from an adult as the **zone of proximal development.** When the adult, or more expert peer, guides a child by providing appropriate help and structure as the child learns new ways of thinking and behaving, we say that the adult provides **scaffolding** for the child (Plumert & Nichols-Whitehead, 1996).

In ideal learning situations, children are moved toward their level of potential development. This goal can be reached only when children complete tasks in interaction with someone whose expertise on the tasks exceeds the child's. Vygotsky's theory supports several educational practices, such as having older children assist in the classrooms of younger children, having peers tutor each other, and having students of mixed levels work cooperatively on projects. The children who are operating at a higher level should pull children operating at lower levels toward higher levels of functioning. Vygotsky used the term **internalization** for the developmental process through which a child absorbs knowledge through social interactions. Children who receive nurturing and care in a democratic setting are well positioned to learn and grow. Given clearly articulated, reasonable expectations, children are more likely to internalize the social and intellectual goals and knowledge that lead to success in school (Wentzel, 1999).

Researchers have found that children who work on a task with a more expert adult, think aloud more about the best strategy to use and participate more actively in the task, compared to those working alone or with another novice (Radziszewska & Rogoff, 1991). Research also indicates that modeling is involved when adults interact with children to help them learn tasks. One technique that emphasizes modeling is called **reciprocal teaching.** The teacher and the students take turns engaging in an activity. When applied to reading comprehension, the teacher and students take turns reading a paragraph. The teacher summarizes the theme of the paragraph, identifies material that needs clarifying, and predicts what might happen next. After reading their paragraph, students then summarize, clarify, and make predictions. Six months after completing 20 reciprocal teaching sessions, the students in one study increased their reading ability from the 20th percentile to the 56th percentile (Brown et al., 1991). Reasoning and learning by analogy or similarity permits increased inferential thinking and the learning of new abstractions. Engaging in these comparison processes also fosters new insights (Gentner & Holyoak, 1997; Gentner & Markman, 1997; Holyoak & Thargard, 1987).

Other researchers, looking specifically at peer tutoring, found that expert children can effectively teach novice children. In one study, children were identified as either experts or novices, based on their experience in building models with Legos. Children were paired to form dyads of two novices, two experts, or one novice and one expert. Each dyad built a Lego model, and then each child built a model. Predictably in terms of Vygotsky's theory, the ability of novices improved significantly when they were paired with an expert, but not when they were paired with another novice (Azmitia, 1988).

Teachers must themselves provide instruction to individuals or small groups of children with a similar level of understanding. For example, they conduct teacher-led minilessons and discussions, or they utilize the reciprocal teaching method described earlier. In these instances, the teacher is the expert tutor and the children are the novices. In some schools, classrooms are organized into grade-level clusters that allow children

Older children as well as adults can guide younger children's development through the zone of proximal development. (*Source:* © Shackman/ Monkmeyer)

from several same-grade classrooms to work together during part of the school day. This arrangement provides a larger pool of children from which teachers can form appropriate dyads and small groups. In some schools, resource teachers often work outside of the regular classroom to organize groups of children to work on special projects, *across* grade levels. A child who is a very expert third-grader might have the opportunity to work as a novice with an older fifth-grader in a special group of this sort. The practice of grouping children across grade levels is based on research that has demonstrated that older children, as well as adults, can guide younger children's cognitive development (e.g., Plumert & Nichols-Whitehead, 1996; Radziszewska & Rogoff, 1991).

It is not enough to provide school-age children with a repertoire of strategies for learning; if left to their own devices, few continue to use the strategies or transfer them to new tasks. For this reason, establishing a school culture of a collaborative community of learners, involving students as well as teachers in reciprocal teaching, is most effective in moving children through the zone of proximal development (Brown, 1997; Bruner, 1996). Indeed, Karpov and Haywood (1998) have indicated that guided discovery, in which peers regulate each other's behavior, is more effective and natural than strict reliance on teacher-student interaction. Guided discovery within the classroom might be accomplished by having children work in dyads (pairs) where both children discuss thoughts and ideas. These ideas are later shared in a group discussion or writing assignment (Wickett, 2000).

Critical to instruction that is based on Vygotsky's theory is the expert's ability to identify the novice's level of understanding (Rogoff, 1998). Vygotsky's ideas solve the problem posed more than 35 years ago by developmental psychologist J. McVicker Hunt (1965), who spoke about the **problem of the match,** or the need to challenge children without overwhelming them.

The changing demands on the social interaction required to develop cognitive skills as children move from complete novice to more experienced learner have been compared to what occurs during the construction of a building. The support in the case of a building is the scaffold. A lot of scaffolding is needed in the early stages of erecting a building, but more and more is removed as the building nears completion. Thus, in speaking metaphorically about adult support of children's learning through social interaction, we often say that the adult provides scaffolding for the child. The adult continually adjusts the amount and kind of guided participation as the child's skill improves. For example, the adult may at first need to direct the child very explicitly as he or she practices. Then, as the child gains skill, the adult removes some of the scaffolding, in order to give the child greater independence. An instructional session might begin with instruction and modeling, progress to feedback to the child about his or her performance, and then conclude with questions that encourage the child to think about the task and to articulate new understandings.

Differences between the Theories of Vygotsky and Piaget

Vygotsky's approach to learning differs in important ways from Piaget's approach. Piaget thought the drive toward higher levels of cognitive development came from within the child, and that the child's need for discovery was universal—exhibited by all children everywhere. In contrast, Vygotsky focused on cognitive change resulting from social interaction with individuals who are capable of guiding the child through the zone of proximal development. Researchers have found individual differences in the **need for cognition** (the tendency to engage in and enjoy effortful cognitive activity), which contradicts Piaget's view that there is a universal drive toward cognitive activity in all children.

What circumstances help determine whether a child will exhibit a strong need for school-related cognition? This question has been the focus of over 100 investigations. In one of these (Cacioppo et al., 1996), children showed increases in their need for cognition in settings where they felt enjoyment, competence, and mastery in thinking as they engaged in cognitive tasks. In contrast, the need for cognition decreased in children who perceived high levels of controlling surveillance, time pressure, and external rewards. Bill's and Desserae's need for cognition was probably increased by the enjoyment they experienced as they worked together and mastered the dice problem-solving tasks their teacher assigned.

Children who exhibit lower levels of the need for cognition, need carefully planned scaffolding to support learning and to increase the need for cognition. Only through experiences that build competence and provide enjoyment in learning will children develop a need for cognition.

Vygotsky and Piaget also disagree about the relationship of language to cognitive development. Piaget stressed language as a *representational* system, as symbols that represent what is *already* known from experience and from thinking about experience. Vygotsky, on the other hand, considered social interaction, including language, essential in guiding children through the zone of proximal development on all learning tasks. Researchers are now applying Vygotsky's theory to find out how social interaction (including language) affects peer learning, observational learning, attention to spatial representations of information (e.g., maps and diagrams), and mathematical representations in everyday life (Bauer & Johnson-Laird, 1993; Hogan & Tudge, 1999; Karpov & Haywood, 1998; Yan, 1999).

Integrating the Theories of Vygotsky and Piaget

One effort to reconcile Vygotsky's emphasis on cognitive development as a function of guided discovery through social interaction with Piaget's focus on independent discovery emerged from the study of human development across cultures. Greenfield

(1999) found that as cultures change over time, approaches to learning and child development also change. Her findings indicate that Vygotsky's scaffolding and guided discovery dominate among cultures that are in a stable, tradition-maintaining period; independent discovery through trial-and-error experimentation is more prevalent when cultures are in a state of change.

Another approach to integrating the theories of Piaget and Vygotsky as they relate to cognitive development has led to the **dynamic systems model** of development (van Geert, 1998). This model adopted Piaget's concepts of assimilation and accommodation as two opposing cognitive processes that result in the developmental mechanism of adaptation. Van Geert (1998) defines **adaptation** as actions and experiences that alternate the conservative mechanism that maintains the present state of development with a progressive mechanism that establishes a future state of development. The model also adopts Vygotsky's concept of the zone of proximal development. The goal of this dynamic systems model is to transform the conceptual models of cognitive development into a quantitative model that will make more accurate predictions about the impact of environmental interventions with individuals with varying levels of experience and at various stages of adaptation.

Defining and Assessing Intelligence

Intelligence tests are frequently administered during the elementary school years to estimate children's ability to learn. Subtests within intelligence tests tap different kinds of thinking, as well as different products of thinking. For example, intelligence tests often include subtests to see how well children can define words (one kind of thinking), how well they can discuss objects in terms of similarities and differences (a second kind of thinking), and how well they can put puzzles together (a product of thinking).

Single-Factor Tests of Intelligence

With the exception of a few researchers who have described specific factors of intelligence, the concept of intelligence throughout the first half of the 20th century was that of a single dimension on which people can be placed. Most of the research on genetic, prenatal, or environmental influences on intelligence have used global scores based on this unidimensional construct.

The first intelligence test was based on the work of Alfred Binet and Theodore Simon. They had been approached by the French minister of instruction to devise a test to identify students who might benefit from instruction outside of the regular classroom. So Binet and Simon chose tasks requiring judgment and reasoning abilities needed for school success in Paris, France, in the early 1900s. By administering the tests to large numbers of children, they were able to establish **norms**—average mental abilities for each age. Binet assumed that his test tapped a variety of abilities that could be altered by introducing different educational experiences.

Terman, who adapted Binet's test for use in the United States, thought intelligence was a stable, unidimensional construct with variability determined largely by genetics, not experience. The intelligence quotient was introduced to compare a child's mental age with his or her chronological age. **Mental age** is the average age at

Many children take intelligence tests. Group differences in IQ scores have been the subject of continuing heated debate. (Source: © Laura Dwight/ Photo Edit)

which children pass the same number of tasks as the child tested. **Chronological age** is the actual age of the child at the time the test is taken. This concept of intelligence as a single number was called the **intelligence quotient.** It was calculated by using the following formula: [MA/CA] × 100 = IQ. (The IQ is now computed as a standardized score with a mean of 100 and a standard deviation of 16.)

The Stanford-Binet Intelligence Scale, published in 1916, became the standard against which other tests of intelligence were validated. It was not until the 1986 revision of the Stanford-Binet that different aspects of intelligence were included as subscales. Thorndike and colleagues (1986) described the new scoring of the Stanford-Binet as having a hierarchical organization in which four broad measures of mental ability are tapped. These include (1) verbal reasoning, (2) quantitative reasoning, (3) visual reasoning, and (4) short-term memory. The new scoring also provided more specific skill scores on four aspects of verbal reasoning, three aspects of quantitative reasoning, four aspects of visual reasoning, and four types of short-term memory.

The most commonly used, individually administered intelligence test is the **Wechsler Intelligence Scale for Children—Third Edition,** often called the WISC-III (Wechsler, 1991). This test, used with children ages 6 to 16, is divided into verbal and performance sections, each of which has six or seven subtests. A child receives three scores on this test, including a verbal IQ, a performance IQ, and a full-scale IQ based on the first two scores.

The verbal part of the WISC-III tests children on information, arithmetic, vocabulary, comprehension, digit span, and the ability to distinguish similarities. The performance part tests them on picture completion, coding, picture arrangement, block design, object assembly, symbol search, and mazes. For an example of the kind of questions that appear on the WISC-III, see Table 13.1.

TABLE 13.1
Paraphrased Wechsler-like questions

General Information

1. How many wings does a bird have?
2. How many nickels make a dime?

General Comprehension

1. What should you do if you see a man forget his hat when he leaves his seat in a restaurant?
2. Why do some people save sales receipts?

Arithmetic

1. Sue had two pieces of candy and Joe gave her four more. How many pieces of candy did Sue have altogether?
2. Three children divided 18 pennies equally among themselves. How many pennies did each child receive?

Similarities

1. In what way are a lion and a tiger alike?
2. In what way are a saw and a hammer alike?

Vocabulary

This test consists simply of asking, "What is a _____?" or "What does _____ mean?"
The words cover a wide range of difficulty or familiarity.

Performance Tests

In addition to verbal tasks of the kinds illustrated in the Vocabulary section, there are a number of performance tasks involving the use of blocks, cutout figures, paper and pencil puzzles, and so on.

Source: Simulated items similar to those in the *Wechsler Intelligence Scale for Children—Third Edition.* Copyright 1949, 1974, 1990, by The Psychological Corporation. Reproduced by permission. All rights reserved. "Wechsler Intelligence Scale for Children" and "WISC-III" are registered trademarks of The Psychological Corporation.

One Intelligence or Multiple Intelligences?

Theorists have debated whether intelligence is a stable attribute reflected by a single number or composed of multiple intelligences that are susceptible to change. Inadequacies with the single-factor concept of intelligence have increased interest in identifying multiple factors of intellect—**multiple intelligences.**

One example of a multiple-factor view of intelligence is J. P. Guilford's structure-of-intellect model (1985). Guilford used factor-analytic techniques to identify multiple factors of intelligence based on memory, convergent thinking (converging on a single correct answer for a problem), and divergent thinking (producing several different answers for a problem) for verbal, quantitative, figural, auditory, and social materials.

More recently, Carroll (1997) factor-analyzed the data from all the mental ability data sets available and developed a hierarchical model of mental ability, with many specific abilities at the lowest level, inductive reasoning and application of previously acquired knowledge at an intermediate level, and general intelligence at a higher level. Researchers have found that the small correlations between specific mental ability tests exist because of a cluster of individuals who score very low on all tests. For example, such performance would be expected of school-age children with fetal alcohol syndrome. If these very low scorers are eliminated, the correlations between tests of different mental abilities disappear (Hunt, 1999; Legree et al., 1996). This makes the use of general intelligence scores questionable. As children gain more experience in a specific domain, their general intelligence scores do not function well as predictors of their performance (Ericsson, 1996).

Another model of multifactor intelligence was developed by Howard Gardner (1991, 1995). Gardner contended that the ability to understand other people or to build something by hand indicates intelligence as much as being able to solve math problems. Gardner identified seven types of intelligence: musical, logico-mathematical, bodily-kinesthetic, linguistic, spatial, interpersonal, and intrapersonal. (See Table 13.2 for a description of each type.)

Another researcher who identified multiple aspects to intelligence is Robert Sternberg, who proposed a **triarchic theory of intelligence** (1995). Sternberg's three components of intelligence are analytical thinking, creative thinking, and practical thinking. **Analytical thinking** involves using strategies that manipulate elements of a problem or the relationships among elements of a problem. This type of thinking is elicited by questions that ask children to analyze, compare, or evaluate. In a mathematics class, students might be asked to evaluate the correctness of a solution to a problem. In music, they might be asked to compare the music of two composers.

TABLE 13.2

Defining and fostering multiple intelligences (Gardner)

Definitions of the Intelligences	Ways to Foster the Intelligences
Musical—Sensitivity to rhythm, pitch, and timbre; appreciating forms of musical expressiveness	Expose children to various types of music; use rhythmic and melodic instruments; encourage singing and songwriting.
Spatial—Accurate perception of the visual-spatial world and the ability to make transformations on those perceptions	Provide opportunities for mapping, exploring spaces, varying arrangements of materials, fitting materials into spaces, working puzzles.
Linguistic—Sensitivity to spoken and written language, meanings, and sounds of words	Read to children; encourage reading, writing, oral expression, and vocabulary development.
Logical-mathematical—Ability to think logically and to explore relationships; sensitivity to numerical patterns	Provide manipulatives for math; encourage puzzle and problem solving; encourage experimentation and prediction.
Bodily-kinesthetic—Mastery over body movements, fine and gross motor coordination	Encourage sports, dancing, making things with hands, running, practicing motor skills.
Interpersonal—Ability to read intentions and emotions of other people and to respond appropriately	Encourage social interactions, personal problem solving; play games figuring out intentions and emotions of others.
Intrapersonal—Self-knowledge of strengths and feelings and ability to guide own behavior	Encourage expression of emotions, preferences, and thinking strategies. Help with understanding of wishes, fears, and abilities.

Source: Adapted from "On multiple intelligence: ECT interview," by H. Gardner, 1995, *Early Childhood Today, 10*(l), pp. 31–32.

Logical-mathematical knowledge is just one kind of intelligence identified by Howard Gardner. Other kinds include musical, spatial, linguistic, bodily-kinesthetic, interpersonal, and intrapersonal. (*Source:* © Will Faller)

Creative thinking involves solving a problem or thinking about its elements in a new way. Creative thinking can be elicited by asking children to design, invent, or create. In a science class, children may be asked to design an experiment to answer a research question. In a social studies class, children might be asked to generate ideas for reducing racial discrimination.

Practical thinking involves applying what is known to solve problems in everyday contexts. To elicit this type of thinking, children can be asked to apply to a new situation knowledge they have learned in another situation. A teacher might ask a class to use knowledge of how geography affected the economic development of a recently studied city in order to hypothesize how geography and economy might interact in a city whose geography only is familiar.

Group Differences in Tested Intelligence

Different groups of people tend to perform differently on tests of mental abilities. The source of these group differences has been hotly debated, because the groups themselves differ in terms of race, ethnicity, and social class. (A family's **social class** is determined by considering several factors, including income level, educational level, and type of occupation.) A great deal of this debate has centered around the 15-point intelligence score difference between Euro-American and African American children, with some people (Herrnstein & Murray, 1994; Jensen, 1969) claiming that these differences are due to racial differences in genetics. But Weinberg (1989) has reported data from adoption studies that indicate the inadequacy of genetics to explain these group differences.

Specifically, African American children who are reared in white middle-class families have an average intelligence of 110. This is about 15 points higher than the average intelligence of similar African American children who are raised by their own parents. The average intelligence of both African American and white adopted children is higher (110) than the average intelligence of their biological parents (about 100). However, adopted children did not score as high as the biological children of the adoptive parents (116.7) nor as high as the adoptive parents

Although as a group, white children of the mainstream culture score higher on IQ tests than other groups do, these results do not necessarily mean that they are more intelligent. The results may instead indicate more experience on tasks similar to those found on IQ tests. If intelligence tests measured the cognitive skills acquired while growing up in a traditional Native American community, this girl might score higher than most of her white peers of the mainstream culture. (*Source:* © Lawrence Migdale/Photo Researchers)

themselves (119). Weinberg concluded that genetics accounts for some of the individual differences *within* a group from similar environments, but that group differences appear to be more related to the typical environments experienced by different groups.

Because racial and ethnic group differences are often compounded by social class differences, people often attribute group differences to race when these should be attributed to factors such as social class. Middle-class children obtain higher scores on intelligence tests than do children from lower-social-class families. Brooks-Gunn and colleagues (1996) reported that differences in intelligence scores between Euro-American and African American children are almost eliminated by adjusting for differences in family poverty, neighborhood economic conditions, maternal education level, and differences in the opportunities children have to learn.

In addition to genetics and environmental explanations for group intelligence score differences, some researchers contend that mental ability tests are **culturally biased**—that test items on intelligence tests reflect the values, experiences, and interests of white middle-social-class culture. Children from the mainstream culture inevitably perform better on the tests than do children whose cultures are different. Some researchers have argued that we need to assess intelligences separately within each of several different cultures.

Roland Good and Vicki Collins (1995) examined the consequences of attributing group differences to genetics, test bias, or social injustice. (For a discussion of their evaluation and analysis, see Knowledge in Action: Policy—Consequences of Various Assumptions about Group Differences in Scores or Intelligence Tests.)

Stability of Intelligence

Parents may wonder whether their child will receive the same score on an intelligence test if tested at age 6 and age 10. Researchers have conducted a number of longitudinal studies to answer questions about the stability of intelligence test scores. Two of these longitudinal studies—the Berkeley Growth Study and the Fels longitudinal studies—found that large changes occurred for many children. In some cases, IQ scores changed by as much as 40 points. Scores for about half of the children changed by 10 or more IQ points over the course of the school years (McCall et al., 1973; McCall, 1984; Sontag et al., 1958). What might cause an IQ score to vary quite a lot from one time to another? Researchers have conducted studies to answer this question.

In one longitudinal study, Sameroff and colleagues (1993) identified some of the environmental factors that account for large changes in IQ. Declines in IQ scores were associated with factors such as parental unemployment, psychological or physical illnesses or deaths among family members, and absence of the father. Scores of children with overly restrictive or highly permissive parents declined as well (Azar, 1996; Baumrind, 1993; Bradley, 1989; Honzik et al., 1948; McCall et al., 1973; Sameroff et al., 1993). Across studies, gains in IQ scores were evident

POLICY

Consequences of Various Assumptions about Group Differences in Scores on Intelligence Tests

Roland Good and Vicki Collins (1995) have examined group differences in intelligence test scores and the potential results of officially adopting each view. They consider three assumptions: (1) the social injustice assumption, (2) the assumption about test bias, and (3) the assumption about genetic differences between racial groups. They indicated the public policy actions that would follow logically from each of these assumptions and the likely consequences of these actions.

The Social Injustice Assumption

The social injustice assumption attributes group differences to variables such as quality of schooling, prenatal care, preschool experiences, age of the mother, and nutrition. It assumes that groups would have the same potential if we could equalize these societal factors. Social injustice explanations also assume that educational achievement drives group differences in intelligence scores.

Social injustice explanations for group differences lead to arguments for improved services and social action. The outcome of actions based on this assumption would be an increase in expectations for all children, an increase in services aimed at eliminating differences in educational opportunity, and increased skills. However, group differences may still appear if tests used to measure intelligence are culturally biased.

The Test Bias Assumption

Those who attribute group differences to test bias assume that groups would get very similar scores on intelligence tests if the tests measured intelligence correctly. Reducing group differences in measured intelligence, given this assumption, requires abandoning tests because they are discriminatory or fixing the tests. The latter action includes efforts to create culture-free tests or to test each intellectual ability with subscales that reflect different cultures.

If differences in group scores are attributed solely to test bias, there is no need to change expectations for achievement, to provide services to ease poverty, or to provide programs designed especially to bring about changes in skills.

The Genetics Assumption

The assumption that group differences are due to genetics carries with it the related assumptions that intelligence determines different levels of school achievement and that different racial, ethnic, and social-class groups have different potentials, no matter what is done for the lower-scoring group. The actions that follow from this assumption include calls to acknowledge stable group differences, withdrawal of funding to reduce group differences, and services matched to expectations for the different groups. The long-term outcome of these actions would be lowered expectations, a decrease in special services, and a decline in the attainment of skills by many children.

Which Assumption Is Valid?

The first two assumptions are not contradictory, although each focuses on a different explanation for group differences in intelligence scores. But both assumptions could be valid, and actions based on both assumptions could be implemented. The genetics explanation is, of course, inconsistent with the other two explanations. But as we have already indicated, the research of Weinberg (1989) and of Brooks-Gunn and colleagues (1996) offers strong evidence against a genetics-only explanation.

Even if genetics contributed to group differences, this conclusion should be considered in light of a statement made in chapter 2. Any discussion of genetics versus the environment in accounting for variability in intelligence must consider the range-of-reaction concept. Weinberg described this concept precisely in the following statement: "There is a myth that if a behavior or characteristic is genetic, it cannot be changed. Genes do not *fix* behavior. Rather, they establish a range of possible reactions to the range of possible experiences that environments can provide" (1989, p. 101). Thus, in terms of action, even a genetic explanation for group differences in intelligence scores does not call for a cessation of efforts to provide all children with adequate opportunities to develop intellectual skill.

---

among independent, academically competitive, and self-initiating children. Intelligence score increases were also found for children whose parents encouraged intellectual development, were verbally and emotionally responsive, made available interesting toys and activities, and provided explanations along with moderation in discipline.

Using verbal measures of mental ability, several researchers have reported increases in ability as a function of exposure to print (e.g., Cipielewski & Stanovich, 1992; Echols et al., 1996; Stanovich et al., 1995). Other studies have explored

TABLE 13.3

Factors associated with increases and decreases
in intelligence test scores

Factors Associated with Increases	Factors Associated with Decreases
1. Parental verbal and emotional responsivity	1. Highly restrictive or permissive parenting
2. Interesting toys and games in the home	2. Absence of father
3. Exposure to reading	3. Maternal psychological or physical illness
4. Amount of mother-child interaction for mothers with more than a high school education	4. Mother did not complete more than the 10th grade of education
5. Connectedness with religion	5. Family and community poverty
6. Parental help with homework	6. Lack of connectedness with peers; rejection by peers
7. Years of schooling completed	7. Parents place low value on completing education

Sources: Azar, 1996; Baumrind, 1993; Brooks-Gunn et al., 1996; Good & Collins, 1995; Guay et al., 1999; Hedges & Nowell, 1995; Jimerson et al., 1999; Masten, 1999; Sameroff et al., 1993; and Stanovich et al., 1995.

changes in the quantitative ability differences between boys and girls over the course of the school years. Meta-analyses of gender differences in mathematical abilities, and analyses from the International Assessment of Educational Progress project, indicate that small gender differences in mathematics during the early elementary grades become larger with increasing years of school. The differences tend to be greatest in the early teen years in complex problem-solving rather than in math computation. (Beller & Gafni, 1996; Benbow, 1990; Hedges & Nowell, 1995; Hyde et al., 1990). (Table 13.3 summarizes the environmental factors that researchers have found to be associated with both increases and decreases in intelligence test scores.)

The relationship between years of schooling and intelligence, noted in Table 13.3, has long been recognized. Until recently, however, researchers assumed that IQ influenced the number of years of education—that individuals with lower IQ scores would choose to complete fewer years of school. But after reexamining this relationship, Stephen Ceci (1991) concluded that the data support the alternative explanation that the amount of education influences intelligence test scores. That is, children who drop out of school or are uninvolved decreased in intelligence scores, compared with a matched stay-in-school sample. Ceci notes that this direction of effect should not be surprising, given that school tasks develop precisely the kind of skills that are tapped on intelligence tests.

Achievement Tests

"What does it say, Grandma?" Molina asks, as she peeks over her grandmother's shoulder.

"It says you are going to be taking some tests next week."

"I don't see why we have to take those tests. Mrs. Fernandes knows what we know. She gives us quizzes and asks us questions all the time."

"I know, but I guess these are special tests. They must be different somehow, or I don't think the school would spend all of this time and money on them."

think about it

What are achievement tests? Why would a school spend considerable time and money on such tests? Don't teachers already know what students know, given the work they do with students day in and day out? What new information could a test possibly provide?

Achievement tests measure knowledge, information, and skills in specific curriculum areas, such as mathematics, reading, science, and social studies. The Iowa Tests of Basic Skills test battery provides an achievement test for each grade level from first through ninth grades (Hieronymous & Hoover, 1986). The tests measure skills in the areas of reading, spelling, vocabulary, language use, work-study, math, social studies, science, writing, and listening.

Of course, most teachers know what their students do and do not know because, as Molina said, they "give them quizzes and ask them questions all the time." But teachers do not always know how to put the performance of children in their class or school district into a larger perspective. Standardized achievement tests provide a bigger context in which Molina's teacher and the administrators in her school district can review how she and her peers are improving in each curriculum area.

The call in recent years for greater accountability by schools in the United States has increased achievement testing. In some cases, the tests are used to determine whether an individual child has attained a grade-appropriate level of knowledge and competence. Standardized achievement tests are also used to assess the success of schools. For example, all fifth-graders in a school district may be tested to determine whether their average performance is above or below a national average. Sometimes achievement tests are used to test children at both the beginning and the end of the year to assess the degree to which one year of schooling has resulted in one year's change in the children's achievement scores.

Achievement tests are also useful in making gender comparisons. By high school, the math achievement of boys and girls diverges. By comparing the achievement of boys and girls through the elementary grades, and analyzing their respective performances on various subtests relating to mathematics, educators can better understand exactly when and where these differences begin and what might be responsible for these gender gaps. (See Knowledge in Action: Education—Explaining Gender Differences in Math and Science Achievement.)

Standardized achievement tests have also been used to assess achievement in different cultures. Recent studies indicate that U.S. school-age children average below the international average in reading and mathematical achievement, whereas children from China, Japan, and Korea have averages considerably above the

EDUCATION

Explaining Gender Differences in Math and Science Achievement

Studies of gender differences in mathematical ability during the school-age years indicate that girls and boys are not different in the early school years, but that boys are better in problem solving, geometry, conceptual understanding, and measurement by about seventh or eighth grade. Similar gender differences emerge during the school-age years in the life, physical, and earth and space sciences (Beller & Gafni, 1996). Studies show that the gender gap begins to emerge during the later school-age years and that the differences become even greater during high school. What might account for these differences in the achievement of boys and girls?

Studies have found that the widening gaps found in high school are related to the variations in the course-taking patterns of boys and girls. That is, boys as a group take more math, as well as higher-level math courses, than girls take. But because courses cannot typically be elected by students until they enter high school, this is not an adequate explanation for differences found before age 13. That is, while in elementary school, girls and boys usually take the same courses. What then might explain differences in math achievement that emerge by late in the elementary years?

One possibility is that more boys than girls are placed in higher-level courses in math. It is typical in some schools for math classes to be offered at different levels during the upper elementary or junior high school years. If more boys are placed in higher levels of the same math course, this could account for the differences in math achievement.

Differences that show up by age 13 might also be due to differences in teaching strategies in the elementary grades, attitudes about potential careers that are communicated to children at home, differential life experiences (e.g., visiting museums, doing mechanical and physical tasks), the lack of available role models for girls in the fields of math and science, or cultural expectations. Some research has suggested that girls who attend all-girls schools achieve better math and science scores. Other studies show conflicting results, with some suggesting that the real difference may lie in these schools' small classes, innovative curricula, and excellent teaching (King, 1999). There are gender differences in children's preferences for different kinds of learning environments. Girls respond more positively to mathematics and science instruction when it is taught in a cooperative rather than competitive manner and when it has a person-centered application perspective. Adjusting elementary-school mathematics classroom environments may narrow the mathematics gender gap that develops late in the school-age years (Eccles & Roeser, 1999).

It is not known at the present time which factors might be responsible for gender differences in achievement in these areas, or if all of them play a part. All of these factors need to be explored in future research (Beller & Gafni, 1996; Byrnes & Wasik, 1991; Cole, 1999; Hyde et al., 1990; Mills et al., 1993).

---

international average. We discuss these cross-cultural differences in achievement later in this chapter.

Academic Motivation and Success in School

"I know he can do better, and that's why I've asked you to come in," the sixth-grade teacher explained to Gregory's parents. "An F in math doesn't reflect Gregory's ability at all. As you know, his IQ is very high. Gregory's problem, I'm afraid, is motivation."

"We're aware that there's a problem," Gregory's father replied. "It's been getting worse for a few years, since about third grade. He has a lot of interests—outdoor sports, playing the drums, collecting baseball cards—but he doesn't seem to care very much about books or school. We just don't know how to motivate him to hit the books."

think about it What exactly does Gregory's teacher mean when she says, "Gregory's problem is motivation"? Does Gregory's lack of dedication to his schoolwork stem from an assumption that he is not very good in math, or does he simply think that achieving in math is not as interesting or important as doing well in other things? How can Gregory's teacher and parents get him to take his schoolwork more seriously?

When a child is underachieving, schools and parents often have a psychologist test the child to see if a learning disability might be interfering with academic performance. It is significant that Gregory's father said that Gregory's grades had been slipping since about third grade because this is the time when children begin to confront a lot of written story problems in math. Perhaps Gregory has a reading problem that limits his performance in math. If testing shows that the child has no learning problems, then the psychologist can help the child place more value on academic achievement or work to improve the child's perceived competence. Ideally, of course, parents and teachers help children to value academic achievement and to learn that with appropriate effort they can be both competent and effective on academic tasks.

Theories of learning and motivation tend to agree that the effort a student shows depends primarily on two factors: (1) the value to the student of particular achievement goals and (2) the student's expectation that he or she can succeed in achieving the goals. This is called **value-expectancy theory.** Students who do not make the effort required to learn in elementary school are thought either to have too little value for school achievement or to have low expectations for their ability to learn. But what causes a child to have a problem in these areas? And what can parents and teachers do if a child exhibits such a problem? These are the questions we discuss next.

Academic Values and Expectations

The first factor in academic motivation is the presence of values for specific achievement goals. If the school psychologist measures Gregory's achievement motivation, she will assess whether he considers it important to do well on academic tasks.

Psychologists who have studied the "need to achieve" (McClelland et al., 1976) have found that it varies significantly from person to person. Children who show a high need for achievement seem to come from environments that stress excelling and accomplishing goals, including academic goals. When parents view education as important and engage themselves in intellectual activities, such as reading books at home, children often behave similarly, demonstrating high achievement (Bradley et al., 1988; Rimm, 1999). When parents value nonacademic activities more highly than academic activities, children are less likely to value education and academic achievement.

An example of how parental values and expectations affect achievement involves comparisons of U.S. schoolchildren who have different cultural backgrounds. One study shows that mathematics scores of Caucasian American students are lower than those of Asian American students. Factors associated with achievement in Asian American children include having parents and peers who hold high standards for

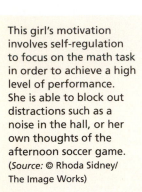

This girl's motivation involves self-regulation to focus on the math task in order to achieve a high level of performance. She is able to block out distractions such as a noise in the hall, or her own thoughts of the afternoon soccer game. (*Source:* © Rhoda Sidney/ The Image Works)

academic achievement, parents who believe that effort is an important determinant of achievement, and positive attitudes about achievement. The high-achieving Asian American students also studied diligently and faced less interference with schoolwork from jobs and informal peer interactions (Chen & Stevenson, 1995). Interestingly, Asian American students reported no greater frequency of maladaptive psychological symptoms than did Caucasian American children, a finding which is inconsistent with the common belief that high expectations for achievement always take a psychological toll. If competing demands are reduced—if jobs do not interfere and peers are supportive of academic pursuits—high expectations for academic performance apparently need not create considerable stress in children.

High-achieving children often have parents who are demanding, evaluate their children's performance, and apply moderate pressure. They also offer praise, get emotionally involved in their children's performance, and provide facilitative rather than intrusive help (Rimm, 1999; Rosen & D'Andrade, 1975).

Parental demands are effective, however, only when the expectations are reasonable and the child perceives herself to be competent. When parental expectations are unrealistic; when the parent's help is dominating, negative, and intrusive; or when the child does not believe herself to be competent, the child's effort and achievement are likely to decline rather than improve (Dweck & Elliot, 1983).

Research in academic achievement motivation has identified two major categories of influences—distal and proximal motivational influences. **Distal motivational influences** determine a child's choice to take on a task or challenge. If the expected effort needed to accomplish a task is high relative to the perceived value of doing the task, motivation will be low. The child's motivation is also influenced by the perceived amount of effort needed to achieve the level of performance expected of him or her. Thus, if parents or teachers do not help children see the value of accomplishing a task, or if they set performance goals far above what children can achieve, children are likely to choose not to engage in the activity. **Proximal motivational influences** determine the amount of attentional effort children make within a task. Proximal motivation involves self-regulation to focus on a task in order to achieve a high level of performance instead of attending to distractions, such as external stimuli or internal thoughts such as worry. Expectation that performance of a task will improve with effort affects proximal motivation. Thus, if parents and teachers provide positive feedback to individual improvement and effort, a child is likely to work to achieve a higher level of performance on a task (Kanfer & Heggestad, 1999).

Achievement Goals

Achievement goals can be focused either on learning and mastery or on performance and ego (MacIver et al., 1995). If students are concerned primarily with developing new skills, understanding something, or improving their level of competence, they are working toward what are called **task-focused goals.** If students are trying only to outperform others or are concerned with being judged as smart rather than dumb, they are said to be working toward **ability-focused goals.**

Different goal orientations can influence students' behavior. For example, students who have adopted primarily task-focused goals are more likely than are students with ability-focused goals to believe that effort leads to success. When they do not at first succeed on a difficult task, they are likely to persevere. Task-focused students also prefer challenging tasks to easy tasks and report more intrinsic interest in learning than do ability-focused students. They also devote more time to tasks and use more effective strategies to approach them (MacIver et al., 1995).

Given the generally positive results found for students who have task-focused rather than ability-focused goals, it is important to consider what goals are fostered by schools. Often, ability-focused goals seem to dominate. Many schools reward normative success rather than individual improvement, bring ability differences into high resolution by publicizing relative performance levels (e.g., posting name charts with stars, putting stars and smiley faces on papers of high-achieving children, and so on), do not reliably reward effort, and do not encourage students to view initial mistakes as part of learning. Some schools do use techniques that develop a more task-focused orientation. These techniques include challenging students to pursue specific short-term, individual improvement goals, using fewer public displays of achievement differences, and rewarding students when their goals are met. Improvement-focused rewards may lead to increased interest in learning because the rewards signal progress and raise perceived competence (Eccles & Roeser, 1999; MacIver et al., 1995).

The achievement goals stressed by parents are usually felt by children as a "need to achieve." These girls' parents have stressed the importance of music, and they have provided music lessons to help them achieve. (*Source:* © Will Hart)

Some children underestimate their actual academic ability. The girl receiving help here may believe she is less competent at schoolwork than her classmates, even if her actual abilities and scores on school tests are comparable to theirs. Perceived competence is a key ingredient in academic motivation, effort, and success.   (*Source:* © Brian Smith)

Perceived Competence

A student's motivation on academic tasks is also affected by **perceived competence**—the child's subjective view of her academic abilities. Some children think they will do poorly in general with schoolwork or will experience difficulty in a certain subject, even though their past history of achievement is good. Why isn't a child's view of her competence always directly related to her actual achievement history? How does perceived competence affect a child's academic motivation?

Perceived competence is often thought to be determined by the child's past history of academic achievement. But even among children with identical academic achievement records, some perceive themselves to be highly competent academically whereas others perceive themselves to be less competent (Phillips, 1987). Thus, self-perception of competence affects academic motivation and effort independent of actual ability.

High-ability children who think they will not perform well are said to have an "illusion of incompetence"—they think they cannot do something when they actually can (Langer, 1979; Phillips & Zimmerman, 1990). Believing that they will not do well, they expend relatively little effort on academic tasks. Over time, they tend to be low achievers. Children with high perceived competence, on the other hand, persist on academic tasks (Carr et al., 1991; Okra & Paris, 1987).

How Perceived Competence Affects Effort   There are at least three ways in which perceived competence can influence effort. High perceived competence increases the expectation that effort will be rewarded, which alone leads to greater effort. It also reduces anxiety in academic situations because fear of failure is lower when children believe that they have some control—believe they are competent enough to master the situation. When children believe they have control, they are less likely to experience anxiety-producing distracting thoughts about negative outcomes, and their performance and concentration are less likely to suffer from the effects of chronic stress, such as exhaustion and depression (Ciaranello, 1988). Finally, children who perceive themselves as competent are able to plan their efforts and rehearse them cognitively—they develop and use metacognitive skills. They believe that such efforts will be rewarded with success, and they are able to deploy mental energy for these tasks, because they are not consumed by anxiety. Thus, increasing perceived competence will enhance both distal and proximal motivation (Bandura, 1989; Kanfer & Heggestad, 1999).

Developmental Changes in Children's Beliefs about Academic Abilities

Children's beliefs about their academic successes and failures become more differentiated and effective with age (Skinner, 1990). At 7 or 8 years of age, children tend to distinguish only two sets of factors to account for their successes and failures. One set consists of "unknown" or "hard to tell" causes ("I don't know what happened"); the other set consists of effort, ability, and other people (e.g., teachers). Children this age think they can control all of these factors through effort. At 9 and 10 years of age, children tend to use one of three sets of factors to account for their successes and failures: (1) unknown causes, (2) internal causes (effort and ability), or (3) external causes (others and luck). At ages 11 and 12, children tend to believe that academic performance is determined by one of four independent factors: (1) effort, (2) ability, (3) external causes, or (4) unknown causes. In other words, at this point, children have differentiated effort and ability. At this age, a tendency to attribute success and failure to external causes (others and luck) is an especially good predictor of poor grades in school (Fincham et al., 1989; Skinner, 1990). The tendency to attribute success and failure to level of effort expended rather than to ability is an especially good predictor of higher grades in school.

As children get older, their improved cognitive abilities enable them to consider the compensatory relationship between effort and ability in determining achievement (Stipek & Daniels, 1988). Even though all children will achieve more if they exert more rather than less effort, the work of childen with greater ability will pay off more handsomely in terms of high achievement. Unlike the 7- or 8-year-old, older elementary school children understand that high effort is not the only factor involved in high

Children have differentiated effort and ability. Sometimes students who are lower in ability disengage themselves from academic tasks, feeling that no matter what they do, they cannot compete with many of their peers. (*Source:* © E. Crews/The Image Works)

achievement. As a result of this increased understanding of the relationship between effort and ability, students who are lower in ability sometimes disengage themselves from academic tasks. They feel that no matter what they do, they cannot get grades as good as those earned by many of their peers. It is in the interest of both the individual learner and the society to keep all students engaged. But what can be done?

School practices that deemphasize public comparisons of grades (e.g., posting charts showing gold stars for children who achieve at high levels, using report cards that report only grades without any narrative) and reward effort, as well as level of achievement, can help maintain the willingness of students with lower levels of ability to expend effort on academic tasks. Increasing student engagement or participation in school tasks is also extremely important and a very good predictor of academic achievement (DeBaryshe et al., 1993).

Home and School Influences on Achievement

"Dad," called 8-year-old Latasha. "I'm starting my homework."

"So, what do we have for homework tonight?"

"Well, I have to review a story in my reading book and answer some questions. I have some subtraction problems and three pages to read in my science book."

"That sounds manageable," said Latasha's father. "I see you are starting with the math problems."

"Yeah. I think I can do them by myself."

"Okay, I'll read the story in your reading book while you do your math. Then I can look over the math problems while you review the story. After that, we can go over any math problems that need double-checking and get to those questions about your story. How does that sound?"

"Okay, and then I can read in my science book."

think about it

Parents and teachers can have a powerful effect on a child's perceived competence and actual performance. What does Latasha's father communicate to her about her competence in doing homework, and about the ease with which the tasks can be managed? Does he exhibit confidence in her ability to work independently, even though she may need his advice and help? If his approach were different—for example, if he communicated to Latasha that he thought the amount of homework was excessive or that it surely was going to be difficult to complete, what effect do you think it would have on Latasha's view of the difficulty of school tasks and on her ability to do them?

A child's perceived competence is strongly influenced by her parents' beliefs about her intellectual abilities and about the difficulty of school-related tasks. Latasha's father's communication increased her actual competence in doing her schoolwork and also built her confidence in her competence. But think for a moment about Ellen, whom we met at the beginning of this chapter. Recall her mother's comments about her own difficulty in math and the difficulty that she thinks girls in general have with this subject. These comments may have made Ellen feel less competent in mathematics because her mother insinuated that girls are not good in math and that math is difficult to understand in the first place.

In this section, we discuss the effects that parental and teachers' beliefs and expectations can have on children's perceived competence and academic performance. We also discuss some strategies that can be used in the classroom to help develop and maintain children's interest and success in cognitive tasks.

Parental Beliefs and Expectations

The power of parental beliefs was demonstrated in one study in which third-graders' views of their academic competence were found to be related more to their parents' beliefs about their abilities than to their actual achievement in the early elementary grades (Phillips, 1987). Parents' beliefs about the difficulty of school tasks also influence children in important ways (Parsons et al., 1982).

Parents' beliefs about tasks and their child's abilities can be particularly powerful when the child initially meets with a failure at a task. Many of the children who persist at a difficult task will probably eventually succeed, and their original perceptions of themselves as being capable of mastering tasks will be confirmed.

Traditional classrooms provide few opportunities for one-on-one scaffolding and practicing basic skill development. Parents can play an especially important role in working with their children to communicate excitement about learning, a belief that tasks can be mastered, and an expectation that effort on a task will lead to higher levels of performance (Kanfer & Heggestad, 1999; Wagner, 1999).

Parents also can affect their children's cognitive performance by creating an environment that leads to positive emotions and mood states. Research demonstrates that a sad or angry mood leads to poorer performance at cognitive tasks like those children perform in school. Creating a positive mood improves problem solving, memory task performance, reading comprehension, and decision making. Neuropsychological investigations attribute these effects to changing levels of brain dopamine that occur with mood fluctuations (Ashby et al., 1999; Ellis et al., 1997; Isen, 1999).

Teachers' Beliefs and Expectations

Children are also influenced by their teachers' expectations. High expectations are associated with higher levels of achievement and a greater feeling of competence among children. Elementary school teachers who believe they are important in children's development and that they can reach all children will increase student motivation and achievement. Those who perceive themselves as "weeders" rather than "cultivators" tend to create a more competitive learning environment and increase the disparities in student motivation and achievement (Eccles & Roesner, 1999; Purkey & Smith, 1983).

Additionally, teachers' different attributions for success and failure seem to be associated with different patterns of achievement. For example, some researchers found that teachers respond differently to failure among boys compared to girls.

If teachers' reactions to boys and girls are different, children are likely to learn to attribute success and failure differently. The boys in this applied math group outnumber the girls, and they look a bit more eager. Girls, more than boys, tend to attribute failures in math to low ability. Boys, more than girls, tend to attribute failure to lack of effort. Teachers can help girls and boys stick with higher-level math work by providing good instruction and telling them to study harder in order to learn difficult concepts. (*Source*: © Brian Smith)

When boys fail, teachers are likely to attribute their poor performance to nonintellectual aspects of their work. When girls fail, teachers tend to attribute the failure to their intelligence—to ability. In one study, teachers attributed boys' failure to motivation problems eight times more often than they did girls' failure (Dweck, 1978). Teachers who behave in this way would probably give boys the message, "You can do anything, if you'll just try." But to girls the message is likely to be, "Well, you can't be good in everything."

Different teacher reactions to boys and girls might account for sex differences in attributions about success and failure. Boys as a group are more likely to attribute success to ability and failure to lack of effort. Girls, on the other hand, tend to attribute success to effort and failure to lack of ability. Thus, girls are likely to respond to failure by decreasing their efforts and their perception of their own competence. Boys, on the other hand, are more likely to believe that when they fail, an increase in effort will help them succeed (Dweck, 1978).

Developmental systems theory, which we discussed in chapter 1, indicates that students also help to create their own environments (Bandura, 1989; Sternberg, 1990). When a child's behavior motivates a teacher to expect and reward achievement, or, conversely, when a student who does not value academic achievement ignores the teacher and looks for attention primarily from other underachieving students, the child is choosing an environment that maintains and develops precisely the values and personality characteristics that led to the initial choice. The challenge for adults is to structure environments and provide guidance to children that will encourage them to "hit the books" rather than choose environments that encourage aimless pursuits.

Fostering Communities of Learners

Engagement in school tasks is closely related to achievement. If students spend little time on school tasks, it stands to reason that they will learn less. Many children spend considerable amounts of their time in the classroom off-task—doing something other than working on their assignments. Some children daydream, others engage in disruptive behavior, others doodle or write notes to each other. What can educators do to increase children's engagement with their schoolwork, in order to improve their learning?

Educators have devised a number of strategies to try to increase children's interest and engagement in learning. Strategies that organize instruction so that children work together on assignments and projects are referred to as cooperative learning techniques. Children typically work together in small groups on problem-solving assignments. When children are in small groups, and when each child has an important job to do, more children tend to become actively engaged in learning. Cooperative learning involves individual accountability, face-to-face interaction among students, appropriate use of group and interpersonal skills, and the ability to assess the effectiveness of the group (Johnson & Johnson, 1999). Group interactions can help children to care for one another, solve their own problems, and feel more in control of their own learning (Harris & Fuqua, 2000).

Many different approaches to cooperative learning have been developed. One of these is known as the jigsaw cooperative learning technique (Aronson, 1999b). When Aronson worked as a consultant in a Texas school system shortly after it had been mandated to desegregate, he became interested in developing better techniques to engage children in learning and to improve the social atmosphere in classrooms. In observing elementary school classrooms, he found environments in which students competed fiercely for the respect and approval of their teacher. He also observed that unsuccessful students were jealous and envious of successful students and that they often ridiculed them. The students who won approval and recognition by the teacher often looked down on the children who did not compete successfully. Aronson, thinking that surely another approach would be more productive for everyone, developed the **jigsaw technique.**

The jigsaw technique involves placing students in independent learning groups. Each child in a learning group becomes the expert on a part of an assignment. Thus, like a jigsaw puzzle, each child has one piece of a puzzle and depends on the others to get the big picture. Students first consult with the students from other learning groups who are becoming experts on the same piece of the total assignment. These like-assignment consultations are often carried out by forming expert groups in which all students who are responsible for a particular portion of the assignment work together in order to understand their assignment and to develop strategies for teaching other children about their area of specialization. In each of the learning groups, each child serves as the teacher for his or her piece of the puzzle. All students are tested on the total assignment.

After several replications of the jigsaw technique, the children learned that they could not succeed without the aid of each person in their learning group. It also took several replications of this procedure with the same groups before children shifted from a competitive to a cooperative orientation. For example, when a child had difficulty communicating her piece of the puzzle, others shifted from ridiculing to asking probing questions that aided communication.

A variety of approaches can be used for cooperative learning. These children are working together on a set of math problems. Each calculates the answer to each problem. When different answers are obtained, they work together to track down errors.   (*Source:* © Bill Aron/ Tony Stone Images)

knowledge *in action*

EDUCATION

Explaining Cross-Cultural Differences in Mathematics Achievement

International comparisons of mathematics achievement show that Japanese, Chinese, and Korean students are unquestionably superior in math performance to students in the United States (Fuson & Kwon, 1992b; Reys & Reys, 1995; Stevenson et al., 1990a).

Language Differences in Names Given to Number Words

As we noted in chapter 9, some researchers (Fuson & Kwon, 1992a) think Asian children's better math achievement might be due to language differences. Specifically, they argue that a child's understanding of the base-ten number system is aided by Asian-language number names. In Japanese, Chinese, and Korean, names for teen numbers are "ten one," "ten two," "ten three," and so on; names for the decades are "two ten," three ten," "four ten," and so on. In English, these numbers have unique names—eleven, twelve, and thirteen; twenty, thirty, and forty.

Differences in Parental Attitudes about Learning

Other researchers have looked for possible explanations in the attitudes and expectations held by parents and teachers. When Stevenson and his colleagues (1990b) interviewed children and their mothers to determine their attitudes toward learning and schooling, they found that Japanese and Chinese mothers were more likely than U.S. mothers to attribute success in math to effort rather than to ability. The percentage of children receiving help with their homework was also 30 points higher in China than in the United States, and the percentage of children who had their own desk for doing homework was 35 points higher in Japan than in the United States. Japanese and Chinese children also devoted much more time to academically related activities *outside* of school than did U.S. children. Even while *in* school, the percentage of time children spent engaging in academic activities was 25 points higher in Asian schools.

Differences in parental and teacher attitudes about learning may cause adults to provide different levels of support for children's engagement in academic tasks. The different attitudes may also influence parents' judgments about the quality of their children's schools. Despite their children's lower academic performance, more negative attitudes toward school, and poorer school-related work patterns, U.S. mothers report more satisfaction with their children's academic achievement than do Asian mothers. In fact, 89 percent of U.S. mothers actually rated their children's academic abilities higher than did Chinese mothers, even though U.S. children's achievement levels were lower. Teacher values and standards for math were also found to be higher in Beijing than in Chicago. Some U.S. fifth-grade teachers were never seen by the researchers to be teaching math. Nor did most profess fondness for it or great skill in it.

Is Lower Math Achievement in the United States a Recent Trend?

Researchers (e.g., Geary et al., 1996) have examined math achievement in older as well as younger Chinese and U.S.

In addition to improving academic achievement for the previously low-achieving children, the jigsaw technique produced other benefits: children came to like one another better, developed a greater liking for school, and developed higher self-esteem than did children in classrooms where teachers used traditional instructional techniques. These positive effects were most evident for minority children. Minority children in classrooms using the jigsaw technique also performed better on exams than did those from traditional classrooms (Aronson, 1999b). The jigsaw technique also increased empathy for others and decreased children's prejudice.

Researchers examining the effect of other approaches to cooperative learning have also reported positive effects (Slavin, 1990). Compared to competitive or individualistic efforts, cooperative learning results in greater effort, more positive interpersonal relationships, and greater self-esteem (Johnson & Johnson, 1999). Cooperative learning seems to be most effective in reducing prejudice and in improving academic achievement in children who are in elementary or middle school.

individuals. They found that younger Chinese students outperform younger U.S. students in arithmetic. But older Chinese and U.S. adults did *not* perform differently. Had the Chinese and U.S. adults they tested been tested during childhood, the researchers suggest that their achievement would not have differed. They argue that the Chinese math advantage is a recent phenomenon and perhaps results from decreased mathematics achievement in U.S. children, rather than from any exceptional natural ability among Asian children.

Complex Interactions May Explain Differences in Achievement

The decline in mathematics achievement in the United States over the past 60 years may be due to the complex interaction of several factors. Perhaps differences in the number names used in Asian languages make the base-ten organization of the number system easier for Asian children to understand. But perhaps before the emergence of more modern theories of development, U.S. teachers simply tried harder to teach mathematics to schoolchildren, regardless of how difficult math was for them.

Another possibility is that cognitive theories of development provided other explanations for U.S. children's difficulties in mathematics, and U.S. teachers were encouraged by various experts to decrease mathematics instruction in the early grades and to delay instruction in topics that seemed most difficult for children to understand (Kamii, 1989).

There are many other differences between schooling in Asian countries and the United States that could produce different achievement levels. For example, the length of the school year is 174 days in Minneapolis, 230 days in Taipei, and 243 days in Sendai (Japan). It is also true that most countries have a national curriculum from which all teachers teach. In the United States, curriculum decisions are left up to individual school districts or individual teachers. It is common in the United States for one teacher's curriculum to be only crudely related to the curriculum of teachers in the same school district who teach at the same grade levels.

School districts and teachers in the United States are given more autonomy over curriculum decisions than are teachers in other countries because the United States has a more individualistic orientation and is more democratic than most Asian countries. Thus, states and local communities have considerable control over all aspects of institutional life. Moreover, the population of the United States is much more diverse than are populations in some Asian countries, especially Japan and Korea. With diversity comes differences of opinion about what to teach, how to teach it, and when to teach it.

National professional organizations in the United States have developed standards for their subject-matter areas. The National Council of Teachers of Mathematics (1999) presented what should be taught at various grade levels and incorporated some of the effective teaching strategies used by Japanese teachers. These include the use of practical examples and concrete models, active involvement of students in solving problems and explaining their solutions, encouraging visualization and spatial reasoning to solve problems, and considering the thinking and strategies of other students.

There is variability, of course, in the success that individual students experience. A review of two decades of research on cooperative peer collaboration indicates that benefits increase based on the degree to which children participate in the collaboration (Ellis & Gauvain, 1992). The teacher's skill in designing cooperative learning projects, in monitoring children's engagement, and in teaching children how to work together is perhaps the most important factor in determining whether all children participate fully in cooperative learning collaborations.

A particularly good program, Fostering Communities of Learning (Brown, 1997), is based on research on developing metacognition and moving children through the zone of proximal development. This program emphasizes reciprocal teaching, the jigsaw technique, self-reflection, cross-age teaching, and tutoring. Karpov and Haywood (1998) have reported high levels of success with a similar program called "guided discovery in a community of learners." **Peer teaching** is a central component of both programs. It involves collaborative problem solving and reciprocal

TABLE 13.4
Some advantages of peer teaching

Older children learn

- perspective-taking.
- how to teach specific skills.
- how to put their knowledge to use.
- how to apply their learning and creativity.
- how to be responsible and caring.
- how to become positive role models for academic and prosocial behavior.

Younger children learn

- to experience success.
- to work at their own pace.

- to have a positive image of older children.
- to see learning in a more positive manner.
- to develop friendships with helping peers.

Teachers can

- maximize one-on-one instruction time.
- increase self-motivation to learn.
- meet the challenge of children who learn faster and slower.
- have more opportunities for individualized interactions with students.
- reduce the professional communication gap between teacher and student.

Sources: Adapted from *A Class of Their Own: When Children Teach Children*, pp. 1–11, by D. Briggs, 1998, Westport, CT: Bergin & Garvey; and *Learning Together and Alone: Cooperative, Competitive, and Individualistic Learning*, pp. 209–211, by D. W. Johnson and R. T. Johnson, 1999, Boston: Allyn & Bacon.

teaching, in which children teach each other. Especially positive results have been achieved when older children teach younger children. Table 13.4 presents some of the advantages of peer teaching. (For a discussion of factors that contribute to peer collaboration effectiveness, see Research Close Up: What Makes a Community of Learners Effective?

Diagnosing and Helping Children with Learning Disabilities

Sometimes, changes in the organization of instruction still does not help some children improve their achievement. Some of these children may suffer from learning disabilities that resist simple solutions. Children with **learning disabilities** have no obvious motor or sensory defect, nor do they suffer from mental retardation or brain damage. They have normal or above-average mental abilities in some areas, but have difficulty in selected areas of encoding, storing, or retrieving information in other mental ability areas. Many have difficulty with working memory rather than long-term memory (Mash & Wolfe, 1999). Usually, they experience difficulty in processing information of a specific kind. This problem makes it extremely difficult for them to learn to do specific things, such as think through math problems, learn to read, or learn to spell words correctly. They may have trouble applying strategies to new problems, distinguishing right from left, distinguishing letters and numbers, concentrating, remembering, organizing, sequencing, or attending to a task (Gallagher, 1994; Smith, 1995). Learning disabilities include **dyslexia** (difficulty in learning how to read), discussed in chapter 14; and **attention deficit disorder** (lack of ability to focus attention), discussed in chapter 12.

Schools have used a number of organizational accommodations to help students with learning disabilities. They have been placed in separate classrooms with specially trained teachers. They have been mainstreamed—integrated into classrooms with other children for much of the school day, and then given special tutoring by special education or remedial reading teachers outside of the regular classroom dur-

RESEARCH

CLOSE-UP   *What Makes a Community of Learners Effective?*

Some researchers have focused on verbalizations to explain the cognitive benefits of peer collaboration. But is the benefit due to sheer quantity of verbalization or to a specific type of verbalization? Information about amount and quality of talk in good and poor problem solvers can shed some light on this question.

Research by Chi and colleagues (1994) suggests that differences in the type rather than amount of talk differentiates good and poor problem solvers. They found that good problem solvers were more likely to articulate rules for their actions, make evaluative statements about hypotheses, and generate more explanations than were poor problem solvers.

Teasley (1995) carried out a study to assess separately the role of talk and the role of peer collaboration on problem-solving performance. Half of her fourth-grade subjects worked at solving a problem alone; the others worked at solving the problem with a peer collaborator. Half of the children in each of these groups received instructions to talk out loud; half of the subjects were asked not to talk as they worked to solve the problem either alone or together with another student.

Teasley found that talking out loud and working together produced an interaction. Talking out loud facilitated performance among peer collaborators, but it did not help those working alone. Peer collaborators talked about three times as much as talkers working alone, and the presence of the peer led to more rapid formulation of correct and more elaborate solutions. The no-talk students working with peers were especially poor in generating correct hypotheses. Talking peer collaborators, on the other hand, gave more interpretive statements and were not as easily distracted by nonessential features of the problem-solving tasks. When Bill and Desserae worked together on their math problems, they probably were better able to formulate hypotheses and to interpret outcomes than if they had been working alone.

Teasley's research suggests that collaborative problem solving with a peer can result in better verbalizations and reasoning. There is an interdependence of cognitive processes with the social context that helps explain the problem-solving benefits of peer collaboration. But as would be predicted by Vygotsky's theory, the less expert students benefit most from this collaboration. However, both expert and novice benefit more than they would in the individual condition (Brown, 1997). Several studies indicate that cooperative groups spend more time on task than do individuals or competitors. This may help explain why cooperation promotes greater productivity (Johnson & Johnson, 1999).

Interestingly, most elementary students report that peer discussions help them to clarify and extend their knowledge about a topic (Pearson & Santa, 1995). For example, one student in this study wrote, "I remembered the most after I read the article about Harper Lee. I believe that the reason for this is because we discussed the article with another classmate. . . . I believe that in order to remember more, you have to be a little more active" (Pearson & Santa, 1995, p. 468).

These two girls are discussing their schoolwork as they work together to complete a homework assignment. Some researchers think that verbalization is the key to the benefit of cooperative learning when a positive effect has been found.   (*Source:* © Will Faller)

---

ing other parts of the day. Currently, many students with learning disabilities are being taught according to an **inclusion** model. Inclusion differs from mainstreaming in that it brings the special education teacher into the classroom to co-teach with the regular teacher. Inclusion brings students with a variety of special needs into the regular classroom. In this model, the regular classroom teacher and the special education teacher share the responsibility for the child's mastery of the subject (Smith, 1995). In the mainstreaming model, the regular teacher did not always know what the child was learning when outside of the classroom or how to adapt the regular classroom curriculum to meet the needs of a special learner. The inclusion model solves some of that problem by having the specialist and the regular classroom teacher work together. Inclusion expands the scope of learning opportunities for all students by encouraging cooperation, tolerance, and acceptance. Children with learning disabilities build confidence in their ability to handle academics, improve their classroom behavior and social interaction, and receive more acceptance by peers (Boyles & Contadino, 1998). However, inclusion is controversial. Some groups of students with special needs do not seem to benefit from inclusion and inclusion is often extremely expensive for school systems to implement. Training and staffing to support regular education teachers who teach special needs children in their classes are often woefully inadequate (Coddington, 1999).

Often, children with learning difficulties in school subjects also have difficulty in the wider arena of social skills. Some of these difficulties can stem directly from the learning disability; others are indirect effects resulting from limited social interaction with a wide array of peers. Because of these general difficulties, special education programs for students with learning disabilities have incorporated several self-management skills, including self-monitoring (becoming aware of one's own impulses); self-regulation (gaining cognitive control over impulsivity); self-evaluation (comparing one's own behavior against a standard); self-reinforcement (rewarding oneself for desirable behavior); and self-instruction (verbally encouraging oneself). They also often include social skills instruction (Gallagher, 1994).

The specific assistance that any individual child with learning disabilities would receive is laid out in what is called an **individualized educational plan,** commonly referred to as a child's IEP. Special education laws mandate that an IEP be developed for each special education student. Services must be provided on an individual basis, and each child should be educated with students who are not disabled (Mash & Wolfe, 1999). The IEP contains a set of goals for the student, strategies that are to be used by various teachers, the student, and parents to meet these goals; and criteria for evaluating the program to make sure it is working for the child. The goals and strategies that make up an IEP are developed by the teachers, principals, various specialists, and the parents. IEP goals are meant to be formulated with the *active participation* of parents, not by teachers and specialists who then present the goals to parents for signing—as often happens (Boyles & Contadino, 1998; Coddington, 1999). This team meets periodically to conduct a **core evaluation** of the student. In most school systems, there must be a core evaluation each year, usually in the late spring. At this time, the current year's IEP is evaluated and revised, if necessary, for the following school year.

Play and Cognitive Development

In addition to enjoying sports and other physical activities discussed in chapter 12, school-age children like to play board, card, and strategy games; read books and magazines; and play video and computer games. Children are able at this age to play strategy games because they can think about what other people are thinking. They even become capable of winning against the adults who taught them the games only a few years earlier.

Games enjoyed by school-age children include checkers, chess, Chinese checkers, Othello, Risk, Scrabble, Master Mind, Battleship, and Stratego—all games that involve second-guessing an opponent. School-age children also enjoy card games such as "oh pshaw," hearts, canasta, and poker, and are able to follow the rules and hierarchy of steps involved.

Many school-age children have video games. Many of these games are violent, sexist, or racist. Video games also keep children indoors rather than engaged in physical activity. Teaching children early how to enjoy other activities can help to curtail the time spent with video games. (*Source:* © Robert Harbison)

Video and Computer Games   Many school-age children have home video games. While some of these games may involve strategy and encourage thinking, many others are violent, as well as sexist and racist. Perhaps due to the content, significantly fewer girls than boys play commercial video games. Girls do not like the violent feedback that usually accompanies good-versus-evil themes, but they do like games based on real goals and ones that involve interpersonal cooperation (Subrahmanyam & Greenfield, 1998). However, the industry is developing more violent-themed games for girls. Girls prefer more constructive themes, such as open-ended challenges, fantasy, and cooperation (Healy, 1998). When 10-year-olds were asked to design video games, the girls' games were more personal, gave gentle feedback, used few evil characters, and were more complex in programming. Most of the boys' games were violent and included a hero fighting off villains (Kafai, 1996). Some findings suggest that the need for entertainment, and especially the long hours of television viewing, may interfere with verbal literacy skills (Calvert, 1999).

Some parents believe in strictly limiting the hours a child can play electronic games each day; other parents allow unlimited play, hoping the child will tire of this kind of activity. Some parents refuse to buy video games at all; others would rather have their child playing at home than spending time in the less desirable arcade environment. A good solution for parents whose children want to spend considerable time with video and computer games is to start early to involve children in a variety of recreational activities, such as sports and playing board games with family members and friends.

Computers can bring new knowledge to children. These children are working with software on geography. If computers are used only for games, the potential for helping children learn via computer is greatly diminished. (*Source:* © Brian Smith)

Many computer games are interactive, allowing the child to make predictions, find solutions, design complicated figures, and so on. *The Logical Journey of the Zoombinis* uses problem-solving skills, *Brain Blaster* incorporates prediction and reasoning skills, *Logic Quest* has mazes

and puzzles, *Draw-A-Story* encourages story writing and illustration, and the *Thinkin' Things* series encourages creativity, logical thinking and reading comprehension. There are literally hundreds of computer games available for all ages, and many aid in developing computer literacy. Unfortunately, as in math skills, girls may not be getting the same level of encouragement and experience in computer literacy as are boys. For example, only 16 percent of children who spend time online are girls (Furger, 1998). In schools, boys are using the computers more than girls are (Furger, 1998; Healy, 1998). Software companies are now targeting girls in their game production—for example, *Laura's Happy Adventures, Madeline's Rainy Day Activities, The Magic Wardrobe* (paper-doll maker), *The American Girls Premiere* (for creating and producing plays), *You Can Be a Woman Engineer,* and the *Carmen Sandiego* adventure series. The Girl Interactive Library, a collaboration of game and software publishers, began broadening the game market for girls in 1997 with their Web site Just4girls (Cassell & Jenkins, 1998).

For some children, however, the computer may substitute for human interactions, may become addictive, or may cause visual, postural, or skeletal problems. For others it may enhance motivation, encourage original thinking, and help develop thinking skills and confidence (Healy, 1998). Programming a computer requires children to use procedural thinking, logical skills, and hierarchical structure, and may have an impact on the way they structure thought (Calvert, 1999). Computer programs have been especially helpful with structuring learning for children with ADHD. Debates will no doubt continue for some time over the advantages, use, and misuse of computers.

Reading for Recreation   Most children become completely fluent readers during the school-age years. Many enjoy selecting their own books and reading them independently. Many families continue to read aloud to their school-age children, with the child often participating in the reading. Some families set aside a quiet time or a reading time for a half hour or so each day to encourage reading by the whole family. School-age children also enjoy magazines. These range from *National Geographic World* and *Ranger Rick* to *Stone Stoup* or *Sports Illustrated for Kids*. Books on tape and video, which many children enjoy, can provide additional literacy experiences. Unfortunately, these materials are relatively high in cost, and not available to borrow from many libraries. This makes them difficult to obtain for children in lower socioeconomic groups.

KEY POINTS

Piaget: The Acquisition of Operations

- The transition from preoperational to concrete operational thought that occurs during the school years allows children to attend to the relationships between physical attributes and to use logical reasoning.
- Tasks of conservation are mastered by children at different ages, although most children master them in the same order.
- Neo-Piagetians are concerned with how task specificity, the role of training, and the roles of culture and education affect the age at which children demonstrate conservation.

Approaches to Cognitive Processing

- Metacognition—the ability to think about thinking—develops during the school-age years. Children become better able to mobilize their thoughts, target a problem, and apply their thoughts to a solution. Metacognitive skills play an important role in many types of cognitive activities.
- As children mature, they develop increasingly sophisticated mental strategies that help them study. Younger children do not have the metacognitive skills to use memory efficiently. The ability to remember is related to knowledge, experience, and

concepts that one can use to organize what has been read or learned.

- The emergence of metacognitive abilities makes it possible for children to develop the study skills and memory strategies critical to success in school, but teachers need to help by teaching these skills directly. Self-referencing is especially useful.

- The information-processing approach to cognitive development examines factors that lead to changes in cognitive task performance abilities.

- Information processing consists of encoding, storage, and retrieval stages of processing.

- Scripts are reconstructed memories that blend many repeated experiences and increase the speed and complexity of information processing.

Social Interaction and Cognitive Development

- Vygotsky's sociocultural cognitive theory proposes that social interaction with more expert persons moves children from their level of actual development through the zone of proximal development toward their level of potential development.

- Reciprocal teaching is one successful example of how teachers can structure a class to move children through the zone of proximal development.

- Children's intrinsic need for cognition (their tendency to engage in effortful cognitive activity) is affected by parenting style and teaching strategies that allow children to enjoy problem-solving tasks.

- New cognitive development models integrate Piaget's and Vygosky's concepts.

Defining and Assessing Intelligence

- The first intelligence test was developed by Binet. It was later adapted by Terman and revised to include subscales.

- The most commonly used IQ test is the Wechsler Intelligence Scale for Children.

- Inadequacies of a single-factor concept of intelligence have led to the identification of multiple factors of intelligence, such as those suggested by Guilford, Gardner, Sternberg, and Carroll.

- Sternberg differentiates between practical, creative, and analytical thinking.

- A major controversy associated with intelligence testing over the past 50 years concerns whether intelligence is determined solely genetically or is influenced greatly by a child's environment. Heredity establishes the range of reaction within which a child's intelligence will fall; environmental factors influence, both positively and negatively, what nature has given the child. Developmentalists study how heredity and environment interact.

- Different groups earn different scores on IQ tests. Experts believe that group differences are due largely to environmental differences. It has also been suggested that IQ tests are somewhat slanted toward the cultural framework of the white middle class.

- Many children's intelligence test scores change during the school years. Developmentalists have identified some of the factors that are associated with increases and decreases in intelligence.

Achievement Tests

- Achievement tests are used to assess students' abilities in specific areas of knowledge. They can be used to compare achievement levels across cultures and to assess the effectiveness of instructional programs.

Academic Motivation and Success in School

- Academic values and perceived competence are important determinants of a child's success in school.

- Parental values—the importance parents place on education, high grades, and intellectual activities such as reading—are a powerful determinant of the value that children place on academic achievement.

- Perceived academic competence increases academic effort by increasing the child's expectancy of success, reducing interference caused by anxiety, and increasing the use of mental strategies for solving problems.

- Distal and proximal motivational systems affect students' engagement in learning tasks.

Home and School Influences on Achievement

- Parents and teachers may convey ideas and feelings to girls that contribute to distorted perceptions of their academic ability in general and mathematics ability in particular. Young girls often believe that they are not competent in math, even though their math achievement equals or surpasses that of boys.

- Children's initial values and expectations are often magnified and confirmed with time. Children low in perceived competence withdraw from situations in which they experience initial failure. As a result, they become even less competent with similar challenges.

- Children whose values are consistent with those of the school are likely to create environments that motivate success; those whose values are inconsistent with academics are likely to place themselves in environments that motivate failure. In this way, they help create their own environment.

- Academic success is associated with certain cultural values. Children perform better on academic achievement tests in societies in which academic achievement is valued, academic success is believed to be the result of effort, and meeting children's basic needs is a high priority.

- Communities of learners that foster collaborative learning can improve academic motivation and achievement and can facilitate social interaction.

- Children with learning disabilities may have trouble with many skills; special programs have been developed for them.

- School-age children now have skills that enable them to play games of strategy and to enjoy board, card, video, and computer games. School-age children also like to read books and magazines. Many children continue to have family reading times.

GLOSSARY

ability-focused goals: goals aimed primarily at trying to outperform others (p. 463)

achievement tests: tests designed to measure knowledge in specific school subject areas, such as math and reading (p. 459)

adaptation: a developmental mechanism regulating alternations of assimilation and accommodation (p. 451)

analytical thinking: thinking that involves manipulating elements in a problem (p. 454)

attentional focus: focusing on just one thought or thing at a time; can include being aware of something else but not engaged in thinking about it (p. 442)

attention deficit disorder: a learning disability in which a child is not able to direct attention in normal ways (p. 472)

chronological age: the actual age at which the child takes an intelligence test (p. 452)

concrete operational thinking: thinking about concrete objects by using reasoning rather than perception (p. 439)

core evaluation: the yearly evaluation of a child's IEP to make sure it is working and to update it (p. 474)

creative thinking: thinking that involves solving a problem or thinking about its elements in a new way (p. 455)

culturally biased tests: tests in which items are thought to be based on the experiences and values common to one cultural group, but not others (p. 456)

depth of processing: various levels of processing that are involved at the encoding stage (p. 447)

distal motivational influences: factors determining whether or not a child will become engaged in a task (p. 462)

dynamic systems model: a quantitative model integrating Piagetian and Vygotskian developmental concepts (p. 451)

dyslexia: the name given to a learning disability in the area of reading (p. 472)

elaboration: linking new information to existing knowledge as a strategy for remembering it (p. 444)

encoding: the process of getting information into memory (p. 446)

formal operational thought: abstract and logical thought that proceeds without the use of concrete referents (p. 441)

horizontal decalage: a gradual progression in which children show mastery on conservation tasks of increasing difficulty (p. 441)

imagery: visualizing an object or event and storing it in a pictorial code (p. 445)

inclusion: placing children with disabilities in regular classrooms and giving the regular and special education teachers joint responsibility for children's learning (p. 473)

individualized educational plan (IEP): a set of goals and strategies for a particular child developed by a team of educators and the child's parents (p. 474)

information-processing approach: a focus on operations of the mind that affect the encoding, storage, and retrieval of information (p. 446)

intelligence quotient (IQ): a number based on the ratio of a child's mental to chronological age, multiplied by 100 (p. 452)

internalization: the process of absorbing knowledge from social interaction in natural contexts (p. 448)

jigsaw technique: a cooperative learning technique in which each child in a group is responsible for one aspect of an assignment or project (p. 469)

learning disability: a difficulty in learning in a specific area in the absence of any obvious physical problem or mental retardation (p. 472)

level of actual development: the level at which a child can function without help (p. 448)

level of potential development: the level at which a child can function when aided by an adult or an expert peer (p. 448)

mental age: the average age at which children pass a set of items on an intelligence test (p. 451)

metacognition: thinking about thinking, and controlling and deploying one's own thinking strategically (p. 443)

metalinguistic awareness: metacognitive activity with language (p. 443)

method of loci: a memory strategy in which the learner attaches each new term to locations along a familiar route (p. 444)

multiple intelligences: a view of intelligence in which more than one factor is described (p. 453)

need for cognition: the tendency to engage in and enjoy effortful cognitive activity (p. 450)

norms: average ages for exhibiting certain behaviors and skills (p. 451)

peer teaching: collaborative problem solving and reciprocal teaching in which children instruct each other (p. 471)

perceived competence: the child's subjective view of his or her ability to succeed on academic tasks (p. 464)

practical thinking: applying what is known to solve problems in everyday contexts (p. 455)

problem of the match: the problem of providing children with a challenge while not overwhelming them (p. 449)

proximal motivational influences: factors determining the amount of attentional effort a child will expend on a task (p. 462)

reciprocal teaching: method in which the teacher models a task, and then students take a turn using the same skills (p. 448)

retrieval: the process of recovering information from memory stores (p. 446)

scaffolding: providing structure to learners when they start to learn something and then removing it gradually as they become more skilled (p. 448)

scripts: reconstructed memories from repeated engagement in a kind of learning task (p. 447)

self-referencing: relating new information to one's life experiences (p. 444)

social class: a classification of family resources based on income level, educational background, and occupation (p. 455)

sociocultural theory: a theory developed by Vygotsky in which social interaction, including language, is emphasized (p. 447)

storage: the maintenance of information in memory (p. 446)

task-focused goals: goals that are related to mastery and improvement in one's learning (p. 463)

triarchic theory of intelligence: a view of intelligence proposed by Sternberg, which conceives of intelligence as consisting of three parts (p. 454)

value-expectancy theory: a theory about motivation that considers the value assigned to a goal and the expectation for success (p. 461)

Wechsler Intelligence Scale—Third Edition: the most commonly used intelligence test (p. 452)

working memory: a short-term memory store (p. 446)

zone of proximal development: the difference between a child's level of independent functioning and his or her performance when aided by an adult or an expert peer (p. 448)

SUGGESTIONS FOR FURTHER READING

Ackerman, P. L., Kyllonen, P. C., & Roberts, R. D. (1999). *Learning and individual differences: Process, trait, and content determinants.* Washington, DC: American Psychological Association. An excellent collection of chapters examining theories and research on cognitive development and factors contributing to the vast individual differences among school-age children.

Brown, A. (1997). Transforming schools into communities of thinking and learning about serious matters. *American Psychologist, 52*(4), 399–413. This address, given in conjunction with Ann Brown's acceptance of the APA Distinguished Award for the Application of Psychology, describes the Fostering Communities of Learners program and its theoretical and research foundation.

Cobb, P., & Bauerfeld, H. (Eds.). (1995). *The emergence of mathematical meaning: Interaction in classroom cultures.* Mahwah, NJ: Erlbaum. This book includes topics such as small group collaboration and learning, mathematics in the classroom, and the relationship between sociocultural processes and individual psychological processes.

Healy, J. M. (1998). *Failure to connect: How computers affect our children's minds—for better and worse.* NY: Simon & Schuster. This is an excellent examination of children's use of computers, covering learning, motivation, and emotional and social issues. Research and examples are very good.

Hughes, F. (1999). *Children, play, and development* (3rd ed.). Boston: Allyn & Bacon. This book examines the influence of play on cognitive development from several different theoretical and cultural perspectives.

Turiel, E. (Ed.). (1999, Spring). Development and cultural change: Reciprocal processes. *New Directions for Child and Adolescent Development, 83*, 5–92. This collection of five articles focuses on cultural factors influencing cognitive development.

14

The Development of Language and Communication in the School-Age Child

"DAD, WHAT DOES 'ano-', 'ano-', . . . 'ano-NY-mous' mean?"

called 9-year-old Alex from her room.

"How do you spell it?" her dad asked.

"A-n-o-n-y-m-o-u-s," she answered.

"Anonymous. It means without a name, someone whose name you

don't know."

A few minutes later, Alex called out again, "Dad, what does 'cat-a-

clysm' mean?"

"A disaster."

"Dad, what about 'in-cap-a-ble'?"

Alex's dad made his way to her room. "Here, use this dictionary," he

said. "What are you reading, anyway?"

"Oh, it's *The Voyages of Doctor Doolittle,* by Hugh Lofting. I got it out

of the library."

Alex is learning many new words from the book she is reading. How many new words do school-age children typically learn in a year? When do they begin to figure out the meaning of new words for themselves by analyzing the meanings of their parts? For example, will Alex realize before long that the prefix *in* means "not" or "without," and use this knowledge to understand the meanings of new words she encounters?

In this chapter, we first describe the advances school-age children make in oral language. Then we look at written language development. In this discussion we focus on children's early spelling strategies and on how children learn to read.

Oral Language Development

Most school-age children speak their language with apparent ease and fluidity, and they delight in the twists of language that make jokes funny. Here we discuss school-age children's difficulties in understanding words in some sentence contexts. Next, we discuss progress in children's awareness of language at the phoneme level. Finally, we take a look at children's appreciation of jokes and riddles and at how they learn a second language.

Expansion of Oral Vocabulary

Children's vocabularies continue to grow at a rapid rate during the school years. In fact, the rate of word learning is even greater than it was during the preschool years. Children learn many new words from the books they read.

Vocabulary Size and Rates of Learning   Because children's vocabularies are so large by age 7, 8, or 10, it is impossible to take inventory of all of the words children know. Instead, researchers test children on a random sample of words found in a good dictionary and then estimate the proportion of the total dictionary entries the child probably knows. Researchers must decide whether to count all of the words a child knows, or to report a child's vocabulary in terms of two groups—the *root* words and the total number of words. If counting the total number of words, *happy, unhappy, happiness,* and *happier* would all be tallied. If counting just root words, *happy* would be tallied, but the derived forms of the word would not. Most reports on school-age children's vocabularies are broken down into these two groups of words.

Over the years, researchers have conducted thorough studies of school-age children's vocabularies to determine their size. Several estimates of word knowledge are available. In one study, Templin (1957) estimated that first-graders knew 7,800 basic words and a total of 13,000 words. Third-graders knew 17,600 basic words and 28,300 total words. In a second study (Aglin 1993), the total vocabulary was estimated to be 10,398 words at first grade, 19,412 words at third grade, and 39,994 words at fifth grade. Using these estimates, we can see that children learn about 20 words a day between first and fifth grade.

The rate of word learning during the period from first through third grades is about 12–17 words a day. This is about double the preschoolers' rate of 6 to 9 words a day. The rate of almost 28 words a day, seen between third and fifth grades, is three or four times the preschoolers' rate. By this time, children can use their basic understanding of morphological information—the meanings of suffixes and prefixes—to infer many word meanings (Anglin, 1993; Carey, 1978). Moreover, because most children have also moved beyond the beginning reading phase to a more fluent reading stage, they no longer need to read books with the number of new words controlled somewhat in order to lighten the burden of reading. Because of improvements in reading skill by third grade, children encounter many more new words in the books they read. This infusion of vocabulary helps increase the number of new words available to children.

Contexts for Word Learning   Although children learn some words through direct instruction at school, much of their word learning during these years occurs in context (Miller & Gildea, 1987). About half of the words children learn during the school-age years are learned by inferring meanings of new words from reading (Nagy et al., 1987). Of course, learning words in this way occurs only if children read, and read a lot. Some children read practically nonstop, once they have learned how. But other children hardly pick up a book. This is one reason why vocabulary size varies considerably from child to child during these and subsequent years.

The number of new words children learn from reading books also varies because children's ability to infer new word meanings from books varies. Two sources of this variation in word inference skill are especially important. First of all, children who already have a good vocabulary tend to learn more new words in the process of reading than do children who have weaker vocabularies (Robbins & Ehri, 1994; Shefelbine, 1990). Initial differences in vocabulary size could be due to different word-learning histories. As we saw in chapter 6, sheer exposure to language influences vocabulary size tremendously. Children who start out with meager vocabularies in infancy and the preschool years would start elementary school at a disadvantage.

But initial differences could also be due to differences in language skill or in basic processing capacity (i.e., working memory and short-term memory). Basic skill in understanding language structure can affect a child's ability to infer word meanings from sentence contexts. While reading, an additional processing burden is imposed because print first must be translated into sounds, then these sounds must be translated into words, then these words must be stored in short-term memory, and so forth. All the while, the reader must continue to integrate what has just been read with what is being read. Children who have difficulty conducting several simultaneous operations and integrating everything do not comprehend text as well as children who have no working or short-term memory storage problems (de Jong, 1998; Nation et al., 1999; Swanson, 1999). Problems in comprehending text will necessarily hinder a child's ability to learn word meanings from reading.

A second group of children—those who are learning English as a second language—also are limited in their ability to learn new English words from context (Elley, 1991; Haynes, 1993; Nagy et al., 1997). Recall that toddlers and young preschoolers begin to use syntax to "bootstrap" word learning and that this ability increases their word-learning rate considerably. (See p. 335 in chapter 10.) Children who are bilingual sometimes rely on syntactic knowledge from their *native* language when they read English, rather than base inferences about new word meanings on English syntactic structure. When the syntax of the native language differs from the syntax of English, bilingual children can be misguided in their inferences about the meanings of new words (Nagy et al., 1997).

Specific study of new words, perhaps in the context of discussions of books themselves, is needed to help children who have difficulty inferring word meanings on their own from books they read. Background experiences related to the topic of books to be read also can help. For children with processing problems related to reading, extra help on phoneme segmentation and letter-sound associations can sometimes decrease the processing load. This then provides more resources in working memory to get to the meaning of what is being read. (See the discussion of dyslexia, p. 501.) For both groups of children, wise decisions about reading materials also are important. Books well beyond a child's comprehension ability do not add to the child's oral vocabulary or reading ability. Obviously, books that are too easy offer no new words and little challenge of any other kind. In today's classrooms, good teachers monitor each individual child's reading progress constantly and have a wide range of books from which to make appropriate choices for the many different reading levels found among the children in a classroom. Bilingual education coordinators, reading specialists, and school librarians usually can help classroom teachers obtain appropriate materials for individual children.

Understanding Syntax

Although children have mastered the basic syntax of their language by 3 or 4 years of age, this does not mean that they understand all linguistic constructions. School-age children still have several difficulties. For example, they confuse words, such as *promise* and *eager,* because they assume that they are used the same way as other words. That is, in the sentence "John told Sara to close the door," John was not to close the door. He directed Sara to do it. But in the sentence "John promised Sara to close the door," John can be expected to close it. Similarly, in the sentence, "John is eager to see Sara," John is the one who is eager. But in the sentence, "Sara is easy to see," Sara is not the one who is seeing. She is the one being seen easily by someone else. These are specific instances of what we have discussed before—children's tendency to exploit the syntax of a sentence to grasp the meanings of words. But because these cases are especially difficult, children take a relatively long time to sort them out.

The critical study of this kind of problem was done by Carol Chomsky (1969). While seated at a table with a blindfolded doll, children were asked, "Is this doll easy to see or hard to see?" If the child answered that the doll was hard to see, Chomsky asked the child to make the doll easy to see. If the child answered that the doll was easy to see, Chomsky asked the child to make the doll hard to see. Children who answered that the doll was hard to see thought they were being asked if it was hard or easy for the *doll* to see, not if it was hard for *them* to see the doll (see Figure 14.1).

Chomsky's doll experiment. Many school-age children do not understand certain subtleties of English usage that adults take for granted. In Carol Chomsky's experiment, a 6½-year-old responded to the request to "make the doll easy to see" by removing the doll's blindfold.

Consider the responses of Lisa, age 6 years, 5 months (Chomsky, 1969, p. 30):

Is this doll easy to see or hard to see?

Hard to see.

Will you make her easy to see?

If I can get this untied.

Will you explain why she was hard to see?

(To doll) Because you had a blindfold over your eyes.

And what did you do?

I took it off.

Ann, a child 8 years and 7 months old (Chomsky, 1969, p. 31), responded differently:

This is Chatty Cathy. Is she easy to see or hard to see?

Easy.

Would you make her hard to see?

So you can't see her at all?

OK.

(Places doll under table.)

Tell what you did.

I put her under the table.

Some school-age children also confuse the words *ask* and *tell*. Consider the example of Samuel, age 8 years, 5 months (Chomsky, 1969, p. 57):

Ask Ellen what to feed the doll.

Feed her hamburgers.

All right now, tell Ellen what to feed her.

Again?

M-hm.

Tomato.

Now I want you to ask Ellen something. I want you to ask her what to feed the doll.

Feed her this thing, whatever it's called.

All right. Now listen very carefully, because I don't want you to tell her anything this time. I want you to ask her what to feed the doll. Can you do that?

Let's see, I don't get it.

OK, just go ahead, and ask her what to feed the doll.

Feed her eggs.

Samuel interpreted *tell* correctly, but he interpreted *ask* the same way. In Chomsky's examples, even 9- and 10-year-olds were confused by the words *ask* and *tell*.

Skill in Manipulating Language at the Phoneme Level

Recall from chapter 10 that preschool children can begin to develop explicit phonological awareness. They learn to recognize words that rhyme and start with the same sound. But preschoolers' ability to isolate or segment the individual phonemes within words is limited. In one study of this ability, researchers (Liberman et al., 1974) asked children to tap with a stick to indicate each sound they heard in words the experimenter pronounced. Preschoolers performed very poorly, as did about 20 percent of the kindergartners. In contrast, about 70 percent of the first-graders did well. The sample used in this study consisted of middle-class children. Low-income children do more poorly on phonemic awareness tasks, although there is wide variation in phonemic awareness within this group, because their specific language experiences have varied (Whitehurst, 1995).

The sharp increase in phoneme-level sensitivity seen during first grade (approximately ages 6 to 7) may make it appear that phoneme segmentation skill is a developmental phenomenon—something that emerges due to maturation. But the sharp increase in this language skill is due to exposure to experiences in first grade. When specific phoneme-related experiences (e.g., language game rhymes, exposure to rhyming stories, segmenting words into phonemes, and so on) are provided before first grade, phoneme segmentation develops earlier than when such experiences are not provided (Lundberg et al., 1988). Without engagement in experiences that engage it, children do not develop phoneme segmentation skill at all (Adams et al., 1998).

Understanding Jokes and Riddles

"Okay, listen to this: 'Knock-knock.'"

"Who's there?"

"Duane."

"Duane who?"

"Duane the tub . . . I'm dwowning."

"Okay, now listen to this one: 'Knock-knock.'"

"No, Eric, I can't. I've heard enough jokes for one day, and, besides, we have errands to run."

"Okay. I'll tell you more in the car."

This "knock-knock" joke, like most jokes and riddles, exploits ambiguity in language. Ambiguity can be located at any level of language. At the phonological level the ambiguity arises from how a word is *pronounced*. At the lexical or word level, ambiguity exploits dual meanings of homonyms. At the syntactic level, ambiguity can arise from different possibilities for the *interpretation of sentences*. A fourth type of ambiguity found in jokes or riddles can play on word boundaries—on departures from the typical strong stress on the first syllable of multisyllabic words.

Examples of Jokes and Riddles　Consider the following riddle:

"Why did the farmer name his hog Ink?"

"Because he kept running out of the pen."

This riddle, based on lexical ambiguity, plays with the two meanings of the word *pen*—(1) an enclosure for animals and (2) an ink-containing writing tool.

The "knock-knock" joke at the beginning of this section utilizes phonological ambiguity. The joke leads the listener to believe that *Duane* is a noun—a person's name—only to learn in the punch line that the word intended *(drain)* had been disguised by mispronouncing one of its phonemes. The mispronunciation is carried over to the final word—*dwowning*—to aid the interpretation of *Duane as drain.*

In the next joke, the structure of the sentence itself—the syntax—is exploited:

"Do you know how long cows should be milked?"

"How long?"

"As long as short ones, of course."

In the initial question, the word *long* can be interpreted either as an adjective modifying cows, or as an adverb indicating how long the cows are to be milked. Common sense tells us to interpret *long* as an adverb. To help prompt an interpretation of the word *long* as an adverb, the joke teller lengthens and stresses this word somewhat. He or she says, "Do you know how *lo-o-n-n-g-g* cows should be milked?" The listener makes the commonsense interpretation that *long* refers to length of time required to milk any or all cows, not to some technique for milking long versus short cows. But the joke—the trick played on the listener—requires *long* to be interpreted as an adjective—to refer to the length of cows.

A fourth kind of trick that can be played with language rests on rhythmic cues that cause the listener to misinterpret word boundaries. Recall from chapter 6 that syllables in English words can be stressed or unstressed, and that stress usually falls on the first syllable in bisyllabic words. This regularity is played on in jokes such as this one:

Be alert! Your country needs lerts!"

Because the word *alert* violates the typical stressed-unstressed pattern, the reader of this joke readily accepts *lerts* as a noun preceded by the article *a,* even though, orig-

Early in the primary grades, children begin to appreciate jokes, riddles, puns, and plays on words. Word play tickles children's imaginations and provides opportunities for them to laugh with friends. This is one of the delights of school-age social life. (*Source:* © Bruce Ayres/Tony Stone Images)

inally, the reader interpreted this same sound pattern to mean being very wide awake and watchful (Cutler & Butterfield, 1992). Of course, *lert* is a nonsense word, which is what makes the whole thing funny.

Development of Language Skills Required to Understand Jokes and Riddles
Children must be able to pay attention to the form of language—to its structure—to appreciate jokes and riddles. To resolve the ambiguity exploited by a joke or riddle—to understand it and to perceive it as funny—the listener must also understand the structure of language. The ability to attend to the structure or form of the language, rather than to its meaning, is called **metalinguistic awareness.**

Children understand ambiguity at the phonological level by the time they are about 6 or 7 years old. Recall that this age corresponds to the norm for fairly high levels of phonemic awareness, as seen in children's ability to segment and manipulate phonemes. Children who achieve this level of phonemic awareness earlier will understand phonologically based jokes earlier. Lexical ambiguity appears next, at 7 or 8, and increases as children learn more and more words that have more than one meaning. Syntactic ambiguity emerges last, usually not until about 11 or 12 years of age (Shultz & Pilon, 1973), after children have mastered complex syntactic structures such as those we discussed earlier in this chapter.

Preschoolers try to interpret and tell jokes, but they lack the linguistic understandings necessary to pull it off. They master the ask-a-question, wait-for-a-response, make-a-statement format of riddles, but what they say is not funny. Not until the school-age years do children begin to grasp the fact that language is being *manipulated* in jokes and riddles and that the overall format does not in itself constitute a joke.

Learning a Second Language

Outside of the United States, it is common for many people to learn more than one language. Many children (and adults) will learn a second language sometime during their lifetime. Perhaps they will move permanently to a new country, visit in a different country for an extended period of time, or study a second language in school. How do children learn a second language? What processes do they use? In this section, we discuss these questions and also how academic learning in limited-English students can be supported in schools until the students become more proficient in English.

Learning the Grammar of a Second Language
Three theories have been proposed to account for the process of learning the grammatical structure of a new language (Macnamara, 1976, p. 46):

1. The child acquires the second language in the same way an infant acquires it as a first language. In other words, learning a second language is **identical in process** to learning the same language as a first language.

2. The child uses the structures from her first language to form structures in the second language. This process assumes that there is interference between the first and second languages, since different languages have different ways of saying things (different grammars) and is termed **interference theory.**

3. The child formulates **unique grammatical structures,** using neither the structures of her first language nor the typical developmental structures of the new language.

To test these hypotheses, researchers compare the language patterns displayed by native speakers of the language during the acquisition phase with the patterns found in persons for whom the language is a second language.

Considerable support has been found for the identical process theory. In one classic study, two Norwegian children learning English as a second language formed questions with *Wh* words the way children learning English as a first language do. They said, "What she is doing?" just as English-speaking toddlers do, rather than "What is she doing?" even though this was not how they formed questions in their native Norwegian (Ravem, 1974). Even when the structure of the child's first language can be applied to English, young children do not use what they already know. When children have well-developed metalinguistic and cognitive abilities, at age 10 or 11, they begin to use what they know about the structure of their native language to learn the structure of a second language. Although younger children, older children, and adults all pass through similar stages in learning a second language, older children and adults perform better on language test items involving "semantic-syntactic relationships." The greater metalinguistic and cognitive abilities of the older child and adult apparently enable them to analyze some of the more complex aspects of language (McLaughlin, 1984, pp. 70–71). In the long run, though, child second-language learners surpass second-language learners who start as adults. Children match native language speakers in all aspects of language, including phonology and syntax, whereas those who begin to learn a second language as adults almost never match native language speakers in either area (Newport, 1990).

The Social Context of Second-Language Learning

People seem to learn a second language most quickly when they spend time routinely communicating with native speakers in a natural way. This approach to learning a new language is called **immersion**. The social conditions for second-language learning typically differ for different age groups. Because preschool children are more likely than older children and adults to spend considerable time playing with other children in a school or neighborhood setting, they are more likely to be exposed to native speakers of the new

When children are interested in playing together, language and cultural differences do not stand in their way. These children seem to be enjoying their recess time together despite the variety of languages and dialects they speak. (*Source:* © Jeffrey Myers/FPG International)

The population of the United States is increasingly diverse due to immigration patterns over recent decades. Any large city contains children who speak a variety of languages, including Chinese, Korean, Vietnamese, Portuguese, Greek, Spanish, Tagalog, and many others. (*Source:* © Robert Harbison)

language in natural contexts. They are also exposed to more language simply because they spend more time interacting socially with peers. Adults must spend a large proportion of their day working; school-age children must spend a lot of time listening to instruction at school, and studying. Thus, older children and adults learn a second language in school or a class, from formal instruction, and may have relatively little time to use the second language while interacting naturally with native speakers. If given the same amount of exposure to the second language through social interaction with native speakers, older children and adults learn a second language *faster* than preschoolers learn it, in the short run, although an earlier start typically pays off in terms of competence in the long run.

Several researchers have documented how children behave in social situations when they are learning a new language. Fillmore (1976, cited in McLaughlin, 1978, pp. 108–11) asked children how they managed to "count themselves in." From their responses, he concluded that they use the following strategies:

- Join a group and act as if you understand what is going on, even if you don't. (a social strategy)

- Assume that people's statements are directly relevant to the situation at hand or to what they or you are experiencing. Metastrategy: Guess! (a cognitive strategy)

- Give the impression that you understand, and start talking. (a cognitive strategy)
- Look for recurring structures in the formulas you know. (a cognitive strategy)
- Work on the big things first; save the details for later. (a cognitive strategy)

With very few exceptions, preschoolers *communicate* with their peers during the first few months of exposure to the new language by using gestures (pointing and mime) and eye contact, and by holding up objects (to elicit object names from adults). They quickly pick up **formulaic utterances**—multiword chunks they hear repeated frequently ("See you tomorrow")—and greetings ("Hi!" and "Good morning"). They also pick up names for classroom areas and scheduled activities ("blocks," "house," "water table"; and "snack time," "cleanup time," and "story time"). With this limited vocabulary, they can participate in routines and appear to know what is going on. By using nonverbal strategies and these bits of language as a start, preschoolers stay engaged socially with peers, and this positions them to learn more language (Tabors & Snow, 1994).

School-age children's strategies are somewhat similar to those used by preschoolers. School-age children spend less time at school in purely social interaction with peers than do preschool children, and they are also expected to achieve more academically while they are acquiring English. Given that more of the contexts in which they must engage in conversation at school are instructional settings, they might be more reluctant than preschoolers to "give the impression" that they understand and "start talking."

School-Based Programs Designed to Support Limited-English Students
The population in the United States is changing, as it has changed in the past. In any large city in the United States there are children whose native tongue is not English. In fact, there is a tremendous variety of native tongues—Chinese, Korean, Vietnamese, Portuguese, Spanish, Greek, Russian, Tagalog, and many others. In one study, researchers found as many as 90 different native languages in a single school district (Porter, 1995).

The number of children in our public schools for whom English is not the native language increased by about 85 percent between 1985 and 1992 (Goldenberg, 1996). In terms of the total elementary and secondary school population, children who are not native speakers of English constitute about 5 to 6 percent. But there is a large concentration of non-native speakers of English in the early grades (i.e., kindergarten through fourth grade). According to one report (Snow et al., 1998), slightly more than half of the non-native speakers of English are in these grades. Non-native English speakers constitute a larger percentage of the school population in large city schools than in suburban and rural schools (Porter, 1995). In *preschool* programs, such as Head Start, designed to serve only low-income children, non-native English speakers constitute about 20 percent of the enrollment (Tabors & Snow, 1994).

At least two difficulties are encountered by students with limited English proficiency (LEP) in the elementary and secondary school. First, a student who does not understand the language of instruction will find it difficult to learn subject matter, such as math, science, and social science. Achievement can decline for a time. Second, the student is faced with the difficulty of learning the new language itself. During the time that students lack even basic oral proficiency in the new language, something must be done to help them learn school subject matter. Otherwise, their achievement will fall behind. On the other hand, if they are not helped to acquire the new language, they are unfairly excluded from participating fully in life in their new country, and they cannot take advantage of many opportunities.

These two goals sometimes compete with each other. Needing the second language to understand what the teacher is saying in the classroom provides high motivation for learning the new language. But it can also reduce achievement in the short run, because, until a certain level of proficiency in the new language is attained, the child cannot understand very much of the teacher's instruction. Two basic approaches have been used in elementary and secondary schools in the United States to teach children whose proficiency with English is very limited. We turn now to a discussion of these approaches.

TEACHING ENGLISH AS A SECOND LANGUAGE.   In the TESL method, children are taught in English-only classrooms. In TESL programs where teachers with no special training in working with limited-English students teach the regular school subjects, students receive help in learning English from other teachers in "pull-out" English classes. In other TESL programs, the regular classroom teachers are trained in strategies that help children acquire a new language. Both of these approaches are called **structured immersion** approaches because children are not simply thrown into classes taught in English without any regard for their special circumstances, even though they are taught their school subjects in the second language from the very start.

TESL programs are often found in schools with many different native language populations, perhaps 8 or 10 or many more. In these cases, it is often not practical to teach in so many languages. Finding teachers can be impossible, and small class sizes for some of the language groups would add considerably to the cost of education. The school provides instruction in the academic subjects in English only and offers other forms of support to limited-English students.

Studies of instructional strategies used in exemplary TESL programs indicate how teachers can help students learn. Results from one study of this kind are listed in Table 14.1 (Tinunoff et al., 1991, adapted by Gersten et al., 1995). Note that many of the strategies that make up Factor 1 constitute good instruction, in general. In other words, all good teachers employ these strategies. But some of the strategies (items 3, 5, 7) listed in Factor 1 are specifically related to second-language learners. Items making up Factors 2 and 3 are directly related to aiding second-language learners.

Data from this study indicate that TESL programs are likely to work well if they are staffed by good teachers. Their success is likely to be greater if teachers have specific knowledge about how to support second-language acquisition in the classroom context. A large number of teachers in successful TESL classrooms embed English-language instruction in regular classroom lessons. In one study (Tinunoff et al., 1991), researchers found that 87 percent of the lessons involved explicit English language teaching "as an integral part of the lesson."

BILINGUAL EDUCATION PROGRAMS.   The second approach used to support limited-English students is called **bilingual education.** In **transitional bilingual programs,** children are taught school subjects in their native language until they become proficient in the second language. These programs teach children at first in their native language, but also prepare children to enter classrooms where only the second language (English) is used.

It is difficult for children to learn subject matter when they do not understand the language in which it is taught. Transitional bilingual education programs are intended to prevent children from falling behind in their achievement levels while they are learning the new language. (For a discussion of issues and programs, see Knowledge in Action: Education—Academic Achievement and English Language Learning among Limited-English Students.)

TABLE 14.1

Three major instructional practice factors and mean percent of teachers (N = 46) using each practice[1]

Instructional Practice Factor	Mean % of Teachers
Factor 1: Facilitating LEP students' comprehension of and participation in academic learning (31% of total variance explained)	
1. Teacher monitors students' progress toward completing instructional tasks.	97.8
2. Teacher adjusts instruction to maximize students' accuracy rates.	97.8
3. Teacher adjusts own use of English to make content comprehensible.	95.6
4. Teacher provides immediate academic feedback individually to students.	95.6
5. Teacher allows students appropriate wait time for responding to questions in English	97.8
6. Teacher perceives that students are capable of learning.	97.8
7. Teacher structures opportunities for students to use English.	97.8
8. Teacher places a clear focus on academic goals.	95.6
9. Teacher spends most of instructional period on subject matter instruction.	97.8
10. Teacher checks students' comprehension during instruction.	93.4
11. Teacher paces instruction briskly.	93.4
12. Teacher expresses high expectations for student achievement.	93.4
13. Teacher uses materials that maximize students' accuracy rates.	95.6
14. Teacher manages classroom well.	93.4
Factor 2: Structuring activities that promote LEP students' active use of language (9%)	
1. Teacher assigns students to collaborate/cooperate on instructional tasks.	47.8
2. Teacher allows students to interact with others to work on assigned tasks.	82.6
3. Student talk dominates lesson.	30.4
4. Teacher does not correct the ungrammatical utterances of students.	89.2
Factor 3: Using LEP students' native languages for English language and concept development (8%)	
1. Teacher uses the students' native languages for concept development/clarification.	26.0
2. Teacher uses students' native language in order to develop competence in English.	23.9
3. Teacher allows students to use their native language to respond to questions asked in English.	54.3

[1]Adopted from *Final Report: A Descriptive Study of Significant Features of Exemplary Special Alternative Instructional Programs,* by W. J. Tinunoff et al., 1991, Los Alamitos, CA: The Southwest Regional Educational Laboratory.

Source: From "Toward an Understanding of Effective Instructional Practice for Language Minority Students: Findings from a Naturalistic Research Study," by R. Gersten, T. J. Keating, and S. U. Brengelman, 1995, *READ Perspectives, 2*(1), 55–82. Reprinted by permission of the Institute for Research in English Acquisition & Development (READ), Amherst, MA.

knowledge *in action*

Academic Achievement and English Language Learning among Limited-English Students

Controversy surrounds the question of the best way to teach limited-English students in the United States. Some people support teaching English as a second language. Others support transitional bilingual programs because they think they do a better job of helping children maintain their native language and culture.

The Relative Effectiveness of TESL versus Transitional Bilingual Programs

Most studies meeting scientific criteria show either no effect or a negative effect on academic subject learning for transitional bilingual programs. Some of the positive effects of bilingual programs have been found in classrooms where all of the instruction has been conducted in English. This occurs frequently, for example, in Chinese bilingual classrooms. Because there are many Chinese dialects, teachers cannot accommodate all of the variations found in a classroom of children (few teachers can read and write in more than one or two dialects). To solve this problem, the teachers use a common language—English—to teach. Thus, these Chinese classes are "bilingual" in name only—for the purpose of meeting laws that require school districts to provide separate "bilingual" classes in a specific language if a certain number of children from that language group attend school in a school district (Rossell & Baker, 1996).

In one study that analyzed data from bilingual classrooms in Massachusetts (Rossell & Baker, 1996), researchers found that almost half of the bilingual classrooms are not transitional bilingual programs. They are TESL programs utilizing either a structured immersion model (teachers teach subject matter in English but are skilled in teaching limited-English students) or a **pull-out model** (academic subjects are taught in English; help in learning English is provided in separate classes that meet several times a week). The most successful programs taught academic subjects in English, making sure that the pace at first allowed students to understand the material. Students entered regular classrooms as soon as possible. The worst results were found in Spanish bilingual classrooms where all of the instruction was conducted in Spanish.

Why Transitional Bilingual Education Sometimes Hinders Second-Language Acquisition

In designing bilingual education programs, educators intend to aid children's school learning during a transitional period when they become proficient in English. Why might these programs sometimes turn out to be relatively ineffective? Several explanations seem to account for their overall low rate of success.

Motivational and Learning Task "Press" Explanations

Basic research on children's learning in several domains suggests that seeing a need to learn something facilitates its acquisition. Children are likely to feel a need to learn new strategies—such as a new language—if the learning tasks they encounter every day at school depend on it. If children can get along in tasks without acquiring new strategies, it is not likely that they will learn the new strategies—there simply is no motivation to do so.

There is interesting evidence for this view in the area of early literacy. Young children pretend-read their familiar storybooks by memorizing the text and recalling it by looking at the pictures. Ehri and Sweet (1991) questioned whether young children actually learn to read merely from reading familiar storybooks whose memorized text they repeat verbatim, using picture clues: " . . . successful pretend reading does not require readers to pay any attention to the print. . . . There is no 'press' from the task itself necessitating further adaptation" (p. 444). Research has confirmed their suspicion. Although pretend-reading of storybooks has many positive benefits, it does not by itself lead directly to actual reading. Other experiences are needed. (See the discussion on pp. 352–353 in chapter 10.)

More support for the idea that tasks must require use of a new strategy, if it is to be acquired, comes from the work of Robert Siegler (1995). Siegler has documented that children actually use several strategies at one time, or are able to solve various problems. But one or a few strategies dominate if the tasks do not require the child to use any others. Thus, teaching children strategies is not enough. Putting children in situations where they need these strategies to succeed in accomplishing a task is also required.

In transitional bilingual education programs, doing well in schoolwork itself does not require rapid acquisition of the new language because school subjects are taught in the native language. Teaching subject matter in the native language also reduces children's exposure to situations in which they actually have opportunities to develop and practice the new language.

Social Interaction Explanations for the Low Success Rate of Transitional Bilingual Programs

Children in transitional bilingual classes are grouped by language—Spanish-speaking children are in one class, Chinese-speaking children are in another class, Russian-speaking children are in a third class. State laws require bilingual education programs when a specified number of children from a specific language group are enrolled in the school district. Thus, peers in bilingual classrooms all speak the same language. Social interaction between second-language children and children who speak the native language, especially in the natural situations that contribute so much to second-language learning, is reduced to a minimum. When peer interaction does not support acquisition of the second language, the rate of acquisition is slowed.

Other Factors to Consider in Program Planning for Limited-English Students

Advocates of the transitional bilingual approach think it helps children maintain their native language and therefore shows respect for a child's culture. They also think that a bilingual or multilingual culture offers greater variety and depth to a society, prevents cultural arrogance, and helps children from diverse backgrounds maintain their cultural heritage.

Proponents of TESL programs also value cultural diversity. But they claim to be more focused on the advancement of equal educational, cultural, political, and economic opportunity for all children. They think that the native language should be maintained at home and in other institutions, such as churches, synagogues, and social/cultural clubs, and at school, too, but not in ways that prevent children from learning English quickly and well. They think children can study their native language as a foreign language in middle school and high school. This kind of study will work for some but not all students, of course, because not all languages are offered in secondary schools as a course of study.

Because bilingual education is a politically sensitive issue, heated debate is likely to continue for some time. Throwing children into English-only classrooms, without any support in learning the new language, slows English language growth and lowers children's achievement in the short run. Providing all of the instruction in the native language, without also teaching English and placing children in positions where they need to use it, hurts children in the long run. Workable solutions will be needed to solve these problems.

Written Language (Literacy) Development

In first grade, Will kept a book in which he could write stories and illustrate them, or to illustrate stories the teacher told the class. Will often asked his teacher to spell words for him because, when he wrote them, they didn't "look right." Sometimes she wrote down in his book what he said. Other times she pronounced the words slowly, emphasizing the individual sounds within them, and helped Will think about how to spell them. Often, these two approaches showed up in the same writing sample. Following are some of the entries from his story journal:

November 14. Tatterhood. This is the castle room where the big Christmas tree is and this is one of the trolls.

January 9. Sno Wit and Ros Rd (Snow White and Rose Red). This is the hows in sprigtim (this is the house in springtime). The first vines from the red rose are starting to bloom.

March 4. The Emperor's New Clothes. This is the emperor sitting in the bedroom. And this is the prim ministr looking at the cloth that the crooks are not reale maeng (And this is the prime minister looking at the cloth that the crooks are not really making).

In second grade, Will kept a log of personal entries. By now, Will was experienced in sounding out words, although he knew his spellings were not always correct.

But Will did not worry because his journal was for himself and no one else, unless he wanted to show it to someone. He did share the following entries:

October 3. Tomareoe I em going to Morgan's huos. After I go to Morgan's hos then the nex day Ryan will cyom ovr. I kant wat.

March 26. I got a crikit. It is a fymale. I hop it has babies.

March 29. Yestrday my criket askapt. It was in the bathroom right wen I cam in. I coght it wen I saw it. I em glad it was in the bathroom at the same time I was.

It looked as if Will's writing had deteriorated from his first-grade level, but that was because he was now more on his own in writing his diary journal. His phonetic spelling is a good reminder of how many unusual spellings there are in English. By third grade, Will's spelling had improved a bit:

September 15. The day before scool started I came back from High Lake. It is a tarifck plaes to go on vacation. I plaed pewe golf. I colekted rocks. I plaed shufllboard. I liked it alott.

April 20. I had a grate Eastre! I woke up and saw a big Eastre basket. I had a milk chocklat bunny, a chickin filled with marchmelo and other candy.

By fourth grade, Will's spelling was more conventional and his ideas about writing had changed a lot also:

November 5. It was Thursday September 17, 3987. The battle raged on. "We got some reinforcements, but still it looks bad" (said Capitan Feragon). "Boss, they are launching an attack on the base." "I wonder why the aliens want to fight. I sent a squad of 5 to get some energy." They were having better luck than we were . . .

Although many spellings still eluded Will, his continuing exposure to books and other written materials, and the word study included in his school's curriculum, would continue to help him master the intricacies of written English.

think about it

Is Will's writing typical of children in the early elementary grades? How do the books and stories children read at home and at school influence the style and content of their writing? How does reading affect children's knowledge of spelling? In this section, we discuss several aspects of learning to read and learning to write. (The development of other writing skills is discussed in chapter 19.)

Learning to Read

Reading involves the integrated use of many different skills. In chapter 10, we discussed some of the components of reading that children should begin to develop during their preschool years (i.e., between 3 and 6 years of age). These components include such things as the very basic understanding that reading involves getting meaning from print, the ability to distinguish among and name the letters of the alphabet, the beginnings of explicit awareness of language at the phoneme level, and knowledge of some specific letter-sound correspondences. The last four of these understandings provide the child with what are commonly called **decoding skills**—the information and understandings that a child needs if he or she is to translate printed words into their oral counterparts.

Children must have some idea of the sound structure of words—be able to think their way through a word, one sound at a time—if they are to understand how an alphabetic system of writing works (Elkonin, 1973). Researchers have found that high levels of explicit **phoneme segmentation** skill (the ability to isolate the individual sounds making up a word when it is pronounced), as well as skill with other kinds of phoneme manipulation (e.g., knowing that "oor" remains when asked, "What would be left if we took the /d/ off of the word *door*?"), are causally related to success in beginning reading (Ball & Blachman, 1991; Byrne & Fielding-Barnsley, 1995; Hatcher & Hulme, 1999; Lundberg et al., 1988; Schneider et al., 1997; Wise et al., 1999). In addition to being able to segment words into phonemes, children must come to understand how letters are used. This insight is called the **alphabetic principle.** Of course, in English orthography, there is not a one-to-one correspondence between sounds and letters. Sometimes the **grapheme** (the letter or letter combination) that codes a sound consists of two letters. Good examples occur in words such as *thin* and *the*, and *chair* and *chicken*. Sometimes a letter appears in words but does not correspond to a sound. For example, in *muscle* the *c* does not correspond to a sound (though it does in the related word *muscular*).

A good vocabulary as well as other understandings about language and extensive background knowledge are essential if a child is to comprehend well the print he or she decodes (Nation & Snowling, 1998; Tunmer & Hoover, 1992). Oral vocabulary, background knowledge, and a good grasp of language also help children with decoding by giving them a sense of which words would fit in a specific sentence structure and in the context of a particular topic. Reading is not, of course, a word "guessing game." Children who take *only* this approach to print will not get very far. However, deciphering the words encoded in print runs more smoothly when both decoding skills and language knowledge (both knowledge of syntax—the structure of sentences and phrases, and semantics—word meanings) work together in an integrated way. Basic language and background knowledge are especially important in instances where straightforward decoding does not yield an accurate pronunciation of the printed word. Due to irregularities in English spelling, beginning readers often encounter situations where even the skilled deployment of good graphic-phonemic knowledge (letter-sound correspondences) simply does not take them far enough. Words such as *knock, love, enough,* and *health* are but a few examples of the many words that fail to yield an accurate pronunciation when sounded out. In such situations, contextual information—thinking about what would make sense in the sentence, given the topic—can carry the day (Nation & Snowling, 1998; Tunmer & Chapman, 1998).

The Transition from Emergent to Beginning Reading   Most children who enter first grade cannot yet actually read, even though they know a lot *about* written language. This is true even of the majority of children who bring extensive literacy-related knowledge with them to first grade, although the road to beginning reading is usually a fairly short and smooth one for them. Their teachers must merely get these students situated in text and help them put into practice all that they know. Children who have not had the benefit of extensive literacy experiences during the preschool years will need to learn decoding skills in first grade, increase their vocabulary, gain an appreciation for stories, develop an understanding of the language used in books, and acquire knowledge about how print is put on a page. It's a tall order, both for the children and their teachers. Major efforts have been mounted to consider how adequate literacy experiences can be provided to all children during the preschool years. (See Snow et al., 1998.) Starting "from scratch" once children arrive in first grade certainly can be done (Whitehurst & Lonigan, 1998), but the burden for all involved would be eased considerably if more children had the benefit of literacy experiences during their preschool years.

How does a first-grade teacher help children break into reading? What special materials and programs are available to help, and what are some of the things a teacher needs to keep in mind when dealing with children who differ dramatically in terms of knowledge and skills?

CONTROLLED VOCABULARY BOOKS.   The highest level of emergent reading, as we indicated in chapter 10, is fingerpoint-reading (i.e., the exact matching of spoken words with their printed forms in the text). Reaching this level of emergent reading depends on alphabet letter knowledge, the ability to segment the beginning phoneme of a word from the rest of the word, and knowledge of some specific letter-sound correspondences.

A child who can fingerpoint-read is virtually on the brink of being able to read unfamiliar text. Helping such a child move into the **beginning reading phase**—the reading of easy, but unfamiliar, texts—is often only a matter of putting appropriate unfamiliar books in the child's hands and supporting and encouraging the child to read them. Support and encouragement consist of coaching the child to "look closely at that word and to think about what makes sense there" when a child says a wrong word that is graphically similar to the word actually printed, but whose meaning does not fit into the context (e.g., reading "house" instead of "horse"). A child who substitutes a word based on meaning without taking graphic cues—the actual print—into account (e.g., reading "apartment" where the printed word is actually "house") can be asked to "look at that word and sound it out."

The teacher encourages a child to use what he or she knows about letter-sound correspondences, language (i.e., what word makes sense in a particular place), and the topic to solve specific word-decoding puzzlements and errors. Specific instruction can help children fill in any missing pieces.

To make it easier for a novice to read unfamiliar text, books designed specifically for beginners often utilize a **controlled vocabulary,** a small set of words repeated

Just as learning to communicate verbally is the hallmark of the years before formal school begins, learning to read is the outstanding achievement of the school-age years.   (*Source:* © Will Hart)

throughout the story. Although these books are not models of good literature, they simplify reading for children when they are just getting started. Controlled vocabulary books provide training wheels of a sort.

ASSISTANCE NEEDED BY FLEDGLING EMERGENT READERS.

Children who arrive in first grade with only the beginnings of emergent reading understandings need more than practice at deploying their graphic-phonemic skills with text. They need instruction on these skills, while being helped to extend their oral vocabulary and other language skills.

Programs and materials designed to help teach children to read use one of three basic approaches: (1) a strong initial emphasis on direct teaching of decoding skills; (2) a strong initial emphasis on language development and getting meaning from text; and (3) a combination of the two, more or less, in some balanced way. The two extreme positions—decoding *or* comprehension/meaning at the start—have been debated so much through the years that a well-known book about these opposing points of view was titled *Learning to Read: The Great Debate* (Chall, 1967). Hardly anyone today takes an extreme position, although there are still differences of opinion about how much emphasis should be placed at the very beginning on decoding skills. Research indicates that basic decoding skills are necessary for children to learn to read (Hatcher & Hulme, 1999; Rack et al., 1994; Vellutino, 1991; Wagner & Torgesen, 1987; and see Adams et al., 1998, for a review), but also that individual programs and teachers sometimes spend more time than necessary on these skills.

A case in point is instruction on letter-sound correspondences. There are about 43 phonemes (depending on how one defines them). Some are represented in more than one way—(e.g., c̲at and k̲itten; p̲h̲one and fi̲l̲ling; s̲eed and imp̲e̲de). Must children be taught all grapheme-phoneme associations directly, or can they use their knowledge of letter names to figure out some of them? Must teachers also teach children every nuance of orthography—all of the spelling rules—or can children get started in reading and then learn more spelling patterns from exposure to the print they read?

Children do not need to be tutored on every single letter correspondence or spelling pattern. Children can infer some of these associations and sequences, as long as they are helped to learn some basics, such as the names of the alphabet letters and how to segment words into phonemes. Consider how a 5½-year-old might be helped to figure out how to spell this message: "The bad monsters were very big, and I told them, 'Go Away!'"

The teacher isolated the first phoneme of the first word and said, "You need *t* and *h* together to spell that sound." The child wrote the letters. The teacher then voiced the tense (long) vowel phoneme, which is the second sound in the word *the*. The child wrote the letter *e*. Then the teacher started on the second word. The child knew immediately that the letter *b* should be used to spell the first sound in the word *bad*. After isolating the next sound in this word, the teacher told him that an *a* was needed to write it, adding, "It's just like the *a* at the beginning of Adam's name [a classmate]." Next, the teacher voiced /d/, and the child shouted out, "W." "W?" the teacher queried, with an expression of puzzlement. "Listen again." She voiced the phoneme again, but the child again said, "W!" "Actually," the teacher said, "We use *d* to write that sound." The teacher and child continued to work together to write the message. The teacher did not seem surprised or perplexed again by the child's dictation of letters until she reached the first phoneme in the word *were*. The child dictated *y*. The teacher asked, "Are you sure about that?" When the child did not respond, the teacher said, "Well, actually, we use *w* to write that sound." "Okay," the child said, as he started to write a *w*.

The child was clearly confident and correct about some associations, not sure about others, and confident but absolutely wrong about still others. This child had not been explicitly taught the letter-sound associations he already knew. The teacher was tutoring him on others, as she helped him spell his message. How did it happen that he had learned some correct associations, without explicit instruction? And why was he confused about others?

Apparently, the child was using his letter-name knowledge to figure out how to code phonemes (Thompson et al., 1999; Treiman et al., 1994, 1997, 1998). Some letter names map very directly onto a phoneme because the phoneme itself is heard right at the beginning when the letter's name is pronounced. The names for *b, k,* and *p* are helpful in this way, as are the names of the letters *t, v, a,* and others. But consider the name for *w.* When this letter is named, the first sound one hears is not the phoneme this letter spells, but /d/. This, no doubt, is why the child dictated *w* when the teacher voiced /d/ in the word *bad,* because he had mapped this letter name onto /d/. A similar explanation accounts for the error in coding *w* in *were* with *y.* When we say the name of the letter *y,* the first sound we hear is actually the phoneme we typically spell with *w* (Treiman, 1998).

When the phoneme to be spelled is not heard at the beginning in the letter's name, children are less likely to map the letter onto the correct phoneme, although they do seem to pick up this information to a considerable extent (Treiman, 1998).

Spelling patterns—the variable but "legal" ways to spell phonemes, including *feet* and *eat* and *repair*—can themselves be learned from reading, once decoding skills are deployed in the service of reading unfamiliar texts. As children look carefully at print when they are sounding out unknown words, they become familiar with spelling, with **orthographic pattern**s—common sequences of letters we use to spell English words. Every spelling pattern need not be taught directly to children, or reviewed again and again on worksheets, for example. Children will learn orthographic (spelling pattern) knowledge as they deploy their basic decoding skills to read books.

This self-teaching hypothesis for the learning of orthographic patterns has been explored extensively and largely confirmed in research by Share (1999). This hypothesis is consistent with the positive correlations researchers have obtained between a child's exposure to print (amount of reading a child does) and the child's orthographic knowledge (Anderson et al., 1988; Barker et al., 1992; Cipielewski & Stanovich, 1992; Cunningham & Stanovich, 1993; Stage & Wagner, 1992). When children first start to read, they do so by sounding words out (Ehri, 1980). At the start, they have little orthographic knowledge, and they do not recognize many words when they see them. But as they read more and more (by sounding words out), they develop images of how words should look. This knowledge of spelling patterns (orthographic information) gradually becomes more automatic, and it begins to contribute independently to reading and spelling skill (Stage & Wagner, 1992; Trieman, 1993). The more children read, the better their orthographic knowledge apparently becomes.

Unfortunately, some children struggle with reading whether they get an early or late start, and no matter, it seems, what a teacher does to help these students. If a child is otherwise able to learn, but has extreme difficulty with reading, we say that the child suffers from **dyslexia.** It is difficult to say just how many children suffer from dyslexia because there are several different kinds, some more debilitating than others. It is also true the some children who have difficulty learning to read are not dyslexic at all, but have not had the benefit of good instruction. (See the Research Close-Up—Dyslexia: When Children Have Trouble Reading, for a discussion of reading problems.)

RESEARCH

CLOSE-UP *Dyslexia: When Children Have Trouble Reading*

Dyslexia is a generic term that refers to extreme difficulty in learning to read when reading achievement is below what would be expected, given the child's age, general ability level, and instructional opportunities. Reading in this case is viewed as a **specific learning disability,** not a problem due to general learning difficulty. In recent years, however, researchers and educators alike have become dissatisfied with this **discrepancy definition of dyslexia.** Reading difficulties seem to occur on a continuum, although different children have different problem profiles (Fletcher et al., 1994).

What Causes Dyslexia?

At one time, reading difficulties were thought by some researchers and educators to be caused by visual or visual-motor problems (Fawcett & Nicolson, 1995; Metzger & Werner, 1984; Regcher & Kaplan, 1988; Riccio & Hynd, 1995). But research has never been able to provide evidence that these factors are the source of reading problems. Instead, language processes of various kinds seem to be the main problem.

Children who have considerable difficulty in learning to read typically have trouble with phonological processing. Phonological processing involves translating graphemes (letters or pairs of letters that represent phonemes) into sounds. These difficulties encompass problems in

(1) articulating words when pronouncing them (Elbro et al., 1998; Swanson, 1999),

(2) breaking words into their sound segments (phoneme segmentation) (Levy et al., 1999),

(3) acquiring letter cluster information (orthographic unit or spelling patterns) as a result of problems in **phonological recoding** (sounding out a printed word to get its oral equivalent) (Elbro et al., 1994; Metsala, 1999),

(4) and in using semantic (i.e., word meanings) information from larger chunks of language (Nation & Snowling, 1998; Nation et al., 1999).

In addition to these phonological processing and other language-related difficulties, there is some evidence that general memory and processing problems also contribute to reading difficulties. Reading requires the short-term storage of some information while other information is being processed (i.e., some words just read are stored temporarily while more words are being sounded out). Problems in memory storage or in some **executive process** (something that directs attention and selects strategies while information is being processed) have been identified as contributing to reading problems (de Jong, 1998; Nation et al., 1999; Swanson, 1999).

Clearly, reading difficulties can be many-faceted problems at various levels. Researchers are still trying to figure out exactly what goes wrong when children have trouble learning to read, which of these problems are independent of one another, and which are actually related such that one causes another.

How Can Dyslexics be Helped?

Considerable success has come from help in the form of training on phonological skills. These are the basic skills involved in decoding text, and they include phoneme segmentation, the alphabetic principle (knowing that letters function to code phonemes) and letter-sound associations (Levy et al., 1999; Scanlon & Vellutino, 1997). Even if memory problems are part of the problem with poor readers, increasing the automaticity of the phonological system can shorten processing time and aid comprehension. Thus, help in the phonological domain may ease load on processing capacities. There may not be any direct way to correct basic processing problems. Instead, learners may need to overcome these problems by learning better the skills used when processing information, and, in this way, reduce processing load.

Some children with reading difficulties have problems with reading comprehension, over and above their phonological skill problems (Nation & Snowling, 1998). Thus, there is also a need to support oral language development, both at the word and larger chunk levels, and to make sure children have good background knowledge about what they read.

Learning to Write

Like reading, writing normally begins during the preschool years. But even though children learn much about writing between the ages of 3 and 6, the development of writing only *begins* during this period. The ability to express ideas and thoughts in writing continues to develop throughout the elementary school years and beyond.

Given the emphasis on writing in the elementary grades over the past several decades, we now know a lot about the composition process in school-age children and the factors that influence it. For example, exposure to content-based curricula in science and social studies seems to influence the extent to which the youngest elementary-age children will produce **expository writing,** writing whose purpose is to convey information. Children in classrooms that stress literature and language arts over science and social studies may be encouraged to write more **narratives**—writing whose purpose is to tell a story about characters or events (Casbergue, 1996). Within the narrative category, we know that the literature children read influences the form and content of the stories they write (Jenkins, 1996).

Researchers have also been interested in how young children manage to write at all. How do they create words before they have learned how to spell all of the words they want to use? As we saw in chapter 10, even 3-, 4-, and 5-year-olds can create "words." But even though preschoolers sometimes use phonemic-based strategies to create words, they use other strategies much of the time, and most of these are not based on sound.

It is the sound-based phonemic approach to creating words that dominates during the early school-age years. Children's decisions about how to code the sounds they hear provide a window on their amazingly fertile minds. Our discussion of school-age children's writing will focus on the decisions that underlie their **invented spellings.**

The Letter-Name Spelling Strategy

The Letter-Name Spelling Strategy As soon as children know the names of letters and can segment words into phonemes, they can begin to associate letters with sounds, as we have seen. This **letter-name strategy** launches children into invented spelling.

Words spelled by using this strategy look quite unusual. We saw some examples in Will's journal—words like *wat (wait), ovr, wen,* and *hop (hope).* Sometimes, the letter-name strategy leads to very peculiar spellings, such as *HKN* for *chicken.* At first glance, it seems that the child was sloppy and failed to include the *c* before the *h.* But, instead, the child has used the letter *h* because, in saying its name, /č/ is produced. Table 14.1 provides a list of spellings that are common among children who are using a letter-name strategy.

Spelling Short-Vowel Phonemes

Spelling Short-Vowel Phonemes Letter names are not of immediate use when the child must code a lax-vowel phoneme because no letter's name contains these. In these cases, children search the phonetic features of the long, or *tense,* vowels to see which ones match most closely each of the lax vowels (Read, 1975). For example, a child might write *then* as *THIN.* The lax *e* in *then* has some phonetic features in common with both tense *i* and long *e.* It shares a similar shape of the vocal track—the height of the tongue in relation to the roof of the mouth—with tense *i.* It shares the specific spot in the vocal track where the sound is formed (front-to-back location) with tense *e.* Apparently, children experience the location of the tongue more than its height. This is why they first represent lax *e* with the letter *i.* The second column in Table 14.2 contains some examples of words created through use of this spelling strategy.

Spelling Words with Other Phonetic Features

Spelling Words with Other Phonetic Features Another phonetic feature sometimes confuses children. Some sounds are *affricated*—spoken with a slow release of air. The sound associated with the spelling *ch* and the soft pronunciation of the letter *g* are examples of affricated sounds. When *d* or *t* is followed by *r,* there is some affrication, even though the phoneme represented by *d* and *t* does not contain this phonetic feature in other contexts. (The /d/ in *dog* and /t/ in *toy* are not affricated, but the /t/ in *train* is.) Because affrication is apparently a fairly dominant phonetic

TABLE 14.2

Examples of children's invented spellings

Words Created Using A Letter-Name Strategy	Words Created by Substituting the Nearest Tense (Long) Vowel for a Lax (Soft) Vowel	Words Created by Focusing on the Affrication in T and D followed by R
Kit (kite)	Fes (fish)	Chran (train)
Da (day)	Pan (pen)	Chra (tray)
Mi (my)	Mas (Mess)	Chri (try)
Kat (Kate)	Git (got)	Griv (drive)
Tabl (table)	Biks (box)	Gri (dry)
Hare (cherry)		
Hrh (church)		
Lade (lady)		
Babe (baby)		
Fas (face)		
Tigr (tiger)		

feature for young children, they tend to spell *train* as CHRAN. (See column 3 in Table 14.2 for other examples.)

Using Morphological Information in Spellings   At first, children phonetically record the endings of past-tense verbs such as *played* and *walked*, using a *d* at the end of *played* and a *t* at the end of *walked*. These letters are used to represent the sounds heard at the ends of these words. Later, children understand the similarity in meaning between these two words and others like them—all express the past tense of a verb. Standard spelling disregards phonetic differences in pronunciation in these cases and uses *-ed* to write this morphological ending no matter how it sounds in a specific word (Nunes et al., 1997).

In a related development, children improve their spelling of words with the same root, such as *sign* and *signal, medicine* and *medical*. In these cases, strict phonetic transcription of one word in a pair is overridden to show that the two words are related in meaning. For example, the *g* in *sign* does not serve as a grapheme; it does not represent a sound. In *signal,* it does. The *g* is retained in *sign* in order to mark that its meaning is related to the meaning of *signal*. In *medicine,* a *c* is used to code the phoneme in the middle of the word because it is found in the same spot in the word *medical*. Once children realize that various words are related in this way, they can use the pronunciation of one word that adheres better to typical sound-letter patterns to recall the atypical spelling of another word (Adams et al., 1998).

The Effects of Invented Spelling   Does allowing children to invent spellings harm their ability to acquire conventional spellings? Data are scant, but one study (Bruck et al., 1998) did find some differences between third-graders who had been in more traditional phonics classrooms and third-graders who had been in whole language classrooms, where invented spelling was encouraged. Children were asked to spell 25 actual words, as well as 25 nonwords that nevertheless sounded as though they could qualify as English words.

The children who had attended the phonics classrooms made fewer errors than children who had attended whole language classrooms, although the kinds of errors, and their proportions, did not differ between the two groups. The children from the whole language classrooms segmented words to spell them just as well as the phonics group, which would be expected, given that invented spelling provides practice in phonemic segmentation. The children who had attended the whole language classrooms also honored basic patterns of English orthography. For example, they never put *ck* at the beginning of a word, where English spelling rules dictate that only *c* or *k* can be used alone. Rather, they used *ck* to code this phoneme only in the middle and at the end of words, where this letter combination is permissible.

In summary, children in the phonics classrooms simply knew more correct spellings than children in the whole language classroom, although the basic processes used to spell words seemed to be the same in both groups. The researchers (Bruck et al., 1998) suggested that if a little instruction on standard letter-sound correspondences (where no obvious letter-sound correspondence exists to guide the child) could be added to the whole language classrooms, the spelling skills of their children would probably equal the spelling skills of their peers in phonics-based classrooms.

The effect of invented spelling on children's spelling development in whole language classrooms probably depends, as well, on how much time is spent each day on reading and on writing. Writing takes considerable time, and in classrooms where children's own stories are revised several times and then published and put in the classroom library, the amount of time spent in reading books is reduced. The combination of rereading one's own spelling errors in a number of drafts and reading fewer books might have a substantial effect on spelling skills. But in a whole language classroom where children read more and write somewhat less, possible negative effects of invented spelling on learning conventional spelling might be diminished considerably. Unless one knows the specific practices actually followed in a classroom, the effect of an instructional program on spelling or anything else cannot be predicted with a great deal of accuracy.

Children Make Gradual Progress in Spelling   As children see more words spelled in standard forms, such as when they read books and study words, they gradually learn which phonetic features are attended to for the sake of spelling, and which ones are ignored. They also use retrieval (i.e., pulling from memory) strategies more as they move from first into second grade, and they rely less on sounding words out, although this approach lingers as a backup for quite some time (Rittle-Johnson & Siegler, 1999). They also begin to use analogies—a spelling pattern known for one word can help them spell another word that sounds the same. In general, children move from strict phonetic transcription of sounds they hear in words to more sophisticated spellings dictated by the conventions of orthography (Treiman, 1985; Treiman et al., 1995). Even children whose dialects cause them at first to spell some words peculiarly seem to take up conventional spelling patterns by age 7½ or so (Treiman et al., 1997).

Supporting Children's Engagement with Reading and Writing

In the classroom and at home, adults can increase children's vocabulary acquisition and awareness of language structure by using such things as crossword puzzles and books of jokes and riddles. They also can play word games such as Scrabble with their children and can help children to discover the pleasures of reading as a recreational activity. Librarians can help children find books of interest and can also give parents ideas for books that they might wish to purchase as gifts.

These boys are enjoying and learning from a magazine. Perhaps they are consulting it to find out how to make or do something at camp. (*Source:* © Bob Daemmrich/ Stock Boston)

A number of magazines are written especially for the school-age child, and subscriptions to these also make appropriate gifts. (See the list in Table 14.3.) Some of these magazines publish children's stories and artwork, and some school-age children enjoy participating in these activities.

Other writing opportunities can be provided through pen-pal projects at school or producing a school newsletter. At home, parents can encourage grandparents or aunts and uncles to correspond with their grandchildren or nieces or nephews.

TABLE 14.3

Magazines for school-age children

Title	Ages	Content
Child Life	9–11	Health, safety, nutrition, fitness
Children's Digest	8–10	Adventure and mysteries, food and health
Cobblestone	8–14	History
Creative Kids	8–14	Stores, poems, art, photos, and music submitted by children
Cricket	9–14	Short stories, poems, and art
Faces	8–14	Cultures and human diversity
Highlights for Children	2–12	Stories, poems, learning activities
Jack and Jill	7–10	Health and fitness
National Geographic World	8–14	Natural science, the outdoors, geography
Odyssey	8–14	Astronomy and space science
Owl	8–14	Environmental education, animals, technology
Ranger Rick	6–12	Nature study
Spider	6–9	Short stories, poems, and art
Stone Soup	6–13	Stories, poems, and art submitted by children
Zillions	8–14	Consumer education, life skills, and decision making

Source: Adapted from *Children's Magazine List,* 1987, Glassboro, NJ: Glassboro State College; and *Magazines for Kids,* edited by O. R. Stoll, 1997, Newark, DE: International Reading Association.

KEY POINTS

Oral Language Development

■ Oral vocabulary develops at a rapid rate over the school-age years, with the rate increasing as children reach the third grade. The increased rate by the middle grades is due to children's ability to understand morphology—the variations on a root word. Much of children's word acquisition during the school-age years takes place as they read books.

■ Young school-age children have mastered the rudiments of language, but they are still confused by certain word usages, such as the distinction between *ask* and *tell*. Even as late as age 9 or 10, some language constructions confuse them.

■ The ability to focus on the structure of language rather than on the literal meaning of specific words is known as metalinguistic awareness. School-age children can understand ambiguity created by the structure of language itself, and they delight in telling jokes and riddles.

■ Schools in the United States have often been filled with children whose native language is not English.

■ Two widely used approaches have been developed to support limited-English students. In TESL programs, children are taught the academic subjects in English and receive help in learning English, either from specially trained teachers in their regular classroom or from other teachers in "pull-out" classes. In transitional bilingual programs, children are taught their academic subjects in the native language and are helped to gain proficiency in the second language. When second-language proficiency is high enough, children enter regular classes.

■ There are three theories about how children (or adults) learn a second language: They learn it the same way as native speakers learn it as toddlers (identical process theory); they use structures from their first language (interference theory); or they de-vise new grammatical structures as they learn (the unique grammatical structure theory). Most research supports the identical process model of learning a second language.

Written Language (Literacy) Development

■ Learning to read requires that children be engaged with print. Preschoolers pretend-read, but they rely on the pictures. Print-related skills that are essential in learning to read include phonemic segmentation, letter recognition, and letter-sound association.

■ Controlled vocabulary books are useful to the beginning reader because they simplify the complex task enough to enable a novice to "get the hang of it."

■ Children vary considerably in terms of the literacy experiences they bring to first grade.

■ Teachers need not waste instructional time teaching what children can figure out by themselves.

■ The content of children's writing is influenced by what they read and by the general curriculum provided in the classroom. Content-rich programs in science and social studies may influence children to do more expository writing, whereas programs dominated by language arts and literature may lead to more narrative writing.

■ School-age children use invented spelling when writing. Their spellings are unusual, but they are systematic and thoughtful. As they read books and study words, they learn to spell words conventionally.

■ Children's engagement with reading and writing can be supported at home as well as in the classroom.

■ There are many good magazines written especially for the school-age child.

GLOSSARY

alphabetic principle: the understanding that alphabetic orthographies code spoken language at the phoneme level and that alphabet letters function, basically, to code phonemes (rather than syllables, for example) (p. 497)

beginning reading phase: the time period in which a child can decode print in unfamiliar books but frequently misreads words because of errors in letter-sound mapping or too much reliance on context clues, rather than graphic-phonemic cues, to recognize words (p. 498)

bilingual education: the general name for a variety of instructional programs that use the native language and English in an attempt to help children whose first language is not English learn at school while also learning English (p. 492)

controlled vocabulary: a characteristic of books with a limited set of new words, designed for children who are learning to read (p. 498)

decoding skills: a cluster of understandings, including letter-name knowledge, phonemic awareness, the alphabetic principle, and letter-sound correspondences, that are needed in order to translate printed words into their oral counterparts (p. 496)

discrepancy definition of dyslexia: dyslexia assessed by looking at the difference between reading ability and general learning ability (p. 501)

dyslexia: a condition in which learning to read is extremely difficult and cannot be accounted for by age or general difficulty in learning (p. 505)

executive process: the process that directs attention and strategy selection while information is being processed in a person's working and short-term memory (p. 501)

expository writing: writing for the purpose of providing information (p. 502)

formulaic utterances: frequently heard, multiword "chunks" of language repeated as heard by a language learner (p. 491)

grapheme: the characters used to code phonemes, consisting of either single letters or letter pairs (pp. 497–501)

identical process theory: a theory suggesting that people learn a new language in the same way as first-language learners learn it (p. 488)

immersion: learning a second language by spending considerable time speaking with native users of the language (p. 489)

interference theory: a theory of second-language learning in which the first language is assumed to interfere with learning the second language (p. 488)

invented spelling: phonemic-based, unconventional spellings created by children (p. 502)

letter-name strategy: letter-sound associations based on phonemes contained in letter names (p. 502)

metalinguistic awareness: ability to attend to the structure of language rather than to meaning (p. 488)

narrative writing: writing for the purpose of telling a story (p. 502)

orthographic patterns: common sequences of letters used in spelling English words (p. 500)

phoneme segmentation: the process of isolating the individual sounds making up a word, in the order that one hears the sounds when the word is spoken (p. 497)

phonological recoding: translating printed words into their spoken counterparts by using letter-sound correspondences, which is to be distinguished from immediate reading of words by sight, without letter-to-sound translation (p. 501)

pull-out model: model of instruction by which academic subjects are taught in English and help in learning English is provided outside the child's regular classroom (p. 494)

specific learning disability: learning difficulties confined to a particular area and unexplained by physical disabilities or low intelligence (p. 501)

spelling patterns: the same as orthographic patterns, which are the conventional ways in which words are to be spelled in a given language (p. 500)

structured immersion: learning a second language by being taught in it, while also being provided with specific instruction in the new language (p. 492)

transitional bilingual program: a program in which academic subjects are taught in children's native language while they are helped to learn English, only later (after a level of proficiency has been achieved) receiving instruction in academic subjects in English (p. 492)

unique grammatical structures theory: a theory suggesting that people learn a new language using structures that do not match those of their own first language or those of someone learning the new language as a first language (p. 488)

SUGGESTIONS FOR FURTHER READING

Genesee, F. (Ed.). (1994). *Educating second language children: The whole child, the whole curriculum, the whole community.* New York: Cambridge University Press. This book contains chapters covering many of the "nuts and bolts" of teaching second-language learners. It covers both oral language and literacy learning. Helpful and very informative.

Jenkins, C. B. (1996). *Inside the writing portfolio: What we need to know to assess children's writing.* Portsmouth, NH: Heinemann. This is a wonderfully descriptive book about school-age children's writing. The book's focus is on a case study of one third-grader, but writing samples from both younger and older children are included.

McGee, L. M., & Richgells, D. J. (1996). *Literacy's beginnings: Supporting young readers and writers.* Boston: Allyn & Bacon. This book discusses literacy development from the preschool years through the third grade. It is rich with examples and suggestions.

Rossell, C., & Baker, K. (1996). *Bilingual education in Massachusetts: The emperor has no clothes.* Boston: Pioneer Institute. This book discusses bilingual education laws and programs and provides important data. It is one of several books published in the 1990s that raise serious questions about the effectiveness of transitional bilingual education programs in helping limited-English children in our public schools.

Stotsky, S. (1999). *Losing our language: How multicultural classroom instruction is undermining our children's ability to read, write, and reason.* New York: Free Press. This provocative book discusses the content of books used in today's classroom. Stotsky contends that the quality and level of books read by children have been jeopardized as attention in schools has shifted to self-esteem and multiculturalism issues and that children's learning is suffering because of this.

15

Social and Emotional Development in School-Age Children

A GROUP OF fourth-graders were huddled together at one end of a table in the lunchroom, talking in hushed tones. They looked for all the world like conspirators hatching a plot—which is exactly what they were doing.

"Look, we've got to have enough time to get the streamers tacked on the wall, the balloons blown up and hung from the windows, the cupcakes on her desk, and 'Happy Birthday, Mrs. Townsend' written on the blackboard," said Paul. "That'll take maybe ten minutes. But how do we get her out of the classroom for that long?" He looked around the circle of intent faces. "Any ideas?"

"How about if we get Mr. Steinberg to call her on the intercom to come to the office to get a message?" suggested Amy.

"No, that won't work," Paul responded. "She always sends one of us to the office to get messages."

"I know!" said David. "We'll have someone fake getting hurt on the playground and have to go to the nurse's office. Then the nurse can call Mrs. Townsend to come see if it's okay for the kid to come back to class. Then on the way back to the classroom, the kid could faint, and Mrs. Townsend would . . . "

"That doesn't make any sense," interrupted Gina. "The nurse always decides if you can come back to the classroom. Teachers don't decide that. Mrs. Townsend would realize something was funny if the nurse asked her to come down."

"Let's tell her we met her husband out front with their baby, and he wants her to come out because he can't make the baby stop crying!" exclaimed Leroy.

"She'd never fall for that!" Paul scoffed. "That's ridiculous!"

"Then you think of something!" retorted Leroy. And they all fell silent for a few minutes . . . waiting for the next idea to surface.

think about it

What abilities enable fourth-graders to make up ruses and imagine how Mrs. Townsend would react? What understandings make it possible for children to put themselves in the place of someone else, and to anticipate what that person might think and do? Are children better at carrying out these sorts of activities in familiar situations, when they are dealing with people whose minds they know reasonably well, or are general understandings about emotions, intentions, and situations enough?

In this chapter, we discuss the growth of **social cognition**—the child's ability to think about a situation from another person's point of view and to understand what causes that person to behave in a certain way. Thinking about another person's thinking involves taking into account a whole host of things, such as the person's desires, intentions, and prior knowledge about a situation. We also discuss children's **social skills**—how children actually behave toward one another and toward adults in their lives. Social cognition is involved here, too, of course, because children's interpretations of other people's behavior influence how they behave toward others. As part of our discussion about social skills, we also consider how children's social behavior affects the regard that other people have for them and how having low status in the eyes of one's peers can affect children's achievement and their tendency later on to engage in delinquent behavior. Finally, we look at cognitive and personality differences between boys and girls, and consider some of the explanations that have been offered to account for them.

Social Role-Taking

We could see the ability to understand the feelings, thoughts, and intentions of another in Paul, Gina, and the other fourth-graders. We also see how they took into account very specific knowledge about the situation, including what their teacher typically does and what the principal (Mr. Steinberg), the school nurse, and their teacher's husband ordinarily do. The children were engaging in an activity called social role-taking. **Social role-taking** involves getting into the mind of another person and trying to think and feel about things as the other person would think and feel about them. Social role-taking ability increases during middle childhood, which is the period from 6 to 10 years of age (Damon & Hart, 1992; Flavell & Miller, 1998). Development in this ability reflects increases in the child's understanding of emotions, intentions, situations, and how all of these relate to a person's behavior. We will consider development in children's understanding of each of these areas.

Social role-taking ability enables children to engage more and more skillfully in strategy games, such as chess and checkers. The chess game played by the two boys pictured here appears to be interesting even to a third child, perhaps because there is so much that he can think about as he anticipates the consequences of each player's move. (*Source:* © Sydney/The Image Works)

Understanding Emotions

The understanding of emotions rests on a series of learnings. As we saw in chapter 5, infants begin to discriminate some basic facial expressions between about 4 and 6 months of age. Then, late in the first year of life, they begin to recognize the meanings of a few basic facial expressions, such as those expressing happy, sad, angry, and worried feelings. During this early period, infants do not have a sophisticated understanding of the meanings of facial expressions, but are able to interpret expressions as either generally positive (i.e., "everything is okay") or generally negative (i.e. "this situation is not okay"). Infants use information displayed on a trusted caregiver's face to determine whether they should judge a new object, person, or situation positively or negatively. Gradually, children learn to distinguish a whole range of emotions (excitement, fear, worry, disappointment, pride, and so on), both within themselves and in other people. The process of learning to differentiate a variety of emotions begins early in the preschool years and continues well into the school-age years (Harris, 1994; Harris et al., 1987).

During the school-age years, children also gradually learn that the emotions that they and other people display are not always their true emotions. In other words, children learn that people often act as if they feel one way when they actually feel quite different (Gnepp & Hess, 1986; Harris & Gross, 1988). In some studies that have probed this aspect of children's understanding of emotions, researchers have told children several stories, each one of which involves a child who feels one way but displays a different emotion (Harris & Gross, 1988). For example, in one story episode, a little girl had a tummy ache, but hid her discomfort (her true emotion) from her mother so that she could go out to play. After being told the story in which the true emotion and the emotion displayed were both described, children were asked to select from among three choices describing how the child in the story really felt and how she acted as if she felt. Four-year-olds could not separate the actual from the displayed emotion, but 6-year-olds could.

In other studies of this behavior, researchers have shown children pictures in which children's faces express an emotion that would not be typical for the situation shown. For example, a child at a birthday party may be depicted with a sad expression, or a child receiving an immunization from a doctor may be smiling (Gnepp, 1983; Reichenbach & Masters, 1983).

Preschoolers and younger school-age children tended to say such things as, "The child's good friends didn't come to the birthday party," and "The shot didn't hurt at all." These responses reveal that preschoolers and young school-age children do not yet understand that the emotions a person displays may not represent true emotions. Thus, they tend to revise or qualify the situation itself in order to increase the match between the emotion they see and what they know about the emotions typically provoked by the situation.

Older children, on the other hand, tend to explain these discrepancies by indicating that the emotion probably does not truly reflect how the person feels. An understanding of the **masking of emotions**—knowing that a person's outward display may not indicate the person's actual feelings—dawns at about 6 years of age and continues to increase throughout the school-age years (Selman, 1980). As a result of this awareness, children begin to respond differently to the pictures that researchers present. By sixth grade, for example, researchers (Reichenbach & Masters, 1983) found that a child responding to the immunization situation, in which a child is shown smiling, was likely to say, "She's really scared about getting the shot, but she doesn't want anyone to know it" or "She's really scared about the shot, but she's trying to act happy to make herself feel better."

These two responses actually reveal somewhat different understandings. The first response involves an understanding that emotions can be masked. The second response indicates knowledge about how we can control, at least to a certain extent, our own emotions. A child who makes this latter kind of response knows that thinking certain thoughts, rather than other ones, can sometimes influence our emotional response to a situation. By late childhood or early adolescence, children also realize that constantly hiding one's feelings, either by masking them from others or by denying them to oneself, might have negative consequences (Saarni, 1988). For example, they realize that a person who does this consistently might have psychological problems and would probably be hard to get to know.

Understanding the Relationship between Situations and Emotions

Another kind of knowledge that helps children understand how other people feel involves understanding situations and the feelings they typically evoke in people. Children learn that some situations are fairly unambiguous or unequivocal in terms of the emotions they evoke, whereas other situations are ambiguous or equivocal. Unambiguous situations evoke quite similar emotions in most people. Almost everyone responds positively, or almost everyone responds negatively, to unambiguous situations. Equivocal or ambiguous situations, on the other hand, are likely to evoke positive reactions in some people and negative reactions in others.

One group of researchers wondered how children's understanding of ambiguous (equivocal) versus unambiguous (unequivocal) situations varies with age (Snepp et al., 1987). To find out, they presented children in kindergarten and in first, second, and third grades with a series of both equivocal and unequivocal situations. Equivocal situations included "a child gets an egg salad sandwich for lunch" and "a child is approached by a small dog while playing." Unequivocal situations included "all the lights go off when a child is playing alone" and "a child drops and breaks a favorite toy" (Gnepp et al., 1987, p. 116).

The children were asked to tell how a hypothetical "story child" would feel about the situation. After stating an emotion they believed the story child would feel, children were asked to explain the answer. Children responded to an equivocal situation by attributing a wider range of emotional reactions to the child pictured. This indicated that children realized that the equivocal situation is more likely to evoke different emotions from people. The researchers also found that older children recognized equivocal situations more clearly than younger children did.

Children also gave different kinds of explanations for their choices of emotion for the equivocal versus the unequivocal situations. In the equivocal situations, children explained why the story child felt the way she did by referring to her supposed interpretation of the event ("She would be happy about an egg salad sandwich because she knows that eggs are good for her"). This behavior indicated that children realized that we cannot know for sure how a person will feel about a particular situation unless we know the meaning of that situation for the person.

As children get older, they also begin to realize that emotions displayed may not be elicited by the immediate situation. Some emotions elicited by previous situations endure and influence people's reactions in a current situation. Thus, when the emotional response displayed in a situation does not fit the specific situation, older children consider not only whether the true emotion might be masked, but also whether the emotion could be authentic, but influenced by lingering emotions from some past experience. In other words, the emotion expressed is the actual emotion felt by the person at the time, although it is not most people's typical reaction to the situation nor this person's reaction to the current situation alone. In these cases, the unusual reaction is caused by emotions the person brings to the situation from past experiences combined with the reaction to the current situation.

One common ambiguous situation is that in which a person expresses displaced aggression, being harsh with one person because she is simply feeling grouchy or worn out from being angry at another person. The man who kicks the cat because his boss yelled at him, and the child who hits her younger sister because she is angry at her mother, are classic examples of this. Similarly, people sometimes respond with general sadness to all situations because they are depressed or because they have suffered specific losses in the recent past. These situations are particularly difficult for 5-year-olds to understand; by 9 years of age, children have less trouble interpreting them. Children improve at understanding displaced aggression or general sadness when they become more aware of the fact and that "life conditions" can create somewhat chronic emotional responses, regardless of the immediate situation (Hoffman, 1988).

Growth in Children's Understanding of Mixed Emotions   Children must also come to understand that people can feel two or more different emotions simultaneously about the same situation. Experiences of emotions can be simple and straightforward, or they can be complex and difficult. For example, a child who opens a birthday present and finds inside the item from the top of his birthday list probably experiences happiness, pure and simple. But a child on his way to a month's stay at an overnight camp might feel several emotions simultaneously. There is the excitement of getting to do everything mentioned in the camp brochure and the videotape. But there also is anxiety about the new experience: "Will I make any friends?" "Will I get homesick?" "What if the food is terrible, and the counselors harsh?" This is a classic example of **mixed emotions**—the experience of feeling both positive and negative emotions about the same experience.

One model for thinking about how children progress in their ability to experience and talk about simultaneous emotions involves **targets**—the object, person, or situation at which an emotion is directed—and **valence**—the positive or negative nature of the emotion (Harter & Buddin, 1987; Harter & Whitesell, 1989). Researchers hypothesized that it might be easier for children to experience two positive emotions directed toward the *same* target simultaneously than a positive and negative emotion toward the same target.

Children aged 4 to 6 could not put feelings together simultaneously. Sometimes they denied that two feelings could be experienced at the same time, or they sequenced two feelings (*"First* I'd feel excited; *then* I'd feel happy"). These children had concepts for separate emotions—they knew the differences between surprise, happiness, anger, and so on—but they did not seem to perceive them as simultaneous—as mixed emotions about the same thing. They sequenced them instead.

By 6 to 8 years of age, children acknowledged that they experienced two emotions at the same time, but they included only same-valence emotions directed toward the same target ("I feel happy and excited about an A on my spelling test"). They still had difficulty feeling two different positive emotions about two different targets ("I felt happy about my new board games and very excited about the tickets to the baseball game") (Harter & Buddin, 1987, p. 392).

Children aged 8 to 9 acknowledged that they experienced two same-valence emotions directed toward different targets at the same time ("I'd feel happy about the spelling test and excited about the class picnic."), but they could not imagine being able to feel two different-valence emotions—one positive, one negative—at the same time. One child said, "I couldn't feel happy and frightened at the same time; I would have to be two people at once!" (Harter & Buddin, 1987, pp. 392–393)

Ten-year-olds reported that they experienced two different-valence emotions at the same time, but only when they were directed at two different targets ("I was scared in the theater watching the movie, but I was happy that I had popcorn to eat"). Even though their range of emotions was quite large by 10 years of age, children could not bring a positive and negative emotion to a *single* target at the same time. Finally, at about 11 years of age, children acknowledged feeling mixed emotions (both positive and negative emotions) about the same target, at the same time ("The movie made me feel both happy and scared").

Development of Empathy　　As we discussed in chapter 11, empathy requires that we go beyond noticing and interpreting the emotions of others to actually responding with emotion ourselves, especially to others' distress. Young children develop in their capacity to be emotionally aroused by the emotions they think other people are experiencing, but this capacity does not appear all at once. Children are first capable of empathic responding at about 18 months of age. But at this young age, empathy is **noninferential** (Flavell, 1985), as we discussed in Chapter 11. During the school-age years, empathy becomes **inferential,** which means that it involves knowing about the mental state of the person who is in distress (Flavell, 1985). As Hoffman (1988) explained it,

> Older children and adults know that they are responding to something happening to someone else, and, based on their knowledge about others and their own past experience, they have an idea of what the other may be feeling; young children who lack the self-other distinction may be empathically aroused without these cognitions. (p. 509)

As children get older, they become more sophisticated in experiencing this kind of empathy, even to the point that they understand that a person's emotional state may not be related to the immediate situation, but to factors that are remote and chronic. As children approach adolescence, they even begin to associate an individual's emotions with that person's membership in some social group (those who live in poverty or those who may face discrimination, for example) (Hoffman, 1988).

These school-age boys are showing considerable empathy toward a friend. School-age children also become distressed when they see that someone else is distressed, and they can think about what might have caused the upset. This ability enables them to console or encourage a friend while they also provide physical comfort. (*Source:* © Will Hart)

The development of empathy appears to be influenced by socialization. For example, parents who point out the effects of their children's behavior on others' feelings when they discipline them have children who show more empathy than children of parents who do not provide this information (Hoffman, 1988). The way that parents help their children deal with their own emotions also appears to affect children's empathic responding. For example, when parents help their children take action in response to anxiety or sadness, try to understand their children's emotions, or explain their own emotions, the children then tend to show more sympathy toward others' distress than do children of parents who do not engage in these practices (Denham & Grout, 1992; Eisenberg et al., 1991, 1993). These practices may also help children learn about ways to respond to distress as they talk with their parents about negative reactions to situations.

These practices may also help children learn to regulate their own emotions, which keeps them from becoming so upset at another's distress that they cannot respond sympathetically (Eisenberg & Fabes, 1998). Children who become overly aroused in the face of another's distress cannot offer support because they are too involved in calming themselves. Some children who show empathy toward others may themselves tend to be aroused too much.

Understanding Other People's Intentions

"Mom, Kelly broke the lid of my treasure box! It's all cracked, and I'm going to break something of hers and see how she likes it!" shouted Sara.

"I didn't break your treasure box. I haven't even seen your treasure box!" Kelly shouted.

"Well, I slept over at Kenika's last night! And when I went into my room this morning, I found it all crushed under my papers. If you didn't do it, who did?"

"Well, maybe I did."

"Then why didn't you tell me?"

"Well, I thought it was only crackers I had stepped on, and, yes, I should have told you about that. But I forgot."

"Mom!!!! It was on my table and she stepped on it! Tell her she's gotta buy me a new one and that she can't sleep in my room ever again!"

Earlier, when Sara emptied her school bag to make room for items for the sleep-over, she tossed some papers on the table in her room, covering the treasure box. Kelly slept in her sister's fancy canopy bed while Sara was gone. When she stepped up on the tabletop to reach a stuffed animal on top of her sister's bookshelf, Sara's treasure box was crushed.

think about it Adults are usually slower than children to jump to conclusions about what has happened in a situation that involves damage. Why are they more thoughtful and forgiving? Is it that adults understand better that unfortunate events, such as breaking something or hurting someone, can occur under a variety of circumstances? Do they also base their responses more on the intentions of the person responsible for the event—on whether it was deliberate or accidental—rather than focus merely on the damage that has been done? It seems that they do.

Young children have difficulty discriminating between the concept of "deliberate" and "accidental." Most adults judge intentions by people's facial expressions and verbalizations. An angry expression accompanied by a sarcastic statement leads most adults to conclude that the speaker's intentions are hostile. A surprised or sad expression accompanied by the statement, "I'm sorry—I was only trying to help," leads most adults to assume a prosocial intention.

Of course, in the case involving the treasure box, Sara had not witnessed the damage. She discovered, after the fact, that the lid was broken. In these situations, the likelihood that something happened accidentally rather than on purpose must be brought into play in the person's thoughts. Given the unlikely scenario that Kelly had stepped on the table, Sara jumped to the somewhat reasonable conclusion that someone—probably her sister—had broken the treasure box on purpose. Only later did Sara learn that Kelly had not realized she had stepped on her sister's treasure box.

In unobserved cases of damage it surely is experience like Sara's and Kelly's that helps children gradually develop a more circumspect approach to these situations. They learn to say to themselves, "If Kelly did it, which she probably did, I'm going to really be mad. Let me find out what I can about how this happened before I jump to conclusions."

Children younger than age 6 or 7 are not very skillful at detecting intentions in situations where they see that damage occurs. In one study, kindergarteners and second and fourth graders were shown videotaped vignettes of a child destroying an object (Dodge et al., 1984). The vignettes showed intentions ranging from hostile to accidental to innocent bystander. The researchers clearly showed that the younger the children, the harder it was for them to identify and distinguish intentions. But children actually vary quite a lot in their ability to judge the intentions of others. Some children routinely see hostile intent where others do not. For example, children who are very aggressive themselves often interpret the intentions of others as hostile in situations where nonaggressive children do not infer hostile intent (Crick & Dodge, 1996; Dodge et al., 1995). It is as if they have learned from their own experience of having been treated harshly by their parents or others to expect that everyone's goal is to harm them (Coie & Dodge, 1998).

Young children have a hard time understanding intention when someone deliberately tries to mislead them. They are virtually defenseless, for example, against the claims of television advertising, as well as actions employed by people who attempt to lure young children into danger. The young child cannot imagine that someone would behave one way in order to make them believe something, when that person's intention is something else entirely. Training films to prepare children to deal with strangers often show scenarios in which a child actor is deceived by the stranger.

Even sixth-graders—10-year-olds—lack skill in taking intentions into account when judging the information given about products in television commercials (Ross et al., 1981). They take the information at face value without allowing for the fact that the advertiser may be trying to mislead them in order to sell the product. Detecting deception is very difficult, even for 11- and 12-year-olds.

Although children younger than 5 or 6 years of age have trouble inferring intentions in situations involving damage, and children as old as 10 or 12 years of age have trouble detecting another's true intentions when the person deliberately tries to mislead them, children younger than 5 years of age do understand somewhat that people have intentions, and that these can differ. This understanding was demonstrated in one investigation of preschoolers' ability to distinguish between lying and giving false information by mistake (Siegal & Peterson, 1998). In one condition in the study (giving false information but not knowing that it is false), the children saw a stuffed bear prepare a snack for a friend and then turn away just as a cockroach crawled over it. Later, when the friend asked the bear if the snack was okay to eat, the bear said, "Yes." Although this was not true, the bear did not know that he had given false information. In the second condition (lying), despite having seen the cockroach crawl over the snack, the bear still told his friend that the snack was okay to eat.

Children in both conditions were told that a person named Laura had seen what the bear had seen and had heard what the bear had said. They were shown two different pictures of Laura, one in which her facial expression indicted disgust or upset, and one in which her facial expression was calm and neutral, as if nothing were amiss. Children were told that Laura felt the same way that they felt about whether the bear had lied or simply been mistaken about what he had told his friend. Children pointed to the picture of Laura that showed how they felt. Even the 3-year-olds judged accurately that the bear had lied when the bear knew about the cockroach and had simply been mistaken when the bear had not seen the cockroach crawl on the snack.

Although this study indicates that an awareness of intentions is present in preschool children, the experimental situation was much easier than what children encounter in real life with their peers. In the study, children observed what the bear knew and what the bear did. In real situations, children must infer intentions to a much greater degree, sometimes under conditions where someone is masking an actual intention in order to deceive them. Often, children (and adults) do not know what other people actually know, and this, too, makes it difficult to judge their intentions.

Understanding Other People's Thinking

A third aspect of social role-taking ability, besides understanding other people's emotions and intentions, is understanding what they know or what they think. Recall the example of the fourth-graders we met at the beginning of the chapter. They were able to generate several different ruses for getting Mrs. Townsend out of the classroom. Then they evaluated each one from *her* point of view, taking into account what she knew.

Children's ability to consider what someone else knows and to think about what someone else might be thinking has been studied in a variety of ways. Some researchers have asked children to play strategy games because these require children to think about other people's thinking. (For a discussion of how children change their strategy as they get older, see the Research Close-Up: Studying Role-Taking Ability with Strategy Games.) Other researchers have asked children to give directions for constructing a design to a second child whose view of the design is blocked (Krauss & Glucksberg, 1969). Still other researchers have presented dilemmas to children and have asked them to think about other people's thinking. A classic study using

---

RESEARCH

CLOSE-UP   *Studying Role-Taking Ability with Strategy Games*

Playing a strategy game with a 5-year-old is an interesting experience. Children this age enjoy the *form* of the game, and they want to try it because they see how it amuses other people. But the content eludes them. They simply cannot think about what someone is thinking that they might be thinking.

To study the development of role-taking ability, Rheta DeVries (1970) asked children of different ages to guess in which hand an adult had concealed a penny. She also gave the children turns concealing the penny from the adult. Skilled players of this game base their guessing and concealing on what they think the other player will think they are thinking. "She hid it in the right hand the last time," a player might think. "She probably thinks I'll choose the left hand this time. But I will choose the right hand again, instead." This sophisticated kind of thinking is rare in children younger than age 6 or 7.

DeVries distinguished five levels of role-taking strategies used by children in this game. In the first two levels (under 4 years), children behave as if they do not even understand that the game involves uncertainty and concealment. They search for the penny in the same hand every time. When they hide the penny, they may extend the hand concealing the penny, or they tell the adult, "Pick this one." They do not seem to understand that the game involves two roles, the concealer and the guesser.

In the third level (ages 4 and 5), children realize that the game is competitive—that there are two players, each trying to outsmart the other. When they hide the penny,

they are delighted when the guesser picks the wrong hand. But apparently they do not realize that the guesser is thinking about their strategy because children hide the penny in a *predictable* pattern, first in one hand, then in the other. Children assume that the adult is also using this strategy when hiding the penny. Thus, they guess alternating hands.

By 5 or 6 years of age, children begin to use an unpredictable pattern when hiding the penny. They are clearly thinking about what their opponents are thinking, and they are trying to outwit them. But when they guess, they revert to the predictable, alternating strategy. Apparently, they do not realize that the other player can think about *their* thinking in the same way that they can think about the other player's.

Finally, around 6 or 7 years of age, children use an unpredictable strategy for both hiding and guessing. They are thinking about their opponent's thinking, and they know their opponent is thinking about their thinking. Therefore, in considering where to guess the penny's place, a child thinks, "He's probably thinking I will think that he's going to hide it in that hand. But because he's probably thinking that, I will try to outsmart him and guess the other hand." And when hiding, the child thinks, "He probably thinks I'll hide it in this hand, because he thinks I will be thinking that he will expect me not to switch hands from the last time. But because that's what he's probably thinking that I'm thinking, I'm going to do something different."

dilemmas was conducted by Selman (1976). The dilemma involved Holly, who had climbed a tree to rescue a kitten:

> Holly is an 8-year-old girl who likes to climb trees. She is the best tree climber in the neighborhood. One day while climbing down from a tall tree, she falls off the bottom branch but does not hurt herself. Her father sees her fall. He is upset and asks her to promise not to climb trees any more. Holly promises. Later that day, Holly and her friends meet Shawn. Shawn's kitten is caught up in a tree and can't get down. Something has to be done right away, or the kitten may fall. Holly is the only one who climbs trees well enough to reach the kitten and get down, but she remembers her promise to her father.

After hearing the dilemma, children are asked, "What does Holly think her father will do if he finds out she climbed the tree?" Selman and his colleagues concluded that children's thinking about other people's thinking evolves through a number of levels, the most rudimentary of which does not include an understanding of two points of view: "Holly likes kittens; Holly's father will be happy because he likes kittens too." When children understand that there are two points of view, they seem to think that the differences are due to differences in information. A child whose thinking is at this level would in essence say, "Holly's father wouldn't object or be upset with Holly, if he knew the circumstances under which Holly climbed the tree."

Somewhat later, children realize that differences in views are not a simple matter of different information. People can have the same information—know the same details—and still have different views or judgments about the course of action one should take. In Selman's research, children's thinking with respect to dilemmas continued to evolve up to about age 14. The oldest and most sophisticated thinkers were able to think about an individual's thinking in terms of that person's membership in a particular social group. They also knew that one would need to know the particular individual to know exactly how the person would react.

In addition to general developmental changes in children's ability to think about what others are thinking, children's specific knowledge about what another person thinks helps them get inside the person's mind (Dunn, 1994). We saw the effect of specific knowledge about what a person knows when the fourth-graders were trying to plan the surprise for Mrs. Townsend. For example, when Amy suggested that they get Mr. Steinberg, the principal, to call her on the intercom to come get a message, Paul said, "No, that won't work. She always sends one of us to the office to get messages." And when David suggested that someone fake getting hurt and that they get the nurse to have Mrs. Townsend come down to decide if the kid could return to class, Gina said, "That doesn't make any sense. The nurse always decides if you can come back to the classroom."

Researchers do not know much about how learning to think about others' thinking is influenced by experience with people whom children know very well. They also have not probed very much how children's knowledge about people from different cultures affects their ability to get inside the mind of another and to think about what that person might be thinking. When children are unfamiliar with a person's knowledge and beliefs, it is unlikely that their ability to understand that person's thoughts will be as effective as it is when they know of a person's knowledge and beliefs (Flavell & Miller, 1998).

Social Role-Taking and Social Behavior

We might expect children's social behavior to improve as they develop higher levels of social role-taking ability. After all, children become capable of more sophisticated interpretations of other people's behavior, and they become more aware of appropriate responses. But even though some studies have shown a positive correlation between social role-taking ability and social behavior (Buckley et al., 1979), others have not (Eisenberg-Berg, 1979; Strayer, 1980).

There is no reason to believe that a child's ability to understand emotions, detect intentions, and think about what another person is thinking would lead inevitably to good social behavior. The ability to see the world through another's eyes *might* lead a child to act on the other's behalf, "but this ability may also be used to one's own advantage at another's expense" (Smith et al., 1983, p. 121). Whether children actually become more prosocial as their social understanding increases depends on children's ideas of what "a good person" would do, and their motivation to live up to those standards. How children actually behave in social situations depends, for example, on whether they have developed a conscience and whether they have learned

TABLE 15.1
Kohlberg's stages of moral development

	Content of Stage		
Level and Stage	*What Is Right?*	*Reasons for Doing Right*	*Social Perspective of Stage*
Level I: Preconventional Stage I—Heteronomous morality	To avoid breaking rules backed by punishment, obedience for its own sake, and avoiding physical damage to persons and property.	Avoidance of punishment, and the superior power of authorities.	*Egocentric point of view.* Doesn't consider the interests of others or recognize that they differ from the actor's; doesn't relate two points of view. Actions are considered physically rather than in terms of psychological interests of others. Confusion of authority's perspective with one's own.
Stage 2—Individualism, instrumental purpose, and exchange	Following rules only when it is to someone's immediate interest; acting to meet one's own interests and needs and letting others do the same. Right is also what's fair, what's an equal exchange, a deal, an agreement.	To serve one's own needs or interests in a world in which you have to recognize that other people have their interests, too.	*Concrete individualistic perspective.* Aware that everybody has his own interest to pursue and these conflict, so that right is relative (in the concrete individualistic sense).
Level II: Conventional Stage 3—Mutual interpersonal expectations, relationships, and interpersonal conformity	Living up to what is expected by people close to you or what people generally expect of people in your role as son, brother, friend, etc. "Being good" is important and means having good motives, showing concern about others. It also means keeping mutual relationships, such as trust, loyalty, respect, and gratitude.	The need to be a good person in your own eyes and those of others. Your caring for others. Belief in the Golden Rule. Desire to maintain rules and authority that support stereotypical good behavior.	*Perspective of the individual in relationship with other individuals.* Aware of shared feelings, agreements, and expectations which take primacy over individual interests. Relates points of view through the concrete Golden Rule, putting yourself in the other guy's shoes. Does not yet consider generalized system perspective.
Stage 4—Social system and conscience	Fulfilling the actual duties to which you have agreed. Laws are to be upheld except in extreme cases when they conflict with other fixed social duties. Right is also contributing to society, the group, or institution.	To keep the institution going as a whole, to avoid the breakdown in the system "if everyone did it," or the imperative of conscience to meet one's defined obligations. (Easily confused with Stage 3 belief in rules and authority.)	*Differentiates societal point of view from interpersonal agreement or motive.* Takes the point of view of the system that defines roles and rules. Considers individual relations in terms of place in the system.

a measure of **self-control**—the ability to deny immediate pleasure for their own or another person's long-term good.

Moral Reasoning

Many people have been interested in moral reasoning as a way of understanding children's behavior. Lawrence Kohlberg's work can be placed within this tradition. His stages of moral reasoning are provided in Table 15.1. In Kohlberg's research, the child is always presented with a moral dilemma, a situation in which hard choices are to be made. Some dilemmas place an action that children have been taught explicitly is wrong in conflict with the legitimate needs of a worthy individual, caught in

	Content of Stage		
Level and Stage	What Is Right?	Reasons for Doing Right	Social Perspective of Stage
Level III: Postconventional, or principled Stage 5—Social contract or utility and individual rights	Being aware that people hold a variety of values and opinions, and that most values and rules are relative to your group. These relative rules should usually be upheld, however, in the interest of impartiality and because they are the social contract. Some nonrelative values and rights such as life and liberty, however, must be upheld in any society and regardless of majority opinion.	A sense of obligation to law because of one's social contract to make and abide by laws for the welfare of all and for the protection of all people's rights. A feeling of contractual commitment, freely entered upon, to family, friendship, trust, and work obligations. Concern that laws and duties be based on rational calculation of overall utility, "the greatest good for the greatest number."	*Prior-to-society perspective.* Perspective of a rational individual aware of values and rights prior to social attachments and contracts. Integrates perspectives by formal mechanisms of agreement, contract, objective impartiality, and due process. Considers moral and legal points of view, recognizes that they sometimes conflict and finds it difficult to integrate them.
Stage 6—Universal ethical principles	Following self-chosen ethical principles. Particular laws or social agreements are usually valid because they rest on such principles. When laws violate these principles, one acts in accordance with the principle. Principles are universal principles of justice: the equality of human rights and respect for the dignity of human beings as individual persons.	The belief as a rational person in the validity of universal moral principles, and a sense of personal commitment to them.	*Perspective of a moral point of view from which social arrangements derive.* Perspective is that of any rational individual recognizing the nature of morality or the fact that persons are ends in themselves and must be treated as such.

Source: "Moral Stages and Moralization," by L. Kohlberg, 1976. In T. Lickona (Ed.), *Moral Development and Behavior: Theory, Research, and Social Issues* (pp. 34–35), New York: Holt, Rinehart & Winston. Reprinted with permission.

unusual circumstances. One dilemma involves a sick woman who needs medicine that can be obtained, according to the story presented, only at a high price from a greedy druggist. Should the man steal it? Another dilemma involves a boy whose father breaks a promise to him. Should the boy disobey his father? Kohlberg was interested in whether the child focused on "higher" moral principles in responding to these dilemmas or was more concerned about the consequences (i.e., punishment or social acceptance) involved in acting one way versus another (Kohlberg, 1969). Kohlberg found that as children get older, they tend to think differently about these dilemmas, more often explaining what should be done in terms of principles rather than in terms of specific social consequences.

The labels for the different levels indicate the extent to which this framework stresses individual judgment—conscious decision-making based on principles—rather than doing specifically what has been learned—following in a straightforward and literal way specific teachings about what is right and wrong. Laws are based on principles. Individual laws, or implementation of them, can conflict with principles, according to Kohlberg. The person with higher moral reasoning ability understands this.

But when a moral dilemma exists—a situation in which choices relating to morality have to be made—factors other than simple moral reasoning must come into play if a person is to perform a particular moral act. This is especially true when the "immoral" choice is a selfish one, bringing personal pleasure or gain. An important factor that helps children make moral choices is self-control (Bandura, 1991).

Self-control, has to do with children's inner feelings of satisfaction and self-respect when they act morally, and of dissatisfaction and guilt when they do not. Children who are high in self-control are more likely to behave consistently with the dictates of their moral reasoning. One theorist suggests that for these children, moral principles have been linked to strong feelings of empathy for others and have become "hot cognitions" (Hoffman, 1991). When a child with this kind of history recognizes a situation as one involving moral principles, she considers alternative actions and their consequences at the same time that she empathizes with any victims in the situation. Morality and empathy are paired because moral principles inherently involve fairness, caring for others, and concern for the general welfare. Repeated pairing of the two leads the child to show fervent feelings in relation to the moral principles themselves. Children prone to strong feelings of empathy can thus be expected to behave most consistently with moral principles. For them, empathy and morality work together to support self-control, which in turn leads to feelings of satisfaction and self-respect.

In addition to variations in self-control, there are also variations in perceptions of whether a situation is one in which moral principles apply. A number of processes can lead children to believe that self-control need not be activated in particular situations (Bandura, 1991). For example, a child may believe an act of violence is necessary to defend herself or her society (using reasoning like that of Kohlberg's Stage 4), when in fact violence is not necessary. Another process involves transforming a deplorable act into an acceptable one by comparing it to other deplorable acts that adults failed to punish. Not understanding consequences and blaming the victim are other processes that undercut the expectation that moral reasoning or moral controls should apply. And, of course, not seeing oneself as a responsible, causal agent—believing that one is "just carrying out orders" and has no choice but to obey—has repeatedly provided the rationale for reprehensible acts by gangs both large and small.

Although lower levels of moral reasoning are roughly associated with higher levels of some kinds of antisocial behavior, such as juvenile delinquency (Nelson et al., 1990), even adults with advanced levels of moral reasoning fail sometimes to do what they think is right. When adults fail, they often feel guilty and experience a conflict between what they have done and what they think of themselves. When a person's morality-related actions elicit the strongest emotions and the deepest anxieties, being moral is central to the person's identity (Blasi, 1984; Davidson & Youniss, 1991). We discuss this topic further in chapter 19, along with considerations of what parents can do to encourage children and teenagers to apply moral controls.

Social Skills and Sociometric Status

Another area of social development that has received considerable attention from researchers involves social behavior with peers, especially in settings such as the elementary school classroom. Middle childhood is a time of friendships and wide-ranging peer interactions that offer opportunities for affection, learning, and just plain fun. How children actually behave in social situations is influenced by a host of factors, such as their developing awareness and understanding of others, their motivations and values, their temperamental predispositions, how they have been socialized by their parents, and many others. By the time children are in elementary school, they usually have a typical way of behaving socially that characterizes how they act with their peers.

But some children's peer interactions during the school years are not positive. Rather than being accepted by other children, they are rejected by their peers. This situation should not be taken lightly because being rejected by peers in childhood is associated with poor achievement in school (DeBaryshe et al., 1993; Wentzel, 1993; Wentzel & Asher, 1995), difficulties in relating to teachers (Birch & Ladd, 1998), a higher probability of dropping out of school (Ladd, 1990), juvenile delinquency, and bad-conduct discharges from the military (Kupersmidt et al., 1990). Of course, these correlational data do not prove that lack of early positive peer relationships *causes* poor achievement or other negative outcomes. In fact, a whole host of factors probably causes both poor peer relationships and some of the negative outcomes associated with them. For example, some children may be more biologically disposed than others to difficulties due to attention deficit disorders, language problems, and so on. These initial vulnerabilities may then be magnified in the home or at school, when adults manage the child poorly (Coie & Dodge, 1998).

But even though the pathways leading to long-term antisocial behavior are likely to be complex, experiences with peers are known to provide an important source of information to children, and there is no question that interactions with peers provide considerable opportunities for practice in relating to others. If a child's peer relationships are problematic, this problem surely contributes to the child's difficulties.

Children's social status among their peers is determined in a variety of ways. For example, teachers can be asked which children are liked by their peers, and which are actively disliked; or researchers can observe children's behavior directly. A common way to determine the social status of children in a classroom, for example, is to ask children themselves to nominate peers who they think represent the best instances of certain behaviors. For example, children might be asked who is friendly, who is co-operative, who is shy, and who is most likely to start fights or disobey classroom rules (Coie et al., 1990). Or they might be asked whom they would like most and least to be their friend (Hinshaw et al., 1997). In yet another approach, children are asked to indicate whom they like a lot, whom they dislike, with whom they spend a lot of time and with whom they spend little time. From information gathered in these ways, researchers can construct a sociogram like the one shown in Figure 15.1.

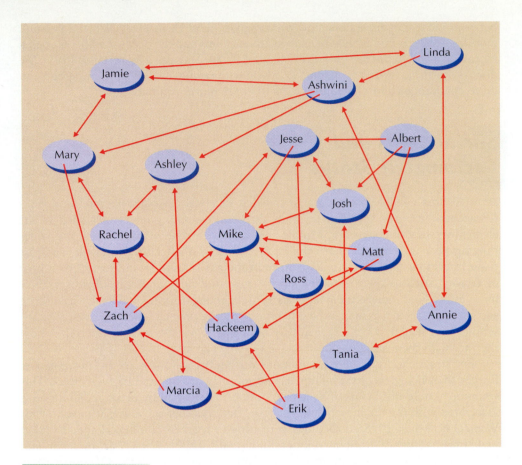

FIGURE 15.1

Example of a sociogram. A sociogram like this one can be constructed from children's responses to questions about which classmates they like the best or want to sit near.

Social status categories include the following: (1) popular, (2) rejected, (3) neglected, (4) controversial, and (5) average (Harrist et al., 1997). **Popular status** is held by children who are nominated often by peers as someone they like or would like to have as friends. **Rejected status** is held by children who receive a lot of nominations for being disliked. **Neglected status** is held by children who receive very few nominations. **Controversial-status** children receive several nominations with equal numbers of liked and disliked nominations (Asher & Dodge, 1986). **Average-status** children are simply those whose scores do not qualify them for any of the other four categories (Harrist et al., 1997).

Social Behavior Associated with Social Status Categories

Specific social behaviors are associated with membership in each of the social status categories. Although the behaviors associated with each category change somewhat with age, there is also a great deal of stability across ages. We will discuss next the typical behavior that is associated with the four major social status categories.

Behaviors Correlated with Popular Status   Children who are popular with their peers are helpful and friendly, and they obey rules (Coie et al., 1990). They will respond aggressively in order to protect themselves, if provoked sufficiently, but they do not engage in unprovoked aggression (Lesser, 1959). When seeking to enter an ongoing play group, popular children might at first engage in parallel play, perhaps as a way to signal the group that they have no intention of changing what the other players are doing. Then, they join in without disrupting the play. Popular children seem to know how to figure out the "frame of reference" of the group they want to enter, and they fit their behavior into that (Putallaz & Wasserman, 1990). If wishing to criticize how a game is played, for example, they do not simply tell others they cannot or should not proceed as they are proceeding. They give reasons and offer ideas for alternative ways to proceed.

Popular children also are competent in processing social information. **Social information-processing** involves encoding, interpreting, generating responses to, and deciding how to respond to social events. Researchers often use videotaped vignettes to assess children's social information-processing ability (Harrist et al., 1997). The child hears and sees a story involving a group-entry dilemma, a situation in which a child is rebuffed by peers, or a situation in which one child is bothered in some way by another child. The experimenter then asks the child to respond to the story by telling what is going on, generating ideas for what the child depicted in the story might do, and what the child would do in similar circumstances. Popular children tend to encode situations fully (they notice all of the relevant details), attribute hostile intentions to children depicted in the stories only when it is quite clear that hostile intentions exist, come up with several ideas for what a child in the situation might do, and make reasonable decisions about what a child should do (Harrist et al., 1997).

Behaviors Correlated with Rejected Status   Many children who are rejected by their peers tend to be aggressive (without provocation), disruptive, and noncompliant (Hinshaw et al., 1997). They are not cooperative, they become angry very easily, they are often inattentive, and they also tend to start fights (Coie et al., 1990; Pope & Bierman, 1999). When entering an ongoing group, rejected children tend to be disruptive and also make statements about themselves (Putallaz & Wasserman, 1990). If unhappy about the ongoing play, they tend to tell others what they cannot or should not do, but they do not offer explanations or provide new ideas for how the players could proceed differently.

There is, however, a subgroup of rejected children who are nonaggressive. These children are instead socially withdrawn (Rubin et al., 1990). They are more aware of their social status than are aggressive-rejected children. Aggressive-rejected children estimate that other children like them more than they actually do, whereas nonaggressive-rejected children have a more realistic picture of others' dislike of them (Zakriski & Coie, 1996).

Researchers have found a number of subtypes within this withdrawn group (Harrist et al., 1997). In one study, children who were withdrawn due to shyness or to anxiety about interacting were not rejected by their peers, at least not in the early grades of school. Children who were sad, depressed, and withdrawn, on the other hand, tended to be rejected by their peers in kindergarten and also neglected in later school years. These sad and depresssed children were judged by their teachers to be immature, and perhaps these immaturity demands extended to peers as well, making them feel burdened. Peers might have rejected these children for this reason. Withdrawn anxious and shy children, on the other hand, were not judged by their

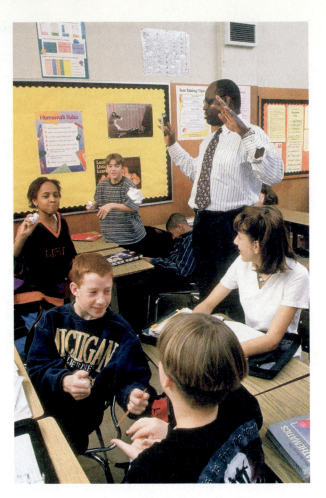

Children who disrupt work or who are aggressive in playing with peers tend to earn a rejected status when their peers complete a sociometric question-naire. The boy in this photo may be involved in a momentary and harmless act of glee. But if he disen-gages frequently from the work of the group, or refuses to cooperate in the fair give-and-take usu-ally required to complete work together, he will not be well-liked by his peers. (*Source:* © Will Hart)

teachers to be immature, and they were not rejected by their peers, at least not during the early grades.

Behaviors Correlated with Neglected Status Neglected children are not aggressive, but they lack some of the friendly, outgoing characteristics of popular children. They may be sad or depressed (Harrist et al., 1997) or quite anxious and shy. Being withdrawn due to anxiety and shyness has not been associated with the neglected sociometric status in kindergarten, but it has been correlated with problematic status in later grades (Bukowski, 1990; Harrist et al., 1997). Perhaps as children get older and participate more in competitive groups (sports, class projects), a shy, anxious, withdrawn child becomes a burden and is therefore neglected or even rejected by peers. When children are younger and have less awareness of or concern about performance, it might not bother them to be in the company of a shy or anxious child.

Neglected children also tend to have more learning difficulties and behavior problems, such as obsessive-compulsive disorders (Coie et al., 1990; Hatzichristou & Hopf, 1996). In terms of group-entry strategies, they tend to hover and watch for a long time, without making additional moves (Putallaz & Wasserman, 1990). Because of their relatively passive behavior and their tendency to remain isolated and withdrawn, they may go unnoticed by the other children. It is not that other children dislike them at first; it is more the case that they are not well known by other children in the class.

Behaviors Correlated with Controversial Status These children have some of the characteristics that rejected children have—they can be aggressive, disruptive, and noncompliant—but they differ from them in having some strengths that rejected children lack. Specifically, controversial children exhibit more leadership qualities than do rejected children, and they may excel in something, such as sports (Coie et al., 1990). Controversial children do not tend to be socially withdrawn (Harrist et al., 1997). Yet, peers often think they are snobbish or arrogant (Hatzichristou & Hopf, 1996).

Stability of Social Status during Childhood

There is some stability in social status throughout childhood, but considerable change as well, except for children with a rejected status (Harrist et al., 1997; Ladd & Burgess, 1999; Pope & Bierman, 1999). Although changes tend not to be dramatic— few popular children later are rejected, for example—they do occur, especially among children who are categorized as neglected. Perhaps this is not surprising, because these children do not have troublesome behavior that is obnoxious to other children. They simply are more withdrawn and shy than popular children. If circumstances change, a neglected child's status could change dramatically from one year to the next. For example, a neglected child in a classroom in which the teacher does not take steps to actively involve everyone might change if he then moves to a class in which the teacher takes special care to mix groups of children for instruction and to employ methods in small-group work that encourage all children to participate. Rejected status is more difficult to change because children in this category are considered obnoxious by their classmates.

In one study of social status stability, children between 9 and 11 years of age (fourth- and fifth-graders) sociometric status data were obtained at four times over a period of two years, in October and April of the year the children were in fourth grade, and in October and April of the year they were in fifth grade (Ollendick et al., 1991). Stability was extremely low in the neglected group, with only 11 percent of the children remaining in the neglected category from Time 1 to Time 4. Rejected status, on the other hand, was quite stable, with over half of the children remaining in this category from Time 1 to Time 4. Popular status was also quite stable, although less so than rejected status. Slightly more than one-third of the children who were popular at Time 1 were also rated as popular at Time 4. These results are consistent with those of another study in which children were studied for four years, from kindergarten through third grade (Harrist et al., 1997). Most children who were initially identified as being rejected by peers in kindergarten maintained this status through third grade.

Of course, even children who earn rejected status can change. Researchers have wondered which of these children change. They have found that aggressive behavior is stable when the social environment reinforces the child's initial aggressive cognitions (Egan et al., 1998). For example, when children are successful in carrying out aggressive acts and receive rewards for their aggressive behavior (i.e., got what they wanted through the use of aggressive means), their initially aggressive behavior is more stable than when a child discovers that aggression does not work.

In a second study (Sandstrom & Coie, 1999), the child's involvement in extracurricular activities and whether the child had a mother who monitored the child's peer experience and was aware of difficulties predicted less stability in the rejected status over time (better outcome) than did lack of involvement in extracurricular activities and having a mother who did not care whether or not her child had positive peer relationships. Within the group of children whose mothers reported to the researchers that they did not place much value on peer relationships, only 7 percent of the children improved in social status. Within the group of children whose mothers reported that peer relationships were important, the social status of 17 percent of the children improved. (See Research Close-Up: Does Early Antisocial Behavior Fade Away? for more discussion about the characteristics and backgrounds of antisocial children and what adults might do to help them.)

RESEARCH

CLOSE-UP *Does Early Antisocial Behavior Fade Away?*

Do children who are disruptive, aggressive, or destructive gradually become as cooperative and productive as their classmates? Unfortunately, the answer is no.

Stability of Antisocial Behavior and Rejected Social Status

Antisocial behavior is very stable over time (Harrist et al., 1997; Howes, 1990; Ladd & Burgess, 1999; Ollendick et al., 1991). It has also been firmly established that generally poor outcomes occur for children who are highly aggressive and rejected. These children tend to achieve poorly in school, engage in acts of juvenile delinquency, commit criminal acts as adults, and experience high levels of marital instability (Caspi et al., 1987; Douglas & Olshaker, 1995; Farrington & West, 1971; Loeber, 1982; Loeber et al., 1989; Roff, 1961; Venezia, 1971). The dynamics of the stability of antisocial behavior are very complex, but researchers have some ideas about how and why this kind of behavior tends to be maintained.

Processes Involved in the Maintenance of Antisocial Behavior

First of all, children, who exhibit these behaviors get off to a bad start in their interactions with other children, who reject and exclude them. Being left out then deprives them of the experience and practice they need to develop the social skills they lack (Dodge et al., 1984; Krantz, 1982; Lieberman, 1977). Thus, early antisocial behavior can set in motion maladaptive social interactions that continue to snowball.

Over time, rejected children may be grouped for instruction with other children who are disruptive, since achievement tends to be low in children who exhibit behavior problems and instructional groups often are based on similarity in achievement levels. These classroom-based groups continue to expose rejected children to problem behaviors, and also isolate them from opportunities to learn subject matter from interactions with higher-achieving peers. It may not, of course, be beneficial to other children to be grouped with children who are disruptive because their achievement may suffer if teachers must spend an inordinate amount of time dealing with disruptive students. But it is also the case that homogeneous grouping based on achievement often isolates children with social problems from children who behave better, thus leaving them with models that maintain their antisocial behavior, or make it worse.

The stability of the rejected status could be due in part to the fact that rejected children tend to have as friends only other children who are rejected. Studies with early elementary grade children have found this largely to be the case (Howes, 1990). Having friends who exhibit problem behav-

ior continually exposes rejected children to deviant behavior. It also exposes them continually to talk about deviant behavior, because considerable talk among friends who display deviant behavior is about deviant behavior (Dishion et al., 1995). As children get older, they spend time in tight-knit social cliques consisting of peers who are very much alike (Sandstrom & Coie, 1999).

The address given by the president of the Society for Research in Child Development at the 1995 biannual meeting in Indianapolis included excerpts from a newspaper article about a 14-year-old boy who, with his best friend, murdered his mother (Hartup, 1996). According to Hartup, the boy had a long history of problem behavior and had been in trouble a number of times, prior to the murder. He had experienced difficulties with peers at school and was described as being disliked. He was often the victim of peer assaults and verbal jeers. He had difficulty learning; physically, he was small. His best friend also had problems, which is probably why they ended up together. The outcome was tragic, but not altogether unpredictable, given the two boys' histories.

Other researchers have also found a relationship between victimization and later highly aggressive acts. Egan and colleagues (1998) found that initially aggressive children who are not able to inflict aggressive behavior on others often became victims of aggression themselves. If these children's initially aggressive way of thinking about interactions does not change, they can become "provocative victims" (Olweus, 1978; Perry et al., 1988). This descriptive label implies that these children continue to incite conflict among their peers and may fall victim to such conflicts, although they are not successful in carrying out aggressive acts themselves. It seems that victimization by peers can keep an initially aggressive child's aggressive acts in check, but often it does not change the way the child thinks or feels about the world. Egan and colleagues have said (1998) that these children "are prone to behave aggressively when situational constraints are relaxed, such as when one is confronted with an opportunity to aggress covertly or is frustrated by a weaker, younger, defenseless person (including, in later years, a defenseless child or spouse)" (p. 1003). These researchers say, "Such children may also be likely to resort to weapons (e.g., guns) to assist them in carrying out aggressive actions" (p. 1003).

This reminds us of the two boys who shot fellow students and teachers at Columbine High School in Colorado in the spring of 1999. From all reports, Dylan and Eric were highly aggressive and were victimized by their peers. They expressed aggression in papers, and they were drawn to aggressive groups on the Internet. Powerless day to day in the face of more powerful peers in their school, these boys armed themselves to increase their power and ensure that their aggressive acts would be successful. Changing emotions appears to be important in changing aggressive behavior (Lemerise & Arsenio, 2000).

Strategies for Changing Antisocial Behavior in Children

The two examples of aggressive behavior involving murder illustrate that it is not enough to curtail aggressive acts. Rather than restrain aggressive behavior while allowing aggressive feelings and ways of thinking to remain intact, adults must find ways to change the cognitions and skills of aggressive children. Allowing other children to keep an aggressive peer's behavior in check only fuels the aggressive child's anger and aggressive views of the world. Although teachers must not allow the aggressive child to make others their victims, they must keep peer responses in check so that initially aggressive but weak children do not become victims themselves. Teachers must make sure that aggressive behavior is not rewarded (Perry et al., 1990) if they expect it to be curtailed and if they expect other children not to retaliate.

Some teaching strategies are more effective than others in engaging difficult students in classroom activities. Successful teachers stay actively involved with children. Such "involved" teachers show appreciation and enjoyment of students, are dependable when students are in need, are understanding, and have knowledge of individual students. They also expend high levels of time and energy on teaching. Teachers who are most effective in keeping children engaged in classroom activities also know how to balance rules, expectations, and routines with appropriate student autonomy—giving choices based on interests (Skinner & Belmont, 1993).

It takes tremendous physical and emotional energy to deal with antisocial children. Teachers need to be able to talk to someone knowledgeable about the situation, and they often need direct help both in the classroom and outside of it. For example, extra help from an aide or other school personnel can enable a teacher to work with children in small groups. This sometimes works better than large groups to keep children engaged, and this in turn can keep behavior problems under control. Small-group instruction is also needed, in many cases, to provide the individualized instruction that some children need. Guidance counselors can sometimes work with difficult children in small groups or individually to coach them in social skills. For example, they can engage them in discussion, role-playing situations, playing a game with another person, brainstorming, and making up endings to unfinished stories. Programs of social skills training have been developed by Oden and Asher (1977) and others (Bierman et al., 1987; Hudley & Graham, 1993; Mize & Ladd, 1990).

Some people think that the school years are too late for intervention with aggressive students and that something should be done early earlier. The first line of defense against the development of severe antisocial tendencies is support for a good attachment between infant and parent. For children who miss out on this earliest of prevention strategies in the home, a good nursery school experience can make a difference. John Douglas, who profiles serial murderers—admittedly a category of extreme antisocial individuals—for the FBI has said that Project Head Start is "one of the most effective, long-term, anticrime programs in history." He thinks there is a need for an "army of social workers" to help women who are battered or homeless and to find good foster homes for children who are caught in intolerable home situations. According to Douglas's studies, these environments spawn the deviant behavior that results in extreme violence (Douglas & Olshaker, 1995, p. 357).

Background and Family Factors Associated with Children's Behavior with Peers

The question arises, of course, as to why there is so much variation among children with respect to their interactions with peers. Why are some children helpful and friendly while others are aggressive, uncooperative, and argumentative? Although the answer is not completely straightforward, early experiences in the family seem to set the stage for children's initial interactions with peers. These initial interactions with peers then set the stage for later peer interactions.

Attachment History and Later Peer Behavior   Early attachment history is related to the pattern of behavior seen in children later in childhood. As we saw in chapter 7, early peer interactions are correlated with attachment history. Children with insecure attachment histories tend to have relationships with peers that are problematic; children who have secure attachment histories tend to have peer relationships that are not problematic. Studies conducted over a considerable span of time are quite consistent in showing that secure attachment history is associated with socially competent play behavior in toddlers and young preschoolers, whereas insecure attachment is associated with various problems (Ware & Cross, 1995).

Some correlations between attachment history and later peer relationships come from research on bullies and victims of bullies. **Bullies** are children who are aggressive toward others, either physically or verbally, without apparent provocation. **Victims** are children targeted by bullies to receive a disproportionate share of their bullying behavior. In studies of bullying and victimization among preschoolers, researchers have found that both being a bully and being a victim are related to insecure attachment history.

According to one study (Troy & Sroufe, 1987), victims tended to have ambivalent attachment histories, whereas bullies had either avoidant or ambivalent histories. Other research has also found that the same child can be both bully and victim (Schwartz, 1995), and that children who are both bullies and victims often are the most problematic and rejected children of all (Hess & Atkins, 1995; Hodges et al., 1995).

Victimization is experienced by about 20 percent of children in newly formed groups, such as kindergarten classes. Somewhat less than half of the children who are victims of bullying in kindergarten remain victims of bullying by the spring of the kindergarten year. Apparently, bullies try out their aggression on a number of victims when groups are first formed. But only some of these children remain victims of bullies. The others let the bullies know somehow that they will not tolerate being victimized (Kochenderfer & Ladd, 1996).

Parenting and Children's Peer Interactions

A child's discipline history within the family is also correlated with peer relationships. Children who are more antisocial and rejected by their peers experience poorer family monitoring, poorer discipline (discipline that is harsher, more controlling, more intrusive, and more authoritarian), and more family stress than average children (Austin & Lindauer, 1990; DeBaryshe et al., 1993; Dishion, 1990; Nix et al., 1999; Pettit et al., 1996; Travillion & Snyder, 1993).

Other studies (Mize & Pettit, 1997) have found that maternal synchrony (coordination of responses with a child's actions and intentions) with preschool children is the best predictor of a child's peer competence. Typically, parental warmth has been thought to be the component of good parent-child relationships that helps most in later peer relationships. But in this study, maternal synchrony was a stronger predictor. This makes some sense because synchrony indicates good reading of a partner's cues and a turn-taking style of interaction. Children may learn this style of interaction from their parents and then generalize it to peer interactions. Paying close attention while interacting allows for good reading of social information, and turn-taking supports the sort of reciprocity that leads to acceptance in social situations. Warmth is surely important too, but warmth may not be sufficient to help children develop actual social skill.

Other researchers have looked directly at how parents prepare their children for playing with other children, and how they facilitate their children's play when the children are in the company of peers. In one study of this kind (Russell & Finnie, 1990), the researchers found that mothers of neglected preschoolers provided them with less group-oriented instruction before they actually played with other children, and fewer ideas for how to play with other children when they were actually in a play group, than did mothers of popular children. Mothers of both rejected and neglected children tended to be disruptive themselves by taking control of the play situation. In a second study, children whose mothers coached them in peer interactions were judged by their teachers to be more socially competent than children who did not receive coaching (Mize & Pettit, 1997).

Other studies of correlations between parental behavior and children's behavior in the peer setting provide more information about the important role of positive, active participation by the parent. In one study, parents who were actively involved with their children—parents who played frequently in reciprocal ways—had children who were more popular and less neglected by peers than those whose parents tended to play little with their children (MacDonald, 1987). In a second study (Travillion & Snyder, 1993), mothers who were involved little with their children at home were again found to have children who earned a neglected status in the peer setting. In this study, maternal involvement in the child's play at home accounted for 25 percent of the variance in neglected peer status among 4-year-olds in the classroom setting. In a third study (Frante & Grass, 1996), researchers looked at specific behaviors of mothers while they worked on a task with their child. Mothers of rejected and neglected children gave fewer suggestions, explanations, and praise than did mothers of average children (i.e., children who did not receive a high number of neglected or rejected peer nominations). Positive interactions between parent and child are consistently associated with higher levels of peer competence than are more negative parent-child interactions (Isley et al., 1999; MacKinnon-Lewis et al., 1999).

Sex Differences and Sex-Role Development

Every culture dictates activities, abilities, social positions, expectations for dress and hairstyles, and other characteristics for women and men. These learned characteristics determine the sex roles in each culture (Angrist, 1969; Block, 1973). **Sex roles** are the characteristic ways of behaving that are associated with men and women in a culture. The fulfillment of these different expectations for behavior, across a vast array of human activity, depends on **sex-role development**—on the acquisition of dispositions and behaviors that are consistent with the expectations the culture holds for how girls and boys and men and women will think, feel, and behave.

Sex-role development depends on complex interactions between biology and socialization. Biological differences associated with being born male or female do not account for all the differences we see in the behavior of men and women and in the social positions they hold. Biological differences are only a starting point. Socialization then magnifies differences or diminishes them. The values in a society help to determine which differences are magnified or are given special importance, and which ones become hardly noticeable at all. For example, in places where there is a subsistence-level economy—where the daily activities of almost all adults are related to acquiring the basic necessities of life, such as food—there is a marked difference in sex roles of men and women, in large part because there are sex differences in physical size and strength and because only women can bear children.

An interesting list of the division of labor in subsistence economies was compiled by D'Andrade. (See Table 15.2.) Some of the activities listed clearly require certain levels of physical strength, and childbearing women might find some inconvenient or difficult to perform. For example, pursuing sea mammals or traveling far from home to hunt would be inconvenient activities for a woman who is about to give birth, and also somewhat dangerous for a newborn. Once relegated to the environment in or near the home, or to the environment away from it, a whole host of activities becomes the domain primarily of men or women, simply because they are placed in a specific environment. As the economy of a group and the tasks adults need to do change over time, sex-role differences that once were sensible—even necessary—are maintained by custom, stereotype, or convenience rather than by necessity. For example, we might compare hunting and fishing to the modern activity of traveling across the country or around the world to meet with business clients. First of all, physical size or strength is usually of little consequence when meeting with business clients. Second, one's physician is just a phone call away. Third, every city has a hospital, were it to be needed for giving birth. Fourth, one can get home very quickly, given the speed of air travel. Yet

TABLE 15.2
Cross-cultural data from 224 societies on subsistence activities and division of labor by sex

	Number of Societies in Which Activity Is Performed by				
Activity	Men Always	Men Usually	Either Sex	Women Usually	Women Always
Pursuit of sea mammals	34	1	0	0	0
Hunting	166	13	0	0	0
Trapping small animals	128	13	4	1	2
Herding	38	8	4	0	5
Fishing	98	34	19	3	4
Clearing land for agriculture	73	22	17	5	13
Dairy operations	17	4	3	1	13
Preparing and planting soil	31	23	33	20	37
Erecting and dismantling shelter	14	2	5	6	22
Tending fowl and small animals	21	4	8	1	39
Tending and harvesting crops	10	15	35	39	44
Gathering shellfish	9	4	8	7	25
Making and tending fires	18	6	25	22	62
Bearing burdens	12	6	35	20	57
Preparing drinks and narcotics	20	1	13	8	57
Gathering fruits, berries, nuts	12	3	15	13	63
Gathering fuel	22	1	10	19	89
Preservation of meat and fish	8	2	10	14	74
Gathering herbs, roots, seeds	8	1	11	7	74
Cooking	5	1	9	28	158
Carrying water	7	0	5	7	119
Grinding grain	2	4	5	13	114

Source: Reprinted from "Sex Differences and Cultural Institutions" by R. G. D'Andrade in *The Development of Sex Differences,* edited by Eleanor E. Maccoby, with the permission of the publishers, Stanford University Press. Copyright 1966 by the Board of Trustees of the Leland Stanford Junior University.

men still tend to occupy positions involving business travel more often than women do, although not to the extent that they did several decades ago.

Convenience—the grouping together of things that easily go together (e.g., child-birth and child care)—helps to maintain divisions of labor that are not actually necessary, resulting in **sex-role stereotypes.** These stereotypes assume differences between the sexes that do not actually exist with respect to the requirements of doing a particular task. Of course, stereotypes and customary ways of doing things help shape views about what is convenient and what is not. Changing the division of labor requires shifts in attitude as well as social structures. Such changes always involve costs to some people and benefits to others. Think for a moment about the possibility of year-round schools for children, as opposed to the current organization of a 10–12-week vacation period in the summer. Think also of an extended school day, one that might extend until 5:00 or 6:00 P.M., rather than to the current 3:00 P.M. These changes would be expensive for school districts (and taxpayers), and they might not benefit children. But such changes might result in major shifts in how women and men think about work and about the options available to both of them. Resistance to making such dramatic changes is often based more on values and on economic consequences than on actual differences found between men and women. Sex-role stereotypes often come into play to explain why current ways of doing things are the best way.

In this section, we consider first some issues in the interpretation of sex-difference data. Then we look at specific sex differences—how boys and girls and men and women actually differ in terms of a number of characteristics. Then we discuss how these differences come into being—what accounts for the differences. Here we meet the age-old question of whether differences are primarily due to initial biological and genetic differences or whether children's experiences are primarily responsible for sex differences.

Interpreting Sex-Difference Data

Accurate interpretation of sex-difference data requires that we understand the nature of distributions and means and that we know that global categories of behavior, such as "verbal ability" or "sociability," consist of a collection of specific behaviors. Misunderstandings concerning these things can lead to misinterpretation of sex-difference data and can make it appear that sex differences are greater than they are. We will discuss first the importance of understanding individual, as opposed to group, differences. Then we will discuss how definitions of characteristics affect what is measured and therefore the results obtained.

Group Means and Individual Differences   It is a well-established fact that the means differ for men and women on height and weight: Men are taller and heavier, on average, than women. But would we be unable to find a woman who is heavier and taller than a man? We know from firsthand experience that this is not impossible, because we know both women who are taller than the average man and men who are shorter. The ease with which we can find an individual that differs from his or her own group's mean depends on how far apart the means are. When the means differ a great deal, the distributions of individuals across characteristics typically overlap less, making it harder to find exceptions. But when means differ by a small amount, which is often the case with sex differences, it is not difficult to find men and women who are more alike than different.

The importance of distinguishing between group means and the characteristics of a specific individual in a group becomes more obvious when one looks at actual distributions. The distributions for verbal ability in men and women obtained in one study (Hyde, 1981) are superimposed in Figure 15.2. The highest point of each distribution is the mean—the average verbal ability in the population of men and women. Women as a group are just a little bit better than men, as a group, in verbal ability. Thus the distribution for verbal ability in women is the one that is slightly to

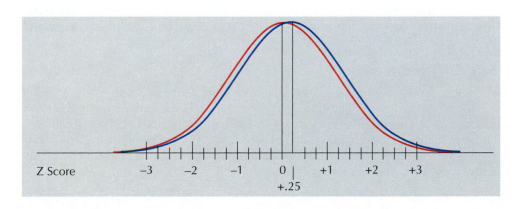

FIGURE   15.2

Two normal distributions with means 0.25 standard derivation apart—that is, with an effect size of 0.25. This is approximately the magnitude of the gender difference in verbal ability.   (*Source:* "How Large Are Cognitive Gender Differences?" by J. S. Hyde, 1981, *American Psychologist, 36,* 892–901. Reprinted with permission.)

the right. Because the means for verbal ability in men and women do not differ a great deal, there is considerable overlap in the distributions. Thus, it would not be difficult to find a man with better verbal ability than most women, nor would it be difficult to find a woman with verbal ability that is worse than the verbal ability of most men. For some behaviors and abilities, the means for men and women are farther apart; for others, they are quite close together.

A serious problem in interpreting sex-difference data occurs when group differences are applied to any particular girl or boy regardless of where the particular individual actually falls within his or her group's distribution. In other words, the danger in talking about group differences is that people can start to assume that individual boys and girls all fall at the mean for their sex group. This is especially problematic when group differences are small and distributions for girls and boys actually overlap considerably.

Definitions of Behavior and Specific versus Global Characterizations of Differences
Reported sex differences rest on specific measurements of various abilities, which, in turn, rest on specific definitions. If we measure verbal ability in terms of vocabulary, we might get one distribution; if we measure it in terms of the ability to make an argument in an essay, we might very well obtain a different distribution. Yet another distribution might be obtained if we simply count the number of words or phrases people utter when they take their turn in a conversation. As another example, we can consider sociability. Judgments about the relative sociability of boys as compared with girls differ, depending on how sociability is defined and measured. If it is defined as making friends or seeking out the company of others, then we are likely to conclude that boys are more sociable than girls (Baumrind & Block, 1967; Whiting & Edwards, 1973). But if sociability is defined as depicting people in drawings or enjoying the company of a few best friends rather than a large group of peers, we are likely to conclude that girls are more sociable (Goodenough, 1957; Waldrop, cited in Maccoby & Jacklin, 1974).

Because the specific definition a researcher chooses can determine what differences a study demonstrates, we might find that the differences often cancel each other out when we compare studies that have used different definitions and measurement contexts or tools. This happens if we try to deal with global categories, such as "verbal ability" or "sociability." To avoid this problem, we must be specific when reporting sex differences. For example, we would want to say that boys and girls differ in terms of vocabulary, or in terms of detecting the phonological aspects of language, and so on, as the case may be. We would not want to say that boys or girls are simply better in terms of a global category of behavior, unless we have evidence of differences across a large number of different measures pertaining to the domain under discussion. Nor is it very useful to claim that there are no differences in some global category, such as verbal or mathematical ability, because each sex is better than the other on an equal number of different subskills in the category. Differences might "cancel each other out" quantitatively, but this kind of approach masks qualitative differences. These are the very differences that sometimes matter to a teacher who wishes to strengthen children's abilities in areas where they might be vulnerable to weakness.

Sex Differences

The research on sex differences is voluminous and somewhat difficult to pull together due to the differences in definitions, measurement tools, and populations studied by different researchers. We have organized several tables in which to list sex differences. The first of these is a modified version of a list first compiled by Halpern (1997). (See Table 15.3.) It summarizes sex differences in cognition and language, and also includes some differences in sensory and motor abilities.

TABLE 15.3

Sex differences in various aspects of cognitive, language, motor, and sensory functioning

General Domain or Basic Characteristic	Specific Test/Task and Studies	Sex Showing the Higher Level of Competence
Rapid access to and use of phonological, semantic, and other information in long-term memory, and in producing speech	Verbal fluency—phonological retrieval (Hines, 1990)	females
	Synonym generation—meaning retrieval (Halpern & Wright, 1996)	females
	Verbal analogies (Lim, 1994)	males
	Spelling and anagrams (Feingold, 1988; Stanley et al., 1992)	females
	Foreign languages (Stanley, 1993)	females
	Tongue twisters (Kimura & Hampson, 1994)	females
Tasks that require dealing with complex prose	Reading comprehension (Feingold, 1993; Hedges & Nowell, 1995; Mullis et al., 1993)	females
	Writing (U.S. Department of Education, 1997)	females
	Interpreting literature (Stanley, 1993)	females
Motor tasks (fine)	Mirror tracing—novel, complex figures (O'Boyle & Hoff, 1987)	females
	Pegboard tasks (Hall & Kimura, 1995)	females
	Matching and coding tasks (Gouchie & Kimura, 1991)	females
Motor tasks (large)	Accuracy in throwing balls or darts (Hall & Kimura, 1995)	males
Tasks that require transformations of information held in visual working memory	Mental (spatial) rotation (Halpern & Wright, 1996; Kerns & Berenbaum, 1991; Levine et al., 1999; Linn & Petersen, 1985; Masters & Sanders, 1993; Voyer et al., 1995)	males
	Piaget's water-level test (Robert & Ohlmann, 1994; Vasta et al., 1996)	males
Tasks involving judgments about moving objects	Dynamic spacio-temporal tasks (Law et al., 1993).	males
Tasks involving knowledge of physical location	Memory for spatial location (Eals & Silverman, 1994)	females
	Geography knowledge (Beller & Gafni, 1996)	males
Mathematical calculations	(Feingold, 1993; Hyde et al., 1990)	females
Math and science reasoning	SAT—Mathematics (Benbow, 1988; Brody, 1992; Byrnes & Takahira, 1993; Willingham & Cole, 1997)	males
	Abstract problem solving (mathematical) (Feingold, 1993; Lummis & Stevenson, 1990)	males
	Mechanical reasoning (Feingold, 1988; Stanley et al., 1992)	males
	Scientific reasoning (Hedges & Nowell, 1995)	males
	Proportional reasoning (Meehan, 1984)	males
Perceptual thresholds (sensitivity to)	Touch (Ippolitov, 1973; Wolff, 1969)	females
	Taste (Nisbett & Gurwitz, 1970)	females
	Odor (Koelega & Koster, 1974)	females
Grades earned in school	(Stricker et al., 1993)	females
Attention deficit disorders	(American Psychiatric Association, 1994)	males
Dyslexia	(DeFries & Gillis, 1993)	males
Stuttering	(Yairi & Ambrose, 1992)	males

TABLE 15.4

Sex differences in various aspects of social and emotional functioning

Characteristic or Behavior	Studies	Sex Showing Higher Levels of the Characteristics
Anxiety	Cohen et al., 1993; Cole et al., 1999, Felson & Trudeau, 1991	females
Confidence in academic ability/ higher expectations for academic success	Cole et al., 1999; Frey & Ruble, 1987; Licht et al., 1989; Pressley et al., 1987; Stipek & Gralinski, 1991	males
Resilience in response to episodes of failure on academic tasks	Dweck, 1986; Dweck & Gilliard, 1975; Kowaleski-Jones & Duncan, 1999	males
Social cues detection (i.e., reading of nonverbal cues)	Hall 1978, 1985	females
Depression	Cole et al., 1999; Petersen et al., 1993; Roberts & Sobhan, 1992	females
Overt (physical) aggression	Berkowitz, 1993; Crick & Grotpeter, 1995; Tomada & Schneider, 1997	males
Relational aggression (spreading rumors, excluding others)	Crick, 1997; Crick & Grotpeter, 1995	females
Delinquent acts	Elliott et al., 1987; Snyder, 1987	males
Conduct disorders	American Psychiatric Association, 1994; Lahey & Loeber, 1994; Offord et al., 1989	males
Nurturance toward children	Berman & Goodman, 1984	females
Use of verbal approaches to conflict resolution	Eisenberg et al., 1994	females
Extensive friendships (larger groups; less exclusion)	Benenson, 1994; Gottman, 1986; Waldrop & Halverson, 1975	males
Intensive friendships (smaller groups; more exclusion)	Benenson, 1994; Gottman, 1986, Waldrop & Halverson, 1975	females
Favorable attitude toward casual sex	Oliver & Hyde, 1993	males

A second table lists sex differences that have been found in several aspects of social and emotional behavior and in achievement motivation and perceptions of ability. (See Table 15.4.)

The items in each list are quite specific. That is, several specific aspects of verbal and mathematical ability, or social or emotional characteristcs, are listed; global categories are avoided. The tables are limited somewhat, however, in that they do not indicate the ages at which the differences have been documented, nor do they indicate the sizes of the differences. These two factors—age of the people involved in a study in which a difference has been found and the size of the difference—are often correlated. For example, boys and girls do not differ in terms of their tendency to overestimate their academic ability prior to third grade. At that point, however, boys begin to overestimate their academic ability more than girls do, and this difference increases as children get older (Cole et al., 1999). If this tendency were studied only among children in first, second, and third grades, no sex difference would be found. If studied in fourth grade, a difference would be found, but it would be smaller than if the study were conducted with sixth- or seventh-graders.

It is very tedious to report all of the variations in the sizes of sex differences found at various ages, and it does not make sense to average the sizes of the difference across ages. The best approach is to report differences that have been found consistently by a number of researchers and seem to persist once they appear.

Explaining Sex Differences

Boys and girls in specific cultures are more similar than they are different, especially in middle childhood. But the small differences that do exist have been well documented. Are these differences inborn or are they learned through experience?

Biology and Sex Differences   Both high levels of spatial ability and high levels of overt aggression are more frequently found in males than in females. For this reason, these traits are often explained in terms of biology. Some people have hypothesized, for example, that spatial ability may be a sex-linked recessive trait. Recall from chapter 2 that girls (with their XX chromosomes) inherit one X chromosome from each parent. Boys (with XY chromosomes), on the other hand, inherit their one X chromosome from their mother. If the gene for spatial ability is carried on the X chromosome and is recessive, it could be overridden in girls by a dominant gene inherited on the X chromosome they receive from their fathers. Because boys receive only one X chromosome, and the trait is carried only on the X chromosome, any recessive gene carried on it can be expressed. (This model is illustrated in Table 15.5.) Thus, boys would have a better chance of inheriting good spatial abilities because they need inherit only one X chromosome that carries the gene. Girls, on the other hand, would need to inherit the gene on each of their X chromosomes.

To explain aggression, researchers have pointed to the male sex hormone testosterone as a possible factor. Evidence in support of a link between male sex hormones and aggression comes from several sources. First, animal studies have shown that female monkeys given testosterone before they were born engage in more aggressive play than untreated females do (Young et al., 1964). Animal studies also have shown that females given testosterone in infancy engage in more fighting than females who have not been given the hormone (Edwards, 1969; Joslyn, 1971).

TABLE 15.5

Possible patterns for spatial ability genes in males and females

Females

Chromosomes		Consequences
X^1	X^2	
s	s	Good spatial ability
s	S	Carrier for good spatial ability but performs poorly
S	s	Carrier for good spatial ability but performs poorly
S	S	Poor spatial ability

This model predicts that one of four females will inherit good spatial ability

Males

Chromosomes		Consequences
X	Y	
s	—	Good spatial ability
S	—	Poor spatial ability

This model predicts that one out of two males will inherit good spatial ability.

Source: From *The Longest War: Sex Differences in Perspective,* by C. Tavris and C. Offir, 1984, pp. 101–102. New York: Harcourt Brace Jovanovich. Reprinted by permission of the publisher.

Biology—heredity—may push the behavior of boys and girls in slightly different directions. Different treatment—socialization—then adds greatly to the differences. The integration of children's sports teams will not alter the physical advantage in size, weight, and strength that older adolescent and adult males, as a group, have over females, as a group. However, differences in physical *skill* will probably decrease as more girls and young women have more opportunities to participate in sports. (*Source:* © Jack Zerht/FPG International)

In humans, testosterone (a predominantly male sex hormone) and aggression have been positively correlated in both adults (Archer, 1991) and adolescents (Olweus et al., 1988; Susman et al., 1987). The direction of the effects—whether testosterone causes aggression to rise or aggression causes testosterone levels to rise—is not known. There is some evidence that testosterone levels rise in response to competition and especially to success in competition (Gladue et al., 1989). One theorist (Archer, 1994) thinks that the effects of testosterone on aggression and aggression on testosterone are reciprocal—testosterone increases aggressive behavior, and aggressive behavior increases testoserone.

Aggression has also been linked to levels of various neurotransmitters. **Neurotransmitters** are enzymes involved in brain activity. Low levels of the neurotransmitter serotonin, for example, have been linked to problems in self-control (emotional regulation) and aggression (Pliszka et al., 1988; Stoff et al., 1987). Here again, though, experience (social conditioning) may affect levels of neurotransmitters, and then levels of these substances may affect behavior. As Coie and Dodge (1998) pointed out, "social conditioning must have some enduring neurobiological structural effects" (p. 811). This means that experience affects the size of brain cells, the branching of dendrites, synapse formation, and brain chemistry (Greenough et al., 1987; Ungerleider, 1995). Therefore, aggressive and generally unregulated behavior, as well as particular experience with respect to parental discipline, affect the brain in ways that maintain certain behaviors.

Some individuals no doubt are born with biological vulnerabilities that make them less responsive to socialization attempts by parents and teachers. Maladaptive interactions and relationships often result as the people responsible for socialization of the child are worn down by the difficulties. As a result, initial biological dispositions gain strength from certain social experiences.

The sociobiological position suggests that the largest gender differences will be those most directly related to sexual selection. The most obvious example is males being considerably more aggressive than females (presumably due to selection pressure to compete aggressively with males for females), which is one of the largest of gender differences. Another general area of large gender difference is predicted by pressure on the female to select males who can provide resources for her and her offspring (e.g., a male who is a good hunter), given her burdensome pregnancy and lactation. And indeed, though other cognitive differences between the genders are relatively small, the difference between genders on spatial rotation ability, an ability essential for hunting and providing for the family, is not. Here the generally preferred male's genes for good spatial ability are most likely to survive; as a result, each generation will tend to increase good spatial ability among men. Evolutionary pressures for females to select a mate who will generate resources (hunt well) is hypothesized to explain the differences between the genders in throwing velocity and accuracy in adulthood (Buss, 1995). Although this sociobiological theory is compelling in its simplicity, psychologists do not agree that it articulates the cause of any sex differences in humans.

In addition, there are explanations other than simple biology for the origins of sex differences. One explanation is that they originate in the historical division of labor into homemaking and occupations outside the home (social role theory) (Wood & Eagly, 1999). According to **social role theory,** this division of labor has resulted in sex-role stereotypes encouraging females to be emotionally supportive and males to be assertive. These supportive versus assertive stereotypes in turn are thought to lead parents to reward daughters who take on supportive roles and sons who take on assertive roles, thus socializing their children to display certain behaviors.

As usual, in a debate about biological and environmental explanations of behaviors, some researchers hold polarized positions that describe the root of behavior as *either* biological *or* environmental. In fact, biology and environment can interact to produce sex-typed effects in the same direction. Rather than arising largely by historical accident, sex-role socialization may be a result of the way cultural learning (behavioral stereotypes) interacts with biological disposition to produce individuals whose social behavior maximizes evolutionary fittness for both cultural and biological/genetic reasons (Archer, 1996; Buss, 1995).

All in all, we know that biology without environmental interaction does not account well for anything. The second possible source for the development of sex differences is children's experiences. What children observe, how they are treated, and what they are taught directly affect sex-role development profoundly.

Socialization and Sex Differences   The learning of sex roles is explained differently by different theories. Social learning theory utilizes principles of reinforcement, punishment, and modeling. Cognitive explanations refer to the child's growing cognitive abilities and the concepts of gender identity and gender constancy. (See the Research Close-Up: The Development of Gender Identity.)

Whatever theory we believe, we can easily see that boys and girls are treated differently. Research focusing on North American children has supported these everyday observations. Fathers play more with their sons than they do with their daughters (Austin & Braeger, 1990; Lamb, 1977; Weinraub & Frankel, 1977), and they play

---

RESEARCH

| **CLOSE-UP**   *The Development of Gender Identity*

"When I'm growed up, I'll have a baby, too," said 3-year-old Jacob, patting his mother's stomach. She looked at him blankly for a few moments, before responding.

"No, Jacob," she finally said. "You're a boy."

"I know," he answered.

"Well . . . boys don't have babies," his mother went on slowly. "Men can be daddies, but only women can be mommies."

"I know. But when I grow up to be a mommy, I'll have a baby."

Should Jacob's mother be alarmed? No. His misunderstanding is fairly typical for children his age. Jacob knows he is a boy, but he does not know that he will *always* be a boy. By age 2½ most children have **gender identity,** meaning that they label themselves correctly as a boy or a girl (Slaby & Frey, 1975). But at this age they do not have **gender constancy,** which is the understanding that they will always be the sex they are now despite changes in appearance. Cut your hair, change your clothes, act a little differently, and you can change your sex, too, according to most 3-year-olds. Most children do not attain a solid understanding that these criteria are not the ones that determine gender until the age of 6 or 7 (Huston, 1983).

Lawrence Kohlberg based a theory of sex-role development on cognitive changes that occur as children get older. He theorized that because until the school years children think they can change sex, they do not pay close attention during the preschool years to same-sex adults who model sex-typed behavior. Therefore, they do not model gender-typed behav-ior systematically themselves. But as gender constancy emerges at about age 6 or 7, children begin to act increasingly like adults of the same sex that they are. In fact, they begin to conform rigidly to their ideas of appropriate behavior for their sex during the school-age period, beginning early in the elementary grades. Later, as they start to observe exceptions to the general rule that men and women behave differently, and begin to be able to think about broader possibilities (in adolescence), they moderate their views (Huston, 1983).

Parents and teachers who made an effort to teach children during their early years that "boys and girls can do the same things" may despair as they see school-age children adopting narrowly stereotyped roles and behaviors. Unless adults can somehow change the world in such a way that males and females do not form gender-related categories of behaviors on which to model their own behavior, children's advancing cognitive abilities will propel them inevitably to make these gender-based distinctions. But just as inevitably, exceptions and even more advanced thinking can gradually make their mark. By exposing children to nonstereotypical sex-role behavior, adults provide models and images that clearly broaden children's understanding of what members of each sex can do (Bigler & Liben, 1990). Children's sex-role attitudes are also affected by traditionalism in parents of the other sex and the amount of time that parent spends with the child (Nelson & Keith, 1990). As children's cognitive abilities continue to advance in adolescence, they are able to attain a greater degree of flexibility in their views of human potential.

with them in more physical ways. Boys under 2 years of age are already provided with more sports equipment, tools, and large and small vehicles than are girls. Girls, on the other hand, have more dolls, toys representing fictional characters, and child's furniture (Pomerleau et al., 1990). Girls of this age also wear more pink clothes and have more pink pacifiers and jewelry than do boys. Toddler boys are also punished more than girls and they misbehave more as well (Minton et al., 1971). Toddler boys also play alone at home more than girls (Smith & Doglish, 1977). In the early elementary grades, teachers expect boys to be more active and unruly than girls (Minuchin & Shapiro, 1983). At home, elementary-school-age boys are given more freedom from parental supervision than are girls (Newson & Newson, 1978).

Boys and girls in North American society are not the only boys and girls in the world to be treated differently. Cross-cultural studies show that parents in many other societies also dress boys and girls differently and assign them different chores. Parents also tend to pay more attention to boys than to girls; to expect more achievement, self-reliance, and autonomy from boys; and to be gentler and more sociable

---

RESEARCH

CLOSE-UP *Socialization of Sex Roles in Different Cultures*

Sex-role differences exist in all cultures, although the particular behaviors viewed as more appropriate for each sex vary. Because we are accustomed to the practices in our own society, we rarely think about them. But practices described in cross-cultural studies are likely to catch our attention. We include here excerpts from a book by Whiting and Edwards (1988), *Children of Different Worlds: The Formation of Social Behavior,* which presents cross-cultural data about many aspects of childhood and child rearing.

The Communities Studied

These researchers and their collaborators collected data in several different countries and cultures, including Kien-taa, Liberia; Kokwet, Kenya; Kisa and Kariobangi, Kenya; Ngega, Kenya; Nyansongo, Kenya; Tarong, Philippines; Juxtlahuaca, Mexico; Taira, Okinawa; Khalapur, India; and Orchard Town, United States.

Differences in How Boys and Girls Are Dressed and Adorned

Adults the world over mark their sex by their dress, hairstyle, and jewelry or other body decorations. Thus, parents can indicate the sex of their children to the community by dressing and adorning boys and girls differently. Whiting and Edwards provide examples of how parents in the communities they studied distinguish between boys and girls:

In several of our communities a clear distinction is made in early childhood. Starting in infancy, the Mixtecan mothers in Juxtlahuaca and the Rajput and Bhubaneswar mothers of North India make it possible to identify the gender of their lap and knee children. For example in Juxtlahuaca the ears of little girls are pierced during the first few weeks of life, and all females wear earrings. Young female knee children already

have miniature rebozas (shawls), and little boys wear their sombreros with pride. In Khalapur the little girls may have a cloth braid worked into the lock of hair at the back of their head, and in addition may have glass beads or glass arm and ankle bracelets. The young girls already have head scarves that they are learning to wear as their mothers do. The little boys all wear a black cord around their navel, a symbol of their Rajput status, and an amulet to ensure that their penis will grow straight. Their hairstyles announce gender and age.

Division of Labor in the Chores Assigned to Boys and Girls

In all societies, children are assigned work to help their parents. Inasmuch as the chores match those carried out by adult men and women, they can train children for adult sex roles. Even if the tasks themselves do not match directly the tasks carried out by men and women in the social group, assigning lower-status chores to girls and higher-status chores to boys, or vice versa, can train children to accept different statuses as adults.

Whiting and Edwards provide interesting observations of how parents in the communities they studied mark differences between boys and girls in the work they assigned to them:

When . . . possible, some of the parents in our samples call attention to the adult division of labor by assigning different types of chores to girls and boys. . . . in preindustrial societies parents ask children to perform tasks beginning as early as age 4, both because the children actually can be of help and because work helps to structure their random activities and channel their boundless energy. . . . Societies differ, however, in the degree to which they are able to replicate in childhood the division of labor by gender that is the norm in the adult world. Children of ages 4 and 5 are not strong enough to perform many of the adult chores, particularly those assigned to men. (p. 222)

with girls (Bronstein, 1984; Zern, 1984). (See the Research Close-Up: Socialization of Sex Roles in Different Cultures for a discussion of how boys and girls are treated differently by parents the world over.)

Within the United States, and probably within all other societies as well, there is some variation in parental treatment of boys and girls, depending on social class and racial group. Sex-typing, particularly of girls, tends to be stronger in working-class families than in middle-class families (McBroom, 1981). Some evidence indicates that African American parents make fewer gender-related distinctions between their sons and daughters, with the result that African American females are socialized more toward employment and economic responsiblity than are Caucasian females (Binion, 1990; Smith, E. J., 1982). Any kind of different treatment can easily lead to different behavior. First, more experience with rough-and-tumble play could make boys more familiar and comfortable with the kinds of behavior used in physical aggression. Second, boys' toys are oriented more toward war and fighting than are girls' toys related to aggression, and boys' toys support aggressive play. When children use toys

Although infant care in all the societies we have studied is in the domain of women, both male and female 4- and 5-year-olds in many cultures are expected to perform child care. However, even in communities where boys may be asked to care for lap children, they are assigned such care infrequently in comparison to girls. . . . there is less distinction by gender in assigning the care of knee children to older siblings. For most of the 4- and 5-year-old girls and boys in our samples, the supervision of knee children is more frequent than responsibility for lap children. The 2- and 3-year-olds tag along after their older brothers and sisters, and even if they are not specifically asked to care for them, they are expected to see that their young siblings are safe. . . . in none of these societies, with the possible exception of Tarong, is the responsibility for knee children considered the work of adult males. (pp. 223–224)

The question arises as to whether there are indeed any tasks that are distinctly male that parents can assign to their young sons. In many societies of the world, the care of large animals is the task that is considered masculine, and young boys can participate in this work beginning at age 4 or 5. In Tarong the care and use of the carabao (water buffalo) are considered to be the domain of men, and all three of the 4- and 5-year-old boys in the sample were observed watering and grazing carabao. No girls were observed caring for these animals.

Parents who emphasize gender from early childhood may . . . try to make distinctions in task assignment even when there is nothing appropriate for males that can be assigned. For example, although the care of pigs and chickens is in the domain of women in Juxtlahuaca, the work is assigned to boys rather than girls in the early years.

Throughout Kenya, the care of cattle is considered the domain of men and boys. The supervision of animals in unfenced pastures adjacent to the homestead is assigned to boys. Although, as in the care of lap children, the task may be assigned to the opposite sex if a child of the appropriate age and gender is lacking, there is a clear preference for

boys. . . . In Khalapur the care of the buffalo is in the domain of men, and the older boys are in charge of taking the animals to the river to be watered and washed. (pp. 224–225)

Direct Observation of Adult Sex-Role Behavior

As the examples illustrate, societies the world over have several means at their disposal to make the sex of their children readily visible to everyone and to train children specifically in sex-appropriate roles. Children also observe the work that adults in their society carry out, and they no doubt notice the different statuses of men and women when these are marked in the culture. Whiting and Edwards (1988) note, for example, that:

All Subsaharan men order their wives around, and probably most children in these societies by age 4 or 5 have witnessed their father, or some other man, beating his wife. For the Rajput child in North India, the picture may be more complicated. The power of the men is obvious when all females lower themselves to the floor and cover their heads when men enter the courtyard; on the other hand, children have also observed that the oldest woman in the courtyard dominates both her married sons and her daughters-in-law. . . . The relative power of men and women is less obvious in Orchard Town, Taira, and Tarong. In these samples the fathers are around more frequently, and in the home setting they are less authoritarian in their relations to their wives. In Taira and Tarong the men and women work together in the fields. In Tarong the fathers prepare meals and take care of their children if, following the birth of a new child, there are no other women living in the house. (p. 226)

Reprinted by permission of the publishers from *Children of Different Worlds* by B. B. Whiting, Cambridge, Mass: Harvard University Press, copyright © 1988 by the President and Fellows of Harvard College.

Children learn considerable sex-role-related behavior from older children and adults. In most cultures, girls are given more responsibility than boys for the care of younger children in the family. Here, a big sister is fixing the hair of her little sister, while the little sister is practicing the same behavior on her doll.
(*Source:* © Kathy Sloane)

related to aggression, they are more likely to be aggressive with each other (Berkowitz & LePage, 1967). Third, since toddler boys more often play alone at home than do girls, their behavior may come under less scrutiny than the behavior of girls, and thus be shaped less frequently into more socialized forms.

At school, teachers praise boys more, give them more help, accept their comments more readily, and permit them to dominate classroom discussions (Sadaker & Sadaker, 1985). Teachers may feel that girls are already better behaved and need less praise and help. They may also think girls are better able to wait for their turn and to listen to others.

Children's learning by direct reinforcement and punishment is supplemented by what children see modeled around them in adults' lives. Their likely observations are summed up in the following excerpt (Huston, 1983, pp. 420–421):

The average child sees women cooking, cleaning, and sewing; working in "female" jobs such as clerical, secretarial, sales, teaching, nursing; choosing to dance, sew, or play bridge for recreation; and achieving in artistic or literary areas more often than in science and engineering. That same child sees men mowing the lawn, washing the car, or doing household repairs; working in "male" occupations; choosing team sports, fishing, and achieving in math, science, and technical areas more often than in poetry or art. In school, the teachers of young children are women; the teachers of older students and the administrators with power are usually men. Peers and siblings pursue sex-stereotyped activities, games, and interests more often than they engage in cross-sex activity.

The mass media and children's books also provide sex-stereotyped versions of life. In one study that analyzed the male and female characters and images in books that had received awards and honors for excellence, the number of male characters in books published between 1981 and 1985 had dropped from the number found in books published between 1976 and 1981 (Dougherty & Engel, 1986). The numbers still did not match the equal proportions found in 1951 to 1955 books. And in books that kindergarten and primary-grade teachers read to children in the classroom, the main character was found to be male over 70 percent of the time (Smith et al., 1987).

Females are typically presented as more dependent than males, as revealed in a study of themes in over 100 books published in the mid-1980s (White, 1986). Females were more likely to receive help; males were more likely to give it. The researchers concluded: "The girls and women in children's fiction do seem to reflect the cultural stereotype of the helpless female, the perennial damsel in distress in need of male protection" (White, 1986, p. 255).

Children can hardly help but get the message: Males and females act differently, are treated differently, and have different kinds of lives. Biological differences that surely do exist certainly have many opportunities to be exaggerated by the subtle and not-so-subtle messages that bombard children from the moment they are born.

KEY POINTS

Social Role-Taking

■ During the school years, children's social role-taking ability—the ability to judge what others are thinking and feeling—improves dramatically. This ability, which is just one aspect of social cognition, gives them greater personal insight and a better understanding of others.

■ During the school years, children begin to understand that facial expressions can sometimes mask actual emotions.

- School-age children begin to understand that some situations are more likely than others to elicit a wider range of emotions from people.

- Older school-age children begin to understand that emotional reactions at the moment may not be elicited by the current situation, and that emotions can linger for a long time. They also begin to realize that "life conditions" can create chronic emotional responses.

- School-age children become better able to identify their own mixed emotions that are elicited in complex situations.

- Inferential empathy emerges during the school-age years. This involves being able to think about what must be going through the other person's mind.

- School-age children begin more often to take intention into account when judging people's actions in situations where something has been damaged or someone has been hurt.

- School-age children become more aware of what other people know, and are more likely when communicating with people to provide information they need. They also begin to understand that people can have different views about the same situation, even if they have exactly the same information.

- Social role-taking ability is not correlated perfectly with prosocial behavior because people can use their skill in thinking what others are thinking to exploit and deceive them. We would expect social role-taking ability to improve social behavior only in children who are motivated to do what is right—in children who have developed a conscience and a measure of self-control.

Moral Reasoning

- Cognitive development affects how children are able to think about complex moral situations.

- Moral reasoning is correlated with moral behavior, but not perfectly. Moral behavior depends not only on moral reasoning ability, but on such things as a person's motivation to do the right thing.

Social Skills and Sociometric Status

- Children vary in terms of their peer interaction skills.

- Social status categories are used to describe variations in how a child is regarded by his or her peers. Popular children are liked by many of their peers; rejected children are disliked by many of their peers; neglected children are relatively unknown by many of their peers; controversial children are liked by about as many peers as dislike them; and average children are those who don't qualify for any other status.

- Specific social behaviors are highly correlated with each social status category.

- Rejected social status is quite stable over the child's school years and beyond. Neglected status is quite unstable.

- A child's attachment history and the history of discipline the child has experienced in the home are correlated with later peer interaction skills and sociometric status.

- Bullies and victims tend to have a history of insecure attachment.

- Antisocial behavior in young children rarely goes away by itself.

- The best approach to solving the problem of antisocial youth is prevention through support programs for parents.

- Interventions for aggressive preschool children include therapeutic nursery schools.

- School-age interventions to help antisocial children include competent and caring classroom teachers and outside intervention programs that teach social skills and changes in the attribution of hostile intent.

Sex Differences and Sex-Role Development

- Sex differences have been documented in children and adults.

- Sex-role stereotyping occurs when people fail to realize that sex differences refer to averages and that specific individuals may be either above or below the average.

- Sex-role teaching occurs in all societies and begins in early childhood.

- Because children tend to form categories for gender-appropriate behavior from everything they see adults do in their society, the modeling and teaching that individual parents provide can seem ineffective. Children adjust their behavior to the central tendency of everything they observe. In adolescence, when children tend to become more flexible in their behavior, family teachings that have not been stereotypic may begin to be seen in behavior, such as career choices.

GLOSSARY

average status: a sociometric status designation given to children who do not qualify for any of the other status categories (p. 524)

bullies: children who are aggressive toward others, either physically or verbally, without apparent provocation (p. 536)

controversial status: a sociometric rating earned by receiving both "liked" and "disliked" nominations from peers (p. 524)

gender constancy: the understanding that one's sex will consistently be the same (p. 539)

gender identity: the categorization of oneself as a boy or a girl (p. 539)

inferential emphathy: empathy that involves knowing the mental state of the other person (p. 514)

masking of emotions: displaying facial expressions and other behavior that do not match how one actually feels (p. 512)

mixed emotions: having both positive and negative feelings about the same thing (p. 513)

neglected status: a sociometric rating earned by receiving a low number of peer nominations of any kind (p. 524)

neurotransmitters: enzymes involved in brain activities (p. 538)

noninferential empathy: empathy that children show without knowing the mental state of the person in distress; that is, not knowing that they are responding to something happening to someone else (p. 514)

popular status: a sociometric rating earned by receiving a lot of "liked" nominations from peers (p. 524)

rejected status: a sociometric rating earned by receiving a lot of "disliked" nominations from peers (p. 524)

self-control: the ability to deny immediate pleasure for one's long-term good or for the good of someone else—behavioral inhibition (p. 521)

sex-role development: the acquisition of dispositions and behaviors that are consistent with the expectations the culture holds for how girls and boys, and men and women, should think, feel, and behave (p. 531)

sex-role stereotypes: expectations, not based on actual differences between the sexes, for how boys and girls, and men and women, should behave and the expectation that every individual boy or girl will match the mean for the sex group (p. 532)

sex roles: characteristic ways of behaving that are associated with men and women in a culture (p. 531)

social cognition: thinking about social phenomena, such as what other people are thinking or feeling (p. 510).

social information-processing: the processing of encoding and evaluating social behavior information (p. 525)

social role-taking: trying to think and feel as another person might think or feel (p. 511)

social role theory: a theory of sex-role development according to which the division of labor in a culture is the source of sex differences (p. 538)

social skills: how children actually behave toward each other and adults (p. 510)

targets: the objects, persons, or situations at which an emotion is directed (p. 513)

valence: the positive or negative nature of an emotion (p. 513)

victims: children targeted by bullies to receive a disproportionate share of their abuse (p. 530)

SUGGESTIONS FOR FURTHER READING

Asher, S., & Coie, J. (1990). *Peer rejection in childhood.* New York: Cambridge University Press. This book integrates existing knowledge about why some children are not accepted by peers, what the consequences of peer rejection are, and how rejected children can be helped.

Beall, A., & Sternberg, R. J. (Eds.). (1993). *Perspectives on the psychology of gender.* New York: Guilford. This book describes several theories of gender typing and discusses the effects of both nature and nurture in creating these differences in behavior.

Grusec, J. E., & Lytton, H. (1988). *Social development.* New York: Springer-Verlag. This book contains thorough chapters on moral development and sex-role development. For the student who wants a readable yet comprehensive briefing on these topics.

Kotlowitz, A. (1991). *There are no children here: The story of two boys growing up in the other America.* New York: Doubleday. This book tells the story of two boys and their family who live in the Henry Horner Housing Projects in Chicago. The author, a journalist, developed a friendship with a family while working on articles about children living in poverty. This book describes in gripping detail the violence experienced by many children in large cities in the United States. The title comes from a comment made by the two boys' mother when the author first suggested that he write a book about children, poverty, and violence: "But you know, there are no children here. They have seen too much to be children."

Kozol, J. (1992). *Savage inequalities: Children in America's schools.* New York: Crown. A penetrating examination of social and economic class inequalities in American schools. The author claims that social policy in public schooling has been turned back in recent years, particularly in urban schools.

Zigler, E. F., Kagan, S. L., & Hall, N. W. (Eds.). (1996). *Children, families, and government.* New York: Cambridge University Press. This book examines the relationship between research and implementation of social policy for children and families. Includes chapters on child-care policy, family leave, and children and television.

MILESTONES *in School-Age Development*

AGE	PHYSICAL	COGNITIVE	LANGUAGE	SOCIAL-EMOTIONAL
6 yrs.	Has 90% of adult-size brain Reaches about two-thirds of adult height Begins to lose baby teeth Moves a writing or drawing tool with the fingers while the side of the hand rests on the table top Can skip Can tie a bow	Begins to demonstrate concrete operational thinking Demonstrates conservation of number on Piaget's conservation tasks Can create series operationally rather than by trial and error	Might use a letter-name spelling strategy, thus creating many invented spellings Appreciates jokes and riddles based on phonological ambiguity	Feels one way only about a situation Has some difficulty detecting intentions accurately in situations where damage occurs Demonstrates Kohlberg's preconventional moral thinking
7 yrs.	Is able to make small, controlled marks with pencils or pens due to more refined finger dexterity Has longer face Continues to lose baby teeth	Begins to use some rehearsal strategies as an aid to memory Becomes much better able to play strategy games May demonstrate conservation of mass and length	Appreciates jokes and riddles based on lexical ambiguity Begins to read using a print-governed approach	May express two emotions about one situation, but these will be same valence Demonstrates Kohlberg's conventional thinking Understands gender constancy
8 yrs.	Plays jacks and other games requiring considerable fine motor skill and good reaction time Jumps rope skillfully Throws and bats a ball more skillfully	Still has great difficulty judging if a passage is relevant to specific theme May demonstrate conservation of area	Sorts out some of the more difficult syntactic difficulties, such as "ask" and "tell" More conventional speller More fluent reader	Expresses two same-valence emotions about different targets Understands that people may interpret situations differently but thinks it's due to different information
9 yrs.	Enjoys hobbies requiring high levels of fine motor skill (sewing, weaving, model building)	May demonstrate conservation of weight		Can think about own thinking or another person's thinking but not both at the same time.
10 yrs.	May begin to menstruate	Begins to make better judgments about relevance of a text Begins to delete unimportant information when summarizing		Can take own view and view of another as if a disinterested third party
11 yrs.	May begin preadolescent growth spurt if female	May demonstrate conservation of volume	Begins to appreciate jokes and riddles based on syntactic ambiguity	Still has trouble detecting deception Spends more time with friends
12 yrs.	Has reached about 80 percent of adult height if male, 90 percent if female Has all permanent teeth except for two sets of molars Plays ball more skillfully due to improved reaction time Begins to menstruate	Shows much greater skill in summarizing and outlining May begin to demonstrate formal operational thinking		May begin to demonstrate Kohlberg's postconventional moral thinking

16

Physical Development in Adolescents

CHRISTY GLANCES IN the full-length mirror to see how she looks in her new sweater. Her breasts started to develop a year ago, before she was 12, and they're about the same size as many of the other girls', but still they don't compare with what she sees in ads and on TV. She'd like them to be bigger, but wants her waist to be smaller.

Christy looks most critically at her legs. "Too pudgy," she thinks. "And too hairy! I wonder if I should start shaving them? They don't look anything like the models' legs in my magazines."

She presses her face close to the mirror and dabs acne lotion on a pimple, while searching her face for signs of new trouble spots. "I'd better get some new lotion," she thinks, "and maybe some make-up, especially something to hide these splotches." Christy sighs, "I wish I could look half as good as those models..."

think about it

What causes young adolescents to spend so much more time in front of the mirror than they did during the elementary school years? Who does Christy think will notice her physique? Why is she dissatisfied with her body? Is the dissatisfaction the same across cultural groups? Becky perceives her physical development to be about the same as that of her classmates. What might be the consequences if she felt she were different—for example, if her physical development were proceeding ahead of, or lagging behind, that of her friends?

Adolescence starts with a burst of physical development that signals the beginning of childhood's end. The school-age years, when growth was slow and steady and changes came in manageable increments, are swept away on a flood of hormones. The child's body grows in every direction, but not evenly. The nose, feet, arms, and hands may grow at different rates for a few years. The skin gets oily, the sweat glands become more active, and hair appears on new parts of the body. Physical signs of sexual maturation appear, but at different times in different children, creating another source of anxiety for the increasingly self-conscious young person.

Some cultures mark the physical transition from childhood to adulthood with rites of passage—rituals and ceremonies that express tangibly and symbolically the end of one stage of life and the start of another. The Bar Mitzvah ceremony celebrating the entry of the Jewish child into a period of religious responsibility at age 13 is one example of such a rite of passage. Confirmation classes and ceremonies are also common in some Christian religious communities. The transition may be more confusing for children who do not have a community experience that affirms their physical or sexual maturation. With the support and understanding of parents, teachers, and friends, adolescents make it through the tumultuous years of puberty and emerge to find their children's bodies and minds transformed into those of young adults.

In this chapter, we focus on physical development changes and their implications. We also see that **body image**—the *idea* of the body—can be as important to some teenagers as physical development itself. The diseases of anorexia and bulimia, and the growing use of anabolic steroids, are related to ideas about how the body *ought* to look. Along with sexual maturation we look at patterns of sexual behavior, pregnancy, and AIDS. We also discuss the growing motor coordination and strength of adolescents, and their need for more physical activity to develop healthy lifestyles. Finally, we discuss factors that make adolescence a time of great risk for health and safety.

Physical Growth

Before the onset of **puberty**, the point at which sexual reproduction becomes possible, tremendous physical change takes place. This period of rapid growth is known as **pubescence**. The increase in height and weight is so dramatic and so fast that it is referred to as the **growth spurt**. Not since infancy has growth been so rapid.

Prepubescent and pubescent girls can be unsure of themselves and their bodies. In just a few years, these girls will have completed their physical transformation into young women.   (*Source:* © Kindra Clineff/Tony Stone Images)

Increases in Height and Weight: The Pubescent Growth Spurt

Starting at about age 9 or 10, girls grow as much as 8 or 9 inches in two or three years, adding a total of about 13 inches on average by the time their growth stops (Tanner, 1991). Boys' growth spurt starts later, at about age 11 or 12. They grow as much as 12 to 14 inches (Malina, 1990; Tanner, 1991). Girls' growth rate reaches a peak at about 12 years and boys grow fastest when they are about 14 years old. Most adolescents continue to grow after they undergo a big spurt, but more slowly. Many adolescents have reached their full adult height by the time the two- or three-year period of pubescence ends. Weight also increases during the adolescent growth spurt.

Figure 16.1 indicates how the growth spurt for girls precedes the growth spurt for boys. Because of this difference in the onset of boys' and girls' growth spurts, it would be typical in the seventh grade for Christy (the girl in the opening vignette) to be taller than most of her male classmates. Differences in height and other physical characteristics often create concern among adolescents.

There are no significant differences in total height at maturity between adolescents who begin the growth spurt early and those who begin late. However, regardless of the age at the beginning of the growth spurt, there is a moderate-to-high correlation between the child's height at the onset of puberty and height at maturity (Tanner, 1991).

The Hormonal Basis for The Growth Spurt   The process of growth and maturation is controlled by a complex interplay of hormones. Under the influence of a "biological clock," and its interactions with the child's history of diet and exercise, the hypothalamus at the base of the brain signals the pituitary gland to send out hormones

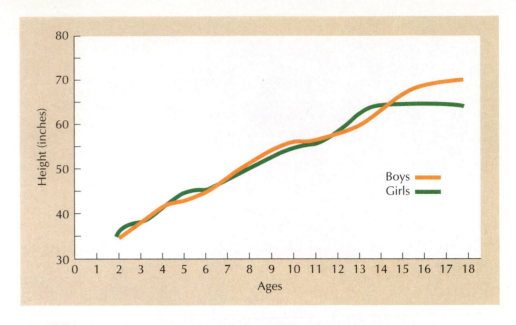

FIGURE 16.1

Growth in height between 2 and 18 years of age. Where the slope of the line is steeper, growth is more rapid. Note that girls have reached their adult height by about 14 or 15 years of age. Boys continue to grow until about 18 years of age.

Seventh- and eighth-grade boys vary considerably in height. Some of this variation is due to inherited differences. But during the early adolescent years, height variation is exaggerated due to differences in the timing of the adolescent growth spurt. (*Source:* © Daemmrich/The Image Works)

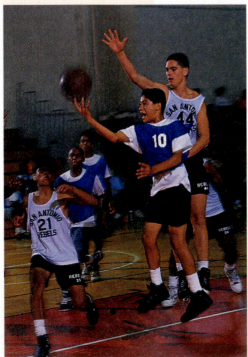

to the **gonads** (sex glands) and to other endocrine glands, such as the thyroid and the adrenals. The awakened ovaries and testes begin to secrete the sex hormones estrogen and testosterone, respectively. These sex hormones then stimulate the hypothalamus. A gonadstat in the hypothalamus senses the presence of circulating hormones. When low levels of certain hormones reach the hypothalamus, signals are sent to the pituitary gland to secrete the hormone. When sufficient levels are reached, signals are sent to stop hormone production. This feedback loop is illustrated in Figure 16.2. These hormones, in turn, trigger the appearance of the secondary sex characteristics, which we describe in the next section. Human growth hormones produce rapid body growth.

Bone Tissue and Organ Growth   The great increases in height (shown in Figure 16.1) are a result of bone growth, first in the legs and then in the trunk. The ratio of head size to body size decreases, and body proportions become more and more like those of an adult. The head does not grow very much during the adolescent growth spurt because the brain achieves almost its entire adult weight by the time the child is age 6. However, the brain and central nervous system continue to develop well into adolescence. For example, although the prefrontal cortex responsible for the regulation of impulsive behaviors goes through a growth spurt at about age 10, the myelination that permits this regulation process is not complete until the 20s. This myelination process occurs later in boys than girls, accounting for some of boys' greater impulsivity and risk taking (Brownlee, 1999; Brooks-Gunn & Reiter, 1990). We discuss their risk taking later in the chapter.

The growth of different parts of the body at different rates is termed **asynchronous growth.** When children first shoot up in height, they are likely to be thin and gawky. Their hands and feet may grow a lot at first and seem to dangle at the ends of long, slender limbs. Some children at this stage stumble over their own feet because of asynchronous growth. The face becomes elongated and some features may seem overly prominent. Gradually, muscle and fat cells catch up, the body and face round out, and proportions become more like those of adults. This asynchronous growth probably contributed to Christy's dissatisfaction with her appearance.

Although both boys and girls add flesh during pubescence, girls add more fat and boys add more muscle. Increases in the layer of subcutaneous fat give girl's bodies the rounded lines of women. Girls gain almost two times as much fatty tissue as boys, whereas boys gain twice as much muscle tissue as girls (Malina & Bouchard, 1991). Boys lose some fat during adolescence, and the proportion of muscle to fat increases. Up to this point, boys and girls have been equally strong, but now boys become stronger than girls. Indeed, the arm strength of males doubles between the ages of 13 and 18 years. The increase in arm strength for girls during this period is less than half that of boys. Boys also have larger hearts and lungs than girls do, which increases their edge in physical strength; a larger supply of oxygen in the blood enables them to metabolize muscle wastes faster. Boys' greater physical prowess, compared to girls, is also due to more experience in physical activities. Although girls' participation in sports has increased substantially in the past 20 years, boys' participation is still higher. Girls are about 20 percent less physically active than boys, and nearly 50 percent of adolescent girls do not reach recommended weekly activity levels (Bialeschki, 1999; McKenzie, 1999).

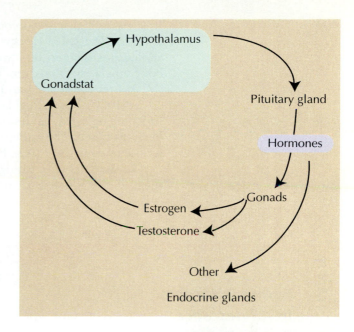

FIGURE 16.2

Feedback loop controlling puberty and sexual maturation.

Body Image

Adolescents are bombarded daily with images of the ideal body. Today's feminine ideal includes large breasts on an otherwise slender figure, a shape exaggerated to the point of caricature in Barbie dolls, cartoons, comic books, teen magazines, and television shows. An increasing number of adolescent girls are getting breast implants, some as gifts from parents (Joas, 1999). Even if girls realize that these figures have impossible dimensions, they still compare their bodies to the slender silhouettes of models. Robust social self-esteem helps adolescents accept their bodies despite the discrepancy between the cultural ideal and their own body image (Pesa, 1999).

Models and media standards for women today are quite thin compared to the more rounded and curvaceous models and stars of past generations. The only other time that popular images of women in the United States were as thin as they are now was during the flapper era of the 1920s. Eating disorders were epidemic among young women then, and unfortunately, history appears to be repeating itself (Cobb, 1998). In today's culture, being slender is valued, especially in females (Madkour & Kuther, 1999; Mancini et al., 1999; Gordon, 2000).

A large majority of adolescent females report that physical attractiveness is very important and that slimness is an important factor in dating and popularity with boys. This belief is stronger among white than African American adolescents and has a basis in fact. Increased body fat, even within a normal range, leads to less dating, greater body dissatisfaction, and more frequent dieting. Adolescent obesity is associated with the completion of fewer years of education and a lower likelihood of marriage in adulthood (Halpern et al., 1999).

Interestingly, African American women are less worried about dieting and fatness than are white females. However, African American women who are assimilated into a predominantly white middle-class culture have more body dissatisfaction and drive for thinness than do African American women who do not interact primarily in a white middle-class cultural group. The drive for thinness is also stronger in higher socioeconomic class adolescents than in lower social class adolescents (Harris, 1994; Schwartz & Abell, 1999; Scott-Johnson et al., 1996). Female adolescents who go on fewer diets and whose weight remains stable have higher body satisfaction and overall self-esteem than their counterparts who diet frequently (McAllister & Caltabiano, 1994).

A study of the eating behaviors of 260 14- and 15-year-old girls in the United Kingdom revealed that Asian girls were more likely to fast and white girls were more likely to binge. The authors concluded that the specific eating abnormality in response to stress appears to be culturally determined (Waller et al., 1995).

Adolescents with eating disorders view their bodies as they believe others see them and internalize an unrealistically thin standard for the ideal body image.

---

knowledge *in action*

HEALTH/SAFETY

Eating Disorders in Adolescence: Anorexia and Bulimia

Anorexia

Anorexia nervosa is not a new disease. In the 19th century, it was identified as a female nervous disorder among adolescent girls in England and France. Papers reported cases of miraculous "fasting girls" who lived without taking any nourishment (Showalter, 1985).

Reports of anorexia have increased worldwide over the past two decades due to changes in cultural norms and concepts of feminine beauty (Murray et al., 1996; Roy & Chrisler, 1997). Anorexia, a disease of intentional self-starvation, affects 1 out of every 100 females between the ages of 12 and 25 (Harris, 1991; Rolls et al., 1991). Most anorectics are middle-class girls or women who are under pressure, are in the public eye, and value thinness very highly. Gymnasts, ballet dancers, public performers, and athletes are especially vulnerable (Gordon, 2000; Stoutjesdyk & Jevne,1993). About 5 percent of all anorectics are male, and many of these have disturbed parental relations, low self-esteem, and sexual identity problems. Males are more resistant to treatment than females and have a poorer prognosis for recovery (Romeo, 1994).

Symptoms of Anorexia

Anorectics often begin as average or slightly above-average-weight girls who start dieting and pursue thinness relentlessly, by starving themselves and by burning a tremendous number of calories through physical exertion. At some point, they develop a distorted body image. Even though they are wasting away, they still think they are fat.

When there is no more fat on the body, the body turns to its own organs in its desperate search for energy. Anorectics become very weak. When body fat drops below a certain level, they develop **amenorrhea**—their men-

strual periods stop. If the disorder is untreated, death can result from heart failure caused by chemical imbalance.

Although the anorectic denies herself food, she is obsessed by it. She may show a sudden interest in preparing food and spend hours poring over recipes. She may hide food or refuse to eat with her family. Even when she looks like a skeleton, she is plagued by anxiety about becoming fat. The symptoms of anorexia include the following:

- Weight loss of 20 to 25 percent of total body weight
- Amenorrhea
- Continual extreme dieting
- Intense fear of weight gain
- Unusual behavior toward food
- Hyperactivity

Causes of Anorexia

Because anorectics are a heterogeneous group (Gowers et al., 1991), a single cause of the disorder is difficult to isolate. The emphasis on slimness in society may prompt a dieting adolescent girl to go overboard. A comparison of *Playboy* models, Miss America pageants, and advertising models shows that the feminine ideal of today is much thinner than in generations past. Adolescents are sensitive to these images for thinner-than-average body shapes. Those who develop eating disorders also show dissatisfaction with their own bodies (Adams et al., 1993).

Many anorectics come from families in which perfection is the only acceptable standard. Parents are often overly concerned about eating habits and appearance (McKinley, 1999). Although anorexia begins with dieting, the disorder is not caused by dieting but by a distortion of body image (Attel & Brooks-Gunn, 1988; Huon, 1996). One of the important psychological issues in anorexia is control. Taking charge of eating habits, even in a self-destructive manner, may allow anorectics to control both their families and their own lives.

Treatment is difficult because anorectics cling to their perceptions of reality and usually deny that they have a

Research has also revealed a correlation between a mother's shame about her own body and her daughters' body dissatisfaction (McKinley, 1999). When concern becomes obsession, the result can be an eating disorder. Anorexia nervosa and bulimia are two serious—in fact, life-threatening—afflictions that physicians see and treat more and more often today. In anorexia, the better known of the two, victims begin with voluntary dieting, but lose emotional and physical control of their eating habits and begin to starve themselves. Bulimia is characterized by binge eating followed by vomiting or use of laxatives to purge the food consumed. For a detailed description of both anorexia and bulimia and how they are treated, see Knowledge in Action: Health/Safety—Eating Disorders in Adolescence: Anorexia and Bulimia, and Table 16.1.

problem. Cognitive behavior therapy, interpersonal psychotherapy, behavioral techniques, family therapy, and pharmacotherapy are often used with anorectics (Link & Bonifazi, 1999; American Psychiatric Association, 2000). About 5 percent of anorectics die from the disease (Harris, 1991).

Bulimia

Bulimia is less visible than anorexia. Like anorectics, bulimics have a distorted body image and an intense fear of becoming fat. But, unlike anorectics, they have an uncontrollable urge to consume huge quantities of food at one sitting. After bingeing, they induce vomiting. They also purge themselves by using laxatives and diuretics. Bulimics may binge and purge several times a week and consume over 6,000 calories in 24 hours (a normal person consumes about 2,500 calories per day) (Kunz & Finkel, 1987). These habits place tremendous stress on the body, often causing kidney failure, loss of vital minerals, and infection. Tooth enamel erodes and teeth decay from constant contact with vomited stomach acids. Frequent purging causes electrolyte and fluid imbalance, and can lead to weakness, lethargy, depression, irregular heartbeat, and even death (Wenar & Kerig, 2000).

Symptoms of Bulimia
Bulimics may eat meals with their families or friends and then gag themselves in the bathroom without anyone else realizing it. Because their weight is relatively normal, they can often keep their disorder a secret for years. Although bulimics have a distorted body image and think they should be thinner than they are, they do not create their own reality to the extent that anorectics do. Bulimics have a relatively normal appearance; they know their eating habits are socially unacceptable and need to be concealed. Symptoms of bulimia may be summarized as follows:

- Low social self-esteem
- Uncontrollable urges to eat
- Cycles of binge eating and self-induced vomiting
- Excessive use of laxatives and diuretics
- Feelings of guilt and depression
- Menstrual irregularities
- Swollen glands
- Large fluctuations in weight
- Dental decay

Causes of Bulimia
Girls who are trying to get or stay thin and who already have underlying emotional problems may be susceptible to cycles in which they binge, fast, and purge. They may be trying to win the approval of others by being thin and wearing more stylish clothes. At the same time they crave the physical and oral satisfactions of eating (Sheppard & Kwavnick, 1999; Wiederman & Pryor, 2000).

Bulimics often come from families who are over-protective, rigid about rules, and high-achieving. Parents in these families typically have high expectations and place great value on attractiveness (Jensen, 1994; Kenny, 1992). Bulimic girls score lower on autonomy than nonbulimics do, and they are unable to claim their own identity within their families. They also believe they have less social support from friends (Gawlick & Bonifazi, 1999; Link & Bonifazi, 1999). Other risk factors include low paternal care, a history of wide weight fluctuation, a slim ideal body image, low self-esteem, and a high level of neuroticism (Engwall & Engwall, 1997; Kendler et al., 1991).

Treatment for Bulimia
Treatment usually involves medical therapy, psychotherapy, and behavior modification techniques. Cognitive-behavior therapy, interpersonal therapy, and nutritional treatments can increase the likelihood of a successful recovery (Fairburn et al., 1999; Treasure et al., 1999). Approximately 20 percent of patients have to be hospitalized (Nemours Foundation, 1999). Most bulimics say that the most difficult aspect to change is their body image distortion and the fear of becoming fat (Rorty et al., 1993).

TABLE   16.1
Factors that protect against eating disorders

- A cultural and social context that accepts a wide range of physical appearances
- A culture that provides support for individuality
- A culture that protects adolescents from abusive experiences
- Good parenting and family support
- Secure attachment
- Absence of parental weight problems or concerns
- Later onset of menarche
- Strong social and coping skills
- Positive temperamental disposition
- Positive self-image and body image

Source: Adapted from Beck et al., 1999; Striegel-Moore & Cachelin, 1999.

The ideal male physique is broad-chested, slim-hipped, and muscular. Exaggerations of this also appear in adolescent pop culture. By the time boys are age 14 or 15, many are eager to develop their new muscles, and they are willing to work out in gyms to do it (Hall, 2000). Others who want even more muscle mass than occurs naturally seek a quick fix through anabolic steroids. Use of these illegal and dangerous drugs has increased alarmingly among adolescent boys trying to build up their bodies to a massive size and improve their athletic performance (Corcoran, 1996). The practice of using these dangerous drugs is detailed in Knowledge in Action: Health/Safety—The Dangers of Anabolic Steroids.

While many adolescents go to extremes to achieve a very thin physique or to build muscles, others struggle with obesity. About one in every six American adolescents is obese (Atwater, 1996; CDC, 1999h). The American Institute of Nutrition reports an increase in obesity among adolescents and also suggests that adolescent obesity is associated with death earlier than would otherwise be expected (Blackburn et al., 1994). Increases in adolescent obesity may be due to increases in television viewing and inactivity (Dietz, 1990; Hodges & Henderson, 1999).

Because obesity is also frequently associated with family conflict, involvement of the family in establishing healthful exercise and eating behaviors usually is more successful than working with the obese adolescent alone (Cobb, 1998). "Given that the number of overweight adolescents is increasing, it is imperative that school personnel (educators, coaches, school nurses, and food service managers) develop coordinated programming to increase physical activity, to increase compliance of school lunches with the U.S. Dietary

This girl has adopted a style of dress she perceives to be fashionable. Models and media standards influence strongly how adolescents think they should look. (*Source:* © Bob Torrez/Tony Stone Images)

knowledge *in action*

The Dangers of Anabolic Steroids

The Fastest Man Alive

The eyes of the world were on runner Ben Johnson when he won the gold medal in the 100-meter sprint at the 1988 Summer Olympics in Seoul, Korea. Johnson's astonishing finish time set a world record that seemed beyond human ability. The press proclaimed him "the fastest man alive."

Just two days later, he was stripped of his medal and sent home in disgrace. Blood tests revealed that he had been taking anabolic steroids, banned by the International Olympic Committee (Janofsky, 1989). The Olympic Committee banned steroids because athletic prowess is supposedly the result of personal effort and discipline. The dangers of using steroids are severe, and sports officials and others have redoubled their efforts to keep them out of the hands of athletes.

According to some experts, athletes have been using anabolic steroids for about 30 years (Johnson, 1990). The use of anabolic steroids among athletes has been increasing (Luetkemeier et al., 1995; Yesalis & Bahrke, 1995). It is estimated that about 10 percent of high school males and about 1 percent of high school females use steroids. This amounts to approximately half a million adolescents (Cobb, 1998).

What Are Anabolic Steroids?

Anabolic-androgenic steroids are synthetic derivatives of testosterone. They are taken in tablets, nasal sprays, transdermal patches, or injection form. Adolescents may share needles, and HIV infection has been reported among users (Yesalis & Bahrke, 1995). Adolescent values of winning in sports and having an attractive physique contribute to the use of anabolic agents (Cobb, 1998; Yesalis and Bahrke, 1995).

Why Are Steroids Dangerous?

Synthetic hormones have many negative side effects. They can cause acne, balding, depression, cancer of the liver and lymph glands, atherosclerosis (hardening of the arteries) and toxic hepatitis. They also affect the male reproductive system, causing atrophy of the testicles, reduced sperm count, and changing levels of testosterone (Anshel, 1998; Shepperd & Kwavnick, 1999). Fluid retention, high blood pressure, high levels of cholesterol, and impaired immune system functioning can all result from their use. Steroids can stop bones from growing, preventing the early adolescent user from attaining full height (National Institute on Drug Abuse, 1999). Although the number of female steroid users is not nearly as great as male steroid users, a number of adverse effects have been found for women. These include menstrual abnormalities, breast shrinkage, increase in body hair, deepening of the voice, and increase in acne (Anshel, 1998; Yesalis & Bahrke, 1995).

Recent data demonstrate a strong association between anabolic steroid use and acts of violence and changes in mood and perception (Yesalis and Bahrke, 1995). Psychiatrists report that using steroids can result in violent crimes, including murder (Daniel, 1989).

How Can the Use of Steroids Be Stopped?

Physicians at one time gave athletes prescriptions for steroids, but when use of these drugs was banned, a thriving underground trade sprang up. Law enforcement officials initially ignored the illicit steroid market. With more attention being focused on their dangers and widespread use, laws have been made more stringent.

Because of the nature of the problem, the American Academy of Pediatrics has alerted physicians to the above dangers and has recommended that they counsel boys who come to them for physical exams. Physicians hope that when young people understand the dangers of steroids early in their athletic careers, they will avoid them altogether (Committee on Sports Medicine, 1989).

Guidelines for Americans, and instruction on appropriate nutritional and weight management practices" (Allensworth, 1996, p. S-20).

Young girls who are concerned about their weight may try to curb their appetites by turning to smoking cigarettes. Adolescent girls who are especially weight-conscious initiate smoking at higher rates than girls with fewer weight concerns (French et al., 1994).

Body image and personal appearance concerns may lead to suntanning, body piercing, and getting tattoos. Adolescents seldom consider the risks of skin cancer from sun exposure. Four out of 5 cases of skin cancer can be prevented by taking

Adolescent boys often are concerned with acquiring an ideal body image. Working out with weights before final height is achieved must be done carefully. Using anabolic steroids to increase body mass is downright dangerous. (*Source:* © Richard Hutchings/ Photo Researchers)

precautions such as using a high-factor sunscreen, wearing a hat, and avoiding the sun between 11:00 A.M. and 3:00 P.M. In 1999 Great Britain began a school sun-safety program, which includes sun-safety education and affordable pouches of sunscreen (Glover, 1999). Adolescents also underestimate the risks of infection, tissue damage, venereal disease, skin disease, and allergic reactions to tattooing and body piercing. Tattoos and body piercing may also lead to family conflicts, social stigma, and employer discrimination (Shepperd & Kwavnick, 1999).

Sexual Maturation and Behavior

The changes visible on the outside of the body are accompanied by important changes inside. In addition to growth hormones that trigger the growth of the skeleton, the pituitary gland also secretes hormones that stimulate the ovaries and testes. When the gonads are stimulated by these hormones, the ovaries become ready to produce mature egg cells and to release them in monthly cycles; the testes become ready to produce sperm.

Primary and Secondary Sex Characteristics

The ovaries produce estrogen, which stimulates the development of secondary sex characteristics in girls, including breast buds, pubic hair, axillary (underarm) hair, larger sex organs, and more rounded contours. Although the **secondary sex charac-**

teristics are not involved in reproduction, they create a greater physical distinction between the sexes. The ovaries also release progesterone, which controls ovulation (release of an egg) and menstruation. The appearance of the **primary sex characteristics**—in girls, ovulation and menstruation—indicates that the reproductive organs have reached maturity.

In boys, the testes start to produce testosterone, which triggers the appearance of male secondary sex characteristics—appearance of body, facial, and pubic hair; growth of the sex organs; and lengthening of the vocal cords, which deepens the voice. The primary sex characteristics in boys are sperm production and ejaculation. Primary and secondary sex characteristics in both males and females are shown in Figure 16.3.

The Sequence of Development in Girls and Boys   The development of sexual characteristics proceeds in a definite sequence. For girls, it starts with the growth spurt around age 9 or 10 and the first stages of breast development. Within the next year or two, the sex organs grow rapidly. Menstruation begins after this rapid physical growth, about two and a half years after the growth spurt begins. In the next two to four years, the breasts and hips continue to fill out to create the adult female body shape.

In boys, the sequence begins with growth of the testes, scrotum, and penis, and the first appearance of pubic hair at about age 13. At this point the growth spurt begins for boys. In the next year or two, the boy's voice starts to change, hair appears on the upper lip, and the sex organs grow rapidly. When ejaculation occurs, often during sleep, the boy has reached sexual maturity. Boys do not reach their maximum growth until two to three years or more after the sequence begins. Even

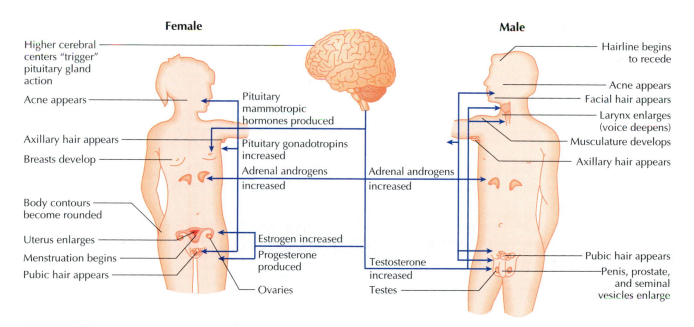

FIGURE 16.3

Physical changes that occur at puberty. These changes result from a complex interaction of hormones released by both the pituitary gland and the sex glands. Body shape and size change, secondary sex characteristics appear, and both males and females become capable of reproduction.

TABLE 16.2
Sequence of maturation in girls

1. Adolescent growth spurt begins.
2. Downy (nonpigmented) pubic hair makes its initial appearance.
3. Elevation of the breasts and rounding of hips begin.
4. The uterus and vagina, as well as labia and clitoris, grow larger.
5. Pubic hair grows rapidly and becomes slightly pigmented.
6. Breasts develop further; nipple pigmentation begins; areola increases in size. Axillary hair becomes slightly pigmented.
7. Growth spurt reaches peak rate.
8. Menarche, or onset of menstruation, occurs.
9. Pubic hair development is completed, followed by mature breast development and completion of axillary hair development.
10. Period of "adolescent sterility" ends, and girls become capable of conception.

later in adolescence, further changes complete development, and physical strength reaches its peak. The sequence of maturation for both girls and boys is summarized in Tables 16.2 and 16.3.

Additional Effects of Increased Glandular Activity   With puberty comes increased activity in the glands in the skin. The sweat glands start to produce substances with a pronounced odor. At the same time, oil-producing glands in the skin, especially those found in the face, start to secrete too much oil. When pores become plugged, blackheads appear, and when blackheads become infected, pimples appear. Acne is usually not a serious medical problem, but adolescents who are acutely conscious of their appearance consider the problem to be relatively traumatic.

The activity of the endocrine glands also affects emotional stability. The mood swings and extreme sensitivity that some adolescents experience may have a physical basis apart from the individual's emotional life (Buchanan, 1991).

TABLE 16.3
Sequence of maturation in boys

1. Testes and scrotum begin to increase in size.
2. Pubic hair begins to appear.
3. Adolescent growth spurt starts; the penis begins to enlarge.
4. Voice deepens as larynx grows.
5. Hair begins to appear under the arms and on the upper lip.
6. Sperm production increases, and nocturnal emission may occur.
7. Growth spurt reaches peak rate; pubic hair becomes pigmented.
8. Prostate gland enlarges.
9. Sperm production becomes sufficient for fertility.
10. Physical strength reaches a peak.

The onset of puberty may have important effects on the individual's self concept. The timing of maturity varies considerably. *(Source:* © Photo Works/Monkmeyer)

Variations in the Onset of Puberty

Although the sequence of development is basically the same for all adolescents, the timing of maturity can vary considerably. Girls begin to mature two to three years earlier than boys. It takes the boys a few years to catch up to and surpass the girls in height.

In addition to this variation in growth between boys and girls, individual boys and girls experience maturation at widely different times. For boys, it may begin as early as age 11 and end as late as age 16, with 13 as the average age of onset. For girls, the growth spurt can start anytime between ages 8 and 11, although it usually begins at about age 10 (Gallahue & Ozmun, 1995).

What Determines When Puberty Begins?
A variety of factors, including nutrition, general health, genetic inheritance, and metabolic rate, determine when puberty begins. The earliest and latest limits for an individual may be established by heredity, but environmental factors influence the timing within this range. For example, girls must have a specific level of body fat in proportion to muscle tissue before their bodies will respond with hormones to start the menstrual periods (Frisch, 1991). When girls burn up a tremendous number of calories daily in activities such as dancing or running, they may not reach this level of fat, and consequently fail to menstruate.

Environmental factors are responsible for the increasingly early onset of puberty today in the United States and other industrialized countries. In 1900, the average age at **menarche** (onset of menstruation) for American girls was 14 years and 2 months. By 1990, it was 12 years and 3 months (Cobb, 1998; Tanner, 1990). This change, known as the **secular growth trend,** has probably been caused by increases over the years in sedentary lifestyles and fat consumption. As nutrition and health reach some upper level, this downward movement in the age of menarche is expected to stop, due to genetic and biological limits on the ages at which individuals can become sexually mature (Graber et al., 1995). The mean age for first ejaculation (**semenarche**) in boys is 12.9 years. Most boys respond with curiosity and confusion, as well as with surprise and pleasure (Stein & Reiser, 1994).

The Effects of Early and Late Maturing   The suspense about physical change can be torturous. When other girls are developing breasts and beginning their periods—or when other boys are growing beards and talking in deeper voices—the adolescents who are showing no signs of development can feel that they have been left behind. On the other hand, girls who look two or three years older than their sixth-grade classmates, and boys who need to shave at age 13, may feel just as uncomfortable. What are the immediate and long-term effects of early and late maturation?

EFFECTS OF EARLY AND LATE MATURING IN GIRLS.   One indicator of the importance of menarche is the finding that girls who have just started to menstruate have higher social self-esteem than those who have been menstruating for a longer time (Lackovic-Grgin et al., 1994). Researchers have found that girls who mature early (in the late elementary grades) often feel out of place because they are taller than their peers and because their sexual development brings some unwanted reactions from boys. Early-maturing girls may experience sexual teasing and harassment. Indeed, 8 percent report having been forced by an older boyfriend to have sex against their will (Zuckerman, 1999). Late-maturing girls also reported negative feelings about themselves during early adolescence, but reported more positive feelings about themselves in later adolescence than did the early-maturing girls. When compared with early-maturing girls, late-maturing girls also tended to complete more years of schooling, be truant less often, and engage less often in troublesome behavior such as smoking and drinking (Magnusson et al., 1985).

EFFECTS OF EARLY AND LATE MATURING IN BOYS.   Boys compare their physical changes to those of other boys and worry about differences. They use avoiding, pretending, and joking as strategies for dealing with embarrassment (Flaming & Morse, 1991). Some studies have found that early-maturing boys are more popular with their peers, more athletic because of their larger size, better coordinated, stronger, and more likely to be leaders in school activities (Gross & Duke, 1980; Jones, 1949; Simmons & Blyth, 1987). Because their level of development more closely matches that of girls the same age, they are more attractive to girls. All of these factors tend to give the early-maturing boy higher social status in early adolescence. However, earlier

The early maturing boys on this team are likely to be more athletic and more popular, giving them a higher social status in early adolescence. (*Source:* © Kopstein/Monkmeyer)

maturation may have some long-range disadvantages. Early-maturing boys often have less self-control and are more inclined than later-maturing boys to smoke, drink, and get into trouble with the law (Duncan et al., 1985; Sussman et al., 1985). It is important when looking at the effects of early maturation to distinguish between "early" with respect to age and "early" with respect to peer group. For example, children held out of kindergarten until more mature, or held back in grade, will mature earlier than classmates, but they do not necessarily mature early for their age.

OTHER INFLUENCES ON THE EFFECTS OF MATURATION.   Whatever the biological timing for an individual boy or girl, other factors influence how comfortable or uncomfortable adolescence actually is. These factors include cultural expectations, parental reaction, and individual perceptions (Hill et al., 1985; Peterson & Taylor, 1980). For example, a late-maturing girl with above-average intellectual ability can often maintain her self-esteem through academic success, whereas a girl with less interest or ability in academics might suffer more from late development. Or a child entering adolescence with a secure sense of self from earlier stages of development might not be affected as much by late development as a less secure child.

Culture can also affect how the age of maturation affects the child's reactions. For example, an early-maturing girl from a family and a culture that value traditional roles for women might fare better than an early-maturing girl whose family and culture expect high academic achievement and a professional career. Even the physical attractiveness of the individual must be considered. Unattractive girls, who presumably base their positive feelings about themselves on other factors, suffer less loss of self-esteem during pubertal change than do attractive girls (Zakin et al., 1984).

An adolescent's self-esteem depends on more than her self-perceived attractiveness, of course. Her perception of her appearance interacts with her self-perceived competencies in other domains to determine her overall self-esteem. The domains of attractiveness, social acceptance, behavioral conduct, scholastic competence, and athletic competence all contribute independently to the overall self-esteem reported by adolescents.

Sexual Attitudes and Behavior

"Aw, come on, Brigita, it's okay to do it if you love me. Who cares what your mom will think—how's she gonna know anyway?"

Brigita pulls away from Josef, folds her arms across her chest, and says softly, "If you really loved me, you wouldn't even ask me to do it right now. I don't care if everyone else is doing it—and, anyway, maybe they aren't. How do you know?"

"Okay," Josef replies. "It's up to you. Maybe I don't want to, anyway. What if you have AIDS or something? I sure don't want to get that!"

think about it

These young teenagers are obviously quite interested in their sexuality and in the exploring and experimenting that often occur during adolescence. Will Brigita submit next time? Does Josef really mean that he's afraid of contracting AIDS? Or was this just a good excuse to make it seem that he wasn't backing off? Do most encounters of this kind between teenagers turn out this way? Or do events usually take a different turn?

Brigita and Josef controlled their sexual interests. However, less controlled outcomes are very frequent, and pregnancy is often the result. More than 1 million teenagers in the United States become pregnant each year, and approximately half of these pregnancies result in births. One-third of all U.S. births involve unwed mothers, and about 85 percent of these mothers did not intend to become pregnant (Coyle et al., 1999).

Changing Attitudes about Sexual Activity

The nature of sexual interactions among teenagers depends on their beliefs about the conditions in which each type of sexual behavior is appropriate. The beliefs of teenagers have changed over the last half of the 20th century, and attitudes towards sex are becoming more permissive (Cobb, 1998).

Adolescent sexual activity has increased over the past 30 years. Fifty percent of 15- to 19-year-old girls have had sexual intercourse, with age 17 being the average age for first intercourse (Zuckerman, 1999). Teenagers today have a relatively high number of sexual partners compared to teenagers in years past, due to the short-term nature of many teenage love relationships and an increase in casual sex—sex outside a love relationship. Researchers have found that teenagers who have intercourse at an early age are more likely to have intercourse with a greater number of partners than those who delay intercourse until they are older (Parrillo et al., 1997).

A report by the Centers for Disease Control and Prevention (CDC, 1995) states that while the percentage of high school adolescents using condoms has increased, only about 50 percent of sexually active high school youth use condoms. About half of all high school youth have had intercourse (Parrillo et al., 1997). When asked why they did not practice safe sex, boys indicated that they thought condom use would decrease the chances that their partner would rate them as good performers. Girls said that being prepared might lead their partners to consider them to be sexually promiscuous. Many also argued that condom use would interrupt spontaneity and affect the romantic mood.

Sexually Transmitted Diseases

Sexually transmitted diseases (STDs) are contagious diseases caused by bacterial and viral organisms that live in the reproductive tract and organs. Contact with an infected person through intercourse exposes an individual to these infections. Common STDs include the bacterial diseases gonorrhea and syphilis, and the viral diseases cytomegalovirus, herpes, and HIV.

The early onset of sexual activity, the high number of sexual partners, and the high incidence of unprotected intercourse (without a condom) put individuals at risk for STDs (Francis, 1999). Adolescents are aware of factors leading to STDs, but do not believe that the relationship with their several partners puts them at risk. Despite having information about STDs, individual adolescents often believe that they will not contract one. One CDC study indicated that 57 percent of adolescents believed birth control pills would protect against STDs, and 84 percent believed having just one partner would protect them from infection (Francis, 1999). Sadly, approximately 4 million adolescents become infected with STDs each year.

Chlamydia is the most frequently reported infectious disease in the United States, and teenage girls have the highest rate of infection (CDC, 1999j). Because approximately 75 percent of women have no symptoms, many do not seek health care. Untreated, this disease can cause pelvic disease, infertility, tubal pregnancy, neonatal conjunctivitis, and pneumonia. Annual chlamydia screening is important and strongly recommended for all sexually active teens (CDC, 1999j).

Many public health professionals, educators, and psychologists consider AIDS the world's most severe health problem for adolescents. HIV infection is the second leading cause of death for people in the United States between the ages of 25 and 44, many of them infected as teenagers. The percentages of AIDS cases reported in the

United States for 13- to 24-year-old males break down as follows: 52 percent homosexual/bisexual, 10 percent injection drug users, and 7 percent heterosexual. Among young women of the same age, 49 percent are infected heterosexually. Although AIDS incidence is declining among young people, the number of newly diagnosed HIV cases is not (CDC, 1998). The HIV infection data provide a clearer picture of the AIDS epidemic because of the long and variable time period between contracting HIV and developing AIDS symptoms (CDC, 1998).

Despite the fact that studies consistently find no correlation between knowledge about STD transmission and safe sex practices (Woodring, 1995), hundreds of millions of dollars continue to be spent on health programs that provide adolescents with information about AIDS transmission and the importance of not engaging in unprotected sexual activity. Although such expenditures are well intentioned, other approaches are needed if adolescent sexual behavior is to change. The assumption underlying most programs designed to persuade adolescents to avoid unsafe sexual practices is that arousing a great deal of fear about contracting AIDS will change the adolescents' sexual behavior (Aronson, 1999b). Unfortunately, many adolescents use the defense mechanisms of denial and defensive attribution to break the association of sexual behavior with death or disease. Adolescents exposed to high-fear-oriented education programs have an even higher level of unsafe sexual behavior. Apparently, this occurs because many adolescents exhibit a high level of risk-taking behavior as a function of the **invincibility fable.** That is, despite their knowledge of the statistics, many adolescents believe "It can't happen to me." These adolescents do not reject the statistics presented, but simply do not believe that the statistics apply to them.

Denial among adolescents also involves **defensive attribution,** whereby adolescents identify individuals who have AIDS as having characteristics that they themselves do not have. For example, the adolescent may attribute AIDS to homosexual behavior, to sexual involvement with individuals who use infected needles to administer drugs, or to engaging in promiscuous sex. Because they list only characteristics that do not describe themselves, these adolescents may believe that they are not at risk because they are heterosexual, do not have sex with people who administer drugs with needles, and limit their sexual partners to a clique who they think would not have sex with people who are likely to be infected.

Other research has uncovered additional beliefs that seem to interfere with safe sex practices among adolescents. Williams and colleagues (1992) found that if sexually active youth know and like their partner, they also believe the partner could not possibly be HIV-positive. Liberman and Chaiken (1992) reported that when a fearful message is relevant to the group to whom it is presented, the members of the group argue that the dangers presented in the message are overstated. The reasoning involved in this form of denial is especially prevalent among the increasing number of adolescents who report that they do not trust adults, the claims of "experts," or government reports.

What can be done to decrease unsafe sex practices among adolescents? Aronson and his associates (Stone et al., 1994) demonstrated in one study the value of applying **cognitive dissonance theory.** Briefly, cognitive dissonance is a state of tension created within an individual who holds two inconsistent attitudes, beliefs, or opinions. The individual can reduce the tension he or she feels by changing one or both of the conflicting views. In this case, some sexually active youth created videos that they believed would be presented to younger adolescent youth. These participants composed arguments advocating abstinence or else condom use "every single time you have sex." Dissonance was created for half of the adolescents by pointing out the hypocrisy of telling younger adolescents to practice safe sex when they themselves had reported incidents in which they found it too difficult or awkward to use condoms. In addition to the video-and-hypocrisy and the video-only groups, a third group of adolescents simply composed a speech, but did not present it on video. To reduce the dissonance, the video-with-hypocrisy participants shifted their behavior to be more consistent with the messages that they presented on the video. Aronson

(1999b) recommends this "saying is believing" paradigm for use in dealing with the unsafe sexual practices that lead to AIDS and teenage pregnancy.

Effective sex education programs must actively involve adolescents in advocating avoidance of unsafe sexual practices and take into account the confusion and denial that characterize adolescent thinking about sex (Aronson, 1999a). Programs other than Aronson's have also involved adolescents in discussing strategies for how to handle hypothetical situations that might lead to unsafe sex. The adolescents in these programs participate in small groups with role-play assignments, modeling, and discussions about assertive responses that adolescents can use in difficult peer situations. These prevention programs focus on strategies for delaying sexual behavior as well as strategies for self-protection (CDC, 1998). The *Safer Choices* intervention is based on social cognitive theory and focuses on the influence of the total school environment on student behavior (Coyle et al., 1999). Many teen-pregnancy deterrent programs are using *Baby Think It Over,* a doll with computerized monitoring and random crying intervals, to give adolescents realistic notions about the demands and responsibilities of child rearing. More efforts must be made to assess the effectiveness of prevention programs. One study of approximately 4,000 adolescent females exposed to a pregnancy prevention program revealed that the majority still did not take appropriate protective steps (Murry, 1999).

The home is another crucial prevention point for adolescents. Parents can encourage and support school health programs, and they can openly discuss with their teenagers the issues of peer pressure, boundary setting, and abstinence (Francis, 1999).

Motor Development and Skills

Serena Williams won the 1999 U.S. Open at age 17. Several Olympic and other athletic championships have been won by adolescents. (*Source:* © Robyn Beck/Corbis)

Olympic and other athletic champions are sometimes as young as 14 or 15 years of age and usually no more than 26 or 28 years old. For example, the winner of the women's 1997 Wimbledon tennis championship was just 16 years old, and Serena Williams won the 1999 U.S. Open at age 17. High school seniors are also being selected for professional sports teams. For example, Tracy McGrady made his NBA debut with the Toronto Raptors at age 18. The physical skills required for athletic events usually reach their peak during adolescence and early adulthood. The strength, stamina, and coordination that emerge during middle childhood continue to develop during the teenage years. Bones harden and become more dense due to the deposition of minerals; muscles become stronger. Even though the adolescent is capable of impressive physical feats, only about half of the adolescents in the United States participate in regular, vigorous, prolonged physical activity of the kind that effectively conditions the cardiorespiratory system. Girls seem especially to become less active once they reach puberty (Ernst et al., 1998; Hodges & Henderson, 1999).

Good physical education programs can help adolescents build body strength and physical fitness. (See Table 16.4 for types of exercise that benefit health.) Tannehill and colleagues (1994) reported that most adolescents think that physical education classes should focus on team sports and improved physical fitness. Sports such as basketball, soccer, volleyball, field hockey, and track also build body strength and physical fitness. The key is to educate and motivate young people to participate in these programs and sports. When they do engage in physical activities outside of school, teenage boys' top choices are bicycling, basketball, football, baseball, and swimming. Girls' top choices are swimming, bicycling, dancing, in-line skating, and walking.

Physical activity is important for the health of both body and mind. Exercise has a direct impact on the brain and can lead to improved cognitive functioning (Etnier & Landers, 1995). Improved skill level in a sport is associated with increased perceived competence, importance, and self-worth. Data from the Institute for Athletics and Education indicate that adolescent girls who play sports are 80 percent less likely to have an unwanted pregnancy and 92 percent less likely to be involved with drugs than their peers who are not in sports. They are also three times more likely to graduate from high school (Neff, 1994). Aerobic running can increase self-esteem, and body esteem and can be a psychotherapeutic aid in helping to alleviate depression and anxiety (Ebbeck, 1994; Selvaggio et al., 1997; Williams & Kuther, 1999). Physical activities also provide adolescents with important opportunities for peer interaction.

Despite the benefits of physical activity, most adolescents in the United States lead a relatively sedentary life. Television, video games, and computers (including computer games, Internet surfing, e-mail, and chatrooms) provide endless hours of passive entertainment. Schools often provide only limited physical education and sports opportunities for adolescents. One study found that only 34 percent of adolescents in grades 9 and 10 were enrolled in daily physical education classes, and even fewer attended physical education classes in grades 11 and 12. In addition, only 38 percent of the high schools offered an opportunity for daily physical activity lasting for 30 minutes or more (Allensworth, 1996). Only 19 percent of adolescents are physically active five days a week for 20 minutes or more in physical education classes (Wright et al., 2000) In recent years, some people have begun to take physical fitness more seriously, but this trend must be expanded if it is

Women's sports are now taken more seriously than in decades past. The experience of playing a team sport provides important opportunities for girls' physical, social, and emotional growth. (*Source:* © Kolvoord/The Image Works)

TABLE 16.4

Types of exercise that benefit health

Aerobic exercises: These raise the rate of heartbeat and breathing, strengthen the circulatory and respiratory systems, and increase the consumption of oxygen.

- Bicycling
- Stationary cycling
- Running/jogging
- Swimming
- Speed walking
- Rowing
- Aerobic dance
- Aerobic classes
- Stair climbing
- Using ski-machine
- Jumping rope
- Cross-country skiing

Flexibility exercises: These help prevent injuries from more strenuous exercise, improve physical performance, and help maintain range of motion and flexibility in joints.

- Static stretching (not bouncing stretches)
- Bending
- Turning and twisting
- Yoga

Strength exercises: These strengthen the muscles.

- Resistence training
- Push-ups, pull-ups, sit-ups
- Exercises with weights
- Using strength-building machines

Progressive relaxation exercises: This training relaxes the basic muscle groups by concentrating on one group at a time. This form of exercise reduces stress.

- Meditation
- Yoga
- Visualization techniques
- Deep breathing

TABLE 16.5
Healthy People 2010 objectives for youth

1. Physical activity and energy expenditure, including leisure time, sustained, and vigorous activities
2. Physical activity for muscular strength, endurance, and flexibility
3. Physical activity in schools, including daily physical education with appropriate requirements and quality
4. Fitness education and access to school physical activity facilities
5. Counseling for physical activity by primary care physicians

Source: Information from Healthy People 2010, 1999, The BeFitNet Alliance, Incorporated. [Online]. Available: *www.befitnet.com/healthy.htm.*

to include a significant proportion of the adolescent population. One goal of the Healthy People 2010 campaign is to help individuals to adopt and maintain physically healthful activities essential for healthy lives. See Table 16.5 for the Healthy People 2010 objectives for youth. Some school physical education programs are becoming more engaging, inclusive, and health-oriented, and are emphasizing lifetime physical activity and fitness (Schnirring, 1999; Welk & Wood, 2000).

Health and Safety during Adolescence

Adolescence is a time of relatively good health. In many ways, adolescence and young adulthood constitute the prime of life. But there are risks to health and safety during adolescence. These include accidents, homicide, suicide, sexually transmitted diseases, drug experimentation, and alcohol abuse (King, 1993).

Keeping the Adolescent Healthy

A number of high schools have health centers for their students. Many have a health curriculum—a course or courses that students take as part of their school programs. What services do health centers provide, and what might be in a high school health curriculum?

The first school-based health center was established in Dallas in 1970. The staff in a typical school-based health center includes a physical health care professional, a mental-health clinician, and dental, nutrition, and health education services. The American Academy of Pediatrics recommends that adolescents see a physician for well-care visits once every two years, up to age 20 (Gullotta & Noyes, 1995). Studies show that students feel comfortable in the school environment and may have fewer medical appointment conflicts with school classes or activities when a health center is located in the school (Gullotta & Noyes, 1995). School-based health centers have the opportunity to change a crisis-oriented, episodic approach to adolescent health and to help less economically advantaged students. Many of the physical health problems that occur during adolescence are directly related to living in poverty and not being able to afford health prevention and health treatment services (Bolig et al., 1999).

In this section we examine a number of issues that affect the health of adolescents. Whether in a school-based health center or in the clinic context of a family pediatrician or general practitioner, each of the following topics must be addressed if the adolescent's health is to be maintained.

Nutrition   Because adolescents are growing more rapidly than at any time since their first year of life, they need a higher caloric intake than at any other time in life. The greatest calorie requirement for girls occurs around 14; for boys, the peak need occurs around age 17 (Malina & Bouchard, 1991). Adolescents need nitrogen, magnesium, zinc, iron, and calcium during their growth spurts. Thus, they need to consume substantial quantities of milk, fruits, vegetables, and proteins that are found in meats, such as chicken and seafood, or in meat substitutes (grains, tofu, eggs, etc.). Adolescent girls need to consume a sufficient amount of calcium to build up bone density. High bone density built early in life helps to prevent osteoporosis at older ages.

Osteoporosis is a disorder that results from loss in bone density. As bones become more porous, the skeleton weakens and bone fractures can occur easily. As a natural part of aging, this disorder affects millions of women, especially after menopause. A calcium-poor diet, sedentary lifestyle, obesity, and smoking all increase the risk of osteoporosis. Initial bone density, established in childhood and adolescence helps to protect against osteoporosis later in life.

Unfortunately, most teenagers do not consume enough calcium or iron, nor do they maintain a balanced diet. Many adolescent girls, for example, do not consume enough milk, cheese, yogurt, and fresh vegetables to achieve the levels of calcium in their bodies required to attain optimum bone density. According to the Centers for Disease Control (1999c), only 29 percent of adolescents in the United States consume the daily recommended five servings of vegetables and fruits; 66 percent consume too many fat calories. Although eating a good breakfast is important for health and development, a survey of young adolescents indicated that 12 percent regularly skipped breakfast. Girls were three times more likely than boys to skip this important meal (Shaw, 1998).

Sleep Needs   Research indicates that adolescents have greater sleep needs than do children, especially during puberty, yet they actually get less sleep (Carskadon, 1999). Sleep deprivation can lead to poorer school performance, moodiness, and accidents and injuries. Sleep is also important to the growing adolescents because growth hormones are secreted during sleep (Weiten, 2000).

Cigarette and Cigar Smoking   At least 4 million adolescents in the United States smoke cigarettes, putting themselves at risk for short- and long-term health consequences (CDC, 1999c). First, cigarette smoke is carcinogenic (capable of producing cancer), and smokers risk contracting cancer of the mouth, throat, esophagus, and lungs. Smoking is also related to heart disease, bronchitis, and impaired lung efficiency, and it reduces the amount of oxygen that gets to the adolescent's body (Merolla, 1994). Smoking impairs driving performance (Spilich et al., 1997), and even secondary smoke increases adolescent respiratory health problems.

Cigars are just as hazardous to health as cigarettes, and one of five adolescents smokes them (Meckler, 1999). Not until 1999 was concern voiced that cigars should carry the same warning label that cigarettes do. Cigar smoking has been glamorized by the media, the entertainment industry, cigar bars and shops, and cigar-smoking celebrities (Meckler, 1999; Woznicki, 1999).

Many adolescents begin to smoke at around age 14. Smoking is supported by favorable attitudes toward smoking, peer influences, social pressure, or curiosity (Christie, 1999; Kelder et al., 1994; Prince, 1995). Initial favorable attitudes might be attributed to observations of parents or peers smoking, to beliefs that smoking will be relaxing, or to media images. Adolescents may be very attentive to image-oriented

Adolescents with friends who smoke are more likely to become smokers, and they vastly underestimate the addictiveness of nicotine.   (*Source:* © Penny Tweedie/Tony Stone Images)

advertisements portraying smoking as a desirable behavior (Covell et al., 1994; Pechmann & Ratneshwar, 1994). Studies also show that the onset of smoking is related to poor academic achievement and the absence of supportive adults (Conrad et al., 1992; Perry et al., 1993). Adolescents who smoke report that the temptation to smoke is greatest after an argument with a friend, when in a restaurant with friends who smoke, and when anxious or frustrated with school or work (Prince, 1995). Adolescents with friends who smoke are more likely to become smokers. "Peer pressure is the tobacco industry's best salesman" (Christie, 1999). See Table 16.6 for tobacco use information.

Although adolescents may want to quit smoking, they have difficulty stopping (Gidding et al., 1995). Nicotine addiction is prevalent among adolescent smokers (Giovino et al., 1993). Because of the level of addiction found among adolescent smokers, and because 89 percent of long-term adult smokers report that they began smoking by age 18, Torrens (1995) advocates a national youth-centered program that encourages children and adolescents to abstain from tobacco use.

Smoking prevention programs provide information about the health risks involved in smoking. In addition to providing this information, one smoking intervention program focuses on immediate consequences, such as smelly breath and hands, stained fingers and fingernails, shortness of breath in sports and recreational activi-

TABLE 16.6

Facts about tobacco use

- Approximately 90 percent of adult smokers start using tobacco before age 18.
- The average youth smoker begins at age 13 or 14.
- Thirteen percent of 11- to 15-year-olds are regular smokers.
- Each year 1 million adolescents become regular smokers.
- Adolescents purchase over $1 billion in tobacco products each year.
- Twenty-seven percent of adolescents (6 million) smoke at least one cigar a year.

- Adolescents vastly underestimate the addictiveness of nicotine.
- Seventy percent of adolescent smokers wish they had never started smoking.
- The earlier people start smoking, the more likely they are to smoke longer and to die early from smoking.
- Tobacco use is the single leading preventable cause of death in industrialized nations.

Source: Adapted from Centers for Disease Control, 1999a, 1999g; Christie, 1999; Reed, 1999.

ties, and the reduced money teens have available to spend on more enjoyable activities because of the amount of money they spend on cigarettes (Prince, 1995).

A program developed by the American Lung Association of Maryland uses worksheets, role playing, and humorous responses called "smart answers" to teach young adolescents how to resist peer pressure to try cigarettes. The American Heart Association program turns cigarette advertising upside-down by depicting smokers as unglamorous and addicted rather than attractive. After legislation to prevent cigarette advertisements on outdoor billboards, the Pennsylvania Department of Health took advantage of the vacated billboards to portray cigarettes as bullets and drug-needles, and smokers as "butt heads." Involving students in antismoking campaigns decreases the likelihood that they will smoke. Life Skills Training and Project TNT (Towards No Tobacco Use) are programs that examine the causes of tobacco use, strategies for not using tobacco, and how the media and advertisers influence teens to use tobacco products (CDC 1999i).

A major court settlement in 1997 required cigarette manufacturers to establish programs to discourage adolescents from using tobacco. In 2000, laws were being proposed to prevent cigarette manufacturers from sponsoring adolescent social or cultural events and using the product identification, from using human or cartoon figures (e.g., Joe Camel) for advertising, from using outdoor ads, and from placing tobacco products in movies, television programs, or video games.

Because adolescents perceive physicians to be credible health experts and may be more likely to heed their advice than that of other adults, physicians could take advantage of this respect to discourage smoking among adolescents. The National Cancer Institute, the American Academy of Pediatrics, the American Medical Association, and other health organizations recommend that physicians actively screen and counsel adolescents about tobacco use (Thorndike et al., 1999).

Alcohol and Drug Abuse   Another threat to the health of adolescents is their abuse of alcohol and other drugs. Just as in the case of unsafe sexual practices and smoking, peer influences have a much stronger effect in determining an adolescent's decision to drink or use drugs than does the adolescent's knowledge about the substances (Roberts, 1995). Programs that elicit fear or shock or those purporting to increase substance avoidance through the enhancement of self-esteem in young children have not had significant long-term effectiveness (Zigler & Hall, 2000; Venturelli, 2000).

ALCOHOL.   Eighty-seven percent of high school seniors have used alcohol, with experimentation beginning around age 13. Seventy percent of teen pregnancies are influenced by alcohol or other drugs, 14 percent of adolescent drivers involved in fatal

Peer influences have a strong effect in determining an adolescent's decision to drink alcohol. When adolescents drink and drive, they are more likely than adults who drink to be involved in an accident. (*Source:* © Jeff Greenberg)

automobile crashes are legally drunk, and adolescents who begin drinking before age 15 are four times more likely to develop alcoholism than those who begin after age 21 (CDC, 1999c; NCADD, 1999a, 1999b). Alcohol contributes to adolescents' injuries, and injuries kill more adolescents than all diseases combined. For example, when adolescents drink and drive, they are more likely than adults to be in an accident, even when drinking less alcohol than adults. Alcohol is involved in about 40 percent of all adolescent drownings, and contributes to other injuries as well (CDC, 2000). Adolescents are drinking at much younger ages than they did 20 years ago, and attending bigger parties which can quickly spiral out of control (Lombardi, 2000).

MARIJUANA.   Although other drugs, including cocaine, LSD, PCP, and amphetamines are used, marijuana is the most widely used psychoactive (mind-altering) drug among adolescents. Twenty-six percent of adolescents report having used marijuana, and older adolescents use more than younger adolescents. Marijuana use among youth has doubled over the past few years (Venturelli, 2000). This increased use appears to be mediated by social learning and the peers with whom adolescents bond (Akers & Lee, 1999; CDC, 1999c). In low doses, marijuana usually creates a pleasant feeling of euphoria and relaxation, a heightening of some sensory experiences, and a slowed-down sense of time. Marijuana slows reaction time, distorts perception, affects memory, impairs motor coordination, increases heart rate, and causes reddening of the eyes and dryness of the mouth. Because of its effects, marijuana impairs driving ability (Cobb, 1998).

COCAINE AND CRACK.   One of the most dangerous and addictive drugs used by adolescents today is cocaine, a powerful stimulant that produces a 10- to 20-minute feeling of euphoria. Like amphetamines (or "speed"), cocaine makes a person more talkative and argumentative, and often deludes users into believing that they are unusually clever or insightful. Because it overstimulates the central nervous system, cocaine can cause paranoia, aggression, tremors or convulsions, vomiting, respiratory collapse, and heart failure. Nine percent of high school seniors have used cocaine at some time, and 1 to 2 percent are current users (Monitoring the Future Study, 1999; NCADD, 1999b).

INHALANTS.   Inhalants are substances found in spray paints, cleaning fluids, paint thinners, gasoline, lighter fluid, aerosols, furniture polish, model glue, rubber cement, and hundreds of other household products. Nitrous oxide (found in "Whippets" for making whipped cream) and butyl nitrite ("bolt") are used as inhalants, as are crushed Ritalin tablets and certain herbal compounds containing stimulants (Hegarty, 1997; Zukerman, 1999). As many as 16 percent of adolescents have used inhalants (CDC, 1999c). Unfortunately, they are inexpensive and easy to obtain. Using inhalants can cause nosebleeds, difficulty in breathing, temporary blindness, severe or permanent damage of major organs, unconsciousness, and even death. Inhalants can cause disturbances in heart rhythm and lead to cardiac arrest. Every time an inhalant is used, death is a risk. Hundreds of people die each year from inhalants and 30 percent of them are first-time users (D'Angelo, 2000; Hegarty, 1997).

WARNING SIGNS AND EDUCATION/AWARENESS PROGRAMS.   Adults should be alert to the signs and symptoms of drug dependency among teenagers. If their grades drop, or they suddenly become withdrawn, emotionally distant, rebellious, or unusually irritable, it may be a sign of trouble. Similarly, if adolescents lose interest in activities or hobbies that they once enjoyed, or suddenly change friends, parents and teachers should look more closely at the possibility that drug use might be involved. As with STDs and cigarette smoking, Aronson (1999a) has demonstrated the value of applying cognitive dissonance theory as an alternative to only dispensing information or using fear-creating techniques to change adolescent substance abuse. His research indicates that substance abuse prevention programs must fully involve adolescents in activities in which they advocate approaches to overcome substance abuse, thereby lowering their favorable attitudes toward alcohol use. A second critical ingredient of programs is having adolescents practice using strategies to resist the peer pressures that lead to substance abuse. D.A.R.E. (Drug Abuse Resistance Education) is one of the most widely used school-based drug prevention programs, in spite of evaluations indicating few positive results in favor of its effectiveness (Ullman et al., 1999). Wysong and colleagues (1994) reported that adolescents judged D.A.R.E. programs to have no lasting influence on their drug-related attitudes or behaviors. Bukstein (1994) claims that substance abuse programs need to use indirect approaches. These approaches increase alternative recreational activities, improve academic skills, and build students' self-esteem. By changing these aspects of adolescents' behaviors, programs can minimize the negative influences of psychological distress, deviant peer cultures, and poor educational performance.

Some programs combine direct and indirect approaches. An example is *Just Kids,* which operates in the Denver, Colorado area. Designed to reach high-risk youth, the program runs for three hours, two days a week, after school. It contains units on communication, problem solving, decision making, and self-esteem. Parents and community volunteers participate as aides, and many of the staff are from university internship programs. The *Just Kids* program contains four components that follow Albert Bandura's (1986) social-cognitive learning theory: (1) information (facts on drug use, AIDS); (2) social and self-regulatory skills; (3) enhancement through guided practice (simulated situations, role play); and (4) social support for social change (Stevens-Smith & Remley, 1994).

Community-based intervention strategies are important in changing risky behaviors. For example, England and Wales have established *Drinkline,* an alcohol helpline that serves as a sounding board for parents and teenagers, offers free confidential advice and booklets, and puts families in contact with specialists (Evans, 1999). Collaboration across agencies can focus on specific problems related to risk-taking behaviors. These efforts should include schools, social services, mental health professionals, and community members, as well as the adolescents and their families (Coddington, 1999).

Programs that target psychosocial factors are also successful in eliminating substance abuse. For example, programs that train teens in the skills they need to understand and resist pressure to take drugs are effective. Programs involving both parents and peers in the intervention, and those including social support, have also had some success (Durlak, 1995).

Various family and personality characteristics are also associated with higher drug and alcohol abuse. For example, adolescents who have parents with ADHD are at higher risk for substance abuse (Samuel et al., 1999). Academic failure beginning in late elementary grades is a risk factor, as are peer pressure and stress (Poinski, 1999). Protective factors such as emotional and social support from parents can help offset the risk factors (Wills et al., 1999). Adolescents who are more involved in risk-taking behavior are also more likely to experiment with alcohol and drugs. Youth who seek thrills in any number of ways also abuse drugs more than youth who do not seek thrills. In this respect, alcohol and drug use are not only health risks for adolescents, but are safety risks as well.

Keeping the Adolescent Safe

Accidents are the leading cause of death during the adolescent years. Fatal accidents most often involve automobiles and motorcycles. Alcohol is often a factor in accidents involving automobiles (Zuckerman & Duby, 1985).

Accidents and Adolescent Risk-Taking Behavior   Risk-taking behavior is responsible for the high number of accidental deaths among teenagers (CDC, 1999c). Risk-taking behavior is related to the typical adolescent feeling of invulnerability—bad things happen to others, but not to me. This belief is called the invincibility fable. Individuals also vary in the extent to which they take risks. Some individuals are less inhibited than others and engage in more risk-taking behavior.

Adolescents as a group minimize the perceived risk of involvement in health-threatening activities, such as drug use or reckless driving, and it is this involvement in health-threatening activities that puts adolescents in jeopardy (Cohn et al., 1995). For example, 19 percent of teenagers rarely or never use a car seat belt, 85 percent rarely use a bicycle helmet, 37 percent have ridden with a driver who has been drinking alcohol, and 14 percent of teenage drivers who were involved in fatal crashes were legally drunk (CDC, 1999c, 1999f). Risk-taking behavior may also lead to occupational accidents. One study indicated that 16- and 17-year-old workers were at a greater risk than adults for fatal accidents due to electrocution, suffocation, drowning, and other environmental dangers (Castillo et al., 1994).

Violence and Accidental Deaths   Homicide now ranks second as a cause of death among 15- to 24-year-olds. Minority youth who live in impoverished areas of cities have a homicide rate 10 times higher than the national average (Nolan et al., 1999). Seventy percent of teenage homicides, and almost as many suicides, are associated with the use of firearms. More than 3,000 American adolescents are killed in gun-related homicides and suicides each year (King, 1993). Youth are the primary victims of homicides by other youth (Nolan et al., 1999). Every two hours, a child or adolescent in the United States is killed with a gun. Many others are injured, require long-term hospitalization, and suffer permanent disabilities (National Crime Prevention Council, 1999).

Acts of violence at school are increasing. Five students were killed in Jonesboro, Arkansas, and 15 were killed in the Littleton, Colorado, shootings in 1999. Surveys show that between 3 and 8 percent of students have carried a gun to school at least once, and 14 percent have carried knives or clubs (Simmons, 1999; Youth Risk Behavior Surveillance, 1998).

Research is ongoing to determine what types of programs can help prevent violence in schools and elsewhere. One national research study indicated that arts programs (Youth ARTS Development Project) can help decrease student involvement in delinquent behavior, improve youths' attitudes, and improve life skills such as an increased ability to express anger appropriately, to communicate more effectively, and to work cooperatively to resolve conflicts (National Endowment for the Arts, 1999). The Centers for Disease Control (1999b) reported that effective strategies for violence prevention include anger management and the development of problem-solving and social skills. Other strategies include family conflict management, family togetherness, and mentoring programs for youth.

Garbarino (1999b) has indicated that adolescence is a time when adversity can lead to aggression and violence. Factors leading to violent behavior toward other adolescents include rejection by social cliques, lack of attachment, inability to control rage, a lack of community connectedness, poverty, and discrimination. Table 16.7 presents the factors contributing to the problem of violence in American schools. Programs to help violent youth have involved the care of animals and spirituality, which have been effective in reclaiming violent adolescents. A 20-year longitudinal study of youth at risk for health, safety, and maladaptive behavior problems identified several factors associated with the adolescents who were resilient. Table 16.8 presents the factors contributing to greater health, safety, and freedom from maladaptive behaviors (Masten, 1999).

Factors that account for violent deaths and injuries of adolescents include peer pressure, substance abuse, impulsive behavior, the adolescent's belief in his or her invincibility, and a general acceptance of violence (King, 1993). The three themes identified by Garbarino (1996) as contributing to greater school-age violence (see chapter 12) also apply to adolescent violence. The percentage of high school juniors who believe adults can be trusted is half of what the percentage was in 1975. There has been a similar reduction in the percentage of adolescents who expect that they will find meaning in life.

Among teenagers, death by violence is increasingly common in urban environments. Violence, both within their families and on the streets, is a fact of life, learned

TABLE 16.7

Factors contributing to the problem of violence in American schools

- Imitation of negative models
- Desire for peer approval through fighting or crime
- Low self-esteem
- History of early aggression
- Inconsistent care as a child; poor monitoring
- Poor emotional attachment to parents
- Gang membership to attain a sense of belonging
- Access to handguns
- Use of alcohol or illicit drugs
- Parents who use alcohol or illicit drugs

- Inability to resolve anger and arguments
- The intent to seek revenge
- Glamorous view of violence provided by the media
- Violence in the family
- Racism resulting in encounter anger
- Association with problem-behavior peers
- No exposure to appropriate coping patterns
- Environmental hazards such as crime and overcrowded, substandard housing

Sources: CDC, 1999b; Garbarino, 1999b; Marcus, 1999; White, 1995.

early and carried into adolescence and adulthood. The increased number of guns on the streets, bought with money from drug sales, has intensified the problem in recent years.

Solutions to these problems require massive efforts to change the social and economic conditions in our cities, to improve the quality of adolescents' lives, and to give people hope for a decent future. By creating educational, recreational, spiritual, and employment opportunities, these changes can be realized. Although the problems are daunting, we can begin to reclaim the lives of urban youth by making these improvements a national priority. The prevalence of violence differs remarkably across countries and across cultures within a country. The likelihood of a 15- to 24-year-old dying is 30 times greater in the United States than in Japan. Within the United States, minorities and those in the lower socioeconomic classes are much more likely than people in higher social classes to suffer violence by guns (Garbarino, 1996, 1999a).

Adolescents' inability to exert self-regulation or self-control is central to most of their safety and health problems, such as alcohol and drug abuse, unsafe sexual practices, automobile accidents, poor diet, and violence. The processes of decision making and controlling emotions deplete self-regulation. More positively, research has shown that self-regulation is a skill that can be learned and developed through practice (Baumeister, 1999). Chapter 19 presents information on conflict resolution and self-regulation.

TABLE 16.8

Resources for fostering resilient adolescents in at-risk environments

- Religious affiliation
- Attending safe and nurturing schools
- Involvement with both parents
- Connectedness with competent, caring adults
- Involvement in community activities

- Having a capacity for self-regulation
- Having social and physical appeal
- Participation in recreation center programs
- Having a good brain capacity for learning
- Close relationships with competent, caring family members

Source: Adapted from Garbarino, 1999b; Masten, 1999.

KEY POINTS

Physical Growth

■ During the period of growth and change known as pubescence, children experience a tremendous growth spurt. Girls grow 8 to 10 inches in two or three years; boys grow 12 to 14 inches.

■ Girls' growth spurt is earlier than boys', beginning at about age 10. Boys start at about age 12. Although some growing continues, adolescents are basically full-grown when pubescence ends.

■ Pubescence occurs as a result of complex hormonal activities initiated by the pituitary gland, which secretes hormones that awaken the gonads. The ovaries begin to secrete estrogen, and the testes begin to secrete testosterone.

■ Bones grow rapidly and harden, terminating growth. Body proportions become more and more adultlike. Girls' bodies increase in fat tissue, and boys' bodies increase in muscle.

■ Teenagers are concerned with how their bodies compare with cultural ideals. Girls who become obsessed with their bodies may develop anorexia or bulimia. These eating disorders are widespread and can be life threatening.

■ Anorexia is characterized by self-starvation and a distorted body image. Bulimia is characterized by cyclic bingeing and purging. Adolescents with either of these disorders need intensive care to get well.

■ Some teenage boys take anabolic steroids to build up muscles and improve athletic performance. These synthetic male hormones have dangerous side effects, including atherosclerosis, atrophy of the testes, high blood pressure, high cholesterol, and impaired immune system functioning.

Sexual Maturation and Behavior

■ Puberty is controlled by a feedback loop. Triggered by the pituitary gland, the sex glands secrete hormones that stimulate the development of primary and secondary sex characteristics. The primary sex characteristics are ovulation and menstruation in girls and sperm production and ejaculation in boys. The secondary sex characteristics are physical traits associated with a distinction between the sexes. In girls, these traits include breasts, pubic hair, and fuller body proportions; in boys, these traits include facial hair, pubic hair, and longer vocal cords.

■ Development proceeds in a definite sequence. In girls, it begins with the growth spurt, followed by the appearance of pubic hair, the development of breasts, the growth of the sex organs, menarche (onset of menstruation), and a tapering off of growth.

■ In boys, the sex organs increase in size, pubic hair appears, the growth spurt begins, the voice deepens, facial hair appears, sperm production begins, and the growth spurt tapers off.

■ Maturation begins as early as age 9 for girls and as early as age 11 for boys.

■ The timing of maturation is determined by genetics and environmental factors, including nutrition, health, and metabolic rate. Girls must have a certain proportion of body fat before they can start menstruating.

■ Puberty has been occurring earlier and earlier in American children since the beginning of the 20th century. The secular growth trend is probably due to improved health and nutrition, but there are biological limits to how early puberty can occur.

■ Girls who mature late seem to have advantages in the long run over girls who mature early. Findings on maturation are mixed for boys.

■ Individual, family, and cultural values and perceptions affect how individual children react to the timing of sexual maturation.

■ A child's self-esteem at puberty is determined by her opinion of her appearance, peer acceptance, scholastic competence, behavioral conduct, athletic competence, and the support of parents and friends.

Sexual Attitudes and Behavior

■ Adolescent sexual activity has increased over the past 30 years.

■ The incidence of sexually transmitted diseases among adolescents is high, and AIDS is of major concern.

■ Effective sex education programs actively involve adolescents rather than just provide information.

Motor Development and Skills

■ Many physical abilities reach their peak in adolescence. Bones and muscles mature, endurance improves, and strength increases.

■ Many adolescents, especially girls, become less active at this time, just when their physical potential is at its height. Because of the benefits to be gained from physical activity, adolescents need to be encouraged to participate in physical activities and sports.

Health and Safety during Adolescence

■ Adolescence is a time of relatively good health and is a critical time to maintain a healthy lifestyle.

■ School-based health centers can provide good adolescent health care.

■ Many adolescents have poor eating patterns, consuming too little calcium and iron.

■ Adolescence is a critical time to prevent the onset of cigarette and cigar smoking.

■ Programs to help adolescents overcome drug and alcohol abuse are based upon social-cognitive learning theory.

■ Accidents are the leading cause of adolescent death. Accidents are often caused by risk-taking behavior and alcohol use.

■ Violence is increasing in high school because of the social acceptance of violence, impulsive behavior, substance abuse, and lack of community connectedness.

GLOSSARY

amenorrhea: the cessation of the menstrual period during years when menstruation is normal (p. 552)

anabolic-androgenic steroids: synthetic derivatives of testosterone used to enhance physical performance and appearance (p. 555)

anorexia nervosa: an eating disorder involving intentional self-starvation (p. 552)

asynchronous growth: the growth of different parts of the body at different rates (p. 550)

body image: the adolescent's idea of his or her body, which may not match reality (p. 548)

bulimia: an eating disorder involving bingeing and purging (p. 553)

cognitive dissonance theory: the idea that a state of tension within an individual who holds two inconsistent attitudes or beliefs will promote change in one or both to reduce the tension (p. 563)

defensive attribution: the tendency to blame victims for their misfortune so that one feels less likely to be victimized by the same things (p. 563)

gonads: sex organs that create sperm and ova (p. 550)

growth spurt: the rapid increase in height and weight during pubescence (p. 548)

invincibility fable: the adolescent's belief that negative outcomes do not apply to him or her (p. 563)

menarche: the onset of menstruation (p. 559)

osteoporosis: a disorder in which bone density is lost, making bones more porous and prone to breakage (p. 567)

primary sex characteristics: the development and functioning of the reproductive organs (p. 557)

puberty: the point in physical maturation when sexual reproduction becomes possible (p. 548)

pubescence: the period before puberty marked by rapid growth and other physical changes (p. 548)

secondary sex characteristics: physical changes that are not directly related to sexual reproduction (p. 556)

secular growth trend: the trend toward earlier maturation with each succeeding generation (p. 559)

semenarche: first ejaculation (p. 560)

sexually transmitted diseases: contagious diseases caused by bacteria and viruses that live in the reproductive organs and are spread through sexual contact (p. 562)

SUGGESTIONS FOR FURTHER READING

Gallahue, D. L., & Ozmun, J. C. (1995). *Understanding motor development: Infants, children, adolescents, adults.* Madison, WI: Brown & Benchmark. Section four of this book includes information on adolescent growth, reproductive maturity, physical development, health-related fitness, and physical activity and socialization.

Gold, M. S. (1995). *Tobacco.* New York: Plenum. This book presents information on neurobiological, physiological, and psychological effects of nicotine and tobacco use.

Johnson, N. G., Roberts, M. C., & Worell, J. (Eds.). (1999). *Beyond appearance: A new look at adolescent girls.* Washington, DC: American Psychological Association. This book has several excellent chapters on disordered eating, health care, dating violence, and sexuality. It provides a thorough and critical review of the literature on adolescent girls.

Kalichman, S. C. (1996). *Answering your questions about AIDS.* Washington, DC: American Psychological Association. Answering a collection of 350 commonly asked questions about HIV and AIDS, this book offers easy-to-understand information based on current knowledge from medical and psychological research. It includes a glossary of terms, directory of resources, and listings of state and national hot lines.

Muuss, R. E., & Porton, H. D. (Eds.). (1998). *Adolescent behavior and society: A book of readings.* New York: McGraw-Hill. This book of readings includes several chapters on health issues of adolescents, such as protecting adolescents from harm, eating disorders, street youth, and risk behaviors.

Thompson, J. K. (Ed.). (1996). *Body image, eating disorders, and obesity: An integrative guide to assessment and treatment.* Washington, DC: American Psychological Association. This book discusses eating disorders and obesity and gives details of intervention programs stressing cognitive-behavioral treatments.

17

Cognitive Development in Adolescents

WHEN 14-YEAR-OLD Latifa came home to find that her apartment building had been fumigated, she got the idea of doing a school science fair study on the effects of pesticides on cockroaches. "Maybe the exterminators didn't need to use so much poison to kill the cockroaches," she thought. "Maybe less poison would do it, and poison humans less in the process. Or maybe less poison would kill a crucial segment of the population—the reproducing females, for example, or the babies. Maybe some kinds of cockroaches are more susceptible to certain poisons than others. If I could find out any of those things, I might even be able to make a difference in how the exterminators used their chemicals."

Later that night Latifa told her mom about her ideas. "I'd like to get a whole bunch of cockroaches down at the pet shop," she explained. "They sell them to people who feed bugs to their snakes and turtles. I know they have the big South American kind and at least two other kinds.

I'll ask Mr. Garvin to help me get some of the pesticide exterminators use. I could use a different concentration of pesticide on each strain of cockroach to see how much you really need to kill them. I could even apply different concentrations of pesticides to cockroaches of different ages. If they laid eggs, I could treat some of the eggs, and then I could treat some of the babies."

"Wait a minute," interrupted her mom. "If you use different concentrations of pesticides on different strains of cockroaches at different points in their life cycle, how will you know which variable you're testing?"

Latifa thought about this for a while and finally said, "Yes, I see what you mean." She sat down at the desk to try to work the problem out on paper. After some time she called out, "Mom, I think I have it. I get the three different strains of roach. I keep them until they have babies. I keep some of the babies until they're 3 weeks old. That gives me three different groups—adults, babies, and juveniles—for each of the three different strains. That's nine groups.

"I also have three different concentrations of pesticide. I'll divide each of the nine groups into three subgroups and treat each subgroup with a different amount of pesticide. I'll end up with 27 different subgroups. Then when a pesticide works, I'll know exactly on which roaches it worked. For example, a certain low concentration might work on South American babies but not on South American adults."

"Excellent thinking, Latifa!"

"And if you killed baby cockroaches, you'd wipe out a whole roach population, wouldn't you? People would just have to wait a little while before they saw results."

"Sounds good to me."

"Then exterminators could use less poison. I think I'll go write this all up as a project proposal. Wait till Mr. Garvin hears about it!"

think about it

How did Latifa's thinking about this science project differ from the way she might have planned such a project as a fourth-grader? How did her mom guide her reasoning through her zone of proximal development to use formal operational thought? How might Latifa's interest in science and the environment have influenced her science project design? How likely is she to demonstrate this level of thinking on an English literature project?

This 15-year-old can think about abstract formulas like the ones written on the chemistry class chalkboard. A younger child would have more difficulty making sense of such diagrams. *(Source: © Will Faller)*

The design of Latifa's science project revealed some very sophisticated rational thinking. Although she had no cockroaches or pesticides in hand, she was able to think about what she would do with them if she had them. She was juggling variables and contemplating possibilities about situations that existed only in her mind. This represents a more advanced approach to problem solving than is evident with concrete operational thought. Figure 17.1 shows all the possible combinations of variables in Latifa's experiment.

Adolescents need to think about their ideas, view events from differing perspectives, understand competing ideas, and consider others' intentions as well as their own. Opportunities must be provided for adolescents to make judgements through discussion and questions that guide them to sound reasoning (Strom, 1999).

This more mature cognitive functioning is apparent in many aspects of adolescents' thinking—whether they are debating social or political issues, formulating abstract ideas, using logic, discussing literature, or solving science problems. Perhaps the best way to characterize this new way of thinking is to say that adolescents are released from concrete interpretations of words and situations. They are able to *imagine* possibilities, build concepts, use metaphors, and solve problems by starting from an exhaustive list of possible hypothetical explanations. Their thinking becomes more logical, more imaginative, and more flexible.

Some researchers think there is an "intellectual growth spurt" that occurs coincidentally with the progression that some adolescents make to formal operational reasoning (Andrich & Styles, 1994). This spurt is apparently due to the effects of both maturation and education or experience. Large

FIGURE 17.1

All the possible combinations of variables in Latifa's experiment. A younger child would be unable to think of all these possibilities.

X Q A	X R A	X S A
Y Q A	Y R A	Y S A
Z Q A	Z R A	Z S A
X Q B	X R B	X S B
Y Q B	Y R B	Y S B
Z Q B	Z R B	Z S B
X Q J	X R J	X S J
Y Q J	Y R J	Y S J
Z Q J	Z R J	Z S J

A, B, J = Adults, babies, and juveniles
X, Y, Z = Three strains of cockroach
Q, R, S = Three concentrations of pesticide

individual differences in the ability to think rationally emerge during adolescence. The following are major factors that may prevent many adolescents from being able to think as Latifa did:

- Poor idea generativity—a failure to think divergently to develop alternative hypotheses

- Premature closure—deciding quickly on a solution without a plan to test the validity of the idea

- Confirmation bias—having a disposition toward looking selectively for information to support an initial idea

- Inefficient hypothesis testing—considering different conditions without realizing that other variables may be confounded with them

- The availability heuristic—relying only on personal experiences to decide how things work

- Computational limitations—failing to follow appropriate computational procedures that correspond to reasoning processes

Generally, adolescents are likely to accept ideas as valid unless they have constructed a mental model of an alternative idea that contradicts the idea being presented (Stanovich & West, 1999).

In this chapter, we discuss the exciting developments in cognition that move the adolescent toward higher levels of reasoning. We begin with Piaget's conception of cognitive activity during adolescence, which he called formal operational thinking. Then we move on to a discussion of some other interpretations of adolescent thinking provided by the information-processing approach to cognitive development. We also describe adolescents' growing ability to think in abstract terms and their creative thinking. Finally, we examine issues related to the education and assessment of the adolescent.

Formal Operational Thinking

Latifa's thinking had only recently advanced to a new level. In fact, when she first told her mother about her idea for the project, she had not designed it in a way that would have produced clear results. But when her mom asked questions about it in a way that led her to discover the problem with her design, she understood the flaw and was able to alter it. She had the ability to consider how multiple variables might interact. Latifa's mom provided questions that guided her to consider the design for her research from a formal operational perspective. Her mom worked with her in the zone of proximal development (see chapter 13), making more sophisticated thinking possible.

Formal operational thinking is characterized by the ability to think in a systematic way—to think of various hypotheses and deduce which one is accurate. Piaget thought of formal operational thinking as the final, integrated stage of intellectual development, one in which a person could perform mental operations on abstract entities, including unusual hypotheses and one's own thinking processes. He thought formal operational thinking was governed by formal logic, the process by which one examines evidence and judges it by comparing it to other abstract propositions.

The formal operational thinker identifies the problem, generates hypotheses that would explain possible outcomes, and designs and carries out a study to test her hypotheses. "The formal-operational thinker makes up a plausible story about what might be going on; figures out what would logically have to happen out there in reality if her story were the right one; checks or does experiments out there to see what does, in fact, happen; and then accepts, rejects, or revises her story accordingly" (Flavell et al., 1993, p. 139). This type of reasoning is called **hypothetico-deductive reasoning.**

Lutz and Sternberg (1999) have differentiated between the concrete operational and formal operational thinker in the following way. Concrete operational thinking involves considering each proposition or possibility as a separate entity and looking for only a factual relationship between a single proposition and reality. In contrast, the formal operational thinker reasons about logical relations that exist between two or more propositions. For example, a concrete operational thinker may simply note that there is a relationship between ethnic group membership and mental ability test performance. The formal operational thinker might add a second proposition concerning cultural bias in testing and a third proposition concerning how environmental or economic conditions may be confounded with particular ethnic groups.

Tasks Used to Assess Formal Operational Thinking

As with the other levels of cognitive development he studied, Piaget devised a number of tasks to test individuals for formal operational thinking. The goal of all these tasks is to isolate the cause of a phenomenon from among several possible factors.

The Pendulum Task   One of the best-known of Piaget's experiments designed to test formal operational thinking is the pendulum task (Inhelder & Piaget, 1958). The adolescent is asked to figure out what determines the period of the pendulum—the time it takes the pendulum to make one full swing. Four factors, or some combination of the four, could be at work: (1) the length of the string, (2) the size of the weight hanging from the string, (3) the height from which the string and weight are released, and (4) the force with which the string and weight are pushed when released (see Figure 17.2).

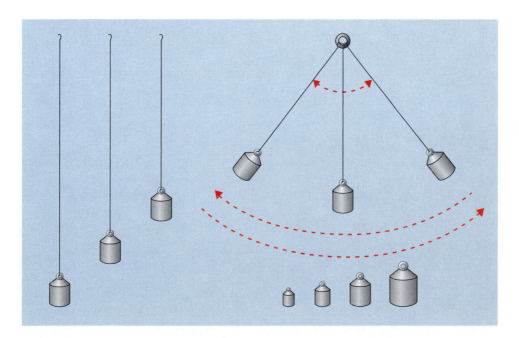

FIGURE 17.2

The Piagetian pendulum. In this task, the child has to think about four variables: the length of the string, the size of the weight, the height from which the weight is let go, and the force with which the weight is let go. Formal operational thinkers can test each variable systematically to arrive at an answer.

To determine which of the variables is responsible for the pendulum's period, the adolescent must vary each one while holding the others constant. If she does not do this—if, for example, she shortens the string at the same time that she decreases the weight—she will not know which change is responsible for any change she observes, or if a change is due to the combined effect.

Concrete operational thinkers change the variables in an unsystematic way and often change more than one at a time. They report the situation ("a long string and a heavy weight versus a short string and a light weight results in a longer period") and the action of the pendulum accurately ("it goes slower now"), but they do not think logically about causation ("the heavy weight and the long string make it go slower"). Formal operational thinkers realize that a more systematic and thorough approach is necessary: "It could be the length of the string or the size of the weight. I must use the same weight while I change the length of the string, or I will not know which one causes the pendulum's period to change." By excluding all competing possibilities, one at a time, they discover that the pendulum's period is determined by the length of the string alone.

The Combination of Chemicals Task   A second task involves combining liquids to produce a liquid of a certain color (Inhelder & Piaget, 1958). The adolescent is shown some beakers and four bottles of clear liquid, labeled 1, 2, 3, and 4. There is also a fifth bottle, labeled g, called an indicator bottle (see Figure 17.3). The chemicals in the bottles are such that combining liquids 1 + 3 + g yields a yellow liquid. If some liquid from bottle 2 is added to liquid 1 + 3 + g, the yellow color remains. If liquid from bottle 4 is added to liquid 1 + 3 + g, the yellow color disappears and the liquid becomes clear.

When the experiment begins, two beakers contain liquid. One contains liquids 1 + 3, and the other contains liquid 2 only. The experimenter adds a drop of liquid from g, the indicator bottle, to beaker 1, and the liquid turns yellow. When the experimenter adds a drop from g to beaker 2, its contents remain clear. The adolescent is then invited to experiment with the liquids to find out which combinations create the yellow liquid.

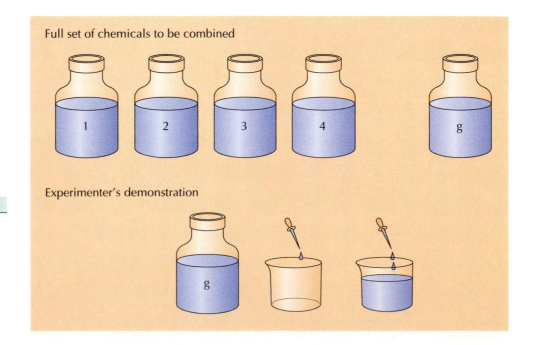

FIGURE   17.3

The combination of chemicals task. This task requires that the child think about more than one liquid at a time and figure out a way to combine them to solve the problem.

Children in the concrete operational stage test the liquids in the bottles one by one, adding a drop of g to each beaker in turn to see if the liquid turns yellow. When none turns yellow, they believe that they have tried everything. If the experimenter suggests that they might try something else, they combine liquids from two bottles and test them, but not in a systematic way. They might try 1 + 4 + g, for example, and then add 3 and then 2. They become confused when they are confronted with so many possibilities.

Adolescents in the formal operational stage also begin by testing one liquid at a time, but when this fails, they realize that they have to mix them. They combine the liquids systematically (1 + 2, 1 + 3, 1 + 4, and so on) and keep track of what they have done until they discover the combination that turns yellow when g is added. Some adolescents even go on to see if combinations of three different liquids from the bottles will turn yellow and to speculate about the relationship of 4 to g because it turns the yellow color clear again.

The Water-Level Task   A third type of task used to test formal operational thinking is the water-level task, a simple perceptual test that involves drawing a line to indicate the water level of a tilted empty container to show that it is half-filled. Recent studies show that as many as 25 to 50 percent of college undergraduates perform poorly on this task (Chronister & Chang, 1999; Vasta & Liben, 1996). This poor showing on a task designed for children presents a challenge to developmentalists. Vasta and Liben concluded that young children do poorly on the task because their spatial system has not yet developed, but that adults who do poorly fail to apply their spatial reasoning system to the task. Chronister and Chang suggest that the inability to solve this problem may be the consequence of how daily information is processed and used. Individual cognitive styles, such as using abstract information in general thinking and being motivated to engage in effortful thinking, may help individuals to figure out the underlying contextual logic presented by the water-level task (Chronister & Chang, 1999).

Do All Adolescents Develop Formal Operational Thinking?

Formal operational thinking is absent in a large proportion of adolescents. Even among well-educated adolescents, only 30 to 40 percent of the students in U.S. schools can solve the Piagetian tasks just described at the formal operational level (Keating, 1980; Linn, 1983). When adults cannot solve these tasks, they are not considered to have attained Piaget's highest cognitive stage (Kuhn, 1988; Overton, 1990; Stanovich, 1993). These findings indicate that formal operational thinking is not a universal developmental milestone.

Those who do not develop such thinking often memorize isolated pieces of information rather than organize and integrate the information as do good scientific thinkers (Atwater, 1996). Concrete operational adolescents may know, and be able to recite, facts and concepts, but often cannot put them to use in solving problems. This is known as **inert knowledge** (Cobb, 1998). That is, the facts are known, but are not transferred or applied to new situations.

Nancy Cobb suggests that problems of inert knowledge can be resolved by teaching students to identify problems, explore alternative solutions, and increase their engagement with the material. Active learning can help students advance from basic knowledge and comprehension to higher levels of analysis, synthesis, and evaluation (McMillan, 1999). In the area of mathematics, Carroll (1994) demonstrated the value of explaining many already-worked word-to-algebraic formula problems rather than using the more conventional technique of giving a model problem with its solution

Because of their experience with scientific activities, these students are likely to demonstrate formal operational thinking. People without scientific experiences often do not use formal operational thinking when presented with problems to think about and solve. (*Source:* © Will Faller)

and having students practice similar problems provided on a worksheet. This instruction was especially effective for students who had lower records of achievement in mathematics. When given only one worked problem, the poorer mathematics students cannot derive the general principle. They then make mistakes as they practice. By following the solutions to several already-worked problems, they can increase their understanding of the general principle involved before moving on to practice.

Why Do the Differences Exist? Why do some people develop formal operational ways of thinking while others do not? Some research suggests that variations in experience account for some of the differences. For example, when adolescents who do not use formal operational thinking are tutored on the Piagetian tasks and similar problems, they often become able to solve problems at this level (Siegler & Liebert, 1975; Stone & Day, 1980; Vasta & Liben, 1996). More adolescent boys than girls show formal operational thinking (Meehan, 1984). Because more boys than girls take science and mathematics courses at the high school level, their greater experience with scientific and mathematical thinking could account for this difference. Benbow and Arjmand (1990) reported that differences in the change in quantitative SAT scores during the high school years, as well as college success in mathematics and science courses, were primarily related to the level of mathematics courses taken. They also reported that significantly fewer females than males identified as mathematically talented in seventh grade took higher-level mathematics and science courses during high school. Similarly, Byrnes and Takahira (1993) found that strategies for problem solving and amount of knowledge accounted for success on SAT math scores and differences in success achieved by male students and female students. Specialized training in spatial tasks as well as encouragement from teachers and parents may help girls achieve higher levels of competence in math and science (Baenninger, 1997). Discrepancies in math performance might also reflect that students live up to expectations (DelCampo & DelCampo, 2000). One study found that mothers who reported a greater liking of math and science had daughters with higher scores on standardized math tests than did daughters of mothers who did not report this interest (Galloway & Balaban, 1998). Several studies show that although U.S. adolescents rank math and computer courses as teaching the most important and useful skills for future success, they continue to test below most other industrialized nations in math (Sullivan, 1999).

Is Formal Operational Thinking Task-Specific? The discovery of differences between adolescent boys' and girls' thinking led some researchers to speculate that the content of the Piagetian tasks, which is oriented predominantly toward math and science, makes them more familiar, appealing, and interesting to some students than to others. They wondered if students who were not math or science oriented would do better if they were given tasks with other content. When they altered the tasks, girls who were not interested in science did better than they did on the standard tasks (Peskin, 1980). In another study, physics majors performed better on the pendulum task while English majors performed better on a task in literary analysis (DeLisi & Staudt, 1980).

Other studies of adolescents indicate that students who know a lot about a subject organize the information in a different way than students who know less. Students who are more knowledgeable also make better use of the information (Cobb, 1998). For example, adolescents with more background knowledge about what they are reading remember better what they have read than do students with less knowledge of what they are reading (Lee, 1990). Students who are knowledgeable in an area of study also organize the information in that area into more abstract categories. Better organization allows students to use strategies more flexibly. "On the subject of expert knowledge, research supports the age-old observation that the rich get richer. The more adolescents know in a given area, the easier it is for them to learn even more" (Cobb, 1998, p. 472).

As mentioned in chapter 13, as children grow older, their metacognitive abilities increase. There are also increases in playing games of strategy, in functional information processing, and in the use of competencies. However, these abilities increase at different rates in different content areas. Thus, a high school junior may be able to apply formal operational thinking in his mathematics class, but continue to approach an English literature course with concrete operational thinking. Research that has provided evidence of domain-specific thinking suggests that formal operational thinking is not an overall pattern of thinking that generalizes to all situations once it is achieved in one area. Instead, the level of thinking seems to depend at least in part on the specific task. Individuals who have had experiences on certain tasks are better able to think at the formal operational level than are individuals who lack knowledge about the specific domain represented by a task (Kuhn, 1989a; Schauble, 1990).

Cultural Considerations in Cognitive Development   Extensive research on cultural factors in cognitive development showed cultural differences in formal operational thinking. These cross-cultural data led Piaget to modify his claim that the stages of thinking were universal. He acknowledged, instead, that the development of formal operational thinking varies across cultures and that its development depends on specific experience with scientific thinking. The cross-cultural research indicated clearly that people are likely to succeed only in tasks that are consistent with the cognitive tasks that are found in their experience. The specific variables that were found to affect performance include familiarity with the objects used in the tasks; similarity of the tasks to experiences provided frequently in the culture; and perceived relevance of new information to day-to-day functioning in familiar cultural contexts (Rogoff & Chavajay, 1995).

During the 1980s, research on cognition and culture shifted to the application of research findings to everyday life and to the functioning of institutions. Rogoff and Chavajay (1995) attribute this shift to a concern in the United States about cultural differences, and to Vygotsky's work on culture and thought. Researchers who have focused on the similarity between tasks required in school and tasks required outside of school have broadened the study of cognition. Now understanding success on cognitive tasks includes an understanding of the complex interactions between the individual, the culture, and the institution (e.g., school).

Adolescents are very interested in social problems, such as those resulting from a multiethnic population. Adolescents can think systematically about racial and cultural problems and apply formal operational thinking to an examination of the causes of

Fewer girls than boys show formal operational thinking, but fewer girls take math courses in high school. Girls like this one, who do take math in high school, are just as likely to use formal operational thinking as their male peers. (*Source:* © Will McIntyre/ Photo Researchers)

and solutions to those problems. Jan Arnow (1995) suggests that high schools should encourage discussion of the processes by which people develop stereotypes and prejudices and that discussions about the effect of family, peers, culture, gender roles, and school activities on school success are important.

An Information-Processing Interpretation of Adolescent Thinking

The **information-processing view** of intellectual development uses the computer as a model of human thinking and views cognitive advances as due not to changes in an overall structure or mode, but to improvements in memory, attention, knowledge, and strategies for solving problems.

Information-processing theorists think that thinking develops continuously, as memory, knowledge, and strategies accumulate (Siegler, 1976, 1986). They do not think that thinking progresses through qualitatively different stages. Information-processing researchers claim that if formal operations were a general way of thinking, we would expect first of all that it would emerge in virtually all people and, second, that individuals would apply it across all situations if they used it in one. But formal operational thinking emerges in only some people, and those who reach it use it to solve certain kinds of problems, but not others.

For example, adolescents are often presented with various types of problems in math and science classes, and some students are better than others in solving these problems. In a study of the comprehension of arithmetic word problems, Hegarty and colleagues (1995) found that successful problem solvers are more likely to use a procedure termed **problem-model strategy.** With this strategy, a mental model of the problem situation is constructed, and a solution is planned on the basis of this model. The unsuccessful problem solvers were more likely to use a **direct-translation strategy,** by basing their solution plan on selected numbers and keywords from the problem. The results of this study indicate that helping adolescents to construct problem-model strategies improves their problem-solving ability.

Characteristics of the Information-Processing Approach

The information-processing approach to understanding the development of cognitive abilities has four major characteristics (Kail & Bisanz, 1992). The first is that computer-like internal mental processes provide the basis of cognitive behavior. The adolescent thinking process consists of symbol manipulation. Thus, information-processing developmentalists use computer programs to simulate the adolescent's development of the ability to manipulate higher-order symbols. An example of using higher-order symbols is Latifa's viewing her study as a three (ages), by three (strains), by three (pesticide concentrations) interaction of factors influencing the results of her study.

A second characteristic of information-processing approaches is the belief that a small set of elementary processes underlies cognitive thought. Thus, researchers taking this approach search for the hierarchical model of fundamental processes that defines an adolescent's thinking.

A third unifying principle of this approach is that the use of the fundamental processes in complex cognitive tasks results in different processes than those present in carrying out lower-level operations. Thus, researchers attempt to learn how fundamental routines are combined to form higher-order thought processes. Finally, information-processing theorists focus on factors internal to the individual. That is, they think that external (environmental) factors, such as the teaching of strategies, have an effect only if they lead to changes in how the adolescent encodes, stores, or indexes information from the environment.

Information-processing research has shifted over the past 25 years from a focus on the study of a limited number of tasks in a laboratory setting to studies focused on understanding the development of social and academic skills in real-world settings. The information-processing approach attempts to provide more precise operational definitions for developmental terms such as assimilation, accommodation, hierarchical thought, schemas, and differentiation.

Information-processing researchers examine the development of more effective strategies to explain how cognitive functioning improves with age. For example, Wood and colleagues (1999) found that adolescents benefit from explicit instruction in a strategy, such as elaboration, and from using that strategy interactively with peers. Information-processing performance also increases when instructional materials provide direction to students in using a self-referencing strategy (Forsyth & Forsyth, 1999).

Having some expertise in a content area helps adolescents gain command of new material in that area. This has been demonstrated in 19 different content areas. Information-processing researchers explain this "expertise effect" as resulting from selective attention being focused economically on the most important characteristics of the new material (Vicente & Wang, 1998).

Developmental studies in information processing also show that adolescence is a period of dramatic improvement in the ability to retain information in the working memory while simultaneously processing other information. This ability increases most rapidly between the ages of 13 and 24, peaks at about age 45, and gradually declines after age 57. The similarity of this pattern across content areas suggests that this is a general improvement in the capacity of working memory during adolescence (Swanson, 1999).

Information-processing researchers also examine short-term factors influencing information processing. For example, Ashby and colleagues (1999) found that increases in the amount of mild positive affect improve performance on cognitive tasks involving working memory, long-term memory, and creative problem solving. These positive effects appear to be related to increased dopamine projection to the prefrontal cortex and anterior cingulate parts of the brain.

Piaget emphasized the assimilation and accommodation processes and direct experiences with problems as the basis for cognitive development. His theory focused on discovery learning rather than learning from instruction by others. The information-processing theorists have added this missing component of learning, which derives from questions and instruction from others. The information-processing researchers are demonstrating ways in which direct instruction and intervention by a teacher can improve performance, not only on the problem for which instruction was offered, but also for a set of similar problems.

Other Dimensions of Adolescent Thinking

Nine-year-old Mark was distracted by a headline he did not understand. After studying the article for a while, he said to his 17-year-old sister, Janice," What does this mean—'Anti-Abortion Demonstrators Close Clinic'?"

Janice glanced at the headline. "It's about a group of people who don't think women should be allowed to have abortions."

"Why are these people against it?"

"Some people think that life begins when the baby is conceived and that taking it out of the mother's womb is the same as killing it. Other people think the woman should have the choice about whether or not she has the baby. What do you think?" Janice asked.

"What do I think about what?" he replied.

"About abortion. Would you think it would be more important to protect the un-born baby or to allow the woman to have control over her body?"

"Well, I don't know, because I don't know anyone who's having a baby right now."

"Well, imagine that Mom is pregnant again. Would you think it would be okay for her to do something so she wouldn't have the baby?"

"But she's not pregnant."

"Well, but you remember when she was pregnant with Molly. Would it have been okay for her not to have had Molly?"

"Well, I don't know, because she did have Molly."

think about it Why do you think Mark cannot discuss this issue? Is he being thick-headed? Why is Janice getting upset with Mark? How does Janice's thinking differ from Mark's? What would be Mark's probable response if Janice had asked him to imagine how he would feel if he had to have a baby he did not want?

Although Mark is a fourth-grader with above-average intelligence, he cannot discuss an issue like abortion with his eleventh-grade sister. He is just not able to think in these sophisticated terms. Janice, on the other hand, has no trouble thinking about this issue. Because she knows her brother is bright, she cannot understand why he is having so much difficulty. Her thinking is fundamentally different from his, and in her conversation we can see several characteristics of adolescents' formal operational thinking that we have not yet discussed.

Hypothetical Thinking and Abstract Ideas

Janice can think in terms of hypothetical situations. She does this by generating problems and considering various ways of addressing them. She is able to "imagine" and "suppose" virtually any set of circumstances, no matter how unrealistic or unlikely. Had she gotten just a little bit further in her conversation with Mark, she might even have asked him to imagine how he would feel if he had to have a baby he did not want. Mark would undoubtedly have answered, "That's impossible! I'm a boy."

Although Mark has no problem pretending—he's been able to pretend-play since he was a toddler—his imagination does not extend to experiences that are very different from his own. Mark also has some social role-taking ability (discussed in chapter 15) and is quite capable of putting himself in someone else's shoes. But again, the shoes have to be a fairly good fit, to start out. What Mark cannot do that Janice can is put all these cognitive abilities together and apply them to a hypothetical situation. During adolescence, children become capable of using and integrating in a systematic way all the achievements of the earlier cognitive stages. They can even argue for a position that contradicts their own knowledge, values, or beliefs (Flavell et al., 1993).

Janice can also think in terms of abstract concepts or ideas about broad principles rather than particular instances. She can think about justice, fairness, rights, and ideas, such as when life may be said to begin or in what ways abortion may be the same as or different from killing any person. Furthermore, she can see ideas about these concepts as points of view or opinions held by different people. Not only can she articulate more than one side of the abortion issue, but she can also argue any side in a formal debate using logical reasoning, no matter her personal convictions. Mark would find it impossible to defend a position opposed to the one he actually holds.

Formal operational thinkers are capable of debating all sides of complex social and political issues. These students are discussing issues as members of a panel.   (*Source:* © M. K. Benny/Photo Edit)

Finally, Janice thinks about important moral, ethical, and political issues. As adolescents' cognitive abilities advance, their interest in complex social and philosophical problems increases. In the later high school years and beyond, they discuss and debate questions of the day: Is nuclear power a viable source of energy? Is surrogate motherhood an acceptable alternative to adoption? What can be done to house the homeless? What can be done to address the fact that 22 percent of U.S. children live in poverty? Adolescents can also discuss the timeless questions that people have been asking for thousands of years: Who or what is God? Why is there evil in the world? What is the meaning of life?

Just as tutoring can elicit improved performances on the Piagetian tasks, carefully designed social interaction can help teenagers think more systematically about complex problems. Debating team coaches, for example, can teach adolescents how to use logical propositions and construct persuasive arguments. English teachers can help students understand sophisticated forms of symbolic communication.

Creative Thinking

J. P. Guilford (1985) distinguished between convergent and divergent thinking in his model of the intellect. Convergent thinking requires the adolescent to apply knowledge in order to converge on a correct answer by narrowing down a list of possible solutions to a problem. Divergent thinking, on the other hand, requires the adolescent to generate many possible solutions to a problem by expanding the number of alternatives. Sternberg (1995) referred to this process of thinking about elements in a new or unique way as **creative thinking.**

Sternberg and his colleagues (Sternberg, 1994) found only moderate correlations between convergent and divergent assessments of thinking. They describe the creative thinker as someone who is good at generating unique ideas, who persists in exploring those ideas, and who moves on to other ideas once her last idea is accepted. Gardner and Sternberg (1994) suggest that the assessment of formal operational

This creative adolescent has found a novel solution for brightening up a drab and dreary student lounge. She is very self-confident and enjoys not being bound to traditional rules. (*Source:* © Bob Daemmrich/ Stock Boston)

thought usually taps convergent problem-solving abilities. They propose that divergent, problem-finding abilities represent an additional stage beyond that of Piaget's formal operational thought. This stage, which occurs after the formal problem-finding stage, recognizes the continuous development of multiple solutions to problems and the evaluation of those solutions (Lutz & Sternberg, 1999).

Creative adolescents can think about something in novel ways and generate unique approaches to thinking about a problem. Researchers have explored some of the characteristics of creative adolescents. They have a high tolerance for ambiguity, enjoy not being bound to rules, are open to experience, and are spontaneous, open-minded, and reflective (Dacey, 1989). Creative adolescents are not easily influenced by other people's opinions, and are more impulsive, more autonomous, more self-confident and self-accepting, less conforming, and less conscientious than less creative people (Barron & Harrington, 1981; Feist, 1998). Sternberg and Lubart (1992) suggest that creative adolescents are willing to change, work at novel solutions for overcoming obstacles, and take risks.

What helps to determine whether an adolescent will be creative? Dacey (1989) found that parents of creative adolescents were very interested in their adolescent's activities but did not set too many rules for behavior. They expected their adolescents to make decisions, and they used family discussions to set expectations. They gave frequent feedback concerning the adolescent's behavior, but seldom used punishment. Humor was highly valued in families of creative adolescents.

The Adolescent at School

As indicated in the chapter 1 presentation of Bronfenbrenner's systems theory of development, an understanding of children or adolescents requires an examination of their relationships with the immediate environment, or microsystem. Because schools play such an important role in the development of adolescents, in this section we examine how transitions in the school environment affect cognitive development.

The Transition to Junior High and High School

At the end of fifth or sixth grade, students typically switch to a junior high or middle school, where they stay for two or three years before entering a senior high school. Junior high and high schools can seem enormous, compared with elementary schools. For the first time since kindergarten, children must meet a whole new set of classmates and adapt to a demanding new schedule.

In most junior high and high schools, subjects are taught by different teachers. Students move from room to room throughout the day, in contrast to elementary school, where they typically spent an entire year in the same classroom. Study periods are also scheduled during the day, and students are expected to allocate their study time as needed to cope with the demands of all their classes. More responsibility for deciding how and what to study falls on the individual student. Other decisions must also be made. In many schools, students are required to take certain core subjects but are free to choose other classes from a group of electives. The number of electives typically increases in high school, as different students decide on different career paths.

Some decisions are made for the student. Ability grouping, a practice sometimes referred to as **tracking,** also becomes commonplace in junior high and high school. Students who excel academically or test high on standardized tests are offered advanced math, science, or English. Students who are less advanced are offered basic math or science. Although some students may have been placed in ability groups in elementary school, being in classes where everyone is basically at the same level in academic skills is usually a new experience for students in junior high school.

Sometimes tracking is carried even further, and whole programs or schools are organized around academic or vocational pursuits. Vocational schools offer basic academic subjects along with classes that train students for specific jobs. Academic schools, on the other hand, offer a wide range of courses in math, social sciences, natural and physical sciences, and humanities, in preparation for college. Tracking can cut short the basic, liberal education a student receives, limiting career and educational options later in school and in life (Fuligni et al., 1995; Oakes, 1985).

Another disadvantage of tracking is that it can create negative attitudes and expectations among students in lower tracks. This can lead these students to expend less effort on schoolwork and to resist learning (Atwater, 1996). These negative expectations and attitudes may contribute to the steep decline in competency self-ratings and academic self-esteem during early adolescence (Seidman et al., 1994). According to **value-expectancy theory,** motivation to work toward success is the product of how much students value the goal of achieving the task and their expectation that they can succeed if they work toward achieving the goal. For many junior high and high school students, the school experience decreases the perceived value of their academic classes and lowers their perceived potential for success, even with hard work. This may be more true for males. One study indicated that extrinsic motivators such as pleasing the teacher and performing well are more prevalent among females than males (DeBacker & Nelson, 1999). Adolescents also have differing perceptions of their academic abilities based on standardized test results. For example, the Center for Talented Youth Program at Johns Hopkins University selects students based on exceptional SAT performance. These students maintain increased levels of self-efficacy in their ability to perform in an academic setting (Galloway & Balaban, 1998). Investigations of the interrelationships of ability, personality, and interest tests suggest that school achievement may be improved through interventions designed to

These students have been tracked into an advanced science class. This placement will have positive outcomes for them. But tracking can limit the intellectual growth of the general high school population if low expectations dominate all but the advanced courses or if motivated students are not allowed to move to higher levels.   (*Source:* © Will Faller)

Larger junior high and high schools can be more impersonal than elementary schools, and can require students to take more responsibility for themselves than they did when they were younger. Very large high schools are often organized into smaller houses in order to create smaller schools within a large school.
(*Source:* © Will Hart)

alter personality or interest characteristics (Ackerman & Heggestad, 1997). Because many students have difficulty with the transition to junior high or middle schools, many school districts are converting back to K–8 elementary schools.

School Size

School size is another factor related to students' school success. Students in smaller schools experience more positive interaction with peers, have a greater sense of belonging, are more engaged in school activities, and are less likely to experience disciplinary action or to drop out of school (Coleman, 1993; Garnier et al., 1997). The positive effects of smaller high schools are especially pronounced as school size decreases from an enrollment of 500 students (Garbarino, 1980). Student participation in activities, the opportunity to assume leadership, and individual attention help to make the school experience more successful for a larger proportion of students in smaller schools (Lindsay, 1984). A longitudinal study by Berk (1992) showed that the greater sense of community in small high schools carries over to greater participation in the community during the adult years.

To reduce some of the adjustment problems found in large junior high schools, **middle schools** offering interdisciplinary teaming are increasingly common. The team organization gives several subject-area teachers responsibility for a common group of students, and they collaborate on instruction (Gallagher, 1994; Lounsbury, 1992). "As middle schools continue to increase in size and complexity, the interdisciplinary team promotes a climate of smallness essential to student success and teacher efficacy" (Lounsbury, 1992, p. vi). Interdisciplinary instruction often enhances understanding through the development of a topic from the perspective of several disciplines, and involves linking and elaborating upon ideas. Working collaboratively in groups aids in the development of positive peer interactions and a greater interest in the subject matter of the courses (Carr et al., 1992; Davies, 1992).

Factors Affecting Academic Success

Numerous variables that might influence academic failure or success in high school come to mind as we reflect about our high school years and the individuals who did and did not succeed. A reliable finding is that participation in school activities is positively correlated with liking school and academic success. The opportunity to participate in cocurricular and extracurricular activities lowers school drop out rates due to increased enjoyment of school and increased social status gained by students who participate actively (Mahoney & Cairns, 1997).

Schools in which teachers believe that students can succeed, in which teachers interact with students, and in which classrooms are friendlier have more students who complete high school. Schools in which teachers hold low expectations for some racial or cultural groups contribute to the failure of those individuals by their differential treatment.

Eccles and Roeser (1999) distinguished between two types of high school teachers. Those with a "weeder" orientation take the view that intelligence is unchangeable and seek to "weed out" less capable students. High school teachers with a "cultivator" orientation emphasize improvement and collaborative learning. The belief system held by a teacher is important to the success of many high school students;

cultivators promote more academic success. Eccles and Roeser also reported that schools with an authoritarian style of control increase student alienation and lower academic success and enjoyment of school.

At the upper grade levels that students reach during adolescence, teachers are less likely to see students' mental health as the teacher's concern and are less likely to notice students' symptoms of distress, such as depression. This change, along with the fact that middle-school teachers feel less efficacious than elementary school teachers, leads to lower academic performance and less expenditure of effort among students in middle school and high school (Roeser & Midgley, 1997).

Characteristics other than mental ability affect students' success in high school and whether they will complete high school. High school dropouts are often victims of **academic disidentification,** meaning that they feel neither positive about their academic success nor disheartened by academic failure. It is a form of self-defense against expectations of poor academic performance (Osborne, 1997).

Family factors such as abuse and interpersonal stress can lead to depression, low self-esteem, decreased school involvement, and running away. A situation often snowballs when abuse and depression go unchecked and the adolescent begins missing school. Parenting methods also affect engagement in academics. For example, one study showed that parenting accounted for more variability in eighth-grade success than did the ability of the adolescent. Authoritative parents enforced schoolwork rules and structure, and their adolescents were above average in their engagement in schoolwork and school activities. But parents whose interactions with their adolescents involved ineffective punitive discipline had sons whose school engagement and success were low (DeBaryshe et al., 1993). (The Knowledge in Action: Education—Parental Support and Achievement discusses parents' roles in school achievement.)

Emotional health is an important factor in school success. Thinking can be disrupted if emotional arousal moves beyond the **window of tolerance,** or the range of emotional arousal that still permits normal functioning. Some adolescents feel comfortable with high degrees of intensity, and their thinking is not affected. For others who have less tolerance, certain emotions such as anger or sadness may disrupt academic functioning (Siegel, 1999). In one study, the combination of adolescent emotional reactivity and hostile parental behavior predicted about 25 percent of the variability in ratings of adolescents' school performance (Shonk et al., 1998).

Some high school students disidentify with academics, and have personal, family and school problems which lead to dropping out of school.   (*Source:* © John Running/Stock Boston)

knowledge *in action*

Parental Support and Achievement

Parent education and encouragement are related to adolescents' academic achievement. Mothers and fathers who take time to talk with their adolescents, are confident in their adolescents' abilities, help them understand and complete homework, listen attentively in discussions about school, and enjoy doing things with their adolescents provide parental support that leads to higher academic success. Parents who expect adolescents to do well academically, and expect a high level of education for them, develop in their adolescent children a higher value for education and higher expectancy for success through effort (Wang & Wildman, 1995). Indeed, the academic success of Asian American students may be related to their relatively problem-free home environments and to the amount of time and money invested by their parents in educational resources (Kao, 1995). Studies comparing Asian American and non-Asian high school students indicate that Asian American students outperform non-Asians and report a greater feeling of responsibility to their families and communities. The non-Asian students had more of an individual-focused orientation and overestimated their ability. The latter appears to result from how non-Asian parents emphasize high self-esteem in contrast to Asian American parents, who emphasize feedback about their adolescents' behavior. The fear-of-failure, performance-oriented motivation of the Asian students appeared to result from parents' stress on academic success and adolescents' concern about not meeting parental standards.

A study of low-income African American youth also suggested that parental beliefs and expectations about their children's future scholastic attainment may play an even more important role in promoting success than do specific parental behaviors (Halle et al., 1997).

Authoritative parenting, coupled with granting of autonomy in adolescence, is positively associated with good college freshman grades, task persistence, and rapport with faculty (Strage & Brandt, 1999). Authoritative parenting is also associated with better deductive reasoning in problem solving (Chapell & Overton, 1998). Even the quality of the early home environment sets a course toward adolescent academic success. For example, a longitudinal study showed that quality of home environment and parents' involvement in school during grades one through three were associated with higher academic performance in high school at age 16 (Jimerson et al., 1999). Attachment style has also been found to relate to information-processing style. Securely attached adolescents were more curious and relied more on new information in making judgments than those with anxious-avoidant attachments (Mikulincer, 1997).

Parental approaches to discipline affect adolescent performance when the adolescents are faced with a difficult challenge. Praise and criticism of specific behaviors, rather than of the adolescent as a person, are more likely to lead to task-mastery motivation and greater persistence in striving to succeed at a challenging task. Adolescents who are criticized as people are more likely to assume that their failure or difficulty in achieving a task is simply the result of an unchangeable personal trait, leading them to quit the task or lose self-efficacy (Kamins & Dweck, 1999).

Also, a parent's academic achievement supports that of the child. The higher the level of a parent's education, the greater the cognitive readiness for parenting. A generational effect is set in motion as the well-educated parent shows the adolescent the importance of prenatal development, good parenting practices, responsibility to children's signals, and the harmful effect of punitiveness (O'Callaghan et al., 1999).

Cairney (1995) argues that a solid partnership between parents and the school should exist for the secondary school as it often does during elementary school years. His research shows that it is not more difficult to involve parents of adolescents in school programs, and that adolescents do appreciate the active involvement of their parents. Cairney's "Effective Partners in Secondary Literacy Learning" (EPISLL) was designed to support and raise parent participation in literacy learning and study skills in grades 7 to 10. Program content covered topics such as the nature of the reading and writing process, strategies for assistance with work (summarizing, note taking, understanding the textbook), learning strategies, and locating community resources. Students in the program acquired new skills as a result of parental involvement, showed evidence of raised expectations, and grew in confidence and self-esteem. In addition, parents and students reported improved communication and better personal relationships.

Research has also indicated that learning environments can be structured to encourage **self-regulated learning,** in which students control their thoughts, motivation, or behaviors in order to achieve educational goals (Hofer & Yu, 1999). Doing group projects, keeping a weekly reflection journal, and working in groups on study skills all aid self-control.

A number of factors differentiate students who successfully complete high school from the large number (over 11 percent of high school students) who drop out. Poverty is the characteristic that best predicts dropping out of school. Table 17.1 pre-

TABLE 17.1

Factors leading to the completion of high school

Adolescent Factors	Family Factors	School Factors
■ Freedom from depression	■ Freedom from abuse	■ Enjoyment of school
■ Good self-esteem	■ Stable home life	■ Involvement in school activities
■ Low anxiety and stress	■ Lack of family stress	■ Passing grades or better
■ Freedom from substance abuse	■ Authoritative parenting	■ No repeated grade levels
■ Avoidance of pregnancy	■ Positive discipline	■ Few absences and tardies
■ Peer acceptance	■ Two-parent household	■ Few disciplinary infractions
■ Connectedness with peers	■ Economic security	■ Few teacher-student difficulties
■ Less than 20 hours employment per week	■ Values education	■ Friendly classrooms
	■ Cultural majority	■ Teachers with high expectations
	■ Positive attitudes toward school	■ Teachers who interact readily with students
	■ Siblings graduated	

Sources: CEPC, 1999; Jacobs et al., 1997; KIDS COUNT, 1999; Osborne, 1997; Shonk et al., 1998; Woods, 1999.

sents the adolescent factors, family factors, and school factors that differentiate those who finish and those who drop out of school.

The consequences of dropping out of high school include limited job opportunities, lower income, and an increased likelihood of delinquency, alcohol and drug abuse, violence, and suicide. By the age range of 25–54 years, the income of dropouts is only half of what high school graduates make (KIDS COUNT, 1999).

Learning disabilities magnify the dropout problem. The unemployment rate is 30 percent higher for those with learning disabilities who drop out of school than for students with learning disabilities who complete high school. They also earn one-third less income (CECP, 1999). Several programs, such as *City-As-School* (New York City), the *Coca Cola Valued Youth Program*, the *Adopt a Student* Program, and *Upward Bound*, have reduced dropout rates (Woods et al., 1999). Table 17.2 presents suggestions for how schools could reduce dropout rates.

TABLE 17.2

What can schools provide to reduce the dropout rate?

■ Tracking of at-risk students	■ Connections with peers
■ Programs addressing risk-taking prevention	■ Parental involvement in school activities
■ Counseling and therapy opportunities	■ Low student-teacher ratios
■ Mentoring programs	■ Smaller programs within large schools
■ Tutoring programs	■ Monitored work experiences (e.g., internships)
■ Career counseling and information	■ Involvement with community role models
■ Mental health development programs	■ Promotion of business partnerships
■ Opportunities to make up work (e.g., summer school)	■ Intercultural sensitivity

Sources: KIDS COUNT, 1999; Woods, 1999.

Cognitive Strategies and Academic Success

Comparisons of academically excelling and regular students indicate differences in the way students use academic strategies. The high-performing students organize more, transform and review notes, and establish self-set consequences for study behavior to a greater extent than do average students. These strategies increase for high-performing individuals as they progress from the fifth to the eleventh grades (Zimmerman & Martinez-Pons, 1990).

The use of effective strategies, ratings of self-efficacy, and actual achievement are not always uniform for students across different academic areas. An examination of self-efficacy (the belief that one has the ability to achieve a specific goal) and high achievement indicated that extreme talent and self-efficacy tend to be specific rather than global. The different areas of excellence and efficacy were consistent with Gardner's (1983) list of multiple intelligences reviewed in chapter 13 (Colangelo & Kerr, 1990).

Students also differ in the academic areas in which they view themselves as capable. In one study, with both high and average academic ability, males had higher confidence than females in their mathematics ability, whereas females had higher confidence in their verbal abilities. Relatedly, males were more interested in taking mathematics and females were more interested in reading and English courses (Galloway & Balaban, 1998).

Students' beliefs about their capabilities are important components of academic motivation and achievement (Bandura, 1997; Pajares & Graham, 1999). Studies seeking explanations for the large variability in adolescents' mathematics achievement and mathematics self-esteem found that mathematics grades were best predicted by students' belief that they would be able to master course concepts if they were to work hard at it. The value placed on understanding mathematics concepts predicted the mathematics course selection by adolescents. These relationships existed for both males and females (Meece et al., 1990). A combination of expectations and the selection of mathematics course level creates the large differences in mathematics achievement between males who finish their high school education with higher mathematics achievements than females. The combination of these two factors has a snowball effect. Higher-level courses not only cover more concepts, but require more higher-order mental reasoning to master the concepts and include exercises or assignments that increase the students' perception that there is value in learning the course content.

Motivational orientation also influences adolescent academic achievement. Intrinsically oriented adolescents (who are motivated by their own need to learn) enjoy challenging tasks and persist longer at them than do extrinsically oriented adolescents (who are motivated by concerns for recognition, reliance on authority, and a preference for easy tasks). These students make self-defeating assessments of their own ability. Intrinsically oriented students have a higher need for cognition, whereas extrinsically oriented students compete compulsively for recognition. Intrinsically oriented students described peak experiences as those in which they enjoyed mastering challenging tasks, while those who are extrinsically motivated described their peaks as heightened experiences of prestige and superiority (Schmalt, 1999; Sturman, 1999).

Whatever their orientation, students who outperform others often experience discomfort. This is a special problem in high school, where the one who outperforms can be perceived as a threat and might experience social isolation. Such negative effects are especially pronounced among extrinsically motivated high school students when in situations requiring them to discuss their superior outcome with those who do less well. Some students avoid the stigma of giftedness by disclaiming their achievements and by effecting a modest self-presentation. In cultures that do not value high academic achievement, outperformers feel a lack of peer support from their racial or ethnic group and begin affiliating with other groups to the exclusion of their own (Exline & Lobel, 1999). Other students experience academic disidentification to maintain ethnic identity and support. This process is especially pronounced for African American high school males (Osborne, 1997).

Information-processing researchers have been using the computer analogy to study the cognitive operations needed for success on the SAT. The **cognitive process approach** analyzes the independent cognitive thought operations (e.g., knowledge skills and cognitive reasoning) needed for academic success. For the mathematics SAT, Byrnes and Takahira (1993) identified six separate cognitive components: correctly defining the problem, accessing prior knowledge related to the problem, putting together an effective strategy, performing computations without error, avoiding being attracted to misleading alternatives, and performing the preceding five operations quickly (less than 1 minute per test item). Prior knowledge and use of an effective strategy accounted for 50 percent of the variability in success on the mathematics SAT scores. This cognitive processing approach suggests that teaching students to use higher-level cognitive strategies will help them achieve greater academic success. This approach is most likely to be effective if steps are also taken to motivate students to value and have high expectations of academic achievement.

Ball and colleagues (1994) found that intellectually gifted adolescents had superior metacognitive abilities and made greater use of efficient strategies. Building on such findings, Pearson and Santa (1995) taught students about organizing, metacognition, and relating new information to background knowledge, and then asked them to experiment with new study strategies as they approached their learning. Such efforts to have adolescents think about thinking help them to achieve a deeper level of understanding and greater success (Dole et al., 1995).

Adolescents' thoughts about their own thinking may have important consequences for motivation to achieve intellectual performance. For example, if they think of intelligence as a fixed trait over which they have no control, they may believe that effort will not matter. This idea is termed **entity theory**. However, if adolescents believe that intelligence is malleable and controllable, they may think that effort and training will matter. This idea is termed **incremental theory** (Flavell, 1999).

Assessing the Adolescent

Three or four generations ago, people would have been mystified by today's talk about SAT scores and the importance they have for so many high school students. Today, these and other test scores are important to millions of young people's lives, influencing where they go to college, how much financial support they receive, and what course their lives will take.

Achievement Tests   Achievement tests measure high school students' accomplishments in various areas of study. The three most frequently used achievement tests are the *School and College Ability Test (SCAT)*, developed by Educational Testing Service (ETS) (1979); the *American College Testing Program (ACT)*, developed by American College Testing Services (1984); and the *Scholastic Assessment Test (SAT)*, developed by the College Entrance Examination Board, and in 1994 changed to *SAT I: Reasoning Test*. The Scholastic Aptitude Test was renamed because of the implication that it measured innate intelligence (Jordan, M., 1993) and that it would be a good predictor of college success. The SAT I: Reasoning Test has an increased emphasis on critical reading and contains longer reading passages. Students produce responses to math problems, rather than respond to multiple choice items. They are also allowed to use calculators (Smith, M. K., 1994).

All the tests include verbal and quantitative (math) parts, although some tests emphasize one more than the other. The SAT and the SCAT, for example, contain just two parts, one verbal and one mathematical. The ACT, on the other hand, has four parts—English usage, mathematics usage, social sciences reading, and natural science reading. The ACT emphasizes reading and other language abilities more than do the SAT and the SCAT. Adolescents who watch a great deal of television perform poorly on standardized achievement tests, perhaps due to less time spent reading (Comstock & Scharrer, 1999).

The SAT and ACT are currently the most commonly used tests for college admissions. Both have low correlations with college grades and neither is as good a predictor of college grades as are high school grades. As additional information, at some schools these test scores improve the prediction of college grades over high school grades alone, for those with a lower percentile rank in high school (Aiken, 1985). Most colleges consider a number of factors in their admissions decisions, giving rank in high school class the most weight. In 1999 the state of New York required students to pass the English Regents exam in order to graduate. By 2003, it is expected that at least 25 states will require high school exit exams (CNN, 1999b).

Intelligence Tests and Interest Tests   The intelligence test used most widely with older adolescents is the *Wechsler Adult Intelligence Scale-Revised (WAIS-R)*. It has six verbal and five performance subtests. The examinee is asked to solve arithmetic problems, give word definitions, complete pictures, make block designs, and assemble objects, for example. The WAIS-R yields a verbal score, a performance

Soon these high school students will be discussing their SAT scores, anxiously waiting to hear from colleges to which they have applied, and thinking about the course their lives will take. It is important for adults to help adolescents consider interest as well as ability profiles in identifying college majors or career choices. *(Source:* © Mark Richards/Photo Edit)

Interest tests can help adolescents discover areas in which they are likely to do well as adults. Many high schools have the facilities to support vocational career exploration. This student is learning to weld. (*Source:* © Michael Rosenfeld/Tony Stone Images)

score, and a full-scale intelligence score. This test is often used to help determine the presence of learning disabilities.

Another type of test helps adolescents identify their inclinations for various fields and vocations. The *Kuder General Interest Survey* measures interest in 10 areas—outdoor, mechanical, computational, scientific, persuasive, artistic, literary, musical, social service, and clerical. Another interest test is the *Strong-Campbell Interest Inventory,* which includes seven parts. Subjects are asked questions such as how they would feel about participating in various occupations, how much they like certain types of people, and what they like to do for recreation. They are also asked to give preferences for pairs of activities, and to choose whether or not certain characteristics describe them well (Aiken, 1991). Either of these tests, when used in conjunction with other measures, such as achievement in specific areas, can help individuals make decisions about careers.

Assessing Specific Cognitive Abilities and Specific Areas of Self-Esteem
As indicated in chapter 13, there has been a shift from labeling children with a single number reflecting their intelligence to assessing multiple cognitive abilities. This shift was reflected in the 1986 revision of the Stanford Intelligence Scale to include four broad areas of mental ability (verbal reasoning, quantitative reasoning, visual reasoning, and short-term memory) with more specific subscales within each area (Thorndike et al., 1986).

In 1993 a massive factor-analytical study was conducted by Carroll to identify all of the types of human cognitive abilities. This analysis clustered many narrow abilities under a smaller number of broader cognitive abilities. Carroll's broad abilities include fluid intelligence (such as reasoning and problem solving), crystallized intelligence (accumulated knowledge), memory processes, visual processing, auditory processing, verbal fluency, and speed of responding. Sternberg (1994) notes the similarity of Carroll's factors to those suggested by Gardner (1995). These include musical (auditory), spatial (visual), linguistic, mathematical, bodily-kinesthetic, and social (personal) intelligence. When these six contents are crossed with memory, practical (convergent), creative (divergent), and analytical (evaluative) thought processes, a profile of 24 different mental abilities results. This profile can help adolescents in their selection of a college major or vocation. Consistent with Guilford's (1985) and Gardner's (1995) theories, Colangelo and Kerr (1990) reported that outstanding performance in one academic area (defined as being in the top 1 percent) was often quite specific. Many of those in the top 1 percent in one academic area tested in the average range in at least one other cognitive ability area.

It is important to consider interest as well as ability profiles in helping adolescents identify college majors or career choices. Colangelo and Kerr (1990) reported that only 1.6 percent of the top 1 percent of verbal ability students planned to major in English, 5 percent of the top 1 percent in mathematics planned to major in mathematics, 0.4 percent of the top 1 percent on the standardized social sciences test planned to major in history or geography, and 19.3 percent of the top 1 percent on the natural sciences standardized test planned to major in the biological or physical sciences.

In addition to these multiple intelligences, there is also a relationship between emotional intelligence and academic achievement in adolescence (Wentzel, 1991). **Emotional intelligence** involves the capacity to reason with emotion in the following ways:

- To be aware of emotions being experienced
- To integrate emotions into cognitive thought
- To understand the reasons for emotions
- To manage or regulate emotion to achieve goals

This aspect of intelligence appears to relate to academic success and the achievement of important life outcomes (Mayer, 1999).

Assessing the many cognitive abilities of adolescents rather than a single IQ provides many more opportunities to indicate areas of special ability and to raise adolescents' self-esteem. Marsh (1992) used factor-analytical techniques to search for the factors of self-esteem present in high schoolers. He found 14 types of self-esteem related to academic areas (e.g., English, mathematics, science, music, art, physical education, foreign languages). Marsh correlated these self-esteem scores with student scores on eight academic achievement tests. Each of the eight achievement scores correlated more highly with the matching academic self-esteem scale than with any other academic self-esteem scale. Indeed, approximately one-third of the variability in an academic subject was accounted for by knowing the adolescents' academic-area self-esteem. In contrast, a general self-esteem measure accounts for an average of less than 5 percent of the variability in academic success scores. A similar pattern of identifying specific achievement motivations to account for success in academic courses was found by Lehman (1993).

In summary, although parental and school interventions prior to adolescence have the greatest effect on adolescent academic achievement, interventions during the high school years can be effective when they help adolescents with organization and higher-order problem-solving strategies, and when they include idiographic feedback and reinforcement for effort as well as for actual achievement (Durlak, 1995). Idiographic feedback focuses on the adolescent's improvement rather than on how she compares to others.

KEY POINTS

Formal Operational Thinking

■ Piaget investigated formal operational thinking with experiments that tested the adolescent's ability to isolate the cause of a phenomenon from among several possible factors.

■ In Piaget's pendulum task, adolescents had to figure out what determined the time it took the pendulum to make one full swing. They had to test each of four factors separately to discover that the length of the string was the only relevant factor. In the combination of chemicals task, they had to figure out how to combine chemicals to produce a liquid of a certain color.

■ The water-level task involves drawing a line to indicate the water level of a tilted empty jar. One fourth to one-half of college students do not perform this task correctly.

■ Because not all adolescents (or adults) attain formal operational thinking, it is not a universal development. Variations in experience may explain why some people attain it and others do not.

■ Formal operational thinking is a task-specific way of thinking, characteristic of people who have had certain experiences.

An Information-Processing View of Adolescent Thinking

■ In the information-processing view of cognition, advances in thinking are attributed to improvements in memory, attention, knowledge, and problem-solving strategies. This view frequently applies the computer analogy to thinking processes. It tends to have difficulty representing the child's thinking about thinking.

■ Information-processing researchers examine the development of more effective thinking strategies with increasing age and environmental support.

■ The information-processing view is not necessarily in conflict with Piaget's view, but it focuses more on the specific experiences that can improve children's performance.

Other Dimensions of Adolescent Thinking

■ Adolescents become capable of thinking in hypothetical terms and imagining all the possibilities inherent in a situation. They put together all the achievements of earlier cognitive stages in a systematic way.

■ Adolescents also become able to think about abstract concepts; to argue different points of view, even if they do not agree with them; and to explore sophisticated political, moral, and philosophical ideas.

■ Good teaching can help teenagers think logically about important issues and appreciate the richness available to them in their cultural heritage.

■ Creative adolescents are able to think about problems in novel ways and to generate unique approaches to solve problems. In the stage following the formal problem-solving task, the development of multiple solutions to problems can be understood.

The Adolescent at School

■ The organization of junior high or middle school is usually quite different from that of elementary school; subjects are departmentalized, students move from room to room throughout the day, and more responsibility is given to the individual.

■ Junior high schools often group students by ability, or track them, based on judgments about what path—college or vocation—different students are likely to take after school. Tracking is thought by some to be detrimental to the goals of creating a well-educated general populace and to keeping a variety of career opportunities open to students.

■ Smaller junior high and high schools generally have advantages over larger schools.

■ Cultural identity, academic disidentification, and parenting styles affect adolescent academic motivation and success.

■ Parents, teachers, peers, self-esteem, and participation in school activities are related to academic success.

■ The use of effective cognitive strategies is important for academic success.

■ Achievement tests commonly used to assess adolescents' knowledge include the SCAT, the SAT, and the ACT. Colleges use students' scores on these tests as well as several other factors in determining whether to accept a student.

■ The most commonly used intelligence test for older adolescents and adults is the Wechsler Adult Intelligence Scale-Revised. The best-known interest tests are the Kuder General Interest Survey and the Strong-Campbell Interest Inventory. Interest tests help individuals make decisions about careers.

■ Specific cognitive abilities, different types of self-esteem, and interests should be considered in helping adolescents identify a college major or a career.

GLOSSARY

academic disidentification: a form of self-defense against expectations of poor academic performance, shown by ambivalent feelings about success or failure (p. 593)

American College Testing Program (ACT): a four-part achievement test emphasizing reading and other language abilities; used for college entrance (p. 597)

cognitive process approach: an approach to information processing that examines knowledge, skills, and cognitive processes needed for academic success (p. 597)

creative thinking: generating many possible solutions to a problem (p. 589)

direct-translation strategy: a solution to a problem based on attention to only certain numbers or key words (p. 586)

emotional intelligence: the capacity to be aware of, understand, and regulate emotions (p. 600)

entity theory: thinking of intelligence as a fixed trait and believing that effort will not matter (p. 597)

formal operational thinking: thinking that involves a logical and systematic formulation of hypotheses-deductive reasoning (p. 580)

hypothetico-deductive reasoning: reasoning in which a problem is identified, hypotheses are generated, and a study is carried out to test the hypotheses (p. 581)

incremental theory: thinking of intelligence as malleable, and believing that effort and training will matter (p. 597)

information-processing view: a view of intellectual functioning and development that stresses memory and rules learned, rather than maturation-induced stages (p. 586)

inert knowledge: knowledge of facts and concepts without the ability to apply them in new situations (p. 583)

Kuder General Interest Survey: a survey used to measure an individual's aptitude for various occupations (p. 599)

middle schools: schools that differ from junior high schools in that they have interdisciplinary teams to bridge the gap between elementary and secondary schools (p. 592)

problem-model strategy: strategy by which a solution to a problem is planned based on making a mental model of the problem (p. 586)

SAT I: Reasoning Test: revised SAT with increased emphasis on critical reading and math responses (p. 597)

Scholastic Assessment Test (SAT): achievement test containing verbal and mathematical sections; used for college entrance (p. 597)

School and College Ability Test (SCAT): a two-part achievement test for college entrance, containing verbal and math sections (p. 597)

self-regulated learning: a process of self-control of thoughts, motivation, or behaviors in order to achieve educational goals (p. 594)

Strong-Campbell Interest Inventory: an inventory used to determine an individual's likes and dislikes as they might relate to different occupations (p. 599)

tracking: substantially different programs of study offered to students who differ in ability and who have different goals for the work they will pursue after high school (p. 591)

value-expectancy theory: the view that motivation for success is based on the value of the goal and the expectation of success (p. 591)

Wechsler Adult Intelligence Scale-Revised (WAIS-R): widely used, individually administered intelligence test used with individuals of age 12 and older (p. 598)

window of tolerance: the range of emotional arousal intensity that still permits normal functioning (p. 593)

SUGGESTIONS FOR FURTHER READING

Coats, E. J. (2000). *Contemporary readings in psychology: A New York Times reader.* Upper Saddle River, NJ: Prentice Hall. This is a special topics reader; including discussion questions for each article. Articles 9 and 10 discuss IQ scores and intelligence in all its interactive aspects.

Crain, W. (2000). *Theories of development: Concepts and applications.* Upper Saddle River, NJ: Prentice Hall. Chapter 6 of this book, written in interesting narrative, discusses Piaget's theory.

Geary, D. C. (1994). *Children's mathematical development: Research and practical applications.* Washington, DC: American Psychological Association. This book discusses cross-national differences in math achievement, gender differences, math giftedness and disabilities, and math anxiety.

Mehler, J., & Franck, S. (Eds.). (1995). *Cognition on cognition*. Cambridge, MA: MIT Press. This series of articles, originally published in *Cognition,* reviews progress of the last 25 years in cognitive research.

Sternberg, R. J., & Wagner, R. K. (Eds.). (1994). *Mind in context: Interactionist perspectives on human intelligence*. New York: Cambridge University Press. Several topics are presented in this book, including novelty and intelligence, academic-task abilities, the effects of context on cognition, and problem solving across age levels. All chapters are very readable.

Ward, T. B., Finke, R. A., & Smith, S. M. (1995). *Creativity and the mind: Discovering the genius within*. New York: Plenum. This book applies insights from research to a variety of creative pursuits and describes the creative processes that led to new endeavors.

CHAPTER 18

Language Development in Adolescents

"MOM, WE'RE HOME! We're back early because Eric was scared by a dog who knocked down a little boy who was playing ball in the park. I told Eric the dog was just a big puppy, not really a mean dog who was going to hurt him. But he wouldn't listen. What a scaredy cat!"

"I'm not a scaredy cat! See, Mom, there was a great big dog. He ran all over the place and jumped up and down. A little boy in the park was playing ball. Then the dog ran over and jumped on him. He fell down, and then he cried. I thought he would knock me down too, and I was scared. So I made Brad bring me home. It was a big, mean dog!"

What are the differences between the sentences used by the two boys? Do they differ in complexity and length? Which boy's language is more efficient, that is, concise and yet at the same time packed with more meaning?

Brad, age 15, and Eric, age 8, tell the same story to their mother, but each tells the story from his own perspective. Of course, this is not what makes their storytelling remarkably different. What separates the two in terms of language development is the level of sophistication found in the sentences they use. Eric uses more sentences, and they are shorter. It takes six separate sentences for him to describe what happened. Each sentence adds another small detail about the incident with the dog. Brad, on the other hand, uses just one sentence to relate all the critical details of the incident. His efficiency illustrates one way that the language of older children differs from the language of younger children. Compared to the language of younger school-age children, adolescent language is often more efficient and coherent in expression.

Although the basics of language learning are virtually complete by the beginning of adolescence, important refinements are made during this period: greater precision in speaking, greater sophistication in writing, the emergence of the ability to comprehend metaphorical as well as literal meaning, and better comprehension of what is read. Many of these advances reflect improvements in cognitive abilities. Others, such as comprehension, reflect increased background knowledge, as well as social, emotional, and cognitive growth. In this chapter, we discuss these characteristics of adolescent language and new aspects of language resulting from various forms of electronic communication.

Cognitive Underpinnings of the Adolescent's Language Advances

Like Eric, most younger children use many sentences to say what adolescents can say in just one or two. When younger children do make longer utterances, they usually accomplish this by combining several simple sentences with the conjunction *and*. Adolescents, on the other hand, use grammatical devices to subordinate some information in the sentence to other information. The ability to relate one piece of information to other pieces allows the adolescent to communicate ideas more precisely and efficiently. The adolescent's improved ability to apply the rules of grammar and to reason logically and analytically also helps to improve language use (deVilliers & deVilliers, 1992). In a complementary way, advances in language acquisition and in the process of applying strategies that help decipher the meanings of new words play important roles in cognitive development (deVilliers & deVilliers, 1999).

Adolescents' greater sophistication in speaking and writing—their ability to create complex sentences containing many clauses—is made possible by their improved intellectual functioning. To use clauses, a person must decide which elements are primary, or superordinate, and which are secondary, or subordinate. Classes or categories must be created and their relationships considered. Because younger school-age children cannot create superordinate and subordinate relationships as readily as the adolescent, they produce many short statements without organizing them hierarchically.

The Emergence of Metaphorical Interpretation

Adolescents' cognitive advances are revealed not only in their speech, but also in their understanding of others' speech. This is seen, for example, in their new ability to understand figurative uses of language. School-age children, on the other hand, are well known for interpreting everything they hear quite literally. They usually interpret things literally because they do not understand something well enough to interpret it at a metaphorical level, even though it often seems that they prefer literal translations of what is said because it gives them a chance to act silly. Tell an 8-year-old to "cut it out" and he is likely to respond, "Let me go get my scissors." Between 5 and 9 years of age, children figure out the meanings of many figures of speech (Geller, 1985). But by 11 or 12 years of age, children begin to appreciate language on a different level—by shifting from literal to **metaphorical interpretations.** When interpreting text or speech metaphorically, as a figure of speech, the adolescent understands the relationship between the ordinary meaning of the words and the implied figurative meaning. For example, the phrases "a copper sky" or "a heart of stone" produce meaning by relating one concept to another in an implied comparison.

With this new ability, older children and adolescents can understand parables and proverbs. One researcher found that children of different ages responded quite differently to proverbs (Saltz, 1979, p. 511). Here are two of the proverbs he asked them to interpret, along with the responses obtained from children of different ages:

Proverb 1: People in glass houses shouldn't throw stones.

Age	Response
5	"Because it breaks the glass."
7	"You know people don't live in glass houses. I don't see no glass houses."
9	"If you buy a glass house, expect to have a broken window."
11	"If you hurt people, you may get hurt yourself."

Proverb 2: When the cat's away, the mice will play.

Age	Response
4	"Cause the mouse scares the cat."
6	"When the cat goes, the mice stay."
7	"Because the cat would eat the mice so they play when the cat is gone."
10	"When parents are away, children will wreck the house."

We see from these examples that by the time children are 10 or 11 years old they begin to escape from literal interpretations of language. These advances in language are also an important aspect of theory-of-mind development and the ability to reflect about the intentions and emotions of those who are communicating with them (Astington & Jenkins, 1999).

EDUCATION

Metaphorical Reasoning and Language

Adolescents' interpretation of literature develops to a higher level when metaphorical reasoning allows them to interpret language figuratively rather than literally. One way to develop this type of reasoning is to give students practice in using the related process of analogical thinking. Analogical thinking is the process of understanding a novel situation in terms of another situation that is already familiar. Analogical thinking includes the following three components. First, several analogs stored in memory are retrieved as candidates for understanding a new situation or problem. Second, each analog accessed from memory is compared to or mapped against the new situation or problem. Third, the analog that most closely resembles the new situation is used to make inferences about what might happen in the new situation.

For example, if an urban high school science class is studying electricity, the teacher's goal may be that students understand the flow of electrons in an electrical circuit. She might ask her students to imagine the flow of people in a crowded subway tunnel and might describe this situation as analogous to electrons in an electrical circuit. Next, she might ask what would happen to the flow of people if they pass through a narrow gate in the tunnel. After the stu-

dents conclude that the gate would decrease the number of people moving through the tunnel, the teacher asks what happens if a resistor is added to an electrical circuit. The students' predictions are then verified by a laboratory demonstration (Gentner & Holyoak, 1997).

Teaching students to use analogical thinking promotes the shift from literal interpretation of language, in which attention is focused on actual object features, to interpretation of language in terms of relational commonalities and metaphors (Gentner & Markman, 1997).

Self-referencing also improves relational thinking. Self-referencing involves relating new material to the learner's life experiences. If a learner uses this encoding process, it improves memory for the newly learned material (Forsyth et al., 1994; Forsyth & Forsyth, 1999). Practice at using self-referencing also improves the relational thinking needed for metaphorical reasoning in both language interpretation and language production (Symons & Johnson, 1997).

Teachers and parents can increase metaphorical reasoning by doing the following:

- Using analogies in explanations
- Using analogies in conversation
- Asking adolescents to develop relationships in language
- Asking adolescents to look for relationships between two different situations
- Modeling the analogy process in problem solving
- Asking adolescents to use self-referencing

Adolescents and younger children may use figures of speech without actually being able to think metaphorically. Correctly explaining the meaning of a specific proverb does not necessarily indicate that the adolescent can think abstractly. The adolescent may simply learn what a proverb means but is not actually able to explain why it has that meaning. Gibbs and Beitel (1995) suggest that it is the use of proverbs in daily discourse—making them up as the situation demands—that illustrates people's ability to think in figurative (metaphorical) rather than literal ways.

Increases in Vocabulary and Refinements in Word Use

Sixteen-year-old Towanda is busy doing her homework when Mike, her younger brother, interrupts with a question: "Towanda, what does 'undercharacterize' mean? I've never seen that word, and it's big!"

"I don't know that word either, but I think I can figure it out," replies Towanda. "Let's see," she continues, talking out loud to herself. "Mmmmmmmm . . . 'under' means 'below' or 'less than.' I think 'characterize' means 'to give a personality to a character in a story'—sort of like you might say Beverly Cleary 'characterizes' Ralph S. Mouse as an adventurer in the story you were reading last night. See what I mean?"

"Yes . . . sort of, so what does it mean? What does 'undercharacterize' really mean?"

"Well," Towanda explains, "I think it means that a writer does less than she should to develop her story characters. You can't tell what the character is really like—for example, whether the character is adventurous, shy, considerate, or whatever."

"Oh, yeah! That makes sense," says Mike. "This movie review I'm reading said that the director undercharacterized the leading role. I guess the director didn't do a good job of building up the person the actor portrayed in the movie. Thanks, Towanda!"

think about it

How are the approaches to understanding a new word different for Mike and Towanda? How does Towanda intuit the meaning of the new word? How might this approach to expanding vocabulary rely on what children are taught in school?

Numerous studies have been conducted to estimate increases in vocabulary during adolescence. The estimates vary a great deal depending on whether they were based on writing, speaking, listening, or reading vocabulary. Studies of reading vocabulary indicate that students typically can read 20,000 to 40,000 words as they enter middle school, and that this range is 40,000 to 80,000 words by the time they complete high school. This increase of 3,000 to 6,700 words per year results in an average daily increase in vocabulary of between 8 and 18 words (Ryder & Graves, 1994).

Much of this vocabulary increase results from hearing new words in context. This auditory approach to forming long-term memory representations of new words is a critical aspect of language development. A **phonological loop** provides a temporary storage of unfamiliar words in the working memory so that a more permanent long-term memory can be constructed. This loop plays a major role in the auditory aspect of increasing vocabulary. Until recently, this phonological loop received little attention except in such tasks as holding telephone numbers in working memory. Adolescents as well as young children depend on auditory processing to learn new words. Differences in attention to this phonological loop in working memory contribute to the individual differences in ability to form long-term memory representations of new words (Baddeley et al., 1998).

Adolescents learn most new words by inferring their meanings from reading as well as listening (Tonjes, 1991), from direct instruction at school, or by using morphological knowledge. When using morphological knowledge, they think about the meanings of prefixes and suffixes and also about the meaning of each part of a compound word. Then they synthesize the meanings of the components to arrive at the meaning of the complex word (Anglin, 1993). Towanda was able to break down *undercharacterize* into two words, identify the meaning of each, and then, by combining these, figure out the meaning of *undercharacterize*.

Adolescents continue to refine their understandings of word meanings as they encounter words in many different contexts. Most words have more than one meaning, and a word's precise meaning in a specific context depends on how it is used. Skill in understanding the various meanings of words increases during adolescence, in part because an increasing appreciation of nonliteral meanings allows the adolescent to understand words at more than one level.

Children's dictionaries typically give only one or two meanings for a word whereas adult dictionaries sometimes give more than half a dozen definitions for one word, including figurative meanings. Consider, for example, the following entries from *The American Heritage First Dictionary* (1998), which is designed for use by young school-age children:

bridge   A bridge is used to cross from one side to the other. Bridges are often built over water.

band   A band is a group of people who play music together. Everyone in the parade marched to the music of the band.

In contrast, *Random House Webster's Dictionary* (1998) Lists the following definitions for the same words:

bridge   1. a structure spanning and providing passage over a river, road, etc. 2. a connection or transition between two adjacent elements, conditions, etc. 3. a raised platform from which a ship is navigated. 4. the ridge of the nose. 5. an artificial replacement for missing teeth. 6. to make a bridge or passage over. 7. a card game in which one partnership plays to fulfill a certain declaration against an opposing partnership.

band   1. a company of persons, animals or things acting together. 2. a group of musicians usually using brass, woodwind and percussion instruments. 3. to unite in a group or company. 4. a thin strip of material. 5. a segment of a phonograph record on which sound is recorded. 6. a specific range of frequencies, as in radio. 7. to mark or furnish with a band.

When asked to define words, adolescents give definitions that are more abstract, and they often include the superordinate category to which the object belongs. For example, an adolescent might define *chair* as a piece of *furniture* on which people sit. A younger child would probably define chair as something for sitting, but would not mention the class—furniture—of which it is a member (Anglin, 1993).

Older children and adolescents are better able than younger children to learn word meanings from formal definitions, such as those found in a dictionary (Dickinson, 1984). Adolescents can also derive meanings from observing how words are used in the books they read (Tonjes, 1991). But adolescents, as well as younger children, need to read elaborate texts—texts in which new words are encountered many times in different contexts—if they are to learn accurate and complete meanings of the words they read (Herman et al., 1987).

While older views of text reading comprehension considered the process to be one of forming a mental representation of the text, more recent research supports a **situational text comprehension model.** This model views text comprehension in terms of the adolescent developing a mental representation of the situations verbally described in the text. Rather than considering text as information to analyze syntactically and semantically for storage, the situation model views language as a set of processing instructions on how to construct a mental representation of the described situation. This model explains the adolescents' ability to integrate information across text segments and explains the

Adolescents can increase their vocabulary by reading. If this 16-year-old regularly chooses a good book over television, she will probably increase her vocabulary considerably over the teenage years. (*Source:* © Bob Daemmrich/ The Image Works)

superior comprehension of new text information by those who already have expertise in the subject matter of the text (Zwaan & Radvansky, 1998). A 1999 report that 40 percent of U.S. adolescents cannot read at grade level clearly indicates the need for more research on improving this skill (CNN, 1999a).

A good vocabulary is important for academic achievement, particularly for reading comprehension. Vocabulary size reflects broad-based, readily retrievable knowledge about the world (Dickinson et al., 1993). Exposure to more sophisticated vocabulary at home is directly related to vocabulary size, perhaps because families who use rarer words usually talk about why people do things and how things work, and discuss predictions or hypotheses (Snow, 1993). One study of young adolescents found that the mother's education, her educational expectations for the adolescent, and the literacy environment of the home were highly correlated with the adolescent's vocabulary and word recognition abilities (Snow, 1993). The adolescent who discusses with her parents at the dinner table why the rain forests need protection or how the new computer chip works is usually exposed to complex vocabulary in the process.

Oral Language Development

The ability to communicate information effectively to someone who knows little about the topic requires **social referential communication** (Whitehurst & Sonnenschein, 1985). For example, an adolescent may describe to his friend, while talking with him on the telephone, how to reach a certain level in a video game. In this case, the teenager must convey the information via language; he cannot show his friend what to do. Younger children are not especially good at this; they usually need to show what they mean, or adults must prompt fuller verbal descriptions with questions. How do children develop this skill? Piaget suggested that the give-and-take of social interaction helps adolescents understand that some messages work better than others. This feedback from listeners facilitates the development of **metacommunication,** or the knowledge and cognitions concerning communication (Flavell et al., 1993).

A major theme of Vygotsky's sociocultural theory is that the higher mental functioning seen during adolescence originates in social life (Wertsch & Kanner, 1992). Adult-adolescent interactions (and adult-child interactions long before that) provide opportunities for **guided participation** in reasoning. Consider, for example, the case of 13-year-old Chris who has misplaced his Nerf basketball and asks his father for help. Asked simply where he last had the ball, Chris responds that he cannot remember. His dad then asks a series of questions designed to help Chris think through where his ball might be and to recall where he actually left it.

His dad first asks Chris to consider a number of contexts: "Did you leave it in the living room, over at your friend's home, or in your bedroom?" Chris responds with a "no" to each of these questions. His dad then helps him think it through: "You use it in your bedroom with the hoop on the back of your door. So, it could be there." Chris agrees that his bedroom is a likely place to find it but says that he has just searched his room and it is not there. "Well," his father continues, "we don't allow you to play with your Nerf ball in the kitchen, but you often play with it in the family room. "With that comment, the light suddenly comes on. Chris remembers that he had practiced pitching it in the wastebasket while watching a television program. He dashes off to retrieve it.

Adolescent-adolescent interactions often lead to **joint discovery** as peers work together to generate ideas and solutions to questions (Newman et al., 1989; McMillan, 1999). For example, by reading the same book, each adolescent can first develop his own understanding. Then, through discussion, each can see how his interpretations are similar to or different than others' interpretations. Literature circles (small groups of students who meet specifically to discuss a chosen author, book, or topic) give students a chance to argue, reflect, and raise questions (Noll, 1994; Rothenberg & Watts, 1997). Active learning exercises help students advance from basic knowledge to higher levels of analysis, synthesis, evaluation, and application (McMillan, 1999). Cooperative learning activities that stress sharing and evaluating information result in an opportunity for children to speak, listen, read, and write. Such involvement enriches the learning process (Erickson, 1998). Small-group discussions and structured peer responses to writing are also helpful in building writing confidence (Medley, 1999).

Vygotsky (1987) also thought **private speech** was an important part of metacognition and self-direction. When adolescents speak to themselves, aloud, in a whisper, or silently it helps them to direct their thinking. See the Research Close-Up: Private Speech for more information. As we noted in earlier chapters, speaking aloud is very effective in fostering metacognition and self-direction. Successful programs intended to promote health and productivity among adolescents involve them in discussions

RESEARCH

CLOSE-UP   *Private Speech*

Vygotsky (1987) thought that individuals use private speech (speaking to themselves privately either aloud, in a whisper, or silently) both to help themselves think and to direct their thinking. Berk and Garvin (1984) classified private speech into nine categories:

- *Egocentric speech*—a result of the inability to take the listener's point of view, such as mumbling, "What an idiot" to an adult's suggestion.
- *Affect expression*—expressions of emotions, such as "Awesome!" or "Check it out!"
- *Word play and repetition*—repeating or playing with words and their multiple meanings, such as saying, "Oh shoot; shoot that ball!"
- *Fantasy play*—making fantasy sounds, such as added sound effects when playing a video game.
- *Remarks to nonhuman objects*—such as telling a bowling ball to go toward the head pin.
- *Describing one's own activity and self-guidance*—such as saying, "I turn the wrench clockwise to tighten the bolt."
- *Self-answered questions*—such as answering a question about a hypothesis in a concept attainment task.
- *Reading aloud*—such as reading instructions aloud while assembling a bike.
- *Inaudible muttering*—vocalizations not understood by the listener.

Self-talk is useful in enhancing performance in tasks, in remembering lists, and in dealing with stressful situations.

Self-talk also improves the ability to concentrate on tasks. In one study adolescents took reasoning and word problem tests with a confederate who used self-talk during the middle part of the half-hour session. Private speech was observed in all but one of the 47 adolescent participants, and private speech increased after hearing the confederate use it.

Most of Berk and Garvin's (1984) categories of private speech were observed in the adolescent participants (though fantasy self-talk was not). Describing one's own activity and self-guidance was positively correlated with test scores, while inaudible muttering was negatively correlated with test scores. Kronk (1994) thinks private speech may help adolescents study or focus on their work, but that it is often suppressed in response to social pressure. Many people respond negatively to others' talking to themselves. Self-talk improves academic performance and skill acquisition, helps change bad habits, creates changes in mood, keeps attention focused, maintains self-regulation, and builds self-efficacy (Healy, 1998; Zinsser et al., 1998).

Chi and colleagues (1994) indicate that the type of verbalizations differentiates good and poor problem-solvers. Good problem-solvers articulate rules for their actions better than poor problem-solvers, make more evaluative statements about hypotheses, and generate more explanations. Teasley (1995) found that talking aloud was especially helpful when working on a problem-solving task with a peer collaborator.

with caring adults. Adolescents are involved in all phases of planning and implementing the projects (Roth et al., 1998).

Improvements in the Ability to Participate in Conversations

Adolescents communicate more effectively if they learn to use several strategies (Martin et al., 1994). For example, it is effective when communicating with others to assert a point of view. The adolescent may express disagreement or argue her point of view. Communication is also aided if the adolescent withholds judgment and does not dismiss another person's opinion without giving the person a chance to explain it. Adolescents also may learn to ignore unpleasant remarks, decide not to argue a position, or simply end the conversation.

Adolescent conversations often lead to joint discoveries as peers work together to generate ideas and work through solutions. *(Source: © MOMATIUK/EASTCOTT/ Woodfin Camp & Associates)*

The conversational strategies an adolescent selects may depend on her perceived intimacy with the person with whom she is conversing. As relationships become more intimate, communication becomes smoother and more efficient. It also develops more breadth and depth, and becomes more personal (Knapp et al., 1980, cited in Martin et al., 1994). Strategy selection may also be influenced by the characteristics of the adolescent, such as the extent to which she is argumentative (challenges the positions of others) and verbally aggressive (challenges people rather than their positions) (Suzuki & Rancer, 1994). Adolescent girls more frequently interrupt their mothers and close friends than do younger girls. This appears to be a change in style of interaction rather than an increase in efforts to dominate or control (Beaumont & Cheyne, 1998).

Improved cognitive abilities also influence adolescents' conversations. For example, they can use probabilistic reasoning—can figure out the extent to which it is likely that others will hold a view, behave in a certain way, and so on. Adolescents often consider probabilities when they justify their own position in response to the position of others, when they challenge another person's position based on what is known about others' positions, and when they attempt to persuade others to change their positions. Probabilistic reasoning and dialogue also influence decisions and the resolution of conflicts (Voss & Wiley, 1995). In communication among culturally, racially, ethnically, and sexually diverse groups, gaining a mutual understanding of different perspectives is important yet challenging (Tatum, 1997). Using language to reduce conflict is especially important in groups, in which polarized thinking has been common. When presented with two conflicting propositions, adolescents often use **polarizing thinking**—establishing one position as correct and the other as wrong. Thinking in Asian cultures, often seeks compromise and attempts to maintain a moderate opinion on each position. American adolescents who hold divergent views need help to move from polarizing thinking to **dialectical thinking.** The latter enables adolescents to understand that several perspectives may have some truth and prompts them to seek reconciliation. Listening to and participating in reasoned dialogue among individuals with different perspectives can help adolescents appreciate contradictions, learn tolerance, and seek negotiation (Peng & Nisbett, 1999).

Adolescents also use irony and sarcasm because they can now think in formal operational terms. For example, on the way out of a particularly boring class, a high schooler may say to his friend: "Hey, dude, was that an exciting class, or what?"

Adolescents realize that using humor when making a presentation makes the audience more interested (Conkell, 1999).

The intended meaning of a verbal statement is likely to be affected by the recipient's perceptions of the speaker (Hilton, 1995). For example, if an adolescent is inaccurate in her perception of her mom's attitude about dating, she may misinterpret her mom's utterances about the topic. A listener may also overestimate the mutual knowledge shared with a speaker (Fussel & Krauss, 1992). This overestimation may lead the adolescent to think that there is consensus when there is not. For example, an adolescent may think that he and his mom both know a lot about drugs (when his mom actually knows very little) and then assume that she would agree with his opinion on their use.

Communication plays a role in social and cognitive development (Budwig et al., 2000). Good interpersonal communication helps adolescents express feelings both verbally and nonverbally and respond to another person's problems and feelings (Johnson, 2000). Adolescents behaving in antisocial ways show improvement when peers trained in "verbal mediation" help them discuss problems rather than act them out (Healy, 1998). See Table 18.1 for communication and social skills.

Language also plays an important role as early adolescents share each other's perspectives and establish close friendships and intimacy through self-disclosure and discussion of important issues. Adolescent girls are more likely than boys to enter such discussions and to disclose their inner psychological states. This gender difference contributes to the fact that boys are less likely than girls to develop close reciprocal friendships. Although the gender difference is maintained, both boys and girls significantly increase self-disclosure communication and discussion of issues during the first two years in high school (McNelles & Connolly, 1999).

Conversational Slang

Slang is "an esoteric body of language created through the novel naming of things not merely for the purpose of denotation, but to provide the language with a creative edge" (Cusatis, 1990, p. 7). Slang is informal, nonstandard, and often composed of novel-sounding synonyms for standard words or phrases. It can add to the richness and texture of speech and has been a defining characteristic of nearly every generation. For example, *lollygag* was popular in 1868 (Kilpatrick, 1999). The dominance

---

TABLE 18.1
Social communication skills

Adolescents who use the following social communication skills effectively are more likely to handle social situations in a positive manner than are adolescents who lack these skills.

- Listening
- Starting a conversation
- Introducing self and others
- Giving a compliment
- Asking for help
- Giving instructions
- Apologizing
- Asking a question

- Convincing others
- Calmly expressing feelings
- Asking permission
- Negotiating
- Responding with humor or teasing
- Making and answering a complaint
- Standing up for rights with reasoning
- Dealing with group pressure

Source: Adapted from *Skillstreaming the Adolescent: New Strategies and Perspectives for Teaching Prosocial Skills,* by A. P. Goldstein and E. McGinnis, 1997, Champaign, IL: Research Press, Chapter 6, pp. 65–117.

An adolescent may prove his affiliation with a group by talking as the group talks. These adolescents greet each other with "Hey, Wha'sup?" or "That ride was da bomb!" (*Source:* © Skjold/The Image Works)

of hip-hop in popular music has created a rich vocabulary for adolescents because rapping evolved from contests of linguistic dexterity. The Internet is providing new slang terms, as are movies, TV shows, and advertisements (Johnson, 1998; Tarlach, 1999). Cusatis (1990) claims that four characteristics of slang make it attractive to adolescents. First and foremost, slang is conspicuous. It draws attention and thus can be used as a social marker. Because using slang is a conscious choice, an adolescent may prove his affiliation with a group by talking as the group talks.

Slang is also novel. To be distinct, young adolescents adopt the latest language. Novel expressions help keep teenagers current and make their separation from adults more visible. Novelty is also refreshing, and new words are fun to use. Adolescents indicated to one reporter that slang "is just a way of talking that's not so formal all the time. . . . I wouldn't talk to my peers the way I'm talking to you. And I wouldn't come up to you and say 'Hey girl, wha'sup?' . . . We just like playing around with words" (Tarlach, 1999, p. 4).

A third characteristic of slang is that it is very evocative. Adolescents find it suitable for expressing feelings. If teens experience social uneasiness, slang may provide them with tools for defense. Slang is also an effective means of communicating aggressive feelings and attitudes. One high school student remarked in this way about peers who had been influenced by rap: "They strut around in those baggy clothes . . . saying 'Yo, don't be dissin' me man; don't be frontin' with me" (Cusatis, 1990, p. 16).

A fourth characteristic that makes slang attractive to adolescents is its informality. Teenagers tend to associate formality with adults, who often chastise them for informality in speech. Adolescents may think that slang liberates them from dreaded formality.

TABLE 18.2
Examples of adolescent slang

Term	Part of Speech	Meaning
'bout it	*verb*	term of bragging; showing off
chill out	*verb*	relax; cool it
cool	*adjective*	good; excellent
da bomb	*adjective*	very good; the best
Don't even go there.	*sentence*	I don't want to talk about it.
dude	*noun*	a person
floss	*verb*	show off
grub on	*verb*	to eat
hottie	*noun*	good-looking girl or boy
I'm down w' that.	*sentence*	It's OK with me.
imho	*phrase*	in my humble opinion
L.O.L.	*phrase*	laughing out loud
my bad	*phrase*	apology; my fault
phat	*adjective*	term of approval; cool
rot-f	*phrase*	rolling on the floor laughing
scope	*verb*	to look at
'Sup?	*sentence*	What's up?; common greeting
tight	*adjective*	very good; cool; attractive
trip out	*verb*	overreact; worry; act crazy
24/7	*phrase*	all the time; 24 hours, 7 days
whacked	*adjective*	boring; uncool
What's the 411?	*sentence*	What's the deal?
yo	*interjection*	attention-getting word
You steppin'?	*sentence*	Are you starting something?

Sources: Jackson, 1998; Sanders, 1998; Tarlach, 1999; author interviews with high school students, October 1999).

Slang can be an effective method of communicating feelings. Many adolescents also consider slang use as liberation from formality. (*Source:* © Goldberg/ Monkmeyer)

Some slang is associated with a particular clique or crowd. Using this language helps adolescents belong to these groups. Other slang simply follows the mainstream teenage culture; it is not associated with any specific group. Although many slang terms might have originated in clique or other subculture slang, the terms are no longer limited to any one subculture. For example, *yo* (a word often preceding a statement as if to say, "Hey, pay attention") was first used in the rap music crowd. Eventually, all teenagers seemed to be using it, whether they were members of a rap crowd or not. Slang changes very quickly, which is part of its novelty and attraction. See Table 18.2 for examples of adolescent slang.

Slang terms differ across the country, often including variations on slang words and phrases. For example, "Talk to the hand, 'cause the face ain't listenin' "; "Talk to the elbow, 'cause you ain't worth the extension"; and "Talk to the left, 'cause you ain't right" are all variations on the same theme (Jackson, 1998). Slang often differs by country, as well. Slang in Great Britain includes "rhyming slang." For example, in "I hit it straight down the British," *British* means "fairway" (golf) because *fairway* rhymes with *airway* (British Airway). Feeling tingly is expressed as "feeling Bradford," since *tingly* rhymes with *Bingley*, (Bradford and Bingley, a popular savings and investment company in the United Kingdom) (Kington, 1999).

Learning a Second Language during Adolescence

Because English is so widely used around the world, children in other countries begin to study it early in the elementary grades. The pressure to learn a second language is not as great in the United States as in many parts of the world. Thus, U.S. schools continue to lag behind schools in other nations in teaching a second language before the high school years.

Elissa Newport (1990) examined the language proficiency in English for individuals whose native language was not English. Her subjects began to learn the English language at ages 3 years to 39 years. English language ability was tested 10 years after they first began learning English. For those who began learning English between ages 3 and 7 years, English proficiency was equal to a control group of native English-speaking individuals. Test scores declined rapidly as a function of age through age 15. There was no significant correlation of English test performance and initial learning age for ages 16 through 39 years.

When studies are conducted for longer periods of time, and when the new language differs markedly from the first language, starting younger seems to provide some advantage. But when both older and younger children are learning the new language in formal classroom settings, older children, not younger ones, seem to have the advantage (McLaughlin, 1984). Adolescents' greater cognitive skill would allow them to take better advantage of classroom instruction in a new language.

It is not simply the lack of ability to learn a second language as we get older that accounts for most of the differences we often see in language proficiency between those who started younger and those who started when older. What differs most across ages are the circumstances under which people learn a second language. The younger the child, the more likely it is that the child learns the new language in social interaction. This immersion approach promotes language learning. Older children and adults usually learn language formally, in a course in school, without extensive application in social situations. Without extensive use of the language that is being learned, the language is not learned as well.

The one aspect of language that is clearly learned less effectively as age increases, no matter the learning conditions, is phonology—how to pronounce the sounds of the language and how to place stress, vary pitch, and so on. The younger the child when a second language is learned, the less likely it is that the child will speak the new language with an accent.

It appears that adolescence is not the optimal time to begin to learn a second language if the language differs a lot from the native language because learning conditions are less likely to be ideal. Several schools in the United States are initiating second language instruction in the early elementary school years.

Written Language Development

Just as their greater use of subordinate clauses allows adolescents to speak more precisely and efficiently than younger children, their grasp of more complex sentences and paragraphs makes their writing more sophisticated. The typical U.S. student does not however meet the writing standards set by U.S. government officials. Writing assessment results released in 1999 showed that only 1 percent of twelfth-graders reached the advanced level (superior performance at a given grade), and 22 percent reached the proficient level (solid performance) or above. The basic level (partial mastery of skills fundamental for proficient work at a given grade) was reached by 78 percent of the twelfth-graders. Even the basic level was not attained by 22 percent of the students. What can be done to improve student's writing? Students who planned their writing, wrote multiple drafts, and saved their work in portfolios had higher scores than students who did not use these techniques. Teachers could help raise students' writing scores by using these techniques. Students who discussed their writing, used computers, had reading materials in the home, and discussed their studies with someone at home had higher scores than students who did not have these advantages (NAEP, 2000). A variety of strategies, games, art, multimedia, and indirect teaching approaches provide "hooks" that interest students and encourage participation in writing (Baines & Kunkel, 2000).

Writing Knowledge and Interests

Music

Music is a glob of sound

People have moved and twisted around

Until it fits right in their ear

The sounds they think they ought to hear.

Scott Forsyth, age 12

think about it

Would the quality of Scott's writing have differed if he had no knowledge about or interest in the topic? Suppose that the topic and type of writing (prose or poetry) had been determined by the teacher. Would this affect his writing? If Scott had written about personal experiences, would he be more motivated to write? Would this motivation lead to more interesting writing?

The Pulitzer Prize–winning writer Donald Murray (1985) believes that writing is one of the most disciplined ways of making meaning and one of the most effective methods for monitoring one's own thinking. Improving the adolescent's writing is an important part of the curriculum in high school. Benton and colleagues (1995) examined the importance of discourse knowledge, topical knowledge, and topic interest in determining the quality of the writing produced by ninth-graders. **Discourse knowledge** is what one knows about writing (e.g., grammatical knowledge, sentence structure, punctuation). **Topical knowledge** refers to what the writer knows about the selected topic. The researchers used a questionnaire to assess the writers' interest in an assigned writing topic. The students' essays were graded in terms of their syntactic and thematic quality, the proportion of relevant to irrelevant actions, and their interest.

Among the ninth-graders, discourse knowledge was significantly correlated with both thematic and syntactic quality assessments. Topical knowledge predicted thematic and syntactic quality. High student interest in the writing topic was also correlated with higher thematic quality evaluations. These findings suggest that high school students will produce higher-quality writing if they are interested in and knowledgeable about the writing topic. Alexander and colleagues (1994) found that readers rate text as more interesting when it contains personally involving details. Thus, inclusion of personal experiences in the theme may increase evaluations of text as being interesting.

Benton and colleagues (1995) and Murray (1985) advise writers to write about topics they know best, with which they have personal experience, and in which they have an interest. Because adolescent writing is better when the topics are those about which the writer is knowledgeable, writing practice and instruction often begin with topics on which the adolescent is an expert. At the next level, the writer learns enough about a topic in order to write to an audience that is unfamiliar with that topic. For example, after a high school health unit on teratogens, students might be asked to write a newspaper advice column to teenagers who do not know about teratogens. Student journal-writing about a specific topic also helps teachers to gain insight into the students' conceptual and procedural knowledge of the topic, as well as their attitudes and feelings about the topic (DiPillo et al., 1997). Creative writing may elicit expressions of social values. For example, when writing stories together, female pairs frequently include prosocial themes whereas male pairs express more aggression (Diriwachter et al., 1999).

However, writing assignments should not be limited only to writing about personal experiences or presenting an informative or persuasive essay. Having adolescents relate autobiographical experiences to constructs in a literary work helps them achieve deeper understandings of the literature, and improves analogical reasoning and analytical writing (Beach, 1990; Symons & Johnson, 1997). Rosenblatt (1978) also emphasized the importance of writing about personal experiences for developing adolescent writing and understanding of literature. Students are stimulated to search for new meanings when they have reflected on their past experiences. This reflection causes restructuring and reevaluating of one's thinking (Saunders, 1997). In one study, researchers found that eighth-grade students who became engaged in reading by describing the relationship between the literary work and their own experiences achieved a deeper understanding of the literature (Nystrand & Gamoran, 1991). Another researcher found that autobiographical writing about relevant personal experiences prior to reading short stories resulted in greater engagement with the literature as well as a more abstract understanding of the story characters (White, B., 1995). Hands-on-activities, relating the lesson or story to their own lives, and developing a personal interpretation of the story can lead students to quite novel interpretations of literary works (Rothenberg & Watts, 1997).

Thus, it appears that four progressive types of writing assignments help develop adolescent writing. First, having students write about their personal experiences provides motivation for writing and leads to more interesting writing in novices. Next, writing informative pieces about topics on which the adolescents perceive themselves to have greater expertise than their audience increases the thematic and syntactic quality of their writing. A third type of writing assignment in which adolescents relate personal experiences to constructs represented in literary works fosters greater understanding of literature. Finally, with sufficient motivation, adequate instruction, and the attainment of formal operational thinking, Stotsky's (1995) proposal suggests a fourth type of writing assignment that focuses on abstract concepts, dealt with analytically.

This student is involved in interpretive writing, and is analyzing the validity of conclusions from her research. Using the computer provides a "hook" that interests her and encourages her participation in writing. (*Source:* © Esbin/Anderson/The Image Works)

Adolescents learn to do both interpretive and reflective writing. When adolescents write interpretively, they indicate the meaning of a text and present justification for the meaning they derived. This type of writing requires thoughtful reading and careful analysis. Examples of **interpretive writing** include interpreting the meaning of a poem, drawing conclusions about the relationships among the characters in a story, making references about the conflict of characters in a book, or analyzing the validity of conclusions drawn from a research study. This type of writing assignment is recommended by Stotsky (1995).

Reflective writing stems from the writer's personal experience or reflections. Reflective essays might show connections between experiences and ideas or indicate thinking about ideas in light of other experiences (Wagner & Larson, 1995). This writing is encouraged by writing about personal experiences that relate to literary constructs. Activities that promote reflective thinking include journal writing, letter writing, examining case studies, compiling portfolios, and writing autobiographies (Brown, 1999; Medley, 1999; Sciutto, 1999).

Writing that expresses and argues a position (**argumentative writing**) can aid in critical thinking (Bensley, 1997). In a study of argumentative writing, adolescents who were personally involved with the topic were better able to argue for a position. Young school-age children did not express a position at all. Older children took a position, but did not justify it, and young adolescents developed minimal arguments. Adolescents 14 to 16 years old not only took a position, but provided elaborate arguments and counterarguments (Coirier & Golder, 1993). Writing a newspaper-style column for a less informed audience is a good exercise for developing this type of writing.

Imaginative writing seems to develop separately from other forms of writing (Ramirez, 1994). Imaginative writing involves divergent thinking about story lines, without using a concrete experiential referent. The ability of some adolescents to think abstractly and to consider events that could be but have never been experienced helps them engage in this type of writing.

Whatever the type of writing, adolescents should be encouraged to make revisions. A study of high school girls' writing revisions that involved combining a series of short sentences into a single nonredundant sentence revealed three different strategies. The poorest products were simply focused on minimizing the number of words. In intermediate level of writing proficiency, writers adhered to a three-step method they had been taught for combining sentences. The best writing was done by those who first combined sentences and then shifted to the task of minimizing words (Zimmerman & Kitsantas, 1999).

The Importance of Instruction and Practice

Writing ability does not improve naturally or spontaneously as thinking ability advances. Children and adolescents must receive instruction and practice if they are to learn to apply their more mature thinking in writing and reading.

What Adolescents Can Understand   As they get older, children and adolescents become increasingly capable of interpreting and remembering written texts. These abilities have wide-ranging implications for academic achievement. The ability to sort out the content of a text or lecture is crucial to learning. Effective studying and note-taking require that students identify the most important material and spend more time on it. When listening to lectures or discussions, for example, effec-

Background experience helps students understand texts. The eagerness of these students to engage in discussion about an assignment may reflect previous work by each individual to relate relevant personal experience to the reading assignment.   (*Source:* © Skjold/The Image Works)

tive note taking includes quick jottings of key phrases, summarizing as soon after the event as possible, and revising. This procedure forces concentration on the meaning of the material (Thaiss & Sanford, 2000).

The most skilled students go beyond **deletion strategies** (removing unimportant information from the focus of their attention) to **invention strategies** (creating new superordinate categories under which to organize and condense material). Skilled readers have a plan for reading comprehension, such as activating prior knowledge, using visual imagery, summing up paragraphs, using mnemonic procedures, and story mapping or study methods such as SQ4R (Salembier, 1999).

Background experience may be crucial for understanding texts, particularly at a deep level. One researcher examined the influence of extensive autobiographical writing before reading literature. He found that students who had written about relevant personal experiences before they read an assignment were more engaged and conversational in their responses to the reading assignment than students who had not written autobiographies. They were also more eager to respond, talked to one another more, and prompted each other to explain their thoughts (White, B., 1995). Having students generate explanations to questions about a text also facilitates comprehension (McMillan, 1999; Pressley et al., 1992). Both reading and writing experience develop metacommunication skills.

Speech, Writing, and Impression Formation   Adolescents' quality of speech and writing can cause other people to form a positive or negative impression of them. One study examined the effects of good versus poor writing and speech quality on such impressions. The presenters of high-quality passages were rated more favorably than the presenters of low-quality passages on attributes such as confidence, competence, success, kindness, and the potential to be befriended (Moyer et al.,

This adolescent girl enjoys communicating with her friends via e-mail. Later she may click on a web site magazine or find information on the Internet for her history project. (*Source:* © David Young Wolff/Photo Edit)

1999). Displaying quality communication skills may be important for the adolescent to be favorably perceived by friends, teachers, and employers.

Recreational Reading   Reading is important throughout life. Recreational reading not only provides pleasure, but improves reading comprehension, writing ability, vocabulary, spelling, and grammatical development (Gallick, 1999). Although adolescent recreational reading has declined significantly in the past few decades, motivation to read may be enhanced by schools that emphasize self-selection, free-choice reading, promoting literary discussions, sharing favorite books with friends, and having teachers read interesting books aloud (Ivey, 1999). Reading aloud models expressive, enthusiastic reading and communicates pleasure in reading (Richardson, 2000). Teachers can make reading experiences rewarding for adolescents. One program, Teens for Literacy, involves adolescents in tutoring peers and elementary children in reading, in reading aloud to others, in coordinating reading contests, and in designing posters to encourage reading (Berger & Shafran, 2000). Many types of reading materials are available, but stories are more interesting if they ask the reader to resolve some inference (Boden & Brodeur, 1999). Adolescents who read for pleasure become better educated and are better students.

Electronic Technology and Language

Today, adolescents must be able to read, write, and converse, and also to use pagers, cell phones, video games, computers, software, electronic mail, and the Internet. They also learn to interpret art, music, drama, film, and videos (Bean et al., 1999). Traditional text-bound, written-word teaching methods sometimes appear slow when compared to the fast-paced digital world in which many adolescents live. Some students may reject the traditional curriculum, viewing traditional, in-school literacy domains as uninteresting (Alverman et al., 1998; Bean et al., 1999; Kaser & Short, 1998). Many students prefer communicating through e-mail and electronic chatrooms (Gallick, 1999). Teachers and parents need to guide students' learning thoughtfully within these electronic environments and may have to decide if and when electronic access should be regulated (Leu, 1999; Stay, 1999).

The use of Web pages, the Internet, and software presentations are gaining popularity, and students should be competent in computer skills (Brunner & Tally, 1999; Poling et al., 1999; Velayo et al., 1999). Web site magazines such as *Cyberkids, Midlink Magazine, KidPub,* and *Reading Online* encourage children and adolescents to write stories; do projects and artwork; publish stories, poems, pictures, and games; and read and communicate interactively online. For example, *The Global Campfire,* a project of the Family Literacy Center at Indiana University, has readers imagine themselves gathered around a campfire where people from all over the world are telling stories. After reading story contributions, readers write and submit their own additions to the story (Anderson-Inman, 1999). One eighth-grader, Maurice Taylor, completing a classroom assignment, used his computer to write and illustrate a book for first graders. His book, *First Words,* was published and is now being used in several schools. Maurice is working on his third book for publication (Fitzgerald, 2000).

On the other hand, studies show that adolescents are not getting enough personal interaction with parents, peers, or mentors (Healy, 1998). Increased use of electronic technology leads to even less interpersonal interaction. A sharp debate was launched by a study examining people who communicate electronically. According to this paradoxical finding, as participants increased in their use of the Internet for communication, they became less socially engaged interpersonally, more lonely, and more depressed (Kraut et al., 1998). Kiesler and Kraut (1999) expressed surprise that technology, which they had assumed would have a positive influence on social well-being, had in fact a negative influence. They did find that Internet communication provided more informational social support but less emotional social support, which is present in interpersonal communication.

Despite the use of words such as *talking* to describe communication on the Internet, there are major differences in language used in speech communication. The latter provides a "melody" along with the content of the message, which is often absent in e-mail. Much research lies ahead to explore the interaction of electronic communication with variables such as social apprehension, social interest, and social self-efficacy across a wide range of contexts and situations.

KEY POINTS

Cognitive Underpinnings of Advances in Adolescent Language

- Adolescents' greater sophistication in speaking and writing is made possible by advances in intellectual functioning.
- Emergence of metaphorical interpretation helps adolescents appreciate language on a whole new level.
- Adolescents continue to increase their vocabularies and begin to appreciate the nonliteral meanings of words they know.

Oral Language Development

- Social referential communication improves during adolescence, and the give-and-take of social interaction helps achieve an understanding that some messages work better than others.
- The adolescent learns to deal successfully with communication issues by conversation improvement strategies.
- Several characteristics of slang make it attractive to adolescents.

Learning a Second Language during Adolescence

- Learning a second language appears from correlational studies to be more difficult if started later in life, but this difficulty is not the result of cognitive ability. Rather, younger children tend to learn a new language more thoroughly because they learn it through extensive social interaction in everyday contexts.
- Some schools are starting to introduce foreign languages earlier in elementary school.

Written Language Development

- Adolescents' improved cognitive skills are also reflected in their written language. Many are capable of writing well-organized essays and stories with complex linguistic constructions and figurative language.
- The improvement of adolescents' writing abilities is an important part of the curriculum in high school. Writing and practice instruction should begin with topics with which the adolescent is very familiar.
- Adolescents learn to do several types of writing, including both interpretive and reflective essays.

■ Adolescents become increasingly capable of interpreting and remembering written text. Effective study skills are important.

Electronic Technology and Language

■ Communication today requires competence with electronic systems such as the Internet.

■ Debate continues on the access students should have to electronic environments.

■ Despite new opportunities made available by this technology, more exploration is needed into its effects on psychological well-being, social interest, and social apprehension.

GLOSSARY

argumentative writing: writing that expresses and argues a position (p. 620)

deletion strategies: removing unimportant information from the focus of one's attention (p. 621)

dialectical thinking: thinking to understand different perspectives and seek reconciliation (p. 613)

discourse knowledge: knowledge about how to write correctly, using correct grammar and language appropriate to the context (p. 618)

guided participation: Vygotsky's terminology for adult interactions that lead adolescents to higher levels of problem solving (p. 611)

imaginative writing: creative and sometimes abstract writing, using divergent thinking (p. 620)

interpretive writing: writing that indicates the meaning of text or data and presents justification for that particular meaning (p. 620)

invention strategies: creating new superordinate categories under which to organize and condense material (p. 621)

joint discovery: finding answers to questions and solutions to problems through discussions with peers (p. 611)

metacommunication: communication affected by knowledge of language and its uses (p. 611)

metaphorical interpretations: understanding the ordinary meanings of words and their implied figurative meanings (p. 607)

phonological loop: a temporary storage of unfamiliar words in working memory while a long-term memory representation is constructed (p. 609)

polarizing thinking: considering two different views as oppositional and accepting one as right and the other as wrong (p. 613)

private speech: speech used by individuals in talking to themselves out loud, in a whisper, or silently (p. 612)

reflective writing: writing stemming from the writer's personal experiences and reflections (p. 620)

situational text comprehension model: views text comprehension as a process of developing a mental representation of situations described in the text (p. 610)

slang: vivid, expressive new words or phrases used among groups of friends, particularly during adolescence (p. 614)

social referential communication: communication in which information is effectively conveyed to someone who is unfamiliar with the topic (p. 611)

topical knowledge: what the writer knows about the topic selected for writing (p. 618)

SUGGESTIONS FOR FURTHER READING

Bly, B. M., & Patterson, M. (1999). Language and the brain. In B. M. Bly & D. E. Rumelhart (Eds.), *Cognitive science.* New York: Academic Press. This chapter presents overviews of the research findings and explorations in the area of brain and language.

Brunner, C., & Tally, W. (1999). *The new media literacy handbook: An educator's guide to bringing new media into the classroom.* New York: Doubleday. In addition to providing an overview and evaluation of new media, this book gives information on how they can be used in several academic disciplines. Chapter 5 discusses language, arts, and the media.

Feldman, L. B. (Ed.). (1995). *Morphological aspects of language processing.* Mahwah, NJ: Erlbaum. This book focuses on morphological processes in word recognition and reading and discusses language processing in general.

Liberman, A. M. (1996). *Speech: A special code.* Cambridge, MA: MIT Press. This book discusses with humor and style the methods and techniques appropriate to the study of speech perception. For example, one section is titled "Reading/Writing Are Hard Just Because Speaking/Listening Are Easy."

Marzano, R. J., & Paynter, D. E. (1994). *New approaches to literacy: Helping students develop reading and writing skills.* Hyattsville, MD: American Psychological Association. Literacy skills for the improvement of reading and writing are discussed in this book.

Thaiss, C., & Sanford, J. F. (2000). *Writing for psychology.* Boston: Allyn & Bacon. This is an excellent book for writing information and includes chapters on writing techniques, critical evaluations of research papers, oral presentations, and a very good, brief APA citation guide.

19

Social and Emotional Development in Adolescents

"MARIA, I FINALLY got through to you! Your line's been busy for almost two hours! Who were you talking to?"

"Hi, Angela!" answers Maria. "I wasn't talking to anyone. Your nephew Carlos was talking to his friends."

"For two hours?"

"That's nothing. One time I found him using both our lines at the same time. He was talking to two different girls, one phone on each ear."

"Well, at least he is popular."

"He doesn't think he's popular! He isn't sure how he is perceived and doesn't have a clear sense of identity. He even said to me, 'I don't know who I am.' At least he is still talking to us, even if he thinks we don't understand him."

think about it What does Carlos mean when he says, "I don't know who I am?" How will he go about finding out who he is in terms of an ideology or a career? What changes will Carlos and his female friends experience during adolescence? How would you characterize Maria's parenting? Over what other issues than phone use might Carlos and his parents experience some conflict?

With his long telephone conversations, his desire for acceptance, and his uncertainty about himself, Carlos is a typical 15-year-old. Along with the physical changes and cognitive advances of this period, there are dramatic changes in social and emotional development. Adolescents' interest in developing friendships and spending time with peers increases. They discover the complexities and satisfactions of deep emotional involvement beyond the family, and they explore the mysteries of love and sex. At the heart of their exploration is the search for self, for a unique identity with which to approach the adult world.

In this chapter we discuss the adolescent's twin quests for independence and intimacy. We look at relationships with peers and with parents, as well as at teenagers' thoughts about sex and sexual behavior. We address adolescents' search for identity and the last major shaping of personality traits. Finally, we discuss problems that can arise for some teenagers as well as the positive aspects of adolescent development.

Relationships with Family: The Quest for Independence

The transition into adolescence is marked by an effort to maintain ties with family members while searching for appropriate levels of individuation and autonomy (Laursen & Collins, 1994). **Individuation** is the process of achieving an identity, independent of one's parents. It is not surprising that conflicts with parents escalate during early adolescence, as adolescents strive to achieve their own identity (Steinberg, 1993).

Adolescent conflict with parents involves verbal disagreements and behavioral opposition over family rules. Parents and adolescents may influence each other in ways that create distress (Ge et al., 1995). For example, parental dissatisfaction with their work or marriage may lead to increased distress for the adolescent (Silverberg & Steinberg, 1990), and the negative affect of adolescents as they experience the transition to adulthood may create further distress for parents. Not all adolescents experience a period of "storm and stress," but, for those who do, this period is critical in determining whether they will establish positive or negative patterns in adjusting to life events (Larson & Ham, 1993). Rather than experiencing storm and stress, many adolescents and their families are likely to negotiate changes through a continuous series of minor yet significant daily hassles. These are "daily, ongoing mundane conflicts and compromises that are made possible by good communications, a strong desire to maintain parental approval, and harmony" (Garrod et al., 1999, p. 147).

Adolescence can be a trying time for parents (Laursen & Collins, 1994), but they are extremely important as their adolescents seek independence. Most teenagers do *not* want to sever relationships with their parents. They want to maintain intimacy and connection with their families at the same time that they search for increased autonomy and independence (Garrod et al., 1999). They want their parents to be willing to expand their relationship with them—to accept their independence, their experimentation, and their mistakes, without rejecting *them*.

Parental Tasks during a Child's Adolescence

One difficult task for parents of teenagers is letting go of their children. When a teenager seeks more freedom and independence, parents must judge whether situations are safe, and whether their child is trustworthy and competent enough to manage them. A teenager's behavior often tries a parent's patience. Teenagers can be irritable, moody, and overly critical of parents whom they previously idolized. Sometimes they take out their insecurities and frustrations on their parents because they consider home to be a safe place to express them.

Although adolescence is a time of change, it need not always be a time of major conflict. Depending on the methods of discipline used by parents, and on the models they provide and the values they support, parents can help their children achieve autonomy and make a smooth transition from adolescence into young adulthood (Gullotta et al., 2000; Kerns et al., 2000; Schulenberg et al., 2000).

The horizons of this adolescent's world are expanding, and she feels the need to keep in constant touch with her friends. Many parents limit or regulate phone time; others have a new line installed. (*Source:* © Laura Dwight/ Corbis)

Stresses Parents Create for Their Adolescents

Young adolescents who perceive their parents as exerting too much control by failing to adjust their restrictiveness report higher levels of storm and stress than adolescents whose parents adjust to their adolescent's increasing competence and independence (Fuligni et al., 1995). The following statements are examples of those given high ratings by adolescents who experience stress because of their parents, and who then turn to peers for advice, belongingness, and escape from control:

1. My parents expect me to do what they say even if I disagree.
2. My parents worry that I will do something they don't want me to do.
3. I cannot do things without getting my parents' permission.
4. My parents get upset if I disagree with them.

In response to being asked what causes stress for them in family relationships, adolescents list the following: unreasonable parental expectations, not being trusted, being nagged, getting the runaround from parents, being stereotyped, and not having their opinions respected (Nelson & Lott, 1990). A major underlying problem seems to be the parents' unwillingness to accept the teenager's differing opinions. An important part of accepting a teenager's new independence is the granting of psychological autonomy. Psychological autonomy refers to whether the parent allows the adolescent to express views within the family and still maintain a close relationship with parents. This is autonomy of expression, not autonomy of action (Allen et al., 1994).

Patterns of Parenting and Adolescent Behavior

Studies have shown that patterns of parenting are strongly related to adolescent independence, social competence, and related behaviors. Baumrind (1989, 1991) examined the outcomes of different **patterns of parenting** on adolescents, using a longitudinal research design. She defined patterns of parenting in terms of two

Controllingness

	Low Control	Average	High Control
High (child-centered)	Permissive	Democratic	Authoritative
Average		Average	
Low (parent-centered)	Rejecting/ neglecting		Authoritarian

Responsiveness

Two-dimensional space defining Baumrind's parenting patterns.

dimensions—demandingness and responsiveness. Fuligni and Eccles (1993) refer to the **demandingness** dimension as parental strictness or control. Parents who are very high in this dimension attempt to control children through status and power, limit what their children are allowed to do, and confront their children when they do not meet expectations. Parents high in **responsiveness** are involved in and supportive of their children's activities. They listen actively to their children, respond to their initiatives, show warmth, and focus on their children's concerns and interests during interactions with them. A mother or father can be placed anywhere in the two-dimensional space depicted in Figure 19.1, depending on his or her levels of demandingness and responsiveness.

Baumrind characterized parents who fall within certain locations in this two-dimensional space in specific ways. **Authoritarian parents** are high in demandingness (controlling) and low in responsiveness. They tend to be restrictive in granting adolescents jurisdiction over decision making, and they are more likely to insist on specific views, without much discussion. **Authoritative parents** are high in both demandingness and responsiveness; **permissive parents** are high in responsiveness, but low in demandingness. Parents who are very low in both demandingness and responsiveness are referred to as **rejecting/neglecting. Democratic parents** represent a fifth category. These parents are high on the responsiveness dimension and average on the demandingness dimension. Not all parents can be classified according to one of these parenting profiles. Indeed, many parents are average on both of Baumrind's dimensions. Maria's tolerance of Carlos's long telephone calls, and her responsiveness to the stress that he is experiencing, suggest that she would be consistent with Baumrind's democratic pattern of parenting.

Table 19.1 summarizes Baumrind's characterization of the four extreme patterns of parenting and the social behavior of adolescents reared by parents of each type. Baumrind (1989) classified adolescents in a two-dimensional space. The first dimension was the adolescent's social confidence (social assertiveness); the second dimension was the degree to which the child demonstrated social responsibility by being friendly and cooperative. Using these two dimensions, Baumrind identified five patterns of adolescent social behavior (1989). Figure 19.2 shows the labels used for these five patterns.

Baumrind also looked for relationships between patterns of parental and child behavior. She found that children of authoritative parents were both socially assertive and socially responsible (competent). At the other end of the spectrum, children of rejecting/neglecting parents were either low on both social responsibility and social assertiveness (incompetent) or low on social responsibility for boys and low on social assertiveness for girls. Children reared by democratic parents were high in social assertiveness and moderate in social responsibility. Children reared by parents classified as authoritarian or permissive were moderately competent (between the extremes produced by authoritative versus rejecting/neglecting parents). The daughters of authoritarian or permissive parents tended to be especially similar to their parents. That is, daughters of

TABLE 19.1

Patterns of parenting and adolescents' social competence

Parenting Pattern	Characteristics of Parenting	Adolescent Social Behavior
Authoritarian	Punitive, restrictive, controlling	Ineffective social interaction; inactive
Authoritative	Encourages independence; warm and nurturing; control with explanation; adolescent expresses views	Social competence and responsibility
Laissez-faire (permissive)	Lack of involvement; nonpunitive; few demands; gives adolescent a lot of freedom	Immature; poor self-restraint; has poor leadership
Rejecting/neglecting	Rejecting, or neglectful of child-rearing responsibilities	Antisocial; immature; psychological problems

Sources: Adapted from "Current Patterns of Parental Authority," by D. Baumrind, 1971, *Developmental Psychology Monographs, 4* (1, pt. 2); and "The Influence of Parenting Style on Adolescent Competence and Substance Use," by D. Baumrind, 1991, *Journal of Early Adolescence, 11* (1), pp. 56–95.

authoritarian parents were more assertive than responsible, while the daughters of permissive parents were more responsible than assertive. These results highlight how patterns of parenting can affect the development of children's competence.

As Baumrind followed her sample into adolescence (1991a), her results were generally consistent with those for childhood. Adolescents of authoritative parents continued to be competent, both socially and cognitively, whereas adolescents from rejecting/neglecting homes were antisocial and lacked self-control, social responsibility, and cognitive competence. Their behavior was also problematic, and they rejected their parents as models for their own behavior and aspirations more than adolescents typically do.

Other studies have found similar relationships for patterns of parenting and adolescent competence. Teenagers who rate highest in autonomy, self-confidence, and independence are more likely to have democratic or authoritative parents who listen actively and explain the basis for their rules or decisions (Elder, 1963; Kurdek & Fine, 1994; Lamborn et al., 1991; Steinberg et al., 1992, 1994). Authoritarian and rejecting/neglecting parenting (high control) is associated with lower self-esteem, lower moral reasoning, poorer psychological adjustment, lower school achievement, and increased problems with substance abuse (Barth, 1989; Boyes & Allen, 1993; Dornbusch et al., 1987; Steinberg, 1999).

Patterns of parenting also seem to influence the adolescent's approach to coping with problems. Dusek and Danko (1994) report that adolescents who view their parents as neglectful tend to be emotion-focused as they face problems. Adolescents who perceive their parents as warm and supportive, on the other hand, tend to be problem-focused. Emotion-focused adolescents express their feelings about the problem that they experience, but do not always take action to solve the problem. Problem-focused adolescents, on the other hand, move more quickly to develop a strategy to solve the problem.

Parents and their adolescents do not always judge similarly what pattern of parenting is being used. Adolescents

FIGURE 19.2

Two-dimensional space defining patterns found in adolescent social behavior.

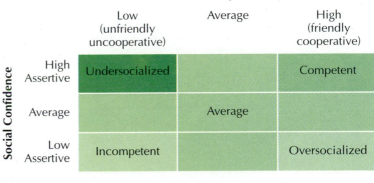

sometimes think their parents are more permissive or more authoritarian than parents themselves think they are (Smetana, 1995). Parents sometimes consider themselves as more authoritative than their adolescents think they are. This research, as well as research by Darling and Steinberg (1993), indicates that parental practices need to be assessed across many different contexts. For example, parents might grant the adolescent more independence with respect to managing homework, but maintain strict control over social schedules and interactions. These differences in parenting across areas, such as schoolwork, clothing, sport activities, and social activities, may account for some of the differences found in how parents and adolescents judge the parenting patterns that are employed. Knowledge in Action: Parenting and Adolescent Autonomy discusses parenting practices that accommodate the adolescent's increasing need for autonomy.

---

knowledge *in action*

PARENTING

Parenting and Adolescent Autonomy

Because adolescents are trying to break away from parental rules and views, they desire more autonomy than their parents grant them (Smetana, 1994). Feldman and Wood (1994) defined separate psychological and behavioral autonomies. The opportunity for adolescents to establish and express their own values, attitudes, and beliefs is referred to as **psychological autonomy.** Freedom to self-regulate behaviors and have privileges and responsibilities is referred to as **behavioral autonomy.** Privileges involve rights and benefits, such as adolescents' access to the car and permission to choose hairstyles, clothes, friends, and leisure activities. Responsibilities involve obligations to others and maturity demands, such as doing chores and homework without being asked.

Adolescents are often concerned about gaining earlier and more extensive privileges, while parents are concerned about the fulfillment of responsibilities (Feldman & Wood, 1994). Parents who grant autonomy early in adolescence may allow more time with peers outside of the home, leaving less time for exposure to the moderating influence of parents (Feldman & Wood, 1994).

Authoritative and democratic parents may be more effective than parents with other patterns of dealing with adolescents in reevaluating and renegotiating the limits they set, because they use reasoning and explanations and respond to adolescents' concerns and views. These parents may facilitate adolescents' understanding of the boundaries or limits of their personal autonomy by clearly articulating the societal concerns that are raised by complex issues (Smetana, 1994). Effectiveness in parenting also appears to be related to flexibility in adapting to the changing autonomy needs of adolescents (Greshler et al., 1994).

The following are some suggestions for achieving positive interactions with adolescents (Caffery & Erdman, 2000; Covey, 1997; Nelson & Lott, 1990; Rimm, 1999; Robertson, 1999):

- Listen empathically, without judging.
- Stop nagging and lecturing.
- Be a "coach" rather than a "judge."
- Remain calm when discussing issues.
- Work on joint problem solving.
- Give choices between acceptable alternatives.
- Avoid overreaction and criticism.
- Develop mutual trust and respect.
- Give undivided attention to communication.
- Keep a sense of humor.
- Ask for the adolescent's opinion and help.
- Support and encourage the adolescent's activities.
- Remember that differences of opinion between parents and adolescents are normal.
- Allow adolescents to make mistakes within limits of health and safety.
- Focus on things the adolescent does well.
- Use deserved praise often.
- Take trips together.
- Do activities planned by the adolescent.
- Tell stories about your own childhood.
- Involve grandparents when possible.
- Plan vacations together.
- Play games together.
- Look at childhood photo albums.
- Hang out with the adolescent.
- Be available.
- Invite the adolescent to see you at your job.
- Schedule regular family meetings.
- Build family traditions.

A strong parent-child relationship is important for adolescents just as it is for younger children. Parents of teenagers must know how to be supportive without stifling their children's developing sense of autonomy. This daughter feels close enough to her mother to share a happy moment. (*Source:* © Dale Durfee/Tony Stone Images)

When parents must exercise power, adolescents who have been raised in a democratic environment react more positively than do adolescents raised by authoritarian or permissive parents. Family members who can listen to each other without prejudice and respond in a way that acknowledges each other's point of view experience fewer conflicts (Bell & Bell, 1983; Bogenschneider et al., 1998; Kurdek & Fine, 1994).

Baumrind's studies are also consistent with others in indicating that troubled or delinquent adolescents often come from families with low levels of emotional expressiveness, positive communication, and help or support for family members (Ary et al., 1999). Parents whose verbal interactions consist mainly of guilt inducement, harsh criticism, or intrusive questions and commands foster in their adolescents low self-esteem, negative attitudes, and poor social competence (West, 1981; Young et al., 1999). Delinquency is related to both problematic relationships with parents and disorganized family environments (Pederson, 1994).

Parents who use harsh discipline and punishment are likely to decrease their influence and provoke hostility and anger (Conger et al., 1995; Noller, 1994). Adolescents who perceive their parents as critical and rejecting may develop a "negative identity"—the adolescent engages in behaviors that are the opposite of those the parent likes. When parents are critical and rejecting, adolescents may seek attention or try to get even with or punish their parents through negative behavior (Cook, 1993; Noller, 1994). On the other hand, when parents and adolescents have a warm and intimate relationship, adolescents have a better sense of well-being, behave in ways that are more socially desirable, and have higher self-esteem (Field et al., 1995). An

PARENTING

Discipline Errors to Avoid

Chamberlain and Patterson (1995) reviewed four types of inadequate discipline that have a negative influence on adolescent adjustment. **Inconsistent discipline** includes parents' indiscriminate reaction to an adolescent's positive and negative behaviors (e.g., rewarding and punishing the same behavior); inconsistent follow-through (e.g., parent requests that the adolescent be home by midnight, but does nothing when the adolescent is late), giving in (e.g., adolescent asks for use of the car, parent refuses, child argues, parent agrees); unpredictably changing expectations and consequences for rule violations; and parents acting at odds with each other on discipline policies or rule monitoring. Inconsistent discipline may lead to adolescent depression, conduct problems, and aggression.

Irritable explosive discipline includes frequent use of high-intensity strategies (e.g., threatening, yelling, and hitting); escalating intensities of punishing; frequent use of negative statements about the adolescent; and high rates of power-assertive commands. This type of discipline may be related to conflict and a likelihood that the adolescent will respond with aggressive or defiant behavior. Child abuse is often an outcome of irritable explosive discipline as parents shift from trying to change the adolescent's behavior to emotional vindictiveness. Other negative effects include adolescent aggression, hyperactivity, irritability, and antisocial and delinquent behavior.

Low supervision and involvement describes parents who are unaware of the adolescent's activities: not knowing with whom the adolescent is associating, being unaware of school adjustment and homework, seldom engaging in joint activities with the adolescent, and not providing supervision. Low supervision and involvement are associated with delinquency, fighting, drug use, lying, poor school achievement, noncompliance, and conduct problems.

Inflexible, rigid discipline involves reliance on a limited range of discipline strategies, failure to take extenuating factors into account, failure to give rationales, and failure to adjust the intensity of the discipline to the severity of the problem. Unfortunately, many parents use one or more of these inadequate techniques. Active listening and reasoning are the most effective disciplinary strategies that parents can use with adolescents.

18-year longitudinal study of family values and adolescent behavior problems identified two family-values factors. The traditional achievement-oriented factor was associated with fewer adolescent behavior problems. The humanistic-egalitarian-oriented factor protected against violent delinquency but was associated with increased drug use (Garnier & Stein, 1998).

Very harsh discipline and punishment may lead to both emotional and physical abuse. (See chapter 11 for a discussion of this topic.) Being abused can in turn cause a host of problems, such as poor social relationships, lack of empathy, drug or alcohol abuse, depression, anxiety, and poor school performance (Noller, 1994; Straus & Kantor, 1994). Many adolescents actually leave home because of abuse in the family. In one study, family violence was cited by 42 percent of homeless youth as a main reason for leaving home (Pears, 1992). Knowledge in Action: Parenting—Discipline Errors to Avoid discusses several types of errors that parents make in disciplining adolescents.

Relationships with Peers: The Quest to Belong

With the arrival of adolescence, social life changes. Friendships, intimate relationships, and group activities become all-important features of the adolescent's life. The boy who was content to spend Friday night watching TV with his parents now wants to be at the school basketball game, shopping mall, or local movie theater where his friends are hanging out. Adolescents sometimes do not even want to be seen with their parents.

Adolescents are awakened to the possibilities of adult life; many begin to think ahead to what it will be like to live as adults in the larger society. They wonder what kind of people they are and what they will become. Facing this challenge, teenagers sense that they must separate themselves from their parents and their past lives as children if they are to become independent people face this challenge. Struggling to differentiate and define themselves, they seek the support of peers.

The influence of peers is greater in early adolescence than it is later (Hill & Holmbeck, 1986), perhaps because in taking their first leap toward independence from their parents, they do not yet have a clear sense of identity. Teenagers look alike, dress alike, talk alike, and go everywhere together. Their extreme conformist behavior represents their strong desire to belong. A few years later, when greater autonomy is attained, adolescents begin to conform less to a peer group.

Baumeister and Leary (1995) define the **need to belong** as a need for frequent, nonaversive interactions within an ongoing relational bond. Belongingness theory states that real or imagined changes in belongingness status cause changes in the adolescent's affect. Positive affect is associated with increases in belongingness; negative affect is associated with decreases in belongingness (Baumeister & Leary, 1995). Because anxiety is associated with perceptions of being excluded, the pressure to conform in order to establish reciprocal belonging relationships is great during early adolescence (Leary, 1990).

Adolescents' happiness and psychological well-being are tied closely to their feelings of belongingness, inclusion, and social support (Ward, 1999). Making friends and identifying with supportive peer groups are important aspects of adolescent social development. It may be difficult for adolescents who move to a new community or school to establish friendships (Vernberg et al., 1994). Wentzel (1993) studied the strategies used by early adolescents for making friends. Those using appropriate prosocial strategies to make friends (e.g., initiating interaction with other-directed questions, cooperating, sharing, actively listening, complimenting, being friendly, and showing social support) had higher ratings for peer acceptance and friendship

Teenagers often try so hard to look like each other that they seem to lose their individuality. Identifying strongly with a peer group is a normal step in the process of forming a personal identity. (*Source:* © David Young Wolff/Photo Edit)

Adolescents engaged in positive leisure activities with others develop a sense of belonging. (*Source:* © Kerbs/Monkmeyer)

formation. But some adolescents have difficulty making friends and belonging to the peer group. Hostile interactions are associated with poor social problem solving, whereas warm and friendly interactions are characteristic of constructive social problem solvers (Rueter & Conger, 1995).

Metacognition influences adolescents' ability to form friendships. Social perspective coordination leads to peer acceptance and friendship. **Social perspective coordination** is the adolescent's ability to differentiate and integrate his or her own views about things with the views of others. Social perspective coordination requires an understanding of both one's own and others' thoughts and feelings (Selman & Schultz, 1989).

Once a friendship is formed, self-disclosure plays a critical role in maintaining and strengthening the relationship. There are three **self-disclosure and liking effects.** First, adolescents who use self-disclosure about intimate matters are liked better than those who do not. Second, adolescents tend to disclose more to peers they initially like, and they increase their liking for those peers as a result of having disclosed much to them. Third, these disclosure–liking effects are stronger in established relationships than in relationships between new acquaintances (Collins & Miller, 1994). The symbolic act of disclosure appears to be more important than the content of the disclosure.

When adolescents are engaged in positive leisure activities with others, they develop social skills and a sense of belonging. They may also understand themselves better by seeing how their peers react to them. Solitary leisure activities can give them a chance to understand themselves, analyze interests, and develop talents (Hughes, 1999). Socialization during adolescence involves less of *doing something* and more of *being together*. For example, adolescents often just want to "hang out" (Hughes, 1999). Males and females rated having close friendships, doing well at school, and being romantically appealing as contributing most to how they feel about themselves (O'Dea & Abraham, 1999).

The adolescent's **peer network** includes best friends, other close friends, cliques or friendship groups, and sometimes a romantic relationship. A **clique** is a small friendship group in which individuals share common backgrounds, live close to each other, and share activities. It is a closely knit peer group based on specific interests, such as music, sports, or physical appearance. As adolescents progress from the sixth through the twelfth grades, they become more selective in naming best and close friends. Best friends continue to be embedded in cliques or friendship groups throughout adolescence. The greater exclusivity of close friends with increasing age is likely to be a function of adolescents' increasing social-cognitive skills and attention to reciprocity and intimacy (Urberg et al., 1995).

Girls are more likely than boys to have a best friend, to be in a clique, and to have a greater number of mutual close friend choices. Girls report a higher level of emotional sharing than boys do, and boys tend to have higher levels of competitiveness and aggression in their relationships than do girls (Windle, 1994). African American and Hispanic adolescents are less connected in peer networks at school than are white adolescents, no matter whether the school has a white, African American, or Hispanic majority. In general, minority racial or ethnic students at a school tend to be less well integrated into the school's peer network (Urberg et al., 1995).

Who becomes a close friend can be influenced by crowd membership. A **crowd** is a group of people with common attitudes, interests, or abilities. Close friends, friendship groups, and crowds serve as the major socialization agents during adolescence. The crowd offers opportunities for exploring identities based on adolescents' varying levels of musical, artistic, intellectual, and athletic abilities and on their physical attractiveness (Kinney, 1999). (See Table 19.2 for descriptions of crowd types.)

Romantic relationships and dating represent one more aspect of peer relationships during adolescence. These relationships normally progress through several overlapping developmental phases. At first, dating often involves simply arranging to be in a situation where members of the opposite sex are present (e.g., hanging out together at the mall, going together as a group to a sports event). This first step is usually followed soon by more organized mixed-sex gatherings, such as school dances

---

TABLE 19.2

Adolescent crowd types and descriptors

Populars (Trendies, Preppies, In Crowd): physically attractive, wear brand-name clothing, attend social events

Brains (Dweebs, Nerds, Geeks): Enjoy academics and computers; nonathletic

Jocks: Like and participate in sports

Normals: Average students who get along with most other students across crowds

Loners: Very small group; feel alone and not accepted by other students

Hippies (Deadheads, Granolas): Traditional "hippy" clothing and music of the 60s and 70s; high level of caring and loyalty; open-minded

Black Crowd: Mostly African American students

Wannabes: Varying ethnicity students who adopt African American dress styles and behavior and may or may not be accepted by the Black crowd

Punk Rockers: Wear ripped, dyed clothing; interested in political and social issues

Headbangers (Metalheads, Druggies): Use drugs, listen to heavy metal rock music, skip school often, and wear concert T-shirts

Troublemakers: Fight, act out, loud, get into trouble with teachers

Rednecks (Grits, Hicks): Tend to have pick up trucks or "muscle cars"; mostly from rural families; many involved in the vocational program

Sources: Stone & Brown, 1999; Strouse, 1999; Youniss et al., 1994.

Romantic relationships progress through several phases. In the fourth stage, pairings are clearly defined before couples go out together. (*Source:* © Tessa Codrington/Tony Stone Images)

or parties, where male-female interaction is expected. The third phase is referred to as multiple or group dating. In these situations, several boys and girls attend an activity together. Early in this stage, individual pairings remain ambiguous. As this stage progresses, the number of pairs in the group decreases, and specific individual pairings become more clearly articulated. In the fourth stage, the double date is common. In the double date, the two pairings are clearly defined before the couples go out. This fourth stage often provides some opportunity for sexual experimentation within mutually acceptable limits. During the fifth stage, a single couple may go out alone (Atwater, 1996). For high school girls, early dating and "going steady" are positively related to self-esteem, perhaps because this relationship validates their sense of attractiveness. However, continuous long-term involvement with one boy is related to lower self-esteem, perhaps indicating insecurity (Bascow & Rubin, 1999).

Dating scripts are cognitive models that guide adolescents through the dating experience and help them evaluate the success of a date. Dating scripts for first two-person dates (as opposed to group dates) follow traditional gender roles. That is, the male script is one of being the initiator in terms of asking the female out, planning the activities, and beginning any sexual interaction. The female's script is a reactive one with a focus on appearance and enjoying the date (Rose & Frieze, 1993).

Dating problems occur during adolescence as a result of differences in the dating scripts for social interaction. Weiten and Lloyd (1994) describe the following scripts of sexual relationships. According to the traditional religious script, sex is acceptable only after the couple is married. In the romantic script, sex is an expression of love and is acceptable if a couple feels they are in love. In one study, 60 percent of adolescent males and 75 percent of adolescent girls who dated only one person with whom they were in love had intercourse (Roche and Ramsby 1993). The sexual friendship script involves friends who enjoy activities together and sometimes end up having sex with no expressed commitment or shared intimacy. The casual/mutual script involves sexual activity among individuals who happen to meet casually and mutually agree to have sex. Finally, the utilitarian/predatory script involves sex for economic gain, job advancement, or power achievement. The majority of the more than 1 million sexual assaults each year on teenagers are date rapes. Failure to recognize the differences in these scripts, or misunderstandings about what script is expected, can make dating unsatisfactory or even dangerous.

The following characteristics are associated with the likelihood of a male committing dating violence: heavy alcohol or drug use, having sexually aggressive peers, acceptance of dating violence, interpersonal violence, acceptance of traditional gender roles, miscommunications about sex, and adversarial attitudes about relationships (CDC, 1999b). Dating violence may affect as many as 10 percent of high school students, increasing the likelihood that they will suffer long-term effects of sexual dysfunction, flashbacks, delayed stress reaction, sexually transmitted disease, and pregnancy (Johnson et al., 1999). Forceful verbal resistance (e.g., screaming) has been found to be a much more effective strategy for stopping an assault than nonforceful verbal resistance, such as pleading or crying (Page, 1997).

Within the many types of peer relationships, and in their social interactions, adolescents begin to identify a place for themselves in society. Peers are central in the adolescent's quest for belonging, and they also are a factor in the adolescent's search for identity.

Knowing the Self: The Quest for Identity

A group of friends are celebrating the end of summer and the senior year in high school that lies ahead. "This year is going to be so busy with field hockey, studying, and deciding what we will do after graduation!" exclaims Tunisha. "This summer, I spent several mornings at the veterinarian's office to see if that is what I might want to do. This fall, Mrs. Moser is going to meet with me before school and let me tutor some of her biology students to see if I'd like to be a high school biology teacher."

"Lighten up, Tunisha. This is your last year in high school. It's a time for fun," says Christy. "I had a great summer and I'm looking forward to a fun-filled senior year. I'll worry about what I'm going to be when the time comes."

"You can't wait till next year, Christy!" chimes in Holly. "You have to send in college applications *this* year. I'll be going to Millersville University. I've always wanted to be an elementary school teacher and my mom says M.U. has a good program for that. Dad and Mom took me there last spring for the get-acquainted program, and they are really excited that I want to go there."

"I used to think I wanted to be a teacher," adds Natasha. "But last year I explored lots of different possibilities just as Tunisha is doing now. That changed my mind. I still want to work with kids or teenagers, but I think I can make more of a difference in their lives by working outside of school. I'm applying to several universities that have graduate programs in community psychology. My cousin told me that psychology majors often do internships and that I could probably get a good field placement at a university where there's a community psychology program. It would be really cool if we could all go to the same university, wouldn't it? I have lots of information about the places I'm applying if anybody wants to see it."

think about it

How would you characterize the status of each of these high schoolers' search for identity? Which girls seemed to be uncertain about the future? This particular conversation focused on the search for identity related to careers. What conversations might reflect the girls' different phases in searching for sexual, political, or religious identity? How might parent-adolescent relationships affect the adolescent's search for identity?

Adolescents are looking for a place among their peers and are developing a sense of who they are. (*Source:* © Kevin Horan/ Stock Boston)

Erikson: The Crisis of Adolescence

Erikson thought adolescent cliques and their stereotyping of themselves and others were defenses against identity confusion. "To keep themselves together they temporarily overidentify, to the point of apparent complete loss of identity, with the heroes of cliques and crowds" (Erikson, 1963, p. 262). According to Erikson, the crisis of adolescence involves establishing a sense of identity. Adolescents are looking for a place among peers and in society at large, and are developing a sense of who they are. When individuals meet these challenges, they achieve the positive sense of self that Erikson terms **psychosocial** or **ego identity.** Tunisha, Christy, Holly, and Natasha are in four distinctly different phases of establishing psychosocial identity.

The concept of psychosocial or ego identity is difficult to define objectively. The American philosopher and psychologist William James described a person's character as an internal state, "which when it came upon him, he felt himself to be most deeply and intensely active and alive" (James, 1920, p. 199). Erikson comments about this: "Thus may a mature person come to the astonished or exuberant awareness of his identity" (Erikson, 1968b, p. 61).

Achieving an identity requires a person to consider society's expectations, as well as her own values and abilities. Finally, the person must make a flexible commitment to occupation, sexuality, religion, and politics. Although the process of forming an identity begins in infancy, many years are required to resolve the identity crisis that occurs when an adolescent seriously considers stepping into society on her own. Even after adolescents and young adults make initial commitments, they often struggle from time to time throughout adulthood with issues related to identity.

If adolescents fail drastically to consider and resolve the identity crisis, they experience **identity confusion**—a lack of focus about who they are and what their place might be in society and among their peers. They may hold on to childish ways, accepting without question the values and life goals their parents set for them. Or they may drift aimlessly, unable to commit themselves to anything substantial. An adolescent may achieve identity in one of the four domains (i.e., occupation, sexuality, values, and politics) while continuing to experience identity confusion in the others. Achieving psychosocial identity in all four domains is a major quest during adolescence.

Marcia: Research on the Quest for Identity

Research in identity development has been led by James Marcia (1980, 1988, 1991). Marcia's "identity status" approach categorizes individuals in terms of whether they have been concerned about exploring alternatives ("identity crisis") and whether they have committed themselves to any specific alternatives. Marcia interviewed young people about their values and career choices and constructed four categories of identity status based on these interviews. Each category reflected a different phase of identity development. These categories are described in Table 19.3, with each student's status identified from the vignette.

Like Erikson, Marcia thinks identity development begins in infancy and continues until old age. In other words, it is a continuing process of incorporating important experiences and fundamental beliefs into a relatively coherent set of ideas about self and society. The first important experience in this process is attachment during infancy. Secure attachment seems to contribute to identity formation. Adolescents labeled "high in identity" were less anxiously attached as infants than those adolescents found to have lower identity status (Kroger, 1985, cited in Marcia, 1988). Anxious or ambivalent attachment of the kind that results in children's clinging behavior is associated with "foreclosed identity" adolescents. They tenaciously hold on to conditionally loving parents (Marcia, 1988). Individuals whose identity status shows diffusion seem to be alienated the most from parental figures.

Some families provide an environment conducive to identity exploration, while others provide environments that inhibit it (Noller, 1994). Extremely close relationships with parents often result in foreclosure, while indifferent, detached, and rejecting relationships with parents often lead to identity diffusion. Parents who provide a moderate level of acceptance and understanding and who emphasize individuality are more likely to encourage identity exploration and achievement (Noller, 1994). What kind of relationships might Natasha, Tunisha, Holly, and Christy have with their parents?

Marcia says that identity formation is useful, in general, because it increases the efficiency with which a person can act in the world (1988). The formation of an identity structure, either achieved or foreclosed, provides an internal organization of previously conflicting ideas and demands. Because the person has already made basic choices, he can make subsequent choices more quickly, easily, and consistently. Identity achievement is positively correlated with making a career decision, while moratorium and diffusion statuses are negatively related to career decisions (Wallace-Broscious et al., 1994).

Current theory and research, like Erikson's original theory, suggest that identity status is determined by a number of cognitive, social, and emotional experiences that occur over the course of childhood. Identity development occurs within the peer context and is experienced differently by adolescents depending upon their niche within the system (Stone & Brown, 1999). Adolescents construct their identity with friends and peers by identifying with some norms and values and rejecting others (Puhj & Hart, 1999). Achieving identity or being in identity moratorium is associated with greater success in freshmen-year academic and interpersonal relations than is experienced

TABLE 19.3

Marcia's identity categories

Category	Description	Student
Identity achievement	Identity crisis is past, and commitments have been made.	Natasha
Identity moratorium	Identity crisis is in progress, and the search for commitments continues.	Tunisha
Identity foreclosure	Commitments are made, but they come from authority figures, not from self-searching.	Holly
Identity diffusion	No specific commitment has been made, and no active search has begun because of unresolved identity or absence of crisis.	Christy

by those in closure or diffusion (Berzonsky & Kuk, 2000). Having clearly defined one's values and goals and having made progress toward realizing them is a major component of happiness, psychological well-being, and identity.

One additional kind of identity confusion is **negative identity.** In this case, instead of standing for particular values, political positions, or sexual scripts, adolescents simply take a position that is in opposition to what their parents or other adults desire. In the area of career identity, negative identity is involved when an adolescent discloses that he will pursue a particular career because he knows it will displease his parents.

Achievement of Identity When Living within Two Cultures

The dramatic increase in racially mixed families has increased attention to **bicultural identity.** For example, the number of children and adolescents living in homes with mixed racial parents has more than tripled in the last quarter of the 20th century, and over 75 percent of African Americans have white ancestors. Based on his studies of human migration and interactions across cultures, sociologist R. E. Park (1928) argued long ago that individuals who live in two cultures may experience identity confusion because of the complexity of dual and often conflicting values and goals. Although Park assumed that an individual's association with two cultures would be uncomfortable for the individual, Park believed that such intermingling had long-term benefits for a society. In his essays in *The Souls of Black Folk* (1903/1961), the American civil rights leader W. E. B. Du Bois termed this simultaneous awareness of self as a member of two cultures as *double consciousness.* Du Bois, the first Black to receive a Ph.D. from Harvard, studied Blacks in American society and was the leading opponent of racial discrimination throughout the first half of the 20th century. Although the majority of biracial youth feel positively about themselves and their biracial identity, some face challenges negotiating their search for identity. Many biracial teens feel pressured to choose one racial group over the other. Continued experiences in two or more cultural groups often lead to bicultural identity later in adolescence for those who accept their multiracial heritage (Tatum, 1997).

Multiculturalism involves achieving a positive sense of self and self-worth in one culture without diminishing or degrading other cultures. When persons achieve a genuine bicultural identity, they do not reject their "home" culture even while also accepting the views of the other culture (Sampson, 1999). According to LaFromboise and colleagues (1993), **cultural competence** within any one culture is gained through achievement in each of the following aspects of social skill and psychosocial adjustment: (1) achieving a clear identity within each culture, (2) knowing the beliefs and values of both cultures, (3) displaying sensitivity to the affective processes of each culture, (4) communicating clearly in the language of both cultural groups, (5) emitting socially sanctioned behavior when interacting with each cultural group, (6) maintaining social interactions within each cultural group, and (7) negotiating the institutional structures found within each culture.

LaFromboise emphasizes the **alternation model** of achieving bicultural identity. In this model, individuals achieve some cultural identity and competence within each of two cultures, and they alter their behavior in accord with the social contexts of each culture when they are operating within it. Individuals who apply the alternation model maintain a positive relationship with both cultures rather than selecting one and rejecting the other. LaFromboise and colleagues (1993) proposed that the achievement of identity in psychosocial development will affect an individual's ability to acquire bicultural competence. Adolescents who are able to achieve bicultural identity and competence tend to be more tolerant of differences and better able to maintain relations with individuals across cultures, than are adolescents who do not achieve bicultural identity.

Another way adolescents achieve identity and bicultural competence within two cultures is through **identity fusion.** Rather than alternate between cultural identities, individuals achieve a fused identity that integrates aspects of the two background cultures into a coherent whole. There is an increasing tendency in the United States and Canada for biracial individuals to have bicultural identity—they do not identify with either of the racial groups as their primary affiliation. Asked if they are black or white, these individuals are likely to respond that they are biracial. In the process of gaining bicultural competence in ways that are consistent with either the alternation or the fusion model, adolescents tend to achieve a values identity and political identity, as well as a career identity.

Not all individuals living within two cultures are successful in achieving identity. Adolescents may devalue their social identities because of discrimination, or they may reject aspects of their identity that are associated with their culture, while emphasizing less threatened aspects. Thus, groups who have suffered repeated discrimination may show disidentification (Cowdry, 1995).

Sexual Preference

Part of one's identity involves sexual preference. Adolescents whose sexual preference is not heterosexual are more likely to be victimized and to feel anxiety about revealing their preference or having learned about it. A substantial number of homosexual adolescents are harassed, physically abused, or verbally abused by peers or adults, and this abuse may help explain their higher rates of suicide, running away, school difficulties, and substance abuse (Faulkner & Cranston, 1998; Steinberg, 1999). Self-acceptance and family support have a moderating effect on victimization and help an adolescent maintain positive psychological well-being despite the challenges inherent in a sexual preference that is nonheterosexual (Bailey & Zucker, 1995). The quest for identity is especially difficult for adolescents who explore identities that interfere with feelings of acceptance and belongingness.

Some high schools encourage clubs for homosexuals or sanction gay-straight alliances. Such steps help decrease social prejudices against homosexuality (Cobb, 1998). Becoming a member of an outgroup viewed as nonnormative or inferior is likely to result in devaluation, discrimination, hostility, and confusion about identity (Mummendey & Wenzel, 1999).

Adolescents' self-concepts can be improved when: (1) the environment is structured to help adolescents perform competently and value competent performance (value-expectancy theory), (2) they experience acceptance and support from individuals who are significant in that self-concept domain, and (3) they learn to face, rather than avoid, problems in that self-concept domain (Harter, 1990). The following self-concept domains have also been identified: athletic, musical, spatial, and physical appearance.

Sexual Behavior: The Quest for Intimacy

The fourth great quest during adolescence is the quest for **intimacy** (closeness, warmth, and sharing in a relationship). Adolescents begin to define themselves as sexual beings and to seek sexual relationships. Over the course of a few years, most adolescents experience romantic love for the first time and explore a variety of sexual behaviors. Emerging sexuality interacts with other changes, such as identity formation, increased independence from parents, and increasingly intimate interactions with peers, to contribute to what Erikson described as the crisis of intimacy versus isolation.

Erikson believed that the conflict between intimacy and isolation cannot be resolved without a sense of identity. Intimate, romantic involvements are important in adolescent emotional development, whether they are platonic or sexual. The love, trust, and honesty of intimate relationships help teenagers evaluate themselves positively.

Most adolescents experience romantic love for the first time. Over the course of the teenage years, adolescents usually become increasingly intimate with peers. (*Source:* © Goldberg/Monkmeyer)

In later adolescence, many of these relationships become sexual. In too many cases, however, early love relationships and sexual experiences lead to teenage pregnancies. Helping adolescents develop healthy, responsible sex lives—whether through birth control or abstinence—is an important task for parents, educators, and adolescents themselves. Parent-adolescent communication quality is a strong predictor of success at this task (Miller, Norton, Fan, & Christopherson, 1998). In this section, we discuss some of the questions and issues related to teenage sexuality.

Teenage Sexual Practices

Most teenagers feel the stirrings of sexuality long before they have an outlet for their desires. The first sexual practice that many regularly engage in is masturbation. One of the most widespread but least talked-about sexual behaviors, it serves to relieve sexual tension without the complications of an emotional relationship with another person. Masturbation has no negative effects and in fact can help adolescents learn about sexual functioning. Nearly all males and most adolescent females report masturbating at some time, although girls vary more than boys in the frequency with which they engage in this behavior.

Teenagers also report other sexual practices, such as kissing, petting, genital touching, and intercourse. We know that teenagers are sexually active at younger ages than ever before. The most common reason for adolescents engaging in sexual intercourse is peer pressure (Bascow & Rubin, 1999). Another is the lack of parent-adolescent communication. Adolescents underestimate their mothers' level of disapproval of sexual behavior, and mothers underestimate the level of sexual activity their teens engage in (Jaccard et al., 1998). More than half of all adolescent boys and girls have engaged in sexual intercourse by age 16, and the likelihood of having sex increases steadily with age. In addition, the average age of first intercourse has been falling steadily over the past four decades. This early sexual activity is reflected in statistics: Approximately 10 percent of U.S. adolescent girls ages 15 to 19 become pregnant each year, and about 85 percent of those did not intend to become pregnant. One-third of all U.S. births are to unwed mothers (Coyle et al., 1999; Donovan, 1999). Socioeconomic status is important in understanding adolescent pregnancy, as low-income families may see motherhood as the major option for identity development (Bascow & Rubin, 1999). The consequences for teenage pregnancies are discussed in the Research Close-up: The Consequences of Teenage Pregnancy.

Effects of Social Trends and the Media

The earlier and more frequent sexual activity of teenagers today, compared with that of earlier generations, reflects an overall trend in our society toward more sexual freedom. Premarital sex is widespread and widely accepted, unmarried couples live together openly, and some live-in couples choose to have children but not to get married. How do these social trends and attitudes filter down to teenagers? Many adolescents read

RESEARCH

CLOSE-UP   *The Consequences of Teenage Pregnancy*

What are the social and medical consequences of adolescent parenthood for teenagers and their babies? First, even though the majority of girls who are in school when they become pregnant are likely to finish high school or obtain a GED, they are highly unlikely to advance their educational standing beyond this basic level (Chase-Lansdale & Brooks-Gunn, 1994). With the arrival of the baby, they also must assume an emotional and economic responsibility for which they are unprepared. The most stable situation probably occurs for those who are able to continue living with their parents. Teenage parents who marry have higher rates of divorce and suicide and are likely to be poor. Obviously, adolescent mothers are at risk for chronic educational, emotional, occupational, and financial problems (Steinberg, 1999). Teenage mothers also have difficulty trying to balance work, school, motherhood, child care, and a social life.

This teenage mother seems proud and pleased with her young baby, but its care will likely direct her energy away from her own development. If she is like many teenage mothers, she may not finish school, and she and her children may live much of their lives in poverty. (*Source:* © Robert Harbison)

Pregnancy and childbirth are also costly to the teenage mother's health. She has a greater risk of anemia and toxemia in pregnancy, prolonged labor, and other birth complications. Some of these problems are related to poor nutrition and prenatal care. Whether she is trying to hide or deny her pregnancy, does not know the importance of eating well during pregnancy, or lacks the financial means to obtain nutritious food, the pregnant teenager often fails to provide herself and her unborn child with the nutrients required for good health.

The infant mortality rate is higher among these babies than it is among babies born to adult mothers, as the likelihood of low birth weight and prematurity are also higher. Babies born to teenage mothers have a greater risk of poor perceptual abilities and motor coordination, as well as a high risk for neurological impairments such as blindness, deafness, and mental retardation. All of these are associated with low birth weight (CPR, 1995). There is also an increased risk of some genetic and chromosomal disorders, such as Down syndrome, among babies of teenage mothers. As school-age children and adolescents, individuals who were born to teenage mothers may have emotional and cognitive problems. For example, 50 percent of adolescents who were born to teenage mothers fail a grade in school (Chase-Lansdale & Brooks-Gunn, 1994). They are also more likely than youth born to older mothers to be delinquents, to have behavior problems in school, and to become involved early in sexual activity. They often become pregnant as teenagers themselves (Chase-Lansdale & Brooks-Gunn, 1994).

The increasing number of teenage mothers whose financial and personal resources are too limited to provide the parental investment needed for infant and toddler development contributes to child abuse in the United States. Indeed, Belsky and Kelly (1994) concluded that poverty, coupled with early and extensive child bearing by teenagers, provides the most fertile soil for child maltreatment.

Many of the medical and physical risks to mothers and babies can be reduced with good prenatal and postnatal care. Some teenage mothers also manage to complete their education, control future pregnancies, and enter stable marriages, thus overcoming some of the difficulties usually encountered by teenage mothers. But nothing supports the healthy development of children as well as having parents who are ready, willing, and able to care for them. Prevention of teenage pregnancy is still the best way to ensure a healthy environment for a child who enters the world.

---

magazines such as *Seventeen, Cosmopolitan*, and *Playboy*. A 20-year study of *Seventeen* magazine showed that recreational sexual activity, homosexuality, oral sex, and masturbation received increased coverage (Carpenter, 1998). Most teenagers listen to rock music and watch music videos that are sexual in nature. Indeed, the typical teenager listens to music four hours a day (Arnett, 1995). Almost all teenagers watch television at a rate of about 23 hours a week. Twenty-nine percent of prime-time television shows involve sexual content (Geier, 1995). Soap operas and talk shows add

Magazines targeted for teenagers are giving increased coverage to recreational sexual activities. TV shows and music show similar increases. (*Source:* © Dorothy Littell Greco/The Image Works)

more sexual content, as does the news. Soap opera program descriptions during one week included "Courtney blackmails Frank into impregnating her"; "A married banker falls for the teenage daughter of his close friend"; "Out of curiosity Paul takes Viagra but misses his scheduled tryst"; and "The father of Roz's baby is but a babe himself" (*TV Guide,* 1999, pp. 53, 76, 124, 190). Talk show topics included "People who suspect their mates of cheating on the Internet"; "Telling unsuspecting mates about summer flings"; "Strippers try to prove they are not prostitutes"; and "People who want to ask their mates for group sex" (*TV Guide,* 1999, pp. 109, 159, 182, 205).

One study of TV sex scenes between unmarried partners found that only 9 percent of the couples in the scenes concluded that having sex would be wrong or inappropriate (Clark, 1995). Another study found that between 14 and 21 intimate sex acts are visually portrayed in a typical R-rated movie (Brown et al., 1993). Sixty percent of children and adolescents polled by a California advocacy group indicated that TV sways them to have sex (Geier, 1995). In addition to the fact that the sexual content of media messages is extremely high, the messages are often unrealistic and misleading. Hardly anyone ever contracts an STD, and practically no one becomes pregnant.

Expectations about the timing of sexual experiences, marriage, and having a child differ across cultures. For example, one survey of 11- to 15-year-old females indicated that Hispanic girls expected these events to occur at a young age and in rapid succession, whereas Asian girls expected each to occur at later ages and in gradual succession. African-American girls had the highest expectation for nonmarital childbearing. Understanding these different cultural expectations is important in addressing problems in adolescent sexual behavior (East, 1998).

Determinants of Contraceptive Use among Adolescents

Although adolescents are vitally interested in sex and engage in various sexual activities, their knowledge about sex is at times simply false. Even when they know the facts, they often do not believe or act on them. Teenage girls often believe they will not get pregnant because it is the wrong time of the month, they are too young, or they have sex only infrequently.

Contraceptive use is also limited by a simple lack of knowledge about the possible consequences of unprotected intercourse. Parent-adolescent discussions about condom use are critical. Adolescents who talk with parents about condom use before their first sexual encounter are 3 times more likely to use a condom than are adolescents who do not discuss the topic. Adolescents who use condoms at first intercourse are 20 times more likely to use them regularly in subsequent acts (Miller, Levine, Whitaker, & Xu, 1998). Much voluntary behavior is determined by a person's beliefs about the consequences of the behavior. Beliefs, as well as associated changes in behavior, are strongly influenced by experience. But teenagers have little experience with the negative consequences of risky behavior. Interviews with adolescents regarding their thoughts about sexual behavior revealed that concern about health risks almost never emerged. Instead, the adolescents focused more on issues of a partner's infidelity and how to control infidelity (Eyre et al., 1998).

Recall from chapter 16 that only about half of sexually active high school youth use condoms. Methods to reduce unintended teen pregnancy include school-based behavioral interventions to delay onset of sexual activity, and contraceptive counseling and assistance to teens who are already sexually active (Wilson & Joffe, 1995). Other approaches focus on improving decision-making skills, improving family communication about sex, reducing peer pressure through training, and providing accurate information about human sexuality in grades K–12 (Chase-Lansdale & Brooks-Gunn, 1994; Haffner, 1992). Aronson's cognitive dissonance theory is also being tried (see chapter 16). In 1999, the U.S. federal government began giving awards of up to $100 million annually for the five states that achieve the greatest decline in out-of-wedlock births and reduce the abortion rate (Donovan, 1999).

Social Factors and Adolescent Problems

Although adolescence is not necessarily a time of trouble or conflict, problems of one kind or another do arise. In one study, adolescents were asked to indicate the most important problem they had faced in the previous year and how they had coped with it. The majority of problems dealt with interpersonal issues involving peers, parents, or romantic relationships, or with problem behavior, school adjustments, or academic stress.

Some problems seem to stem from teenagers' increasing independence, their curiosity and interest in new experiences, their inclination to take risks, and their tendency not to foresee the consequences of their actions. For example, one survey estimated that there are over 1 million compulsive gamblers between the ages of 12 and 18, and approximately 80 percent of all teenagers have done some type of gambling before graduation (Keynes, 1999). Adolescents involved in lottery gambling are more likely to smoke, drink alcohol, and use drugs (Griffiths & Sutherland, 1998).

A heightened level of **sensation seeking** (a need for seeking out novel and intense experiences) contributes to adolescents' reckless behavior (Arnett, 1995), as does adolescent **egocentrism** (a belief that thoughts of others are directed toward the self) (Elkind, 1967). One consequence of adolescent egocentrism is that young people tend to believe that others are as admiring or as critical of them as they are of themselves. Consequently, adolescents are continually constructing or reacting to an **imaginary audience** (adolescents' belief that they are the focus of attention in social situations, even when this is not the case). This concept probably contributes to the adolescent's self-consciousness, wish for privacy, reluctance to share revealing thoughts, faddish dress, and "showing off" behaviors.

A second consequence of adolescent egocentrism is the **personal fable** (a sense of invulnerability by imagining their life as having a special existence, and a belief that

These teenagers are doing what over 90 percent of American adolescents do at one time or another—experimenting with alcohol. Alcohol, the most frequently used drug among teenagers, is used to increase sociability and to celebrate special occasions. Alcohol use is associated with automobile accidents and sexual offenses. *(Source:* © Will Hart)

unfortunate events will happen to others but never to them). Other problems seem to result from inadequate ways of handling anger and aggression and alienation from family and society. In fact, rates of adolescent emotional and behavioral problems have increased in the past 15 years. Adolescent resilience is strengthened by the following factors: high intelligence, strong sense of identity, high feelings of self-efficacy, "easy" temperament, good coping skills, material and financial resources, a positive family environment, a close relationship with a parent, opportunities for change and growth, and social support (Striegel-Moore & Cachelin, 1999).

Drug and Alcohol Abuse

Like sexual behavior, the use of drugs and alcohol among teenagers reflects adult behavior in the larger society. Law enforcement agencies seem unable to stop the flow of drugs, even to elementary school children. Many communities focus instead on educating young people about the dangers of addiction. The availability of alcohol and illegal drugs, along with society's permissive view toward the use of legal, mood-altering chemicals, clearly contributes to widespread drug and alcohol abuse. The excessive use of alcohol and other drugs presented in chapter 16 has led to a search for the factors that contribute to these problems. For example, adolescents whose parents are responsive to them, monitor them closely, and make clear their opposition to alcohol abuse, drink less and associate less with alcohol-using youth (Bogenschneider et al., 1998). Being supervised after school cuts in half the risk that adolescents will smoke, drink, or abuse drugs (Boyle, 1999). Moreover, those adolescents who like school and those who are committed to a religion are less likely to abuse drugs (Evans, 1999; Larson, D. B., 1998).

Interventions that encourage parents to be warm and supportive in their relationships with adolescents, and those that provide parents with skills and strategies to talk with their children, minimize adolescents' risk for problem behavior (CDC, 1999d; Repinski et al., 1998). Programs such as The Life Skills Training help adolescents cope with social anxiety and develop greater self-mastery and social confidence (Castro, 1999).

Home, School, and Social Pressures

Dropping Out of School Sometimes the demands of or problems at school seem so intense that teenagers believe they would be better off by dropping out. This is almost never true. Without skills or education, high school dropouts usually face a lifetime of social and economic hardship. Yet 10 to 15 percent of American adolescents fail to complete high school (Atwater, 1996; Cobb, 1998). At least half of them are estimated to be of average or above-average intelligence. Why do they drop out? The most common reasons for dropping out of school are a dislike for school, low or failing grades, pregnancy, life stresses, home responsibilities, or a desire to earn money. Females are less likely to drop out of school and to get into trouble than are male students (Eccles et al., 1999). Adolescents who have experienced poor peer relationships in earlier years are more likely to drop out than their better-accepted peers because without close ties to peers, they lack the in-school support and resources that facilitate academic achievement (Kobus, 1999). The school dropout rate among at-risk adolescents is much lower for students who participate in extracurricular activities (Mahoney & Cairns, 1997).

Running Away from Home   Runaways are persons under 18 years of age who leave home at least for one night, without the permission of parents or guardians. In the United States there are close to 1.2 million runaways. Problems include emotional conflicts at home, parental physical abuse, parental neglect, parental strictness, parental drug or alcohol problems, depression, poor school attendance, bad grades, drug and alcohol abuse, and inability to get along with teachers (Lopez & Gary, 1995; Wolfe et al., 1999). Runaways are at risk for malnutrition, prostitution, sexually transmitted diseases, HIV infection, substance use, respiratory problems, mental health problems, and accidents (Lopez & Gary, 1995).

Homeless and Latchkey Youth   Adolescents who have no place for care and supervision are identified as homeless. Some homeless adolescents have run away, but many have been forced out of their homes or abandoned by parents. Still others are the children of homeless parents. Homeless youth in the United States tend to come from severely dysfunctional families who offer no guidance, structure, or encouragement (Smollar, 1999). They stand at risk of being misused by others, making unhealthy choices, and becoming further cast out from society (Fitzgerald, 1995). They are sometimes concerned with the lack of attention and respect they receive from their teachers (Daniels, 1995). Altering the developmental pathways of homeless youth is not an easy task. Increased advocacy and increased research would lead to services to help homeless youth develop along more positive pathways (Smollar, 1999).

Many youth are left by themselves for much of the time. These latchkey youth must fend for themselves, and many spend time at home alone because most service programs are for younger children (Nash & Fraser, 1998). Many are boys who have opted out of school activities and engage in problem behavior after school. During the period from 3:00 to 6:00 P.M., adolescents are twice as likely to abuse drugs and alcohol, get pregnant, join a gang, or become a criminal (Gurian, 1998). The amount of unmonitored time adolescents spend engaged in activities such as driving around or "hanging out" is associated with this "risky time" of encountering negative developmental experiences (Larson, R., 1998). Adolescents are missing valuable time for socializing, making contributions to the community, and being recognized for personal accomplishment.

Delinquency   The criminal activities of juveniles are a serious problem in the United States. Sometimes teenage delinquency is the continuation of behavior begun as early as the preschool years and remains stable into adulthood. In other cases, the delinquency appears only during adolescence. Moffitt (1993) refers to the latter as "adolescent-limited" delinquency.

Adolescent delinquency is common for males and may serve as an expression of autonomy. One-third of U.S. males have been involved in crimes by the time they reach adulthood, and four-fifths have been involved in minor offenses. One New Zealand study indicated that 93 percent of its male adolescents were involved in some delinquent activity (Moffitt, 1993).

The juvenile delinquent's profile often includes the following characteristics: nonempathic; egocentric, impersonal, and manipulative behavior; attentional problems; and a lack of impulse control (John et al., 1994). Shoplifting, for example, often occurs in response to peer pressure and is engaged in for "fun and thrills" (Lo, 1994).

Peer rejection, parental violence or negative discipline, inability to self-regulate, and aggression are predictive of adolescent behavior problems (Ary et al., 1999;

Ianniello, 1999; Wheeler et al., 1999). A study of over 13,000 Native American adolescents revealed that resilient youth differed from maladaptive youth in that the former suffered from physical abuse and family rejection (Blum et al., 1997). A longitudinal study of adolescents showed that antisocial behaviors were predicted by school-age withdrawal, inability to self-regulate, and aggression. Difficulty learning to regulate negative affect appears to be the underlying source for later adolescent problem behavior (Baumeister et al., 1998; Dale & Baumeister, 1999; Pope & Bierman, 1999).

Individual characteristics identified as possible causes of delinquency include poor social skills, sensation seeking, learning disabilities, educational and problem-solving deficits, and problems in the socialization of conventional norms and values (Brown, 1999). Alcohol and drug use account for almost half of the variability in aggressive delinquent adolescent behavior, particularly such behavior directed at peers and family (Durant et al., 1997). There is also an association between engaging in delinquent behaviors and affiliating with deviant peers. Family management practices during childhood, such as fewer family activities and coercive interactions, lead to adolescent associations with deviant peers (Ary et al., 1999; Irvine et al., 1999; Wiener, 1999). In East Asian postindustrial societies, such as Japan, Korea, and Taiwan, parents more closely monitor their adolescents, limiting their freedom to be away from home and to stay out late. In northern Europe, adolescents have fewer nighttime activities and spend more time doing things with their families than is true of youth in the United States. (Larson, R., 1998a).

The best approach to juvenile delinquency appears to be prevention—it is more effective to intervene with children before they reach adolescence. Teachers and other adults should identify at-risk children no later than early elementary school. Preventive steps can be taken at that time (Ary et al., 1999). Families and communities can work together to create a more positive environment in which to raise healthy children and adolescents, concentrating on developmental assets they need in order to succeed, social support, constructive use of time, commitment to learning, positive values, and social competencies (Benson, 1997).

America's Promise—The Alliance for Youth (1999), led by Colin Powell, is dedicated to building and strengthening the character and competence of our youth by providing these basics for adolescents:

- An ongoing relationship with a caring adult—parent, mentor, tutor, or coach

- A safe place with structured activities during nonschool hours

- Good health care

- A marketable skill through effective education

- An opportunity to give back through community service

Suicide   Suicide is the second leading cause of death for adolescents aged 15 to 24. One in 9 adolescents reports at least one suicide attempt, and approximately 5,000 youth die each year from suicide. Suicide attempts are twice as high for Native American and Alaska Native youth and six times higher for homosexual youth. Social stigma hinders gay adolescents from gaining identity achievement and leads to more depression, isolation, and loneliness (Borowksy, 1999; Garofalo & Wolf, 1999; Radkowsky & Siegel, 1997). Males account for about 85 percent of suicides among adolescents, and males are committing suicide at younger ages than ever before (Kindlon & Thompson, 1999). Of all problem behaviors in adolescence, teenage suicide is, understandably, the most troubling to adults.

Adolescents often fail to think ahead to consider what the possibilities of the future may be. If adolescents are severely depressed or anxious, if they feel helpless or worthless, they may see suicide as the only escape from despair.

Adolescents at high risk for suicide are those who are depressed, isolated, and who tend to strike out without thinking (angry-impulsive). The loss of a family member or friend, lower status, lower self-esteem or poor health, failure in school, failure in social situations, failure in romantic relationships, and exposure to a peer's suicide all contribute to suicidal thoughts. Physical, sexual, and emotional abuse of adolescents contributes to suicide attempts, as do high levels of parent-parent or parent-adolescent conflict (Borowsky, 1999; Norton, 1994; Rowe et al., 1999). Depression is the number one risk factor for suicide. One study indicated that although 57 percent of adolescents who attempted suicide had major depression, only 13 percent of the parents thought their teenagers were depressed (Velting, 1999). Signs of depression include a drop in school grades, not caring about school, dropping friends and activities, abusing drugs, changing eating habits, experiencing sleep problems, giving away possessions, thinking about dying, and having fantasies about suicide (Arbetter, 1995; Norton, 1994). Protective factors for adolescents include family connectedness, discussing problems with family or friends, church attendance, and positive emotional health (Borowsky, 1999; Rowe et al., 1999; Larson, R., 1998).

Many factors combine to put adolescents at risk for suicide. Family problems, drug or alcohol abuse, and perceived inadequacy in some highly valued area are often involved when a teenager attempts suicide. This girl may feel lonely and isolated if she has few friends or is unpopular, but highly values social success. (*Source:* © Rosanne Olson/Tony Stone Images)

Positive Aspects of Adolescent Development

Although we are concerned with adolescent problems and stresses, one survey indicates that 83 percent of adolescents report few if any problems (Rowe et al., 1999). Adolescents' ability to carry out higher levels of social perspective-taking and their increases in cognitive and social maturity provide a foundation for positive aspects of social emotional development. A greater sensitivity to the needs and perspectives of others can lead to an increase in prosocial behavior. Youthful idealism also contributes to a greater concern with humanitarianism and social justice.

Prosocial Reasoning and Identity

As adolescents achieve an understanding of themselves as distinct from others, they may become more sensitive to other's needs (social cognition) and realize that they can take action to reduce others' distress. Eisenberg (1986) developed a set of social vignettes in which individuals were faced with a prosocial dilemma. In each vignette the needs of one individual are in conflict with the needs of others. After describing each dilemma, the adolescent is asked to say what the focus individual should do, and why. Based on these dilemmas, Eisenberg identified five levels of prosocial reasoning. At each successive stage, there is an increased concern for others and a decreased concern for self.

Hedonistic reasoning involves a preoccupation with the individual's needs at the expense of satisfying others' needs. With **needs-oriented prosocial reasoning**, the person recognizes the physical and psychological needs of others and knows that they conflict with one's own. The person with an **approval and interpersonal orientation** takes into consideration the reactions of others to help or refusal to help those in need. At the **empathic reasoning** level, the target person puts herself or himself in the shoes of persons in need. At the **internalized reasoning** level, the person lives up to internalized values concerning obligations to society. This final level is characteristic of individuals who experience happiness and pride when they live up to their standards.

A longitudinal investigation of these levels of prosocial reasoning (Eisenberg et al., 1995) indicated that there are both gender and developmental differences in responses. Overall, females generally use higher levels of prosocial reasoning than males. Changes in development included a decline in hedonistic reasoning up to adolescence but an increase in it again toward the end of adolescence. Throughout adolescence, needs-oriented reasoning declined, while approval, empathic, and internalized reasoning increased. During adolescence, increases in higher-level, internalized prosocial reasoning appear to be due to an increase in formal operational reasoning and exposure to experiences requiring thinking about others.

Helwig (1995) found a shift upward in judgments about civil liberties with increasing age. Forsyth and colleagues (1997) found that empathic reasoning correlated negatively with the perceived humorousness of jokes in which racial, ethnic, or religious groups were the target of the humor. Empathic reasoning, social competence, and responsive parenting are all predictors of adolescent prosocial behaviors (Eisenberg, 1991).

This period of transition provides many opportunities for establishing a positive developmental trajectory into adulthood. Lerner (1996) points out the need for research-based programs that capitalize on the plasticity of adolescent development. The adolecent's search for career, political, religious, and sexual identities relies heavily on the successful integration of social support provided by family, peers, schools, community organizations, and cultural dynamics.

An example of this integrative approach is Taylor's (1996). This study found that kinship and family-management practices influenced the development of African American adolescents. Kin-social support was associated with an absence of adolescent problem behaviors, greater self-reliance, and better psychological well-being. Greater organization in the home environment and greater parental involvement in school-related activities were usually correlated with extended family kinship support. They resulted in better grades, increased psychological well-being, and more involvement in community and school organizations.

Another study of African American families reported positive influences of parental religious belief on adolescent-parent relationships, adolescent self-regulation, and prosocial attitudes such as concern for others, love, forgiveness, and tolerance. The social support processes across family, church, and community systems appear to be extremely important in the adolescent's positive prosocial development (Brody et al., 1996).

Thus, the greater the integration of social support in the adolescent's ecosystem, the more likely she will contribute to a positive family and community system through activities such as volunteer services and expressions of concern for others. Adolescents report that it is important and personally satisfying to help others. Females judged helping others to be more important than did males (Killen & Turiel, 1999). Also, having a high self-regard gives adolescents the freedom and generosity to defend others, such as going to the aid of someone who is being bullied (Salmivalli, 1999). The application of principles such as those involved in cognitive dissonance theory, along with social support programs for adolescents, can lead to greater empathic reasoning and higher self-regulation (Garbarino, 1996; Sampson, 1999).

Approximately 25 percent of high school seniors report being involved in volunteer service on a regular basis, and about 50 percent are involved occasionally. The more important religion is in adolescents' lives, the more likely they are to do service. In fact, students who believe that religion is important in their lives are almost three times more likely to do service than those who do not believe religion is important (Youniss et al., 1999).

Adolescent participation in community service builds skills and discipline, provides self-respect, elicits respect from others, and strengthens work values (Johnson et al., 1999; Takanishi et al., 1997). It is important to raise young people to learn to give without need for reward (Gurian, 1998). Some adolescents are involved in the Volunteers in Career Awareness program, serving as mentors to younger students and exposing them to a variety of career options (VICA, 1999). Another program, Assets in Motion, trains adolescents to work with younger children, ranging from calming traumatized children to mentoring elementary youth in after-school programs (Alexander, 1999). Volunteering to help with Boy Scout or Girl Scout activities is another service choice. Kaps for Kids involves students obtaining hats from celebrities, firefighters, and others to give to children with cancer. In another program, students make early-literacy books for families in need. Many other volunteer programs, sponsored by participants in America's Promise, encourage youth to volunteer. The Prudential Spirit of Community Awards recognize youth who have demonstrated exemplary community service (America's Promise, 1999).

Research indicates that adolescents are concerned about social issues, such as discrimination, racial unity, community violence, war, and the environment. Adolescents who receive community and family support are more likely to find a responsible course of action for dealing with these issues (Davis, 1999; Frydenberg & Lewis, 1996).

Time Windows and Personality Stability

Rovee-Collier's (1995) concept of **time windows** is analogous to the idea of critical periods in biological development. The difference is that time windows relate to psychological experience. The adolescent years can be viewed as a critical time window when an individual's major personality traits can be shaped. Based on longitudinal studies conducted over 20 years, McCrae and Costa (1994) indicated that the following five personality traits remain quite stable from late adolescence or early adulthood:

- Openness to experience versus cautiousness

- Conscientiousness versus irresponsibility

- Extroversion versus introversion

- Agreeableness versus disagreeableness

- Neurotic problems versus psychological well-being

Openness to experience increases dramatically between ages 12 to 17 (Brener & Collins, 1998), and males develop higher self-esteem than females as they approach the end of adolescence (Kling et al., 1999). A universal pattern of adolescent-to-adulthood personality change was found in Croatia, Germany, Italy, Portugal, South Korea, and the United States, with increases in conscientiousness and agreeableness and decreases in openness to experience, extroversion, and neuroticism (McCrae et al., 1999).

KEY POINTS

Relationships with Family: The Quest for Independence

- Adolescents continue to want their parents' involvement in their lives, even while going through the process of individuation.

- Parents can experience their children's teenage years as stressful and changes of their own, such as divorce or a change in career, contribute to their adolescents' stress.

- Parents can support their teenagers' healthy social and emotional development by their parenting methods. The most competent and independent teenagers come from authoritative or democratic families in which parents give rational explanations for their actions and listen to their children's point of view. The authoritarian pattern of parenting is associated with low social competence. The permissive pattern is associated with immaturity. Families with poor communication and negative interactions foster low self-esteem and poor social skills in adolescents.

Relationships with Peers: The Quest to Belong

- Friends and peers become increasingly important to teenagers. They spend more and more time with peers in a clique or crowd. They prefer peers who are like themselves.

- Teenagers rely on peers to help them become emotionally independent from their families and discover a clear sense of identity. They often seem to merge completely with their peer group for a time before they become autonomous. Several different crowd types dominate the high school social structure.

- Metacognition and self-disclosure play critical roles in forming and maintaining peer relationships, and cliques and crowds are major socialization agents.

- Romantic relationships and dating represent another aspect of changing peer relationships, normally progressing through several overlapping phases and following dating scripts.

Knowing the Self: The Quest for Identity

- According to Erikson, the crisis of adolescence involves establishing a sense of identity and overcoming role confusion.

- Research in identity development categorizes adolescents on the basis of whether they have been concerned about exploring alternatives and what commitments have been made.

- Family factors affect the process of identity formation, as do a number of cognitive, social, and emotional experiences.

- Bicultural competence is gained by biracial and bi-ethnic adolescents through increased achievement in several aspects of social skill and psychosocial adjustment.

- The quest for identity is especially difficult for adolescents who explore identities that interfere with feelings of acceptance and belongingness, such as sexual preference. Non-normative outgroups are devalued and face discrimination.

Sexual Behavior: The Quest for Intimacy

- The first sexual behavior many teenagers engage in is masturbation. Nearly all males and most adolescent females report masturbating at some time.

- Teenagers are becoming sexually active at an earlier age than ever before. Many have had sexual intercourse by the time they are age 14 or 15.

- Adolescent sexual behavior reflects the trend toward greater sexual freedom that has dominated U.S. society for the past 30 years, resulting in 10 percent of 15- to 19-year-old girls becoming pregnant each year.

- Adolescents are often unrealistic in their thinking about sex and do not use contraceptives until well after they become sexually active. They think pregnancy cannot happen to them. Their babies are at greater risk for medical problems than are babies of adult mothers. Adequate prenatal and postnatal care can reduce many medical and physical risks associated with teenage motherhood.

- Both media and subculture influence views about appropriate sexual behavior.

Social Factors and Adolescent Problems

- Adolescent egocentrism, sensation seeking, and their beliefs in the imaginary audience and the personal fable put them at risk for alcohol and drug use, injury, and emotional problems.

- The widespread use of drugs and alcohol among adolescents reflects the acceptance and availability of these substances in the larger society.

- About 10 to 15 percent of all adolescents drop out of school, many of them of average or above-average intelligence. Dropouts come from all socioeconomic classes.

- In the United States there are close to 1.2 million individual runaway youth, as well as homeless and latchkey youth.
- Juvenile delinquency is often characterized by unempathetic, egocentric, and manipulative behavior, and is related to several poor social and learning skills as well as to associations with deviant peers. The best approach to juvenile delinquency is to prevent it before it occurs.
- Suicidal teenagers are attempting to express and communicate their need for help. Adolescents at high risk are those who are depressed and isolated. Protective factors include family connectedness, church attendance, and discussing problems with friends and family.

Positive Aspects of Adolescent Development

- As adolescents achieve an understanding of self, they may become more sensitive to other's needs, leading to increases in social interest, self-regulation, and volunteer activities.
- Eisenberg has identified five levels of prosocial reasoning and has found developmental changes in their use.
- Empathic reasoning, high self-esteem, social competence, and responsive parenting are all predictors of adolescent prosocial behaviors.
- The adolescent years might be viewed as the period of the last open time window in shaping an individual's major personality traits.

GLOSSARY

alternation model: achieving bicultural identity by altering behavior in accord with the context of each culture (p. 642)

approval and interpersonal orientation: taking into consideration the reactions of others whether or not providing help to someone (p. 652)

authoritarian parenting: a pattern of parenting in which parents are high on demandingness and low on responsiveness (p. 630)

authoritative parenting: a pattern of parenting in which parents are high in both demandingness and responsiveness (p. 630)

behavioral autonomy: the granting of privileges and responsibilities to adolescents by their parents (p. 632)

bicultural identity: simultaneous awareness of self as a member of two cultures (p. 642)

clique: a small friendship group of close peers based on common interests or activities (p. 636)

crowd: a relatively large group of teenagers whose interests and backgrounds may be somewhat more varied than those of a clique (p. 637)

cultural competence: demonstration of knowledge of the beliefs, values, language, social interactions, and so on, of a culture (p. 642)

dating scripts: cognitive models that guide adolescents through the dating experience (p. 638)

demandingness: a dimension of parenting pertaining to the level of strictness and control exerted by the parent (p. 630)

democratic parenting: a pattern of parenting in which parents are high in responsiveness and average on demandingness (p. 630)

egocentrism: a belief that thoughts of others are directed toward the self (p. 647)

empathic reasoning: putting one's self in the shoes of a person in need and expressing concern for that person (p. 652)

hedonistic reasoning: reasoning that involves a preoccupation with one's own needs at the expense of responding to others' needs (p. 651)

identity achievement: commitments made to the type of person one wants to be, to peer groups, and to a vocation, all of which have been produced by searching (p. 641)

identity confusion: a lack of focus concerning who one is and what place one should seek within society and a social group (p. 640)

identity diffusion: a lack of identity commitment combined with lack of effort to resolve the identity crisis; lack of concern for not having an identity (p. 641)

identity foreclosure: a premature ending of the search for identity by making decisions without first exploring and thinking through the options (p. 641)

identity fusion: forming an identity that integrates aspects of two cultures (p. 642)

identity moratorium: a delay in commitment to identity while experimenting with alternative identities (p. 641)

imaginary audience: adolescents' belief that they are the focus of attention, even when this is not the case (p. 647)

inconsistent discipline: indiscriminate reaction to an adolescent's positive and negative behaviors; unpredictable changing of expectations and consequences (p. 634)

individuation: the process of achieving an identity of one's own, independent of one's parents (p. 628)

inflexible, rigid discipline: failure to take extenuating circumstances into account, to give rationales, or to adjust the intensity of consequences to the severity of the problem (p. 634)

internalized reasoning: living up to internalized values about fulfilling societal obligations (p. 652)

intimacy: closeness, warmth, and sharing in a relationship (p. 643)

irritable explosive discipline: use of high-intensity strategies, power-assertive commands, and negative statements about the adolescent (p. 634)

low supervision and involvement: unawareness of and infrequent engagement in adolescents' activity (p. 634)

multiculturalism: achieving a positive sense of self in one culture without diminishing one's respect for other cultures (p. 642)

needs-oriented prosocial reasoning: recognizing the needs of others but knowing that they conflict with one's own needs (p. 651)

need to belong: a desire for frequent, positive interactions within an ongoing relationship (p. 635)

negative identity: engaging in intentional behaviors that are the opposite of those that the parents expect of the adolescent (p. 642)

patterns of parenting: different child-rearing methods used to discipline and guide children (p. 629)

peer network: a friendship group that includes best friends, other close friends, and cliques (p. 636)

permissive parenting: a pattern of parenting in which parents are low on demandingness and high in responsiveness (p. 630)

personal fable: a sense of invulnerability arising from adolescents' imagining their life as having a special existence, and believing that unfortunate events will not happen to them (p. 647)

psychological autonomy: opportunity given by parents to adolescents to express their values, attitudes, and beliefs (p. 632)

psychosocial (ego) identity: a positive sense of self that is achieved by establishing values and commitment to self and society (p. 640)

rejecting/neglecting parenting: a pattern of parenting in which parents are low in both demandingness and responsiveness (p. 630)

responsiveness: a dimension of parenting pertaining to the level of support, warmth, and child involvement provided by the parent (p. 630)

self-disclosure and liking effects: liking better those who share intimate matters (p. 636)

sensation seeking: a need to seek out novel and intense experiences (p. 647)

social perspective coordination: the ability to differentiate and integrate one's views in relationship to the views of others (p. 636)

time windows: a limited time during which psychosocial systems are developing rapidly (p. 653)

SUGGESTIONS FOR FURTHER READING

Brooks, J. B. (1999). *The process of parenting.* Mountain View, CA: Mayfield. This book includes theories and practical strategies for how parents can establish close relationships with their children and adolescents. There are separate chapters on early and late adolescence, working parents, special needs, and support systems for parents.

Carroll, P. S. (Ed.). (1999). *Using literature to help troubled teenagers cope with societal issues.* Westport, CT: Greenwood. This reference provides guidance on how to use literature to encourage adolescents to cope with issues such as body image, sexuality, and leaving home.

Davis, N. J. (1999). *Youth crisis: Growing up in the high-risk society.* Westport, CT: Praeger. This is a very readable book that looks at the social condition of adolescents in modern society. Topics include endangered youth, gang participation, youth addictions, homelessness, and violence in the home or on the streets.

Johnson, N. G., Roberts, M. C., & Worell, J. (1999). *Beyond appearance: A new look at adolescent girls.* Washington, DC: American Psychological Association. This book includes research on girls from a variety of racial, ethnic, and socioeconomic backgrounds, exploring topics such as gender role, relationships with family and peers, sexual decision making, and experiences at school and in the community.

Kerns, K. A., Contreras, J. M., & Neal-Barnett, A. (Eds.). (2000). *Family and peers: Linking two social worlds.* Westport, CT: Praeger. This book discusses factors that account for continuities across family and peer relationships and the developmental issues that have an impact on these relationships.

Kindlon, D., & Thompson, M. (1999). *Raising Cain: Protecting the emotional life of boys.* New York: Ballantine. Using research and case studies, this book discusses the forces that threaten boys and suggests ways of building compassion, sensitivity, and warmth. A very readable book.

Raffaelli, M., & Larson, R. W. (Eds.). (1999). Homeless and working youth around the world: Exploring developmental issues. *New Directions for Child and Adolescent Development,* No. 85, Fall 1999. San Francisco: Jossey-Bass. Several excellent articles within this collection include developmental issues of homeless youth, research with street children, and the historical, political, economic, and societal forces that influence these youth.

MILESTONES *in Adolescent Development*

AGE	PHYSICAL	COGNITIVE	LANGUAGE	SOCIAL-EMOTIONAL
13 yrs.	Has reached and passed peak of growth spurt if female Has probably reached puberty (begun menstruation) if female Has begun growth spurt if male Experience heightened concern about appearance	May demonstrate formal operational thinking Begins to imagine several possibilities for solving problems May become a self-regulated learner	Speaks in longer sentences, uses principles of subordination. Understands metaphors, multiple levels of meaning Increases vocabulary	Still has weak sense of individual identity, is easily influenced by peer group Spends more time with friends, usually same sex Might begin sexual relationships, especially with early maturation
14 yrs.	Is reaching peak of growth spurt if male Is gaining muscle cells if male, fat cells if female May develop anorexia or bulimia, especially if female Is getting deeper voice if male Has probably reached the conclusion of the growth spurt if female	Continues to gain metacognitive abilities and improve study skills Begins to generate hypotheses to explain possible outcomes May have more advantages if in a small high school	Improves reading comprehension abilities and study skills Writes longer, more complex sentences Likely to be very involved in electronic communication	Seeks increasing emotional autonomy from parents Fewer parent-adolescent conflicts with authoritative or democratic parenting Involvement in volunteer activities leads to higher levels of prosocial reasoning
15 yrs.	Has probably reached puberty (begun sperm production) if male May reach fastest reaction time	Can think in terms of abstract principles If creative, can think about problems in novel ways and generate unique approaches to solve problems	Improves analogical reasoning of self-referencing strategies. Language is more efficient and coherent in expression	Seeks intimate friendships and relationships May have had sexual intercourse but may not use contraception
16 yrs.	Has probably reached the conclusion of the growth spurt if male May reach peak performance level in some sports Body image concerns lead some to eating disorders and steroid use	Can argue either side in a debate Shows growing interest in social and philosophical problems Better able to organize studies and establish self-set study behavior	May fail to develop writing ability if not instructed Continues interest in electronic communications	Is actively involved in search for personal identity Is likely to be sexually active May use alcohol, cigarettes, and marijuana Romantic relationships are influenced by dating scripts
17 yrs.	Is still gaining muscle strength if male Is likely to have had an automobile accident Is likely to have had a sexual relationship	Shows hypothetico-deductive reasoning Can think in terms of abstract concepts about broad principles May take SAT or ACT test as part of college admissions process	With instruction and practice, metalinguistic abilities and study skills continue to improve May have learned a second language	Likely to be involved in continuing process of identity formation May have part-time job May make decisions that bear on later occupational choices May be preparing to leave home, separate from parents

Understanding Research in Child and Adolescent Development

Staying current in our understanding of children and adolescents requires reading and interpreting empirical research reports. Incorrect interpretations of psychological research are prevalent, but they can be corrected. Specifically, research is more likely to be understood correctly when readers have a set of questions, which provides a template for interpreting the research, and a strategy for answering each question (Forsyth & Bohling, 1999). In this appendix, we introduce seven questions to guide the interpretation of research, along with some basic strategies for answering each. Table A.1 lists the seven questions to be answered when interpreting any research study of child and adolescent development.

1. What Are the Independent and Dependent Variables?

Empirical studies of child and adolescent development usually identify some aspect of behavior (e.g., quantitative mental ability, bodily-kinesthetic ability, openness to experience, social interest, or aggressiveness) that differs greatly among children or adolescents. Researchers try to explain, predict, or control differences in the behavior of interest. The **dependent variable** is the behavior of interest to the researcher. In the method section of a research article, the researchers describe how they will measure the dependent variable. The specific technique for measuring the behavior of interest is called the **operational definition** of the dependent variable. One researcher who studies social interest might count affirming comments and helping behaviors emitted by adolescents. Another researcher might assess social interest with a survey that asks adolescents to rate the degree to which each of several social interest statements describes them.

In order to explain, predict, or control differences in the dependent variable, researchers manipulate and measure something separately from (independent of) measuring the dependent variable. That other variable, called the **independent variable,** is some characteristic of the environment or of individuals that might be related to or cause differences in the dependent variable. For example, the degree to which individuals were involved in church or service organizations such as Girl Scouts or Boy Scouts

TABLE A.1
Questions to answer when interpreting a developmental research study

1. What are the independent and dependent variables?

2. Was a relationship found between the independent and dependent variables? That is, was the relationship statistically significant?

3. To what extent can the results be generalized to other youth than those in the study?

4. How appropriate is it to conclude that changes in the independent variable caused changes in the dependent variable?

5. How strong is the relationship between the independent and the dependent variables?

6. Is the research finding important? That is, to what degree are you likely to act on the research findings?

7. What additional research questions are raised by this study?

would be an aspect of adolescents (an independent variable) that might predict differences on a dependent variable such as social interest. When the independent variable is an already-existing characteristic of the individual, it is called a non-manipulated or classificatory independent variable. Other non-manipulated independent variables might include age and gender.

When the researchers vary some aspect of the environment, they use a manipulated independent variable. For example, researchers might involve one group of youth in peer mediation training and give no such training to a control group. These two treatments represent the two levels of the manipulated independent variable. Both groups would complete the same social interest (dependent variable) survey at the end of the experiment.

Some research studies employ two or more independent variables. For example, researchers might study if peer mediation versus no peer mediation training (manipulated independent variable) affects social interest (dependent variable) differently for males and females (non-manipulated independent variable).

2. Is There a Relationship between Independent and Dependent Variables?

The second question to be addressed in interpreting a research report is whether or not the relationship between the independent and dependent variables is statistically significant. If the researchers state that they found a **statistically significant** relationship, they have concluded that the dependent variable scores differ across levels of the independent variable more than one would expect to find by chance. For example, a results section of a journal article might report that the difference between the mean social interest scores for a group receiving peer mediation training was significantly higher than the mean for those not receiving training, with an obtained $p = .02$. This number signifies that the difference between the two means was so large that if 100 independent researchers compared one group of no-peer-mediation children with another group of no-peer-mediation children, only two of the researchers would find a difference between group means as large as or larger than the difference found in this study. The researchers and the readers must also understand that the difference between the means of their experimental groups might just be one of the two in 100 cases that would occur by chance.

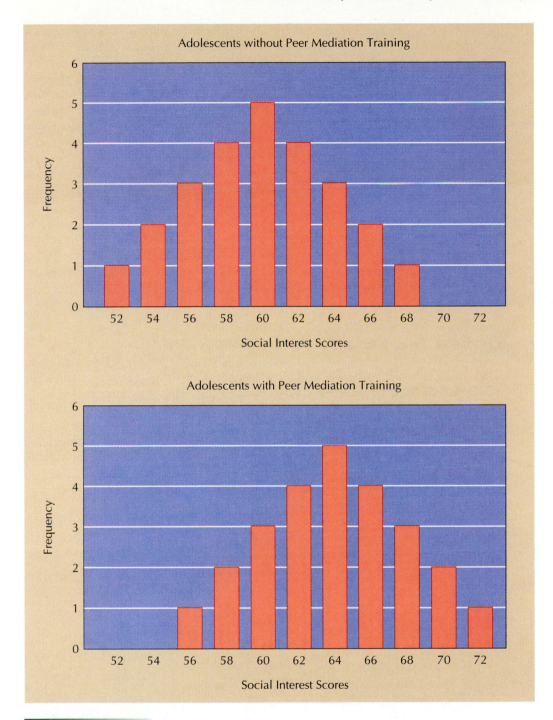

FIGURE A.1

Frequency distributions of scores for adolescents with and without peer mediation training.

According to one typical misinterpretation of research, every student from one level of the independent variable ought to rank higher on the dependent variable than every student from the other level of the independent variable if the results are to be considered statistically significant. The overlap of results from the trained and untrained students in Figure A.1 shows that some of the untrained children had higher social interest scores than the average score for the group with peer mediation.

Because of this overlap, a teacher at the school where the study was done might say that she knows a child who received no peer mediation training who seems to have more social interest than another child who did receive peer mediation training. Relying on those two cases, the teacher might argue that the peer mediation program failed to increase social interest. The researchers must help the teacher understand that statistical significance means that, on average, the two groups differ more than would be expected if the peer mediation program had no effect. It does not represent two non-overlapping frequency distributions.

This distinction is important. Most people rely on examples from their life experiences to judge the validity of relationships between independent and dependent variables. Indeed, Aronson (1999b) indicates that one clear, vivid personal example will affect people more than an abundance of statistical data and claims of statistical significance. The **availability heuristic** refers to judgments about independent/dependent variable relationships based on how easy it is to bring supporting examples to mind. Understanding that statistical significance reflects results like those depicted in Figure A.1 can help overcome reliance on the availability heuristic. Carefully designed developmental research with tests of statistical significance can help overcome this bias.

3. Can the Results Be Generalized?

The degree to which a study's results can be generalized to children or adolescents other than those included in the study is referred to as the study's **external validity**. Suppose that the children in the peer mediation study represented a group available only at one middle school. The reader of the journal article would not feel very confident in thinking that the findings would be the same at some other middle school. The greater the number of ways that the students at the two middle schools differ, the lower the confidence in generalizing the findings.

One way to increase the external validity of a research study is to use random sampling to select participants from the population of children or adolescents to which the findings are to be generalized. For example, if the researchers wanted to generalize the results of the study to all seventh-graders in Pennsylvania, they would have taken a random sample of all seventh-graders in the state. This would give every seventh-grader in the state an equal chance to be selected for the study. As indicated in Figure A.2, ran-

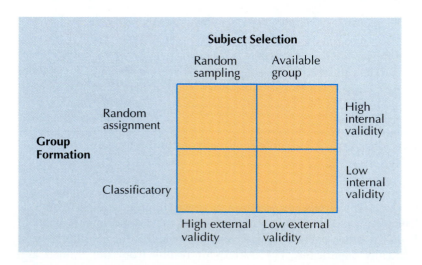

FIGURE A.2

Basic Methodology
Taxonomy

dom sampling of participants increases external validity—the degree to which the results can be generalized to the population from which the sample was drawn.

Although increasing external validity through random sampling is desirable, most studies use only an available group. Such studies do not permit statistical inferences or generalizations. External validity can be increased by replicating such studies, which works best if the new participants are like those in the first study in terms of demographics, such as economic status, ethnic or racial composition, and education level of parents. Because so few developmental research studies use random sampling to select participants, replication of findings across studies is an important alternative for increasing external validity. Such research should include a detailed procedure section, providing other researchers with all information needed to replicate the study. Articles summarizing the findings across many replications are referred to as meta-analyses.

4. Are Cause-and-Effect Conclusions Appropriate?

Certainty that differences in the independent variable caused the differences in the dependent variable is referred to as **internal validity**. As indicated in Figure A.2, random assignment of participants to levels of the independent variable increases confidence in drawing cause-and-effect conclusions. In the peer mediation study, the researchers could have randomly assigned students to groups by writing the name of each participant on a Ping-Pong ball and mixing the balls in a large container. Without looking, a researcher could pull out one of the balls. That person would be assigned to the peer mediation group. The second ball drawn would send a different person to the group with no peer mediation. This alternating procedure would continue until each participant was assigned to one of the groups.

Random assignment produces two groups that, on average, are alike on all characteristics except the independent variable. Matching participants on some extraneous variable also increases internal validity of the study. For example, if each participant in one group was matched by someone in the other group based on family income, the two groups overall would not differ in average family income, and this extraneous variable could not explain differences in the social interest differences between the two groups. Some studies increase internal validity by holding an extraneous variable constant at just one level. But this approach usually increases internal validity at the expense of external validity. For example, if the researchers decided to use only female seventh-graders, group differences in social interest could not be explained by differences in gender across groups. However, the results could not be generalized to males.

5. How Strong Is the Relationship between Independent and Dependent Variables?

An independent/dependent variable relationship can exist but be weak, not strong. Also, the probability of getting by chance a difference as large as or larger than the one obtained should not determine the strength of the relationship between variables. Studies of how people interpret research reports indicate that this is a common error (Forsyth et al., 1998). Both the American Psychological Association and the American

Educational Research Association have recommended approaches to communicate relationship strength (Azar, 1997; Thompson, 1996).

One frequently used index is the proportion of variability in the dependent variable accounted for by the independent variable. For example, the amount children are read to accounts for about 22 percent of the variability in elementary school language-arts performance. This accountable variability reflects the differences between the mean language-arts scores for groups experiencing different amounts of reading. The remaining 78 percent of the variability reflects differences between individuals who have experienced the same amount of reading. This unaccountable variability is due to other variables not examined in the study (e.g., quality of language spoken in the home, amount of alcohol consumed by the mother during pregnancy). Other independent variables may account for less variability in a behavior of interest. For example, the percentage of variability accounted for in freshman college grades by knowing students' SAT scores is about 4 percent. The percent of variability in heart dysfunction that is accountable by knowing whether or not individuals are using aspirin is less than 1 percent. In the hypothetical example of the social interest study represented in Figure A.1, approximately 20 percent of the variability in social interest is accounted for by knowing which children experienced the peer mediation training. Twenty percent would be very good considering how many other independent variables might be related to childrens' social interest scores. The differences among children within each group shown in Figure A.1 comprise the 80 percent of variability in social interest scores that is not accounted for by the peer mediation independent variable. Although ideally an independent variable would account for 100 percent of the variability in a dependent variable, this ideal is seldom approached. Knowing the proportion of variability that is accounted for by a specific variable alerts the journal reader to consider other independent variables in addition to the one of interest in a specific study.

Because most people understand percentage, a second way of expressing strength of relationship is to indicate the percentage of one group scoring above the mean of the other group. For example, in Figure A.1's hypothetical data, 19 of the 25 children (76 percent) in the peer mediation training group scored above the mean social interest score of the other group. Jeanne Brooks-Gunn (1998) used this index of strength of relationship when she reported that 84 percent of children reared in poverty have intelligence test scores below the average child not reared in poverty.

In a third approach a range of values is presented to show how much the dependent variable scores would increase if the entire population were treated with one condition rather than the other. For example, if the obtained data were like those in Figure A.1, the researchers might report that they are 95 percent confident that the interval from 1.7 to 6.3 encompasses the population social interest increase that would occur if children were shifted from no training to peer mediation training. This strength-of-relationship index is especially useful when the reader is familiar with the numbers on the dependent variable.

6. Is the Research Finding Important?

The sixth step in interpreting a research study is to determine the importance of the finding. That is, after studying the research report, readers should ask how the findings will affect their future actions. For example, if a school counselor were to read the hypothetical study on how peer mediation affects social interest, the findings could be considered important if the counselor decided to implement a peer mediation training program like the one in the study. The information presented in a research study might not have any effect on readers if they do not explore how the findings are important to them personally.

Clinchy (1995) suggests that simply being exposed to the results of a study is unlikely to have a long-term effect unless readers translate the findings into a personally relevant story with clear implications. Positive effects of taking this step resulted when school leaders and parents read about the better social and academic behavior found in seventh- and eighth-grade students attending small K–8 grade schools rather than large middle schools. Acting on the findings, two south central Pennsylvania school districts phased out middle schools and increased the number of K–8 schools. Looking for personal meaning while reading a developmental research study produces greater retention and use of information, as shown in studies of students who use a self-referencing study strategy.

7. What Additional Questions Are Raised by the Research?

Most research studies not only answer the questions posed but raise new questions as well. Consumers of research should examine multiple articles for alternative interpretations and be careful not to accept conclusions uncritically. The following cases show how new questions are identified by a thorough investigation of procedure and results.

In studies involving a manipulated independent variable, readers should determine whether the variability within each group of participants is the same. Figure A.1 presents an outcome in which the variability within each group is identical. Often, this is not the case in experimental studies because a treatment condition affects people differently. For example, if a treatment helps only individuals who are initially low on the dependent variable, that treatment group may have less dependent variable variability compared to other groups. Conversely, if a single treatment has a positive effect on some individuals and a negative effect on others, that treatment group would have more variability than other groups in the study. The assumption that a treatment has a constant effect on all individuals is seldom warranted.

Care should be taken to consider the cultural background of participants in the study before assuming that the same pattern of findings would exist within another cultural group. For example, if a study included primarily high-achievement, family-oriented Asian American adolescents, an independent variable found to have an effect may not have a similar effect with adolescents from a more individualistic culture.

When a study uses a non-manipulated independent variable, readers must consider extraneous variables that may affect the dependent variable. Studies show that if readers initially believe the independent and dependent variables are causally related, they will err in drawing cause-and-effect conclusions when reading a study using a non-manipulated independent variable. For example, a classificatory study may report more attention problems among children exposed to secondhand smoke than among children not so exposed. Because the independent variable was classificatory (non-manipulated), the reader must exercise caution in drawing cause-and-effect conclusions. Conversely, readers who do not initially believe that there is a causal relationship tend to attribute statistical significance to extraneous variables that are confounded with the independent variable.

The practice of generating alternative explanations for findings should lead interpreters of research to a search of the literature addressing these new hypotheses. A good discussion section helps this process by presenting the limitations of the reported study.

GLOSSARY

availability heuristic: judgments about independent/dependent variable relationships based on how easy it is to bring specific examples to mind (p. 662)

dependent variable: the aspect of children's or adolescents' behavior that the researcher is trying to explain, predict, or control (p. 659)

external validity: the degree to which results of a study can be generalized to youth other than those participating in the study (p. 662)

independent variable: some characteristic of individuals or the environment that might be systematically related to differences in the dependent variable (p. 659)

internal validity: the degree to which one can be confident that differences in the independent variable caused differences in the dependent variable (p. 663)

operational definition: the specific technique for measuring the dependent variable (p. 659)

statistical significance: the conclusion that the dependent variable scores are more different across levels of the independent variable than would be expected by chance (p. 660)

REFERENCES

AAHCC. (1999). Childbirth goals: The Bradley method of natural childbirth. *American Academy of Husband Coached Childbirth*. Retrieved March 2000 from the World Wide Web: www.bradleybirth.com

Abbott, S. (1992). Holding on and pushing away: Comparative perspectives on an Eastern Kentucky child-rearing practice. *Ethos, 20*, 35–65.

Ackerman, P. L., & Heggestad, E. D. (1997). Intelligence, personality, and interests: Evidence for overlapping traits. *Psychological Bulletin, 121*(2), 219–245.

Acredolo, L. P. (1978). Development of spatial orientation in infancy. *Developmental Psychology, 14*, 224–234.

Ad Hoc Work Group on Child Abuse and Neglect. (1999). Oral and dental aspects of child abuse and neglect. *Pediatrics, 104*, 348–350.

Adams, M. J. (1990). *Beginning to read: Thinking and learning about print.* Cambridge: MIT Press.

Adams, M. J., Treiman, R., & Pressley, M. (1998). Reading, writing, and literacy. In W. Damon (Editor-in-Chief) and I. E. Sigel & K. A. Renninger (Vol. Eds.), *Handbook of child psychology* (5th ed.): Vol. 4. *Child psychology in practice* (pp. 275–355). New York: Wiley.

Adams, P. J., Katz, R. C., Beauchamps, K., & Cohen, E. (1993). Body dissatisfaction, eating disorders, and depression: A developmental perspective. *Journal of Child and Family Studies, 2*(1), 37–46.

Adams, R. J., Courage, M. L., & Mercer, M. E. (1994). Systematic measurement of human neonatal color vision. *Vision Research, 34*, 1691–1701.

Adolf, K. E. (1997). Learning in the development of infant locomotion. *Monographs of the Society for Research in Child Development, 62*(3, Serial No. 251).

Adolf, K. E., Bereijken, B., & Denny, M. A. (1998). Learning to crawl. *Child Development, 69*, 1299–1312.

Aguiar, A., & Baillargeon, R. (1998). Eight-and a-half-month-old infants' reasoning about containment events. *Child Development, 69*(3), 636–653.

Aiken, L. R. (1985). Review of ACT Assessment Program. In J. V. Mitchell (Ed.), *The ninth mental measurement yearbook*. Lincoln, NB: University of Nebraska Press.

Aiken, L. R. (1991). *Psychological testing and assessment.* Boston, MA: Allyn & Bacon.

Ainsworth, M. D. S., Blehar, M. D., Waters, E., & Wall, S. (1978). *Patterns of attachment*. Hillsdale, NJ: Erlbaum.

Ainsworth, M. D. S. (1990). Some considerations regarding theory and assessment relevant to attachments beyond infancy. In M. T. Greenberg, D. Cicchetti, & E. M. Cummings (Eds.), *Attachment in the preschool years: Theory, research, and intervention* (pp. 463–488). Chicago: University of Chicago Press.

Akers, R. L., & Lee, G. (1999). Age, social learning and social bonding in adolescent substance use. *Deviant Behavior, 20*(1), 1–25.

Akhtar, N., Dunham, F., & Dunham, P. J. (1991). Directive interactions and early vocabulary development: The role of joint attentional focus. *Journal of Child Language, 18*, 41–49.

Akhtar, N., & Tomasello, M. (1996). Twenty-four-month-old children learn words for absent objects and actions. *British Journal of Developmental Psychology, 14*, 79–93.

Alexander, B. (1999). Youth-driven project AIM delivers new services the teen way. *Youth Today, 8*(5), 9.

Alexander, P. A., Kulikowich, J. M., & Schulze, S. K. (1994). How subject matter knowledge affects recall and interest. *American Educational Research Journal, 31*, 313–337.

Allen, J. P., Hauser, S. T., Bell, K. L., & O'Connor, T. G. (1994). Longitudinal assessment of autonomy and relatedness in adolescent-family interactions as predictors of adolescent ego development and self-esteem. *Child Development, 65*(1), 179–194.

Allen, K. (1996, August 15). Olympic family expands. *USA Today*, p. 3C.

Allen, K. E., & Marotz, L. R. (1999). *Developmental profiles: Pre-birth through eight*. Albany, NY: Delmar.

Allensworth, D. (1996). Cardiovascular objectives for youth in Healthy People 2000: Update on the status of risk factors. *Journal of Health Education, 27*(5), 5–19-S–23.

Altemeier, W. A. (1998). Immunization rates: Where is the help when we need it? *Pediatric Annals, 27*(6), 325–327.

Alverman, D. E., Hinchman, K. A., Moore, D. W., Phelps, S. E., & Waff, D. R. (Eds.). (1998). *Reconceptualizing the literacies in adolescents' lives* (pp. 3–26). Mahwah, NJ: Erlbaum.

Aman, Christine J., Roberts, R. J., Jr., & Pennington, B. F. (1998). A neuropsychological examination of the underlying deficit in attention deficit hyperactivity disorder: Frontal lobe versus right parietal lobe theories. *Developmental Psychology, 34*(5), 956–969.

America's Promise. (1999). The Alliance for Youth. Retrieved March 2000 from the World Wide Web: www.americaspromise.org

American Academy of Pediatrics, Committee on Communications (1995). Media violence. *Pediatrics, 95*, 949–951.

American College Testing Program (1984). *Counselor's handbook*. Iowa City, IA: Author.

American Medical Association. (1996). *Physician guide to media violence*. Chicago: Author.

American Psychiatric Association (1994). Diagnostic and Statistical Manual of Mental Disorders (4th ed.). Washington, DC, Author.

American Psychiatric Association (2000). Practice guideline for the treatment of patients with eating disorders. *The American Journal of Psychiatry: 157*(1), 1–39.

American Psychological Association (1993). *Violence and youth: Psychology's response*. Washington, DC: Author.

American Public Health Association and American Academy of Pediatrics (1992). *Caring for our children: National health and safety performance standards: Guidelines for out-of-home child care programs*. Washington, DC: Author.

Ames, L. B. (1937). The sequential patterning of prone progression in the human infant. *Genetic Psychology Monographs, 19*, 409–460.

Anderson, D. R., Field, D. E., Collins, P. A., Lorch, E. P., & Nathan, J. C. (1985). Estimates of young children's time with television: A methodological comparison of parent reports with time-lapse video home observation. *Child Development, 56*, 1345–1357.

Anderson, R. C., Wilson, P. T., & Fielding, L. C. (1988). Growth in reading and how children spend their time outside of school. *Reading Research Quarterly, 23*, 285–303.

Anderson-Inman, L. (1999). Interactive stories and books. *Reading online: Web watch*. International Reading Association. Retrieved March 2000 from the World Wide Web: http://readingonline.org/electronic/watch.

Andrich, D., & Styles, I. (1994). Psychometric evidence of intellectual growth spurts in early adolescence. *Journal of Early Adolescence, 14*(3), 328–344.

Anglin, J. M. (1983). Extensional aspects of the preschool child's word concepts. In T. Seiler & W. Wannenmacher (Eds.), *Concept development and the development of word meaning*. Berlin: Springer Verlag.

Anglin, J. N. (1993). Vocabulary development: A morphological analysis. *Monographs of the Society for Research in Child Development, 58*(10, Serial No. 238).

Angrist, S. S. (1969). The study of sex roles. *Journal of Social Issues, 25*, 215–232.

Anisfeld, E. (1982). The onset of social smiling in preterm and full-term infants from two ethnic backgrounds. *Infant Behavior and Development, 5*, 387–395.

Anisfeld, E., Casper, V., Nozyce, M., & Cunningham, N. (1990). Does infant carrying promote attachment? An experimental study of the effects of increased physical contact on the development of attachment. *Child Development, 61*(5), 1617–1627.

Anisfeld, M., Rosenberg, E. S., Hoberman, M. J., & Gasparini, D. (1998). Lexical acceleration coincides with the onset of combinatorial speech. *First Language, 18*, 165–184.

Anshel, M. H. (1998). Drug abuse in sport: Causes and cures. In J. M. Williams (Ed.), *Applied sport psychology* (pp. 372–397). Mountain View, CA: Mayfield.

Anslin, R. N., & Smith, L. B. (1988). Perceptual development. *Annual Review of Psychology, 39*, 435–473.

Apgar, V. (1953). Proposal for a new method of evaluating the newborn infant. *Anesthesia and Analgesia, 52*, 260–267.

Appel, M., & Campos, J. J. (1977). Binocular disparity as a discriminable stimulus parameter for young infants. *Journal of Experimental Child Psychology, 23*, 47–56.

Arbetter, S. (1995). Am I normal? *Current Health, 21*(8), 6–12.

Archer, J. (1991). The influence of tetosterone on human aggression. *British Journal of Psychology, 82*, 1–28.

Archer, J. (1994). Testosterone and aggression: A theoretical review. *Journal of Offender Rehabilitation, 21*, 3–39.

Archer, J. (1996). Sex differences in social behavior: Are the social role and evolutionary explanations compatible? *American Psychologist, 51*, 909–917.

Ariagno, R. L., & Glotzbach, S. F. (1996). Sudden infant death syndrome. In A. M. Rudolph (Senior Ed.), *Rudolph's pediatrics* (pp. 868–878). Stamford, CT: Appleton & Lange.

Arnett, J. (1995). The young and the reckless: Adolescent reckless behavior. *Current Directions in Psychological Science, 4*(3), 67–70.

Arnold, A. (1972). *The world book of children's games*. Greenwich, CT: Fawcett Publications, Inc.

Arnold, D. H., Lonigan, C. J., Whitehurst, G. J., & Epstein, J. N. (1994). Accelerating language development through picture book readings: Replication and extension to a videotape training format. *Journal of Educational Psychology, 86*(2), 235–243.

Arnow, J. (1995). *Teaching peace*. New York: The Berkeley Publishing Group.

Aronson, E. (1999a). Dissonance, hypocrisy, and the self-concept. In E. Harmon-Jones & J. Mills (Eds.), *Cognitive dissonance: Progress on a pivotal theory in social psychology* (pp. 103–126). Washington, DC: American Psychological Association.

Aronson, E. (1999b). *The social animal*. (8th ed.), New York: Worth Publishers.

Arvin, A. M. (1997). Live attenuated varicella vaccine. *Pediatric Annals, 26*(6), 384–387.

Ary, D. V., Duncan, T. E., Duncan, S. C., & Hops, H. (1999). Adolescent problem behavior: the influence of parents and peers. *Behavior Research and Therapy, 37*, 217–230.

Asendorpf, J. B., & Nunner-Winkler, G. (1992). Children's moral motive strength and temperament inhibition reduce their immoral behavior in real moral conflicts. *Child Development, 63*, 1223–1235.

Ashby, F. G., Isen, A. M., & Turken, U. (1999). A neuropsychological theory of positive affect and its influence on cognition. *Psychological Review, 106*(3), 529–550.

Asher, S. R., & Dodge, K. A. (1986). Identifying children who are rejected by their peers. *Developmental Psychology, 22*(4), 444–449.

Aslin, R. N. (1987). Visual and auditory development in infancy. In J. D. Osofsky (Ed.), *Handbook of infant development* (2nd ed.). New York: Wiley.

Aslin, R. N., & Smith, L. B. (1988). Perceptual development. *Annual Review of Psychology, 39*, 435–473.

Aslin, R. N., & Shea, S. L. (1990). Velocity thresholds in human infants: Implications for the perception of motion. *Developmental Psychology, 26*, 589–598.

Astington, J. W. (1993). *The child's discovery of the mind*. Cambridge, MA: Harvard University Press.

Astington, J. W. (1995). Talking it over with my brain. In J. Flavell, F. Green, & E. Flavell (Eds.), *Monographs of the Society for Research in Child Development, 60*(1), 104–113. Serial No. 243.

Astington, J. W., & Jenkins, J. M. (1999). A longitudinal study of the relation between language and theory-of-mind development. *Developmental Psychology, 35*(5), 1311–1320.

Attel, I., & Brooks-Gunn, J. (1988). Development of eating problems in adolescent girls: A longitudinal study. *Developmental Psychology, 25*(1), 70–79.

Atwater, E. (1996). *Adolescence*. Upper Saddle River, NJ: Prentice-Hall.

Au, T. K., Dapretto, M., & Song, Y. (1994). Input vs. constraints: Early word acquisition in Korean and English. *Journal of Memory and Language, 33*, 567–582.

Austin, A. M., & Lindauer, S. L. (1990). Parent–child conversation of more-liked and less-liked children. *Journal of Genetic Psychology, 15*, 5–23.

Austin, A., & Braeger, T. J. (1990). Gendered differences in parents' encouragement of sibling interaction: Implications for the construction of a personal premise style. *First Language, 10*, 181–197.

Avis, J., & Harris, P. L. (1991). Belief–desire reasoning among Baka children: Evidence for a universal conception of mind. *Child Development, 62*, 460–467.

Azar, B. (1996, June). People are becoming smarter—why? *The APA Monitor*, p. 20.

Azar, B. (1997, March). APA task force urges a harder look at data. *APA Monitor*, pp. 1–2.

Azmitia, M. (1988). Peer interaction and problem-solving: When are two heads better than one? *Child Development, 59*, 87–96.

Backscheider, A. G., Shatz, M., & Gelman, S. A. (1993). Preschoolers' ability to distinguish living kinds as a function of regrowth. *Child Development, 64*, 1242–1257.

Baddeley, A., Gathercole, S., & Papagno, C. (1998). The phonological loop as a language learning device. *Psychological Review, 105*(1), 158–173.

Baenninger, M. (1997). *The case for an environmental model of sex-related differences in spatial ability*. Paper presented at the annual meeting of The Eastern Psychological Association, Washington, DC.

Bailey, J. M., & Zucker, K. J. (1995). Childhood sex-typed behavior and sexual orientation: A conceptual analysis and quantitative review. *Developmental Psychology, 31*, 43–55.

Baillargeon, R. (1993). The object concept revisited: New directions in the investigation of infants' physical knowledge. In C. Granrud (Ed.), *Visual perception and cognition* (pp. 265–315). Hillsdale, NJ: Erlbaum.

Baillargeon, R. (1994). Physical reasoning in young infants: Seeking explanations for impossible events. *British Journal of Developmental Psychology, 12*, 9–33.

Baillargeon, R., & Hanko-Summers, S. (1990). Is the top object adequately supported by the bottom object? Young infants' understanding of support relations. *Cognitive Development, 5*, 29–53.

Baines, L., & Kunkel, A. J. (2000). *Going Bohemian: Activities that engage adolescents in the art of writing well*. Newark, DE: International Reading Association.

Baka, S. P., Fowler, C., Guohua, L., Watner, M., & Dannenberg, A. L. (1994). Head injuries incurred by children and young adults during informal recreation. *American Journal of Public Health, 84*, 649–652.

Bakeman, R., & Adamson, L. (1984). Coordinating attention to people and objects in mother-infant and peer-infant interactions. *Child Development, 55*, 1278–1289.

Baker-Ward, L., Orstein, P. A., & Holden, D. J. (1984). The expression of memorization in early childhood. *Journal of Experimental Child Psychology, 37*, 555–575.

Baldwin, D. (1993). Infants' ability to consult the speaker for clues to word reference. *Journal of Child Language, 2*, 395–418.

Baldwin, D. A., Markman, E. M., & Melartin, R. L. (1993). Infants' ability to draw inferences about nonobvious object properties: Evidence from exploratory play. *Child Development, 64*, 711–728.

Ball, C., Mann, L., & Stamm, C. (1994). Decision-making abilities of intellectually gifted and non-gifted children. *Australian Journal of Psychology, 46*(1), 13–20.

Ball, E., & Blachman, B. A. (1991). Does phoneme awareness training in kindergarten make a difference in early word recognition and developmental spelling? *Reading Research Quarterly, 26*, 49–66.

Ballard, B. D., Gipson, M. T., Guttenberg, W., & Ramsey, K. (1980). Palatability of food as a factor in influencing obese and normal-weight children's eating habits. *Behavior Research and Therapy, 18*, 598–600.

Balogh, R. D., & Porter, R. M. (1986). Olfactory preferences resulting from mere exposure in human neonates. *Infant Behavior and Development, 9*, 395–401.

Bamford, F. N., Bannister, R. P., Benjamin, C. M., Hillier, V. F., Ward, B. S., & Moore, W. M. O. (1990). Sleep in the first year of life. *Developmental Medicine and Child Neurology, 32*, 718–724.

Banchoff, T. F. (2000). The mathematician as a child and children as mathematicians. *Teaching children mathematics, 6*(6), 350–356.

Bandura, A. (1973). *Aggression: A social learning analysis*. Englewood Cliffs, NJ: Prentice-Hall.

Bandura, A. (1977). *Social learning theory*. Englewood Cliffs, NJ: Prentice-Hall.

Bandura, A. (1986). *Social foundations of thought and action: A social cognitive theory*. Englewood Cliffs, NJ: Prentice-Hall.

Bandura, A. (1989). Human agency in social cognitive theory. *American Psychologist, 44*, 1175–1184.

Bandura, A. (1991). Social cognitive theory of moral thought and action. In W. Kurtines & J. Gewirtz (Eds.), *Handbook of moral behavior and development: Vol. 1. Theory* (pp. 45–104). Hillsdale, NJ: Erlbaum.

Bandura, A. (1994). Social cognitive theory of mass communication. In J. Bryant & D. Zillman (Eds.), *Media effects: Advances in theory and research* (pp. 61–90). Hillsdale, NJ: Erlbaum.

Bandura, A. (1997). *Self-efficacy: The exercise of control*. New York: Freeman.

Bandura, A. (Ed.). (1995). *Self-efficacy in changing societies*. New York: Cambridge University Press.

Bandura, A., & Walters, R. (1963). *Social learning and personality development*. New York: Holt, Rienhart & Winston.

Banks, M. S. (1980). The development of early infancy. *Child Development, 51*, 646–666.

Banks, M. S., & Crowell, J. A. (1993). A re-examination of two analyses of front-end sensitivity to infant vision. In K. Simons (Eds.), *Early visual development: Normal and abnormal* (pp. 91–116). New York: Oxford University Press.

Banks, M. S., & Salapatek, P. (1976). Contrast sensitivity function of the infant visual system. *Vision Research, 16*, 867–869.

Bar-Or, O., Foreyt, J., Bouchard, C., Brownell, K. D., Dietz, W. H., Ravussin, E., Salbe, A. D., Schwenger, S., St. Jeor, S., & Torun, B. (1998). Physical activity, genetic, and nutritional considerations in childhood weight management. *Medicine and Science in Sports and Exercise, 30*(1), 2–10.

Barabas, G., & Taft, L. T. (1986). The early signs and differential diagnosis of cerebral palsy. *Pediatric Annals, 15*(3), 203–214.

Baranowski, T., Davis, M., Resnicow, K., & Barnanoski, J. (2000). Gimmie 5 fruit, juice and vegetables for fun and health: Outcome evaluation. *Health Education and Behavior, 27*(1), 96–111.

Barcus, E. F., & McLaughlin, L. (1978). *Food advertising on children's television: An analysis of appeals and nutritional content*. Newtonville, MA: Action for Children's Television.

Barker, T. A., Torgesen, J. K., & Wagner, R. K. (1992). The role of orthographic processing skills on five different reading tasks. *Reading Research Quarterly, 27*(4), 335–345.

Barkley, R. A. (1997). Behavioral inhibition, sustained attention, and executive functions: Constructing a unifying theory of ADHD. *Psychological Bulletin, 121*, 65–94.

Baron-Cohen, S. (1989). Perceptual role-taking and protodeclarative pointing in autism. *British Journal of Developmental Psychology, 7*, 113–127.

Baroody, A. (1987). *Children's mathematical thinking*. New York: Teachers College Press.

Barr, R. G., McMullan, S. J., Heinz, S., Leduc, D. G., Yaremko, J., Barfield, R., Francoeur, E., & Hunziker, U. A. (1991). *Pediatrics, 87*(5), 623–630.

Barret, K. C., & Campos, J. J. (1987). Perspectives on emotional development: II. A functionalist approach to emotions. In J. D. Osofsky (Ed.), *Handbook on infant development* (pp. 555–578). New York: Wiley.

Barrett, M. S., & Roach, R. A. (1995). Early interactive processes: Parenting by adolescent and adult single mothers. *Infant Behavior and Development, 18*, 97–109.

Barron, F., & Harrington, D. M. (1981). Creativity, intelligence, and personality. *Annual Review of Psychology, 32*, 439–476.

Barry, H. III, & Paxson, L. M. (1971). Infancy and early childhood: Cross-cultural codes 2. *Ethology, 10*, 466–508.

Barth, J. M. (1989, April). *Parent-child relationships and children's transition to school*. Paper presented at the Biennial Meeting of the Society for Research in Child Development, Kansas City, MO.

Bartoshuk, L. M. (1990). Distinctions between taste and smell relevant to the role of experience. In E. D. Capaldi & T. L. Powley (Eds.), *Taste, experience, and feeding*. Washington, DC: American Psychological Association.

Bascow, S. A., & Rubin, L. R. (1999). Gender influences on adolescent development. In N. G. Johnson, M. C. Roberts, & J. Worell (Eds.), *Beyond appearance: A new look at adolescent girls* (pp. 25–52). Washington, DC: American Psychological Association.

Bast, J., & Reitsma, P. (1998). Analyzing the development of individual differences in terms of Matthew effects in reading: Results from a Dutch longitudinal study. *Developmental Psychology, 34*(6), 1374–1399.

Bates, E. (1976). *Language in context*. New York: Academic Press.

Bates, E. (1979). *The emergence of symbols*. New York: Academic Press.

Bates, E., Benigni, L., Bretherton, I., Camaioni, L., & Volterra, V. (1979). *The emergence of symbols: Cognition and communication in infancy*. New York: Academic Press.

Bates, E., Camaioni, L., & Volterra, V. (1975). The acquisition of performatives prior to speech. *Merrill-Palmer Quarterly, 21*, 205–224.

Bates, E., Dale, P. S., & Thal, D. (1995). Individual differences and their implications for theories of language development. In P. Fletcher & B. MacWhinney (Eds.), *The handbook of child language*. Oxford: Blackwell.

Bates, E., Marchman, V., Thal, D., Fenson, L., Dale, P., Reznick, J. S., Reilly, J., & Hartung, J. (1994). Developmental and stylistic variation in the composition of early vocabulary. *Journal of Child Language, 21*, 85–123.

Bates, J. E. (1994). Introduction. In J. E. Bates, & T. D. Wachs (Eds.), *Temperament: Individual differences at the interface of biology and behavior* (pp. 1–14). Washington, DC: American Psychological Association.

Bates, J. E., Dodge, K. A., Pettit, G. S., & Ridge, B. (1998). Interaction of temperamental resistance to control and restrictive parenting in the development of externalizing behavior. *Developmental Psychology, 34*(5), 982–995.

Batten, S., Hirschman, J., & Thomas, D. (1990). Impact of the special supplemental food program on infants. *The Journal of Pediatrics, 117*(2), S101–S109.

Bauer, M. I., & Johnson-Laird, P. N. (1993). How diagrams can improve reasoning. *Psychological Science, 4*(6), 372–378.

Bauer, P. J. (1995). Recalling past events: From infancy to early childhood. In R. Vasta (Ed.), *Annals of child development* (Vol. 11, pp. 25–71). London: Jessica Kingsley.

Bauer, P. J., & Thal, D. J. (1990). Scripts or scraps: Reconsidering the development of sequential understanding. *Journal of Experimental Child Psychology, 50*, 287–304.

Baumeister, R. F. (1999, April 17). *Ego depiction, self-control, failure, and the nature of self.* Invited address presented at the Annual Meetings of the Eastern Psychological Association, Boston, MA.

Baumeister, R. F., & Heatherton, T. F. (1996). Self-regulation failure: An overview. *Psychological Inquiry, 7*, 1–15.

Baumeister, R. F., & Leary, M. R. (1995). The need to belong: Desire for interpersonal attachments as a fundamental human motivation. *Psychological Bulletin, 117*(3), 497–529.

Baumeister, R. F., Leith, K. P., Muraven, M., & Bratslavsky, E. (1998). Self-regulation as a key to success in life. In D. Pushkar & W. M. Bukowski (Eds.), *Improving competence across the lifespan: Building interventions based on theory and research* (pp. 117–35). New York: Plenum.

Baumrind, D. (1967). Child care practices anteceding three patterns of preschool behavior. *Genetic Psychology Monograph, 75*, 43–88.

Baumrind, D. (1972). Socialization and instrumental competence in young children. In W. W. Hartup (Ed.), *The young child: Reviews of research* (Vol. 2, pp. 202–274). Washington, DC: The National Association for the Education of Young Children.

Baumrind, D. (1989). Rearing competent children. In W. Damon (Ed.), *Child development today and tomorrow* (pp. 23–32). San Francisco: Jossey-Bass.

Baumrind, D. (1991a). The influence of parenting style on adolescent competence and substance use. *Journal of Early Adolescence, 11*(1), 56–95.

Baumrind, D. (1991b). Parenting styles and adolescent development. In R. M. Lerner, A. C. Peterson, & J. Brooks-Gunn (Eds.), *Encyclopedia of adolescence* (Vol. 2, pp. 746–758). New York: Garland.

Baumrind, D. (1993). The average expectable environment is not good enough: A response to Scarr. *Child Development, 64*, 1299–1317.

Baumrind, D., & Block, A. E. (1967). Socialization and practices associated with dimensions of competence in pre-school boys and girls. *Child Development, 38*, 291–329.

Bayley, N. (1993). *Bayley scales of infant development.* (2nd ed.). New York: The Psychological Corporation.

Beach, R. (1990). The creative development of meaning: Using autobiographical experiences to interpret literature. In D. Boydan & S. Straw (Eds.), *Beyond communication: Reading comprehension and criticism* (pp. 211–236). Portsmouth, NH: Boynton/Cook.

Beals, D. E., & Tabors, P. O. (1995). Arboretum, bureaucratic and carbohydrates: Preschoolers' exposure to rare vocabulary at home. *First Language, 15*, 57–76.

Bean, C. (1990). *Methods of childbirth.* New York: Morrow.

Bean, T. W., Bean, S. K., & Bean, K. F. (1999). Intergenerational conversations and two adolescents' multiple literacies: Implications for redefining content area literacy. *Journal of Adolescent & Adult Literacy, 42*(6), 438–448.

Bearman, P. S., Jones, J., & Udry, J. R. (1997). *The national longitudinal study of adolescent health: Research design.* Retrieved March 2000 from the World Wide Web: http://www.cpc.unc.edu/projects/add health/design.html

Beauchamp, G. K., Cowart, B. J., Mennella, J. A., & Marsh, R. R. (1994). Infant salt taste: Developmental, methodological, and contextual factors. *Developmental Psychobiology, 27*(6), 353–365.

Beaumont, S. L., & Cheyne, J. A. (1998). Interruptions in adolescent girls' conversations: Comparing mothers and friends. *Journal of Adolescent Research, 13*(3), 272–292.

Beck, B. L., Jara, D., Astor-Stetson, E., Zarecky, A., & Starks, M. (1999, August). *The effects of body image, social support, and media sensitivity on self-esteem, psychological well-being, and restrained eating.* Paper presented at the annual American Psychological Association meeting, Boston, MA.

Becker, H. C., Randall, C. L., Salo, A. L., Saulnier, J. L., & Weathersby, R. T. (1994). Animal research: Charting the course for FAS. *Alcohol Health and Research World, 18*(1), 10–16.

Becker, J. (1989). Preschoolers' use of number words to denote one-to-one correspondence. *Child Development, 60*, 1147–1157.

Beers, M. H., & Berko, R. (Eds.). (1999). *The Merck manual of diagnosis and therapy.* Whitehouse Station, NJ: Merck & Company.

Beeson, J. H. (1989). Controversies surrounding antepartum RH Immune globulin prophylaxis. In M. I. Evans, J. C. Fletcher, A. D. Dixler, & J. D. Schulman (Eds.), *Fetal diagnosis and therapy: Science, ethics, and the law.* Philadelphia: Lippincott.

Behl-Chadha, G. (1996). Basic-level and superordinate-like categorical representations in early infancy. *Cognition, 60*, 105–141.

Beilin, H. (1994). Jean Piaget's enduring contribution to developmental psychology. In R. D. Parke, P. A. Ornstein, J. J. Rieser, & C. Zahn-Waxler (Eds), *A century of developmental psychology.* Washington, DC: American Psychological Association.

Belka, D. E. (1998). Strategies for teaching tag games. *Journal of Physical Education, Recreation and Dance, 69*(8), 40–46.

Bell, D. C., & Bell, L. G. (1983). Parental validation and support in the development of adolescent daughters. In H. D. Grotevant & C. R. Cooper (Eds.), *Adolescent development in the family.* San Francisco: Jossey-Bass.

Bell, T. W. (1971). Stimulus control of parent or caretaker behavior by offspring. *Developmental Psychology, 4*, 63–72.

Beller, M., & Gafni, N. (1996). The 1991 international assessment of educational progress in mathematics and sciences: The gender differences perspective. *Journal of Educational Psychology, 88*, 365–377.

Bellinger, D., Sioman, J., Leviton, A., Rabinowitz, M., Needleman, H. L., & Waternaux, C. (1991). Low-level lead exposure and children's cognitive functioning in the pre-school years. *Pediatrics, 87*(2), 219–226.

Belsky, J. (1980). Child maltreatment: An ecological integration. *American Psychologist, 35*, 320–335.

Belsky, J. (1984). The determinants of parenting: A process model. *Child Development, 55*, 83–96.

Belsky, J. (1997). Theory testing, effect-size evaluation, and differential susceptibility to rearing influence: The case of mothering and attachment. *Child Development, 64*, 598–600.

Belsky, J., Goode, M. K., & Most, R. K. (1980). Maternal stimulation and infant exploratory competence: Cross-sectional, correlational, and experimental analyses. *Child Development, 51*, 1163–1178.

Belsky, J., & Kelly, J. (1994). *The transition to parenthood.* New York: Dell.

Belsky, J., & Rovine, M. (1988). Non-maternal care in the first year of life and infant–parent attachment security. *Child Development, 59*, 157–167.

Belsky, J., & Vondra, J. (1989). Lessons from child abuse: The determinants of parenting. In D. Cicchetti & V. Carlson (Eds.), *Child maltreatment: Theory and research on the causes and consequences of child abuse and neglect.* New York: Cambridge University Press.

Beltramini, A. V., & Hertzig, M. E. (1983). Sleep and bedtime behavior in preschool-aged children. *Pediatrics, 71*(2), 153–158.

Benbow, C. P. (1990). Sex differences in mathematical reasoning ability among the intellectually talented: Further thoughts. *Behavioral and Brain Sciences, 13*, 196–198.

Benbow, C. P., & Arjmand, O. (1990). Predictors of high academic achievement in mathematics and science by mathematically talented students: A longitudinal study. *Journal of Educational Psychology, 82*(3), 430–441.

Benenson, J. F. (1994). Ages four to six years: Changes in the structures of play networks of girls and boys. *Merrill-Palmer Quarterly, 40*, 478–487.

Bengston, K. A. (1999). Inhalant use. *Child Health Talk.* Wilmington, DE: duPont Hospital for Children.

Bensley, D. A. (1997). *Improving students' critical thinking through writing.* Symposium presented at the annual meeting of The Eastern Psychological Association, Washington, DC.

Benson, P. L. (1997). *All kids are our kids: What communities must do to raise caring and responsible children and adolescents.* San Francisco: Jossey-Bass.

Bentin, S., Hammer, R., & Cahan, S. (1991). The effects of aging and first grade schooling on the development of phonological awareness. *Psychological Science, 2*, 271–274.

Benton, S. L., Corkill, A. J., Sharp, J. M., Downey, R. G., & Khramtsova, I. (1995). Knowledge, interest, and narrative writing. *Journal of Educational Psychology, 87*(1), 66–79.

Berenbaum, S. A., & Hines, M. (1992). Early androgens are related to childhood sex-typed toy preferences. *Psychological Science, 3*, 203–206.

Berg, W. K., & Berg, K. M. (1987). Psychophysiological development in infancy: State, startle, and attention. In J. D. Osofsky (Eds.), *Handbook of infant development.* (2nd ed., pp. 238–317). New York: Wiley.

Berg, W. K., & Richards, J. E. (1997). Attention across time in infant development. In P. J. Lang, R. P. Simons, & M. T. Bolsken (Eds.), *Attention and orienting: Sensory and motivational processes* (pp. 347–368). Mahwah, NJ: Erlbaum.

Berger, A., & Shafran, E. (2000). *Teens for literacy: Promoting reading and writing in schools and communities.* Newark, NJ: International Reading Association.

Berger, M. J., & Goldstein, D. P. (1980). Impaired reproductive performance in DES-exposed women. *Obstetrics and Gynecology, 55*, 25–27.

Berk, L. E. (1992). The extracurriculum. In P. W. Jackson (Ed.), *Handbook of research on curriculum* (pp. 1002–1043). New York: Macmillan.

Berk, L. E., & Garvin, R. A. (1984). Development of private speech among low-income Appalachian children. *Developmental Psychology, 20*, 271–286.

Berkowitz, L. (1993). *Aggression: Its causes, consequences, and control.* New York: Academic Press.

Berkowitz, L., & LePage, A. (1967). Weapons as aggression—eliciting stimuli. *Journal of Personality and Social Psychology, 1*, 202–207.

Berman, P. W., & Goodman, V. (1984). Age and sex differences in children's responsiveness to babies: Effects of adults' caretaking requests and instructions. *Child Development, 55*, 1071–1077.

Bernstein-Ratner, N. (1984). Patterns of vowel modification in mother–child speech. *Journal of Child Language, 11*, 557–578.

Bernstein-Ratner, N. (1986). Durational cues which mark clause boundaries in mother–child speech. *Journal of Phonetics, 14*, 303–309.

Bertoncini, J., & Mehler, J. (1981). Syllables as units in infant speech perception. *Infant Behavior and Development, 4*, 247–260.

Berzonsky, M. D. & Kuk, L. S. (2000). Identity status, identity processing style, and the transition to university. *Journal of Adolescent Research, 15*(1), 81–98.

Besharov, D. J. (1990). *Recognizing child abuse: A guide for the concerned.* New York: The Free Press.

Besharov, D. J., & Laumann, L. A. (1996). Child abuse reporting. *Social Science and Modern Society, 33*(4), 40–46.

Bever, T. G. (1970). The cognitive basis for linguistic structures. In J. R. Hayes (Ed.), *Cognition and the development of language.* New York: Wiley.

Bialeschki, M. D. (1999). Physical activity for women: What park and recreation departments can do. *Journal of Physical Education, Recreation, and Dance, 70*(3), 36–39.

Bidell, T. B., & Fisher, K. W. (1992). Beyond the stage debate. In R. J. Sternberg, & C. Berg (Eds.), *Intellectual development*. New York: Cambridge University Press.

Bierman, K. L., Miller, C. L., & Stabb, S. D. (1987). Improving the social behavior and peer acceptance of rejected boys: Effects of social skills training with instructions and prohibitions. *Journal of Consulting and Clinical Psychology, 55,* 194–200.

Bigelow, A. E. (1992). Locomotion and search behavior in blind infants. *Infant Behavior and Development, 15,* 179–189.

Bigler, R., & Liben, L. (1990). The role of attitudes and interventions in gender-schematic processing. *Child Development, 61,* 1440–1452.

Binion, V. (1990). Psychological androgyny: A black female perspective. *Sex Roles, 22,* 487–507.

Birch, L. L., & Fisher, J. A. (1995). Appetite and eating behavior in children. *Pediatric Clinics of North America, 42*(4), 931–952.

Birch, S. H., & Ladd, G. W. (1998). Children's interpersonal behaviors and the teacher-child relationship. *Developmental Psychology, 34*(5), 934–946.

Biringen, Z., Emde, R. N., Campos, J. J., & Applebaum, M. L. (1995). Affective reorganization in the infant, the mother, and the dyad: The role of upright locomotion and its timing. *Child Development, 66,* 499–514.

Bisgard, K. M., & Wenger, J. D. (1997). Recommendations for the use of Haemophilus influenzae type b vaccines among children in the United States. *Pediatric Annals, 26*(6), 361–366.

Bishop, P. R., & Nowicki, M. J. (1999). Defecation disorders in the neurologically impaired child. *Pediatric Annals, 28*(5), 322–328.

Blackburn, G. L., Dwyer, J., Flanders, W. D., Hill, J. O., Kuller, L. H., Pi-Sunyer, F. X., St. Jeor, S. T., & Willett, W. C. (1994). Report of the American Institute of Nutrition (AIN) Steering Committee on Healthy Weight. *Journal of Nutrition, 124,* 2240–2243.

Blasi, A. (1984). Moral identity: Its role in moral functioning. In W. Kurtines & J. Gewirtz (Eds.), *Morality, moral behavior, and moral development*. New York: Wiley.

Blass, E. M., & Ciaramitaro, V. (1994). A new look at some old mechanisms in human newborns: Taste and tactile determinants of state, affect, and action. *Monographs of the Society for Research in Child Development, 59*(1, Serial No. 239).

Blass, E. M., Ganchrow, J. R., & Steiner, J. E. (1984). Classical conditioning in newborn humans 2–48 hours of age. *Infant Behavior and Development, 7,* 223–235.

Blass, E. M., & Shah, A. (1995). Pain-reducing properties of sucrose in human newborns. *Chemical Senses, 20*(1), 29–35.

Bloch, M., & Adler, L. (1994), African children's play and the emergence of the sexual division of labor. In J. Roopnarine, J. Johnson, & F. Hooper (Eds.), *Children's play in diverse cultures* (pp. 148–178). Albany: SUNY Press.

Bloch, M. N. (1989). Young boys' and girls' play at home and in the community: A cultural-ecological framework. In M. N. Bloch & A. D. Pellegrini (Eds.), *The ecological context of children's play* (pp. 120–154). Norwood, NJ: Ablex.

Block, J. H. (1973). Conceptions of sex role: Some cross-cultural and longitudinal perspectives. *American Psychologist, 28,* 512–576.

Bloom, A. B. (1968). *The republic of Plato*. New York: Basic Books.

Bloom, K. (1977). Patterning of infant vocal behavior. *Journal of Experimental Child Psychology, 23,* 367–377.

Bloom, K., & Esposito, A. (1975). Social conditioning and its proper control procedures. *Journal of Experimental Child Psychology, 19,* 209–222.

Bloom, L. (1970). *Language development: From function to emerging grammars*. Cambridge, MA: MIT Press.

Bloom, L. (1973). *One word at a time: The use of single-word utterances before syntax*. The Hague: Mouton.

Bloom, L. (1993). *The transition from infancy to language: Acquiring the power of expression*. Cambridge, UK: Cambridge, University Press.

Bloom, L. (1998). Language acquisition in its developmental context. In W. Damon (Editor-in-chief) and D. Kuhn & R. S. Siegler (Vol. Eds.), *Handbook of child psychology (5th ed.): Vol. 2, Cognition, perception, and language* (pp. 371–420). New York: Wiley.

Bloom, L., Lightbown, P., & Hood, L. (1975). Imitation in language development. *Monographs of the Society for Research in Child Development, 40*(Serial No. 160).

Bloom, L., Rocissano, L., & Hood, L. (1976). Adult-child discourse: Developmental interaction between information processing and linguistic knowledge. *Cognitive Psychology, 8,* 521–552.

Blum, R. W., Potthoff, S. J., & Resnick, M. D. (1997). The impact of chronic conditions on Native American adolescents. *Families, Systems, and Health, 15*(3), 275–282.

Boden, C., & Brodeur, D. A. (1999). Visual processing of verbal and nonverbal stimuli in adolescents with reading disabilities. *Journal of Learning Disabilities, 32,* 121–126.

Bogenschneider, K., Wu, M., Raffaelli, M., & Tsay, J. C. (1998). Parent influences on adolescent peer orientation and substance use: The interface of parenting practices and values. *Child Development, 69*(6), 1672–1688.

Bohannon, J. N., MacWhinney, B., & Snow, C. (1990). No negative evidence revisited: Beyond learnability or who has to prove what to whom. *Developmental Psychology, 26*(2), 221–226.

Bohannon, J. N., & Stanowicz, L. (1988). The issue of negative evidence: Adult response to children's language errors. *Developmental Psychology, 24*(5), 684–689.

Bolig, E. E., Borkowski, J., & Brandenberger, J. (1999). Poverty and health across the life span. In T. L. Whitman et al. (Eds.), *Lifespan perspectives on health and illness* (pp. 67–84). Mahwah, NJ: Erlbaum.

Bookstein, F. L., Sampson, P. D., Streissguth, A. P., & Barr, H. M. (1996). Exploiting redundant measurement of dose and developmental outcome: New methods from the behavioral teratology of alcohol. *Developmental Psychology, 32,* 404–415.

Borke, H. (1975). Piaget's mountains revisited: Changes in the egocentric landscape. *Developmental Psychology, 11*(2), 240–243.

Bornstein, M., & Sigman, M. (1986). Continuity in mental development from infancy. *Child Development, 57*(2), 251–274.

Bornstein, M. H., & Arterberry, M. E. (1999). Perceptual development. In M. H. Bronstein & M. E. Lamb (Eds.), *Developmental psychology: An advanced text* (pp. 231–274). Mahwah, NJ: Erlbaum.

Bornstein, M. H., & Tamis-LeMonda, C. S. (1995). Parent-child symbolic play: Three theories in search of an effect. *Developmental Review, 15,* 382–400.

Borowsky, I. W. (1999, June). Teens and suicide attempts: Who is at risk? *Archives of Pediatrics and Adolescent Medicine,* pp. 573–580.

Bower, T. G. R. (1974). *Development in infancy*. San Francisco: W. H. Freeman.

Bower, T. G. R. (1977). *A primer of infant development*. San Francisco: W. H. Freeman.

Bowerman, M. (1985). Reorganizational processes in lexical and syntactic development. In E. Wanner & L. R. Gleitman (Eds.), *Language acquisition: The state of the art* (pp. 319–346). Cambridge, UK: Cambridge University Press.

Bowlby, J. (1969) *Attachment and loss: Vol. 1. Attachment*. London: Hogarth.

Bowlby, J. (1980). *Attachment and loss: Vol. 3. Loss, sadness, and depression*. New York: Basic Books.

Bowlby, J. (1988). *A secure base: Parent-child attachment and healthy human development*. New York: Basic Books.

Boyes, M. C., & Allen, S. G. (1993). Styles of parent-child interaction and moral reasoning in adolescence. *Merrill-Palmer Quarterly, 39,* 551–570.

Boyle, P. (1999). Tobacco funds: Kids get stale butt. *Youth Today, 8*(7), 14–20.

Boyles, N. S., & Contadino, D. (1998). *The learning differences sourcebook*. Los Angeles, CA: Lowell House.

Bracey, G. W. (1995). Curing teen violence. *Phi Delta Kappan, 77*(2), 185–186.

Brackbill, Y., Kane, J., Manniello, R. L., & Abramson, D. (1974). Obstetric premedication and infant outcome. *American Journal of Obstetrics and Gynecology, 118,* 377–384.

Bradley, R. H., Caldwell, B. M., & Rock, S. L. (1988). Home environment and school performance: A ten-year follow up and examination of three models of environmental action. *Child Development, 59*(1), 852–867.

Braham, C. G. (Ed.). (1998). *Random House Webster's dictionary*. (3rd ed.). New York: Ballentine.

Brazelton, T. B. (1961). Psychophysiologic reactions in the neonate. *The Journal of Pediatrics, 58,* 513–518.

Brazelton, T. B. (1969). *Infants and mothers*. New York: Delacorte/Seymour Lawrence.

Brazelton, T. B. (1970). Effects of prenatal drugs on the behavior of the neonate. *American Journal of Psychiatry, 126,* 95–100.

Brazelton, T. B. (1984). *Neonatal behavioral assessment scale*. Philadelphia: Lippincott.

Brazelton, T. B., Tronick, E., Adamson, L., Als, H., & Weise, S. (1975). Early mother–infant reciprocity. In *Parent–infant interaction* (Ciba Foundation Symposium No. 33, new series). Amsterdam: Elsevier.

Bredekamp, S. (1987). *Accreditation criteria and procedures of the National Academy of Early Childhood Programs*. Washington, DC: NAEYC.

Bregman, J., & Kimberlin, V. S. (1993). Developmental outcome in extremely premature infants: Impact of surfactant. *Pediatric Clinics of North America, 40*(5), 937–953.

Brehm, S. S. (1981). Oppositional behavior in children: A reactance theory approach. In S. S. Brehm, S. M. Kassin, & F. X. Gibbons (Eds.), *Developmental social psychology theory* (pp. 96–121). New York: Oxford University Press.

Brener, N. D., & Collins, J. L. (1998). Co-occurrence of health-risk behaviors among adolescents in the United States. *Journal of Adolescent Health, 22*(3), 209–213.

Brenner, J., & Mueller, E. (1982). Shared meaning in boy toddlers' peer relations. *Child Development, 53*(2), 380–391.

Bretherton, I. (1984). *Representing the social world in symbolic play* (pp. 3–41). New York: Academic Press.

Bretherton, I. (1992). The origins of attachment theory: John Bowlby & Mary Ainsworth. *Developmental Psychology, 28,* 759–775.

Bretherton, I., Fritz, J., Zahn-Waxler, C., & Ridgeway, D. (1986). Learning to talk about emotions: A functionalist perspective. *Child Development, 57,* 529–548.

Breznitz, Z., & Sherman, T. (1987). Speech patterning of natural discourse of well and depressed mothers and their young children. *Child Development, 58,* 395–400.

Bridges, A. (1986). Actions and things: What adults talk about to 1-year-olds. In S. Kuczaj & M. Barrett (Eds.), *The development of word meaning* (pp. 225–255). Berlin: Springer-Verlag.

Briere, J., & Runtz, M. (1990). Differential adult symptomatology associated with three types of child abuse histories. *Child Abuse and Neglect, 14,* 357–364.

Briscoe, J., Gathercole, S. E., & Marlow, N. (1998). Short-term memory and language outcomes after extreme prematurity at birth. *Journal of Speech, Language, and Hearing Research, 41*(3), 654–666.

Brody, G. H., Stoneman, Z., & Flor, D. (1996). Parental religiosity, family processes, and youth competence in rural, two-parent African-American families. *Developmental Psychology, 32,* 696–706.

Brody, N. (1992). *Intelligence* (2nd ed.). San Diego: Academic Press.

Broerse, J., & Elias, G. (1994). Changes in the content and timing of mothers' talk to infants. *British Journal of Developmental Psychology, 12,* 131–145.

Bronfenbrenner, U. (1977). Toward an experimental ecology of human development. *American Psychologist, 32,* 513–531.

Bronfenbrenner, U. (1979). *The ecology of human development: Experiments by nature and design*. Cambridge: Harvard University Press.

Bronfenbrenner, U. (1989). Ecological systems theory. In R. Vasta (Ed.), *Annals of child development: Vol. 6*. London: Kingsley.

Bronfenbrenner, U. (1993). The ecology of cognitive development: Research models and fugitive findings. In R. W. Wozniak & K. W. Fischer (Eds.), *Development in context: Acting and thinking in specific environments* (pp. 3–44). Hillsdale, NJ: Erlbaum.

Bronfenbrenner, U., & Morris, P. A. (1998). The ecology of developmental processes. In W. Damon & R. Lerner (Eds.), *Handbook of child psychology: Vol. 1. Theoretical models of human development* (pp. 993–1028). New York: Wiley.

Bronson, W. (1981). *Toddlers' behaviors with agemates: Issues of interaction, cognition, and affect.* Norwood, NJ: Ablex.

Bronstein, P. (1984). Differences in mothers' and fathers' behaviors toward children: A cross-cultural comparison. *Developmental Psychology, 20*(6), 995–1003.

Brookhart, J., & Hock, E. (1976). The effects of experimental context and experiential background on infants' behavior toward their mothers and a stranger. *Child Development, 47,* 333–340.

Brooks-Gunn, J. (1998). *Poor families, poor outcomes: Income, education, and parenting practices.* The American Psychological Association Distinguished Scientist Lecture. Presented at the annual meeting of the Midwestern Psychological Association, Chicago.

Brooks-Gunn, J., Klebanov, P. K., & Duncan, G. J. (1996). Ethnic differences in children's intelligence test scores: Role of economic deprivation, home environment, and maternal characteristics. *Child Development, 67,* 396–408.

Brooks-Gunn, J., & Reiter, E. O. (1990). The role of pubertal processes. In S. S. Feldman & G. R. Elliott (Eds.), *At the threshold: The developing adolescent.* Cambridge, MA: Harvard University Press.

Brown, A., & Kane, M. (1988). Preschool children can learn to transfer: Learning to learn and learning by example. *Cognitive Psychology, 20,* 493–523.

Brown, A. L. (1997). Transforming schools into communities of thinking and learning about serious matters. *American Psychologist, 52*(4), 399–413

Brown, A. L., Campione, J. C., Reeve, R. A., Ferrara, R. A., & Palincsar, A. S. (1991). Interactive learning and individual understanding: The case of reading and mathematics. In L. T. Landsmann (Ed.), *Culture, schooling and psychological development* (pp. 136–170). Norwood, NJ: Ablex.

Brown, B. B. (1999). Measuring the peer environment of American adolescents. In S. L. Friedman & T. D. Wachs (Eds.), *Measuring environment across the life span* (pp. 59–90). Washington, DC: American Psychological Association.

Brown, D. (1999). Promoting reflective thinking: Preservice teachers' literacy autobiographies as a common text. *Journal of Adolescent & Adult Literacy, 42*(5), 402–410.

Brown, J. D., Greenberg, B. S., & Buerkel-Rothfuss. (1993). Media, sex and sexuality. *Adolescent Medicine: State of the Art Reviews, 4*(31), 511.

Brown, J. V., & Bateman, R. (1978). Relationships of human mothers with their infants during the first year of life: Effects of prematurity. In R. W. Bell & W. P. Smotherman (Eds.), *Maternal influences and early behavior.* Holliswood, NY: Spectrum.

Brown, L. F. (1994). Research in dental health education and health promotion: A review of the literature. *Health Education Quarterly, 21,* 83–102.

Brown, R. (1973). *A first language.* Cambridge, MA: Harvard University Press.

Brown, R., & Hanlon, C. (1970). Derivational complexity and order of acquisition in child speech. In J. R. Hayes (Ed.), *Cognition and the development of language.* New York: Wiley.

Brown, R. W., Cazden, C. B., & Bellugi, U. (1969). The child's grammar from I to III. *Minnesota Symposium on Child Psychology: Vol. 2.* Minneapolis: University of Minnesota Press.

Brownell, K. D., Kelman, J. H., & Stunkard, A. J. (1983). Treatment of obese children with and without their mothers. Changes in weight and blood pressure. *Pediatrics, 71,* 515–523.

Brownlee, S. (1999, August 9). Inside the teen. *U.S. News & World Report* pp. 44–54.

Bruck, M., Treiman, R., Caravolas, M., Genesee, F., & Cassar, M. (1998). Spelling skills of children in whole language and phonics classrooms. *Applied Psycholinguistics, 19,* 669–634.

Bruner, J. S. (1975). From communication to language—a psychological perspective. *Cognition, 3,* 255–287.

Bruner, J. S. (1977). Early social interaction and language acquisition. In H. R. Schaffer (Ed.), *Studies in mother-infant interaction.* London: Academic Press.

Bruner, J. S. (1996). *The culture of education.* Cambridge, MA: Harvard University Press.

Brunner, C., & Tally, W. (1999). *The new media literacy handbook: An educator's guide to bringing new media into the classroom.* New York: Doubleday.

Bryant, P. E., Bradley, L., Maclean, M., & Crossland, J. (1989). Nursery rhymes, phonological skills and reading. *Journal of Child Language, 16,* 407–428.

Bryk, A. S., & Randenbush, S. W. (1988). Toward a more appropriate conceptualization of research on school effects: A three-level hierarchical linear model. *American Journal of Education, 97,* 65–108.

Bryn, S., & Gallagher, S. (1999). Report of the ASHA National injury and violence prevention task force: An executive summary. *Journal of School Health, 69*(5), 177–180.

Buchanan, C. M. (1991). Pubertal status in early-adolescent girls: Relations to moods, energy, and restlessness. *Journal of Early Adolescence, 11*(2), 185–200.

Buckley, N., Siegel, L. S., & Ness, S. (1979). Egocentrism, empathy, and altruistic behavior in young children. *Developmental Psychology, 15,* 329–330.

Budwig, N., Wertsch, J. V., & Uzgiris, I. C. (2000). Communication, meaning, and development. In N. Budwig & I. C. Uzgris (Eds.) *Communication: An arena of development: Advances in applied developmental psychology* (pp. 1–14). Stanford, NJ: Ablex.

Bukowski, W. (1990). Age differences in children's memory of information about aggressive, socially withdrawn, and prosociable boys and girls. *Child Development, 61,* 1326–1334.

Bukstein, O. G. (1994). Treatment of adolescent alcohol abuse and dependence. *Alcohol Health and Research World, 18*(4), 296–301.

Bullock, M. (1985). Animism in childhood thinking: A new look at an old question. *Developmental Psychology, 21*(2), 217–225.

Bumpers, D. (1984). Securing the blessings of liberty for posterity: Preventive health care for children. *American Psychologist, 39*(8), 896–900.

Burger, L. K., & Miller, P. J. (1999). Early talk about the past revisited: Affect in working-class and middle-class children's narrations. *Journal of Child Language, 26*(1), 133–162.

Burnett, D. J. (1999). *Positive coaching: A behavior checklist for youth sports coaches.* Retrieved March 2000 from the World Wide Web: http://youth-sports.com/topics/052298-1.html

Burnham, D. K., Earnshaw, L. J., & Clark, J. E. (1991). Development of categorical identification of native and non-native bilabial stops: Infants, children, and adults. *Journal of Child Language, 18,* 231–260.

Bus, A. G., van IJzendoorn, M. H., & Pellegrini, A. D. (1995). Joint book reading makes for success in learning to read: A meta-analysis on intergenerational transmission of literacy. *Review of Educational Research, 65*(1), 1–21.

Bushnell, E. W., & Boudreau, J. P. (1993). Motor development and the mind: The potential role of motor abilities as a determinant of aspects of perceptual development. *Child Development, 64*(4), 1005–1021.

Buss, D. M. (1995). Psychological sex differences: Origins through sexual selection. *American Psychologist, 50,* 164–168.

Butler, R. A. (1953). Discrimination learning by rhesus monkeys to visual exploration motivation. *Journal of Comparative Physiological Psychology, 46,* 95–98.

Butterworth, G. E., & Franco, F. (1993). Motor development: Communication and cognition. In L. Kalverboer, B. Hopkins, & R. H. Gueze (Eds.), *A longitudinal approach to the study of motor development in early and later childhood.* Cambridge: Cambridge University Press.

Butterworth, G. E., & Grover, L. (1988). Social cognition in infancy: Joint visual attention, manual pointing, and the origins of referential communication. *Revue Internationale de Psychologie Sociale, 2,* 9–22.

Butterworth, G. E., & Grover, L. (1990). Joint visual attention, manual pointing and preverbal communication in human infancy. In M. Jeannerod (Ed.), *Attention and Performance XIII* (pp. 605–624). Hillsdale, NJ: Erlbaum.

Butterworth, G. E., & Jarret, N. (1991). What minds have in common is space: Spatial mechanisms serving joint visual attention in infancy. *British Journal of Developmental Psychology, 9,* 55–72.

Byrne, B., & Fielding-Barnsley, R. (1995). Evaluation of a program to teach phonemic awareness to young children: A 2- and 3-year follow-up and a new pre-school trial. *Journal of Educational Psychology, 87,* 488–503.

Byrnes, J. P., & Takahira, S. (1993). Explaining gender differences on SAT-math items. *Developmental Psychology, 29,* 805–810.

Byrnes, J. P., & Wasik, B. A. (1991). Role of conceptual knowledge in mathematical procedural learning. *Developmental Psychology, 27*(5), 777–786.

Byrnes, J. P., Miller, D. C., & Shafer, W. D. (1999). Gender differences in risk taking: A meta-analysis. *Psychological Bulletin, 125*(3), 367–383.

Cacioppo, J. T., Petty, R. E., Feinstein, J. A., & Jarvis, W. B. G. (1996). Dispositional differences in cognitive motivation: The life and times of individuals varying in need for cognition. *Psychological Bulletin, 119,* 197–253.

Cadoret, R. J., Leve, L. D., & Devor, E. (1997). Genetics of aggressive and violent behavior. *Psychiatric Clinics of North America, 20*(2), 301–322.

Caffery, T., & Ercman, P. (2000). Conceptualizing parent-adolescent conflict: Applications from systems and attachment theories. *Family Journal, 8*(1), 14–21.

Cairney, T. H. (1995). Developing parent partnership in secondary literacy learning. *Journal of Adolescent and Adult Literacy, 38,* 520–526.

Cairns, R. B. (1998). The making of developmental psychology. In W. Damon & R. Lerner (Eds.) *Handbook of child psychology: Vol. 1. Theoretical models of human development* (pp.25–105). New York: Wiley.

Caldera, V. M., Huston, A. C., & O'Brien, M. (1989). Social interactions and play patterns of parents and toddlers with feminine, masculine, and neutral toys. *Child Development, 60,* 70–76.

Caliandro, C. K. (2000). Children's inventions for multidigit multiplication and division. *Teaching children mathematics, 6*(6), 420–426.

Callister, L. C. (1995). Cultural meanings of childbirth. *Journal of Obstetric Gynecologic and Neonatal Nursing, 24*(4), 327–331.

Calvert, S. (1999). *Children's journeys through the information age.* New York: McGraw-Hill.

Calvert, S. L., & Wright, J. C. (1982). *Relation of age, sex, and SES to children's patterns of home television viewing.* Paper presented at the Biennial Meeting of the Southwestern Society for Research in Human Development, Galveston, TX.

Campbell, F. A., & Ramey, C. T. (1994). Effects of early intervention on intellectual and academic achievement: A follow-up study of children from low-income families. *Child Development, 65,* 684–698.

Campos, J. J., Barret, K. C., Lamb, M. E., Goldsmith, H. H., & Stenberg, C. (1983). Socioemotional development. In P. H. Mussen (Ed.), *Handbook of child psychology* (4th ed.). New York: Wiley.

Campos, J. J., Hiatt, S., Ramsay, D., Henderson, C., & Svejda, M. (1978). The emergence of fear on the visual cliff. In M. Lewis & L. Rosenblum (Eds.), *The development of affect,* (pp. 149–182). New York: Plenum Press.

Campos, J. J., Langer, A., & Krowitz, A. (1970). Cardiac responses on the visual cliff in prelocomotor human infants. *Science, 170,* 196–197.

Capirci, O., Iverson, J. M., Pizzuto, E., & Volterra, V. (1996). Gestures and words during the transition to two-word speech. *Journal of Child Language, 23,* 645–673.

Cara, J. F., & Johanson, A. J. (1990). Growth hormone for short stature not due to classic growth hormone deficiency. *Pediatric Clinics of North America, 37*(6), 1229–1254.

Cardon, L. R. (1994). Height, weight, and obesity. In J. C. DeFries, R. Plomin, & D. W. Fulker (Eds.), *Nature and nurture during middle childhood.* Oxford: Blackwell.

Carey, S. (1978). The child as a word learner. In J. Bresnan, G. Miller, & M. Halle (Eds.), *Linguistic theory and psychological reality.* Cambridge, MA: MIT Press.

Carlson, C. L., Tamm, L., & Gaub, M. (1997). Gender differences in children with ADHD, ODD, and co-occurring ADHD/ODD identified in a school population. *Journal of the American Academy of Child and Adolescent Psychiatry, 36*(12), 1706–1714.

Carlson, K., & Cunningham, J. L. (1990). Effect of pencil diameter on the graphomotor skill of preschoolers. *Early Childhood Research Quarterly, 5*(2), 279–293.

Carlsson, S. G., Fagerberg, H., Horneman, G., Hwange, C. P., Larsson, K., Rodgab, M., Schaller, J., Danielsson, B., & Gundewall, C. (1978). Effects of amount of contact between mother and child on the mother's nursing behavior. *Developmental Psychology, 11,* 143–150.

Caron, A. J., Caron, R. C., & Antell, S. E. (1988). Infant understanding of containment: An affordance perceived or a relationship conceived? *Developmental Psychology, 24,* 620–627.

Caron, A. J., Caron, R. F., & MacLean, D. J. (1988). Infant discrimination of naturalistic emotional expressions: The role of face and voice. *Child Development, 59,* 604–616.

Caron, R. F., Caron, A. J., & Myers, R. S. (1982). Abstraction of invariant face expressions in infancy. *Child Development, 53,* 1008–1015.

Carpenter, L. M. (1998). From girls into women: Scripts for sexuality and romance in *Seventeen magazine, 1974–1994. Journal of Sexual Research, 35*(2), 158–168.

Carpenter, M., Nagell, K., & Tomasello, M. (1998). Social cognition, joint attention, and communicative competence from 9–15 months of age. *Monographs of the Society for Research in Child Development,* Vol. 63 (4, Serial No. 255).

Carr, J., Eppig, P., & Monether, P. (1992). Learning by solving real problems. In J. H. Lounsbury (Ed.), *Connecting the curriculum through interdisciplinary instruction* (pp. 121–128). Columbus, OH: National Middle School Association.

Carr, M., Borkowski, J. G., & Maxwell, S. E. (1991). Motivational components of underachievement. *Developmental Psychology, 27*(1), 108–118.

Carr, M., Kurtz, B. E., Schneider, W., Turner, L. A., & Berkowski, J. G. (1989). Strategy acquisition and transfer among American and German children: Environmental influences on metacognitive development. *Developmental Psychology, 25,* 765–771.

Carroll, J. B. (1993). *Human cognitive abilities: A survey of factor-analytic studies.* Cambridge, England: Cambridge University Press.

Carroll, J. B., (1997). Psychometrics, intelligence, and public perception. *Intelligence, 24,* 24–52.

Carroll, W. M. (1994). Using worked examples as an instructional support in the algebra classroom. *Journal of Educational Psychology, 86*(3), 360–367.

Carskadon (1999). Sleep needs. *Indiana Education.* Retrieved March 2000 from the World Wide Web: http://education.indiana.edu/cas/sleep.html

Carson, J. (1995). A black tie affair. *Exceptional Parent, 25*(3), 25–26.

Carter, A. (1975). The transformation of sensorimotor morphemes into words: A case study of the development of "more" and "mine." *Journal of Child Language, 2,* 233–250.

Casaer, P. (1993). Old and new facts about perinatal brain development. *Journal of Child Psychiatry and Allied Disciplines, 50*(3), 716–721.

Casbergue, R. (1996). *The Chrojen Hors: Emergence of expository writing.* Paper presented at the Annual Meeting of the International Reading Association, April 30–May 5, New Orleans, LA.

Case, R. (1992). *The mind's staircase.* Hillsdale, NJ: Erlbaum.

Case, R. (1993). *Central conceptual structures and their manifestation in specific task performance.* Paper presented at the Biennial Meeting of the Society for Research in Child Development, March 1993, New Orleans, LA.

Case, R. (1998). The development of conceptual structures. In W. Damon (Series Ed.) and D. Kuhn & R. S. Siegler (Vol. Eds.) *Handbook of child psychology (5th ed.): Vol. 2. Cognition, perception, and language* (pp. 745–800). New York: Wiley.

Caselli, C., Casadio, P., & Bates, E. (1999). A comparison of the transition from first words to grammar in English and Italian. *Journal of Child Language, 26,* 69–111.

Cashore, W. J., & Stern, L. (1982). Neonatal hyperbilirubinemia. *Pediatric Clinics of North America, 29*(5), 1191–1203.

Caspi, A., Bem, D. J., & Elder, G. H. (1987). Moving against the world: Life-course patterns of explosive children. *Developmental Psychology, 23*(2), 308–313.

Cassell, J., & Jenkins, H. (Eds.). (1998). *From Barbie to Mortal Kombat.* Cambridge, MA: The MIT Press.

Cassidy, J. (1994). Emotion regulation: Influences of attachment relationships. In N. Fox (Ed.), The development of emotion: Biological and behavioral considerations. *Monographs of the Society for Research in Child Development, 59*(2–3, Serial No. 240), 228–249.

Cassidy, J., & Berlin, L. J. (1994). The insecure/ambivalent pattern of attachment: Theory and research. *Child Development, 65,* 971–991.

Cassidy, K. W., Ball, L. V., Rourke, M. T., Werner, R. S., Feeny, N., Chu, J. Y., Lutz, D. J., & Perkins, A. (1998). Theory of mind concepts in children's literature. *Applied Psycholinguistics, 19,* 463–470.

Castillo, D. N., Landen, D. D., & Layne, L. A. (1994). Occupational injury deaths of 16–17-year-olds in the United States. *American Journal of Public Health, 84,* 646–649.

Castro, C. (1999). Description of *Life Skills Training.* Retrieved March 2000 from the World Wide Web: www.lifeskillstraining.com/lstinfo.htm

Caudill, W., & Weinstein, H. (1962). Maternal care and infant behavior in Japan and America. *Psychiatry, 32,* 12–43.

Ceci, S. J. (1991). How much does schooling influence general intelligence and its cognitive components? A reassessment of the evidence. *Developmental Psychology, 27,* 703–722.

Centers for Disease Control and Prevention (CDC). (1995). *Pediatric AIDS Report.* Rockville, MD: National AIDS Information Clearinghouse.

CDC. (1997). Sexually transmitted disease surveillance. *Morbidity and Mortality Report, 46w.*

CDC. (1998). Conversion trends '98. Retrieved March 2000 from the World Wide Web: www.cdc.gov/hiv/stats/trends98.pdf

CDC. (1999a). Cigarette smoking among high school students. *MMWR Weekly.* Retrieved March 2000 from the World Wide Web: www.cdc.gov/epo/mmwr/preview

CDC. (1999b). *Facts about violence among youth and violence in schools.* Retrieved March 2000 from the World Wide Web: www.cdc.gov/od/oc/media/pressrel/r990421.htm

CDC. (1999c). Facts about youth risk behavior surveillance. Retrieved March 2000 from the World Wide Web: www.cdc.gov/od/oc/media/fact/youthrisk.htm

CDC (1999d). Fact sheet on dating violence. *National Center for Injury Prevention and Control.* Retrieved March 2000 from the World Wide Web: www.cdc.gov/ncipc/dvp/datviol.htm

CDC. (1999e). Health effects of smoking among young people. *Tobacco Information and Prevention Source: Office on Smoking and Health.* Retrieved March 2000 from the World Wide Web: www.cdc.gov/tobacco

CDC. (1999f). Impaired driving fact sheet. *National Center for Injury Prevention and Control.* Retrieved March 2000 from the World Wide Web: www.cdc.gov/ncipc/duip/drving.htm

CDC. (1999g). Incidence of initiation of cigarette smoking among U.S. teens: Fact sheet. *Tobacco information and prevention service.* Retrieved March 2000 from the World Wide Web: www.cdc.gov/tobacco/initfact.htm

CDC. (1999h). New study finds overweight children and adolescents are at risk for cardiovascular problems. Retrieved March 2000 from the World Wide Web: www.cdc.gov/od/oc/media/pressrel/r990607.htm

CDC. (1999i). Preventing tobacco use and addiction among young people. *Tobacco Information and Prevention Source.* Retrieved March 2000 from the World Wide Web: www.cdc.gov/nccdphp/osh

CDC. (1999j). Some facts about chlamydia. Retrieved March 2000 from the World Wide Web:www.cdc.gov/nc\hstp/dstd/chlamydia

CDC. (1999k). Youth violence in the United States. *National Center for Injury Prevention and Control.* Retrieved March 2000 from the World Wide Web: www.cdc.gov/ncipc/dvp/yvfacts.htm

CDC. (2000). Facts on adolescent injury. Retrieved March 2000 from the World Wide Web: htp://www.cdc-gov/ncipc/elui/adoles

CEPC. (1999). Paying now or paying later. Center for Effective Collaboration and Practice. Retrieved March 2000 from the World Wide Web: http://cecp.air.org/resources/schfail/paying

Cernoch, J., & Porter, R. H. (1985). Recognition of maternal axillary odors by infants. *Child Development, 56*(6), 1593–1598.

Chall, J. S., (1967). *Learning to read: The great debate.* New York: McGraw-Hill.

Chamberlain, P., & Patterson, G. R. (1995). Discipline and child compliance in parenting. In M. H. Bornstein, *Handbook of parenting: Vol. IV. Applied and practical parenting* (pp. 205–266). Mahwah, NJ: Erlbaum.

Chandler, M., & Hala, S. (1994). The role of personal involvement in the assessment of early false belief skills. In C. Lewis & P. Mitchell (Eds.), *Children's early understanding of mind: Origins and development* (pp. 403–423). Hillsdale, NJ: Erlbaum.

Chao, R. K. (1994). Beyond parental control and authoritarian parenting style: Understanding Chinese parenting through the cultural notion of training. *Child Development, 65,* 1111–1119.

Chappell, M. S., & Overton, W. F. (1998). Development of logical reasoning in the context of parental style and test anxiety. *Merrill-Palmer Quarterly, 44*(2), 141–156.

Charlesworth, W. R., & Kreutzer, M. A. (1973). Facial expressions of infants and children. In P. Ekman (Ed.), *Darwin and facial expressions: A century of research in review* (pp. 11–89). New York: Academic Press.

Chartrand, S. A., & Pong, A. (1998). Acute otitis media in the 1990s: The impact of antibiotic resistance. *Pediatric Annals, 27*(2), 85–95.

Chase-Lansdale, P. L., & Brooks-Gunn, J. B. (1994). Correlates of adolescent pregnancy and parenthood. In C. B. Fisher & R. M. Lerner (Eds.), *Applied developmental psychology* (pp. 205–215). New York: McGraw-Hill.

Chen, C., & Stevenson, H. W. (1995). Motivation and mathematics achievement: A comparative study of Asian-American, Caucasian-American, and East Asian high school students. *Child Development, 66,* 1215–1234.

Chess, S., & Thomas, A. (1984). *Origins and evolution of behavior disorders.* New York: Bruner/Mazel.

Chi, M., deLeeuw, N., Chiu, M., & LaVancher, C. (1994). Eliciting self-explanations improves learning. *Cognitive Science, 18,* 439–477.

Chi, M. T. H., Hutchinson, J. E., & Robin, A. F. (1989). How inferences about novel domain-related concepts can be constrained by structured knowledge. *Merrill-Palmer Quarterly, 35,* 27–61.

Chi, M. T. H., & Rees, E. (1983). A learning framework for development. *Contributions to Human Development, 9,* 71–107.

Child Protection Report, 21 (17), 1995, August 18.

Children Affected by AIDS Foundation. (1999). Children with AIDS statistics. Retrieved March 2000 from the World Wide Web: http://www.CAAF4kids.org/hyh/hg_body.html

Chomsky, C. (1969). *The acquisition of syntax in children from 5 to 10.* Cambridge, MA: MIT Press.

Chomsky, N. (1959). A review of *Verbal behavior,* by B. F. Skinner. *Language, 35,* 26–58.

Chomsky, N. (1965). *Aspects of the theory of syntax.* Cambridge, MA: MIT Press.

Christie, S. (1999). Schools urged to sharpen up smoking policies. *Health Education Authority.* Retrieved March 2000 from the World Wide Web: www.hea.org.uk/press/1479929.html

Chronister, M. J., & Chang, P. (1999, April). Cognitive styles and performance on Piaget's water-level task. Paper presented at the annual convention of the Eastern Psychological Association, Providence, RI.

Ciaranello, R. (1988). Neurochemical aspects of stress. In N. Garmezy & M. Rutter (Eds.), *Stress, coping, and development in children.* Baltimore: Johns Hopkins University Press.

Cicero, T. J. (1994). Effects of paternal exposure to alcohol on offspring development. *Alcohol Health and Research World, 18*(1), 37–41.

Cipielewski, J., & Stanovich, K. E. (1992). Predicting growth in reading ability from children's exposure to print. *Journal of Experimental Child Psychology, 54*, 74–89.

Clancy, P. (1985). Acquisition of Japanese. In D. I. Slobin (Ed.), *The cross-linguistic study of language acquisition.* Hillsdale, NJ: Erlbaum.

Clark, C. S. (1995). Sex, violence and the media. *Congressional Quarterly Research, 5*(43), 1019–1039.

Clark, E. V. (1975). Knowledge, context, and strategy in the acquisition of meaning. In D. P. Dato (Ed.), *Developmental psycholinguistics: Theory and applications.* Georgetown University Round Table on Languages and Linguistics 1975. Washington, DC: Georgetown University Press.

Clark, E. V. (1978). Non-linguistic strategies and the acquisition of word meaning. In L. Bloom (Ed.), *Readings in language development.* New York: Wiley.

Clark, E. V. (1990). On the pragmatics of contrast. *Journal of Child Language, 17*, 417–431.

Clarke-Stewart, A., & Fein, G. (1983). Early childhood programs. In M. M. Haith & J. J. Campos (Eds.), P. H. Mussen (Series Ed.), *Handbook of child psychology: Vol. 2. Infancy and developmental psychobiology.* New York: Wiley.

Clarke-Stewart, K. A., Vanderstoep, L. P., & Killian, G. A. (1979). Analysis and relocation of mother-child relations at two years of age. *Child Development, 50*, 777–793.

Clarkson, M. G. (1992). Infants' perception of low pitch. In L. A. Werner & E. W. Rubel (Eds.), *Developmental Psychoacoustics.* Washington: APA.

Clavadetscher, J. E., Brown, A. M., Ankrum, C., & Teller, D. Y. (1988). Spectral sensitivity and chromatic discrimination in 3- and 7-week-old infants. *Journal of the Optical Society of America, 5*, 2093–2105.

Clay, M. (1983). Getting a theory of writing. In B. M. Kroll & G. Wells (Eds.), *Explorations in the development of writing* (pp. 259–284). New York: Wiley.

Clay, M. (1987). *Writing begins at home.* Portsmouth, NH: Heinemann.

Clifton, R. K., Muir, D. W., Ashmead, D. H., & Clarkson, M. G. (1993). Is visually guided reaching in early infancy a myth? *Child Development, 64*,(4), 1099–1110.

Cline, V. B., Croft, R. G., & Courrier, S. (1972).The desensitization of children to television violence. *Proceedings of the American Psychological Association, 80*, 99–100.

Clyman, R. B., Emde, R. N., Kempe, J. E., & Harmon, R. J. (1986). Social referencing and social looking among twelve-month-old infants. In T. B. Brazelton & M. W. Yogeman (Eds.), *Affective development in infancy* (pp. 75–94). Norwood, NJ: Ablex.

CNN. (1999a). Affordable drug reduces mother-to-child HIV Transmission. Retrieved March 2000 from the World Wide Web: www.cnn.com/health/aids/1997/14/preventing.baby.hiv/index

CNN. (1999b). High school exit exam tests limits of education. *Cable News Network.* www.cnn.com

CNN. (1999c). Report urges parents to read to kids early and often. *Cable News Network.* Retrieved March 2000 from the World Wide Web: http://cnn.com/US/9907/26/reading.assessment.

Cobb, N. J. (1998). *Adolescence: Continuity, change, and diversity.* Mountain View, CA: Mayfield.

Coddington, D. G. (1999). Review of the book *Understanding children and adolescents* for Allyn & Bacon, (pp. 6–7).

Cohen, J. A., & Mannarino, A. P. (1998). Factors that mediate treatment outcome of sexually abused preschool children: Six- and 12-month follow-up. *Journal of the American Academy of Child & Adolescent Psychiatry, 37*, 44–51.

Cohen, L., & Gelber, E. (1975). Infant visual memory. In L. B. Cohen & P. Salapatek (Eds.), *Infant perception: From sensation to cognition* (Vol. 1). New York: Academic Press.

Cohen, L. B., & Oakes, L. M. (1993). How infants perceive a simple causal event. *Developmental Psychology, 29*, 421–433.

Cohen, L. B., & Strauss, M. S. (1979). Concept acquisition in the human infant. *Child Development, 50*, 419–424.

Cohen, P., Cohen, J., Kasen, S., Velez, C. H., Hartmark, C., Johnson, J., Rojas, M., Brook, J., & Streuning, E. L. (1993). An epidemiological study of disorders in late adolescence: I. Age- and gender-specific prevalence. *Journal of Child Psychology and Psychiatry, 6*, 851–867.

Cohen, S. E., & Parmelee, A. H. (1983). Prediction of five-year Stanford-Binet scores in preterm infants. *Child Development, 54*, 1242–1253.

Cohn, L. D., Macfarlane, S., Yanez, C., & Imai, W. K. (1995). Risk perception: Differences between adolescents and adults. *Health Psychology, 14*(3), 217–222.

Coie, J. D., & Dodge, K. A. (1998). Aggression and antisocial behavior. In W. Damon (Editor-in-Chief) and N. Eisenberg (Vol. Ed.), *Handbook of child psychology,* (5th ed.): Vol. 3. Social, emotional, and personality development (pp. 779–862). New York: Wiley.

Coie, J. D., Dodge, K. A., & Kupersmidt, J. B. (1990). Peer group behavior and social status. In S. Asher & J. D. Coie (Eds.), *Peer rejection in childhood* (pp. 17–59). New York: Cambridge University Press.

Coirier, P., & Golder, C. (1993). Writing argumentative text: A developmental study of the acquisition of supporting structures. *European Journal of Psychological Education, 8*(2), 169–181.

Colangelo, N., & Kerr, B. A. (1990). Extreme academic talent: Profiles of perfect scorers. *Journal of Educational Psychology, 82*, 404–409.

Cole, D. A., Martin, J. M., Lachlan, A., Peeke, A. D., Seroczynski, A. D., & Fier, J. (1999). Children's over- and underestimation of academic competence: A longitudinal study of gender differences, depression, and anxiety. *Child Development, 70*(2), 459–473.

Cole, M. (1999). Culture in development. In M. H. Bornstein & M. E. Lamb (Eds.), *Developmental psychology: An advanced textbook* (4th ed., pp. 73–123). Mahwah, NJ: Erlbaum.

Coleman, P. (1993). Testing the school system: Dropouts, accountability, and social policy. *Curriculum Inquiry, 23*, 329–342.

Collett, J. P., Burtin, P., Kramer, M. S., Floret, D., Bossard, N., Ducruet, T. (1994). Type of day-care setting and risk of repeated infections. *Pediatrics, 94*(Suppl. 6), 997–999.

Collias, N. E. (1956). The analysis of socialization in sheep and goats. *Ecology, 37*, 228–239.

Collins, N. W., & Miller, L. C. (1994). Self-disclosure and liking: A meta-analytic review. *Psychological Bulletin, 116*(3), 457–475.

Colombo, J. (1995). On the neural mechanisms underlying development and individual differences in visual fixation in infancy: Two hypotheses. *Developmental Review, 15*, 97–135.

Colombo, M., de la Para, A., & Lopez, I. (1992). Intellectual and physical outcome of children undernourished in early life is influenced by later environmental conditions. *Developmental Medicine and Child Neurology, 34*, 611–622.

Committee on Sports Medicine (1989). Anabolic steroids and the adolescent athlete. *Pediatrics, 83*(1), 127–128.

Comstock, G., & Scharrer, E. (1999). *Television. What's on, who's watching, and what it means.* San Diego: Academic Press.

Condon, W. S. (1979). Neonatal entrainment and enculturation. In M. Bullowa (Ed.), *Before speech: The beginning of interpersonal communication.* Cambridge: Cambridge University Press.

Conger, R. D., Patterson, G. R., & Ge, X. (1995). It takes two to replicate: A mediational model for the impact of parents' stress on adolescent adjustment. *Child Development, 66*, 80–97.

Conkell, C. S. (1999). The effects of humor on communicating fitness concepts to high school students. *The Physical Educator, 56*(1), 8–18.

Connell, J. P., & Goldmith, H. H. (1982). A structural modeling approach to the study of attachment and strange situation behaviors. In R. J. Emde & R. J. Harmon (Eds.), *The development of attachment and affiliative systems.* New York: Plenum.

Conrad, K., Flay, B. R., & Hill, D. (1992). Why children start smoking cigarettes: Predictors of onset. *British Journal of Addiction, 87*, 1711–1724.

Conway, E. E. (1998). Nonaccidental head injury in infants: "The Shaken Baby Syndrome Revisited." *Pediatrics, 27*(10), 677–690.

Conway, E. E., & Bello, J. (1996). Intracranial pathology and outcome of patients admitted to the PICU with non-accidental head trauma. *Archives of Pediatric and Adolescent Medicine, 316*, 150 A.

Cook, W. L. (1993). Interdependence and the interpersonal sense of control: An analysis of family relationships. *Journal of Personality and Social Psychology, 64*, 587–601.

Cooley, M. L., & Unger, D. G. (1991). The role of family support in determining developmental outcomes in children of term mothers. *Child Psychiatry and Human Development, 21*, 217–234.

Cooper, R. P., & Aslin, R. N. (1990). Preference for infant-directed speech in the first month after birth. *Child Development, 61*, 1584–1595.

Corcoran, K. J. (1996, August). *Understanding anabolic steroid use: A social learning theory perspective.* Paper presented at the 104th Annual Convention of the American Psychological Association. Toronto, Ontario.

Corkum, V., & Moore, C. (1995). Development of joint visual attention in infants. In C. Moore & P. Dunham (Eds.), *Joint attention: Its origins and role in development.* Hillsdale, NJ: Erlbaum.

Covell, K., Dion, K. Z., & Dion, K. K. (1994). Gender differences in evaluations of tobacco and alcohol advertisements. *Canadian Journal of Behavioural Science, 26*(3), 404–420.

Covey, S. R. (1997). *The 7 habits of highly effective families.* New York: Golden Books.

Cowdry, R. W. (1995). Basic behavioral science research for mental health: A national investment. A report of the National Advisory Mental Health Council. Behavioral Science Task Force. *Psychological Science, 6*(4), 192–202.

Coyle, K., Basen-Enquist, K., Kirby, D., Parcel, G., Banspach, S., Harrist, R., Baumler, E., & Weil, M. (1999). Short-term impact of *Safer Choices:* A multicomponent, school based HIV, other STD, and pregnancy prevention program. *Journal of School Health, 69*(5), 181–188.

Cozbyk, P. C. *Methods in behavioral research* (6th ed.). Mountain View, CA: Mayfield Publishing Company.

CPR. *See* Child Protection Report.

Craik, F. I. M., & Tulving, E. (1975). Depth of processing and the retention of words in episodic memory. *Journal of Experimental Psychology: General, 104*, 268–294.

Crain-Thoreson, C., & Dale, P. S. (1992). Do early talkers become early readers? Linguistic precocity, preschool language, and emergent literacy. *Developmental Psychology, 28*(3), 421–429.

Crall, J. J. (1986). Promotion of oral health and prevention of common pediatric dental problems. *Pediatric Clinics of North America, 33*(4), 887–898.

Cratty, B. J. (1986). *Perceptual and motor development in infants and children.* (3rd ed.). Englewood Cliffs, NJ: Prentice-Hall.

Crick, N. R. (1997). Engagement in gender normative versus nonnormative forms of aggression: Links to social-psychological adjustment. *Developmental Psychology, 33*(4), 610–617.

Crick, N. R., & Dodge, K. A. (1996). Social information-processing mechanisms in reactive and proactive aggression. *Child Development, 67*, 993–1002.

Crick, N. R., & Grotpeter, J. K. (1995). Relational aggression, gender, and social-psychological adjustment. *Child Development, 66*, 710–722.

Crittenden, P., & Ainsworth, M. D. S. (1989). Child maltreatment and attachment theory. In D. Circhetti & V. Carlson (Eds.), *Child maltreatment: Theory and research on the causes and consequences of child abuse and neglect* (pp. 432–463). New York: Cambridge University Press.

Crnic, K., & Acevedo, M. (1995). Everyday stress and parenting. In M. H. Bornstein. *Handbook of parenting: Vol. IV. Applied and practical parenting* (pp. 277–298). Mahwah, NJ: Erlbaum.

Crnic, K. A., Ragozin, A. S., Greenberg, M. T., Robinson, M. M., & Basham, R. B. (1983). Social interaction and developmental competence of preterm and full-term infants during the first year of life. *Child Development, 54,* 1199–1210.

Crockenberg, S. B. (1981). Infant irritability, mother responsiveness, and social support influences on the security of infant-mother attachment. *Child Development, 52,* 856–865.

Crockenberg, S. B. (1985). Toddlers' reactions to maternal anger. *Merrill-Palmer Quarterly, 31*(4), 361–373.

Crockenberg, S. B., & Litman, C. (1990). Autonomy as competence in two-year-olds: Maternal correlates of child defiance, compliance, and self-assertion. *Developmental Psychology, 26,* 961–971.

Crowley, K., & Siegler, R. S. (1999). Explanation and generalization in young children's strategy learning. *Child Development, 70*(2), 304–316.

Cruttenden, A. (1970). A phonetic study of babbling. *British Journal of Disorders in Communication, 5,* 110–118.

Culp, A. M., Osofsky, J. D., & O'Brien, M. (1996). Language patterns of adolescent and older mothers and their one-year-old children: A comparison study. *First Language, 16,* 61–75.

Culp, R. E., Applebaum, M. L., Osofsky, J. D., & Levy, J. A. (1988). Adolescent and older mothers: Comparison between prenatal maternal variables and newborn interaction measures. *Infant Behavior and Development, 11,* 353–362.

Culp, R. E., Culp, A. M., Osofsky, J. D., & Osofsky, H. J. (1991). Adolescent and older mothers' interaction patterns with their six-month-old infants. *Journal of Adolescence, 14,* 353–362.

Cummings, E. M., & Zahn-Waxler, C. (1992). Emotions and the socialization of aggression: Adults' angry behavior and children's arousal and aggression. In A. Fraezek & H. Zumkley (Eds.), *Socialization and aggression* (pp. 61–84). Berlin: Springer-Verlag.

Cunningham, A. E., & Stanovich, K. E. (1993). Children's literacy environments and early word recognition skills. *Reading and Writing: An Interdisciplinary Journal, 5,* 193–204.

Cunningham, A. S., Jelliffee, D. B., & Jelliffee, E. F. P. (1991). Breast-feeding and health in the 1980s: A global epidemiological review. *The Journal of Pediatrics, 118*(5), 659–665.

Cunningham, J., Dockery, D. W., & Speizer, F. E. (1994). Maternal smoking during pregnancy as a predictor of lung function in children. *American Journal of Epidemiology, 139,* 1139–1152.

Curtis, G. B. (1997). *Your pregnancy week by week.* Tucson, AR: Fisher Books.

Cusatis, J. (1990). *The nature of modern slang.* Unpublished MA thesis, Millersville University, Millersville, PA.

Cutler, A., & Butterfield, S. (1992). Rhythmic cues to speech segmentation: Evidence from juncture misperception. *Journal of Memory and Language, 31,* 218–236.

Cutler, A., & Carter, D. M. (1987). The predominance of strong initial syllables in the English vocabulary. *Computer Speech and Language, 2,*133–142.

Cutler, A., & Norris, D. G. (1988). The role of strong syllables in segmentation for lexical access. *Journal of Experimental Psychology: Human Perception and Performance, 14,* 113–121.

Dacey, J. S. (1989). *Fundamentals of creative thinking.* Lexington, MA: D. C. Heath.

Dale, K. L., & Baumeister, K. T. (1997). Self-regulation and psychopathology. In R. M. Kowalski & M. R. Leary (Eds.), *The social psychology of emotional and behavioral problems.* pp. 139–166. Washington, DC: American Psychological Association.

Dale, P. S. (1976). *Language development: Structure and function.* (2nd ed.). New York: Holt, Rinehart & Winston.

D'Angelo, L. (2000). Danger: Inhalant hazards. *Science World, 56*(10), 8–11.

Damon, W., & Hart, D. (1992). Self-understanding and its role in social and moral development. In M. H. Bornstein & M. E. Lamb (Eds.), *Developmental psychology: An advanced textbook.* Hillsdale, NJ: Erlbaum.

Daniel, J. (1989, March 14). Fatal attraction: Steroids—the athlete's drug. *The Tab,* pp. 40–41.

Dargassies, S. (1966). Neurological maturation of the premature infant of 28 to 41 weeks' gestation age. In F. Faulkner (Ed.), *Human development.* London: Saunders.

Darling, N., & Steinberg, L. (1993). Parenting styles as context: An integrative model. *Psychological Bulletin, 113,* 487–496.

Darwin, C. (1859). *The origin of the species.* London: Murray.

Dasen, P. (1984). The cross-cultural study of intelligence: Piaget and the Baoule. *International Journal of Psychology, 19,* 407–434.

Davidson, P., & Youniss, J. (1991). Which comes first: Morality or identity? In K. Kirtines & J. Gewirtz (Eds.), *Handbook of moral behavior and development: Vol. 1. Theory* (pp. 105–121). Hillsdale, NJ: Erlbaum.

Davies, M. A. (1992). Are interdisciplinary units worthwhile? Ask students. In J. H. Lounsbury (Eds), *Connecting the curriculum through interdisciplinary instruction* (pp. 37–44). Columbus, OH: National Middle School Association.

Davis, K. L., Roberts, T. C., Smith, R. R., Ormond, F., Pfohl, S. Y., & Bowling, M. (1994). North Carolina children and youth fitness study. *Journal of Physical Education, Recreation and Dance, 65*(8), 65–74.

Davis, N. J. (1999). *Youth crisis: Growing up in the high-risk society.* Westport, CT: Praeger.

Dawe, H. C. (1934). An analysis of two hundred quarrels of preschool children. *Child Development, 5,* 139–157.

Day, N. L., & Richardson, G. A. (1994). Comparative teratogenicity of alcohol and other drugs. *Alcohol, Health, and Research World, 18*(1), 42–48.

Dean, A. L. (1994). Instinctual affective forces in the internalization process: Contributions of Hans Loewald. *Human Development, 37,* 42–57.

Deater-Deckard, K., & Dodge, K. A. (1997). Externalizing behavior problems and discipline revisited: Nonlinear effects and variation by culture, context, and gender. *Psychological Inquiry, 8,* 161–175.

DeBaryshe, B. D. (1993). Joint picture-book reading correlates of early oral language skill. *Journal of Child Language, 20,* 455–461.

DeBaryshe, B., Paterson, G., & Capaldi, D. (1993). A performance model for academic achievement in early adolescent boys. *Developmental Psychology, 29,* 795–804.

deBoysson-Bardies, B. (1993). Ontogeny of language-specific phonetic and lexical productions. In de Boysson-Bardies, B., de Schonen, D., Jusczyk, P., MacNeilage, P., & Morton, J. (Eds.), *Developmental neurocognition: Speech and face processing in the first year of life.* Dordrecht, The Netherlands: Kluwer.

deBoysson-Bardies, B. (1999). *How language comes to children from birth to two years.* Cambridge, MA: The MIT Press.

deBoysson-Bardies, B., Sagart, L., & Durand, C. (1984). Discernable differences in the babbling of infants according to target language. *Journal of Child Language, 11,* 1–15.

deBoysson-Bardies, B., Vihman, M. M., Roug-Hellichuis, L., Durand, C., Landberg, I., & Arao, F. (1992). Material evidence of infant selection from the target language: A cross-linguistic phonetic study. In C. A. Ferguson, L. Menn, & C. Stoel-Gamnan (Eds.), *Phonological development: Models, research, implications.* Timonium, MD: York Press.

Debucker, T. K., & Nelson, R. M. (1999). Variations on an expectancy model of motivation in science. *Contemporary Educational Psychology, 24*(2), 71–94.

DeCasper, A. J., & Carstens, A. A. (1981). Contingencies of stimulation: Effects on learning and emotion in neonates. *Infant Behavior and Development, 4,* 19–35.

DeCasper, A. J., & Fifer, W. P. (1980). Of human bonding: Newborns prefer their mother's voices. *Science, 208,* 174–176.

DeCasper, A. J., & Spence, M. J. (1986). Newborns prefer a familiar story over an unfamiliar one. *Infant Behavior and Development, 9,* 133–150.

DeFries, J. C., & Gillis, J. J. (1993). Genetics of reading disability. In R. Plomin & G. E. McClearn (Eds.), *Nature, nurture, and psychology* (pp. 121–145). Washington, DC: American Psychological Association.

DeGroot, A. (1966). Perception and memory versus thought: Some old ideas and recent findings. In B. Kleinmuntz (Ed.), *Problem solving.* New York: Wiley.

deHann, M., & Nelson, C. D. (1999). Brain activity differentiates faces and object processing in 6-month-old infants. *Developmental Psychology, 35*(4), 1113–1121.

deJong, P. (1998). Working memory deficits of reading disabled children. *Journal of Experimental Child Psychology, 70,* 75–96.

DelCampo, D. S., & DelCampo, R. L. (2000). *Taking sides: Clashing views on controversial issues in childhood and society.* Guilford, CT: Dushkin/McGraw Hill.

D'Elio, M. A., Mundt, D. J., Bush, P. J., & Iannotti, R. J. (1993). Healthful behaviors: Do they protect African-American urban preadolescents from substance abuse? *American Journal of Health Promotion, 7*(5), 354–363.

DeLisi, R., & Staudt, J. (1980). Individual differences in college students' performance on formal operations tasks. *Journal of Applied Developmental Psychology, 1,* 201–208.

Deloache, J. S., Miller, K. F., & Pierroutsakos, S. L. (1998). Reasoning and problem-solving. In W. Damon, (Editor-in-Chief) and D. Kuhn & R. S. Siegler (Vol. Eds.), *Handbook of child psychology* (5th ed.): *Vol. 2. Cognition, perception, and language* (pp. 801–849). New York: Wiley.

deMarrais, K. B., Nelson, P. A., & Baker, J. H. (1994). Meaning in mud: Yup'ik Eskimo girls at play. In J. L. Roopnarine, J. E. Johnson, & F. H. Hooper (Eds.), *Children's play in diverse cultures* (pp. 179–209). Albany, NY: State University of New York Press.

Demos, V. (1986). Crying in early infancy: An illustration of the motivational function of affect. In T. B. Brazelton & M. W. Yogman (Eds.), *Affective development in infancy.* Norwood, NJ: Ablex.

Dempsey, P., & Gesse, T. (1995). Beliefs, values and practices of Navajo childbearing women. *Western Journal of Nursing Research, 17*(16), 591–604.

Demuth, K. (1990). Subject, topic and Sesotho passive. *Journal of Child Language, 17,* 67–84.

Denham, S. A., & Grout, L. (1992). Mothers' emotional expressiveness and coping: Relations with preschoolers' social-emotional competence. *Genetic, Social, and General Psychology Monographs, 118,* 75–101.

Dennis, W. (1960). Causes of retardation among institutional children: Iran. *Journal of Genetic Psychology, 96,* 47–59.

Desmond, M. M., Franklin, R. R., Vallbona, C., Hilt, R. H., Plumb, R., Arnold, H., & Watts, J. (1963). The clinical behavior of the newly born I. *Journal of Pediatrics, 12,* 307–325.

Desor, J. A., Maller, O., & Andrews, K. (1975). Ingestive responses of human newborns to salty, sour, and bitter stimuli. *Journal of Comparative and Physiological Psychology, 89,* 966–970.

deVilliers, J., & deVilliers, P. (1973). Development of the use of word order in comprehension. *Journal of Psycholinguistic Research, 2,* 331–341.

deVilliers, J. G., & deVilliers, P. A. (1999). Language development. In M. H. Bornstein & M. E. Lamb (Eds.), *Developmental psychology: An advanced textbook* (4th ed., pp. 313–373). Mahwah, NJ: Erlbaum.

DeVries, R. (1970). The development of role-taking as reflected by behavior of bright, average, and retarded children in a social guessing game. *Child Development, 41,* 759–770.

Dewey, J., & Bentley, A. F. (1949). *Knowing and the known.* Boston: Beacon.

deWolff, M. S., & Ijzendoorn, M. H. (1997). Sensitivity and attachment: A meta-analysis on parental antecedents of infant attachment. *Child Development, 68,* 571–591. Dickinson, D. K. (1984). First impressions: Children's knowledge of words gained from a single exposure. *Applied Psycholinguistics, 5,* 359–373.

Dickinson, D. K. (1991). Teacher agenda and setting: Constraints on conversation in preschools. In A. McCabe & C. Peterson (Eds.), *Developing narrative structure* (pp. –301). Hillsdale, NJ: Erlbaum.

Dickinson, D. K., Cote, L., & Smith, M. W. (1993). Learning vocabulary in preschool: Social discourse contexts affecting vocabulary growth. *New Directions for Child Development, 61,* 67–78.

Dickinson, D. K., & Smith, M. W. (1994). Long-term effects of preschool teachers' book readings on low-income children's vocabulary and story comprehension. *Reading Research Quarterly, 29*(2), 105–122.

Dietz, W. H. (1986). Prevention of childhood obesity. *Pediatric Clinics of North America, 33*(4), 823–833.

Dietz, W. (1990). You are what you eat: What you eat is what you are. Conference: Teens and television. *Journal of Adolescent Health Care, 11*(1), 76–81.

DiPillo, M., Sovchik, R., & Moss, B. (1997). Exploring middle graders' mathematical thinking through journals. *Mathematics Teaching in the Middle School, 2,* 308–314.

Diriwachter, R., Strough, J., & Schnall, S. (1999, April). *Gender differences in prosocial and aggressive story themes in creative writing.* Paper presented at the annual Eastern Psychological Association meeting, Providence, RI.

Dishion, T. (1990). The family ecology of boys' peer relations in middle childhood. *Child Development, 61,* 874–892.

Dishion, T. J., Andrews, D. W., & Crowby, L. (1995). Antisocial boys and their friends in early adolescence: Relationship characteristics, quality, and interactional processes. *Child Development, 66,* 139–151.

Dobbing, J. (1984). Infant nutrition and later achievement. *Nutrition Reviews, 42*(1), 1–7.

Dobbing, J. (Ed.). (1987). *Early nutrition and later achievement.* London: Academic Press.

Dodge, K. A. (1990). Nature versus nurture in childhood conduct disorder: It is time to ask a different question. *Developmental Psychology, 26*(5), 698–701.

Dodge, K. A., Murphy, R. R., & Buchsbaum, K. (1984). The assessment of intention-cue detection skills in children: Implications for developmental psychopathology. *Child Development, 55,* 163–173.

Dodge, K. A., Pettit, G. S., & Bates, J. E. (1994). Socialization mediators of the relation between socioeconomic status and child conduct problems. *Child Development, 65,* 649–665.

Dodge, K. A., Pettit, G. S., Bates, J. E., & Valente, E. (1995). Social-information processing patterns partially mediate the effect of early physical abuse on later conduct problems. *Journal of Abnormal Psychology, 104,* 632–643.

D'Odorico, L. (1984). Nonsegmental features in prelinguistic communication: An analysis of some types of infant cry and non-cry vocalization. *Journal of Child Language, 11,* 17–27.

DOE. (U.S. Department of Energy) (1999a). U.S. Human Genome Project 5-year research goals. *Human Genome Project.* Retrieved March 2000 from the World Wide Web: www.ornl.gov/TechResources/Human_Genome/hg5yp

DOE. (1999b). Protein structures central to cystic fibrosis solved. *Lawrence Berkeley National Laboratory.* Retrieved March 2000 from the World Wide Web: www.doe.gov/cysticfibro

Dole, J. A., Sloan, C., & Trathen, W. (1995). Teaching vocabulary within the context of literature. *Journal of Reading, 38*(6), 452–460.

Doleys, D. M., & Dolce, J. J. (1982). Toilet training and enuresis. *Pediatric Clinics of North America, 29*(2), 297–312.

Dollaghan, C. (1985). Child meets word: "Fast mapping" in preschool children. *Journal of Speech and Hearing Research, 28,* 449–454.

DONA. (1999). What is a doula? *Doulas of North America.* Retrieved March 2000 from the World Wide Web: www.dona.com

Donovan, P. (1999). The "illegitimacy bonus" and state efforts to reduce out-of-wedlock births. *Family Planning Perspectives, 31,* 94–100.

Dornbusch, S. M., Ritter, P. L., Leiderman, P. H., Rogerts, D. F., & Fraleigh, M. J. (1987). The relation of parenting style to adolescent school performance. *Child Development, 58,* 1244–1257.

Dougherty, W. H., & Engel, R. E. (1986). An 80s look at sex equality in Caldecott winners and honor books. *The Reading Teacher, 40*(4), 394–398.

Douglas, J., & Olshaker, M. (1995). *Mind hunter: Inside the FBI's elite serial crime unit.* New York: Scribner.

Downs, M. P. (1978, Fall). That a child may hear. *Deafness Research Foundation Receiver.*

Doyle, A. (1975). Infant development in day care. *Developmental Psychology, 11,* 655–656.

Drabman, R. S., & Thomas, M. H. (1974). Does media violence increase children's toleration of real-life aggression? *Developmental Psychology, 10,* 3–13.

Dreher, N. (1995). Women and smoking. *Current Health, 21*(8), 16–19.

Du Bois, W. E. B. (1903/1961). *The souls of black folk: Essays and sketches.* New York: Fawcett.

Duncan, P. D., Ritter, P. L., Dornbusch, S. M., Gross, R. T., & Carlsmith, J. M. (1985). The effects of pubertal timing on body image, school behavior, and deviance. *Journal of Youth and Adolescence, 14,* 227–235.

Dunham, P. J., Dunham, F., & Curwin, A. (1993). Joint-attentional states and lexical acquisition at 18 months. *Developmental Psychology, 29,* 827–831.

Dunn, J. (1998). Young children's understanding of other people: Evidence from observations within the family. In M. Woodhead, D. Faulkner, & K. Littleton (Eds.), *Cultural worlds of early childhood* (pp. 101–116). New York: The Open University.

Durant, R. H., Knight, J., & Goodman, E. (1997). Factors associated with aggressive and delinquent behaviors among patients attending an adolescent medicine clinic. *Journal of Adolescent Health, 21*(5), 303–308.

Durlak, J. A. (1995). *School-based prevention programs for children and adolescents.* Thousand Oakes, CA: Sage.

Dusek, J. B., & Danko, M. (1994). Adolescent coping styles and perceptions of parental child rearing. *Journal of Adolescent Research, 9*(4), 412–426.

Dweck, C. S. (1978). Achievement. In M. E. Lamb (Ed.), *Social and personality development* (pp. 114–130). New York: Holt, Rinehart & Winston.

Dweck, C. S. (1986). Motivation processes affecting learning. *American Psychologist, 41,* 1040–1048.

Dweck, C. S., & Elliot, E. S. (1983). Achievement motivation. In P. H. Mussen (Series Ed.), *Handbook of child psychology* (4th ed.). E. Mavis Hetherington (Ed.), *Vol. 4: Socialization, personality, and social development* (pp. 643–692). New York: Wiley.

Dweck, C. S., & Gilliard, D. (1975). Expectancy statements as determinants of reaction to failure: Sex differences in persistence and expectancy change. *Journal of Personality and Social Psychology, 32*(6), 1077–1084.

Dykman, R., & Ackerman, P. (1993). Behavioral subtypes of attention deficit disorder. *Exceptional Children, 60,* 132–141.

Dyson, F. J. (1999). *The sun, the genome, and the Internet.* New York: Oxford University Press.

Eals, M., & Silverman, I. (1994). The hunter-gatherer theory of spatial sex differences: Proximate factors mediating the female advantage in recall of object arrays. *Ethology and Sociobiology, 15*(2), 95–105.

East, P. L. (1998). Racial and ethnic differences in girls' sexual, marital, and birth expectations. *Journal of Marriage and the Family, 60*(1), 150–162.

Easterbrook, M. A. (1999). Faceness or complexity: Evidence from newborn visual tracking of facelike stimuli. *Infant Behavior and Development, 22*(1), 17–35.

Ebbeck, V. (1994). Self-perception and motivational characteristics of tennis participants: The influence of age and skill. *Journal of Applied Sport Psychology, 6,* 71–86.

Eccles, J., Barber, B., Jozefowicz, D., Malenchuk, O., & Vida, M. (1999). Self-evaluations of competence, task values, and self-esteem. In N. G. Johnson, M. C. Roberts, & J. Worell (Eds.), *Beyond appearance: A new look at adolescent girls* (pp. 53–84). Washington, DC: American Psychological Association.

Eccles, J. S., & Roeser, R. W. (1999). School and community influences on human development. In M. H. Bornstein & M. E. Lamb (Eds.), *Developmental psychology: An advanced textbook.* (4th ed. pp. 503–553). Mahwah, NJ: Erlbaum.

Echols, L. D., West, R. F., Stanovich, K. E., & Zehr, K. S. (1996). Using children's literacy activities to predict growth in verbal cognitive skills: A longitudinal investigation. *Journal of Educational Psychology, 88,* 296–304.

Eckerman, C., Whatley, J., & Kutz, S. (1975). Growth of social play with peers during the second year of life. *Developmental Psychology, 11,* 42–49.

Eckerman, C. O., Oehler, J. M., Medvin, M. B., & Hannan, T. E. (1994). Premature newborns as social partners before term age. *Infant Behavior and Development, 17,* 55–70.

Edelman, G. M. (1987). *Neural Darwinism.* New York: Basic Books.

Edwards, D. A. (1969). Early androgen stimulation and aggressive behavior in male and female mice. *Physiology and Behavior, 4,* 333–338.

Edwards, P. (1989). Supporting lower SES mothers' attempts to provide scaffolding for book reading. In J. B. Allen & J. M. Mason (Eds.), *Risk makers, risk takers, and risk breakers* (pp. 222–250). Portsmouth, NH: Heinemann.

Egan, M. C. (1977). Federal nutrition support programs for children. *Pediatric Clinics of North America, 24,* 229–239.

Egan, S. K., Monson, T. C., & Perry, D. G. (1998). Social-cognitive influences on change in aggression over time. *Developmental Psychology, 34*(5) 996–1006.

Egan, S. K., Monson, T. C., & Perry, D. G. (1998). Social-cognitive influences on change in aggression over time. *Developmental Psychology, 68*(5), 996–1006.

Ehri, L. C. (1980). The development of orthographic images. In U. Frith (Ed.), *Cognitive processes in spelling* (pp. 311–338). London: Academic Press.

Ehri, L. C., & Sweet, J. (1991). Fingerpoint-reading of memorized text: What enables beginners to process the print? *Reading Research Quarterly, 26*(4), 442–462.

Eiden, R. D., & Leonard, K. E. (1996). Paternal alcohol use and the mother-infant relationship. *Development and Psychopathology, 8,* 307–323.

Eilers, R. E., Gavin, W., & Wilson, W. R. (1979). Linguistic experience and phonemic perception in infancy: A crosslinguistic study. *Child Development, 50,* 14–18.

Eimas, P. D. (1974). Auditory and linguistic processing of cues for place of articulation by infants. *Perception and Psychophysics, 16,* 513–521.

Eimas, P. D., Siqueland, E. R., Jusczyk, P., & Vigorito, J. (1971). Speech perception in infants. *Science, 171,* 303–306.

Eimas, P. J., & Quinn, P. C. (1994). Studies on the formation of perceptually based basic-level categories in young infants. *Child Development, 65,* 903–917.

Eisenberg, A., Murkoff, H., & Hathaway, S. (1996) *What to Expect When You're Expecting.* New York: Workman.

Eisenberg, N. (1986). *Altruistic emotion, cognition, and behavior.* Hillsdale, NJ: Erlbaum.

Eisenberg, N. (1991). Prosocial development in adolescence. In R. M. Lerner, A. C. Petersen, & J. Brooks-Gunn (Eds.), *Encyclopedia of adolescence.* Vol. 1. (pp. 845–855). New York: Garland.

Eisenberg, N., Carlo, G., Murphy, B., & Van Court, P. (1995). Prosocial development in late adolescence: A longitudinal study. *Child Development, 66,* 1179–1197.

Eisenberg, N., & Fabes, R. A. (1998). Prosocial development. In W. Damon (Editor-in-Chief) and N. Eisenberg (Vol. Ed.), *Handbook of child psychology,* (5th ed.): *Vol. 3. Social, emotional, and personality development* (pp. 701–778). New York: Wiley.

Eisenberg, N., Fabes, R. A., Carlo, G., Speer, A. L., Switzer, G., Karbon, M., & Troyer, D. (1993). The relations of empathy-related emotions and maternal practices to children's comforting behavior. *Journal of Experimental Child Psychology, 55,* 131–150.

Eisenberg, N., Fabes, R. A., Nyman, M., Bernzweig, J., & Pinuelas, A. (1994). The relations of emotionality and regulation to children's anger-related reactions. *Child Development, 65,* 109–128.

Eisenberg, N., Fabes, R. A., Schaller, M., Carlo, G., & Miller, P. A. (1991). The relations of parental characteristics and practices to children's vicarious emotional responding. *Child Development, 62,* 1393–1408.

Eisenberg-Berg, N. (1979). Development of children's pro-social judgment. *Developmental Psychology, 15,* 128–137.

Eizenman, D. R., & Bertenthal, B. I. (1998). Infants' perception of object unity in translating and rotating displays. *Developmental Psychology, 34*(3), 426–434.

Elder, G. H. (1963). Parental power legitimation and its effects on the adolescent. *Sociometry, 26,* 50–65.

Elkind, D. (1967). Egocentrism in adolescence. *Child Development, 38,* 1025–1034.

Elkonin, D. B. (1973). Methods of teaching reading. In. J. Downing (Ed.), *Comparative reading* (pp. 551–579). New York: MacMillan.

Elley, W. B. (1989). Vocabulary acquisition from stories. *Reading Research Quarterly, 24*(2), 174–187.

Elley, W. (1991). Acquiring literacy in a second language: The effect of book based programs. *Language Learning, 41,* 375–411.

Elliot, R., & Vasta, R. (1970). The modeling of sharing: Effects associated with vicarious reinforcement, symbolization, age and generalization. *Journal of Experimental Child Psychology, 10,* 8–15.

Elliott, D. S., Huizinga, D., & Morse, B. J. (1987). Self-reported violent offending: A descriptive analysis of juvenile violent offenders and their offending careers. *Journal of Interpersonal Violence, 1,* 472–514.

Ellis, G. T., & Kekyra, F. (1972). The effect of aggressive cartoons on the behavior of first grade children. *Journal of Psychology, 81,* 37–43.

Ellis, H. C., Ottaway, S. A., Varner, L. J., Becker, A. S., & Moore, B. A. (1997). Emotion, motivation, and text comprehension: The detection of contradictions in passages. *Journal of Experimental Psychology, General, 126,* 131–146.

Ellis, S., & Gauvain, M. (1991). Social and cultural influences on children's collaborative interactions. In L. T. Winnegar & J. Valsiner (Eds.), *Children's development within social contexts* (pp. 155–180). Hillsdale, NJ: Erlbaum.

Elman, J. L., Bates, E. A., Johnson, M. H., Karmiloff-Smith, A., Parisi, D., & Plunkett, K.(1998). *Rethinking innateness: A connectionist perspective on development.* Cambridge, MA: The MIT Press.

Emde, R. N., Biringen, Z., Clyman, R. B., & Oppenheim, D. (1991). The moral self of infancy: Affective core and procedureal knowledge. *Developmental Review, 11,* 251–270.

Emde, R. N., & Gaensbauer, T. (1981). Some emerging models of emotion in human infancy. In K. Immelmann, G. W. Barlow, L. Petrinovich, & M. Main (Eds.), *Behavioral development: The Bielefeld interdisciplinary project* (pp. 568–588). New York: Cambridge University Press.

Emde, R. N., Gaensbauer, T. J., & Harmon, R. J. (1976). Emotional expression in infancy: A behavioral study. *Psychological Issues, A Monograph Series, 10*(7, 37). New York: International Press.

Engleberts, A. C., & deJong, G. A. (1990). Choice of sleeping position for infants: Possible association with cot death. *Archives of Disease in Children,* 65, 462.

Engwall, K. B., & Engwall, D. (1997). *A comparison of eating disorders among student athletes and general college students.* Paper presented at the annual meeting of the Eastern Psychological Association, Washington, DC.

Eppler, M. A. (1995). Development of manipulatory skills and the deployment of attention. *Infant Behavior and Development, 18,* 391–405.

Epstein, L. H., Valoski, A., Wing, R. R., & McCurley, J. (1994). Ten-year outcomes of behavioral family-based treatment for childhood obesity. *Health Psychology, 13*(5), 373–383.

Epstein, L. H., Valoski, A. M., Vara, S. McCurley, J., Wisniewski, L., Kalarchian, M. A., Klein, K. R., & Shrager, L. R. (1995). Effects of decreasing sedentary behavior and increasing activity on weight change in obese children. *Health Psychology, 14,* 109–115.

Epstein, L. H., Wing, R. R., & Valoski, A. (1985). Childhood obesity. *Pediatric Clinics of North America, 32*(2), 363–379.

Erb, T. O. (1992). What team organization can do for teachers. In J. H. Lounsbury (Eds.), *Connecting the curriculum through interdisciplinary instruction* (pp. 7–14). Columbus, OH: National Middle School Association.

Erhardt, D., & Hinshaw, S. P. (1994). Initial sociometric impressions of attention-deficit hyperactivity disorder and comparison in boys: Predictions from social behaviors and from nonbehavioral variables. *Journal of Consulting and Clinical Psychology, 62*(4), 833–842.

Erickson, D. (1998). Informational literacy in the middle grades. *The Helen Dwight Reid Educational Foundation.* Electric Library Document.

Ericsson, K. A. (Ed.). (1996). *The road to excellence: The acquisition of expert performance in the arts and sciences, sports, and games.* Mahwah, NJ: Erlbaum.

Erikson, E. H. (1950). *Childhood and society.* New York: Norton.

Erikson, E. H. (1963). *Childhood and society* (2nd edition). New York: Norton.

Erikson, E. H. (1968). Psychosocial identity. In *International encyclopedia of social sciences* (pp. 61–65). New York: Crowell-Collier.

Erikson, P. S., Gennser, G., Lofgran, O., & Nilsson, K. (1983). Acute effects of maternal smoking on fetal breathing and movements. *Obstetrics and Gynecology, 61*(3), 367–372.

Eriksson, M., & Berglund, E. (1999). Swedish early communicative development inventories: Words and gestures. *First Languge, 19*(55), 055–090.

Ernst, M. P., Pangrazi, R. P., & Corbin, C. B. (1998). Physical education: Making a transition toward activity. *Journal of Physical Education, Recreation, and Dance, 69*(9), 29–32.

Eron, L. D., Walder, L. O., & Lefkowitz, M. M. (1971). *Learning of aggression in children.* Boston: Little, Brown.

Erting, C., Prezioso, C., & Hynes, M. O. (1990). The interactional context of deaf mother-infant communication. In V. Volterra & C. Erting (Eds.), *From gesture to language in deaf and hearing children.* Berlin: Springer-Verlag.

Escarce, M. E. W. (1989). A cross-cultural study of Nepalese neonatal behavior. In J. K. Nugent, B. M. Lester, & T. B. Brazelton (Eds.), *The cultural context of infancy: Vol. 1: Biology, culture, and infant development* (pp. 65–86). Norwood, NJ: Ablex.

Etnier, J. L., & Landers, D. M. (1995). Brain function and exercise: Current perspectives. *Sports Medicine, 19*(2), 81–85.

Evans, K. (1999a). Help at hand for drink problems. *Health Education Authority.* Retrieved March 2000 from the World Wide Web: www.hea.org.uk/press/275998.html

Evans, K. (1999b). School children and health: New Survey shows the bullied also bully. *Health Education Authority.* Retrieved March 2000 from the World Wide Web: www.hea.org.uk/press/949910.html

Exline, J. J., & Lobel, M. (1999). The perils of outperformance: Sensitivity about being the target of a threatening upward comparison. *Psychological Bulletin, 125*(3), 307–337.

Eyre, S. L., Auerswald, C., Hoffman, V., & Millstein, S. G. (1998). *Journal of Health Psychology, 3*(3), 393–406.

Fagot, B. I. (1997). Attachment, parenting, and peer interactions of toddler children. *Developmental Psychology, 33,* 489–499.

Fairburn, C. G., Shafran, R., & Cooper, Z. (1999). A cognitive behavioral theory of anorexia nervosa. *Behaviour Research and Therapy, 37*(1), 1–13.

Fantz, R. L. (1963). Pattern vision in newborn infants. *Science, 140,* 296–297.

Fantz, R. L., Ordy, J. M., & Udelf, M. S. (1962). Maturation of patterns of vision in infants during the first six months. *Journal of Comparative and Physiological Psychology, 55,* 907–917.

Farrar, M. J. (1990). Discourse and the acquisition of grammatical morphemes. *Journal of Child Language, 17,* 607–624.

Farrar, M. J. (1992). Negative evidence and grammatical morpheme acquisition. *Developmental Psychology, 28*(1), 90–98.

Farrington, D. P., & West, D. J. (1971). A comparison between early delinquents and young aggressives. *British Journal of Criminology, 11,* 341–358.

Farrior, E. S., & Ruwe, C. H. (1987). Women, Infants, and Children Program prenatal participation and dietary intakes. *Nutrition Research, 7,* 451–459.

Farver, J. (1993). Cultural differences in scaffolding play: A comparison of American and Mexican mother-child and sibling-child pairs. In K. MacDonald (Ed.), *Parent-child play: Description and implications.* Albany, NY: State University of New York Press.

Farver, J., & Wimbarti, S. (1995). Indonesian toddlers' social play with their mothers and older siblings. *Child Development, 66*(5), 1493–1503.

Farver, J. A., & Shin, Y. L. (1997). Social pretend play in Korean- and Anglo-American Preschoolers. *Child Development, 68,* 544–556.

Faukner, A. H., & Cranston, K. (1998). Correlates of same-sex sexual behavior in a random sample of Massachusetts high school students. *American Journal of Public Health, 88*(2), 262–266.

Fein, G. G. (1975). A transformational analysis of pretending. *Developmental Psychology, 11*(3), 291–296.

Fein, G. G. (1981). Pretend play in childhood: An integrative review. *Child Development, 52,* 1095–1118.

Fein, G. G. (1984). The self-building potential of make-believe play, or "I got a fish, all by myself. " In T. D. Yawkey & A. D. Pellegrini (Eds.), *Child's play: Developmental and applied* (pp. 125–142). Hillsdale, NJ: Erlbaum.

Fein, G. G., Johnson, D., Kosson, N., Stork, L., & Wasserman, L. (1975). Sex stereotypes and preferences in the toy choices of 20-month-old boys and girls. *Developmental Psychology, 11*(4), 527–528.

Fein, G. G., & Apfel, N. (1979). Some preliminary observations on knowing and pretending. In N. Smith & M. Franklin (Eds.), *Symbolic functioning in childhood.* Hillsdale, NJ: Erlbaum.

Fein, G. G., & Fryer, M. G. (1995). Maternal contributions to early symbolic play competence. *Developmental Review, 15,* 367–381.

Fein, G., & Rivkin, M. (Eds.). (1986). *The young child at play: Reviews of research* (Vol. 4). Washington, DC: National Association for the Education of Young Children.

Feingold, A. (1988). Cognitive gender differences are disappearing. *American Psychologist, 43,* 95–103.

Feingold, A. (1993). Cognitive gender differences: A developmental perspective. *Sex Roles, 29,* 91–112.

Feinman, S., & Lewis, M. (1983). Social referencing at ten months: A second-order effect on infants' responses to strangers. *Child Development, 54*(4), 878–887.

Feist, G. J. (1998). A meta-analysis of personality in scientific and artistic creativity. *Personality and Social Psychology Review, 2*(4), 290–309.

Feldman, H. M., Dollaghan, C. A., Campbell, T. E., Kurs-Lasky, M., Janosky, J. E., & Paradise, J. L. (2000). Measurement properties of the MacArthur Communicative Development Inventories at ages one and two years. *Child Development, 71*(2), 310–322.

Feldman, R., Greenbaum, C. W., Mayes, L. C., & Erlich, S. H. (1997). Change in mother-infant interactive behavior: Relations to change in the mother, the infant, and the social context. *Infant Behavior and Development, 20,* 151–163.

Feldman, S. S., & Wood, D. N. (1994). Parents' expectations for preadolescent sons' behavioral autonomy: A longitudinal study of correlates and outcomes. *Journal of Research on Adolescence, 4*(1), 45–70.

Felson, R. B., & Trudeau, L. (1991). Gender differences in mathematics performance. *Social Psychology Quarterly, 54,* 113–126.

Fenson, L. (1984). Developmental trends for action and speech in pretend play. In I. Bretherton (Ed.), *Symbolic play* (pp. 249–270). New York: Academic Press.

Fenson, L., Dale, P. S., Reznick, J. S., Bates, E., Thal, D. J., & Pethick, S. J. (1994). Variability in early communicative development. *Monographs of the Society for Research in Child Development, 59*(5), Serial No. 242.

Fenson, L., Kagan, J., Kearsley, R., Zelazo, P. (1976). The developmental progression of manipulative play in the first two years. *Child Development, 47,* 232–236.

Fenson, L., & Ramsay, D. S. (1980). Decentration and integration of the child's play in the second year. *Child Development, 51,* 171–178.

Ferguson, C. A. (1964). Baby talk in six languages. *American Anthropologist, 66,* 103–114.

Ferguson, C. A. (1978). Talking to children: A search for universals. In J. H. Greenberg (Ed.), *Universals of human language.* Standard, CA: Stanford University Press.

Ferguson, C. A., & Farwell, C. B. (1975). Words and sounds in early language acquisition. *Language, 51*(2), 419–439.

Fernald, A. (1993). Approval and disapproval: Infant responsiveness to vocal affect in familiar and unfamiliar languages. *Child Development, 64*(3), 657–674.

Fernald, A., & Kuhl, P. K. (1987). Acoustic determinants of infant preference for motherese speech. *Infant Behavior and Development, 10,* 279–293.

Fernald, A., & Morikawa, H. (1993). Common themes and cultural variations in Japanese and American mothers' speech to infants. *Child Development,* 637–656.

Fernald, A., Pinto, J. P., Swingley, D., Weinberg, A., & McRoberts, G. W. (1998). Rapid gains in speed of verbal processing by infants in the 2nd year. *Psychological Science, 9*(3), 228–231,

Fernald, A., & Simon, T. (1984). Expanded intonation contours in mothers' speech to newborns. *Developmental Psychology, 20,* 104–113.

Fernald, A., Taeschner, T., Dunn, J., Papousek, M., deBoysson-Bardies, B., & Fukui, L. (1989). A cross-language study of prosodic modifications in mothers' and fathers' speech to preverbal infants. *Journal of Child Language, 16,* 477–501.

Ferrara, R. A., & Palinesar, A. S. (1991). Interactive learning and individual understanding: The case of reading and mathematics. In L. T. Landsmann (Ed.), *Culture, Schooling and psychological development* (pp. 136–170), Norwood, NJ: Ablex.

Ferreiro, E., & Teberosky, A. (1982). *Literacy before schooling.* Portsmouth, NH: Heinemann.

Field, T., Demsey, J., & Shuman, H. H. (1983). Five-year follow-up of preterm respiratory distress syndrome and post-term postmaturity syndrome infants. In T. Field & A. Sostek (Eds.), *Infants born at risk: Physiological, perceptual, and cognitive processes* (pp. 317–335). New York: Grune & Stratton.

Field, T., Healy, B., & LeBlanc, W. P. (1989). Sharing and synchrony of behavior states and heart rate in non-depressed versus depressed mother-infant interactions. *Infant Behavior and Development, 12,* 357–376.

Field, T., Lang, C., Yando, R., & Bendell, D. (1995). Adolescents' intimacy with parents and friends. *Adolescence, 30*(117), 133–140.

Field, T., Schanberg, S. M., Scafidi, F., Bauer, C. R., Vega-Lahr, N., Garcia, N., Nystrom, J., & Kuhn, C. M. (1986). Tactile/kinesthetic stimulation effects on preterm neonates. *Pediatrics, 77,* 654–658.

Field, T. M., Cohen, D., Garcia, R., & Greenberg, R. (1984). Mother-stranger face discrimination by the newborn. *Infant Behavior and Development, 7,* 19–25.

Fiese, B. M. (1990). Playful relationships: A contextual analysis of mother-toddler interaction and symbolic play. *Child Development, 61,* 1648–1656.

Figueroa-Colon, R., Mayo, M. S., Aldridge, R. A., Winder, T., & Weinsier, R. (1998). Body composition changes in Caucasian and African American children and adolescents with obesity using dual-energy X-ray absorptiometry measurements after a 10-week weight loss program. *Obesity Research, 6,* 326–331.

Fincham, F., Hokoda, A., & Sanders, R. (1989). Learned helplessness, test anxiety, and academic achievement: A longitudinal analysis. *Child Development, 60*(1), 138–145.

Fishbein, H. D., Lewis, S., & Keiffer, K. (1972). Children's understanding of spatial relations: Coordination of perspectives. *Developmental Psychology, 7,* 21–33.

Fisher, C. (1996). Structural limits on verb mapping: The role of analogy in children's interpretations of sentences. *Cognitive Psychology, 31,* 41–81.

Fisher, C., & Tokura, H. (1996). Prosody in speech to infants: Direct and indirect acoustic cues to syntactic structure. In J. L. Morgan & K. Demuth (Eds.), *Signal to syntax.* Mahwah, NJ: Erlbaum.

Fisher, C., Hall, D. G., Rakowitz, S., & Gleitman, L. R. (1994). When it is better to receive than to give: Syntactic and conceptual constraints on vocabulary growth. *Lingua, 92,* 333–375.

Fisher, L., Harris, V. G., & VanGuren, J. (1980). Assessment of a pilot child playground injury prevention project in New York State. *American Journal of Public Health, 70,* 1000–1007.

Fitzgerald, N. (2000). Teen author *Scholastic Action, 23*(8), 14–16.

Fivush, R. (1984). Learning about school: The development of kindergartners' school scripts. *Child Development, 55,* 1697–1709.

Fivush, R., Gray, J. T., & Fromhoff, F. A. (1987). Two-year-olds talk about the past. *Cognitive Development, 2,* 393–409.

Fivush, R., Kuebli, J., & Clubb, P. A. (1992). The structure of events and event representations: A developmental analysis. *Child Development, 63,* 188–201.

Flaming, D., & Morse, J. M. (1991). Minimizing embarrassment: Boys' experiences of pubertal changes. *Issues in Comprehensive Pediatric Nursing, 14*(4), 211–230.

Flavell, J. H. (1985). *Cognitive development.* Englewood Cliffs, NJ: Prentice-Hall.

Flavell, J. H. (1999). Cognitive development: Children's knowledge about the mind. In J. T. Spence (Ed.), *Annual review of psychology,* (Vol. 50, pp. 21–45). Palo Alto, CA: Annual Reviews.

Flavell, J. H., Green, F. L., & Flavell, E. R. (1995). Young children's knowledge about thinking. *Monographs of the Society for Research in Child Development, 60*(1, Serial No. 243).

Flavell, J. H., & Miller, P. H. (1998). Social cognition. In W. Damon (Editor-in-Chief) and D. Kuhn & R. S. Siegler (Vol. Eds.), *Handbook of child psychology* (5th ed.): *Vol. 2. Cognition, perception, and language* (pp. 851–892). New York: Wiley.

Flavell, J. H., Miller, P. H., & Miller, S. A. (1993). *Cognitive development.* Englewood Cliffs, NJ: Prentice-Hall.

Forsyth, G. A., Altermatt, T. W., & Bohling, P. H. (1998). *Improving strength-of-relationship interpretations of research reports.* Paper presented at the Annual Meetings of the Eastern Psychological Association, Boston, MA.

Forsyth, G. A., Altermatt, E. R., & Forsyth, P. D. (1997). *Humor, emotional empathy, creativity, and cognitive dissonance.* Paper presented at the annual convention of The American Psychological Association, Chicago, Illinois.

Forsyth, G. A., & Bohling, P. H. (1999). *Understanding statistics and behavioral research.* Acton, MA: Copley Publishing.

Forsyth, G. A., & Forsyth, P. D. (1999, August). *Improving general psychology performance with SQ4R support materials.* Paper presented at the Annual Meeting of the American Psychological Association. Boston, MA.

Forsyth, G. A., Woodring, T., & Forsyth, P. D. (1994, August). *The effect of SQ4R training on retention: Developmental psychology.* Paper presented at the Annual Meetings of the American Psychological Association, Los Angeles.

Fox, N. (Ed.). (1994). The development of emotion: Biological and behavioral considerations. *Monographs of the Society for Research in Child Development, 59*(2–3, Serial No 240), 208–227.

Fox, N. A., Kimmerly, N. L., & Schafer, W. D. (1991). Attachment to mother/attachment to father: A meta-analysis. *Child Development, 62,* 210–225.

Fox, N. A., & Stifter, C. A. (1989). Biological and behavior differences in infant reactivity and regulation. In G. A. Kohnstamm, J. E. Bates, & M. K. Rothbart (Eds.), *Temperament in childhood.* Chichester, England: Wiley.

Fraiberg, S. (1975). Intervention in infancy: A program for blind infants. In B. Z. Friedlander, G. M. Steritt, & G. E. Kirk (Eds.), *Exceptional infant* (Vol. 1). New York: Brunner/Mazel.

Fraiberg, S. (1977). *Insights from the blind: Comparative studies of blind and sighted infants.* New York: Plenum.

Francis, S. (Ed.). (1999). Building a healthy child. *National PTA.* Retrieved March 2000 from the World Wide Web: http://www.pta.org/programs/ourhealth/9904/building.htm

Francis, S. (Ed.). (1999). HIV prevention for our kids: Our Health. *National PTA* Retrieved March 2000 from the World Wide Web: www.pta.org

Franco, F., & Butterworth, G. (1996). Pointing and social awareness: Declaring and requesting in the second year. *Journal of Child Language, 23,* 307–336.

Frank, D., & Zeisel, S. (1988). Failure-to-thrive. *Pediatric Clinics of North America, 35,* 1187–1206.

Frank, D., Zuckerman, B., Reece, H., Amaro, H., Hingson, R., Fried, L., Cabral, H., Levenson, S., Kayne, H., Vinci, R., Bauchnmer, H., & Parker, S. (1988). Cocaine use during pregnancy: Prevalence and correlates. *Pediatrics, 82,* 888–895.

Frederici, A. D., & Wessels, J. M. I. (1993). Phonotactic knowledge and its use in infant speech perception. *Perception and Psychophysics, 54,* 287–295.

Frederiksen, N. (1994). The integration of testing with teaching: Applications of cognitive psychology in instruction. *American Journal of Education, 102,* 527–564.

Freed, G. E. (1999). Apnea of prematurity and risk for sudden infant death syndrome. *Pediatrics, 104* 297–298.

Freed, G. E., Steinschneider, A., Glassman, M., & Winn, K. (1994). Sudden infant death syndrome prevention and an understanding of selected clinical issues. *Pediatric Clinics of North America, 41*(5), 967–985.

Freedland, R. L., & Bertenthal, B. I. (1994). Developmental changes in interlimb coordination: Transition to hands-and-knees climbing. *Psychological Science, 5,* 26–32.

Freedman, D. S., Srinivasan, S. R., Valdez, R. A., Williamson, D. F., & Berenson, G. S. (1997). Secular increases in relative weight and adiposity among children over two decades: the Bogalusa heart study. *Pediatrics, 88,* 420–426.

French, S. A., Perry, C. L., Leon, G. R., & Fulkerson, J. A. (1994). Weight concerns, dieting behavior, and smoking initiation among adolescents: A prospective study. *American Journal of Public Health, 84,* 1818–1820.

Freud, S. (1925). Instincts and their vicissitudes. In S. Freud, *Collected papers* (Vol. 4). London: Institutes for Psychoanalysis & Hogarth Press.

Freund, L. S., Baker, L., & Sonnenschein, S. (1990). Developmental changes in strategic approaches to classification. *Journal of Experimental Child Psychology, 49,* 343–362.

Frey, K. S., & Ruble, D. N. (1987). What children say about classroom performance: Sex and grade differences in perceived competence. *Child Development, 58,* 1066–1078.

Fried-Cassorla, A. (1995). *In-line skating.* Rocklin, CA: Prima.

Friedlander, S. (1994). Does your school's physical education program measure up? *Parents playbook: Sports illustrated for kids supplement, 6,* 12–13.

Friedman, S. C., Jacobs, B. S., & Wertmann, A. W. (1981). Preterms of low medical risk: Spontaneous behaviors and soothability at expected date of birth. *Infant Behavior and Development, 5*(1), 3–10.

Friedrich, L. K., & Stein, A. H. (1973). Aggressive and prosocial television programs and the natural behavior of preschool children. *Monographs of the Society for Research in Child Development, 38*(151).

Frisch, J. L. (1977). Sex stereotypes in adult-infant play. *Child Development, 48,* 1671–1675.

Frisch, R. E. (1991). Puberty and body fat. In R. M. Lerner, A. C. Peterson, & J. Brooks-Gunn (Eds.), *Encyclopedia of adolescence* (Vol. 2, pp. 884–892). New York: Garland.

Frodi, A. M., & Lamb, M. E. (1978). Fathers' and mothers' responses to the face and cries of normal and premature infants. *Developmental Psychology, 14*(5), 490–498.

Frydenberg, E., & Lewis R. (1996). Social issues: What concerns young people and how they cope? *Peace and conflict: Journal of Peace Psychology, 2*(3), 271–283.

Fuligni, A. J., & Eccles, J. S. (1993). Perceived parent-child relationships and early adolescents' orientation toward peers. *Developmental Psychology, 29,* 622–632.

Fuligni, A. J., Eccles, J. S., & Barber, B. L. (1995). The long term effects of seventh-grade ability grouping in mathematics. *Journal of Early Adolescence, 15*(1), 58–59.

Furger, R. (1998). *Does Jane compute? Preserving our daughters' place in the cyber revolution.* New York: Warner.

Furrow, D., & Nelson, K. (1984). Environmental correlates of individual differences in language acquisition. *Journal of Child Language, 11,* 523–534.

Furrow, D., Nelson, K., & Benedict, H. (1979). Mothers' speech to children and syntactic development: Some simple relationships. *Journal of Child Language, 6,* 423–442.

Furstenberg, F. F. (1993). How families manage risk and opportunity in dangerous neighborhoods. In W. J. Wilson (Ed.), *Sociology and the public agenda* (pp. 231–258). Newbury Park, CA: Sage.

Fuson, K. C. (1992). Research on learning and teaching addition and subtraction of whole numbers. In G. Leinhardt, R. T. Putnam, & R. A. Hattrup (Eds.), *The analysis of arithmetic for mathematics teaching* (pp. 53–187). Hillsdale, NJ: Erlbaum.

Fuson, K. C., & Kwon, Y. (1992a). Korean children's understanding of multidigit addition and subtraction. *Child Development, 63,* 491–506.

Fuson, K. C., & Kwon, Y. (1992b). Korean children's single-digit addition and subtraction: Numbers structured by ten. *Journal for Research in Mathematics Education, 23,* 148–165.

Fussel, S. R., & Krauss, R. M. (1992). Coordination of knowledge in communications: Effects of speakers' assumptions about what others know. *Journal of Personality and Social Psychology, 62,* 378–391.

Gallagher, J. J. (1994). Teaching and learning: New models. *Annual Review of Psychology, 45,* 171–195.

Gallahue, D. L., & Ozmun, J. C. (1995). *Understanding motor development: Infants, children, adolescents, adults.* Madison, WI: Brown & Benchmark.

Gallahue, D. L., & Ozmun, J. C. (1998). *Understanding motor development.* New York: McGraw Hill.

Galler, J. R. (1987). The interaction of nutrition and the environment in behavioral development. In J. Dobbing (Ed.), *Early nutrition and later achievement,* (pp. 125–207).

Gallick, J. D. (1999). Do they read for pleasure? Recreational reading habits of college students. *Journal of Adolescents & Adult Literacy, 42*(6), 480–488.

Galligan, R. (1986). Intonation with single words: Purposive and grammatical use. *Journal of Child Language, 14,* 1–21.

Galloway, M. K., & Balaban, M. T. (1998, February). *Home and school influences on the academic environment of adolescents.* Paper presented at the annual meeting of the Eastern Psychological Association meeting, Boston, MA.

Galton, F. (1869). *Hereditary genius: An inquiry into its laws and consequences.* London: Macmillan.

Garbarino, J. (1980). Some thoughts on school size and its effects on adolescent development. *Journal of Youth and Adolescence, 9,* 19–31.

Garbarino, J. (1982). Sociocultural risk: Dangers to competence. In C. B. Kopp & J. B. Krako (Eds.), *The child: Development in a social context.* Reading, MA: Addison-Wesley.

Garbarino, J. (1996, August). *Children in war and peace: At home and abroad.* Invited address presented at the 104th Annual Convention of the American Psychological Association, Toronto, Ontario.

Garbarino, J. (1999a). *Lost boys: Why our sons turn violent and how we can save them.* New York: The Free Press.

Garbarino, J. (1999b, August). *Reclaiming lost boys: From survival to resilience.* Presentation in the Fostering Resilient Children and Families symposium at the Annual Meetings of the American Psychological Association. Boston, MA.

Garcia Coll, C. T., Hoffman, J., & Oh, W. (1987). The social ecology and early parenting of Caucasian adolescent mothers. *Child Development, 58*(4), 955–963.

Gardner, H. (1980). *Artful scribbles.* New York: Basic Books.

Gardner, H. (1983). *Frames of mind: The theory of multiple intelligences.* New York: Basic Books.

Gardner, H. (1991). *The unschooled mind: How children think and how schools should teach.* New York: Basic Books.

Gardner, H. (1995). On multiple intelligences: ECT interview of the month. *Early Childhood Today, 10*(1), 30–332.

Gardner, M. K., & Sternberg, R. J. (1994). Novelty and intelligence. In R. J. Sternberg & R. K. Wagner (Eds.), *Mind in context: Interactionist perspectives on human intelligence* (pp. 38–73). New York: Cambridge University Press.

Garnier, H. E., & Stein, J. A. (1998). Values and the family: Risk and protective factors for adolescent problem behaviors. *Youth and Society, 30*(1), 89–120.

Garnier, H. E., & Stein, J. A., & Jacobs, J. K. (1997). The process of dropping out of high school: A 19-year perspective. *American Educational Research Journal, 34* 395–419.

Garofalo, R., & Wolf, R. C. (1999, May). Sexual orientation and risk of suicide attempts among a representative sample of youth. *Archives of Pediatrics & Adolescent Medicine,* pp. 487–493.

Garrod, A., Smulyan, L., Powers, S. I., & Kilkenny, R. (1999). *Adolescent portraits: Identity, relationships and challenges.* Boston: Allyn & Bacon.

Garver, K. L., & Garver, B. (1994). The human genome project and eugenic concerns. *American Journal of Human Genetics, 54,* 148–158.

Garvey, C. (1990). *Play* (expanded version). Cambridge, MA: Harvard University Press.

Gaskins, S. (1994). Symbolic play in a Mayan village. *Merrill-Palmer Quarterly, 40,* 344–359.

Gathercole, V. C. (1985). More and more and more about more. *Journal of Experimental Child Psychology, 40,* 73–104.

Gawlick, M., & Bonifazi, D. Z. (1999, April). *Bulimia nervosa, impulsivity, addictive personality, and social support.* Paper presented at the annual meeting of the Eastern Psychological Association, Providence, RI.

Ge, A., Conger, R. D., Lorenz, F. O., Shanahan, M., & Elder, G. H. (1995). Mutual influences in parent and adolescent psychological distress. *Developmental Psychology, 31*(3), 406–419.

Ge, X., Conger, R. D., & Elder, G. H., Jr. (1996). Coming of age too early: Pubertal influences on girls' vulnerability to psychological distress. *Child Development, 67,* 3386–3400.

Geary, D. C., Salthouse, T. A., Chen, G. P., & Fan, L. (1996). Are East Asian versus American differences in arithmetic ability a recent phenomenon? *Developmental Psychology, 32*(2), 254–262.

Geier, T. (1995, September 11). Sex and violence on TV. *U.S. News and World Report, 119*(10), 62–67.

Geller, L. G. (1985). *Word play and language learning for children.* Urbana, IL: National Council of Teachers of English.

Gelman, R. (1969). Conservation acquisition: A problem of learning to attend to relevant attributes. *Journal of Experimental Child Psychology, 7,* 167–187.

Gelman, R., & Baillargeon, R. (1983). A review of some Piagetian concepts. In P. H. Mussen, J. H. Flavell, & E. M. Markman (Eds.), *Handbook of child psychology.* (4th ed, Vol. 3, pp. 167–221). New York: Wiley.

Gelman, R., & Brenneman, K. (1994). Domain specificity and cultural variation are not inconsistent. In L. A. Hirschfeld & S. Gelman (Eds.), *Mapping the mind: Domain specificity in cognition and culture.* New York: Cambridge University Press.

Gelman, R., & Gallistel, C. R. (1978). *The child's understanding of number.* Cambridge, MA: Harvard University Press.

Gelman, R., & Meck, E. (1983). Preschoolers' counting: Principles before skill. *Cognition, 13,* 343–359.

Gelman, S. A., Croft, W., Fu, P., Clausner, T., & Gottfried, G. (1998). Why is a pomegranate an apple? The role of shape, taxonomic relatedness, and prior lexical knowledge in children's overextensions of apple and dog. *Journal of Child Language, 25,* 267–291.

Gelman, S. A., & Gottfried, G. M. (1996). Children's causal explanations of animate and inanimate motion. *Child Development, 67,* 1970–1987.

Gentner, D., & Holyoak, K. (1972). Meaning and learning by analogy: Introduction. *American Psychologist, 52*(1), 32–34.

Gentner, D., & Holyoak, K. (1997). Reasoning and learning by analogy: Introduction. *American Psychologist, 52*(1), 32–34.

Gentner, D., & Markman, A. B. (1997). Structure mapping in analogy and similarity. *American Psychologist, 52,* 45–56.

Gentner, D., & Rattermann, M. J. (1992). Language and the career of similarity. In S. A. Gelman & J. P. Byrnes (Eds.), *Perspectives on thought and language: Interrelations in development* (pp. 225–227). Cambridge, UK: Cambridge University Press.

George, C., & Main, M. (1981). Social interactions of young abused children: Approach, avoidance, aggression. In E. M. Hetherington & R. D. Parke (Eds.), *Contemporary readings in child psychology* (2nd ed.). New York: McGraw-Hill.

Gersten, R., Keating, T. J., & Brengelman, S. U. (1995). Toward an understanding of effective instructional practices for language minority students: Findings from naturalistic research. *Read Perspectives, 2*(1), 55–79.

Gesell, A., & Thompson, H. (1929). Learning and growth in identical infant twins: An experimental study of the method of co-twin control. *Genetic Psychology Monographs, 6,* 1–124.

Gibbs, R. W., & Beitel, D. (1995). What proverb understanding reveals about how people think. *Psychological Bulletin, 118,* 133–154.

Gibson, E. (1969). *Principles of perceptual learning and development.* Englewood Cliffs, NJ: Prentice-Hall.

Gibson, E. J., & Walk, R. (1960). The "visual cliff." *Scientific American, 202,* 64–72.

Gibson, J. (1979). *The ecological approach to visual perception.* Boston: Houghton Mifflin.

Gidding, S. S., Deckelbaum, R. J., Strong, W., & Moller, J. H. (1995). Improving children's heart health: A report from the American Heart Association's children's heart health conference. *Journal of School Health, 65*(4), 129–132.

Gil, D. G. (1970). *Violence against children: Physical child abuse in the United States.* Cambridge, MA: Harvard University Press.

Gilligan, C. (1977). In a different voice: Women's conceptions of the self and of morality. *Harvard Educational Review, 47,* 481–517.

Ginsberg, G. P., & Kilbourne, B. K. (1988). Emergence of vocal alternation in mother-infant interchanges. *Journal of Child Language, 15,* 221–235.

Ginsberg, H. P., & Opper, S. (1988). *Piaget's theory of intellectual development* (3rd ed.). Englewood Cliffs, NJ: Prentice-Hall.

Giovino, G. A., Shelton, D. M., & Schooley, M. W. (1993). Trends in cigarette smoking cessation in the United States. *Tobacco Control, 2*(Suppl.), 53–510.

Gjone, H., & Stevenson, J. (1997). A longitudinal twin study of temperament and behavior problems: Common genetic or environmental influences? *Journal of the American Academy of Child and Adolescent Psychiatry, 36*(10), 1448–1456.

Gladue, B. A., Boechler, M., & McCaul, K. D. (1989). Hormonal responses to competition in human males. *Aggressive Behavior, 17,* 313–326.

Gleason, J. B. (1973). Code switching in children's language. In T. E. Moore (Ed.), *Cognitive development and the acquisition of language.* New York: Academic Press.

Gleitman, L. (1990). The structural sources of verb meanings. *Language Acquisition, 1,* 3–5.

Gleitman, L., Newport, E. L., & Gleitman, H. (1984). The current status of the motherese hypothesis. *Journal of Child Language, 11,* 43–79.

Gleitman, L. R., & Gillette, J. (1995). The role of syntax in verb learning. In P. Fletcher & B. MacWhinney (Eds.), *The handbook of child language* (pp. 413–427). Oxford: Basil Blackwell.

Glover, L. (1999). Schools get sun know how. *Health Education Authority.* Retrieved March 2000 from the World Wide Web: www.hea.org.uk/press/172997.html

Glucksberg, S., Krauss, R. M., & Higgins, E. T. (1975). The development of referential communication skills. In F. D. Horowitz (Ed.), *Reviews of child development research* (Vol. 4). Chicago: University of Chicago Press.

Gnepp, J. (1983). Children's social sensitivity: Inferring emotions from conflicting cues. *Developmental Psychology, 19,* 805–814.

Gnepp, J., & Hess, D. L. R. (1986). Children's understanding of verbal and facial display rules. *Developmental Psychology, 22,* 103–108.

Gnepp, J., McKee, E., & Domanic, J. A. (1987). Children's use of situational information to infer emotion: Understanding emotionally equivocal situations. *Developmental Psychology, 22*(1), 114–123.

Gold, R. (1978). On the meaning of non-conservation. In A. M. Lesgold, J. W. Pelligrino, S. D. Fokkema, & R. Glaser (Eds.), *Cognitive psychology and instruction.* New York: Plenum.

Goldberg, L., Brinkley, G., and Kukar, J. (1998). *Pregnancy to parenthood.* Garden City Park, NY: Avery.

Goldberg, R. M. (1995). *The vaccines for children program: A critique.* Washington, DC: American Enterprise Institute.

Goldberg, S. (1982). Some biological aspects of early parent-infant interaction. In S. Moore & C. Cooper (Eds.), *The young child: Reviews of research* (Vol. 3, pp. 35–36). Washington, DC: National Association for the Education of Young Children.

Goldberg, S. (1983). Parent-infant bonding: Another look. *Child Development, 54*(6), 1355–1382.

Goldfield, B. A. (1993). Noun bias in maternal speech to one-year-olds. *Journal of Child Language, 20,* 85–99.

Goldfield, E. C. (1995). *Emergent forms: Origins and early development of human action and perception.* New York: Oxford University Press.

Goldman, A. S., & Smith, C. W. (1973). Host resistance factors in human milk. *Journal of Pediatrics, 82,* 1082.

Goldsmith, H. H., Buss, K. A., and Lemery, K. S. (1997). Toddler and childhood temperament: Expanded content, stronger genetic evidence, new evidence for the importance of the environment. *Developmental Psychology, 33*(6) 891–905.

Golinkoff, R. M., Hirsch-Pasek, K., Cauley, K. M., & Gordon, L. (1987). The eyes have it: Lexical and syntactic comprehension in a new paradigm. *Journal of Child Language, 14,* 23–45.

Golinkoff, R. M., Shuff-Baley, M., Olguin, R., & Runa, W. (1995). Young children extend novel words at the basic level: Evidence for the principle of categorical scope. *Developmental Psychology, 31*(3), 494–507.

Golomb, C. (1992). *The child's creation of a pictorial world.* Berkeley: University of California Press.

Goncu, A. (1998). Development of intersubjectivity in social pretend play. In M. Woodhead, D. Faulkner, & K. Littleton (Eds.), *Cultural worlds of early childhood* (pp. 117–132). New York: The Open University.

Good, R. H., & Collins, V. (1995). *Evaluating latent assumptions of group differences.* Paper presented at the Annual Meetings of the American Psychological Association. New York, August 11–15.

Goodale, M. A., & Milner, A. D. (1992). Separate visual pathways for perception and action. *Trends in Neuroscience, 15,* 20–25.

Goodenough, E. (1957). Interest in persons as an aspect of sex differences in the early years. *Genetic Psychology Monographs, 55,* 287–323.

Gopnik, A., & Astington, J. W. (1988). Children's understanding of representational change and its relation to the understanding of false belief and the appearance reality distinction. *Child Development, 59*(1), 26–37.

Gopnik, A., & Choi, S. (1990). Relation of maternal language to variation in rate and style of language acquisition. *Journal of Child Language, 20,* 313–342.

Gopnik, A., & Graf, P. (1988). Knowing how you know: Young children's ability to identify and remember the sources of their beliefs. *Child Development, 59*(5), 1366–1371.

Gopnik, A., & Meltzoff, A. N. (1992). Categorization and naming: Basic-level sorting in eighteen-month-olds and its relation to language. *Child Development, 63,* 1091–1103.

Gopnik, A., & Meltzoff, A. N.(1997). *Words, thoughts, and theories.* Cambridge, MA: The MIT Press.

Gordon, R. (2000). *Eating Disorders: Anatomy of a social epidemic.* Boston: Blackwell.

Gosden, R. (1999). *Designing babies! The brave new world of reproductive technology.* New York: W. H. Freeman.

Gottesman, I. (1974). Developmental genetics and ontogenetic psychology: Overdue detente and propositions from a matchmaker. In A. Pick (Ed.), *Minnesota symposium on child psychology.* Minneapolis: University of Minnesota Press.

Gottlieb, G. (1998). Normally occurring environmental and behavioral influences on gene activity: From central dogma to probabilistic epigenesis. *Psychological Review, 105*(4), 792–802.

Gottlieb, G., Wahlsten, G., & Lickliter, R. (1998). The significance of biology for human development: A developmental psychobiological systems view. In W. Damon & R. Lerner (Eds.), *Handbook of child psychology: Vol. 1. Theoretical models of human development* (pp. 233–273). New York: Wiley.

Gottman, J. M. (1986). The world of coordinated play: Same- and cross-sex friendship in young children. In J. M. Gottman & J. G. Parker (Eds.), *Conversations of friends: Speculations on affective development* (pp. 139–191). Cambridge, UK: Cambridge University Press.

Goubet, N., & Clifton, R. K. (1998). Object and event representation in 6 ½-month-old infants. *Developmental Psychology, 34*(1), 63–76.

Gouchie, C., & Kimura, D. (1991). The relationship between testosterone levels and cognitive ability patterns. *Psychoneuroendocrinology, 16,* 323–334.

Gould, J. L., & Marler, P. (1987). Learning by instinct. *Scientific American, 256,* 62–73.

Gowers, S. G., Crisp, A. H., Joughin, N., & Bhat, A. (1991). Premenarcheal anorexia nervosa. *Journal of Child Psychology and Psychiatry, 32*(3), 515–524.

Graber, J. A., Brooks-Gunn, J., & Warren, M. P. (1995). The antecedents of menarchal age: Heredity, family environment, and stressful life events. *Child Development, 66,* 346–359.

Gralinski, J. H., & Kopp, C. B. (1993). Everyday rules for behavior: Mothers' requests to young children. *Developmental Psychology, 29,* 573–584.

Granott, N., & Gardner, H. (1994). When minds meet: Interactions, coincidence, and development in domains of ability. In R. J. Sternberg & R. K. Wagner (Eds.), *Mind in context* (pp. 171–201). New York: Cambridge University Press.

Granrud, C. E., Haake, R. J., & Yonas, A. (1985). Infants' sensitivity to familiar size: The effect of memory on spatial perception. *Perception & Psychophysics, 37*(5), 459–466.

Granrud, C. E., & Yonas, A. (1984). Infants' perception of pictorially specified interposition. *Journal of Experimental Child Psychology, 37*(3), 500–511.

Granthem-McGregor, S., Powell, C., Walker, S., Chang, S., & Fletcher, P. (1994). The long-term follow-up of severely malnourished children who participated in an intervention program. *Child Development, 65*(2), 428–439.

Granucci, P. (1986). *A case study of one child's literacy development from 24 to 36 months.* Unpublished doctoral dissertation, Boston University.

Green, A. H., Gaines, R. W., & Sandgrund, A. (1974). Child abuse: Pathological syndrome of family interaction. *American Journal of Psychiatry, 131,* 882–886.

Greenfield, P. M. (1999, Spring). Cultural change and human development. *New Directions for Child and Adolescent Development, 83.*

Greenough, W., T., Black, J. E., & Wallace, C. S. (1987). Experience and brain development. *Child Development, 58,* 539–559.

Greensher, J., & Mofenson, H. C. (1985). Injuries at play. *Pediatric Clinics of North America, 32*(1), 127–139.

Greshler, S. N., Weis, C. M., and Shapiro, C. (1994, March). *Adolescent social competencies and academic achievement: Correlates of authoritative parenting.* Paper presented at the Eastern Psychological Association Annual Meeting, Providence, R.I.

Grether, J. K., & Schulman, J. (1989). Sudden infant death syndrome and birth weight. *The Journal of Pediatrics, 114*(4), 561–567.

Grieser, D. L., & Kuhl, P. K. (1988). Maternal speech to infants in a tonal language: Support for universal prosodic features in motherese. *Developmental Psychology, 24,* 14–20.

Griffiths, M., & Sutherland, I. (1998). Adolescent gambling and drug use. *Journal of Community and Applied Social Psychology, 8*(6), 423–427.

Grin, T. R., Nelson, L. B., & Jeffers, J. B. (1987). Eye injuries in childhood. *Pediatrics, 80*(1), 13–17.

Grodstein, F., Goldman, M. B., & Cramer, D. W. (1994). Infertility in women and moderate alcohol use. *American Journal of Public Health, 84,* 1429–1432.

Gross, R. T., & Duke, P. M. (1980). The effect of early versus late physical maturation in adolescent behavior. *Pediatric Clinics of North America, 27,* 71–77.

Grunau, R. V., Johnston, C. C., & Craig, K. D. (1990). Neonatal facial and cry response to invasive and non-invasive procedures. *Pain, 42*(3), 295–305.

Grunau, R. V., Whitfield, M. F., & Petrie, J. H. (1994). Pain sensitivity and temperament in extremely low-birth-weight premature toddlers and preterm and full controls. *Pain, 58*(3), 341–346.

Grusec, J. E. (1991). Socializing concern for others in the home. *Developmental Psychology, 27,* 338–342.

Grusec, J. E., & Goodnow, J. J. (1994). Impact of parental discipline methods on the child's internalization of values: A reconceptualization of current points of view. *Developmental Psychology, 30,* 4–19.

Grusec, J. E., Kuczynski, L., Rushton, J. P., & Simutis, Z. M. (1978). Modeling, direct instruction, and attributions: Effects on altruism. *Developmental Psychology, 14,* 51–57.

Grusec, J. E., & Skubinski, S. (1970). Model nurturance, demand characteristics of the modeling experiment, and altruism. *Journal of Personality and Social Psychology, 14,* 352–359.

Guay, F., Boivin, M., & Hodges, E. V. E. (1999). Predicting change in academic achievement: A model of peer experiences and self-system processes. *Journal of Educational Psychology, 91*(1), 105–115.

Guilford, J. P. (1985). The structure-of-intellect model. In B. B. Wolman (Ed.), *Handbook of intelligence* (pp. 225–266). New York: Wiley.

Gullotta, T. P., Adams, G. R., & Markstrom, C. A. (2000). *The adolescent experience.* San Diego: Academic Press.

Gullotta, T. P., & Noyes, L. (1995). The changing paradigm of community health: The role of school-based health centers. *Adolescence, 30*(117), 107–115.

Gunter, B. (1994). The question of media violence. In J. Bryant & D. Zillman (Eds.), *Media effects.* Hillsdale, NJ: Erlbaum.

Guntheroth, W. G., Lohmann, R., & Spiers, P. S. (1990). Risk of sudden infant death syndrome in subsequent siblings. *The Journal of Pediatrics, 116*(4), 520–524.

Gurian, M. (1998). *A fine young man: What parents, mentors and educators can do to shape adolescent boys into exceptional men.* New York: Tarcher/Putnam.

Gustafson, G. E. (1984). Effects of the ability to locomote on infants' social and exploratory behaviors: An experimental study. *Developmental Psychology, 20*(93), 397–405.

Guttmacher, A. (1999). Teratology: A primer. *Vermont Pregnancy Risk Information Service.* Retrieved March 2000 from the World Wide Web: www.vtmed-net.org/~m145037

Haaf, R. (1974). Complexity and facial resemblance as determiners of response to face-like stimuli by 5- and 10-week-old infants. *Journal of Experimental Child Psychology, 18,* 580–587.

Haaf, R. (1977). Visual response to complex face-like patterns by 15- and 20-week-old infants. *Developmental Psychology, 13,* 77–78.

Haaf, R. F., & Bell, R. Q. (1967). A facial dimension in visual discrimination by human infants. *Child Development, 38,* 893–899.

Hack, M., Horbar, J. D., & Malloy, M. H. (1991). Very low birthweight outcomes of the National Institute of Child Health and Human Development Neonate Network. *Pediatrics, 87,* 587–597.

Haden, C. A., Reese, E., & Fivush, R. (1996). Mothers' extratextual comments during storybook reading: Stylistic differences over time and across texts. *Discourse Processes, 21,* 135–169.

Haffner, D. W. (1992). Sexuality education in public schools. *Education Digest, 58*(1), 53–57.

Hagerman, R. J. (1996). Biomedical advances in developmental psychology: The case of Fragile X Syndrome. *Developmental Psychology, 32*(3), 416–424.

Haight, W., & Miller, P. J. (1992). The development of everyday pretend play: A longitudinal study of mothers' participation. *Merrill-Palmer Quarterly, 38*(3), 331–349.

Hainline, L., Riddell, P., Grose-Fifer, J., & Abramov, I. (1992). Development of accommodation and convergence in infancy. Special Issue: Normal and abnormal visual development in infants and children. *Behavioral Brain Research, 49*(10), 33–50.

Haith, M. M. (1980). *Rules that babies look by.* Hillsdale, NJ: Erlbaum.

Haith, M. M., & Benson, J. B. (1998). Infant cognition. In W. Damon (Editor-in-Chief) and D. Kuhn & R. Siegler (Vol. Eds.), *Handbook of child psychology* (5th ed.): Vol. 2. *Cognition, perception, and language* (pp. 199–254). New York: Wiley.

Haith, M. M., Bergman, T., & Moore, M. J. (1977). Eye contact and face scanning in early infancy. *Science, 198,* 853–855.

Hales, D. J., Lozoff, B., Sosa, R., & Kennel, J. H. (1977). Defining the limits of the maternal sensitive period. *Developmental Medicine and Child Neurology, 19,* 454–461.

Halford, G. S. (1993). *Children's understanding: The development of mental models.* Hillsdale, NJ: Erlbaum.

Hall, J. A. Y. (1978). Gender effects in decoding nonverbal cues. *Psychological Bulletin, 85,* 845–857.

Hall, J. A. Y. (1985). *Nonverbal sex differences: Communication accuracy and expressive style.* Baltimore: Johns Hopkins University Press.

Hall, J. A. Y., & Kimura, D. (1995). Sexual orientation and performance on sexually dimorphic motor tasks. *Archives of Sexual Behavior, 24,* 395–407.

Hall, S. S. (2000). Obsession for men. *New York Times Up Front, 132*(12), 12–15.

Halle, P. A., & de Boysson-Bardies, B. (1994). Emergence of an early receptive lexicon: Infants' recognition of words. *Infant Behavior and Development, 17,* 119–129.

Halle, T. G., Kurtz-Costes, B., & Mahoney, J. L. (1997). Family influences on school achievement in low-income African-American children. *Journal of Educational Psychology, 89*(3), 527–537.

Halliday, H. I., Robertson, B., Saugstad, O. D., Speer, C. P., & Curstedt, T. (Eds.). (1998). Recent advances in surfactant research. *Biology of the Neonate: Foetal and Neonatal Research, 74,* 1–58.

Halliday, M. (1975). *Learning how to mean: Explorations in the development of language.* London: Edward Arnold.

Hallman, M., & Gluck, L. (1982). Respiratory distress syndrome—update 1982. *Pediatric Clinics of North America, 29*(5), 1057–1075.

Halpern, C. T., Udry, J. R., Campbell, B., & Suchindran, C. (1999). Effects of body fat on weight concerns, dating, and sexual activity: A longitudinal analysis of Black and White adolescent girls. *Developmental Psychology, 35*(3), 721–736.

Halpern, D. F., & Wright, T. (1996). A process-oriented model of cognitive sex differences (Special issue). *Learning and Individual Differences, 8,* 3–24.

Halpern, D. F. (1997). Sex differences in intelligence. *American Psychologist, 52*(10), 1091–1102.

Hamosh, M. (1998). Protective function of proteins and lipids in human milk. *Biology of the Neonate, 74,* 163–176.

Hampson, J., & Nelson, K. (1993). Relation of maternal language to variation in rate and style of language acquisition. *Journal of Child Language, 20,* 313–342.

Harlow, H. F. (1958). The nature of love. *American Psychologist, 13,* 673–685.

Harris, D. B. (1963). *Children's drawing as measures of intellectual maturity.* New York: Harcourt Brace Jovanovich.

Harris, D. V. (1991). Exercise and fitness during adolescence. In R. M. Lerner, A. C. Peterson, & J. Brooks-Gunn (Eds.), *Encyclopedia of adolescence* (Vol. 1, pp. 324–327). New York: Garland.

Harris, G., Thomas, A., & Booth, D. A. (1990). Development of salt taste in infancy. *Developmental Psychology, 26,* 534–538.

Harris, M., Jones, D., Brookes, S., & Grant, J. (1986). Relations between nonverbal context of maternal speech and rate of language development. *British Journal of Developmental Psychology, 4,* 261–268.

Harris, P. L., & Gross, D. (1988). Children's understanding of real and apparent emotions. In J. W. Astington, P. L. Harris, & D. R. Olson (Eds.), *Developing theories of mind* (pp. 295–314). Cambridge, UK: Cambridge University Press.

Harris, P. L., & Kavanaugh, R. D. (1993). Young children's understanding of pretense. *Monographs of the Society for Research in Child Development, 58*(1, Serial No. 231).

Harris, P. L., Olthof, T., Meerum, T. M., & Hardman, C. E. (1987). Children's knowledge of the situations that provoke emotion. *International Journal of Behavioral Development, 10,* 319–344.

Harris, S. M. (1994). Racial differences in predictors of college women's body image attitudes. *Women and Health, 21,* 89–104.

Harris, T. T., & Fuqua, J. D. (2000). What goes around comes around: Building a community of learners. *Young Children, 55*(1), 44–47.

Harris-Schmidt, G., & Fast, D. (1998). Fragile X syndrome: Genetics, characteristics, and educational implications. In A. F. Rotatori & J. O. Schwenn (Eds.), *Advances in special education: Vol. 11. Issues, practices, and concerns in special education* (pp. 187–222). Greenwich, CT: JAI Press.

Harrist, A. W., Zaia, A. F., Bates, J. E., Dodge, K. A., & Pettit, G. S. (1997). Subtypes of social withdrawal in early childhood: Sociometric status and social-cognitive differences across four years. *Child Development, 68*(2), 278–294.

Harste, J. C., Burke, C. L., & Woodward, V. A. (1981). *Children, their language and world: Initial encounters with print.* Bloomington, IN: College of Education. (NIE Research Grant #NIE-G-79-0132)

Hart, B., & Risley, T. R. (1992). American parenting of language-learning children: Persisting differences in family-child interactions observed in natural home environments. *Developmental Psychology, 28,* 1096–1105.

Hart, B., & Risley, T. (1995). *Meaningful differences in the everyday experiences of young American children.* Baltimore: Brookes.

Harter, S. (1990). Processes underlying adolescent self-concept formation. In R. Montemayor, G. R. Adams, & T. P. Gulotta (Eds.), *From childhood to adolescence: A transitional period*? Newburg Park, CA: Sage.

Harter, S., Alexander, P., & Neimeyer, R. (1988). Long-term effects of incestuous child abuse in college women. Social adjustment, social cognition, and family characteristics. *Journal of Consulting and Clinical Psychology, 56*(1), 5–8.

Harter, S., & Buddin, B. J. (1987). Children's understanding of the simultaneity of two emotions: A five-stage developmental acquisition sequence. *Developmental Psychology, 22*(3), 388–399.

Harter, S., & Whitesell, N. R. (1989). Developmental changes in children's understanding of single, multiple, and blended emotion concepts. In C. Saarni & P. L. Harris (Eds.), *Children's understanding of emotion.* Cambridge, UK: Cambridge University Press.

Hassink, S. (1999). *Is my child obese?* Retrieved March 2000 from the World Wide Web Kidshealth.org.http://kidshealth.org/parent/nutrition/child-obese.html

Hatcher, P. J., & Hulme, C. (1999). Phonemes, rhymes, and intelligence as predictors of children's responsiveness to remedial reading instruction: Evidence from a longitudinal intervention study. *Journal of Experimental Child Psychology, 72,* 130–153.

Hatzichristou, C., & Hopf, D. (1996). A multiperspective comparison of peer sociometric status groups in childhood and adolescence. *Child Development, 67,* 1085–1102.

Hauser, P., Zametkin, A. J., Martinez, P., Vitello, B., Matochik, J. A., Marxson, A. J., & Weintraub, B. D. (1993). Attention deficit hyperactivity disorder in people with generalized resistance to thyroid hormone. *New England Journal of Medicine, 328,* 997–1001.

Haviland, J. (1982). Sex-related pragmatics in infants. *Journal of Communication, 27,* 80–84.

Haviland, J. M., & Lelwica, M. (1987). The induced affect response: 10-week-old infants' responses to three emotion expressions. *Developmental Psychology, 23,* 97–104.

Hawdon, J. M., Key, E., Kolvin, I., & Fundudis, T. (1990). Born too small—is outcome still affected? *Developmental Medicine and Child Neurology, 32,* 943–953.

Haynes, H., White, B. W., & Held, R. (1965). Visual accommodation in human infants. *Science, 148,* 528–530.

Healy, J. M. (1998). *Failure to connect: How computers affect our children's minds—for better and worse.* New York: Simon & Schuster.

Hedges, L. V., & Nowell, A. (1995). Sex differences in mental test scores, variability, and numbers of high scoring individuals. *Science, 269,* 41–45.

Hegarty, M., Mayer, R. E., & Monk, C. (1995). Comprehension of arithmetic word problems: A comparison of successful and unsuccessful problem solvers. *Journal of Educational Psychology, 87*(1), 18–32.

Hegarty, M. P. (1997). Use of inhalants among teens on the rise. *Counseling Today.* Retrieved March 2000 from the World Wide Web: www.uncg.edu/edu/ericcass/substnce/docs/inhalant/htm.

Held, R., Birch, E. E., & Gwiazda, J. (1980). Stereoacuity of human infants. *Proceedings of the National Academy of Sciences, 77.*

Held, R., & Hein, A. (1963). Movement-produced stimulation in the development of visually guided behavior. *Journal of Comparative and Physiological Psychology, 56,* 822–876.

Helwig, C. C. (1995). Adolescents' and young adults' conceptions of civil liberties: Freedom of speech and religion. *Child Development, 66,* 152–166.

Herbst, A. L. (1972). Vaginal and cervical abnormalities after exposure to stilbestrol in utero. *Obstetrics and Gynecology, 40,* 287–298.

Herbst, A. L., Scully, R. E., & Robboy, S. J. (1975). Problems in the examination of DES-exposed females. *Obstetrics and Gynecology, 46,* 353–355.

Herman, P. A., Anderson, R. C., Pearson, P. D., & Nagy, W. E. (1987). Incidental acquisition of word meanings from expositions with varied text features. *Reading Research Quarterly, 22*(3), 263–284.

Herman-Giddens, M. E., Slora, E. J., Wasserman, R. C., Bourdony, C. J., Bhapkar, M. V., Koch, T. G., & Hassemeier, L. M. (1997). Secondary sexual characteristics and menses in young girls seen in office practice: A study from the Pediatric Research in Office Settings Network. *Pediatrics, 99,* 505–512.

Herrman, H. J., & Roberts, M. W. (1987). Preventive dental care: The role of the pediatrician. *Pediatrics, 80*(1), 107–110.

Herrnstein, R. J., & Murray, C. (1994). *The bell curve: Intelligence and class structure in American life.* New York: The Free Press.

Hersher, L., Moore, A. U., & Richmond, R. B. (1958). Effects of modified maternal care in the sheep and goat. *Science, 128,* 1342–1343.

Hess, L. E., & Atkins, M. C. (1995). *Correlates of aggression and victimization in school-age children.* Paper presented at the Biennial Meeting of the Society for Research in Child Development, Indianapolis, IN.

Hewlett, B. S., Lamb, M. E., Shannon, D., Leyendecker, B., & Scholmerich, A. (1998). Culture and early infancy among central African foragers and farmers. *Developmental Psychology, 34,* 653–661.

Hiatt, S., Campos, J., & Emde, R. M. (1979). Facial patterning and infant emotional expressions: Happiness, surprise, and fear. *Child Development, 50,* 1020–1035.

Hickman, M., Hendriks, H., Roland, F., & Liang, J. (1996). The marking of new information in children's narratives: A comparison of English, French, German, and Mandarin Chinese. *Journal of Child Language, 23,* 591–619.

Hieronymous, A., & Hoover, H. (1986). *Iowa tests of basic skills, form H.* Chicago: Riverside Publishing Company.

Hill, J. P., & Holmbeck, G. (1986). Attachment and autonomy during adolescence. In G. Whitehurst (Ed.), *Annals of child development* (Vol. 3). Greenwich, CT: Jai Press.

Hill, J. P., Holmbeck, G. N., Marlow, L., Green, T. M., & Lynch, M. E. (1985). Menarchal status and parent-child relations in families of seventh-grade girls. *Journal of Youth and Adolescence, 14,* 301–316.

Hilton, D. J. (1995). The social context of reasoning: Conversational inference and rational judgment. *Psychological Bulletin, 118*(2), 248–271.

Hines, M. (1990). Gonadal hormones and human cognitive development. In J. Balthazart (Ed.), *Brain and behaviour in vertebrates: 1. Sexual differentiation, neuroanatomical aspects, neurotransmitters, and neuropeptides* (pp. 51–63). Basel, Switzerland: Karger.

Hinshaw, S. P., Zupan, B. A., Simmel, C., Nigg, J. T., & Melnick, S. (1997). Peer status in boys with and without attention-deficit hyperactivity disorder: Predictions from overt and covert antisocial behavior, social isolation, and authoritative parenting beliefs. *Child Development, 68*(5), 880–896.

Hirschfeld, L. A., & Gelman, S. A. (Eds.) (1994). *Mapping the mind: Domain specificity in cognition and culture.* New York: Cambridge University Press.

Hirschman, R., & Katkin, E. S. (1974). Psychophysiological functioning, arousal, attention, and learning during the first year of life. In H. W. Reese (Ed.), *Advances in child development and behavior.* (Vol. 9) (pp. 116–150) New York: Academic Press.

Hirsh-Pacek, K., & Golinkoff, R. M. (1996). *The origins of grammar: Evidence from early language comprehension.* Cambridge, MA: MIT Press.

Hirsh-Pasek, K., Nelson, D. G. K., Jusczyk, P. W., Cassidy, K. W., Druss, B., & Kennedy, L. (1987). Clauses are perceptual units for young infants. *Cognition, 26,* 269–286.

Hirshberg, L., & Svejda, M. (1990). When infants look to their parents: Infants' social referencing of mothers compared to fathers. *Child Development, 61,* 1175–1186.

Hodges, E. V. E., Malone, M. J., & Perry, D. G. (1995). *Behavioral and social antecedents and consequences of victimization by peers.* Paper presented at the Biennial Meeting of the Society for Research in Child Development, Indianapolis, IN.

Hodges, J. S., & Henderson, K. A. (1999). Promoting the physical activity objectives in the Surgeon General's report: A Summary. *Journal of Physical Education, Recreation and Dance, 70*(3), 40–41.

Hofer, B. K., & Yu, S. L. (1999, August). *Learning to learn: The development of self-regulated learning.* Paper presented at the annual meeting of the American Psychological Association, Boston, MA.

Hoff-Ginsberg, E., & Krueger, W. M. (1991). Older siblings as conversational partners. *Merrill-Palmer Quarterly, 37,* 454–482.

Hoffman, M. (1982). Development of prosocial motivation: Empathy and guilt. In N. Eisenberg (Ed.), *The development of prosocial behavior* (pp. 281–313). San Diego, CA: Academic Press.

Hoffman, M. (1988). Moral development. In M. H. Bornstein & M. E. Lamb (Eds.), *Developmental psychology: An advanced textbook* (2nd ed.). Hillsdale, NJ: Erlbaum.

Hoffman, M. (1991). Empathy, social cognition, and moral action. In W. Kurtines & J. Gewirtz (Eds.), *Handbook of moral behavior and development: Vol. 1 Theory.* Hillsdale, NJ: Erlbaum.

Hoffman, M. L. (1993). Affective and cognitive processes in moral internalization. In E. T. Higgins, D. Ruble, & W. Hartup (Eds.), *Social cognition and social development: A social cultural perspective* (pp. 236–274). Cambridge: Cambridge University Press.

Hofsten, C. von (1982). Eye-hand coordination in newborns. *Developmental Psychology, 18,* 450–461.

Hofsten, C. von, & Ronnquist, L. (1988). Preparation for grasping an object: A developmental study. *Journal of Experimental Psychology: Human Perception and Performance, 14,* 610–621.

Hogan, D. M., & Tudge, J. (1999). Implications of Vygotsky's Theory for peer learning. In A. M. O'Donnell & A. King (Eds.), *Cognitive perspectives on peer learning,* (pp. 201–226). Mahwah, NJ: Erlbaum.

Hohnen, B., & Stevenson, J. (1999). The structure of genetic influences on general cognitive, language, phonological, and reading abilities. *Developmental Psychology, 35*(2), 590–603.

Holden, G. E. (1983). Avoiding conflict: Mothers as tacticians in the supermarket. *Child Development, 54,* 233–240.

Holden, G. W., & West, M. J. (1989). Proximate regulation by mothers: A demonstration of how differing styles affect young children's behavior. *Child Development, 60,* 64–69.

Holyoak, K. J., & Thagard, P. (1997). The analogical mind. *American Psychologist, 52*(1), 35–44.

Hopkins, B. (1991). Facilitating early motor development: An intracultural study of West Indian Infants living in Britain. In J. K. Nugent, B. M. Lester, & T. B. Brazelton (Eds.), *The cultural context of infant,* Vol. 2 (pp. 93–143). Norwood, NJ: Ablex.

Hotchner, T. (1995). *Pregnancy pure and simple.* New York: Avon Books.

Hotchner, T. (1997). *Pregnancy and childbirth.* New York: Avon.

Howard, B. J. (1996). Eating. In A. W. Rudolph (Senior Ed.), *Rudolph's pediatrics* (pp. 103–105). Stamford, CT.: Appleton & Lange.

Howes, C. (1990). Social status and friendship from kindergarten to third grade. *Journal of Applied Developmental Psychology, 11,* 321–330.

Hudley, C., & Graham, S. (1993). An attributional intervention to reduce peer-directed aggression among African-American boys. *Child Development, 64,* 124–138.

Hudson, J. A. (1990). The emergence of autobiographical memory in mother-child conversation. In R. Fivush & J. A. Hudson (Eds.), *Knowing and remembering in young children* (pp. 166–196). Cambridge, UK: Cambridge University Press.

Hudson, J. A. (1993). Reminiscing with mothers and others: Autobiographical memory in young two-year-olds. *Journal of Narrative and Life History, 3,* 1–32.

Huesmann, L. R. (1988). An information-processing model for the development of aggression. *Aggressive Behavior, 14,* 13–24.

Hughes, F. P. (1999). *Children, play, and development.* Boston: Allyn & Bacon.

Human genome project. Retrieved March 2000 from the World Wide Web: www.ornl.gov/TechResources/Human_

Humiston, S., & Atkinson, W. (1998). 1998 immunization schedule changes and clarifications. *Pediatric Annals, 27*(6), 338–348.

Hunt, E. (1999). Intelligence and human resources: Past, present and future. In P. L. Ackerman, P. C. Kyllonen, & R. D. Roberts (Eds.), *Learning and individual differences* (pp. 3–28). Washington, DC: American Psychological Association.

Hunt, J. McV. (1965.) Intrinsic motivation and its role in psychological development. *Nebraska Symposium on Motivation, 13,* 189–282.

Hunt, R. R., & Ellis, H. C. (1999). *Fundamentals of cognitive psychology,* (6th ed.). Boston: McGraw Hill.

Hunter, J., Mullen, J., & Dallas, D. V. (1994). Medical considerations and practice guidelines for the neonatal occupational therapist. *The American Journal of Occupational Therapy, 48*(6), 546–549.

Huntsinger, C. S., Liaw, F., Schoeneman, J., & Ching, W. (1995). *Cultural differences in young children's drawing skills.* Paper presented at the Biennial Meeting of the Society for Research in Child Development. Indianapolis, March 30–April 2.

Hunziker, U. A., & Barr, R. G. (1986). Increased carrying reduces infant crying: A randomized controlled trial. *Pediatrics, 77*(5), 641–647.

Huon, G. F. (1996). Health promotion and the prevention of dieting-induced disorders. *Eating Disorders: The Journal of Treatment and Prevention, 4*(1), 27–32.

Hurwitz, E. S., Deseda, C. C., Shapiro, C. N., Nalin, D. R., Freitg-Koontz, M. J., & Hayashi, J. (1994). Hepatitis infections in the day-care setting. *Pediatrics, 94*(Suppl. 6), 1023–1024.

Hurwitz, E. S., Gunn, W. J., Pinsky, P. F., & Schonberger, L. B.(1991). Risk of respiratory illness asssociated with day-care attendance: A nationwide study. *The Journal of Pediatrcs, 87,* 62–69.

Huston, A., McLoyd, V. C., & Coll, C. G. (1997). Poverty and behavior: The case for multiple methods and levels of analysis. *Developmental Review, 17*(3), 376–393.

Huston, A. C. (1983). Sex-typing. In P. H. Mussen (Ed.), *Handbook of child psychology* (4th ed., Vol. 4, pp. 387–467). New York: Wiley.

Huston, A. C., Donnerstein, E., Fairchild, H., Feshbach, N. D., Katz, P. A., Murray, J. P., Rubenstein, E. A., Wilcox, B. L., & Zuckerman, D. (1992). *Big world, small screen: The role of television in American society.* Lincoln, NE: University of Nebraska Press.

Huston, A. C., Wright, J. C., Marquis, J., & Green, S. B. (1999). How young children spend their time: Television and other activities. *Developmental Psychology, 35*(4), 912–925.

Huttenlocher, J. (1994). The origins of language comprehension. In R. L. Slobin (Ed.), *Theories in cognitive development.* New York: Wiley.

Huttenlocher, J. (1995). *Input and language.* Paper presented at the Biennial Meeting of the Society for Research in Child Development, Indianapolis, IN, March 30–April, 2.

Huttenlocher, J., Haight, W., Bryk, A., Seltzer, M., & Lyons, T. (1991). Early vocabulary growth: Relation to language input and gender. *Developmental Psychology, 27*(3), 236–248.

Huttenlocher, J., & Presson, C. B. (1973). Mental rotation and the perspective problem. *Cognitive Psychology, 4,* 277–299.

Hyde, J. S. (1981). How large are cognitive gender differences? A meta-analysis using w^2 and d. *American Psychologist, 36,* 892–901.

Hyde, J. S., Fennema, E., & Lamon, S. J. (1990). Gender differences in mathematics performance attitudes/affect: A meta-analysis. *Psychological Bulletin, 107,* 139–155.

Hyman, I. A. (1995). Corporal punishment, psychological maltreatment, violence, and punitiveness in America: Research advocacy and public policy. *Applied and Preventive Psychology, 4,* 113–130.

Hymes, J. (1982). *Early childhood education. The year in review: A look at 1981.* Carmel, CA: Hacienda Press.

Hymes, J. L. (1995). The Kaiser Child Service Centers—50 years later: Some memories and lessons. *Journal of Education, 177*(3), 23–28.

Ianniello, E. (1999, April). *Violence in schools: Concerns, causes, and possible solutions.* Paper presented at the annual meeting of the Eastern Psychological Association meeting, Providence, RI.

ICBD (International Clearinghouse for Birth Defects). (1999). Who we are and what we do. Retrieved March 2000 from the World Wide Web: www.icbd.org/who

Iconis, R. (1995). A rash of childhood diseases hits young adults. *Current Health, 21*(7), 27–29.

Ingersall, B. D., & Goldstein, S. (1993). *Attention deficit disorder and learning disabilities: Realities, myths, and controversial treatments.* New York: Doubleday.

Ingram, D. (1995). The cultural bias of prosodic modifications to infants and children: A response to Fernald's universalist theory. *Journal of Child Language, 22,* 223–233.

Inhelder, B., & Piaget, J. (1958). *The growth of logical thinking from childhood to adolescence.* New York: Basic Books.

Inhelder, B., & Piaget, J. (1969). *The early growth of logic in the child.* (E. A. Lunzer & D. Papert, Trans.) New York: Norton.

Ippolitov, F. W. (1973). Internal differences in the sensitivity-strength parameter for vision, hearing, and cutaneous modalities. In V. D. Nebylitsyn & J. A. Gray (Eds.), *Biological bases of individual behavior* (pp. 43–61). New York: Academic Press.

Irvine, A. B., Biglan, A., Smolkowski, K., & Ary, D. V. (1999). The value of the Parenting Scale for measuring the discipline practices of parents of middle school children. *Behavior Research and Therapy, 37*, 127–142.

Isabella, R. A., & Belsky, J. (1991). Interactional synchrony and the origins of infant-mother attachment: A replication study. *Child Development, 62*(2), 373–384.

Isen, A. M. (1999). Positive affect. In T. Dalgleish & M. Powers (Eds.), *The handbook of cognition and emotion* (pp. 521–539). New York: Wiley.

Isley, S. L., O'Neil, R., Chatfelter, D., & Parke, R. D. (1999). Parent and child expressed affect and children's social competence: Modeling direct and indirect pathways. *Developmental Psychology, 35*(2), 547–560.

Itons-Peterson, M. J., & Reddel, M. (1984). What do people ask about the neonate? *Developmental Psychology, 20*(3), 358–359.

Ivey, G. (1999). Reflections on teaching struggling middle school readers. *Journal of Adolescent & Adult Literacy, 42*(5), 372–381.

Jaccard, J. D., Hus, P. J., & Gordon, V. V. (1998). Parent-adolescent congruency in reports of adolescent sexual behavior and in communications about sexual behavior. *Child Development 69*(1), 247–261.

Jackson, B., & Rokosz, F. (1995). Superkids day: Two field days for elementary schools. *Journal of Physical Education, Recreation, and Dance, 66*(3), 56–72.

Jackson, J. F. (1993). Human behavioral genetics, Scarr's theory, and her views on interventions: A critical review and commentary on their implications for African American children. *Child Development, 64*, 1318–1332.

Jackson, K. (1998, October 31). Word? Teen slang may be hard to follow, but it serves a purpose. *The Tampa Tribune*, p. 3.

Jacobs, J. K., Garnier, H. E., & Weisner, T. (1996, March). *The impact of family life on the process of dropping out of high school.* Paper presented at the meeting of the Society for Research on Adolescence. Boston, MA.

Jacobson, J. L., & Jacobson, S. W. (1996). Methodological considerations in behavioral toxicology in infants and children. *Developmental Psychology, 32*, 390–403.

Jacobson, J. L., & Willie, D. E. (1984). Influence of attachment and separation experience on separation distress at 18 months. *Developmental Psychology, 20*(3), 330–353.

Jacobson, M. (1995, September). Folic acid: For the young and heart. *Nutrition Action Newsletter, 22*(7), 4–6.

Jacobvitz, D., & Sroufe, L. A. (1987). The early caregiver-child relationship and attention-deficit disorder with hyperactivity in kindergarten: A prospective study. *Child Development, 58*(6), 1488–1495.

Jakobson, R. (1941). *Child language, aphasia, and phonological universals* (A. R. Keiler, trans.). The Hague: Mouton (English translation, 1968).

James, P., & Thorpe, N. (1994). *Ancient inventions.* New York: Ballantine Books.

James, W. (1920). *Letters.* (Vol. 1). Boston: Atlantic Monthly Press.

Jang, K. L., Livesley, W. J., Vernon, P. A., & Jackson, D. N. (1996). Heritability of personality disorder traits: A twin study. *Acta Psychiatrica*

Janofsky, M. (1989, March 6). Coach's drug use shaped philosophy. *The New York Times*, p. C7.

Jantz, J. W., Blosser, C. D., & Fruechting, L. A.(1997). A motor milestone change noted with a change in sleep position. *Archives of Pediatric and Adolescent Medicine, 151*, 565–568.

Jeffrey, H. E., Megevand, A., & Page, M. (1999). Why the prone position is a risk factor for sudden infant death syndrome. *Pediatrics, 104*(2), 263–268.

Jenkins, C. B. (1996). *Inside the writing portfolio: What we need to know to assess children's writing.* Portsmouth, NH: Heinemann.

Jensen, A. (1969). How much can we boost IQ and scholastic achievement? *Harvard Educational Review, 39*, 1–123.

Jensen, H. (1994). Bulimia and anorexia nervosa: Predictors of recovery and treatment intervention. *Journal of Health Education, 25*(6), 338–340.

Jensen, R., & Moore, S. G. (1977). The effect of attribute statements on cooperativeness and competitiveness in schoolaged boys. *Child Development, 48*, 305–307.

Jesse, P. O., Nagy, M. C., & Poteet-Johnson, D. (1995). Children with AIDS. In E. N. Junn & C. J. Boyatzis (Eds.), *Annual editions: Child growth and development* (pp. 236–240). Guilford, CT:Dushkin.

Jimerson, S., Egeland, B., & Teo, A. (1999). A longitudinal study of achievement trajectories: Factors associated with change. *Journal of Educational Psychology, 91*(1), 116–126.

Joas, R. (1999, May 23). For more teens today, bigger breasts are better. *Sunday News*, Lancaster, PA, A-17.

John, D. P., Caspi, A., Robins, R. W., Moffitt, T. E., & Stouthamer-Loeber, M. (1994). The "little five": Exploring the nomological network of the five-factor model of personality in adolescent boys. *Child Development, 65*, 160–178.

Johnson, D. (2000). *Reaching out: Interpersonal effectiveness and self-actualization.* Boston: Allyn & Bacon.

Johnson, D. W., & Johnson, R. T. (1999). *Learning together and alone: Cooperative, competitive, and individualistic learning.* Boston: Allyn & Bacon.

Johnson, H. R., Mykre, S. A., Ruvalcaba, R. H. A., Thuline, H. C., & Kelley, V. C. (1970). Effects of testosterone on body image and behavior in Klinefelter's syndrome: A pilot study. *Developmental Medicine and Child Neurology, 12*, 454–460.

Johnson, K. E., Scott, P., & Mervis, C. B.(1997). Development of children's understanding of basic-subordinate inclusion relations. *Developmental Psychology, 33*, 745–763.

Johnson, M. D. (1990). Anabolic steroid use in adolescent athletes. *Pediatric Clinics of North America, 37*(5), 1111–1123.

Johnson, M. H. (1999). Developmental neuroscience. In M. H. Bornstein & M. E. Lamb (Eds.), *Developmental psychology: An advanced text* (pp. 199–230). Mahwah, NJ: Erlbaum.

Johnson, M. H. (2000). Functional brain development in infants: Elements of an interactive spcialization framework. *Child Development, 71*(1), 75–81.

Johnson, M. K., Becbe, T., Mortimer, J. T., & Snyder, M. (1999). Volunteerism in adolescence: A process perspective. *Journal of Research on Adolescence, 8*(3), 309–332.

Johnson, N. G., Roberts, M. C., & Worell, J., (Eds.). (1999). *Beyond appearance: A new look at adolescent girls.* Washington, DC: American Psychological Association.

Johnson, R. (1998, September 1). Radical pop-cult speak leaves older folks exclaiming 'Duh'; Colorful phrases from TV, movies make up dialect. *The Washington Times*, p. A2.

Johnson, S. C., & Solomon, G. E. (1997). Why dogs have puppies and cats have kittens: The role of birth in young children's understanding of biological origins. *Child Development, 68*, 404–419.

Johnson, S. P., & Anslin, R. N. (1995). Perception of object unity in 2-month-old infants. *Developmental Psychology, 31*, 739–745.

Johnston, F. E., Low, S. M., deBaessa, Y., & MacVean, R. B. (1987). Interaction of nutritional and socioeconomic status as determinants of cognitive development in disadvantaged urban Guatemalan children. *American Journal of Physical Anthropology, 73*, 501–506.

Johnston, J. R., & Slobin, D. I. (1979). The development of locative expressions in English, Italian, Serbo-Croation, and Turkish. *Journal of Child Language, 16*, 532–547.

Jones, C. (1957). *Childbirth choices today.* New York: Citadel Press.

Jones, H. F. (1949). Adolescence in our society. In Anniversary Papers of the Community Service Society of New York: *The family in a democratic society* (pp. 70–82). New York: Columbia University Press.

Jones, M. (1998). *Motherhood after 35.* Tuscon, AZ: Fisher Books.

Joos, S. K., Pollitt, E., Mueleer, W. H., & Albright, D. L. (1983). The Bacon Chow study: Maternal nutritional supplementation and infant behavioral development. *Child Development, 54*, 669–676.

Jordan, B. (1993). *Birth in four cultures* (4th ed.). Prospect Heights, NJ: Waveland Press.

Jordan, M. (1993, March 27). SAT changes name, but it won't score 1,600 with critics. *Washington Post*, p. A7.

Joslyn, W. D. (1971). Androgen-induced social dominance in infant female rhesus monkeys. *Journal of Child Psychology and Psychiatry, 84*, 35–44.

Judd, S. A., Mervis, C. B. (1979). Learning to solve class-inclusion problems: The roles of quantification and recognition of contradiction. *Child Development, 50*, 163–169.

Juel, C. (1988). Learning to read and write: A longitudinal study of 54 children from first through fourth grades. *Journal of Educational Psychology, 80*(4), 417–447.

Jusczyk, P. W. (1985). On characterizing the development of speech perception. In J. Mehler & R. Fox (Eds.), *Neonate cognition: Beyond the blooming, buzzing confusion.* Hillsdale, NJ: Erlbaum.

Jusczyk, P. W. (1993). From general to language specific capacities: The WRAPSA model of how speech perception develops. *Journal of Phonetics, 21*, 3–28.

Jusczyk, P. W. (1997). *The discovery of spoken language.* Cambridge, MA: The MIT Press.

Jusczyk, P. W., Cutler, A., & Redanz, N. (1993a). Preference for the predominant stress patterns of native language words. *Journal of Memory and Language, 32*, 402–420.

Jusczyk, P. W., Friederici, A., Wessels, J., Svenkerud, V., & Jusczyk, A. M. (1993b). Infants' sensitivity to the sound patterns of native language words. *Journal of Memory and Language, 32*, 402–420.

Jusczyk, P. W., Hirsh-Pasek, K., Kemler Nelson, D. G., Kennedy, L. J., Woodward, A., Piwoz, J. (1992). Perception of acoustic correlates of major phrasal units by young infants. *Cognitive Psychology, 24*, 252–293.

Jusczyk, P. W., Charles-Luce, J. (1994). Infants' sensitivity to phonotactic patterns in the native language. *Journal of Memory and Language, 33*, 630–645.

Kafai, Y. B. (1996). Gender differences in children's constructions of video games. In P. M. Greenfield & R. R. Cocking (Eds.), *Interacting with video* (pp. 39–66). Norwood, NJ: Ablex.

Kagan, J. (1971). *Change and continuity in infancy.* New York: Wiley.

Kagan, J. (1987). Introduction. In J. Kagan & S. Lamb (Ed.), *The emergence of morality in young children* (pp. ix–xx). Chicago: University of Chicago Press.

Kagan, J. (1997). Temperament and reactions to unfamiliarity. *Child Development, 68*, 139–143.

Kagan, J. (1998). Biology and the child. In W. Damon (Editor-in-Chief) & N. Eisenberg (Vol. Ed.), *Handbook of child psychology* (5th ed.): Vol. 3. *Social, emotional, and personality development* (pp. 177–235). New York: Wiley.

Kagan, J., Kearsley, R. B., & Zelazo, P. R. (1978). *Infancy: Its place in human development.* Cambridge, MA: Harvard University Press.

Kagan, J., & Snidman, N. (1991). Temperamental factors in human development. *American Psychologist, 46*(8), 856–862.

Kagan, J., Snidman, N., & Arcus, D. (1998). Childhood derivatives of high and low reactivity in infancy. *Child Development, 69*, 1483–1493.

Kail, R. (1991). Developmental change in speed of processing during childhood and adolescence. *Psychological Bulletin, 109*, 490–501.

Kail, R., & Bisanz, J. (1992). The information-processing perspective on cognitive development in childhood and adolescence. In R. J. Sternberg & C. A. Berg (Eds.), *Intellectual development* (pp. 229–269). Cambridge: Cambridge University Press.

Kalish, C. W. (1998). Young children's predictions of illness: Failure to recognize probabilistic causation. *Developmental Psychology, 34*, 1046–1058.

Kamhi, A. G. (1986). The elusive first word: The importance of the naming insight for the development of referential speech. *Journal of Child Language, 13,* 155–161.

Kamii, C. (1989). *Young children continue to reinvent arithmetic—2nd grade: Implications of Piaget's theory.* New York: Teachers College, Columbia University Press.

Kamins, M. L., & Dweck, C. S. (1999). Person vs. process praise and criticism: Implications for contingent self-worth and coping. *Developmental Psychology, 35*(3), 835–847.

Kandel, D. B., Wu, P., & Davies, M. (1994). Maternal smoking during pregnancy and smoking by adolescent daughters. *American Journal of Public Health, 84,* 1407–1413.

Kanfer, R., & Heggestad, E. D. (1999). Individual differences in motivation: Traits and self-regulatory skills. In P. L. Ackerman, P. C. Kyllonen, & R. D. Roberts (Eds.), *Learning and individual differences* (pp. 293–309). Washington, DC: American Psychological Association.

Kao, G. (1995). Asian Americans as model minorities? A look at their academic performance. *American Journal of Education, 103,* 121–153.

Kaplan, H., & Dove, M. H. (1987). Infant development among the Ache of Eastern Paraguay. *Developmental Psychology, 23,* 190–198.

Kaplan, P. S., Bashorowski, J., & Zorlengo-Strouse, P. (1999). Child-directed speech produced by mothers with symptoms of depression fails to promote associative learning in 4-month-old infants. *Developmental Psychology, 70*(3), 560–570.

Kappas, A., Drummond, G. S., Manola, T., Petmezoki, S., & Valaes, T. (1988). Sn-protoporphyrin use in management of hyperbilirubinemia in term newborns with direct Coombs-Positive ABO incompatibility. *Pediatrics, 81*(4), 485–497.

Karniol, R. (1989). The role of manual manipulative stages in the infant's acquisition of perceived control over objects. *Developmental Review, 9,* 205–233.

Karpov, Y. V., & Haywood, H. C. (1998). Two ways to elaborate Vygotsky's concept of mediation: Implications for instruction. *American Psychologist, 53*(1), 27–36.

Kaser, S., & Short, K. G. (1998). Exploring culture through children's connections. *Language Arts, 75,* 185–192.

Kataria, S., Swanson, M. S., & Trevathon, G. E. (1987). Persistence of sleep disturbances in preschool children. *Journal of Pediatrics, 110*(4), 642–646.

Katz, L., & Hamilton, J. R. (1974). Fat absorption in infants of low birth weight less than 1,300 gm. *Journal of Pediatrics, 85,* 6081.

Kaufman, J., & Zigler, E. (1989). The intergenerational transmission of child abuse. In D. Cicchetti & V. Carlson (Eds.), *Child maltreatment: Theory and research on the causes and consequences of child abuse and neglect* (pp. 129–152). New York: Cambridge University Press.

Kaye, K. (1982a). *The mental and social life of babies.* Chicago: The University of Chicago Press.

Kaye, K. (1982b). Organism, apprentice, and person. In E. Z. Tronick (Ed.), *Social interchange in infancy: Affect, cognition, and communication.* Baltimore: University Park Press.

Kaye, K., & Fogel, A. (1980). The temporal structure of face-to-face communication between mothers and infants. *Developmental Psychology, 16*(5), 454–464.

Keating, D. (1980). Thinking processes in adolescence. In J. Adelson (Ed.), *Handbook of adolescent psychology.* New York: Wiley.

Keats, E. J. (1977). *Whistle for Willie.* New York: Puffin Books.

Keefer, C. H., Dixon, S., Tronick, E. Z., & Brazelton, T. B. (1991). Cultural mediation between newborn behavior and later development: Implications for methodology in cross-cultural studies. In J. K. Nugent, B. M. Lester, and T. B. Brazelton (Eds.), *The cultural context of infancy: Vol. 2. Multicultural and interdisciplinary approaches to parent-infant relations* (pp. 39–61). Norwood, NJ: Ablex.

Keil, F. (1979). The development of the young child's ability to anticipate the outcomes of simple causal events. *Child Development, 50,* 455–462.

Keith, C. G., & Doyle, L. W. (1995). Retinopathy of prematurity in extremely low birth weight infants. *Pediatrics, 95,* 42–45.

Kelder, S. H., Perry, C. L., Klepp, K. I., & Lytle, L. L. (1994). Longitudinal tracking of adolescent smoking, physical activity, and food choice behaviors. *American Journal of Public Health, 84*(7), 1121–1126.

Kellman, P. J., & Arterberry, M. E. (1998). *The cradle of knowledge: Development of perception in infancy.* Cambridge, MA: The MIT Press.

Kellman, P. J., & Banks, M. S. (1998). Infant visual perception. In W. Damon (Editor-in-Chief) and D. Kuhn & R. S. Siegler (Vol. Eds.), *Handbook of child psychology* (5th ed.): Vol. 2. *Cognition, perception, and language* (pp. 103–146). New York: Wiley.

Kellman, P. J., & Short, K. R. (1987). Development of three-dimensional form perception. *Journal of Experimental Psychology: Human Perception and Performance, 13*(4), 545–557.

Kellman, P. J., & Spelke, E. S. (1983). Perception of partly occluded objects in infancy. *Cognitive Psychology, 15,* 483–524.

Kellogg, R. (1967) *The psychology of children's art.* New York: CRM—Random House.

Kelly, D. H., & Shannon, D. C. (1982). Sudden infant death syndrome and near sudden death syndrome: A review of the literature, 1964–1982. *Pediatric Clinics of North America, 29*(5), 1241–1261.

Kemler-Nelson, D. G., Hirsh-Paseck, K., Jusczyk, S. W., & Cassidy, K. W. (1989). How the prosodic cues in motherese might assist language learning. *Journal of Child Language, 16,* 55–58.

Kemp, J. S., Livine, M., White, D. K., & Arfken, C. L.(1998). Softness and potential to cause rebreathing: Differences in bedding used by infants at high and low risk for sudden infant death syndrome. *The Journal of Pediatrics, 132,* 234–239.

Kempe, C. H., Silverman, F. N., Steele, B. F., Droegemueller, W., & Silver, H. K. (1962). The battered child syndrome. *Journal of the American Medical Association, 181,* 4–11.

Kendler, K. S., MacLean, C., Neale, M., & Kessler, R. C. (1991). The genetic epidemiology of bulimia nervosa. *American Journal of Psychiatry, 148*(12), 1627–1637.

Kenny, M. E. (1992, August). *Parental attachment, psychological separation, and eating disorder symptoms among college women.* Paper presented at the Meeting of the American Psychological Association, Washington, DC.

Kent, R. D., & Bauer, H. R. (1985). Vocalizations of one-year-olds. *Journal of Child Language, 12,* 491–526.

Kerkay, J., Zsako, S., & Kaplan, A. (1971). Immunoelectrophoretic serum patterns associated with mothers of children affected with the G_1-trisomy syndrome (Down's syndrome). *American Journal of Mental Deficiency, 75,* 729–732.

Kerkman, D., Wright, J. C., Huston, A. C., Rice, M., & Bremer, M. (1983). *Preschoolers who get cable TV: Family patterns, media orientations, and media use.* Paper presented at the Biennial Meeting of the Society for Research in Child Development, Detroit, MI.

Kerns, K. A., & Brerenbaum, S. A. (1991). Sex differences in spatial ability: An early sex difference. *Developmental Psychology, 58,* 725–740.

Kerns, K. A., Contreras, T. M., & Neal-Barnett, A. (Eds.). (2000). *Family and peers: Linking two social worlds.* Westport, CT: Praeger.

Keynes, A. (1999). Take no chances on teen gamblers. *Youth Today, 8*(7), 10–11.

KIDS COUNT. (1999). The Annie E. Casey Foundation. Retrieved March 2000 from the World Wide Web: www.aecf.org/kidscount/kc1999/findings2

Kiesler, S., & Kraut, R. (1999). Internet use and ties that bind. *American Psychologist, 54*(9), 783–784.

Kilbride, J. E., & Kilbride, P. L. (1975). Sitting and smiling behavior of Baganda infants. *Journal of Cross-Cultural Psychology, 6,* 88–107.

Killen, M., & Turiel, E. (1999). Adolescents' and young adults' evaluations of helping and sacrificing for others. *Journal of Research on Adolescence, 8*(3), 355–375.

Kilpatrick, J. (1999, September 21). J. E. Lighter's Work last word in defining American slang. *Denver Rocky Mountain News,* p. 3.

Kimmerle, M., Mick, L. A., & Michel, G. F. (1995). Bimanual role-differentiated toy play during infancy. *Infant Behavior and Development, 18,* 299–307.

Kimura, D., & Hampson, E. (1994). Cognitive pattern in men and women is influenced by fluctuations in sex hormones? *Psychological Science, 3* 57–61.

Kindlon, D., & Thompson, M. (1999). *Raising Cain: Protecting the emotional life of boys.* New York: Ballentine.

King, C. R. (1993). *Children's health in America: A history.* New York: Twayne.

King, P. A. (1999, June). Science for girls only. *Newsweek.* Retrieved March 2000 from the World Wide Web: http://www.Newsweek.com

Kington, M. (1999, July 21). Rally round the Melvyn, I'm right out of the Ryans. *Independent,* p. 2.

Kinney, D. A. (1999). From "headbangers" to "hippies": Delineating adolescents' active attempts to form an alternative peer culture. *New Directions for Child and Adolescent Development, 84,* 21–35.

Kisilevsky, B. S., Stach, D. M., & Muir, D. W. (1991). Fetal and infant response to tactile stimulation. In M. J. S. Weiss & P. R. Zelazo (Eds.), *Newborn attention: Biological constraints and the influence of experience* (pp. 63–98). Norwood, NJ: Ablex.

Kitzinger, S. *The complete book of pregnancy and childbirth.* New York: Knopf, 1997.

Klaus, M. H., & Fanaroff, A. A. (1973). *Care of the high-risk neonate.* Philadelphia: Saunders.

Klaus, M. H., Jerazauld, R., Kreger, N. C., McAlpine, W., Steffa, M., & Kennell, J. H. (1972). Maternal attachment importance of the first post-partum days. *New England Journal of Medicine, 286,* 460–463.

Klaus, M. H., & Kennell, J. H. (1976). *Maternal-infant bonding.* St. Louis: Mosby.

Kliegman, R. M. (1996). The fetus and the neonate infant: Overview of mortality and morbidity. In W. E. Nelson (Senior Ed.) *Nelson textbook of pediatrics* (pp. 431–432). Philadelphia: Saunders.

Kline, C. M. (1995). Violence in children's lives: Fighting back. *Childhood Education, 71*(5), 288–291.

Kling, K. C., Hyde, J. S., Showers, C. J., & Buswell, B. N. (1999). Gender differences in self-esteem: A meta-analysis. *Psychological Bulletin, 125*(4), 470–500.

Klinnert, M. (1981). *The regulation of infant behavior by maternal facial expression.* Unpublished doctoral dissertation, University of Denver, Denver, CO.

Klinnert, M., Campos, J. J., Sorce, J. F., Emde, R. N., & Svejda, M. (1983). Emotions as behavior regulators: Social referencing in infancy. In R. Plutchick & H. Kellerman (Eds.), *Emotion in early development: Vol. 1. The emotions* (pp. 57–86). New York: Academic Press.

Kloth, S., Janssen, P. Kraaimaat, F., & Brutten, G. J. (1998). Communicative styles of mothers interacting with their preschool-age children: A factor analytic study. *Journal of Child Language, 25,*149–168.

Kobus, K. (1999, April). *Academic and psychological correlates of membership in adolescent peer groups.* Paper presented at the annual meeting of the Eastern Psychological Association, Providence, RI.

Kochanska, G. (1991). Socialization and temperament in the development of guilt and conscience. *Child Development, 62,* 1374–1392.

Kochanska, G. (1993). Toward a synthesis of parental socialization and child temperament in early development of conscience. *Child Development, 64,* 325–347.

Kochanska, G. (1994). Beyond cognition: Expanding the search for the early roots of internalization and conscience. *Developmental Psychology, 30,* 20–22.

Kochanska, G. (1995). Children's temperament, mothers' discipline, and security of attachment: Multiple pathways to emerging internalization. *Child Development, 66,* 597–615.

Kochanska, G., Casey, R. J., & Fukumoto, A. (1995). Toddlers' sensitivity to standard violations. *Child Development, 66,* 643–656.

Kochanska, G., Murray, K., & Coy, K. C. (1997). Inhibitory control as a contributor to conscience in childhood: From toddler to early school age. *Child Development, 68*(2), 263–277.

Kochanska, G., Murray, K., Jacques, T. Y., Koenig, A. L., & Vandegeest, K. A. (1996). Inhibitory control in young children and its role in emerging internalization. *Child Development, 67,* 490–507.

Kochenderfer, B. J., & Ladd, G. W. (1996). Peer victimization: Cause or consequence of school maladjustment? *Child Development, 67,* 1305–1317.

Kochenderfer, B. J., & Ladd, G. W. (1997). Victimized children's responses to peers' aggression: Behaviors associated with reduced versus continued victimization. *Development and Psychopathology, 9*(1), 59–73.

Koelega, H. S., & Koster, E. P. (1974). Some experiments on sex differences in odor perception. *Annals of the New York Academy of Sciences, 237,* 234–246.

Koepke, J. E., & Bigalow, A. E. (1997). Observations of newborn suckling behavior. *Infant Behavior and Development, 20,* 93–98.

Kogon, D. P., Oulton, M., Gray, J. H., Liston, R. M., Luther, E. R., Peddle, L. J., & Young, D. C. (1986). Amniotic fluid phosphatdylglycerol and phosphyatidylcholine phosphorus as predictors of fetal lung maturity. *American Journal of Obstetrics and Gynecology, 154*(2), 226–230.

Kohlberg, L. (1969). Stage and sequence: The cognitive developmental approach to socialization. In D. A. Goslin (Ed.), *Handbook of socialization theory and research* (pp. 347–480). Chicago: Rand McNally.

Komner, M., & Shostak, M. (February, 1987). Timing and management of birth among the !Kung: Biocultural interaction and reproductive adaptation. *Cultural Anthropology, 2*(1), 11–28.

Konig, A. (1995, March/April). *Maternal discipline and child temperament as contributors to the development of internalization in young children.* Paper presented at the Biennial Meetings of the Society for Research in Child Development, Indianapolis, March 30–April.

Konner, M. (1982). Biological aspects of the mother-infant bond. In R. N. Emde & R. J. Harmon (Eds.), *The development of attachment and affiliative systems* (pp. 137–159, 237–259). New York: Plenum Press.

Konopczynski, G. (1995). *A developmental model of acquisition of rhythmic patterns: Results from a cross-linguistic study.* Paper presented at the Biennial Meeting of the Society for Research in Child Development, Indianapolis, March 30–April 2.

Korbin, J. E., Coulton, C. J., Chard, S., Plat-Houston, C., & Su, M. (1998). Impoverishment and child maltreatment in African American and European American neighborhoods. *Development and Psychopathology, 10,* 215–233.

Korean speakers: Nouns are not always learned before verbs. In M. Tomasello & W. Merriman Eds.), *Beyond names for things: Young children's acquisition of verbs.* Hillsdale, NJ: Erlbaum.

Korner, A., & Grobstein, R. (1966). Visual alertness as related to soothing in neonates: Implications for maternal stimulation and early deprivation. *Child Development, 37,* 867–876.

Korner, A., & Thoman, E. B. (1972). The relative efficacy of contact and vestibular-proprioceptive stimulation on soothing neonates. *Child Development, 43,* 443–453.

Kouba, V. L., Brown, C. A., Carpenter, T. P., Lindquist, M. M., Silver, E. A., & Swafford, J. O. (1988). Results of the fourth NAEP assessment of mathematics: Number, operations, and word problems. *Arithmetic Teacher, 35,* 14–19.

Kouba, V. L., Franklin, K. (1995). Multiplication and division: sense making and meaning. *Teaching Children Mathematics, 1*(9), 574–577.

Kowaleski-Jones, L., & Duncan, G. J. (1999). The structure of achievement and behavior across middle childhood. *Child Development, 70*(4), 930–943.

Krantz, M. (1982). Sociometric awareness, social participation, and perceived popularity in preschool children. *Child Development, 53,* 376–379.

Krauss, R. M., & Glucksberg, S. (1969). The development of communication: Competence as a function of age. *Child Development, 42,* 255–266.

Kraut, R., Patterson, M., Lundmark, V., Kiesler, S., & Mukhopadhyay, T., & Scherlis, W. (1998). Internet paradox: A social technology that reduces social involvement and psychological well- being. *American Psychologist, 54*(9), 1017–1031.

Kronk, C. M. (1994). Private speech in adolescents. *Adolescence, 29*(116), 781–804.

Kuchuk, A., Vibbert, M., & Bornstein, M. H. (1986). The perception of smiling and its experiential correlates in three-month-old infants. *Child Development, 57*(4), 1054–1061.

Kuczynski, L., & Kochanska, G. (1995). Function and content of maternal demands: Developmental significance of early demands for competent action. *Child Development, 66,* 616–628.

Kuhl, P. K., Williams, K. A., Lacerda, F., Stevens, K. N., & Lindblom, B. (1992). Linguistic experience alters phonetic perception in infants by 6 months of age. *Science, 255,* 606–608.

Kuhn, D. (1988). Cognitive development. In M. H. Bernstein & M. E. Lamb (Eds.), *Developmental psychology: An advanced textbook* (2nd ed., pp. 205–260). Hillsdale, NJ: Erlbaum.

Kuhn, D. (1989a). Children and adults as intuitive scientists. *Psychological Review, 96*(4), 674–689.

Kuhn, D. (1989b). Making cognitive development research relevant to education. In W. Damon (Ed.), *Child development today and tomorrow* (pp. 261–287). San Francisco: Jossey-Bass.

Kumra, S., Wiggs, E., Krasnewich, D., Meck, J., Smith, A. C. M., Bedwell, J., Fernandez, T., Jacobsen, L. K., Leslie, K., Lenane, M., & Rapoport, J. L. (1998). Association of sex chromosome anomalies with childhood-onset psychotic disorders. *Journal of the American Academy of Child and Adolescent Psychiatry, 37*(3), 292–296.

Kunz, J. R., & Finkel, A. J. (Eds.) (1987). *The American Medical Association family medical guide.* New York: Random House.

Kupersmidt, J. B., Coie, J. D., & Dodge, K. A. (1990). The role of poor peer relationships in the development of disorder. In S. R. Asher & J. D. Coie (Eds.),

Peer rejection in childhood (pp. 274–308). New York: Cambridge University Press.

Kurdek, L. A., & Fine, M. A. (1994). Family acceptance and family control as predictors of adjustment in young adolescents: Linear, curvilinear, or interactive effects? *Child Development, 65,* 1137–1146.

Kurzweil, S. (1988). Recognition of mother from multisensory interactions in early infancy. *Infant Behavior and Development, 11,* 235–243.

Laborde, D. J., Weigle, K. A., Weber, D. J., Sobsey, M. D., & Kotch, J. B. (1994). The frequency, level, and distribution of fecal contamination in day-care center classrooms. *Pediatrics, 94*(Suppl. 6), 1008–1011.

Lackovic-Grgin, K., Dekovic, M., & Opacic, G. (1994). Pubertal status, interaction with significant others, and self-esteem of adolescent girls. *Adolescence, 19*(15), 691–700.

Ladd, G. (1990). Having friends, keeping friends, making friends, and being liked by peers in the classroom: Predictors of children's early school adjustment? *Child Development, 61,* 1081–1100.

Ladd, G. W., & Burgess, K. B. (1999). Charting the relationship trajectories of aggressive, withdrawn, and aggressive/withdrawn children during early grade school. *Child Development, 70*(4), 805–1046.

LaFromboise, T., Coleman, H. L. K., & Gerton, J. (1993). Psychological impact of biculturalism: Evidence and theory. *Psychological Bulletin, 114*(3), 395–412.

Lahey, B., & Loeber, R. (1994). Framework for a developmental model of oppositional defiant disorder and conduct disorder. In D. Routh (Ed.), *Disruptive behavior disorders in childhood* (pp. 139–180). New York: Plenum Press.

Lamb, M. E. (1977). The development of parental preference in the first two years of life. *Sex Roles, 3,* 495–497.

Lamb, M. E. (1982). Parent-infant interaction, attachment, and socioemotional development in infancy. In R. M. Emde & R. J. Harmon (Eds.), *The development of attachment and affiliative systems* (pp. 195–211). New York: Plenum Press.

Lamb, M. E. (1998). Nonparental child care: Context, quality, correlates, and consequences. In W. Damon (Editor-in-Chief) and I. E. Sigel & K. A. Renninger (Vol. Eds.), *Handbook of child psychology* (5th ed.) Vol. 4: *Child psychology in practice* (pp. 999–1058). New York: Wiley.

Lamb, M. E., Hwang, C. P., Ketterlinus, R. D., & Fracasso, M. P. (1999). Parent-child relationships: Development in the context of the family. In M. H. Bornstein & M. E. Lamb (Eds.), *Developmental psychology: An advanced textbook* (4th ed., pp. 411–450). Mahwah, NJ: Erlbaum.

Lamborn, S. D., Mounts, N. S., Steinberg, L., & Dornbusch, S. M. (1991). Patterns of competence and adjustment among adolescents from authoritative, authoritarian, indulgent, and neglectful families. *Child Development, 62,* 1049–1065.

Landau, B., Smith, L. B., & Jones, S. S. (1988). The importance of shape in early lexical learning. *Cognitive Development, 3,* 299–321.

Landau, B., & Stecker, D. (1990). Objects and places: Geometric and syntactic representations in early lexical learning. *Cognitive Development, 5,* 287–312.

Landers, C. (1989). A psychobiological study of infant development in South India. In J. K. Nugent, B. M. Lester, & T. B. Brazelton (Eds.), *The cultural context of infancy: Vol. 1: Biology, culture, and infant development* (pp. 169–208). Norwood, NJ: Ablex.

Landrigan, P. (1981, December). *Report of the 84th Ross Conference on Pediatric Research.*

Langer, E. J. (1979). The illusion of incompetence. In L. C. Perlmutter & R. A. Monty (Eds.), *Choice and perceived control* (pp. 301–313). Hillsdale, NJ: Erlbaum.

Larsen, J. S. (1971). The sagittal growth of the eye: IV. Ultra-sonic measurement of the axial length of the eye from birth to puberty. *Acta Ophthalmologica, 49,* 873–886.

Larson, D. B. (1998). Have faith: Religion can heal mental ills. In B. Slife (Ed.), *Taking sides: Clashing views on controversial psychological issues* (pp. 292–296). Guilford, CT: Dushkin/McGraw Hill.

Larson, R. (1998). Implications for policy and practice: Getting adolescents, families, and communities in sync. *New Directions for Child and Adolescent Development, 82,* 83–88.

Larson, R., & Ham, M. (1993). Stress and "storm and stress" in early adolescence: The relationship of negative events with dysphoric affect. *Developmental Psychology, 29*(1), 130–140.

Laurence, J. (1999). The usual state of emergency. *AIDS Patient Care and STDS, 13*(11), 3–5.

Laursen, B., & Collins, W. A. (1994). Interpersonal conflict during adolescence. *Psychological Bulletin, 115*(2), 197–209.

Lavine, L. (1977). Differentiation of letterlike forms in pre-reading children. *Developmental Psychology, 13*(2), 89–94.

Law, B., Fitzsimon, C., Ford-Jones, L., MacDonald, N., Dery, P., Vaudry, W., Mills, E., Haperiin, S., Michaliszyn, A., & Riviere, M. (1999). Cost of chickenpox in Canada: Part II. Cost of complicated cases and total economic impact. *Pediatrics, 104*(1), 7–14.

Law, D., Pellegrino, J. W., & Hunt, E. B. (1993). Comparing the tortoise and the hare: Gender differences and experience in dynamic spatial reasoning tasks. *Psychological Science, 4,* 35–41.

Leary, M. R. (1990). Responses to social exclusion: Social anxiety, jealousy, loneliness, depression, and low self-esteem. *Journal of Social and Clinical Psychology, 9,* 221–229.

Lecanuet, J. P., & Granier-Deferre, C. (1993). Speech stimuli in the fetal environment. In deBoysson-Bardies, B., de Schonen, S., Jusczyk, P., MacNeilage, P., & Morton, J. (Eds.), *Developmental neurocognition: Speech and face processing in the first year of life.* Dordrecht, The Netherlands: Kluwer.

Lecanuet, J. P., Granier-Deferre, C., & Schaal, B. (1993). Continuite sensorielle transnatale. In Pouthas and Jouen, *Les comportements du bébé.* (Cited in deBoysson-Bardies, B., 1999. *How language comes to children.* Cambridge, MA: MIT Press, p. 24.)

Lee, S. H. (1990). Influence of metacognitive knowledge and aptitude on problem solving. *Journal of Educational Psychology, 82,* 306–314.

Lee, T. F. (1993). *Gene future: The promise and perils of the new biology.* New York: Plenum.

Leehan, J., & Wilson, L. (1985). *Grown-up abused children.* Springfield, IL: Charles C. Thomas.

Legree, P. J., Pifer, M. E., & Grafton, F. C. (1996). Correlations among cognitive abilities are lower for higher-ability groups. *Intelligence, 23,* 45–58.

Lehman, G. (1993, March). *Academic achievement motivation and time management as predictors of academic success.* Paper presented at the Annual Meetings of the Eastern Psychological Association. Crystal City, VA.

Leifer, A. D., Leiderman, P. H., Barnett, C. R., & Williams, J. A. (1972). Effects of mother-infant separation on maternal attachment behavior. *Child Development, 43,* 1203–1218.

Lemerise, E. A., & Arsenio, W. F. (2000). An integrated model of emotion processes and cognition in social information processing. *Child Development, 71*(1), 107–118.

Lempers, J. D. (1979). Young children's production and comprehension of nonverbal deictic behaviors. *The Journal of Genetic Psychology, 135,* 93–102.

Lenz, W. (1966). Malformations caused by drugs in pregnancy. *American Journal of Diseases of Children, 112,* 99–106.

Leonard, C. H., Clyman, R. I., Piecuch, R. E., Juster, R. P., Ballard, R. A., & Behle, M. B. (1990). Effect of medical and social risk factors on outcome of prematurity and very low birthweight. *The Journal of Pediatrics, 116*(4), 620–626.

Leont'ev, A.V. (1981). In J. V. Wertsch (Ed.). The problem of activity in psychology. *The concept of activity in Soviet psychology* (pp. 37–71). Armonk, NY: M. E. Sharpe.

Lepper, M. (1973). Dissonance, self-perception, and honesty in children. *Journal of Personality and Social Psychology, 13,* 495–507.

Lerner, R. M. (1986). *Concepts and theories of human development.* (2nd ed.). New York: Random House.

Lerner, R. M. (1996). Relative plasticity, integration, temporality, and diversity in human development: A developmental contextual perspective about theory, process, and method. *Developmental Psychology, 32,* 781–786.

Leslie, A. M. (1984). Spatiotemporal continuity and the perception of causality in infants. *Perception, 13,* 287–305.

Leslie, A. M., & Keeble, S. (1987). Do 6-month-olds perceive causality? *Cognition, 25,* 265–288.

Lesser, G. S. (1959). The relationship between various forms of aggression and popularity among lower-class children. *Journal of Educational Psychology, 50,* 20–25.

Leu, D. J. (1999). Sarah's secret: Social aspects of literacy and learning in a digital information age. *International Reading Association.* Retrieved March 2000 from the World Wide Web: www.readingonline.org/electronic

Leung, E. H. L., & Rheingold, H. L. (1981). Development of pointing as a social gesture. *Developmental Psychology, 17*(2), 215–220.

Levin, I., & Korat, O. (1993). Sensitivity to phonological, morphological, and semantic cues in early reading and writing in Hebrew. *Merrill-Palmer Quarterly, 39,* 213–232.

Levin, J. (1980). *The mnemonic '80's: Keywords in the classroom. Theoretical paper No. 86.* Wisconsin Research and Development Center for Individualized Schooling. Madison, WI.

Levine, S. C., Huttenlocher, J., Taylor, A., & Langroch, A. (1999). Early sex differences in spatial skill. *Developmental Psychology, 35*(4), 940–949.

Levitt, A. G., & Wang, Q. (1991). Evidence for language-specific rhythmic influences in the reduplicative babbling of French- and English-learning infants. *Language and Speech, 34,* 235–249.

Lewis, C. (1994). Episodes, events, and narratives in the child's understanding of mind. In C. Lewis & P. Mitchell (Eds.), *Children's early understanding of mind: Origins and development* (pp. 457–478). Hillsdale, NJ: Erlbaum.

Lewis, M. D. The promise of Dynamic Systems approaches for an integrated account of human development. *Child Development, 71,* 36–43.

Liberman, A., & Chaiken, S. (1992). Defensive processing of personality relevant health messages. *Personality and Social Psychology, 18,* 669–679.

Liberman, I. Y., Shankweiler, D., Fisher, F. W., & Carter, B. (1974). Explicit syllable and phoneme segmentation in the young child. *Journal of Experimental Child Psychology, 18,* 201–212.

Licht, B. G., Stader, S. R., & Swenson, C. C. (1989). Children's achievement-related beliefs: Effects of academic area, sex, and achievement level. *Journal of Educational Research, 82*(5), 253–260.

Lieberman, A. F. (1977). Preschoolers' competence with a peer: Relations with attachment and peer experience. *Child Development, 48,* 1277–1287.

Lieberman, A. F., & Pawl, J. H. (1990). Disorders of attachment and secure base behavior in the second year of life: Conceptual issues and clinical intervention. In M. T. Greenberg, D. Cichetti, E. M. Cummings (Eds.), *Attachment in the preschool years: Theory, research and intervention* (pp. 375–347). Chicago: University of Chicago Press.

Lieberman, E., Gremy, I., Lang, J. M., & Cohen, A. (1994). Low birthweight at term and the timing of fetal exposure to maternal smoking. *American Journal of Public Health, 84,* 1127–1131.

Liebert, R. M. (1986). Effects of television on children and adolescents. *Journal of Development and Behavioral Pediatrics, 7*(1), 43–48.

Liebert, R. M., & Baron, R. A. (1972). Some immediate effects of televised violence on children's behavior. *Developmental Psychology, 6,* 469–475.

Light, P., & Perrett-Clermont, A. (1989). Social context effects in learning and testing. In A. R. H. Gellatly, D. Rogers, & J. Sloboda (Eds.), *Cognition and social worlds* (pp. 99–112). Oxford: Clarendon Press.

Lilienfeld, A. M. (1969). *Epidemiology of mongolism.* Baltimore: Johns Hopkins Press.

Lim, T. K. (1994). Gender-related differences in intelligence: Application of confirmatory factor analysis. *Intelligence, 19,* 179–192.

Lin, B. H., Guthrie, J., & Blaylock, J. R. (1999). The diets of America's children: Influence of dining out, household characteristics, and nutrition knowledge. *USDA Agricultural Economic Report* No. 746.

Lindsay, P. (1984). High school size, participation in activities, and young adult social participation: Some enduring effects of schooling. *Educational Evaluation and Policy Analysis, 6,* 73–83.

Link, D. D., & Bonifazi, D. Z. (1999, April). *The role of family environment and expressed emotion in eating disorders.* Paper presented at the annual meeting of the Eastern Psychological Association, Providence, RI.

Linn, M. C. (1983). Content, context, and process in reasoning. *Journal of Early Adolescence, 3,* 63–82.

Linn, M. C., & Petersen, A. C. (1985). Emergence of characteristics of sex-differences in spatial ability: A meta-analysis. *Child Development, 56,* 1479–1498.

Lipsitt, L. P., & Behl, G. (1990). Taste-mediated differences in the sucking behavior of human newborns. In E. D. Capaldi & T. L. Powley (Eds.), *Taste experience, and feeding* (pp. 74–93). Washington, DC: American Psychological Association.

Lipsitt, L. P., Engen, T., & Kaye, H. (1963). Developmental changes in the olfactory threshold of the neonate. *Child Development, 34,* 371–376.

Lipsitt, L. P., & Levy, N. (1959). Electrotactual threshold in the neonate. *Child Development, 30,* 547–554.

Lloyd, B., & Goodwin, R. (1995). Let's pretend: Casting the characters and setting the scene. *British Journal of Developmental Psychology, 13,* 261–270.

Lo, L. (1994). Exploring teenage shoplifting behavior: A choice and constraint approach. *Environmental Behavior, 26*(5), 612–639.

Lobel, M., Dunkel-Schetter, C., & Scrimshaw, S. C. M. (1992). Prenatal maternal stress and prematurity: A prospective study of socio-economically disadvantaged wowen. *Health Psychology, 11,* 32–40.

Locke, J. L. (1996). Why do infants begin to talk? Language as an unintended consequence. *Journal of Child Language, 23,* 251–268.

Loeber, R. (1982). The stability of antisocial and delinquent child behavior: A review. *Child Development, 53,* 1431–1446.

Loeber, R., Tremblay, R., Gagnon, R., & Charlesbois, P. (1989). Continuity and desistance in disruptive boys' early fighting at school. *Development and Psychopathology, 1,* 39–50.

Loehlin, J. C. (1997). Genes and environment. In D. Magnusson (Ed.), *The lifespan development of individuals: Behavioral, neurobiological, and psychosocial perspectives* (pp. 38–51). New York: Cambridge University Press.

Lombardi, K. S. (2000, January 16). Underage drinkers getting younger and drinking more. *The New York Times,* pp. 1–4.

Londerville, S., & Main, M. (1981). Security of attachment, compliance, and maternal training methods in the second year of life. *Developmental Psychology, 17,* 289–299.

Lonigan, C. J., & Whitehurst, G. J. (1998). Relative efficacy of parent and teacher involvement in a shared reading intervention for preschool children from low-income backgrounds. *Early Childhood Research Quarterly, 13*(2), 263–290.

Lopez, L. R., & Gary, F. (1995). Logical response to youth who run away from home: Implications for psychiatric mental health nursing. *Journal of Psychological Nursing, 33*(3), 9–15.

Lounsbury, J. H. (1992). Interdisciplinary instruction: A mandate for the nineties. In J. H. Lounsbury (Ed.), *Connecting the curriculum through interdisciplinary instruction.* Columbus, OH: National Middle School Association.

Lowrey, G. H. (1978). *Growth and development of children* (7th ed.) Chicago: Year Book.

Lucas, A., Morley, R., Cole, T. J., Lister, G., & Leeson-Payne, C. (1992). Breast milk and subsequent intelligence quotient in children born preterm. *Lancet, 339,* 261–264.

Luetkemeier, M. J., Bainbridge, C. N., Walker, J., Brown, D. B., & Eisenman, P. A. (1995). Anabolic-androgenic steroids: Prevalence, knowledge, and attitudes in junior and senior high school students. *Journal of Health Education, 26*(1), 4–9.

Lummis, M., & Stevenson, H. W. (1990). Gender differences in beliefs and achievement: A cross-cultural study. *Developmental Psychology, 26,* 254–263.

Lundberg, I., Frost, J., & Peterson, O. (1988). Effects of an extensive program for stimulating phonological awareness. *Reading Research Quarterly, 23,* 263–284.

Lundberg, L., & Torneus, M. (1978). Nonreaders' awareness of the basic relationship between spoken and written words. *Journal of Experimental Child Psychology, 25,* 404–412.

Lundy, B., Field, T., & Pickens, J. (1996). Newborns of mothers with depressive symptoms are less expressive. *Infant Behavior and Development, 19,* 419–424.

Luoma, L., Herrgard, E., Martikainen, A., & Ahonen, T. (1998). Speech and language development of children born at <=32 weeks' gestation: A 5-year prospective follow-up study. *Developmental Medicine and Child Neurology, 40*(6), 380–387.

Lutz, D., & Sternberg, R. J. (1999). Cognitive development. In M. H. Bornstein & M. E. Lamb (Eds.) *Developmental psychology: An advanced textbook* (4th ed., pp. 275–312). Mahwah, NJ: Erlbaum.

Lyle, J., & Hoffman, H. (1972). Children's use of television and other media. *Television in everyday life: Patterns of use.* Washington, DC: U.S. Government Printing Office.

Lynam, D. R., Milich, R., Zimmerman, R., Novak, S. P., Logan, T. K., Martin, C., Leukefeld, C., & Clayton, R. (1999). Project DARE: No effects at 10-year follow-up. *Journal of Consulting and Clinical Psychology, 67,* 590–593.

Lynch, M. P. (1996). The case of total deafness: I. Phrasing in the prelinguistic vocablization of a child with congenital absence of cochleas. *Applied Psycholinguistics, 17,* 293–312.

Lytton, H. (1990). Child and parent effects in boys' conduct disorders. *Developmental Psychology, 26 (5),* 683–697.

Ma, G. X., Toubbeh, J., Cline, J., & Chisholm, A. (1998). Fetal alcohol syndrome among Native American adolescents: A model prevention program. *Journal of Primary Prevention 19*(1), 43–55.

Maccoby, E. E. (1992). The role of parents in the socialization of children: An historical overview. *Developmental Psychology, 28,* 1006–1018.

Maccoby, E. E., & Jacklin, C. N. (1974). *The psychology of sex differences.* Stanford, CA: Stanford University Press.

Maccoby, E. E., & Martin, J. A. (1983). Socialization in the context of the family: Parent-child interaction. In P. H. Mussen (Series Ed.) & E. M. Hetherington (Vol. Ed.), *Handbook of child psychology: Vol. 4. Socialization, personality, and social development* (4th ed., pp. 1–101). New York: Wiley.

MacDonald, K. (1987). Parent-child physical play with rejected, neglected, and popular boys. *Developmental Psychology, 23,* 705–711.

MacIver, D. J., Reuman, D. A., & Main, S. R. (1995). Social structuring of the school: Studying what is, illuminating what could be. *Annual Review of Psychology, 46,* 375–400.

MacKinnon-Lewis, C., Rabiner, D., & Starnes, R. (1999). Predicting boys' social acceptance and aggression: The role of mother-child interaction and boys' beliefs about peers. *Developmental Psychology, 35*(3), 632–639.

Macksound, M. S., & Aber, J. L. (1996). The war experience and psychosocial development of children in Lebanon. *Child Development, 67,* 70–88.

MacLean, D. J., & Schuler, M. (1989). Conceptual development in infancy: The understanding of containment. *Child Development, 60,* 1126–1137.

Macnamara, J. (1976). First and second language learning: Same or different? *Journal of Education, 158,* 39–54.

Maddi, S. R. (1976). *Personality theories.* Homewood, IL: Dorsey.

Madkour, J., & Kuther, T. L. (1999, April). *Gender differences in the relation of self-esteem and eating disordered attitudes.* Paper presented at the annual meeting of the Eastern Psychological Association, Providence, RI.

Maes, H. H.M., Neale, M. C., & Eaves, L. J. (1997). Genetic and environmental factors in relative body weight and human adiposity. *Behavior Genetics, 27*(4), 32!5–351.

Magai, C., & McFadden, S. H. (1995). *The role of emotions in social and personality development: History, theory, and research.* New York: Plenum Press.

Maggioni, A., & Lifshitz, F. (1995). Nutritional management of failure to thrive. *Pediatric Clinics of North America, 42*(2), 791–807.

Magnuson, D. (1988). *Individual development from an interactional perspective: A longitudinal perspective.* Hillside, NJ: Erlbaum.

Magnusson, D., Stattin, H., & Allen, V. L. (1985). Biological maturation and social development: A longitudinal study of some adjustment processes from mid-adolescence to adulthood. *Journal of Youth and Adolescence, 14,* 267–283.

Mahoney, J. L., & Cairns, R. B. (1997). Do extracurricular activities protect against early school dropout? *Developmental Psychology, 33,* 241–253.

Main, M. (1981). Avoidance in the service of attachment: A working paper. In K. L. Immelmenn, G. W. Barlow, L. Petrinovitch, & M. Main (Eds.), *Behavioral development.* Cambridge, UK: Cambridge University Press.

Main, M., & Hesse, E. (1990). Parents' unresolved traumatic experiences are related to infant disorganized attachment status. Is frightened and/or frightening parental behavior the linking mechanism? In M. T. Greenberg, D. Cicchetti, & E. M. Cummings (Eds.), *Attachment in the preschool years: Theory, research, and intervention* (pp. 161–182). Chicago: University of Chicago Press.

Main, M., & Solomon, J. (1990). Procedures for identifying infants as disorganized/disoriented during the Ainsworth Strange Situation. In M. T. Greenberg, D. Cicchetti, & E. M. Cummings (Eds.), *Attachment in the preschool years: Theory, research, and intervention* (pp. 121–160). Chicago: University of Chicago Press.

Malina, R. M. (1990). Physical growth and performance during the transitional years (9–16). In R. Montemayor, G. R. Adams, & T. P. Gullotta (Eds.), *From childhood to adolescence* (pp. 41–62). Newbury Park, CA: Sage.

Malina, R. M., & Bouchard, C. (1991). *Growth, maturation, and physical activity.* Champaign, IL: Human Kinetics Books.

Mancini, J., Beckman, G., Grella, J., & Pruzinsky, T. (1999, April). *Gender differences in body-image and reasons for exercise.* Paper presented at the annual meeting of the Eastern Psychological Association, Providence, RI.

Mandler, J. M., Bauer, P. J., & McDonough, L. (1991). Separating the sheep from the goats: Differentiating global categories. *Cognitive Psychology, 23*(2), 263–298.

Mandler, J. M., Fivush, R., & Reznick, J. S. (1987). The development of contextual categories. *Cognitive Development, 2,* 339–354.

Mandler, J. M., & McDonough, L. (1998). On developing a knowledge base in infancy. *Developmental Psychology, 34*(2), 1274–1288.

Mann, D. (1997). Caffeine during pregnancy linked to lower birth weight. *Medical Tribune.* Retrieved March 2000 from the World Wide Web: www.thriveonline.com/newsstand/todays/times

Maratsos, M., Kuczaj, S. A., Fox, D. E. C., & Chalkley, M. A. (1979). Some empirical studies in the acquisition of transformational relations: Passives, negatives, and the past tense. In W. A. Collins (Eds.), *Children's language and communication.* Hillsdale, NJ: Erlbaum.

Marcia, J. E. (1980). Identity in adolescence. In J. Adelson (Ed.), *Handbook of adolescent psychology* (pp. 159–187). New York: Wiley.

Marcia, J. E. (1988). Common processes underlying ego identity, cognitive/moral development, and individuation. In D. Lapsky and F. C. Power (Eds.), *Self, ego, and identity: Integrative approaches* (pp. 211–225). New York: Springer-Verlag.

Marcia, J. E. (1991). Identity and self development. In R. M. Lerner, A. C. Petersen, E. J. Brooks-Gunn (Eds.), *Encyclopedia of adolescence* (Vol. 1) (pp. 527–5331). New York: Garland.

Marcus, G. F., Pinker, S., Ullman, M., Hollander, M., Rosen, T. J., & Zu, F. (1992). Overregularization in language acquisition. *Monographs of the Society for Research in Child Development, 57*(4, Serial No. 228).

Marcus, R. F. (1999). A gender-linked exploratory factor analysis of antisocial behavior in young adolescents. *Adolescence, 34,* 17–23.

Margolis, H. S., Coleman, P. J., Brown, R. E., Mast, E. E., Sheingold, S. H., & Aravelo, J. A. (1995). Prevention of hepatitis B virus transmission by immunization. *Journal of the American Medical Association, 274*(15), 1201–1208.

Marin, M. C., DeTomas, M. E., Serres, C., & Mercuri, O. (1995). Protein-energy malnutrition during gestation and lactation in rats affects growth rate, brain development and essential fatty acid metabolism. *Journal of Nutrition, 125,* 1017–1024.

Marlier, L., Schall, B., & Soussignan, R. (1998). Neonatal responsiveness to the odor of amniotic and lacteal fluids: A test of perinatal chemosensory continuity. *Child Development, 69,* 611–623.

Marotz, L. R., Cross, M. Z., & Rush, J. M. (1993). *Health, safety, and nutrition for the young child.* Albany, NY: Delmar.

Marsh, H. W. (1992). Content specificity of relations between academic achievement and academic self-concept. *Journal of Educational Psychology, 84,* 135–142.

Martin, J. N., Hecht, M. L., & Larkey, L. K. (1994). Conversational improvement strategies for interethnic communication: African American and European American perspectives. *Communication Monographs, 61,* 236–255.

Martinez, F. D., Wright, A. L., & Taussig, L. M. (1994). The effect of paternal smoking on the birthweight of newborns whose mothers did not smoke. *American Journal of Public Health, 84,* 1489–1491.

Masataka, N. (1992). Motherese in a signed language. *Infant Behavior and Development, 15,* 453–460.

Masataka, N. (1992). Pitch characteristics of Japanese maternal speech to infants. *Journal of Child Language, 19,* 213–224.

Mash, E. J., & Wolfe, D. A. (1999). *Abnormal child psychology.* Belmont, CA: Wadsworth.

Massaro, D. W., & Cowan, N. (1993). Information processing models: Microscopes of mind. In L. W. Porter & M. R. Rosenzweig (Eds.), *Annual Review of Psychology, 34,* 383–425.

Masten, A. S. (1999, August 21). *Ordinary magic, extraordinary lives: Growing up competent in hazardous environments.* Address presented at the Annual Meetings of the American Psychological Association. Boston, MA.

Masters, M. S., & Sanders, B. (1993). Is the gender difference in mental rotation disappearing? *Behavioral Genetics, 23,* 337–341.

Matas, L., Arend, R. A., & Sroufe, L. A. (1978). Continuity of adaptation in the second year: The relationship between quality of attachment and later competence. *Child Development, 49,* 547–556.

Matthews, D. B., & Simpson, P. E. (1998). Prenatal exposure to ethanol disrupts spatial memory: Effect of the training-testing delay period. *Physiology and Behavior, 64*(1), 63–67.

Mattys, S. L., Jusczyk, P. W., Luce, P. A., & Morgan, J. L. (1999). Phonotactic and prosodic effects on word segmentaton in infants. *Cognitive Psychology, 38,* 465–494.

Maugh, T. H. (1996, July 26). Study blames tobacco smoke in crib deaths. *Austin American-Statesman,* pp. A1; A7.

Maurer, D. (1985). Infants' perception of facedness. In T. M. Field & N. A. Fox (Eds.), *Social perception in infants* (pp. 73–100). Hillsdale, NJ: Ablex.

Mayer, J. D. (1999, September). Emotional intelligence: Popular or scientific psychology? *APA Monitor,* p. 50.

McAllister, R., & Caltabiano, M. L. (1994). Self-esteem, body image, and weight in non-eating-disordered women. *Psychological Reports, 75,* 1339–1343.

McAnarney, E. R., Lawrence, R. A., Ricciuti, H. N., Polley, J., & Szilagyi, M. (1986). Interactions of adolescent mothers and their 1-year-old children. *Pediatrics, 78,* 585–590.

McBroom, W. H. (1981). Parental relationships, socioeconomic status, and sex role expectations. *Sex Roles, 7,* 1027–1033.

McCall, R. B. (1984). Developmental changes in mental performance: The effect of birth of a sibling. *Child Development, 55,* 1317–1321.

McCall, R. B., Appelbaum, M. I., & Hogarty, P. S. (1973). Developmental changes in mental performance. *Monographs of the Society for Research in Child Development, 38*(3, Serial No. 150).

McCall, R. B., & Carriger, M. S. (1993). Recognition memory performance as predictors of late IQ. *Child Development, 64,* 57–79.

McCartney, J. S., Fried, P. A., & Watkinson, B. (1994). Central auditory processing in school-age children prenatally exposed to cigarette smoke. *Neurotoxicology and Teratology, 16*(3), 269–276.

McCarty, M. E., & Ashmead, D. H. (1999). Visual control of reaching and grasping in infants. *Developmental Psychology, 35,* 620–631.

McCatcheon, S. (1996). *Natural childbirth the Bradley way.* New York: Plume.

McCaughey, K., McCaughey, B., & Lewis, D. (1998). *Seven from heaven:* The miracle of the McCaughey septuplets. New York: Nelson.

McClelland, D. C., Atkinson, I. W., Clark, R. A., & Lowell, E. L. (1976). *The achievement motive.* New York: Halsted Press.

McCormick, C. E., & Mason, J. M. (1989). Fostering reading for Head Start children with little books. In J. B. Allen & J. M. Mason (Eds.), *Risk makers, risk takers, risk breakers* (pp. 154–177). Portsmouth, NH: Heinemann.

McCormick, M., Gortmaker, S., & Sobol, A. (1990). Very low birthweight children. Behavior problems and school difficulty in a national sample. *The Journal of Pediatrics, 117,* 687–693.

McCrae, R. R., & Costa, P. T. (1994). The stability of personality: Observations and evaluations. *Current Directions in Psychological Science, 3,* 173–175.

McCrae, R. R., Costa, P. T., deLima, M. P., Simoes, A., Ostendorf, F., Angleitner, A., Marusic, I., Bratko, D., Caprara, G. V., Barbanelli, C., Chae, J. H., & Piedmont, R. L. (1999). Age differences in personality across the adult life span: Parallels in five cultures. *Developmental Psychology, 35,* 466–477.

McCune, L. (1995). A normative study of representational play at the transition to language. *Developmental Psychology, 31*(2), 198–206.

McCune-Nicolich, L. (1981). Toward symbolic functioning: Structure of early pretend games and potential parallels with language. *Child Development, 52,* 785–797.

McCune-Nicolich, L., & Fenson, L. (1984). Methodological issues in studying early pretend play. In T. Yawkey & T. Pellegrini (Eds.), *Child's play.* Hillsdale, NJ: Erlbaum.

McGarrigle, J., & Donaldson, M. (1975). Conservation accidents. *Cognition, 3,* 341–350.

McGivern, R. F., Huston, J. P., Byrd, D., King, T., Siegle, G. J., & Reilly, J. (1997). Sex differences in visual recognition memory: Support for a sex-related difference in attention in adults and children. *Brain and Cognition, 34*(3), 323–336.

McHugh, E. (1995). Going beyond the physical: Social skills and physical education. *Journal of Physical Education, Recreation and Dance, 66*(4), 18–21.

McKenzie, T. L. (1999). School health-related physical activity programs: What do the data say? *Journal of Physical Education, Recreation, and Dance, 70*(1), 16–19.

McKinley, N. M. (1999). Women and objectified body consciousness: Mothers and daughters' body experience in cultural, developmental, and familial context. *Developmental Psychologist. 35*(3), 760–769.

McLaughlin, B. (1984). *Second language acquisition in childhood* (Vol. 1). Hillsdale, NJ: Erlbaum.

McMahon, K. C. (1998). *Interaction of goal orientation, coach's feedback, and level of competition on an athletic's intrinsic motivation.* Paper presented at the Eastern Psychological Association meeting, Boston, MA.

McMillan, D. K. (1999, August). *The personality portfolio: A structured journal increases learning and enjoyment.* Paper presented at the annual meeting of the American Psychological Association, Boston.

McNeill, D. (1966). Developmental psycholinguistics. In F. Smith & G. A. Miller (Eds.), *The genesis of language: A psycholinguistic approach* (pp. 15–84). Cambridge, MA: The MIT Press.

McNeill, D. (1985). Holophrastic noun phrases within grammatical clauses. In M. D. Barrett (Ed.), *Children's single-word speech.* Chichester: Wiley.

McNeill, D., & McNeill, N. B. (1968). What does a child mean when he says "no"? In E. E. Zales (Ed.), *Language and language behavior.* New York: Appleton-Century- Crofts.

McNelles, L. R., & Connolly, J. A. (1999). Intimacy between adolescent friends: Age and gender differences in affect and intimate behaviors. *Journal of Research on Adolescence, 9*(2), 143–160.

Mead, M., & Newton, N. (1967). Cultural patterning of perinatal behavior. In S. A. Richardson & A. F. Guttmacher (Eds.), *Childbearing.* Baltimore: Williams & Wilkins.

Meckler, L. (1999). Antismoking forces take aim at cigars. *Detroit Free Press.* Retrieved March 2000 from the World Wide Web: www.detroitfreepress.com/news/health/qcigar27.htm

Medansky, D., & Edelbrock, C. (1990). Cosleeping in a community sample of 2- and 3-year-olds. *Pediatrics, 86,* 197–203.

Medley, R. M. (1999). Channel effects: Two methods of letter writing in the classroom. *Journal of Adolescent & Adult Literacy, 42*(8), 668–673.

Meece, J. L., Wigfield, A., & Eccles, J. S. (1990). Predictors of math anxiety and its influence on young adolescents' course enrollment intentions and performance in mathematics. *Journal of Educational Psychology, 82,* 60–70.

Meehan, A. M. (1984). A meta-analysis of sex differences in formal operational thought. *Child Development, 55,* 1110–1124.

Mehler, J., Jusczyk, P., Lambertz, G., Halsted, N., Bertoncini, J., & Amiel-Tison, C. (1988). A precursor of language acquisition in young infants. *Cognition, 198,* 143–178.

Mehlman, M. J., & Botkin, J. R. (1998). *Access to the genome: The challenge to equality.* Washington, DC: Georgetown University Press.

Meichenbaum, D., & Turk, D. (1976). The cognitive-behavioral management of anxiety, anger, and pain. In P. O. Davison (Ed.), *The behavioral management of anxiety, depression, and pain.* New York: Brunner/Mazel.

Mennella, J. A., & Beauchamp, G. K. (1991). Maternal diet alters the sensory qualities of human milk and the nursling's behavior. *Pediatrics, 88,* 737–744.

Meredith, H. V. (1975). Relation between tobacco smoking of pregnant women and body size of progeny. *Human Biology, 47,* 451–472.

Merolla, C. (1994). Five solid reasons your teenager shouldn't smoke. *Family Safety and Health, 53*(4), 28–29.

Mervis, C. B. (1987). Child-basic object categories and early lexical development. In U. Neisser (Ed.), *Concepts and conceptual development: Ecological and intellectual factors in categorization* (pp. 201–233). Cambridge, MA: Cambridge University Press.

Messer, D. J., McCarthy, M. E., McQuiston, S., MacTurk, R. H., Yarrow, L. J., & Vietze, P. M. (1986). Relations between mastery behavior in infancy and competence in early childhood. *Developmental Psychology, 22,* 366–372.

Messinger, D. S., Dickson, K. L., & Fogel, A. (1999). What's in a smile? *Developmental Psychology, 35,* 701–708.

Mestayan, G., & Varga, R. (1960). Chemical thermoregulation of full-term and premature newborn infants. *Journal of Pediatrics, 56,* 623–629.

Metcalfe, J., & Mischel, W. (1999). A hot/cool system analysis of delay of gratification: Dynamics of willpower. *Psychological Review, 106*(1), 3–19.

Metsala, J. A., & Walley, A. C. (1998). Spoken vocabulary growth and the segmental restructuring of lexical representations: Precursors to phonemic awareness and early reading ability. In J. L. Metsala & L. C. Ehri (Eds.), *Word recognition in beginning literacy* (pp. 89–120). Mahwah, NJ: Erlbaum.

Metsala, J. L. (1999). Young children's phonological awareness and nonword repetition as a function of vocabulary development. *Journal of Educational Psychology, 91*(1), 3–19.

Meyer, L. A., Wardrop, J. L., Stahl, S. A., & Linn, R. L. (1994). Effects of reading storybooks aloud to children. *Journal of Educational Research, 88*(2), 69–85.

Michael, E. D. (1990). Physical development and fitness. In R. M. Thomas (Ed.), *The encyclopedia of human development and education: Theory, research, and studies* (pp. 223–225). Oxford: Pergamon.

Michelsson, K., Rinne, A., & Paajanen, S. (1990). Crying, feeding, and sleeping patterns in 1 to 12-month-old infants. *Child: Care, Health, and Development, 16,* 99–111.

Mikulincer, M. (1997). Adult attachment style and information processing: Individual differences in curiosity and cognitive closure. *Journal of Personality and Social Psychology, 72*(5), 1217–1230.

Milano, S. (1995). Don't believe it! Three sports myths. *Parents playbook: Sports illustrated for kids supplement, 7,* 11.

Millar, W. S. (1974). Conditioning and learning in early infancy. In B. Foss (Ed.), *New perspectives in child development.* Harmondsworth, England: Penguin.

Miller, B. C., Norton, M. C., Fan, X., & Christopherson, C. R. (1998). Pubertal development, parental communication, and sexual values in relation to adolescent sexual behaviors. *Journal of Early Adolescence, 18*(1), 27–52.

Miller, E. M. (1998). Evidence from opposite-sex twins for the effects of prenatal sex hormones. In L. Ellis & L. Eberts (Eds.), *Males, females, and behavior: Toward biological understanding* (pp. 27–57). Westport, CT: Praeger.

Miller, G. A., Galanter, E. H., & Pribram, K. H. (1960). *Plan and the structure of behavior.* New York: Holt, Rinehart and Winston.

Miller, G. A., & Gildea, P. N. (1987, September). How school children learn words. *Scientific American, 257,* 94–98.

Miller, J. G. (1971). The nature of living systems. *Behavioral Science, 16,* 277–301.

Miller, J. L., & Eimas, P. D. (1979). Organization in infant speech perception. *Canadian Journal of Psychology, 33,* 353–365.

Miller, K. E., Levine, M. L., Whitaker, D. J., & Xu, X. (1998a). Patterns of condom use among adolescents: The impact of maternal-adolescent communication. *American Journal of Public Health, 88*(10), 1542–1544.

Miller, K. E., Sabo, D. F., Farrell, M. P., Barnes, G. M., & Melnick, M. J. (1998b). Athletic participation and sexual behavior in adolescents: The different worlds of boys and girls. *Journal of Health and Social Behavior, 39*(2), 108–123.

Miller, L. S., Hoffman, R. E., Baron, A. E., Marine, W. M., & Melinkovich, P. (1994). Risk factors for delayed immunization against measles, mumps, and rubella in Colorado two-year-olds. *Pediatrics, 94*(2), 213–219.

Miller, P. J., & Sperry, L. L. (1988). Early talk about the past: The origins of conversational stories of personal experience. *Journal of Child Language, 15,* 293–315.

Miller, P. J., Wiley, A. T., Fung, H., & Liang, C. (1997). Personal storytelling as a medium of socialization in Chinese and American families. *Child Development, 68*(3), 557–568.

Miller, R. E., & Rosenstein, D. J. (1982). Children's dental health: Overview for the physician. *Pediatric Clinics of North America, 29*(3), 429–438.

Miller, R. L., Brickman, P., & Bolen, D. (1975). Attribution versus persuasion as a means for modifying behavior. *Journal of Personality and Social Psychology, 21*(3), 430–441.

Miller, S., & Garvey, D. (1984). Mother-baby role play: Its origins in social support. In I. Bretherton (Ed.), *Symbolic play: The development of social understanding* (pp. 101–130). New York: Academic Press.

Mills, C. J., Ablard, K. E., & Stumpf, H. (1993). Gender differences in academically talented young students' mathematical reasoning: Patterns across age and subskills. *Journal of Educational Psychology, 85,* 340–346.

Mills, J. K., & Andrianopoulos, G. D. (1993). The relationship between childhood onset obesity and psychopathology in adulthood. *Journal of Psychology, 127*(5), 547–551.

Milunsky, A. (1992). *Heredity and your family's health.* Baltimore: Johns Hopkins University Press.

Minami, M. (1996). Japanese preschool children's narrative development. *First Language, 16,* 339–363.

Mindell, J. A., Moline, M. L., Zendell, S. M., Brown, L. W., & Fry, J. M. (1994). Pediatricians and sleep disorders: Training and practice. *Pediatrics, 94*(2), 194–196.

Minton, C., Kagan, J., & Levine, J. A. (1971). Maternal control and obedience in the two-year-old. *Child Development, 42,* 1873–1894.

Minuchin, P. P., & Shapiro, E. K. (1983). The school as a context for social development. In P. H. Mussen (Ed.), *Handbook of child psychology* (4th ed., Vol. 4). New York: Wiley.

Mischel, W. (1976). *Introduction to personality.* New York: Holt, Rinehart & Winston.

Mischel, W., & Baker, N. (1975). Cognitive transformation of reward objects through instructions. *Journal of Personality and Social Psychology, 16,* 329–337.

Mischel, W., & Ebbesen, E. (1970). Attention in delay of gratification. *Journal of Personality and Social Psychology, 16,* 329–337.

Miura, I. T., Okamoto, Y., Kim. C. C., Chang, C.M., Steere, M., & Fayol, M. (1994). Comparisons of children's cognitive representation of number: China, France, Japan, Korea, Sweden, & the U.S. *International Journal of Behavioral Development, 17,* 401-411.

Miura, I. T., Okamoto, Y., Kim, C. C., Steer, M., & Fayol, M. (1993). First graders' cognitive representation of number and understanding of place value: Cross-national comparisons—France, Japan, Korea, Sweden, and the United States. *Journal of Educational Psychology, 85*(1), 24–30.

Miyake, K., Chen, S., & Campos, J. (1985). Infant temperament, mother's mode of interaction, and attachment in Japan: An interim report. In I. Bretherton & E. Waters (Eds.), Growing points of attachment theory and research (pp. 276–297). *Monographs of the Society for Research in Child Development, 50* (Serial No. 209).

Mize, J., & Ladd, G. W. (1990). Toward the development of successful social skills training for preschool children. In S. R. Asher & J. D. Coie (Eds.), *Peer rejection in childhood* (pp. 338–364). New York: Cambridge University Press.

Mize, J., & Pettit, G. S. (1997). Mothers' social coaching, mother-child relationship style, and children's peer competence: Is the medium the message? *Child Development, 68*(2), 312–332.

Mizukami, K., Kobayashi, N., Ishii, T., & Iwata, H. (1990). First selective attachment begins in early infancy: A study using telethermography. *Infant Behavior and Development, 13,* 257–271.

MOD. (March of Dimes) (1999a). Accutane. *March of Dimes Health Library.* Retrieved March 2000 from the World Wide Web: www.modimes.org/HealthLibrary2/factsheets/Accutane

MOD. (1999b). Birth defects information. *March of Dimes Health Library.* Retrieved March 2000 from the World Wide Web: www.modimes.org/HealthLibrary2/BirthDefects

MOD. (1999c). Deliver the best. *March of Dimes Health Library.* Retrieved March 2000 from the World Wide Web: www.modimes.org/HealthLibrary2/healthybaby/deliver

MOD. (1999d). Diabetes in pregnancy. *March of Dimes Health Library.* Retrieved March 2000 from the World Wide Web: www.modimes.org/HealthLibrary2/factsheets/Diabetes_in_pregnancy

MOD. (1999e). Think ahead. *March of Dimes Health Library.* Retrieved March 2000 from the World Wide Web: www.modimes.org/HealthLibrary2/HealthyBaby/think.

Moerk, E. L. (1991). Positive evidence for negative evidence. *First Language, 11,* 219–251.

Moffit, A. R. (1971). Consonant cue perception by twenty-to-twenty-four-week-old infants. *Child Development, 42,* 717–731.

Moffitt, T. E. (1993). Adolescence-limited and life-course-persistent antisocial behavior: A developmental taxonomy. *Psychological Review, 100,* 674–701.

Monitoring the Future Study (1999). *Cocaine.* Retrieved March 2000 from the World Wide Web: www.whitehousedrugpolicy.gov/drugfact

Moon, C., Cooper, R. P., Fifer, W. P. (1993). Two-day-olds prefer their native language. *Infant Behavior and Development, 16,* 495–500.

Moore, C., & Frye, D. (1991). The acquisition and utility of theories of mind. In D. Frye & C. Moore (Eds.), *Children's theories of mind: Mental states and social understanding.* Hillsdale, NJ: Erlbaum.

Moore, C. A., Khoury, M. J., & Liu, Y. (1997). Does light to moderate alcohol consumption during pregnancy increase the risk for renal anomalies among offspring? *Pediatrics 99,* Retrieved March 2000 from the World Wide Web: http//www.pediatrics.org/cgi/content/full/99/4/e

Moore, K. A. (1993). The effect of exercise on body image, self-esteem, and mood. *Mental Health in Australia, 5*(1), 38–40.

Moore, K. L., & Persaud, T. V. N. (1993). *Before we are born.* Philadelphia: Saunders.

Morgan, J. L. (1986). *From simple input to complex grammar.* Cambridge, MA: MIT Press.

Morgan, J. L., Bonamo, K. M., & Travis, L. L. (1995). Negative evidence on negative evidence. *Developmental Psychology, 31*(2), 180–197.

Morgan, J. L., & Saffran, J. R. (1995). Emerging integration of sequential and suprasegmental information in preverbal speech segmentation. *Child Development, 66,* 911–936.

Morissette, P., Ricard, M., & Decarie, G. (1995). Joint visual attention and pointing in infancy: A longitudinal study of comprehension. *British Journal of Developmental Psychology, 13,* 163–175.

Morphett, M. V., & Washburne, C. (1931). When should children begin to read? *Elementary School Journal, 31,* 496–503.

Mosier, C. E., & Rogoff, B. (1994). Infants' instrumental use of their mothers to achieve their goals. *Child Development, 65,* 70–19.

Moss, E. (1992). The social affective context of joint cognitive activity. In L. T. Winegar & J. Valsiner (Eds.), *Children's development with social context: Vol, 2: Research and methodology* (pp. 117–154). Hillsdale, NJ: Erlbaum.

Moyer, M. D., Shumway, E. A., & Specht, S. M. (1999, August). *Impression formation is influenced by the quality of speech and writing.* Paper presented at the American Psychological Annual Meeting, Boston, MA.

Msall, M. E., Rogers, B. T., & Buck, G. M. (1991). Risk factors for major neurodevelopmental impairments and need for special education resources in extremely premature infants. *Journal of Pediatrics, 119,* 606–614.

Mueller, E., & Brenner, J. (1977). The origins of social skills and interaction among playgroup toddlers. *Child Development, 48,* 854–861.

Mulhern, S., Dworkin, P. H., & Bernstein, B. (1994). Do parental concerns predict a diagnosis of attention-deficit hyperactivity disorder? *Journal of Developmental and Behavioral Pediatrics, 15*(5), 348–352.

Mullis, I. V. S., & Others (1993). *NAEP 1992—reading report card for the nation and the states: Data from the national and trial state assessments.* Princeton, NJ: National Assessment of Educational Progress.

Mummendey, A., & Wenzel, M. (1999). Social discrimination and tolerance in intergroup relations: Reactions to intergroup difference. *Personality and Social Psychology Review, 3*(2), 158–174.

Munakata, Y., McClelland, J. L., Johnson, M. H., & Siegler, R. S. (1997). Rethinking infant knowledge: Toward an adaptive process account of successes and failures in object permanence tasks. *Psychological Review, 104*(2), 686–713.

Munck, H., Mirdal, G. M., & Marner, L. (1991). Mother-infant interaction in Denmark. In J. K. Nugent, B. M. Lester, & T. B. Brazelton (Eds.), *The cultural context of infancy,* (Vol. 2, pp. 169–199). Norwood, NJ: Ablex.

Muret-Wagstaff, S., & Moore, S. G. (1989). The Hmong in America: Infant behavior and rearing practices. In J. K. Nugent, B. M. Lester, & T. B. Brazelton (Eds.), *The cultural context of infancy. Vol. 1: Biology, culture, and infant development* (pp. 319–340). Norwood, NJ: Ablex.

Murphy, C. M. (1978). Pointing in the context of a shared activity. *Child Development, 49,* 371–380.

Murphy, C. M., & Messer, D. J. (1977). Mothers, infants, and pointing: A study of gesture. In H. R. Schaffer (Ed.), *Studies in mother-infant interaction.* London: Academic Press.

Murray, A. D. (1988). Newborn auditory brain stem evoked response (ABRs): Prenatal and contemporary correlates. *Child Development, 59*(3), 571–588.

Murray, A. D., Johnson, J., & Peters, J. (1990). Fine-tuning of utterance length to preverbal infants: Effects on later language development. *Journal of Child Language, 17,* 511–525.

Murray, D. M. (1985). *A writer teaches writing.* Boston: Houghton Mifflin.

Murray, S. H., Touyz, S. W., & Beaumont, P. J. (1996). Awareness and perceived influence of body ideals in the media: A comparison of eating disorder patients and the general community. *Eating Disorders: The Journal of Treatment and Prevention, 4*(1), 33–46.

Murry, V. M. (1999). Variation in adolescent pregnancy status: A national tri-ethnic study. In H. I. McCubbin et al. (Eds.), *Resiliency in African-American families* (pp. 179–205). Thousand Oaks, CA: Sage Publications.

Musick, J. S., Clark, R., & Cohler, B. (1981). The Mothers' Project: A program for mentally ill mothers of young children. In B. Weissbourd & J. Musick, (Eds.), *Infants: Their social environments.* Washington, DC: National Association for the Education of Young Children.

Muter, V., Hulme, C., Snowling, M., & Taylor, S. (1997). Segmentation, not rhyming, predicts early progress in learning to read. *Journal of Experimental Child Psychology, 65,* 370–396.

NAEP (National Assessement of Educational Progress). (2000). U.S. student writing falls short of NAEP goals. *Reading Today, 17*(3), 3–4.

Naeye, R. (1983). Maternal age, obstetric complications, and the outcome of pregnancy. *Obstetrics and Gynecology, 61*(2), 210–216.

Naeye, R. L., Blanc, W., & Paul, C. (1973). Effects of maternal nutrition on the human fetus. *Pediatrics, 52,* 494–503.

Nafstad, P., Hagen, J. A., Leif, O., Magnus, P., & Jaakkola, J. J. K. (1999). Day care centers and respiratory health. *Pediatrics, 103*(4), 753–757.

Nagell, K. (1995). *Joint attention and gestural and verbal communication in 9- to 15-month-olds.* Paper presented at the bienniel Meeting of the Society for Research in Child Development, Indianapolis, March 30–April 2.

Nagy, W., Anderson, R., & Herman, P. (1987). Learning word meanings from context during normal reading. *American Educational Research Journal, 24,* 237–270.

Nagy, W. E., McClure, E. F., & Mir, M. (1997). Linguistic transfer and the use of context by Spanish-English bilinguals. *Applied Psycholinguistics, 18,* 431–452.

Nahmias, M. L. (1995). Including a child who has ADHD. *Scholastic Early Childhood Today, 10*(1), 21–22.

Naigles, L., & Hoff-Ginsbert, E. (1995). Input to verb learning: Evidence for the plausibility of syntactic bootstrapping. *Devlopmental Psychology, 31,* 827–837.

Naigles, L. G., & Gelman, S. A. (1995). Overextensions in comprehensioin and production revisited: Preferential looking in a study of dog, cat, and cow. *Journal of Child Language, 22,* 19–46.

Naito, M., Komatsu, S., & Fuke, T. (1994). Normal and autistic children's understanding of their own and others' false belief: A study from Japan. *British Journal of Developmental Psychology, 12,* 403–416.

Nash, J. K., & Fraser, M. W. (1998). After-school care for children: A resilience-based approach. *Families in Society, 79*(4), 370–383.

Nation, K., Adams, J. W., Bowyer-Crane, C. A., & Snowling, M. J. (1999). Working memory deficits in poor comprehenders reflect underlying language impairments. *Journal of Experimental Child Psychology, 73,* 139–158.

National Association for the Education of Young Children (1991). Public Policy Report: 101st Congress: The children's congress. *Young Children, 46*(2), 78–81.

National Association for the Education of Young Children (1996). Washington update: Children's television agreement. *Young Children, 51*(6), 84.

National Center for Health Statistics (1988). *Vital statistics of the United States 1986: Vol. 1 Natality* (DHHS Publication No. PHS88–1123). Washington, DC: U.S. Government Printing Office.

National Center for Health Statistics (1995). Ectopic pregnancy—United States, 1990–1992. *Pregnancy and infant health.*

National Council of Teachers of Mathematics (1999). *Principles and standards for school mathematics.* Retrieved March 2000 from the World Wide Web: http://standards-e.nctm.org

National Crime Prevention Council. (1999). Guns and other weapons. Retrieved March 2000 from the World Wide Web: www.ncpc.org/10adu6.htm

National Endowment for the Arts. (1999). Retrieved March 2000 from the World Wide Web: http://arts.endow.gov/endownews/news99/YouthARTS.html

National Institute of Mental Health. (1982). *Television and behavior: Ten years of scientific progress and implications for the 80's.* Washington, DC: U.S. Government Printing Office.

National Institute on Drug Abuse. (1999). Do anabolic steroids really make the body stronger? Retrieved March 2000 from the World Wide Web: 165.112.78.61/MOM/ST/MOMST2.html

NCADD (National Council on Alcohol and Drug Dependence). (1999a). Alcohol use among teenagers. Retrieved March 2000 from the World Wide Web: www.neosoft.com~hcada/teen

NCADD. (1999b). Youth, alcohol, and other drugs. Retrieved March 2000 from the World Wide Web: www.ncadd.org/youthalc.html

Neff, V. (1994, March). Opening tips. *Parents playbook. Supplement to Sports Illustrated for kids, 6,* 10–11.

Nelson, C., & Keith, J. (1990). Comparison of female and male early adolescent sex-role attitude and behavior development. *Adolescence, 25,* 183–204.

Nelson, C. A. (1987). The recognition of facial expressions in the first two years of life: Mechanisms of development. *Child Development, 58,* 889–909.

Nelson, C. A., & Dolgin, K. (1985). The generalized discrimination of facial expressions by 7-month-old infants. *Child Development, 56,* 58–61.

Nelson, J., & Lott, L. (1990). *I'm on your side.* Rocklin, CA: Prima.

Nelson, J. R., Smith, D. J., & Dodd, J. (1990). The moral reasoning of juvenile delinquents. *Journal of Abnormal Child Psychology, 18,* 231–239.

Nelson, K. (1981). Individual differences in language development: Implications for development and language. *Developmental Psychology, 17,* 170–187.

Nelson, K. (1993). The psychological and social origins of autobiographcal memory. *Psychological Science, 4*(1), 7–13.

Nelson, K. E. (1973). Structure and strategy in learning to talk. *Monographs of the Society for Research in Child Development, 38*(1 & 2, Serial No. 149).

Nelson, K. E. (1987). Some observations from the perspective of the Rare Event Cognitive Comparison Theory of Language Acquisition. In K. E. Nelson & A. Van Kleek (Eds.), *Children's language* (Vol. 6.) Hillsdale, NJ: Erlbaum.

Nelson, K. E. (1988). Strategies for first language teaching. In R. Scheifelbusch & M. Rice (Eds.), *The teachability of language* (pp. 263–310). Baltimore, MD: Dan Brooks.

Nelson, K. E., & Lucariello, J. (1985). The development of meaning in first words. In M. D. Barrett (Ed.), *Children's single-word speech* (pp. 59–86). Chichester: Wiley.

Nelson, K. E., & Nelson, K. (1978). Cognitive pendulums and the linguistic realization. In K. E. Nelson (Ed.), *Children's language* (Vol. 1). New York: Gardner Press.

Nemours Foundation. (1999a). Exercise. Retrieved March 2000 from the World Wide Web: http:/kidshealth.org/parent/nutrition/exercise.html

Nemours Foundation. (1999b). The pain of eating disorders. Retrieved March 2000 from the World Wide Web: www.kidsheath.org

Nevitt, A. (1998). *Fetal alcohol syndrome.* New York: Rosen Publishing Group.

New, R. S. (1988). Parental goals and Italian infant care. In R. A. LeVine, P. M. Miller, & M. M. West (Eds.), *Parental behaviors in diverse societies.* (*New Directions in Child Development* No. 40 pp. 51–63). San Francisco: Jossey-Bass.

Newcombe, N., & Huttenlocher, J. (1992). Children's early ability to solve perspective-taking problems. *Developmental Psychology, 28*(4), 635–643.

Newell, A., Shaw, J. C., & Simon, H. A. (1958). Elements of a theory of human problem solving. *Psychological Review, 65,* 151–166.

Newman, D., Griffin, P., & Cole, M. (1989). *The construction zone: Working for cognitive change in school.* Cambridge, MA: Cambridge University Press.

Newport, E. L. (1990). Maturational constraints on language learning. *Cognitive Science, 14,* 11–28.

Newport, E. L., Gleitman, H. A., & Gleitman, L. R. (1977). Mother, I'd rather do it myself: Some effects and non-effects of maternal speech style. In C. Snow & C. Ferguson (Eds.), *Talking to children: Language input and acquisition.* Cambridge: Cambridge University Press.

Newson, J., & Newson, E. (1978). *Seven years old in the home environment.* London: Penguin.

NICHD Early Child Care Research Network. (1997). The effects of infant child care on infant-mother attachment security: Results of the NICHD Study of Early Child Care. *Child Development, 68,* 860–879.

Nicolich, L. (1977). Beyond sensorimotor intelligence: Assessment of symbolic maturity through analysis of pretend play. *Merrill-Palmer Quarterly, 23,* 89–99.

Niestroj, B. H. E. (1991). Fetal nutrition: A study of its effect on behavior in Zulu newborns. In J. K. Nugent, B. M. Lester, & T. B. Brazelton (Eds.), *The cultural context of infancy* (Vol. 2, pp. 321–352). Norwood, NJ: Ablex.

Ninio, A., & Bruner, J. (1978). The achievement and antecedents of labeling. *Journal of Child Language, 5,* 1–15.

Nisbett, R. E., & Gurwitz, S. B. (1970). Weight, sex, and the eating behavior of human newborns. *Journal of Comparative and Physiological Psychology, 73,* 245–253.

Nissen, H. J. W. (1930). A study of exploratory behavior in the white rat by means of the obstruction method. *Journal of Genetic Psychology, 37,* 361–376.

Nix, R. L., Pinderhughes, E. E., Dodge, K. A., Bates, J. E., Pettit, G. S., & McFadyen-Ketchum, S. A. (1999). The relation between mothers' hostile attribution tendencies and children's externalizing behavior problems: The mediating role of mothers' harsh discipline practices. *Child Development, 70*(4), 896–909.

Nolan, R. F., Dai, Y., & Benefield, R. (1999, August). *Peer conflict resolution training in a middle school.* Paper presented at the annual meeting of the American Psychological Association meeting, Boston, MA.

Noll, E. (1994). Social issues and literature circles with adolescents. *Journal of Reading, 38*(2), 88–96.

Noller, P. (1994). Relationships with parents in adolescence: Process and outcome. In R. Montemayor, G. R. Adams & T. P. Gullotta (Eds.), *Personal relationships during adolescence.* Thousands Oakes, CA: Sage.

Norcia, A. M., & Tyler, C. W. (1985). Spatial frequency sweep VEP: Visual acuity during the first year of life. *Vision Research, 25*(10), 1399–1408.

Norcia, A. M., Tyler, C. W., & Hamer, R. D. (1990). Development of contrast sensitivity in the human infant. *Vision Research, 30*(10), 1475–1486.

Norton, R. D. (1994). Adolescent suicide: Risk factors and countermeasures. *Journal of Health Education, 25*(6), 358–361.

NSKC (National Safe Kids Campaign). (1997). *Bicycle injury fact sheet.* Washington, DC: Author.

Nunes, T., Bindman, M., & Bryant, P. (1997). Morphological spelling strategies: Developmental stages and processes. *Developmental Psychology, 33*(4), 637–649.

Nystrand, M., & Gamoran, A. (1991). Instructional discourse, student engagement, and literature achievement. *Research in the Teaching of English, 25,* 261–290.

Oakes, J. (1985). *Keeping track: How schools structure inequality.* New Haven, CT: Yale University Press.

Oakes, L. M. (1994). The development of infants' use of continuity cues in their perception of causality. *Developmental Psychology, 30,* 869–879.

Oakes, L. M., & Cohen, L. B. (1990). Infant perception of a causal event. *Cognitive Development, 5,* 193–207.

Oakes, L. M., Coppage, D. J., & Dingel, A. (1997). By land or by sea: The role of perceptual similarity in infants' categorization of animals. *Developmental Psychology, 33*(3), 396–407.

Obonai, T., Yasuhara, M., Nakamura, T., & Takashima, S. (1998). Catecholamine neurons alteration in the brainstem of sudden infant death syndrome victims. *The Journal of Pediatrics, 101,* 285–288.

O'Boyle, M. W., & Hoff, E. J. (1987). Gender and handedness differences in mirror-tracing random forms. *Neuropsychologia, 25,* 977–982.

O'Callaghan, M. F., Borkowski, J. G., Whitman, T. L., Maxwell, S. E., & Keogh, D. (1999). A model of adolescent parenting: The role of cognitive readiness to parent. *Journal of Research on Adolescents, 9*(2), 203–225.

O'Connell, B., & Bretherton, I. (1984). Toddlers' play, alone and with mother: The role of maternal guidance. In I. Bretherton (Ed.), *Symbolic play* (pp. 337–368). New York: Academic Press.

O'Dea, J., & Abraham, S. (1999). Association between self-concept and body weight, gender, and pubertal development among male and female adolescents. *Adolescence, 34,* 121–128.

Oden, S., & Asher, S. R. (1977). Coaching children in social skills for friendship making. *Child Development, 48,* 495–506.

Oetting, J., Rice, M., & Swank, L. (1995). Quick Incidental Learning (QUIL) of words by school-aged children with and without SLI. *Journal of Speech and Hearing Research, 38,* 434–445.

Offord, D. R., Boyle, M. H., & Racine, Y. A. (1989). Ontario Child Health Study: Correlates of conduct disorder. *Journal of the American Academy of Child and Adolescent Psychiatry, 28,* 856–860.

Okra, E. R., & Paris, S. G. (1987). Patterns of motivation and reading skills in underachieving children. In S. J. Ceci (Ed.), *Handbook of cognitive, social, and neuropsychological aspects of learning disabilities* (Vol. 2, pp. 115–146). Hissdale, NJ: Erlbaum.

Oliver, J. E., & Taylor, A. (1971). Five generations of ill-treated children in one family pedigree. *The British Journal of Psychiatry, 119,* 473–480.

Oliver, M. B., & Hyde, J. S. (1993). Gender differences in sexuality: A meta-analysis. *Psychological Bulletin, 114,* 29–51.

Ollendick, T. H., Greene, R. W., Francis, G., & Baum, C. G. (1991). Sociometric status: Stability and validity among neglected, rejected, and popular children. *Journal of Child Psychology and Psychiatry, 32*(3), 525–534.

Oller, D. K., & Eilers, R. E. (1988). The role of audition in infant babbling. *Child Development, 59*(1), 441–449.

Oller, D. K., Eilers, R. E., Basinger, D., Steffins, M. L., & Urbano, R. (1995). Extreme poverty and the development of precursors to the speech capacity. *First Language, 15,* 167–187.

Oller, D. K., & Lynch, M. P. (1992). Infant vocalizations and innovations in infraphonology: Toward a broader theory of development and disorders. In C. A. Ferguson, L. Menn, & C. Stoel-Gammon (Eds.), *Phonological development: Models, research, implications.* Timonium, MD: York Press.

Oller, D. K., Wieman, L. A., Doyle, W. J., & Ross, C. (1976). Infant babbling and speech. *Journal of Child Language, 3,* 1–11.

Olson, H. C., Feldman, J. J., Streissguth, A. P., Sampson, P. D., & Bookstein, F. L. (1998). Neuropsychological deficits in adolescents with fetal alcohol syndrome: clinical findings. *Alcoholism: Clinical and Experimental Research. 22*(9) 1998–2012.

Olson, R. (Ed.). (1986). The manipulation of children's eating preferences. *Nutrition Reviews, 44*(10), 327–328.

Olvera-Ezzell, N., Power, T. G., & Cousins, J. H. (1990). Maternal socialization of children's eating habits. Strategies used by obese Mexican-American mothers. *Child Development, 61*(2), 395–400.

Olweus, D. (1978). *Aggression in the schools: Bullies and whipping boys.* Washington, DC: Hemisphere, with New York: Wiley.

Olweus, D., Mattison, A., Schalling, D., & Low, H. (1988). Circulating testosterone levels and aggression in adolescent males: A causal analysis. *Psychosomatic Medicine, 50,* 261–272.

Osborne, J. W. (1997). Race and academic disidentification. *Journal of Educational Psychology, 89*(4), 728–735.

Osofsky, H. J., & Osofsky, J. D. (1970). Adolescents as mothers: Results of a program for low-income pregnant teenagers with emphasis upon infants' development. *American Journal of Orthopsychiatry, 40,* 825–834.

Overby, K. J. (1996). Physical growth. In A. M. Rudolph (Senior Ed.), *Rudolph's pediatrics* (pp. 3–8). Stamford, CT.: Appleton & Lange.

Overton, W. E. (Ed.). (1990). *Reasoning, necessity and logic: Developmental perspectives.* Hillsdale, NJ: Erlbaum.

Page, R. M. (1997). Helping adolescents avoid date rape: The role of secondary education. *The High School Journal, 80,* 75–80.

Paik, H., & Comstock, G. (1994). The effects of television violence on antisocial behavior: A meta-analysis. *Communications Research, 21,* 516–546.

Pajares, F., & Graham, L. (1999). Self-efficacy, motivation constructs, and mathematics performance of entering middle school students. *Contemporary Educational Psychology, 24,* 124–139.

Palmer, C. F. (1989). The discriminating nature of infants' exploratory actions. *Developmental Psychology, 25,* 885–893.

Pan, H. L. W. (1994). Children's play in Taiwan. In J. L. Roopnarine, J. E. Johnson, & F. H. Hooper (Eds.), *Children's play in diverse cultures* (pp. 31–50). Albany, NY: State University of New York Press.

Paneth, N. (1986). Etiologic factors in cerebral palsy. *Pediatric Annals, 15*(3), 191–201.

Papageorgiou, A., Zelkowitz, P., & Allard, M. (1991). Comparison of cognitive performance of children with birth weight 600–1000g and 1000–15000g. *Pediatric Research, 25,* 1552.

Papousek, H. (1967). Experimental studies of appetitional behavior in human newborns and infants. In H. Stevenson, E. Hess, & H. Rheingold (Eds.), *Early behavior: Comparative and developmental approaches.* New York: Wiley.

Papousek, M. (1992). Early ontogeny of vocal communication in parent-infant interactions. In H. Papousek, U. Jurgens, & M. Papousek (Eds.), *Nonverbal and vocal communication.* Cambridge, UK: Cambridge University Press.

Papousek, M., Bronstein, H., Nuzzo, C., Papousek, H., & Symmes, D. (1990). Infant responses to prototypical melodic contours of parental speech. *Infant Behavior and Development, 1,* 163–224.

Papousek, M., Papousek, H., & Symmes, D. (1991). The meanings of melodies in motherese in tone and stress languages. *Infant Behavior and Development, 14,* 415–440.

Paratore, J. (1991). *An investigation of an intergenerational approach to literacy.* Boston University Intergenerational Literacy Project. School of Education, Boston University.

Parillo, A. V., Felts, W. M., & Mikow-Porto, V. (1997). Early initiation of sexual intercourse and its co-occurrence with other health-risk behaviors in high school students. *Journal of Health Education, 28*(2), 85–93.

Park, R. E. (1928). Human migration and the marginal man. *American Journal of Sociology, 5,* 881–893.

Parke, R. D., & Buriel, R. (1998). Socialization in the family: Ethnic and ecological perspectives. In W. Damon (Editor-in-Chief), and N. Eisenberg (Vol. Ed.), *Handbook of child psychology* (5th ed.): Vol. 3. *Social, emotional, and personality development* (pp. 463–552). New York: Wiley.

Parke, R. D., & Lewis, N. G. (1981). The family in context: A multilevel interactional analysis of child abuse. In R. W. Henderson (Ed.), *Parent-child interaction: Theory, research, and prospects* (pp. 169–204). New York: Academic Press.

Parke, R. D., & Suomi, S. J. (1980). Adult male-infant relationships: Human and nonprimate evidence. In K. L. Immelmann, G. Barlow, M. Main, & L. Petrinovitch (Eds.), *Behavioral development: The Bielefeld interdisciplinary project.* New York: Cambridge University Press.

Parker, P. H. (1999). To do or not to do? That is the question. *Pediatric Annals, 28*(5), 283–290.

Parmalee, A., & Stern, E. (1972). Development of states in infants. In C. B. Clemente, D. P. Purpura, & F. E. Mayer (Eds.), *Sleep and the maturing nervous system.* New York: Academic Press.

Parsons, J. E., Adler, T. F., & Kaczala, C. M. (1982). Socialization of achievement attitudes and beliefs: Parental influences. *Child Development, 53*(2), 310–321.

Parten, M. (1932). Social play among preschool children. *Journal of Abnormal and Social Psychology, 27,* 243–269.

Pascalis, O., DeSchoenen, S., Morton, J., Deruelle, C., & Fabre-Grenet, M. (1995). Mother's face recognition by neonates: A replication and an extension. *Infant Behavior and Development, 18,* 79–85.

Pasman, R. L., Naatman, R., & Alho, K. (1991). Auditory evoked responses in prematures. *Infant Behavior and Development, 14,* 129–135.

Pasquariello, P. S.(Ed.). (1999). *The Children's Hospital of Philadelphia book of pregnancy and child care.* New York: Wiley.

Pastor, D. L. (1981). The quality of mother-infant attachment and its relationship to toddler's initial sociability with peers. *Developmental Psychology, 17,* 326–338.

Patterson, C. (1982). Self-control and self-regulation in childhood. In T. Field & A. Huston-Stein (Eds.), *Review of human development.* New York: Wiley.

Patterson, C., & Mischel, W. (1976). Effects of temptation-inhibiting and task-facilitating plans on self-control. *Journal of Personality and Social Psychology, 33,* 209–217.

Patterson, G. L., Litman, R. A., & Bricker, W. (1967). Assertive behavior in children: A step toward a theory of aggression. *Monographs of the Society for Research in Child Development, 32,* 1–43.

Patterson, G. R. (1995). Coercion–A basis for early age of onset for arrest. In J. McCord (Ed.), *Coercion and punishment in long-term perspective* (pp. 81–105). New York: Cambridge University Press.

Patterson, G. R., & Reid, J. B. (1984). Social interaction processes within the family: The study of moment-by-moment family transactions in which human social development is embedded. *Journal of Applied Developmental Psychology, 5,* 237–262.

Pears, J. (1992). *Youth homelessness: Abuse, gender, and the process of adjustment to life on the streets.* Unpublished manuscript, University of Queensland, Australia.

Pearson, B. Z., & Basinger, D. (1995, March 30–April 2). *Criteria for language delay in 3 populations of two-year-olds.* Paper presented at the biennial Meeting of the Society for Research in Child Development. Indianapolis, IN.

Pearson, J. W., & Santa, C. M. (1995). Students as researchers of their own learning. *Journal of Reading, 38*(6), 462–469.

Pechmann, C., & Ratneshwar, S., (1994). The effects of antismoking and cigarette advertising on young adolescents' perceptions of peers who smoke. *Journal of Consumer Research, 21*(2), 236–251.

Peck, C. (1994). What Abby did on her summer vacation. *Exceptional Parent, 25*(3), 50–51.

Peck, M. N., & Lundberg, O. (1995). Short stature as an effect of economic and social conditions in childhood. *Social Science and Medicine, 41,* 733–738.

Pederson, D. R., Gleason, K. E., Moran, G., & Bento, S. (1998). Maternal attachment representations, maternal sensitivity, and the infant-mother attachment relationship. *Developmental Psychology, 34,* 925–933.

Pederson, W. (1994). Parental relations, mental health, and delinquency in adolescents. *Adolescence, 29*(116), 975–990.

Peeples, D. R., & Teller, D. Y. (1975). Color vision and brightness discrimination in two-month-old human infants. *Science, 189,* 1102–1103.

Pegg, J. E., Werker, J. F., & McLeod, P. J. (1992). Preference for infant-directed over adult-directed speech: Evidence from 7-week-old infants. *Infant Behavior and Development, 15,* 325–345.

Pelligrini, A. D., Bartini, M., & Brooks, F. (1999). School bullies, victims, and aggressive victims: Factors relating to group affiliation and victimization in early adolescence. *Journal of Educational Psychology, 91*(2), 216–224

Pemberton, E. F.,& Watkins, R. V. (1987). Language facilitation through stories: Recasting and modeling. *First Language, 7,* 79–89.

Peng, K., & Nisbett, R. E. (1999). Culture, dialectics, and reasoning about contradiction. *American Psychologist, 54*(9), 741–754.

Perlstein, P. H., Hersch, C., Glueck, C. J., & Sutherland, J. M. (1974). Adaptation to cold in the first three days of life. *Pediatrics, 54,* 411.

Perner, J. (1988). Developing semantics for theories of mind: From propositional attitudes to mental representation. In J. W. Astington, P. J. Harris, & D. R.

Olson (Eds.), *Developing theories of mind* (pp. 141–172). Cambridge, UK: Cambridge University Press.

Perner, J. (1991). *Understanding the representational mind.* Cambridge, MA: Bradford Books/M.I.T. Press.

Perry, C. L., Kelder, S. H., & Komro, K. A. (1993). The social world of adolescents: Family, peers, schools, and the community. In Milstein, S. G., Petersen, A. C., & Nightingale, E. O. (Eds.), *Promoting the health of adolescents: New directions for the twenty-first century* (pp. 153–157). New York: Oxford University Press.

Perry, D., Williard, J., & Perry, L. (1990). Peers' perceptions of the consequences that victimized children provide aggressors. *Child Development, 61,* 1310–1325.

Perry, D. G., Kusel, S. J., & Perry, L. C. (1988). Victims of peer aggression. *Developmental Psychology, 24,* 807–814.

Pesa, J. (1999). Psychosocial factors associated with dieting behaviors among female adolescents. *Journal of School Health, 69*(5), 196–200.

Peskin, J. (1980). Female performance and Inhelder's and Piaget's tests of formal operations. *Genetic Psychology Monographs, 101,* 245–256.

Peters, A. M., & Menn, L. (1993). False starts and filler syllables: Ways to learn grammatical morphemes. *Language, 69*(4), 742–777.

Petersen, A. C., Compas, B. C., Brooks-Gunn, J., Stemmler, M., Ey, S., & Grant, K. E. (1993). Depression in adolescence. *American Psychologist, 48,* 155–168.

Peterson, A. C., & Taylor, B. (1980). The biological approach to adolescence: Biological change and psychological adaptation. In J. Adelson (Ed.), *Handbook of adolescent psychology* (pp. 117–155). New York: Wiley.

Peterson, C., Jesso, B., & McCabe, A. (1999). Encouraging narratives in preschoolers: An intervention study. *Journal of Child Language, 26,* 49–67.

Peterson, C., & McCabe, A. (1992). Parental styles of narrative elicitation: Effect on children's narrative structure and content. *First Language, 12,* 299–321.

Petitto, L. A., & Marentette, P. F. (1991). Babbling in the manual mode: Evidence for the ontogeny of language. *Science, 251,* 1493–1496.

Petrill, S. A., Saudino, K., Cherny, S. S., Emde, R. N., Fulker, D. W., Hewitt, J. K., & Plomin, R. (1998). Exploring the genetic and environmental etiology of high general cognitive ability in fourteen- to thirty-six-month-old twins. *Child Development 69*(3), 611–623.

Pettit, G. S., Clawson, M. A., Dodge, K. A., & Bates, J. E. (1996). Stability and change in peer-rejected status: The role of child behavior, parenting, and family ecology. *Merrill-Palmer Quarterly, 42*(2), 267–294.

Phillips, D. (1974). Neonatal heat loss in heated cribs versus mothers' arms. *Child and Family, 4,* 307–314.

Phillips, D. A. (1987). Socialization of perceived academic competence among highly competent children. *Child Development, 58,* 1308–1320.

Phillips, D. S., & Zimmerman, M. (1990). The developmental course of perceived competence. In R. J. Sternberg & J. Kolligian (Eds.), *Competence considered.* New Haven: Yale University Press.

Phipps, R. H. (1996). Multiple births. In A. M. Rudolph (Senior Ed.) *Rudolph's pediatrics* (pp. 243–245). Stamford, CT.: Appleton & Lange.

Piaget, J. (1926). *The language and thought of the child.* London: Kegan Paul. (Original published in 1923)

Piaget, J. (1952). *The origins of intelligence in children* (M. Cook, Trans.). New York: International Universities Press. (Original published in 1936.)

Piaget, J. (1954). *The construction of reality in the child* (M. Cook, Trans.). New York: Ballantine Books.

Piaget, J. (1960). *The child's conception of the world.* London: Routledge & Kegan Paul Ltd. (Original published in 1929.)

Piaget, J. (1962). *Play, dreams, and imitation* (C. Gattegno & F. M. Hodgson, Trans.). New York: Norton.

Piaget, J. (1963). *The origins of intelligence in children* (M. Cook, Trans.). New York: Norton. (Original published in 1936)

Piaget, J. (1969). *The child's conception of the world.* (J. Tomlinson & A. Tomlinson, Trans.). Totowa, NJ: Littlefield, Adams.

Piaget, J. (1972). *The child's conception of physical causality* (M. Gabain, Trans.). Totowa, NJ: Littlefield, Adams.

Piaget, J., & Inhelder, B. (1967). *The child's conception of space* (F. J. Langdon & J. L. Lunger, Trans.). New York: Norton. (Original published in 1948)

Piessens, P. W. (1991). Newborn behavior and development in Indonesia. In J. K. Nugent, B. M. Lester, & T. B. Brazelton (Eds.), *The cultural context of infancy* (Vol. 2, pp. 271–298. Norwood, NJ: Ablex.

Pine, J. M. (1992). How referential are 'referential' children? Relationships between maternal report and observational measures of vocabulary composition and usage. *Journal of Child Language, 19,* 75–86.

Pine, J. M., Lieven, E. V. M., & Rowland, C. F. (1997). Stylistic variation at the "single-word" stage: Relations between maternal speech characteristics and children's vocabulary composition and usage. *Child Development, 68*(5), 807–819.

Platt, S. A., & Stanislow, C. A. III, (1988). Norm of reaction: Definition and misinterpretation of animal research. *Journal of Comparative Psychology, 102,* 254–261.

Pliszka, S. R., Rogeness, G. A., Renner, P., Sherman, J., & Broussard, T. (1988). Plasma neurochemistry in juvenile offenders. *Journal of the American Academy of Child and Adolescent Psychiatry, 27,* 588–594.

Plomin, R., Fulker, D. W., Corley, R., & DeFries, J. C. (1997b). Nature, nurture, and cognitive development from 1 to 16 years: A parent-offspring adoption study. *Psychological Science, 8*(6), 442–447.

Plomin, R., DeFries, J. C., McClearn, G., & Rutter, M. (1997a). *Behavioral Genetics* (3rd ed.) New York: W. H. Freeman.

Plumert, J. M., & Nichols-Whitehead, P. (1996). Parental scaffolding of young children's spatial communication. *Developmental Psychology, 32*(3), 523–532.

Plummer, G. (1952). Anomalies occurring in children exposed in utero to the atomic bomb in Hiroshima. *Pediatrics, 10,* 687.

Plunkett, K. (1993). Lexical segmentation and vocabulary growth in early language acquisition. *Journal of Child Language, 20,* 43–60.

Poinski, M. (1999). New federal guidelines on teen drug abuse. *Youth Today, 8*(4), 7–8.

Poling, D. A., Mull, M. S., & Evans, E. M. (1999, August). *Computing across the curriculum: The Internet as an educational tool.* Paper presented at the Annual meeting of the American Psychological Association. Boston, MA.

Polka, L., & Werker, J. F. (1994). Developmental changes in perception of non-native vowel contrasts. *Journal of Experimental Psychology: Human Perception and Performance, 20,* 421–435.

Pollitt, E., Gorman, K. S., Engle, P. L., Martorell, R., & Riverea, J. (1993). Early supplementary feeding and cognition. *Monographs of the Society for Research in Child Development, 58*(7, Serial No. 235).

Pomerleau, A., Bolduc, D., Malcuit, G., & Cossette, L. (1990). Pink or blue: Environmental gender stereotypes in the first two years of life. *Sex Roles, 22,* 359–367.

Pope, A. W., & Bierman, K. (1999). Predicting adolescent peer problems and antisocial activities: The relative roles of aggression and dysregulation. *Developmental Psychology, 35*(2), 335–346.

Pope, A. W., & Bierman, K. L. (1999). Predicting adolescent peer problems and antisocial activities: The relative roles of aggression and dysregulation. *Developmental Psychology, 35*(2), 335–346.

Popkin, B. M., & Udry, J. R. (1998). Adolescent obesity increases significantly for second and third generation U.S. immigrants: The National Longitudinal Study of Adolescent Health. *Journal of Nutrition, 128,* 701–706.

Porges, S. W., Doussard-Roosevelt, J. A., & Maiti, A. K. (1994). Vagal tone and the physiological regulation of emotion. In N. A. Fox (Ed.), Emotion regulation: Behavioral and biological considerations. *Monographs of the Society for Research in Child Development, 59*(Serial No. 240), 167–186.

Porter, F. S., Blick, L. C., & Sgroi, S. (1982). Treatment of the sexually abused child. In S. Sgroi (Ed.), *Handbook of clinical intervention in child sexual abuse.* Lexington, MA: Lexington Books.

Porter, R. P. (1995). A review of the U.S. General Accounting Office study on limited English students. *Read Perspectives, 2*(1), 9–23.

Posner, J. K., & Vandell, D. L. (1999). After-school activities and the development of low-income urban children: A longitudinal study. *Developmental Psychology, 35*(3), 868–879.

Power, T. G., & Chapiewski, M. L. (1986). Child rearing and impulse control in toddlers: A naturalistic investigation. *Developmental Psychology, 22,* 271–275.

Power, T. G., & Parke, R. D. (1982). Play as a context for early learning. In L. M. Laosa & I. E. Siegel (Eds.), *Families as learning environments for children* (pp. 147–178). New York: Plenum Press.

Prechtl, H. F. R. (1977). *The neurological examination of the full-term newborn infant* (2nd ed.). London: Heinemann.

Prechtl, H. F. R. (1982). Assessment methods for the newborn infant: A critical evaluation. In P. Stratton (Ed.), *Psychobiology of the human newborn* (pp. 21–52). New York: Wiley.

Prechtl, H. F. R., & Beintema, D. J. (1964). *The neurological examination of the full-term newborn infant: Clinics in developmental medicine,* No. 12. London: Heinemann.

Prechtl, H. F. R., & O'Brien, M. J. (1982). Behavioral states of the full-term newborn: The emergence of a concept. In P. Stratton (Ed.), *Psychobiology of the human newborn* (pp. 53–73). New York: Wiley.

Premack, D., & Woodruff, G. (1978). Does the chimpanzee have a theory of mind? *The Behavioral and Brain Sciences, 1,* 515–526.

Pressley, M., Levin, J. R., Ghatala, E. S., & Ahmad, M. (1987). Test monitoring in young grade school children. *Journal of Experimental Child Psychology, 43*(1), 96–111.

Pressley, M., Wood, E., Woloshyn, V. E., Martin, V., King, A., & Menke, D. (1992). Encouraging mindful use of prior knowledge: Attempting to construct explanatory answers facilitates learning. *Educational Psychology, 27*(1), 91–109.

Prevots, D. R., & Strebel, P. M. (1997). Poliomyeltis prevention in the United States: New recommendations for routine childhood vaccinations place greater reliance on inactivated poliovirus vaccine. *Pediatric Annals, 26*(6), 378–383.

Prince, F. (1995). The relative effectiveness of a peer-led and adult-led smoking intervention program. *Adolescence, 30*(117), 187–194.

Prosser (Eds.), *Indicators of children's well-being* (pp. 428–441). New York: Russell Sage Foundation.

Pugh, M. J. V., & Hart, D. (1999). Identity development and peer group participation. *New Directions for Child and Adolescent Development, 84,* 55–70.

Purkey, S. C., & Smith, M. S. (1983). Effective schools: A review. *The Elementary School Journal, 83*(4), 427–452.

Putallaz, M., & Wasserman, A. (1990). Children's entry behavior. In S. R. Asher & J. D. Coie (Eds.), *Peer rejection in childhood* (pp. 60–89). New York: Cambridge University Press.

Querleu, D., Renard, X., & Versyp, F. (1981). Les perceptions auditives du foetus humain. *Médecine et Hygiène, 39,* 2101–2110. (Cited in deBoysson-Bardies, B., 1993. *How children come to language.* Cambridge, MA: The MIT Press, p. 23.)

Quinn, P. C., Eimas, P. D., & Rosenkrantz, S. L. (1993). Evidence for representation of perceptually similar natural categories by 3-month-old and 4-month-old infants. *Perception, 23,* 463–475.

Rack, J., Hulme, C., Snowling, M., & Wightman, J. (1994). The role of phonology in young children learning to read words: The Direct-Mapping Hypothesis. *Journal of Experimental Child Psychology, 57,* 42–71.

Radke-Yarrow, M., Cummings, E. M., Kuczynski, L., & Chapman, M. (1985). Patterns of attachment in two- and three-year-olds in normal families and families with parental depression. *Child Development, 56,* 854–893.

Radke-Yarrow, M., Zahn-Waxler, C., & Chapman, M. (1983). Children's prosocial dispositions and behavior. In P. H. Mussen (Ed.), *Handbook of child psychology:* Vol. 4 *Socialization, personality, and social development* (4th ed., pp. 469–545). New York: Wiley.

Radkowsky, M., & Siegel, L. (1997). The gay adolescent: Stressors, adaptations, and psychosocial interventions. *Clinical Psychology Review, 17*(2), 191–216.

Radziszewska, B., & Rogoff, B. (1991). Children's guided participation in planning imaginary errands with skilled adult or peer partners. *Developmental Psychology, 27*(3), 381–389.

Raiti, S., Kaplan, S. L., Vliet, V., & Moore, W. V. (1987). Short-term treatment of short stature and subnormal growth rate with human growth hormone. *Journal of Pediatrics, 119*(3), 357–361.

Rakison, D. H., & Butterworth, G. E. (1998). Infants' use of object parts in early categorization. *Developmental Psychology, 34*(1), 49–62.

Ramirez, A. G. (1994). Literacy acquisition among second-language learners. In B. M. Ferdman, R. Weber, & A. G. Ramirez (Eds.), *Literacy across languages and cultures* (pp. 75–101). Albany, NY: State University of New York Press.

Randt, R. D. (1985). Ball-catching proficiency among 4-, 6-, and 8-year-old girls. In J. E. Clark & J. H. Humprey (Eds.), *Motor development: Current selected research* (Vol. 1). Princeton, NJ: Princeton Book.

Ratcliffe, S. G., Masera, N., Pan, H., & Mekie, M. (1994). Head circumference and IQ of children with sex chromosome abnormalities. *Developmental Medicine and Child Neurology, 36*(6), 533–544.

Rathbun, M. (1995). Does exercise help make children smarter? *Parents playbook: Sports illustrated for kids supplement, 7,* p. 12.

Ratner, C. (1991). *Vygotsky's sociohistorical psychology and its contemporary applications.* New York: Plenum Press.

Ratner, N. B., & Pye, C. (1984). Higher pitch in BT is not universal: Acoustic evidence from Qu'iche Mayan. *Journal of Child Language, 5,* 391–401.

Rauh, V., Wasserman, G., & Brunelli, S. (1990). Determinants of maternal child-rearing attitudes. *American Academy of Child and Adolescent Psychiatry, 26,* 375–381.

Ravem, R. (1974). The development of Wh—questions in first and second language learners. In J. C. Richards (Ed.), *Error analysis: Perspectives on second language acquisition.* London: Longman.

Read, C. (1975). *Children's categorization of speech sounds in English.* Urbana, IL: National Council of Teachers of English.

Read, C. (1986). *Children's creative spelling.* London: Routledge & Kegan Paul.

Read, C., Zhang, Y., Ne, H., & Ding, B. (1986). The ability to manipulate speech sounds depends on knowing alphabetic spelling. *Cognition, 24,* 31–44.

Reece, E. A., Assimakopoulos, E., Zheng, X., Hagay, Z., & Hobbins, J. (1990). The safety of obstetric ultrasonography: Concern for the fetus. *Obstetrics and Gynecology, 76,* 139–146.

Reed, J. (1999). Regulating tobacco ads protects children. In B. L. Stay (Ed.), *Mass media: Opposing viewpoints* (pp. 72–77). San Diego, CA: Greenhaven Press.

Reese, E. (1995). Predicting children's literacy from mother-child conversations. *Cognitive Development, 10,* 381–405.

Reese, E., & Cox, A. (1999). Quality of adult book reading affects children's emergent literacy. *Developmental Psychology, 35*(1), 20–28.

Reese, H. W., & Lipsitt, L. P. (1970). *Experimental child psychology.* New York: Academic Press.

Reichelderfer, T. E., Overbach, A., & Greensher, J. (1979). Unsafe playgrounds. *Pediatrics, 64,* 962–963.

Reichenbach, L., & Masters, J. (1983). Children's use of expressive and contextual cues in judgments of emotion. *Child Development, 54,* 993–1004.

Reif, F., & Allen, S. (1992). Cognition for interpreting scientific concepts: A study of acceleration. *Cognition Instructor, 9*(1), 1–44.

Reilly, J. S., & Bellugi, U. (1996). Competition on the face: Affect and language in ASL motherese. *Journal of Child Language, 23,* 219–239.

Reiss, A. J., & Roth, J. A. (1993). *Understanding and preventing violence.* Washington, DC: National Academy Press.

Reissland, N., & Snow, D. (1996). Maternal pitch height in ordinary and play situations. *Journal of Child Language, 23,* 269–278.

Repinski, D. J., Boyce, M. L., Kucharczak, K., & Laing, R. (1998, February). *Relations between parent and sibling behavior and adolescent problem behavior.* Paper presented at the annual meeting of the Eastern Psychological Association, Boston.

Rescorla, L. (1989). The Language Development Survey: A screening tool for delayed language in toddlers. *Journal of Speech and Hearing Disorders, 54,* 587–599.

Resnick, L. B. (1989). Developing mathematical knowledge. *American Psychologist, 44,* 162–169.

Reys, B. J., & Reys, R. E. (1995). Japanese mathematics education: What makes it work? *Teaching Children Mathematics,* April, 474–475.

Ricciuti, H. N. (1965). Object grouping and selective ordering behavior in infants 12 to 24 months old. *Merrill-Palmer Quarterly, 11*(2), 129–148.

Rice, M. L., & Woodsmall, L. (1988). Lessons from television: Children's word learning when viewing. *Child Development, 59,* 420–429.

Richards, J. E., & Holley, F. B. (1999). Infant attention and the development of smooth pursuit tracking. *Developmental Psychology, 35*(3), 856–867.

Richards, M. P., & Bernal, J. F. (1972). An observational study of mother-infant interactions. In N. B. Jones (Ed.), *Ethological studies of child behavior.* London: Cambridge University Press.

Richardson, G., Day, N., & Goldschmidt, L. (1995). *A longitudinal study of prenatal cocaine exposure: Infant development at 12 months.* Paper presented at Biennial Meetings of the Society for Research in Child Development, Indianapolis, March 30–April 2.

Richardson, J. (2000). *Read it aloud! Using literature in the secondary content classroom.* Newark, NJ: International Readings Association.

Ricks, M. H. (1985). The social transmission of parental behavior: Attachment across generations. In I. Bretherton & E. Waters (Eds.), Growing points of attachment theory and research. *Monographs of the Society for Research in Child Development, 50*(1–2).

Rieser, J., Yonas, A., & Wikner, K. (1976). Radial localization of odors by human newborns. *Child Development, 47*, 856–859.

Rimm, S. (1999). *See Jane win*. New York: Crown Publishers.

Rittle-Johnson, B., & Siegler, R. S. (1999). Learning to spell: Variability, choice, and change in children's strategy use. *Child Development, 70*(2), 332–348.

Rivara, F. P., Reay, D. T., & Bergman, A. B. (1989). Analysis of fatal pedestrian injuries in King County, WA, and prospects of prevention. *Public Health Reports, 104*(3), 293–297.

Robbins, C., & Ehri, L. C. (1994). Reading storybooks to kindergartners helps them learn new vocabulary words. *Journal of Educational Psychology, 86*(1), 54–64.

Robert, M., & Ohlmann, T. (1994). Water-level representation by men and women as a function of rod-and-frame test proficiency and visual and postural information. *Perception, 23*, 1321–1333.

Roberts, J. E., Sanyal, M. A., Burchinal, M. R., Collier, A. M., Ramey, C. T., & Henderson, F. W. (1986). Otitis media in early childhood and its relationship to later verbal and academic performance. *Pediatrics, 78*(3), 423–430.

Roberts, K. (1988). Retrieval of a basic-level category in prelinguistic infants. *Developmental Psychology, 24*(1), 21–27.

Roberts, R. E., & Sobhan, M. (1992). Symptoms of depression in adolescence: A comparison of Anglo, African, and Hispanic Americans. *Journal of Youth and Adolescence, 21*, 639–651.

Roberts, S. (1995). Effectiveness of drug education components: Knowledge, attitudes, decision-making, motivations, and self-esteem. *Journal of Health Education, 26*(3), 146–150.

Roberts, W., & Strayer, J. (1987). Parents' responses to the emotional distress of their children: Relations with children's competence. *Developmental Psychology, 23*(3), 415–422.

Robertson, A. (1999). Communicating with your teen. *Kidsource*. Retrieved March 2000 from the World Wide Web: www.kidsource.com/kidsource/content4/

Robertson, L. S. (1985). Motor vehicles. *Pediatric Clinics of North America, 32*(1), 87–94.

Robeson, W. W. (1995). *The relationship between verbal feedback from mothers and their children's language development*. Paper presented at the Biennial Meeting of the Society for Research in Child Development, Indianapolis, March 30–April 2.

Robinson, S. S., & Dixon, R. G. (1992, May). *Language concepts of low- and middle-class preschoolers*. Paper presented at the 1992 Meeting of the International Reading Association, May, Orlando, Fl.

Robinson, T. N., & Killen, J. D. (1995). Ethnic and gender differences in the relationships between television viewing and obesity, physical activity, and dietary fat intake. *Journal of Health Education, 26*(Suppl. 2), S–91-S–98.

Robson, K. S. (1967). The role of eye-to-eye contact in maternal-infant attachment. *Journal of Child Psychology and Psychiatry and Allied Disciplines, 8*, 13–25.

Rochat, P. (1989). Object manipulation and exploration in 2- to 5-month-old infants. *Developmental Psychology, 25*(6), 871–884.

Rochat, P., & Goubet, N. (1995). Development of sitting and reaching in 5- to 6-month-old infants. *Infant Behavior and Development, 18*, 53–68.

Roche, J. P., & Ramsby, T. W. (1993). Premarital sexuality: A five-year follow-up study of attitudes and behavior by dating stage. *Adolescence, 28*, 67–80.

Rock, A. M. L., Trainor, L. J., & Addison, T. L. (1999). Distinctive messages in infant-directed lullabies and play songs. *Developmental Psychology, 35*, 527–534.

Rode, S. S., Chang, P. N., Fisch, P. O., & Stroufe, L. A. (1981). Attachment patterns of infants separated from birth. *Developmental Psychology, 17*, 188–191.

Rodriguez-Tome, H., Bariaud, F., Cohen-Zardi, M. F., & Delmas, C. (1993). The effects of pubertal changes on body image and relations with peers of the opposite sex in adolescence. *Journal of Adolescence, 16*(4), 421–438.

Roedell, W. C., Slaby, R. C., & Robinson, H. B. (1977). *Social development in young children*. Belmont, CA: Wadsworth.

Roeser, R. W., & Midgley, C. M. (1997). Teachers views of aspects of student mental health. *Elementary School Journal, 98*(2), 115–133.

Roff, J. (1961). Childhood social interactions and young adult bad conduct. *Journal of Abnormal and Social Psychology, 63*, 333–337.

Rogoff, B. (1990). *Apprenticeship in thinking*. New York: Oxford University Press.

Rogoff, B. (1998). Cognition as a collaborative process. In D. Kuhn & R. S. Siegler, (Eds.), *Handbook of child psychology: Vol. 2. Cognition, perception and language.* (5th ed., pp. 523–574). New York: Wiley.

Rogoff, B., & Chavajay, P. (1995). What's become of research on the cultural basis of cognitive development? *American Psychologist, 50*, 859–877.

Rolls, B. J., Fedoroff, I. C., & Guthrie, J. F. (1991). Gender differences in eating behavior and body weight regulation. *Health Psychology, 20*, 133–142.

Rome, E. S. (1995). Sports-related injuries among adolescents: When do they occur, and how can we prevent them? *Pediatrics in Review, 16*(5), 184–187.

Romeo, F. F. (1994). Adolescent boys and anorexia nervosa. *Adolescence, 29*(115), 643–647.

Rorty, M., Yager, J., & Rossotto, E. (1993). Why and how do women recover from bulimia nervosa? The subjective appraisals of 40 women recovered for a year or more. *International Journal of Eating Disorders, 14*(3), 249–260.

Rose, S., & Frieze, I. R. (1993). Young singles' contemporary dating scripts. *Sex Roles, 28*, 499–509.

Rose, S. A., & Blank, M. (1974). The potency of context in children's cognition: An illustration through conservation. *Child Development, 45*, 499–502.

Rosen, B. C., & D'Andrade, R. (1975). The psychosocial origins of achievement motivation. In U. Bronfenbrenner & M. H. Mahoney (Eds.), *Influences on human development* (2nd ed., pp. 438–450). Hinsdale, IL: Dryden Press.

Rosen, K. S., & Burke, P. B. (1999). Multiple attachment relationships within families: Mothers and fathers with two young children. *Developmental Psychology, 35*(2), 436–444.

Rosenblatt, J. S. (1969). The basis of synchrony in the behavioral interaction between the mother and her offspring in the laboratory rat. In B. M. Foss (Ed.), *Determinants of infant behavior* (Vol. 3). London: Methuen.

Rosenblatt, L. (1978). *The reader, the text, the poem: The transactional theory of the literary work*. Carbondale, IL: Southern Illinois University Press.

Rosenblum, O., Mazet, P., & Benony, H. (1997). Mother and infant affective involvement states and maternal depression. *Infant Mental Health Journal, 18*, 350–363.

Rosenzweig, M. R. (1984). Experience, memory, and the brain. *American Psychologist, 39*(4), 365-376.

Ross, E. (2000). *Health ahead/heart smart: Curriculum*. Retrieved March 2000 from the World Wide Web: http://www.tmc.tulane.edu/cardiohealth/htsmt.htm

Ross, G., Lipper, E., & Auld, P. A. (1990). Social competence and behavior problems in premature children at school-age. *Pediatrics, 86*, 391–397.

Ross, R. P., Campbell, T., Huston-Stein, A., & Wright, J. C. (1981). Nutritional misinformation of children: A developmental and experimental analysis of the effects of televised food commercials. *Journal of Applied Developmental Psychology, 1*, 329–347.

Rossell, C., & Baker, K. (1996). *Bilingual education in Massachusetts: The emperor has no clothes*. Boston, MA: Pioneer Institute.

Rosser, P. L., & Randolph, S. M. (1989). Black American infants: The Howard University Normative Study. In J. K. Nugent, B. M. Lester, & T. B. Brazelton (Eds.), *The cultural context of infancy: Vol. 1 Biology, culture, and infant development* (pp. 133–165). Norwood, NJ: Ablex.

Roth, J., Brooks-Gunn, J., Murray, L., & Foster, W. (1998). Promoting healthy adolescents: Synthesis of youth development program evaluations. *Journal of Research on Adolescence, 8*(4), 423–460.

Rothbart, M. K. (1989a). Temperament and development. In G. A. Kohnstamm, J. A. Bates, & M. K. Rothbart (Eds.), *Temperament in childhood* (pp. 187–247). New York: Wiley.

Rothbart, M. K.(1989b). Temperament in childhood: A framework. In G. A. Kohnstamm, J. A. Bates, & M. K. Rothbart (Eds.), *Temperament in childhood* (pp. 59–73). New York: Wiley.

Rothbart, M. K., & Bates, J. E. (1998). Temperament. In W. Damon (Editor-in-Chief) & N. Eisenberg (Vol. Ed.), *Handbook of child psychology (5th ed.): Vol. 3. Social, emotional, and personality development* (pp. 105–176). New York: Wiley.

Rothenberg, S. S., & Watts, S. M. (1997). Students with learning difficulties meet Shakespeare: Using a scaffolded reading experience. *Journal of Adolescent and Adult Literacy, 40*(7), 532–539.

Rothman, B. K. (1998). *Genetic maps and human imaginations*. New York: Norton.

Rotter, J. G., Liverant, B., & Crowne, D. P. (1961). The growth and extinction of expectancies in change controlled and skilled tests. *Journal of Psychology, 52*, 161–177.

Rovee-Collier, C. (1995). Time windows in cognitive development. *Developmental Psychology, 31*, 147–169.

Rovee-Collier, C. K., & Lipsitt, L. P. (1982). Learning, adaptation, and memory in the newborn. In P. S.tratton (Ed.), *Psychobiology of the human newborn* (pp. 147–190). New York: Wiley.

Rowe, E. W., Abelkop, A. S., & Kamphaus, R. W. (1999, August). *An empirical typology of adolescent adjustment*. Paper presented at the annual meeting of the American Psychological Association, Boston, MA.

Roy, R. E., & Chrisler, J. C. (1997). *Media effects on body image and eating attitudes in girls and women*. Paper presented at the annual meeting of the Eastern Psychological Association, Washington, DC.

Rubenstein, J., & Howes, C. (1976). The effects of peers on toddler interaction with mother and toys. *Child Development, 47*, 597–605.

Rubin, J. Z., Provenzano, F. J., & Luria, Z. (1974). The eyes of the beholder: Parents' views on sex of newborns. *American Journal of Orthopsychiatry, 44*, 512–519.

Rubin, K. H., LeMare, L. J., & Lollis, S. (1990). Social withdrawal in childhood: Developmental pathways to peer rejection. In S. R. Asher & J. D. Coie (Eds.), *Peer rejection in childhood* (pp. 217–249). New York: Cambridge University Press.

Rudd, A., & Stoll, S. K. (1998). Understanding sportsmanship. *Journal of Physical Education, Recreation, and Dance.* 69(9), 38–42.

Ruddy, M. G., & Adams, S. (1995, June). *Responsiveness to crying: How mothers' beliefs vary with infants' sex*. Paper presented at the Meeting of the American Psychological Society, New York.

Rueter, M. A., & Conger, R. D. (1995). Interaction styles, problem-solving behavior, and family problem-solving effectiveness. *Child Development, 66*, 98–115.

Ruffman, T., Perner, J., Naito, M., Parkin, L., & Clements, W. A. (1998). Older (but not younger) siblings facilitate false belief understanding. *Developmental Psychology, 34*, 161–174.

Rule, B. G., & Ferguson, T. J. (1986). The effects of media violence on attitudes, emotions, and cognitions. *Journal of Social Issues, 42*, 29–50.

Russell, A., & Finnie, V. (1990). Preschool children's social status and maternal instructions to assist group entry. *Developmental Psychology, 26*(4), 603–611.

Russell, M. (1994). New assessment tools for risk drinking during pregnancy. *Alcohol Health and Research World, 18*(1), 55–61.

Rutter, D. R., & Durkin, K. (1987). Turn-taking in mother-infant interaction: An examination of vocalizations and gaze. *Developmental Psychology, 23*(1), 54–61.

Rutter, M. (1981). Socioemotional consequences of day care for preschool children. *American Journal of Orthopsychiatry, 51*, 4–28.

Rutter, M. L. (1997). Nature-nurture integration: The example of antisocial behavior. *American Psychologist, 52*(4) 390–398.

Ryder, R. J., & Graves, M. F. (1994). *Reading and learning in content areas*. New York: Macmillan.

Saarni, C. (1988). Children's understanding of the interpersonal consequences of dissemblances of nonverbal emotional-expressive behavior. *Journal of Nonverbal Behavior, 12*, 275–294.

Sabbagh, M. A., & Callanan, M. A.(1998). Metarepresentation in action: 3-, 4-, and 5-year-olds' developing theories of mind in parent-child conversations. *Developmental Psychology, 34*, 491–502.

Sachs, J. J., Holt, K. W., Holmgreen, P., Colwell, L. S., & Brown, J. M. (1990). Playground hazards in Atlanta child-care centers. *American Journal of Public Health, 80*, 986–988.

Sadaker, M., & Sadaker, D. (1985). Sexism in the schoolroom of the '80s. *Psychology Today, 19*(3), 54–56.

Saffici, C. (1998). Conducting a coaching session. *Journal of Physical Education, Recreation, and Dance. 69*(8), 44–46.

Salembier, G. B. (1999). SCAN and RUN: A reading comprehension strategy that works. *Journal of Adolescent & Adult Literacy, 42*(5), 386–394.

Salmivalli, C. (1999). Intelligent, attractive, well-behaving, unhappy: The structure of adolescents' self-concept and its relations to their social behavior. *Journal of Research on Adolescence, 8*(3), 333–354.

Saltz, R. (1979). Children's interpretation of proverbs. *Language Arts, 56*, 508–514.

Sameroff, A. J. (1972). Learning and adaptation in infancy. In H. W. Reese (Ed.), *Advances in child development and behavior* (Vol. 7). New York: Academic Press.

Sameroff, A. J. (1981). Longitudinal studies of preterm infants: A review of chapters 17–20. *Developmental Psychology, 387–394.*

Sameroff, A. J., Seifer, R., Baldwin, A., & Baldwin, C. (1993). Stability of intelligence from preschool to adolescence: The influence of social and family risk factors. *Child Development, 64*, 80–97.

Sampson, E. E. (1999). *Dealing with differences: An introduction to the social psychology of prejudice*. New York: Harcourt Brace.

Samuel, V. J., George, P., Thornell, A., Curtis, S., Taylor, A., Brome, D., Mick, E., Faraone, S. V., & Biederman, J. (1999). *Journal of the American Academy of Child and Adolescent Psychiatry, 38*(1), 34–39.

Samuel, V. J., George, P., Thornell, A., Curtis, S., Taylor, A., Brome, D., Mick, E., Faraone, S. V., & Biederman, J. (1999). A pilot controlled family study of DSM III R and DSM IV ADHD in African-American children. *Journal of the American Academy of Child and Adolescent Psychiatry, 38*(1), 34–39.

Sanders, J. (1998). Top 20 college slang terms. Cal Poly, Pomona. *The College Slang Research Project.* Retrieved March 2000 from the World Wide Web: www.intranet.csupomona.edu/~jasanders/slang/top20

Sandstrom, M. J., & Coie, J. D. (1999). A developmental perspective on peer rejection: Mechanisms of stability and change. *Child Development, 70*(4), 955–966.

Saunders, L. S. (1997). Lingering with Dicey: Robin's Song. *Journal of Adolescent and Adult Literacy, 40*(7), 548–557.

Saxe, G. B., Guberman, S. R., & Gerhart, M. (1987). Social processes in early number development. *Monographs of the Society for Research in Child Development, 52*(2, Serial No. 215).

Saxon, T. F. (1997). A longitudinal study of early mother-infant interaction and later language competence. *First Language, 17*, 271–281.

Saxton, M. (1997). The contrast theory of negative input. *Journal of Child Language, 24*, 139–161.

Saxton, M., & Towse, J. N. (1998). Linguistic relativity: The case of place value in multi-digit numbers. *Journal of Experimental Child Psychology, 69*, 66–79.

Saxton, M., Kulcsar, B., Marshall, G., & Rupra, M. (1998). Longer-term effects of corrective input: An experimental approach. *Journal of Child Language, 25*, 701–721.

Scafidi, F., Field, T., Schanberg, S., Bauer, C., Tucci, K., Roberts, J., Morrow, C., & Kuhn, C. (1990). Massage stimulates growth in preterm infants: A replication. *Infant Behavior and Development, 13*, 167–188.

Scaife, M., & Bruner, J. (1975). The capacity for joint visual attention in human infancy. *Nature, 253*, 265–266.

Scarr, S. (1992). *Developmental theories for the 1990s: Developmental and individual differences.* Presidential address to the biennial meetings of the Society for Research in Child Development, April 20, 1991. Seattle, WA. *Child Development, 63*, 1–19.

Scarr, S., & McCartney, K. (1983). How people make their own environments: A theory of genotype environment effects. *Child Development, 54*, 424–435.

Schaffer, H. R., & Emerson, P. E. (1964). The development of social attachments in infancy. *Monographs of the Society for Research in Child Development, 29*(Serial No. 94).

Schaffer, H. R., Collis, G. M., & Parsons, G. (1977). Vocal interchange and visual regard in verbal and pre-verbal children. In H. R. Schaffer (Ed.), *Studies in mother-infant interaction.* London: Academic Press.

Schall, E. (1994). School-based health education: What works? Special issue: Medicine in the twenty-first century: Challenges in personal and public health promotion. *American Journal of Preventive Medicine, 10*(Suppl. 3), 30–32.

Schauble, L. (1990). Belief revision in children: The role of prior knowledge and strategies for generating evidence. *Journal of Experimental Child Psychology, 49*, 31–57.

Schickedanz, J. (1986). *More than the ABCs: The early stages of reading and writing.* Washington, DC: National Association for the Education of Young Children.

Schickedanz, J. (1990). *Adam's righting revolutions: A case study of one child's writing development from one to seven.* Portsmouth, NH: Heinemann.

Schickedanz, J. (1998). What is developmentally appropriate practice in early litereacy? Considering the alphabet. In S. B. Neuman & K. A. Roskos (Eds.), *Children achieving: Best practices in early literacy* (pp. 20–37). Newark, DE: IRA.

Schieber, R. A., & Branch-Dorsey, C. M. (1995). In-line skating injuries. *Sports Medicine, 19*(6), 427–432.

Schieffelin, B. B. (1986). Teasing and shaming in Kaluli children's interactions. In B. B. Schieffelin & E. Ochs (Eds.), *Language socialization across cultures* (pp. 165–181). New York: Cambridge University Press.

Schleifer, M. J. (1987). Toothbrush adaptations. *Exceptional Parents, 17*(5), 22–24.

Schlesinger, I. M. (1974). Relational concepts and underlying language. In R. Schiefelbusch & L. L.loyd (Eds.), *Language perception: Acquisition, retardation, and intervention.* Baltimore: University Park Press.

Schmalt, H. D. (1999). Assessing the achievement motive using the grid technique. *Journal of Research in Personality, 33*, 109–130.

Schneider, P. E., & Peterson, J. (1982). Oral habits: Considerations in management. *Pediatric Clinics of North America, 29*(3), 653–668.

Schneider, W., & Bjorklund, D. F. (1998). Memory. In W. Damon (Editor-in-Chief) & D. Kuhn & R. S. Siegler (Vol. Eds.), *Handbook of child psychology* (5th ed.): Vol. 2. Cognition, perception, and language pp. 467–521). New York: Wiley.

Schneider, W., Kuspert, P., Roth, H., Mechtild, V., & Marx, H. (1997). Short- and long-term effects of training phonological awareness in kindergarten: Evidence from two German studies. *Journal of Experimental Child Psychology, 66* 311-340.

Schneirla, T. (1957). The concept of development in comparative psychology. In D. Harris (Ed.), *The concept of development.* Minneapolis: University of Minnesota Press.

Schnirring, L. (1999). Can school PE make fitter kids? *The Physician and Sports Medicine, 27*(13), 23–28.

Schulenberg, J., O'Malley, P. M., Bachman, J. G., & Johnson, L. D. (2000). Spread your wings and fly: The course of well-being and substance use during the transition to young adulthood. In L. J. Crockett & R. K. Silbereisen (Eds.), *Negotiating adolescence in times of social change* (pp. 224–255). New York: Cambridge University Press.

Schulte, E. E., Birkhead, G. S., Kondracki, S. F., Morse, & D. L. (1994). Patterns of Haemophillus influenzae type b invasive disease in New York State, 1987 to 1991: The role of vaccination requirements for day care attendance. *Pediatrics, 94*(Suppl. 6), 1014–1016.

Schwartz, D. (1995). *The behavioral correlates of peer victimization.* Paper presented at the Biennial Meetings of the Society for Research in Child Development, Indianapolis.

Schwartz, D., Dodge, K. A., Pettit, G. S., & Bates, J. E. (1997). The early socialization of aggressive victims of bullying. *Child Development, 68*(4) 665–675.

Schwartz, M. S., & Abell, S. C. (1999, August). Body shape satisfaction and self-esteem: Exploring racial differences. Paper presented at the annual meeting of the American Psychological Association, Boston, MA.

Schwartz, P. (1983). Length of day-care attendance and attachment behavior in eighteen-month-old infants. *Child Development, 54*, 1073–1078.

Sciutto, M. J. (1999, August). *The use of a student-generated portfolio in a methods-statistics course.* Paper presented at the Annual meeting of the American Psychological Association, Boston, MA.

Scott-Johnson, P. E., Lee, J. S., & Thomas, S. F. (1996, August). *Drive for thinness, body dissatisfaction, and self-esteem among African-Americans.* Paper presented at the 104th Annual Conference of the American Psychological Association, Toronto, Ontario.

Seidel, R. W., & Reppucci, N. D. (1995). Organized youth sports and the psychological development of nine-year-old males. *Journal of Child and Family Studies, 2*(3), 229–248.

Seidman, E., Allen, L., Aber, J. L., Mitchell, C., & Feinman, J. (1994). The impact of school transitions in early adolescence on the self-esteem and perceived social content of poor urban youth.*Child Development, 65*, 507–522.

Seifer, R., Schiller, M., Sameroff, A. J., Resnick, S., & Riordan, K. (1996). Attachment, maternal sensitivity and infant temperament during the first year of life. *Developmental Psychology, 32*, 12–25.

Select Committee on Hunger, U.S. House of Representatives. (1988, October). *Strategies for expanding the special supplemental food program for women, infants, and children (WIC) participation: A survey of WIC directors.* Washington, DC: U.S. Government Printing Office.

Selman, R. (1976). Social-cognitive understanding: A guide to educational and clinical practice. In T. Lickona (Ed.). *Moral development and behavior: Theory, research, and social issues* (pp. 219–240). New York: Holt, Rinehart & Winston.

Selman, R. L., & Schultz, L. H. (1989). Children's strategies for interpersonal negotiation with peers: An interpretive empirical approach to the study of social development. In T. J. Berndt & G. W. Ladd (Eds.), *Peer relationships in child development* (pp. 371–406). New York: Wiley.

Selvaggio, A., Kordula, M., Church, R., Guelce, S. S., Woodall, A., & Sieman, J. (1997). *The role of exercise duration, exercise frequency, and gender on self-reported anxiety.* Paper presented at the annual meeting of The Eastern Psychological Association, Washington, DC.

Senechal, M. (1997). The differential effect of storybook reading on preschoolers' acquisition of expressive and receptive vocabulary. *Journal of Child Language, 24*(1), 123–138.

Senechal, M., & Cornell, E. H. (1993). Vocabulary acquisition through shared reading experiences. *Reading Research Quarterly, 28*(4), 361–376.

Senechal, M., Thomas, E., & Monker, J. (1995). Individual differences in 4-year-old children's acquisition of vocabulary during storybook reading. *Journal of Educational Psychology, 87*(2), 218–229.

Shank, R. C., & Abelson, R. (1977). *Scripts, plans, goals, and understanding.* Hillsdale, NJ: Erlbaum.

Share, D. L. (1999). Phonological recoding and orthographic learning: A direct test of the Self-Teaching Hypothesis. *Journal of Experimental Child Psychology, 72*, 95–129.

Shaw, M. E. (1998). Adolescent breakfast skipping: An Australian study. *Adolescence, 33*(132), 851–861.

Shefelbine, J. L. (1990). Student factors related to variability in learning word meanings from context. *Journal of Reading Behavior, 22*, 71–97.

Shelton, P. G., Ferratti, G. H., & Dent, M. (1982). Maintaining oral health. *Pediatric Clinics of North America, 29*(3), 653–668.

Shepperd, J. A., & Kwavnick, K. D. (1999). Maladaptive image maintenance. In R. M. Kowalski & M. R. Leary (Eds.), *The social psychology of emotional and behavioral problems* (pp. 249–277). Washington, DC: American Psychological Association.

Shirley, M. M. (1933). *The first two years: A study of twenty-five babies* (Vol. 2). Minneapolis: University of Minnesota Press.

Shonk, S. M., Repinski, D. J., O'Loughlin, C., Miller, K., & Kent, A. (1998, February). *Parenting behavior and adolescents' emotional reactivity: Predictors of academic performance and problem behavior.* Paper presented at the annual meeting of the Eastern Psychological Association, Boston, MA.

Showalter, E. (1985). *The female malady: Women, madness, and English culture, 1830–1980.* New York: Penguin.

Shu, X., Ross, J. A., Pendergrass, T. W., Reaman, G. H., Lampkin, B., & Robinson, L. L. (1996). Prenatal alcohol consumption, cigarette smoking, and risk of infant leukemia: A children's cancer group study. *Journal of the National Cancer Institute, 88*, 24–31.

Shultz, T. R., & Pilon, R. (1973). Development of the ability to detect linguistic ambiguity. *Child Development, 44*, 728–733.

Shure, M. B. (1994). Alternatives to violence. *Children Today, 23*(1), 14–15.

Siedentop, D. (1999). Physical activity programs and policies. *Journal of Physical Education, Recreation, and Dance, 70*(3), 32–35.

Siegal, M., & Peterson, C. C. (1998). Preschoolers' understanding of lies and innocent and negligent mistakes. *Developmental Psychology, 34*(2), 332–341.

Siegel, D. J. (1999). *The developing mind: Toward a neurobiology of interpersonal experience.* New York: Guilford Press.

Siegel, M., Fuerst, H., & Guinee, J. V. (1971). Rubella epidemicity and embryopathy. *American Journal of Diseases of Children, 121*, 469–473.

Siegler, R. S. (1976). Three aspects of cognitive development. *Cognitive Psychology, 8*, 481–520.

Siegler, R. S. (1986). *Children's thinking.* Englewood Cliffs, NJ: Prentice-Hall.

Siegler, R. S. (1991). *Children's thinking* (2nd ed.). Englewood Cliffs, NJ: Prentice-Hall.

Siegler, R. S. (1995). How does change occur?. A microgenetic study of number conservation. *Cognitive Psychology, 28*, 225–273.

Siegler, R. S. (1998). *Children's thinking* (3rd ed.). Upper Saddle River, NJ: Prentice Hall.

Siegler, R. S., & Liebert, R. M. (1975). Acquisition of formal scientific reasoning by 10- and 13-year-olds. Designing a factorial experiment. *Developmental Psychology, 11*, 401–402.

Sierra, J., & Kaminski, R. (1995). *Children's traditional games.* Phoenix, AR: The Oryx Press.

Sigman, M. (1995). Nutrition and child development: More food for thought. *Current Directions in Psychological Science, 4*(2), 52–55.

Sigman, M., Newmann, C., Janse, A. A. J., & Bwibo, N. (1989). Cognitive abilities of Kenyan children in relation to nutrition, family characteristics, and education. *Child Development, 60*(6), 1463–1473.

Silver, L. M. (1998). *Remaking Eden.* New York: Avon Books.

Silverberg, S. B., & Steinberg, L. (1990). Psychological well-being of parents with early adolescent children. *Developmental Psychology, 26*, 658–666.

Simmons, R. G., & Blyth, D. A. (1987). *Moving into adolescence: The impact of pubertal change in school context.* New York: A. de Gruyter.

Simmons, T. (1999). More middle-school students carry weapons. Retrieved March 2000 from the World Wide Web: www.news-observer.com/daily/1999/01/15/nc06.html

Simon, F., & Butterworth, G. (Eds.). (1998). *The development of sensory, motor, and cognitive capacities in early infancy: From perception to cognition.* Philadelphia: Psychology Press.

Simons, R. L., Whitbeck, L. B., Conger, R. D., & Chyi-In, W. (1991). Intergenerational transmission of harsh parenting. *Developmental Psychology, 27*, 159–171.

Sinclaire, J. C. (1975). The effect of the thermal environment on neonatal mortality and morbidity. In K. Adamson & H. A. Fox (Eds.), *Preventability of perinatal injury.* New York: A. R. Liss.

Siqueland, E. R., & DeLucia, C. (1969). Visual reinforcement of non-nutritive sucking in human infants. *Science, 165*, 1144–1146.

Siqueland, E. R., & Lipsitt, L. P. (1966). Conditioned headturning in human newborns. *Journal of Experimental Child Psychology, 3*, 356–376.

Sitskoorn, M. M., & Smitsman, A. W. (1995). Infants' perception of dynamic relations between objects: Passing through or support? *Developmental Psychology, 31*(3), 437–447.

Skadberg, B. T., Morild, I., & Markestad, T. (1998). Abandoning prone sleeping: Effect on the risk of sudden infant death syndrome. *The Journal of Pediatrics, 132*, 340–343.

Skinner, E. (1990). Age differences in the dimensions of perceived control during middle childhood: Implications for developmental conceptualizations and research. *Child Development, 61*(6), 1882–1890.

Skinner, E. A., & Belmont, M. J. (1993). Motivation in the classroom: Reciprocal effects of teacher behavior and student engagement across the school year. *Journal of Educational Psychology, 85*(4), 571–581.

Slaby, R. G., & Frey, R. S. (1975). Development of gender constancy and selective attention to same-sex models. *Child Development, 46*, 849–856.

Slade, A. (1987). Quality of attachment and early symbolic play. *Developmental Psychology, 23*(1), 78–85.

Slade, A., Belsky, J., Aber, J. L., & Phelps, J. L. (1999). Mothers' representations of their relationships with their toddlers: Links to adult attachment and observed mothering. *Developmental Psychology, 35*, 611–619.

Slade, S. (1999). Why do we teach sports? *Journal of Physical Education, Recreation and Dance, 70*(3), 15–16.

Slater, A. M., & Findlay, J. M. (1975). Binocular fixation in the newborn baby. *Journal of Experimental Child Psychology, 20*, 248–273.

Slavin, R. (1990). Research on cooperative learning: Consensus and controversy. *Educational Leadership, 452–54.*

Sleek, S. (July, 1996). Competition: Who's the real opponent? *The APA Monitor, 27*(7), 8.

Slobin, D. I. (1982). Universal and particular in the acquisition of language. In E. Wanner & L. R. Gleitman (Eds.), *Language acquisition: The state of the art.* Cambridge, UK: Cambridge University Press.

Smetana, J. G. (1994). Parenting styles and beliefs about parental authority. *New Directions for Child Development, 66*, 21–36.

Smith, C., & Lloyd, B. (1978). Maternal behavior and perceived sex of infant: Revisited. *Child Development, 49*, 1263–1265.

Smith, C. B., Adamson, L. B., & Bakeman, R. (1988). Interactional predictors of early language. *First Language, 8*, 143–156.

Smith, C. L., Leinbach, M. D., Stewart, B. J., & Blackwell, J. M. (1983). Affective perspective-taking, exhortation, and children's prosocial behavior. In D. L. Bridgeman (Ed.), *The nature of prosocial development* (pp. 113–134). New York: Academic Press.

Smith, E. E., & Jonides, J. (1997). Working memory: A view from neuroimaging. *Cognitive Psychology, 33*, 5–42.

Smith, E. J. (1982). The black female adolescent: A review of the educational, career, and psychological literature. *Psychology of Women Quarterly, 6*(3), 261–288.

Smith, F. T. (1997). *Obesity in Childhood.* New York: Basic Books.

Smith, H. (1992). The detrimental health effects of ionizing radiation. *Nuclear Medicine Communications, 13*, 4–10.

Smith, M. K. (1994). *Repugnant* is to *aversion* . . . A look at ETS and the new SAT I. *Phi Delta Kappan,* June, 752–757.

Smith, N. (1983). *Experience and art.* New York: Teachers College Press.

Smith, N. J., Greenlaw, M. J., & Scott, C. J. (1987). Making the literate environment equitable. *The Reading Teacher, 40*(4), 400–407.

Smith, P. B., & Pederson, D. R. (1988). Maternal sensitivity and patterns of infant-mother attachment. *Child Development, 59*, 1097–1101.

Smith, P. K., & Doglish, L. (1977). Sex differences in parent and infant behavior in the home. *Child Development, 48*, 1250–1254.

Smith, R. E., Smoll, F. L., & Barnett, N. P. (1995). Reduction of children's sport performance through social support and stress-reduction training for coaches. *Journal of Applied Developmental Psychology, 16*, 125–142.

Smith, S. (1995). Enabling the learning disabled. In M. Cauley, F. Linder, & J. H. McMillan (Eds.), *Annual Editions: Educational Psychology* (pp. 68–70). Guildford, CT: Dushkin.

Smith, T. (Ed.). (1998). *The baby guide.* Auburn, CA: Hazen Publishing.

Smoll, F. L., Smith, R. E., Barnett, N. P., & Everett, J. J. (1993). Enhancement of children's self-esteem through social support training for youth sport coaches. *Journal of Applied Psychology, 78*(4), 602–610.

Smollar, J. (1999). Homeless youth in the United States: Description and developmental issues. *New Directions for Child and Adolescent Development, 85*, 47–58.

Snow, C. E. (1972). Mothers' speech to children learning language. *Child Development, 43*, 549–565.

Snow, C. E. (1977a). Mothers' speech research: From input to interaction. In C. E. Snow & C. A. Ferguson (Eds.), *Talking to children: Language input and acquisition.* Cambridge: Cambridge University Press.

Snow, C. E. (1977b). The development of conversation between mothers and babies. *Journal of Child Language, 4*, 1–22.

Snow, C. E. (1991). The theoretical basis for relationships between language and literacy in development. *Journal of Research in Childhood Education, 6*(1), 5–10.

Snow, C. E. (1993). Families as social contexts for literacy development. *New Directions for Child Development, 61*, 11–24.

Snow, C. E. (1995). Issues in the study of input: Finetuning, universality, individual and developmental differences, and necessary causes. In P. Fletcher & B. MacWhinney (Eds.), *The handbook of child language* (pp. 180–193). Cambridge, MA: Blackwell.

Snow, C. E., Burns, M. S., & Griffin, P. (Eds.) (1998). *Preventing reading difficulties in young children.* Washington, DC: National Academy Press.

Snow, C. E., & Dickinson, D. K. (1990). Social sources of narrative skills at home and at school. *First Language, 10*, 87–103.

Snow, C., & Ferguson, C. (Eds.). (1977). *Talking to children.* New York: Cambridge University Press.

Snyder, H., Finnegan, T., Nimick, E., Sickmund, D., Sullivan, D., & Tierney, N. (1987). *Juvenile court statistics, 1984.* Pittsburgh: National Center for Juvenile Justice.

Snyder, J. J., & Patterson, G. R. (1995). Individual differences in social aggression: A test of a reinforcement model of socialization in the natural environment. *Behavior Therapy, 26*, 371–391.

Snyder, L., Schonfeld, M., & Offerman, E. (1945). The Rh factor and feeblemindedness. *Journal of Heredity, 36*, 9–10.

Soja, N., Carey, N., & Spelke, E. S. (1991). Ontological categories guide young children's inductions of word meanings: Object terms and substance terms. *Cognition, 38*, 179–211.

Somer, E. (1995). *Nutrition for a healthy pregnancy.* New York: Henry Holt.

Sontag, L. W., Baker, C. T., & Nelson, V. L. (1958). Mental growth and personality development: A longitudinal study. *Monographs of The Society for Research in Child Development, 23* (Serial No. 68).

Sorce, J. F., Emde, R. N., Campos, J. J., & Klinnert, M. D. (1985). Maternal emotional signalling: Its effects on the visual cliff behavior of 1-year-olds. *Developmental Psychology, 21*, 195–200.

Spearman, C. (1927). *The abilities of man.* New York: Macmillan.

Spelke, E. S. (1991). Physical knowledge in infancy: Reflections on Piaget's theory. In S. Carey & R. Gelman (Eds.), *The exigenesis of mind: Essays on biology and cognition* (pp. 133–170). Hillsdale, NJ: Erlbaum.

Spelke, E. S., Breinlinger, K., Jacobson, K., & Phillips, A. (1993). Gestalt relations and object perception: A developmental study. *Perception, 22*, 1483–1501.

Spelke, E. S., Breinlinger, K., Macomber, J., & Jacobson, K. (1992). Origins of knowledge. *Psychological Review, 99*, 605–632.

Spelke, E. S., Katz, G., Purcell, S. E., Ehrlich, S. M., & Breinlinger, K. (1994). Early knowledge of object motion: Continuity and inertia. *Cognition, 51*, 131–176.

Spelke, E. S., & Van de Walle, G. (1993). Perceiving and reasoning about objects. N. Eilan, W. Brewer, & R. McCarthy (Eds.), *Spatial representations.* New York: Blackwell.

Spence, M. J., & DeCasper, A. D. (1987). Prenatal experience with low-frequency maternal-voice sounds influence neonatal perception of maternal voice samples. *Infant Behavior and Development, 10*, 133–142.

Spilich, G. J., Hartman, J., & Hartsock, A. (1997). *Does nicotine affect driving performance?* Paper presented at the Eastern Psychological Association annual meeting, Washington, DC.

Spireck, M. M. (1993). Parent and child perceptions of strategy effectiveness for reducing children's television-induced fear. *Journal of Social Behavior and Personality, 8*(6), 51–65.

Spock, B., & Rothenberg, M. B. (1992). *Dr. Spock's baby and child care.* New York: Pocket Books.

Spreen, O., Tupper, D., Risser, A., Tuokko, H., & Edgell, D. (1984). *Human developmental neuropsychology.* New York: Oxford University Press.

Sroufe, L. A. (1981, October). *Infant caregiver attachment and patterns of adaptation in preschool: The roots of maladaptation and competence.* Paper presented at the Minnesota Symposium.

Sroufe, L. A. (1982). Attachment and the roots of competence. In H. E. Fitzgerald and T. H. Carr (Eds.), *Human development: Annual editions.* Guildford, CA: Dushkin.

Sroufe, L. A. (1983). Infant-caregiver attachment and patterns of adaptation in preschool: The roots of maladaptation and competence. In M. Perlmutter (Ed.), *Minnesota symposium in child psychology* (Vol. 16, pp. 41–83). Hillsdale, NJ: Erlbaum.

Sroufe, L. A. (1988). The role of infant-caregiver attachment in development. In J. Belsky & T. Nezworksi (Eds.), *Clinical implications of attachment.* Hillsdale, NJ: Erlbaum.

Sroufe, L. A. (1990). An organizational perspective on the self. In D. Cicchetti & M. Beeghly (Eds.), *The self in transition: Infancy to childhood* (pp. 281–308). Chicago: The University of Chicago Press.

Sroufe, L. A., Fox, N. E., & Pancake, V. R. (1983). Attachment and dependency in developmental perspective. *Child Development, 54*, 1615–1627.

St. James-Roberts, I., Bowyer, J., Varghese, A., & Sawdon, J. (1994). Infant crying patterns in Manali and London. *Child: Care, Health, and Development, 20*, 323–337.

Stage, S. A., & Wagner, R. K. (1992). Development of young children's phonological and orthographic knowledge as revealed by their spellings. *Developmental Psychology, 28*(2), 287–296.

Stager, C. L. (1995). *Phonetic similarty influences learning word-object associations in fourteen-month-old infants.* Unpublished doctoral dissertation, University of British Columbia.

Stanley, J. C. (1993). Boys and girls who reason well mathematically. In G. R. Bock & K. Ackrill (Eds.), *The origin and development of high ability* (pp. 119–138). New York: Wiley.

Stanley, J. C., Benbow, C. P., Brody, L. E., Dauber, S., & Lupkowski, A. (1992). Gender differences on eighty-six nationally standardized aptitude and achievement tests. In N. Colangelo, S. G. Assouline, & D. L. Ambroson (Eds.), *Talent development: Vol. 1. Proceedings from the 1991 Henry B. and Jocelyn Wallace National Research Symposium on Talent Development* (pp. 42–65). Unionville, NY: Trillium Press.

Stanne, M. B., Johnson, D. W., & Johnson, R. T. (1999). Does competition enhance or inhibit motor performance: A meta-analysis. *Psychological Bulletin, 125*(1), 133–154.

Stanovich, K. E. (Ed.). (1993). The development of rationality and critical thinking (Special issue). *Merrill-Palmer Quarterly, 39*(1), 47–103.

Stanovich, K. E., & West, R. F. (1999). Individual differences in reasoning and the heuristics and biases debate. In P. L. Ackerman, P. C. Kyllonen, & R. D. Roberts (Eds.), *Learning and individual differences* (pp. 389–407). Washington, DC.: American Psychological Association.

Stanovich, K. E., West, R. F., & Harrison, M. R. (1995). Knowledge growth and maintenance across the life span: The role of print exposure. *Developmental Psychology, 31*, 811–826.

Starkey, D. (1981). The origins of concept formation: Object sorting and object preference in early infancy. *Child Development, 52*, 489–497.

Starling, S. P., Holden, J. R., & Jenny, C. (1995). Abusive head trauma: The relationship of perpetrators to their victims. *Pediatrics, 95*, 259–262.

Staub, E. (1971). A child in distress: The influence of nurturance and modeling on children's attempts to help. *Developmental Psychology, 5*, 124–132.

Staub, E. (1975). *The development of prosocial behavior in children.* Morristown, NJ: General Learning Press.

Stay, B. L. (Ed.). (1999). *Mass media: Opposing viewpoints.* San Diego, CA: Greenhaven Press.

Steckel, R. (1997, June 2). 2000: The millennium notebook. *Newsweek,* p. 10.

Steen, R. G. (1996). *DNA and destiny: Nature and nurture in human behavior.* New York: Plenum Press.

Stein, J. H., & Reiser, L. W. (1994). A study of white middle-class adolescent boys' responses to "semenarche" (the first ejaculation). *Journal of Youth and Adolescence, 23*(3), 373–384.

Stein, L., Ozdamar, O., Kraus, N., & Paton, J. (1983). Followup of infants screened by auditory brainstem response in the neonatal intensive care unit. *Journal of Pediatrics, 103*(3), 447–453.

Steinberg, L. (1993). *Adolescence.* New York: McGraw-Hill.

Steinberg, L. (1999). *Adolescence.* New York: McGraw-Hill.

Steinberg, L., Lamborn, S. D., Darling, N., Mounts, N. S., & Dornbusch, S. M. (1994). Over-time changes in adjustment and competence among adolescents from authoritative, authoritarian, indulgent, and neglectful families. *Child Development, 65*, 754–770.

Steinberg, L., Lamborn, S. D., Dornbusch, S. M., & Darling, N. (1992). Impact of parenting practices on adolescent achievement: Authoritative parenting, school involvement, and encouragement to succeed. *Child Development, 63*, 1266–1281.

Steinberg, L., & Silverberg, S. B. (1986). The vicissitudes of autonomy in early adolescence. *Child Development, 57*(4), 841–851.

Steiner, J. (1977). Facial expressions of the neonate infant indicating hedonics of food-related chemical stimuli. In J. M. Weiffenbach (Ed.), *Taste and development: The genesis of sweet preference* (pp. 173–188). Bethesda, MD: U.S. Department of Health, Education, and Welfare (HEW).

Stenberg, C., Campos, J., & Emde, R. (1983). The facial expression of anger in seven-month-old infants. *Child Development, 54*, 178–184.

Stern, D., Jaffe, J., Beebe, B., & Bennett, S. L. (1975). Vocalizing in unison and in alternation: Two modes of communication within the mother-infant dyad. *Annals of the New York Academy of Sciences, 263*, 89–100.

Stern, G. (1973). *Principles of human genetics* (3rd ed.). San Francisco: W. H. Freeman.

Stern, M., & Karraker, K. H. (1989). Sex stereotyping of infants: A review of gender labeling studies. *Sex Roles, 20*, 501–522.

Sternberg, R. J. (1990). *Metaphors of mind: Conceptions of the nature of intelligence.* New York: Cambridge University Press.

Sternberg, R. J. (1992). Intellectual development: A satiric fairy tale. In R. J. Sternberg, & C. B.erg (Eds.), *Intellectual development.* New York: Cambridge University Press.

Sternberg, R. J. (1994). 468 factor-analyzed data sets: What they tell us and don't tell us about human intelligence. *Psychological Science, 5*, 63–65.

Sternberg, R. J. (1995). *In search of the human mind.* New York: Harcourt Brace.

Sternberg, R. J., & Lubart, T. I. (1992). Buy low and sell high: An investment approach to creativity. *Current Directions in Psychological Science, 1*(1), 1–5.

Sternberg, S. (1999, June 23). Lead exposure linked to bad teeth in children. *USA Today,* p. 10D.

Stevens, B. J., Johnson, C. C., & Horton, L. (1994). Factors that influence the behavioral pain response of premature infants. *Pain, 59*(1), 101–109.

Stevens-Smith, P., & Remley, T. P. (1994). Drugs, AIDS, and teens: Intervention and the school counselor. *The School Counselor, 41*, 180–184.

Stevenson, H., and Shin-ying, L., in collaboration with Chen, C., Stigler, J., Hsu, C., and Kitamura, S. (1990a). Contexts of achievement: A study of American, Chinese, and Japanese children. With Commentary by G. Hatans: and a Reply by H. Stevenson and S. Lee. *Monographs of the Society for Research in Child Development, 55*(1–2, Serial No. 221).

Stevenson, H., Shin-ying, L., Chuansheng, C., Lummis, M., Stigler, J., Fan, C., & Fang, G. (1990b). Mathematics achievement of children in China and the United States. *Child Development, 61*, 1053–1066.

Stipek, D., & Gralinski, H. (1991). Gender differences in children's achievement-related beliefs and emotional responses to success and failure in math. *Journal of Educational Psychology, 83*, 361–371.

Stipek, D. J., & Daniels, D. H. (1988). Declining perceptions of competence: A consequence of changes in the child or in the educational environment? *Journal of Educational Psychology, 80*(3), 352–356.

Stoff, D. M., Pollock, L., Vitiello, B., Behar, D., & Bridger, W. H. (1987). Reduction of (3H)—Imipramine binding sites on platelets of conduct-disordered children. *Neuropsychopharmacology, 1*, 55–62.

Stone, C. A., & Day, M. C. (1980). Competence and performance models and the characterization of formal operational skills. *Human Development, 23*, 323–353.

Stone, J., Aronson, E., Crain, A. L., Winslow, M. P., & Fried, C. B. (1994). Inducing hypocrisy as a means of encouraging young adults to use condoms. *Personality and Social Psychology Bulletin, 20*, 116–128.

Stone, M. R., & Brown, B. B. (1999). Identity claims and projections: Descriptions of self and crowds in secondary school. *New Directions for Child and Adolescent Development, 84*, 7–20.

Stoner, L. J. (1978). Selecting physical activities for the young child, with an understanding of bone growth and development. *Reviews of Research for Practitioners and Parents, 1*, 32–42.

Stoppard, M. (1998), *Healthy pregnancy.* New York: D. K. Publishing Inc.

Stotsky, S. (1995). The uses and limitations of personal or personalized writing in writing theory, research, and instruction. *Reading Research Quarterly, 30*(4), 758–777.

Stoutjesdyk, D., & Jevne, R. (1993). Eating disorders among high performance athletes. *Journal of Youth and Adolescence, 22*, 271–282.

Strachan, T., and Read, A. P. (1996). *Human molecular genetics.* New York: Wiley.

Strage, A., & Brandt, T. S. (1999). Authoritative parenting and college students' academic adjustment and success. *Journal of Educational Psychology, 91*(1), 146–156.

Strand, B., Scantling, E., & Johnson, M. (1998). Guiding principles for implementing fitness education. *Journal of Physical Education, Recreation, and Dance, 69*(8), 35–39.

Strasburger, V. C. (1992). Children, adolescents, and television. *Pediatric Review, 13,* 144–151.

Stratford, B. (1994). Down syndrome is for life. *International Journal of Disability Development and Education, 41*(1), 3–13.

Stratton, P. (1982). Rhythmic functions in the newborn. In P. Stratton (Ed.), *Psychobiology of the human newborn* (pp. 119–145). New York: Wiley.

Straus, M. A., & Kantor, G. K. (1994). Corporal punishment of adolescents by parents: A risk factor in the epidemiology of depression, suicide, alcohol abuse, child abuse, and wife beating. *Adolescence, 29*(115), 543–561.

Strayer, F. F. (1980). Social ecology of the preschool peer group. In W. A. Collins (Ed.), *Development of cognition, affect, and social relations: Minnesota Symposium in Child Development* (Vol. 3). Hillsdale, NJ: Erlbaum.

Strear, W. B. (1995). Youth sports contexts: Coaches' perceptions and implications for intervention. *Journal of Applied Sport Psychology, 7,* 23–37.

Streissguth, A. P., Barr, H. M., Bookstein, F. L., Sampson, P. D., & Olson, H. C. (1999). The long-term neurocognitive consequences of prenatal alcohol exposure: A 14-year study. *Psychological Science, 10*(3), 186–190.

Streissguth, A. P., Bookstein, F. L., Sampson, P. D., Olson, H. C., & Barr, H. M. (1995, March). *Measurement and analysis of main effects, covariates, and moderators in the behaviorial teratology of alcohol.* Paper presented at the Biennial Meetings of the Society for Research in Child Development, Indianapolis, March 30–April 2.

Strelau, J., & Angleitner, A. (1991). Introduction. Temperament research: Some divergences and similarities. In J. Strelau and A. Angleitner (Eds.), *Explorations in temperament: International perspectives on theory and measurement* (pp. 1–12). New York: Plenum Press.

Stricker, L. J., Rock, D. A., & Burton, N. W. (1993). Sex differences in predictions of college grades from Scholastic Aptitude scores. *Journal of Educational Psychology, 85,* 710–718.

Striegel-Moore R. H., & Cachelin F. M. (1999). Body image concerns and disordered eating in adolescent girls: Risk and protective factors. In N. G. Johnson, M. C. Roberts, & J. Worell (Eds.), *Beyond appearance: A new look at adolescent girls* (pp. 85–108). Washington, DC: American Psychological Association.

Strohner, H., & Nelson, K. E. (1974). The young child's development of sentence comprehension: Influence of event probability, nonverbal context, syntactic form, and strategies. *Child Development, 45,* 567–576.

Strom, M. S. (1999). Raising a moral child. *The Brown University Child and Adolescent Behavior Letter, 15*(4), 8.

Strouse, D. L. (1999). Adolescent crowd orientations: A social and temporal analysis. *New Directions for Child and Adolescent Development, 84,* 37–54.

Stunkard, A. J., & Sobol, J. (1995). Psychosocial consequences of obesity. In K. D. Brownell & C. G. Fairburn (Eds.), *Eating disorders and obesity: A comprehensive handbook* (pp. 417–421). New York: Guilford Press.

Sturman, T. S. (1999). Achievement motivation and Type A behavior as motivational orientations. *Journal of Research in Personality, 33,* 189–207.

Subrahmanyam, K., & Greenfield, P. (1998). Computer games for girls: What makes them play? In J. Cassell & H. Jenkins (Eds.), *From Barbie to Mortal Kombat* (pp. 46–71). Cambridge, MA: The MIT Press.

Sullivan, S. A., & Birch, L. L. (1994). Infant dietary experience and acceptance of solid foods. *Pediatrics, 93,* 271–277.

Sullivan, T. J. (1999). Surveys reveal becalmed youngsters. *Youth Today, 8*(8), 35–36.

Sulzby, E. (1985). Children's emergent reading of favorite storybooks: A developmental study. *Reading Research Quarterly, 20*(4), 458–481.

Super, C. M. (1981). Behavioral development in infancy. In R. H. Monroe, R. L. Monroe, & B. B. Whiting (Eds.), *Handbook of cross-cultural human development* (pp. 181–270). New York: Garland.

Super, C. M., Herrera, M. G., & Mora, J. O. (1990). Long-term effects of food supplementation and psychosocial intervention on the physical growth of Columbian infants at risk of malnutrition. *Child Development, 61,* 29–49.

Susman, E. J., Inoff-German, G., Nottelmann, E. D., Loriaux, L., Cutler, G. B., & Chrousos, G. P. (1987). Hormones, emotional dispositions, and aggressive attributes in young adolescents. *Child Development, 58,* 1114–1134.

Sussman, E. J., Nottelmann, E. D., Inhoff-Germain, G. E., Dorn, L. D., Cutler, G. B., Jr., Loriaux, D. L., & Chrousos, G. P. (1985). The relation of development and social-emotional behavior in young adolescents. *Journal of Youth and Adolescence, 14,* 245–264.

Sutton-Smith, B. (1972). *The folkgames of children.* Austin, TX: The University of Texas Press.

Suzuki, S., & Rancer, A. S. (1994). Argumentativeness and verbal aggression: Testing for conceptual and measurement equivalence across cultures. *Communication Monographs, 61,* 256–279.

Svejda, M. J., Pannabecker, B. J., & Emde, R. N. (1982). Parent-to-infant attachment: A critique of the early "bonding" model. In R. M. Emde & R. J. Harmon (Eds.), *The development of attachment and affiliative systems* (pp. 83–94). New York: Plenum Press.

Swanson, H. L. (1999a). Reading comprehension and working memory in learning-disabled readers: Is the phonological loop more important than the executive system? *Journal of Experimental Child Psychology, 72,* 1–31.

Swanson, H. L. (1999b). What develops in working memory? A life span perspective. *Developmental Psychology, 35*(4), 986–1000.

Symons, C. S., & Johnson, B. T. (1997). The self-reference effect in memory: A meta-analysis. *Psychological Bulletin, 121* 371–394.

Tabors, P. O., & Snow, C. E. (1994). English as a second language in preschool programs. In F. Genesee (Ed.), *Educating second language children* (pp. 103–126). Cambridge: University of Cambridge Press.

Takanishi, R., Mortimer, A. M., & McGourthy, T. J. (1997). Positive indicators of adolescent development: Redressing the negative image of American Adolescents. In R. M. Houser, B. V. Brown & W. R. Prosser, (Eds.), *Indicators of children's well-being* (pp. 428–441). New York: Russell Sage Foundation.

Takeuchi, M. (1994). Children's play in Japan. In J. L. Roopnarine, J. E. J.ohnson, & F. H. Hopper (Eds.), *Children's play in diverse cultures* (pp. 51–72). Albany, NY: State University of New York Press.

Tamis-LaMonda C., & Bornstein, M. H. (1994). Specificity in mother-toddler language-play relations across the second year. *Developmental Psychology, 30,* 283–292.

Tamis-LeMonda, C. S., Albright, M. B., Damast, A. M., & Fox, T. (1995, March 28–April 2). *A longitudinal incatipation of first- to second-year play: Efforts toward validating an 18-level scale.* Paper presented at the bienniel meeting of the Society for Research in Child Development, Indianapolis.

Tannehill, D., Romar, J. E., O'Sullivan, M., & England, K. (1994). Attitudes toward physical education: Their impact on how physical education teachers make sense of their work. *Journal of Teaching in Physical Education, 13*(4), 406–420.

Tanner, J. M. (1970). Physical growth. In P. H. Mussen (Ed.), *Carmichael's Manual of Child Psychology* (Vol. 1, 3rd ed.). New York: Wiley.

Tanner, J. M. (1978). *Education and physical growth* (2nd.ed.). New York: International Universities Press.

Tanner, J. M. (1990). *Foetus into man: Physical growth from conception to maturity.* (2nd ed.). Cambridge, MA: Harvard University Press.

Tanner, J. M. (1991). Adolescent growth spurt. In R. M. Lerner, A. C. Peterson, & J. Brooks-Gunn (Eds.), *Encyclopedia of adolescence* (Vol. 1, pp. 419–424). New York: Garland.

Tardif, T. (1996). Nouns are not always learned before verbs: Evidence from Mandarin speakers' early vocabularies. *Developmental Psychology, 32,* 492–504.

Tardiff, T., Gelman, S. A., & Yu, F. (1999). Putting the "noun bias" in context: A comparison of English and Mandarin. *Developmental Psychology, 70*(3), 537–804.

Tarlow, G. (1999, February 23). Hip-hop, Internet give teenagers new vocabulary. *The Washington Times,* p. E4.

Tatum, B. D. (1997). *Why are all the black kids sitting together in the cafeteria?* New York: Basic Books.

Taylor, H. G., Klein, N., Schatschneider, C., & Hask, M. (1998). Predictors of early school age outcomes in very low birthweight children. *Developmental and Behavioral Pediatrics, 19*(4), 235–239.

Taylor, I. (1981). Writing systems and reading. In G. E. Mackinnon & T. G. Waller (Eds.), *Reading research: Advances in theory and practice* (Vol. 2, pp. 1–47). New York: Academic Press.

Taylor, M., & Carlson, S. M.(1997). The relation between individual differences in fantasy and theory of mind. *Child Development, 68,* 436–455.

Taylor, R. D. (1996). Adolescents' perceptions of kinship support and family management practices: Association with adolescent adjustment in African-American families. *Developmental Psychology, 32,* 687–695.

Teale, W., & Sulzby, E. (1986). Emergent literacy as a perspective for examining how young children become writers and readers. In W. Teale and E. Sulzby (Eds.), *Emergent literacy.* Norwood, NJ: Ablex.

Teasley, S. D. (1995). The role of talk in children's peer collaborations. *Developmental Psychology, 31,* 207–220.

Teele, D. W., Klein, J. O., & Rosner, B. A. (1984). Otitis media with effusion during the first three years of life and development of speech and language. *Pediatrics, 74*(2), 282–287.

Teitz, C. C. (1982). Sports medicine concerns in dance and gymnastics. *Pediatric Clinics of North America, 29*(6), 1399–1421.

Teller, D. Y., Peeples, D. R., & Sekel, M. (1978). Discrimination of chromatic from white light by 2-month-old human infants. *Vision Research, 18,* 41–48.

Templin, M. C. (1957). *Certain language skills in children.* Minneapolis: University of Minnesota Press.

Terman, L. M. (1916). *The measurement of intelligence.* Boston: Houghton Mifflin.

Termine, N. T., & Izard, C. E. (1988). Infants' responses to their mothers' expressions of joy and sadness. *Developmental Psychology, 24,* 223–229.

Thaiss, C., & Sanford, J. F. (2000). *Writing for psychology.* Boston: Allyn & Bacon.

Thapar, A., & McGuffin, P. (1997). Anxiety and depressive symptoms in childhood: A genetic study of comorbidity. *Journal of Child Psychology and Psychiatry and Allied Disciplines, 38*(6), 651–656.

Thelen, E., Corbetta, D., Kamm, K., & Spencer, J. P. (1993). The transition to reaching: Mapping intention and intrinsic dynamics. *Child Development, 64*(4), 1058–1098.

Thelen, E., & Smith, L. B. (1997). Dynamic systems theory. In W. Damon & R. Lerner (Eds.), *Theoretical models of human development: Vol. 1. Handbook of child psychology,* (5th ed., pp. 637–655). New York: Wiley.

Thelen, E., & Ulrich, B. D. (1991). Hidden skills. *Monographs of The Society for Research in Child Development.* Vol. 56(1, Serial No. 223).

This week's TV programs. (1999, September 18–24). *TV Guide, 47*(3), issue 2425.

Thompson, B. (1996). AERA editorial policies regarding statistical significance testing: Three suggested reforms. *Educational Researcher, 25,* 26–30.

Thompson, F. E., & Dennison, B. A. (1994). Dietary sources of fats and cholesterol in U.S. children aged 2 through 5 years. *American Journal of Public Health, 84*(5), 799–806.

Thompson, G. B., Fletcher-Flinn, C. M., & Cottrell, D. S. (1999). Learning correspondences between letters and phonemes without explicit instruction. *Applied Psycholinguistics, 20,* 21–50.

Thompson, R. (1988). The effects of infant day care through the prism of attachment theory: A critical appraisal. *Early Childhood Research Quarterly, 3*(3), 273–282.

Thompson, R. A. (1998). Early sociopersonality development. In W. Damon (Series Ed.) & N. Eisenberg (Vol. Ed.), *Handbook of child psychology (5th ed.):*

Vol. 3. Social, emotional, and personality development (pp. 25–104). New York: Wiley.

Thompson, R. A. (1999). The individual child: Temperament, emotion, self, and personality. In M. H. Bornstein & M. E. Lamb (Eds.), *Developmental psychology: An advanced text* (pp. 377–409). Mahwah, NJ: Erlbaum.

Thorndike, A. N., Ferris, T. G., Stafford, R. S., & Rigotti, N. A. (1999). Rates of U.S. physicians counseling adolescents about smoking. *Journal of the National Cancer Institute, 91*(21), 1857–1862.

Thorndike, R. L., Hagen, E. P., & Sattler, J. M. (1986). *The Stanford Binet Intelligence Scale: Fourth edition technical manual.* Chicago: Riverside Publishing Company.

Tikunoff, W. J., Ward, B. A., van Broekhuizen, L. D., Romero, M., Castaneda, L. V., Luca, T., & Katz, A. (1991). *Final report: A descriptive study of significant features of exemplary special alternative instructional programs.* Los Alamitos, CA: The Southwest Regional Educational Laboratory.

Tincoff, R., & Jusczyk, P. W. (1999). Some beginnings of word comprehension in 6-month-olds. *Psychological Science, 10*(2), 172–175.

Tishler, P. V., Henschel, C. E., Ngo, T. A., Walters, E. E., & Worobec, T. G. (1998). Fetal alcohol effects in alcoholic veteran patients. *Alcoholism: Clinical and Experimental Research, 22*(8), 1825–1831.

Tomada, G., & Schneider, B. H. (1997). Relational aggression, gender, and peer acceptance: Invariance across culture, stability over time, and concordance among informants. *Developmental Psychology, 33*(4), 601–609.

Tomasello, J., & Todd, J. (1983). Joint attention and acquisition style. *First Language, 4,* 197–212.

Tomasello, M. (1988). The role of joint attentional processes in early language development. *Language Sciences, 10,* 69–88.

Tomasello, M. (1992). *First verbs: A case study of early grammatical development.* Cambridge, UK: Cambridge University Press.

Tonjes, M. J. (1991). *Secondary reading, writing and learning.* Boston: Allyn & Bacon.

Torrens, P. R. (1995). Growing up tobacco free. *Journal of the American Medical Association, 273*(17), 1326.

Travillion, K., & Snyder, J. (1993). The role of maternal discipline and involvement in peer rejection and neglect. *Journal of Applied Developmental Psychology, 14,* 37–57.

Treasure, J. L., Katzman, M., Schmidt, V., Troop, N., Todd, G., & deSilva, P. (1999). Engagement and outcome in the treatment of bulimia nervosa. *Behavior Research and Therapy, 37,* 405–418.

Trehub, S. (1973). Infants' sensitivity to vowel and tonal contrasts. *Developmental Psychology, 9,* 91–96.

Trehub, S. E., & Rabinovitch, M. S. (1972). Auditory-linguistic sensitivity in early infancy. *Developmental Psychology, 6,* 74–77.

Trehub, S. E., Trainor, L., & Unyk, A. M. (1993). Music and speech processing in the first year of life. In H. W. Reese (Ed.), *Advances in child development and behavior.* (Vol. 24, pp. 1–35). New York: Academic Press.

Trehub, S. E., Unyk, A. M., & Henderson, J. L. (1994). Children's songs to infant siblings: Parallels with speech. *Journal of Child Language, 21,* 735–744.

Treiman, R. (1985). Phonemic awareness and spelling: Children's judgments do not always agree with adults'. *Journal of Experimental Child Psychology, 39,* 182–201.

Treiman, R. (1993). *Beginning to spell: A study of first-grade children.* New York: Oxford University Press.

Treiman, R., Goswami, U., Tincoff, R., & Leevers, H. (1997). Effects of dialect on American and British Children's Spelling. *Child Development, 68*(2), 229–245.

Treiman, R., Tincoff, R., & Richmond-Welty, E. D. (1996). Letter names help children to connect print and speech. *Developmental Psychology, 32*(3), 505–514.

Treiman, R., Tincoff, R., & Richmond-Welty, E. D. (1997). Beyond zebra: Preschoolers' knowledge about letters. *Applied Psycholinguistics, 18,* 391–409.

Treiman, R., Tincoff, R., Rodriguez, K., Mouzaki, A., & Francis, D. J. (1998). The foundations of literacy: Learning the sounds of letters. *Child Development, 69*(6), 1524–1540.

Treiman, R., Weatherston, S., & Berch, D. (1994). The role of letter names in children's learning of phoneme-grapheme relations. *Applied Pscholinguistics, 15,* 97–122.

Treiman, R., Zukowski, A., & Richmond-Welty, E. D. (1995). What happened to the "n" of sink? Children's spellings of final consonant clusters. *Cognition, 55,* 1–38.

Trevarthen, C. (1977). Descriptive analysis of infant communicative behavior. In H. R. Schaffer (Ed.), *Studies in mother-infant interaction* (pp. 227–270). London: Academic Press.

Trickett, P. K., & Kuczynski, L. (1986). Children's misbehavior and parental discipline strategies in abusive and non-abusive families. *Developmental Psychology, 8,* 240–260.

Trickett, P. K., & McBridge-Chang, C. (1995). The developmental impact of different forms of child abuse and neglect. *Developmental Review, 15,* 311–337.

Tronick, E. Z., Frank, D. A., Cabral, H., Mirochnick, M., & Zuckerman, B. (1996). Late-dose response effects of prenatal cocaine exposure on newborn neurobehavioral performance. *Pediatrics, 98,* 76–83.

Troy, M., & Sroufe, L. A. (1987). Victimization among preschoolers: Role of attachment relationship history. *Journal of the American Academy of Child and Adolescent Psychiatry, 26*(2), 166–172.

Trudel, P., & Cote, J. (1994). Sports education and learning conditions. *Enfance, 2–3,* 285–297.

Tseng, M., & Cermak, S. A. (1993). The influence of ergonomic factors and perceptual-motor abilities on handwriting performance. *American Journal of Occupational Therapy, 47*(10), 919–926.

Tseng, M., & Murray, E. A. (1994). Differences in perceptual-motor measures in children with good and poor handwriting. *Occupational Therapy Journal of Research, 14*(1), 19–36.

Tunmer, W. E., & Chapman, J. W. (1998). Language prediction skill, phonological recoding ability and beginning reading. In M. Joshi & C. Hulme (Eds.), *Reading and spelling: Development and disorders* (pp. 33–67). Hillsdale, NJ: Erlbaum.

Tunmer, W. E., & Hoover, W. (1992). Cognitive and linguistic factors in learning to read. In P. B. Gough, L. C. Ehri, & R. Treiman (Eds.), *Reading acquisition* (pp. 175–214). Hillsdale, NJ: Erlbaum.

Turner, R. B. (1998). The common cold. *Pediatric Annals, 27*(12), 790–795.

Ullman, J. B., Stein, J. A., & Dukes, R. L. (1999, August). *Multilevel model of moderators of D. A. R. E. effectiveness.* Paper presented at the annual meeting of the American Psychological Association, Boston, MA.

Ungerer, J. A., Zelazo, P. R., Kearsley, R. B., & O'Leary, K. (1981). Developmental changes in the representation of objects in symbolic play from 18 to 35 months of age. *Child Development, 52,* 186–195.

Ungerleider, L. D. (1995). Functional brain imaging studies of cortical mechanisms for memory. *Science, 270,* 769–775.

Urberg, K. A., DeGirmencioglu, S. M. Tolson, J. M., & Halliday-Scher, K. (1995). The structure of adolescent peer networks. *Developmental Psychology, 31*(4), 540–547.

U.S. Department of Education. (1997). *National assessment of educational progress* (Indicator 32: Writing Proficiency; prepared by the Educational Testing Service). Washington, DC.: Author. Retrieved March 2000 from the World Wide Web: http://www.ed.gov/nces

Valenzuela, M. (1997). Maternal sensitivity in a developing society: The context of urban poverty and infant chronic undernutrition. *Developmental Psychology, 33*(5), 845–855.

Valsiner, J. (1998). The development of the concept of development: Historical and epistemological perspectives. In W. Damon (Series Ed.) & R. Lerner (Vol. Eds.), *Handbook of child psychology: Vol. 1. Theoretical models of human development* (pp.189–232). New York: Wiley.

Van de Walle, G. A., & Spelke, E. S. (1996). Spatiotemporal integration and object perception in infancy: Perceiving unity versus form. *Child Development, 67,* 2621–2640.

Van den Boom, D. (1989). Neonatal irritability and the development of attachment. In G. Kohnstamm, J. Bates, & M. Rothbart (Eds.), *Temperament in childhood.* New York: Wiley.

Van den Boom, D. C. (1991). The influence of infant irritability on the development of the mother-infant relationship in the first 6 months of life. In J. K. Nugent, B. M. Lester, & T. B. Brazelton (Eds.), *The cultural context of infancy* (Vol. 2, pp. 63–89). Norwood, NJ: Ablex.

van den Boom, D., & Gravenhorst, J. B. (1995). Prenatal and perinatal correlates of neonatal irritability. *Infant Behavior and Development, 18,* 117–121.

van der Veer, R., & Valsiner, J. (1991). *Understanding Vygotsky: A quest for synthesis.* Cambridge, MA: Basil Blackwell.

van Ijzendoorn, M. H., Goldberg, S., Kroonenberg, P. M., & Frenkel, O. J. (1992). The relative effects of maternal and child problems on the quality of attachment: A meta-analysis of attachment in clinical samples. *Child Development, 63,* 840–858.

van Ijzendoorn, M. H., & Krooneberg, P. M. (1988). Cross-cultural patterns of attachment: A meta-analysis of the strange situation. *Child Development, 59,* 147–156.

vanGeert, P. (1998). A dynamic systems model of basic developmental mechanisms: Piaget, Vygotsky, and beyond. *Psychological Review 105*(4), 634–677.

Vasta, R., & Liben, L. S. (1996). The water-level task: An intriguing puzzle. *Current Directions in Psychological Science, 5,* 171–177.

Vasta, R., Knott, J. A., & Gaze, C. E. (1996). Can spatial training erase the gender differences on the water-level task? *Psychology of Women Quarterly, 20,* 549–568.

Vaughn, B., Engeland, B., Sroufe, L. A., & Waters, E. (1979). Individual differences in infant-mother attachment at twelve and eighteen months: Stability and change in families under stress. *Child Development, 50,* 971–975.

Vaughn, B., Gove, R. L., & Egeland, B. (1980). The relationship between out-of-home care and the quality of infant-mother attachment in an economically disadvantaged population. *Child Development, 51,* 971–975.

Velayo, R. S., Quirk, C., & Pollini, S. (1999). *Tips on teaching psychology through presentation programs and home pages.* Paper presented at the annual meeting of the American Psychological Association, Boston, MA.

Vellutino, F. R. (1991). Introduction to three studies on reading acquisition: Convergent findings on throretical foundations of code-oriented versus whole-language approaches to reading instruction. *Journal of Educational Psychology, 83*(4), 437–443.

Velting, D. M. (1999). Teen suicides. In L. P. Lipsitt (Ed.), *The Brown University Child and Adolescent Behavior Letter, 15*(4), 3.

Venezia, P. A. (1971). Delinquency prediction: A critique and suggestion. *Journal of Research in Crime and Delinquency, 8,* 108–117.

Venturelli, P. J. (2000). Drugs in Schools: Myths and realities. *Annals of the American Academy of Political and Social Science, 567,* 72–87.

Verhulst, F. C., Van Der Lee, J. H., Akkerhuis, G. E., Sanders-Woudstra, J. A. R., Timmer, F. C., & Donkhorst, I. D. (1985). The prevalence of nocturnal enuresis: Do DSM III criteria need to be changed? A brief research report. *Journal of Child Psychology, 26*(6), 989–993.

Vernberg, E. M., Ewell, K., Beery, S. H., & Abwender, D. T. (1994). Sophistication of adolescents' interpersonal negotiation strategies and friendship formation after relocation: A naturally occurring experiment. *Journal of Research on Adolescence, 4* (1), 5–19.

VICA (Volunteers in Career Awareness). (1999). Retrieved March 2000 from the World Wide Web: www.vica.org/aboutmentoring.html

Viham, M. M., Macken, M. A., Miller, R., Simmons, H., & Miller, J. (1985). From babbling to speech: A re-assessment of the continuity issue. *Language, 61*(2), 397–445.

Vincente, K. J., & Wang, J. H. (1998). An ecological theory of expertise effects in memory recall. *Psychological Review, 105*(1), 33–57.

Vogel, E. T. (1968). *Japan's new middle class: The salary man and his family in a Tokyo suburb.* Berkeley: University of California Press.

Volpe, J. J. (1992). Effect of cocaine use on the fetus. *New England Journal of Medicine, 327*(6), 399–407.

von Hofsten, C., & Spelke, E. S. (1985). Object perception and object-directed reaching in infancy. *Journal of Experimental Psychology: General, 114,* 198–212.

Vondra, J. I., & Barnett, D. (1999). Atypical attachment in infancy and early childhood among children at developmental risk. *Monographs of the Society for Research in Child Development, 64*(3, Serial No. 258).

Vondra, J., & Belsky, J. (1989). Exploration and play in social context: Developments from infancy to early childhood. In J. J. Lockman & N. L. Hazen (Eds.), *Action in social context: Perspectives on early development* (pp. 173–203). New York: Plenum.

Vondra, J. I., Shaw, D. S., & Kevenides, M. C. (1995). Predicting infant attachment classifications from multiple contemporaneous measures of maternal care. *Infant Behavior and Development, 18,* 415–425.

Voss, J. F., & Wiley, J. (1995). Acquiring intellectual skills. *Annual Review of Psychology, 46,* 155–181.

Voyer, D., Voyer, S., & Bryden, M. P. (1995). Magnitude of sex differences in spatial abilities: A meta-analysis and consideration of critical variables. *Pyschological Bulletin, 117,* 250–270.

Vygotsky, L. (1926). The methods of reflexological and psychological investigation. In R. Van der Veer & J. Valsiner (1994), *The Vygotsky reader* (pp. 27–45). Cambridge, MA: Basil Blackwell.

Vygotsky, L. (1978). *Mind in society: The development of higher psychological processes.* Cambridge: Harvard University Press.

Vygotsky, L. (1987). *Thinking and speech.* (N. Minick, Trans.). New York: Plenum.

Wachtel, A. (1998). *The attention deficit answer book.* New York: Penguin Putnam.

Wagner, B. J., & Larson, M. (1995). *Situations: A casebook of virtual realities from the English teacher.* Portsmouth, NH: Boynton/Cook Publishers.

Wagner, R. K. (1999). Searching for determinants of performance in complex domains. In P. L. Ackerman, P. C. Kyllonen, & R. D. Roberts (Eds.), *Learning and individual differences* (pp. 371–385). Washington, DC: American Psychological Association.

Wagner, R. K., & Torgesen, J. K. (1987). The nature of phonological processing and its causal role in the acquisition of reading skills. *Psychological Bulletin, 101,* 192–212.

Wahler, R. G. (1990). Who is driving the interactions? A commentary on "Child and parent effects in boys' conduct disorders. " *Developmental Psychology, 26*(5), 702–704.

Walden, T. A., & Baxter, A. (1989). The effect of context and age on social referencing. *Child Development, 60*(6), 1511–1518.

Walden, T. A., & Ogden, T. A. (1988). The development of social referencing. *Child Development, 60*(6), 1511–1518.

Waldrop, M. F., & Halverson, C. F., Jr. (1975). Intensive and extensive peer behavior: Longitudinal and cross-sectional analysis. *Child Development, 46,* 19–26.

Walker, D., Greenwood, C., Hart, B., & Carta, J. (1994). Prediction of school outcomes based on early language production and socioeconomic factors. *Child Development, 65*(2), 606–622.

Walkers-Andrew, A. S. (1986). Intermodal perception of expression behaviors: Relation to eye and voice? *Developmental Psychology, 22,* 373–377.

Wallace-Broscious, A., Serafica, F. C., & Osipow, S. H. (1994). Adolescent career development: Relationships to self-concept and identity status. *Journal of Research on Adolescence, 4*(1), 122–149.

Waller, G., Coakley, M., & Richards, L. (1995). Bulimic attitudes among Asian and Caucasian schoolgirls. *European Eating Disorders Review, 3*(1), 24–34.

Walma Van Der Molen, J. H., & van Der Voort, T. H. (2000). The impact of television, print, and audio on children's recall of the news: A study of three alternative explanations for the dual-coding hypothesis. *Human Communication Research, 26*(1), 3–26.

Walters, J. (1975). Birth defects and adolescent pregnancies. *Journal of Home Economics, 67,* 23–27.

Walton, G. E., Bower, N. J. A., & Bower, T. G. R. (1992). Recognition of familiar faces by newborns. *Infant Behavior and Development, 15,* 265–269.

Wang, J., & Wildman, L. (1995). The effects of family commitment in education on student achievement in seventh grade mathematics. *Education, 115,* 317–319.

Ward, G. (1999). Friends can be good for your health. *Health Education Authority.* Retrieved March 2000 from the World Wide Web: www.hea.org.uk/press/2969942.html

Ware, A. M., & Cross, D. R. (1995). *Early development of social competence in the peer group: A lag sequential analysis of toddler and preschool social play.* Poster presented at the Biennial Meeting of the Society for Research in Child Development, Indianapolis.

Waters, E., & Cummings, E. M. (2000). A secure base from which to explore close relationships. *Child Development, 71*(1), 164–172.

Waters, E., & Deane, K. E. (1982). Infant-mother attachment: Theories, models, recent data, and some tasks for comparative developmental analysis. In L. W. Hoffman, R. Gandelman, & H. R. Schiffman (Eds.), *Parenting: Its causes and consequences.* Hillsdale, NJ: Erlbaum.

Watson, A. C., Nixon, C., Wilson, A., & Capage, L. (1999). Social interaction skills and theory of mind in young children. *Developmental Psychology, 35,* 386–391.

Watt, J. (1990). Interaction, intervention, and development in small-for-gestation-age infants. *Infant Behavior and Development, 13,* 273–286.

Wechsler, D. (1991). *Wechsler Intelligence Scale for Children* (3rd ed.). San Antonio, TX: Psychological Corporation.

Weese-Mayer, D. E.(1998). Modifiable risk factors for sudden infant death syndrome: When will we ever learn? *Journal of Pediatrics, 132,* 197–198.

Weinberg, R. A. (1989). Intelligence and IQ. *American Psychologist, 44*(2), 98–104.

Weinraub, M., & Frankel, J. (1977). Sex differences in parent-infant interactions during free play, departure, and separation. *Child Development, 48,* 1240–1249.

Weiss, M. L., & Mann, A. E. (1981). *Human biology and behavior.* Boston: Little Brown.

Weiten, W. (2000). *Psychology: Themes and variations.* (briefer edition). Pacific Grove, CA: Brooks Cole.

Weiten, W., & Lloyd, M. A. (2000). *Psychology applied to modern life: Adjustment at the turn of the century.* Pacific Grove, CA: Brooks/Cole.

Weiten, W., & Lloyd, M. (1994). *Psychology applied to modern life: Adjustment in the 90's.* Pacific Grove, CA: Brooks/Cole.

Welk, G. J., & Wood, K. (2000). Physical activity assessments in physical education. *Journal of Physical Education, Recreation, and Dance, 71*(1), 30–40.

Wellman, H. M. (1990). *The child's theory of mind.* Cambridge, MA: The MIT Press.

Wellman, H. M., & Gelman, S. A. (1998). Knowledge acquisition in foundational domains. In W. Damon, (Editor-in-Chief) and D. Kuhn & R. S. Siegler (Vol. Eds.), *Handbook of child psychology* (5th ed.): *Vol. 2. Cognition, perception, and language.* (pp. 523–573). New York: Wiley.

Wenar, C., & Kerig, P. (2000). *Developmental psychopathology: From infancy through adolescence.* New York: McGraw-Hill.

Wendland-Carro, J., Piccinini, C. A., & Millar, W. S. (1999). The role of an early intervention on enhancing the quality of mother-infant interaction. *Child Development, 70,* 713–721.

Wennberg, R., Woodrum, D., & Hodson, A. (1973). The perinate. In D. Smith & E. Bierman (Eds.), *The biologic ages of man.* Philadelphia: W. B. Saunders.

Wentzel, K. R. (1991). Social competence at school: Relations between social responsibility and academic achievement in early adolescence. *Child Development, 62,* 1066–1078.

Wentzel, K. R. (1993). Does being good make the grade? Social behavior and academic competence in middle school. *Journal of Educational Psychology, 85*(2), 357–364.

Wentzel, K. R. (1999). Social-motivational processes and interpersonal relationships: Implications for understanding motivation at school. *Journal of Educational Psychology, 91*(1), 76–97.

Wentzel, K. R., & Asher, S. (1995). The academic lives of neglected, rejected, popular, and controversial children. *Child Development, 66,* 754–763.

Werker, J. F., & Lalonde (1988). Cross-language speech perception: Initial capabilities and developmental change. *Developmental Psychology, 24,* 672–683.

Werker, J. F., & McLeod, P. J. (1989). Infant preference for both male and female infant-directed talk: A developmental study of attentional and affective responsiveness. *Canadian Journal of Psychology, 43,* 230–246.

Werker, J. F., Pegg, J. E., & McLeod, P. J. (1994). A cross-language investigation of infant preference for infant-directed communication. *Infant Behavior and Development, 17*(3), 323–333.

Werker, J. F., & Tees, R. C. (1984). Cross-language speech perception: Evidence for perceptual reorganization during the first year of life. *Infant Behavior and Development, 7,* 49–63.

Werner, H., & Kaplan, E. (1952). The acquisition of word meanings: A developmental study. *Monographs of the Society for Research in Child Development, 15*(1, Serial No. 51).

Wertsch, J. V. (1985). *Vygotsky and social formation of mind.* Cambridge, MA: Harvard University Press.

Wertsch, J. V. (Ed.). (1981). *The concept of activity in Soviet psychology.* Armonk, NY: M. E. Sharp.

Wertsch, J. V., & Kanner, B. G. (1992). A sociocultural approach to intellectual development. In R. J. Sternberg & C. A. Berg, *Intellectual development* (pp. 328–349). Cambridge, MA: Cambridge University Press.

Wertz, R. W., & Wertz, D. C. (1977). *Lying-in: A history of childbirth in America.* New York: Free Press.

West, K. L. (1981). Assessment and treatment of disturbed adolescents and their families: A clinical research perspective. In M. Lasky (Ed.), *Major psychopathology and the family.* New York: Grune & Stratton.

West, M. L., & Sheldon-Keller, A. E. (1994). *Patterns of relating: An adult attachment perspective.* New York: Guilford Press.

Wheeler, R., Alloy, L. B., & Abramson, L. Y. (1999, August). *Parenting style and late adolescents' personality dimensional scores.* Paper presented at the annual meeting of the Eastern Psychological Association, Providence, RI.

White, B. (1995). Effects of autobiographical writing before reading on students' responses to short stories. *Journal of Educational Research, 88*(3), 173–184.

White, B. L. (1971). *Human infants: Experience and psychological development.* Englewood Cliffs, NJ: Prentice-Hall.

White, H. (1986). Damsels in distress: Dependency themes in fiction for children and adolescents. *Adolescence, 21,* 251–256.

White, J. (1995). Violence prevention in the schools. *Journal of Health Education, 26*(1), 52–53.

White, J., & Labarba, R. C. (1976). The effects of tactile and kinesthetic stimulation on neonatal development in preterm infants. *Developmental Psychology, 9,* 569–577.

White, R. W. (1959). Motivation reconsidered: The concept of competence. *Psychological Review, 66,* 297–333.

Whitehurst, G. J. (1995, May). *Levels of reading readiness and predictors of reading success among children from low-income families.* Paper presented at the Biennial Meeting of the Society for Research in Child Development, Indianapolis, IN.

Whitehurst, G. J. (1997, April). *Long-term effects of an emergent literacy intervention in Head Start.* Presented as part of a symposium, Child and Family Literacy in the Context of Intervention Programs, at the Meeting of the Society for Research in Child Development, Washington, D.C.

Whitehurst, G. J., & Lonigan, C. J. (1998). Child development and emergent literacy. *Child Development, 69*(3), 848–872.

Whitehurst, G. J., & Sonnenschein, S. (1985). The development of communication: A functional analysis. In G. T. Whitehurst (Ed.). *Annals of child development* (Vol. 2). Greenwich, CT: JAI Press.

Whiting, B. B., & Edwards, C. E. (1973). A cross-cultural analysis of sex differences in the behavior of children aged three through eleven. *The Journal of Social Psychology, 91,* 171–188.

Whiting, B. B., & Edwards, C. E. (1988). *Children of different worlds: The formation of social behavior.* Cambridge, MA: Harvard University Press.

Whiting, B. B., & Whiting, J. W. M. (1975). *Children of six cultures: A psychological analysis.* Cambridge, MA: Harvard University Press.

Whiting, H. T. (1969). *Acquiring ball skills: A psychological interpretation.* London: Prentice-Hall.

Whitley, R., & Goldenberg, R. (1990). Infectious disease in the prenatal period and recommendations for screening. In I. R. Merkatz & J. E. Thompson (Eds.), *New perspectives on prenatal care.* New York: Elsevier.

Wickett, M. S. (2000). Nurturing the voices of young mathematics with dyads and group discussions. *Teaching children Mathematics, 6*(6), 412–415.

Wiederman, M. W., & Pryor, T. L. (2000). Body dissatisfaction, bulimia, and depression among women: The mediating role of drive for Thinness. *International Journal of Eating Disorders, 27*(1), 90–95.

Wiener, V. (1999). *Winning the war against youth gangs: A guide for teens, families, and communities.* Westport, CT: Greenwood.

Wiley, A. R., Rose, A. J., Burger, L. K., & Miller, P. J. (1998). Constructing autonomous selves through narrative practices: A comparative study of working-class and middle-class families. *Child Development, 69*(3), 833–847.

Will, J. A., Self, P. A., & Datan, N. (1976). Maternal behavior and perceived sex of infant. *American Journal of Orthopsychiatry, 46*(1), 135–139.

Williams, B. F., Howard, V. F., & McLaughlin, T. F. (1994). Fetal alcohol syndrome: Developmental characteristics and directions for further research. *Education and Treatment of Children, 17*(1), 86–97.

Williams, G. (1989). Lead paint alert. *Practical Homeowner, 4*(5), 24–26.

Williams, H. (1983). *Perceptual and motor development.* Englewood Cliffs, NJ: Prentice-Hall.

Williams, N. (1994). The physical education hall of shame, part II. *Journal of Physical Education, Recreation and Dance, 65*(2), 17–20.

Williams, S. S., Kimble, D. L., Cowell, N. H., Weiss, L. H., Newton, K. J., Fisher, J. D., & Fisher, W. A. (1992). College students use implicit personality theory instead of safe sex. *Journal of Applied Social Psychology, 22,* 921–933.

Williams, T., & Kuther, T. (1999, April). *The relation of exercise and body esteem.* Paper presented at the annual meeting of the Eastern Psychological Association, Providence, RI.

Willingham, W. W., & Cole, N. S. (1997). *Gender and fair assessment.* Hillsdale, NJ: Erlbaum.

Wills, J. (1998). *The food bible.* New York: Simon & Schuster.

Wills, T. A., McNamara, G., Vaccaro, D., and Hirkey, E. (1999). Escalated substance use: A longitudinal grouping analysis from early to middle adolescence. *Journal of Abnormal Psychology, 105*(2), 166–180.

Wilson, G., & Terence, G. (1994). Behavioral treatment of childhood obesity: Theoretical and practical implications. *Health Psychology, 13*(5), 371–372.

Wilson, H. R. (1993). Theories of infant visual development. In K. Simons (Ed.), *Early visual development: Normal and abnormal.* New York: Oxford University Press.

Wilson, M. D., & Joffe, A. (1995). Adolescent medicine. *Journal of the American Medical Association, 273*(21), 1657–1658.

Wimmer, H., & Perner, J. (1983). Beliefs about beliefs: Representation and constraining function of wrong beliefs in young children's understanding of deception. *Cognition, 13,* 103–128.

Windle, M. (1994). A study of friendship characteristics and problem behaviors among middle adolescents. *Child Development, 65,* 1764–1777.

Winick, M., Meyer, K. K., & Harris, A. C. (1975). Malnutrition and environmental enrichment by early adoption. *Science, 190,* 1173–1175.

Winitz, H., & Irwin, O. (1958). Syllabic and phonetic structure of infants' early words. *Journal of Speech and Hearing Research, 1,* 250–256.

Winn, S., Tronick, E. Z., & Morelli, G. A. (1989). The infant and the group: A look at Efe caretaking practices in Zaire. In J. K. Nugent, B. M. Lester, & T. B. Brazelton (Eds.), *The cultural context of infancy: Vol. 1. Biology, culture, and infant development* (pp. 87–110). Norwood, NJ: Ablex.

Wise, B. W., Ring, J., & Olson, R. K. (1999). Training phonological awareness with and without explicit attention to articulation. *Journal of Experimental Child Psychology, 72,* 271–304.

Wisot, A., and Meldrum, D. (1998). *Conceptions and misconceptions.* New York: Hartley and Marks Publishers.

Wolf, A. W., Lozoff, B., Latz, S., & Paludetto, R. (1996). Parental theories in the management of young children's sleep in Japan, Italy, and the United States. In S. Harkness & C. S.uper (Eds.), *Parents' cultural belief systems: Their origins, expressions, and consequences* (pp. 364–384). New York: The Guilford Press.

Wolfe, S. M., Toro, P. A., & McCaskill, P. A. (1999). A comparison of homeless and matched housed adolescents on family environment variables. *Journal of Research on Adolescence, 91*(1), 53–66.

Wolfe, W. S., Campbell, C. C., Frongillo, E. A., Hass, J. D., & Melnik, T. A. (1994). Overweight schoolchildren in New York State: Prevalence and characteristics. *American Journal of Public Health, 84,* 807–813.

Wolff, P. (1965). The development of attention in young infants. *Annals of the New York Academy of Sciences, 118,* 815–830.

Wolff, P. (1966). The causes, controls, and organizations of behavior in the newborn. *Psychological Issues, 5,* 1–105.

Wolff, P. (1969a). The natural history of crying and other vocalizations in early infancy. In B. Foss (Ed.), *Determinants of infant behavior* (Vol. 4, pp. 113–138). London: Methuen.

Wolff, P. (1969b). Observations of the early development of smiling. In B. Foss (Ed.), *Determinants of infant behavior* (Vol. 2). London: Methuen.

Wood, E., Willoughby, T., McDermott, C., Motz, M., Kaspar, V., & Ducharme, M. J. (1999). Developmental differences in study behavior. *Journal of Educational Psychology, 91*(3), 527–536.

Wood, W., & Eagly, A. H. (1999). Sex differences in interaction style as a product of perceived sex differences in competence. *Journal of Personality and Social Psychology, 50,* 341–347.

Wood, W., Wong, F. Y., & Chachere, G. (1991). Effects of media violence on viewers' aggression in unconstrained social interaction. *Psychological Bulletin, 109,* 371–383.

Woodring, T. (1995). *Effects of peer education programs on sexual behavior, AIDS knowledge, and attitudes.* Paper presented at the Annual Meetings of the Eastern Psychological Association, Boston.

Woods, E. G. (1999). Reducing the dropout rate. *School Improvement Research Series,* Northwest Regional Educational Laboratory. Retrieved March 2000 from the World Wide Web: www.nwrel.org/scpd/sirs/9/c017.html

Wooley, J. D., & Bruel, M. J. (1996). Young children's awareness of the origins of their mental representations. *Developmental Psychology, 32,* 335-346.

Woroby, J. (1993). Effects of feeding method on infant temperament. In H. W. Reese (Ed.), *Advances in child development and behavior* (Vol. 24, pp. 37–61). San Diego, CA: Academic Press.

Woznicki, K. (1999). Government wants cigar warning labels. *On health.* Retrieved March 2000 from the World Wide Web: http://onhealth.com/ch1/briefs/item

Wright, H. F. (1960). Observational child study. In P. H. Mussen (Ed.), *Handbook of research methods in child development.* New York: Wiley.

Wright, J. C., & Huston, A. C. (1995). *Effects of educational TV viewing on low income preschoolers on academic skills, school readiness, and school adjustment one to three years later: A report to Children's Television Workshop.* Lawrence, KS: University of Kansas, Department of Human Development.

Wright, M. T., Patterson, D. L., & Cardinal, B. J. (2000). Increasing children's physical activity. *Journal of Physical Education, Recreation, and Dance, 71*(1), 26–29.

Wysong, E., Aniskiewicz, R., & Wright, D. (1994). Truth and DARE: Tracking drug education to graduation and as symbolic politics. *Social Problems, 41* (3), 448–472.

Xanthou, M. (1998). Immune protection of human milk. *Biology of the Neonate, 74,* 121–133.

Yairi, E., & Ambrose, N. (1992). Onset of stuttering in preschool children: Selected factors. *Journal of Speech and Hearing Research, 35,* 782–788.

Yan, Z. (1999, August). *Measuring the zone of proximal development with individual growth model.* Paper presented at the Annual Meeting of the American Psychological Association, Boston, MA.

Yarrow, M. R., Scott, P. M., & Waxler, C. Z. (1973). Learning concern for others. *Developmental Psychology, 8,* 240–260.

Yazigi, R. A., Odem, R. R., & Polakoski, K. L. (1991). Demonstrations of specific binding of cocaine to human spermatozoa. *Journal of the American Medical Association, 266,* 1956–1959.

Yesalis, C. E., & Bahrke, M. S. (1995). Anabolic-androgenic steroids. *Sports Medicine, 19*(5), 326–340.

Yonas, A. (1981). Infants' responses to optical information for collision. In R. N. Aslin, J. R. Alberts, & M. R. Peterson (Eds.), *Development of perception: Psychobiological perspectives* (Vol. 2 pp. 313–334). New York: Academic Press.

Yonas, A., & Hartman, B. (1993). Perceiving the affordance of contact in 4- and 5-month-old infants. *Child Development, 64*(1), 298–308.

Yonas, A., & Owsley, C. (1987). Development of visual space perception. In P. Salapatek & L. B. Cohen (Eds.), *Handbook of infant perception: Vol. 2. From perception to cognition* (pp. 80–117). New York: Academic Press.

Yopp, H. K. (1988). The validity and reliability of phonemic awareness tests. *Reading Research Quarterly, 23*(2), 159–177.

Young, K. A., & Thomas, A. M. (1999). *Relation of parents' marital status, family communication, and conflict to late adolescent self-esteem.* Paper presented at the annual meeting of the Eastern Psychological Association, Providence, RI.

Young, S. K., Fox, N. A., & Zahn-Waxler, C. (1999). The relations between temperament and empathy in 2-year-olds. *Developmental Psychology, 35*(5), 1189–1197.

Young, W. C., Goy, R. W., & Phoenix, C. H. (1964). Hormones and sexual behavior. *Science, 143,* 212–218.

Youngblade, L., & Belsky, J. (1990). Social and emotional consequences of child maltreatment. In R. Hammerman & M. Hersen (Eds.), *Children at risk: An evaluation of factors contributing to child abuse and neglect.* New York: Plenum Press.

Younger, B. (1990). Infants' detection of correlations among feature categories. *Child Development, 61,* 614–620.

Younger, B. A., & Cohen, L. B. (1983). Infant perception of correlations among attributes. *Child Development, 54,* 858–867.

Younger, B. A., & Cohen, L. B. (1986). Developmental change in infants' perception of corrrelations among attributes. *Child Development, 57,* 803–815.

Youniss, J., McLeellan, J. A., & Strouse, D. (1994). "We're popular, but we're not snobs": Adolescents describe their crowds. In R. Montemayor, G. R. Adams, & T. P. Gullotta (Eds.), *Personal relationships during adolescence* (pp. 101–122). Thousand Oaks, CA: Sage.

Youniss, J., McLellan, J. A., & Yates, M. (1999). Religion, community service, and identity in American youth. *Journal of Adolescence, 22,* 243–253.

Youth Risk Behavior Surveillance (August 1, 1998). Number E G003-837493-711017.

Zahn-Waxler, C., Radke-Yarrow, M., & King, R. A. (1979). Child-rearing and children's prosocial initiations towards victims of distress. *Child Development, 50,* 319–330.

Zahn-Waxler, C., Radke-Yarrow, M., Wagner, E., & Chapman, M. (1992). Development of concern for others. *Developmental Psychology, 28*(1), 126–136.

Zakin, D. F., Blyth, D. A., & Simmons, R. G. (1984). Physical attractiveness as a mediator of the impact of early pubertal changes for girls. *Journal of Youth and Adolescence, 13,* 439–450.

Zakriski, A. L., & Coie, J. D. (1996). A comparison of aggressive-rejected and nonaggressive-rejected children's interpretations of self-directed and other-directed rejection. *Child Development, 67,* 1048–1070.

Zerin, E., Zerin, M., & Cuiran, Z. (1997). A comparative study of Chinese and American high school students' responses to stress under pressure. *Transactional Analysis Journal, 27*(4), 241–255.

Zern, D. S. (1984). Relationships among selected child-rearing variables in a cross-cultural sample of 110 societies. *Developmental Psychology, 20*(4), 683–690.

Zeskind, P. S., & Ramey, C. T. (1978). Fetal malnutrition: An experimental study of its consequences on infant development in two caregiving environments. *Child Development, 49,* 1155–1162.

Zigler, E. F., & Hall, N. W. (2000). *Child development and social policy.* New York: McGraw-Hill.

Zimmerman, B. J., & Kitsantas, A. (1999). Acquiring writing revision skill: Shifting from process to outcome self-regulatory goals. *Journal of Educational Psychology, 91*(2), 241–250.

Zimmerman, B. J., & Martinez-Pons. (1990). Student differences in self-regulated learning: Relating grade, sex, and giftedness to self-efficacy and strategy-use. *Journal of Educational Psychology, 82,* 51–59.

Zinsser, N., Bunker, L., & Williams, J. M. (1998). Cognitive techniques for building confidence and enhancing performance. In J. M. Williams (Ed.), *Applied sport psychology,* (pp. 270–295). Mountain View, CA: Mayfield.

Zuckerman, B. S., & Dubey, J. C. (1985). Developmental approach to injury prevention. *Pediatric Clinics of North America, 32*(1), 17–29.

Zuckerman, D. (1999). Research watch: Girls just aren't having fun. *Youth Today, 8*(4), 10–12.

Zwaan, R. A., & Radvansky, G. A. (1998). Situation models in language comprehension and memory. *Psychological Bulletin, 123*(2), 162–185.

NAME INDEX

SUBJECT INDEX